THE EC MERGER REGULATION: SUBSTANTIVE ISSUES

AUSTRALIA
Law Book Co
Sydney

CANADA and USA
Carswell
Toronto

HONG KONG
Sweet & Maxwell Asia

NEW ZEALAND
Brookers
Wellington

SINGAPORE and MALAYSIA
Sweet & Maxwell Asia
Singapore and Kuala Lumpur

THE EC MERGER REGULATION: SUBSTANTIVE ISSUES

ALISTAIR LINDSAY
Partner, Allen & Overy

LONDON
SWEET & MAXWELL
2006

Published in 2006 by Sweet & Maxwell Limited of
100 Avenue Road,
London NW3 3PF
www.sweetandmaxwell.co.uk
Typeset by YHT Ltd, London
Printed by MPG Books Ltd, Bodmin, Cornwall

No natural forests were destroyed to make this product; only farmed
timber was used and replanted

A CIP catalogue record for this book is available from the British Library

ISBN   0 421 930802

ISBN-13 978-0-421-93080-3

CONTENTS

CONTENTS

6. MARKET OPERATION

7. HORIZONTAL MERGERS: NON-COORDINATED EFFECTS

8. COORDINATED EFFECTS

PREFACE

The treatment of substantive issues in EC merger control has continued to evolve rapidly since the publication of the first edition of this text in 2003. The most important developments include the publication by the European Commission (the "Commission") of a Notice on Horizontal Mergers differing substantially from the draft discussed in the first edition; the adoption of a new substantive test with effect from May 1, 2004; a shift in the Commission's approach to vertical and conglomerate mergers; publication of the Merger Remedies Study, which contains a wealth of information about the practical implementation of remedies, and seems set to presage a tightening of policy in this area; and the decisions of the European Court of Justice in *Tetra Laval* and the Court of First Instance in *General Electric*.

In addition to the normal updating process, the text has been reorganised to follow more closely the structure of the Commission's Notice on Horizontal Mergers and to split the old "Unilateral Effects" chapter into more easily navigable text.

The text is up to date to January 31, 2006.

I would like to thank: Eithne McCarthy, Richard Wainwright, Julie Lacey, Emma Lafferty, Lynne Arnold, Jayne Ball, Andy Betton and Nigel Stevenson for their assistance and support; my PhD examiners (Professors Richard Whish and Alan Dashwood) for their helpful comments on the first edition; Sarah Watt at Sweet & Maxwell for her support, responsiveness and enthusiasm; the document checkers at Allen & Overy LLP; and all of my colleagues at Allen & Overy LLP for continuing to provide a dynamic home from which to practise competition law. All errors are, of course, my responsibility.

The views expressed in this edition are personal and do not represent those of Allen & Overy LLP or its clients.

I would be very pleased to receive comments or suggestions on the text by email to *alistair.lindsay@allenovery.com*.

Dr Alistair Lindsay
Allen & Overy LLP
February 1, 2006

TABLE OF LEGISLATION

A. TABLE OF EC TREATIES, SECONDARY LEGISLATION AND NOTICES

Commission Guidelines

Notices

TABLE OF CASES

B. ECJ AND ECFI DECISIONS

C. MERGER DECISIONS (NUMERICAL)

C. MERGER DECISIONS (NUMERICAL)

D. MERGER DECISIONS (ALPHABETICAL)

E. JOINT VENTURES AND ECSC DECISIONS

Joint Ventures

ECSC

F. TABLE OF NATIONAL CASES

G. GUIDELINES

H. UK LEGISLATION

CHAPTER 1

THE ECONOMIC JUSTIFICATION FOR MERGER CONTROL

1.1 INTRODUCTION

In analysing the treatment of substantive issues under the EC Merger **1–001** Regulation (the "ECMR"),[1] it will be necessary to return time and again to the objectives underlying the Regulation. This is scarcely surprising. If antitrust policy is to be applied coherently, its goals must be clear. Accordingly, this Chapter describes in outline the economic justification for merger control.[2] In particular, it examines the criteria available for appraising market performance (s.1.2), the effects of structural change through merger on market performance (s.1.3), the extent to which the predicted effects of mergers can be measured (s.1.4) and empirical evidence on the effects of mergers (s.1.5). The final section (s.1.6) provides an overview of the analysis set out in the remainder of the book.

1.2 CRITERIA FOR ASSESSING MARKET PERFORMANCE

Economists typically use one of three criteria[3] for assessing market perfor- **1–002** mance: *consumer welfare* considers whether the market delivers benefits to consumers; *total welfare* takes account of the interests of producers as well

---

[1] Council Regulation (EC) No 139/2004 on the control of concentrations between undertakings [2004] O.J. L24/1.
[2] The objectives of EC merger control are analysed in s.2.2 below.
[3] In addition, market performance is commonly examined using equitable or distributional criteria (although, in this context, it is noteworthy that the use of a consumer welfare standard in preference to a total welfare standard reflects a distributional policy decision to accord decisive weight to consumers' interests ahead of producers').

as consumers; and *efficiency* focuses on the way the market operates. This section considers those three criteria separately before examining their suitability for assessing market performance.[4]

(a) Consumer welfare

1–003 There are four components[5] of consumer welfare.[6] Consumer welfare is enhanced if the *price* of goods or services is reduced or the *quality* of those goods is increased whilst the price is not changed. Price and quality are treated as two separate aspects of consumer welfare (although they can be regarded as differing aspects of a single criterion—*value for money*—because the concept of *price* only has any meaning as a sum payable for a good or service *of a particular quality*).[7] Criteria for measuring value for money are examined below. The third component is *consumer choice*: if consumers have

---

[4] Politicians may design systems of merger control to promote policy objectives other than market performance; see the discussion in Areeda & Hovenkamp, *Antitrust Law* (2nd edn, Aspen Law & Business, 2000) Vol.I, s.1B and the International Competition Network, Analytical Framework Sub-group, "The Analytical Framework for Merger Control" (available at *www.internationalcompetitionnetwork.org/afsguk.pdf*), paras 14 to 16. See also OFT Economic Discussion Paper, "Innovation and Competition Policy", Charles River Associates, March 2002 (note that the views in the paper do not necessarily reflect those of the OFT), paras 4.60 to 4.66.

[5] The four components are recognised in the Commission Notice on the appraisal of horizontal mergers under the Council Regulation on the control of concentrations between undertakings [2004] O.J. C31/5, para.8. In the Foreword to the XXXIst Report on Competition Policy, 2001, Mario Monti, then the Commissioner for Competition Policy, stated: "Our objective is to ensure that competition is undistorted, so as to permit wider consumer choice, technological innovation and price competition". Similarly, in Case IV/M.430 *Procter & Gamble / VP Schickedanz (II)* [1994] O.J. L354/32, the Commission found, at para.182, that the proposed merger was likely to harm consumers in relation to price, quality, innovation and choice. See also Mario Monti, then the Commissioner for Competition Policy, "A Global Competition Policy?", speech of September 17, 2002 (www.europa.eu.int/comm/competition/speeches/index_2002.html) ("Somebody must check that a merger does not result in excessive market power and thus ensure that consumers will continue to benefit from a competitive environment in terms of innovation, quality, choice and prices") and European Commission, "Glossary of Terms Used in EU Competition Policy", July 2002, (note that this document is not binding on the Commission) (*www.europa.eu.int/comm/competition/publications/glossary_en.pdf*), definition of a "dominant position". The four components are also reflected in the UK's Enterprise Act 2002.

[6] See generally Tirole, *The Theory of Industrial Organization* (The MIT Press, 1988), pp.7 to 12; Besanko, Dranove & Shanley, *Economics of Strategy* (2nd edn, John Wiley & Sons Inc, 2000), pp.391 to 395 (and, for discussion of methods for estimating and characterising perceived benefits to consumers, see pp.437 to 441); Clarke, *Industrial Economics* (Blackwell, 1985), p.227; and Porter, "Competition and Antitrust: Toward a Productivity-Based Approach to Evaluating Mergers and Joint Ventures", [2001] *The Antitrust Bulletin* 919 (arguing that productivity growth ought to be adopted as the basic goal of antitrust policy in place of consumer welfare on the grounds that antitrust policy would then focus on increasing a nation's standard of living; Porter contends that focusing on short run consumer welfare measured by price-cost margins fails to recognise the broader significance of healthy competition for consumers).

[7] Similarly, the quality of a good or service is of no interest to a consumer unless the consumer also knows its price. For this reason, it is common to refer to a product's price/value or price/performance ratio. The "quality" component of the analysis is important because if prices in a market exceed marginal cost, this may lead customers to "quality downshift", i.e. to switch from higher quality to lower quality goods because of the prices of the former.

differing tastes then consumer welfare may be enhanced if they are able to choose from a wider product range.[8] Fourthly consumers generally benefit if new products are developed through *innovation*.[9]

In considering whether a market provides *value for money* to consumers it is common to use the concept of *consumer surplus*. For example, if I were willing to pay 75p for a bag of apples which is priced at 50p then I would buy it, as my *maximum willingness to pay* exceeds the price, and my consumer surplus would be 25p, i.e. the difference between my maximum willingness to pay[10] and the monetary price. Individual consumer surpluses can be aggregated to provide market data. Consumer surplus may therefore be regarded as the *gains from trade* enjoyed by consumers,[11] i.e. the gains from purchasing goods in the market compared with making no purchases.

(i) Consumer surplus—single market price The consumer surplus available to **1–004** purchasers in a market can be illustrated using the industry demand curve.[12]

Fig.1.1 shows a normal downward-sloping industry demand curve: at low prices there is high demand for the product but, as price increases, demand falls. Assume that the market price is P_1 and market demand Q_1.[13] The consumer surplus is the area beneath the demand curve but above the market price, XP_1E. There are some customers who would have been willing to pay prices at or approaching X[14] and, for these customers, the gains from trade (i.e. consumer surplus) are very high (X minus P_1). Equally, there are some customers who were only willing to pay P_1 or a price very slightly in excess of P_1 and, for those customers, the gains from trade (i.e. consumer surplus) are slight.[15]

---

[8] Whether a wider product range in fact enhances consumer welfare is a difficult question: see Eaton & Lipsey, "Product Differentiation", in *Handbook of Industrial Organization* (Schmalensee & Willig edn, 1989) Vol.1, p.723, at 760. Further, when there are economies of scale in production, increasing variety may be inefficient: see Oster, *Modern Competitive Advantage* (3rd edn, Oxford UP, 1999), p.265. For a discussion of US cases involving a reduction in consumer choice through vertical integration, see Areeda, Hovenkamp & Solow, *Antitrust Law* (2nd edn, Aspen Law & Business, 1998), Vol.IVA, para.1010.

[9] Assuming that there is actual or potential consumer demand for the new products. For an explanation as to why static performance has been accorded greater weight by antitrust authorities than dynamic performance (and in particular innovation), see Areeda, Hovenkamp & Solow, *Antitrust Law* (2nd edn, Aspen Law & Business, 1998), Vol.IV, para.918.

[10] More particularly, a consumer's maximum willingness to pay is the perceived gross benefit of the product to the customer less user costs (e.g. installation and operation costs) and transaction and purchasing costs: see Besanko, Dranove & Shanley, *Economics of Strategy* (2nd edn, John Wiley & Sons Inc, 2000), pp.392 and 393.

[11] Consumer surplus measures gains from trade *as perceived by customers*, i.e. a subjective standard is applied.

[12] A *demand curve* shows how customers' demand for a product or service varies depending on its price, i.e. it measures willingness to pay (which is sometimes described as a reservation price).

[13] The graph illustrates a perfectly competitive market: see paras 1–015 to 1–016 below.

[14] Demand at prices approaching X is very limited, as illustrated by the fact that the demand curve is very close to the price axis at such prices.

[15] If the demand curve were to remain unchanged whilst the market price increased above P_1, then consumer surplus would fall.

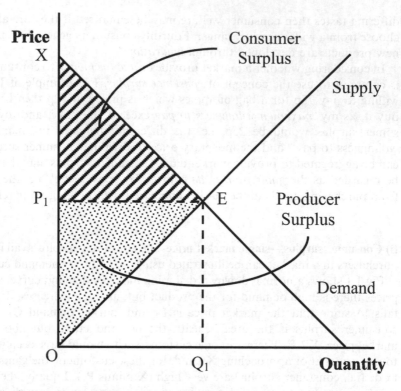

Fig.1.1: Consumer and Producer Surplus

1–005 **(ii) Consumer surplus—price discrimination** The example given above assumed that there was a single market price, P_1. In this section, by contrast, it is assumed that suppliers are able to price discriminate,[16] i.e. to charge different prices to different customers for the same product.[17] In a broader sense, price discrimination arises in the sale of *different* products when the ratio of the *prices* of two products differs from the ratio of the *marginal costs* of producing those products.[18]

---

[16] See generally Tirole, *The Theory of Industrial Organization* (The MIT Press, 1988), Ch.3; Phlips, *The Economics of Price Discrimination* (Cambridge UP, 1981); and OFT Economic Discussion Paper, "*Innovation and Competition Policy*" (Charles River Associates, March 2002), para.5.58 (discussing the welfare consequences of price discrimination) (note that the views in the paper do not necessarily reflect those of the OFT).

[17] Or charging the same price to different customers in different positions. Price discrimination by a dominant firm may be unlawful under Art.82.

[18] Cabral gives the example of hardback and paperback books where the costs of production are different, but the difference in the prices charged for the two types of book is out of proportion to the differences in cost of production: Cabral, *Introduction to Industrial Organization* (The MIT Press, 2000), p.168. See also Phlips, *The Economics of Price Discrimination* (Cambridge UP, 1981), p.6: "price discrimination should be defined as implying that two varieties of a commodity are sold (by the same seller) to two buyers at different *net* prices, the net price being the price (paid by the buyer) corrected for the cost associated with the product differentiation".

Price discrimination is *possible* when the supplier has at least some market power (otherwise no customer would be willing to pay more than the perfectly competitive price)[19] and the supplier is able to prevent or limit resale or arbitrage (otherwise customers charged lower prices would sell on to customers charged higher prices).[20] (The expression "market power" is used in two main senses.[21] In its wide sense, "market power" refers to the ability of a supplier to make sales at prices above marginal cost. In its narrow sense, "market power" involves the ability to profitably price significantly above the competitive level[22] for a substantial period[23] (and is sometimes treated as synonymous with dominance).[24] A supplier may be able to engage successfully in price discrimination without enjoying market power in the narrow sense.[25] For example, many shops price discriminate in favour of students or the elderly without conceivably holding a dominant position.)[26]

Discriminatory pricing policies can be categorised as follows[27]:   **1–006**

---

[19] See paras 1–015 to 1–016 below.

[20] See Carlton & Perloff, *Modern Industrial Organization* (4th edn, Addison-Wesley, 2005), p.294 and, for a more detailed account, ABA Section of Antitrust Law, *Econometrics* (ABA Publishing, 2005), Ch.X.

[21] See generally ABA Section of Antitrust Law, *Market Power Handbook* (ABA Publishing, 2005); Areeda, Hovenkamp & Solow, *Antitrust Law* (2nd edn, Aspen Law & Business, 2000), Vol.IIA, s.5A; Werden, "Demand Elasticities in Antitrust Analysis" (1998) 66 *Antitrust Law Journal* 363, pp.370 and 371; Daskin & Wu, "Observations on the Multiple Dimensions of Market Power", *Antitrust*, Summer 2005, p.53; and the Canadian Merger Guidelines, 2004 (*www.competitionbureau.gc.ca/PDFs/2004%20MEGs.Final.pdf*), para.2.3. The expression "market power" is generally used in the wide sense by economists and the narrow sense for competition policy purposes.

[22] The use of the perfectly competitive level as a benchmark does not imply that perfect competition is a desirable outcome for the market (see para.1–016 below). In applying systems of merger control, the use of benchmarks can commonly be avoided by comparing the position following the merger with the pre-merger situation.

[23] Areeda, Hovenkamp & Solow, *Antitrust Law* (2nd edn, Aspen Law & Business, 2000), Vol.IIA, para.501, note that "Market power exists in degrees ... For antitrust purposes ..., market power is the ability (1) to price substantially above the competitive level *and* (2) to persist in doing so for a significant period without erosion by new entry or expansion". The US Horizontal Merger Guidelines, 1992 (amended in 1997) (*www.usdoj.gov/atr/public/guidelines/hmg.htm*), para.0.1, state that "Market power to a seller is the ability profitably to maintain prices above competitive levels for a significant period of time". See also ABA Section of Antitrust Law, *Market Power Handbook* (ABA Publishing, 2005), p.1.

[24] See s.2.4(e) below for discussion of the meaning of "dominance".

[25] Areeda, Hovenkamp & Solow, *Antitrust Law* (2nd edn, Aspen Law & Business, 2000), Vol.IIA, para.517, note that "price discrimination seldom shows the amount of market power, and many instances of price discrimination are quite consistent with robust but imperfect competition. As a result, price discrimination evidence has very limited utility for proving power." For discussion of mechanisms for identifying price discrimination with market power in the narrow sense, see CRA, "Price Discrimination—An Unreliable Indicator of Market Power" (*www.crai.com/.%5Cpubs%5Cpub_3343.pdf*).

[26] See Phlips, *The Economics of Price Discrimination* (Cambridge UP, 1981), p.16.

[27] See Cabral, *Introduction to Industrial Organization* (The MIT Press, 2000), pp.169 and 170; Carlton & Perloff, *Modern Industrial Organization* (4th edn, Addison-Wesley, 2005), pp.299, 303, 313 and 314; and Shapiro & Varian, *Information Rules: A Strategic Guide to the New Economy* (Harvard Business School Press, 1999), p.39. Note that economists use "second-degree" and "third-degree" price discrimination in different ways. Carlton & Perloff define second-degree price discrimination as charging different customers different prices without knowing the demands of each individual customer. Others define second-degree price discrimination as arising when different prices are charged depending on the quantity purchased.

(a) First-degree price discrimination or *personalised* pricing involves charging *each* customer the maximum amount which that customer is willing to pay.

(b) Second-degree price discrimination or *versioning*[28] involves allowing customers to *self-select* between different offerings. For example, suppliers of mobile telephony services in the United Kingdom offer a wide range of packages to customers, suppliers of books delay the release of cheaper paperback books to protect hardback sales, and films are shown in cinemas before they are released on DVD. Such discrimination is based on non-observable characteristics.

(c) Third-degree price discrimination or *group pricing* involves charging *different groups* of customers different prices. In this case, the *seller* makes the selection based on customer indicators, for example, discounts for students or the elderly or charging different prices in different territories. Such discrimination is based on observable characteristics. When third-degree price discrimination is used, sellers seek to charge higher prices in segments with lower price sensitivity.

A producer seeks to price discriminate in order to capture some or all of the consumer surplus. In other words, those customers who place relatively greater value on the goods are required to pay more. The advantage to the producer of price discrimination is that it can raise the price for some customers without losing the business of other customers who continue to purchase at lower prices.[29]

1–007 This can be illustrated[30] with reference to *two-part tariffs* under which a

---

[28] For a summary of product dimensions susceptible to versioning, see Shapiro & Varian, Information Rules: A Strategic Guide to the New Economy (Harvard Business School Press, 1999), p.62.

[29] See also the discussion of Ramsey pricing in Carlton & Perloff, *Modern Industrial Organization* (4th edn, Addison-Wesley, 2005), p.702.

[30] Other examples of price discrimination include the following.

(a) *Quantity discounts*—for example, "buy one get one free" or reductions for large purchases. (Such differences may be objectively justified with reference to cost.)

(b) *Voucher discounts*—US department stores commonly advertise in regional newspapers by printing vouchers offering reductions for customers shopping several days after the date of publication of the newspaper. The rationale is that price-sensitive customers will cut out the vouchers and shop when the vouchers are redeemable, whereas customers who are less sensitive to price will make more spontaneous shopping decisions. Similarly, in the UK, discounts frequently involve collecting large numbers of tokens from newspapers or product packages, which deters the money-rich but not the time-rich customer.

(c) *Quality discrimination*—airlines offer first, business and economy class seats. Similarly, some suppliers disable particular features on a product in order to sell *damaged goods* at lower prices. (For examples, see Cabral, *Introduction to Industrial Organization* (The MIT Press, 2000), pp.176 and 177). The rationale is to distinguish customers who are willing to pay a premium price for a premium product.

(d) *Trade-in discounts*—some software producers offer substantial discounts to customers who "trade-in" licences to use preceding versions of the programme.

(e) *Peak-load pricing*—charging more for use at peak-time (e.g. telephone charges, train tickets). (In many cases the products are in different antitrust markets because they fall into different temporal markets: see s.3.10 below.)

customer must pay a fixed fee, irrespective of consumption, and a variable fee proportional to consumption. For example, many utilities companies charge a fixed "connection" fee in addition to charges for usage. A monopolist charging a single price will restrict output below the perfectly competitive level (i.e. the level where price is set at marginal cost) in order to maximise profits.[31] If the monopolist can use a two-part tariff, then its profit-maximising strategy (leaving to one side the practicability of implementation) is to extract the consumer surplus using the fixed component of the charges and maximise sales by increasing output until the price of the variable component is equal to the marginal cost of production. This is illustrated in Fig.1.2 (see below) where a monopolist not engaging in price discrimination would charge P_1, corresponding to a consumption of Q_1; but an optimal[32] two-part tariff would involve charging a fixed component, raising the sums identified in the shaded area (i.e. extracting the entirety of the consumer surplus which would have arisen had a single price been set at P_2),[33] and a variable component at P_2, where P_2 is equal to marginal cost.[34] This results in the same output as in a perfectly competitive market[35] but eliminates all consumer surplus (whereas in the case of a monopoly which does not price discriminate, consumer surplus is the area above P_1 but below the demand curve).[36]

(b) Total welfare

Total welfare takes account not only of the interests of consumers but also **1–008** producers. Producer welfare is commonly assessed using the concept of *producer surplus*, which measures producers' gains from trade, *i.e.* the gains from selling goods in the market compared with making no sales. It is the difference between the sums which would have induced producers to supply the product and the sums they actually receive. Fig.1.1 above shows a

---

(f) *Tying*—when a purchaser of one good is required to purchase a second in circumstances in which the first and second goods may be consumed in variable proportions. For example, a manufacturer of packaging systems may require customers purchasing the system to buy containers from that supplier.

(g) *Pure bundling*—when two goods are sold as a single package but not separately.

(h) *Mixed bundling*—when two goods are sold as a package *and* are sold separately, for

[31] See para.1–016.

[32] In practice, it is very difficult to extract the entirety of the consumer surplus through a fixed charge, as the fixed charge needs to be higher for those customers who place relatively greater value on consumption of the product.

[33] This implies that the fixed component varies depending on customers' willingness to pay.

[34] For further discussion, see Cabral, *Introduction to Industrial Organization* (The MIT Press, 2000), p.173.

[35] See para.1–009 below for a discussion of allocative efficiency.

[36] For a more detailed discussion of the pros and cons of price discrimination, see Cabral, *Introduction to Industrial Organization* (The MIT Press, 2000), pp.180 to 183 and Phlips, *The Economics of Price Discrimination* (Cambridge UP, 1981), especially pp.1 to 19.

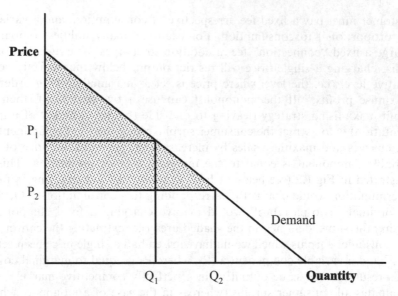

Fig.1.2: Two-part tariffs and consumer surplus

normal upward-sloping industry supply curve,[37] i.e. at low prices there is low supply of the product but, as price increases, supply increases. Assume that the market price is P_1 and market demand Q_1.[38] The producer surplus is the area above the supply curve but below the market price, OP_1E. *Total surplus* is the sum of consumer and producer surplus. *Total welfare* takes account of total surplus and consumer choice and innovation.[39]

(c) Efficiency

1–009 There are numerous categories of efficiencies but the four principal ones are allocative, productive, dynamic and transactional.[40]

Allocative efficiency arises when suppliers produce goods and services that consumers want, as evidenced by their willingness to pay. More formally, it arises in a trading relationship when the value of the product to consumers at the margin is equal to the value of the resources expended in supplying the product, i.e. when prices could not be reduced and output could not be increased without producers making economic losses.[41]

---

[37] A *supply curve* shows how producers' willingness to provide a product or service varies depending on its price.

[38] The graph illustrates a perfectly competitive market: see paras 1–015 to 1–016 below.

[39] See para.1–003 above.

[40] For a taxonomy of efficiencies, see the Appendix to Kolasky & Dick, "The Merger Guidelines and the Integration of Efficiencies into Antitrust Review of Horizontal Mergers", 2002 (available at *www.usdoj.gov/atr/hmerger/11254.pdf*). See also Areeda, Hovenkamp & Solow, *Antitrust Law* (2nd edn, Aspen Law & Business, 2000), Vol.IIA, para.402b.

[41] A "Pareto improvement" can be made if someone can be made better off without someone else being made worse off. When no Pareto improvements are possible a situation is described as "Pareto efficient".

Productive efficiency arises when actual production cost is at its lowest achievable level. In other words, productive efficiency occurs when the factors of production (machinery, labour and raw materials) could not be reorganised to increase the output of at least one product whilst keeping the output of all other products constant. If a producer is not subject to external competitive pressures (for example, from rival suppliers, potential entrants or its customers) it may not need to minimise costs and maximise profits in order to survive and, as a result, *X-inefficiency* or organisational slack can creep in. X-inefficiency, which involves a failure to make optimal use of resources, is a form of productive inefficiency.[42]

Dynamic efficiency includes technical change (leading to improvements over time in products and production techniques) and learning-by-doing (when unit costs decline with cumulative output because the producer has greater experience of the production process).

Transactional efficiency reflects the extent to which the costs of purchasing can be reduced. Transaction costs tend to be high when opportunistic behaviour is likely (for example if a company is dependent on a monopoly supplier of an essential input) and/or extensive coordination is required between the parties to a cooperative agreement (e.g. certain joint ventures). Transactional efficiencies constitute the broadest of the four categories of efficiencies and commonly facilitate companies' efforts to achieve allocative, productive and dynamic efficiencies.[43]

(d) Analysis of criteria

There are several points to note about the three criteria for assessing market **1–010** performance identified in para.1–002 above.[44] First, they are inter-connected. In particular, in order to achieve allocative efficiency, it is necessary to maximise the sum of consumer and producer surplus, otherwise both producers and consumers could be made better off by redistributing resources to produce the welfare-maximising outcome and dividing the increased surplus. Further, the connection between innovation (an aspect of consumer welfare) and dynamic efficiency is obvious. Equally, an improvement in productive efficiency may lead to more and/or better goods and services, i.e. an enhancement in consumer welfare.[45]

---

[42] For a discussion of X-inefficiency, see Martin, *Advanced Industrial Economics* (2nd edn, Blackwell, 2002), pp.392 to 399.

[43] See Kolasky & Dick, "The Merger Guidelines and the Integration of Efficiencies into Antitrust Review of Horizontal Mergers", 2002, Appendix (available at *www.usdoj.gov/atr/hmerger/11254.pdf*).

[44] The determination of particular cases is also influenced by the antitrust authority's choices between competing economic theories; see generally Areeda & Hovenkamp, *Antitrust Law* (2nd edn, Aspen Law & Business, 2000), Vol.1, para.112d.

[45] Vickers commented in a speech to the Social Market Foundation, "Competition is for Consumers", February 21, 2002 (*www.oft.gov.uk/News/Speeches + and + articles/2002/index.htm*): "Productivity, like competition, is not an end in itself, but a means of promoting the goal of the economic well being of the public. Higher productivity means more / better goods and services—so more consumer satisfaction—for the same input of effort ... So higher productivity is desirable precisely because it serves the public".

Secondly, the policy choice in administering a system of merger control between a consumer welfare and a total welfare standard may have important implications for the efficiency of the economy. Imagine a system that prohibits mergers if they have *any* detrimental effect on consumer welfare. A transaction that would lead to small price rises in a minor market (totalling, say, £10,000) would, on this criterion, be blocked even if it led to cost savings to the merging parties of, say, £10 million.

Thirdly, there may be trade-offs between the components of consumer welfare. In particular, increasing consumer choice and innovation may reduce value for money. Imagine a technology-driven market with five suppliers each holding market shares of 20 per cent. A merger between two of the suppliers may enable the merged group to combine research and development expertise leading to the development of new products (i.e. increasing *consumer choice* and facilitating *innovation*) but it is equally plausible that the merger will result in price increases and therefore reductions in *value for money*. Similarly, product differentiation (which is *capable* of increasing *consumer choice*) is associated with an ability to increase prices,[46] which may involve reductions in *value for money*.

1–011   Fourthly, the effects of price discrimination are ambiguous.[47] Taking first-degree price discrimination[48] as a paradigm,[49] it is clear that a monopolist practising first-degree price discrimination will produce the same output as a perfectly competitive industry and the performance of the two markets, measured solely in terms of allocative efficiency[50] or total surplus, will therefore be identical. By contrast, first-degree price discrimination eliminates *all* consumer surplus and market performance would therefore be regarded as problematic if judged against the consumer welfare criterion. But it is noteworthy that all consumers who were willing to pay a price at or in excess of the perfectly competitive price have made purchases in this scenario and none would have done so unless they perceived there was at least a marginal benefit from trading. By contrast, in the case of a monopoly with a restricted output charging a single market price, consumer surplus is not eliminated but the output restriction means that those customers who were not willing to pay the monopoly price but were willing to pay a price at least equal to the perfectly competitive market price did not trade. This raises the question of whether, in assessing the value for money element of consumer welfare in cases of price discrimination, it is more important to

---

[46] Porter, *Competitive Advantage* (The Free Press, 1998 edn), p.11, identifies two basic types of sustainable competitive advantage, i.e. low cost or differentiation.
[47] See generally Cooper, Froeb, O'Brien and Tschantz, "Does Price Discrimination Intensify Competition? Implications for Antitrust" (2005) 72 *Antitrust Law Journal* 327.
[48] See para.1–006 above.
[49] First degree price discrimination is rarely observed in practice.
[50] See para.1–009 above.

examine whether output is maintained (or increased) or consumer surplus[51] maximised.[52]

Fifthly, some commentators[53] argue that consumer welfare is affected by producer welfare since many consumers own shares directly or, through pension funds and the like, indirectly and, other things being equal, an increase in producer surplus would be likely to lead to an increase in share price. This argument seeks to collapse the distinction between consumer surplus and producer surplus and is sometimes used to resist arguments that consumer welfare should be used as the criterion in appraising market performance.

1.3 THE EFFECTS OF MERGERS ON MARKET PERFORMANCE

One of the basic premises of merger control[54] is that the *structure* of the **1–012** market has an effect on the *conduct* of participants and ultimately on market performance.[55] An historic view[56] has been that there is a one-way chain of causation from the *structure* of the market (the number of producers active in the market, barriers to entry, cost structures, product differentiation, etc.) to the *conduct* of the producers in that market (in terms of pricing and output decisions, advertising and product differentiation, research and development, collusion, etc.) to the *performance* of the market (consumer welfare, total welfare, efficiency and firm profitability). It is now clear that the chain of causation is not just one-way as there are *feedback* effects from *conduct* to *structure*—in particular producers may be able to eliminate competitors through predatory pricing or tying, or reduce or eliminate the

---

[51] In Case COMP/M.2187 *CVC / Lenzing* [2004] O.J. L82/20 the Commission found, at para.182, that a merger created or strengthened a dominant position because it would enable the merged group to engage in price discrimination.

[52] Consumer surplus is almost impossible to measure because it is only rarely possible to esti-mate the demand curve. By contrast, output is clearly measurable (even if predicting the effects of mergers on output is far from straightforward).

[53] e.g. Varian, *Intermediate Microeconomics: A Modern Approach* (5th edn, W W Norton & Co, 1999), p.257.

[54] All systems of merger control proceed on the basis of a number of premises. Indeed, Bork in *The Antitrust Paradox* (1993 edn, The Free Press, 1978), p.3, went so far as to describe antitrust as a subcategory of ideology.

[55] See generally Scherer & Ross, *Industrial Market Structure and Economic Performance* (3rd edn, Houghton Mifflin Co, 1990), pp.4 to 7; Viscusi, Vernon & Harrington, *Economics of Regulation and Antitrust* (3rd edn, The MIT Press, 2000), pp.63 to 67; Carlton & Perloff, *Modern Industrial Organization* (4th edn, Addison-Wesley, 2005), pp.2 to 4 and Ch.8; Areeda, Hovenkamp & Solow, *Antitrust Law* (2nd edn, Aspen Law & Business, 1998), Vol.IV, para.930c; Cabral, *Introduction to Industrial Organization* (The MIT Press, 2000), p.156; and Martin, *Advanced Industrial Economics* (2nd edn, Blackwell, 2002), pp.119 and 121. The premise is basic to merger control because, without it, there would be no basis for intervening in the merger process (i.e. on the occasion of proposed structural change) in order to influence market performance.

[56] See, e.g. Bain, *Barriers to New Competition* (Harvard UP, 1956).

scope for new entry by investing heavily in advertising, excess capacity or research and development. Accordingly, the recent focus of industrial economists has been on modelling the operation of markets with particular characteristics—particularly but not exclusively using game theory[57]—rather than pursuing a rigid structure-conduct-performance analysis. However, these alternative analyses routinely include structural variables, such as the number of suppliers in the market, as important predictors of market performance, corroborating the broad contention that market structure ultimately affects performance.

Mergers may generate efficiencies (see s.(a) below) and may create or enhance market power (see s.(b) below). The possible trade-off between efficiency and market power is discussed in s.(c) below.

(a) Efficiencies

1–013 The efficiencies which may be generated by mergers are considered in detail in Ch.18 and the following list is therefore illustrative.

(a) Mergers may improve *allocative efficiency* by eliminating the "double marginalisation" problem. This arises when the output of a monopoly is used as an input by an independently controlled downstream monopoly. As each successive monopoly seeks to maximise its profits by reducing output to establish high prices, the end result is a double restriction of output. If the two monopolies merge, there will only be a single restriction of output and total output will be increased, leading to an improvement in allocative efficiency.[58]

(b) Mergers commonly improve *productive efficiency* through economies of scale (reductions in average cost as output is increased) or economies of scope (cost savings arising from producing different products together).

(c) *Dynamic efficiencies* may arise, e.g. through the combination of research and development expertise or learning-by-doing.

(d) Finally, *transactional efficiencies* may be attained by purchasing an upstream monopoly supplier which, prior to the merger, had an incentive to engage in opportunistic behaviour, or by combining research and development activities which, if carried out under a joint arrangement, would have been difficult to coordinate.

---

[57] See paras 6–005 and 6–006 below.
[58] See paras 11–008 and 11–009 below.

(b) Market power

On the other hand,[59] mergers may[60] create or enhance market power.[61] There **1–014** are two types of market power. First, *original market power* is the direct ability of a company (either alone or by tacitly coordinating[62] with other suppliers) to increase price or reduce quality, variety or innovation significantly relative to the competitive level for a substantial period. The most common form of original market power arises when a company is able profitably to restrict output significantly and therefore increase prices in the light of its substantial market share and the limited constraint posed by actual and potential rivals and its customers. Secondly, *exclusionary market power* is the ability of a company to exclude or marginalise one or more of its competitors from the market thereby enabling it, as a result of the weakening of the competitive constraints imposed by rivals, to increase price or reduce quality, variety or innovation significantly relative to the competitive level for a substantial period. The existence of market power may prevent the market, through the process of competition, from ensuring that social resources are efficiently allocated and consumer and total welfare maximised.

Much of the remainder of this book is devoted to determining whether a merger will create or enhance original or exclusionary market power. For the purposes of illustrating the trade-off between efficiency and market power, this section contrasts the text-book economic models of perfect competition and monopoly and, since the vast majority of mergers occur in oligopolistic markets, provides an overview of the key predictions of two of the principal models of oligopoly, the Cournot and Bertrand models.

(i) Perfect competition and monopoly contrasted A system of *perfect com-* **1–015** *petition* exists when each supplier assumes that the market price is independent of its own level of output.[63] A perfectly competitive market is shown diagrammatically in Fig.1.3 below.

---

[59] See generally Areeda, Hovenkamp & Solow, *Antitrust Law* (2nd edn, Aspen Law & Business, 2000), Vol.IIA, s.5A.

[60] The UK Office of Fair Trading's Substantive Merger Guidelines, May 2003 (*www.oft.gov.uk*), para.3.6, note that "some mergers are either pro-competitive (because they positively enhance levels of rivalry) or are competitively neutral".

[61] In this context, "market power" is used in its narrow sense as meaning the ability to price significantly above the competitive level for a substantial period (see para.1–005 above).

[62] See Ch.8.

[63] Varian, *Intermediate Microeconomics: A Modern Approach* (5th edn, W W Norton & Co, 1999). The assumptions underlying the model of perfect competition are sometimes spelled out in more detail (see, e.g. Carlton & Perloff, *Modern Industrial Organization* (4th edn, Addison-Wesley, 2005), p.57):

    (a)   all companies supply *homogenous* goods, so that customers regard goods supplied by one company as perfect substitutes for those supplied by another;

    (b)   there is *perfect information*, i.e. customers and suppliers have all relevant knowledge about the operation of the market, including the prices at which goods and services are being sold;

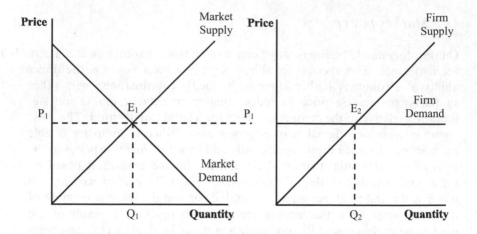

Fig.1.3: A Perfectly Competitive Market

The market price is set by the intersection of the market supply[64] and market demand[65] curves.[66] Since each supplier is small relative to the total size of the market, none is able to increase the market price by decreasing its output and each therefore faces a horizontal *firm* demand curve. The economic model is important because perfect competition results in allocative efficiency, in the sense that producers would make economic losses if prices were reduced or output increased.[67] The efficient outcome occurs when the market price is equal to the cost incurred by producers in making the

---

(c)   there are no *transaction costs*, i.e. customers and suppliers do not incur costs (such as the payment of fees or the expenditure of time, which has an economic value) through participating in the market;

(d)   the companies active in the market are *price takers*, i.e. they can sell at or below the prevailing market price or not at all; in this sense, each company faces a horizontal own demand curve; and

(e)   there is *freedom of entry and exit* into the market, i.e. if the market price were to rise so that suppliers could earn economic profits (i.e. returns above the opportunity cost of investing), then companies would enter the market until those economic profits were eliminated. The opportunity cost of investing includes an element of accounting profit to reflect the fact that, had the resources been invested elsewhere, they could have been used to generate a return.

[64] In general, the supply curves for a market and a company slope upwards, reflecting the fact that suppliers are incentivised to increase output if the market price increases.

[65] In general, the demand curve for a *market* is downward sloping, reflecting the fact that customer demand falls as price rises. A company's demand curve (sometimes described as a *residual demand curve*) will be horizontal if the company has no market power and therefore cannot raise its price even slightly without losing all of its customers—this is characteristic of a *perfectly competitive market*. More commonly, a company's demand curve is downward sloping, reflecting the fact that the company has some scope to raise price without losing all of its customers—this is characteristic of companies operating in *monopoly*, *oligopoly* and *monopolistically competitive* markets.

[66] This is the *equilibrium* point, i.e. the point at which each of the economic agents is choosing the best action for itself and each agent's actions are consistent with all other agents' actions.

[67] This would lead to exit from the market.

14

marginal or final unit of output.[68] A perfectly competitive market also maximizes total surplus, namely the sum of consumer surplus and producer surplus as shown in Fig.1.1 above.

In reality, there are few perfectly competitive markets.[69] Their rarity is no **1–016** bad thing because markets which are characterised by significant economies of scale would suffer from substantial productive inefficiency if all output were supplied by companies whose output was so small that they were unable to exercise any influence over the market price. As Bork observed, "A determined attempt to remake the American economy into a replica of the textbook model of competition would have roughly the same effect on national wealth as several dozen strategically placed nuclear explosions."[70]

The polar opposite of the model of perfect competition is the *monopoly* model.[71] This exists when a single producer faces no competition and is able to fix price or output.[72] In monopoly markets a company's own demand curve *is* the market demand curve. In general, the market demand curve is downward-sloping. This is shown in Fig.1.4 below. It has the consequence that the supplier's *marginal revenue*[73] curve also slopes downwards but with a gradient that is twice as steep.[74] The gradient is steeper because each additional (or marginal) unit sold results in *increased* revenue from the sale of that unit but also *decreases* revenue from the sales of *other* units, as the

---

[68] It should, however, be emphasised that producers are rarely, if ever, able to plot their marginal cost curve on a graph: see Bork, *The Antitrust Paradox* (1993 edn, The Free Press, 1978), p.126.

[69] The typical example is agricultural produce, such as wheat.

[70] Bork, *The Antitrust Paradox* (1993 edn, The Free Press, 1978), p.92. For discussion of "second best" problems see Areeda, Hovenkamp & Solow, *Antitrust Law* (2nd edn, Aspen Law & Business, 2000), Vol.IIA, para.412.

[71] Economic monopolies tend to arise following government grants of exclusive rights or through intellectual property rights.

[72] This may involve setting the price at a level above the perfectly competitive level.

[73] The following *revenues* may be distinguished.

(a) *Total revenue*—if all output is sold at the same price, total revenues are calculated by multiplying sales by price.

(b) *Marginal revenue*—which is the revenue generated by the sale of the last unit of output. In markets in which the decision to increase output does not affect the market price (in particular in a perfectly competitive market in which a company faces a horizontal demand curve), marginal revenue is equal to the market price. In markets in which companies face downward-sloping individual demand curves, the calculation is more complicated. If there is a single market price (i.e. if the company cannot sell its output at different prices to different customers), then the effect of increasing output will be to reduce the market price, with the result that the marginal revenue will comprise the sums received for the sale of the additional unit of output less the reduction in sums received for the sale of all other units of output arising from the fall in market price. The concept of marginal revenue is crucial because a profit-maximising company will seek to increase its output for so long as the marginal revenue is greater than the marginal cost; but when marginal revenue is equal to marginal cost, the company is operating at its profit-maximising output. It should be noted that firms are rarely aware of their marginal cost curves but, since the profit-maximising strategy is to produce the output which equates marginal cost and marginal revenue, it is assumed that companies strive to achieve this result using the performance indicators which are available to them.

[74] This applies assuming that the demand function is linear. See Shy, *Industrial Organization* (The MIT Press, 1995), p.52.

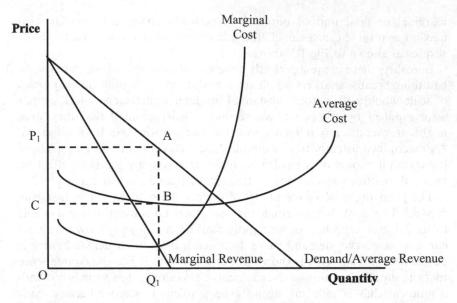

Fig. 1.4: Monopoly

price of *all* units must be reduced in order to induce the marginal customer to purchase. A profit-maximising company will set its output at the level, Q_1, where marginal revenue is equal to marginal cost[75]: the firm has an

---

[75] A cost function is the minimum cost of achieving a specified level of output. The following *costs* faced by a company may be distinguished:

(a) *Total costs*—all costs incurred by a company during the period under analysis, i.e. the sum of fixed and variable costs.

(b) *Fixed costs*—those costs which do not vary with output in the short run (i.e. the period of time in which at least one input is not variable) and must be paid whether or not the firm produces any output. The question of whether costs are fixed or not depends on the period under analysis (e.g. if the company's lease requires one year's notice of termination then rental payments are fixed over a one year period) and the circumstances of the company (and costs which are fixed for one company may be variable for another, e.g. if the period of notice in contracts of employment is longer in one than the other). Costs may be semi-fixed, i.e. fixed over certain ranges of output but variable over other ranges (e.g. a company may be able to deliver 100 units per week using a single van but increasing deliveries beyond 100 units may require investment in a second van). In the long run, all costs are variable.

(c) *Variable costs*—those costs which change with the company's level of output, i.e. costs which would be zero if output were zero. Categorisation of costs as fixed or variable may be difficult, e.g. maintenance may have fixed and variable components.

(d) *Marginal costs*—the additional costs incurred in producing one additional unit of output. (More generally, marginal cost measures a *rate of change*, namely the change in costs associated with a specific change in output.) Marginal costs typically fall initially as output is increased but later rise as *diminishing returns* are obtained (i.e. if more and more of a variable factor of production is added to a fixed factor or factors, eventually the increase in output caused by the addition of the last unit of the variable factor will begin to decline).

(e) *Avoidable costs*—costs, including fixed costs, which are not incurred if operations cease (e.g. if a lease is assigned to a third party). In other words, avoidable costs are the opposite of *sunk costs* and, in deciding how to act, a company should focus on its avoidable costs as it can do nothing to influence its sunk costs.

incentive to continue to increase output for so long as marginal revenue exceeds marginal cost, as the increase will be profitable. Market price, P_1, is identified by reading up from the output, Q_1, to the demand curve. Profit is shown by the box P_1ABC (i.e. the difference between price and average cost multiplied by output).

Fig.1.5 below, compares consumer welfare and total welfare in monopoly **1–017** and perfect competition. Assume that a monopolist's marginal revenue equals its marginal cost at output Q_2, which is below that under perfect competition, Q_1. The prevailing price at output Q_2 is read off the demand curve and, at P_2, is higher than P_1, which would be set in a perfectly competitive market at the intersection of market demand and supply curves. This means that monopoly is characterised by a restriction of output relative to a perfectly competitive market. The reason why monopolists have an incentive to reduce output is that by doing so they can raise market price and increase their profits (bearing in mind that increasing output reduces revenue across *all* sales and not just sales of the marginal product). This means that monopoly results in allocative inefficiency and lower levels of consumer welfare than perfect competition.

Monopoly also results in a *deadweight welfare loss*. This is illustrated in **1–018** Fig.1.5 below, which shows consumer surplus, XP_2Y (which is lower than in perfect competition because the price is higher and output lower) and producer surplus, $0P_2YZ$. The shaded area, YZE, is welfare which is not enjoyed by either consumers or producers and is therefore lost: this is the deadweight welfare loss.

Monopoly is also associated with other forms of inefficiency. First, *X-inefficiency*[76] arises when the producer, lacking the discipline of competition, fails to make the optimal use of its resources, reflecting the adage that the "best of all monopoly profits is a quiet life".[77] Secondly, companies in competitive markets often learn from their competitors and use their competitors as comparators to measure achievements. Monopolists lack this facility, which may result in inefficiency.[78] Thirdly, monopoly profits may result in *rent-seeking* by companies which expend resources seeking to obtain or create monopolies in circumstances in which there is no welfare gain from such expenditure.[79]

These observations are the foundation-stone of the justification for the

---

It is common to refer to *average* total costs, average fixed costs and average variable costs. In general, a firm's average total costs determine whether it produces and its marginal costs determine how much it produces.

[76] Scherer & Ross, *Industrial Market Structure and Economic Performance* (3rd edn, Houghton Mifflin Co, 1990), pp.668 to 672.

[77] JR Hicks, "Annual Survey of Economic Theory: The Theory of Monopoly" (January 1935) Vol.3, *Econometrica*, p.8.

[78] Carlton & Perloff, *Modern Industrial Organization* (4th edn, Addison-Wesley, 2005), p.94.

[79] Posner, *Antitrust Law* (2nd edn, The University of Chicago Press, 2001), pp.13 and 14. See also Varian, *Intermediate Microeconomics: A Modern Approach* (5th edn, W W Norton & Co, 1999), p.407.

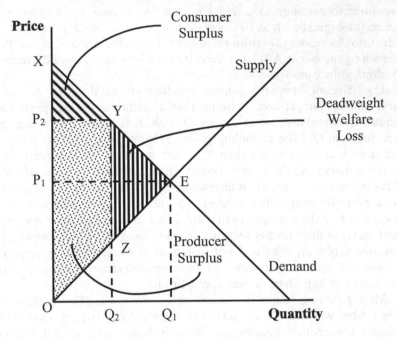

Fig. 1.5: Economic Welfare in Monopoly and Perfect Competition

use of merger control (and other aspects of competition law) to promote competition over monopoly.[80]

1–019 **(ii) Oligopoly** In reality, merger control authorities review few transactions involving mergers between firms operating in perfectly competitive markets or involving merger to monopoly. Most mergers occur in *oligopolistic* markets, i.e. markets with limited numbers of suppliers, each of which can exercise some influence over the market price but none of which can determine the market price.[81] Oligopolistic markets differ from markets characterised by perfect competition or monopoly[82] in that each producer's

---

[80] On the other hand, monopoly may generate efficiencies, e.g. when the minimum efficient scale of a business is larger than market demand.

[81] There is a great deal of economic research into the question why certain industries (e.g. salt) are highly concentrated in most markets around the world. See, for example, Sutton, *Sunk Costs and Market Structure: Price Competition, Advertising, and the Evolution of Concentration* (The MIT Press, 1991).

[82] The key distinction between oligopolistic markets and monopolistically competitive markets is that in the former there is assumed not to be freedom of entry and exit which is present in the latter. Oligopolistic markets and markets characterised by perfect competition or monopoly differ in that in oligopolistic markets, each producer's decisions affect the market outcome not only for itself but also its competitors; and commensurately, in taking its market decisions, a producer has to factor in the consequences of decisions taken or to be taken by its competitors, i.e. there is a situation of interdependence or *strategic interaction*. The interaction which characterises oligopoly makes it more difficult to model the way in which oligopolistic

decisions affect the market outcome not only for itself but also its competitors. Commensurately, in taking its market decisions, a producer in an oligopolistic market has to factor in the consequences of decisions taken or to be taken by its competitors, i.e. there is a situation of interdependence or *strategic interaction*. There are numerous economic models of oligopoly, but the most prominent are Cournot's and Bertrand's.

The *Cournot model*[83] of oligopoly proceeds on the basis that each producer makes its *output* decisions (i.e. sets quantities) at the same time as other producers and seeks to maximise its profits in the light of *predictions* of the quantities others will produce. This means that rather than focusing on its own demand curve (which is uncertain because it will be affected by the output decisions of its competitors), the Cournot oligopolist focuses on its *reaction function* or *best-response function*, which describes its best (i.e. most profitable) output decision given different output decisions of its competitors.[84] In a duopoly, both producers' reaction functions (i.e. the quantities produced for given quantities produced by the competitor) can be plotted diagrammatically, as shown in Fig.1.6 below. This shows that as the output produced by one company increases, the profit-maximising output of the second falls, reflecting the fact that it is generally profitable to restrict industry output below the competitive level. The *equilibrium* in this model is the point at which the reaction functions intersect. This is because each producer will predict that the other will produce the quantity relating to the intersection point as this is the *best response* to the other's output decision.

The model predicts that each producer will limit its output to an extent, **1–020** resulting in a market price which is above the perfectly competitive level, but that each producer will produce more than the output which, aggregated to form an industry output, would be the monopoly (and therefore joint profit-maximising) output. This is because each producer is concerned only about its own profits and not those of the industry. In Fig.1.6 below, the monopoly output is shown by the *imaginary* straight line XY[85] (which joins the outputs that each would produce if its rival produced nothing) and the perfectly competitive output by the *imaginary* straight line WZ[86] (which joins the outputs of each which would lead the rival supplier to produce nothing). The Cournot equilibrium, Q_AQ_B, lies between the imaginary lines, reflecting

---

markets operate because producers have conflicting incentives—if all restrict output then the market price (and economic profits across the industry) will be higher; but if market price is above the level of perfect competition, then each producer has an incentive to increase its individual output as doing so will generally increase its sales and profits in the period in question.

[83] See in particular Scherer & Ross, *Industrial Market Structure and Economic Performance* (3rd edn, Houghton Mifflin Co, 1990), pp.200 and 201 and Viscusi, Vernon & Harrington, Economics of Regulation and Antitrust (3rd edn, The MIT Press, 2000), pp.102 to 108.

[84] This can be plotted by identifying total market demand and calculating the profit-maximising output for each residual demand curve (the residual demand curve shifts towards the origin as the conjectured output of the rival is increased). See Martin, *Advanced Industrial Economics* (2nd edn, Blackwell, 2002), pp.14 and 15.

[85] i.e. a line not shown in Fig.1.6.

[86] i.e. a line not shown in Fig.1.6.

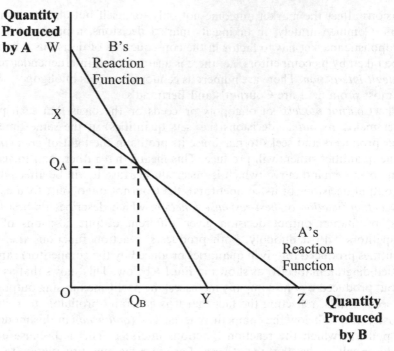

Fig. 1.6: Reaction Functions in a Cournot Duopoly

an output which exceeds the monopoly output but falls short of the perfectly competitive output.[87]

The Cournot model is particularly apposite when suppliers compete to install sunk productive capacity[88] or, more generally, when suppliers must make production decisions in advance and face high costs in holding inventories.[89]

---

[87] See generally Martin, *Advanced Industrial Economics* (2nd edn, Blackwell, 2002), pp.15 to 17.
[88] Shapiro, "Theories of Oligopoly Behaviour", in *Handbook of Industrial Organization* (Schmalensee & Willig, edns, 1989), Vol.1, p.329 at 351, comments: "The choice between a pricing game and a quantity game cannot be made on a priori grounds. Rather, one must fashion theory in a particular industry to reflect the technology of production and exchange in that industry. For example, competition via sealed bids between firms without capacity constraints fits the Bertrand model quite nicely, whereas competition to install sunk productive capacity corresponds to Cournot". Similarly, Varian comments in *Microeconomic Analysis* (3rd edn, W W Norton & Co, 1992), at p.301: "The Cournot model seems appropriate when quantities can only be adjusted slowly. This is especially appealing when 'quantity' is interpreted as 'capacity'. The idea is that each firm chooses, in secret, a production capacity, realizing that once the capacity is chosen they will compete on price—i.e. play a Bertrand game". The Bertrand model is discussed in para.1–022 below.
[89] See Besanko, Dranove & Shanley, *Economics of Strategy* (2nd edn, John Wiley & Sons Inc, 2000), pp.255 and 256: "In such settings, prices will adjust more quickly than quantities, and each firm will set a price that lets it sell all that it produces. Under these circumstances, each firm expects that its competitors will instantaneously match any price change that the firm might make, so that competitors can keep their sales equal to their planned production volumes. Thus, if a firm lowers its price, it cannot expect to steal customers from its rivals." See also Ivaldi *et al*, "The Economics of Unilateral Effects", 2003, Interim Report for

The Cournot model draws a strong correlation between the number of **1–021** producers in the industry and the market price: as the number of producers falls, the market price increases towards the monopoly level. Conversely, as the number of producers rises, the market price falls towards the perfectly competitive level (so long as there are no economies of scale).[90] Indeed, when all firms have the same marginal costs and market shares, the Cournot model draws a direct correlation between market price and market concentration as measured by the Herfindahl-Hirschman Index.[91] The model therefore has two implications of general importance. First, it identifies a direct link (under the specified circumstances) between an increase in market concentration arising from a horizontal merger and an increase in market price. More particularly, merger in Cournot oligopoly will lead the merged group to reduce its output (relative to the sum of the two merging firms' outputs) and rivals to increase their output.[92] Farrell & Shapiro comment, on the basis of a model of mergers in Cournot oligopoly: "We found that mergers do indeed, typically, raise price. In particular any merger that generates no synergies ... raises price. And for a merger to lower price requires considerable economies of scale or learning. This result is only strengthened if the merger causes behaviour in the industry to shift from Cournot to something less competitive".[93] Secondly, it postulates that increases in concentration below the levels which typically lead to transactions being blocked will nevertheless lead to increases in price.[94]

However, the practical utility of the Cournot model is limited by the fact that mergers between Cournot competitors are generally unprofitable[95]; this means that the model is inconsistent with the observation that mergers in fact occur.[96] Further, the key assumption in the Cournot model,[97] namely that oligopolists focus on their output in deciding how to compete, is

---

DG Competition (available via *http://europa.eu.int/comm/competition/mergers/review/the_ economics_of_unilateral_effects_en.pdf*), p.12 (noting that glass, cement and package holidays have been said to fall within this category).

[90] See Martin, *Advanced Industrial Economics* (2nd edn, Blackwell, 2002), p.39.

[91] See s.4.3 below and Europe Economics, "Study on Assessment Criteria for Distinguishing between Competitive and Dominant Oligopolies in Merger Control", Report for the European Commission, p.52.

[92] See Europe Economics, "Study on Assessment Criteria for Distinguishing between Competitive and Dominant Oligopolies in Merger Control", Report for the European Commission, pp.11 and 53 and Farrell & Shapiro, "Horizontal Mergers: an equilibrium analysis" (1990) 80 *American Economic Review* 107.

[93] Farrell & Shapiro, "Horizontal Mergers: an equilibrium analysis" (1990) 80 *American Economic Review* 107. See also Martin, *Advanced Industrial Economics* (2nd edn, Blackwell, 2002), pp.401 to 403.

[94] i.e. companies may have *some* market power and therefore *some* influence over prices in circumstances falling short of dominance—see para.1–005 above.

[95] See Salant, Switzer & Reynolds, "Losses from Horizontal Merger: The Effects of an Exogenous Change in Industry Structure on Cournot-Nash Equilibrium" (1983) 98 Q.J. Econ. 185.

[96] Except to the extent that firms act irrationally in merging.

[97] There are numerous variants on the model: for a description of a Cournot model with *differentiated* products, see Martin, *Advanced Industrial Economics* (2nd edn, Blackwell, 2002), p.59. Empirical economics now suggests that profits (which assuming uniform costs are a

inconsistent with empirical observation—many oligopolists seem to decide on the prices at which they sell and adjust output to accommodate actual demand.[98]

1–022   The *Bertrand model* of oligopoly proceeds on the assumption that each producer of homogeneous goods makes its *pricing* decision in the light of *predictions* of what other producers will do. In its simplest form it assumes that the producers do not face any capacity constraints. In a two-firm Bertrand model, each producer will have an incentive to undercut the other on the basis that this will enable the producer setting the lowest price to supply the whole market (whereas overpricing relative to the competitor will result in the producer making no sales). In turn, each producer will deduce that its competitor has the same incentive. The outcome of the model is that each producer will price at the lowest level possible (i.e. the marginal cost of production) and the prevailing market price will be identical to that in perfect competition. It follows that Bertrand rejects the Cournot relationship between market structure and prices.[99] More generally, if competitors compete on prices rather than quantities, outputs are greater and prices lower.[1]

In its simplest form, the model proceeds on three important assumptions. First, the product is homogeneous. If the products are differentiated (either in product characteristics[2] or geographic space),[3] the producer is likely to have some market power and prices will not be driven down to marginal cost.[4] In welfare terms, there is a trade-off between the number of brands available to consumers of differentiated products and the price of each product.[5] Secondly, the suppliers do not face capacity constraints. If they do, they will not seek to cut prices to win the whole of the market.[6] Thirdly, the parties compete in just one period, i.e. a failure to price at or below the level of the rival will lead to a loss of all customers in the single period under

---

reasonable proxy for prices) are weakly correlated with industry concentration but strongly correlated with market share: Scherer & Ross, *Industrial Market Structure and Economic Performance* (3rd edn, Houghton Mifflin Co, 1990), p.430.

[98] Or use both price and output as variables: see Martin, *Advanced Industrial Economics* (2nd edn, Blackwell, 2002), p.66.

[99] See ABA Section of Antitrust Law, *Market Power Handbook* (ABA Publishing, 2005), p.48.

[1] See Martin, *Advanced Industrial Economics* (2nd edn, Blackwell, 2002), pp.65 and 81 and Ivaldi *et al*, "The Economics of Unilateral Effects", 2003, Interim Report for DG Competition (available via *http://europa.eu.int/comm/competition/mergers/review/the_economics_of_unilateral_effects_en.pdf*), p.15.

[2] e.g. the sweetness of breakfast cereal.

[3] e.g. the locations of ice cream sellers.

[4] See Martin, *Advanced Industrial Economics* (2nd edn, Blackwell, 2002), p.63.

[5] For a discussion of optimal diversity which measures the trade-off between these factors see Carlton & Perloff, *Modern Industrial Organization* (4th edn, Addison-Wesley, 2005), pp.218 and 219.

[6] Bertrand competition with capacity constraints has been modelled by Edgeworth: see Shy, *Industrial Organization* (The MIT Press, 1995), pp.111 to 112.

review.[7] If suppliers can factor in future earnings and the scope for retaliation, a different outcome may occur.

(c) The trade-off between efficiency and market power

There is a general trade-off between the fact that mergers may (and many **1–023** commentators assume that they generally do)[8] generate efficiencies and the fact that they may[9] create or enhance market power.[10] Williamson[11] identified a "naive" trade-off model, noting that market power will enable the merged group to reduce output and increase price,[12] leading to a shift in welfare from consumers to producers and a deadweight welfare loss.[13] He applied a *total welfare* standard (and therefore treated the shift in welfare from consumers to producers as neutral) and recommended that mergers should be approved if the efficiency savings which benefit producers outweigh the deadweight welfare loss. He also recognised that the welfare analysis may be complicated if price increases introduced by the merged group result in competitors raising their prices.

From a *consumer welfare* perspective, a merger which results in market **1–024** power without efficiency savings is unambiguously objectionable, whereas a merger which results in efficiency savings without market power is at least

---

[7] Varian comments in *Microeconomic Analysis* (3rd edn, W W Norton & Co, 1992), at p.292: "One way to think about Bertrand competition is that it is a model of competitive bidding. Each firm submits a sealed bid stating the price at which it will serve all customers; the bids are opened and the lowest bidder gets the customers. Viewed in this way, the Bertrand result is not so paradoxical. It is well-known that sealed bids are a very good way to induce firms to compete vigorously, even if there are only a few firms".

[8] e.g. Areeda, Hovenkamp & Solow, *Antitrust Law* (2nd edn, Aspen Law & Business, 1998), Vol.IVA, para.970a states: "*every* merger presumably produces certain efficiencies. Indeed, in the absence of opportunities for the exercise of market power the attainment of efficiencies is the principal if not the only reason that firms merge".

[9] Ivaldi *et al*, "The Economics of Unilateral Effects" 2003, Interim Report for DG Competition (available via *http://europa.eu.int/comm/competition/mergers/review/the_economics_of_unilateral_effects_en.pdf*), assume that *all* mergers lead to increases in prices in the absence of offsetting efficiencies. They state, at p.22: "Whether firms compete in prices or quantities (or capacities), a merger between competitors increases the remaining firms' market power (both for the merged firm and its competitors), thereby leading (absent any offsetting efficiency gain) to higher prices and lower output. This is so because the merged entity is acting in a less competitive way than the two uncoordinated firms would have done."

[10] The Commission acknowledged the trade-off in its XXIInd Annual Report on Competition Policy, 1992, paras 7 and 8: "Merger control . . . aims to reconcile two imperatives. Firstly, the mergers envisaged by industry will generally help to adapt industrial structures to the single market so that the market can in fact generate the desired efficiency gains . . . Secondly, it is likewise vital that mergers should not be allowed to establish dominant positions in the Community, with the holders of such positions no longer exposed to sufficient competitive pressure".

[11] Williamson, "Economies as an antitrust defense: the welfare trade-offs" (1968) 58 *American Economic Review* 18 to 31 and Williamson, "Economies as an antitrust defense revisited" (1977) 125 U Pa Law Rev 699.

[12] For discussion of the trade-off between increased *procurement* power and efficiencies generated by the merger, see Peter Carstensen, "Buyer Power and Merger Analysis—The Need for Different Metrics" (*www.ftc.gov/bc/mergerenforce/presentations/040217carstensen.pdf*).

[13] See Fig.1.5 above.

neutral and may be beneficial.[14] The more difficult case in policy terms is when the merger results in both market power and efficiency savings. Imagine a merger which will enable the merged group to restrict output and profitably increase prices in a market by, in aggregate, £5 million, whilst creating production efficiencies valued at £10 million. In contrast to the position under Williamson's model, when a *consumer welfare* standard is applied, the only issue is whether price will rise following the merger. On the stylised facts presented in this paragraph, the merged group will have the *power* profitably to raise prices and, in order to obtain approval for its transaction, would need to establish that it would have no *incentive* to exercise that power because the *more profitable* strategy, taking account of the efficiency gains, would be to increase output, making more sales but at a lower price.[15] If an *efficiency* standard is applied to such a hypothetical merger, then allocative efficiency is reduced, on the assumption that the merged group restricts output to increase price using its market power, but productive efficiency is enhanced, creating a need to balance the two effects or identify one as paramount.

1–025   In the example given above, the process of trading-off was straightforward because monetary values for the price increase and efficiency gains were specified. In the vast majority of cases such data is not available (see s.1.4 below). This has led to suggestions that merger control involves an *assumption* that mergers generate certain efficiencies. The argument is that merging companies must be assumed to be acting rationally and, in cases not creating or enhancing market power, the only benefits from the merger are the generation of efficiencies. On this approach, mergers between companies that do not create or enhance market power are assumed to generate efficiencies and are therefore declared lawful whilst mergers which create or enhance market power are assumed to be unlawful unless the merger generates especial efficiencies, going beyond the norm, that are likely to eliminate any incentive to increase prices.[16]

If the "presumed efficiencies" analysis is correct, it helps to explain the treatment of mergers by antitrust authorities in comparison with the treatment of agreements between competitors and internal growth. Bork, in his classic study of US antitrust policy, *The Antitrust Paradox*, started by seeking to identify why mergers are treated more benignly than cartels (notwithstanding that both reduce or eliminate competition between previously independent entities) but less benignly than organic growth (notwithstanding that both may result in a company holding a high market share). He argued that the only relevant point of distinction between mergers and cartels is that mergers are capable of generating efficiencies that ultimately benefit customers whereas cartels comprise naked restraints that can only serve to increase prices paid by customers without any counter-

---

[14] See s.7.6 below.
[15] For a more detailed discussion of efficiency gains, see Ch.18.
[16] See Areeda, Hovenkamp & Solow, *Antitrust Law* (2nd edn, Aspen Law & Business, 1998), Vol.IVA, para.976d.

vailing benefits.[17] Conversely, internal growth arises from the creation of efficiency by the firm, and is therefore always to be welcomed by antitrust policy, whereas mergers may have the negative effect of conferring market power, which can be used to earn monopoly profits, as well as the positive effect of generating efficiencies.[18]

1.4 MEASUREMENT OF THE PREDICTED EFFECTS OF MERGERS ON MARKET PERFORMANCE

Sections 1.2 and 1.3 identified, in descriptive terms, a trade-off between the **1–026** market power and efficiency effects of mergers, and described three criteria which could be used to judge the effects of mergers on market performance. The issue considered in this section is the extent to which it is possible *in practice* to measure the effects of mergers in carrying out the trading-off process.

There are two reasons why precise measurement is rarely, if ever, possible. First, all merger control is to a greater or lesser extent forward-looking or *prophylactic*.[19] It follows that in almost all cases the Commission has to make predictions about the likely effect of the merger on competition in the market.[20] The prospective nature of this task means that merger control is a speculative, uncertain exercise.

Secondly, seeking to place financial values on the market power and efficiency effects is extremely difficult. Whilst it is possible to make direct estimates of the price increases likely to result from a merger in rare cases when sufficient data is available,[21] it is necessary to rely exclusive on a structural analysis in the vast majority of cases, predicting as a qualitative matter whether price increases are likely, in the light in particular of an

---

[17] Bork, *The Antitrust Paradox* (1993 edn, The Free Press, 1978), p.67. For a contemporary attempt to draw an analytical distinction between the treatment of cartels and mergers, see the US FTC and DOJ, "Antitrust Guidelines for Collaborations Among Competitors", April 2000 (available via *www.ftc.gov/os/2000/04/ftcdojguidelines.pdf*), s.1.3: "Most mergers completely end competition between the merging parties in the relevant market(s). By contrast, most competitor collaborations preserve some form of competition among the participants. The remaining competition may reduce competitive concerns, but also may raise questions about whether participants have agreed to anti-competitive restraints on the remaining competition. Mergers are designed to be permanent, while competitor collaborations are more typically of limited duration. Thus, participants in a collaboration typically remain competitors, even if they are not actual competitors for certain purposes (e.g. research and development) during the collaboration. The potential for future competition between participants in a collaboration requires antitrust scrutiny different from that required for mergers".

[18] Bork, *The Antitrust Paradox* (1993 edn, The Free Press, 1978), p.68.

[19] Subject to very limited exceptions, parties to mergers requiring notification under the ECMR are not permitted to implement them before clearance is obtained.

[20] This has the advantage that the competition authorities may be able to prevent the emergence of market structures which facilitate coordinated effects, notwithstanding the fact that, if such a market structure existed, the participants would not infringe Art.81 by acting in a tacitly coordinated manner.

[21] See para.19–006 below.

analysis of actual and potential rivalry and buyer power. A precise analysis of the effects of a merger on customer choice and innovation is even more difficult.[22] Finally, whilst merging parties commonly place a financial value on the efficiencies available through merger these are often not verifiable and do not always materialise.

1–027   There are four main models which could be used to assess the effects of mergers on market performance: "direct analysis", "bright-line models", "rules-based appraisal" and "all-encompassing appraisal".

(a)   *Direct analysis* seeks to quantify the financial effects of the merger. For example, the Canadian authorities sought to ascribe monetary values to the effects of the *Superior Propane* merger.[23] However, such an approach is not suitable for the majority of cases because the exercise of assigning monetary values is too speculative to be meaningful.[24]

(b)   A *bright-line model* recognises the difficulties of direct estimates of the effects of individual transactions and instead seeks to use economic principles to formulate a *single rule* to be applied to all transactions. For example, Bork used as the basis for a bright-line model his empirical observation that restrictions of output decrease greatly from one-firm to two-firm markets and his conjecture that mergers may very well create substantial new efficiencies. Bork's conclusion on the trade-off was that in a fragmented market the maximum market share attainable by merger ought to be 40 per cent and, to take account of oligopoly concerns, when one company already has a share of 50 per cent the maximum ought to be 30 per cent.[25]

(c)   A *rules-based appraisal* also recognises that direct analysis of the trade-offs is impossible but rejects a bright-line approach as inflexible. For example, a market share in excess of Bork's bright-line criteria would not enable the merged group profitably to raise prices

---

[22] See Jacquemin & Slade, "Cartels, Collusion, and Horizontal Merger", published in *Handbook of Industrial Organization* (Schmalensee & Willig edns, 1989), Vol.1, p.415, at p.463 (and see the discussion at pp.459 to 463 and, in the same volume, Eaton & Lipsey, "Product Differentiation", p.724, at p.760). The question of whether Schumpeter was right to argue in *The Theory of Economic Development: An inquiry into profits, capital, credit, interest and the business cycle* (Harvard UP, 1934), that market power is conducive to innovation remains a live one: see Jacquemin & Slade, at p.462.

[23] *The Commissioner of Competition v Superior Propane*, April 4, 2002. (The decision was upheld on appeal by the Canadian Federal Court of Appeal on January 31, 2003).

[24] See para.1–026 above.

[25] Bork, *The Antitrust Paradox* (1993 edn, The Free Press, 1978), pp.221 and 222. The US Horizontal Merger Guidelines of the National Association of Attorneys General 1993 (available at *www.naag.org/issues/pdf/at-hmerger_guidelines.pdf*) come close to advocating a bright-line model at s.5: "The present state of economic theory, especially where there is an absence of supporting empirical work, is generally insufficient to overcome the usual presumption that increases in market concentration will increase the likelihood and degree to which industry performance is adversely affected".

if new entry would be timely, likely and sufficient to prevent the exercise of market power.[26] A rules-based appraisal system recognises that:

(i) mergers may raise issues at or beyond the boundary of cutting-edge economics research, but it disregards such research for the purposes of deciding whether or not to approve a transaction because: it is of uncertain quality, as it has not been accepted generally by the profession and (usually) has not been verified empirically[27]; those adjudicating on mergers are rarely well-placed properly to appraise such research; and taking contemporary theory into account introduces uncertainty and cost to the merger appraisal process[28];

(ii) considerations of legal certainty and due process require that

---

[26] See Ch.16. Areeda, Hovenkamp & Solow, *Antitrust Law* (2nd edn, Aspen Law & Business, 1998) Vol.IV, para.905g, propose a set of presumptions and burdens of proof for use in the US as a rules-based appraisal system. See also Shepherd, Shepherd & Shepherd, "Sharper Focus: Market Shares in the Merger Guidelines" [2000] *The Antitrust Bulletin* 835, criticising the proliferation of theories and relevant factors identified in the US Horizontal Merger Guidelines, 1992 (amended in 1997) (*www.usdoj.gov/atr/public/guidelines/hmg.htm*) and urging an approach focused on market shares.

[27] Kantzenbach, Kottmann & Krüger, "New Industrial Economics and Experiences From European Merger Control—New Lessons About Collective Dominance", March 1995, (prepared on behalf of the Commission but not necessarily representing the Commission's official position), note, at p.79, the dangers of deriving policy recommendations from game-theoretical papers.

[28] Areeda & Hovenkamp, *Antitrust Law* (2nd edn, Aspen Law & Business, 2000), Vol.1, para.112b state: "The cutting edge of any discipline is always marked by relative controversy, while the core is generally much more stable. Nearly all of the economic issues relevant to antitrust policy lie at the core. The issues at the cutting edge are beyond the management capabilities of our antitrust tribunals. Thus, for example, most of merger policy has little to do with the more refined mathematical debates over theories of oligopoly ... In sum, antitrust economics employs what academic economists sometimes denigrate as 'applied economics'. The relation of applied economics to economics as an intellectual discipline is a little like the relationship of the tonsillectomy to the science of surgery or the oil change to the science of automotive engineering. Applied economics as a general matter is hardly at the frontier of economic science, but its very banality supplies the consensus needed to make it a useful antitrust tool". See also para.112c3. William Kolasky, Deputy Assistant Attorney General, US DOJ, stated in a speech, " 'Sound Economics and Hard Evidence': The Touchstones of Sound Merger Review", June 14, 2002 (available at *www.usdoj.gov*): "The first element of sound decision making is a sound analytical framework grounded in economic science. I use the term 'economic science,' rather than 'economic theory,' to draw a distinction I believe was first noted by George Stigler. As Stigler and others have observed, the minds of economists are extremely fertile. It is very easy to come up with theories of competitive harm. The difference between theory and science is that science requires hypotheses to be testable empirically. By economic science, I refer to those economic theories that have been tested empirically and not yet disproven." Similar sentiments are reflected in comments (expressed in a personal capacity) by Lars-Hendrik Röller, Chief Competition Economist at DG COMP, in "Economic Analysis and Competition Policy Enforcement in Europe" (available at *http://europa.eu.int/comm/competition/speeches/text/sp2005_011_en.pdf*), who observed: "The development of new theories (such as de novo models, which are based on alternative assumptions, leading to radically different results) are likely to be less influential in the context of case proceedings for a number of reasons, including the difficulty of communicating a new theory in a rather short period of time. As a result, one is tempted to conclude that the analysis of the merit of new theories is best left to the academic journals, where a long and rigorous peer review will ensure consistency and ultimately empirical relevance."

the criteria applied in assessing mergers are publicised in advance whilst providing flexibility for individual appraisal of each transaction; the necessary publicity may occur through the promulgation of guidelines (as in the cases, for example, of the EC, US, Canada, the UK, Australia, New Zealand, France and Ireland) and/or the publication of decisions so that merging parties can identify the principles being applied.

(d) An *all-encompassing appraisal* seeks to make the best prediction of the likely effects of a transaction taking into account *any* relevant available materials including cutting-edge economics research and direct analysis. The rationale for such an approach is that, provided the decision-maker has economics expertise, the merger appraisal process is more likely to reach the "right" result if all evidence is taken into account than if certain categories are a priori excluded. Such an approach is roundly criticised by Areeda, Hovenkamp & Solow[29]:

"Unfortunately, the world we live in is characterized by flawed and incomplete information and decision processes that are both imperfect and very costly. To be sure, we may be able to articulate numerous factors that could be relevant to the competitive consequences of any merger. Such articulations are quite common, and any text on industrial organization will list numerous such factors. But assigning weight or significance to individual factors in a real case poses enormous difficulties, both empirical and conceptual. For that reason, the effort to employ many factors often degenerates into a focus on a key fact supplemented by loose and usually unpersuasive talk about other evidence, some relevant and some not."

1.5 EMPIRICAL EVIDENCE OF THE EFFECTS OF MERGERS ON CONSUMERS

1-028 A working paper[30] from 2000 co-authored (prior to his appointment) by Lars-Hendrik Röller, the first Chief Competition Economist at DG COMP, reached the following relatively tentative conclusions: "the empirical literature does provide some support for the fear that horizontal mergers

---

[29] *Antitrust Law* (2nd edn, Aspen Law & Business, 1998), Vol.IV, para.905c; see also paras 940, 944e and 950b and Vol.IVA, para.960.

[30] See also Schmalensee, "Inter-industry Studies of Structure and Performance", in *Handbook of Industrial Organization* (Schmalensee & Willig edns, 1989), Vol.1, p.951; Scherer & Ross, *Industrial Market Structure and Economic Performance* (3rd edn, Houghton Mifflin Co, 1990), pp.97 to 141; Pautler, "Evidence on Mergers and Acquisitions" [2003] *The Antitrust Bulletin* 119; and PriceWaterhouseCoopers, "Ex Post Evaluation of Mergers", Report Prepared for the OFT, DTI and Competition Commission, March 2005 (available via *www.oft.gov.uk/NR/rdonlyres/4E8F41F9-5D96-4CD4-8965-8DDA26A64DA8/0/oft767.pdf*), Annex B.

increase market power ... [The] empirical evidence suggests that controlling mergers is important".[31] The paper emphasises that there are relatively few studies assessing the effects of mergers on prices and consumers although the small number of direct studies (e.g. of the effect of mergers between airlines on prices on particular routes) "unambiguously indicate that price tends to rise as a result of merger".[32] This conclusion is supported by indirect studies finding that there is a positive relationship between concentration and price levels (implying that horizontal mergers increase prices)[33] and by assessments of the effects of mergers on market shares[34] (the available evidence suggesting that the market shares of companies engaged in horizontal mergers tend to decline, implying that the merger was driven by the objective of obtaining market power).[35]

1.6 OVERVIEW OF ANALYSIS

(a) Theories of competitive harm

(i) **Introduction** The ECMR seeks to prevent mergers which are likely to lead **1–029** to material harm to consumers in the form of higher prices or reduced quality, innovation or variety. The Commission has identified several methods—known as "theories of competitive harm"—through which mergers can adversely affect consumers. In each case, the Commission identifies any reasonably credible, testable theory of competitive harm and seeks to determine whether the merger is likely, as a result, materially to harm consumers.[36]

For the purposes of identifying relevant theories of competitive harm, it is useful to divide mergers into the following broad categories. *Horizontal mergers* involve parties which are active or potentially active in the same market. The merger reduces the number of players in the market and increases the merged group's market share. A *vertical merger* involves a combination of companies active in two or more successive stages of the

---

[31] Röller, Stennek & Verboven, "Efficiency Gains from Mergers", The Research Institute of Industrial Economics, Working Paper No.543, 2000 (available at *www.iui.se/wp/Wp543/IUIWp543.pdf*), pp.9, 35 and 36.

[32] p.43.

[33] pp.45 and 46.

[34] p.47.

[35] If the merger created sufficient variable cost synergies, the merged group would be expected to increase its share as it would have an incentive to lower prices.

[36] The theories of competitive harm are not closed, and new theories are developing all the time. However, after dabbling unsuccessfully in the development of new theory in Case COMP/M.2220 *GE / Honeywell* [2004] O.J. L48/1 (the conglomerate aspects of the decision were overturned in Case T-210/01 *General Electric Company v Commission*, not yet reported, judgment of December 14, 2005), the Commission appears to regard its role as a merger control authority as limited to the application of relatively well-established theory. See generally para.1–027(c)(i) above.

production or distribution process. *Conglomerate mergers*[37] occur between parties which are not actual or potential competitors of one another (horizontal mergers) and when neither produces a good which is, or could be, used by the other (vertical mergers).

1–030 **(ii) Horizontal mergers: non-coordinated effects** There is a range of theories of competitive harm associated with horizontal mergers, including the following. First, the larger the merged group's market share, the more likely it is to enjoy market power and the larger the increment in market share arising from the merger, the more likely the merger is to significantly increase the merged group's market power[38] (see s.7.2). Secondly, if the merging parties supply differentiated products (i.e. products which consumers perceive to have different attributes from rival products), then a merger may allow the merged group profitably to raise prices if the parties are close competitors to one another because the merger removes an important competitive constraint which each merging party was exercising on the other (this is discussed in s.7.3). Thirdly, if the merging parties' competitors are unlikely to increase supply if price increases (for example, if they face *capacity constraints*) then the merged group may be able profitably to raise prices by reducing its own output (see s.7.4). Fourthly, if one of the merging parties would have been likely, in the absence of the merger, to have entered a market, then the merger may harm consumers by depriving them of the benefits of such *potential competition* (this is discussed in Ch.9). Fifthly, consumers may be harmed by increases in the merged group's buyer power, for example if a merged supermarket group reduces its purchases of carrots in order to obtain a better price then it will have fewer carrots to sell

---

[37] If the merging parties are active in neighbouring markets, it is necessary to consider four issues:

  (a) "associative links"—if a company has power in market A, then the main constraint on its pricing may come from suppliers in market B and a merger between a company active in market A and a company active in market B may enable the merged group to increase its prices in market A (see s.9.3 below);

  (b) "leveraging"—if a company has power in market A, then it may be able to leverage that market power into market B by tying, bundling, predatory pricing etc. (see Ch.12 below);

  (c) "concentric markets"—as well as separate markets for A and B, there may be a "concentric" market comprising both A and B (e.g. there may be a market for banking services as well as markets for personal current accounts and personal savings accounts) (see para.3–002(b) below); and

  (d) coordinated effects—if a company is active in several product or geographic markets and competes against the same competitors in those markets, then it may have an incentive not to compete aggressively in one market in case it faces retaliation in the second (see Ch.8 below).

[38] Imagine a market with two suppliers, one with a market share of 85% and the other 15%; a 10% reduction in industry output would increase the market price by 10%. The smaller supplier has no incentive to seek to increase the market price because its sales would drop by two-thirds (from 15% to 5% of the original market) if it sought to bid up the market price by 10%. By contrast, the larger supplier may have an incentive to reduce its output as it would benefit from a price increase of 10% across retained sales representing 75% of the original market and, presumably, would save costs by reducing output.

and might increase the price at which it sells carrots (see Ch.10 below). These five theories of harm are described as *non-coordinated effects*; they arise when, as a result of the merger, the merged group is able profitably to increase price or reduce quality, choice or innovation through its own acts *without the need for a cooperative response from competitors*.[39] However, this does not mean that the effects of the merger are only felt by customers of the merged group; if the merged group changes its prices or other aspects of its competitive strategy, this may create an incentive for rivals to change their competitive strategies. Most obviously, if the merged group raises its prices then this will often create an incentive for rivals to raise their own prices. In this way, any anti-competitive effects of a merger may be felt across the whole market (and it is to capture this point that the Commission uses the term "non-coordinated effects" to describe such theories of competitive harm, rather than "unilateral effects").

(iii) Horizontal mergers: coordinated effects Horizontal mergers may also **1–031** harm consumers through *coordinated effects*. If a merger enables the companies remaining in the market to increase their profits through actions which depend for their success on cooperative reactions from other suppliers[40] (i.e. tacitly to coordinate[41] their activities),[42] then they may be able profitably to increase prices or reduce quality standards, thereby mimicking wholly or partly the monopoly or cartel[43] outcome. Such a situation is commonly referred to as one of collective or joint dominance. The Guidelines on the assessment of horizontal mergers under the Council Regulation on the control of concentrations between undertakings[44] summarise the position as follows, stating that a merger may significantly impede effective competition "by changing the nature of competition in such a way that firms that previously were not coordinating their behaviour, are now significantly more likely to coordinate and raise prices or otherwise ham effective com-

---

[39] See also the discussion of the scope of "non-coordinated effects" in the UK Office of Fair Trading's Substantive Merger Guidelines, May 2003 (*www.oft.gov.uk*), para.4.7 and n.21. In a narrow sense, non-coordinated effects arise when the actions of the merged group and the impediment of effective competition occur in a single antitrust market. In this narrow sense, non-coordinated effects are distinct from vertical effects and conglomerate effects (see Chs 11 and 12) as those theories of competitive harm arise when power in one market is leveraged into a second. In a broader sense, non-coordinated effects arise when effective competition is significantly impeded by the merged group *in its own right* whether or not the market power and competitive harm arise in the same or different markets.

[40] See the US Horizontal Merger Guidelines, 1992 (amended in 1997) (*www.usdoj.gov/atr/public/guidelines/hmg.htm*), s.2.1.

[41] Through independent decision-taking, i.e. without expressly colluding with competitors. Tacit coordination is generally not regarded as infringing antitrust rules.

[42] Coordination may relate to, e.g. price, fixed price differentials, capacity, down-time, market shares or customer or territorial restrictions.

[43] On the question of whether a merger may be prohibited because it increases the likelihood of *express* collusion, see Areeda, Hovenkamp & Solow, *Antitrust Law* (2nd edn, Aspen Law & Business, 1998), Vol.IV, para.917.

[44] [2004] O.J. C31/5.

petition. A merger may also make coordination easier, more stable or more effective for firms which were coordinating prior to the merger".[45] Coordinated effects are discussed in Ch.8 below.

1–032 **(iv) Vertical and conglomerate mergers** Vertical and conglomerate mergers both raise concerns about the scope for the merged group to leverage market power from one market into a second by excluding or marginalising rivals in the second market (for example, by refusing to supply or to purchase in the case of vertical mergers or through tying or bundling in the case of conglomerate mergers). Vertical and conglomerate effects are discussed in Chs 11 and 12 below.

(b) Framework for analysis

1–033 In assessing mergers, the Commission takes account of a range of factors which provide a framework for its substantive analysis. The substantive test for the assessment of concentrations contained in the ECMR is discussed in Ch.2. By defining relevant antitrust markets (Ch.3), the Commission is able to identify in a systematic way those suppliers, if any, which provide, or could readily provide, genuine alternative choices for customers of the merging parties and whose activities are directly relevant to a determination of whether the merged group will enjoy market power. Once the relevant antitrust market has been defined, the Commission is able to calculate market shares and concentration levels (Ch.4). Market share data can provide useful information about the market positions of the merging parties and their competitors whilst concentration data may cast light on the overall structure of the market (and in particular on the extent to which a few large firms control supplies or purchases).

The Commission seeks to identify whether consumers will be harmed *by the merger*, which involves distinguishing the effects of the merger from changes in the marketplace that would have occurred in any event (the "counterfactual", which is analysed in Ch.5). Finally, in carrying out its analysis, the Commission examines *the way in which the market operates* (Ch.6). For example, the effect of a merger may vary depending on the way in which a market is changing (e.g. whether it is growing rapidly), how customers make their purchasing decisions, how suppliers make their pricing decisions and the types of goods or services supplied in the market.

(c) Rebutting theories of competitive harm

1–034 In the same way that there is a number of recognised theories of competitive harm which, if applicable, might result in the merger causing harm to

---

[45] Para.22(b).

consumers, there are several factors which, if present, are likely to ensure that consumers are not harmed by the merger or contribute to their protection.

(a) If competitors provide an effective competitive constraint then the merged group will not have the ability to act to the detriment of consumers (Ch.14).

(b) The Commission analyses whether *customers* would act as a constraint on the merged group's ability to exercise market power (Ch.15). Customers enjoy buyer power when they have viable alternatives to the merged group or can make other credible threats to obtain advantage in negotiations with their suppliers.[46]

(c) The Commission examines potential rivalry from *new entrants* (Ch.16). If it is established that new entry would defeat any attempt by the merged group to exercise market power—and in particular, that such entry would be likely, timely and sufficient in magnitude and scope—then the Commission is likely to clear a transaction even if it results in a merged group holding a high market share.

(d) If it can be shown that one of the merging parties would probably have exited from the market if the merger did not proceed, then it may be possible to show that any harm to consumers was not *caused* by the merger. The "failing firm defence" is discussed in Ch.17.

(e) If a merger results in efficiencies, then it is possible that those efficiencies will counteract any potential harm to consumers which would otherwise have arisen (Ch.18). For example, if the merger lowers the merged group's marginal costs, then it will have an incentive to increase its output (reducing prices) even though it may face less intense competition following the elimination of rivalry from its merger partner.

Ch.19 discusses categories of evidence which relate generally to the question of whether the merger is likely to harm consumers. Ultimately, if the merger is likely to cause harm to consumers then it will be prohibited unless the merging parties offer remedies (i.e. undertakings or commitments) to eliminate or address the competitive concern (Ch.20).

(d) Unifying principles—incentives and abilities

The remainder of this book has been arranged in a further 19 chapters in an **1–035** attempt to organise a disparate yet overlapping set of principles in a way

---

[46] Generally, if the merged group has a high share of a properly defined antitrust market, then customers will lack viable alternatives and, in such cases, it is rare for buyer power issues taken in isolation to "trump" the presumption that high market shares confer market power.

which is practical and accessible. However, merger control is essentially aiming to answer a question which can be stated quite shortly, namely whether, as a result of the merger, the merged group will have the *incentive and ability* to act in ways which[47] are likely to *harm consumers*[48] (in particular by increasing price or reducing quality, variety or innovation).

The merged group's *incentives* are important because merger control is a real world exercise and regulators need only concern themselves with matters which might credibly occur. They can therefore leave to one side strategies that the merged group could theoretically adopt, but which it is unlikely in practice to pursue because there are more profitable alternatives. At one stage, the Commission lost sight of the importance of assessing in detail the merged group's incentives in vertical and conglomerate mergers (where it is easy to hypothesise that the merged group might adopt a particular strategy).[49] The Commission's failure to recognise the role of incentives also led to its refusing for a long time to grant positive weight to efficiencies in merger analysis: the fact that the merged group *could* act in ways which harm consumers as a result of the merger is irrelevant if the merged group *would not* do so because the merged group's more profitable strategy would benefit consumers (e.g. even if the merged group could increase its profits by reducing output and increasing price, it would nevertheless be unlikely to adopt this strategy if its *most* profitable strategy was to increase its output and benefit from efficiencies generated by the merger).[50] However, the crucial role of incentives has been emphasised by the Community Courts, most prominently in *General Electric Company v Commission*,[51] and the Commission now focuses carefully on the merged group's incentives.[52]

(e) Relevance of economic theory

1–036   It follows from the discussion in this section that EC merger control is *not* principally about identifying the economic model of oligopoly that most closely corresponds to the market in question[53] and determining whether that model predicts that consumers would be harmed by the merger. The exercise of assessing the merged group's abilities and incentives is less dogmatic. There is no single unifying model in play, but at the same time the

---

[47] In assessing whether the merger is likely to harm consumers, it is necessary to take account of the responses of other suppliers to any change in strategy by the merged group. This holds true whether the Commission is investigating coordinated effects or non-coordinated effects.
[48] See s.2.2 below for discussion of the role of consumer surplus under the ECMR.
[49] See generally Chs 11 and 12 below.
[50] See generally Ch.18.
[51] Case T-210/01, judgment of December 14, 2005, not yet reported.
[52] See para.11–13 below.
[53] Contrast the draft Commission Notice on the appraisal of horizontal mergers under the Council Regulation on the control of concentrations between undertakings, [2002] O.J. C331/18, which placed great weight on whether competition was on output (Cournot) or price (Bertrand). These passages were not included in the final version of the Notice.

Commission takes account of modern theory of industrial organisation, provided that the theory in question is widely accepted by economists and is administrable.[54]

---

[54] See para.1–027(c)(i) above.

CHAPTER 2

THE SIEC TEST AND OTHER LEGAL AND METHODOLOGICAL ISSUES

2.1 INTRODUCTION

2–001 The substantive test[1] under the ECMR is whether the merger "would significantly impede effective competition in the common market or in a substantial part of it, in particular as a result of the creation or strengthening of a dominant position".[2] If it would, the merger should be blocked or cleared only following the provision of suitable commitments. The current test came into force on May 1, 2004[3] and differs from the original provisions of the ECMR that were adopted in 1989[4] and required the Commission to determine whether the merger "creates or strengthens a dominant position as a result of which effective competition would be significantly impeded in the common market or a substantial part of it".[5]

The Commission provided guidance on its approach to substantive issues under the ECMR by publishing Guidelines[6] on the assessment of horizontal

---

[1] See generally OECD, "Substantive Criteria Used for the Assessment of Mergers", DAFFE/ COMP (2003) 5.

[2] Council Regulation (EC) No 139/2004 on the control of concentrations between undertakings [2004] O.J. L24/1, Arts 2(2) and 2(3).

[3] The amended ECMR was adopted following a proposal that the Commission published on December 12, 2002 (the "2002 Proposed Amended and Re-stated ECMR") [2003] O.J. C20/4. See also the Commission press release IP/02/1856, December 11, 2002.

[4] Council Regulation 4064/89 on the control of concentrations between undertakings [1989] O.J. L395/1 (subsequently corrected and amended). For a history of EC merger control from 1951 to 1989, see Fountoukakos & Ryan, "A New Substantive Test for EU Merger Control" [2005] E.C.L.R. 277, pp.277 to 280.

[5] Regulation 4064/89, Art.2(3).

[6] The Notice on Horizontal Mergers is binding on the Commission (although it is drafted in terms which are intended to retain for the Commission a good deal of discretion). This appears from Case T-114/02 *BaByliss v Commission* [2003] E.C.R. II-1279, in which the Court of First Instance rejected the Commission's argument that the Notice on remedies acceptable under Regulation 4064/89 and under Regulation 447/98 [2001] O.J. C68/3, was not binding on the grounds that: "The Commission is bound by notices which it issues in the area of supervision of concentrations, provided they do not depart from the rules in the Treaty and

mergers under the Council Regulation on the control of concentrations between undertakings (the "Notice on Horizontal Mergers").[7]

The remainder of this Chapter identifies the overall objectives of EC **2–002** merger control[8] (since an understanding of the overall objectives sheds light on the meaning and application of the substantive test under the revised ECMR) (s.2.2), explains the evolution of the change to the substantive test (s.2.3), discusses a number of legal issues regarding the interpretation of the new test (s.2.4), describes the burden and standard of proof under the ECMR (s.2.5), discusses the period over which the predicted effects of the merger are examined under the ECMR (s.2.6), examines the relationship between the ECMR and Articles 81 and 82, national regulatory systems, contractual restrictions and State aids (s.2.7), describes the methodology adopted by the Commission in gathering evidence (s.2.8) and concludes by analysing issues of international comity (s.2.9).

2.2 THE OBJECTIVES OF EC MERGER CONTROL

On its face,[9] the substantive test under the revised ECMR could be applied **2–003** using consumer welfare, total welfare or efficiency as the criterion for determining the effect of mergers on market performance.[10] In other words, the decision on the criterion to be used is one for the Commission (subject to review by the Community Courts) and *not* one which was pre-determined by the Council in framing the ECMR[11] or the Member States in drafting the EC Treaty.[12]

---

from Regulation No 4064/89 [the original EC Merger Regulation] ... Moreover, the Commission cannot depart from rules which it has imposed on itself". The same reasoning appears equally applicable to the Notice on Horizontal Mergers. The decision in *BaByliss* was effectively confirmed by the Court of First Instance (without referring to the *BaByliss* decision or the reasoning contained in it) in Case T-210/01 *General Electric Company v Commission*, not yet reported, judgment of December 14, 2005, para.516 ("As regards the alleged failure to comply with the notice on market definition, it is appropriate to observe at the outset that the Commission may not depart from rules which it has imposed on itself ... Thus, to the extent that the notice on market definition lays down in mandatory terms the method by which the Commission intends to define markets in the future and does not retain any margin of assessment, the Commission must indeed take account of the provisions of the notice").

[7] [2004] O.J. C31/5. The Commission also issued a press release (IP/04/70) and a set of "Frequently Asked Questions" (MEMO/04/9). The Notice was adopted following an extensive consultation on a draft Commission Notice on the appraisal of horizontal mergers under the Council Regulation on the control of concentrations between undertakings ("the 2002 draft Commission Notice on Horizontal Mergers") [2002] O.J. C331/18.

[8] The analysis in this Chapter builds on the general discussion in Ch.1 above.

[9] See generally Pera & Auricchio, "Consumer Welfare, Standard of Proof and the Objectives of Competition Policy" [2005] *European Competition Journal* 153.

[10] See s.1.2 above.

[11] The obligations imposed by Art.2(1) of the ECMR on the Commission to take account, in appraising concentrations, of "intermediate and ultimate consumers" and technical and economic progress provided that "it is to consumers' advantage" point towards a consumer welfare test (see also recital 29 focusing on the position of consumers) but are not decisive as they do not unambiguously exclude a total welfare or efficiency criterion.

[12] Recital 2 of the ECMR refers to Arts 3(1)(g) and 4(1) of the EC Treaty and recital 23 refers to Art.2 of the EC Treaty and Art.2 of the Treaty on European Union. Art.2 of the EC Treaty identifies a range of economic objectives, including promoting harmonious, sustainable and

The former Commissioner for Competition Policy, Mario Monti, made several statements during his term of office emphasising that the only objective of EC competition policy was to protect consumer welfare[13]:

"the goal of competition policy, in all its aspects, is to protect consumer welfare by maintaining a high degree of competition in the common market. Competition should lead to lower prices, a wider choice of goods, and technological innovation, all in the interest of the consumer."[14];

"Our objective is to ensure that competition is undistorted, so as to permit wider consumer choice, technological innovation and price competition."[15];

"when competitive forces are at play, producers make greater efforts to attract consumers by offering them lower prices, higher quality and better service than when the market is controlled by a monopolist or a handful of companies."[16];

"I would like ... to refute the assertion that the European Commission, when dealing with conglomerate mergers, is in fact applying what has been dubbed an 'efficiency offence'. Indeed, we distinguish clearly between—on the one hand—mergers leading to price reductions that are the result of strategic behaviour on the part of a dominant firm, the purpose of which is to eliminate or marginalize competitors with a view to

---

balanced development and raising the standard of living. Art.3(1)(g) of the EC Treaty provides the Community with the objective of instituting a system ensuring that competition in the internal market is not distorted. Art.4(1) of the EC Treaty provides that the activities of Member States and the Community are to be conducted in accordance with the principle of an open market economy with free competition. Art.2 of the Treaty on European Union identifies a range of objectives, including the promotion of economic progress.

[13] See also:

(a) Philip Lowe, Director General of DG Competition, "Competition Policy in the European Union", speech to the American Antitrust Institute, July 1, 2002 (*www.antitrustinstitute.org/activities.cfm*): "The interest of consumers in the broad sense—individuals and businesses—is the primary concern. The concerns of competitors are relevant to the extent, and only to the extent, that they provide evidence of actual or potential harm to competition and consumer interests".

(b) Philip Lowe, Director General of DG Competition, "The interaction between the Commission and Small Member States in Merger Review", speech in Dublin, October 10, 2003 (*http://europa.eu.int/comm/competition/speeches/*): "Merger control is about protecting the competitive process in the market and aims at ensuring consumers a sufficient choice of products at competitive prices. By preventing a merger from creating a dominant position in a small country the Commission protects the customers who live there."

(c) "Media Mergers", OECD, DAFFE/COMP(2003)16, p.296, in which the Commission's discussion paper states: "Consumer welfare considerations are decisive in the final assessment of the cases".

[14] "The Future for Competition Policy", speech of July 9, 2001 at Merchant Taylor's Hall, London (*www.europa.eu.int/comm/competition/speeches/index_2001.html*).

[15] Foreword to the Commission's XXXIst Annual Report on Competition Policy, 2001.

[16] Speech of February 26, 2002 at Casino de Madrid, "What are the aims of European Competition Policy?" (*www.europa.eu.int/comm/competition/speeches/index_2002.html*).

exploiting consumers in the medium term, and—on the other—mergers which will objectively lead to significant and durable efficiency gains that are likely to be passed on to the consumer."[17];

"Preserving competition, in merger control as in all areas of competition policy, is not ... an end in itself. The ultimate policy goal is the promotion of economic performance, and in particular the protection of consumer welfare. By seeking to preserve the competitive process, merger control plays an important role in guaranteeing efficiency in production, in preserving the incentive for enterprises to innovate, and in ensuring the optimal allocation of resources within the economy. Our customers are the beneficiaries of a properly conducted enforcement policy, enjoying lower prices and a wider choice of products and services as a result."[18];

the EU and US "both agree that the ultimate purpose of our respective intervention in the market-place should be to ensure that consumer welfare is not harmed"[19]; and

"Merger control ensures a diversity of mass-market consumer goods and low prices for the final consumer."[20]

These policy objectives are reflected in the Commission's decisions in merger **2–004** cases.[21] Further, the Notice on Horizontal Mergers is drafted in terms which focus exclusively on the protection of consumer welfare[22]: "Effective competition brings benefits to consumers, such as low prices, high quality products, a wide selection of goods and services, and innovation. Through its

---

[17] Speech of November 14, 2001, "Antitrust in the US and Europe: a History of Convergence" (*www.europa.eu.int/comm/competition/speeches/index_2001.html*). The Commissioner repeated the statement that there is no "efficiency offence" under the ECMR in a subsequent speech, "Review of the EC Merger Regulation—Roadmap for the reform project", Brussels, June 4, 2002 (*www.europa.eu.int/comm/competition/speeches/index_2002.html*).

[18] Speech at the International Competition Network Conference of September 28 and 29, 2002, "Analytical Framework for Merger Review" (*www.europa.eu.int/comm/competition/speeches/index_2002.html*).

[19] Speech at the UCLA Law First Annual Institute on US and EU Antitrust Aspects of Mergers and Acquisitions of February 28, 2004, "Convergence in EU-US antitrust policy regarding mergers and acquisitions: an EU perspective" (*http://europa.eu.int/rapid/pressReleasesAction.do?reference=SPEECH/04/107&format=HTML&aged=0&language=EN&guiLanguage=en*). See also comments by Mario Monti in response to a speech by Hew Pate in Brussels on June 7, 2004 (*http://europa.eu.int/comm/competition/speeches/text/sp2004_005_en.pdf*) emphasising that consumer welfare is the ultimate objective of both US and EU competition policy.

[20] Speech at the European Competition Policy Day, Amsterdam, October 22, 2004 "Competition for Consumers' Benefit" (*http://europa.eu.int/comm/competition/speeches/text/sp2004_016_en.pdf*).

[21] In addition to the examples in the text below, the use by the Commission of consumer welfare as the standard for appraising mergers is clear from the cases considering whether a transaction would create competition concerns on a market for the *procurement* of goods or services; the Commission does not consider directly the implications of the transaction for suppliers (who are not consumers) but focuses exclusively on the implications of the enhancement of buyer power for consumers in the markets *supplied* by the merged group; see, e.g. Case IV/M.784 *Kesko / Tuko* [1997] O.J. L110/53 (and, generally, Ch.10 below).

[22] Para.8. See also paras 76 to 88 (dealing with efficiencies) and the Commission's XXXIVth Annual Report on Competition Policy, 2004, para.176.

control of mergers, the Commission prevents mergers that would be likely to deprive customers of these benefits by significantly increasing the market power of firms."

Nevertheless,[23] there have been *hints* that Mario Monti's successor as Commissioner for Competition Policy, Neelie Kroes, does not regard the protection of consumer welfare as the *sole* objective of EC competition policy. Although she has described consumer welfare as "the standard" for the assessment of mergers, she added: "Our aim is simple: to protect competition in the market as a means of enhancing consumer welfare and ensuring an efficient allocation of resources."[24] The word "efficiency" is used in different senses[25] and Neelie Kroes may have used it as a synonym for "consumer welfare".[26] However, as explained further below, maximising consumer welfare does not necessarily maximise allocative efficiency (or productive efficiency) and, if EC merger control is to have a single policy

---

[23] Hildebrand, *The Role of Economic Analysis in the EC Competition Rules* (Kluwer, 2002), argues in Chs 1 to 3 that EC competition policy serves a broader range of objectives than consumer welfare in the light, in particular, of the terms of the EC Treaty and the approach in Germany (which can be regarded as the historic root of EC competition law).

[24] Speech of September 15, 2005, "European Competition Policy—Delivering Better Markets and Better Choices" (*http://europa.eu.int/rapid/pressReleasesAction.do?reference = SPEECH/ 05/512&format = HTML&aged = 0&language = EN&guiLanguage = en*). Further, in a speech of September 23, 2005, "Preliminary Thoughts on Policy Review of Article 82" (*http:// europa.eu.int/rapid/pressReleasesAction.do?reference = SPEECH/05/537&format = HTML&aged = 0&language = EN&guiLanguage = en*) the Commissioner described the objective of Art.82 as the protection of competition as a means of enhancing consumer welfare *and* ensuring an efficient allocation of resources. The Commissioner has also emphasised the role which competition policy can play in contributing to growth in the context of the Lisbon agenda (see, e.g. speech, "Effective Competition Policy—a Key Tool for Delivering the Lisbon Strategy", February 3, 2005 (*http://europa.eu.int/rapid/pressReleasesAction.do?reference = SPEECH/05/73&format = HTML&aged = 0&language = EN&guiLanguage = en*)); although there is no inherent contradiction in focusing on consumer welfare as the sole objective of merger control policy whilst regarding competition policy as contributing to growth, the Commissioner's speeches on this topic raise the question of whether the Commission would treat consumers' interests as paramount (as required by the use of a consumer welfare standard) if doing so would significantly harm producers (e.g. by restricting their ability to grow). (By contrast, former Commissioner for Competition Policy, Mario Monti, when discussing the Commission Communication, "A Pro-Active Competition Policy for a Competitive Europe", April 20, 2004 (*http://europa.eu.int/comm/competition/publications/proactive/en.pdf*), emphasised that the fact that competition policy can bring about gains in productivity and innovation "should not deflect from the positive impact of competition policy on consumer welfare": speech, "Proactive Competition Policy and the role of the Consumer", April 29, 2004 (*http://europa.eu.int/rapid/pressReleasesAction.do?reference = SPEECH/04/212&format = HTML&aged = 0&language = EN&guiLanguage = en*). The then Commissioner added: "The ultimate objective of productivity growth and global competitiveness is, and should be in the long term, prosperity and increased living standards. This happens when the winds of competition are in full swing: producers make greater efforts to attract customers by offering them lower prices, higher quality and better service than when the market is controlled by a cartel, a monopolist or a small number of companies.")

[25] See the discussion in Gifford & Kudrle, "Rhetoric and Reality in the Merger Standards of the United States, Canada and the European Union" (2005) 72 *Antitrust Law Journal* 423 (adopting the maximisation of aggregate consumer and producer surplus as the definition of "efficiency" at p.428).

[26] Compare Hildebrand, *The Role of Economic Analysis in the EC Competition Rules* (Kluwer, 2002), p.14: "The objective [of EC competition law] is to enhance efficiency, in the sense of maximizing consumer welfare and achieving the optimal allocation of resources."

objective,[27] it is necessary to choose *either* consumer welfare or *efficiency* as that objective. Nevertheless, for the time being, since Ms Kroes has described consumer welfare as "the standard", the working assumption must be that the single policy objective of EC merger control is indeed the promotion of consumer welfare.[28]

This conclusion has five important implications for the application of the **2–005** ECMR. First, the objective of the ECMR is *not*, as such, to maximise total welfare (i.e. the sum of consumer welfare and producer welfare). For example, in *SCA / Metsä Tissue*[29] the Commission stated that "even if the largest customers would be able to exercise some countervailing buyer power this would not protect smaller customers, and the new entity would still be able to raise prices above the pre-merger level." Similarly, in *Nestlé / Perrier*[30] the Commission said: "In the enforcement of the competition rules, the Commission must also pay attention to the protection of the weaker buyers. Even if some buyers might have a certain buying power, in the absence of sufficient competitive pressure on the market, it cannot be excluded that Nestlé and BSN apply different conditions of sale to the various buyers." In both passages quoted, the Commission focused exclusively on the position of consumers to the exclusion of producers and its reasoning is therefore inconsistent with the use of a total welfare standard.

Secondly, the objective of the ECMR is *not*, as such, to maximise allocative efficiency.[31] This can be tested by imagining that the merging parties admit that, following the transaction, they would be able to practise first-degree price discrimination, i.e. to charge to each customer the maximum price which that customer is willing to pay for the product.[32] A company which could discriminate in this way would produce the same quantity of goods as a perfectly competitive industry because producing an additional unit of output would have no effect on the revenues generated by previous units of output, meaning that it would be profitable to continue increasing output up until the point at which the price charged for the marginal unit is

---

[27] If EC merger control has a single ultimate policy objective, then the Commission does not need to make difficult decisions in hard cases reconciling competing aims.

[28] The Commissioner for Competition Policy, Neelie Kroes, in a speech, "Introductory remarks at press conference on Choline Chloride cartel and EDP/ENI/GDP merger decisions", December 9, 2004 (*http://europa.eu.int/rapid/pressReleasesAction.do?reference=SPEECH/04/526&format=HTML&aged=0&language=EN&guiLanguage=en*) stated: "The Commission must ensure that consumers benefit from more effective competition, in terms of choice of supplier and lower prices, following mergers". Three points arise. First, in this statement, the Commissioner focuses on consumer welfare as the exclusive objective of merger control policy. Secondly, in horizontal mergers, consumers will never benefit from greater choice of supplier because, by definition, the merger reduces the number of suppliers by one. Thirdly, the Commissioner appears to require an unduly demanding standard, i.e. merging parties should not be required to demonstrate that their merger *benefits* consumers, but simply that the merger does not cause any material *harm* to consumers.

[29] Case COMP/M.2097.

[30] Case IV/M.190 [1992] O.J. L356/1, para.78.

[31] Although see the statements of the Commissioner for Competition Policy, Neelie Kroes, cited above. Allocative efficiency would be maximised by maximising total welfare (i.e. the sum of consumer welfare and producer welfare): see para. 1–010 above.

[32] See para.1–006 above.

equal to the marginal cost of producing that unit. Such an outcome is one of allocative efficiency. But the Commission has in its decisions[33] established that an ability to engage in price discrimination is a ground for finding that the transaction significantly impedes effective competition.[34]

2–006   Thirdly, productive efficiency (for example, reducing production costs by allowing the merging parties to run dedicated machines) is not *directly* relevant to the assessment of the transaction under the ECMR. In particular, a transaction which significantly impeded effective competition would *not* be cleared even if the prejudice to consumer welfare were significantly smaller than the gains in productive efficiency (assuming that the welfare and efficiency effects can be assessed and compared). However, productive efficiency may serve to improve consumer welfare, most obviously by reducing the merged group's marginal cost, thereby creating an incentive for it to increase output (because a firm will increase output until its marginal revenue is equal to its marginal cost), since increases in output lead to reductions in price. Gains in productive efficiency are therefore *indirectly* relevant insofar as the merging parties can satisfy the criteria for ascribing positive weight to efficiencies in the merger appraisal process.[35]

Fourthly, there is no objective measure of how far a merger may reduce consumer welfare without being prohibited under the ECMR. The Commission's methodology is scientific but its decisions are unavoidably *qualitative*, i.e. every decision involves a subjective assessment of whether the effects of the transaction on consumer welfare are sufficiently serious to justify blocking it or clearing it only following the provision of undertakings.

2–007   Finally, in applying the consumer welfare criterion, the Commission clearly rejects the bright-line model espoused in particular by Bork.[36] The Commission believes that the question of whether the merged group will enjoy market power is one which is susceptible to more refined analysis, taking account of a whole range of factors, such as concentration levels, barriers to entry and buyer power. Whilst some of these issues are capable of objective measurement, many are not and the analysis of each of the relevant factors taken together is necessarily a *complex, subjective* one. Indeed, the Commission's approach has elements of both a rules-based appraisal and an all-encompassing appraisal.[37] For example, in predicting whether a merger will result in coordinated effects, the Commission takes account of *all* evidence potentially bearing on the issue.[38] By contrast, Areeda,

---

[33] Compare the discussion of this issue at para.1–007 above.
[34] See Case IV/M.190 *Nestlé / Perrier* [1992] O.J. L356/1 para.78; Case IV/M.1069 *WorldCom / MCI* [1999] O.J. L116/1 (the Commission found that the merged group could reinforce its market position by pricing selectively to attract customers from competing networks, i.e. price discriminating; para.118); Case COMP/M.2097 *SCA / Metsä Tissue*; and Case IV/M.1672 *Volvo / Scania* [2001] O.J. L143/74 para.90.
[35] See generally Ch.18.
[36] See sub-para.1–027(b) above.
[37] See sub-paras 1–027(c) and (d) above.
[38] See Ch.8 below.

Hovenkamp & Solow[39] comment, as regards coordinated effects: "Our own conclusion is that identifying these criteria in the specific case, making the relevant measurements and assigning weights, and predicting the true 'likelihood' that collusion will occur in the postmerger market are nearly impossible in most situations. If that is so, adding the criteria offers little or no promise of increased accuracy while making merger legality much less predictable than it would be if simpler criteria were used."

2.3 THE CHANGE TO THE SUBSTANTIVE TEST IN THE ECMR

(a) The Commission's 2001 consultation and 2002 proposals

In December 2001, the Commission commenced a consultation exercise to **2–008** determine whether the substantive test under the ECMR should be amended to a "substantial lessening of competition" standard,[40] which, if proposed by the Commission and adopted by the Council, would have brought the ECMR's standard for review into line with US law. Following the initiation of the consultation exercise, the Court of First Instance handed down its judgment in *Airtours plc v Commission*[41] which appeared to establish that, in the absence of single firm dominance, the Commission was entitled to prohibit a merger (or clear it subject to undertakings) only if it could establish that the criteria for coordinated effects were satisfied. This decision was perceived by some within the Commission to create a possible "gap" in the Commission's powers which needed to be filled; the concern was that mergers in oligopolistic markets that did not create or strengthen a position of single firm dominance and did not satisfy the onerous criteria necessary for a finding of coordinated effects in the light of the *Airtours* judgment might nevertheless result in harm to consumers (through price increases or reductions in service quality, innovation or choice) in circumstances in which the Commission arguably lacked the necessary legal powers to intervene. The 2002 Proposed Amended and Re-stated ECMR accordingly included a new provision, designed to clarify the meaning of "dominance", namely: "For the purposes of this Regulation, one or more undertakings shall be deemed to hold a dominant position if, with or without coordinating, they hold the economic power to influence appreciably and sustainably the parameters of competition, in particular, prices, production,

---

[39] Areeda, Hovenkamp & Solow, *Antitrust Law* (2nd edn, Aspen Law & Business, 1998), Vol.IV, para.916a.
[40] Green Paper on the Review of Council Regulation (EEC) No. 4064/89, COM (2001) 745/6 final, December 11, 2001, pp.38 to 40.
[41] Case T-342/99 [2002] E.C.R. II 2585. See generally Ch.8 below.

quality of output, distribution or innovation, or appreciably to foreclose competition."[42]

(b) Possible deficiencies in the "dominance" test

2–009 The Commission's consultation and proposals prompted an extensive debate regarding the suitability of the "dominance" test. At a conceptual level, concerns were expressed that the "dominance" test is not well suited to an assessment of the *effects* of a merger on conditions of competition in a market.[43] It was also claimed that the Commission was "expanding" the concept of dominance under the ECMR and its merger decisions were effectively broadening the scope of Art.82. More practically, there was extensive discussion about the existence and extent of any "gap" in the Commission's powers to prohibit mergers.[44] Commentators sought to identify categories of mergers which would be likely to lead to material harm to consumers but could not be prohibited under the text of the ECMR as it then stood.

---

[42] Proposed Amended and Re-stated ECMR, Art.2(2). See also recitals 20 and 21, press release IP/02/1856 and the explanatory memorandum accompanying the Proposed Amended and Re-stated ECMR.

[43] More particularly, the issue was whether "dominance" is to be construed in a *structural* context, such that (leaving coordinated effects to one side) it applies only to suppliers which are the largest in the market and hold significant market shares (normally in excess of 40%) or whether it is instead to be construed as synonymous with *substantial market power*, so that it applies whenever the merged group has the ability profitably to price significantly above the competitive level for a substantial period (or reduce service quality, innovation or variety) irrespective of its market share and the shares of its rivals. Levy, "Dominance vs. SLC: A Subtle Distinction", paper presented to the EC Merger Control Conference on November 8, 2002, considered whether there was a distinction between the dominance test and the question of whether the merged group would enjoy substantial market power and concluded that in practice the dominance test had evolved towards a market power standard.

[44] The literature includes Bishop & Ridyard, "Prometheus Unbound: Increasing the Scope for Intervention in EC Merger Control" [2003] E.C.L.R. 356; Thompson, "Goodbye to 'the Dominance Test'? Substantive Appraisal Under the New UK and EC Merger Regimes" [2003] Comp Law 332; Selvam, "The EC Merger Control Impasse: is there a Solution to this Predicament?" [2004] E.C.L.R. 52; Voigt & Schmidt, "Switching to Substantial Impediments of Competition (SIC) can have Substantial Costs—SIC!" [2004] E.C.L.R. 584; Schmidt, "The New ECMR: 'Significant Impediment' or 'Significant Improvement'" [2004] C.M.L.Rev. 1555; Kokkoris, "The Reform of the European Control Merger Regulation in the Aftermath of the *Airtours* Case—the Eagerly Expected Debate: SLC v Dominance Test" [2005] E.C.L.R. 37; Fountoukakos & Ryan, "A New Substantive Test for EU Merger Control" [2005] E.C.L.R. 277; and Baxter & Dethmers, "Unilateral Effects Under the European Merger Regulation: How Big is the Gap" [2005] E.C.L.R. 380. See also Neven & Röller, "Discrepancies Between Markets and Regulators: An Analysis of the First Ten Years of EU Merger Control", published as Ch.2 of *The Pros and Cons of Merger Control* by the Swedish Competition Authority in 2002 (and available at *www.kkv.se/bestall/pdf/skrift_proscons.pdf*), which stated, at p.13: "Significant price increases may indeed take place without leading to the creation or strengthening of a dominant position".

At a particular level, several scenarios were identified.[45]   **2–010**

(a) The merging parties have relatively low combined market shares but are close competitors in the supply of *differentiated products* (i.e. products which are regarded by customers as different)[46] and will be able profitably to raise prices following the transaction. The issue is whether a transaction can be regarded as creating or strengthening a dominant position when the merged group has market power in a *particular segment* of a market but not in other segments and its share of the market as a whole is below the levels generally regarded as conferring sole-firm dominance. Philip Lowe, Director General of DG Competition, focused on this particular issue when describing the rationale for the amendment to the substantive test, observing that "there were particular concerns that the Regulation might not be able to tackle all situations of oligopoly in markets for differentiated products, when the merger would involve the elimination of a significant competitive constraint, but would neither result in the creation or strengthening of the paramount firm in the market, nor in a likelihood of coordination between the oligopolists".[47]

(b) The number of players in the market is reduced from three to two but the non-merging party remains by far the leading player and there is no indication that coordinated effects will occur following the

---

[45] See generally the Irish Competition Authority's "Guidelines for Merger Analysis", December 2002 (available at *www.tca.ie*), para.4.14 (the document also raises the question of whether a transaction may be prohibited on the grounds that it reduces the number of suppliers in a market in which Cournot competition occurs (see paras 1–019 to 1–021) or eliminates a competitor in a market in which competition depends on the number of suppliers, e.g. if competition in an auction market is determined by the number of bidders); the UK House of Lords Select Committee on the European Union, Thirty-second Report, "The Review of the EC Merger Regulation", July 23, 2002, HL Paper 165 (available at *www.parliament. the-stationery-office.co.uk/pa/ld200102/ldselect/ldeucom/165/165.pdf*) (paras 147 to 150); the International Competition Network Analytical Framework Sub-group, "The Analytical Framework for Merger Control" (available at *www.internationalcompetitionnetwork.org/ afsguk.pdf*) (paras 41 to 43); Levy, "Dominance vs. SLC: A Subtle Distinction", paper presented to the EC Merger Control Conference on November 8, 2002; Vickers, "How to reform the EC merger test", speech of November 8, 2002 (www.oft.gov.uk/News/Speeches+and+articles/2002/index.htm); and the Australian Merger Guidelines, June 1999 (*www.accc.gov.au/content/item.phtml?itemId=719436&nodeId=file43a1f42c7eb63&fn=Merger %20Guidelines.pdf*) (contemplating, at para.5.97, that transactions falling beneath the Australian concentration thresholds may be prohibited "in auction type situations, where two small suppliers of (product or spatially) differentiated products provide the closest substitute to each other, or where an incumbent acquires a small innovative new entrant".) For discussion of whether the substantive test under the ECMR as it then stood was capable of covering some or all of the scenarios identified in the text, see para.1–32 of the first edition of this text.
[46] See s.7.3 below.
[47] "Current Issues of EU Competition Law—The New Competition Enforcement Regime", speech at Barcelona, October 2, 2003 (available at *http://europa.eu.int/comm/competition/ speeches/text/sp2003_035_en.pdf*).

transaction.[48] A traditional analysis under the ECMR is that the merger does not result in the creation or strengthening of a dominant position since the second largest firm in a market cannot hold a position of sole-firm dominance and the transaction therefore cannot be prohibited. These stylised facts are drawn from those in the US *Baby Foods*[49] transaction, in which the second and third largest players in the US commercial baby foods market, Heinz and Beech-Nut, planned to merge. The market leader, Gerber, had a market share of around 65 per cent and the merging parties shares of around 17 and 15 per cent. The DC Circuit Court granted a preliminary injunction restraining the transaction (reversing the decision of the district court). Retail grocers generally carried two ranges of baby foods, Gerber's and either Heinz's or Beech-Nut's, and Heinz and Beech-Nut competed to win the second position, in particular, by paying slotting fees. In issuing the injunction, the DC Circuit Court took into account the fact that the merger would eliminate that competition for second position, the increase in the Herfindahl-Hirschman Index[50] from 4,775 to 5,285 and the high barriers to entry, and rejected an argument based on efficiency gains. Analytically, the case is best regarded as one of non-coordinated effects arising in a segment of the market, namely the provision of baby foods to retail grocers to occupy the second slot, as the principal concern about the transaction was the elimination of competition between Heinz and Beech-Nut rather than the way that the merged group would compete with Gerber.[51]

(c) The merging parties have relatively low combined market shares measured by sales or total capacity, but their *competitors are capacity constrained*, which may enable the merged group profitably to reduce its output and raise prices following the merger.[52]

---

[48] The Commission has doubted the significance in practice of this scenario: see the Green Paper on the Review of Council Reg. 4064/89, December 11, 2001, COM (2001) 745/6 final, para.166. However, for an example of a case affecting European consumers involving a merger which would have created a stronger second (but not leading) supplier and which was found to harm consumers, see *Cendant Corporation / RAC Holdings Limited*, UK Monopolies and Mergers Commission (now Competition Commission), 1999 (*www.competition-commission.org.uk/rep_pub/reports/1999/423cendant.htm#full*).

[49] *FTC v H J Heinz Co* 246 F.3d 708 (DC Cir 2001).

[50] See s.4.3 below.

[51] The case is not authority for the proposition that US courts will issue preliminary injunctions to prevent mergers which reduce the number of players in an oligopoly *notwithstanding* the absence of non-coordinated or coordinated effects. Although the US applies a substantial lessening of competition test, the only theories of competitive harm identified by the US agencies in their Horizontal Merger Guidelines, 1992 (amended in 1997) (*www.usdoj.gov/atr/public/guidelines/hmg.htm*) are unilateral (i.e. non-coordinated) and coordinated effects. In other words, the US agencies have not identified a third theory of competitive harm (based on a reduction in the number of players in an oligopoly notwithstanding the absence of non-coordinated or coordinated effects) which can be applied in the US under its statutory provisions.

[52] See s.7.4 below.

(d) The merging parties have relatively low combined market shares measured by sales or total capacity but are in a position to make "*all-or-nothing*" offers to a small group of large customers because their competitors face *capacity constraints* or *differential costs*.[53] Imagine a market with ten suppliers, each having a capacity of 100 units per year; five of the suppliers have production costs of £10 per unit and five of £12 per unit; the largest customer in the market purchases 400 units per year; prior to the merger, the largest customer negotiates a price of £10 per unit by playing off against one another the five lower-cost suppliers since it needs to deal with just four of them; if two of those suppliers merge they may be able to make an "all-or-nothing" offer to the customer for the supply of 200 units at £2,199; as the customer requires 400 units and can only acquire 300 units from other lower-cost suppliers it would have to buy 100 units from the higher-cost suppliers unless it accepted the merged group's "all-or-nothing" offer and, by doing so, it saves £1. The merger may therefore facilitate an increase in the merged group's price of almost 10 per cent even though the merged group's share by capacity is just 20 per cent.

(e) One of the merging parties is a "maverick" whose activities prior to the merger had prevented other suppliers from profitably raising prices.[54]

(c) The adoption by the Council of "compromise" text

Discussion on the substantive test in the Council of Ministers began in **2–011** Summer 2003.[55] The Commission obtained agreement in principle that "non-collusive oligopolies" ought to be caught by the ECMR, but there was no consensus on the formulation of any new test. The compromise "significant impediment to effective competition" test was proposed by the French and Spanish delegations and appears to have won favour[56] because it

---

[53] See Areeda, Hovenkamp & Solow, *Antitrust Law* (2nd edn, Aspen Law & Business, 1998), Vol.IV, para.915; Baker, "Non-coordinated Competitive Effects Theories in Merger Analysis", Spring 1997, *Antitrust*, Vol.11, p.21; and the US Horizontal Merger Guidelines, 1992 (amended in 1997) (*www.usdoj.gov/atr/public/guidelines/hmg.htm*), n.21.

[54] See s.7.5(c) below. Fingleton, "Does Collective Dominance Provide Suitable Housing for All Anti-Competitive Oligopolistic Mergers?" published in the 2002 *Annual Proceedings of the Fordham Corporate Law Institute*, p.181 at p.183, distinguishes two categories of "gap": first, cases of unilateral market power arising at market shares lower than the normal levels associated with dominance; and secondly multilateral effects where the emphasis is not on the market power of the merging parties, but instead on the equilibrium outcome, as in the case of the loss of a maverick.

[55] See Fountoukakos & Ryan, "A New Substantive Test for EU Merger Control" [2005] E.C.L.R. 277 for details of the political discussions.

[56] On November 27, 2003, the Council of Ministers finally reached agreement on the text of the revised ECMR, including the adoption of the "compromise" "significant impediment to effective competition" test.

shifted the focus of attention to the effects of the merger on competition (the main objective of the delegations which had pressed for a switch to a substantial lessening of competition test) whilst retaining the concept of dominance and providing for continuity (as it did not introduce any concepts which were not already present in the text of the ECMR).

2.4 INTERPRETING THE SIEC TEST

(a) Formally, the new test broadens the Commission's jurisdiction

2–012 The new substantive test under the ECMR uses the same core concepts ("significant impediment to effective competition" and "dominance") as the original text, but the effect of re-ordering the words is to broaden the Commission's jurisdiction to prohibit mergers. Under the original text, the Commission could prohibit a merger (or clear it subject to undertakings) only if it established that the merger would create or strengthen a dominant position. However, a merger that would lead to a significant impediment to effective competition *without* creating or strengthening a dominant position may be prohibited under the new test. This has implications for horizontal mergers[57] as the changes to the substantive test allow the Commission to challenge certain transactions not raising coordinated effects concerns, even though the merged group's market share is below the level giving rise to a dominant position.

The change to the substantive test also arguably[58] removes the need, in vertical and conglomerate cases, for the Commission to establish that a dominant position has been created or strengthened (an issue that is not straightforward, for example, when the theory of competitive harm is that the merged group will leverage its power in a market in which it holds a dominant position into a second market in which it does not hold and will not obtain a dominant position).[59] A broader point remains to be determined, namely whether the shift to a "significant impediment to effective competition test" will result in the Commission intervening in vertical and conglomerate cases when the merged group will not hold a dominant position in *any* of the markets affected.[60]

---

[57] The extent to which this *formal* broadening of the test is of *practical* significance depends on the meaning of "significant impediment to effective competition" (which is discussed in s.(b) below) and the extent to which the Commission would have been able to "stretch" the dominance test had the substantive test not been amended.

[58] The counter-argument to the proposition in the text is based on recital 25 of the ECMR and is discussed in para.2–015 below.

[59] See para.11–017 below.

[60] See para.11–018 below.

(b) What is meant by "significant impediment to effective competition"?

(i) Textual analysis The starting point in interpreting the phrase "significant   **2–013** impediment to effective competition" is a textual analysis. The words "significant impediment" imply that a merger will be prohibited only if it materially reduces or lessens the extent of "competition" within the market. "Competition" is the commercial interaction between actual and potential suppliers and their customers and "effective competition" is competition that delivers material benefits to consumers. This means that a merger which does not materially harm consumers (e.g. because the target is ineffectual, the acquirer and target do not compete directly to any material extent, or customers possess sufficient buyer power to prevent any attempt to exercise market power) could not be prohibited, even though it reduces rivalry by removing an independent supplier from the market.[61]

(ii) Decisions of the Community Courts Decisions of the Community Courts   **2–014** interpreting the words "significant impediment to effective competition" under the original ECMR support this textual interpretation and shed further light on the meaning of the new test. Under Regulation 4064/89, a merger could be prohibited only if it *both* created or strengthened a dominant position *and* thereby significantly impeded effective competition.[62] Whilst the Commission focused in its decisional practice on the dominance test, the Community Courts emphasised that the substantive test involved

---

[61] On this reading, the word "effective" largely duplicates the materiality concept included through the words "significant impediment".

[62] Some of the older cases draw a distinction between the short-term focus of the dominance test and the longer-term perspective of the significant impediment of competition test. In Case IV/ M.53 *Aerospatiale / Alenia / de Havilland* [1991] O.J. L334/42, para.53 (see also para.72), the Commission distinguished the dominance and effective competition provisions stating that "a concentration which leads to the creation of a dominant position may however be compatible with the common market within the meaning of Art.2(2) of the Merger Regulation if there exists strong evidence that this position is only temporary and would be quickly eroded because of the high probability of strong market entry. With such market entry the dominant position is not likely to significantly impede competition within the meaning of Art.2(3) of the Merger Regulation". (See also the discussion of *de Havilland* in the Commission's XXIst Annual Report on Competition Policy, 1991, p.362). In Case IV/M.222 *Mannesmann / Hoesch* [1993] O.J. L114/34, paras 92, 112 to 114, the Commission found that "there is strong evidence that the parties concerned may achieve upon completion of the concentration a liberty of action that is not immediately fully controlled by existing competitors" but cleared the transaction on the grounds that it would not result in a significant impediment of effective competition because of the high probability of new entry which would quickly erode the merged group's position on the market. However, the approach taken in these cases has not generally been followed. Further, the decisions are inconsistent with the cases discussed in s.2.6 below, which identify a two to three year period for analysis under the ECMR without distinguishing between the dominance and significant impediment of competition tests.

two separate limbs ("a bifurcated test")[63] and characterised the second part of the test (i.e. the significant impediment to effective competition limb) as raising the question of "whether the remaining competition would be significantly weakened".[64] This formulation focuses on the competitive process and the significant impediment to effective competition test is therefore a *dynamic* one, examining the *effects*[65] of the merger on competition within the market (not just on the merged group's market position). Importantly, by focusing on the effect of the merger on competition in the market *as a whole*, the Commission appears[66] able to intervene in cases in which the alleged harm to competition arises when the merger creates or strengthens market power *held by a third party*. Whilst the Commission interpreted the dominance test to apply to such cases,[67] its approach was controversial and might not have withstood scrutiny by the Community Courts.

2–015 **(iii) Recitals to the revised ECMR** The opening three sentences of recital 25 to the ECMR describe the rationale for adopting the significant impediment to effective competition test in terms which focus on the need to close any perceived "gap" in the Commission's jurisdiction to prohibit mergers which materially harm consumers:

"In view of the consequences that concentrations in oligopolistic market structures may have, it is all the more necessary to maintain effective competition in such markets. Many oligopolistic markets exhibit a healthy degree of competition. However, under certain circumstances, concentrations involving the elimination of important competitive constraints that the merging parties had exerted upon each other, as well as a

---

[63] The existence of a bifurcated test is supported by the judgments of the Court of First Instance in Case T-2/93 *Air France v Commission* [1994] E.C.R. II-323, para.79; Case T-290/94 *Kayserberg v Commission* [1997] E.C.R. II-2137; Case T-5/02 *Tetra Laval BV v Commission* [2002] E.C.R. II-4381, paras 120, 128, 146 and 285 (the decision was upheld on appeal on the basis of reasoning not relating to this issue in Case C-12/03P *Commission v Tetra Laval BV*, not yet reported, judgment of February 15, 2005); Case T-158/00 *ARD v Commission* [2003] E.C.R. II-3825, para.130; Case T-87/05 *EDP v Commission*, not yet reported, judgment of September 21, 2005, para.45; and Case T-210/01 *General Electric Company v Commission*, not yet reported, judgment of December 14, 2005, para.84. Furthermore, the substantive test under Regulation 4064/89 was finalised in the light of criticism by ECOSOC of a 1988 draft which proposed a straightforward dominance test ([1988] O.J. C208/14): "The Regulation must make it clear that a merger is not incompatible with the Common Market merely because it gives rise to or strengthens a dominant position".

[64] Case T-5/02 *Tetra Laval BV v Commission* [2002] E.C.R. II-4381, para.285 (the decision was upheld on appeal on the basis of reasoning not relating to this issue in Case C-12/03P *Commission v Tetra Laval BV*, not yet reported, judgment of February 15, 2005).

[65] See the Commission Communication, "A Pro-Active Competition Policy for a Competitive Europe", April 20, 2004 (*http://europa.eu.int/comm/competition/publications/proactive/en.pdf*), emphasising, at p.12, that the "new Regulation now contains a clear and unambiguous, effects-based competition test".

[66] The caveat to the analysis in the text arises from recital 25 of the ECMR which is discussed in para.2–015 below.

[67] See para.2–023 below.

reduction of competitive pressure on the remaining competitors, may, even in the absence of a likelihood of coordination between the members of the oligopoly, result in a significant impediment to effective competition."

The final sentence of recital 25 purports to limit the extent to which the Commission's jurisdiction to prohibit mergers is extended by the change to the substantive test, stating: "The notion of 'significant impediment to effective competition' in Article 2(2) and (3) should be interpreted as extending, beyond the concept of dominance, only to the anti-competitive effects of a concentration resulting from the non-coordinated behaviour of undertakings which would not have a dominant position on the market concerned."[68] This recital means that the significant impediment to effective competition test applies to mergers which *either* create or strengthen a dominant position[69] *or* result in anti-competitive effects through "non-coordinated behaviour" of undertakings. However, the practical effect of the recital is quite limited. This is because every theory of competitive harm which does not involve an allegation of coordinated effects within the *Airtours* test can reasonably be characterised as "non-coordinated behaviour" (i.e. behaviour which does not depend, for its success, on accommodating responses from rivals)[70] and the recital allows the Commission to intervene in any such case provided that the merger results in "anti-competitive effects", a concept which can reasonably be construed to apply to all situations in which consumers are materially harmed.[71] Certainly, recital 25 does not, on its face, appear to limit the ability of the Commission to intervene in any of the five cases identified in para.2–010 above of possible "gaps" in the Commission's powers to prohibit mergers which are likely materially to harm consumers.

The more complex question is whether the Commission can rely on the significant impediment to effective competition test in cases of vertical or conglomerate effects without needing to establish that the merger creates or

---

[68] The importance of recital 25 is bolstered by a joint statement by the Council and Commission that the significant impediment to effective competition test should be interpreted in the light of the objectives of the ECMR as referred to in Article 2(1) "and in the recitals to the Regulation, in particular recital 25"; see the minutes of the 2557th meeting of the Council of the European Union (Economic and Financial Affairs), January 20, 2004 (available via *http://register.consilium.eu.int/pdf/en/04/st05/st05501-ad01.en04.pdf*).

[69] The *de minimis* exception, which is discussed in para.2–020 below, is relevant in cases involving the creation or strengthening of a dominant position.

[70] See the discussion of the meaning of non-coordinated effects in OECD, "Substantive Criteria Used for the Assessment of Mergers", DAFFE/COMP 2003 5, pp. 22 and 23.

[71] See also Fountoukakos & Ryan, "A New Substantive Test for EU Merger Control" [2005] E.C.L.R. 277, who comment as follows on the final sentence of recital 25: "this sentence places no meaningful boundary on the substantive test. Coordinated and non-coordinated effects encompass the totality of possible anti-competitive effects flowing from a merger, and so no further gap is apparent". Contrast Völcker, "Mind the Gap: Unilateral Effects Analysis Arrives in EC Merger Control" [2004] E.C.L.R. 395, p.404, who states at n.64, that the effect of recital 25 is that the Commission has no greater powers to challenge vertical or conglomerate mergers.

strengthens a dominant position. As these cases involve the leveraging of market power from one market into a second, it is not always straightforward to establish that a transaction creates or strengthens a dominant position, since the principal effects of the strategy are felt in the leveraged market and may occur without creating or strengthening a dominant position in that market.[72] The Commission itself does not appear to have treated this issue as one which affects its ability to intervene in mergers when it predicts material harm to consumers, but the change to the legislation resolves this issue so long as vertical and conglomerate effects are treated as "non-coordinated effects" for the purposes of interpreting recital 25.

2–016   Recital 26 also limits the Commission's freedom to challenge mergers. Its opening sentence provides: "A significant impediment to effective competition generally results from the creation or strengthening of a dominant position." The use of the word "generally" implies that relatively few cases will fall within the "significant impediment to effective competition" test without also creating or strengthening a dominant position. Such an interpretation would not prevent the "significant impediment to effective competition" test from being applied in the "gap" cases identified in para.2–010 above,[73] but would appear to prevent the Commission from intervening more generally to prohibit mergers which do not create or strengthen a dominant position (for example in reliance on models of competition in oligopoly markets which suggest that "8 to 7" or "7 to 6" mergers generally lead to material increases in prices).[74]

Recital 26 also states that the "significant impediment to effective competition" test was adopted "With a view to preserving the guidance that may be drawn from past judgments of the European courts and Commission decisions pursuant to Regulation (EEC) No 4064/89, while at the same time maintaining consistency with the standards of competitive harm which have been applied by the Commission and the Community courts regarding the compatibility of a concentration with the common market". This sentence implies that the Commission should apply the new test in a similar way to the previous test.

2–017 **(iv) Statements by Commission officials** The interpretation of recital 26 set out above is supported by statements by senior Commission officials who took the view that the change to the substantive test served to eliminate uncertainty regarding the *breadth* of the Commission's jurisdiction and did not in substance *lower* the threshold for intervention. In other words, under the new substantive test, the Commission is required to establish to the

---

[72] See generally para.11–019 below.

[73] In the Commission's Frequently Asked Questions (MEMO/04/9), the Commission stated that the effect of the amendments is to make clear that "all anti-competitive mergers resulting in higher prices, less choice or innovation are covered", i.e. there are no remaining cases caught within the "gap".

[74] See paras 1–019 to 1–021 above for discussion of the Cournot model.

requisite legal standard[75] that the merger is likely materially to harm consumers (through higher prices, lower quality or reductions in choice or innovation) in exactly the same way as under the old law, the only change being that a notifying party can no longer take the "technical" point that, notwithstanding that material harm to consumers is likely, the transaction must be approved because it does not create or strengthen a dominant position. Consistently with this approach, Mario Monti, then Commissioner for Competition Policy, observed that the new test would not alter the Commission's approach to the analysis of the competitive impact of mergers.[76] Further, Philip Lowe, Director General of DG Competition, stated: "The test should not be interpreted as a lowering of the intervention threshold ... The standard of incompatibility of mergers will therefore remain the same as before, as would the underlying rationale for EC merger control, that is, to prevent undertakings from acquiring significant market power through mergers."[77] He also observed: "By keeping the concept of dominance unaltered, the new test will preserve the acquis and, thus, the guidance that can be drawn from past decisional practice and case law. As a result, previous decisions and judgements could still be relied upon as precedents when considering whether a merger is likely or not to create or strengthen a dominant position".[78]

(v) **Comparison with the substantial lessening of competition test** When the **2–018** Commission commenced its consultation exercise on possible reform to the substantive test under the ECMR, it raised the possibility of switching to the "substantial lessening of competition" test which is used in numerous merger control systems, in particular the US.[79] The question arises whether the "significant impediment to effective competition" test is in any material

---

[75] See s.2.5(b) below.
[76] Competition Policy Newsletter, Special Edition, "The EU gets new competition powers for the 21st century" (*http://europa.eu.int/comm/competition/publications/cpn/special_edition.pdf*), p.2.
[77] "Implications of the recent reforms in the antitrust enforcement in Europe for National Competition Authorities", Speech at Italian Competition/Consumer Day, Rome, December 9, 2003 (*http://europa.eu.int/comm/competition/speeches/text/sp2003_067_en.pdf*). See also Mr Lowe's speech, "The future shape of European merger control", Brussels, February 17, 2003 (*http://europa.eu.int/comm/competition/speeches/*), arguing that the dominance test was capable of covering the same issues as a substantial lessening of competition test because the Commission had interpreted the dominance test dynamically with the objective of protecting consumers from the potentially negative effects of mergers on the competitive process. See also Fountoukakos & Ryan, "A New Substantive Test for EU Merger Control" [2005] E.C.L.R. 277, 288 and 291 to 293 ("the new test does not signal a 'lowering of the intervention threshold'").
[78] "Implications of the recent reforms in the antitrust enforcement in Europe for National Competition Authorities", Speech at Italian Competition/Consumer Day, Rome, December 9, 2003 (*http://europa.eu.int/comm/competition/speeches/text/sp2003_067_en.pdf*).
[79] See para.2–008 above.

respects different from the "substantial lessening of competition" test.[80] At a purposive level, both are intended to focus on the effect of the merger on the competition process (rather than on a structural analysis). From a textual perspective, both tests focus on the effects on competition, direct attention to the reduction (if any) in competition arising from the merger (through the terms "impediment"[81] and "lessening") and include a materiality threshold so that mergers having a trivial effect on competition are not caught (through the terms "substantial" and "significant"). It is difficult to identify any material differences between the two tests arising from the use of marginally different words to address two of the three concepts (the *reduction* in competition and the *materiality* threshold) and the practical conclusion is that the two tests are materially the same.[82] This interpretation receives support from the Commission's evidence to the United Kingdom House of Lords Select Committee on the European Union.[83] The Committee reports that, "The Commission ... emphasised that, in the [old] Regulation, dominance was 'surrounded by other wording' [the significant impediment to effective competition test] which was 'quite similar to the SLC [substantial lessening of competition] test'".[84] Further, Mario Monti, when Commissioner for Competition Policy, observed that if there were ever a gap between the US system (which has a substantial lessening of competition test) and the EU system, that gap disappeared following the adoption of the significant impediment to effective competition test in the ECMR.[85]

(c) The "significant impediment to effective competition" test in practice

2–019   Initial experience with the "significant impediment to effective competition" test suggests that little has changed. First, the nature of the Commission's

---

[80] The decision by the legislature not to adopt the "substantial lessening of competition" test does not imply that the legislature must have intended the "significant impediment to effective competition" test to bear a different meaning as the choice of words can be explained on the basis of a wish to preserve the language from Regulation 4064/89 and to maintain a distinctive "European character" to the test (see Fountoukakos & Ryan, "A New Substantive Test for EU Merger Control" [2005] E.C.L.R. 277, at p.288).

[81] As discussed above, the reference to "effective" competition also appears to connote a materiality threshold.

[82] Even if the tests were identical, this would not provide an assurance of actual convergence in decision making.

[83] Thirty-second Report, "The Review of the EC Merger Regulation", July 23, 2002, HL Paper 165 (available at *www.parliament.the-stationery-office.co.uk/pa/ld200102/ldselect/ldeucom/165/16501.htm*), para.103. See also para.170.

[84] See also Fountoukakos & Ryan, "A New Substantive Test for EU Merger Control" [2005] E.C.L.R. 277, 295 describing the two tests as "for all intents and purposes synonymous".

[85] Speech at the UCLA Law First Annual Institute on US and EU Antitrust Aspects of Mergers and Acquisitions of 28 February, 2004, "Convergence in EU-US antitrust policy regarding mergers and acquisitions: an EU perspective" (*http://europa.eu.int/rapid/pressReleases Action.do?reference=SPEECH/04/107&format=HTML&aged=0&language=EN&gui Language =en*). See also Voigt & Schmidt, "The Commission's Guidelines on Horizontal Mergers: Improvement or Deterioration?" (2004) 41 C.M.L.Rev. 1583, describing the differences between the two tests as semantic rather than substantive.

analysis has not materially altered (reflecting the fact that the Commission had in practice applied the dominance test in a way which focused on the effects of the merger on consumer welfare). For this reason, decisions taken prior to the adoption of the "significant impediment to effective competition" test remain relevant precedents, reflecting the objective identified in recital 26 of the revised ECMR of preserving under the new test the guidance that could be drawn from past judgments of the Community Courts and decisions of the Commission. This is consistent with Philip Lowe's prediction that the adoption of the new test would not change the standard of incompatibility of mergers[86] and with a paper prepared by the German Bundeskartellamt which concluded that the fact that antitrust authorities might reach different conclusions in particular cases could not be attributed to the fact that some used a substantial lessening of competition test and others a dominance test.[87] Secondly, few if any cases have been identified which fell within the "gap". In its decisions since the coming into force of the "significant impediment to effective competition" test on May 1, 2004, the Commission has drafted its merger decisions using a range of different verbal formulations (sometimes setting out the full substantive test, sometimes simply referring to the issue of dominance and sometimes referring only to the question of significant impediment to effective competition). In general, it cannot be inferred from such variations in drafting style that the Commission has intervened in cases using the significant impediment to effective competition test. However, in *Syngenta CP / Advanta*[88] the Commission identified serious doubts in certain markets regarding the possible creation of a dominant position and identified separate concerns regarding "the creation of non-coordinated effects in an oligopolistic market for sugar beet seeds in Belgium and France", implying that the Commission did not have serious doubts that the merger would create or strengthen a dominant position in such markets. The commitments accepted by the Commission nevertheless included undertakings regarding the market for sugar beet seeds in Belgium and France and the inference is that this market might have fallen within the "gap" under the old substantive test. Further, in *EDF / AEM / Edison*[89] the Commission examined whether the merged group would be able to influence the price of electricity, despite having shares well below those which typically connote dominance, although, following an investigation, it concluded that this was no more likely after the transaction than before.

---

[86] See para.2–017 above.
[87] See OECD, "Substantive Criteria Used for the Assessment of Mergers", DAFFE/COMP (2003) 5, pp. 19 and 20.
[88] Case COMP/M.3465.
[89] Case COMP/M.3729, paras 73, 80 and 85 to 88.

(d) "De minimis" exception

2–020 The reference to a "significant" impediment to effective competition implies that a trivial or non-material reduction in competition will not lead to the prohibition of a merger.[90] This reading is consistent with the interpretation of the original substantive test in Regulation 4064/89 by the Court of First Instance which ruled that a merger may only be prohibited if it results in a "substantial alteration" to competition[91] which significantly and lastingly impedes competition in the relevant market.[92]

The existence of a "de minimis" exception is also clear[93] from numerous decisions in which the Commission has approved transactions involving small increments in market share.[94]

In addition, the Commission has taken account of the total value of the market in approving transactions involving relatively high combined shares of *very small markets*. For example,[95] in *CVC / Ruhrgas Industries*[96] the Commission emphasised, in clearing the transaction, that the combined shares of 50 to 60 per cent and 65 to 75 per cent arose in markets that were comparatively small (total market sizes of €16,000 and €390,000 respectively).

(e) "Dominant position"

2–021 The meaning of a "dominant position" is less important under the revised ECMR, as the focus is now on the "significant impediment to effective competition" test. Nevertheless, in practice, most cases will depend on whether the merger creates or strengthens a dominant position. This is clear from recital 26 to the revised ECMR,[97] which states that a significant impediment to effective competition will "generally" arise from the creation or strengthening of a dominant position[98] and the Notice on Horizontal Mergers which refers to the creation or strengthening of a dominant position as the "primary" form of competitive harm[99] and states that "it is

---

[90] See, e.g. Case T-210/01 *General Electric Company v Commission*, not yet reported, judgment of December 14, 2005, para.543.

[91] Case T-2/93 *Air France v Commission* [1994] E.C.R. II-323 (paras 78 and 79); Case T-102/96 *Gencor v Commission* [1999] E.C.R. II-753 (paras 170, 180 and 193); and Case T-342/99 *Airtours plc v Commission* [2002] E.C.R. II-2585 (paras 58 and 82).

[92] Case T-342/99 *Airtours plc v Commission* [2002] E.C.R. II-2585, para.58.

[93] The 1991 version of the Canadian Merger Guidelines, para.2.4, defined a *substantial* lessening of competition as arising when prices were likely to be at least 5% greater in a substantial part of the relevant market. However, this version has now been replaced and the 2004 Guidelines (*www.competitionbureau.gc.ca/PDFs/2004%20MEGs.Final.pdf*) state, at para.2.14, that the Bureau does *not* apply a numerical threshold for material price increases.

[94] See para.4–030 below.

[95] See, e.g. Case COMP/M.3751 *Novartis / Hexal*, pp.6 and 12.

[96] Case COMP/M.3874, para.39.

[97] See para.2–016 above.

[98] The Commission's Frequently Asked Questions (MEMO/04/9) state that dominance will remain the "main scenario".

[99] Para.2.

expected that most cases of incompatibility of a concentration with the common market will continue to be based upon a finding of dominance".[1]

A "dominant position" has been defined by the European Court of Justice as "a position of economic strength enjoyed by an undertaking which enables it to hinder the maintenance of effective competition on the relevant market by allowing it to act to an appreciable extent independently of its competitors and customers and ultimately of consumers."[2] In *General Electric Company v Commission*[3] the Court of First Instance made a number of observations about the operation of the dominance test:

(a) there is no need to show that competition will be eliminated in order to establish that a supplier holds a dominant position;

(b) if an undertaking is compelled to lower its own prices by the pressure of price reductions by rivals, this is generally incompatible with its holding a dominant position;

(c) however, the making of financial concessions in a tender market is not inconsistent with a supplier holding a dominant position; the Court identified a distinction between everyday consumer products and high value products sold through bidding processes;

(d) "even the existence of lively competition on a particular market does not rule out the possibility that there is a dominant position on that market, since the predominant feature of such a position is the ability of the undertaking concerned to act without having to take account of this competition in its market strategy and without for that reason suffering detrimental effects from such behaviour".[4]

---

[1] Para.4. See also Fountoukakos & Ryan, "A New Substantive Test for EU Merger Control" [2005] E.C.L.R. 277, who comment at p.291, that it is "likely that the notion of dominance will continue to be a central feature of EC merger analysis for some time to come".

[2] Case 322/81 *Michelin v Commission* [1983] E.C.R. 3461, para.30 (a case under Art.82). See also Case 85/76 *Hoffmann-La Roche* [1979] E.C.R. 461, para.38; Case 27/76 *United Brands v Commission* [1978] E.C.R. 207, para.65; Case T-30/89 *Hilti v Commission* [1991] E.C.R. II-1439, para.90; Case T-102/96 *Gencor v Commission* [1999] E.C.R. II-753, para.200; and Case T-282/02 *Cementbouw Handel & Industrie v Commission*, not yet reported, judgment of February 23, 2006, para.195. Case T-87/05 *EDP v Commission*, not yet reported, judgment of September 21, 2005, para.48. The European Court of Justice's definition is criticised in Azevedo & Walker, "Dominance: Meaning and Measurement" [2002] E.C.L.R. 363 (see also Dobbs & Richards, "Output Restriction as a Measure of Market Power" [2005] E.C.L.R. 572). For a detailed account of the adoption and evolution of the dominance test under the ECMR, see Levy, "Dominance vs. SLC: A Subtle Distinction", paper presented to the EC Merger Control Conference on November 8, 2002, pp.4 to 21.

[3] Case T-210/01, not yet reported, judgment of December 14, 2005, paras 114, 116, 117 and 215 (see also paras 85, 184, 243 and 249).

[4] See also Case COMP/M.2187 *CVC / Lenzing* [2004] O.J. L82/20 in which the Commission observed, at para.137: "Such a position [i.e. a dominant position] does not exclude the existence of some competition but enables the undertaking which profits from it, if not to determine, at least to have an appreciable influence on the conditions under which that competition will develop, and in any case to act largely in disregard of it so long as such conduct does not operate to its detriment".

In *GE / Instrumentarium*[5] the Commission "glossed" this test by adding that the issue was whether the merged group would be able to "significantly raise prices charged to customers."

Finally, the Commissioner for Competition Policy, Neelie Kroes, has said: "naturally I identify dominance with substantial market power".[6]

2–022 **(i) "Dominance" involves an assessment of the merged group's incentives and abilities** The definition of dominance in Art.82 cases must be treated with some caution for the purposes of the ECMR because merger control is a prospective exercise whereas Art.82 cases involve an assessment of historic behaviour.[7] The cases under Art.82 focus on the undertaking's *ability* to act to an appreciable extent independently of competitors, customers and ultimately consumers,[8] whereas merger control is concerned not so much with conduct that the merged group *could* adopt as with conduct that it is *likely* to adopt.[9] Merger control therefore involves an assessment of the merged group's ability *and incentive*[10] to harm consumers. This appears most clearly from the cases on coordinated effects, vertical effects and conglomerate effects[11] and the Notice on Horizontal Mergers.[12] The merged group's incentives are most obviously relevant when the theory of competitive harm is that the merged group might adopt a particular course of conduct but this can be ruled out as a practical concern if the strategy would not be profit-maximising. The merged group's incentives are less often relevant when the theory of competitive harm is based on non-coordinated effects arising from horizontal overlaps, although they were crucial in *BASF / American Cyanamid (AHP)*.[13] In that case, the merged group sold the same product into

---

[5] Case COMP/M.3083 [2004] O.J. L109/1, para.217.

[6] Speech of September 23, 2005, "Preliminary Thoughts on Policy Review of Article 82" (*http://europa.eu.int/rapid/pressReleasesAction.do?reference=SPEECH/05/537&format=HTML&aged=0&language=EN&guiLanguage=en*). See also Case COMP/M.3245 *Vodafone / Singlepoint*, para.24 (equating significant market power with dominance) and Götz Drauz, "Conglomerate and Vertical Mergers in the Light of the Tetra Judgment", *Competition Policy Newsletter*, Summer 2005, p.35, at p.36, arguing that the purpose of merger control is to assess whether a merger will result in the creation or enhancement of market power.

[7] The Commission observed in its XXIst Annual Report on Competition Policy, 1991, p.362, that: "In its decisions, the Commission has basically followed the definition of a dominant position given by the Court of Justice for the application of Article [82] ... In the context of mergers this test is, however, more structure and future-oriented than under Article [82], which deals with abuses by firms having already acquired a dominant position".

[8] This appears from the words "which enables it to hinder" (see para.2–021 above).

[9] See s.2.5(b) below for discussion of the standard of proof.

[10] The merged group's intentions (as opposed to its incentives) are irrelevant to the determination of whether the merger will significantly impede effective competition: see Case COMP/M.2187 *CVC / Lenzing* [2004] O.J. L82/20, paras 163 to 168.

[11] See Chs 8, 11 and 12.

[12] See, e.g. paras 36 and 77. See also OECD, "Substantive Criteria Used for the Assessment of Mergers", DAFFE/COMP (2003) 5, p.311 (the Commission's paper stated that mergers may be prohibited if the merged group has the "ability and incentive" to increase its prices following the merger).

[13] Case COMP/M.1932, paras 46 to 48.

several separate antitrust markets but was unable to price discriminate, i.e. it had to set a single price for sales across all markets. Following the merger, the merged group would have had high shares in two markets and, presumably, could profitably have increased prices in those markets if it disregarded sales of the same product into other markets. However, the Commission found that no competition concerns arose in the markets in question because it would not have been profitable[14] for the merged group to increase prices, taking account of the loss of sales of the same product in other competitive and more significant markets.[15] An assessment of the merged group's incentives is also relevant when considering non-profit organisations which may not have the incentive to harm consumers as profit-maximising firms even if they have the ability to do so.[16]

(ii) **Dominant position held by a third party** Applying the substantive test under 2–023 Regulation 4064/89, the Commission concluded in *Exxon / Mobil*[17] that a transaction may be prohibited under the ECMR if it creates or strengthens a dominant position held by a third party or third parties (i.e. one which is not held by the parties to the concentration) for the following reasons:

"It can be noted that Article 2(3) of the Merger Regulation states that a concentration which creates or strengthens a dominant position is to be declared incompatible with the common market. Article 2(3) is thus, in terms, not limited to the prohibition of an operation which will give rise to the creation or reinforcement of a dominant position on the part of one or more of the parties to the concentration—see also recitals 1, 5 and 7 in the preamble to the Regulation ... The Commission considers that the creation or reinforcement of a dominant position by a third party is not excluded from the scope of application of Article 2(3) of the Merger Regulation."

The Commission also derived support for its conclusion from the reasoning of the European Court of Justice in *Kali und Salz*[18] and of the Court of First

---

[14] In the sense of being the profit-maximising strategy.
[15] See also Case COMP/M.2547 *Bayer / Aventis Crop Science* [2004] O.J. L107/1, paras 175 to 177, 584, 662 and 707 and Case COMP/M.2706 *Carnival Corporation / P&O Princess* [2003] O.J. L248/1 (in which the Commission relied, in finding that the transaction would not create a dominant position, on the parties' incentives to expand sales because the high fixed costs of the cruise industry meant that the profit-maximising strategy was to arrive at, or close to, 100% capacity utilisation; paras 238 and 251).
[16] See s.6.4(j) below.
[17] Case IV/M.1383 [2004] O.J. L103/1, paras 225 to 229.
[18] Joined Cases C-68/94 and C-30/95 *France and Others v Commission* [1998] E.C.R. I-1375. At para.171, the Court stated: "A concentration which creates or strengthens a dominant position on the part of the parties concerned with an entity not involved in the concentration is liable to prove incompatible with the system of undistorted competition which the Treaty seeks to secure. Consequently, if it were accepted that only concentrations creating or strengthening a dominant position on the part of the parties to the concentration were covered by the Regulations, its purpose ... would be partially frustrated. The Regulation would thus be deprived of a not insignificant aspect of its effectiveness without being necessary from the perspective of the general structure of the Community system of control of concentrations".

Instance in *Gencor v Commission*,[19] whilst acknowledging that the support was indirect as the merged group was in both cases found to be one of the parties which would jointly hold a dominant position. The Commission has subsequently found that other transactions created or strengthened a dominant position held by a third party[20] and the Notice on Horizontal Mergers provides that a merger may create or strengthen a dominant position held by a third party.[21]

As noted above, the switch from the "dominance" test to the "significant impediment to effective competition" test (with the attendant focus on the effect of the merger on competition in the market rather than on the position of the merged group itself) appears to establish the Commission's power to intervene to prohibit mergers which create or strengthen a dominant position held by a third party or third parties.[22] This ought, therefore, to render moot the debate about whether the Commission was correct in its view that the dominance test itself extended to such situations.

---

[19] Case T-102/96 *Gencor v Commission* [1999] E.C.R. II-753.

[20] In Case COMP/M.2434 *Grupo Villar Mir / EnBW / Hidroélectrica del Cantábrico* [2004] O.J. L48/86, the Commission found that the merger strengthened a position of collective dominance held by two electricity companies which were not involved in the transaction. The parties argued that the Commission's decision in *Exxon* was distinguishable as there were structural links in that case between the merging parties and the undertaking holding a dominant position, the decisions on coordinated effects were distinguishable as in each case the merged group was part of the set of collectively dominant undertakings, and the construction of Arts 2(3) and 8(3) of the ECMR pointed against its application to cases involving the creation or strengthening of a dominant position held by a third party or third parties not involved in the concentration. The Commission rejected these arguments and confirmed that structural links between the merging parties and the company or companies holding a dominant position were *not* required. (In any event, the Commission identified structural links on the facts of the case.) Similarly, in Case COMP/M.2684 *EnBW / EDP / Cajastur / Hidrocantábrico* the Commission found, at paras 33 and 37, that the acquisition by EnBW, EDP and Cajastur of joint control over the Spanish utility company, Hidrocantábrico would strengthen the existing dominant position held collectively by Endesa and Iberdrola (neither of which companies was involved in the notified concentration) because EDF, which jointly controlled EnBW, would, as a result of the transaction, no longer have the incentives which existed beforehand to expand the electricity interconnection capacity between France and Spain, which would eliminate the existing Spanish electricity generators' main potential independent competitor. In Case COMP/M.2876 *NewsCorp / Telepiù* [2004] O.J. L110/73, paras 269 to 281, the Commission considered a related point, namely whether a merger could be prohibited because it created or strengthened a dominant position held by an entity which was not itself an undertaking concerned but which had agreed to acquire a minority, non-controlling stake in the merged entity. The parties argued that the ECMR did not apply to the creation or strengthening of a dominant position held by a third party and pointed out that the Commission would have had no jurisdiction to examine such issues if NewsCorp acquired a 100% interest and, through a separate transaction, subsequently sold a stake not conferring decisive influence to Telecom Italia. The Commission rejected these arguments on the grounds that any decision under the ECMR must cover the entirety of any transaction bringing about a concentration, including minority shareholdings. See also Case COMP/M.2845 *Sogecable / Canalsatélite / Via Digital*.

[21] n.2.

[22] The only reservation regarding this analysis relates to cases of collective dominance and is derived from recital 25 which limits the expansion of the Commission's jurisdiction (arising from the switch to a significant impediment to effective competition test) to cases of non-coordinated effects.

(f) Mergers involving existing monopolies

In *EDP v Commission*[23] the Court of First Instance ruled that a merger could **2–024**
not be prohibited because of its effects on a market in which one of the
merging parties already had a monopoly, reasoning that a monopoly
represents "the ultimate dominant position, which for that reason cannot be
strengthened on that market" and "in the total absence of competition,
there was no competition that could be significantly impeded by the concentration".[24] The decision may[25] be important for at least two categories of
cases. The first is markets which are subject to statutory monopolies, but
where liberalisation is proposed. This was the situation in *EDP / ENI /
GDP*[26] in which the Commission was concerned that the merger would
reduce the extent of competition in the market following liberalisation. The
second, more general, category is cases involving a loss of potential competition. The Court's decision appears to contemplate[27] that a monopolist
which acquires a potential competitor would automatically be granted
approval, but a supplier with a 99 per cent market share entering such a
transaction would be subject to a normal review in the light of the principles
described in Ch.9 even though, other things being equal, the first merger is
marginally more problematic than the second.

(g) "Substantial part of the common market"

In *Suiker Unie*,[28] when determining whether a particular territory was large **2–025**
enough to amount to a "substantial part of the common market", the
European Court of Justice took into account "the pattern and volume of the
production and consumption of the ... product as well as the habits and
economic opportunities of vendors and purchasers". The Commission
applied these criteria under the ECMR in *Exxon / Mobil*[29] when concluding

---

[23] Case T-87/05, not yet reported, judgment of September 21, 2005.
[24] Paras 116 to 120.
[25] The precise rationale for the decision (and therefore the proper limits of its application) are
not clear from the Court of First Instance's reasoning at paras 113 to 133. In particular, the
principles may be applicable generally to all cases involving pre-existing monopolies (indeed,
paras 116 to 120 are drafted in terms which appear on their face to be of general application)
or they may be limited to situations involving derogations under EC law from liberalisation
obligations (see paras 122, 126 and 127), markets in which national law has eliminated any
competition (see para.126), markets in which any reduction in potential competition will not
occur as a direct and immediate effect of the merger or in the near future (see para.124) and/or
cases in which the Commission fails to accord proper weight to remedies packages that would
have the effect of bringing forward liberalisation if the merger were approved (para.125).
[26] Case COMP/M.3440. This decision was challenged in the *EDP* appeal.
[27] It may be possible to distinguish *EDP* on the bases discussed in n.25 above. Compare Case
COMP/M. 3696 *E.ON/MOL*, paras 459 and 460.
[28] Cases 40/73 etc., *Coöperatieve Verenigin "Suiker Unie" SA and others v Commission* [1975]
E.C.R. 1663.
[29] Case IV/M.1383 [2004] O.J. L103/1, para.813.

that Gatwick airport constituted a substantial part of the common market because it was the fifth largest airport in the EEA and represented 25 per cent of United Kingdom consumption of the product in issue (aviation fuels) and 6 per cent of EEA sales.[30] In its earlier decision in *Holdercim / Cedest*[31] the Commission had stated that markets representing "less than one per cent. of the Community consumption of the product" constitute an insubstantial part of the common market. However, the apparently decisive nature of this test is inconsistent with the approach in the Commission's subsequent decision in *TotalFina / Elf*,[32] which took account of the *physical dimensions* of the geographic market and the fact that the products were partly constituted by *imports* (but did not mention the criterion identified in *Holdercim*), in concluding that each of six zones in France for wholesale supply of fuels separately comprised a substantial part of the common market.[33] The better view is that no single factor is determinative of whether the effects on competition of a transaction occur in a "substantial part of the common market"; rather, a range of factors, including economic criteria, physical characteristics, the presence or absence of international trade and

---

[30] Similarly, in considering markets for groundhandling services, the Commission has generally defined the geographic market as the area of the airport: see, e.g. Case IV/M.1035 *Hochtief / Aer Rianta / Düsseldorf Airport* and Case IV/M.1124 *Maersk Air / LFV Holding*.

[31] Case IV/M.460.

[32] Case COMP/M.1628 [2001] O.J. L143/1, para.28.

[33] In that case, the Commission also concluded, at para.189, that fuel sales on three separate groups of motorways each comprised a substantial part of the common market: "First, they cover very extensive areas of French territory. Second, each of them connects with the motorway networks of neighbouring Member States. They are therefore of prime importance for trade in goods and the movement of people within the European Union. 79% of France's trade in goods transported by land is carried by road. Goods transported by road accounted for 92% by value of trade with other Member States. Lastly, general statistics ... show that, on average, 10% of light vehicles and 30% of heavy goods vehicles using the French motorway network are from abroad". See also Case COMP/M.2530 *Südzucker / Saint Louis Sucre* [2003] O.J. L103/1, para.44; Case COMP/M.2596 *RMC / UMA / JV* (the supply of aggregates; Isle of Wight found not to be a substantial part of the common market, in the light of its area, population, GDP and the volume and value of aggregates supplied; in relation to each of these parameters, the Commission considered the absolute value for the Isle of Wight and the relative share of the UK as a whole; para.26); Case COMP/M.2822 *EnBW / ENI / GVS* [2003] O.J. L248/51 (supply of gas; the Commission found that Baden-Württemberg was a substantial part of the common market for these purposes as the quantities supplied in the area corresponded to those in the whole of Austria or Denmark; para.32); Case COMP/M.3669 *Blackstone (TBG CareCo) / NHP* (the provision of care homes; Arbroath, Nottingham and Port Talbot were not considered to be a substantial part of the common market either separately or together; the Commission took into account the economic importance of the services and territories concerned, the volume of cross-border trade and "general geographic factors"; see paras 34 and 35); Case COMP/M.3754 *Strabag / Walter Bau* (the supply of asphalt in Hamburg did not constitute a substantial part of the common market); Case COMP/M.3817 *Wegener / PCM / JV* (areas in the Randstad in the Netherlands where the parties' regional newspapers overlapped were found not to be a substantial part of the common market either individually or jointly, but no reasons were given; para.50; see also para.54); Case COMP/M.3905 *Tesco / Carrefour* (grocery retailing; three Czech cities were not regarded as a substantial part of the common market as each constituted less than 0.1% of total grocery sales in the common market, para.32); and Case COMP/M.3943 *Saint-Gobain / BPB* (Ile de France was found to be a substantial part of the common market for the purposes of the distribution of fitting-out products, in the light of total sales of the product in Ile de France and its geographic area and population; para.117).

the significance of the activity to trade within the Community[34] may be relevant.[35]

The question arises whether the same geographic area or location may comprise a substantial part of the common market for the supply of certain goods, but not others. The reasoning in the cases discussed above suggests that the assessment is specific to the goods in issue, implying that the outcome might be different if the Commission examined the supply of different goods in the same area. However, in *Lagardère / Natexis / VUP*,[36] when assessing the retail supply of books, the Commission relied on the findings in another case, not involving the retail supply of books, that the largest French airports constituted a substantial part of the common market.[37]

2.5 BURDEN AND STANDARD OF PROOF

(a) Burden of proof

The judgment of the Court of First Instance in *EDP v Commission*[38] states **2–026** that "it is for the Commission to demonstrate that a concentration cannot be declared compatible with the common market". Similarly, the Court's earlier decision in *Airtours plc v Commission*[39] emphasised that the Commission is required to provide convincing evidence before proceeding to a prohibition decision. These judgments therefore indicate that the burden of proof is, in a general sense, on the Commission, but important issues relating to the allocation of the burden of proof remain to be litigated.

Five features of the ECMR process are relevant to a more particularised allocation of the burden of proof. First, the Commission's investigation is inquisitorial and the Commission determines whether a merger should be approved (subject to any appeals to the Community Courts). Secondly,

---

[34] The significance of the activity has contributed to findings in a number of Art.82 cases that ports, airports and air routes comprise substantial parts of the common market; see, e.g. Case C-179/90 *Merci convenzionali porto di Genova SpA v Siderurgica Gabrielli SpA* [1991] E.C.R. 5889 and Case C-18/93 *Corsica Ferries Italia Srl v Corpo dei Piloti del Porto di Genova* [1994] E.C.R. I-1783. Contrast Case COMP/M.3554 *Serco / NedRailways / Northern Rail*, finding that five passenger point-to-point flows in the north west of England did *not* constitute a substantial part of the common market as they accounted for only a small percentage of total rail passenger train operating services; paras 13 and 14.

[35] For discussion of the meaning of "common market" when markets cover both EEA Member States and non-Member States, see Case COMP/M.3764 *Belgacom / Swisscom / JV*, para.20 (Belgium-Switzerland route).

[36] Case COMP/M.2978 [2004] O.J. L125/54 (appeal pending in Case T-279/04 *Editions Odile Jacob SAS v Commission*), para.400.

[37] Case COMP/M.1628 *TotalFina / Elf* [2001] O.J. L143/1.

[38] Case T-87/05, not yet reported, judgment of September 21, 2005, para.61. The Court also ruled that if the notifying party submits commitments, the burden of showing that the concentration as amended by the commitments should be prohibited remains on the Commission (paras 62 to 69).

[39] Case T-342/99 [2002] E.C.R. II-2585, para.63.

there are numerous ways of establishing that a transaction significantly impedes effective competition and issues which are relevant in one case may be wholly irrelevant in others. Thirdly, some evidence which would be material to the Commission's investigation might be known only to the merging parties (for example, the parties' plans for expansion, whether the target is a failing firm and the efficiencies which may be generated through the transaction). Fourthly, under the procedural rules applicable under the ECMR, the merging parties do not have any rights to obtain evidence from third parties, but the Commission has extensive powers. Fifthly, it is in general terms artificial to speak of "defences" in an ECMR investigation. Certainly, high market shares create a presumption of market power which may be rebutted, for example, by evidence showing that new entry would be timely, likely and sufficient to constrain the merged group's conduct, but the assessment of potential competition may be regarded as part of the Commission's general analysis of the market. Further, whilst it is common to speak of an "efficiency defence", the Notice on Horizontal Mergers makes clear that an analysis of the efficiencies generated by the merger forms an integral part of the assessment of the merger's likely effects on consumers.[40] Similarly, the "failing firm defence" is better regarded as part of the determination of whether there is a causal link between the transaction and the creation or strengthening of a dominant position.[41]

2–027 These observations lead to the following suggested conclusions.

(a) The "ultimate burden"[42] of establishing that the transaction will significantly impede effective competition in the common market or a substantial part of it, lies on the Commission ("the ultimate issue"). This follows from the Court's decisions in *EDP* and *Airtours*.

(b) The notifying party bears an "evidential burden"[43] (i.e. an obligation to provide sufficient evidence to raise an issue) in relation to any issues which it believes are material to a decision on the ultimate issue. This follows because it cannot be open to a notifying party to keep to itself information which it believes is relevant to the appraisal, for example as to potential entry by company X, and bring an appeal on the grounds that the Commission has not proven that entry by X would not be timely, likely and sufficient to defeat an

---

[40] For example, the merging parties may be able to show that there is no significant impediment to effective competition because the transaction will generate sufficient savings that the merged group's *profit-maximising* strategy would be to increase output (reducing price) even if it has the *ability* profitably to raise price and increase profits relative to the pre-merger level by reducing output and that there is therefore no significant impediment to effective competition; see generally Ch.18.

[41] See Ch.17.

[42] Lord Denning explains the concept of an "ultimate burden" as follows: "Where the ultimate decision of a case depends on the determination of a number of separate issues, the burden on the ultimate issue needs to be distinguished from the burden on the separate issues" (1945) 61 L.Q.R. 380.

[43] See Phipson, "The Law of Evidence" (16th edn, Sweet & Maxwell, 2005), para.6–02.

attempt by the merged group to exercise market power. As noted above, the factors relevant to the ultimate issue vary significantly from case to case and the Commission cannot be expected to identify all issues of possible relevance on its own initiative.[44]

(c) The Commission bears the "persuasive burden"[45] (i.e. to prove the facts, whether positive or negative, which are necessary for its determination on the ultimate issue) on *all* issues[46] except the "failing firm defence" and "efficiency gains" arising from the merger,[47] on which the notifying party bears the persuasive burden because[48] it alone has access to the *majority* of the relevant evidence. However, this analysis is subject to a *proviso*, namely that the Commission does not neglect its investigative role by rejecting such submissions on the basis that the burden of proof has not been discharged[49] when the

---

[44] On the contrary, the starting point for the Commission's analysis is information provided by the merging parties on Form CO. In Case COMP/M.2547 *Bayer / Aventis Crop Science* [2004] O.J. L107/1 the Commission found that the notifying party had failed to discharge an evidential burden on one of the issues; the Commission stated, at para.336: "As the parties have not provided any evidence that supply contracts will be withdrawn, the Commission assumes for the purposes of this assessment that the supply contracts will continue". See also paras 446, 483 and 496.

[45] See Phipson, "The Law of Evidence" (16th edn, Sweet & Maxwell, 2005), para.6–02.

[46] In Case IV/M.165 *Alcatel / AEG Kabel* the Commission stated at para.22: "Where three companies have a combined market share exceeding 50% there is a legal presumption under German law that no substantial competition exists between these companies and that consequently they form a dominant oligopoly. Under the Regulation such a presumption which amounts to a reversal of the burden of proof does not exist. On the contrary, the Commission would have to demonstrate in all cases that effective competition could not be expected on structural grounds between the leading companies in a highly concentrated market". Contrast Case COMP/M.2547 *Bayer / Aventis Crop Science* [2004] O.J. L107/1, para.659 (the parties had not provided any evidence to contradict *submissions* by third parties and the Commission therefore made a finding against the parties; whilst this passage suggests that the notifying party bears a persuasive burden on issues other than the failing firm defence and efficiency gains, it is best rationalised as one in which the Commission made a finding on the balance of probabilities based on the uncontradicted *evidence* supplied by third parties).

[47] The Commission considers that the burden of proof in relation to a "failing firm defence" and "efficiency gains" is on the notifying party. See the Notice on Horizontal Mergers, paras 87 (efficiency gains) and 91 (failing firm defence). The Commission has stated that there is a presumption that a creation or strengthening of dominance that would follow a merger is caused by that merger, with the consequence that the burden of proof for the existence of the requirements of a "rescue merger" lies with the merging firms: OECD Best Practice Roundtable, "Failing Firm Defence", OCDE/GD(96)23, p.91. (It is not clear that the Commission is correct in identifying such a presumption, although the proposition that the burden of proof in relation to the failing firm defence lies on the notifying party does not depend on establishing the presumption).

[48] The point that the merging parties uniquely have access to much of the information relevant to the "failing firm defence" and the "efficiency defence" seems more significant in allocating the burden of proof than the (nevertheless important) observation that the analytical distinction between the two "defences" and other issues relevant to the ultimate issue is imprecise.

[49] The Commission rarely relies on the burden of proof in its analysis but in Case IV/M.1157 *Skanska / Scancem* [1999] O.J. L183/1, the Commission found that sales of concrete produced by Scancem as sub-contractor for other suppliers ought to be attributed to Scancem in calculating market shares for two reasons: "First, no objective reason has been provided why the parties, in the absence of the subcontracting agreements, would not be able to supply the same volumes under their own brands. Secondly, no evidence has been submitted to indicate

ground for rejection relates to the general operation of the market[50] as opposed to the particular position of the merged group, since the Commission has powers to obtain evidence from third parties which the notifying party does not.

(b) Standard of proof

2–028 The standard of *proof*[51] describes the evidential[52] threshold that the Commission must satisfy before it can prohibit a transaction (or clear it only subject to commitments).[53]

The proper formulation of the standard of proof is complicated by four matters.[54] First, a merger appraisal may be based on thousands of pieces of

---

that the parties' subcontracting partners would be able to supply these volumes without recourse to the production facilities of the parties. As such it must be concluded that the parties produce these volumes because they have the production facilities most suitable for this activity".

[50] The failing firm defence involves predicting how the market share held by the failing firm would be reallocated if the firm went out of business which depends on the reactions of customers and competitors. An assessment of efficiency gains may involve predicting the strategies of competitors in order to determine whether the profit-maximising strategy for the merged group is to increase output (thereby reducing prices) or reduce output (thereby increasing prices).

[51] See Vesterdorf, "Standard of Proof in Merger Cases: Reflections in the Light of Recent Case Law of the Community Courts" (2005) 1 *European Competition Journal*, issue 1, p.3; Prete & Nucara, "Standard of Proof and Scope of Judicial Review in EC Merger Cases: Everything Clear after *Tetra Laval?*" [2005] E.C.L.R. 692; Bailey, "Standard of Proof in EC Merger Proceedings: A Common Law Perspective" [2003] C.M.L.Rev. 845; and Bellamy in "Judicial Enforcement of Competition Law", OECD, OCDE/GD(97)200 (available via *www.oecd.org/dataoecd/34/41/1919985.pdf*), p.105 (distinguishing primary or basic facts, economic facts and policy).

[52] The Commission does not apply rules excluding on *a priori* grounds certain categories of evidence (in contrast, for example, to many systems of litigation which exclude or restrain the admissibility of hearsay evidence). For example, the Commission commonly relies in its appraisal on the findings of national competition authorities: see, e.g. Case COMP/M.1628 *TotalFina / Elf* [2001] O.J. L143/1, para.44 (and see also para.168).

[53] This is *different* from the question of the standard of *review* applied by the Court of First Instance on an appeal (for discussion of the standard of review on appeal, see Vesterdorf, "Judicial Review in EC Competition Law: Reflections on the Role of the Community Courts in the EC System of Competition Law Enforcement" (2005) *Competition Policy International*, Vol.1, No.2, p.3), although the two are related in the sense that if the standard of *review* is lax (i.e. on an appeal, the Commission is given significant leeway in its assessment of the case) then the effect is to lower the standard of *proof* because a decision might be upheld on appeal notwithstanding that the evidence was not especially convincing.

[54] Notwithstanding the changes in approach and procedure in merger cases that followed the Commission's defeats in *Airtours, Schneider* and *Tetra Laval*, there remain concerns about the quality of the evidential analysis carried out by the Commission. These concerns were voiced by Jonathan B Baker, a US professor who formerly held senior positions in the US DOJ and FTC, and who spent part of Summer 2005 at the Commission. In "My Summer Vacation at the European Commission", *The Antitrust Source*, September 2005 (*www.abanet.org/antitrust/source/09-05/Sep05-Baker9 = 27.pdf*) he reported: "My impression is that DG-Comp case teams do not feel subject to the same pressure to test and support their conclusions as do their U.S. counterparts, and may not go to the same lengths in uncovering and analyzing evidence ... Although [the decisions in *Airtours, Schneider* and *Tetra Laval*] have increased the care with which evidence is discussed while decisions are drafted, they do not appear to have

evidence, relating to the numerous issues discussed in this book, all of which ultimately relate to the question of the merger's predicted effect on consumers. The multifaceted nature of this appraisal is different from most issues which arise in litigation (was the defendant present at the scene of the crime? what did the parties agree at the meeting to discuss the proposed contract?). Secondly, the vast majority of decisions of courts on questions of fact involve investigating historic events but an important part of the Commission's function under the ECMR involves predicting the future. Thirdly, the Commission's role is not limited to determining historic facts and predicting the future. It also applies economic theory. Finally, the Commission both investigates the merger and determines whether it is compatible with the common market.

The Community Courts have formulated the standard of proof in a **2–029** variety of different terms.

(a) In *Kali & Salz*[55] the European Court of Justice stated that the Commission must rely on a "rigorous analysis", demonstrating the merger's effects with "a sufficient degree of probability", and must identify a "sufficiently cogent and consistent body of evidence".

(b) In *Airtours plc v Commission*[56] the Court of First Instance referred to the need to provide "convincing" and "cogent" before the Commission may prohibit a transaction.

(c) Subsequently, in *Tetra Laval BV v Commission*[57] the Court of First Instance adopted a balance of probabilities test, rejecting the Commission's argument that it was sufficient to show that there was a "possibility" of harm and referring to the need to establish that competitive harm was "likely" to arise.[58] The Court also stated[59] that the Commission had failed to base its conclusions on a "solid coherent body of evidence obtained by it through its market investigation" and that the Commission's analysis of the future market structure ought to have been "particularly plausible" because the

---

altered fundamentally how case teams uncover and evaluate evidence ... My suspicion, based on limited observations, is that DG-Comp could benefit from increasing its effort to develop and test evidence". These observations give rise to material concerns: if the Commission is not analysing the evidence adequately, it is likely to be making avoidable errors when appraising mergers.

[55] Joined Cases C-68/94 and C-30/95 *France and others v Commission* [1998] E.C.R. I-1375, paras 228 and 246.

[56] Case T-342/99 [2002] E.C.R. II-2585, paras 63 and 294.

[57] Case T-5/02 [2002] E.C.R. II-4381, para.212.

[58] Case T-5/02 [2002] E.C.R. II-4381, paras 153 ("in all likelihood") and 251 ("likely"), rejecting the Commission's approach, namely that a "possibility" of harm to competition was sufficient (para.45). Mario Monti, then Commissioner for Competition Policy, "EU Competition Policy", speech at the Fordham Annual Conference on International Law & Policy, October 31, 2002 (*www.europa.eu.int/comm/competition/speeches/index_2002.html*), stated that "the level of proof required by the CFI is high, which implies that the Commission's enquiries should be more extensive and detailed than at present".

[59] Para.162.

dominant position would be created a significant time after completion of the merger.

(d) Prior to the European Court of Justice's decision in *Tetra Laval*, the Court of First Instance in *BaByliss v Commission*[60] stated that the Commission was bound to accept commitments which were "likely" to prevent the creation or strengthening of a dominant position and found that the remedy accepted by the Commission was "likely" to enable licensees to migrate customers to their own brands. The Court also referred to the need for the Commission to base its decisions on "specific and consistent" evidence[61] and overturned the Commission's reasoning when its interpretation was "no more plausible" than a contrary view of the facts.[62]

(e) In *Commission v Tetra Laval BV*[63] the European Court of Justice[64] upheld the Court of First Instance's decision insofar as "it specified the quality of the evidence which the Commission is required to produce in order to demonstrate" that a transaction may be prohibited.[65]

   (i) The European Court of Justice stated that the Court of First Instance had *not* added a condition to the *Kali & Salz* case relating to the standard of proof,[66] but had simply specified that the evidence must be "convincing".[67]

   (ii) The Court emphasised the prospective nature of a merger control process and stated that it was therefore necessary to examine various chains of cause and effect to ascertain which are "the most likely".[68]

---

[60] Case T-114/02 [2003] E.C.R. II-1279, paras 173 and 193.
[61] Para.353.
[62] Para.357. If the issue is whether one interpretation is "more plausible" than another, then the Court is adopting a "balance of probabilities" test.
[63] Case C-12/03P, not yet reported, judgment of February 15, 2005.
[64] Advocate General Tizzano's opinion of May 25, 2004 argued, at paras 73 to 81, that a merger could be prohibited only if the harm to competition was "very probable" on the basis that: (a) the provisions in the ECMR deeming a concentration to be compatible with the common market if the Commission did not take decisions within the specified time limits showed that the Council intended that mergers should be cleared in cases of uncertainty; and (b) the Commission and competent national authorities could intervene post-merger using the powers under Art.82. The Advocate General's inference about the legislature's intentions (point (a) above) seems clearly incorrect because the deeming provisions in Art.10.6 of the ECMR can readily be explained on the basis that they are intended to promote a system of good administration by creating an incentive on the Commission to adhere to the specified timetables.
[65] Para.45.
[66] Para.41. This is an observation which is difficult to reconcile with the passages from the Court of First Instance's judgment which are discussed in sub-para.(c) of the text above. See also Prete & Nucara, "Standard of Proof and Scope of Judicial Review in EC Merger Cases: Everything Clear after *Tetra Laval*?" [2005] E.C.L.R. 692, at p.697, noting that the European Court of Justice had neither openly upheld nor disputed the Court of First Instance's test, but had re-interpreted the lower court's ruling.
[67] Para.41.
[68] Paras 42 and 43.

(iii) Finally, the Court stated: "The analysis of a 'conglomerate-type' concentration is a prospective analysis in which, first, the consideration of a lengthy period of time in the future and, secondly, the leveraging necessary to give rise to a significant impediment to effective competition mean that the chains of cause and effect are dimly discernible, uncertain and difficult to establish. That being so, the quality of the evidence produced by the Commission in order to establish that it is necessary to adopt a decision declaring the concentration incompatible with the common market is particularly important, since that evidence must support the Commission's conclusion that, if such a decision were not adopted, the economic development envisaged by it would be plausible."

(f) Subsequently, in *General Electric Company v Commission*[69] the Court of First Instance followed the conclusions of the Community Courts in the *Tetra Laval* cases in describing the standard of proof.[70] In analysing the facts of the case, the Court used a series of formulations to refer to the standard of proof, namely "likely",[71] "convincing evidence"[72] and "sufficient degree of probability",[73] but in general the Court did not purport to be developing the *Tetra Laval* jurisprudence.[74]

The position on the general standard of proof applicable in merger proceedings is somewhat obscure in the light of the Court of Justice's opaque reasoning in *Tetra Laval*.[75] However, the observations made above, read with the decisions of the Community Courts, lead to the following suggested conclusions. **2–030**

(a) Legal certainty requires that the Commission applies an *objective* standard of proof, for example the balance of probabilities (i.e. more likely than not) or beyond reasonable doubt (i.e. sure) as opposed to apparently subjective standards (such as a "sufficient degree of certainty").

---

[69] Case T-210/01, not yet reported, judgment of December 14, 2005.
[70] Paras 61, 64, 65, 66 and 76.
[71] Paras 297 (purporting to summarise a finding of the Commission), 327 (referring to the *Tetra Laval* judgments), 339, 432 ("likelihood"), 449 ("real likelihood") and 555.
[72] Paras 332, 340, 429, 433, 462 and 464.
[73] Paras 331, 340, 429, 462 and 464.
[74] When discussing a remedies proposal from the notifying party, the Court stated, at para.555, that the Commission needed to conclude that as a result of the implementation of the remedies, the competition problem "would not be likely" to materialise in the relatively near future. The Court also stated that the Commission needed to conclude "with certainty" that the commitments would be implemented, but this statement simply confirms that commitments must be implemented (and does not alter the standard of proof in this area).
[75] See Prete & Nucara, "Standard of Proof and Scope of Judicial Review in EC Merger Cases: Everything Clear after *Tetra Laval?*" [2005] E.C.L.R. 692, at p.697.

(b) The standard of proof comprises two cumulative conditions.[76]

    (i) The evidence deployed by the Commission must be cogent and coherent (a criterion also reflected in the use by the Community Courts of the words "consistent", "convincing" and "rigorous"). As the Commission controls the investigation and has extensive powers to obtain evidence, it is obliged to obtain sufficient evidence (proportionate to the complexity of the issues) to enable it to make a decision which is cogent and coherent. In particular, the Commission is not free to take a lackadaisical approach to the collation of evidence and then determine whether, on the balance of probabilities, the inadequate and incomplete evidence which it has collated points towards a prohibition decision.

    (ii) Having collated sufficient evidence to enable it to adopt a cogent and coherent decision, the Commission should then make that decision on the balance of probabilities (a criterion reflected in the use of the words "likely", "most likely" and "more plausible" in the Community Courts' judgments).[77] This reflects the ECMR's status as a civil proceeding. If the standard were set at beyond reasonable doubt (i.e. certainty), mergers would be permitted which were likely or even very likely to harm consumers—which would not respect the Treaty objective of maintaining undistorted competition in the common market. It would also be difficult for the Commission to prohibit any transactions if this standard of proof were applicable because of the need to collate evidence on a very wide range of matters in the short time periods allowed under the ECMR. Conversely, mergers are not presumed to be unlawful[78] and any

---

[76] The formulation in the text can be compared with that proposed by Bo Vesterdorf, writing extra-judicially, "Standard of Proof in Merger Cases: Reflections in the Light of Recent Case Law of the Community Courts" (2005) 1 *European Competition Journal*, issue 1, p.3: "The Commission, under the judicial control of the Courts, would have to decide that it was satisfied at a high degree [more than a pure balance of probabilities but less than a criminal standard] whether the concentration would be likely to result in significant anti-competitive effects and would have to prove that its conclusion was based on a body of solid, cogent and convincing evidence and was not vitiated by any errors of fact, law or manifest errors of appreciation".

[77] See also the Notice on Horizontal Mergers, para.2 ("the Commission must take into account any significant impediment to effective competition likely to be caused by a concentration"). Contrast Case COMP/M.3436 *Continental / Phoenix* in which a competition issue arose because Continental had an interest in Vibracoustic and the Commission stated that, even if it were likely that a third party would, following the merger, exercise a call option over Continental's interest in Vibracoustic, this was by no means certain, and the Commission therefore accepted a commitment by Continental to sell its interest in Vibracoustic.

[78] The fact that post-merger conduct can be controlled, to an extent, by Art.82 is a weak factor pointing against setting the standard of proof at too low a level. This point was made by Advocate General Tizzano in Case C-12/03P *Commission v Tetra Laval BV*, not yet reported, at para.81 of his opinion, arguing for a test of "very probable" (i.e. a higher standard of proof than the balance of probabilities).

suggestion that the standard of proof should be less than the balance of probabilities would indirectly introduce such a presumption.[79] Finally, the formulations of the tests in the ECMR for clearing a transaction (Art.2(2)) and prohibiting a transaction (Art.2(3)) are symmetrical (using exactly the same language, except that Art.2(2) includes the word "not"), suggesting that the standard to be satisfied for reaching each type of decision is the same, i.e. the balance of probabilities. This approach receives support from Götz Drauz, then Deputy Director-General of DG Competition, who stated: "The recent Tetra judgment [of the European Court of Justice] positively confirms, in our view, that our standard should indeed be one of 'balance of probabilities'."[80]

(c) The ultimate issue which must be proved by the Commission is that the transaction would significantly impede effective competition in the common market or a substantial part of it. If the Commission is able to establish its primary facts to this standard but concludes that there is a 40 per cent chance that the merger would lead to material increases in prices, then the upshot is that there is a 40 per cent chance that the merger will result in a significant impediment to effective competition and the Commission has *not* satisfied the standard of proof.[81]

The question arises whether the standard of proof *varies*.[82] In particular, the 2–031 Community Courts, in their decisions in *Kali & Salz*, *Airtours*, *Tetra Laval* and *General Electric* emphasised, when discussing the standard of proof, that the first two cases involved coordinated effects and the last two con-

---

[79] The reference by the European Court of Justice in Case C-12/03P *Commission v Tetra Laval BV*, not yet reported, judgment of February 15, 2005, para.44, to the Commission's analysis being "plausible" could be read as creating a standard of proof which is less than the balance of probabilities. On the other hand, the Court also referred to a need to assess which of the chains of cause and effect were the "most likely" (which is certainly consistent with a balance of probabilities standard) (para.43).

[80] "Conglomerate and Vertical Mergers in the Light of the Tetra Judgment", *Competition Policy Newsletter*, Summer 2005, p.35.

[81] In other words, economic theory is simply a tool for predicting the likely factual operation of the market in the same way as, for example, historic market operation and interviews with customers.

[82] The President of the Court of First Instance, Bo Vesterdof, speaking extra-judicially, has apparently suggested that the standard of proof should be higher for events which have already occurred than for events which have yet to occur; see Bailey, "Standard of Proof in EC Merger Proceedings: A Common Law Perspective" [2003] C.M.L.Rev. 845, pp.864 and 865. However, these comments relate more naturally to the standard of *review* applied by the Court of First Instance since the Court can generally itself determine the facts with reasonable certainty (as most factual assessments in merger cases are based on an analysis of documentation, rather than an assessment of the credibility of witnesses in the light of the delivery of their evidence) allowing it to apply an intense process of review, but it has repeatedly stated that the Commission has a margin of discretion in economic matters (which may require expertise not necessarily held by the Court and commonly involve predictions as to the future operation of the market).

glomerate effects,[83] raising the question whether a different standard would be applicable in other cases (e.g. a horizontal non-coordinated effects case). Further, the Commission has stated that "the [standard][84] of proof is certainly heavier for the merging firms in the case of a 'failing division' than in the case of a 'failing firm';" because otherwise, "every merger involving the sale of an allegedly unprofitable division could be justified under merger control by the seller's declaring that, without the merger, the division would cease trading."[85] In addition, in *BASF / Eurodiol / Pantochim*[86] the Commission identified as one of the criteria required to establish a "failing firm" defence that the assets to be acquired would *inevitably* exit the market if not taken over by another undertaking.[87]

However, the better view is that the standard of proof does *not* vary according to the theory of competitive harm[88] or the issue under consideration for four reasons.[89]

(a) The balance of probabilities standard *is* capable of addressing concerns about the inherent implausibility of certain events (e.g. a claim that a division of an otherwise healthy firm is failing and is likely to close if the merger does not proceed or that, following a conglomerate merger, a merged group will adopt a novel leveraging strategy after an interval of some time). In a speech in the UK House of Lords, Lord Hoffman stated:

> "some things are inherently more likely than others. It would need more cogent evidence to satisfy one that the creature seen walking in Regent's Park was more likely than not to have been a lioness than to be satisfied to the same standard of probability that it was an Alsatian. On this basis, cogent evidence is generally required to satisfy a tribunal that a person has been fraudulent or behaved in some other reprehensible manner. But the question is always whether the tribunal thinks it more probable than not."[90]

Applying Lord Hoffman's analogy in the merger control sphere, the leveraging theory in *Tetra* was a lioness which needed to be justified

---

[83] The *General Electric* case also raised horizontal and vertical issues.
[84] The Commission used the word "burden" but the context demonstrates that it was discussing the standard of proof.
[85] Commission paper for OECD Best Practice Roundtable, "Failing Firm Defence", OCDE/GD(96)23, p.91 at p.94. See Ch.17 below; Case IV/M.1221 *Rewe / Meinl* [1999] O.J. L274/1 para.65; and Case COMP/M.2876 *NewsCorp / Telepiù* [2004] O.J. L110/73, para.212.
[86] Case COMP/M.2314 [2002] O.J. L132/45.
[87] The test of "inevitability" is included in the Horizontal Merger Guidelines, at para.90.
[88] When considering whether a merger may be prohibited on coordinated effects grounds when coordinated effects were not present prior to the merger, it is necessary to determine whether the Commission must demonstrate that post-merger coordinated effects are likely or, instead, that the merger is likely to increase significantly the prospect that coordination will occur; this is discussed in para.8–055 below.
[89] See generally Bailey, "Standard of Proof in EC Merger Proceedings: A Common Law Perspective" [2003] C.M.L.Rev. 845, at p.859.
[90] *Secretary of State for the Home Department v Rehman* [2003] 1 A.C. 153, at para.55.

with "particularly plausible" evidence (using the words of the Community Courts), whilst a claim that a merged group with a high market share will harm consumers through the exercise of market power is an Alsatian. But both mergers can be analysed satisfactorily under a balance of probabilities standard.

(b) It would be anomalous if the question of whether a merger were cleared or not turned on its categorisation (e.g. whether it is treated as horizontal or conglomerate), as the substantive question of whether consumers are likely to be harmed as a result of the transaction is not affected by the label placed on the merger.[91]

(c) It would also be anomalous if a merger were prohibited even though the notifying party could show at a 95 per cent level of certainty that the assets being acquired would otherwise exit from the market (assuming the other criteria for the failing firm defence are satisfied). In that situation, far and away the most likely outcome is that the merger would not cause any detriment to competition and yet consumers would be deprived of the benefits of the transaction because the standard of proof is set at a very high level.[92]

(d) It is difficult to articulate principles that can be used in practice to determine which issues are subject to a higher standard of proof. There can be no justification for arbitrary decisions, altering the standard of proof on an ad hoc basis.

Some issues are enormously complex and the Commission may lack the **2–032** expertise to resolve them. For example, in *Pfizer / Pharmacia*[93] the question arose whether Pfizer's attempts to enforce patents in relation to the erectile dysfunction drug, Viagra, would be successful. The Commission found that if Pfizer's patent claims were upheld, then the number of potential competitors would fall significantly as many rivals' pipeline products would be affected by the ruling. The Commission might reasonably regard itself as not well placed in terms of resources or expertise to predict the likely outcome of complex litigation.[94] In its decision, the Commission took account of the "uncertainty" regarding the patent litigation in identifying serious doubts regarding the loss of potential competition in the erectile dysfunction market. It is submitted that such a finding would be acceptable even at the

---

[91] See Götz Drauz, "Conglomerate and Vertical Mergers in the Light of the Tetra Judgment", *Competition Policy Newsletter*, Summer 2005, p.35, at p.36 (emphasising the need for a practical approach, keeping in mind the basic principles of merger control).
[92] See s.17.5 below.
[93] Case COMP/M.2922, paras 79 to 91.
[94] See also Bacchiega, Dionnet, Todino & MacEwen, "Johnson & Johnson / Guidant: Potential Competition and Unilateral Effects in Innovative Markets", *Competition Policy Newsletter*, Autumn 2005, p.87 at p.90.

end of a second phase inquiry because the Commission is only required to take reasonable steps to investigate the case.[95]

2–033   A further issue arises, namely whether two or more findings by the Commission which do not separately satisfy the standard of proof can be considered together to support a finding of fact or a conclusion on the ultimate issue.[96] For example, imagine that the Commission's findings of fact are that there is: a 40 per cent chance that the merged group's first competitor, A, will exit the market in the year following the transaction; a 40 per cent chance that the merged group's second competitor, B, will exit the market in the year following the transaction; and that the chances of A and B leaving the market are not dependent on one another or on whether the merger proceeds. If the Commission concludes that the merger will not create a dominant position provided that both A and B remain in the market one year after the transaction, the question arises as to whether the Commission must take as separate issues the chances of A and B remaining in the market (leading to conclusions in each case on the balance of probabilities that the competitor will remain in the market) or whether the Commission is entitled to consider the issues together (leading to a conclusion that it is more likely than not that the merged group will face fewer than two competitors one year after the merger)?[97] Similarly, imagine that the Commission concludes that there is a 40 per cent chance that the transaction will result in coordinated effects and a 40 per cent chance that it will result in non-coordinated effects in the same market; is the Commission entitled to prohibit the transaction on the grounds that it is more likely than not to result in either non-coordinated or coordinated effects? The following conclusion is offered, namely that it is not necessary that each item of evidence relied on by the Commission is established on the balance of probabilities; rather, the Commission ought to be entitled to analyse the evidence as a whole in order to determine whether the ultimate issue is made out on the balance of probabilities, for two reasons. First, a requirement to establish each item of evidence on the balance of probabilities could result in the approval without commitments of mergers which are more likely than not to result in a significant impediment to effective competition (or to lead to the prohibition or clearance subject to commitments of mergers which

---

[95] Whilst the European Court of Justice's decision in *Commission v Tetra Laval BV* Case C-12/03P, not yet reported, judgment of February 15, 2005, is somewhat unclear, it appears to have had a similar point in mind in ruling that the Commission was required to take account of any duties owed by the merged group under Art.82 without having to carry out a detailed appraisal of, for example, the penalties that might be imposed by national competition authorities (the Commission clearly has expertise in the application of Art.82, but the resourcing issue identified in the text is equally applicable). This issue is discussed in s.2.7(a) below.

[96] See Areeda & Turner, *Antitrust Law* (Aspen Law & Business, 1980), Vol.V, para.1147.

[97] The probability of both competitors remaining is 0.36 (i.e. 0.6 x 0.6) and, accordingly, the probability of one or both of the competitors leaving the market is 0.64 (1 - 0.36).

probably will not be anti-competitive),[98] consequences which are at odds with the objective of protecting consumer welfare. Secondly, the broad-ranging analyses essential to many ECMR investigations are particularly unsuited to an item-by-item appraisal in which each strand must be established on the balance of probabilities or excluded from the review. This means that in the first example given in the text, where the issue was whether both A and B would remain in the market one year after the merger, the transaction may be blocked. However, on the stylised facts of the second example, involving a merger with a 40 per cent chance of non-coordinated effects and a 40 per cent chance of coordinated effects, the Commission does *not* have sufficient evidence to block the transaction because non-coordinated and coordinated effects are mutually exclusive and it therefore cannot be concluded, without more evidence, that it is more likely than not that the merger will lead to either non-coordinated or coordinated effects.[99]

Finally, the standard of proof loses its practical significance if the Commission fails to comply with the principles of *logic* in reaching its decision. A failure of logic strikes at the internal consistency of the Commission's analysis and provides a ground for challenge before the Court of First Instance which does not require an analysis of the evidence collated by the Commission. For example, in *Schneider Electric SA v Commission*[1] the Court of First Instance struck down a prohibition decision in part because the Commission found that the geographic markets were national but took account, as indicators of economic power, of information collated on an international basis (i.e. not separated out by geographic market).[2]   **2–034**

---

[98] For an example of a situation in which a merger might wrongly be prohibited even though it is unlikely to be anti-competitive, see Tom, "Market Definition Under the Merger Guidelines: Some Modest Proposals" (*www.usdoj.gov/atr/public/workshops/docs/202597.htm#N_4_*), s.I(B).

[99] See Areeda & Turner, *Antitrust Law* (Aspen Law & Business, 1980), Vol.V, para.1147d, emphasising that cumulating possibilities is permissible only when the theories of anti-competitive harm are consistent with one another. The non-applicability of probability theory to the second example can be illustrated with a further example. Imagine that a horse has a 40% chance of winning race A and a 40% chance of winning race B. If races A and B are run at different places at the same time (i.e. participation in one race excludes participation in the second) the chances of the horse winning either race A or race B are 40%, assuming that it participates in one of the races.

[1] Case T-310/01 [2002] E.C.R. II-4071, paras 170, 171, 243, 256, 405 and 409.

[2] See also Case T-114/02 *BaByliss v Commission* [2003] E.C.R. II-1279 in which the Court of First Instance considered an appeal against the Commission's decision in Case COMP/ M.2621 *SEB / Moulinex*, ruling out concerns in Member States in which the sales of the merged group in product markets with shares exceeding 40% accounted for less than 10% of the merged group's total sales in that Member State. The Court stated, at para.353, that "the fact remains that the principle is that each market is to be assessed independently and any exception to or modification of that principle must be based on specific and consistent evidence showing the existence of such interactions".

2.6 PERIOD OVER WHICH THE PREDICTED EFFECTS OF THE MERGER ARE EXAMINED UNDER THE ECMR

2–035 The Court of First Instance has stated that the Commission may prohibit a merger when it has a "direct and immediate effect" of significantly impeding effective competition or when the effects are likely in "the near future".[3]

The Commission has adopted a *general* practice of focusing on the development of the market over the *two to three years*[4] following the decision, as the following cases illustrate.[5]

(a) In *Procter & Gamble / VP Schickedanz (II)*[6] the Commission examined possible developments in the market "within the foreseeable future (e.g. within three years)" and stated that analysis of

---

[3] See Case T-342/99 *Airtours plc v Commission* [2002] E.C.R. II-2585, para.58; Case T-5/02 *Tetra Laval BV v Commission* [2002] E.C.R. II-4381, para.153 (the decision was upheld on appeal on the basis of reasoning not relating to this issue in Case C-12/03P *Commission v Tetra Laval BV*, not yet reported, judgment of February 15, 2005); and Case T-87/05 *EDP v Commission*, not yet reported, judgment of September 21, 2005, para.124. In *EDP* the Court did not rule on an argument that the Commission acted unlawfully in projecting its analysis of the gas markets beyond five years after the concentration (see paras 134 to 141).

[4] See Hildebrand, *The Role of Economic Analysis in the EC Competition Rules* (Kluwer, 2002), p.380.

[5] See also Case IV/M.1229 *American Home Products / Monsanto* (para.34); Case COMP/ M.1601 *Allied Signal / Honeywell* [2001] O.J. L152/1 (the Commission rejected, at para.76, an argument that a product would be susceptible to technological leap-frogging on the grounds that it would take at least 10 years for the new product to be brought to market); and Case COMP/M.2706 *Carnival Corporation / P&O Princess* [2003] O.J. L248/1 (decision of July 2002 analysing how the market would develop in the years up to 2004; para.133; see also the analysis of barriers to expansion at para.200). By contrast, in Case COMP/M.2861 *Siemens / Drägerwerk / JV* [2003] O.J. L291/1, para.105, the Commission disregarded possible repositioning by a competitor on the grounds that it was not likely to occur over the one to two year time period relevant for the competition assessment. It is unclear whether the Commission was suggesting that the merger appraisal (either generally or in that case, which involved ventilation equipment) should focus on the one to two year period following the merger or (more likely) the Commission took the view that, in order to form an effective competitive constraint, repositioning by competitors in the context of a differentiated products analysis (see s.7.3 below) must take place within a period not longer than the normal period for a new entry analysis (see Ch.16). The Commission will also take into account effects of the merger which are temporary, in particular if they are likely to have a strong detrimental effect on competition and, possibly, long lasting effects; see Case COMP/M.3440 *ENI / EDP / GDP* [2005] O.J. L302/69, para.383 and n.284 (prohibition upheld on appeal in Case T-87/05 *EDP v Commission*, not yet reported, judgment of September 21, 2005). The International Competition Network Analytical Framework Sub-group, "The Analytical Framework for Merger Control" (available at *www.internationalcompetitionnetwork.org/afsguk.pdf*), raises several questions, at para.65: "How should effects on future competition be weighed alongside the short-term effects of the merger? For example, if a merger increases rivalry (and reduces prices) in the short-term but might reduce rivalry (and increase prices) over the long-term (e.g. by foreclosing the market or reducing incentives to innovate), how are these effects to be weighed against each other? Do limitations on decision-makers' predictive powers diminish the weight that should be accorded to potential long-term effects and if so, how should future effects be weighed?"

[6] Case IV/M.430 [1994] O.J. L354/32.

events outside that period "exceeds the relevant perspective to be established by the Commission under the Merger Regulation".[7]

(b) In *Alcoa / Reynolds*,[8] which was decided in May 2000, the Commission noted that production at a new plant was scheduled to commence in 2005 at the earliest and commented: "This is clearly outside the time frame used by the Commission to assess the impact of potential competition on a proposed merger".

(c) In *Astra Zeneca / Novartis*[9] the Commission, in examining the significance of pipeline products under development by the merging parties' competitors, considered only those products due to be introduced on the market between the date of the decision, July 2001, and 2003.

(d) In *Glaxo Wellcome / SmithKline Beecham*[10] the Commission focused on developments in the market over the three years following the merger.[11]

(e) In the *Hutchinson / RCPM / ECT*[12] decision of July 3, 2001 the Commission stated that it had "taken the year 2005 as the cut-off date for taking account of developments in the market. Developments beyond that date are generally too uncertain to be relied on in the present assessment."

However, the specific circumstances of a case may justify analysing the **2–036** effects of the concentration over a different period.[13] In particular, when the Commission is able with reasonable confidence to predict the way in which the market will operate over a period longer than two to three years, it tends to do so. This arises, for example, when there are long lead times in the construction of new plants (and the likely emergence of new capacity can therefore be predicted for a longer period) or the market is characterised by long term contracts. For example,[14] in *Gaz de France / Ruhrgas / Slovensky*[15] the Commission found that the joint venture, whose parents were active in

---

[7] Para.104.
[8] Case COMP/M.1693 [2002] O.J. L58/25, para.31.
[9] Case COMP/M.1806 [2004] O.J. L110/1, para.270.
[10] Case COMP/M.1846.
[11] The Commission focused on Phase III compounds, which are likely to be launched on the market within the next three years, to the exclusion of Phase II compounds, which are likely to be launched within four to five years; see para.190.
[12] Case COMP/JV.55, n.70 of the Commission's decision.
[13] A shorter period may be appropriate in dynamic industries.
[14] See also Case COMP/M.3486 *Magna / New Venture Gear* (decision of September 24, 2004, considering the effects on the market until 2008; para.29); Case COMP/M.3576 *ECT / PONL / Euromax* (decision of December 22, 2004, considering the effects on the market in the period to 2010; paras 29 to 34); and Case COMP/M.3625 *Blackstone / Acetex* [2005] O.J. L312/60 (decision of July 13, 2005, considering the development of the market for acetic acid over the period to 2009 and, in particular, assessing whether capacity would grow more quickly than demand over that period for the purposes of a non-coordinated effects analysis).
[15] Case COMP/M.2791, paras 15 to 21.

the EU gas markets, would control a pipeline accounting for around 75 per cent of Russian natural gas supply into the EU, but that typical contracts to use the pipeline were for durations of 15 to 25 years with no early termination provisions. The Commission therefore concluded that the joint venture could not use its control over the pipeline to impede gas imports into the EU over the following *one or two decades* and cleared the transaction after finding that alternative pipelines would be operative by the years 2006 to 2010 (*four to eight years* after the Commission's decision). Similarly, in *Shell / Enterprise Oil*[16] the Commission considered how the market for gas pipelines from the Northern North Sea would develop over the *ten years* following the merger, noting that the parties' share of spare pipeline capacity would fall during this period, expected new demand could be satisfied by spare capacity not controlled by the parties and, over the period 2005 to 2012, available independent spare capacity would be at least twice the expected demand.

In *ABB / Daimler-Benz*[17] the Commission accepted that the "peculiarities of railway technology" meant that a five year forecast period was appropriate in place of the "usual two or three years" but dismissed the possibility of a further extension on the grounds that "the purpose of merger control is to prevent market-dominating structures. Too long an extension of the relevant forecast period would not only lead to greater uncertainty in the forecast itself but would also be tantamount to accepting market dominance over a considerable period. That would be at variance with the purpose of merger control, which is to safeguard competitive structures on the Community's markets. What is more, in the case of dominant positions which are accepted in the medium term, the forecasts about any opening up of markets are unreliable. It cannot be ruled out that dominant undertakings might avail themselves of their market position so as to achieve a portioning of the markets by economic means, thereby countering the Community's attempts to open up markets."

Finally, in *NewsCorp / Telepiù*[18] the remedies package (which was designed to facilitate new entry and the subsistence of actual competition) applied from April 2003 until the end of 2011, over eight years. The Commission justified the duration on the grounds that it was necessary to allow effective competition to be restored (following a merger to near monopoly in circumstances in which customers benefited from allowing the merger subject to commitments, rather than prohibiting the transaction and risking one of the two suppliers going out of business).[19]

---

[16] Case COMP.M.2745, para.21. See also paras 28, 34 and 44.
[17] Case IV/M.580 [1997] O.J. L11/1, para.43.
[18] Case COMP/M.2876, para.260.
[19] See the Commission's XXXIIIrd Annual Report on Competition Policy, 2003, para.270. This case is discussed in detail in s.17.4(a) below.

2.7 RELATIONSHIP BETWEEN THE ECMR AND ARTS 81 AND 82, NATIONAL REGULATORY SYSTEMS, CONTRACTUAL RESTRICTIONS AND STATE AIDS

(a) Arts 81 and 82

The question arises whether the Commission is entitled to prohibit a **2–037** transaction if the theory of competitive harm is that the merged group may adopt a particular course of conduct, if the merged group's doing so would infringe Arts 81 or 82 of the EC Treaty.[20] The Court of First Instance considered this issue in *Tetra Laval BV v Commission*[21] and stated:

"when the Commission, in assessing the effects of ... a merger, relies on foreseeable conduct which in itself is likely to constitute abuse of an existing dominant position, it is required to assess whether, despite the prohibition of such conduct, it is none the less likely that the entity resulting from the merger will act in such a manner or whether, on the contrary, the illegal nature of the conduct and/or the risk of detection will make such a strategy unlikely. While it is appropriate to take account, in its assessment, of incentives to engage in anti-competitive practices ... the Commission must also consider the extent to which those incentives would be reduced, or even eliminated, owing to the illegality of the conduct in question, the likelihood of its detection, action taken by the competent authorities, both at Community and national level, and the financial penalties which could ensue."[22]

The Commission appealed against the Court's judgment,[23] claiming that the requirement to take account of the likelihood of compliance with Art.82

---

[20] Compare the discussion of whether a merger may be prohibited because it increases the likelihood of *express* collusion in Areeda, Hovenkamp & Solow, *Antitrust Law* (2nd edn, Aspen Law & Business, 1998), Vol.IV, para.917. In the United Kingdom, the Director General of Fair Trading's advice in *Orica UK / Exchem plc*, April 25, 2002 (*www.oft.gov.uk/Business/Mergers + FTA/Decisions/index.htm*), noted that the merger might increase the parties' incentives to engage in express collusion, but concluded: "This theoretical risk is not on its own sufficient to warrant [opening a detailed second-phase investigation]. Conduct such as collusion or price fixing, or abuse by a dominant supplier, would in any event be subject to investigation under the Competition Act 1998".

[21] Case T-5/02 [2002] E.C.R. II-4381, para.159.

[22] The Court of First Instance also ruled, at para.161, that the Commission ought to have taken into account, in applying the principles quoted above, the fact that Tetra Laval had offered commitments regarding its future conduct. See also paras 220 and 221 and, generally, s.20.6 below.

[23] The Commission made its decision in Case COMP/M.3440 *ENI / EDP / GDP* [2005] O.J. L302/69 (prohibition upheld on appeal in Case T-87/05 *EDP v Commission*, not yet reported, judgment of September 21, 2005) after the Court of First Instance's ruling in *Tetra Laval*, but prior to the decision of the European Court of Justice. In *ENI*, at paras 414, 424, 425 and 497, the Commission considered whether the prohibition on price discrimination under Art.82 would prevent the merged group from implementing a raising rivals' costs strategy but found that such a strategy would not necessarily (or obviously) constitute price discrimination if the

would be "impossible to meet in practice" and was inconsistent with the focus under the ECMR on structural issues.[24]

2–038   The European Court of Justice[25] started its analysis by stating that, since the Commission's decision depended on a prediction that the merged group would adopt a specific course of conduct, the Court of First Instance was right to find that the likelihood of such conduct being adopted needed to be examined comprehensively, taking account of both the incentives to adopt such conduct and the factors liable to reduce or even eliminate those incentives "including the possibility that the conduct is unlawful".[26] The judgment continued:

"However, it would run counter to the Regulation's purpose of prevention to require the Commission ... to examine, for each proposed merger, the extent to which the incentives to adopt anti-competitive conduct would be reduced, or even eliminated, as a result of the unlawfulness of the conduct in question, the likelihood of its detection, the action taken by the competent authorities, both at Community and national level, and the financial penalties which could ensue. An assessment such as that required by the Court of First Instance would make it necessary to carry out an exhaustive and detailed examination of the rules of the various legal orders which might be applicable and of the enforcement policy practised in them ... It follows that, at the stage of assessing a proposed merger, an assessment intended to establish whether an infringement of Article 82 EC is likely and to ascertain that it will be penalised in several legal orders would be too speculative and would not allow the Commission to base its assessment on all of the relevant facts with a view to establishing whether they support an economic scenario in which a development such as leveraging will occur. Consequently, the Court of First Instance erred in law in rejecting the Commission's conclusions as to the adoption by the merged entity of anti-competitive conduct capable of resulting in leveraging on the sole ground that the Commission had, when assessing the likelihood that such conduct might be adopted, failed to take account of the unlawfulness of that conduct and, consequently, of the likelihood of its detection, of action by the competent authorities, both at Community and national level, and of the financial penalties which might ensue."[27]

---

terms of the contracts differed, for example regarding technical or external conditions; further, it was likely that neither the rivals nor the national regulator would be able to identify such a pricing strategy in due time and the incentive to pursue the strategy was therefore unlikely to be eliminated by Art.82.

[24] Commission Press Release, IP/02/1952, December 20, 2002. The Commission also stated that commitments not to engage in specified commercial practices are difficult, if not impossible, to monitor.

[25] Case C-12/03P *Commission v Tetra Laval BV*, not yet reported, judgment of February 15, 2005. In an Opinion of May 25, 2004, Advocate General Tizzano argued that the Court of First Instance's judgment was correct on this point and in particular that the Court's requirements were practicable (see paras 122 to 125).

[26] Para.74.

[27] Paras 75 to 78.

It appears[28] therefore that the Commission is bound to take account of **2–039** Art.82 when assessing whether a merged group has the incentive and the ability to adopt a particular course of conduct, but the inquiry must be a pragmatic one, proportionate to the fact that the Commission is investigating a merger under short time limits. On this reading, the European Court of Justice in *Tetra Laval* ruled that the Court of First Instance placed the Commission under an excessive and unrealistic burden in formulating the extent of the obligation to take account of Art.82 in merger control proceedings but, by stating that the Court of First Instance was correct to rule that the Commission has to consider the merged group's incentives to adopt a particular course of conduct, "including the possibility that the conduct is unlawful", it maintained a duty on the Commission to carry out a certain assessment of the position under Art.82. For example, if it can readily be established that Art.82 imposes an unambiguous obligation on the merged group not to adopt the conduct in question and that obligation is likely to be enforced in the case of breach, this ought to be taken into account in the merger control analysis. On the other hand, the Commission is not required to carry out a speculative assessment of the likelihood of enforcement by different authorities, predicting the likely penalties if infringements are found and determining whether the merged group would be likely to be deterred by these risks from adopting the course of conduct.

In *General Electric Company v Commission*,[29] the Court of First Instance adopted this interpretation,[30] stating:

"the Commission must, in principle, take into account the potentially unlawful, and thus sanctionable, nature of certain conduct as a factor which might diminish, or even eliminate, incentives for an undertaking to engage in particular conduct. That appraisal does not, however, require an exhaustive and detailed examination of the rules of the various legal orders which might be applicable and of the enforcement policy practised within them, given that an assessment intended to establish whether an infringement is likely and to ascertain that it will be penalised in several legal orders would be too speculative.

Thus, where the Commission, without undertaking a specific and detailed investigation into the matter, can identify the unlawful nature of the conduct in question, in the light of Article 82 EC or of other provi-

---

[28] The interpretation of the judgment is not straightforward; see also the discussion in Prete & Nucara, "Standard of Proof and Scope of Judicial Review in EC Merger Cases: Everything Clear after *Tetra Laval?*" [2005] E.C.L.R. 692, at pp.701 and 702. In contrast to the position adopted in the text, Götz Drauz, "Conglomerate and Vertical Mergers in the Light of the Tetra Judgment", *Competition Policy Newsletter*, Summer 2005, p.35 at p.38, writing before the Court of First Instance handed down its judgment in *General Electric Company v Commission*, stated: "In our view this clearly means that an Art.82 assessment does not have to be integrated into a merger assessment".

[29] Case T-210/01, not yet reported, judgment of December 14, 2005, paras 73 to 75.

[30] See also Case COMP/M.3680 *Alcatel / Finmeccanica / Alcatel Alenia Space & Telespazio*, para.102 and Case COMP/M.3696 *E.ON/MOL*, para.442.

sions of Community law which it is competent to enforce, it is its responsibility to make a finding to that effect and take account of it in its assessment of the likelihood that the merged entity will engage in such conduct ...

It follows that, although the Commission is entitled to take as its basis a summary analysis, based on the evidence available to it at the time when it adopts its merger-control decision, of the lawfulness of the conduct in question and of the likelihood that it will be punished, it must none the less, in the course of its appraisal, identify the conduct foreseen and, where appropriate, evaluate and take into account the possible deterrent effect represented by the fact that the conduct would be clearly, or highly probably, unlawful under Community law."

The Court of First Instance found in that case that the Commission had made an error of law in failing to take into account General Electric's duties under Art.82.[31]

(b) National regulatory systems

2–040 Many Member States have regulatory systems which operate in certain markets, in particular those for the public utilities.[32] This raises the question of whether and, if so, to what extent, such regulatory systems are relevant in the assessment under the ECMR of mergers in those markets. More particularly, the issue is whether the judgment of the European Court of Justice in *Commission v Tetra Laval BV*[33] applies to national regulatory obligations in the same way that it applies to Arts 81 and 82. In order to determine this, it is necessary to identify the rationale for the Court's ruling. The European Court of Justice expressly approved the Court of First Instance's judgment that it was relevant to examine comprehensively the *likelihood* that the merged group would adopt the conduct in question.[34] The likely conduct of the merged group could be affected just as much by national regulatory obligations as by the duty to comply with Arts 81 and 82, and the reasoning of the European Court of Justice and the Court of First Instance therefore implies that the principles that the Commission must now apply when

---

[31] See paras 302 to 312, 424, 425 and 468.
[32] See also the Australian Merger Guidelines, June 1999 (*www.accc.gov.au/content/item. phtml?itemId=719436&nodeId=file43a1f42c7eb63&fn=Merger%20Guidelines.pdf*), para.5.178
[33] C-12/03P, not yet reported, judgment of February 15, 2005.
[34] Para.74, referring to para.159 of the judgment of the Court of First Instance in Case T-5/02 *Tetra Laval BV v Commission* [2002] E.C.R. II-4381. The European Court of Justice and the Court of First Instance did *not* base their decisions on the Commission's duty to avoid inconsistencies that might arise in the implementation of the various provisions of *EC law*, in particular merger control and other provisions of EC competition law which have as their objective the maintenance of undistorted competition in the common market; compare Case T-156/98 *RJB Mining PLC v European Commission* [2001] E.C.R. II-337, para.112, which is discussed in s.(d) below.

analysing whether the merged group is likely to comply with Arts 81 and 82 are equally applicable when considering national regulations (although in the latter case, the Commission would presumably need also to consider, in particular, the territorial limits of national regulatory systems and the prospect that national regulations may be amended or repealed). Indeed,[35] in *Apax / Travelex*,[36] *BT / Radianz*,[37] *Verizon / MCI*[38] and *Apax / Mölnlycke*,[39] each of which was decided after the European Court of Justice delivered its judgment in *Tetra Laval*, the Commission took account of national regulatory constraints in assessing whether the merger was likely to result in a significant impediment to effective competition.

(c) Contractual restrictions

For the reasons given above in s.(b) above, the principles identified by the European Court of Justice in *Commission v Tetra Laval BV*[40] seem to apply equally to contractual restrictions (although the Commission would presumably need also to consider the scope for the parties to terminate, renegotiate or simply not comply with the contract). Indeed, in *General Electric Company v Commission*[41] the Court of First Instance emphasised the importance of a contractual restriction in limiting the merged group's commercial freedom. Further, in its decisions in *Telefónica / Cesky Telecom*[42] and *ADM Poland / Cefetra / BTZ*,[43] which post-date the European Court of Justice's decision in *Tetra Laval*, the Commission took account of contractual provisions (respectively, the rules governing the FreeMove alliance and contractual commitments owed to the Gdynia Port Authority) when assessing whether the merger would significantly impede effective competition.[44]

2–041

---

[35] However, in a decision which post-dates the judgment of the Court of First Instance, the Commission in Case COMP/M.1378 *Hoechst / Rhône-Poulenc* (decision of January 30, 2004, on an application to amend the commitments given in that case) rejected arguments that national company law provisions could be relied on to prevent the passing of information by individuals who were on the boards of two or more rival suppliers; paras 30 to 32. See also Case COMP/M.3099 *Areva / Urenco / ETC JV*, n.115.

[36] Case COMP/M.3762, paras 27 and 31.

[37] Case COMP/M.3695, para.42.

[38] Case COMP/M.3752, paras 90 to 92 and 126.

[39] Case COMP/M.3816, para.47 (and see also press release IP/05/743).

[40] Case C-12/03P, not yet reported, judgment of February 15, 2005.

[41] Case T-210/01, not yet reported, judgment of December 14, 2005, paras 346, 347 and 349.

[42] Case COMP/M.3806 (and see also press release IP/05/713).

[43] Case COMP/M.3884, para.30.

[44] For other cases post-dating the European Court of Justice's ruling in which the Commission took account of contractual restrictions, see Case COMP/M.3729 *EDF / AEM / Edison*, para.57 and Case COMP/M.3762 *Apax / Travelex*, para.32 (the Commission found that confidentiality clauses in contracts would prevent the leaking of information).

(d) State aids

2–042 The Commission is required, at least in certain cases, to have regard to any State aid in analysing the competitive position of the merged group under the ECMR[45] because it must, as a matter of principle, avoid inconsistencies that might arise in the implementation of the various provisions of EC law, in particular provisions on State aids and merger control, which both have as their objective the maintenance of undistorted competition in the common market.[46] The Court of First Instance's judgment in *RJB Mining*[47] establishes three principles to be applied by the Commission in its appraisal (although some doubt is cast on the applicability of these principles by the subsequent decision of a different chamber of the Court of First Instance in *BaByliss*,[48] which is discussed below).

(a) The Commission is required to take into account State aid which affects competitive conditions in the market and which is *not* directly linked to the merger; such aid is relevant in particular in determining the commercial strength of the parties to the merger.[49]

(b) Secondly, the Commission must *also* examine any aid which *is* directly linked to the merger. In *RJB Mining* the Court of First Instance found that the Commission had wrongly failed to take account of the fact that the consideration for the transfer of the business had been fixed substantially below its market value. In particular, the sale at an undervalue may have strengthened the

---

[45] Case T-156/98 *RJB Mining PLC v European Commission* [2001] E.C.R. II-337 in which the Court of First Instance annulled the decision in COMP/ECSC.1252 *RAG / Saarbergwerke / Preussag Anthracite*. The Court stated, at para.114, that "in adopting a decision on the compatibility of a concentration between undertakings with the common market the Commission cannot ignore the consequences which the grant of State aid to those undertakings has on the maintenance of effective competition on the market". *RJB Mining* arose under the ECSC Treaty but the Commission has subsequently applied the principles in that case to transactions arising under the EC Treaty: see, e.g. Case COMP/M.2125 *Hypo Vereinsbank / Bank Austria* and Case COMP/M.2772 *HDW / Ferrostaal / Hellenic Shipyard*.

[46] Case T-156/98 *RJB Mining PLC v European Commission* [2001] E.C.R. II-337, para.112 (citing Case C-225/91 *Matra v Commission* [1993] E.C.R. I-3203, paras 41 and 42, Case C-164/98P *DIR International Film v Commission* [2000] E.C.R. I-447, paras 21 and 30 and Case T-49/93 *SIDE v Commission* [1995] E.C.R. II-2501, para.72). The rationale cited in the text for taking account of State aids does not extend directly to benefits conferred by non-Member States but, as a matter of principle, the Commission ought to take such funding into account as it may affect the financial and commercial strength of the recipient and is therefore a relevant circumstance in the merger appraisal.

[47] Case T-156/98 *RJB Mining PLC v European Commission* [2001] E.C.R. II-337. The principles in *RJB Mining* were applied by the Commission in Case COMP/M.3440 *ENI / EDP / GDP* [2005] O.J. L302/69, para.298 (prohibition upheld on appeal in Case T-87/05 *EDP v Commission*, not yet reported, judgment of September 21, 2005).

[48] Case T-114/02 *BaByliss v Commission* [2003] E.C.R. II-1279.

[49] Case T-156/98 *RJB Mining PLC v European Commission* [2001] E.C.R. II-337, paras 117 and 118. In Case COMP/M.2772 *HDW / Ferrostaal / Hellenic Shipyard*, the Commission found, at para.77, that the state funding was unlikely to affect the competitive position of the recipient. See also Case COMP/M.2908 *Deutsche Post / DHL (II)*, paras 29 to 38 (State aid to the *acquirer*).

financial and commercial power of the purchaser, allowing it, for example, to support those parts of its business which were subject to international competition.[50] In applying this second principle, the Commission has:

(i) sought to identify whether there is a causal link between the granting of State aid and the concentration; and

(ii) tended to consider whether, on a "worst case scenario", the possible State aid would result in a significant impediment to effective competition in the light of the financial resources available to the merged group's competitors.

In *HDW | Ferrostaal | Hellenic Shipyard*[51] the state funding was intended to facilitate privatisation and was not dependent on the identity of the buyer, with the consequence that any advantage arising from the state funding was not caused by the concentration.[52] In *Metronet | Infraco*[53] the Commission stated that it "needs to assess whether any financial strengthening has a direct impact in markets directly affected by the operation such that the impact of the operation, combined with any increase in the financial strength of the companies involved, threatens to create or strengthen any dominant position as a result of which competition would be significantly impeded". In carrying out this assessment in *Metronet*, the Commission considered both the parties' positions on the market and, separately, whether, if the alleged aid (calculated on a "worst case scenario") were divided equally between Metronet's shareholders, this would substantially change their position in relation to their major competitors on markets related to the joint venture's operations.[54] Finally, in *RAG | Saarbergwerke | Preussag Anthrazit II*,[55] the

---

[50] Case T-156/98 *RJB Mining PLC v European Commission* [2001] E.C.R. II-337, paras 122 to 125. The transaction was then reconsidered by the Commission in Case COMP/ECSC.1350 *RAG | Saarbergwerke | Preussag Anthrazit II* and approved on the basis that, even if the sale involved state subsidies, the transaction would not enable RAG to evade the ECSC competition rules as a result of its increased financial, and therefore commercial, power.

[51] Case COMP/M.2772, para.77.

[52] The Commission also carried out a "worst case scenario" analysis, finding that the aid was unlikely to have a material effect on competitive conditions because it did not affect the purchaser's competitive position in other markets and was likely to have a limited effect on the target's competitive position as most of its capacity was committed to orders from the Greek navy. See also Case COMP/M.2125 *Hypo Vereinsbank | Bank Austria* (in which the Commission found that a municipal guarantee of the target's liabilities would remain in force after the transaction but would not improve the merged group's position as it would not be extended to the remainder of the purchaser's corporate group) and Case COMP/M.2908 *Deutsche Post | DHL (II)* (in which the Commission found, at para.33 and n.12, that there was no causal link between State aid which had previously been paid to Deutsche Post and the purchase of DHL as that purchase was made at market value; the Commission also emphasised that Deutsche Post's rivals were of similar or greater financial strength). (See also Case COMP/M.3971 *Deutsche Post | Exel*, paras 79 to 81).

[53] Case COMP/M.2694, para.66.

[54] Paras 67 to 71.

[55] Case COMP/ECSC.1350.

Commission calculated the aid on a "worst case scenario" basis,[56] but found that any increase in financial power would not enable the merged group to marginalise its competitors, as those competitors were well capitalised and the merged group would not have an incentive to engage in predatory pricing because doing so would affect the subsidies received by the merged group and re-entry into the German imported coal market was relatively straightforward.

(c)   Thirdly, in carrying out its merger review, the Commission is *not* required to await the outcome of the parallel, but independent, inquiry into the compatibility with the common market of any State aids.[57] In *Metronet / Infraco*[58] the UK Government had notified certain arrangements connected with the concentration, contending that they did not amount to State aid, although the Commission had received a complaint that State aid was involved and was difficult to justify. At the time of its decision on the merger, a conclusion had not been reached on the State aid notification, but the Commission concluded that it was bound by *RJB Mining*[59] to determine whether and, if so, to what extent, the financial strength of the parties was increased by the financial support provided by the supposed aid. It described its methodology as follows: "For the purposes of this decision it is not necessary or appropriate to determine whether or not the ... arrangements involve the payment of State aid. Indeed, it is important to emphasize that this assessment is entirely without prejudice to the Commission's eventual position on the existence and, if relevant, the legality of such State aid. The Commission has therefore taken the figures presented by the complainant and has assessed whether those payments would be likely to increase the financial and commercial strength of the parties to the operation, and if so, whether such a strengthening raises competition policy problems under the ECMR".[60] By contrast, in *RAG / Saarbergwerke / Preussag Anthrazit II*,[61] the decision made following the successful appeal in *RJB Mining*, the Commission *did* await the outcome of the parallel State aid application[62] (although, because the decision was

---

[56] It is noteworthy that the Commission carried out this calculation even though the merger decision was taken on the same day as a finding that the purchase price did not involve any State aid (see press release IP/02/674) *and* the Commission had commissioned an accountancy firm to provide a report which appears to have concluded that the merger did not have a positive effect on the purchaser's balance sheet.

[57] Case T-156/98 *RJB Mining Plc v European Commission* [2001] E.C.R. II-337, para.115. In Case COMP/M.2772 *HDW / Ferrostaal / Hellenic Shipyard*, the Commission stated, at para.78: "The present decision does not prejudice the outcome of the Commission's investigation under the State aid rules". See also Case COMP/M.3150 *SNCF / Trenitalia*, para.15.

[58] Case COMP/M.2694.

[59] Case T-156/98 *RJB Mining Plc v European Commission* [2001] E.C.R. II-337.

[60] Paras 65 and 66.

[61] Case COMP/ECSC.1350.

[62] Press release IP/02/674 of May 7, 2002 discusses both decisions.

made under the ECSC, the Commission was not bound by the time limits in the ECMR).

In *BaByliss*,[63] the Court of First Instance considered an appeal against the **2–043** Commission's decision in *SEB / Moulinex*.[64] Before the Commission, BaByliss argued that SEB had been sold at undervalue and the French state had assumed liability for redundancy costs which would otherwise ultimately have been the responsibility of the purchaser. The Commission rejected these points in summary form on the basis that the actions by the French state were not for SEB's benefit.[65] The Court of First Instance considered them in more detail[66] but rejected both on the facts. The argument that the sale was at undervalue was rejected, as the price had been approved by the French court in the context of the insolvency proceedings and the (higher) price which BaByliss had been willing to pay was not comparable as it related to a different transaction.[67] Furthermore, the evidence was that an insurance company was liable to pay, rather than the French state,[68] and even if the French state *had* agreed to pay, this would not have affected the value of the assets acquired by SEB.[69] In making these findings, the Court's judgment is consistent with the principles set out in the *RJB Mining* decision. However, two passages in the Court's reasoning could be read as limiting the application of *RJB Mining*. First, in rejecting the argument based on redundancy costs (and before discussing the factual points identified above), the Court observed:

"contrary to the situation in the case of *RJB Mining* v *Commission*, cited above, upon which the applicant relies, the Commission asked the French authorities, by letters of 27 September and 9 November 2001, for information concerning any action by the French Republic in connection with the petition for voluntary liquidation and the acquisition of the Moulinex group. Second, the French Republic replied, by a note of 16 November 2001, that no State assistance to the Moulinex group was being considered and that only redeployment measures of direct benefit to employees were envisaged."[70]

It is unclear whether the facts set out in the quoted passage would, in themselves, have been sufficient to lead to the rejection of BaByliss's appeal on this point. If so, then the mere process of asking the Member State about the alleged State aid and receiving a response denying that there is aid would be sufficient for the Commission to reject concerns based on *RJB Mining*.

---

[63] Case T-114/02 *BaByliss v Commission* [2003] E.C.R. II-1279.
[64] Case COMP/M.2621.
[65] Para.10.
[66] Paras 435 to 442.
[67] Paras 436 to 439.
[68] Not, it appears, the French state.
[69] Para.440.
[70] Para.440.

However, Member States routinely deny the existence of State aid in cases in which a finding of aid is subsequently made and it ought not to be open to the Commission to abdicate all responsibility for assessing whether there is possible aid by delegating that assessment to a Member State with a clear conflict of interest. It is submitted, therefore, that the true basis for the rejection of the allegation of aid through state responsibility for redundancy payments lay in the factual analysis described above.

2-044   Secondly, the Court ended its analysis of the State aid arguments by stating:

"Finally, the Commission cannot be required to conduct a State aid procedure in connection with every concentration procedure, which must be completed within strict time-limits. Although the Court annulled the Commission's decision in the judgment in *RJB Mining* v *Commission*, cited above, on the ground that the Commission had not considered whether the level of the purchase price was such as to strengthen the new entity's position, this was by reason of the particular circumstances of that case, where the purchase price itself had been notified as aid by the German authorities. That situation cannot be compared with a concentration of two private companies, such as that in the present case."[71]

This paragraph can be read as making at least three points. First, the Court of First Instance may be read as criticising or limiting the scope of the principles set out in *RJB Mining*. However, the Court did not examine how the line of cases commencing with *Matra* could be distinguished[72] and, at most, therefore, the passage could be said to act as an invitation for the European Court of Justice to examine these issues in the future, should an opportunity arise.[73] Secondly, the passage suggests that the Commission is not under a duty to consider State aid issues in all cases. This seems correct in principle: the duty to examine these issues should arise only if the Commission is on notice of a potential concern, whether because there is a State aid notification, it is in receipt of a complaint, or it is aware of other facts which raise the question of whether State aid is involved. Thirdly, the Court contemplates that the Commission cannot carry out a full State aid analysis as part of its merger appraisal. This is consistent with the approach adopted by the Commission in *Metronet*, cited above.

---

[71] Para.441.

[72] In Case T-374/00 *Verband der freien Rohrwerke v Commission* [2003] E.C.R. II-2275, a decision which post-dates *BaByliss*, a Chamber of the Court of First Instance comprising the same three judges who decided *BaByliss* referred to the *Matra* principles as "settled case-law" but described the *RJB Mining* case as involving an "inference" from those principles (see para.169).

[73] A merger between two private companies could involve State aid if, for example, the target has received rescue or restructuring aid.

2.8 INVESTIGATIVE TECHNIQUES

When the Commission exercises its powers under the ECMR, it is almost **2–045** invariably seeking to predict the effects of a merger and in particular to determine whether the merger will materially harm consumers by increasing prices or reducing quality, innovation or choice. This exercise is complex: every market is unique and predicting the future is complicated, especially when there is a large number of interdependent variables, as in the case of most antitrust markets. It is generally impossible to predict with assurance the precise effects of a merger on price (or quality, innovation or choice).[74] Accordingly, the Commission will rarely conclude that if a merger were allowed to proceed, then prices would rise by, say, 8 per cent. when compared with the situation if the merger did not occur.[75] Equally, as the Commission is not generally able to make reliable predictions of the effects of mergers on price, it has not identified a threshold for unacceptable post-merger price increases.[76]

The Commission relies on a range of techniques when investigating **2–046** mergers.[77] First, it requires a great deal of information to be created specifically for the purposes of the appraisal process through responses to the notification form (Form CO) and answers by the notifying party to questionnaires. There is a risk that the information that is provided is biased or skewed because the notifying party wishes to obtain a clearance decision or a decision which is subject to less onerous undertakings. However, the notifying party is incentivised to provide a full and accurate account by the fact that the Commission will "market test" the notifying party's case (i.e. consult extensively with customers, competitors and other interested third parties), which generally exposes any flaws or omissions. Further, the Commission may impose sanctions if the information provided is incomplete or inaccurate: there is power to impose fines in such circumstances[78]

---

[74] See further para.1–026 above.

[75] Compare the discussion of merger simulations in para.19–006 below (and see also the use of econometric techniques in cases involving mergers of suppliers of differentiated products which is described in s.7.3 below).

[76] Any "acceptable" level is clearly below 5% because the SSNIP test contemplates that a hypothetical monopolist could profitably raise prices by 5 or 10% and a merger to monopoly, which would allow the merged group to impose such a price increase, would be prohibited. If a hypothetical monopolist could profitably raise prices by 5% (but no more), then a merged group with less than a monopoly position would be expected to be able profitably to raise prices by a lower percentage (if at all) and yet the Commission commonly prohibits mergers (or clears them only subject to commitments) in cases of horizontal mergers involving shares well below 100%.

[77] See generally the International Competition Network, "Developing Reliable Evidence in Merger Cases" (*www.internationalcompetitionnetwork.org/Reliable.pdf*); the International Competition Network, "Report on Investigative Techniques Employed by Member Agencies in the Area of Merger Review" (*www.internationalcompetitionnetwork.org/ReportIT.pdf*); and the International Competition Network, "ICN Investigative Techniques Handbook for Merger Review", June 2005 (*www.internationalcompetitionnetwork.org/handbook_5-5.pdf*).

[78] ECMR, Art.14(1).

but, more commonly, notifying parties are penalised because the notification is rejected, the clock is stopped or the Commission concludes that it is necessary to take the case into a detailed second phase investigation in order to assess the issues which were not raised properly in the original notification.

Secondly, the Commission requires the notifying parties to provide certain "internal documents", i.e. documents created by or for the notifying party for its own purposes (as opposed to being produced for the purposes of seeking merger approval from the Commission).[79] The advantage of such documents from the perspective of the Commission is that they may provide an insight into the notifying party's own assessment of the operation of the market, whether in terms of facts or analysis, untainted by any wish to obtain approval for the merger.[80]

2–047   Thirdly, the Commission relies heavily on evidence from third parties (customers, competitors, suppliers, trade associations and others) which is obtained through public invitations to comment, unsolicited submissions, responses to written questionnaires[81] and meetings and telephone calls.[82] In particular, as noted above, the Commission will test the central claims made by the notifying parties regarding the operation of the market through questions to third parties.[83] It may rely on the absence of serious objections as a pointer towards clearing a merger,[84] although in some markets—in particular those for consumer goods—customers are unlikely to complain because the value of their transactions is too small to justify the time and cost involved[85] and the absence of customer complaints regarding mergers in such markets is therefore not an indicator that a transaction does not raise substantive competition concerns. On the other hand, the Commission is sceptical of the value of customer testimonials solicited by the merging

---

[79] Form CO, s.5.4. The Commission also has power to obtain evidence by surprise inspection of the company's premises: ECMR, Art.13.

[80] For the use of internal documents, see, e.g. Case COMP/M.3099 *Areva / Urenco / ETC JV*, para.173.

[81] The Commission's investigation is "mainly" conducted in the form of written requests for information; see DG Competition Best Practices on the Conduct of EC Merger Control Proceedings, para.27.

[82] For the power to obtain evidence by interview, see the ECMR, Art.11(7).

[83] For concerns about the use of hypothetical questions in surveys, see Hughes & Beale, "Customer Surveys in UK Merger Cases—the Art and Science of Asking the Right People the Right Questions" [2005] E.C.L.R. 297, at pp.302 and 303 and Dubow, "Understanding Consumers: The Value of Stated Preferences in Antitrust Proceedings" [2003] E.C.L.R. 141. See also Tom, "Market Definition Under the Merger Guidelines: Some Modest Proposals" (*www.usdoj.gov/atr/public/workshops/docs/202597.htm#N_4_*), s.I(C). For a general discussion of the way in which questions to third parties should be formulated, see International Competition Network, "Developing Reliable Evidence in Merger Cases" (*www.international competitionnetwork.org/Reliable.pdf*), pp. 9, 10, 13 and 14.

[84] See para.19–010 below.

[85] In addition, consumers in such markets may lack expertise about the operation of the market and/or antitrust law.

parties[86]; this is in marked contrast to the position in the US, where it is routine to gather such statements (reflecting the fact that, in the absence of settlement or abandonment, cases to which the agencies object will be subject to court litigation on an application for an interlocutory injunction). The Commission ought to be sceptical of statements provided by competitors to the merging parties.[87] For example, a competitor may[88] be motivated to object to a transaction because it would generate efficiency savings which would lead to more intense competition in the market. Further, competitors may object to a transaction in the hope of "shaking out some cheap assets" if the merging parties are required to offer commitments to make disposals in order to obtain clearance. For this reason, evidence on ultimate issues for determination by the Commission (e.g. whether the third party agrees with the Commission's proposed definition of the product market[89] or the Commission's conclusion that barriers to entry are high) needs to be treated very carefully. By contrast, factual evidence which can be used by the Commission to reach its own conclusions on the ultimate issues may be highly persuasive (e.g. data on prices and volumes supplied by a competitor). Indeed, Mario Monti, when the Commissioner for Competition Policy, said that: "The test for considering a complaint is not whether it originates from a customer or a competitor but rather whether it is based on accurate factual information and well-supported and acceptable economic reasoning".[90]

Fourthly, the Commission will rely, when possible, on direct evidence of **2–048**

---

[86] In Case IV/M.938 *Guinness / Grand Metropolitan* [1998] O.J. L288/24, the Commission stated, at para.110: "The parties provided a number of statements supplied by customers, which implied that the customers concerned did not believe the merger would have adverse impacts on their business. However, only limited reliance can be placed on those statements, in view of the fact that those customers have an important commercial relationship with the parties, which asked them to make this statement".

[87] Nevertheless, the suspicion remains on the part of some companies that the ECMR process is skewed in favour of competitors; see, e.g. the article written by the chairman of Tetra Laval Group and the chairman and CEO of Schneider Electric SA in the *Financial Times*, December 6, 2001.

[88] Complaints by competitors may be motivated by a variety of other concerns, some of which would, if well-founded, be evidence of competition concerns arising from the transaction (in particular the scope for the merged group to refuse to supply or otherwise foreclose the complainant or for the merged group to exclude the complainant other than through the normal competitive process) and others of which are neutral on the question of whether the transaction will harm consumers (e.g. the complainant wishes to pick up staff or customers from the merging parties and believes that this is more likely the longer and more uncertain the merger review process, or the complainant wishes itself to acquire the target).

[89] In Case COMP/M.2842 *Saipem / Bouygues Offshore* the Commission described its methodology as follows at paras 9 to 11: "Third parties have generally confirmed the suggested product market definition [for offshore construction] ... Third parties have generally supported the view of the parties that subsea pipelaying should be divided into trunklines and flowlines respectively ... Third parties have generally supported the parties' view that onshore construction constitutes a separate product market..."

[90] Mario Monti, then the Commissioner for Competition Policy, speech of July 9, 2001 at the Merchant Taylor's Hall, London (*www.europa.eu.int/comm/competition/speeches/index_2001.html*).

the conduct and performance of suppliers in the market.[91] For example, in a market in which contracts are awarded through a tender process, it may be possible to carry out a bidding study to identify for each contract which suppliers were invited to tender, which supplier won, and why.[92] This may reveal, for example, whether the merging parties are close competitors (e.g. if both are invited to bid for the same contracts and one or the other generally wins).

Fifthly, the Commission is increasingly seeking to model markets with the objective of predicting the effects of the merger on price.[93] It may instruct outside experts to carry out the modelling exercise[94] (although, with the appointment of a Chief Competition Economist, the Commission is building its own capabilities in this area). Generally, it can be said that the Commission's methodology in merger cases is currently in a period of evolution, with a shift from an emphasis on third party views (in particular polling customers and competitors) to greater use of econometric techniques in cases which raise difficult issues.[95]

Finally, the Commission may consult with eminent experts in the field. In *Johnson & Johnson / Guidant*,[96] which involved cardiovascular medical products, the Commission interviewed a small number of eminent physicians in carrying out its review.

2.9 INTERNATIONAL COMITY

2-049 Many mergers are subject to review by two or more merger authorities. When different authorities consider the same or similar issues arising from a transaction (e.g. in cases involving global or other international markets) there is a potential inefficiency (duplicating the same inquiry) and a risk of inconsistent decisions. The inefficiency risk is partly addressed through liaison between authorities,[97] involving both communication of information and, occasionally, joint meetings. The question arises whether the risk of inconsistent decisions should be "managed" by informal arrangement between antitrust authorities, allowing one to "lead" the analysis. Certainly, in *Oracle / Peoplesoft*[98] the Commission delayed its investigation sub-

---

[91] Evidence of this type may give rise to *revealed* preferences (in contrast to responses to hypothetical questions, which result in *stated* preferences).
[92] See s.7.3 below.
[93] See para.19–006 below.
[94] See DG Competition Best Practices on the Conduct of EC Merger Control Proceedings, para.28.
[95] The "difficult" issues are often identified on the basis of third party views.
[96] Case COMP/M.3687, para.70.
[97] The merging parties can facilitate such liaison by granting waivers; see the model Commission confidentiality waiver at *http://europa.eu.int/comm/competition/mergers/others/npwaivers.pdf* and, more generally, the International Competition Network, "Waivers of Confidentiality in Merger Investigations" (*www.internationalcompetitionnetwork.org/NPWaiversFinal.pdf*).
[98] Case COMP/M.3216.

stantially[99] to enable it to reach its conclusions *after* the final resolution of the US proceedings and the Commission ultimately reached the same substantive conclusion as the US district court. The Deputy Assistant Attorney General in the Antitrust Division of the DOJ, Thomas O. Barnett, commented, in relation to *Oracle*:

> "We believe that when a competent authority in a jurisdiction with which the parties to a transaction have a strong connection rules in a case, generally speaking the global antitrust system should respect such a decision. The alternative would be a highly inefficient system of seriatim review of controversial matters in which each agency to use Hew Pate's phrase lines up to take its own whack at the piñata. While the EC, as it should, made up its own, independent decision in the Oracle case, the result is consistent with this view of comity."[1]

Several issues arise from this statement. First, it is far from clear that the **2–050** Commission would characterise its decision in *Oracle / Peoplesoft* as a manifestation of a principle of international comity. It might say that the decision to suspend the inquiry under the ECMR simply enabled the Commission to take into account in its final decision important evidence from the US trial that would not otherwise have been available. Secondly, as Mr Barnett recognised, under the ECMR, the Commission is required to take decisions based on its own analysis of the effect of the merger on consumer welfare. Thirdly, however, the rationale articulated by Mr Barnett seems reasonably sound and, notwithstanding the second point made above, decisions of other governmental bodies reviewing mergers are of persuasive authority and the Commission would be expected to take them into account in reaching its own conclusions.[2]

---

[99] Generally, the Commission is bound by tight timetables under the ECMR (in contrast to the position in the US).

[1] "Antitrust Enforcement Priorities: A Year in Review", speech of November 19, 2004 (*www.usdoj.gov/atr/public/speeches/206455.htm*).

[2] It remains to be seen whether the US agencies will apply the comity principle proposed by Mr Barnett when the transaction is closely connected with another jurisdiction but the US officials believe that the transaction is likely to harm US consumers.

CHAPTER 3

MARKET DEFINITION

3.1 INTRODUCTION

3–001 The purpose of market definition[1] is to identify in a systematic way those suppliers, if any, which provide, or could readily provide, genuine alternative *choices* for customers of the merging parties and whose activities are directly relevant to a determination of whether the merged group will enjoy

[1] See generally Bellamy & Child, *European Community Law of Competition* (eds Roth & Rose) (6th edn, Oxford UP, forthcoming) (Chapter on "Market Definition" by Lindsay & Scola); Struys & Robinson (eds), *EC Merger Decisions Digest* (2005, Kluwer); Baker & Wu, "Applying the Market Definition Guidelines of the European Commission" [1998] E.C.L.R. 273; Werden, "Demand Elasticities in Antitrust Analysis" (1998) 66 *Antitrust Law Journal* 363; Kaserman & Zeisel, "Market Definition: Implementing the Department of Justice Merger Guidelines" [1996] *The Antitrust Bulletin* 665; Huettner, "Product Market Definition in Antitrust Cases when Products are Close Substitutes or Close Complements" [2002] *The Antitrust Bulletin* 133; Baumann & Godek, "Could and Would Understood: Critical Elasticities and the Merger Guidelines" [1995] *The Antitrust Bulletin* 885; Werden, "The 1982 Merger Guidelines and the Ascent of the Hypothetical Monopolist Paradigm", June 4, 2002 (available at *www.usdoj.gov/atr/hmerger/11256.htm*); Denis, "An Insider's Look at the New Horizontal Merger Guidelines" [1992] *Antitrust* 6; Scheffman, "Statistical Measures of Market Power: Uses and Abuses" (1992) 60 *Antitrust Law Journal* 901; Keyte, "Market Definition and Differentiated Products: the Need for a Workable Standard" (1995) 63 *Antitrust Law Journal* 697; OFT Economic Discussion Paper, "Innovation and Competition Policy", Charles River Associates, March 2002 (note that the views in the paper do not necessarily reflect those of the OFT); "Market Definition in the Media Sector—Economic Issues", Report by Europe Economics for the European Commission, DG Competition, November 2002 (available via *http://europa.eu.int/comm/competition/publications/studies/european_economics.pdf*); the International Competition Network, "Analysis of Merger Guidelines", Ch.2, "Market Definition" (available via *www.internationalcompetitionnetwork.org/seoul/amg_chap2_mktdefn.pdf*); ABA Section of Antitrust Law, *Market Power Handbook* (ABA Publishing, 2005), Ch.IV; Motta, *Competition Policy Theory and Practice* (2004, Cambridge UP), Ch.3; Porter, *Competitive Advantage* (1998 edn, The Free Press, Chs 7 and 8; Porter, *Competitive Strategy* (1998 edn, The Free Press), pp.23 and 24; Bishop & Walker, *The Economics of EC Competition Law* (2nd edn, Sweet & Maxwell, 2002); OFT Research Paper "Quantitative Techniques in Competition Analysis", LECG (note that the views in the paper do not necessarily represent those of the OFT); Langenfield & Li, "Critical Loss Analysis in Evaluating Mergers" [2001] *The Antitrust Bulletin* 299; Niels, "The SSNIP Test: Some

market power.[2] This is generally[3] achieved by delineating the *narrowest* product, geographic and temporal markets on which economic power can be exercised.[4]

Market definition appears to be a necessary pre-condition for the assessment of a concentration[5] but it is a starting point for a competitive analysis[6] and not an end. It must be recognised for what it is, namely an exercise in *drawing lines* to *assist* the Commission's understanding of how competition operates in a market.[7] Indeed, Mario Monti, then the Commissioner for Competition Policy, emphasised the importance of market definition, but also its limitations: "market definition is not an end in itself but a tool to identify situations where there might be competition concerns ... We use market definition and market shares as an easily available proxy for the measurement of the market power enjoyed by firms. In effect, the main objective of defining a market is to identify the competitors of the

---

Common Misconceptions" [2004] Comp Law 267; Kokkoris, "The Concept of Market Definition and the SSNIP Test in Merger Appraisal" [2005] E.C.L.R. 209; Federal Trade Commission and Department of Justice, "Commentary on the Horizontal Merger Guidelines", 2006 (available via *www.ftc.gov/os/2006/03/CommentaryontheHorizontalMergerGuide linesMarch2006.pdf*), Ch.1; and Copenhagen Economics, *The internal market and the relevant geographical market*, Report prepared for the European Commission (available at *http://Europa.Eu.Int/Comm/Enterprise/Library/Lib-Competition/Doc/Marketdef_Final_Report.Pdf*) (which analyses the Commission's decisions and identifies a proposed framework for market definition).

[2] Case T-342/99 *Airtours plc v Commission* [2002] E.C.R. II-2585, para.20. The process of market definition may also determine whether a transaction is a horizontal merger or a vertical or conglomerate merger; this is important as vertical and conglomerate mergers are treated more benignly than horizontal mergers (compare Chs 11 and 12 with Ch.7).

[3] However, see para.3–002(b) discussing the scope to identify concentric markets.

[4] See the Commission notice on the definition of the relevant market for the purposes of Community competition law [1997] O.J. C372/3 ("the Notice on Market Definition"), para.2. See also the Notice on Horizontal Mergers, para.10. If markets are defined too narrowly, transactions which do not harm (and may benefit) consumer welfare may be blocked. Conversely, if markets are defined too widely, transactions which harm consumer welfare may be cleared.

[5] See Case T-2/93 *Air France v Commission* [1994] E.C.R. II-323, para.80; Joined Cases C-68/94 and C-30/95 *France v Commission* [1998] E.C.R. I-1375, para.143 ("a proper definition of the relevant market is a necessary precondition for any assessment of the effect of a concentration"); and Case T-342/99 *Airtours plc v Commission* [2002] E.C.R. II-2585, para.19. Market definition is of little value in cases involving differentiated products if a reliable means of assessing directly the merged group's ability profitably to raise prices (or otherwise to harm consumer welfare) is available and it may be questioned as to whether, in such cases, the Commission is required to define an antitrust market as a pre-condition of its analysis; see Epstein & Rubinfeld, "Technical Report—Effects of Mergers Involving Differentiated Products", 2004, Report for DG Competition (available via *http://europa.eu.int/comm/competition/mergers/others/effects_mergers_involving_differentiated_products.pdf*), p.19.

[6] The process of market definition would be redundant if it were possible to estimate directly the effect of the merger on price (see n.5 above). Since this is not generally practicable (see s.7.3 and para.19–006 below), markets are defined in part to facilitate the calculation of market shares which provide a proxy for market power. See the International Competition Network, "Analysis of Merger Guidelines", Ch.2, "Market Definition" (available via *www.international competitionnetwork.org/seoul/amg_chap2_mktdefn.pdf*), paras 1.3 to 1.6.

[7] In theory, therefore, even if the Commission defines the market incorrectly, the outcome of the case will be unaffected *provided* that the Commission fully analyses the way the market operates. However, in practice, market shares play a significant role in the Commission's decision making.

undertakings concerned by a particular case that are capable of constraining their behaviour ... What is ultimately important is to understand the nature of the competitive situation facing the firms involved in a ... proposed merger. The market definition is a first—and very important—step in the analysis".[8]

3–002   The Commission is not bound to follow its previous decisions on issues of market definition.[9] Indeed, the proper definition of the market may differ depending on the activities of the merging parties or the effects of the merger.

(a)   If a product faces competition from two or more other products, it may be necessary to consider the parties' activities before defining the relevant antitrust market. For example, if products B and C each comprise partial substitutes for product A then it may be that a hypothetical monopoly supplier of A could not profitably increase its prices by 5 to 10 per cent,[10] but a hypothetical monopoly supplier of either A and B *or* A and C could do so, in which case a merger between suppliers of A and B should be assessed using a product market comprising A and B, whereas a merger between suppliers of A and C should be assessed using a product market comprising A and C.[11]

(b)   A merger between companies active in neighbouring markets, A and B, may raise issues in those markets *and* in a separate, concentric market comprising the supply of both A and B. If a hypothetical monopoly supplier of either product A or product B could profitably increase prices by 5 to 10 per cent (indicating that A and B comprise separate markets), then a hypothetical monopoly supplier of both A and B could also profitably increase prices by 5 to 10 per cent.

---

[8] Mario Monti, then the Commissioner for Competition Policy, "Market Definition as a cornerstone of EU Competition Policy", speech of October 5, 2001 (*www.europa.eu.int/comm/competition/speeches/index_2001.html*).

[9] See Cases T-125 & 127/97 *Coca-Cola v Commission* [2000] E.C.R. II-1733, paras 81 and 82 and Case T-210/01 *General Electric Company v Commission*, not yet reported, judgment of December 14, 2005, paras 118 to 120, 252 and 514. See also, e.g. Case COMP/M.2337 *Nestlé / Ralston Purina*, para.21 (departing from two previous decisions); Case COMP/M.2851 *Intracom / Siemens / STI*, para.28; Case COMP/M.3333 *Sony / BMG* [2005] O.J. L62/30 (appeal pending in Case T-464/04 *Impala v Commission*), para.29 (finding that online music markets were national despite an earlier finding that they were international); and Case COMP/M.3401 *Danish Crown / Flagship Foods*, para.19.

[10] The Australian Merger Guidelines, June 1999 (*www.accc.gov.au/content/item.phtml?item Id=719436&nodeId=file43a1f42c7eb63&fn=Merger%20Guidelines.pdf*), para.5.47, state, "it is the collective effect of substitution which determines what is in or out of the relevant market. A number of substitution possibilities, each of which is insufficient alone to defeat a SSNIP, may collectively have that effect".

[11] See Baker & Wu, "Applying the Market Definition Guidelines of the European Commission" [1998] E.C.L.R. p.273, at p.274; the UK OFT's Guidelines on Market Definition, December 2004 (*www.oft.gov.uk/NR/rdonlyres/972AF80C-2D74-4A63-84B3-27552727B89A/0/OFT403.pdf*), n.32; and "Market Definition in the Media Sector—Economic Issues", Report by Europe Economics for the European Commission, DG Competition, November 2002 (available via *http://europa.eu.int/comm/competition/publications/studies/european_economics.pdf*), paras A1.76 to A1.79.

Although antitrust markets are generally defined as the *narrowest* market in which market power may be exercised,[12] this principle is intended to ensure that market power is not overlooked as a result of erroneously wide market definitions and is not intended to exclude from the analysis possible original market power in a wider, concentric[13] market (arising, e.g. from a merger between suppliers of neighbouring products). Furthermore, the Commission could investigate, as alternative theories of competitive harm which might result from a merger, possible non-coordinated effects arising from horizontal overlaps in a wider cluster market[14] *and* conglomerate or leveraging issues arising from the use of market power in the supply of one product in the cluster into a second. For example, a hypothetical monopoly supplier of personal current accounts may be able profitably to raise prices by 5 to 10 per cent but so too might a monopoly provider of personal banking services. In analysing a merger between two banks, it may be necessary to examine the scope to exercise original market power in the narrow market (personal current accounts) and the wider market (personal banking services) *and* to consider whether the merged group would be able to leverage market power in any individual market into a second.

(c) The parties' activities may influence the product market definition in cases of one-way markets.[15] For example, if consumers of product A regard product B as a perfect substitute but consumers of product B do not regard product A as an adequate substitute, the proper market definition in the case of a merger between producers of product A may be A and B, but in the case of a merger between producers of product B may be B alone. In the first case, product B is a demand-side substitute for product A but in the second case there is no demand-side substitute for product B. Similarly, if production costs in area A are £90 and in area B are £100 and the costs of transporting goods between the two areas is £10 then the proper geographic market definition in the case of a merger between producers in area B may be areas A and B, whereas the proper geographic market definition in the case of a merger between producers in area A may be A alone because producers in area B could not sell economically in area A even if prices in area A rose by 5 to 10 per cent.

(d) The parties' activities may influence the product market definition when there is no clear dividing line in the market. For example, in cases involving differentiated products, a merger between A and B

---

[12] See the Notice on Market Definition, para.17.
[13] See Areeda, Hovenkamp & Solow, *Antitrust Law* (2nd edn, Aspen Law & Business, 1998), Vol.IV, para.929d.
[14] See s.3.5(h) below.
[15] See s.3.5(i) below.

may lead to one relevant market definition whereas a merger between C and D may lead to a second.[16]

(e) In *Industri Kapital (Nordkem) / Dyno*[17] the Commission found that the geographic market was *regional* but defined the region for analysis in the transaction *in the light of the activities of the parties*,[18] stating: "Given that the activities of [the parties] overlap in the Nordic area . . ., for the purposes of this Decision, this area will be considered to constitute the relevant geographic market". The implication of the Commission's approach is that if the parties' activities had overlapped in, say, Germany and Denmark then the relevant geographic market would have comprised those two states.[19] This approach is reflected in *Owens-Illinois / BSN Glasspack*[20] in which the Commission departed from previous decisions finding that the geographic markets for glass containers were not wider than national, and instead identified geographic markets for Barcelona / South-Western France and Northern Italy / South-Eastern France. The Commission took account of the locations of the parties' plants and import and export data showing that trade occurred across borders.

(f) In *Telia / Telenor*[21] the Commission noted that a merger between two national telecoms companies could have the effect of broadening markets which were national into two-country markets, although it proceeded on the basis of national markets because the development of two-country markets was not the "automatic consequence" of the merger.[22]

---

[16] See s.3.5(d) below and the UK OFT's Guidelines on Market Definition, December 2004 (*www.oft.gov.uk/NR/rdonlyres/972AF80C-2D74-4A63-84B3-27552727B89A/0/OFT403.pdf*), para.5.10 and n.41.

[17] Case COMP/M.1813 [2001] O.J. L154/41, para.88.

[18] Such an approach is supported by the Notice on Market Definition, para.16.

[19] Such an approach is possible so long as the regional markets are not unique (perhaps because a series of overlapping markets can be identified but the connections between the markets are not sufficiently strong to justify a wider market definition on the basis of a continuous chain of substitution). However, if it is clear that conditions of competition in one region are not significantly influenced by suppliers in another, then the two regions cannot be regarded as comprising part of the same market. Nevertheless, the observation in the text means that definitions of regional markets in previous cases are of limited weight as persuasive authorities.

[20] Case COMP/M.3397, paras 24 to 26.

[21] Case IV/M.1439 [2001] O.J. L40/1, para.117.

[22] In Case COMP/M.2416 *Tetra Laval / Sidel* [2004] O.J. L43/13 (decision of October 30, 2001) the Commission contemplated, at para.163, that markets may evolve over time. This part of the Commission's decision was referred to by the Court of First Instance in Case T-5/02 *Tetra Laval BV v Commission* [2002] E.C.R. II-4381, at para.34, without criticism (and the Court of First Instance's decision was upheld on appeal on the basis of reasoning not relating to this issue in Case C-12/03P *Commission v Tetra Laval BV*, not yet reported, judgment of February 15, 2005). The Commission repeated its conclusions on this point in Case COMP/M.2416 *Tetra Laval / Sidel* (decision of January 13, 2003), paras 46 and 70. See also the Notice on Market Definition, para.12 ("the scope of the geographic market might be different when analysing a concentration, where the analysis is essentially prospective, from an analysis of past behaviour").

Notwithstanding these points of principle, in practice previous decisions of the Commission on market definition are of substantial persuasive authority under the ECMR.[23]

When possible, the Commission seeks to avoid reaching any concluded **3–003** view on the definition of the antitrust market: "in view of our limited resources, we define markets only when strictly necessary. In merger cases ... if none of the conceivable alternative market definitions for the operation in question give rise to competition concerns, the question of market definition will normally be left open".[24] This means that where the parties can demonstrate that a transaction does not significantly impede effective competition *on any reasonably credible candidate antitrust market*, the Commission will issue a clearance decision leaving open the issue of the definition of the antitrust market. Indeed, in a survey published in 2001 of decisions over a five year period, the Commission left open the definition of geographic market in 71.4 per cent of cases.[25]

The Commission's approach to market definition is summarised in Fig.3.1 **3–004** below.

---

[23] Compare Baker & Wu, "Applying the Market Definition Guidelines of the European Commission" [1998] E.C.L.R. 273 at 274. The Commission also takes account of the outcome of preliminary investigations in relation to notifications which are withdrawn prior to the Commission publishing its decision: see, e.g. Case COMP/M.2567 *Nordbanken / Postgirot*, paras 14, 16 and 18. Decisions of national competition authorities are of persuasive authority: see, e.g. Case IV/M.1383 *Exxon / Mobil* [2004] O.J. L103/1, para.79; Case COMP/M.2300 *YLE / TDF / Digita / JV*, para.16; Case COMP/M.2567 *Nordbanken / Postgirot*, para.32; Case COMP/M.3178 *Bertelsmann / Springer / JV*, para.18; and Case COMP/M.3184 *Wolseley / Pinault Bois & Matériaux*, para.21. However, decisions on market definition in anti-dumping procedures are of limited persuasive authority: see Case IV/M.774 *Saint-Gobain / Wacker-Chemie / NOM* [1997] O.J. L247/1, paras 45 to 47.

[24] Mario Monti, then the Commissioner for Competition Policy, "Market Definition as a cornerstone of EU Competition Policy", speech of October 5, 2001 (*www.europa.eu.int/comm/competition/speeches/index_2001.html*). See also the Notice on Market Definition, para.27 and the International Competition Network, "Project on Merger Guidelines", April 2004, Ch.1 (available via *www.internationalcompetitionnetwork.org/seoul/amg_chap1_overview.pdf*), which states, at para.17: "it is rarely the case that markets can be easily delineated, and taking too strong a position on the limits of a market might in fact exclude some constraints that do affect competition in that market. In reality, there is normally a spectrum of substitution possibilities that the analytical framework needs to accommodate". This point is reflected in the UK OFT Guidelines on Market Definition, December 2004 (*www.oft.gov.uk/NR/rdonlyres/972AF80C-2D74-4A63-84B3-27552727B89A/0/OFT403.pdf*), para.2.6, which describe the relevant market as no more than a frame of reference for analysis of the competitive effects.

[25] This information was revealed in a speech by Mario Monti, then the Commissioner for Competition Policy, "Market Definition as a cornerstone of EU Competition Policy", speech of October 5, 2001 (*www.europa.eu.int/comm/competition/speeches/index_2001.html*). See also the Commission's XXXIst Annual Report on Competition Policy, 2001, para.253.

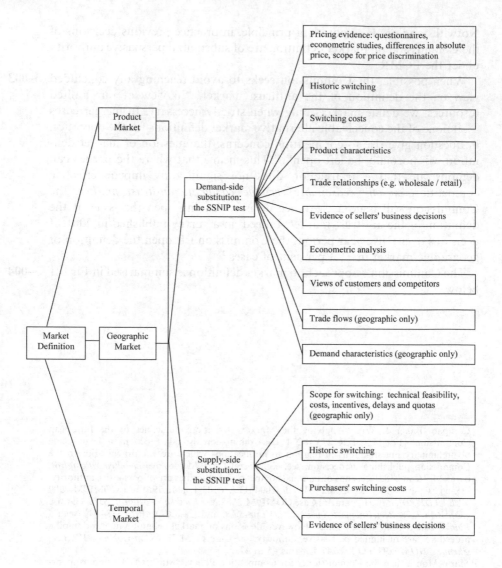

Fig. 3.1: Overview of the Commission's Approach to Market Definition

3.2 PRODUCT MARKET DEFINITION: INTRODUCTION

The Notice on Market Definition[26] defines a relevant product market as **3–005** comprising all those products and/or services which are regarded as interchangeable or substitutable[27] by the consumer, by reason of the products' characteristics, their prices and their intended use.[28] Product market definition involves analysing demand-side substitution and supply-side[29] substitution.[30]

3.3 PRODUCT MARKET DEFINITION: DEMAND-SIDE SUBSTITUTION

(a) The SSNIP test

Demand-side substitution depends on whether customers would switch to **3–006** other products in response to a price rise and involves identifying products

---

[26] The Notice on Market Definition is binding on the Commission. This appears from Case T-114/02 *BaByliss v Commission* [2003] E.C.R. II-1279 in which the Court of First Instance rejected the Commission's argument that the Notice on remedies acceptable under Reg 4064/89 and under Reg 447/98, [2001] O.J. C68/3, was not binding on the grounds that: "The Commission is bound by notices which it issues in the area of supervision of concentrations, provided they do not depart from the rules in the Treaty and from Regulation No 4064/89 [the original EC Merger Regulation] ... Moreover, the Commission cannot depart from rules which it has imposed on itself". The same reasoning is equally applicable to the Notice on Market Definition as the Court of First Instance confirmed in Case T-210/01 *General Electric Company v Commission*, not yet reported, judgment of December 14, 2005, para.516 ("As regards the alleged failure to comply with the notice on market definition, it is appropriate to observe at the outset that the Commission may not depart from rules which it has imposed on itself ... Thus, to the extent that the notice on market definition lays down in mandatory terms the method by which the Commission intends to define markets in the future and does not retain any margin of assessment, the Commission must indeed take account of the provisions of the notice".)

[27] This depends on the *choices open to customers*.

[28] The Notice on Market Definition, para.7.

[29] Under the US Horizontal Merger Guidelines, 1992 (amended in 1997) (*www.usdoj.gov/atr/public/guidelines/hmg.htm*), supply-side substitution does not result in a widening of the product market but instead results in the inclusion of the potential entrants in calculating market shares.

[30] The Commission's approach is as follows (per the Notice on Market Definition, para.26): "The process of defining relevant markets may be summarized as follows: on the basis of the preliminary information available or information submitted by the undertakings involved, the Commission will usually be in a position to broadly establish the possible relevant markets within which, for instance, a concentration ... has to be assessed. In general, and for all practical purposes when handling individual cases, the question will usually be to decide on a few alternative possible relevant markets. For instance, with respect to the product market, the issue will often be to establish whether product A and product B belong or do not belong to the same product market. It is often the case that the inclusion of product B would be enough to remove any competition concerns".

which are regarded by customers as good substitutes. Under the ECMR, the SSNIP ("small but significant non-transitory increase in price") test[31] is applied.[32]

(a) The issue in considering a candidate market is whether a hypothetical monopolist would find it profitable[33] to increase the prevailing[34] market price of the product by 5 to 10[35] per cent.[36] In shorthand, *an antitrust market is something worth monopolising*.

(b) The test is applied iteratively. The first iteration is applied to a nar-

---

[31] Mario Monti, then the Commissioner for Competition Policy, "Market Definition as a cornerstone of EU Competition Policy", speech of October 5, 2001 (*www.europa.eu.int/comm/ competition/speeches/index_2001.html*), has summarised the test as follows: "The question that this test asks is whether the parties' customers would switch to readily available substitutes or to suppliers located elsewhere in response to a hypothetical small (in the range 5%–10%), permanent relative increase in the products and areas being considered. If substitution would be enough to make the price increase unprofitable, because of the resulting loss of sales, additional substitutes and areas are included in the relevant market. This theoretical test allows us to identify a set of products and a geographic area small enough to allow permanent increases in relative prices that would be profitable".

[32] See paras 3–009 and 3–011 below for discussion of whether the SSNIP test is the exclusive methodology when defining markets in merger cases. The SSNIP test is now widely used internationally and has been adopted, for example, in the Merger Guidelines of the US Agencies and the Canadian, Australian, New Zealand and Irish authorities as well as those of the UK Office of Fair Trading and UK Competition Commission. However, the US Horizontal Merger Guidelines of the National Association of Attorneys General, 1993 (available at *www.naag.org/issues/pdf/at-hmerger_guidelines.pdf*), use an alternative approach, stating, at s.3.1, that: "A comparably priced substitute will be deemed substitutable and thereby expand the product market definition if, and only if, considered substitutable by customers accounting for seventy-five per cent of the purchases".

[33] More accurately, the issue is whether the hypothetical monopolist's profits would *increase* as a result of the increase in price. For discussion of the importance of focusing on the effect of the hypothetical price increase on profitability, see Case COMP/M.2947 *Verbund / EnergieAllianz*, [2004] O.J. L92/91 (appeal pending in Case T-350/03 *Wirschaftskammer Karnten and best connect Ampere Strompool v Commission*), para.75. Werden, "Beyond Critical Loss: Tailored Application of the Hypothetical Monopolist Test" [2005] Comp Law 69 argues that even if a price increase of 5 to 10% would be *profitable*, the relevant market ought to be defined more broadly if the profit-*maximising* price increase is less than 5%, because competition policy should only properly be concerned with rational exercises of market power.

[34] The Notice on Market Definition, para.19.

[35] A hypothetical monopolist may find it profitable to increase prices by more than 5 to 10% but *not* by 5 to 10%. The Notice on Market Definition makes no reference, at para.17, to taking account of increases in price in excess of 10% (in contrast to the position under the US Horizontal Merger Guidelines, 1992 (amended in 1997) (*www.usdoj.gov/atr/public/guidelines/ hmg.htm*) which refer to price increases "at least" as great as the significance threshold: see Werden, "Market Delineation and the Justice Department's Merger Guidelines" [1983] Duke LJ 514, at pp.543 and 544 and Langenfield & Li, "Critical Loss Analysis in Evaluating Mergers" [2001] *The Antitrust Bulletin* 299, at p.323; see also the UK OFT's Guidelines on Market Definition, December 2004 (*www.oft.gov.uk/NR/rdonlyres/972AF80C-2D74-4A63- 84B3-27552727B89A/0/OFT403.pdf*), n.12). However, the Commission guidelines on market analysis and the assessment of significant market power under the Community regulatory framework for electronic communications networks and services [2002] O.J. C165/3, state, at para.40: "While the significance of a price increase will depend on each individual case, in practice, NRAs [National Regulatory Authorities] should normally consider customers' (consumers or undertakings) reactions to a permanent increase in price of 5 to 10%". This implies that price increases of different magnitudes may be relevant in certain cases.

[36] The prices and terms of sale of all other products are held constant in applying the SSNIP test.

row candidate market and, if a hypothetical monopolist would *not* find such a price increase profitable, products are added to the candidate market and the test is repeated[37] until[38] a price increase of 5 to 10 per cent would be profitable.[39]

(c) The profitability of the increase in price will depend on whether the increased revenues on sales which are retained by the hypothetical monopolist but are made at the higher price, together with any cost savings arising from the reduction in output associated with falling demand, are greater than the revenues lost as a result of falling demand.

Under the SSNIP test, products which are treated as sufficiently strong **3–007** substitutes to form part of the same market must be *very close* substitutes, i.e. it must be easy for consumers to switch to the alternatives if they are to be included in the market.[40]

The test focuses attention on the reactions of *marginal* customers to the hypothetical price increase and not *captive* customers.[41] Marginal customers are those which are the first to switch in response to small increases in price. Captive customers are those which are unable to switch to an alternative product or, at least, have a strong preference not to switch. Even if a majority of customers is captive—and therefore unable or unwilling to switch to an alternative product—the fact that a small proportion of marginal customers can switch may make it unprofitable to increase prices. If

---

[37] For discussion of whether, when a candidate market comprising product A is widened to cover two products, A and B, it is necessary for the hypothetical monopolist to be able profitably to increase the price of one of the merging parties' products in A, A alone, or both A *and* B, see the Canadian Merger Guidelines, 2004 (*www.competitionbureau.gc.ca/PDFs/2004%20MEGs.Final.pdf*), para.3.5; the UK OFT Market Definition Guidelines, 2004 (*www.oft.gov.uk/NR/rdonlyres/972AF80C-2D74-4A63-84B3-27552727B89A/0/OFT403.pdf*), para.2.12; Niels, "The SSNIP Test: Some Common Misconceptions", [2004] Comp Law 267, pp.271 and 272; Tom, "Market Definition Under the Merger Guidelines: Some Modest Proposals" (*www.usdoj.gov/atr/public/workshops/docs/202597.htm#N_4_*), s.I(B); and Church & Ware, *Industrial Organization A Strategic Approach* (McGraw-Hill, 2000), p.603.

[38] The iterative nature of the SSNIP test is sometimes expressed by saying that the product market is the *smallest* group of products in relation to which a hypothetical monopolist could profitably increase price by 5 to 10 per cent. However, this raises the question of whether each product is part of a *unique* product market or whether, instead, products may be part of two or more *overlapping* or *concentric* markets. In principle the latter analysis is to be preferred: see para.3–002(b) above.

[39] It is therefore important to identify the criteria used to identify: the product or group of products to which the first iteration is applied; the products to be added in subsequent iterations; and the order in which such products are introduced into the iterative process. The Notice on Market Definition, paras 16 and 17, indicates that the starting point is the type of products sold by the undertakings involved. Whilst the Notice on Market Definition provides no guidance on the choice of products to be added to the iterative process and the order in which such additions should occur, in principle the next-best substitute should be added at each iteration: see Werden, "Demand Elasticities in Antitrust Analysis" (1998) 66 *Antitrust Law Journal*, 363 at 402 to 406.

[40] Products which are not sufficiently close substitutes to form part of the same product market may nevertheless exercise an important competitive constraint.

[41] Contrast Case COMP/M.3779 *Pernod Ricard / Allied Domecq*, para.12.

such a price increase would be unprofitable and it is not possible to price discriminate between the captive and non-captive customers, then the market should be defined on a wider basis.[42]

3–008 The test includes in the market not only goods and services which are currently sold but also those which *would* be sold if price were to increase on a lasting basis by 5 to 10 per cent. Identifying goods or services which are not currently sold but would be sold in particular circumstances is a difficult hypothetical exercise and the Commission inevitably focuses on information about past market behaviour.

The *time period* for the application of the SSNIP test is important because market power may be greater when measured over a shorter period and, accordingly, the shorter the period taken in applying the test, the narrower the likely market definition. The period within which switching has to occur in order to qualify for the purposes of demand-side substitution is "the short term"[43] (which is generally taken as one year,[44] although the precise period selected depends on the way in which the market operates).[45]

There are suggestions in the academic literature,[46] which were adopted in a US decision,[47] that the *percentage price increase* used for the purposes of the SSNIP test should vary depending on the significance of purchases of the

---

[42] See Case IV/M.970 *TKS / ITW Signode / Titan* [1998] O.J. L316/33, para.40, noting that, whilst 3 to 10 per cent of consumption of product A was captive, price discrimination seemed not to be feasible and, accordingly, a wider market definition including both A and B was adopted. See also Baker & Wu, "Applying the Market Definition Guidelines of the European Commission" [1998] E.C.L.R. 273, at pp.275 and 276, criticising decisions of the Commission which seemed to require complete substitution for all applications as a condition for finding a wider product market.

[43] The Notice on Market Definition, para.16.

[44] In Case COMP/M.2420 *Mitsui / CVRD / Caemi* [2004] O.J. L92/50 the Commission agreed with a statement by the economics consultancy, NERA, in the context of the SSNIP test, that "in general the competitive assessment of mergers considers time periods of at least one year and in some instances up to two years" (see n.29 to para.111). A two year period would generally be excessive though, because new entry is normally considered "timely" only if it occurs within two years (Notice on Horizontal Mergers, para.74) and substitution on the supply-side requires that the constraint be more direct and immediate than in the case of new entry. The UK OFT's Guidelines on Market Definition, December 2004 (*www.oft.gov.uk/NR/rdonlyres/972AF80C-2D74-4A63-84B3-27552727B89A/0/OFT403.pdf*), para.3.6, adopt a one year period as a "rough rule of thumb" and the Canadian Merger Guidelines, 2004 (*www.competitionbureau.gc.ca/PDFs/2004%20MEGs.Final.pdf*), para.3.4, adopt a one year period in "most cases". For further comparative data, see the International Competition Network, "Analysis of Merger Guidelines", Ch.2, "Market Definition" (available via *www.internationalcompetitionnetwork.org/seoul/amg_chap2_mktdefn.pdf*), para.1.37.

[45] Denis, "An Insider's Look at the New Horizontal Merger Guidelines" [1992] *Antitrust* 6, comments, at p.7: "The length of the 'foreseeable future' will depend on the nature of the industry. For example, in industries where technological change is rapid or there are relatively frequent product cycles, the foreseeable future may be quite short. In other, more stable industries, the foreseeable future may be relatively long".

[46] Scherer & Ross, *Industrial Market Structure and Economic Performance* (3rd edn, Houghton Mifflin Co, 1990), p.180.

[47] *Marathon Oil Co v Mobil Corp* 530 F.Supp 315, 322 (N.D. Ohio 1981), affirmed, 669 F.2d 378 (6th Cir. 1981). The US Horizontal Merger Guidelines, 1992 (amended in 1997) (*www.usdoj.gov/atr/public/guidelines/hmg.htm*), para.1.11 indicate that a price increase which is larger or smaller than 5% may be used.

good in question.[48] In particular, when an input is a substantial cost for customers the percentage in question should, on this approach, be set at a lower level (1 per cent in the case of the US decision) than cases in which the input is a small part of overall cost for customers (when customers might be expected to be less sensitive to small changes in price). The Commission would find it difficult to adopt this suggestion whilst the Notice on Market Definition remained in its current terms.[49]

In merger control, the SSNIP test is applied with reference to the *pre-merger market price*.[50] The use of the pre-merger market price may result in an incorrect analysis because a monopolist—or a group of firms tacitly or expressly operating as if they were a monopolist—will price at a level at which any further price increases would not be profitable. It follows that if there is already an actual or effective monopoly, then applying the SSNIP test will result in an unduly wide market definition. This is known as the "cellophane fallacy" after a much criticised decision of the US Supreme Court finding that cellophane was part of a wider product market comprising flexible wrapping materials including aluminium foil, brown paper etc.[51] This issue tends to be of greater concern in behavioural cases than mergers because most mergers occur in markets in which there is competition and the price is below the monopoly level.[52] If the SSNIP test cannot be used, markets will be defined with particular reference to product characteristics and intended use.[53]

In addition to the "cellophane fallacy", there may be other situations in which the SSNIP test is not directly applicable. In particular[54]:

3–009

---

[48] See the International Competition Network, "Analysis of Merger Guidelines", Ch.2, "Market Definition" (available via *www.internationalcompetitionnetwork.org/seoul/amg_chap2_mktdefn.pdf*), para.1.32.

[49] The Notice on Market Definition states, at para.17, that the percentage increase to be considered is "in the range 5% to 10%".

[50] The Notice on Market Definition, para.19. The US Horizontal Merger Guidelines, 1992 (amended in 1997) (*www.usdoj.gov/atr/public/guidelines/hmg.htm*), para.1.11, note that the pre-merger prevailing price is generally used but reserve the right to use the competitive price if there is evidence of coordinated interaction and to use future prices, absent the merger, if changes in the prevailing prices can be predicted with reasonable reliability.

[51] *United States v EI du Pont de Nemours & Co*, 351 US 377, 76 S.Ct. 994, 100 L.Ed. 1264 (1956). See generally Posner, *Antitrust Law* (2nd edn, The University of Chicago Press, 2001), p.151.

[52] The "cellophane fallacy" is nevertheless relevant in merger cases, in particular if there are pre-merger coordinated effects. See further Church & Ware, *Industrial Organization A Strategic Approach* (McGraw-Hill, 2000), p.618.

[53] There are suggestions that an *inverse* cellophane fallacy may operate in markets with network effects as suppliers engage in very low pricing to seek to be the successful supplier when the market "tips" and market definitions may therefore be unduly *narrow*; see "Merger Review in Emerging High Innovation Markets", OECD, DAFFE/COMP(2002)20, p.8 and OFT Economic Discussion Paper, "Innovation and Competition Policy", Charles River Associates, March 2002 (note that the views in the paper do not necessarily reflect those of the OFT), paras 4.53 to 4.59.

[54] See also paras 3–010 and 3–011 below. There are suggestions that the SSNIP test may not be appropriate in markets with high *switching costs*; see Harkrider, "Operationalizing the Hypothetical Monopolist Test" (available via *www.usdoj.gov/atr/public/workshops/docs/202598.pdf*), p.11. It has also been argued that the use of the SSNIP test is less appropriate in

(a) in *bidding markets* where suppliers tender for bespoke pieces of work, it may not be possible to identify a market price to which a hypothetical price increase can be added[55];

(b) the SSNIP test cannot be applied when the supplier is subject to *price regulation*[56];

(c) the SSNIP test is also difficult to apply when there is *no current trade*[57];

(d) many media products, such as television channels and newspapers, are supplied *free of charge*, making it difficult to apply the SSNIP test[58] to determine whether the free products compete with paid for products.

3–010 Further, by focusing on a hypothetical monopolist's ability profitably to raise prices, the SSNIP test is closely aligned to the concept of *original market power*, i.e. the direct ability of a company to increase price or reduce quality, variety or innovation significantly relative to the competitive level. Indeed, the notion underlying the SSNIP test is that market shares are a reliable proxy for market power only if a 100 per cent market share would confer significant market power.[59] The most common form of original market power arises when a company is able profitably to restrict output and thereby increase prices in the light of its significant market share and the limited constraints posed by rivals, new entry and customers.[60] By contrast, the SSNIP test is not so obviously aligned to the concept of *exclusionary market power*, i.e. the ability of a company to exclude or marginalise one or more of its competitors from the market, enabling it profitably to increase

---

high innovation markets when customers may focus on product performance to a greater extent than price (see "Merger Review in Emerging High Innovation Markets" OECD, DAFFE/COMP(2002)20, p.8).

[55] However, it may be possible to assess the extent to which customers are sensitive to small changes in relative prices.

[56] See the Commission guidelines on market analysis and the assessment of significant market power under the Community regulatory framework for electronic communications networks and services [2002] O.J. C165/3, para.42 and the US Horizontal Merger Guidelines, 1992 (amended in 1997) (*www.usdoj.gov/atr/public/guidelines/hmg.htm*), para.1.0.

[57] See "Market Definition in the Media Sector—Economic Issues", Report by Europe Economics for the European Commission, DG Competition, November 2002 (available via *http://europa.eu.int/comm/competition/publications/studies/european_economics.pdf*), paras 2.5.21 to 2.5.26.

[58] For discussion of the scope to apply the hypothetical monopolist test to changes in relative *quality* in such cases, see "Market Definition in the Media Sector—Economic Issues", Report by Europe Economics for the European Commission, DG Competition, November 2002 (available via *http://europa.eu.int/comm/competition/publications/studies/european_economics.pdf*), paras 2.4.21 and 3.4.81 to 3.4.85.

[59] See Werden, "The 1982 Merger Guidelines and the Ascent of the Hypothetical Monopolist Paradigm", June 4, 2002 (available at *www.usdoj.gov/atr/hmerger/11256.htm*).

[60] The US Horizontal Merger Guidelines, 1992 (amended in 1997) (*www.usdoj.gov/atr/public/guidelines/hmg.htm*), para.1.0, make clear that the SSNIP test is employed solely as a methodological tool for the analysis of mergers and not as a tolerance level for price increases. See also Bishop, "The Modernisation of DGIV" [1997] E.C.L.R. 481.

price or reduce quality, variety or innovation. This raises the question of whether the SSNIP test is apposite in defining markets in which the Commission anticipates the possible exercise of *exclusionary* market power.[61] First, the clear alignment between the SSNIP test and the concept of original market power enables the Commission to infer, in the absence of any other evidence, that companies holding high shares of properly defined antitrust markets enjoy original market power and that the degree of market power is proportionate to the market share. Secondly, the absence of a clear alignment between the SSNIP test and the concept of exclusionary market power means that no such similar inference about the existence of exclusionary market power can be drawn from the merged group's market share. In particular, determining whether the merged group will enjoy exclusionary market power requires a careful analysis of whether it will have the incentive and ability to adopt an exclusionary strategy.[62] But, thirdly, a company which lacks market power will not have the ability to pursue an exclusionary strategy because such a strategy would be defeated by rivals, new entry and customers. Therefore, one of the several conditions for the exercise of exclusionary market power is (or at least ought to be)[63] that the merged group holds a dominant position in a market defined according to the SSNIP test.

The question arises whether the SSNIP test is applied generally[64] when **3–011** defining relevant antitrust markets under the ECMR or whether other tests are also used and, if so, in what circumstances. The issue is material because[65]:

(a) the Notice on Market Definition refers to the SSNIP test as "one way" of defining the relevant market[66];

(b) the Notice on Market Definition expressly adopts definitions of the relevant product and geographic markets from earlier decisions of

---

[61] Lind & Muysert, "Innovation and Competition Policy: Challenges for the New Millenium" [2003] E.C.L.R. 87, at pp.88 and 89, argue that markets should be defined on the basis of power to exclude as well as power to raise price.

[62] See Chs 11 and 12.

[63] See para.11–018 below.

[64] Subject to the exceptions already discussed in para.3–009 above.

[65] The DG Competition Discussion Paper on the Application of Article 82 of the Treaty to Exclusionary Abuses, December 2005, para.14, states that the SSNIP test constitutes a "central part" of the Commission's approach to market definition in merger cases.

[66] See para.15. However, the Notice on Market Definition does not refer to any *other* overarching coherent test for determining relevant antitrust markets. See also the "Commission guidelines on market analysis and the assessment of significant market power under the Community regulatory framework for electronic communications networks and services" [2002] O.J. C165/6, n.26 (referring to the SSNIP test as "but one example of methods used for defining the relevant market) and para.40 ("One possible way of assessing the existence of any demand and supply-side substitution is to apply the so-called 'hypothetical monopolist test' [i.e. the SSNIP test]"). In addition, the UK OFT Guidelines on Market Definition (December 2004) (*www.oft.gov.uk/NR/rdonlyres/972AF80C-2D74-4A63-84B3-27552727B89A/0/OFT403. pdf*), state, at para 2.5, that the SSNIP test is "usually" employed.

the Community Courts[67] which do not refer to the SSNIP test and do not use the SSNIP methodology,[68] and those definitions continue to be referred to by the Community Courts[69];

(c) the Commission's own merger decisions refer expressly to the SSNIP test relatively rarely[70]; and

(d) the Commission's guidelines on market analysis and the assessment of significant market power under the Commission regulatory framework for electronic communication networks and services state[71] that when "consumer choice is influenced by considerations other than price increases, the SSNIP test may not be an adequate measurement of product substitutability" and cite the decision of the Court of First Instance in *Roberts*[72] in support.

However, the use of the SSNIP test, at least in merger cases, was endorsed by the Court of First Instance in *Airtours plc v Commission*,[73] where the arguments of the parties and the analysis of the Court all proceeded on the basis that, in defining relevant markets, the focus is on the scope for substitution at the margins which is the hallmark of the SSNIP test.[74] Further,

---

[67] See, e.g. Case 6/72 *Europemballage and Continental Can v Commission* [1973] E.C.R. 215; Case 27/76 *United Brands v Commission* [1978] E.C.R. 207; Case 85/76 *Hoffmann La-Roche v Commission* [1979] E.C.R. 461; and Case 322/81 *Michelin v Commission* [1983] E.C.R. 3461.

[68] See paras 8 and 9.

[69] See, e.g. Case T-374/00 *Verband der freien Rohrwerke v Commission* [2003] E.C.R. II-2275, para.141 (geographic market) and Joined Cases T-346/02 and T-347/02 *Cableuropa SA and others v Commission* [2003] E.C.R. II-4251, para.115.

[70] Copenhagen Economics, *The internal market and the relevant geographical market*, Report prepared for the European Commission (available at *http://Europa.Eu.Int/Comm/Enterprise/Library/Lib-Competition/Doc/Marketdef_Final_Report.Pdf*), found, at p.59, that the Commission referred expressly to the use of the SSNIP test in 4% of geographic market definitions and 11% of product market definitions in a large sample of phase II ECMR cases.

[71] [2002] O.J. C165/3, n.28.

[72] Case T-25/99 *Colin Arthur Roberts and Valerie Ann Roberts v Commission* [2001] E.C.R. II-1881, para.40. Two points should be noted. First, almost all products are differentiated at least to an extent and there is therefore nothing unusual about products in high technology or media markets; products which appear to be truly homogenous are usually differentiated in some respects (e.g. on geographic location). Secondly, the operation of the SSNIP test does not depend on price being the only parameter which influences consumers' choices; its essential insight is that if consumers would not switch away from a particular group of products in sufficient numbers to defeat a hypothetical price increase, then products outside that group are not sufficiently close competitive constraints to fall within the same antitrust market; this insight holds true when customers also take account of other factors in making their purchasing decision.

[73] See Case T-342/99 *Airtours plc v Commission* [2002] E.C.R. II-2585, paras 31 and 32.

[74] Little weight can be placed on formulations of the test for market definition in judgments of the Community Courts reached before the SSNIP test was widely recognised by the global antitrust community as material to market definition in antitrust cases and/or in cases in which it was not argued that the SSNIP test should be preferred to qualitative analysis of product characteristics and intended use.

the decisions of the Court of First Instance in *BaByliss v Commission*[75] and *General Electric Company v Commission*[76] have established that the Notice on Market Definition (which focuses on the use of the SSNIP test for defining relevant antitrust markets) *is* binding[77] on the Commission to the extent that it does not depart from the rules of the Treaty. Finally, as Copenhagen Economics point out: "the only alternative to the SSNIP-methodology is lack of consistency and transparency".[78]

The predominance of the SSNIP test in defining antitrust markets can be reconciled with the fact that it is not mentioned frequently in the Commission's decisions if the Commission is regarded as applying a "first screen" test (assessing the needs of marginal consumers in the light of product characteristics, intended use and price), to be followed by a full application of the SSNIP test if there are doubts as to whether the "first screen" test correctly identified the market. On this analysis, the SSNIP test provides the ultimate conceptual basis for the process of market definition but it is only applied in its full panoply in cases which merit the necessary application of resources. Indeed, the DG Competition Discussion Paper on the Application of Article 82 of the Treaty to Exclusionary Abuses,[79] emphasises that an assessment of product characteristics and intended use should be carried out *paying particular regard to the needs of marginal consumers*, i.e. the paper emphasises that a qualitative assessment (focusing on product characteristics and intended use) is effectively a *proxy* for the more precise methodology inherent in the SSNIP test and is not a separate, independent exercise. If this paragraph is correct, then the Commission is in each case seeking to make the best assessment of the reactions of marginal consumers to small but significant changes in relative prices and it is

---

[75] Case T-114/02 [2003] E.C.R. II-1279, in which the Court of First Instance stated, at para.143: "The Commission is bound by notices which it issues in the area of supervision of concentrations, provided they do not depart from the rules in the Treaty and from [the ECMR] ... Moreover, the Commission cannot depart from rules which it has imposed on itself". The decision in *BaByliss* related to the Commission Notice on Remedies Acceptable Under Council Regulation (EEC) No.4064/89 and under Commission Regulation (EC) No.447/98 [2001] O.J. C68/3 (see Ch.20), but the same principles apply to the Notice on Market Definition.

[76] Case T-210/01, not yet reported, judgment of December 14, 2005, para.516 ("As regards the alleged failure to comply with the notice on market definition, it is appropriate to observe at the outset that the Commission may not depart from rules which it has imposed on itself ... Thus, to the extent that the notice on market definition lays down in mandatory terms the method by which the Commission intends to define markets in the future and does not retain any margin of assessment, the Commission must indeed take account of the provisions of the notice").

[77] The Notice on Market Definition does *not* provided that the SSNIP test will be applied in all cases (see sub-para.(a) above), with the consequence that a challenge to a particular decision on the grounds that the Commission failed to apply the SSNIP test is likely to fail (because the Commission can point to the fact that it retained for itself a discretion whether to apply the SSNIP test).

[78] *The internal market and the relevant geographical market*, Report prepared for the European Commission (available at *http://Europa.Eu.Int/Comm/Enterprise/Library/Lib-Competition/Doc/Marketdef_Final_Report.Pdf*), p.65.

[79] December 2005, para.18.

ultimately arid to debate whether the Commission is applying the SSNIP test or an approximation of it.

(b) Evidence: introduction

3–012 The Notice on Market Definition[80] and the Commission's previous decisions indicate that a range of categories of evidence[81] may be relevant in determining the product market on the demand side.[82]

(c) Pricing evidence

3–013 **(i) Commission questionnaires** In applying the SSNIP test, the Commission commonly sends questionnaires to customers in the market asking them how they would react if prices were to rise permanently by 5 per cent and, separately, by 10 per cent.[83] The Commission may use the responses to calculate the likely loss of sales if the price of one product were increased by 5 to 10 per cent by weighting the customer responses according to their volumes of purchases.[84] The use of such questionnaires in applying the SSNIP test was criticised by the notifying party in *CVC / Lenzing*[85] on the grounds that the results are subjective, arbitrary and unreliable.[86] However,

---

[80] The Notice on Market Definition notes, at para.25, that the Commission adopts an open approach to empirical evidence, making use of all available and relevant material.

[81] See also Porter, *Competitive Advantage* (1998 edn, The Free Press), p.278.

[82] In very general terms, the Commission's methodology is to identify the products sold by the parties and their uses, customers, distribution channels and prices and then to examine whether any of the differences identified are relevant to the definition of the market.

[83] The Commission published an extract from a typical questionnaire in Case COMP/M.2187 *CVC / Lenzing* [2004] O.J. L82/20, n.17.

[84] For an example, see Case COMP/M.2187 *CVC / Lenzing* [2004] O.J. L82/20, para.40. Critical loss analysis is discussed in para.3–031 below.

[85] Case COMP/M.2187, [2004] O.J. L82/20, para.25.

[86] For concerns about the use of hypothetical questions in surveys, see Hughes & Beale, "Customer Surveys in UK Merger Cases—the Art and Science of Asking the Right People the Right Questions" [2005] E.C.L.R. 297, at pp.302 and 303 and Hildebrand, *The Role of Economic Analysis in the EC Competition Rules* (Kluwer, 2002), pp. 329 and 334. Dubow, "Understanding Consumers: The Value of Stated Preferences in Antitrust Proceedings" [2003] E.C.L.R. 141 and Hildebrand, pp.329 to 331 advocate the use of "conjoint" analysis to *reveal* preferences (rather than using respondents' *stated* preferences) relevant to the SSNIP test. In "conjoint" analysis, customers are asked to make choices between different products and, by asking a series of real-world questions, the analyst can build up a detailed model of demand using a preference model. See also the UK OFT's Guidelines on Market Definition, December 2004 (*www.oft.gov.uk/NR/rdonlyres/972AF80C-2D74-4A63-84B3-27552727B89A/0/OFT403. pdf*), para.3.7, noting that answers to hypothetical questions may need to be treated with a degree of caution. The Commission, in its Notice on Market Definition, para.40, states that reasoned answers to such hypothetical questions "are taken into account when they are sufficiently backed by factual evidence". However, highly probative evidence may be obtained by asking customers open questions about their previous purchasing choices and the reasons for them and, in asking about the customer's reaction to a hypothetical future price increase, focusing on the customer's reasons for regarding particular options as viable or not. Scheffman, Coate & Silva, "20 Years of Merger Guidelines Enforcement at the FTC: An

the Commission rejected the criticism, emphasising that the SSNIP test is by definition a hypothetical, prospective analysis.[87]

(ii) Price correlation studies Price correlation studies identify statistically **3–014** whether, and the extent to which, the prices of two products track one another over time.[88] The underlying idea is that the prices of products which form part of the same product market are likely to move together.[89] Such studies require detailed pricing data for the relevant products and produce a result—the correlation—between −1 and +1. A correlation of +1 shows that the prices move in parallel. A correlation of 0 shows that the prices move independently. A correlation of −1 shows that the prices move in opposite directions. If there is a high positive correlation (i.e. prices tend to track one another) this *suggests*[90] that the products form part of the same market since it is possible that pricing decisions of one are constrained by the prices of the other. The Commission regularly considers evidence from such studies.[91] The following points arise when applying the test.

Economic Perspective" (available at *www.usdoj.gov/atr/hmerger/11255.htm*), state that: "In the 1980s and into the early 1990s ... legal staff investigations placed considerable emphasis on the answers of customers to the hypothetical price increase question. In retrospect, it is clear that customers had difficulty understanding the hypothetical question and that staff did not appreciate the importance of determining whether there were customers at the margin and the volume of business they represented. (The use of the hypothetical price increase was eventually significantly improved by the addition of 'critical loss' analysis.)"

[87] Paras 26 to 29. The Commission also emphasised that the results of the SSNIP test had been corroborated by empirical data regarding market movements in the past using price correlation analysis.

[88] See Bishop & Walker, *The Economics of EC Competition Law* (2nd edn, Sweet & Maxwell, 2002), Ch.11; ABA Section of Antitrust Law, *Market Power Handbook* (ABA Publishing, 2005), pp.62 to 64 (noting, at p.64, criticisms of the use of price correlations in defining markets); Ivaldi *et al*, "The Economics of Unilateral Effects", 2003, Interim Report for DG Competition (available via *http://europa.eu.int/comm/competition/mergers/review/the_economics_of_unilateral_effects_en.pdf*), p.97; Motta, *Competition Policy Theory and Practice* (2004, Cambridge UP), pp.107 to 110; OFT Research Paper "Quantitative Techniques in Competition Analysis", LECG, Ch.5 (note that the views in the paper do not necessarily represent those of the OFT); Kaserman & Zeisel, "Market Definition: Implementing the Department of Justice Merger Guidelines" [1996] *The Antitrust Bulletin* 665, at pp.672 to 674; and the International Competition Network, "ICN Investigative Techniques Handbook for Merger Review", June 2005 (*www.internationalcompetitionnetwork.org/handbook_5-5.pdf*), pp.59 and 60.

[89] If the products formed part of the same market and their relative prices diverged, customers would be likely to switch to the relatively lower priced option which, in turn, would be likely to contribute to the elimination of the divergence in prices.

[90] Price correlations are not used in isolation to define antitrust markets. In all cases, the results of price correlation studies form part of an overall analysis of competitive conditions.

[91] See the Commission's XXIVth Annual Report on Competition Policy, 1994 para.291. Examples include: Case IV/M.190 *Nestlé / Perrier* [1992] O.J. L356/1, para.16; Case IV/M.430 *Procter & Gamble / VP Schickedanz (II)* [1994] O.J. L354/32; Case IV/M.619 *Gencor / Lonrho* [1997] O.J. L11/30 (upheld on appeal in Case T-102/96 *Gencor v Commission* [1999] ECR II-753); Case IV/M.938 *Guinness / Grand Metropolitan* [1998] O.J. L288/24; Case IV/M.997 *Swedish Match / KAV*; Case IV/M.1383 *Exxon / Mobil* [2004] O.J. L103/1, para.552; Case COMP/M.1628 *TotalFina / Elf* [2001] O.J. L143/1, paras 256 to 258; Case COMP/M.1939 *Rexam / American National Can*, paras 11 to 13; Case COMP/M.2187 *CVC / Lenzing* [2004] O.J. L82/20, paras 21, 73, 74, 77 and 108 to 115; Case COMP/M.2420 *Mitsui / CVRD / Caemi*

(a) Any apparent correlation needs to be tested carefully for *false correlation*. This may arise if the prices of the two products move together because both have a common input (e.g. oil), both are seasonal, or the price series move along a trend, as in the case of high inflation, leading the prices of both products to increase over the period.[92] The latter effect can be eliminated by running the analysis using the changes between the data for each period (rather than using the actual data). In *Rexam / American National Can*[93] the Commission examined whether aluminium and steel beverage cans formed part of the same product market. To test for false correlation arising from changes in metal costs, the Commission identified the correlation between the prices of steel beverage cans and aluminium beverage cans and, separately, the prices of aluminium beverage cans and aluminium sheet and the prices of steel beverage cans and steel sheet. The study showed that there was a high correlation in the prices of aluminium beverage cans and steel beverage cans and in the prices of steel beverage cans and steel sheet but a low correlation in the prices of aluminium beverage cans and aluminium sheet. The implication of the analysis was that changes in the price of aluminium sheet could not be passed through to aluminium beverage can customers, which indicated that the price of aluminium beverage cans was constrained by the presence of another product competing in the market (namely steel beverage cans).[94] Spurious correlations caused by common costs can be eliminated by more sophisticated econometric analysis using co-integration and unit root tests.[95] The Commission applied both techniques in *CVC / Lenzing*.[96]

(b) If a change in the price of one product is likely to affect demand for the second only after a time-delay (e.g. if prices are negotiated at discrete intervals), then the data will need to be time-lagged. A failure to time-lag properly may result in a false negative, i.e. a failure to identify a positive correlation between the two data sets which would have been revealed by proper lagging. In *CVC / Lenzing*[97] the Commission stated that, "In order to confirm the appropriate periodicity of the data, the Commission has tested the correlation analysis through different lags".[98]

[2004] O.J. L92/50, paras 118 and 119; Case COMP/M.2498 *UPM-Kymmene / Haindl* [2002] O.J. L233/38, para.17; and Case COMP/M.2972 *DSM / Roche Vitamins* [2004] O.J. L82/73, para.43.

[92] In Case COMP/M.2187 *CVC / Lenzing* [2004] O.J. L82/20 the Commission noted, at paras 109 and 110, that certain correlation coefficients were inflated due to common costs and, to an extent, a common trend.

[93] Case COMP/M.1939.

[94] Paras 11 to 13.

[95] See Kennedy, *A Guide to Econometrics* (4th edn, Blackwell, 1998), pp.268, 269 and 283 to 286.

[96] Case COMP/M.2187, n.83.

[97] Case COMP/M.2187.

[98] Para.115.

(c) There is no statistical significance to any particular level of correlation and it is therefore difficult to determine the level at which a correlation is sufficiently high to be regarded as significant evidence regarding the question of market definition.[99] It is therefore common to *benchmark*, a process which involves calculating the correlation between two products which are indisputably in the same market and comparing the results of the benchmarking exercise with the correlation in the actual test. For example, if the issue is whether fizzy orange drinks form part of the same product market as fizzy colas, a price correlation study comparing the two products might be benchmarked against a price correlation study comparing the prices of two cola brands which are indisputably part of the same product market. If the actual correlation is higher than the benchmarked correlation, this suggests that the result is significant. However, notwithstanding the absence of statistical significance to any particular level of correlation, in *CVC / Lenzing*[1] the Commission referred to the fact that it had previously regarded correlations of above 0.80 as high and correlations below 0.65 as low,[2] as a basis for rejecting an argument that a correlation of 0.44 was sufficient to support a finding that the two products formed part of the same market.[3]

The Commission clarified its approach to price correlation analysis in *CVC / Lenzing*[4] stating: **3–015**

"the Commission's product market definition in the present case does not rely primarily on an analysis of price correlations and cross-price elasticities ... [The] results of the analysis have merely been found to support the findings of separate product markets which are themselves based on considerations of demand-side and supply-side substitutability and therefore on a lack of sufficient numbers of examples of switching ... [The] Commission has never exclusively relied on an analysis of price correlations and cross-price elasticities but has used these analyses as a supplementary element to support the results of its market investigation. The Commission has always clearly indicated that a high degree of correlation between two price series is neither a necessary nor a sufficient condition for two products to belong to the same market. The Commission rather regards correlations as an indicator of the degree of competition in given markets. Moreover ... a correlation analysis has to be examined cautiously. In particular ... there can be inappropriately high correlations (false positive correlation or spurious correlation) if the

---

[99] See Carlton & Perloff, *Modern Industrial Organization* (4th edn, Addison-Wesley, 2005), p.647.
[1] Case COMP/M.2187.
[2] In Case COMP/M.1939 *Rexam / American National Can*, para.12.
[3] Paras 74 and 110 and n.59 and 84.
[4] Case COMP/M.2187.

prices of two products are subject to a common input (meaning common costs) and/or a common trend. Similarly, correlations can be inappropriately low, for instance due to significant lags in response. Drawbacks of this kind can, however, be avoided by using a co-integration test or a unit-root test".[5]

3-016 **(iii) Stationarity tests** *Stationarity tests* determine whether the *ratio of the prices* of two goods remains reasonably stable or tends to change over time. If the ratio is stable (i.e. it tends to return towards a constant to an extent which is statistically significant), this suggests that the two products form part of the same market. In such cases, the time series is said to be *stationary* as the effects of shocks are temporary. By contrast, if the ratio is not stable (i.e. it follows a "random walk"), then the effects of shocks are permanent and the time series is *non-stationary*.[6] The advantages of stationarity tests over price correlation analysis are that they are not vulnerable to false positives arising from changes in the prices of common inputs (e.g. oil) because they measure the *ratio* of prices rather than the absolute levels of price, and they are less vulnerable to issues of time-lags (where low correlations arise because, whilst prices do track one another closely, they do so after a time-lag which has not been incorporated into the statistical analysis).[7] Further, the results of stationarity tests can be tested for statistical significance (in contrast to price correlation studies where benchmarking is used). Finally, stationarity tests can be used to analyse more than two products. In the case of three products, this is achieved by testing whether the two relative prices are simultaneously and jointly stationary.[8]

3-017 **(iv) Own-price and cross-price elasticities** As noted above, the profitability of a 5 to 10 per cent increase in price by a hypothetical monopolist will depend on whether the increased revenues on sales which are retained by the hypothetical monopolist, but are made at the higher price, together with any cost savings arising from the reduction in output associated with falling demand are greater than the revenues lost as a result of falling demand. It is therefore important to determine the proportion of sales which would be lost by the hypothetical monopolist if it were to increase prices by 5 to 10 per

---

[5] Paras 79 and 113.
[6] Evidence from stationarity tests was relied on by the UK Competition Commission in *Nutreco Holding NV / Hydro Seafood GSP Ltd*, December 2000, Cm 5004, in analysing whether Scottish salmon and Norwegian salmon formed part of the same product market. The analysis showed that the price of Scottish salmon relative to Norwegian salmon was stationary (i.e. tended to return to a constant level after any shocks) and the Competition Commission relied on this in finding that the product market included both Scottish and Norwegian salmon.
[7] See Wills, "Market Definition: How Stationarity Tests Can Improve Accuracy" [2002] E.C.L.R. 4 at p.5.
[8] See Wills, "Market Definition: How Stationarity Tests Can Improve Accuracy" [2002] E.C.L.R. 4.

cent, holding constant the terms of sale of all other products.[9] This involves estimating or calculating the *own-price elasticity of demand*[10] for the product or products comprising the candidate market.[11] In *Gencor / Lonrho*[12] the Commission found that the own-price elasticity of platinum was numerically smaller than 1 and concluded that "an inelastic price elasticity of demand indicates that platinum is a separate relevant product market".[13]

[9] See the Notice on Market Definition, para.39; Areeda, Hovenkamp & Solow, *Antitrust Law* (2nd edn, Aspen Law & Business, 2000) Vol.IIA, para.507; Werden, "Demand Elasticities in Antitrust Analysis" (1998) 66 *Antitrust Law Journal* 363; Rubinfeld, "Market Definition with Differentiated Products: The Post / Nabisco Cereal Merger" (2000) 68 *Antitrust Law Journal* 163; Kaserman & Zeisel, "Market Definition: Implementing the Department of Justice Merger Guidelines" [1996] *The Antitrust Bulletin* 665, at 674 to 678; and the International Competition Network, "ICN Investigative Techniques Handbook for Merger Review", June 2005 (*www.internationalcompetitionnetwork.org/handbook_5-5.pdf*), pp.57 and 58. Own-price and cross-price elasticities may be estimated using econometric techniques; see para.19–006. For the use of such techniques in defining markets, see e.g. Case COMP/M.2187 *CVC / Lenzing* [2004] O.J. L82/20, n.83. Econometric analysis is not a substitute for a proper analysis of the structure of the market. Baker, "Econometric analysis in *FTC v. STAPLES*", speech of July 17, 1997 (revised March 31, 1998) (available at *www.ftc.gov/speeches/other/stspch.htm*), comments, "econometric analyses are more persuasive when key modeling choices are consistent with economic theory, informed by quantitative or qualitative information about the market, and tested against plausible alternatives".

[10] "Elasticity" is a measure of the proportionate effect of a change in price on demand for a product. For example, an "own-price elasticity of demand" of -2 means that if the market price increased by 1%, market demand for that product would fall by 2%. Formally, the elasticity of demand is calculated by dividing the change in demand by the change in price; dividing the original price by the original demand; and multiplying the two numbers. When the numerical value of the elasticity exceeds 1, it is said to be elastic (in which case the quantity demanded changes proportionately more than the change in price) and when it is below 1 it is inelastic (in which case the quantity demanded changes proportionately less than the change in price). When a demand curve is linear, the elasticity ranges from zero to infinity along its length. The proportion of sales which is lost by a supplier for a given increase in price depends on the company's residual elasticity of demand. This is a measure of the proportionate effect of a change in a company's selling price for a product on the demand for supplies of that product which are not met by other suppliers in the market. In applying the SSNIP test, the supplier is assumed to have a monopoly of supplies of a particular product with the consequence that, within the monopoly area, the supplier's residual elasticity of demand is identical to the market elasticity of demand.

[11] The estimation of own-price elasticity of demand may be particularly important in cases involving differentiated consumer products (where consumers make purchase decisions on the basis of taste) as opposed to producer goods where the purchasing decision is based on objective cost issues (which are well-suited to critical loss analysis, which is described in para.3–031 below).

[12] Case IV/M.619 [1997] O.J. L11/30 (upheld on appeal in Case T-102/96 Gencor v Commission [1999] E.C.R. II-753).

[13] Para.57. The International Competition Network, "ICN Investigative Techniques Handbook for Merger Review", June 2005 (*www.internationalcompetitionnetwork.org/handbook_5-5.pdf*) states, at p.58: "a finding that the own-price elasticity of the narrowly defined market (good A) ... is less than one (in absolute value) is a sure indication that no additional goods need to be included in the market definition. An own-price elasticity greater than one (in absolute value) will require a consideration of costs, which can be carried out via a critical loss analysis". See also Case IV/M.934 *Guinness / Grand Metropolitan* (the Commission identified "insecure elements" in the econometric evidence of own-price elasticities and discounted their significance; para.126) and Case IV/M.1313 *Danish Crown / Vestjyske Slagterier* [2000] O.J. L20/1 (low own-price elasticities for beef, pork and poultry meat indicated that each constituted a separate relevant product market; para.29). Own price elasticities tend to be higher when the product has few unique features, is a significant item of expenditure for customers or is used as an input for a good which is sold in a competitive downstream market; conversely,

The Commission commonly refers in its decisions on market definition to cross-price elasticities of demand, which measure the change in demand for a product, A, in response to a change in the price of a second product, B.[14]

Notwithstanding this practice, cross-price elasticities are not *directly* relevant to market definition as they describe the relationship between two products, whereas the SSNIP test seeks to determine customers' reactions to changes in price in the candidate market without determining the product or products to which customers switch or, indeed, whether they choose not to purchase at all. However, cross-price elasticities are *indirectly* relevant to market definition using the SSNIP test because a product's own-price elasticity is, in general terms, a weighted sum of the cross-price elasticities of demand for other products with respect to the first product's price.[15] In *Gencor / Lonrho*[16] the Commission stated that a "price elasticity numerically smaller than 1 implies that the cross-price substitution elasticities to other metals are even smaller, i.e. the competitive impact of other metals is not very high".[17] Further, in markets involving differentiated products, cross-

---

own price elasticities tend to be lower when comparisons between rival products are difficult, buyers' purchasing decisions are subsidised by the state or insurance companies, switching costs are high or the product is used with a second product which buyers have already acquired: see Besanko, Dranove & Shanley, *Economics of Strategy* (2nd edn, John Wiley & Sons Inc, 2000), p.27.

[14] Cross-price elasticities provide information about the extent to which products are substitutes on the demand-side. More formally, the cross-price elasticity of demand between products A and B measures the responsiveness of demand for product A to changes in the price of product B. For any pair of products there will be two cross-price elasticities of demand, which may differ radically. In general terms, a cross-price elasticity of less than +1 strongly suggests that product A is not an effective substitute for product B: Case COMP/M.2187 *CVC / Lenzing* [2004] O.J. L82/20, para.76. However, it does not follow that a cross-price elasticity in excess of +1 means that the products are in the same market: see Areeda, Hovenkamp & Solow, *Antitrust Law* (2nd edn, Aspen Law & Business, 2000), Vol.IIA, para.534c, and Kaserman & Zeisel, "Market Definition: Implementing the Department of Justice Merger Guidelines" [1996] *The Antitrust Bulletin* 665, at p.667.

[15] See Werden, "Demand Elasticities in Antitrust Analysis" (1998) 66 *Antitrust Law Journal* 363, at p.398; Areeda, Hovenkamp & Solow, *Antitrust Law*, (2nd edn, Aspen Law & Business, 2000), Vol.IIA, para.507a; and the International Competition Network, "ICN Investigative Techniques Handbook for Merger Review", June 2005 (*www.internationalcompetition network.org/handbook_5-5.pdf*), p.58.

[16] Case IV/M.619 [1997] O.J. L11/30 (upheld on appeal in Case T-102/96 *Gencor v Commission* [1999] E.C.R. II-753).

[17] Para.57. The implication of the passage quoted is that own-price elasticities of demand are relevant to the exercise of market definition only insofar as they can be used to infer cross-price elasticities of demand. This is incorrect for the reasons given in the text. For a fierce criticism of the use of cross-price elasticities of demand (as opposed to own-price elasticities of demand) see Werden, "Demand Elasticities in Antitrust Analysis" (1998) 66 *Antitrust Law Journal* 363, at pp.401 and 402 (cross-price elasticities provide no direct information about market power; they focus on the question of whether two products form part of the same market rather than the more relevant question of whether the group of products in question comprises a separate market; and they fail adequately to take account of the fact that a hypothetical monopolist may be constrained by a number of substitute products none of which taken individually has a high cross-price elasticity of demand); Kaserman & Zeisel, "Market Definition: Implementing the Department of Justice Merger Guidelines" [1996] *The Antitrust Bulletin* 665, at pp.671 and 672 (cross-price elasticities are difficult to calculate and are directly influenced by the prices charged by the existing firms); and Scheffman, "Statistical Measures of Market Power: Uses and Abuses" (1992) 60 *Antitrust Law Journal* 901, at p.903.

price elasticities may be instructive as they assist in identifying chains of substitution between different products (whereas own-price elasticities do not provide any information about the closeness of competitors).[18]

(v) Price discrimination If sellers can distinguish different customers or **3–018** customer groups in their pricing decisions *and* prevent resale between those groups, then the groups may comprise different markets, as a hypothetical monopolist supplying one of the groups may be able profitably to increase price by 5 to 10 per cent.[19] For example, in *Hutchison / RCPM / ECT*[20] the Commission found that stevedoring services for hinterland and transhipment traffic were "essentially the same", but that there were separate product markets because prices for handling containers for transhipment were lower than those for handling hinterland containers.[21]

The Commission clarified its general approach to the use of cross-price elasticities in Case COMP/M.2187 *CVC / Lenzing* [2004] O.J. L82/20 in the passage quoted in para.3–015 above. See also Case IV/M.430 *Procter & Gamble / VP Schickedanz (II)* [1994] O.J. L354/32 (the Commission identified a number of weaknesses with a univariate cross-price elasticity analysis (analysing the effect of changes in the price of tampons on sales of sanitary towels) carried out by the parties, stating that a multivariate approach (i.e. an approach seeking to model the effect of as many variables as possible) was better as it could take account of seasonal variations, promotions, etc.; see paras 55 to 61) and Case IV/M.754 *Anglo American Corporation / Lonrho* [1998] O.J. L149/21, paras 71, 72, 83 and 84.

[18] See Torre, "The Use of Own Price Elasticity of Demand in Competition Law" [2005] E.C.L.R. 468, at p.469.

[19] See Case C-12/03P *Commission v Tetra Laval BV*, not yet reported, judgment of February 15, 2005, para.103 (contrast the Opinion of Advocate General Tizzano of May 25, 2004, paras 141 to 143, advocating an approach to market definition in cases involving price discrimination which does not involve an application of the SSNIP test) and the Notice on Market Definition, para.43. The existence of different markets may be evidenced by price or margin variations which are inconsistent with competitive arbitrage. See also the Commission guidelines on market analysis and the assessment of significant market power under the Community regulatory framework for electronic communications networks and services [2002] O.J. C165/3, para.46. In markets where price discrimination is possible and there are switching costs, it may be necessary to identify separate markets for old and new customers: see OFT Economic Discussion Paper 5, "Switching Costs", NERA, April 2003 (note that the views in the paper do not necessarily reflect those of the OFT), para.7.7. For discussion of possible complexities when defining markets on the basis of price discrimination (in particular if the groupings used for the discrimination overlap and if a product which is priced differently between groups competes with a product for which price discrimination is not attempted), see "Market Definition in the Media Sector—Economic Issues", Report by Europe Economics for the European Commission, DG Competition, November 2002 (available via *http://europa.eu.int/comm/competition/publications/studies/european_economics.pdf*), paras 2.2.15, 2.2.16, 2.2.33 and 2.2.34.

[20] Case COMP/JV.55 [2003] O.J. L223/1, paras 31, 33 and 35. There is a greater choice of ports for transhipment.

[21] In Case IV/M.1293 *BP / Amoco*, the Commission identified separate markets for the supply of additives to, respectively, the additives and industrial sectors, emphasising that the customer groups were clearly identifiable (permitting suppliers to charge different prices) and additives customers regarded selling PIB to industrials customers as outside the scope of their business (ruling out arbitrage): see para.25. See also Case COMP/M.2416 *Tetra Laval / Sidel* (decision of January 13, 2003), paras 26 to 32. See further the discussion of trade relationships in s.(h) below.

3–019 **(vi) Differences in levels of absolute price** Differences in *levels of absolute price*[22] are an indicator[23] that products are in separate markets[24] since, generally, products which compete in the same market have similar prices.[25] However, products with different prices *will* be in the same market if the relative price of product A significantly constrains the price of product B.[26] The constraint could be significant even though prices are different, in particular if the relative *price/value* of the two products is comparable, e.g. if product A has a higher operating cost than product B.[27]

---

[22] Wholesale prices are generally compared net of VAT and discounts ("net net"): see, e.g. Case IV/M.190 Nestlé / Perrier [1992] O.J. L356/1, para.16.

[23] See the discussion in "Market Definition in the Media Sector—Economic Issues", Report by Europe Economics for the European Commission, DG Competition, November 2002 (available via *http://europa.eu.int/comm/competition/publications/studies/european_economics. pdf*), para.2.2.40.

[24] See Case COMP/M.2420 *Mitsui / CVRD / Caemi* [2004] O.J. L92/50, para.117. In some cases the Commission has defined product markets by reference to price brackets, e.g. Case IV/ M.57 *Digital / Kienzle* (mini-computers); Case IV/M.1157 *Skanska / Scancem* [1999] O.J. L183/1 (division of construction projects into small and large projects using SEK 40 million as a threshold; paras 53 and 54); Case COMP/M.2223 *Getronics / Hagemeyer / JV*; Case COMP/ M.2503 *HBG / Ballast Nedam / Baggeren JV* (distinguishing large international dredging projects and small national projects using a project value of Euros 5 million; para.10); Case COMP/M.2609 *HP / Compaq* (server market divided into low-end servers below US$100,000, mid-range servers priced between US$100,000 and US$1 million and high-end servers priced above US$1 million; the Commission noted, at paras 20 and 21, that: "Although this market definition cannot fully capture all competitive interactions in the technologically highly dynamic market, alternative market definitions capture the market dynamics to a much lesser degree ... The price bands serve as proxies which reflect the different functionalities offered by entry-level servers as opposed to medium level and large servers"); and Case COMP/M.3216 *Oracle / PeopleSoft* [2005] O.J. L218/6 (licence values used as one of a complementary set of proxies for defining the market; paras 116 to 124). In Case IV/M.1578 *Sanitec / Sphinx* [2000] O.J. L294/1, the Commission did not define markets by price point as all the major competitors offered products at different price levels (see para.28).

[25] See the discussion of goods which are interchangeable but have substantial price differences in Areeda, Hovenkamp & Solow, *Antitrust Law* (2nd edn, Aspen Law & Business, 2000), Vol.IIA, para.562b.

[26] In Case COMP/M.2706 *Carnival Corporation / P&O Princess* [2003] O.J. L248/1 the Commission stated, at n.40: "It is of course possible that two products with very different prices are in competition with each other". Further, the Commission guidelines on market analysis and the assessment of significant market power under the Community regulatory framework for electronic communications networks and services [2002] O.J. C165/3, state, at para.46: "in order for products to be viewed as demand-side substitutes it is not necessary that they are offered at the same price. A low quality product or service sold at a low price could well be an effective substitute to a higher quality product sold at higher prices. What matters in this case is the likely responses of consumers following a relative price increase". See also the UK OFT's Guidelines on Market Definition, December 2004 (*www.oft.gov.uk/NR/rdonlyres/ 972AF80C-2D74-4A63-84B3-27552727B89A/0/OFT403.pdf*), para.3.5 and Baker & Wu, "Applying the Market Definition Guidelines of the European Commission" [1998] E.C.L.R. 273, pp.278 and 279.

[27] Porter, *Competitive Advantage* (1998 edn, The Free Press), pp.280 to 285, identifies the following sources of adjustment to identify the price/value ratio of a product: usage rate, delivered and installed costs, financing cost, relative variability of price or availability, direct costs of use, indirect costs of use, buyer performance, number of functions, cost and performance of complementary products, uncertainty and perception of value.

The approach of the Commission is as follows.[28]   **3–020**

(a) In *Airtours / First Choice*[29] the Commission relied on the fact that the
     average brochure prices of long-haul and short-haul package holi-
     days differed by over 100 per cent in finding that such holidays
     formed separate markets. It also noted that prices overlapped to a
     limited extent for certain destinations at certain times of the year but
     concluded that "it is not to be expected that this very limited overlap
     would suffice to constrain prices throughout the short-haul market,
     since the long-haul holidays concerned would not be regarded as
     effective substitutes—either on price or other grounds—by more
     than a very small proportion of customers".[30] On appeal to the Court
     of First Instance,[31] Airtours argued that average prices were irrele-
     vant to the analysis and the Commission ought to have focused on
     "customers at the margin".[32] The Commission defended its decision
     on the grounds that when "the differences [in average price] are so
     significant, it is unlikely that a sufficient range of genuinely com-
     parable long-haul package holidays is available at prices which are
     sufficiently similar to constrain prices of short-haul packages, since
     the long-haul packages concerned are regarded as genuine substitutes
     by only a very small proportion of customers".[33] The Court found
     that the Commission's assessment that only a small proportion of
     customers regarded the two types of holidays as substitutes was not
     manifestly incorrect.[34] The implication of the Court's judgment is
     that the focus of attention in defining the market ought to be on the
     marginal and not the average customer, but that differences in
     average price may be relevant as one part of an analysis of whether
     the scope for substitution at the margin is sufficiently substantial that
     an attempt to raise prices of one of the products would be unprofi-
     table because of switching to the second.[35]

(b) In *UPM-Kymmene / Haindl*[36] the Commission identified a 20 per cent
     difference in price between two grades of paper but nevertheless
     found that they formed part of a single product market because there
     was a broad spectrum of partly overlapping qualities and prices

---

[28] See also Case IV/M.582 *Orkla / Volvo* [1996] O.J. L66/17 (differences in the prices of beer,
wine and carbonated soft drinks); Case IV/M.906 *Mannesmann / Vallourec* (differences in the
prices of seamless and welded tubes); and Case COMP/M.3722 *Nutreco / Stolt-Nielsen /
Marine Harvest JV* (absolute differences in price between wild and farmed salmon; para.12).
[29] Case IV/M.1524 [2000] O.J. L93/1.
[30] Para.24.
[31] Case T-342/99 *Airtours plc v Commission* [2002] E.C.R. II-2585.
[32] Para.31.
[33] Para.31.
[34] Para.41.
[35] In other words, to determine whether there are sufficient numbers of marginal customers to
protect the infra-marginal customers from price increases.
[36] Case COMP/M.2498 [2002] O.J. L233/38.

within the two grades and there were examples of customers switching between them.[37]

(c) In *SmithKline Beecham / Block Drug*[38] the Commission found that prices of toothpaste varied, but there was low price-sensitivity amongst customers as they tended to make purchases on the basis of suitability of particular types of toothpaste for their specific or overall needs, and therefore concluded that there was an overall market for toothpaste.

(d) By contrast, in *Nestlé / Perrier*[39] the Commission examined the ex-works price lists and retail prices of bottled water and soft drinks and found that a price difference of 200 to 300 per cent was an indicator that the two products were in separate markets: "A price-ratio of between two and three is of such a magnitude that it cannot be reasonably expected that an appreciable, non-transitory increase in the price of source waters, would lead to a significant shift of demand from source waters to soft drinks for reasons of price only".

(e) Similarly, in *Saint-Gobain / Wacker-Chemie / NOM*[40] the Commission stated that: "Persistent price differences between [products] for the same applications serve as a strong indication that, from a customer's point of view, these [products] have different performance characteristics and do not serve as direct and effective substitutes".

(f) In *Metso / Svedala*[41] the Commission emphasised the importance of absolute price differences, stating that "the price differences between the two types of equipment clearly show that customers do not view them as economically substitutable".

3–021 **(vii) Comparisons of prices between regions** If a supplier is able to charge higher prices for a product in areas where there it has a higher share of supply, this suggests that the relevant market is limited to that product (because if other products formed part of the same market they would be expected to prevent the merged group from profitably raising its prices in areas where it has a higher share of supply).[42]

---

[37] Para.21.
[38] Case COMP/M.2192, paras 9 and 11. The Commission also took account of supply-side substitutability at para.10.
[39] Case IV/M.190 [1992] O.J. L356/1, para.13(1).
[40] Case IV/M.774 [1997] O.J. L247/1, para.83.
[41] Case COMP/M.2033 [2004] O.J. L88/1, para.205.
[42] See DG Competition Discussion Paper on the Application of Article 82 of the Treaty to Exclusionary Abuses December 2005, para.19.

(d) Shock analysis or event studies and other evidence of historic switching

The SSNIP test involves an analysis of a *hypothetical* question, namely **3–022** whether a hypothetical monopolist could profitably raise price by 5 to 10 per cent. In some cases, a great deal of probative evidence directly relevant to this hypothetical question may be available by observing *natural experiments* arising, for example, if: the price of one product in the candidate market changes but that of a second does not (e.g. as a result of exchange rate changes)[43]; industry capacity alters; new products are launched; or the costs facing one or some but not all suppliers change.[44] This is known as *shock analysis* or an *event study*.[45]

(a) In *Procter & Gamble / VP Schickedanz (II)*[46] the Commission examined the impact of the launch of a new brand of sanitary towels on prices of sanitary towels and tampons and on the share of female hygiene supplies accounted for by sanitary towels. The data showed that, following the launch of the new brand, prices of tampons rose but prices of sanitary towels remained constant and the new brand won share from other sanitary towel brands but did not reduce the share of female hygiene supplies represented by tampons. This evidence supported the conclusion that there were separate product markets for sanitary towels and tampons.

(b) In *Coca-Cola Enterprises / Amalgamated Beverages Great Britain*[47] the Commission considered whether colas formed a product market separate from other carbonated soft drinks. In the United Kingdom, a number of new cola brands had been introduced and the Commission was able to establish that the new brands had won share predominantly at the expense of other colas and that The Coca-Cola Company had, in response, increased its expenditure in advertising colas but not its other carbonated soft drinks. The Commission found that colas constituted a separate market.

(c) In *Alcoa / Reynolds*[48] the Commission analysed the impact on the market of an explosion at a smelter-grade alumina plant, noting that the plant's capacity represented 7 per cent of Western third party

---

[43] In dealing with imported goods, it is possible to map the ratio of the prices of imported goods to the prices of domestically produced goods; the shock alters the ratio from its base level of 100 and the issue is whether it returns reasonably rapidly to parity or remains permanently out of step.

[44] See the Notice on Market Definition, para.38.

[45] The Commission has described evidence from shock analysis as "fundamental" and "determinant": see the Notice on Market Definition, para.38. See also Areeda, Hovenkamp & Solow, *Antitrust Law* (2nd edn, Aspen Law & Business, 2000), Vol.IIA, para.538.

[46] Case IV/M.430 [1994] O.J. L354/32, paras 62 to 71.

[47] Case IV/M.794, paras 64 to 79.

[48] Case COMP/M.1693 [2002] O.J. L58/25, para.24.

sales but its removal from the market led to an immediate increase in price of 34 per cent and that the price continued to rise thereafter, indicating that there was very limited scope for switching on the demand side.

(d) In *Rexam / American National Can*[49] the Commission found, through a price correlation analysis, that prices of aluminium beverage cans were sensitive to changes in the price of steel beverage cans but did not change substantially in response to changes in the price of aluminium sheet, demonstrating that aluminium beverage cans faced close competition from steel beverage cans.[50]

(e) In *Carnival Corporation / P&O Princess*[51] one issue was whether a narrow market definition should be adopted; the notifying party noted that capacity in that candidate market had expanded significantly without depressing yields and argued that the ability of the candidate market to absorb such capacity demonstrated that the relevant product market was wider; the Commission rejected the argument on the facts because there were other possible explanations for the failure of the expansion in capacity to depress yields.

3–023 At a qualitative level, falling short of shock analysis or event studies, it is important, in seeking to define the market, to identify whether there is any evidence of actual switching by customers between products or suppliers or of credible threats to switch made during commercial negotiations.[52]

(a) The existence of such switching or threats does not of itself show that the two products are sufficiently close substitutes that a small increase in the price of one would be unprofitable because customers would switch to the rival[53]; but a claim that such switching would occur is more credible if at least some customers have changed between the products.

(b) Sellers which bid against one another for a particular contract are generally in the same antitrust market. In *Oracle / PeopleSoft*[54] the Commission examined bidding behaviour to identify the suppliers

---

[49] Case COMP/M.1939.
[50] If aluminium beverage cans had not faced close competition, it is likely that suppliers would have altered their prices in response to changes in the price of aluminium sheet.
[51] Case COMP/M.2706 [2003] O.J. L248/1, paras 61 to 63, 65 and 66.
[52] The Commission is cautious about the weight to be attributed to surveys purporting to identify customers' willingness to switch: see Case IV/M.430 *Procter & Gamble / VP Schickedanz (II)* [1994] O.J. L354/32, para.49 and Case IV/M.794 *Coca-Cola Enterprises / Amalgamated Beverages Great Britain*, paras 85 to 87.
[53] For example, in Case COMP/M.2187 *CVC / Lenzing* [2004] O.J. L82/20 the Commission found at paras 62, 63 and 67 that the evidence of switching by customers provided by the parties was not sufficient to justify finding a wider product market because the responses to the Commission's questionnaires showed that the examples were not representative of the overall customer response.
[54] Case COMP/M.3216 [2005] O.J. L218/6, paras 98, 129, 136 and 144.

which customers invited to tender for particular projects and undertook an econometric analysis to investigate whether there was a difference in bidding behaviour depending on the identity of the competitors in the final bidding round (as this might have revealed that certain competitors were regarded as peripheral and not sufficiently close competitive constraints to be included in the relevant product market).

(c) If customers purchase two different goods, it is important to analyse whether the goods are complements or substitutes.[55] Goods generally form part of the same product market only if they are close substitutes; complementary products generally do not form part of the same market.[56] For example, in *Kesko / Tuko*[57] the Commission found that the fact that some customers used both classic wholesalers and cash-and-carry outlets did not indicate that there was a single product market, because the evidence suggested that the services were *complementary*, with dual-users tending to obtain their main supplies from classic wholesalers and using cash-and-carry outlets for "top up" volumes.[58]

(d) Evidence of *long-term* switching is not sufficient to justify a conclusion that two products form part of the same antitrust market[59] as the SSNIP test requires that demand for product A is highly sensitive to changes in the price of product B over a short period, if A and B are to be treated as forming part of the same antitrust market.

(e) Switching costs

The existence of *financial costs* associated with switching[60] between two **3–024** products[61] which are substantial relative to the price of the product (and, more particularly, relative to the 5 to 10 per cent increase in price contemplated by the SSNIP test) is an indicator that the two products are in separate markets.[62] For example, rival computer games cartridges may not

---

[55] See also Case IV/M.1221 *Rewe / Meinl* [1999] O.J. L274/1, para.14.
[56] For an exception to the general rule, see the discussion of cluster goods in s.3.5(h) below.
[57] Case IV/M.784 [1997] O.J. L110/53, para.30.
[58] See also Case COMP/M.3396 *Group 4 Falck / Securicor*, para.25 and Case COMP/M.3732 *Procter & Gamble / Gillette* (dental floss was identified as a separate market from toothbrushes as flossing is complementary to brushing; para.50).
[59] See, e.g. Case COMP/M.2187 *CVC / Lenzing* [2004] O.J. L82/20, para.45.
[60] See the Notice on Market Definition, para.42. Switching costs were taken into account, e.g. in Case COMP/M.1628 *TotalFina / Elf* [2001] O.J. L143/1, para.248. For examples of switching costs in network industries, see Shy, *The Economics of Network Industries* (Cambridge UP, 2001), pp.4 and 5.
[61] In addition to switching to other products, customers may defeat an attempted price increase by choosing not to purchase, lowering the usage of the product, using second-hand or recycled goods or commencing self-supply.
[62] See Porter, *Competitive Advantage* (1998 edn, The Free Press), p.278.

form part of the same product market if they operate on different and relatively expensive computer games consoles.[63]

(a) It is important, in analysing switching costs, to identify the *customer* who would switch. In *Enso / Stora*[64] the issue was whether liquid packaging board formed part of a market including other packaging materials. The Commission emphasised that the customers of the liquid packaging board suppliers were converters (who used the board to produce cartons and had high switching costs) and not final customers such as dairies.[65]

(b) The fact that switching costs are high is not decisive regarding the question of market definition: if a sufficient proportion of customers makes a decision each year whether to switch between systems, this may result in the price of a product used on one system effectively constraining the price charged for a product used on a rival system.[66]

(f) Functional interchangeability

3–025 For two products to form part of the same product market it is necessary, but not sufficient, that they are *functionally interchangeable*.[67] A finding of functional interchangeability is not sufficient because customers may, nevertheless, not regard the products as sufficiently good substitutes to defeat an attempt by a hypothetical monopolist supplying one of the products to impose a SSNIP (e.g. because of switching costs or brand loyalty).[68] For example, in *Procter & Gamble / VP Schickedanz (II)*[69] the Commission

---

[63] Porter, *Competitive Advantage* (1998 edn, The Free Press), pp.286 to 288, identifies the following categories of switching costs: identifying and quantifying sources, costs of redesign or reformulation, retraining or relearning costs, changing role of the user, risk of failure, new ancillary products and switching costs versus switching back costs. When customers purchase very substantial quantities of consumables for a product, a proper assessment of the financial costs of switching requires an analysis of the total relative costs of the consumables over the lifetime of the new product, since a customer would spread the cost of switching across its total expenditure on consumables. There may be *temporal* costs associated with switching, e.g. if alterations to filling equipment could be implemented only by taking the filling line out of operation for a time.

[64] Case IV/M.1225 [1999] O.J. L254/9, para.33.

[65] See also Case IV/M.1109 *Owens-Illinois / BTR Packaging* (switching by fillers from glass packaging to other types of packaging "usually requires significant changes and investment in filling and packaging lines"; para.15).

[66] OFT Research Paper, "Market Definition in UK Competition Policy", NERA, 1992, p.54 (note that the views in the paper do not necessarily represent those of the OFT). It is important to examine whether customers take account of the prices of consumables or after-market goods in deciding on original purchases.

[67] See "Market Definition in the Media Sector—Economic Issues", Report by Europe Economics for the European Commission, DG Competition, November 2002 (available via *http://europa.eu.int/comm/competition/publications/studies/european_economics.pdf*), para.3.4.10.

[68] The Notice on Market Definition, para.36.

[69] Case IV/M.430 [1994] O.J. L354/32, para.42.

identified separate markets for tampons and sanitary towels, even though both "broadly perform the same function", because customers did not regard them as substitutable once an established preference or pattern of usage had been established.[70] Similarly, in *Bertelsmann / Springer / JV*[71] catalogues and advertisements could be printed using either offset or roto-gravure machines (i.e. they were functionally interchangeable), but the evidence was that larger orders almost invariably used rotogravure reflecting its greater cost effectiveness. The Commission therefore identified a separate market for rotogravure printing of high volume printing orders.

(g) Product characteristics

In assessing the extent of substitutability from customers' perspectives, the **3–026** Commission examines the product's *characteristics*. Commonly, substantial differences in product characteristics will contribute to a finding that the products are in separate antitrust markets.[72] But this is by no means inevitable[73]: for example, on certain routes, customers may be able to defeat attempts to increase air fares by switching to train travel and vice versa.[74] In such cases, the products are regarded by customers as close and effective alternatives notwithstanding the differences in characteristics. The real issue in each case is whether the relative price of product A constrains the price of product B and therefore whether any differences in characteristics imply that there is little scope for demand- or supply-side substitution between the different products, thereby suggesting that they are in separate markets.[75]

However, the Court of First Instance in *General Electric Company v Commission*[76] placed relatively greater weight on the significance of product

---

[70] See also Case IV/M.190 *Nestlé / Perrier* [1992] O.J. L356/1 (several products serving the broad function of "thirst quenching" were found not to be in the same antitrust market; para.9) and Case IV/M.774 *Saint-Gobain / Wacker-Chemie / NOM* [1997] O.J. L247/1, para.83. Clearly, the more broadly a product's functionality is defined, the greater the number of potential substitutes.

[71] Case COMP/M.3178, paras 40, 41 and 44.

[72] e.g. in Case IV/M.1439 *Telia / Telenor* [2001] O.J. L40/1, the fact that mobile telephones did not provide the same functionality as fixed lines, in particular in providing internet access, was relied on in finding that mobile telephone services formed a separate market; (para.94). Similarly, in Case COMP/M.3333 *Sony / BMG* [2005] O.J. L62/30 (appeal pending in Case T-464/04 *Impala v Commission*), paras 22 and 23, differences in characteristics between online music and physically recorded music meant that online music formed part of a separate market.

[73] The Notice on Market Definition, para.36.

[74] See also the Commission guidelines on market analysis and the assessment of significant market power under the Community regulatory framework for electronic communications networks and services, [2002] O.J. C165/3, para.45.

[75] OFT Economic Discussion Paper No. 2, "The Role of Market Definition in Monopoly and Dominance Inquiries", NERA, 2001 (note that the views in the paper do not necessarily represent those of the OFT). For examples of markets defined with specific reference to product characteristics see: Case IV/M.53 *Aerospatiale / Alenia / de Havilland* [1991] O.J. L334/42 (aircraft by numbers of seats; para.11) and Case COMP/M.1980 *Volvo / Renault VI* (trucks by weight category; paras 10 and 16).

[76] Case T-210/01, not yet reported, judgment of December 14, 2005, para.524.

characteristics in product market definition, stating: "inasmuch as point 36 of the notice on market definition states that '[f]unctional interchangeability or similarity in characteristics may not, in themselves, provide sufficient criteria, because the responsiveness of customers to the relative price changes may be determined by other considerations as well...', it follows from that citation, a contrario, that in certain cases, indeed as a general rule (save where particular circumstances indicate otherwise, such as those mentioned in the example relating to spare parts given later in point 36), products which are functionally interchangeable and which have similar characteristics are substitutes".

Evidence of product characteristics may be available:

(a) by inspection[77];

(b) through *surveys*; for example, if customers are asked to identify the characteristics they consider when choosing a product and the characteristics identified by customers as important in making a purchasing decision are common to two products, this suggests that both form part of the same product market[78]; and

(c) by examining *marketing and promotional activity*; for example, in *Nestlé / Perrier*[79] the Commission found that suppliers of bottled waters sought to portray their product as natural, pure and healthy with the result that consumers did not recognise soft drinks, which were marketed differently, as substitutes.

The Commission may also take into account the product's *occasions for use*.[80]

(h) Trade relationships

3–027 If conditions of competition differ as between different trading relationships[81] (e.g. by categories of buyer[82] or distribution channels),[83] the

---

[77] See, e.g. Case COMP/M.2187 *CVC / Lenzing* [2004] O.J. L82/20, paras 33 to 35.

[78] See the Notice on Market Definition, para.41. In Case COMP/M.2706 *Carnival Corporation / P&O Princess* [2003] O.J. L248/1 the Commission considered, at para.33, survey evidence in which travel agents described their customers' top reasons for booking a cruise.

[79] Case IV/M.190 [1992] O.J. L356/1, para.13(2).

[80] e.g. gin and whisky are both spirits but gin is commonly drunk before a meal and whisky afterwards; compare Case IV/M.938 *Guinness / Grand Metropolitan* [1998] O.J. L288/24.

[81] Market definition may differ substantially at different stages in a distribution chain, e.g. a German television company procuring content to display on afternoon television may regard highlights of Argentinian league football and a Canadian soap opera as ready substitutes but advertisers and viewers will not.

[82] In Case IV/M.469 *MSG Media Service* the Commission stated, at para.33, that: "The decisive factor is whether trade relationships exist in respect of a good or a service". In that case separate markets were identified for pay-TV and free TV on the grounds that in the case of pay-TV the broadcaster has a contractual relationship with the viewer, whereas in the case of free TV the relationship is solely between the broadcaster and any advertisers.

[83] The New Zealand Merger Guidelines, 2004 (*www.comcom.govt.nz/Publications/ContentFiles/Documents/MergersandAcquisitionsGuidelines.PDF*), state, at para.3.4: "In assessing the appropriate functional levels of markets, the Commission considers factors such as: [1] the

Commission may identify different product markets, even if the products themselves are fully inter-changeable or even identical.[84] The issue is whether the differences in conditions of competition are such that a hypothetical monopolist serving one of the groups of customers could profitably impose a SSNIP.

Trade relationships have frequently been relied on[85] by the Commission in identifying separate antitrust markets.[86] For example in relation to tissue-paper products, separate markets have been identified for domestic consumption and away from home ("AFH") use "as they are sold via different distribution channels and to different customers and are therefore not substitutable".[87] Similarly, in *Air Liquide / BOC*[88] the Commission distinguished separate markets for the different means of distributing industrial gases (tonnage supplies, bulk supplies and supply in cylinders) on the grounds that price, cost of transport and rent and possible safety and other charges differed depending on the choice of delivery mechanism. The Commission has also identified separate markets for: sales of food to the retail sector (in which the customers are mainly supermarkets and food retail operators) and the food service sector[89]; the on-trade and off-trade

---

observed structures of seller-buyer relationships; [2] the possible presence of economies of scope between adjacent functional levels, such that vertical integration might be efficient; [3] evidence of substitution between vertical layers, for example, a retailer moving into wholesaling in response to an increase in wholesale prices; [4] the scope for non-integrated businesses to compete; [5] likely future developments. Generally, the Commission identifies separate relevant markets at each functional level affected by an acquisition, and assess the impact of the acquisition on each".

[84] See the Commission's XXIst Annual Report on Competition Policy, 1991, p.347. Porter, *Competitive Advantage* (1998 edn, The Free Press), identifies the following channel segments, at p.245: direct versus distributors, direct mail versus retail (or wholesale), distributors versus brokers, types of distributors or retailers and exclusive versus non-exclusive outlets. Compare the Australian Merger Guidelines, June 1999 (*www.accc.gov.au/content/item.phtml?itemId = 719436&nodeId = file43a1f42c7eb63&fn = Merger%20Guidelines.pdf*), paras 5.66 and 5.67 and the New Zealand Merger Guidelines, 2004 (*www.comcom.govt.nz/Publications/ ContentFiles/Documents/MergersandAcquisitionsGuidelines.PDF*), para.3.4.

[85] It is not always clear from the Commission's decisions whether, having identified different trading relationships, the Commission has taken the necessary additional step of applying the SSNIP test. See in particular Case T-5/02 *Tetra Laval BV v Commission* [2002] E.C.R. II-4381, paras 258 to 269 (finding that the Commission's decision did not provide sufficient evidence to justify the definition of a product market by end use) (upheld on appeal in Case C-12/03P *Commission v Tetra Laval BV*, not yet reported, judgment of February 15, 2005, paras 102 to 105).

[86] Areeda, Hovenkamp & Solow, *Antitrust Law* (2nd edn, Aspen Law & Business, 2000), Vol.IIA, para.566, comment, adopting a different approach from the Commission: "A mode of distribution might occasionally give a firm or group of firms a cost advantage over others who cannot readily copy this mode. In that case, placing the former firms in a distinct relevant market makes sense. In the great majority of cases, however, distribution modes confer no cost advantage that cannot readily be duplicated by others".

[87] Case COMP/M.2097 *SCA / Metsä Tissue*, para.17. See also Case IV/M.623 *Kimberly-Clark / Scott* [1996] O.J. L183/1, para.33.

[88] Case COMP/M.1630 [2004] O.J. L92/1, paras 12 to 27. See also Case COMP/M.3314 *Air Liquide / Messer Targets*, paras 17 to 25.

[89] See, e.g. Case COMP/M.1990 *Unilever / Bestfoods*, paras 9 to 11 and Case COMP/M.3658 *Orkla / Chips*, para.9. See also Case IV/M.1313 *Danish Crown / Vestjyske Slagterier* [2000] O.J. L20/1 (separate retail and catering markets; para.38).

supply of alcohol[90]; sales of paper to merchants and directly to end customers[91]; the distribution of electronic components as opposed to direct supply by manufacturers[92]; sales of sugar to industrial customers and retailers[93]; fuel retailing on motorways[94]; mail-order and other forms of retailing[95]; digital interactive television services and traditional high street retailing of goods and services[96]; the provision of audit and accounting services to quoted or large companies as opposed to non-quoted or smaller companies[97]; the supply of electricity to larger and smaller customers[98]; sales of airline seats to tour operators (for incorporation into package tours) and individuals[99]; sales of viscose staple fibres for tampons as opposed to commodity viscose staple fibres[1]; the supply of outbound cross-border *business* mail as opposed to outbound cross-border personal mail[2]; the provision of food service to the commercial and social segments[3]; outgoing and incoming distance payment systems[4]; the distribution of office supplies to *larger customers*[5]; and sales of daily consumer goods through retail and cash-and-carry outlets.[6]

3–028   By contrast,[7] in *Gerling / NCM*[8] the Commission rejected a possible distinction between supplies of *del credere* insurance to small and medium sized enterprises on the one hand and large multinational companies on the other, on the basis that the main features of the policies for both groups were the

[90] Case C-234/89 *Stergios Delimitis v Henninger Bräu* [1991] E.C.R. I-977; Case IV/M.582 *Orkla / Volvo* [1996] O.J. L66/17; and Case COMP/M.2044 *Interbrew / Bass*, para.24.
[91] Case IV/M.884 *KPN BT / Bunzl / Wilhelm Seiler*; Case COMP/M.1728 *CVC / Torraspapel*; Case COMP/M.2020 *Metsä-Serla / Modo*, para.17; and Case COMP/M.2245 *Metsä-Serla / Zanders*, para.13.
[92] Case COMP/M.3820 *Avnet / Memec*, paras 12 to 17.
[93] Case IV/M.62 *Eridania / ISI*.
[94] Case IV/M.1383 *Exxon / Mobil* [2004] O.J. L103/1, para.437.
[95] Case IV/M.80 *Redoute / Empire Stores*.
[96] Case COMP/JV.37 *BSkyB / KirchPayTV*, para.37.
[97] Case IV/M.1016 *Price Waterhouse / Coopers & Lybrand* [1999] O.J. L50/27, para.32.
[98] Case IV/M.1557 *EDF / Louis Dreyfus* and Case COMP/JV.36 *TXU Europe / EDF-London Investments*, para.27.
[99] Case IV/M.1354 *Sair Group / LTU*.
[1] Case COMP/M.2187 *CVC / Lenzing* [2004] O.J. L82/20. At para.96 the Commission noted that the former was sold directly to manufacturers of end products whereas the latter was sold to intermediate producers.
[2] Case COMP/M.1915 *The Post Office / TPG / SPPL* [2004] O.J. L82/1. The Commission found, at paras 35 and 36, that business customers could negotiate special agreements for the provision of rebates or additional services which were not available to private customers.
[3] Case COMP/M.1990 *Unilever / Bestfoods*, para.42. The commercial segment comprises restaurants, snack-bars, hotels, fast-food chains, the leisure sector, etc. and the social segment canteens, schools, hospitals, etc.
[4] Case COMP/M.2567 *Nordbanken / Postgirot*, para.46.
[5] Case COMP/M.2286 *Buhrmann / Samas Office Supplies*, para.18. See also Case IV/M.27 *Promodes / DIRSA* (retail markets distinguished by size of shop).
[6] Case IV/M.784 *Kesko / Tuko* [1997] O.J. L110/53, para.16.
[7] See also Case IV/M.1517 *Rhodia / Donau Chemie / Albright & Wilson* (Commission divided amphoterics surfactants into markets by chemical type and not by sectors served; para.40) and Case COMP/M.1882 *Pirelli / BICC* [2003] O.J. L70/35 (single market for general wiring, not divided into sales to wholesalers, distributors, installers or OEMs; para.12).
[8] Case COMP/M.2602, para.15.

same.[9] In *Agfa-Gevaert / Du Pont*[10] the Commission found that sales to both dealers and end-users formed part of a single market, on the grounds that sales were on similar terms and there was little competition between producers and dealers, in part because of the existence of exclusive territories. In *Masterfoods / Royal Canin*[11] the Commission found that sales of pet food through grocery outlets, such as supermarkets, and specialist outlets, such as pet shops, formed part of a single market at a retail level because shoppers had significant opportunities to purchase in either channel and suppliers' sales and marketing strategies aimed to attract customers regardless of channel. Finally, in *TotalFina / Elf*[12] the Commission found that sales of fuels to retailers formed part of the same market as sales to major end-users, on the grounds that any price differential between the two categories of customer would be eroded by arbitrage.

Further, market definition may be affected by the conditions of competition in markets *downstream* of the market in question. *Derived demand* arises when a company's requirements for a product are determined by the requirements of its customers, e.g. demand by retailers for pet food is derived from the requirements of shoppers. The Commission has considered issues of derived demand in the following cases.[13]

(a) In *General Electric / Honeywell*[14] the Commission noted that: "the demand for engines derives from the demand for jet aircraft. In this

---

[9] Further, from the supply-side, the necessary know-how and resources for writing both types of business did not differ significantly.

[10] Case IV/M.986 [1998] O.J. L211/22, para.12. Similarly, in Case COMP/M.1601 *Allied Signal / Honeywell* [2001] O.J. L152/1, the Commission noted the distinction between buyer-furnished equipment ("BFE", which is fitted to aircraft by airlines) and supplier-furnished equipment ("SFE", which is fitted to aircraft by airframe suppliers). However, it did not distinguish separate markets since different customers might characterise products differently and the characterisation of products might vary over time (paras 17 to 22). However, in Case COMP/ M.2220 *GE / Honeywell* [2004] O.J. L48/1 (prohibition decision upheld on appeal in Case T-210/01 *General Electric Company v Commission*, not yet reported, judgment of December 14, 2005) the Commission identified separate markets for BFE and SFE because of the existence of different purchasers (paras 236 to 239).

[11] Case COMP/M.2544, paras 18 to 23.

[12] Case COMP/M.1628 [2001] O.J. L143/1, para.28.

[13] In Case IV/M.938 *Guinness / Grand Metropolitan* [1998] O.J. L288/24, the Commission, in considering markets for the manufacture and wholesale distribution of spirits, noted, at para.13, that: "The strongest determinant of product market boundaries in spirits appears to be that of consumer demands and preferences, since they will drive the stocking and marketing policies of retailers, wholesalers and ultimately manufacturers". In Case IV/M.1109 *Owens-Illinois / BTR Packaging*, in considering the market for the supply of glass packaging from producers to fillers, the Commission took account of customer preferences and image in the downstream market for drinks and in particular the fact that if a filler were to switch packaging materials it might need to relaunch the product, with associated market research and advertising costs (paras 16 to 18). In Case COMP/M.2544 *Masterfoods / Royal Canin* the Commission took account, at para.14, of the competitive situation in retailing pet foods in considering whether the merged group, which produced pet foods, would be able to exercise market power in its relations with retailers.

[14] Case COMP/M.2220, [2004] O.J. L48/1, para.9 (prohibition decision upheld on appeal in Case T-210/01 *General Electric Company v Commission*, not yet reported, judgment of December 14, 2005).

sense, an engine is a complementary product to the aircraft, the sale of the one being of no value without the sale of the other. As a consequence, in defining the relevant jet engines product markets one needs to take into account also competition between the end-use applications—that is, between the types of aircraft that final buyers consider suitable".

(b) In *De Beers / LMVH*[15] the Commission noted that: "As the demand for diamonds at the polishing level is derived from consumers' demand for jewellery it is also necessary to examine the competitive conditions at the retail level before reaching conclusions about the relevant market upstream".

(i) Evidence of sellers' business decisions

3–029 Evidence that *sellers* of product A base their business decisions on the prospect of customers switching to product B in response to small changes in the relative price of product A, corroborates a conclusion that products A and B are in the same product market, although it is clearly not decisive, as the focus in each case must be on the willingness of customers to switch to alternative products. This evidence might arise, for example, from pre-merger marketing studies or evidence that suppliers of product A monitor the prices of product B and set prices primarily by reference to the price of product B.[16] In *Aerospatiale / Alenia / de Havilland*[17] the Commission concluded that a manufacturer of commuter aircraft was unlikely to develop a new type of aircraft to compete against an existing product range, with the consequence that proposed product market definitions, under which two types of de Havilland aircraft would have been classified as competing against one another, were not considered realistic.[18] More generally, in *ENI / EDP / GDP*[19] the Commission stated that it was relevant, in defining a market, to take into account the perceptions of parties and their competitors regarding the grouping of the market in commercial terms, especially if there was a consensus.

(j) Sellers' relative costs

3–030 In *T-Online International / TUI / C&N Touristic / JV*[20] the Commission *provisionally*[21] concluded that on-line travel agencies formed a separate

---

[15] Case COMP/M.2333, para.17.
[16] See the Notice on Market Definition, para.41.
[17] Case IV/M.53 [1991] O.J. L334/42.
[18] Para.13.
[19] Case COMP/M.3440 [2005] O.J. L302/69, para.267 (prohibition upheld on appeal in Case T-87/05 *EDP v Commission*, not yet reported, judgment of September 21, 2005).
[20] Case COMP/M.2149.
[21] The parties withdrew their notification whilst the case was subject to a Phase II investigation but the Commission reported its provisional conclusions in *Competition Policy Newsletter*, June 2002, p.57.

market from "bricks and mortar" travel agencies on the grounds that "the variable costs of an online agency operating at efficient scale are likely to be significantly lower than in the traditional sector. This systematic cost advantage would, in a competitive market, be passed on to the consumer. Conversely, a hypothetical monopolist could capture the cost advantage. Such an online monopolist would be constrained in its pricing power by the traditional travel agency sector only at supra-competitive prices".

(k) Critical loss analysis

Critical loss analysis[22] can be used to provide analytical rigour in carrying **3–031** out the hypothetical exercise required by the SSNIP test.[23] It involves two stages.[24]

---

[22] For an example of a critical loss calculation, see Case COMP/M.2187 *CVC / Lenzing* [2004] O.J. L82/20, n.56. See generally Epstein & Rubinfeld, "Technical Report—Effects of Mergers Involving Differentiated Products", 2004, Report for DG Competition (available via *http://europa.eu.int/comm/competition/mergers/others/effects_mergers_involving_differentiated_products.pdf*), Ch.II; the UK OFT's Guidelines on Market Definition, December 2004 (*www.oft.gov.uk/NR/rdonlyres/972AF80C-2D74-4A63-84B3-27552727B89A/0/OFT403.pdf*), para.3.7; Harris & Simons, "Focusing Market Definition: How Much Substitution is Necessary?" (1989) 12 *Research in Law and Economics* 207; Werden, "Demand Elasticities in Antitrust Analysis" (1998) 66 *The Antitrust Law Journal* 363, at pp.391 to 394; Langenfield & Li, "Critical Loss Analysis in Evaluating Mergers" [2001] *The Antitrust Bulletin* 299; Danger & Frech, "Critical Thinking About 'Critical Loss' in Antitrust" [2001] *The Antitrust Bulletin* 339; Werden & Froeb, "Calibrated Economic Models Add Focus, Accuracy and Persuasiveness to Merger Analysis", published as Ch.4 of *The Pros and Cons of Merger Control* by the Swedish Competition Authority in 2002 (and available at *www.kkv.se/bestall/pdf/skrift_proscons.pdf*), pp.64 to 69 (emphasising, at p.66, the assumption in critical loss analysis that the hypothetical monopolist has constant marginal costs); Katz & Shapiro, "Critical Loss: Let's Tell the Whole Story", *Antitrust*, Spring 2003, p.49; O'Brien & Wickelgren, "A Critical Analysis of Critical Loss Analysis" (2003) 71 *Antitrust Law Journal* 161; Scheffman & Simons, "The State of Critical Loss Analysis: Let's Make Sure We Understand the Whole Story", *The Antitrust Source*, November 2003 (available at *www.abanet.org/antitrust/source/11-03/scheffman.pdf*); Harris & Veljanovski, "Critical Loss Analysis: Its Growing Use in Competition Law" [2003] E.C.L.R. 213; Harris, "Recent Observations About Critical Loss Analysis" (*www.usdoj.gov/atr/public/workshops/docs/202599.htm#N_4_*); the International Competition Network, "ICN Investigative Techniques Handbook for Merger Review", June 2005 (*www.international competitionnetwork.org/handbook_5-5.pdf*), pp.58 and 59; and Kokkoris, "Critical Loss Analysis: Critically Ill" [2005] E.C.L.R. 518. Scheffman, Coate & Silva, "20 Years of Merger Guidelines Enforcement at the FTC: An Economic Perspective" (available at *www.usdoj.gov/atr/hmerger/11255.htm*), comment that the operation of the SSNIP test in the US has significantly improved by the use of critical loss analysis. Werden, "The 1982 Merger Guidelines and the Ascent of the Hypothetical Monopolist Paradigm", June 4, 2002 (available at *www.usdoj.gov/atr/hmerger/11256.htm*), notes that critical loss analysis is now widely used in the US in the investigation and litigation phases of mergers.

[23] It is also possible to calculate critical *elasticities* (i.e. the maximum own-price elasticity of demand which would still result in a price increase being profitable): see, e.g. Langenfield & Li, "Critical Loss Analysis in Evaluating Mergers" [2001] *The Antitrust Bulletin* 299 at 309 to 312, and Baumann & Godek, "Could and Would Understood: Critical Elasticities and the Merger Guidelines" [1995] *The Antitrust Bulletin* 885.

[24] Mathematically, the critical loss percentage is $(Y \times 100\%) / (Y + CM)$, where Y is the hypothesised price increase and CM is the contribution margin of the producers in the group (i.e. the difference between the original price and average variable cost stated as a percentage of the original price); see Harris, "Recent Observations About Critical Loss Analysis" (*www.usdoj.gov/atr/public/workshops/docs/202599.htm#N_4_*).

(a) The first is to identify the *critical loss*, i.e. the percentage loss of sales which would render a price increase of 5 to 10 per cent unprofitable[25] for the producer. This involves estimating the hypothetical monopolist's per unit *margins* over the relevant output range prior to the price increase and calculating the percentage of sales which could be lost before the price increase would be unprofitable.[26] The profitability of the increase in price will depend on whether the increased revenues on sales which are retained by the hypothetical monopolist but are made at the higher price, together with any cost savings arising from the reduction in output associated with falling demand, are greater than the revenues lost as a result of falling demand. The critical loss will be lower, the higher the hypothetical monopolist's margins because the monopolist will be more reluctant to give up high-margin sales than low-margin sales.[27] Conversely, if markets are competitive and prices are close to marginal cost then margins will be lower and the critical loss may be very large.[28]

(b) The second stage is to determine whether an increase in price of 5 to 10 per cent in the hypothesised market would lead to a loss of sales in excess of the critical loss.[29] If not, then the hypothesised market is a

---

[25] The question of whether the increase in price would be profitable is assessed relative to the pre-SSNIP level of profitability. Compare the discussion about the relative merits of profit-maximising critical loss and break-even critical loss in Langenfield & Li, "Critical Loss Analysis in Evaluating Mergers" [2001] *The Antitrust Bulletin* 299, at p.303, n.6 and Danger & Frech, "Critical Thinking About 'Critical Loss' in Antitrust" [2001] The Antitrust Bulletin 339, at p.341, n.6.

[26] See Langenfield & Li, "Critical Loss Analysis in Evaluating Mergers" [2001] *The Antitrust Bulletin* 299, at p.302.

[27] The critical loss is around 5% if margins are high (80 to 100%), around 7.5% on margins of 50 to 60%, and more than 15% if margins are low (less than 25%); see Werden & Froeb, "Calibrated Economic Models Add Focus, Accuracy and Persuasiveness to Merger Analysis", published as Ch.4 of *The Pros and Cons of Merger Control* by the Swedish Competition Authority in 2002 (and available at *www.kkv.se/bestall/pdf/skrift_proscons.pdf*), p.65.

[28] Commensurately, the critical loss will be lower, the lower the hypothetical monopolist's marginal costs because the loss of sales caused by the increase in price will lead to lower cost savings. For example, in an industry with high fixed costs and low marginal costs, a loss of, say, 6% of sales may render a 5% increase in price unprofitable. By contrast, if marginal costs are high, a price increase of 5% may be unprofitable only if 10% of sales are lost. In the former case, other things being equal, the supplier would be more cautious about raising its price. Danger & Frech, "Critical Thinking About 'Critical Loss' in Antitrust" [2001] *The Antitrust Bulletin* 339, at pp.346 and 354, point out that the use of critical loss analysis in highly competitive sectors may therefore result in narrow market definitions and in relatively uncompetitive markets may lead to unduly wide market definitions; they also note that arguments that the antitrust market is wide may be inconsistent with claims that the merging parties face intense competition. See also the UK OFT's Guidelines on Market Definition, December 2004 (*www.oft.gov.uk/NR/rdonlyres/972AF80C-2D74-4A63-84B3-27552727B89A/0/OFT403.pdf*), para.3.7, emphasising that high mark ups may be evidence that the customer base is not particularly price sensitive.

[29] For discussion of four categories of evidence relevant to this inquiry, see Harkrider, "Operationalizing the Hypothetical Monopolist Test" (available via *www.usdoj.gov/atr/public/workshops/docs/202598.pdf*).

separate antitrust market; if so, then the hypothesised market is too narrow, and the exercise must be repeated with a wider definition.[30]

(l) Demand characteristics

If the merging parties and their competitors hold materially different shares of supply for different types of products, this suggests that the different products comprise separate markets.[31] Further, if purchasing decisions for two products are taken by different individuals or departments, this suggests that the two products form parts of separate markets,[32] because the scope for, and likelihood of, substitution is much reduced.

3–032

(m) Previous cartel activity

If suppliers of a group of products are, or have previously, engaged in unlawful cartel activity, this suggests strongly that the relevant product market is no wider than the group of products in question (because otherwise the cartel would have been defeated by customers switching to suppliers of products not within the cartel).[33]

3–033

(n) Evidence from customers and competitors

The Commission will solicit the views of customers, competitors[34] and other third parties.[35] The views of customers are important[36] because the process

3–034

---

[30] In addition to evidence of actual or potential switching by customers, it is instructive at the second stage to examine the merging parties' margins because higher margins are associated with lower own-price elasticities of demand and such elasticities suggest that a given price increase will result in a smaller actual loss of sales: see Langenfield & Li, "Critical Loss Analysis in Evaluating Mergers" [2001] *The Antitrust Bulletin* 299, at pp.308 and 309. Further, it may be possible to identify "contestable" geographic areas or customer groups and focus attention on determining the proportion of customers within the "contestable" groups which would switch in the event of a 5 to 10% price increase.

[31] See Case COMP/M.3083 *GE / Instrumentarium* [2004] O.J. L109/1, para.29.

[32] See, e.g. Case COMP/M.3083 *GE / Instrumentarium* [2004] O.J. L109/1, para.23.

[33] See Harkrider, "Operationalizing the Hypothetical Monopolist Test" (available via *www.us doj.gov/atr/public/workshops/docs/202598.pdf*), pp.6 and 7.

[34] See para.2–047 above.

[35] The process is described in the Notice on Market Definition at paras 33 and 34 as follows: "When a precise market definition is deemed necessary, the Commission will often contact the main customers and the main companies in the industry to enquire into their views about the boundaries of product and geographic markets and to obtain the necessary factual evidence to reach a conclusion. The Commission might also contact the relevant professional associations, and companies active in upstream markets, so as to be able to define, in so far as necessary, separate product and geographic markets, for different levels of production or distribution of the products/services in question. It might also request additional information to the undertakings involved. Where appropriate, the Commission will address written requests for information to the market players mentioned above. These requests will usually include questions relating to the perceptions of companies about reactions to hypothetical price increases and their views of the boundaries of the relevant market. They will also ask for provision of the factual information the Commission deems necessary to reach a conclusion on the extent of the relevant market". See also See Baker & Wu, "Applying the Market Definition Guidelines of the European Commission" [1998] E.C.L.R. 273 at 279 and 280.

[36] For discussion of the use of Commission questionnaires when applying the SSNIP test, see para.3–013 above. Also, for discussion of the significance of responses by customers to a merger, see para.19–010 below

of defining markets on the demand-side depends to a substantial extent on buyers' propensity to substitute.[37]

(o) International categorisations

3–035 The Commission may take account of product categorisations by international organisations in defining antitrust markets. For example, in pharmaceutical cases, the ATC classification is used.[38] In *Mercedes-Benz / Kässbohrer*[39] the Commission relied in part on the product classification in an EEC Regulation to define the product market.

3.4 PRODUCT MARKET DEFINITION: SUPPLY-SIDE SUBSTITUTION

(a) The SSNIP test

3–036 Supply-side substitution[40] arises when suppliers (which might be described as "near competitors"[41] or "uncommitted entrants")[42] are able to switch production to the relevant products and market them *in the short term* without incurring significant additional costs or risks[43] in response to a

---

[37] Porter, *Competitive Advantage* (1998 edn, The Free Press), pp.288 and 289, identifies the following factors influencing buyers' propensity to substitute: resources, risk profile, technological orientation, previous substitutions, intensity of rivalry and generic strategy.

[38] See, e.g. Case COMP/M.1846 *Glaxo Wellcome / SmithKline Beecham*, para.12. See also Case IV/M.950 *Hoffmann-La Roche / Boehringer Mannheim* [1998] O.J. L234/14 (following the European Diagnostics Manufacturers Association classification; para.32) and Case COMP/M.1681 *Akzo Nobel / Hoechst Roussel Vet* (adopting the segmentation adopted by the Animal Health Industry and consultants (e.g. Wood Mackenzie); para.13).

[39] Case IV/M.477 [1995] O.J. L211/1, para.15.

[40] See, e.g. Case COMP/M.3197 *Candover / Cinven / BertelsmannSpringer* (finding that a demand-side analysis would result in large numbers of small markets for the analysis of a merger affecting academic and professional publishing; however, the market was expanded significantly as a result of a supply-side analysis; paras 13 to 29); Case COMP/M.3431 *Sonoco / Ahlstrom* [2005] O.J. L159/13, para.47; Case COMP/M.3687 *Johnson & Johnson / Guidant* (supply-side substitution amongst different types of endovascular accessories; para.49); and Case COMP/M.3805 *Crompton / Great Lakes* (chemicals; paras 25 to 28).

[41] Following the New Zealand Merger Guidelines, 2004 (*www.comcom.govt.nz/Publications/ ContentFiles/Documents/MergersandAcquisitionsGuidelines.PDF*), para.3.2.

[42] Following the US Horizontal Merger Guidelines, 1992 (amended in 1997) (*www.usdoj.gov/atr/ public/guidelines/hmg.htm*), para.1.0.

[43] The UK OFT's Guidelines on Market Definition, December 2004 (*www.oft.gov.uk/NR/ rdonlyres/972AF80C-2D74-4A63-84B3-27552727B89A/0/OFT403.pdf*), para.3.18, adds a further criterion, namely that the possibility of supply-side substitution "already" has an impact on the market by constraining suppliers of the products in question.

SSNIP.[44] The then Commissioner for Competition Policy, Mario Monti, said that: "Supply substitutability is only taken into account when its effects are equivalent to those of demand substitution in terms of effectiveness and immediacy. That requires that the alternative producer has already all of the important assets (fixed inputs and distribution networks) required".[45] The period in which switching has to occur in order to qualify for the purposes of supply-side substitution is the "short term",[46] namely "such a period that does not entail a significant adjustment of existing tangible and intangible assets".[47] This period is generally taken as

---

[44] The Notice on Market Definition states at paras 20 to 22: "Supply-side substitutability may also be taken into account when defining markets in those situations in which its effects are equivalent to those of demand substitution in terms of effectiveness and immediacy. This means that suppliers are able to switch production to the relevant products and market them in the short term without incurring significant additional costs or risks in response to small and permanent changes in relative prices. When those conditions are met, the additional production that is put on the market will have a disciplinary effect on the competitive behaviour of the companies involved. Such an impact in terms of effectiveness and immediacy is equivalent to the demand substitution effect. These situations typically arise when companies market a wide range of qualities or grades of one product; even if, for a given final customer or group of customers, the different qualities are not substitutable, the different qualities will be grouped into one product market, provided that most of the suppliers are able to offer and sell the various qualities immediately and without the significant increases in costs described above. In such cases, the relevant product market will encompass all products that are substitutable in demand and supply, and the current sales of those products will be aggregated so as to give the total value or volume of the market. A practical example of the approach to supply-side substitutability when defining product markets is to be found in the case of paper. Paper is usually supplied in a range of different qualities, from standard writing paper to high quality papers to be used, for instance, to publish art books. From a demand point of view, different qualities of paper cannot be used for any given use, i.e. an art book or a high quality publication cannot be based on lower quality papers. However, paper plants are prepared to manufacture the different qualities, and production can be adjusted with negligible costs and in a short time-frame. In the absence of particular difficulties in distribution, paper manufacturers are able therefore, to compete for orders of the various qualities, in particular if orders are placed with sufficient lead time to allow for modification of production plans. Under such circumstances, the Commission would not define a separate market for each quality of paper and its respective use. The various qualities of paper are included in the relevant market, and their sales added up to estimate total market value and volume". For a case involving paper, see Case IV/M.166 *Torras / Sarrio*.

[45] Mario Monti, then the Commissioner for Competition Policy, "Market Definition as a cornerstone of EU Competition Policy", speech of October 5, 2001 (*www.europa.eu.int/comm/ competition/speeches/index_2001.html*). On the other hand, there are suggestions that supply-side substitution should be the main determinant of market definition in mergers affecting "cultural goods"; see Boeshertz, Kleiner, Nouet, Petit, Von Koppenfels & Rabassa, "Lagardère / Natexis / VUP: big deal in a small world", *Competition Policy Newsletter*, Spring 2004, p.8, at p.10.

[46] The Notice on Market Definition, para.20. See also the Commission guidelines on market analysis and the assessment of significant market power under the Community regulatory framework for electronic communications networks and services [2002] O.J. C165/3, n.37 (time frame to be fixed on a case-by-case basis).

[47] The Notice on Market Definition, n.4.

one year,[48] although the precise period selected depends on the way in which the market operates.[49]

(b) Evidence

3–037　As in the case of the demand-side analysis, a range of categories of evidence may be relevant in determining the product market from the supply side.

(a)　Supply-side substitution can be *ruled out* if switching by suppliers is not *technically feasible*. Technical feasibility may be demonstrated, for example, by the fact that certain producers currently use the same machinery to manufacture both products.[50] However, if two or more products are produced simultaneously using a *joint production process*, this suggests that supply-side substitution is *not* feasible (since the producer would otherwise switch to producing the more profitable product rather than producing two or more products).[51]

(b)　The SSNIP test requires that switching should occur in response to a small but significant change in price. This means that it is important

---

[48] In Case COMP/M.2420 *Mitsui / CVRD / Caemi* [2004] O.J. L92/50 the Commission agreed with a statement by the economics consultancy, NERA, in the context of the SSNIP test, that "in general the competitive assessment of mergers considers time periods of at least one year and in some instances up to two years" (see n.29 to para.111). However, the Notice on Horizontal Mergers provides, at para.74, that for new entry to be timely, it must normally occur within two years (see Ch.16); this implies that the period for analysis of supply-side substitutability (which involves closer and more direct constraints than new entry) should be shorter (as explained in the UK OFT's Guidelines on Market Definition, December 2004 (*www.oft.gov.uk/NR/rdonlyres/972AF80C-2D74-4A63-84B3-27552727B89A/0/OFT403.pdf*), para.3.15). In Case IV/M.053 *Aerospatiale-Alenia / de Havilland* [1991] O.J. L334/42, the Commission disregarded possible supply-side substitution which would take over three to four years (see para.14). In Case IV/M.149 *Lucas / Eaton*, the Commission used one year as the dividing line. See also the European Commission, "Glossary of Terms Used in EU Competition Policy", July 2002, (note that this document is not binding on the Commission) (*www.europa.eu.int/comm/competition/publications/glossary_en.pdf*), definition of "potential competitor" and Guidelines on Vertical Restraints [2000] O.J. C291/1, para.26.

[49] If switching will take longer, the relevant product market is defined more narrowly but the potential for new entry in the long run is taken into account in analysing market operation. Delays in switching might arise, e.g. from product testing or existing long-term supply contracts constraining capacity.

[50] In Case COMP/M.2498 *UPM-Kymmene / Haindl* [2002] O.J. L233/38, the Commission found that most suppliers of paper were able to handle different grades of paper without costly adjustments to their machines (para.13 and n.8). See also Case COMP/M.2926 *EQT / H&R / Dragoco*, paras 19, 28 and 30.

[51] See Case IV/M.619 *Gencor / Lonrho* [1997] O.J. L11/30 (upheld on appeal in Case T-102/96 *Gencor v Commission* [1999] E.C.R. II-753); Case IV/M.774 *Saint-Gobain / Wacker-Chemie / NOM* [1997] O.J. L247/1, paras 29 and 41; and Case COMP/M.1671 *Dow Chemical / Union Carbide* [2001] O.J. L245/1 (several products were produced in a fixed ratio in the production process; the Commission confirmed, at para.155, that this did not mean that the products were supply-side substitutes; quite the contrary: if the products are produced in fixed ratios then there is no scope to switch from production of one to another). For a discussion of the general rule and possible exceptions, see Areeda, Hovenkamp & Solow, *Antitrust Law* (2nd edn, Aspen Law & Business, 2000) Vol.IIA, para.534b.

to identify in particular[52]: the costs incurred by suppliers in adjusting[53] to the supply of the new product (such as altering the production process,[54] establishing a distribution network,[55] marketing[56] or obtaining a release from existing contractual commitments)[57]; the costs which would be incurred by suppliers in switching back from production of the candidate product[58]; the costs incurred by *buyers* in switching from products supplied by incumbents to those of the near competitor (since a new entrant would generally need to absorb these costs in order to win business from the incumbents); whether the near competitor can make supplies out of spare capacity (i.e. without sacrificing existing margins) and, if not, the relative margins earned on current production as compared with supply as a new entrant in the candidate market (assuming that entry occurs at a price 5 to 10 per cent above the pre-merger market level).[59]

(c) Shock analysis (or event studies), which was described above in para.3–022 in relation to demand-side substitutability, is equally applicable in assessing supply-side issues. Further, at a qualitative level, falling short of shock analysis, the process of market definition is assisted by evidence of actual switching by suppliers between products. The existence of such switching does not of itself show that the two products are sufficiently close supply-side substitutes that a small increase in the price of one would lead to producer switching; but a claim that such switching would occur is more credible if at least some producers have changed between the products.

(d) Evidence[60] that *sellers* base their business decisions on the prospect of switching by producers of other products in response to small changes in price may corroborate the analysis described above.

---

[52] If no producer currently supplies both products, it is important to establish the explanation for this as the reasons may reveal important impediments to switching.

[53] See the UK Competition Commission's Guidelines on Merger References, March 2003 (*www.competition-commission.org.uk*), para.2.23.

[54] e.g. if switching requires extensive product development and testing, the purchase of new machinery or fittings, or extensive down-time. If production is by way of *batch* process (as opposed to continuous production), it may be easier to make changes to product specifications; see, e.g. Case IV/M.1467 *Rohm and Haas / Morton*, para.32.

[55] e.g. if the producer cannot use its existing distribution structure and has to set up new arrangements either itself or through third parties.

[56] In particular, if the producer needs to spend money on advertising or sales to persuade customers to buy the new product. See Case IV/M.986 *Agfa-Gevaert / Du Pont* [1998] O.J. L211/22, para.29.

[57] If switching would prevent the producer from complying with existing long-term contracts, the costs in terms of damages payments and reputational issues would need to be factored in.

[58] Costs of exit are a barrier to entry: see Ch.16.

[59] Successful entry will depress the price.

[60] This evidence might arise, e.g. from pre-merger marketing studies.

3.5 SPECIFIC ISSUES IN PRODUCT MARKET DEFINITION

(a) Continuous chains of substitution

3–038 Products A and D, which are not themselves in direct competition, may form part of a single product market if there is a continuous chain of substitution between them, i.e. if product A competes in a market with product B, B in a market with product C, and C in a market with product D. The pricing decisions of the producer of product A may affect the ability of the producer of product D profitably to increase its prices through a "ripple effect". It is necessary to determine whether the relative prices of products A and D have diverged and, if so, with what effect on demand: if products A and D form part of the same market there should be evidence that an increase in the price of one resulted in an increase in demand for the other.[61]

The Commission has frequently considered the connected issue of whether the existence of a continuum of different product characteristics means that there is a single antitrust market.[62]

(a) In *Pernod Ricard | Diageo | Seagram Spirits*[63] the Commission observed: "while it is possible to identify separate segments for different quality levels within each spirit category such as premium, secondary brands, private labels, low price, etc. the Commission has concluded that there is a continuous price spectrum ranging from the most expensive to the cheapest".

---

[61] The Australian Merger Guidelines, June 1999 (*www.accc.gov.au/content/item.phtml?item Id=719436&nodeId=file43a1f42c7eb63&fn=Merger%20Guidelines.pdf*), state, at para.5.56, that "the relevance of ripple effects depends on whether they constrain the price and output decisions of the merged firm". If, for example, the merged group will hold a monopoly in one of the markets, then the "ripple effect" will break down.

[62] See also Case IV/M.477 *Mercedes-Benz | Kässbohrer* [1995] O.J. L211/1, para.13; Case IV/M.984 *Du Pont | ICI* (possible single market for different grades of titanium dioxide; issue ultimately left open; paras 33 to 42); Case IV/M.1133 *Bass plc | Saison Holdings BV* (the Commission considered the market for hotels and identified a "continuum of prices at all levels from the cheapest to the dearest, with no 'break points' at which there were no hotels on offer. The relevant market may therefore be one for all hotels (except perhaps the very cheapest and the most expensive) on the basis of a chain of substitution".); Case IV/M.1571 *New Holland | Case* (possible chains of substitution between (separately): (i) tractors of different power, specification and weight; (ii) heavy excavators; and (iii) heavy loaders; paras 9, 10, 60 and 61); Case COMP/M.1806 *Astra Zeneca | Novartis* [2004] O.J. L110/1, para.60; Case COMP/M.1882 *Pirelli | BICC* [2003] O.J. L70/35, para.17; Case COMP/M.2498 *UPM-Kymmene | Haindl* [2002] O.J. L233/38, para.21; and Case COMP/M.2861 *Siemens | Drägerwerk | JV* [2003] O.J. L291/1 (products could be divided by performance category and use but there were clear overlaps pointing to an overall market for ventilation equipment for critical care; the Commission also emphasised that the merging parties and their competitors offered a broad range of different models and that breaking the market down by models would not alter the assessment (implying that if either of these factors were not present, it might have identified a narrow product market); paras 15 to 19).

[63] Case COMP/M.2268, para.16.

(b) In *Ciba-Geigy / Sandoz*[64] the Commission found that, in view of the fluid dividing lines between certain products, it was impossible to draw up a hard-and-fast product market definition. In its subsequent decision in *Astra Zeneca / Novartis*[65] the Commission identified a chain of substitution between the products identified in *Ciba-Geigy* as forming part of a single market because a hypothetical monopolist supplying one of the products would not find it profitable to increase prices by 5 to 10 per cent since customers would switch to other, overlapping products.

(c) In *Masterfoods / Royal Canin*[66] the Commission found that there was a continuum of increasing quality and price in pet foods without clear break points, and concluded that there was a single market for pet food, but added that an appropriate assessment of the parties' market power would require analysis of their strengths in the various quality segments.

(d) In *Carnival Corporation / P&O Princess*[67] the Commission stated: "If there were a clear distinction between premium and economy cruises, then this would be likely to be reflected in differences in pricing. However, if there was a continuum of prices, then this would be an indication that there is not a clear quality / price distinction between premium and economy cruises and therefore that they belong to the same relevant product market". It concluded: "There is not a clear dividing line between premium and economy offerings ... The Commission considers that evidence points to a single market for oceanic cruises. If there were a clear enough distinction between the quality of economy and of premium cruises such that they did not exert any competitive impact on each other, then this would be reflected in an obvious discontinuity of prices. Such a discontinuity could not be established with sufficient certainty".[68]

(e) By contrast,[69] in *Volvo / Scania*[70] the Commission stated that: "The difficulty in determining a precise demarcation of the market within a broad and highly differentiated product range cannot be accepted as the basis for dispensing with a market definition altogether despite the obvious lack of substitutability between particular products".

---

[64] Case IV/M.737 [1997] O.J. L201/1.
[65] Case COMP/M.1806 [2004] O.J. L110/1, para.60.
[66] Case COMP/M.2544, paras 15 to 17. See also Case COMP/M.2337 *Nestlé / Ralston Purina*.
[67] Case COMP/M.2706, paras 78, 91 and 112.
[68] See the discussion of differentiated products in s.7.3 below.
[69] See also Case COMP/M.2201 *MAN / Auwärter* [2002] O.J. L116/35, in which the Commission stated, at para.17: "The fact that some overlaps may occur between the individual product markets (for example, some types of bus can be used both in intercity transport and for touring) is not enough in itself to indicate any sufficient degree of substitutability".
[70] Case COMP/M.1672 [2001] O.J. L143/74, para.220.

(b) Own label goods

3–039 The question of whether own label goods form part of the same market as branded goods turns on whether a hypothetical monopoly supplier of branded goods would find it profitable to impose a SSNIP.[71] If switching by customers would render such a price increase unprofitable, then there is a single product market comprising both branded and own label goods. The Commission has considered this issue in numerous cases.[72]

(a) *SCA / Metsä Tissue*[73] involved a merger between producers of tissue products. The Commission found that in the consumer market for sales to retailers there were separate markets for branded and own label goods because there were clear distinctions in the way in which the main buyers, supermarkets, purchased the two types of product[74] and, furthermore, different sets of competitors served the two markets and had only limited economic incentives and financial capabilities to seriously challenge each other's product markets.[75] However, in the Away From Home ("AFH") market for supplies to

---

[71] It may also be necessary to consider the separate question of whether a hypothetical monopoly provider of own label goods could profitably impose a SSNIP; see para.3–002(b) above for discussion of concentric markets and para.3–048 below for discussion of one-way markets.

[72] See also Case IV/M.330 *McCormick / CPC / Rabobank / Ostmann* (dried spices; paras 53 to 55, 68 and 70); Case IV/M.431 *Medeol / Elosua*, para.24; Case IV/M.445 *BSN / Euralim*, paras 19 and 34; Case IV/M.458 *Electrolux / AEG*, para.25; Case IV/M.492 *Klöckner & Co AG / Computer 2000 AG* (branded hardware and software for computers competed with unbranded goods; para.12); Case IV/M.623 *Kimberly-Clark / Scott* [1996] O.J. L183/1 (branded and private label goods formed part of the same markets for consumer tissue papers because in retail stores private label products are priced relative to leading branded products and some consumers, at least, are willing to switch between branded and private label products, paras 48 to 52; compare Case COMP/M.2097 *SCA / Metsä Tissue*, which is discussed in sub-para.(a) of the text); Case IV/M.997 *Swedish Match / KAV* (merger between producers of matches; the Commission stated at para.12: "private label products are in the same market as branded products both for lighters and for matches, in line with the conclusions of previous cases in the field of utilitarian consumer products, as opposed to more sophisticated and taste distinguishable consumer products, such as spirits"; the Commission contrasted Case IV/M.623 *Kimberly-Clark / Scott* [1996] O.J. L183/1, with Case IV/M.938 *Guinness / Grand Metropolitan* [1998] O.J. L288/24); Case COMP/M.1740 *Heinz / United Biscuits Frozen and Chilled Foods* (branded and own label frozen and chilled foods found to form part of the same market; para.14); Case COMP/M.1802 *Unilever / Amora-Maille*; Case COMP/M.1990 *Unilever / Bestfoods* (branded and own label retail food products found to form part of the same product market; para.61); Case COMP/M.2072 *Phillip Morris / Nabisco* (no distinction drawn between branded and private label chocolate tablets in the Netherlands; para.14); Case COMP/M.2530 *Südzucker / Saint Louis Sucre* [2003] O.J. L103/1, para.18; and Case COMP/M.3693 *TPV / Philips (Monitors)*, para.13.

[73] Case COMP/M.2097. See also Case COMP/M.2522 *SCA Hygiene Products / Cartoinvest* (the Commission anticipated that an in-depth investigation would lead to the same conclusion as in *SCA / Metsä Tissue* but left the issue open; paras 8 and 9).

[74] In purchasing branded goods, supermarkets could only realistically select brands currently marketed in the state in question and made purchasing decisions on the basis of consumer loyalty to the brand, price and promotional activity. By contrast, in purchasing own label goods, supermarkets determined the quality and quantity of the product and the supplier produced to order.

[75] Paras 23 to 28.

hotels, restaurants and catering firms and other corporate customers, the Commission found that branded and own label goods formed part of the *same* product market because an AFH customer was more likely to choose products based on quality and price than to be influenced by brand image.[76]

(b) In *Nestlé | Ralston Purina*[77] the Commission found that branded and own label pet foods competed with one another at the retail level[78] but were in separate markets at a wholesale level (because the retailers, who comprised the purchasers at the wholesale level, could not substitute branded and unbranded goods if they wished to offer products under their own label).[79]

(c) In *Procter & Gamble | VP Schickedanz (II)*[80] the Commission relied on the sizeable price difference between branded and own-label sanitary towels as evidence that there was only limited competition between branded and unbranded products.

(d) In *Sarah Lee | Courtaulds*[81] the Commission found that branded and own label hosiery and intimate apparel formed part of a single market as own label products had won share from branded goods and both had identical characteristics and intended uses; were often displayed next to one another in shops; had overlapping price ranges; and, on the supply-side, were made on the same equipment with the same processes and personnel.

(c) Original equipment | replacement goods

Although original equipment and replacement goods may be *physically* **3–040** *identical* they may nevertheless form separate product markets, the issue in each case being whether a monopoly supplier could profitably increase the price of one category of goods by 5 to 10 per cent. This may be possible, in particular if the different means of distribution prevent arbitrage. The Commission has stated that: "Functional interchangeability or similarity in characteristics may not, in themselves, provide sufficient criteria, because the responsiveness of customers to relative price changes may be determined by other considerations as well. For example, there may be different

---

[76] Para.33.
[77] Case COMP/M.2337, paras 15 to 17, 32 and 33.
[78] This conclusion was confirmed in Case COMP/M.2544 *Masterfoods | Royal Canin* (whilst emphasising that the competitive constraint from private label products was stronger at the lower end of the market and that the absence of clear distinctive quality categories meant that all producers of branded pet foods were subject to some competitive constraint from private label suppliers; paras 12 to 14). See also Case IV/M.554 *Dalgety PLC | The Quaker Oats Company* (branded and own branded pet foods formed part of the same market; para.13).
[79] Paras 15 to 19.
[80] Case IV/M.430 [1994] O.J. L354/32, para.44.
[81] Case COMP/M.1892, paras 18 to 21.

competitive constraints in the original equipment market for car components and in spare parts, thereby leading to a separate delineation of two relevant markets".[82]

(d) Differentiated products

3–041 Differentiated products[83] are products which consumers perceive to have attributes[84] differing from those of rivals. Since the intensity of competition between differentiated products generally varies across the market, the process of defining the relevant product market may be misleading because market shares calculated on the basis of such a definition will ascribe equal weight to every unit of sales of products within the market but no weight to

---

[82] The Notice on Market Definition, para.36. Cases on this issue include Case IV/M.12 *Varta / Bosch* [1991] O.J. L320/26, paras 12 to 16; Case IV/M.43 *Magneti Marelli / CEAC* [1991] O.J. L222/38, paras 8 to 10; Case IV/M.134 *Mannesmann / Boge* (distinguishing the markets on the grounds that: they comprised separate customers; prices were different; different distribution systems were required; and R&D cooperation with the motor vehicle industry was required to compete in the OEM market but not the IAM market; paras 9 to 13); Case IV/M.337 *Knorr-Bremse / Allied Signal* (relying in part in drawing the distinction on the fact that: "Prices of parts sold to independent resellers are much higher than to OEMs ... The reasons given for the differences include: lower volumes per customer than for OEMs; the requirement for rapid delivery which necessitates stockholding; marketing support; packaging; additional sales personnel and technical training on maintenance and repairs"; paras 25 and 26); Case IV/M.358 *Pilkington-Techint / SIV* [1994] O.J. L158/24 (distinguishing sales to vehicle manufacturers and to the independent aftermarket on the grounds that there are different conditions of competition in the two markets; para.19); Case IV/M.360 *Avin / Sofegi* (basing the distinction on differences in "customers (OE—a few large car manufacturers; AM—numerous wholesalers, distributors and fitters); production (OE suppliers produce large numbers of small parts for a limited number of models; AM suppliers produce a vast range of components for a wide range of different makes and models); product (AM exhausts are generally made to lower material specification than OE exhausts); and delivery (just-in-time delivery to a car manufacturer's plant as opposed to a sophisticated distribution system to numerous customers)"; para.15); Case IV/M.726 *Bosch / Allied Signal* (relying on differences in prices and customers in finding separate markets; para.12); Case IV/M.861 *Textron / Kautex*; Case IV/M.818 *Cardo / Thyssen*, para.19; Case IV/M.937 *Lear / Keiper* (s.IV); Case IV/M.1093 *ECIA / Bertrand Faure*; Case IV/M.1207 *Dana / Echlin* (s.4); Case IV/M.1230 *Glaverbel / PPG*, para.10; Case IV/M.1245 *Valeo / ITT Industries* (s.IV(a)(i)); Case IV/M.1335 *Dana / Glacier Vandervell* (thinwall and dry bearings; para.11); Case IV/M.1342 *Knorr Bremse / Robert Bosch*; Case IV/M.1363 *Du Pont / Hoechst / Herberts*, para.14; Case COMP/M.1481 *Denso / Magneti Marelli*; Case COMP/M.1491 *Robert Bosch / Magneti Marelli*, para.9; Case COMP/M.1629 *Knorr-Bremse / Mannesmann*, para.17; Case COMP/M.1778 *Freudenberg / Phoenix JV*; Case COMP/M.1789 *INA / LUK*, para.7; Case COMP/M.1907 *Woco / Michelin*, para.12; Case COMP/M.1929 *Magneti Marelli / Semia*; Case COMP/M.1959 *Meritor / Arvin*, para.7; Case COMP/M.2366 *Denso / MMCL*, paras 7 to 9; Case COMP/M.2608 *INA / FAG*, paras 12 and 13; Case COMP/M.3436 *Continental / Phoenix*, paras 14 and 15; and Case COMP/M.3789 *Johnson Controls / Robert Bosch / Delphi SLI*, para.8. By contrast, in Case IV/M.164 *Mannesmann / VDO* the Commission found, at para.15, that there was not a separate independent aftermarket for certain components because more than 95% of sales were to OEMs and the "segment would be too small to create distinct, competitive features significantly different from the competitive structure of the original equipment market".
[83] See s.7.3 below.
[84] Whether relating to the products themselves or their geographic location.

those outside the market.[85] It is therefore commonly argued that in the case of mergers between suppliers of differentiated products, the focus of attention should be on a direct analysis of whether the merged group will be able profitably to increase its prices[86] and not on the process of market definition.[87] Nevertheless, in the cases involving differentiated products, the Commission has defined antitrust markets and, when it has used direct analysis, has done so to supplement an orthodox structural analysis of the antitrust markets identified. The discussion in this section about continuous chains of substitution, own label goods and original equipment/replacement goods may be regarded as an application of the principles of market definition to differentiated products.[88]

(e) Captive production/in-house supplies

As a matter of principle, the question of whether actual or potential captive production[89] (i.e. production by vertically integrated companies for their own use) should be included in the market depends on whether an increase **3–042**

---

[85] See Shapiro, "Mergers with Differentiated Products" [1996] *Antitrust* 23; Rubinfeld, "Market Definition with Differentiated Products: The Post / Nabisco Cereal Merger" (2000) 68 *The Antitrust Law Journal* 163, at p.181; Baker & Coscelli, "The Role of Market Shares in Differentiated Product Markets" [1999] E.C.L.R. 412, at pp.413 and 414; and Baker & Wu, "Applying the Market Definition Guidelines of the European Commission" [1998] E.C.L.R. 273, at p.277. Vickers, "Competition Economics and Policy", speech of October 3, 2002 (*www.oft.gov.uk/News/Speeches + and + articles/2002/index.htm*), refers to the "pitfall [of] the 'zero-one' fallacy—the tendency, once 'the market' is defined, to think of all products within it as extremely substitutable for the products at the centre of concern, and those products beyond the boundaries as irrelevant. In reality matters are of varying degrees, and the useful tool of market definition must be employed with this in mind".

[86] Or reduce quality, variety or innovation. See, e.g. Werden & Rozanski, "The Market Delineation Dilemma" [1994] *Antitrust* 40, at p.42.

[87] The counter-argument is that if a hypothetical monopolist supplying the products sold by the merging parties (and, if necessary, any products supplied by rivals which lie between the merging parties' products in product or geographic space) could not profitably raise prices by 5 to 10%, with the consequence that a separate antitrust market is not identified, then the merged group will not be able to raise prices by that level and its impact on the value for money aspects of consumer welfare is therefore not substantial. This argument is fallacious for two reasons. First, the SSNIP test is used for defining the antitrust market and does not provide a tolerance level for acceptable post-merger price increases. Secondly, the SSNIP test is not a substitute for a direct analysis of the merged group's ability profitably to increase its prices, e.g. a merger of suppliers of products A and B may allow the merged group profitably to raise the price of A in circumstances in which an attempt to raise the prices of both A and B might have been defeated by switching to C.

[88] See Keyte, "Market Definition and Differentiated Products: the Need for a Workable Standard" (1995) 63 *Antitrust Law Journal* 697, at pp.705 to 729, for a detailed analysis of the sources of product differentiation. The dilemma surrounding market definition in cases of differentiated products is most acute when there is a continuous chain of substitution and the Commission is unable to identify a clear break in the chain but the merger is likely to lead to significant increases in price. If the Commission is required in all cases to define a relevant antitrust market and to ascribe substantial weight to market shares, even in the case of differentiated products, then acceding to the chain of substitution argument may deprive the Commission of jurisdiction to prohibit the transaction.

[89] See generally Baker, "The Treatment of Captive Sales in Market Definition: Rules or Reason?" [2003] E.C.L.R. 161.

in price by a hypothetical monopolist in the free market would be defeated, in particular:

(a) by *supplies* which had been ear-marked for in-house use being diverted into the free market,[90] in-house *suppliers* increasing production and selling into the free market, or *customers* developing in-house capability[91]; or

(b) because a price increase would not be profitable unless the price of the downstream product also rose.[92]

For example, if company X is a vertically integrated producer of product A and its downstream business can use either A or B as inputs and the market price of both A and B is 100 then X might use its own production of A in the downstream market; but if the price of A rose to 105, X might sell its output of A and buy B in the market as its input in the downstream market. Conversely, whilst a company supplying the merchant market may be willing to divert output to supply customers willing to pay higher prices, a company producing exclusively for its own consumption may be less willing to divert its output into the merchant market because this may deprive the downstream business of supplies, and entering the merchant market may involve costs, in particular in marketing and distribution.

The US Horizontal Merger Guidelines[93] provide that captive producers will be included in the market to the extent that such inclusion accurately reflects their competitive significance. In determining whether captive production is competitively significant, the US authorities consider not merely whether such producers would be willing to sell the relevant product in the merchant market but *also* whether they might increase production of both the relevant product and the downstream product.[94] (Analytically, the scope for captive producers to increase self-supply of the relevant product in order to increase their output of the downstream product does *not* alter the boundaries of the market for the relevant product—since the essence of a

---

[90] OFT Research Paper: "Market Definition in UK Competition Policy", NERA, 1992, (note that the views in the Paper do not necessarily reflect OFT policy), p.96. Compare the Australian Merger Guidelines, June 1999 (*www.accc.gov.au/content/item.phtml?itemId=719436 &nodeId=file43a1f42c7eb63&fn=Merger%20Guidelines.pdf*) (para.5.68). See also the UK OFT's Substantive Merger Guidelines, May 2003 (*www.oft.gov.uk*), para.3.21.

[91] See Case COMP/M.3216 *Oracle / PeopleSoft* [2005] O.J. L218/6, para.115 (finding that customers would not develop the products in-house in response to a SSNIP).

[92] See the UK Competition Commission report on *DS Smith plc / Linpac Containers Ltd* (*www.competition-commission.org.uk/rep_pub/reports/2004/fulltext/492.pdf*), 2004, paras 4.14 and 4.15 (finding a market for the supply of corrugated sheet which included both third party and intra-group supply because an increase in the price of corrugated sheet sold to third parties would not be profitable unless the price of corrugated cases (which are made from corrugated sheet) also increased).

[93] The US Horizontal Merger Guidelines, 1992 (amended in 1997) (*www.usdoj.gov/atr/public/ guidelines/hmg.htm*), para.1.31.

[94] See Arquit, "Perspectives on the 1992 U.S. Government Horizontal Merger Guidelines" (1992) 61 *Antitrust Law Journal* 121, at p.126.

market is the actual or potential presence of trade which is absent in the case of self-supply—but it is clearly relevant in determining whether the merged group has the incentive and ability profitably to increase its prices.)[95]

However, in large numbers of cases[96] prior to the decision of the Court of **3–043** First Instance in *Schneider Electric SA v Commission*[97] the Commission excluded captive production from the market without further analysis. For example, in *Preussag / Thomson*[98] the Commission stated that: "It has been

---

[95] Compare Denis, "An Insider's Look at the New Horizontal Merger Guidelines" (1992) 3 *Antitrust* 6, at p.7: "The new Guidelines no longer require that vertically integrated firms change their behaviour in response to a SSNIP in order to be counted as market participants. Vertically integrated firms are as important to the pre- and post-merger competitive interaction as firms selling into the merchant market and should be given equal weight in identifying market participants. If any portion of productive capacity, captive or not, were withdrawn from production without a change in demand for the relevant product, the price of the relevant product would rise".

[96] See, e.g. Case IV/M.126 *Accor / Wagons-Lits* [1992] O.J. L204/1, para.15; Case IV/M.134 *Mannesmann / Boge*, para.19; Case IV/M.139 *VIAG / EB Brühl*, para.19(i); Case IV/M.149 *Lucas / Eaton*, para.22; Case IV/M.197 *Solvay-Laporte / Interox* (free markets for chemicals; para.23); Case IV/M.214 *Du Pont / ICI* [1993] O.J. L7/13 (captive production of nylon fibres excluded from the market; para.4.1); Case IV/M.361 *Neste / Statoil*, paras 27, 29 and 31; Case IV/M.553 *RTL / Veronica / Endemol* [1996] O.J. L294/14, paras 24, 89 and 90 (upheld on appeal in Case T–221/95 *Endemol Entertainment Holding BV v Commission* [1999] E.C.R. II–1299, para.107); Case IV/M.603 *Crown Cork & Seal / Carnaud Metalbox* [1996] O.J. L75/38, para.84; Case IV/M.678 *Minorco / Tilcon* (non-captive market for quicklime; para.27); Case IV/M.726 *Bosch / Allied Signal*, para.24; Case IV/M.774 *Saint-Gobain / Wacker-Chemie / NOM* [1997] O.J. L247/1 (the Commission focused on the fact that the merged group would have only minor activities in non-captive trade, notwithstanding that the parties' shares *including* captive use in the two relevant markets were 50 to 60% and 80 to 90% respectively; see paras 166 and 167); Case IV/M.779 *Bertelsmann / CLT*, para.17; Case IV/M.931 *Neste / IVO* (electricity produced for own consumption excluded from the market for wholesale sales of electricity; para.21; see also para.39); Case IV/M.1182 *Akzo Nobel / Courtaulds*, para.33; Case COMP/M.1225 *Enso / Stora* [1999] O.J. L254/9 (the Commission considered, at para.10, the parties' production excluding "captive" supplies); Case COMP/M.1341 *Westdeutsche Landesbank / Carlson / Thomas Cook*, para.13; Case COMP/M.1502 *Kuoni / First Choice*, para.10; Case COMP/M.1574 *Kirch / Mediaset*, para.14; Case COMP/M.1711 *Tyco / Siemens*, para.12; Case COMP/M.1741 *MCI WorldCom / Sprint* [2003] O.J. L300/1 ("self provision in itself does not constitute part of the market"; para.85); Case COMP/M.1751 *Shell / BASF / JV—Project Nicole*, para.30 and Table 1; Case COMP/M.1492 *Hyundai Electronics / LG Semicon*, para.12; Case COMP/M.1849 *Solectron / Ericsson Switches* (captive production by Ericsson of switching hardware excluded from the market; para.10); Case COMP/M.1943 *Telefónica / Endemol*, para.8; Case COMP/M.1958 *Bertelsmann / GBL / Pearson TV* (market for television productions not put to captive use; para.11); Case COMP/M.2097 *SCA / Metsä Tissue* (the Commission defined the relevant product market, at para.16 (see also para.75), as "the supply of parent reels to third parties", i.e. excluding captive supplies); Case COMP/M.2277 *Degussa / Laporte*, paras 39 and 43; Case COMP/M.2314 *BASF / Eurodiol / Pantochim* [2002] O.J. 2002 L132/45 (the Commission examined, at paras 62 and 84, the shares of the "free market" or "merchant market"); Case COMP/M.2389 *Shell / DEA* [2003] O.J. 2003 L15/35 (market shares for ethylene calculated on the basis of sales into the merchant market; para.22); Case COMP/JV.55 *Hutchison / RCPM / ECT* [2003] O.J. L223/1, paras 71, 76 and 78; Case COMP/ JV.56 *Hutchison / ECT* ("These volumes represent captive production, which should not be included in the market when determining market shares"; para.22; see also para.27); Case COMP/M.2413 *BHP / Billiton* (distinct market for the sale of copper concentrate to third party smelters/refiners; para.40); Case COMP/M.2479 *Flextronics / Alcatel*, para.14; Case COMP/M.2533 *BP / E.ON* [2002] O.J. L276/31, para.19; and the Guidelines on Vertical Restraints [2000] O.J. C291/1, para.98.

[97] Case T-310/01 [2002] E.C.R. II-4071.

[98] Case COMP/M.2002, para.11.

the Commission's general practice to exclude self-supply from the relevant market, and to assess the impact of a concentration on the 'third-party' or 'free' procurement market". Similarly, in *EDF | EnBW*[99] the Commission noted that "auto-production ... does not form part of the market". Nevertheless, in *Alcoa | Reynolds*[1] the Commission examined whether captive-use aluminium would be made available to the merchant market if the market price were to increase. It found on the facts that captive producers had a strong economic incentive not to make supplies into the merchant market and therefore excluded captive production from the market. However, the implication of the Commission's analysis is that if captive producers would have commenced supplies into the market in response to a permanent increase in market price of 5 to 10 per cent then such supplies would have been treated as part of the market.[2]

In *Schneider Electric SA v Commission*[3] the Court of First Instance analysed a market for electrical distribution panels in which some suppliers were vertically integrated (and therefore competed for appointment as electrical contractors on large-scale construction projects) and others were not. The Court found that the vertically integrated and the non-vertically integrated suppliers in fact competed either directly or indirectly and, by excluding from its market share calculation captive sales by the vertically integrated suppliers, the Commission had under-estimated the economic power of the vertically integrated suppliers and over-estimated the economic power of the non-vertically integrated suppliers. It follows from this decision that the Commission can no longer adopt a blanket "rule" of disregarding captive

---

[99] Case COMP/M.1853, para.26.

[1] Case COMP/M.1693 [2002] O.J. L58/25, para.13.

[2] Similarly, in Case COMP/M.2220 *GE | Honeywell* [2004] O.J. L48/1 (prohibition decision upheld on appeal in Case T–210/01 *General Electric Company v Commission*, not yet reported, judgment of December 14, 2005) the Commission noted, at para.338, that Hamilton Sundstrand supplied engine starters exclusively to an affiliated company (but compare para.421—"mainly" for its own use) and its starters were therefore not made available to the market; but the Commission also considered whether a small but significant, non-transitory price increase in engine starters would induce it to sell to the free market (see also para.421). In Case IV/M.1101 *Hermes | Sampo | FGB—FCIC* the Commission stated, at para.41: "Captive production should, according to the normal economic practice, be excluded from the market share calculations. However, the investigation suggests that, while the captive insurers operating in the Finnish credit insurance market are themselves restricted as to the choice of their customers, their customers appear to be somewhat free to seek insurance coverage on the open market. A tentative conclusion may therefore be drawn that, from the demand side, both captive and non-captive insurers compete, at least to some extent, for the same customers. Given this, it appears that captive insurers operate, at least partly, on the same market as non-captive insurers". The Commission examined the market shares both including and excluding captive insurers. In some cases the Commission has calculated shares both including and excluding captive production in order to demonstrate that it is not necessary to determine the correct way to calculate market shares in order for the transaction to be cleared; see, e.g. Case COMP/M.2358 *Flextronics | Ericsson*, para.12; Case COMP/M.2629 *Flextronics | Xerox*, para.13; and Case COMP/M.2815 *Sanmina-SCI | Hewlett Packard*, paras 6 and 7. In Case COMP/M.1913 *Lufthansa | Menzies | LGS | JV* the Commission calculated market shares in ground handling services by using aircraft movements, thereby *including* self-supply in the market (see para.14).

[3] Case T–310/01 [2002] E.C.R II-4071, paras 282, 283 and 296.

sales and must instead examine the competitive significance of captive sales in each case. For example,[4] in *Celanese / Degussa / European Oxo Chemicals*[5] the Commission found that market shares were not a reliable indicator of competitive strength because most output was used internally and only a small amount was sold on the merchant market (3 per cent in the case of butyraldehyde) and competitors had sufficient spare capacity to increase their sales if the merged group sought to raise its prices to third parties.

(f) Secondary markets

Secondary markets are markets for products, such as spares, maintenance **3–044** services and accessories, which are purchased[6] only if a customer has already purchased a primary product.[7] In principle,[8] there could be: a *single*

---

[4] See Case COMP/M.2854 *RAG / Degussa*, para.50; Case COMP/M.2978 *Lagardère / Natexis / VUP* [2004] O.J. L125/54 (appeal pending in Case T-279/04 *Editions Odile Jacob SAS v Commission*) (excluding self-supply from the calculation of market shares but taking them into account in assessing the merged group's market position; paras 154 to 156; but compare paras 521 and 522); Case COMP/M.3060 *UCB / Solutia*, para.31; Case COMP/M.3396 *Group 4 Falck / Securicor* (excluding self-supply because a customer which had outsourced its requirements could not credibly threaten to switch back to in-house provision; paras 15 and 31; the Commission did not consider whether in-house providers might commence third party supply in response to a SSNIP); Case COMP/M.3431 *Sonoco / Ahlstrom* [2005] O.J. L159/13 (calculating market shares both for the merchant market and, separately, including sales by a competitor to its parent and recognising that, on the facts, the competitor was more significant than its merchant share would have suggested; paras 84 and 104 and n.12); Case COMP/M.3579 *WPP / Grey* (the Commission took account of the scope for advertisers to deal directly with suppliers of advertising time and space and therefore cleared a merger creating relatively high shares in the merchant supply of media buying services in Denmark and Sweden; paras 102 and 124); and Case COMP/M.3695 *BT / Radianz*, paras 24 and 25.
[5] Case COMP/M.3056 [2004] O.J. L38/47, paras 55 and 77.
[6] If products are invariably sold together, they will usually be treated as a single market, e.g. shoes and shoelaces. In Case COMP/M.3687 *Johnson & Johnson / Guidant*, the Commission found that stents were "generally" sold together with their delivery system and analysed the effects of the merger on markets for the supply of the system as a whole; para.12. By contrast, in Case COMP/M.3972 *TRW Automotive / Dalphi Metal España*, para.10, the fact that a limited number of customers continued to purchase two products separately meant that a separate market was identified for one of the two products.
[7] See generally Areeda, Hovenkamp & Solow, *Antitrust Law* (2nd edn, Aspen Law & Business, 2000), Vol.IIA, paras 519 and 564b; OFT Economic Discussion Paper 5, "Switching Costs", NERA, April 2003 (note that the views in the paper do not necessarily reflect those of the OFT), paras 7.10 to 7.17; "Market Definition in the Media Sector—Economic Issues", Report by Europe Economics for the European Commission, DG Competition, November 2002 (available via *http://europa.eu.int/comm/competition/publications/studies/european_economics.pdf*), paras 2.3.33 to 2.3.44; and DG Competition Discussion Paper on the Application of Article 82 of the Treaty to Exclusionary Abuses, December 2005, s.10.2.
[8] See the UK OFT Guidelines on Market Definition (December 2004) (*www.oft.gov.uk/NR/rdonlyres/972AF80C-2D74-4A63-84B3-27552727B89A/0/OFT403.pdf*), Ch.6. The UK Notice is more detailed on this point than the Notice on Market Definition published by the Commission (see the Notice on Market Definition, para.56). (See also the OFT Research Paper: "Market Definition in UK Competition Policy", NERA, 1992, pp.xii, xiii and 87 to 91 (note that the views in the paper do not necessarily represent those of the OFT)). Contrast Case COMP/M.2861 *Siemens / Drägerwerk / JV* [2003] O.J. L291/1, paras 30 to 33, dispensing with an analysis of secondary markets on the basis that the parties' positions in the supply of accessories was linked with their competitive positions in the supply of the primary products.

"system" market for all brands of the primary and secondary products; *dual markets*, in which there are product markets for all brands of the primary products and, separately, all brands of the secondary products; or *multiple markets*, in which there is a single market for all brands of the primary products and separate markets for each brand of the secondary product.[9]

In determining the relevant market in such cases, the approach is to identify the narrowest candidate market definitions (e.g. separate markets for each brand in the secondary market and a further market for the primary product) and apply the SSNIP test. If a SSNIP in relation to *any* of those candidate markets would not be profitable, then that candidate market should be expanded and the exercise repeated. For example, it may be that a SSNIP in the primary product would be profitable, but SSNIPs in each of the secondary products would not, so a second iteration would involve determining whether a SSNIP in relation to the secondary products taken together would be profitable; if so, there is a dual market; if not, there may be both a single system market *and*, separately, a market for the primary product.[10]

When applying the SSNIP test in cases where the same supplier provides a primary and a secondary product (e.g. a supplier of printers which also sells printer cartridges), the profitability of a SSNIP in the primary product[11] ought[12] to be determined taking account only of the effect of the price increase on sales of the primary product and *not* also taking account of the profit lost through reduced sales of the secondary product. This is because the SSNIP test is a "thought experiment" based on an assessment of whether a SSNIP by a hypothetical monopoly supplier of the products in the candidate market would be profitable.

(a) *Single "system" markets* are more likely to arise when sufficient[13] customers engage in "whole-life costing", by factoring in expenditure

---

[9] See Case COMP/M.2803 *Telia / Sonera* (distinct markets for the provision of call termination services on each of Telia's and Sonera's mobile telephony networks; paras 29 to 31).

[10] See para.3–002(b) above for discussion of concentric markets.

[11] The same analysis applies *vice versa* in relation to market definition for the secondary products.

[12] Compare DG Competition Discussion Paper on the Application of Article 82 of the Treaty to Exclusionary Abuses, December 2005, para.247. Contrast the approach in the UK OFT Guidelines on Market Definition, December 2004 (*www.oft.gov.uk/NR/rdonlyres/972AF80C-2D74-4A63-84B3-27552727B89A/0/OFT403.pdf*), para.6.3. The issue is controversial. The counter-argument to the position adopted in the text is that the SSNIP test is intended to convey meaningful information about the competitive position in the market and if a hypothetical monopolist with the characteristics of the merging parties (i.e. with activities in the supply of both primary and secondary products) would not raise the prices of its primary product because of concerns about loss of profits in the sale of the secondary product then it is somewhat abstruse to find that there is nevertheless a separate market for the primary product because a hypothetical monopolist taking account only of its interests in the supply of primary products would find a SSNIP profitable. See more generally the discussion in OFT Economic Discussion Paper 5, "Switching Costs", NERA, April 2003 (note that the views in the paper do not necessarily reflect those of the OFT), paras 7.16 and 7.17.

[13] See the UK OFT Guidelines on Market Definition, December 2004 (*www.oft.gov.uk/NR/rdonlyres/972AF80C-2D74-4A63-84B3-27552727B89A/0/OFT403.pdf*), para.6.6, final bullet point.

on secondary products when making the decision to purchase the primary product (e.g. mainframe computers and maintenance services) with the result that changes in the price of the secondary product would result in a loss of primary product sales, reducing demand for (and therefore sales of) the secondary product.[14] Customers are more likely to *whole-life cost* if: the costs of secondary products over the life of the primary product are high relative to the price of the primary product; customers are sophisticated; customers have information about likely future prices for secondary products at the time of purchasing the primary product[15]; and customers can make reasonable predictions about their requirements for secondary products.[16]

(b) *Dual markets* are more likely to arise when the link between primary purchasing decisions and secondary product pricing is weaker but there is competition between different suppliers of secondary products, i.e. it is possible for a customer which has already purchased the primary product readily to switch between different suppliers of secondary products without incurring material switching costs *or* to switch to another primary product to avoid higher prices for a particular brand in the secondary market.

(c) *Multiple markets* may arise if the primary product suppliers control the secondary product market through intellectual property rights, locking customers who have purchased the primary product into using a limited number of compatible secondary products. Such markets are more likely if the primary product is replaced infrequently and there are substantial costs in switching between primary products supplied by different companies.

In *Cardo / Thyssen*[17] the Commission reviewed a proposed combination of **3–045** the parties' railways businesses. The Commission found that the after-

---

[14] See the discussion in OFT Economic Discussion Paper 5, "Switching Costs", NERA, April 2003 (note that the views in the paper do not necessarily reflect those of the OFT), para.7.14.
[15] See the UK OFT Guidelines on Market Definition, December 2004 (*www.oft.gov.uk/NR/rdonlyres/972AF80C-2D74-4A63-84B3-27552727B89A/0/OFT403.pdf*), para.6.5.
[16] See Case IV/M.17 *Aérospatiale / MBB*; Case IV/M.913 *Siemens / Elektrowatt* [1999] O.J. L88/1 (leaving open the issue of whether servicing of fire alarms formed part of a systems market and noting that the fact that servicing was often carried out by the manufacturer pointed towards a single market whilst the existence of smaller firms carrying out maintenance services pointed in the opposite direction); Case COMP/M.2694 *Metronet / Infraco* (the Commission left open the issue of market definition, at para.30, but noted that its market test had supported the view that the supply of new rolling stock could be analysed together with the maintenance of that rolling stock; the parties had indicated that over 80% of railway vehicles ordered in the United Kingdom since privatisation had ongoing maintenance contracts); and Case COMP/M.3687 *Johnson & Johnson / Guidant* (the Commission identified a single system market for beating-heart stabilisation systems on the grounds that there was no interoperability between components supplied by different suppliers, certain components were low value and sometimes provided without charge, and the choice of stabiliser was the main factor that determined the choice of supplier; para.58).
[17] Case COMP/M.818, para.19.

market for brakes, which comprised the supply of spare parts, had to be distinguished from the market for original equipment, as most of the contracts for spare parts were concluded separately from the contracts for original equipment. In particular, contracts for spare parts were normally not concluded with assemblers, which purchased the original equipment, but with the end user of the rolling stock, i.e. the national, regional and local railway authorities. In *General Electric / Honeywell*[18] the Commission found that there was a separate antitrust market for maintenance, repair and overhaul services for jet engines, since these services might be provided not only by the original equipment manufacturers but also by various airlines' maintenance departments and independent service shops. Similarly, in *Agfa-Gevaert / Du Pont*[19] the existence of providers of services independent of equipment sales was relied on in finding a separate market for servicing.

(g) Two-sided markets

3–046 Two-sided markets[20] arise when a product is valuable to a consumer only if at least two groups of consumers purchase the product. For example, a man would not join a heterosexual dating agency if there were no female members; similarly, advertisers would not purchase space in newspapers without readers and consumers would not purchase credit cards which were not accepted by merchants. The issue which arises here is whether the SSNIP test is applied taking account only of the effects of the price increase on the group of customers in question, or whether the overall effect on profitability is considered. For example, a SSNIP for female membership of a dating agency may be profitable in terms of its impact on female members, but a reduction in female membership may reduce male membership leading to a loss of profits on the second side of the market. In principle, for the reasons given in s.(f) above, the SSNIP test is applied taking account only of the effect on profits of the products which form part of the candidate market.[21]

(h) Range and cluster goods

3–047 In some cases a range or cluster of goods, which are not themselves substitutes for one another, may be grouped together to form a single product

---

[18] Case COMP/M.2220 (prohibition decision upheld on appeal in Case T-210/01 *General Electric Company v Commission*, not yet reported, judgment of December 14, 2005), para.35. See also para.96.

[19] Case IV/M.986 [1998] O.J. L211/22, para.36.

[20] See generally Evans, "The Antitrust Economics of Multi-Sided Platform Markets", 20(2) *Yale Journal on Regulation*, Summer 2003, 325 and "Market Definition in the Media Sector—Economic Issues", Report by Europe Economics for the European Commission, DG Competition, November 2002 (available via *http://europa.eu.int/comm/competition/publications/studies/european_economics.pdf*). For discussion of the effect on the substantive analysis of the existence of a two-sided market, see para.6–028.

[21] For a contrary view, see Evans, "The Antitrust Economics of Multi-Sided Platform Markets", 20(2) *Yale Journal on Regulation*, Summer 2003, 325.

market.[22] The issue is whether the number of customers requiring the provision of a range or cluster of goods or services *and* the costs of unbundling[23] are such that a monopoly full range supplier would be able profitably to increase its prices by 5 to 10 per cent even though rival suppliers could offer one or some (but not all) of the goods or services.[24] There is more likely to be a separate market for a bundle of products if the bundle is sold at a significant discount to the separate components or if there are quality advantages in buying the bundle.[25]

If a hypothetical monopoly supplier of the range could profitably raise prices by 5 to 10 per cent *and* a hypothetical monopoly supplier of one or more of the products separately could also profitably raise prices by the same amount, then, as a matter of principle, there will be separate antitrust markets both for the range *and* some or all of the individual products. This implies that a product may belong to two or more markets (as is recognised in the case of one-way markets).[26] Different markets may be relevant to the investigation of different theories of competitive harm.[27]

---

[22] See the discussion in ABA Section of Antitrust Law, *Market Power Handbook* (ABA Publishing, 2005), pp.111 and 112 (describing cluster markets as involving "transactional complements" and noting that the US courts have identified cluster markets in a variety of contexts including hospital services, banking, pet products and fire protection services).

[23] The Australian Merger Guidelines, June 1999 (*http://www.accc.gov.au/content/item.phtml?itemId=719436&nodeId=file43a1f42c7eb63&fn=Merger%20Guidelines.pdf*), state, at para.5.60, that "it may be appropriate to define 'cluster' markets, comprising a bundle of related products, where the costs of unbundling mean that suppliers of the component parts are unable to defeat a SSNIP by a hypothetical monopolist supplying the whole bundle of products. These unbundling costs could be costs incurred directly by the consumer of unbundled products, e.g. additional transaction costs, or additional costs incurred by the suppliers of single products, e.g. diseconomies of scope, which are then reflected in the relative prices of bundled and unbundled products".

[24] Areeda, Hovenkamp & Solow, *Antitrust Law* (2nd edn, Aspen Law & Business, 2000), Vol.IIA, para.565c, also note that a cluster market can be defined if "economies of joint provision (economies of scope) make distribution of the cluster good cheaper per good than distribution of each separately, *and* ... the firms supplying one of the products in the cluster could not easily add the others as well".

[25] See "Market Definition in the Media Sector—Economic Issues", Report by Europe Economics for the European Commission, DG Competition, November 2002 (available via *http://europa.eu.int/comm/competition/publications/studies/european_economics.pdf*), para.2.3.22.

[26] i.e. relevant antitrust markets may be "concentric". See further para.3–002(b) above and the discussion in "Market Definition in the Media Sector—Economic Issues", Report by Europe Economics for the European Commission, DG Competition, November 2002 (available via *http://europa.eu.int/comm/competition/publications/studies/european_economics.pdf*), paras 2.3.23 to 2.3.25, emphasising the sequential nature of the SSNIP test analysis, with the consequence that if there is not a separate market for the bundle A + B, the next question is whether there is a market for the bundle *and* A (or the bundle *and* B). The Report also discusses in detail the circumstances in which bundled goods compete with unbundled goods; see paras 2.3.66 to 2.3.69, 2.3.74 to 2.3.78 and 2.3.87 to 2.3.89.

[27] e.g. in principle the Commission might investigate possible non-coordinated effects arising from horizontal overlaps in a cluster market *and* conglomerate issues arising from the leveraging of market power in the supply of one product into a second within the cluster.

The Commission has applied these principles in the following cases.[28]

(a) In *BP / Mobil*[29] the Commission stated, in considering whether there were separate product markets for different types of industrial lubricants (which served different functions): "Some industrial customers demand the full range of lubricants for their operations from their lubricant supplier, rather than sourcing individual lubricants from different suppliers. This range effect, combined with the very strong supply side substitutability would seem to indicate a single market for industrial lubricants despite the specific products which are produced for different uses".

(b) In *Cardo / Thyssen*[30] the Commission found that there was an antitrust market for complete brake systems even though many smaller suppliers could only supply components and not the complete system: "Given that most of the customers' purchases of brakes relate to complete brake systems and that the trend is to buy complete brake systems, it appears reasonable therefore to conclude in favour of the existence of markets for complete brake systems. However, the customers have still the ability to buy the different components separately where necessary".

(c) In *Sanitec / Sphinx*[31] the Commission found that there were "strong indications" that there was a single market for the supply of ceramic

---

[28] See also Case IV/M.315 *Mannesmann / Vallourec / Ilva* [1994] O.J. L102/15, para.20; Case IV/M.580 *ABB / Daimler Benz* [1997] O.J. L11/1 (rejecting a cluster goods argument on the grounds that "procurement of some of the products but not others cannot be ruled out, so that it must not necessarily be assumed that there is an autonomous market for entire systems"; para.14); Case IV/M.913 *Siemens / Elektrowatt* [1999] O.J. L88/1 (some customers preferred to purchase all of their security technology from the same manufacturer but the Commission assumed that there were separate markets for different categories of equipment because other customers attached importance to buying from several suppliers: para.21); Case IV/M.1383 *Exxon / Mobil* [2004] O.J. L103/1 (single market for retail sales of motor fuels even though there was no demand-side substitutability between petrol and diesel; the Commission relied on supply-side substitutability, the fact that at the distribution level, both products were always available at the same point of sale, and the fact that market shares for each type of fuel would roughly coincide with the aggregate market share; para.436); Case IV/M.1439 *Telia / Telenor* [2001] O.J. L40/1 (the Commission treated call origination (i.e. outgoing telephone calls) and call termination (i.e. incoming telephone calls) as part of a single market because it was difficult to unbundle the costs of the two services from a single bill; and, whilst a customer could in theory have two lines, one for call origination and one for call termination, it would be unlikely to be cost efficient because of the need to pay two line-rental charges; paras 86 and 87); Case COMP/M.1628 *TotalFina / Elf* [2001] O.J. L143/1 (fuel retailing considered as a single market; para.157); Case COMP/M.1632 *Reckitt + Colman / Benckiser* (the Commission found, at para.10, that the granting by suppliers of group rebates was not sufficient to constitute a cluster market because the products in question were selected individually on their merits and not as part of a "portfolio"); Case COMP/M.1741 *MCI WorldCom / Sprint*, paras 85 and 86; and Case COMP/M.1838 *BT / Esat* (market for the distribution in Ireland of pan-European or global end-to-end network services, including managed data networks, frame relay services and voice virtual private networks including call centre services; para.17).

[29] Case IV/M.727, para.32. See also Case COMP/M.1891 *BP Amoco / Castrol*, para.11.

[30] Case IV/M.818, para.17.

[31] Case IV/M.1578 [2000] O.J. L294/1, paras 19 to 29.

sanitary ware (including WCs, WC cisterns, washbasins and bidets made out of ceramics) because final customers commonly required whole ranges (for new construction and refurbishment) and distributors and wholesalers therefore typically demanded a full range of each producer's product portfolio.

(d) In *KNP / Bührmann-Tetterode / VRG*[32] the Commission noted that manufacturers and distributors both supplied a complete range of printing press equipment and found that the market should not be broken down by type of machine, in part because "the activity of the parties consists in the provision of a service (distribution and serving of printing presses) rather than in the manufacture of goods". The implication, clearly, is that a different approach might be appropriate in a merger between manufacturers.

(e) In *Hoffmann-La Roche / Boehringer Mannheim*[33] the Commission found that there was a single market for classical clinical chemistry reagents, even though they were not substitutable from a demand-side perspective, because they had common characteristics, customers regularly bought almost all their requirements from one source and, on the supply-side, all major suppliers offered the same range.

(f) In retailing markets it is common to identify a market for the provision of a basket or range of goods. In *Kesko / Tuko*[34] the Commission identified a market for a "one-stop shopping" service for the provision of a basket of daily consumer goods in a supermarket environment. In *Buhrmann / Samas Office Supplies*[35] the Commission found that the market was the provision of office supplies to customers employing a large number of office workers. Similarly, in *Blokker / Toys 'R' Us (II)*[36] the Commission examined the market for retail outlets which sold a broad assortment of toys throughout the year. The Commission has also found stockholding of steel products to be a single market.[37] Finally, the US Supreme Court has defined a market to include a *cluster* of banking services, including current and savings accounts, loans and related banking services.[38]

---

[32] Case IV/M.291 [1993] O.J. L217/35, para.12.
[33] Case IV/M.950 [1998] O.J. L234/14, para.36 (compare the discussion of immunochemistry reagents at para.39).
[34] Case IV/M.784 [1997] O.J. L110/53.
[35] Case COMP/M.2286, para.18. See also Case COMP/M.3108 *Office Depot / Guilbert*, n.4.
[36] Case IV/M.890 [1998] O.J. L316/1, para.28.
[37] Case IV/M.73 *Usinor / ASD* and Case IV/M.239 *Avesta / British Steel / NCC*.
[38] *United States v Philadelphia National Bank* 374 U.S. 321, 356–357, 83 S.Ct. 1715, 10 L.Ed.2d 915 (1963).

(i) One-way markets

3–048 If both merging parties supply product A but do not supply product B, then the fact that customers using product B can readily switch to product A does *not* result in both products being included in the market if customers using product A cannot readily switch to product B.[39] However, if the merging parties both supply product B, then the relevant market is the supply of products A and B if a hypothetical monopolist in the supply of product B seeking to apply a SSNIP would be defeated by switching to product A. In *Crown Cork & Seal / Carnaud Metalbox*[40] the Commission found that there was one-way substitution from aluminium to tinplate cans but, since both parties supplied tinplate cans and not aluminium cans and there was no evidence of substitution from tinplate to aluminium, the relevant product market was the provision of tinplate cans. Further, in *Mitsui / CVRD / Caemi*[41] the Commission indicated that in cases of one-way substitution it may be necessary to consider two markets: a separate market for product A if customers of product A cannot readily switch to product B and a combined market for products A and B, if customers of product B can readily switch to product A. Finally, in *Group 4 Falck / Securicor*[42] the Commission found that suppliers of service X could readily commence the supply of service Y, although suppliers of service Y could not readily commence supply of service X. The Commission identified a market comprising X and Y since the merger involved the supply of service Y (and not service X), although the Commission stated that a different market definition might be appropriate in a merger affecting the supply of service X.

---

[39] See para.3–002(c) above and Areeda, Hovenkamp & Solow, *Antitrust Law* (2nd edn, Aspen Law & Business, 2000), Vol.IIA, para.535f.

[40] Case IV/M.603 [1996] O.J. L75/38, paras 21 to 26. See also Case IV/M.950 *Hoffmann-La Roche / Boehringer Mannheim* [1998] O.J. L234/14, para.41; Case IV/M.1383 *Exxon / Mobil*, [2004] O.J. L103/1 (noting the one-way substitution and defining separate product markets; paras 794 and 795); Case IV/M.1621 *Pakhoed / Van Ommeren (II)* (a distinction was drawn between tanks for speciality chemicals which could be used to store speciality or easy chemicals and tanks for easy chemicals which could not be used to store speciality chemicals; there was one-way substitutability between speciality and easy chemical tanks; the Commission found that there was a single market because chemical terminals were usually equipped for both types of chemicals but took the difference into account in its market appraisal; see para.10); Case COMP/M.2547 *Bayer / Aventis Crop Science* [2004] O.J. L107/1 (one-way substitution from foliar and soil applications of fungicides and insecticides to seed treatment); Case COMP/M.2597 *Vopak / Van der Sluijs* (the merging parties both supplied product A and not product B; customers using product A could switch to product B subject to substantial costs; but customers using product B could not switch to product A; the Commission found that product A formed a separate market; although the Commission emphasised, at para.14, that "Substitutability is only possible one way", this is not a reason for adopting a narrow market definition when consumers affected by the merger have the choice of substituting; the case is therefore best regarded as one in which the high costs of switching from product A to product B meant that product B should be excluded from the market); and Case COMP/M.3431 *Sonoco / Ahlstrom* [2005] O.J. L159/13, paras 26 and 27.

[41] Case COMP/M.2420 [2004] O.J. L92/50, para.210.

[42] Case COMP/M.3396, para.16 and n.1.

(j) Outsourcers or resellers who sub-contract to actual suppliers

In some markets actual suppliers of goods or services compete against **3–049** outsourcers or resellers, which compete to win business at a retail level but then sub-contract delivery of goods or services to an actual supplier. In principle, outsourcers do not form part of the market for the supply of the goods or services in question at a retail level if they lack an assured long-term source of supply and could not readily commence self supply. This is because a hypothetical monopoly supplier of the actual goods or services could increase price, notwithstanding the presence of outsourcers, by simply refusing to supply the outsourcers or supplying them at an increased price.[43]

(a) In *WorldCom / MCI*[44] the Commission stated that: "If the top-level networks increased the price of their Internet connectivity services by, say, 5 per cent, then in principle the cost base of resellers would be increased by the same amount, and that increase would have to be passed on to the customer. Therefore the pure resellers cannot provide a competitive constraint on the prices charged by the top level network".[45]

(b) Similarly, in *Deutsche Post / ASG*,[46] DHL, a subsidiary of one of the merging parties, Deutsche Post, acted as subcontractor in a market for ASG, the other merging party. The Commission found: "Although ASG offers express delivery services to its customers, it doesn't have its own dedicated network for these services and is therefore unable, alone, to provide effective constraints to the competitive behaviour of other service providers. Thus, the acquisition of ASG will not remove an active and viable competitor to DHL from the market".[47]

---

[43] There may be separate markets for:

(a) the provision of outsourced services: see, e.g. Case IV/M.126 *Accor / Wagons-Lits* [1992] O.J. L204/1; Case COMP/M.1972 *Granada / Compass*, para.9; Case COMP/M.2373 *Compass / Selecta*, paras 11 and 12; and Case COMP/M.2466 *Sodexho / Abela (II)*, para.10; and

(b) the provision of prime contracting services as opposed to sub-contracting services: see, e.g. Case IV/M.580 *ABB / Daimler Benz* [1997] O.J. L11/1 (noting the distinction between an ability to provide components and an ability to participate in the market for the supply of a product as a system, and concluding that an ability to provide components could not be regarded as participation in the market for rail vehicles; paras 19 and 70) and Case COMP/M.2095 *Sextant / Diehl* (the merger of a prime contractor and a sub-contractor did not raise any horizontal concerns as the sub-contractor lacked sufficient expertise to act as prime contractor; para.27).

[44] Case IV/M.1069 [1999] O.J. L116/1, para.67. See also paras 69, 70, 75 and 76.

[45] The Commission reached a similar conclusion in Case COMP/M.1741 *MCI WorldCom / Sprint* [2003] O.J. L300/1, para.102.

[46] Case IV/M.1549.

[47] Para.24. See also Case IV/M.1585 *DFDS / FLS Industries / Dan Transport* and Case COMP/M.3216 *Oracle / PeopleSoft*, [2005] O.J. L218/6, para.102.

(c) By contrast, in *Vopak / Van der Sluijs*[48] the issue was whether broker services formed part of an overall market for shipping by inland mineral oil tanker. The Commission found that the brokers entered contracts with customers and were responsible for arranging transport (which they did using ships which were owned by the broker or leased on the basis of one to five year contracts or in the spot market). The Commission concluded that brokering services formed part of an overall shipping market, because customers were indifferent to the ultimate ownership of the barges. The decision appears to be explicable on the basis that the brokers had capacity in place (through ownership and leases) in advance of negotiating contracts and, therefore, an attempt by a hypothetical ship-owners' monopoly profitably to increase the price of transport services would have been defeated by the brokers.

(d) In *Vodafone / Singlepoint*[49] the Commission considered the distinction between suppliers of mobile communication services which operated their own networks and independent cellular service providers (known as ISPs) which resold airtime services that they purchased from operators of networks. It found that there was a separate market for "wholesale access" because the ISPs would not have been able to defeat an attempt by a hypothetical monopoly supplier of wholesale access to impose a SSNIP since the barriers to entry at a network level were very high. However, the Commission also analysed an overall retail market in which ISPs competed against owners of networks. This finding can be reconciled with the principles described above on the assumption that the ISPs had capacity in place (through existing agreements) that would have enabled them to defeat a SSNIP at a retail level by the owners of the networks.

(k) Durable goods

3–050 Durable goods are goods which last over several periods.[50] In principle, second hand goods[51] should be included in markets for durable goods if they

---

[48] Case COMP/M.2597, paras 11 and 12.
[49] Case COMP/M.3245, para.10.
[50] When a company sells a durable good, its pricing decisions may be affected by:

  (a) the scope for customers to defer new purchases by extending the use of their existing goods, e.g. a supplier of a new version of a computer programme has to take account of the fact that, subject to their licence terms, existing customers are free to continue to use their existing versions; equally, the owner of a piece of machinery may be able to extend its useful life by increasing its spending on maintenance and repair; and
  (b) the scope for customers to purchase a second hand good rather than a new durable good, e.g. a purchaser of a new car always has the option of purchasing a nearly new one with very similar product characteristics.

[51] See the discussion in ABA Section of Antitrust Law, *Market Power Handbook* (ABA Publishing, 2005), pp.108 and 109.

would defeat a SSNIP imposed by a hypothetical monopoly supplier of new goods.[52] This is recognised by the US Horizontal Merger Guidelines which provide that second hand or reconditioned goods may be included in the market if they satisfy the SSNIP test.[53]

(1) Recycled goods

In determining whether recycled goods form part of the product market, the **3–051** issue is whether a supplier of original goods holding a hypothetical monopoly would be able profitably to increase price by 5 to 10 per cent in the face of competition from recycled goods.[54] The US Horizontal Merger Guidelines recognise that recycled goods may be included in the product market if

---

[52] See Case IV/M.53 *Aerospatiale / Alenia / de Havilland* [1991] O.J. L334/42, para.50; Case IV/ M.877 *Boeing / McDonnell Douglas* [1997] O.J. L336/16, paras 17 to 19 and 47; Case IV/ M.1379 *Valmet / Rauma* (leaving open the question of whether new and second hand pulp driers, grinders and refiners formed part of the same market; para.7); Case IV/M.1448 *MAN Roland / Omnigraph (II)* (leaving open the question of whether new and second hand printing presses formed part of the same market; paras 8 and 9); Case COMP/M.1709 *Preussag / Babcock / Celsius* (leaving open the question of whether the supply of new submarines, used submarines and mid-life conversions could be combined into a single market; the parties argued for a wider market noting that new and used submarines were functionally substitutable and relying on evidence of bids where both new and used submarines had been offered; the Commission noted, however, that new and used submarines differed in terms of price, performance and duration and new submarines were sold by manufacturers whereas used submarines were sold by Governments; see paras 30 to 34); Case COMP/M.1980 *Volvo / Renault VI* (where the Commission noted that sales in Portugal of second hand trucks produced by high quality manufacturers exceeded sales of new trucks produced by those suppliers and seemed to take this into account in determining that the transaction did not raise competition concerns in Portugal; para.38); and Case COMP/M.2033 *Metso / Svedala* [2004] O.J. L88/1 (concluding that there were separate markets for new and used rock crushers because competitors did not consider that used crushers acted as a competitive constraint on sales of new crushers; used equipment in a satisfactory condition was scarce; few customers had recently purchased used crushers; customers were risk averse; and customers who said that they were willing to purchase used equipment were only willing to do so for relatively new equipment and used machines in the market were usually old and outdated; paras 69 to 73). The issue was raised in Case IV/M.1571 *New Holland / Case* but the transaction was approved on conventional grounds: see Lexecon Competition Memo, "Mergers with Durable Goods", February 7, 2000 (*www.lexecon.co.uk/assets/mergers_durable_goods.pdf*). See also Carlton & Perloff, *Modern Industrial Organization* (4th edn, Addison-Wesley, 2005), pp.508 and 509.

[53] The US Horizontal Merger Guidelines, 1992 (amended in 1997) (*www.usdoj.gov/atr/public/ guidelines/hmg.htm*), para.1.31. Compare Scheffman, Coate & Silva, "20 Years of Merger Guidelines Enforcement at the FTC: An Economic Perspective" (available at *www.usdoj.gov/ atr/hmerger/11255.htm*) (used products had not, as at the date of the article, been included in an antitrust market defined using the principles set out in the US Agencies' Horizontal Merger Guidelines).

[54] See the analysis in Case IV/M.619 *Gencor / Lonrho* [1997] O.J. L11/30, paras 91 to 95 (findings upheld on appeal in Case T-102/96 *Gencor Ltd v Commission* [1999] E.C.R. II-753 paras 254 to 263); Case IV/M.754 *Anglo American Corporation / Lonrho* [1998] O.J. L/149, p.21, paras 104 and 116; Case IV/M.1225 *Enso / Stora* [1999] O.J. L254/9; Case IV/M.1356 *Metsä-Serla / UK Paper* (confirming that pulp made from wood and pulp made from waste paper / recycled fibres formed part of a single market; para.11); and Case COMP/M.2314 *BASF / Eurodiol / Pantochim* [2002] O.J. L132/45, para.105.

their sale would be a competitive constraint on the activities of a hypothetical monopolist.[55]

(m) New markets

3–052 The Commission has in several cases identified markets for products or services which have yet to be supplied on the grounds that there is a clear customer demand for the product and a reasonable likelihood of the product becoming available in the reasonably foreseeable future.[56] For example, in *Vodafone Airtouch / Mannesmann*[57] the Commission found that there was a distinct market for the provision of advanced seamless pan-European mobile telecommunication services (even though no such services were being supplied) on the grounds that a number of mobile operators had been approached by corporations for the provision of such services and the Commission's investigation had confirmed that certain customers would prefer such services to a patchwork of national services.[58] Similarly, in *Allied Signal / Honeywell*[59] the Commission found that a future market existed because one of the merging parties had announced its intention to develop a product and the Commission's market investigation had established that there would be a clear demand for it.

(n) Innovation markets

3–053 When merger control authorities are concerned that a merger may reduce the parties' incentives to innovate,[60] potentially depriving consumers of the benefits of new or improved products, they may define markets for

---

[55] The US Horizontal Merger Guidelines, 1992 (amended in 1997) (*www.usdoj.gov/atr/public/ guidelines/hmg.htm*), para.1.31.

[56] A distinction may be drawn between competition in current goods, future goods (i.e. new markets) and pure research. The Commission has identified numerous "emerging" markets including portals (Case COMP/JV.48 *Vodafone / Vivendi / Canal+*), on-line music (Case COMP/M.2050 *Vivendi / Canal+ / Seagram*, paras 15 and 26 to 32; see also Case COMP/ M.1845 *AOL / Time Warner* [2001] O.J. L268/28, para.26), interactive video networks (Case COMP/M.2048 *Alcatel / Thomson Multimedia / JV*, para.16), one-stop integrated supply of broadband content via the internet (Case COMP/M.1845 *AOL / Time Warner* [2001] O.J. L268/28, para.35), bottled water in Norway (Case IV/M.582 *Orkla / Volvo* [1996] O.J. L66/17, para.39), internet book sales in Spain (Case IV/JV.24 *Bertelsmann / Planeta / BOL Spain*, para.26), and the collection of used catalytic converters, the outfitting / pounding of those converters and the extraction of precious metals from catalysts (Case IV/M.615 *Rhone-Poulenc / Engelhard*, para.25).

[57] Case COMP/M.1795.

[58] Para.21. See also Case COMP/M.2016 *France Telecom / Orange*, para.14 and Case COMP/ JV.37 *BSkyB / KirchPayTV*, para.30.

[59] Case COMP/M.1601 [2001] O.J. L152/1, paras 57 and 58.

[60] See generally Davis, "Innovation Markets and Merger Enforcement: Current Practice in Perspective" (2003) 71 *Antitrust Law Journal* 677 and ABA Section of Antitrust Law, *Market Power Handbook* (ABA Publishing, 2005), pp.113 and 114. The substantive concerns arising from a loss of innovation competition are discussed in para 7–014 below.

innovation.[61] In some respects, this is an artificial exercise,[62] because the real concern is the potential reduction in competition in the market for the new or improved product. Nevertheless, the Commission routinely examines loss of innovation competition[63] in pharmaceutical mergers,[64] basing the market definition in such cases on existing ATC classes or being guided primarily by the characteristics of future products and the indications to which they are to be applied.[65]

(o) Technology

The Commission has in numerous cases identified separate antitrust markets **3–054** for the licensing of technology.[66] In *CVC / Lenzing*[67] the Commission found

---

[61] See Gilbert & Sunshine, "Incorporating Dynamic Efficiency Concerns in Merger Analysis: The Use of Innovation Markets" (1995) 63 *Antitrust Law Journal* 569 and the 1995 US Department of Justice and Federal Trade Commission "Antitrust Guidelines for the Licensing of Intellectual Property", 1995 (*www.usdoj.gov/atr/public/guidelines/0558.htm#t323*), s.3.2.3, which states that, "An innovation market consists of the research and development directed to particular new or improved goods or processes, and the close substitutes for that research and development".

[62] The argument against the use of innovation markets is that antitrust markets exist only if there is actual or potential scope for trade, and research and development is generally a function which is internal to the firm and therefore not aptly characterised as forming part of a "market": see Rapp, "The Misapplication of the Innovation Market Approach to Merger Analysis" (1995) 64 *Antitrust Law Journal* 19.

[63] Rapp, "Innovation Market Analysis—Lessons from the *Genzyme-Novazyme* Acquisition", NERA, Antitrust Insights, January/February 2004, states that the US authorities have applied innovation market analysis to the pharmaceutical industry, truck and bus transmissions, retail anti-theft devices, chemical or crop protection, defence contracting, software and large-scale storage vessels.

[64] See, e.g. Case IV/M.737 *Ciba-Geigy / Sandoz* [1997] O.J. L201/1 (identifying concerns about a future market but concluding that it could not ultimately be said with sufficient probability that the merger would on any future market lead to the creation or strengthening of a dominant position; paras 101 to 106) and Case COMP/M.1846 *Glaxo Wellcome / SmithKline Beecham* (paras 70 to 72, 175 to 178, 194, 195 and 222). In *Glaxo Wellcome* the Commission noted, at para.70, that, in the pharmaceuticals market, research and development projects pass through three phases of clinical testing. Phase I marks the start of clinical testing on humans and occurs eight to ten years before the product is marketed; Phase I projects have no more than a 10% chance of success. Phase II involves working out the proper dose for the patient and defining areas of application and occurs four to five years before marketing; Phase II projects have around a 30% chance of success. Phase III involves establishing a product's effectiveness on larger groups of patients and starts three years before marketing; Phase III projects have around a 50% chance of success.

[65] Case COMP/M.1846 *Glaxo Wellcome / SmithKline Beecham*, para.72. The geographic market for future pharmaceutical products tends to be at least the EC and possibly global because such products have normally not been registered and are therefore not subject to national regulatory systems: see para.75.

[66] See, e.g. Case IV/M.269 *Shell / Montecatini* [1994] O.J. L332/48, para.44; Case IV/M.550 *Union Carbide / Enichem*, para.36; Case IV/M.1007 *Shell / Montell*, para.7; Case IV/M.1671 *Dow Chemical / Union Carbide* [2001] O.J. L245/1 (identifying several markets for polyethylene technology; paras 69 to 95); Case COMP/M.1751 *Shell / BASF / JV—Project Nicole*, para.15; Case COMP/M.2187 *CVC / Lenzing* [2004] O.J. L82/20, para.124; Case COMP/M.2128 *ABB Lummus / Engelhard / Equistar / Novolen* (polypropylene technology package licensing; para.10); Case COMP/M.2297 *BP Chemicals / Solvay-PP* (licensing of polypropylene process technology; para.14); Case COMP/M.2299 *BP Chemicals / Solvay / HDPE JV* (licensing of polyethylene technology; para.16); Case COMP/M.2345 *Deutsche BP / Erdölchemie* (acrylonitrile technology licensing; para.12); Case COMP/M.2396 *Industri Kapital / Perstorp (II)*, paras 33 and 34. See also the Commission Guidelines on Horizontal Cooperation Agreements [2001] O.J. C3/2.

[67] Case COMP/M.2187.

such a market because: certain licences had already been granted; a second type of technology had yet to enter commercial production, with the consequence that competition could take place only at the level of production and processing technology; and there was clear demand for licences of the new technology.

(p) Procurement markets

3–055 When assessing the merged group's buyer power (see Ch.10), it will be necessary to define a relevant market for the *purchase* of goods.[68] In principle, the SSNIP test is applied in the same way as in markets for the *supply* of goods, except that the question is whether a hypothetical monopoly *purchaser* would be able profitably to *reduce* the price paid for the purchase of goods by 5 or 10 per cent.[69]

(q) Exploration, production and supply

3–056 In *BP Amoco / Arco*[70] the Commission left open the question of whether there was a market for exploration of crude oil and natural gas separate from their development and production. Similarly, in *De Beers / LVMH*[71] the Commission left open the question of whether there was a market for the exploration and production of rough diamonds separate from their supply. The argument that exploration constitutes a separate economic activity is that clients procure exploration services, in particular through the granting of concessions by host countries and the sale by the company carrying out the exploration of rights to develop and produce resources.[72]

(r) Spot and long-term contracts

3–057 In *Alcoa / Reynolds*[73] one issue was whether spot contracts for smelter-grade alumina formed part of the same antitrust market as medium term contracts

---

[68] See, e.g. Case COMP/M.2876 *NewsCorp / Telepiù* [2004] O.J. L110/73 (purchase of audio-visual TV content; paras 49 to 77); Case COMP/M.3579 *WPP / Grey*, para.36 (purchase of advertising time or space); Case COMP/M.3605 *Sovion / HMG* (appeal pending in Case T-151/05 *Nederlandse Vakbond Varkenshouders v Commission*), para.12 (purchasing of live pigs and sows for slaughtering); Case COMP/M.3935 *Jefferson Smurfit / Kappa* (purchasing of recovered paper); and the cases discussed in Ch.10 below.

[69] Peter Carstensen, "Buyer Power and Merger Analysis—The Need for Different Metrics" (*www.ftc.gov/bc/mergerenforce/presentations/040217carstensen.pdf*) argues that procurement markets are particularly prone to price discrimination, which may necessitate the use of narrow market definitions (see para.3–018 above).

[70] Case IV/M.1532 [2001] O.J. L18/1, paras 13 to 15. See also Case IV/M.1383 *Exxon / Mobil* [2004] O.J. L103/1, paras 15 to 39.

[71] Case COMP/M.2333 [2003] O.J. L29/40, para.16.

[72] The counter-argument is that exploration is too closely intertwined with production and supply to be considered meaningfully as a separate economic activity.

[73] Case COMP/M.1693 [2002] O.J. L58/25, paras 14 to 17. See also Case COMP/M.2413 *BHP / Billiton*, para.40 (market including both spot sales and sales pursuant to long-term contracts).

(typically of two to five years) and long-term contracts (typically of five to ten years but which could run for up to 20 years). The Commission found that all three categories of contract formed part of a single market, in particular because prices in long-term contracts were normally tied to spot prices.

(s) Physical and paper trading

In *Archer Daniels Midland Company / Alfred C. Toepfer International* **3–058** *GmbH*[74] both parties were active in paper trading of agricultural commodities and also sold physical quantities of oil. The Commission calculated the market share figures based on the volume physically delivered to third parties, *excluding* paper trade.

(t) Wholesale markets

Suppliers of a product, X, which is an essential input into a downstream **3–059** product, Y, may not be able profitably to raise the price of the input, X, if the downstream product's competitors include a product, Z, which does not use the input, X.[75] This is because any attempt to raise the price of X may be rendered unprofitable if sales of Y (and therefore demand for X) fall as a result.

(u) Use of demand- and supply-side analysis

It may be possible to define a market using demand- *and* supply-side ana- **3–060** lysis. If A and B are demand-side substitutes and B and C are supply-side substitutes, A, B and C may be part of a single market.[76] Further, it is possible in principle to imagine situations in which there is both demand- and supply-side substitution and, whilst neither effect, taken in isolation, is sufficient to defeat a SSNIP, taken together they would; in this situation the hypothetical monopolist's price increase would fail (i.e. it would be unprofitable) and a wider market definition is required.

---

[74] Case COMP/M.2693, para.13.
[75] See the UK OFT's Guidelines on Market Definition, December 2004 (*www.oft.gov.uk/NR/ rdonlyres/972AF80C-2D74-4A63-84B3-27552727B89A/0/OFT403.pdf*), para.5.12.
[76] See the decision of the UK Competition Commission in *Icopal Holdings / Icopal*, Cm 5089, April 2001, paras 2.79 and 4.98.

(v) Programme and catalogue sales

3–061 In the defence sector, the Commission has distinguished programme and catalogue sales. Programme sales involve the design, development and production of new products meeting specifications of national defence ministries. By contrast, catalogue sales arise when customers buy existing products (which have generally been developed through earlier programmes).[77]

3.6 GEOGRAPHIC MARKET DEFINITION: INTRODUCTION

3–062 In principle,[78] the definition of a geographic market is identical to the definition of a product market, because the location of an item is simply one characteristic amongst many, and physically identical goods in different locations can be seen as different economic products. More specifically, the Commission has defined a relevant geographic market as follows[79]: "The relevant geographic market comprises the area in which the undertakings concerned are involved in the supply and demand of products or services, in which the conditions of competition are sufficiently homogeneous and which can be distinguished from neighbouring areas because the conditions of competition are appreciably different in those areas".

3.7 GEOGRAPHIC MARKET DEFINITION: DEMAND-SIDE SUBSTITUTION

(a) The SSNIP test

3–063 Demand-side substitution involves identifying areas within which suppliers are regarded by customers as substitutes.[80] This depends on the *choices open to customers*. The SSNIP test is applied to geographic market definition in

---

[77] See, e.g. Case COMP/M.1745 *EADS* and Case COMP/M.2079 *Raytheon / Thales / JV*, para.19.

[78] See Epstein & Rubinfeld, "Technical Report—Effects of Mergers Involving Differentiated Products", 2004, Report for DG Competition (available via *http://europa.eu.int/comm/competition/mergers/others/effects_mergers_involving_differentiated_products.pdf*), Ch.III and Dobson, Breen & Hurdle, "Geographic Market Definition: A Review of Theory and Method for Domestic and International Markets", Federal Trade Commission.

[79] The Notice on Market Definition, para.7.

[80] i.e. consumers who substitute on the demand side do so by purchasing at other locations.

the same way as product market definition.[81] Essentially, the starting point is to take a narrow hypothetical geographic market and consider whether a monopoly supplier in that area could profitably raise prices. If a price increase would not be profitable because too many customers would switch to suppliers outside the area in the short term,[82] then the hypothetical geographic market definition needs to be widened and the analysis repeated.[83]

Product and geographic markets ought to be determined simultaneously and not sequentially as both are interacting dimensions of a single market.[84]

(b) Evidence: introduction

The Notice on Market Definition and the Commission's previous decisions **3–064** indicate that a range of categories of evidence may be relevant in determining the geographic market on the demand side.

---

[81] The SSNIP test is widely used internationally: see n.32 to para.3–006 above. The US Horizontal Merger Guidelines of the National Association of Attorneys General, 1993 (available at *www.naag.org/issues/pdf/at-hmerger_guidelines.pdf*), adopt a different approach, at s.3.2: "Utilizing the locations from which supplies of the relevant products are obtained by members of the protected interest group, the geographic market will be defined as the area encompassing the product locations from which this group purchases seventy-five per cent of their supplies of the relevant period".

[82] The Notice on Market Definition, para.29.

[83] The Commission has described its approach as follows in the Notice on Market Definition, para.28: "The Commission's approach to geographic market definition might be summarized as follows: it will take a preliminary view of the scope of the geographic market on the basis of broad indications as to the distribution of market shares between the parties and their competitors, as well as a preliminary analysis of pricing and price differences at national and Community or EEA level. This initial view is used basically as a working hypothesis to focus the Commission's enquiries for the purposes of arriving at a precise geographic market definition". For the application of this methodology, see, e.g. Case COMP/M.3099 *Areva / Urenco / ETC JV*, para.75. Copenhagen Economics, *The internal market and the relevant geographical market*, Report prepared for the European Commission (available at *http:// Europa.Eu.Int/Comm/Enterprise/Library/Lib-Competition/Doc/Marketdef_Final_Report.Pdf*), identified, at p.60, the following factors as most influential in geographic market definition: regulatory barriers, transport costs, distribution costs and national preferences. At p.61, the survey found that the types of evidence most frequently relied on were trade flow data and simple price comparisons, and that relatively more advanced techniques, such as estimations of price correlations and price elasticities, were used very rarely.

[84] The US Horizontal Merger Guidelines, 1992 (amended in 1997) (*www.usdoj.gov/atr/public/ guidelines/hmg.htm*), recognise, at n.8, that "product market definition and geographic market definition are inter-related. In particular, the extent to which buyers of a particular product would shift to other products in the event of a 'small but significant and nontransitory' increase in price must be evaluated in the context of the relevant geographic market". See also the UK OFT's Guidelines on Market Definition, December 2004 (*www.oft.gov.uk/NR/rdon lyres/972AF80C-2D74-4A63-84B3-27552727B89A/0/OFT403.pdf*), para.2.9 and the UK OFT's Substantive Merger Guidelines, May 2003 (*www.oft.gov.uk*), which state, at para.3.16: "The product and geographic dimensions of a market are often inter-linked. For example, an airline route has a geographic dimension".

(c) Pricing

3–065 **(i) Commission questionnaires** In determining geographic markets, the Commission relies heavily on the responses of customers to questionnaires, sent by the case team, asking whether customers would switch to suppliers located in different geographic areas if prices in a specified area were to rise permanently by 5 to 10 per cent.[85]

3–066 **(ii) Price correlation studies** Price correlation studies[86] were described above at paras 3–014 and 3–015 above in relation to product market definition. The same principles apply to geographic market definition: if the prices of the goods in the two areas[87] tend to track one another for reasons not related to common factors,[88] this suggests that they may form part of the same geographic market since it is possible that pricing decisions in one area are constrained by prevailing prices in the other.[89] For example,[90] in

---

[85] For discussion of the use of customer questionnaires, see para.2–047 above.

[86] See generally Copenhagen Economics, *The internal market and the relevant geographical market*, Report prepared for the European Commission (available at *http://Europa.Eu.Int/ Comm/Enterprise/Library/Lib-Competition/Doc/Marketdef_Final_Report.Pdf*), Ch.4 (advocating the greater use of price correlation or co-integration techniques when defining geographic markets) and Epstein & Rubinfeld, "Technical Report—Effects of Mergers Involving Differentiated Products", 2004, Report for DG Competition (available via *http://europa. eu.int/comm/competition/mergers/others/effects_mergers_involving_differentiated_products.pdf*), pp.37 and 38.

[87] Price correlation analysis is usually used to compare prices in two different areas. However, if there are several areas, A, B, C and D, that together exercise an effective competitive constraint on prices in area E, then measuring correlations between any pair of areas (e.g. A and E) is likely to give a low correlation and may falsely suggest that A comprises a separate geographic market; see Epstein & Rubinfeld, "Technical Report—Effects of Mergers Involving Differentiated Products", 2004, Report for DG Competition (available via *http://europa. eu.int/comm/competition/mergers/others/effects_mergers_involving_differentiated_products.pdf*), pp.37 and 38.

[88] Spurious correlations can arise from common factors not relating to competitive forces (e.g. if all producers face a significant change in input costs, this is likely to lead all of them to increase their prices, increasing the calculated correlation); see Copenhagen Economics, *The internal market and the relevant geographical market*, Report prepared for the European Commission (available at *http://Europa.Eu.Int/Comm/Enterprise/Library/Lib-Competition/ Doc/Marketdef_Final_Report.Pdf*), pp.80 and 81. For the use of Granger causality tests to overcome this, see Epstein & Rubinfeld, "Technical Report—Effects of Mergers Involving Differentiated Products", 2004, Report for DG Competition (available via *http://europa. eu.int/comm/competition/mergers/others/effects_mergers_involving_differentiated_products.pdf*), p.38.

[89] If the price series is non-stationary, price correlations will be unreliable and alternative techniques, such as cointegration analysis, must be adopted; see Copenhagen Economics, *The internal market and the relevant geographical market*, Report prepared for the European Commission (available at *http://Europa.Eu.Int/Comm/Enterprise/Library/Lib-Competition/ Doc/Marketdef_Final_Report.Pdf*), pp.75 and 80; see also Epstein & Rubinfeld, "Technical Report—Effects of Mergers Involving Differentiated Products", 2004, Report for DG Competition (available via *http://europa.eu.int/comm/competition/mergers/others/effects_ mergers_involving_differentiated_products.pdf*), pp.38 to 40.

[90] In Case IV/M.1313 *Danish Crown / Vestjyske Slagterier* [2000] O.J. L20/1, the Commission considered, at para.84, whether the market for fresh pork sold through supermarkets was limited to Denmark. A price correlation study showed correlation coefficients for prices in

Mannesmann | Vallourec | Ilva[91] the Commission emphasised that, whilst the absence of price correlations between two areas was a strong indicator that those areas formed part of separate geographic markets, the existence of price correlations did not necessarily indicate that the areas formed part of the same market in the absence of other elements, such as mutual inter-penetration or similar structures of supply and demand in the different areas. In *Blackstone | Acetex*[92] the Commission disregarded correlation analysis on the grounds that there might be a spurious correlation caused by the presence of common factors.

There are technical difficulties which make it more difficult to carry out a price correlation analysis to determine the extent of a geographic market which may cross exchange rate regimes.[93]

(iii) Stationarity tests Stationarity tests were described above at para.3–016 **3–067** in relation to product market analysis.[94] The same principles apply to geographic market definition: if the ratio of the prices in two areas tends to be stationary over time, this suggests that the two areas form part of the same geographic area. One advantage of stationarity tests compared with price correlation studies is that they can be applied to prices in different currencies.[95]

(iv) Uniformity in prices If prices are uniform between two areas (after the **3–068** adjustments described below), this is *consistent with* the areas forming part

---

Denmark and various other states generally exceeding 0.9. However, the Commission rejected this evidence because: it related to sales by one of the parties and not the market as a whole; the correlations reflected, at least partly, changes in the prices of common input factors; and "Danish prices are to a certain extent automatically correlated with export prices due to the way the Danish slaughterhouses optimise their revenue stream. According to the parties, the sales department of a slaughterhouse will always sell a given quantity of meat wherever it will receive the best price". See also Case COMP/M.1628 *TotalFina | Elf* [2001] O.J. L143/1, para.164; Case COMP/M.2314 *BASF | Eurodiol | Pantochim* [2002] O.J. L132/45 (the Commission relied, at para.39, on the fact that prices in Eastern European countries tended to follow EEA prices as evidence that those territories formed part of a single market, including also the EEA); Case COMP/M.3268 *Sydkraft | Graninge* (the Commission noted that price correlation analysis suggested that the relevant geographic market was international but ultimately the issue was left open; para.27); and Case COMP/M.3440 *ENI | EDP | GDP* [2005] O.J. L302/69, para.92 (the Commission relied on low price correlations in finding narrower geographic markets) (prohibition upheld on appeal Case T-87/05 *EDP v Commission*, not yet reported, judgment of September 21, 2005).

[91] Case IV/M.315 [1994] O.J. L102/15.
[92] Case COMP/M.3625 [2005] O.J. L312/60, paras 35 and 77. The Commission did not identify any candidate "common factors". The parties responded on one of these two markets by providing cointegration and Granger causality analyses to seek to overcome the Commission's concerns (para.35; see also para.56).
[93] See Bishop & Walker, *The Economics of EC Competition Law* (2nd edn, Sweet & Maxwell, 2002), pp.400 to 402.
[94] See generally Copenhagen Economics, *The internal market and the relevant geographical market*, Report prepared for the European Commission (available at *http://Europa.Eu.Int/Comm/Enterprise/Library/Lib-Competition/Doc/Marketdef_Final_Report.Pdf*), Ch.4.
[95] Wills, "Market Definition: How Stationarity Can Improve Accuracy" [2002] E.C.L.R. 4, at p.5.

of the same geographic market. It is clearly not decisive as prices may be uniform by coincidence. Conversely, if prices are not uniform (after the adjustments described below), this is a strong indicator that the two areas are parts of separate geographic markets because prices (as adjusted) would be expected to converge if the two areas form part of the same geographic market.[96] The following points should be taken into account in comparing prices.[97]

(a) Prices should be compared *after allowing for transport costs and tariffs at a prevailing exchange rate.* For example, if product A is priced at 100 units in territory X and 50 units in territory Y and transports costs from Y to X are 50 units, there may be vigorous competition in territory X from suppliers in territory Y.[98] The Commission recognised the importance of allowing for transport costs in *Nestlé / Ralston Purina*[99] when it stated that "in the absence of significant transport costs accounting for these differentials/margins, significant price differences provide clear evidence on the cap-

---

[96] See, e.g. Case IV/M.623 *Kimberly-Clark / Scott* [1996] O.J. L183/1, paras 72 to 80; Case IV/M.950 *Hoffmann-La Roche / Boehringer Mannheim* [1998] O.J. L234/14, para.52; Case COMP/M.1628 *TotalFina / Elf* [2001] O.J. L143/1 ("Despite being partly justified by the higher costs ... this price difference would not be sustainable if motorway service stations were actually in competition with other service stations near the motorway. If the consumer had a genuine choice between the two alternative refuelling possibilities, prices would even out around a single market price that reflected supply both on and off motorways"; para.163); Case COMP/M.2033 *Metso / Svedala* [2004] O.J. L88/1, para.89; Case COMP/M.2621 *SEB / Moulinex* (emphasising that prices differed by national markets and followed different trends; para.27(e) (not challenged on this point on appeal in Case T-119/02 *Royal Philips Electronics NV v Commission* [2003] E.C.R. II-1433; see paras 89 to 91)); Case COMP/M.3083 *GE / Instrumentarium* [2004] O.J. L109/1, paras 82 and 92; Case COMP/M.3687 *Johnson & Johnson / Guidant*, para.68(c); and Case COMP/M.3732 *Procter & Gamble / Gillette*, para.17. In Case COMP/M.1672 *Volvo / Scania* [2001] O.J. L143/74, the Commission relied on the fact that price lists differed between countries as an indicator that there were national markets, on the grounds that this suggested that conditions of competition differed in different states (para.39). The Commission summarised the position as follows in Case COMP/M.2097 *SCA / Metsä Tissue*, at para.47: "If customers can buy at the same prices as customers located in other areas, such areas should be included in the geographic market definition. If, however, customers buying from suppliers located in other areas cannot necessarily buy at the same prices as the customers located in those areas, such areas should not necessarily be included in the geographic market definition. In other words, there can be situations where the fact that customers are being supplied from a plant in a certain area does not mean that those customers are getting the prevailing 'market' prices in that area. This could, for instance, be the case when the suppliers deliver the products to the premises of the customers. If arbitrage between customers is not possible, suppliers can then charge different prices to customers in different areas". In Case T-374/00 *Verband der freien Rohrwerke and others v Commission* [2003] E.C.R. II-2275, the Court of First Instance stated, at para.145, that price differences of 10 to 15% between Member States did not rule out the existence of a Community market. See also the decision of the UK Competition Commission in *Nutreco Holding NV / Hydro Seafood*, Cm 5004 December 2000, para.4.224.

[97] It is essential that the comparisons are between transactions with equivalent specifications and quantities: Case COMP/M.1882 *Pirelli / BICC* [2003] O.J. L70/35, para.42.

[98] For discussion of one-way markets, see para.3–086 below.

[99] Case COMP/M.2337, para.26.

ability of incumbent firms to apply different prices in different countries, depending on the local conditions of competition".[1]

(b) Wholesale prices are generally compared net of all discounts and rebates ("net net prices").[2]

(c) If prices fluctuate depending on raw material costs (e.g. copper in the case of cable), it may be appropriate to carry out the comparisons on a "hollow" basis, i.e. stripping out fluctuations in the raw material price.[3]

In *Lagardère / Natexis / VUP*[4] the Commission compared the *discounts* offered by Lagardère to dealers in different Member States and analysed[5] whether the level of discount differed depending on the Member State where the sale occurred, taking into account other variables affecting discounts, in particular quantities supplied and quality of service provided. When there was no "country effect", this suggested an international market; but the presence of a "country effect" suggested that there was a national market.

(v) Price discrimination If sellers can distinguish customers in different areas 3–069 *and* prevent resale between those customers, then the areas may comprise separate geographic markets, as a hypothetical monopoly supplier in one of the areas may be able profitably to impose a SSNIP. In *Volvo / Scania*[6] the Commission relied on evidence that Volvo and other suppliers of heavy trucks had applied significantly different prices and margins for comparable products in different Member States, as evidence that the geographic market was national. In *Mitsui / CVRD / Caemi*[7] certain areas of the world, including Western Europe, were dependent on imports of iron ore ("seaborne" customer areas), whilst the remainder of the world was able to rely on domestic production ("domestic" customer areas). The Commission considered carefully whether the relevant geographic market was Western Europe or wider, comprising all seaborne customer areas. As most seaborne suppliers sold in most seaborne customer areas, the Commission indicated that: "Narrower geographic markets can ... only exist if iron ore suppliers have the ability and incentives to discriminate between customer areas". It concluded that there was insufficient evidence of discrimination to justify

---

[1] In Case COMP/M.3149 *Procter & Gamble / Wella*, the Commission stated, at para.27: "Persistent price differences that are not due to transport costs are a strong indicator that hair care products in one Member State do not exercise a competitive constraint on hair products in other Member States". See also para.34.
[2] See, e.g. Case IV/M.430 *Procter & Gamble / VP Schickedanz (II)*, [1994] O.J. L354/32, para.79 and Case IV/M.1578 *Sanitec / Sphinx* [2000] O.J. L294/1, para.83.
[3] Case COMP/M.1882 *Pirelli / BICC* [2003] O.J. L70/35, n.16.
[4] Case COMP/M.2978 [2004] O.J. L125/54 (appeal pending in Case T-279/04 *Editions Odile Jacob SAS v Commission*), paras 353, 374 and 383.
[5] Using an econometric model.
[6] Case COMP/M.1672 [2001] O.J. L143/74, paras 35 to 49 and 91 to 93.
[7] Case COMP/M.2420 [2004] O.J. L92/50, paras 146 to 148, 158 and 159.

adopting the narrower market definition. Similarly, in *SCA / Metsä Tissue*[8] the Commission stated: "In a prospective analysis, as is carried out in investigations of concentrations, the possibility of future price discrimination by undertakings which through a concentration can achieve a very strong position among the suppliers that can supply to a certain area, may be a crucial factor in delineating the relevant geographic market to take into consideration. The extent of the geographic market may thus be affected by the existence of customers in a certain area, which could be subject to price discrimination by a firm controlling most of the supply into that area. This will usually be the case when two conditions are met: (a) it is possible to identify clearly which area an individual customer belongs to at the moment of selling the relevant products to him, and (b) trade among customers or arbitrage by third parties should not be feasible. Such arbitrage is particularly difficult where the product is sold on a delivered basis and where the transportation costs are a significant percentage of the final cost".

3–070 **(vi) Absolute price levels** The New Zealand Merger Guidelines[9] note that: "Generally, the higher the value of the product to be purchased, in absolute terms or relative to total buyer expenditure as appropriate, the more likely that buyers will travel and shop around for the best buy, and the wider the likely geographic extent of the market".[10]

(d) Trade flows and buying patterns

3–071 **(i) Evidence of market operation** In analysing trade flows[11] and buying patterns, it is important first to analyse the way in which the market operates.[12] In particular, if the market operates by customers visiting suppliers (e.g. physical shopping in retail outlets or contracts for delivery ex-works), then the relevant geographic market depends on customers' willingness to travel.[13] If the market operates by suppliers delivering to customers, then

---

[8] Case COMP/M.2097, paras 47 and 48. The Commission found that, since manufacturers delivered tissue products to customers' warehouses, a manufacturer controlling all supplies to one or more of the Nordic countries could target a price increase on customers in one country without affecting prices in other countries: see para.51.

[9] 2004 (*www.comcom.govt.nz/Publications/ContentFiles/Documents/MergersandAcquisitionsGuidelines.PDF*), para.3.3.

[10] See also the UK OFT's Guidelines on Market Definition, December 2004 (*www.oft.gov.uk/NR/rdonlyres/972AF80C-2D74-4A63-84B3-27552727B89A/0/OFT403.pdf*), para.4.3 (noting, in addition, the potential relevance of customer mobility).

[11] See the Notice on Market Definition, para.45.

[12] The UK OFT's Substantive Merger Guidelines, May 2003 (*www.oft.gov.uk*), para.3.16, state: "The more willing customers are to switch demand to firms located in a neighbouring area (or the more willing firms are to supply customers in neighbouring areas), the wider the geographic market is likely to be".

[13] This may be established by survey evidence of the locations from which a sample of customers visiting a particular store travelled or more general evidence about customers' willingness to travel (if customers are willing to drive for 30 minutes to visit a supermarket this can be plotted on a "drive-time" chart).

demand-side analysis is important only to establish whether customers are sensitive to the geographic source of supply (e.g. because of concerns about *delays in delivery* in the case of customers using *just-in-time* production techniques, cost of delivery if this is paid directly by customers, or *security of supply* if delivery is to occur over substantial distances or across frontiers)[14] and attention is focused on the supply-side issue of whether suppliers from particular areas are willing to incur the costs of delivery.

(ii) Trade flow data The absence of trade flows[15] between two areas[16] is **3–072** *consistent* with the areas forming parts of separate geographic markets but does not in itself *prove* this. For example, if the price in area A is £100 and in area B is £100 and transport costs between the two areas are £3 per unit then there may be no exports but an increase in price in area A to £105 might result in significant trade and the SSNIP test might therefore indicate that area A is not a separate geographic market.[17]

Conversely, the presence of trade flows between two areas is *consistent* with the two areas forming part of the same geographic market but does not prove this.[18] For example, if the price in area A is set at a monopoly level it may be profitable for suppliers in area B to ship to area A, but this is

---

[14] See, e.g. Case IV/M.358 *Pilkington-Techint / SIV* [1994] O.J. L158/24, para.23; Case COMP/ M.1630 *Air Liquide / BOC* [2004] O.J. L92/1, para.44; Case COMP/M.3178 *Bertelsmann / Springer / JV* (printing of magazines found to be time critical; para.63); and Case COMP/ M.3687 *Johnson & Johnson / Guidant*, para.68(d). The occasional blockades of the Channel Tunnel and French ports mean that some UK customers are concerned about relying on supplies from Continental Europe; see, e.g. Case IV/M.1109 *Owens-Illinois / BTR Packaging*, para.28. However, in Case COMP/M.2608 *INA / FAG* the Commission indicated, at para.20, that: "Even as regards just-in-time ('JIT') deliveries it is considered irrelevant whether the bearing suppliers' plants are in their proximity if suitable logistics can be put in place. JIT may therefore not be excluded by lack of proximity".

[15] See the Notice on Market Definition, paras 31 and 49 (noting that trade flow data is not conclusive and it is necessary in each case to look behind the data to identify the rationale for the trade flows). For a detailed analysis of the relationship between transport costs, trade flow data and geographic market definition, see Areeda, Hovenkamp & Solow, *Antitrust Law* (2nd edn, Aspen Law & Business, 2000), Vol.IIA, para.552.

[16] Trade flow data between the EU Member States may be available from EU customs data at *www.europa.eu.int/comm/eurostat*. Eurostat data was used, e.g. in Case IV/M.774 *Saint-Gobain / Wacker-Chemie / NOM* [1997] O.J. L247/1, para.99. Trade flow data may also be available from trade associations: see, e.g. Case COMP/M.2187 *CVC / Lenzing* [2004] O.J. L82/20, para.151.

[17] See also Areeda, Hovenkamp & Solow, *Antitrust Law* (2nd edn, Aspen Law & Business, 2000), Vol.IIA, para.534a.

[18] It is also necessary to consider whether the trade flows are explicable by price discrimination (see Kaserman & Zeisel, "Market Definition: Implementing the Department of Justice Merger Guidelines" [1996] *The Antitrust Bulletin* 665, at 670) and whether any existing trade flows will continue. For example, if the trade flows arise because of temporary overcapacity in the exporting market or short-term changes in currency exchange rates, they may not persist after the overcapacity is eliminated or the exchange rate changes. See also the Notice on Market Definition, paras 48 and 49.

evidence that the suppliers in area A hold market power and *not* that areas A and B comprise a single market.[19]

The real question is whether levels of imports are sensitive to domestic prices (or, more accurately, the ratio of domestic to foreign prices), i.e. whether they *increase* as domestic prices become relatively higher.[20] With adequate data, this can be measured through *import penetration tests*.[21] In measuring imports, the Commission *excludes* intra-company sales and sales between competitors and, when the products are differentiated, it prefers import data by value rather than volume.[22]

The Commission's approach is exemplified by the following cases.[23]

(a) In *Enso / Stora*[24] the Commission noted that imports of liquid packaging board into Western Europe were around 8 per cent, but found that the market was not wider than the EEA in part because of "the relatively low level of imports".

(b) In *UPM-Kymmene / Haindl*[25] the Commission found that the newsprint market was not wider than the EEA and Switzerland, in part because imports "accounted for only 9.3 per cent of the total EEA consumption".

(c) In *Shell / Montecatini*[26] the Commission emphasised that transport costs may be substantially affected by the availability of return loading of the vehicle (i.e. the possibility of back-hauling).

(d) In *Blackstone / Acetex*[27] the Commission relied on *fluctuations* in international trade flows as evidence of a global market, on the

---

[19] The UK OFT's Guidelines on Market Definition, December 2004 (*www.oft.gov.uk/NR/rdonlyres/972AF80C-2D74-4A63-84B3-27552727B89A/0/OFT403.pdf*), para.4.6, state that imports may not be evidence of an international market, in particular if the imports are from the international operations of domestic suppliers (and may therefore not comprise an independent constraint on domestic suppliers), if the international suppliers would need to make significant investments to increase the scale of their trade, or if there are quotas which limit imports.

[20] If imports are sensitive to relative prices and there are no quotas, this is strong evidence of a wider geographic market irrespective of actual levels of imports.

[21] OFT Research Paper "Quantitative Techniques in Competition Analysis", LECG, Ch.11 (note that the views in the paper do not necessarily represent those of the OFT).

[22] See Case IV/M.12 *Varta / Bosch* [1991] O.J. L320/26, para.43. The Commission's approach to calculations of import figures is analogous to its approach to calculating market shares: see Ch.4 below.

[23] See also Case COMP/M.3178 *Bertelsmann / Springer / JV*, para.62 (the fact that imports accounted for less than 4% of German demand was regarded by the Commission as a pointer towards a national market).

[24] Case IV/M.1225 [1999] O.J. L254/9, paras 54 and 59. However, the Commission found that board tended to be imported from North America for strategic reasons and also took account, in reaching its decision, of duties, transport costs, non-tariff barriers and evidence that the supply structure in North America differed from that in Europe.

[25] Case COMP/M.2498 [2002] O.J. L233/38, paras 25 and 30.

[26] Case IV/M.269 [1994] O.J. L332/48, para.47.

[27] Case COMP/M.3625 [2005] O.J. L312/60, paras 32, 33, 54 and 55.

grounds that the fluctuations showed that supplies moved easily across regions to satisfy changes in demand, regardless of location.

(iii) **Shipping distances** The Commission may examine the average distance 3–073 between the supplier and its customers and the radius within which a large proportion of customers is located. For example,[28] in *Sonoco / Ahlstrom*[29] the Commission identified the proportions of the parties' sales by volume to customers within particular radii and rejected the parties' argument that the relevant geographic market covered the EEA in part because the proportions of sales shipped more than 600 km was very small.

(iv) **Shock analysis or event studies** Shock analysis (or event studies), which 3–074 was described in para.3–022 above in relation to product market definition, is equally applicable to geographic market definition. For example, shock analysis may be carried out by examining changes in currency valuations,[30] e.g. by assessing the impact of the United Kingdom's exit from the ERM. In *Blackstone / Acetex*[31] the Commission examined the effect of unexpected plant outages (losses of production due to breakdowns or shortages of raw materials) on prices and trade flows; it found that unexpected outages in the EEA caused a surge in imports from North America, indicating that the geographic market included at least the EEA and North America.

At a qualitative level, falling short of "shock analysis", the process of market definition is assisted by evidence of actual switching by customers between suppliers from different areas (or credible threats to switch made during commercial negotiations).[32] The existence of such switching does not of itself show that the two areas are sufficiently close substitutes that a small increase in the price in one area would be unprofitable because customers would switch to the other; but a claim that such switching would occur is more credible if at least some customers have switched between suppliers in different areas.

(v) **Bidding studies** If customers invite bids from throughout an area and 3–075 suppliers do not bid differently depending on the locations of rival bidders, this suggests that the area in question comprises a relevant geographic market. For example, in *Oracle / PeopleSoft*[33] the Commission examined bidding behaviour to identify the locations of the suppliers which customers

---

[28] See also Case COMP/M.3314 *Air Liquide / Messer Targets*, para.37 (considering the average shipping distance and the radius within which 80% of customers were located).
[29] Case COMP/M.3431 [2005] O.J. L159/13, paras 58, 59 and 61 (see also para.74).
[30] See Case COMP/M.3099 *Areva / Urenco / ETC JV*, para.90 (depreciation of the dollar).
[31] Case COMP/M.3625 [2005] O.J. L312/60, paras 36 to 41 and 59 to 62.
[32] See the Notice on Market Definition, para.45.
[33] Case COMP/M.3216 [2005] O.J. L218/6, paras 175 and 176

invited to tender for particular projects and undertook an econometric analysis to investigate whether there was any difference in Oracle's bidding behaviour depending on the location of the competitor (as this might have revealed that competitors from certain areas were regarded as peripheral and not sufficiently close competitive constraints to be included in the relevant geographic market).

(e) Transport and other transaction costs

3–076 If *transport costs*[34] are high relative to the price of the product, this suggests that the geographic market is relatively small. This is not, however, decisive.[35] If the price[36] in area A is £50 and in area B is £100 and transport costs between the two areas are £50 per unit, then a small price increase in area B may result in substantial exports from area A.[37]

The importance of transport costs can be measured using *shipment and transport cost tests*.[38] The Elzinga-Hogarty test[39] suggests that a candidate area is a separate geographic market if it meets two criteria: first, the "little in from outside" criterion is satisfied if 1-(imports / consumption) is greater than 0.9; and secondly, the "little out from inside" criterion is satisfied if 1-(exports / production) is greater than 0.9. This is a very approximate measure[40] and in all cases it is necessary to analyse:

(a) why the trade patterns arise;

(b) whether shipments would occur if prices rose in the area in question; and

---

[34] See the Notice on Market Definition, paras 29 (switching must occur "at a negligible cost") and 50.

[35] See the Notice on Market Definition, para.50 ("The impact of transport costs will usually limit the scope of the geographic market for bulky, low-value products, bearing in mind that a transport disadvantage might also be compensated by a comparative advantage in other costs").

[36] If there is evidence of production costs in different locations and the costs of transportation between the two regions, it may be possible for the Commission to examine the incentives on producers in one area to export to a second if the price in the second were to increase.

[37] In this example, in the case of a merger between producers in area A, the geographic market is area A, and in the case of a merger between producers in area B, the geographic market is areas A and B. One example is fertilizers, where transport costs are high relative to the value of the good, but exports have occurred from Trinidad to the United Kingdom because the main input, natural gas, is effectively free in Trinidad: see the OFT Research Paper: "Market Definition in UK Competition Policy", NERA, 1992, p.53 (note that the views in the paper do not necessarily represent those of the OFT).

[38] Bishop & Walker, *The Economics of EC Competition Law* (2nd edn, Sweet & Maxwell, 2002), Ch.12.

[39] See para.3–077(e) below for the Commission's views on the Elzinga-Hogarty test.

[40] See the criticism in Areeda, Hovenkamp & Solow, *Antitrust Law* (2nd edn, Aspen Law & Business, 2000), Vol.IIA, para.550b3 and ABA Section of Antitrust Law, *Market Power Handbook* (ABA Publishing, 2005), pp.65 to 68.

(c) whether the reduction in demand in the area in question following a price increase would affect shipments from outside the area.

The Commission has analysed these issues in the following cases.[41]   **3–077**

(a) In *KNP / Bührmann-Tetterode / VRG*[42] the Commission examined market shares within "the area where transport costs represent between 5 and 10 per cent of the price of" the goods.

(b) In *Pirelli / BICC*[43] the Commission found that intra-Community transport costs[44] were "relatively low" at 3 to 7 per cent of production cost and concluded that local production capacity was not a prerequisite for successful market entry as transport costs "lie in the same range as in other industries with well-established European production systems".[45]

(c) In *Crown Cork & Seal / Carnaud Metalbox*[46] the Commission noted that the economically feasible distance for shipping food cans was less than 500 km, but that if the market price were to rise by 5 per cent, the maximum shipping range, based on transport costs alone, would have increased to between 700 km and 1,000 km.

(d) In *Solvay / Montedison-Ausimont*[47] transport costs were significant and accounted for up to 10 per cent of the delivered price for transportation of 1,000 km. However, the Commission found that the geographic market was the EEA because of the absence of trade barriers between Member States, the existence of common European standards and rules for transportation, and the fact that supply and

---

[41] See also, e.g. Case IV/M.623 *Kimberly-Clark / Scott* [1996] O.J. L183/1 (the Commission found, at paras 83 and 104, that transport costs of tissue products were high relative to the value of the goods and concluded that the United Kingdom and Ireland constituted a single separate geographic market); Case COMP/M.1813 *Industri Kapital (Nordkem) / Dyno* [2001] O.J. L154/41, para.57; Case COMP/M.1854 *Emerson Electric / Ericsson Energy Systems* (the Commission noted, at para.7, that transport costs within the EEA were "relatively low" at less than 3% of product value and relied on this in finding that the market was at least EEA-wide); and Case COMP/M.1671 *Dow Chemical / Union Carbide* [2001] O.J. L245/1 (the Commission considered, at para.46, that transport costs of 6 to 7% for a distance of 1,000 km were "relatively low" and took this, together with substantial trade flows, as an indicator that the market was western Europe).

[42] Case IV/M.291 [1993] O.J. L217/35, para.53.

[43] Case COMP/M.1882 [2003] O.J. L70/35.

[44] Data on "intra-Community transport costs" is meaningless because transport costs can be calculated only for transportation of a particular cargo between particular locations. For this reason, calculating transport costs over a specified distance (say, 1,000 km) is more meaningful, although even in this case, transport costs may vary significantly depending on the locations between which transport is occurring, with the consequence that attention should properly focus on the costs facing those suppliers whose presence in the market is being examined.

[45] Para.53. The Commission also found that a local presence was not necessary for "just in time" delivery or to provide maintenance or installation services (see para.54).

[46] Case IV/M.603 [1996] O.J. L75/38, para.42.

[47] Case COMP/M.2690, paras 72 and 73.

demand were organised on a pan-European basis. This demonstrates that transport costs are not decisive in defining a geographic market.

(e) In *Mannesmann / Vallourec / Ilva*[48] the Commission expressed scepticism about the Elzinga-Hogarty test, stating that "this test is widely regarded as questionable in particular because it does not give any indication with respect to mutual interpenetration between the different areas considered. Only if there is mutual interpenetration can purchasers arbitrage price differences by buying in other areas. In the present case, even though the 10 per cent export threshold is met, interpenetration is very low".

(f) In *Celanese / Degussa / European Oxo Chemicals*[49] the Commission stated: "Transport costs are not an argument for accepting narrower market definitions than the EEA market ... [The] parties' main competitors are at a 3 per cent to 6 per cent transport cost disadvantage. This narrow gap has no significant negative effect on foreign suppliers selling ... in Germany".

In *Blackstone / Acetex*[50] the Commission sought to analyse *all transaction costs* involved in inter-regional trade, including not only transport costs but also storage costs and duties. It also compared *production costs* in different regions to assess whether the gross margins were sufficient to allow trade flows between regions.

(f) Legal restrictions and capacity constraints

3–078 Legal restrictions and capacity constraints may prevent customers in one area from switching to a supplier in another area.[51] Legal restrictions include quotas, tariffs[52] and regulatory barriers, technical standards,[53] legal monopolies and requirements for administrative authorisations.[54] In *EDF / EnBW*[55] the Commission found that the market for electricity was national because of the lack of capacity of cross-border interconnectors.

---

[48] Case IV/M.315 [1994] O.J. L102/15, para.33. See also the Commission's XXIVth Annual Report on Competition Policy, 1994, para.292.
[49] Case COMP/M.3056 [2004] O.J. L38/47, para.89.
[50] Case COMP/M.3625 [2005] O.J. L312/60, paras 42 to 46, 63 to 67 and 78.
[51] Legal restrictions and capacity constraints are also relevant on the supply side when considering the scope for suppliers to commence supply to a particular area.
[52] See, e.g. Case COMP/M.1671 *Dow Chemical / Union Carbide* [2001] O.J. L245/1, para.47 and Case COMP/M.1751 *Shell / BASF / JV—Project Nicole*, para.27.
[53] See Case COMP/M.1672 *Volvo / Scania* [2001] O.J. L143/74, paras 56 and 57.
[54] See Case COMP/M.1932 *BASF / American Cyanamid (AHP)*.
[55] Case COMP/M.1853. See also Case COMP/M.1673 *VEBA / VIAG* [2001] O.J. L188/1.

(g) Customer requirements for local support services

The need to provide services to customers on a local basis may limit the **3–079** scope of the geographic market. In particular, in cases in which customers require after-sales services (such as the provision of maintenance, overhaul and spare parts) provided through a local presence, the geographic market may be narrower than would be suggested from the perspective purely of production[56]:

(a) in *Volvo / Scania*[57] a need for after-sales service on a local basis was one of the factors pointing towards a national (rather than an international) geographic market for the supply of heavy trucks;

(b) in *GE / Instrumentarium*[58] the Commission identified national markets in part because of the need for after-sales service, maintenance and training; it relied on the results of a survey asking customers to assess the significance of numerous different factors in selecting a product; and

(c) in *Gerling / NCM*[59] the Commission found that the market for credit insurance was national because personal contacts through a local presence were required during the customer acquisition phase and for policy handling.

(h) Conditions of competition

Conditions of competition are generally the same throughout a geographic **3–080** market. It is common for the *same suppliers to be active* throughout the same

---

[56] See also Case IV/M.950 *Hoffmann-La Roche / Boehringer Mannheim* [1998] O.J. L234/14 (need for rapid and reliable service through a local presence; para.51); Case IV/M.1286 *Johnson & Johnson / Depuy* (national market for reconstructive implants for hips and knees as customers required training and assistance which required national representation); Case COMP/M.1571 *New Holland / Case* (need for suppliers of agricultural products to have an effective distribution network because customers could not afford to wait in the event of a breakdown; para.29); Case COMP/M.2033 *Metso / Svedala* [2004] O.J. L88/1 (geographic market for rock crushing equipment was national because customers depended on producers' distributors or agents for almost all specialised key services or parts; paras 75 and 80); Case COMP/M.2300 *YLE / TDF / Digita / JV* (national market because of the need for after-sales repair and maintenance services for smaller customers); and Case COMP/M.2861 *Siemens / Drägerwerk / JV* [2003] O.J. L291/1, para.47. By contrast, in Case IV/M.1381 *Imetal / English China Clays* the Commission found that the market for kaolin for coating applications was global, observing, at para.47, that: "The circumstance that distribution facilities would be needed to compete in Europe does not alter this conclusion, to the extent that these imports do effectively take place and are economically justified, given the substantial production cost advantage enjoyed by non-European producers and the availability of high quality kaolin which is not available in Europe".
[57] Case COMP/M.1672 [2001] O.J. L143/74, paras 61 to 63.
[58] Case COMP/M.3083 [2004] O.J. L109/1, paras 75, 84 and 96 and nn.52, 58 and 66.
[59] Case COMP/M.2602, para.23.

geographic market and to have similar *shares of supply*[60] and *brands*[61] in each part of the market.

(a) In *Air Liquide / BOC*[62] the Commission stated that its investigation had "shown that while the conditions of competition in the tonnage market are homogeneous within the EEA, those conditions are appreciably different in other areas of the world. The EEA must therefore be distinguished from other regions of the world".

(b) In *Areva / Urenco / ETC JV*[63] the Commission stated: "The fact that suppliers are able to maintain for a long period high and stable market positions in a particular geographic area is an element indicating that they may not face substantial competitive pressure from forces outside that area. This pleads in favour of the definition of the area in question as a distinct geographic market from the competition point of view. On the other hand market share differences can be explained by historic reasons and are not in themselves incompatible with a broader market definition".

(c) In *Procter & Gamble / VP Schickedanz (II)*[64] the Commission emphasised that none of the suppliers used the same brand name across Western Europe, adding that: "The existence of some 'Euro-brands' does, in any case, not automatically prevent the market from being essentially national".

(d) In *Guinness / Grand Metropolitan*[65] differences in tax regimes between Member States were taken as a pointer towards national markets.

---

[60] See the Notice on Market Definition (para.28); Case IV/M.950 *Hoffmann-La Roche / Boehringer Mannheim* [1998] O.J. L234/14, para.53; COMP/M.1672 *Volvo / Scania* [2001] O.J. L143/74 (para.65; in that case the Commission also took account of variations in profit margins between states: para.66); Case COMP/M.2033 *Metso / Svedala* [2004] O.J. L88/1, para.89; Case COMP/M.2337 *Nestlé / Ralston Purina* (the Commission relied on asymmetries in market shares between states as evidence that they comprised separate markets; para.29); Case COMP/M.2621 *SEB / Moulinex*, para.27(c) (not challenged on this point on appeal in Case T-119/02 *Royal Philips Electronics NV v Commission* [2003] E.C.R. II-1433; see paras 89 to 91); Case COMP/M.2706 *Carnival Corporation / P&O Princess* [2003] O.J. L248/1, para.26(a); Case COMP/M.2947 *Verbund / EnergieAllianz* [2004] O.J. L92/91 (appeal pending in Case T-350/03 *Wirschaftskammer Karnten and best connect Ampere Strompool v Commission*), para.58; Case COMP/M.3083 *GE / Instrumentarium* [2004] O.J. L109/1, paras 80 and 81; Case COMP/M.3149 *Procter & Gamble / Wella*, para.25; Case COMP/M.3436 *Continental / Phoenix*, paras 41 and 42; and Case COMP/M.3732 *Procter & Gamble / Gillette*, para.17. By contrast in Case COMP/M.2978 *Lagardère / Natexis / VUP* [2004] O.J. L125/54 (appeal pending in Case T-279/04 *Editions Odile Jacob SAS v Commission*) the Commission stated that differences in market shares by region were not sufficient in themselves to identify separate geographic markets; para.362.
[61] See Case COMP/M.3149 *Procter & Gamble / Wella* (the existence of different brand names in different Member States was regarded by the Commission as a pointer towards national markets; para.23).
[62] Case COMP/M.1630 [2004] O.J. L92/1, para.34.
[63] Case COMP/M.3099, para.76. See also para.83.
[64] Case IV/M.430 [1994] O.J. L354/32, paras 89 and 90.
[65] Case IV/M.938 [1998] O.J. L288/24.

The Commission also expects suppliers to have knowledge of the conditions of competition in the markets in which they compete. If suppliers make radically different estimates of total sales in a particular region, this suggests that the relevant geographic market is smaller than the region in question.[66]

(i) Customers' procurement policies

The Commission has considered customers' procurement policies in a **3–081** number of cases. If procurement processes differ significantly between Member States, this is an indicator that they comprise separate geographic markets. For example,[67] the geographic market for pharmaceuticals is national, in part because different national health authorities have different purchasing policies.[68]

Further, if international companies choose to purchase from international suppliers on a national basis, this is an indicator that the geographic markets are not wider than national.[69] For example, the Commission found there was a Western European market for satellites procured by space agencies because the European Space Agency, which was the primary purchaser of institutional satellites in the area, purchased on a geographic *juste retour* principle.[70] Similarly, when states adopt policies of purchasing military hardware from domestic prime contractors to support their national suppliers, and thereby the country's military independence, the geographic market is national.[71]

---

[66] In Case COMP/M.2033 *Metso / Svedala* [2004] O.J. L88/1 the Commission relied on discrepancies in global market volume estimates provided by suppliers as evidence that the geographic market was smaller than global, concluding that suppliers were not aware of a substantial number of projects worldwide (para.112).

[67] In Case COMP/M.1915 *The Post Office / TPG / SPPL* [2004] O.J. L82/1 the Commission noted, at paras 51 and 52, that there was a trend by customers towards demanding global accounts for outbound cross-border business mail and that this could result, in the future, in the Commission identifying a global rather than a national market.

[68] See, e.g. Case COMP/M.1846 *Glaxo Wellcome / SmithKline Beecham*, para.73, which also mentions other factors which point towards national markets. See also Case IV/M.1286 *Johnson & Johnson / Depuy* (national market for reconstructive implants for hips and knees in the light, in particular, of public reimbursement systems) and Case COMP/M.3687 *Johnson & Johnson / Guidant*, para.68(b).

[69] See Case COMP/M.1672 *Volvo / Scania* [2001] O.J. L143/74, paras 58 to 60 and Case COMP/ M.2602 *Gerling / NCM*, para.24. For the converse situation (procurement of pan-European services), see Case COMP/M.1795 *Vodafone Airtouch / Mannesmann*, paras 18 and 21.

[70] Case COMP/M.1636 *MMS / DASA / Astrium* [2003] O.J. L314/1 and Case COMP/M.1745 *EADS*, para.78.

[71] See, e.g. Case IV/M.945 *Matra BAe Dynamics / DASA / LFK*; Case IV/M.1198 *British Aerospace PLC / Saab AB*; Case COMP/M.1745 *EADS*, para.129; Case COMP/M.3418 *General Dynamics / Alvis*, para.15; Case COMP/M.3491 *BAE Systems / Alvis*, para.13; and Case COMP/M.3680 *Alcatel / Finmeccanica / Alcatel Alenia Space & Telespazio*, para.54. (See also Case COMP/M.3649 *Finmeccanica / BAES Avionics and Communications*, paras 18 to 22, Case COMP/M.3735 *Finmeccanica / AMS*, paras 18 to 22 and Case COMP/M.3985 *EADS / BAES / FNM / NLFC*, paras 9 to 11, in which the parties argued for a wider geographic market but the Commission ultimately left the definition open). Markets for military equipment are generally global if no domestic supplier exists: Case COMP/M.1745 *EADS*, para.129. Even if a domestic supplier exists, the market *may* be global if there is no restriction on the domicile of the prime contractor: see Case COMP/M.1797 *Saab / Celsius*, paras 28 to 33.

(j) EU harmonisation and procurement legislation

3–082 EU harmonisation and procurement legislation has played a significant role in market definition.[72] In *Pirelli / BICC*[73] the Commission concluded that the market for power cables was EC-wide following the liberalisation of the electricity markets and the implementation of EU public procurement legislation (in contrast to a pre-liberalisation decision in 1991,[74] finding that the geographic market was national). The Commission noted that "cross-border bids are increasingly frequent and a number of European cable manufacturers regularly participate in tenders across various Member States ... Competitive pressure is ... exerted by foreign suppliers, because utilities would face no obstacles in switching to foreign suppliers if local prices rose above competitive levels".[75]

---

[72] See the Notice on Market Definition, para.32. See also Case COMP/M.2690 *Solvay / Montedison-Ausimont* (noting a "tendency to a European market, which will be reinforced by the adoption of the European Biocide Products Directive"; para.109) and Case COMP/M.3440 *ENI / EDP / GDP* [2005] O.J. L302/69, paras 16 and 122 (taking account of existing and foreseen liberalisation of energy markets when defining the relevant antitrust market) (prohibition upheld on appeal in Case T-87/05 *EDP v Commission*, not yet reported, judgment of September 21, 2005). However, Copenhagen Economics, *The internal market and the relevant geographical market*, Report prepared for the European Commission (available at *http:// Europa.Eu.Int/Comm/Enterprise/Library/Lib-Competition/Doc/Marketdef_Final_Report.Pdf*) showed, at p.8, that relevant geographic markets had not increased in size between 1990 and 2001 despite the implementation of the Single Market Programme.

[73] Case COMP/M.1882 [2003] O.J. L70/35.

[74] Case IV/M.165 *Alcatel / AEG Kabel*.

[75] Paras 43 to 48. Mario Monti, then the Commissioner for Competition Policy, "Market Definition as a cornerstone of EU Competition Policy", speech of October 5, 2001 (*www.europa.eu.incomm/competition/speeches/index_2001.html*), placed great emphasis on this: "The opening up to competition of markets as a result of EU liberalisation efforts or harmonising results from EU harmonisation directives will normally result in the widening of the scope of markets at some point in time. The telecommunications sector is a very good example of the above ... As regards equipment, markets were defined as national in early merger cases. However, today, several years after liberalisation of the equipment market, many parts of the industry are being assessed on the basis of cross-border markets that may be regional, EU-wide or even worldwide ... The Pirelli-BICC case illustrates the result of a process where deregulation and harmonisation of the power supply industry has effectively led to a widening of the relevant antitrust markets. In this case, the market was indeed confirmed to be EEA-wide because customers increasingly source power cables at a European level on the basis of the procedures provided for in the Community public procurement directives. The case contrasted with earlier cases involving the same industry. In 1992, markets were still considered to be national in scope. In 1998 a transition was recognised, but the assessment was still [made] at the national level". See also the Notice on Market Definition, para.32 and Case IV/M.222 *Mannesmann / Hoesch* [1993] O.J. L114/34. By contrast, in Case COMP/JV.54 *Smith & Nephew / Beiersdorf / JV* implementation of the Medical Device Directive was not sufficient to justify a finding of an international market because of national purchasing, the existence of national specifications, price differences between Member States, and divergent market shares between Member States. See also Case IV/M.706 *GEC Alsthom NV / AEG* (in which the Commission identified an EEA market in the light, in particular, of public procurement legislation); Case IV/M.1339 *ABB / Elsag Bailey* (the geographic market was found to be at least Europe-wide in the light in particular of legislative harmonisation of standards and the public procurement obligations); and Case COMP/M.1672 *Volvo / Scania* [2001] O.J. L143/74 (there was no evidence that public tendering would enable other city bus suppliers to provide the same level of competition as Scania then provided; para.325).

(k) Other harmonisation of product standards

Other harmonisation of product standards may facilitate international **3–083** competition. For example,[76] in *Pirelli / BICC*[77] the Commission noted that most power cables were covered by European standards ("ENs"); 90 per cent of ENs and harmonised documents ("HDs") were implemented at the national level within a year of adoption by the European Committee for Electro-technical Standardisation; and most utilities applied ENs, international standards or national standards compliant with European standards. The Commission concluded that different product standards had been largely harmonised at a European level and existing national specifications were no longer obstacles to market entry. Conversely, if goods are procured on the basis of national specifications, this may point towards a national market.

(l) National preferences, language and culture

The then Commissioner for Competition Policy, Mario Monti, emphasised **3–084** the importance of demand characteristics in defining geographic markets, stating that: "Factors such as national preferences or preferences for national brands, language [and] culture and life style ... are all important factors in defining the relevant geographic market".[78]

If customers in different states prefer products with markedly different characteristics, this is an indicator that the geographic market is national.[79] National preferences[80] or preferences for national brands may appear from survey evidence.[81] For example, in *SCA / Metsä Tissue*[82] survey evidence showed that spontaneous awareness of one of SCA's brands varied substantially between different Nordic countries, indicating that "brand

---

[76] See also Case IV/M.580 *ABB / Daimler-Benz* [1997] O.J. L11/1, para.28 and Case COMP/M.2851 *Intracom / Siemens / STI* (telecommunications equipment standards published by ETSI contributed to a finding that the geographic market was at least EEA-wide; para.29).

[77] Case COMP/M.1882 [2003] O.J. L70/35, paras 36 to 41.

[78] Mario Monti, then the Commissioner for Competition Policy, "Market Definition as a cornerstone of EU Competition Policy", speech of October 5, 2001 (*www.europa.eu.int/comm/competition/speeches/index_2001.html*). See also the Notice on Market Definition, para.46.

[79] See the Notice on Market Definition (para.46); Case IV/M.430 *Procter & Gamble / VP Schickedanz (II)* [1994] O.J. L354/32, para.78; and Case COMP/M.1672 *Volvo / Scania* [2001] O.J. L143/74, paras 50 to 55. In Case IV/M.938 *Guinness / Grand Metropolitan* [1998] O.J. L288/24, differing consumption patterns between states were taken as an indicator of national markets.

[80] See Case IV/M.222 *Mannesmann / Hoesch* [1993] O.J. L114/34, para.78; Case IV/M.1313 *Danish Crown / Vestjyske Slagterier* [2000] O.J. L20/1 (the Commission identified a strong preference by Danish consumers for Danish pork; para.82); and Case COMP/M.2817 *Barilla / BPL / Kamps* (the Commission stated that a "brand reputation in the relevant sector must be built up on a country-by-country basis" and identified a national market; para.19).

[81] See the Notice on Market Definition, para.41. It may also be apparent from an analysis of the distribution of market shares; see para.3–080 above.

[82] Case COMP/M.2097, para.55.

building exercises in one Nordic country appear to have no effect on recognition in any neighbouring country, supporting the hypothesis that markets for branded consumer goods are national even when the same brand is used in different countries". Language may determine the geographic market.[83]

3.8 GEOGRAPHIC MARKET DEFINITION: SUPPLY-SIDE SUBSTITUTION

3–085 Producers who substitute on the supply-side do so by selling at other locations (and, more particularly, by selling in the area served by the merging parties). In assessing the impact of supply-side substitutability, the Commission applies the SSNIP test,[84] which was described in ss.3.3 and 3.7 above.[85] In applying the SSNIP test, the issue is whether the long run returns from diverting some production to area B in response to a SSNIP in area B are more attractive than continuing to focus on serving area A. In examining this question it is relevant to consider:

(a) quotas, tariffs and regulatory barriers[86];

(b) the local set-up costs[87] incurred by suppliers (e.g. establishing a distribution network,[88] marketing, or obtaining a release from existing contractual commitments)[89]; the costs which would be incurred by suppliers if they ceased to supply in the area in question[90]; the costs incurred by *buyers* in switching from products supplied by incumbents to those of the near competitor (since a new entrant would generally need to absorb these costs in order to win business from the incumbents); and whether the near competitor can make supplies out of spare capacity (i.e. without sacrificing existing margins) and, if not, the relative margins earned on current sales as compared with supply as a new entrant in the candidate market (assuming that entry

---

[83] See the Notice on Market Definition (para.46); Case IV/M.469 *MSG Media Service*, para.46; and Case COMP/M.2300 *YLE / TDF / Digita / JV*.

[84] For discussion of whether demand-side substitution should be given relatively greater prominence when defining geographic markets for consumer products, see Copenhagen Economics, *The internal market and the relevant geographical market*, Report prepared for the European Commission (available at *http://Europa.Eu.Int/Comm/Enterprise/Library/Lib-Competition/Doc/Marketdef_Final_Report.Pdf*), p.70.

[85] See Areeda, Hovenkamp & Solow, *Antitrust Law* (2nd edn, Aspen Law & Business, 2000), Vol.IIA, para.551.

[86] The Notice on Market Definition, para.30.

[87] See also the Notice on Market Definition, para.30.

[88] e.g. if the producer cannot use its existing distribution structure and has to set up new arrangements either itself or through third parties.

[89] If switching would prevent the producer from complying with existing long-term contracts, the costs in terms of damages payments and reputational issues would need to be factored in.

[90] Costs of exit are a barrier to entry: see Ch.16.

occurs at a price 5 to 10 per cent above the pre-merger market level)[91];

(c)   shock analysis[92]; and, at a qualitative level, falling short of shock analysis, the process of market definition is assisted by evidence of suppliers switching between areas; the existence of such switching does not of itself show that the two areas are sufficiently close supply-side substitutes, that a small increase in the price in one area would lead to producers switching from the other area; but a claim that such switching would occur is more credible if at least some producers have changed between the areas;

(d)   evidence[93] that *sellers* base their business decisions on the prospect of switching by producers in other areas in response to small changes in price corroborates the arguments described above.

3.9 SPECIFIC ISSUES IN GEOGRAPHIC MARKET DEFINITION

(a) "One-way" markets

A geographic market may be "one-way" if, for example, the price in area A   **3–086** is £110 and in area B is £100 and transport costs between the two areas are £10 per unit.[94] If the price in area A were to rise to £115, there might be significant exports from area B; but a rise in price in area B of £5 would not result in exports from area A. In this situation, area B may be a separate market but area A may be part of a market comprising areas A and B.[95] A similar analysis may apply if producers in one area are capacity-constrained. For example, in *Rexam / American National Can*[96] the Commission found that beverage can prices were higher in the United Kingdom than in the remainder of Northern Europe (Germany, Benelux, Northern France and Austria), but producers in Northern Europe were capacity-constrained and therefore could not export to the United Kingdom, whilst the UK producers

---

[91] Successful entry will depress the price.
[92] See para.3–022 above.
[93] This evidence might arise, e.g. from pre-merger marketing studies.
[94] See Areeda, Hovenkamp & Solow, *Antitrust Law* (2nd edn, Aspen Law & Business, 2000), Vol.IIA, para.535f.
[95] A merger between suppliers in area B would be assessed using area B as the relevant geographic market whereas a merger between suppliers in area A would be assessed using areas A and B as the relevant geographic market.
[96] Case COMP/M.1939, para.19. In that case, market shares were measured by capacity: see paras 21 and 22. In Case COMP/M.2533 BP / E.ON, [2002] O.J. L276/31, the Commission found, at para.16, that there was "one way price influence" from the ARG+ ethylene pipeline to other areas. The Commission concluded: "This pricing influence which only leads out of the ARG+ cannot be said to extend the scope of the ARG+ geographic market". See also Case COMP/M.2838 *P&O Stena Line (Holdings) Ltd*, para.14.

had excess capacity and were competing to make sales in Northern Europe. The Commission found that the United Kingdom comprised a separate geographic market but the capacity represented by production facilities in the United Kingdom should also be counted as forming part of the Northern European market.

(b) Continuous chains of substitution

3–087 A continuous chain of substitution arises when suppliers draw customers from particular areas but the areas served by different suppliers overlap, with the consequence that demand in one area is sensitive to changes in price in another because of a "ripple effect". The Commission has stated that: "From a practical perspective, the concept of chains of substitution has to be corroborated by actual evidence, for instance related to price inter-dependence at the extremes of the chains of substitution, in order to lead to an extension of the relevant market in an individual case. Price levels at the extremes of the chain would have to be of the same magnitude as well".[97] The following cases exemplify the Commission's approach to continuous chains of substitution in geographic market definition.[98]

---

[97] The Notice on Market Definition, para.58 (see also para.57). However, in Case COMP/ M.2706 *Carnival Corporation / P&O Princess* [2003] O.J. L248/1 the Commission stated, at n.40: "It is of course possible that two products with very different prices are in competition with each other". Similarly, a product sold in one location may be in competition with a product sold in a second location, even though they are sold at different prices.

[98] In Case IV/M.1524 *Airtours / First Choice* [2000] O.J. L93/1, in considering the geographic market for foreign package holidays, the Commission noted that customers preferred to fly from airports near to their homes but found that the market was national, in part because: "This relative uniformity of pricing and cost suggests that there is a sufficient degree of overlap between possible regional or local markets for them to be regarded for the present purpose as constituting a single, national one on the demand side, on a 'chain of substitution' basis" (see para.45). (The Commission's analysis was referred to by the Court of First Instance in Case T-342/99 *Airtours plc v Commission* [2002] E.C.R. II-2585, at para.238, without criticism.) See also Case IV/M.242 *Promodes / BRMC* (the Commission considered whether continuous chains of substitution existed in retail distribution markets and stated, at para.11: "Overlappings between areas affect the homogeneity of the conditions of competition. These effects depend on the following factors: [1] [T]he overlapping depends on the density of points of sales and the housing density. Overlapping is more frequent in urban areas and more rare in the rural areas. [2] [T]he overlapping effect is proportionate to the share of the areas for which there is overlapping, which is increasingly smaller the more one moves away from the cities".); Case IV/M.623 *Kimberly-Clark / Scott* [1996] O.J. L183/1, para.68; Case IV/M.890 *Blokker / Toys 'R' Us (II)* [1998] O.J. L316/1 (the Commission found, at paras 38 to 42, that the geographic market for specialised toy retailing was national because pricing decisions, advertising strategy and choices of product range were made centrally; but the Commission did not rely on "chain of substitution" arguments in reaching this conclusion); Case IV/M.784 *Kesko / Tuko* [1997] O.J. L110/53 (merger of supermarkets; the Commission noted the chain of substitution argument, at para.21, but concluded that it was not necessary to define the geographic market; see para.23); Case IV/M.914 *Tesco / ABF* (the Commission relied on "knock-on" effects to define the geographic market for retail outlets as national or regional (as opposed to local as the parties had argued); see para.12); Case IV/ M.1256 *OK Ekonomisk Förening / Kuwait Petroleum Sverige AB* (the Commission contemplated that a market comprising deliveries to consumers would be national because it consisted of a continuous chain of overlapping zones, although the point was left open; see

(a) In *Rewe / Meinl*[99] the Commission found that the market for food retailing was national in the case of Austria in particular because "a large number of local markets affected by the concentration are connected in such a way as to overlap and seamlessly cover a larger area or even a whole Member State".[1]

(b) In *Pilkington-Techint / SIV*[2] 80 to 90 per cent of deliveries were within 500 km of the plant but the geographic market was found to comprise the EC because of the existence of a continuous chain of substitution: "given the dispersion of the individual float plants and the varying degrees of overlap for the natural supply areas, so that effects can be transmitted from one circle to another, it seems appropriate to consider that the geographical reference market is the Community as a whole".

(c) In *Air Liquide / BOC*[3] the Commission found that it was not eco-

---

paras 24 and 25; contrast Case IV/M.511 *Texaco / Norsk Hydro*); Case IV/M.1383 *Exxon / Mobil* [2004] O.J. L103/1 (national market for motor fuel retailing because of continuous chains of substitution; para.441); Case COMP/M.1628 *TotalFina / Elf* [2001] O.J. L143/1 (the Commission noted that if the hinterlands behind each supply point for wholesale fuels for retailers overlapped in terms of demand, the result might be a uniformity in conditions of competition; however, on the facts, the Commission accepted that the hinterlands were limited and did not overlap, with the consequence that the regions in question comprised separate markets; see paras 33 and 34; the Commission also found that there was a single geographic market for motorway fuel sales in France because of a chain of substitution, given that the average distance between service stations was around 40 km and most motorways intersect one another, giving rise to a chain reaction extending from one motorway to another; see paras 177 to 188; the Commission also found that LPG was generally transported over short distances but the geographic market was national because of chains of substitution; see para.273); Case COMP/JV.29 *Lafarge / Readymix* (national market for ready mixed concrete possible if "the local areas overlap to such an extent as to lead to equivalent conditions of competition throughout the country"; para.14); Case COMP/M.2032 *SCA Packaging / Metsä Corrugated* (an ability to price discriminate precludes a continuous chain of substitution argument; para.19); Case COMP/M.2271 *Cargill / Agribrands* (animal feed could be transported economically up to 150 to 300 km, but the Commission found that the geographic market was at least national and possibly EU wide because of a chain effect; para.10); Case COMP/M.2333 *De Beers / LVMH* [2003] O.J. L29/40 (the Commission found that there was a *global* market for retailing branded jewellery "because the brand is sold the same way in the Community as in the United States or Japan"; para.36); Case COMP/M.2502 *Cargill / Cerestar* (chain effect led to a finding of international markets in glucose: para.18); Case COMP/M.2854 *RAG / Degussa* (an ability to price discriminate precludes a continuous chain of substitution argument; para.36); and Case COMP/M.3314 *Air Liquide / Messer Targets*, para.37. Baker, Coscelli & Van Dijk, "Non-coordinated Effects in Retail Chain Mergers: An Application to Supermarkets" [2002] E.C.L.R. 180, note that continuous chains of substitution operate on the demand side and identify the following supply-side factors which may point towards national markets in retail cases: the setting of uniform national or regional prices; a focus on national advertising; frequency and ease of alterations in the existing pattern of outlets; and a need for any entrant to operate a certain number of outlets in order to be a viable competitor in the light of economies of scale in the market.

[99] Case IV/M.1221 [1999] O.J. L274/1.

[1] Paras 18 to 20. The Commission also took account of the fact that the major retail chains advertised and took stocking decisions on a national basis.

[2] Case IV/M.358 [1994] O.J. L158/24, para.16.

[3] Case COMP/M.1630 [2004] O.J. L92/1, para.39. In addition, the Commission was influenced by the existence of swaps between suppliers to reduce transport costs.

nomic to distribute bulk and cylinder gases more than 200 kilometres from the production facility, but in the larger Member States the catchment areas were normally overlapping, pointing to a national market.

(d) In *Exxon / Mobil*[4] the Commission stated that: "there is no natural barrier between the eastern and the western parts of Germany. This means that a uniform price increase in the western part would be defeated through marginal competition at the limit between the eastern part and the western part, through a sort of ripple effect".

(e) In *Owens-Illinois / BSN Glasspack*[5] and *Group 4 Falck / Securicor*[6] a continuous chain of substitution was ruled out because suppliers could price discriminate.

(f) In *Sonoco / Ahlstrom*[7] a continuous chain of substitution was ruled out because the degree of inter-penetration of market shares into different countries and regions was fairly limited.

(c) "Route by route" markets

3–088 Some markets, in particular those involving transport, are defined on a "route by route" basis, e.g. flights from London to Frankfurt. In *KLM / Alitalia*[8] the Commission found, in relation to air transport, that each point-of-origin / point-of-destination pair constituted a relevant market and that the market included non-stop flights between the two airports, non-stop flights between airports with significantly overlapping catchment areas and indirect flights provided that such flights were substitutable.[9] Route by route markets are also used in cases involving containerised liner shipping services.[10] Finally, in *BP / E.ON*[11] the Commission found that the geographic market for the supply of ethylene was the pipeline system of the ARG+ ethylene pipeline (since it was neither profitable nor practical to transport ethylene overland by road or rail).

---

[4] Case IV/M.1383 [2004] O.J. L103/1, para.588.
[5] Case COMP/M.3397, para.25 and n.6.
[6] Case COMP/M.3396, para.34.
[7] Case COMP/M.3431 [2005] O.J. L159/13, paras 53 and 75. The Commission did not address directly the question of whether demand in one area was sensitive to changes in price in another.
[8] Case IV/JV.19.
[9] See also Case IV/M.157 *Air France / Sabena*, para.25; Case IV/M.616 *Swissair / Sabena*, paras 18 and 19; Case IV/M.857 *British Airways / Air Liberté*, para.15; Case IV/M.1354 *SAirGroup / LTU*; Case IV/M.1494 *Marine-Wendel / SAirGroup / AOM*; Case COMP/M.1855 *Singapore Airlines / Virgin Atlantic*, para.16; Case COMP/M.2041 *United Airlines / US Airways*, paras 9 and 10; Case COMP/M.2672 *SAS / Spanair*, para.10; Case COMP/M.3280 *Air France / KLM* (appeal pending in Case T-177/04 *easyJet Airline Company v Commission*), para.9; and Case COMP/M.3770 *Lufthansa / Swiss*, para.12.
[10] See, e.g. Case COMP/M.3829 *Maersk / PONL*, paras 7 and 14.
[11] Case COMP/M.2533 [2002] O.J. L276/31, paras 12 to 17.

(d) Suppliers competing in both national and local markets

Certain markets, in particular retailing, have both national and local 3–089 characteristics. For example, retailers may compete at a national level (through national pricing strategies and the development of national brands) and at a local level (as customers choose between particular stores on a high street or within a particular drive time isochrone). In order properly to assess the effects of the transaction, it may be necessary to examine its effects at both a national and a local level.[12]

(e) Smaller Member States

In relation to *smaller Member States* there has been some criticism of the 3–090 Commission's decisions in certain high profile cases (notably *Volvo / Scania*,[13] *FöreningsSparbanken / SEB*[14] and *SCA / Metsä Tissue*)[15] to define the geographic market as national rather than international. The Swedish Prime Minister, Mr Persson, stated that "the present rules are disadvantageous to us since we tend to dominate our market fraction to such a great extent".[16] The argument is that the relatively lower demand in smaller Member States means that such states cannot support large numbers of suppliers each benefiting from economies of scale. However, preventing such undertakings from merging places them at a competitive disadvantage internationally, relative to suppliers from larger Member States which have been able to merge and therefore benefit from economies of scale. The Commission has emphatically rejected this criticism. Essentially, the rebuttal is that: the decisions in the cases in question were consistent with other decisions; a lower than average proportion of cases from the Nordic countries involve markets being defined nationally; customers in smaller Member States require protection against market power just as much as customers in larger Member States; operating a different policy for cases involving smaller

---

[12] See, e.g. Case COMP/M.2978 *Lagardère / Natexis / VUP* [2004] O.J. L125/54 (appeal pending in Case T-279/04 *Editions Odile Jacob SAS v Commission*) (the Commission found that retail sales of books occur in local markets but it is necessary also to analyse the strategies and positions of the different players at a national level; para.403); Case COMP/M.3068 *Ascott Group / Goldman Sachs / Oriville* (the Commission noted that the hotel sector has both national and local characteristics, although the precise market definition was left open; paras 18 to 20); Case COMP/M.3184 *Wolseley / Pinault Bois & Matériaux* (a merger affecting builders merchanting was assessed by the Commission on both national and local markets; para.22); and Case COMP/M.3314 *Air Liquide / Messer Targets* (the Commission identified national and local components to the distribution of cylinders; para.37).

[13] Case IV/M.1672 [2001] O.J L143/74.

[14] Case COMP/M.2380; notification withdrawn; see press release IP/01/1290 of September 19, 2001 (stating that "customers in smaller markets deserve the same level of protection as customers in larger economies").

[15] Case COMP.M/2097.

[16] Quoted in *Dagens Industri*, September 20, 2001. See also Bernitz & Gutu, "The Effect of EU Merger Policy on Large Multinationals Based in Sweden and Other Smaller Member States: Is the Policy Discriminatory?" [2003] E.C.L.R.19.

Member States would lead to discrimination against consumers in such states; and international competitiveness is more likely to be achieved by suppliers facing a competitive environment at home.[17]

(f) Multi-plant operations

3–091   Cases in which a producer operates a single plant involve more straightforward issues of geographic market definition than those involving multi-plant operations. For example, if the issue is whether the market for widgets is limited to England and Wales or also includes Scotland it would be relevant on the supply-side to consider whether the owner of a single widget plant in Glasgow sells to customers in England and Wales or would make such sales if the price in England and Wales were to increase by 5 to 10 per cent. However, if the owner of the widget plant in Glasgow also owns a widget plant in Birmingham, the question of whether the company supplies customers in England and Wales from its plant in Glasgow may not be relevant. The reason for this is that one of the economies of multi-plant operations is the ability to run dedicated lines, reducing down-time. So the widget producer may choose to produce in Glasgow for shipping to customers in England and Wales, purely because the savings available from running dedicated lines exceed the additional costs of transport; and yet that producer may not have shipped to England and Wales had it only owned the Glasgow widget plant.

3–092   In *Sanitec / Sphinx*[18] the Commission noted that imports into the EEA were increasing. However, a large proportion of these imports involved transactions between members of the same group. The Commission stated: "In assessing the flow of bathroom products into the EEA, the Commission considers that these imports should be excluded. Intra-group imports are merely logistical trade flows based on more favourable production costs and, therefore, imports which do not originate from third parties do not impose any competitive constraint on the behaviour of the market players already active in the EEA". Similarly, in *Nestlé / Ralston Purina*[19] the Commission stated: "The existence of significant petfood trade flows could be interpreted as evidence of a EU-wide geographical market, if it would be customer-driven (i.e. if retailers are significant importers) or if producers

---

[17] Mario Monti, then the Commissioner for Competition Policy, "Market Definition as a cornerstone of EU Competition Policy", speech of October 5, 2001 (*www.europa.eu.int/comm/competition/speeches/index_2001.html*) and Philip Lowe, Director General of DG Competition, "The interaction between the Commission and Small Member States in Merger Review", Dublin, October 10, 2003 (*http://europa.eu.int/comm/competition/speeches/*). See also the Commission's XXXIst Annual Report on Competition Policy, 2001 paras 250 to 252 and Lindsay, Lecchi & Williams, "Econometrics Study into European Commission Merger Decisions Since 2000" [2003] E.C.L.R. 673, p.681 (finding from a study of ECMR decisions from January 1, 2000 to June 30, 2002 that there was no evidence of bias against Nordic incorporated parties).

[18] Case IV/M.1578 [2000] O.J. L294/1, para.51.

[19] Case COMP/M.2337, para.27.

would not face significant impediments to commercialize imported products on countries of destination. However, it appears that trade flows respond to a geographic specialization carried out by petfood producers as a result of economies of scale in production and relatively low transport costs rather than evidence on retailers' European wide procurement policies ... Such figures cannot be seen as an indication of a market that is wider than national, as the trade-flows are generally not directed towards the customers, but normally reach subsidiaries or platforms for distribution within the supplier's own business organisation (being thus mainly intra-company trade, where companies do not have manufacturing facility, in a specific country)". In *BP / Amoco*[20] a market was defined as not wider than the EEA, notwithstanding that imports amounted to 12 per cent of EEA demand, in part because the only successful "importer" had been making intra-group supplies, and other exporters had been selling into the EEA on a spot rather than a systematic basis. Finally, in *Continental / Phoenix*,[21] the fact that the foreign manufacturer which was exporting to Europe was in the process of setting up its own plant in Europe pointed towards a European market, rather than a global one.

In *Sanitec / Sphinx*[22] the Commission also considered more generally the **3–093** implications for geographic market definition of multi-plant operation within the EEA. In that case, it found that production facilities tended to supply the country of production with exports mainly directed to neighbouring countries, stating that "the fact that production has not been geographically particularly centralised and that the parties have a number of production outlets all over Europe with a tendency to supply home markets and the neighbouring markets is taken as evidence that the supply of bathroom products is optimised in order to minimise the transport distance". The Commission relied on this evidence in support of its finding that geographic markets were national or at most covered a few countries. Similarly, in *Procter & Gamble / VP Schickedanz (II)*[23] the Commission took account of the fact that producers had production facilities in several locations across the EEA as evidence that markets were national adding: "In any event, the mere centralization of plants would not, in itself, be incompatible with separate national markets".[24] By contrast,[25] in *Agfa-Gevaert / Du Pont*[26] the fact that there was a limited number of production sites in the EEA, and dealers bought directly from those sites, was taken as an indicator

---

[20] Case IV/M.1293, paras 29 to 33.
[21] Case COMP/M.3436, paras 38 to 40.
[22] Case IV/M.1578 [2000] O.J. L294/1, paras 69 and 115.
[23] Case IV/M.430 [1994] O.J. L354/32, para.85.
[24] See also Case IV/M.603 *Crown Cork & Seal / CarnaudMetalbox*, para.43 and Case COMP/M.3149 *Procter & Gamble / Wella*, para.24.
[25] See also Case IV/M.214 *Du Pont / ICI* [1993] O.J. L7/13; Case IV/M.358 *Pilkington-Techint / SIV* [1994] O.J. L158/24; and Case COMP/M.3431 *Sonoco / Ahlstrom* [2005] O.J. L159/13, para.30.
[26] Case IV/M.986 [1998] O.J. L211/22, paras 39 to 41.

of an EEA-wide market. Similarly, in *Solutia / Viking Resins*[27] the Commission regarded the fact that producers generally supplied the whole EEA from a single plant as an indicator that the market was the EEA or wider. Finally, in *Blackstone / Acetex*[28] the fact that new capacity was being added in the Middle East and East Asia (which were likely to show substantial surpluses) and not in the EEA (which was already in deficit), tended to show that the geographic market was global, as it was likely that the EEA would absorb this additional capacity.

(g) Competitive tenders and inplants

3–094 In *Framatome / Siemens / Cogema / JV*[29] the Commission stated: "It should be noted that the mere fact that a supplier has the ability to provide certain goods world-wide is not in itself sufficient to demonstrate that the market is global in scope. In a market in which big contracts are often put to tender, the assessment should also concentrate on whether suppliers really do compete for such contracts in the same geographic area, and whether suppliers compete under homogeneous conditions in such an area".

In some markets, customers appoint suppliers to construct a production facility on the customer's premises (sometimes known as an "inplant").[30] In *Air Liquide / BOC*[31] the parties argued that an on-site separation plant could be constructed anywhere in the world. However, the Commission indicated that this was not sufficient to justify a finding of a global market for the reasons given in the *Framatome* case.[32]

3.10 TEMPORAL MARKET DEFINITION

3–095 A temporal market arises when there are particular periods when suppliers are able to raise prices profitably relative to supply during other periods. The issue involves determining whether the same physical good can be a different *economic good* depending on the date or time of delivery. Such

---

[27] Case COMP/M.1763, para.12.
[28] Case COMP/M.3625 [2005] O.J. L312/60, paras 48 and 69.
[29] Case COMP/M.1940 [2001] O.J. L289/8, para.114.
[30] In Case IV/M.1157 *Skanska / Scancem* [1999] O.J. L183/1, the Commission considered the geographic market for house and infrastructure projects (which are built on-site) and found, at para.60, that it was national for large projects on the grounds that it "is still rare for non-Swedish construction companies to take on construction projects in Sweden".
[31] Case COMP/M.1630 [2004] O.J. L92/1.
[32] In *Air Liquide* the Commission stated, at para.29 that: "the mere fact that a supplier has the technological ability to provide certain goods worldwide is not in itself sufficient to justify [a finding of a global market]. Rather, in a market in which long-term supply contracts are put out to tender, the analysis should focus on whether suppliers do actually compete for such contracts in the same geographic area, and whether suppliers compete under homogeneous conditions in different geographic areas".

markets typically arise when consumers are unable to switch between periods (e.g. workers who have to travel to arrive at a particular time and who cannot use off-peak travel) or producers' ability to supply varies over time (e.g. certain fruits and vegetables are seasonal and difficult to store). Temporal markets may also arise in *inter-generational products* when customers delay spending on goods currently on the market in the expectation that a better product will become available in the future.[33] Temporal markets are defined using demand- and supply-side substitution. The techniques are described above.

---

[33] See the UK OFT Guidelines on Market Definition, December 2004 (*www.oft.gov.uk/NR/ rdonlyres/972AF80C-2D74-4A63-84B3-27552727B89A/0/OFT403 pdf*), para.5.1.

CHAPTER 4

MARKET SHARES AND CONCENTRATION LEVELS

4.1 INTRODUCTION

4–001 The Commission relies on data about market shares and concentration levels[1] as "useful first indications" about the market structure and the competitive importance of the merging parties and their competitors.[2] Market share information[3] is relevant to the market positions of the merging parties and their competitors (see s.4.2 below), whilst concentration data provides information about the overall structure of the market and in particular the extent to which a few large firms control supplies or purchases (see s.4.3 below).

4.2 MARKET SHARE DATA

(a) Units for measuring market shares

4–002 Having defined the market,[4] the next step in the antitrust analysis is to identify the shares of that market held by the merging parties.[5] From a merger control perspective, the objective in measuring the merging parties' market shares is to provide the best proxy of the ability of the merged group profitably to raise prices above the pre-merger prevailing level or to reduce the quality of goods or services, the variety or choice available for customers

---

[1] See generally ABA Section of Antitrust Law, *Market Power Handbook* (ABA Publishing, 2005), Ch.V.
[2] Notice on Horizontal Mergers, para.14.
[3] See generally Werden, "Assigning Market Shares" (2002) 70 *The Antitrust Law Journal* 67.
[4] See Ch.3 above.
[5] The market shares held by competitors are also relevant, as explained in para.14–003 below.

or the rate of innovation.[6] This means that the best way of calculating market shares may vary depending on the characteristics of the market, a point which is acknowledged in the Notice on Market Definition[7]: "If sales are usually the reference to calculate market shares, there are nevertheless other indications that, depending on the specific products or industry in question, can offer useful information such as, in particular, capacity, the number of players in bidding markets, units of fleet as in aerospace, or the reserves held in the case of sectors such as mining. As a rule of thumb, both volume sales and value sales provide useful information. In cases of differentiated products, sales in value and their associated market share will usually be considered to better reflect the relative position and strength of each supplier". The remainder of this section describes the different measures of market share currently used by the Commission.

(i) **Value data** Use of value data[8] is particularly appropriate[9] in cases **4–003** involving differentiated products[10] as market share information calculated by value adjusts for these differences[11] and ascribes greater significance to sales of more expensive goods.[12]

---

[6] See s.7.2 below. The New Zealand Merger Guidelines, 2004 (*www.comcom.govt.nz/Publica tions/ContentFiles/Documents/MergersandAcquisitionsGuidelines.PDF*), para.5.2, raise the possibility of selecting the measure which provides the *highest* market share and analysing the way in which the market operates at subsequent stages in the inquiry.

[7] Para.54.

[8] Value data is seen as particularly important by the Commission—the Form CO requires the provision of such data in all cases when there is an affected market (subject to a decision by the case team to waive the requirement to provide such data).

[9] For discussion of the circumstances in which the use of value data for the calculation of market shares is not appropriate or is impractical, see ABA Section of Antitrust Law, *Market Power Handbook* (ABA Publishing, 2005), pp.73 and 74.

[10] Products which are perceived by customers to be different. Contrast Areeda, Hovenkamp & Solow, *Antitrust Law* (2nd edn, Aspen Law & Business, 2000), Vol.IIA, para.535a.

[11] This applies in particular if the products differ according to their intensity of usage, e.g. if one brand of kitchen roll has more sheets or greater absorbency than others; see ABA Section of Antitrust Law, *Market Power Handbook* (ABA Publishing, 2005), p.73. More generally, value data is preferable if physical units are not comparable—for example long-lasting light bulbs require replacement less frequently than normal bulbs: see Areeda, Hovenkamp & Solow, *Antitrust Law* (2nd edn, Aspen Law & Business, 2000), Vol.IIA, para.535a. Compare Werden, "Assigning Market Shares" (2002) 70 *Antitrust Law Journal* 67, at p.75 (arguing for greater use of "efficiency units", such as sweetness per pound, to take account of differing product characteristics).

[12] See the Notice on Market Definition, para.55. See also Case T-221/95 *Endemol Entertainment Holding BV v Commission* [1999] E.C.R. II-1299, para.130 (upholding the Commission's decision to calculate market shares by value of programmes and not number of hours produced); Case IV/M.214 *Du Pont / ICI* [1993] O.J. L7/13 (the Commission stated, at para.30: "In a market where products are differentiated in terms of price and quality, the appropriate method of calculation of market shares has to be based on value rather than volume. In this way, high value items are given their correct weight relative to low value items. A calculation based on volumes would not reflect the real market position of the players".); Case IV/M.315 *Mannesmann / Vallourec / Ilva* [1994] O.J. L102/15 (the Commission preferred value data to take into account the different value mixes of the various suppliers; para.47); Case COMP/M.1990 *Unilever / Bestfoods* (the Commission preferred value data in measuring sales of food products at a retail level because the multiplicity of packaging formats and consequent stock

(a) In *Nestlé / Perrier*[13] the Commission stated, in relation to the French water market: "The market shares in value terms better reflect the real market strength in this market than the market shares in volume terms because the French water market is composed of two categories of products which are very different in terms of price, i.e. the nationally distributed mineral waters and the local waters, which are mainly spring waters".

(b) In *Procter & Gamble / VP Schickedanz (II)*[14] the parties argued that volume data should be used to measure shares of the sanitary towel market. Branded products commanded a significant price premium in that market. The Commission rejected the parties' argument: "The ability of a manufacturer to command a higher price for its products than for competing products, whether as a result of product innovation, advertising, branding or marketing, is an important indication of the relative market power of that company compared with its competitors. This ability is reflected in value market shares but not in volume".[15]

(c) Finally, in *Air Liquide / BOC*[16] the Commission stated that: "Due to the nature of the tonnage contracts, value data represent the market position of suppliers more accurately than volume data. For instance, given that take-or-pay arrangements or non-volume related facility fees are often used, the actual strength of a supplier in relation to its customers and competitors is better reflected by the revenue earned than by the quantities of gases supplied".

If products are highly differentiated, then market share data is of less significance because it does not reflect the closeness of competition between the products.[17] However, if products are only moderately differentiated, market shares remain a good indicator of market power because closeness of substitution does not play a decisive role.[18]

4–004 (ii) Volume data Market shares in cases of homogeneous products[19] are

keeping units meant that volume data was less meaningful; para.60); and Case COMP/M.2396 *Industri Kapital / Perstorp (II)* (use of value data as the products forming the market were regarded by the notifying party as not comparable in volume terms; para.61). See also the Commission Guidelines on Vertical Restraints [2000] O.J. C291/1, para.97.

[13] Case IV/M.190 [1992] O.J. L356/1, para.40.
[14] Case IV/M.430 [1994] O.J. L354/32.
[15] Para.115. See also Case IV/M.190 *Nestlé/Perrier* [1992] O.J. L356/1, para.40.
[16] Case COMP/M.1630 [2004] O.J. L92/1, para.53, n.16.
[17] See s.7.3 below.
[18] See Case COMP/M.3687 *Johnson & Johnson / Guidant*, para.192.
[19] Areeda, Hovenkamp & Solow, *Antitrust Law* (2nd edn, Aspen Law & Business, 2000), Vol.IIA, para.535a, argue, contrary to the Commission's practice, that volume data is more meaningful than value data even in markets involving differentiated goods because most substitutions occur in a one-to-one ratio, e.g. a consumer purchasing a refrigerator will acquire just one item and units of different prices compete equally for the consumer's business.

commonly measured using volume data.[20] In such cases, shares by value are likely to be very similar to those by volume in any event.[21] In *SNECMA / TI*[22] the Commission measured the shares of the global landing gear market by volume (and by value) but *weighted* the volume calculation according to the physical weight of the aircraft for which the landing gear was supplied, to take account of the greater size and complexity of landing gear units supplied for larger aircraft. In *Carnival Corporation / P&O Princess*[23] the Commission chose not to measure shares of a cruises market by numbers of passengers as this would overstate the market position of companies offering shorter cruises; instead it used passenger cruise days.

(iii) Capacity data Measurement of market shares using capacity data[24] is **4–005** most relevant in cases of homogeneous products when customers can easily switch supplier *but* suppliers face capacity constraints.[25] In such a case, historic volume and value data may be a weaker indicator of market power than capacity data. For example,[26] in *Rexam / American National Can*[27] the

---

[20] See, e.g. Case IV/M.157 *Air France / Sabena* (shares on airline routes calculated by numbers of passengers; para.35); Case IV/M.490 *Nordic Satellite Distribution* [1996] O.J. L53/20 (number of smart cards sold; para.136); Case COMP/JV.55 *Hutchinson / RCPM/ECT*, paras 48 and 60; Case COMP/M.2315 *The Airline Group / NATS*, para.31; and Case COMP/M.2803 *Telia / Sonera* (numbers of mobile telephony subscribers, para.59). In Case IV/M.986 *Agfa-Gevaert / Du Pont* [1998] O.J. L211/22, the Commission used volume data in calculating market shares, having established that there were no significant price differences between competitors which would render the use of volume data less reliable than value data (para.44).

[21] Volume data is seen as particularly important by the Commission—the Form CO requires the provision of such data in all cases when there is an affected market (subject to a decision by the case team to waive the requirement to provide such data).

[22] Case IV/M.368, para.23.

[23] Case COMP/M.2706 [2003] O.J. L248/1, para.130. The Commission accepted that value data would also be relevant but was unable to obtain reliable calculations based on value.

[24] See the detailed discussion in Areeda, Hovenkamp & Solow, *Antitrust Law* (2nd edn, Aspen Law & Business, 2000), Vol.IIA, para.535c.

[25] ABA Section of Antitrust Law, *Market Power Handbook* (ABA Publishing, 2005), states, at p.75: "If a firm can easily supply more output at or below its current costs, its competitive significance (assuming homogeneous demand) may be better represented by its capacity to supply additional units than by its actual sales or output". In Case COMP/M.1671 *Dow Chemical / Union Carbide* [2001] O.J. L245/1, shares of a market for the licensing of technology were calculated using the capacity of the licences: para.99. (Contrast the earlier decision in Case IV/M.269 *Shell / Montecatini* [1994] O.J. L332/48, in which shares of a market for the licensing of technology were calculated on the basis of the number of licences granted to date; para.61.) The Australian Merger Guidelines, June 1999 (*www.accc.gov.au/content/item.phtml?itemId=719436&nodeId=file43a1f42c7eb63&fn=Merger%20Guidelines.pdf*), n.68, provide: "Capacity can also be a useful measure of concentration in some markets for differentiated products. The Commission has indicated that in considering acquisitions of radio stations, it will attach particular significance to the number of licences held by the merged firm in relation to the total number of licences available in the market, because of the volatility of individual audience and revenue shares". Werden, "Assigning Market Shares" (2002) 70 *Antitrust Law Journal* 67, at p.78, characterises value and volume data as *performance* indicators and capacity data as a *structural* indicator.

[26] See also Case COMP/M.3060 *UCB / Solutia*, paras 36 and 37 (capacity data used for calculating market shares in a case involving relatively homogeneous products, where all suppliers supply for all applications and the same production capacity is used for all grades).

[27] Case COMP/M.1936, paras 21, 22 and 24. Similarly, in Case COMP/M.2498 *UPM-Kymmene / Haindl* [2002] O.J. L233/38, the Commission considered capacity data in relation to the newsprint market.

Commission measured shares of the beverage can market by capacity, having found that beverage cans were homogeneous. Similarly, in *World-Com / MCI*[28] the Commission, in considering the market for top level or "universal" Internet connectivity, stated that the "size of installed capacity links ... might well provide an indication of the potential of a network in terms of performance, and also of size, on the assumption that capacity would not be purchased and installed unless there were some reasonable expectation of using it". However, capacity data is less appropriate as a measure of market share if costs vary as output increases (e.g. because additional capacity is less efficient or because of the need to add overtime or additional shifts),[29] if additional capacity is not readily available (e.g. because it has been leased to third parties), or if some suppliers lack other assets which are necessary to compete effectively (e.g. a sales and distribution network or a service team).[30]

Capacity data may also be used in cases of new, growing markets as the most reliable indicator of market power.[31]

4–006 **(iv) Numbers of credible bidders** In bidding markets[32] shares may be calculated using the number of credible bidders.[33] The rationale is that if customers regard suppliers as interchangeable and can easily switch between them *and* suppliers do not face capacity constraints, then each credible supplier has as much chance as the others of winning contracts in the future. In such cases, historic sales figures are a much weaker predictor of market operation than the number of credible players in the market. Indeed, in cases of truly homogeneous products, non-coordinated effects should *not* be expected in markets in which there is *at least one* credible competitor to the merged group, provided there are no capacity constraints. Such an approach to calculating market shares is consistent with the US Horizontal Merger Guidelines which state: "Where all firms have, on a forward-looking basis,

---

[28] Case IV/M.1069 [1999] O.J. L116/1, para.98.
[29] Werden, "Assigning Market Shares" (2002) 70 *Antitrust Law Journal* 67, at p.84, discusses the circumstances in which high-cost capacity might be ignored in calculating market shares.
[30] See further ABA Section of Antitrust Law, *Market Power Handbook* (ABA Publishing, 2005), pp.75 and 76.
[31] Case T-5/02 *Tetra Laval BV v Commission* [2002] E.C.R. II-4381. (The Court of First Instance's decision was upheld on appeal on the basis of reasoning not relating to this issue in Case C-12/03P *Commission v Tetra Laval BV*, not yet reported, judgment of February 15, 2005.)
[32] See generally paras 6–029 and 6–030 below. It is important to distinguish two uses of the expression "bidding market": first, as described in this paragraph; and secondly to refer to any market in which contracts are awarded by competitive tender.
[33] Contrast the Commission guidelines on market analysis and the assessment of significant market power under the Community regulatory framework for electronic communications networks and services [2002] O.J. C165/3, para.76 (contemplating the use of the number of *bids won and lost* in bidding markets as an approximation of market shares).

an equal likelihood of securing sales, the Agency will assign firms equal shares".[34]

The Commission's approach is similar in substantive terms, although it tends not to calculate market shares by the number of bidders. Instead, when considering bidding markets, it generally calculates market shares using sales, capacity or installed base and states that limited weight can be placed on those shares and the main issue is whether a sufficient number of bidders will remain in the market after the merger.[35]

(a) In *Boeing / Hughes*[36] the Commission accepted that satellite markets were bidding markets in which the conditions of competition were determined by the presence of credible suppliers.

---

[34] The US Horizontal Merger Guidelines, 1992 (amended in 1997) (*www.usdoj.gov/atr/public/ guidelines/hmg.htm*) at n.15. In *Compass Group PLC / Rail Gourmet Holding AG, Restorama AG and Gourmet Nova AG*, July 2002, Cm 5562, the UK Competition Commission cleared a transaction even though the post-merger share of supply was 83% (an increment of 3%). The UK Competition Commission regarded the supply of on-train food services as a bidding market and was clear, at para.2.15, that market share was not relevant in an assessment of a true bidding market: "it would not matter for the purposes of competition if one company held all the contracts at any point in time, as long as this or other factors did not restrain or prevent the possible entry of a competitor, each time one of those contracts was tendered, or else act to restrain or prevent the regular tendering of the contracts". Similarly, at para.2.32, the UK Competition Commission stated: "In a bidding market of this kind it may only be necessary for one genuine and serious competitor to remain for competition to be maintained". The UK Competition Commission therefore focused its investigation not on market share but on whether the merger would discourage market entry: "The acquisition could discourage entry if it increased the merged entity's market power, in relation to competitors and [customers], compared with the power previously exercised by [the target]. This could happen if the acquisition created conditions that discouraged competitors from bidding, or if it gave the merged entity a new and unique advantage in bidding or such as would increase its market power in relation to the [customers]" (para.2.33).
[35] In Case COMP/M.1745 *EADS* the Commission found, at para.146, that "programme markets are bidding markets, where the conditions of competition are determined by the presence of competitors with the capability to offer credible alternatives to the parties products" and reached a similar conclusion in relation to export markets at para.155. In Case COMP/ M.2201 *MAN / Auwärter* [2002] O.J. L116/35, the Commission stated, at para.32, that "market shares in procurement markets are of only limited evidential value". In Case COMP/ M.2111 *Alcoa / British Aluminium* the Commission noted, at para.13, that: "The relevant market is a bidding market characterised by a lumpy demand and as a result the relative market positions of the various suppliers may fluctuate according to the number of tenders that each of them has been or will be able to win". In Case COMP/M.2694 *Metronet / Infraco*, the Commission stated, at para.47, that: "in markets where contracts are awarded through bidding procedures, it is insufficient to examine market share figures alone. This is because market shares in bidding markets are by their nature, lumpy, and they only take into account the activity of the winners of a given contract but do not show how many credible competitors actually participated as bidders and thus created competitive constraints". In Case COMP/ M.2816 *Ernst & Young France / Andersen France*, the Commission stated, at para.60: "for a bidding market to be competitive, the main requirement is that there exist a sufficient number of credible bidders that are willing to compete. The Commission's investigation showed that the respective market shares among the Big Five in this case did not fully reflect the ability to win a tender. The market investigation has shown that any of the Big Five could possibly win or lose a competitive tender". See also paras 65 to 67 of that decision. In Case COMP/M.3641 *BT / Infonet*, the Commission stated that in bidding markets the level of market shares was less relevant than the ability of customers to choose alternative suppliers. It made similar statements in Case COMP/M.3752 *Verizon / MCI*, para.74.
[36] Case COMP/M.1879 [2004] O.J. L63/53, para.42.

(b) In *Framatome / Siemens / Cogema JV*[37] the Commission described the market for spent-fuel racks as a bidding market,[38] noting that: "As such, a high combined market share is not necessarily a good indication of the market power that the NewJV will obtain as a result of the merger". However, if the market were a true "bidding market" in the sense described in this paragraph, the market share analysis would properly be carried out on the basis of the number of bidders.

(c) In *Siemens / Alstom Gas and Steam Turbines*[39] the Commission stated that market shares may be an unreliable proxy for the competitive strength of the players in the market as they only reflect previous wins. Instead, the Commission focused on whether a sufficient number of bidders would remain in the market after the merger.

(d) In *Raytheon / Thales / JV*[40] the Commission noted that the military equipment in issue in that case is "procured through bidding markets, where the conditions of competition are determined by the presence of credible suppliers, able to offer competitive alternatives to the parties' products. In that context, even relatively high market shares may not translate into market power, and it would be necessary to examine whether the competitive behaviour of the joint venture would remain sufficiently constrained by the presence of other competitive bidders".

(e) The 2002 draft Commission Notice on Horizontal Mergers stated that: "In bidding markets, market shares may not be informative of the likely competitive impact of a merger. In these cases it is preferable to obtain direct information about the role of market players in the bidding processes, for example by means of win/loss analysis. The more precise the customer preference information is, the less weight should be placed on market shares as indicators of the possible competitive effects of a given merger".[41]

4–007 The Commission's approach was supported by the Court of First Instance in *General Electric Company v Commission*,[42] which stated:

"market shares as at a given date are less significant for the analysis of a market such as the market for jet engines for large commercial aircraft than, for example, for the analysis of a market for everyday consumer goods ... On [a market involving the award of a limited number of high-value contracts] the fact that a particular company has had a number of

---

[37] Case COMP/M.1940 [2001] O.J. L289/8.
[38] Para.143.
[39] Case COMP/M.3148, paras 24 and 35.
[40] Case COMP/M.2079, para.40 (see also para.50).
[41] Para.14. See also n.9. The treatment of market shares in cases of bidding markets is not addressed in the final version of the Notice on Horizontal Mergers.
[42] Case T-210/01, not yet reported, judgment of December 14, 2005, paras 148 to 151.

recent 'wins' does not necessarily mean that one of its competitors will not be successful in the next competition. Provided that it has a competitive product and that other factors are not heavily weighted in the first company's favour, a competitor can always win a valuable contract and increase its market share considerably at one go.

However, such a finding does not mean that market shares are of virtually no value in assessing the strength of the various manufacturers on a market of that kind, especially where those shares remain relatively stable or reveal that one undertaking is tending to strengthen its position ... Even on a bidding market, the fact of a manufacturer maintaining, or even increasing, its market share over a number of years in succession is an indication of market strength".

The Commission has on several occasions rejected arguments that markets **4–008** are bidding markets when customers have a preference for dealing with suppliers with a track-record of successfully winning contracts.[43] For example, the Commission found that tonnage sales of industrial gases did not occur in a bidding market in *Air Liquide | BOC*,[44] stating that "unless there is specific evidence that the pattern of the past no longer reflects the present situation, it is reasonable to assume that a supplier's market share is indicative of its strength". Similarly, in *General Electric | Honeywell*[45] the parties argued that competition amongst suppliers for the provision of engine starters[46] took place whilst the engine was under development with the consequence that market shares were not indicative of market power. The Commission rejected this: "As a detailed knowledge of the engine and airframe systems that interface with the component / sub-system are fundamental in this business, a sound track record in applying the technology in aerospace jet engine applications is a key discriminator for being selected as an engine starter supplier. Market share is therefore a measure of the experience of suppliers and, provided that sufficient resources are attributed to R&D, market share is a direct indicator of market power". In *Dow Chemical | Union Carbide*[47] the parties argued that the market for polyethylene technology packages was a bidding market, but the Commission rejected this because potential licensees sought licensors with a track record of production using the technology and of licensing, with research and development and back-up resources to ensure the plant remained effective,

---

[43] In Case IV/M.580 *ABB | Daimler Benz* [1997] O.J. L11/1, the Commission surveyed competitors to identify the parameters which determined the winner of a tender and noted the importance placed on a long-term relationship with customers and familiarity with customers' requirements; para.36. See also Case COMP/M.3436 *Continental | Phoenix*, paras 124 to 133.

[44] Case COMP/M.1630 [2004] O.J. L92/1, para.57. See also Case COMP/M.3314 *Air Liquide | Messer Targets*, paras 47 and 48.

[45] Case COMP/M.2220 [2004] O.J. L48/1, para.339 (prohibition decision upheld on appeal in Case T-210/01 *General Electric Company v Commission*, not yet reported, judgment of December 14, 2005).

[46] The passage from the Court of First Instance's judgment quoted above in para.4–007 above related to the market for jet engines.

[47] Case COMP/M.1671 [2001] O.J. L245/1, paras 129 to 131.

and with the ability to protect the licensed intellectual property rights. The Commission found that the merged group would be in a much better position to satisfy these criteria than its competitors.

Further, when large numbers of contracts are awarded through tenders each period, the Commission tends to place greater weight on market shares as they provide a strong indication of the merged group's market power and are not distorted by the small sample size.[48]

4–009 **(v) Uncommitted reserves** In markets in which a supplier's ability to compete depends on access to finite natural resources, market shares may be calculated on the basis of uncommitted reserves (i.e. reserves which the controller is not already contractually committed to supply). In the typical case of a merger of mining companies, the rationale is that, without uncommitted reserves, a mining company will not be a credible competitor for future business, and its elimination through merger will therefore make little or no difference to the operation of competition in the market. The US Supreme Court ruled in a merger of two coal producers that market shares ought to have been measured on the basis of uncommitted coal reserves needed to win new long-term contracts from electrical utilities—rather than current coal production shares—with the consequence that the merger in issue in that case ought not to have been blocked since one of the merging parties had very limited reserves.[49] The Commission has followed this approach in mining cases.[50] However, the use of reserves is less appropriate if some suppliers lack other assets which are necessary to compete effectively (e.g. a sales and distribution network or a service team).[51]

4–010 **(vi) Installed base and firm orders** In markets in which there are substantial costs in using two or more suppliers (in terms of training staff to use an additional supplier's products and stocking an additional set of spare parts), customers have an incentive to purchase from a single supplier. This applies in particular to purchases of expensive durable goods,[52] such as aircraft, lorries and coaches. In such markets, a supplier's market power depends in a large part on whether it is an incumbent supplier, i.e. on its historic sales. For this reason, it is common to calculate market shares in such cases on the

---

[48] See, e.g. Case COMP/M.3083 *GE / Instrumentarium* [2004] O.J. L109/1, paras 122 and 262.
[49] *United States v General Dynamics* 415 US 486, 94 S.Ct. 1186, 39 L.ED.2d 530 (1974).
[50] See Case IV/M.619 *Gencor / Lonrho* [1997] O.J. L11/30, paras 79 to 85a (decision upheld on appeal in Case T-102/96 *Gencor v Commission* [1999] E.C.R. II-753) and Case IV/M.1532 *BP Amoco / Arco* [2001] O.J. L18/1, para.25.
[51] See further ABA Section of Antitrust Law, *Market Power Handbook* (ABA Publishing, 2005), pp.76 and 77.
[52] See para.6–023 below for discussion of durable goods.

basis of installed base and firm orders.[53] The following cases illustrate the Commission's approach.[54]

(a) In *Aerospatiale / Alenia / de Havilland*,[55] a merger between producers of commuter aircraft, the Commission calculated market shares on the basis of firm orders to date (including all deliveries to date and orders placed but not yet delivered) for each commuter type currently manufactured or developed. The Commission's methodology also eliminated distortions in a low volume market,[56] excluded aircraft no longer produced as such craft did not affect the market power analysis, and excluded options to purchase—as opposed to firm orders—as they could easily be cancelled.

(b) In *General Electric / Honeywell*[57] the parties contested the methodology used in *de Havilland* but the Commission concluded that it remained the best proxy in measuring and interpreting the position of competitors given: "the fact that incumbency plays a role in the decisions of customers (that is, airlines) concerning their future buys. As the cost curve of an airline is in part influenced by fleet and engine commonality, engine suppliers expect to increase their market penetration more or less proportionately to their current degree of incumbency within an airline".[58]

(vii) Total stock Where customer relationships are ongoing and new business **4–011**

---

[53] For discussion of the choice between sales or production in measuring market shares, see Areeda, Hovenkamp & Solow, *Antitrust Law* (2nd edn, Aspen Law & Business, 2000), Vol.IIA, para.535b.

[54] See also Case IV/M.50 *AT&T / NCR* (the Commission measured shares of a market for automatic teller machines on the basis of installed units (supplemented by annual shipments data; see para.14) but did not explain the rationale for adopting this approach); Case IV/ M.950 *Hoffmann-La Roche / Boehringer Mannheim* [1998] O.J. L234/14 (the installed base had a strong influence over the way competition occurred in the market, but the Commission took this factor into account *in addition* to considering market shares, rather than by calculating market shares using the installed base; para.74); Case COMP/M.2416 *Tetra Laval / Sidel* (decision of January 13, 2003) (the Commission took account of the installed base of aseptic PET filling machines as well as shares of new sales by value; para.73); and Case COMP/ M.3148 *Siemens / Alstom Gas and Steam Turbines* (the Commission took account of the installed base of industrial steam turbines in addition to shares by sales, because a significant proportion of total gross profits was generated by aftermarket services and the market was "lumpy", with variations in demand).

[55] Case IV/M.53 [1991] O.J. L334/42, paras 21 to 24.

[56] See also Case IV/M.877 *Boeing / McDonnell Douglas* [1997] O.J. L336/16, para.28.

[57] Case COMP/M.2220 [2004] O.J. L48/1, para.41 (prohibition decision upheld on appeal in Case T-210/01 *General Electric Company v Commission*, not yet reported, judgment of December 14, 2005). The Commission examined the market for jet aircraft as demand for aircraft engines was derived from demand for aircraft.

[58] The Court of First Instance upheld the Commission's decision to exclude from its calculation of the installed base aircraft which were no longer in production; see Case T-210/01 *General Electric Company v Commission*, not yet reported, judgment of December 14, 2005, para.162.

represents a very small proportion of the market it may be appropriate to measure market share on the basis of total stock rather than new business.[59]

4–012 **(viii) Other measurements** Other measurements of market share commonly used by the Commission include: number of contracts won[60]; numbers of mobile telephone subscribers[61]; traffic flow[62]; capital expenditure and/or expected production in a (possible) market for exploration for crude oil and natural gas[63]; and numbers of companies willing to commit themselves to long-term supply contracts.[64] The Commission has measured shares in investment banking markets using league tables.[65]

4–013 **(ix) Combinations of measurements** The Commission has commonly relied on a *combination of measurements* of market share to provide an overall picture.[66]

---

[59] Compare OFT Economic Discussion Paper 5, "Switching Costs", NERA, April 2003 (note that the views in the paper do not necessarily reflect those of the OFT), para.7.103, arguing that in markets with switching costs, share of new business may be a better reflection of the importance of competitors than total stock.

[60] In Case COMP/M.1630 *Air Liquide / BOC* [2004] O.J. L92/1 the Commission took account, at para.55 and n.17, of the number of contracts won during the preceding five years. See also Case COMP/M.2069 *Alstom / Fiat Ferroviaria*, para.22 and Case COMP/M.2079 *Raytheon / Thales / JV*, para.39.

[61] See Case COMP/M.1795 *Vodafone Airtouch / Mannesmann*, para.32 and Case COMP/M.2016 *France Telecom / Orange*.

[62] This was used in Case IV/M.1069 *WorldCom / MCI* [1999] O.J. L116/1, in relation to the market for top level or "universal" internet connectivity paras 107 to 113.

[63] Case IV/M.1532 *BP Amoco / Arco* [2001] O.J. L18/1, paras 21 to 23 (but note the criticisms of the use of capital expenditure at para.22).

[64] In Case COMP/M.1693 *Alcoa / Reynolds* [2002] O.J. L58/25, the Commission was unable to calculate market shares for capacity or production of P0404 and therefore took as the best proxy the fact that only two companies were willing to commit themselves to long-term supply contracts, allocating a 50% share to each of the companies in question: see paras 100 and 101.

[65] See, e.g. Case IV/M.642 *Chase Manhattan / Chemical Banking*, para.13; Case COMP/M.2158 *Credit Suisse Group / Donaldson, Lufkin & Jenrette*, para.12; and Case COMP/M.2982 *Lazard / IntesaBCI / JV*, para.23.

[66] See also Case IV/M.1383 *Exxon / Mobil* [2004] O.J. L103/1 (market shares calculated by nameplate capacity, effective production and Group I production; para.334); Case COMP/M.1630 *Air Liquide / BOC* [2004] O.J. L92/1 (market shares calculated by value and by number of contracts won; paras 53 and 55); Case COMP/M.1845 *AOL / Time Warner* [2001] O.J. L268/8 (shares of internet dial-up market assessed in terms of revenues and numbers of subscribers; para.79); Case COMP/M.2314 *BASF / Eurodiol / Pantochim* [2002] O.J. L132/45 (the Commission analysed capacity and volume data; para.84 and Table 4); Case COMP/M.2420 *Mitsui / CVRD / Caemi* [2004] O.J. L92/50 (sales and capacity; para.174; the Commission also took account of the merged group's reserves in assessing the merged entity's competitive advantages; para.177); Case COMP/M.2498 *UPM-Kymmene / Haindl* [2002] O.J. L233/38 (the Commission considered capacity and value data; para.113); Case COMP/M.2533 *BP/E.ON* [2002] O.J. L276/31, paras 44 and 47; Case COMP/M.2681 *Conoco / Philipps Petroleum*, para.18; Case COMP/M.2772 *HDW / Ferrostaal / Hellenic Shipyard* (value and volume data; para.63); Case COMP/M.2816 *Ernst & Young France / Andersen France* (market for audit and accounting services for quoted and large companies; market shares calculated by number of statutory audit mandates and turnover figures; paras 55 and 56); and Case COMP/M.3746 *Tetra Laval / SIG* (market shares calculated by fillers ordered and installed fillers; paras 20, 21, 34, 35, 47 and 48).

(a) In *General Electric / Honeywell*[67] the Commission assessed the implications of the transaction for competition in the supply of engines for jet aircraft and took as its main indicators the installed base and the order backlog of engines on aircraft that were still in production, but considered also the net present value of the future income stream generated by the aftermarket of engines forming part of the overall installed base, an analysis of recent platform competitions and an analysis of engine exclusivity competitions over the preceding ten years.

(b) In *BP Amoco / Arco*[68] the Commission took account of market capitalisation, oil and gas production and proven reserves.

(c) In *WorldCom / MCI*[69] the Commission took account of capacity data, revenue and traffic flows in analysing the market for top level or universal internet interconnection.

(d) It is common for the Commission to consider value and/or volume data together with capacity data.[70]

(e) If there is a substantial time lag between order and delivery, the Commission may wish to analyse market share data for both deliveries and orders. In *Allied Signal / Honeywell*,[71] which involved a merger of suppliers of commercial avionics, the parties provided market share data based on deliveries. The Commission stated: "In order to properly evaluate the market strength of the competitors in the market, the Commission considers it appropriate to look also at orders placed, given that these would better indicate the current competitive potential of the producers".

(b) Calculating market shares

This section explains the Commission's approach to calculating market shares and in particular attributing sales to the correct supplier. **4–014**

(i) Exclusion of certain transactions from the market Certain transactions ought to be excluded from the market. **4–015**

(a) Sales between the merging parties should not be taken into account in calculating market shares as this would provide a misleading

---

[67] Case COMP/M.2220 [2004] O.J. L48/1, para.44 (prohibition decision upheld on appeal in Case T-210/01 *General Electric Company v Commission*, not yet reported, judgment of December 14, 2005).
[68] Case IV/M.1532 [2001] O.J. L18/1, para.28.
[69] Case IV/M.1069 [1999] O.J. L116/1.
[70] See Case COMP/M.1741 *MCI WorldCom / Sprint* [2003] O.J. L300/1, para.123.
[71] Case COMP/M.1601 [2001] O.J. L152/1, para 65

impression of the post-merger position.[72] In *Telecom Italia / News Television / Stream*[73] the Commission disregarded one of the parties' substantial pre-merger sales on the grounds that almost all were to a company over which it was acquiring joint control, noting that "the proposed concentration will have no market effects beyond the relationship of the involved parties".

(b) Intra-group sales by the target to the vendor are not included in market shares calculated by value or volume. In *Solectron / Nortel*[74] the purchaser acquired a Nortel unit which had produced exclusively for internal consumption by Nortel and had not sold on the merchant market. The Commission concluded that: "the activities being acquired have not been generating turnover directly on any market. Consequently, their acquisition does not in itself entail any market share acquisition downstream by Solectron, but rather an acquisition of additional capacity".

(c) Sales by joint ventures to their parents[75] and sales by the parties to their affiliates[76] should be excluded as they have not been subject to market conditions or any competition.

(d) Sales between competitors should be excluded to avoid double-counting.[77]

---

[72] See, e.g. Case IV/M.2095 *Sextant / Diehl* (prior to the merger, a subsidiary of Diehl supplied goods to Sextant; the Commission stated, at para.27, that "this vertical integration will not modify the competitive situation since, even before the operation, BGT only sells ... to Sextant and does not have the ability to sell directly to Airbus"); Case COMP/M.2314 *BASF / Eurodiol / Pantochim* [2002] O.J. L132/45, para.123; and Case COMP/M.2628 *Koch / Kosa* (the Commission noted, at para.13, that after "the transaction will have taken place roughly [...] of Koch's present market share ... will be considered as inter-company sales thereby reducing Koch's merchant market share to about [0–10%]"). When the target company has won business only through a consortium in which the purchaser is a member, there is no real addition of market shares through the merger: see Case COMP/M.2069 *Alstom / Fiat Ferroviaria*, para.25.
[73] Case COMP/M.1978, para.17.
[74] Case COMP/M.1968, para.10. See also Case COMP/M.1711 *Tyco / Siemens* (the transaction was a disposal by Siemens of a business unit which, prior to the concentration, transferred nearly half its output to Siemens group; notwithstanding that any sales from the unit to Siemens following the transaction would occur in the market, the Commission excluded from the market share calculation those units which were the subject of internal transfers; see para.12); Case COMP/M.1849 *Solectron / Ericsson Switches*; and Case COMP/M.3571 *IBM / Maersk Data / DMData*, para.18. In Case COMP/M.2389 *Shell / DEA* [2003] O.J. L15/35, the Commission emphasised, at para.31, that it is necessary in each case: "to individually assess restructuring operations which may lead to an increase in market shares without leading to a corresponding direct and immediate increase of market power. Such a situation may in particular occur if, in the case of a divestiture of some activities in downstream production, intra-group supplies of ethylene are replaced by long-term supply agreements with third parties. As a consequence of the new third party supply agreements, the former captive use is accounted for the merchant market and may generate additional market shares. However, such additional market shares may not necessarily be considered as a full reflection of new market power. Such operations and their particularities have to be assessed on a case-by-case basis".
[75] Case COMP/M.2420 *Mitsui / CVRD / Caemi* [2004] O.J. L92/50, para.172.
[76] Case IV/M.1383 *Exxon / Mobil* [2004] O.J. L103/1, para.337.
[77] Case IV/M.970 *TKS / ITW Signode / Titan* [1998] O.J. L316/33, notes to Table 1.

(e) Sales by companies owned by a merging party but not controlled by that party may be excluded. In *Orkla / Volvo*[78] Volvo had given an undertaking to a Swedish court, backed by a substantial penalty in the event of default, not to integrate a business. The Commission took account of the undertaking and indications in Volvo's strategic plan that the business would be sold within the next few years, in *excluding* the sales by that business from the calculation of Volvo's market shares.

(ii) Data sources The Commission uses the most reliable data available in **4–016** calculating market shares.

(a) *Third party research* is generally preferred when available.[79]

(b) When it is not, the Commission will generally[80] verify the parties' estimates[81] or, if no estimates are provided, the Commission will carry out its own assessment. It does this by contacting the main suppliers in the market[82] to obtain details of their sales, enabling the Commission to calculate accurately[83] the total size of the market and each supplier's shares.[84]

---

[78] Case IV/M.582 [1996] O.J. L66/17, para.113.

[79] See, e.g. Case COMP/M.1846 *Glaxo Wellcome / SmithKline Beecham*, para.100 and Case COMP/M.3779 *Pernod Ricard / Allied Domecq* (the market test was used to confirm the reliability of a particular third party source; see n.6). In Case COMP/M.2544 *Masterfoods / Royal Canin* the Commission accepted the parties' evidence that the third party databases contained some significant errors and preferred the parties' estimates: paras 28 and 29. In Case COMP/M.2558 *Havas / Tempus* the Commission considered, at para.16, shares of media billings on the grounds that such data were available from third party research organisations, even though the relevant product markets were the provision of marketing communications and advertising. In Case COMP/M.3149 *Procter & Gamble / Wella* the Commission used share estimates derived from data compiled by AC Nielsen, IRI and Euromonitor (see n.15).

[80] In Case COMP/M.2416 *Tetra Laval / Sidel* (decision of January 13, 2003), the parties were unable to provide market share estimates but the Commission appears not to have investigated this in detail (beyond stating that there appeared to be a number of other suppliers) as no concerns were raised in the market investigation; see para.85.

[81] The Commission may ask the notifying parties for greater specification regarding any "others" category, in particular asking them to identify the suppliers within this group and to explain how the residual value was arrived at; see, e.g. Case COMP/M.2861 *Siemens / Drägerwerk / JV* [2003] O.J. L291/1, para.77.

[82] The Commission may also verify with third parties the methodology used by the notifying party in calculating market shares: see, e.g. Case COMP/M.1794 *Deutsche Post / Air Express International*, para.15 and Case COMP/M.3579 *WPP / Grey*, paras 50 to 52 and 58 to 61.

[83] So long as all parties supplying sales information understand and properly apply the market definition identified by the Commission.

[84] The Notice on Market Definition, para.53. See, e.g. Case IV/M.890 *Blokker / Toys 'R' Us (II)* [1998] O.J. L316/1, para.53; Case COMP/M.2050 *Vivendi / Canal + / Seagram*, paras 37 and 38; Case COMP/M.2547 *Bayer / Aventis Crop Science* [2004] O.J. L107/1, para.20; Case COMP/M.2861 *Siemens / Drägerwerk / JV* [2003] O.J. L291/1, paras 83 and 116; Case COMP/M.2978 *Lagardère / Natexis / VUP* [2004] O.J. L125/54 (appeal pending in Case T-279/04 *Editions Odile Jacob SAS v Commission*), para.563; Case COMP/M.3083 *GE / Instrumentarium* [2004] O.J. L109/1, paras 109 and 259; Case COMP/M.3314 *Air Liquide / Messer Targets*, nn.19, 21, 27, 28, 32, 52 and 54; Case COMP/M.3396 *Group 4 Falck /*

(c) The Commission may use two or more methods of calculation if there is uncertainty about their accuracy.[85]

(d) The Commission is willing to use proxies when necessary.[86] For example, in *Unilever / Bestfoods*[87] the Commission considered the market for the supply at a *wholesale* level of foods to retail outlets, but used *retail* sales data on the grounds that such data was the only available indication of wholesale market shares and was the source used by suppliers to monitor movements in market shares.[88] Similarly, in *VEBA / VIAG*[89] the Commission calculated market shares on the basis of electricity generated (even though electricity generation is not a market but an industrial activity) on the grounds that this was a good proxy for the calculation of market shares in the wholesale supply of electricity (since imports were of marginal importance).

4–017 **(iii) Period for calculating market shares** Data is generally collated on an *annual basis*.[90] The use of annual data avoids distortions through short-term fluctuations and shifts in supplies, but the Commission takes account of

---

Securicor, para.103; and Case COMP/M.3595 *Sony / MGM*, paras 46, 50, 53, 57 and 60. In Case T-221/95 *Endemol Entertainment Holding BV v Commission* [1999] E.C.R. II-1299, paras 131 and 132, the Court of First Instance upheld the calculation of market shares carried out by the Commission on the basis of written evidence and a series of telephone calls to rival producers. The Commission may also adopt complainants' estimates: see Case COMP/ M.1838 *BT / Esat*, para.18.

[85] See, e.g. Case COMP/JV.15 *BT / AT&T* (separate surveys of suppliers and customers to estimate market shares; paras 106 and 107); Case COMP/M.1741 *MCI WorldCom / Sprint* [2003] O.J. L300/1, para.230; and Case COMP/M.2810 *Deloitte & Touche / Andersen (UK)* (different samples of companies used in assessing the market for audit and accounting services for quoted and large companies; para.33).

[86] See also Case IV/M.950 *Hoffmann-La Roche / Boehringer Mannheim* [1998] O.J. L234/14 (the Commission took the parties' shares for clinical chemistry reagents as representative of their shares of clinical chemistry instruments in the expectation that the shares in the two markets would correspond closely; para.61); Case COMP/M.2978 *Lagardère / Natexis / VUP* [2004] O.J. L125/54 (appeal pending in Case T-279/04 *Editions Odile Jacob SAS v Commission*) (when assessing the market for publishing rights, the Commission was unable to calculate shares by the amounts paid annually in advances for books; it therefore obtained data on the advances paid by the different publishing houses to the authors of the 100 best-selling titles in certain categories; paras 424, 425 and 491); and Case COMP/M.3216 *Oracle / PeopleSoft* [2005] O.J. L218/6, paras 184 to 186.

[87] Case COMP/M.1990, para.61.

[88] The use of retail sales data to assess market power at manufacturer level is not straightforward. Scheffman, "Statistical Measures of Market Power: Uses and Abuses" (1992) 60 *Antitrust Law Journal* 901, at pp.912 and 913, notes that demand conditions may differ substantially between the wholesale and retail markets given the scope for retailers to engage in sophisticated purchasing (such as requiring payment of slotting allowances), inventorying and forward-purchasing. See also Steiner, "The Third Relevant Market" [2000] *The Antitrust Bulletin* 719.

[89] Case COMP/M.1673 [2001] O.J. L188/1, para.50.

[90] The US Horizontal Merger Guidelines, 1992 (amended in 1997) (*www.usdoj.gov/atr/public/ guidelines/hmg.htm*) suggest, at para.1.43, that calculations over a period longer than one year may be appropriate if exchange rates fluctuate significantly so that comparable dollar calculations on an annual basis may be unrepresentative.

more recent data if it reflects important recent changes that are likely to be permanent.[91]

The use of annual data may be inappropriate when the market involves a small number of transactions per year, as the following cases illustrate.[92]

(a) In *General Electric / Honeywell*[93] the Commission examined the evolution of the installed base of aircraft engines over a five-year period.

(b) In *Framatome / Siemens / Cogema JV*[94] the Commission measured the parties' shares of fuel assemblies for nuclear reactors over a three-year period and of spent-fuel racks over a ten-year period.[95]

(c) In *Shell / BASF / JV—Project Nicole*[96] the Commission calculated shares of the market for licensing polypropylene technology by capacity licensed over a 15-year period.

(d) Finally, in *Preussag / Babcock / Celsius*[97] the Commission calculated market shares for the supply of submarines over a ten-year period considering both contracts concluded in that period, and actual deliveries.

(iv) Adjustments to market shares The Commission may *discount or adjust* **4–018** market share data if it does not properly reflect the future significance of the

---

[91] Case COMP/M.3130 *Arla Foods / Express Dairies*, para.64.

[92] The Notice on Horizontal Mergers provides, in para.15: "Historic data may be used if market shares have been volatile, for instance when the market is characterised by large, lumpy orders". In addition to the cases cited in the text, see, e.g. Case IV/M.269 *Shell / Montecatini* [1994] O.J. L332/48 (technology licensing; market shares were calculated on the basis of *licences granted to date*; para.61); Case IV/M.580 *ABB / Daimler Benz* [1997] O.J. L11/1 (three-year period for assessing rail technology products and services because demand varied over time; shares were calculated on the basis of flow of new orders "since these are the direct result of competition between the various suppliers in the relevant period"; para.55); Case COMP/M.1671 *Dow Chemical / Union Carbide* [2001] O.J. L245/1 (technology licensing; periods of 15 years were used in calculating market shares; paras 105 and 132); Case COMP/M.1930 *Ahlström / Andritz* (market shares for chemical pulp mill equipment were calculated over a ten-year period; para.58); Case COMP/M.2033 *Metso / Svedala* [2004] O.J. L88/1 (sales of mining crushers were calculated on the basis of a ten-year period because of the low volume of sales; para.172); and Case COMP/M.2079 *Raytheon / Thales / JV* (sales of military equipment were calculated over a seven-year period; para.39). See also Case COMP/M.3091 *Konica / Minolta* (noting, at para.48, that market shares in markets with very small numbers of transactions would not reflect the market situation, but not adopting an alternative mechanism for calculating market shares). In the United Kingdom, see *Alcatel Cable SA / STC Limited*, Cm. 2477, February 24, 1994, para.4.21. See generally Werden, "Assigning Market Shares" (2002) 70 *Antitrust Law Journal* 67, at pp.90 to 93.

[93] Case COMP/M.2220 [2004] O.J. L48/1, paras 74 and 75 (prohibition decision upheld on appeal in Case T-210/01 *General Electric Company v Commission*, not yet reported, judgment of December 14, 2005).

[94] Case COMP/M.1940 [2001] O.J. L289/8, para.37.

[95] The Commission stated, at para.142, that "a shorter period may not be reflective of the true market position given the relatively small number of contracts annually (two or three)".

[96] Case COMP/M.1751, para.46.

[97] Case COMP/M.1709, para.68.

supplier in question.[98] The Notice on Horizontal Mergers states that "current shares may be adjusted to reflect reasonably certain future changes, for instance in the light of exit, entry or expansion".[99] For example, in *BASF / Eurodiol / Pantochim*[1] Eurodiol and Pantochim were placed under a pre-bankruptcy regime in September 2000. In calculating market shares, the Commission used 1999 data on the grounds that the financial difficulties facing Eurodiol and Pantochim in 2000 severely limited their output.[2]

In a merchant market in which a producer is both buying and selling, shares may be calculated on a "net basis".[3]

The same principles are applied in calculating the market shares of competitors. For example, in *Gencor / Lonrho*[4] apparently substantial sales from Russia were regarded as a short-term factor as they were to a large extent from stocks.

If other parties in the market have announced agreements to merge, the Commission may be willing to treat the companies as if they had already merged in calculating market shares.[5]

4–019 **(v) Currencies** If all prices in a market are expressed in the same currency, then that currency should be used in calculating market shares by value.[6] If

---

[98] See also the discussion of post-merger shrinkage in para.4–033 below and Case COMP/ M.2547 *Bayer / Aventis Crop Science* [2004] O.J. L107/1 (an EC Directive was likely to result in the withdrawal from the market of large numbers of plant protection products; para.22; illegal sales were discounted because of their illegal status and the uncertainty relating to such supplies; para.415). For discussion of possible adjustments of market shares in two-sided media markets, see "Media Mergers", OECD, DAFFE/COMP(2003)16, p.7.

[99] Para.15. Similarly, the UK Office of Fair Trading's Substantive Merger Guidelines, May 2003 (*www.oft.gov.uk*), state, at para.4.3: "Current market shares may be adjusted to reflect expected and reasonably certain future changes, such as a firm's likely exit from the market or the introduction of additional capacity".

[1] Case COMP/M.2314 [2002] O.J. L132/45, para.5.

[2] Paras 59 and 60. The implication is that any purchaser of the businesses would be able to inject funds, increase output and win back market share.

[3] In Case COMP/M.2533 *BP / E.ON* [2002] O.J. L276/31, the Commission calculated market shares on a "net basis" as regards sales and purchases of ethylene on the ARG+ pipeline system (para.20). The rationale for netting was: "In case a producer is at the same time selling and purchasing on the merchant market, it is appropriate to consolidate sales and purchases to a net position as either net buyer or net seller. The Commission's investigation has shown that swaps among producers as well as sales and purchases on the (spot) market in the same year are mainly carried out for operational reasons and not for the purposes of a systematic and large scale on-sale. Furthermore, swaps do not reflect independent market power on the part of the participating undertaking and cannot be compared to sales". In that case, imports were attributed to the undertaking selling the imports within the ARG+ catchment area (para.21). See also Case COMP/M.2389 *Shell / DEA* [2003] O.J. L15/35, para.37 (discussing whether sales to a joint venture jointly controlled by Shell should be treated as captive sales for the purposes of netting-off; the Commission counted the joint venture as a separate entity as it was full function). The use of such a "net merchant market rule" is discussed in RBB Economics Brief 03, July 2002 (*www.rbbecon.com/publications/downloads/rbb_brief03.pdf*).

[4] Case IV/M.619 [1997] O.J. L11/30 (upheld on appeal in Case T-102/96 *Gencor v Commission* [1999] E.C.R. II-753).

[5] See Case IV/M.986 *Agfa-Gevaert / Du Pont* [1998] O.J. L211/22, para.46. See generally s.5.3 below on the Commission's approach to "parallel" or "overlapping" mergers.

[6] Case IV/M.877 *Boeing / McDonnell Douglas* [1997] O.J. L336/16 (all aircraft priced in US dollars; para.28)

conversion of currencies is required, conversion should be carried out using European Central Bank average exchange rates.[7]

(vi) Captive production The question of whether *captive production*[8] and, **4–020** separately, *own label supplies* should be included in the market share calculation depends on issues of market definition discussed in Ch.3. If own label supplies *are* included in the market, then the Commission analyses the implications of the transaction both at a retail level (allocating sales of own label goods to the retailer) *and* at producer level (to determine whether own label suppliers might face difficulties in obtaining competitive terms in contracting out their production requirements).

(a) In *Kaysersberg v Commission*[9] the Court of First Instance considered an appeal against the Commission's decision in *Procter & Gamble / Schickedanz (II)*.[10] The transaction involved a combination of manufacturers of sanitary towels and the Commission had, in analysing market shares at a retail level, allocated own label sales to the retailer and not the manufacturer. The Court stated: "When assessing the market strength of an undertaking which is party to a concentration, the market shares of the products which it manufactures as sub-contractor for retailers which resell those products under their own labels cannot, in principle, be imputed, in whole or in part, to the market share held by that undertaking in regard to similar products which it sells under its own brand. Since the retailers sell those products under their own-labels in order to compete with the products sold under the manufacturers' brands, the market share which they hold as a result of those sales must therefore, as a general rule, be attributed to them for the purpose of assessing the competition to which the manufacturers of premium and secondary brands are subject".[11] However, the Court emphasised that if the merging parties produced a substantial proportion of products sold under own labels in a particular market then a failure to take account of the

---

[7] Case COMP/M.1915 *The Post Office / TPG / SPPL* [2004] O.J. L82/1, para.66 and n.14.
[8] Even if production for own consumption by captive producers is excluded from the market, captive producers may be an important source of potential competition: in Case IV/M.1293 *BP / Amoco* the Commission found that the transaction did not create or strengthen a dominant position in the supply of a product (PIB) to additives customers, even though the merged group's market share exceeded 65%, because customers self-supplied, making them potential entrants into the merchant market (para.37). For the US position, see Areeda, Hovenkamp & Solow, *Antitrust Law* (2nd edn, Aspen Law & Business, 2000), Vol.IIA, para.535e. (For the treatment of market shares when the effect of the merger is to convert some intra-group sales to third party sales, see para.4–015(b) above.)
[9] Case T-290/94 [1997] E.C.R. II-2137.
[10] Case IV/M.430 [1994] O.J. L354/32.
[11] Para.176. See also para.161.

share of production would result in an underestimate of the market position of the merged group.[12]

(b) In *Kimberly-Clark / Scott*[13] the Commission stated: "The essential question is whether retailers would be able to seek valid alternative suppliers for their private-label sales if the merger were allowed to proceed. If this is the case, then in terms of normal competitive assessment, it would be correct to disregard the fact that a high proportion of private-label sales are manufactured by [the merging parties]".

(c) In *Sarah Lee / Courtaulds*,[14] which involved a merger between *manufacturers* of hosiery and intimate apparel, the Commission examined the implications of the transaction both in the downstream retail market and the upstream production market. In calculating market shares in the downstream *retail* market, the Commission allocated sales of own label products to the retailers and not the producers.[15] In calculating market shares in the upstream *production* market, the Commission allocated sales of own label products to the producers.[16]

(d) *Unilever / Bestfoods*[17] involved a combination of producers of food service products for the retail market. The Commission used *retail* shares, seemingly on the basis that they were the best *proxy* of wholesale shares, and allocated sales of own label products to the retailer (and not the manufacturer) whilst noting that the decision on allocation would not have materially affected the position.

(e) In *Imperial Tobacco / Reemtsma Cigarettenfabriken GmbH*[18] the purchaser was a major supplier of own label tubes[19] but the Commission allocated those sales to the distributors because they enjoyed buyer power, had the ability easily and quickly to change supplier,

---

[12] Paras 161 and 177. On the facts of that case, the evidence was that the merging parties had a low share of production of own label goods in the market in question (para.178).

[13] Case IV/M.623 [1996] O.J. L183/1, para.123.

[14] Case COMP/M.1892, paras 46 and 73.

[15] Para.28. See also Case COMP/M.1802 *Unilever / Amora-Maille*.

[16] Para.51. The Commission adopted the same approach in relation to branded and own label biscuits in Case COMP/M.1920 *Nabisco / United Biscuits*, paras 14 and 15. In Case COMP/M.2337 *Nestlé / Ralston Purina* the Commission found that, whilst branded and own label pet food formed part of a single market at a retail level, they did not at a wholesale level, as a retailer wishing to offer own label goods could not use branded supplies: paras 15 to 19. In analysing the market in that case the Commission focused on the market shares at a retail level *including* private label supplies and allocated those sales to the retailer (and not the manufacturer) but *also* took account of the extent to which the parties were suppliers to the private label owners and whether the private label sector would be dependent on the commercial strategy of the merged entity: paras 47 and 50.

[17] Case COMP/M.1990, paras 60 and 61.

[18] Case COMP/M.2779.

[19] Pre-formed paper tubes used by smokers to consume roll-your-own tobacco.

and could enter the market or expand capacity.[20] However, in the UK market for cigarettes, the Commission allocated sales of own label products *to the manufacturers* because own label cigarettes were generally not branded with reference to the retailer (in contrast to the normal position with own label goods) and the target had acquired the trademarks for a large proportion of own label cigarettes sold in the United Kingdom and incurred promotional expenditure in relation to some of the trademarks.[21]

(vii) Market share calculations in cases of supply-side substitution If the **4–021** Commission defines a market to include products A and B on the grounds that B is a supply-side substitute for A, then the market share calculations generally include *all*[22] sales, or capacity[23] held, by producers of products A or B.

Such an approach seems appropriate in the paradigm case of supply-side substitution in which consumers cannot switch between different grades of paper but suppliers can switch readily, leading to a conclusion that the relevant product market comprises paper of all grades. However, in the paradigm case, A is also a supply-side substitute for B (i.e. the substitution is two-way) and all suppliers of paper may compete for contracts of any grade, i.e. a single set of assets can be used to produce a range of products. A more difficult situation arises if the supply-side substitutability operates only one-way and producers of product B would, at pre-merger prices, not consider bidding for contracts to supply product A. Imagine, in such a situation, that the merging parties both supply product A and not product B and suppliers in segment B have existing customer relationships, supported by long-term contracts, tying up a large part of their capacity, raising the question of whether, in calculating shares of the market comprising A and B, *all* of the sales or capacity in segment B should be included or only part and, if so, how that part should be identified. It seems clear in principle that including in the market share calculation all sales or capacity in segment B would fail to provide an accurate proxy for the merged group's market power because it would face effective competition only from other suppliers of product A and the capacity which producers in segment B would divert to production of A if the price of A were to be increased by 5 to 10 per cent. This analysis is

---

[20] Para.30. It is doubtful whether the Commission focused on the right criteria in choosing to allocate own label sales to the distributors. Once it is accepted that own label sales form part of the same antitrust market as branded sales, own label sales should in general be allocated to the party who controls the terms of supply (price, etc.) since that party's actions affect the nature of competition in the market; see para.4–023 below.

[21] Paras 43 to 45.

[22] This is implicit in Case COMP/M.2498 *UPM-Kymmene / Haindl* [2002] O.J. L233/38, paras 13 and 80. The analysis in relation to geographic markets is identical.

[23] "Market Definition in the Media Sector—Economic Issues", Report by Europe Economics for the European Commission, DG Competition, November 2002 (available via *http://europa.eu.int/comm/competition/publications/studies/european_economics.pdf*), para.A.1.69 argues that it is more appropriate to use *capacity* data in such cases.

consistent with the indication in the US Horizontal Merger Guidelines[24] that market shares will generally be calculated on the basis of sales or capacity currently devoted to the market together with the sales or capacity that would be likely to be devoted to the relevant market in response to a small but significant and non-transitory price increase.

4–022 **(viii) Calculation of market shares when a merging party has an interest falling short of sole control in a rival supplier** When a merging party, X, has an *interest falling short of sole control*[25] in another supplier, Y, which is not a merging party,[26] it is necessary to determine whether all, part or none of Y's sales are *attributed* to X in calculating market shares. The issue of how to deal with such links between the merging parties and their competitors is considered in detail in s.14.4 below. On the specific question of the attribution to the merging parties of sales by third parties for the purposes of calculating market shares, in principle the proportion, if any, to be attributed depends on the theory of competitive harm under investigation by the Commission (i.e. how it is hypothesised that the merged group may be able to exercise market power) and whether, and if so, to what extent, X's interest in Y will enable X to act in a manner which causes such harm.[27]

(a) In *General Electric / Honeywell*[28] the Commission considered how to allocate the market shares held by several joint ventures. For each of the joint ventures, it identified which of the parents were independent prime contractors and shared the joint venture's sales equally between those parents (allocating none of the sales to parents which were not independent prime contractors, on the grounds that such companies could not be regarded as independent competing undertakings). The Commission's reasoning on this issue was upheld by

---

[24] 1992 (amended in 1997) (*www.usdoj.gov/atr/public/guidelines/hmg.htm*), para.1.41.

[25] When a merging party, X, has sole control over another supplier, Y, the shares of X and Y are aggregated for the purposes of calculating market shares, even if Y is given management autonomy; see e.g. Case COMP/M.2978 *Lagardère / Natexis / VUP* [2004] O.J. L125/54 (appeal pending in Case T-279/04 *Editions Odile Jacob SAS v Commission*), paras 404 to 414.

[26] If X acquires joint control of Y, then *all* of Y's share is attributed to X for the purposes of examining the effects of the joint venture; see Case IV/JV.1 *Telia / Telenor / Schibsted*; Case COMP/JV.42 *Asahi Glass / Mitsubishi / F2 Chemicals*; Case COMP/M.1915 *The Post Office / TPG / SPPL* [2004] O.J. L82/1; Case COMP/M.2420 *Mitsui / CVRD / Caemi* [2004] O.J. L92/50; and Case COMP/M.3161 *CVRD / Caemi*, para.37.

[27] See also Case COMP/M.1628 *TotalFina / Elf* [2001] O.J. L143/1 (the Commission, in calculating market shares, identified separately capacity which was solely controlled and capacity which was jointly controlled; para.110) and Case COMP/M.3294 *ExxonMobil / BEB*, para.25. See also Council Regulation on the application of Art.81(3) of the Treaty to categories of specialisation agreements [2000] O.J. L304/3, Art.6(1)(c) (providing for shares to be apportioned equally between those undertakings holding joint control over the joint venture when calculating market shares for the purposes of determining whether an agreement benefits from the block exemption).

[28] Case COMP/M.2220 [2004] O.J. L48/1, paras 46, 49 and 67. See also Case IV/M.92 *RVI / VBC / Heuliez*; Case IV/M.390 *Akzo / Nobel Industrier*; and Case IV/M.1157 *Skanska / Skancem* [1999] O.J. L183/1.

the Court of First Instance[29] which stated that the Commission's attribution of shares reflected the commercial realities of the market.[30]

(b) By contrast, in *BP Amoco / Arco*[31] the Commission considered how to attribute market shares in the case of joint ventures operating UK gas pipelines and processing facilities. It noted that the joint ventures generally required unanimity amongst their parents on major decisions, including the conditions of third party access, and that the main competition concern in the case arose from the possibility that the owners of the pipelines would constrain the development of competing gas fields. Since each joint venture parent had a veto right over the grant of third party access, the Commission concluded that market shares should be calculated on the basis of "total capacity, and especially spare capacity, of the infrastructure in which it has an interest".[32] *General Electric / Honeywell* and *BP Amoco / Arco* can be reconciled on the basis that, in the former, the area of competitive concern arose from a reduction in the number of prime contractors, leading the Commission to focus on the influence held by such companies. In that case, if *all* of the sales made by companies in which a prime contractor held a minority stake had been attributed to that prime contractor, then there would have been double counting in the cases of companies jointly controlled by two or more prime contractors, which would have distorted the market share

---

[29] Case T-210/01 *General Electric Company v Commission*, not yet reported, judgment of December 14, 2005, paras 127 to 146. However, the Court found, in paras 147, 458 and 459, that the Commission had erred in failing to recognise that a joint venture partner would have no interest in making financial sacrifices to allow the merged group to favour its own products.

[30] Para.144. This indicates that the Court of First Instance agreed with the Commission's conclusion (and did not decide the appeal on this point on the basis of the margin of discretion accorded to the Commission in the course of a review).

[31] Case IV/M.1532 [2001] O.J. L18/1.

[32] Para.56. The Commission followed the reasoning in *BP Amoco / Arco* in Case COMP/M.2681 *Conoco / Philipps Petroleum*, paras 20 and 21. In Case COMP.M.2745 *Shell / Enterprise Oil* the Commission identified as its main competition concern the possibility that the merged group would foreclose third parties from access to gas pipeline capacity and calculated shares in terms of pipeline *spare* capacity which could be vetoed by the parties (see para.20; see also paras 33, 34, 43 and 44); the Commission also considered the parties' shares of *total* gas pipeline capacity, again on the basis of capacity which could be vetoed by the parties (para.19). A similar issue of "negative control" was identified in Case COMP/M.2883 *Bertelsmann / Zomba*. The Commission stated, at para.37: "during the Time Warner/EMI investigation, the Commission considered that 'basic' market shares such as the ones analysed so far do not reflect accurately by themselves a publisher's true market position, given the overall control enjoyed by a publisher over co-owned or co-administered musical compositions. Whilst partial ownership or administration gives rise only to partial receipts from the composition in question, it nevertheless gives the publisher total (negative) control over the commercial exploitation of that composition. Since the exploitation requires the consent of all right-holders, any partial owner or administrator of a composition have [*sic*] the power to prevent the licensing of that work and thus exercises 100% control over its commercial exploitation. The Commission has therefore addressed as well the issue of negative control during its investigation in the present case".

calculations. By contrast, in *BP Amoco* the issue of competitive concern was whether the merged group might prevent third party access to pipelines and, accordingly, it was necessary to determine the proportion of capacity which could be foreclosed by the merged group from third parties, irrespective of whether other parties also had an interest in those pipelines. Double counting was therefore not a concern.

(c) In *Vodafone Airtouch / Mannesmann*[33] the merged group would have had joint control, by virtue of shareholdings of 25 per cent and 50 per cent, in two of the three holders of Belgian mobile telecommunications licences. The Commission carried out the market share calculation on the basis that the *entirety* of the shares held by the two joint venture companies should be attributed to the merged group.[34] The inference is that the Commission concluded that the merged group would be able to eliminate or substantially reduce competition between the two licensees and, therefore, that the competitive effects of the transaction should be treated as analogous to a full merger of the two licensees.

(d) In *Mitsui / CVRD / Caemi*[35] the merging parties were members of joint ventures with both financial institutions and, separately, a competitor. The Commission included in the market shares of the

---

[33] Case COMP/M.1795.

[34] Paras 31 and 32. See also Case COMP/ECSC.1351 *Usinor / Arbed / Aceralia*, para.231; Case IV/M.1383 *Exxon / Mobil* [2004] O.J. L103/1, paras 446 to 458 (joint control by Mobil of a joint venture with BP; the Commission rejected arguments that the market shares of the joint venture should not be attributed to Mobil); Case IV/M.1430 *Vodafone / AirTouch* (the Commission attributed to the merging parties the entire market shares of those companies in which the parties held joint control; see paras 19, 20 and 26); Case COMP/M.1673 *VEBA / VIAG* [2001] O.J. L188/1 (the Commission allocated to a merging party all sales by a joint venture jointly controlled by that party; para.66); Case COMP/M.1879 *Boeing / Hughes* [2004] O.J. L63/53, paras 60, 78 and 79 (joint control by Boeing over Sea Launch; the market shares of Sea Launch were attributed in their entirety to Boeing); Case COMP/M.1980 *Volvo / Renault VI* (the target was active in the Finnish truck markets but was party to a 50/50 distribution joint venture with a major competitor in those markets; the Commission concluded that the market shares of the target and the competitor should be combined in assessing the competitive effect of the concentration on the markets for trucks in Finland; paras 30 and 31); Case COMP/M.2495 *Haniel / Fels* [2003] O.J. L103/36, paras 69 and 70; Case COMP/M.2568 *Haniel / Ytong* [2003] O.J. L111/1, paras 92 and 93; Case COMP/ M.2690 *Solvay / Montedison-Ausimont* (in which one of the merging parties was active in a market only through a 50/50 joint venture with a rival suppliers and the Commission attributed the *entire* sales of the joint venture to the merged group; paras 83 and 84); Case COMP/M.2947 *Verbund / EnergieAllianz* [2004] O.J. L92/91 (appeal pending in Case T-350/03 *Wirschaftskammer Karnten and best connect Ampere Strompool v Commission*) (share of a supplier which was jointly controlled by a merging party attributed in whole to that merging party; para.131); and Case COMP/M.3431 *Sonoco / Ahlstrom* [2005] O.J. L159/13 (the Commission attributed to the merging parties *all* of the sales of suppliers over which they held joint control, but *none* of the sales of suppliers in which they had non-controlling minority interests, although it stated that adding the sales of such companies would not have altered the competitive assessment; paras 14 to 22).

[35] Case COMP/M.2420 [2004] O.J. L92/50, nn 36, 37 and 38 to the Table at para.169. See also nn 39, 40 and 41.

merging parties *all* output of any company over which they had joint or sole control (irrespective of the identities of the other parties having joint control) *except* that sales by the joint venture to the joint venture partner were excluded.[36] In calculating the shares of competitors, the Commission adopted the same methodology, allocating to the competitors 100 per cent of sales by companies they jointly controlled. This leads to double counting.

(e) In *ECT / PONL / Euromax*[37] the Commission examined a joint venture to construct, develop and operate a container terminal.[38] In calculating market shares, the Commission disregarded conferences in which either of the parents was a member (because *conferences* did not restrict the carrier's choice of ports and/or terminal operators), but took account of *consortia* and *alliances* as they affected the choice of ports and terminal operators.[39]

(f) By contrast, in *Wallenius Lines / Wilhelmsen / Hyundai Merchant Marine*,[40] when considering the effects of a merger on the market for the deep-sea transportation of vehicles, the Commission attributed to the acquirer the share held by a competitor which was part of the same *conference* because the two companies operated as a "collective entity" in providing services on the route in question.[41] The same analysis applies in cases involving *airline alliances*[42] when the merger eliminates competition not only between the merging parties but also with their respective alliance partners.[43]

(g) Similarly, in *DSM / Roche Vitamins*[44] the merging parties were each party to an alliance agreement (with different third parties) covering production, sales and distribution. The Commission calculated shares of both production and sales *for the two alliances* (implicitly attributing sales or production by the alliance partner to the merging party).[45]

---

[36] See para.4–015(c) above.

[37] Case COMP/M.3576.

[38] See also Case COMP/JV.55 *Hutchison / RCPM / ECT* [2003] O.J. L223/1 in which the capacity at a port terminal was allocated in accordance with the breakdown of throughput; one terminal was jointly controlled by two parties and the Commission allocated the capacity in proportion to the parents' shareholdings, 66.6% and 33.3%; the inference is that the Commission concluded that market power was correlated with the ability to control the *use* of the terminal; see paras 72 and 73.

[39] Paras 38 and 39.

[40] Case COMP/M.2879, paras 41 and 42.

[41] See also Case COMP/M.3829 *Maersk / PONL*, para.31 and Case COMP/M.3863 *TUI / CP Ships*, paras 21 and 29.

[42] See, e.g. Case COMP/M.3280 *Air France / KLM* (appeal pending in Case T-177/04 *easyJet Airline Company v Commission*), para.62 and Case COMP/M.3770 *Lufthansa / Swiss*, paras 22, 23 and 116.

[43] See also Case COMP/M.4035 *Telefónica / O2* (mobile telephony alliances).

[44] Case COMP/M.2972 [2004] O.J. L82/73, paras 51 to 62.

[45] Separately, in para.69, the Commission treated two competitors' sales together for the purposes of calculating market shares because one had a 42.7% shareholding in the other (which the Commission concluded was likely to lead to an alignment of their economic interests) and there were distribution agreements between them.

4–023 **(ix) Attribution of market shares in cases of exclusive distribution, toll production and supply of top-up volumes** The issue of attribution of market shares also arises in relation to the appointment of exclusive distributors, the use of third parties to produce goods (under toll-production or subcontracting arrangements) and sales by producers of top-up volumes purchased from rivals.[46] In general, sales by a third party should be attributed to a company if the company can *control* those sales in seeking to exercise market power (i.e. the question is whether, after the company has reduced its own output, it can prevent sales by the third party of the units in issue).[47] If it can, then a proper analysis of its market power requires the attribution of the third party's sales to the company. If it cannot, the sales should be attributed to the third party. In analysing the issue of control, it is important to identify which entity operates on the market, winning business and setting the terms of trade, and to determine whether the arrangements are exclusive and long-term.

(a) If a company, X, has appointed a long-term exclusive distributor, Y, in a territory, sales made by Y are generally properly allocated to Y and not X for the purposes of the market share analysis because it is Y's decisions which determine how competition occurs in the market and a decision by Y to reduce its output could not be defeated by X because Y's appointment is exclusive and long-term.[48] (However, in *Astra Zeneca / Novartis*[49] the Commission found that the merger would create or strengthen a dominant position in a market in which Novartis was active only as a *non-exclusive* distributor for UniRoyal. The Commission relied on the fact that Novartis was the only distributor of the product and that Astra Zeneca had appointed Uni-

---

[46] See generally Werden, "Assigning Market Shares" (2002) 70 *Antitrust Law Journal* 67, at pp. 99 and 100.

[47] See Areeda, Hovenkamp & Solow, *Antitrust Law* (2nd edn, Aspen Law & Business, 2000), Vol.IIA, para.535g.

[48] See Case COMP/M.1925 *Scottish & Newcastle / Groupe Danone* (favouring the attribution of sales of beer produced under licence to the licensee as the licensee was responsible for marketing, but ultimately leaving the point open; paras 14 to 16); Case COMP/M.2044 *Interbrew / Bass* (the Commission considered, at para.43, a licence to brew and distribute certain beer brands and concluded that, because the licensor could determine the price at which the beer was sold by the distributor, the licensee would pose a significantly reduced competitive threat); Case COMP/M.2547 *Bayer / Aventis Crop Science* [2004] O.J. L107/1 (paras 169, 170, 206 and 207); Case COMP/M.2569 *Interbrew / Beck's* (para.30, although this passage is not decisive as the Commission did not express a concluded view; furthermore, the description of the arrangement between the parties was redacted from the public version of the decision on confidentiality grounds); Case COMP/M.2825 *Fortis AG SA / Bernheim-Comofi SA* (the parties were both active in the provision of car parking facilities in Brussels but the Commission examined the parties' activities in the *management* of car parks as opposed to their ownership and, since the car parks owned by the target were already managed by the purchaser, the transaction was regarded as not modifying the competitive situation in the market; para.17); and Case COMP/M.3182 *Scottish & Newcastle / HP Bulmer* (an exclusive distributor of beer brands was treated as the "supplier" of those brands; para.22). For the allocation of market shares in cases of franchised hotels, see Case COMP/M.2197 *Hilton / Accor / Forte / Travel Services JV*.

[49] Case COMP/M.1806 [2004] O.J. L110/1, paras 440 and 442.

Royal its exclusive licensee for a separate product which "means that it would become more delicate for UniRoyal to change distributor" after the merger.)

(b) If a company toll-produces or produces as sub-contractor for an actual supplier, the sales[50] in question should be allocated to the actual supplier which negotiates the terms with the customer and not the toll-producer or sub-contractor *unless* a decision by the actual supplier to reduce its output would be defeated by customers turning to the toll-producer or sub-contractor.[51] In *Framatome / Siemens / Cogema JV*[52] the parties argued that, in calculating shares of the market for spent-fuel racks, the value added by sub-contractors in the respective consortia should not be attributed to the "lead company". The Commission found, however, that such attribution was appropriate as it better reflected the role and market position of the "lead company".[53] In *Skanska / Scancem*[54] the Commission found that sales of concrete produced by Scancem as sub-contractor for other suppliers ought to be attributed to Scancem in calculating market shares for two reasons: "First, no objective reason has been provided why the parties, in the absence of the subcontracting agreements, would not be able to supply the same volumes under their own brands. Secondly, no evidence has been submitted to indicate that the parties' subcontracting partners would be able to supply these volumes without recourse to the production facilities of the parties. As such it must be concluded that the parties produce these volumes because they have the production facilities most suitable for this activity".

(c) If a company, X, produces 100 units and buys 20 top-up units from a rival supplier, Y, sales of the 20 top-up units are generally allocated to Y because, if X sought to exercise market power by reducing its sales from 120 units to 100, Y would simply sell the 20 units directly, i.e. X cannot control the sales of the 20 units after it has reduced its own output and they are to be attributed to Y. In *Ciba-Geigy /*

---

[50] If market shares are calculated by *capacity* it may be necessary to examine the terms of the toll-production agreement to determine whether the capacity is controlled by the owner of the plant or (e.g. through a long-term exclusive arrangement) the counterparty to the agreement.

[51] Case IV/M.1578 *Sanitec / Sphinx* [2000] O.J. L294/1, para.191. In Case IV/M.1182 *Akzo Nobel / Courtaulds* the Commission attributed to Courtaulds sales made on a toll-manufacturing basis to a third party but added, at para.34, that "it could be argued that Courtaulds is not really active in this market at all. In any case it is clear that Courtaulds is not a significant player in this market".

[52] Case COMP/M.1940 [2001] O.J. L289/8.

[53] Para.142. Similarly, in Case COMP/M.1932 *BASF / American Cyanamid (AHP)* the parties argued that American Cyanamid's sales of plant growth regulators should be attributed to BASF because BASF supplied one of the two active ingredients to American Cyanamid. The Commission rejected this as American Cyanamid could have sourced the ingredient from an alternative, generic supplier and American Cyanamid had freedom as to price and marketing because of its well-established brand name.

[54] Case IV/M.1157 [1999] O.J. L183/1, para.151.

Sandoz[55] the merging parties sold some of their fungicides and herbicides through other suppliers of plant protection products; the Commission allocated such sales to the producer (not the rival supplier) in part because the appointments were *short-term*, with termination generally permitted on 12 months' notice.

(d) If a company, X, grants company Y a licence to use X's patent for the purpose of producing a specified number of goods for delivery to Z, Y's sales are properly allocated to X because X controls the sales through its patent licence.[56]

4–024 **(x) Attribution to a merging party of sales by a competitor** The Commission may in certain circumstances attribute to a merging party sales *by a competitor* if the links between the merging party and the competitor provide a strong incentive for the competitor to align its commercial strategy with the merged group. In *AOL / Time Warner*[57] AOL was party to a 50/50 joint venture with Bertelsmann and the two companies had also concluded a joint promotion, distribution and sales agreement. The Commission found that the structural links in particular and, to a lesser extent, the contractual links gave Bertelsmann a "strong incentive" to make its content available preferentially through AOL with the conclusion that sales by Bertelsmann were attributed to AOL in calculating shares of the market for licensing performance and mechanical rights.

(c) The use by the Commission of market share data

4–025 Data about the combined market share of the parties is, by some way, the single most important piece of evidence considered by the Commission in the course of an inquiry under the ECMR. A regression analysis of a large sample of ECMR decisions taken during the period January 1, 2000 to June 30, 2002 concluded that market share data was very significant in determining whether a merger would be blocked or cleared by the Commission.[58]

---

[55] Case IV/M.737 [1997] O.J. L201/1, para.137. The Commission also took into account, in reaching its conclusion, that the merger would broaden the distribution networks of the two companies, reducing the need to use rival suppliers. The Commission noted, however, that when the rival suppliers sold the parties' products as part of a package, sales might fall if the appointment was terminated, with the consequence that the market shares might be overstated.

[56] The example is taken from Areeda, Hovenkamp & Solow, *Antitrust Law* (2nd edn, Aspen Law & Business, 2000), Vol.IIA, para.535g.

[57] Case COMP/M.1845 [2001] O.J. L268/28, paras 44 and 49.

[58] Lindsay, Lecchi & Williams, "Econometrics Study into European Commission Merger Decisions Since 2000" [2003] E.C.L.R. 673, at p.681.

(i) The principal uses of market share data Market share data has three **4–026** principal uses.

(a) Substantial market shares may themselves be evidence of the existence of a dominant position.[59] The Notice on Horizontal Mergers provides: "According to well-established case law, very large market shares—50% or more—may in themselves be evidence of the existence of a dominant market position. However, smaller competitors may act as a sufficient constraining influence if, for example, they have the ability and incentive to increase their supplies".[60]

(b) Data on the parties' combined market share is used by the Commission as a *filter* to enable it to focus on those cases which require careful review. The Notice on Horizontal Mergers provides that: "Market shares and concentration levels provide useful first indications of the market structure and of the competitive importance of both the merging parties and their competitors".[61] The ECMR[62] itself provides that there is a presumption that a merger will not significantly impede effective competition when the market shares of the undertakings concerned do not exceed 25 per cent.[63] However, the

---

[59] See the discussion about whether there is a "critical market share" which enables a supplier to exercise market power in ABA Section of Antitrust Law, *Market Power Handbook* (ABA Publishing, 2005), p.83.

[60] Para.17. The case law includes Case 85/76 *Hoffmann-La Roche v Commission* [1979] E.C.R. 461, para.41; Case C-62/86 *AKZO v Commission* [1991] E.C.R. I-3359, para.60; Case T-221/95 *Endemol v Commission* [1999] E.C.R. II-1299 ("a particularly high market share may in itself be evidence of the existence of a dominant position, in particular where, as here, the other operators on the market hold only much smaller shares"; para.134); Case T-210/01 *General Electric Company v Commission*, not yet reported, judgment of December 14, 2005, paras 115 and 571; and Case T-282/02 *Cementbouw Handel & Industrie v Commission*, not yet reported, judgment of February 23, 2006, para.201. The Notice on Horizontal Mergers also states, at para.17: "A merger involving a firm whose market share will remain below 50% after the merger may also raise competition concerns in view of other factors such as the strength and number of competitors, the presence of capacity constraints or the extent to which the products of the merging parties are close substitutes". In Case T-374/00 *Verband der freien Rohrwerke and others v Commission* [2003] E.C.R. II-2275, the Court of First Instance stated, at para.112, that the mere fact that the merged group would have a combined market share of 30.5% did not mean that the merger had the effect of creating or strengthening a dominant position.

[61] Para.14.

[62] In Germany there is a presumption of dominance in cases involving the merger of companies with a combined market share of 33%.

[63] ECMR, recital 32 (formerly recital 15). See also the Notice on Horizontal Mergers, para.18 and n.24 (pointing out that the indication does not apply to cases in which the proposed merger creates or strengthens a position of collective dominance). In Case T-5/02 *Tetra Laval BV v Commission* [2002] E.C.R. II-4381, the Court of First Instance referred to recital 15 of Regulation 4064/89 in stating, at para.232, that "it is clear that a market share of [10–20%] is far short of amounting to a dominant position on that market". (The Court of First Instance's decision was upheld on appeal on the basis of reasoning not relating to this issue in Case C-12/03P *Commission v Tetra Laval BV*, not yet reported, judgment of February 15, 2005.) See also Case COMP/M.3779 *Pernod Ricard / Allied Domecq* (ruling out concerns when the combined market share did not exceed 25%; para.27) and the UK Competition Commission's Guidelines on Merger References, March 2003 (*www.competition-commission.org.uk*) (combined share of 25% or above would be sufficient to raise potential concerns; para.3.23).

Commission has also emphasised that "there is no formal threshold in Community merger control for potential market dominance".[64]

(c) The merged group's market share is taken by the Commission as the best working proxy of its market power.[65] This means that, other things being equal, the higher the merged group's combined market share, the more compelling the evidence of competitive constraints that will be required by the Commission before granting approval.[66]

4–027 (ii) **Limitations on the usefulness of market share data** However, it is clear that, whilst the practical significance of data about the merged group's

---

[64] The Commission's XXIXth Annual Report on Competition Policy, 1999, box 7 on p.66. It is noteworthy that, earlier in the history of the ECMR, the Commission applied a filtering threshold at a 50% level, but the Commission has in recent years gradually expanded its substantive jurisdiction by investigating more carefully cases which would historically have been approved. See the UK House of Lords Select Committee on the European Union, Thirty-second Report, "The Review of the EC Merger Regulation", July 23, 2002, HL Paper 165 (available at *www.parliament.the-stationery-office.co.uk/pa/ld200102/ldselect/ldeucom/165/16501.htm*), para.139: "Mr Götz Drauz, the Director of the Merger Task Force, admitted that the Commission had 'developed and exploited progressively' its interpretation of dominance since 1989, when there was a presumption that dominance could only occur in cases where an individual company had more than 50% of the market. The Commission had since found dominance in market shares as low as 27%". For cases in which the Commission identified competition concerns in markets in which the merged group would have had a relatively low market share see, e.g. Case COMP/M.1684 *Carrefour / Promodes* (combined share below 30%) and Case IV/M.1412 *Hutchinson Whampoa / RMPM / ECT* (share of 36%). Götz Drauz, then the Director of the Merger Task Force, "Recent Developments in the Assessment of Dominance", published in *EC Merger Control: Ten Years On* (International Bar Association, 2000), p.109, at 120 stated: "I think we cannot stick to static interpretations of the case law as if they were carved in stone. Just because there have been situations where we have accepted a combined market position of 50% in the past, that does not guarantee that such an operation will necessarily be cleared today".

[65] See Areeda, Hovenkamp & Solow, *Antitrust Law* (2nd edn, Aspen Law & Business, 2000), Vol.IIA, para.532a. See also DG Competition Discussion Paper on the Application of Article 82 of the Treaty to Exclusionary Abuses, December 2005, para.32: "Market share is only a proxy for market power, which is the decisive factor".

[66] The Commission stated in its XXIst Report on Competition, 1991, at p.362, that "high market shares can be an indication of the existence of a dominant position". See also Case IV/M.68 *Tetra Pak / Alfa Laval* [1991] O.J. L290/35 ("A market share as high as 90% is, in itself, a very strong indicator of a dominant position. However, in certain rare circumstances even such a high market share may not necessarily result in dominance".); Case IV/M.222 *Mannesmann / Hoesch* [1993] O.J. L114/34 (in which the Commission stated, at para.91: "High market shares represent an important factor as evidence of a dominant position provided they not only reflect current conditions but are also a reliable indicator of future conditions. If no other structural factors are identifiable which are liable in due course to change the existing conditions of competition, market shares have to be viewed as a reliable indicator of future conditions".); Case IV/M.477 *Mercedes-Benz / Kässbohrer* [1995] O.J. L211/1 ("High market shares do not in themselves justify the assumption of a dominant position. At any rate, they do not allow a dominant position to be assumed if other structural factors are detectable which, in the foreseeable future, may alter the conditions of competition and justify a more relative view of the significance of the market share of the merged companies"; see para.65); Case IV/M.1439 *Telia / Telenor* [2001] O.J. L40/1 (Telia had a market share of 90 to 100% and the Commission regarded this as decisive: "With a market share of this size, Telia is clearly dominant"; para.183); and Case COMP/M.2187 *CVC / Lenzing* [2004] O.J. L82/20 (the Commission stated, at para.138, that: "The existence of a dominant position may derive from several factors which, taken separately, are not necessarily determinative; amongst these factors, a highly important one is the existence of large market shares").

market share should not be understated, it forms only one component of the Commission's analysis of the transaction.

(a) The Commission is willing to consider a wide range of evidence which tends to show that, following the transaction, the merged group will not enjoy market power, notwithstanding its high market share. This is clear from numerous cases approving transactions involving high market shares[67] and is corroborated by the Commission's indication that: "Since the adoption of the Merger Regulation in 1989, the application of the notion of dominance has evolved, allowing it to be adapted both to developments in economic theory and to refinements of the now available econometric tools to measure market power. This implies that merger assessment today can be less reliant on the rather blunt and imprecise market share test than it was 10 years ago".[68]

(b) Conversely, market shares may *understate* the competitive significance of one or more of the merging parties, in particular if the company is innovating, expanding, cutting prices or generally independent when compared with the rest of the market.[69] For example,

---

[67] See, e.g. Case IV/M.468 *Siemens / Italtel* [1995] O.J. L161/27 (share of 60% cleared; see para.38); Case IV/M.477 *Mercedes-Benz / Kässbohrer* [1995] O.J. L211/1 (share of 73.7% cleared; paras 61 and 99); Case COMP/M.1225 *Enso / Stora* [1999] O.J. L254/9 (combined share of EEA liquid packaging board between 50 and 70% cleared in the light in particular of countervailing buyer power); Case IV/M.1293 *BP / Amoco* (share of supply of PIB to additives customers in excess of 65% cleared because customers self-supplied, giving them buyer power and making them potential entrants into the merchant market; para.37); Case IV/M.1313 *Danish Crown / Vestjyske Slagterier* [2000] O.J. L20/1 (share of 80% cleared); Case IV/M.1578 *Sanitec / Sphinx*, [2000] O.J. L294/1 (shares in the region of [< 60%] and, for one product, exceeding [< 70%] cleared; see paras 161 and 164); Case COMP/M.1882 *Pirelli / BICC* [2003] O.J. L70/35 (combined shares in the United Kingdom and Italy of 75 to 95% cleared); Case COMP/M.1915 *The Post Office / TPG / SPPL* [2004] O.J. L82/1 (share of 60 to 70% of outbound cross-border business mail including franking machines cleared; see paras 66 and 99 and Table 1a); Case COMP/M.2201 *MAN / Auwärter* [2002] O.J. L116/35 (shares of 48 to 50% in the supply of city buses cleared; see Table 1); Case COMP/M.2602 *Gerling / NCM* (share of 60 to 70% cleared; see para.44); Case COMP/M.2922 *Pfizer / Pharmacia* (combined share of 60 to 70% cleared because the merger did not remove a main competitor and the target's product was off-patent with a small and declining share; paras 65 to 67); Case COMP/M.3431 *Sonoco / Ahlstrom* [2005] O.J. L159/13 (share of 80 to 90% of a putative market cleared because the market was very small in terms of volume supplied compared with the European total and there were credible rival suppliers with the capacity to serve the market; para.95); Case COMP/M.3687 *Johnson & Johnson / Guidant* (share of 85 to 95% in a national market with an increment of 25 to 35% cleared because there were other strong suppliers in the EEA as a whole; paras 178 and 181) Case COMP/M.3751 *Novartis / Hexal* (share of 70 to 75% cleared in the light of likely new entry; p.17); and Case COMP/M.3789 *Johnson Controls / Robert Bosch / Delphi SLI* (share of 50 to 60% cleared; see para.15).

[68] Commission Green Paper on the Review of Council Regulation (EEC) No. 4064/89, December 11, 2001, COM (2001) 745/6 final, p.39.

[69] See s.7.5 below. See also the Australian Merger Guidelines, June 1999 (*www.accc.gov.au/merger/fr_mer gers.html*) (paras 5.139 and 5.164); the New Zealand Merger Guidelines, 2004 (*www.comcom.govt.nz/Publications/ContentFiles/Documents/MergersandAcquisitionsGuidelines. PDF*), para.7.2; the UK Office of Fair Trading's Substantive Merger Guidelines, May 2003 (*www.oft.gov.uk*) (noting, at para.4.8, that non-coordinated effects may arise if one of the merging firms is a "'maverick'—an important rivalrous force in the market representing a

in *Hoffmann-La Roche / Boehringer Mannheim*[70] the Commission emphasised that Roche had been one of the most dynamic competitors, enjoying the highest growth in the market. Similarly, in *Metso / Svedala*[71] the purchaser had developed a prototype of a new product and the Commission identified concerns about the combination of the target's leading market position with the purchaser's promising technology, which was expected to become more successful than the purchaser's existing products.

(d) Interpreting market share data

4–028 There are six particular points to note in interpreting market share data.

4–029 **(i) Changes in market shares** Evidence about changes in market shares and customer contracting patterns may provide strong evidence of the merged group's likely market power. The Notice on Horizontal Mergers states: "Changes in historic market shares may provide useful information about the competitive process and the likely future importance of various competitors, for instance, by indicating whether firms have been gaining or losing market shares".[72]

    (a) If the merging parties have held consistently high market shares over several years, this suggests that they enjoy market power.[73] In *General Electric / Honeywell*[74] the Commission stated that: "The fact that GE's market shares have been not only high but steadily increasing over time ... at the expense of [the two leading competitors] is as such indicative of dominance".[75]

    (b) Volatile market shares over time suggest that market share is not indicative of market power.[76]

---

competitive constraint greater than its market share indicates, whose elimination may thus be an important change in competitive dynamics"); the UK House of Lords Select Committee on the European Union, Thirty-second Report, "The Review of the EC Merger Regulation", July 23, 2002, HL Paper 165 (available at *www.parliament.the-stationery-office.co.uk/pa/ ld200102/ldselect/ldeucom/165/16501.htm*), para.148; the US Horizontal Merger Guidelines of the National Association of Attorneys General, 1993 (available at *www.naag.org/issues/pdf/at-hmerger_guidelines.pdf*), Appendix D; and Areeda & Hovenkamp, *Antitrust Law* (2nd edn, Aspen Law & Business, 2002), Vol.III, para.701c.

[70] Case IV/M.950 [1998] O.J. L234/14, para.91.
[71] Case COMP/M.2033 [2004] O.J. L88/1, paras 185 and 188.
[72] Para.15.
[73] Case IV/M.68 *Tetra Pak / Alfa-Laval* [1991] O.J. L290/35.
[74] Case COMP/M.2220 [2004] O.J. L48/1 (prohibition decision upheld on appeal in Case T-210/ 01 *General Electric Company v Commission*, not yet reported, judgment of December 14, 2005).
[75] Para.83.
[76] See, e.g. Case IV/M.9 *Fiat Geotech / Ford New Holland*; Case IV/M.235 *Elf Aquitaine-Thyssen / Minol*; Case IV/M.781 *Schering / Gehe-Jenapharm*; Case COMP/M.1672 *Volvo / Scania* [2001] O.J. L143/74, paras 270 and 294; Case COMP/M.2036 *Valeo / Labinal*, para.29; Case COMP/M.2199 *Quantum / Maxtor*, para.16; and Case COMP/M.3486 *Magna / New Venture Gear*, para.41.

(c) Equally, a high turnover of customers or "churn" (i.e. frequent switching or volatility in customers) suggests that competition is dynamic even if market share and concentration ratios appear constant.[77]

(d) If contracts for supply in *future periods* have already been switched away from the merging parties, this may indicate that they will not enjoy market power.[78]

(c) Finally, market shares may not be indicative of market power if they are dependent on substantial volumes of business from one or a small number of customers which could switch to alternative suppliers. For example,[79] in *Sampo | Varma Sampo | If Holding | JV*[80] the Commission took account, in clearing the transaction, of the fact that a large share of one of the merging parties' sales could be attributed to one large customer and, if that customer were lost, its market share would drop significantly. However, the Commission will generally not *exclude* sales to significant customers from the market share calculations. For example, in *General Electric Company v Commission*[81] the Court of First Instance rejected a challenge to the inclusion in the market share figures of contracts for the supply of engines to a single plane (the second and third generation Boeing B737), stating that the Commission could properly take the view that the applicant's large market share, which in part resulted from that success, was liable to alter the state of competition in the market in a way favourable to General Electric.

(ii) Increment in market share The Commission examines the *increment* in **4–030** market share arising as a result of the merger. The Court of First Instance has confirmed that a merger may be prohibited under the ECMR only if it has the "direct and immediate"[82] effect, through a "substantial alteration" to competition,[83] of significantly impeding effective competition.[84] In gen-

---

[77] For discussion, see Scherer & Ross, *Industrial Market Structure and Economic Performance* (3rd edn, Houghton Mifflin Co, 1990), p.89. In Case IV/M.1551 *AT&T | Mediaone* the Commission relied, at para.19, on high levels of customer churn and strong variations in market shares as evidence of strong competition in the market when considering whether coordinated effects were likely.

[78] Although the Commission will examine whether the merging parties may win share from other sources to make up for the lost contracts: Case COMP/JV.55 *Hutchison | RCPM | ECT* [2003] O.J. L223/1, paras 56 and 57.

[79] See also Case COMP/M.1745 *EADS* (a large part of one of the merging parties' turnover was derived from a single customer with the consequence that the party's market power ultimately depended on that customer's ability to turn to other competitive suppliers (and, on the facts, it could not): paras 87 and 94); Case COMP/M.3486 *Magna | New Venture Gear*, para.41; and Case COMP/M.3571 *IBM | Maersk Data | DMData*, para.32.

[80] Case COMP/M.2676, para.26.

[81] Case T-210/01, not yet reported, judgment of December 14, 2005, paras 173 to 180.

[82] Case T-102/96 *Gencor v Commission* [1999] E.C.R. II-753, para.94 and Case T-342/99 *Airtours plc v Commission* [2002] E.C.R. II-2585, para.58.

[83] Case T-2/93 *Air France v Commission* [1994] E.C.R. II-323, paras 78 and 79; Case T-102/96 *Gencor v Commission* [1999] E.C.R. II-753, paras 170, 180 and 193; and Case T-342/99 *Airtours plc v Commission* [2002] E.C.R. II-2585, paras 58 and 82.

[84] Case T-342/99 *Airtours plc v Commission* [2002] E.C.R. II-2585, para.58.

eral, the Commission accepts that increments in market share of less than 1 per cent do not satisfy this test. For example,[85] in *Glaxo Wellcome / SmithKline Beecham*[86] the Commission noted that in "7 markets, the combined market share is above 40% but with an accretion of less than 1%" and did not discuss these markets further. In *Mercedes-Benz / Kässbohrer*[87] the Commission regarded an increment in market share of 1.6 per cent as insignificant. Similarly, in *Nestlé / Ralston Purina*[88] the Commission found that an increment in market share of 1 to 5 per cent would not significantly strengthen a dominant position. Finally, in *Sanitec / Sphinx*[89] the Commission noted that "the increment of market share resulting from the operation is relatively low, only some [< 10 per cent]".

However, this approach is not inflexible: it is possible to envisage

---

[85] In Case T-114/02 *BaByliss v Commission* [2003] E.C.R. II-1279, the Court of First Instance considered markets where the acquirer had a share of more than 40% and there was some overlap. The Court stated, at paras 320 and 321, that serious doubts (for the purposes of phase I approval) can be ruled out only when the overlap is "really insignificant", adding: "Although it may be true that there is no significant overlap where a market share is close to 0%, the same cannot be true where it is close to 10%". See also Case IV/M.17 *Aérospatiale / MMB* (increment represented five helicopters per year); Case IV/M.57 *Digital / Kienzle* (increment of 4%); Case IV/M.256 *Linde / Fiat* (increment of 1%); Case IV/M.289 *PepsiCo / KAS* (increment of 1%); Case IV/M.317 *Degussa / Ciba-Geigy*; Case IV/M.580 *ABB / Daimler Benz* [1997] O.J. L11/1 (increments of 1 and 2% regarded as "marginal"); Case IV/M.812 *Allianz / Vereinte*; Case IV/M.1082 *Allianz / AGF*; Case COMP/M.1932 *BASF / American Cyanamid (AHP)* (combined market share of 70 to 80% and increment of *more* than 5% cleared because "Cyanamid adds only a very small percentage to BASF's market share, suggesting that ... the market structure will hardly change as a result of the proposed merger operation"; para.53); Case COMP/M.1980 *Volvo / Renault VI* (increment of 3% to 40% cleared as the main competition seemed to take place between the acquirer and companies other than the target; para.31); Case COMP/M.2192 *SmithKline Beecham / Block Drug* (increment of less than 1% cleared: para.40); Case COMP/M.2495 *Haniel / Fels* [2003] O.J. L103/36, paras 85 to 87; Case COMP/M.2517 *Bristol Myers Squibb / Du Pont* (combined share of 50 to 60% but increment below 5%; transaction cleared; paras 30 and 31); Case COMP/M.2922 *Pfizer / Pharmacia* (markets involving increments of less than 1% disregarded; separately, pre-existing market share of 70 to 80% and increment of less than 5% approved on the basis that the increment was small and the product accounting for the increment was off-patent; paras 20 and 93); Case COMP/M.3060 *UCB / Solutia* (increment of less than 5%; transaction cleared; para.57); Case COMP/M.3062 *IBM / Rational* (increment of 1% not sufficient to create or strengthen a dominant position; para.29); Case COMP/ M.3083 *GE / Instrumentarium* [2004] O.J. L109/1 (the Commission found that overlaps were significant when the merged group's combined share was close to or in excess of 50% and the increment exceeded 5%; para.115); Case COMP/M.3465 *Syngenta CP / Advanta* (increments of not above 2%; paras 65, 69, 70 and 83); COMP/M.3593 *Apollo / Bakelite* (parties had shares of 60 to 70% and 0 to 10%, but there was no significant impediment to effective competition because the smaller player was "relatively marginal"; para.98); and Case COMP/ M.3732 *Procter & Gamble / Gillette*, para.55. In Case COMP/M.2569 *Interbrew / Beck's* the Commission cleared without undertakings a transaction in which (see para.21): "In Belgium, Interbrew/Beck's' combined share in the Belgian all-beer on-trade market is [50–60]%, of which the Beck's increment is [< 1]%". In Case COMP/M.2602 *Gerling / NCM* the Commission stated, at para.57, that, following implementation of the remedies offered by the parties, "the remaining overlap, created by the transaction, of below 1% on the Dutch market and below 0.5% on the Danish market will not significantly impede competition on these markets".

[86] Case COMP/M.1846, para.82

[87] Case IV/M.477 [1995] O.J. L211/1, paras 59, 60 and 102.

[88] Case COMP/M.2337, para.38.

[89] Case IV/M.1578 [2000] O.J. L294/1, para.163.

circumstances in which a small player has a substantial impact on the market,[90] e.g. through an aggressive bidding strategy[91]; similarly, the acquirer may have such a substantial market position[92] that the elimination of *any* competition is regarded as problematic. For example, in *Blokker / Toys 'R' Us (II)*[93] an increment in market share of 3 to 10 per cent led to the transaction being prohibited because "the combination of the increase in market share with a number of factors which together demonstrate that the potential of the acquired business is much greater than is reflected in its actual market share, further strengthens the dominant position of Blokker".[94]

(iii) Gap in market share If the merged group will be the largest supplier in the market, the Commission will examine the *gap* between its share and that of its next largest rival. Other things being equal, the larger the gap, the greater the likelihood of non-coordinated effects.[95]   **4–031**

(iv) Directions of shifts in market shares The Commission reviews the directions of shifts in market shares. If shifts in the market shares held by one of the merging parties tend to correspond to equal and opposite shifts in the market shares held by the other merging party,[96] this suggests that the merging parties are close competitors (since, in the absence of any other evidence, they appear to win business from one another).   **4–032**

(v) Shrinkage effects arising from the merger In calculating the predicted market share of the merged group by adding the pre-merger market shares of the merging parties, it is assumed[97] that none of the parties' customers will switch to other suppliers in response to the merger. However, this   **4–033**

---

[90] See s.7.5 below.

[91] See Case COMP/M.2568 *Haniel / Ytong* [2003] O.J. L111/1, para.126.

[92] See Case T-210/01 *General Electric Company v Commission*, not yet reported, judgment of December 14, 2005, para.551 (rejecting an argument that a merger to monopoly did not involve a significant impediment to effective competition when the target was relatively weak prior to the merger). See also Case IV/M.68 *Tetra Pak / Alfa-Laval* [1991] O.J. L290/5 (in which the Commission noted, in s.4, that: "When faced with ... a high degree of dominance, the Commission must be particularly vigilant, because in such circumstances even a very small increase in market power can have a disproportionately large negative effect on the competitive conditions in the market place".) and Case COMP/M.3829 *Maersk / PONL* (emphasising that the limited competition between the parties was important in a market characterised by the absence of competition; para.108).

[93] Case IV/M.890 [1998] O.J. L316/1, para.88.

[94] See also Case COMP/M.1741 *MCI WorldCom / Sprint* [2003] O.J. L300/1 ("it is incumbent on the Commission to investigate any creation or strengthening of a dominant position in a notified operation. Increase in the market share of the parties is one of the indicators looked at to assess the changes in the market power detained by the notifying parties"; para.247).

[95] See para.14–003 below.

[96] Case COMP/M.1672 *Volvo / Scania* [2001] O.J. L143/74, para.82.

[97] See the Notice on Horizontal Mergers, para.15.

assumption may be rebutted as some customers may switch to maintain leverage over the merged group, and competitors are likely to change their price and output decisions to take account of the merger. Evidence of likely customer and competitor reaction may help to show that high market shares will be rapidly eroded following the merger. The Commission is willing to take account of such *shrinkage*[98] effects when the merger "can be safely predicted to lead to market share losses that will significantly change the competitive situation"[99] (i.e. when the effects are both likely and material). For example,[1] in *Pirelli / BICC*[2] the Commission concluded that the merged group was unlikely to sustain the combined share of the two companies separately as the main customers were likely to diversify their supplier-base. This conclusion was supported by evidence from rival suppliers and internal guidelines of certain of the main customers indicating that they would maintain at least three suppliers of the products in question. In *Ernst & Young France / Andersen France*[3] the Commission found that the parties' market shares would inevitably be reduced following the merger because of conflicts of interest since, under the French regulatory regime, a single firm could not act as both of the two statutory auditors required by companies.[4]

---

[98] Compare Areeda, Hovenkamp & Solow, *Antitrust Law* (2nd edn, Aspen Law & Business, 1998), Vol.IV, para.932a.

[99] Case COMP/M.1672 *Volvo / Scania* [2001] O.J. L143/74, para.116. The Commission also noted, at para.129, that "it is doubtful whether effects which only materialise after four years can be defined as 'immediate', which is what Volvo contends in this case". In Case IV/M.986 *Agfa-Gevaert / Du Pont* [1998] O.J. L211/22, as well as losing sales through the merger, the merged group was expected to acquire new customers because a parallel merger in the industry was also likely to lead to shrinkage effects; para.48. In Case COMP/M.2676 *Sampo / Varma Sampo / If Holding / JV* the Commission took account, at para.26, in clearing the transaction, of the fact that one of the parties was planning to run down completely the business which created the overlap. See also Case IV/M.737 *Ciba-Geigy / Sandoz* [1997] O.J. L201/1, para.138.

[1] See Case IV/M.42 *Alcatel / Telettra* [1991] O.J. L122/48 (the merged group's high market share in Spain arose because a single customer, Telefonica, had chosen the merging parties as its main suppliers; the Commission found that: "Since Telefonica has maintained a diversified purchasing policy up to now, it is not probable that the new combined entity will sustain the same market share as achieved by the parties as competitors"); Case IV/M.477 *Mercedes-Benz / Kässbohrer* [1995] O.J. L211/1 (the Commission noted, at para.64, that the parties had similar market positions in terms of brand and models and added: "Experience has shown that, precisely in such a situation, a merger produces significant shrinkage effects. Such an effect could, for example, be seen in the UK following the acquisition of British Leyland by Volvo".); and Case COMP/M.3431 *Sonoco / Ahlstrom* [2005] O.J. L159/13 (the Commission found that the market share of the merged group would probably be lower than the sum of the individual shares as customers sought to avoid over-dependence on one supplier; it relied on evidence from both customers and competitors; nevertheless, it found that this share shifting would not be sufficient to deprive the merged group of market power; para.91). See also the Commission's XXIst Annual Report on Competition Policy, 1991, p.363: "If two important suppliers merge in an industry where customers follow a dual or triple sourcing policy, it may not be acceptable for customers to maintain past volumes with the new firm. In such a case a mere addition of market shares could overstate the real strength of the new entity".

[2] Case COMP/M.1882 [2003] O.J. L70/35, para.71 and n.33.

[3] Case COMP/M.2816, para.62. The Commission also took account of the fact that clients would continue to be lost as a result of the Enron scandal.

[4] See also Case COMP/M.3579 *WPP / Grey* (possible shrinkage in media buying because of conflict issues in representing two or more clients in the same industry; paras 71 and 88).

(vi) Small markets or small numbers of transactions per year In cases in which **4–034** a merger involves a very small market or a small number of transactions per year, the Commission may be willing to accept that high market shares in one year are a result of statistical accident rather than being indicative of market power. For example,[5] in *Unicredito / HVB*[6] the Commission cleared a transaction involving a combined share of 50 to 60 per cent, in particular on the grounds that there was a limited number of highly sophisticated purchasers and the market shares might change significantly even if only one customer (in particular one of the larger customers) were to change its supplier.

4.3 CONCENTRATION DATA

Concentration data seeks to convey information about the degree to which **4–035** production (or procurement) is concentrated in the hands of a few large firms.[7] Such data is a useful supplement to an analysis of the merged group's market share and the gap between the shares held by the merged group and its nearest rival. In particular, if the competitors are all very small it is more likely that the merged group will have substantial market power.[8] From a merger control perspective, the objective in measuring market concentration in an inquiry into possible non-coordinated effects is to provide the best proxy of the ability of the merged group profitably to raise prices beyond the pre-merger prevailing level.[9] This means that the best way of calculating market concentration may vary depending on the characteristics of the market.[10] There are three main measures of concentration: the Herfindahl-Hirschman Index, concentration ratios, and the Lerner Index.

---

[5] See also Case COMP/M.1672 *Volvo / Scania* [2001] O.J. L143/74, paras 271 and 294 and Case COMP/M.3820 *Avnet / Memec*, para.40. See also para.4–017 above on the scope in such cases to calculate market shares on the basis of sales over periods exceeding one year.

[6] Case COMP/M.3894, paras 47 and 48.

[7] See Clarke, *Industrial Economics* (Blackwell, 1985), pp.9 to 19. Areeda, Hovenkamp & Solow, *Antitrust Law* (2nd edn, Aspen Law & Business, 1998), Vol.IV, note, at para.927a, that, whilst the links between price and high concentration are fairly robust, those between innovation and concentration are much weaker.

[8] By contrast, if the post-merger market will be populated by a few, large firms, non-coordinated effects are less likely but there may be greater scope for coordinated effects (i.e. collective dominance); see Ch.8.

[9] Concentration data is also commonly used as an aid in determining the susceptibility of the market to coordinated effects. However, see Kühn, "Closing Pandora's Box? Joint Dominance After the Airtours Judgment", published as Ch.3 of *The Pros and Cons of Merger Control* by the Swedish Competition Authority in 2002 (and available at *http://www.kkv.se/ bestall/pdf/skrift_proscons.pdf*), p.46, who explains that the use of HHI data in examining coordinated effects can be misleading because a merger which increases the asymmetry in asset distribution between the colluding firms can reduce the likelihood of coordinated effects even though it increases the HHI score.

[10] There is substantial debate about the extent to which different measures of concentration provide a proxy for the merged group's power profitably to raise price. For example, Demsetz contends that high price-cost margins are associated with high concentration (when more

4–036   First, the *Herfindahl-Hirschman Index* ("HHI")[11] takes account of the relative sizes of companies in the market as a whole. The HHI increases as the number of firms falls and the variance of the market shares increases. The HHI is calculated[12] by summing the squares of the market shares (measured in percentages) held by each of the participants in the market, e.g. if the market comprises five suppliers, A, B, C, D, and E with respectively 30, 20, 20, 18 and 12 per cent of the market and suppliers A and B propose to merge, the pre-merger HHI is 2,168 and the post-merger HHI is 3,368, an increment ("delta") of 1,200. If the shares of some of the participants are unknown, a *range* can be calculated, e.g. if it is known that the shares of the three largest suppliers A, B and C are 50, 20 and 10 per cent, then the top of the HHI range is calculated by assuming that there are two other suppliers each with shares of 10 per cent and the bottom by assuming that the unaccounted 20 per cent is represented by numerous small suppliers (the square of whose market shares is approximately nil). The range in such a case is 3,000 to 3,200. *If* the Cournot model accurately describes an oligopolistic market, then the HHI is an accurate predictor of pricing behaviour.[13] If it does not, the predictive power of the HHI is reduced.[14] This was recognised by the Director General of DG Competition, Philip Lowe, who emphasised[15] that the 2002 draft Commission Notice on Horizontal Mergers used the HHI index as a threshold in the context of homogeneous goods and market shares as a threshold in the context of differentiated goods (however, the final version of the Notice does not draw such a rigorous distinction between competition in homogeneous goods and competition in differentiated goods).

The Commission uses the HHI as part of its analysis and the Form CO now requires notifying parties to identify pre- and post-merger HHIs and the delta for affected markets.[16] Historically, the Commission used[17] the

---

efficient producers prevail) but that high concentration levels do not result in high price-cost margins. See the discussion in Viscusi, Vernon & Harrington, *Economics of Regulation and Antitrust* (3rd edn, The MIT Press, 2000), pp.149, 150; Scherer & Ross, *Industrial Market Structure and Economic Performance* (3rd edn, Houghton Mifflin Co, 1990), especially at p.430; and Areeda, Hovenkamp & Solow, *Antitrust Law* (2nd edn, Aspen Law & Business, 2000), Vol.IIA, para.404d.

[11] See Areeda, Hovenkamp & Solow, *Antitrust Law* (2nd edn, Aspen Law & Business, 1998), Vol.IV, para.931a2, noting in particular that the effect of a merger on the HHI is the same irrespective of the remaining structure of the market.

[12] See the Notice on Horizontal Mergers, para.16.

[13] See paras 2–019 to 2–021 above and Carlton & Perloff, *Modern Industrial Organization* (4th edn, Addison-Wesley, 2005), p.283.

[14] See Areeda, Hovenkamp & Solow, *Antitrust Law* (2nd edn, Aspen Law & Business, 1998), Vol.IV, para.931b.

[15] Speech, "The future shape of European merger control", Brussels, February 17, 2003 (*http://europa.eu.int/comm/competition/speeches/*).

[16] Form CO, para.7.3.

[17] See, e.g. Case COMP/JV.55 *Hutchison / RCPM / ECT* [2003] O.J. L223/1, para.50 and n.51; Case COMP/M.1628 *TotalFina / Elf* [2001] O.J. L143/1, paras 199 and 217; Case COMP/M.2044 *Interbrew / Bass*, para.65; and Case COMP/M.2498 *UPM-Kymmene / Haindl* [2002] O.J. L233/38, para.115.

HHI thresholds in the US Horizontal Merger Guidelines.[18] However, the Notice on Horizontal Mergers uses marginally different thresholds, stating that the Commission is unlikely to identify horizontal competition concerns in cases in which the aggregate HHI following the transaction is below 1000.[19] The Notice also provides that horizontal competition concerns are unlikely to be identified if the post-merger HHI is between 1,000 and 2,000 and the delta is below 250, or if the post-merger HHI is above 2,000 but the delta is below 150, except in either case, when special circumstances are identified.[20] The Notice does *not* state that competition concerns arise in cases above these thresholds (there is simply no presumption in such cases that the Commission is unlikely to identify horizontal competition concerns).[21] The Commission is now applying the criteria in the Notice.[22]

Vincent Verouden, a Commission official, has provided an explanation for the approach to HHI data in the Notice.[23] In selecting the thresholds, the Commission carried out an analysis of a large number of its previous decisions and found that it was difficult to identify thresholds which applied

---

[18] The US Horizontal Merger Guidelines, 1992 (amended in 1997) (*www.usdoj.gov/atr/public/guidelines/hmg.htm*), distinguish the following cases:

(a) the post-merger HHI is below 1,000: such mergers generally require no further analysis;
(b) the post-merger HHI is between 1,000 and 1,800: mergers within this range producing an increment of less than 100 ordinarily require no further analysis; mergers producing an increment of more than 100 "potentially" raise significant competitive concerns depending on the operation of the market; and
(c) the post-merger HHI is above 1,800: mergers producing an increment of less than 50 ordinarily require no further analysis; mergers producing an increment of more than 50 "potentially" raise significant competitive concerns depending on the operation of the market; and when the increment is over 100 it is "presumed" that the merger is likely to create or enhance market power or facilitate its exercise.

The US Horizontal Merger Guidelines, para.1.5.1, make clear that the object in looking at HHI data is to *filter* out cases which do not require further review. When cases are not filtered out, an analysis of market operation is required in all cases, i.e. a calculation of the HHI is the *starting point* and not the end of an assessment of a merger.
[19] Para.19.
[20] Para.20. The special circumstances identified are that: the merger involves a potential entrant or a recent entrant with a small market share; one or more merging parties are important innovators in ways not reflected in market shares; there are significant cross-shareholdings between competitors; one of the merging parties is a maverick firm with a high likelihood of disrupting coordinated conduct; there is evidence of past or ongoing coordination or of facilitating practices; or one of the merging parties has a pre-merger share of 50% or more.
[21] By contrast, the 2002 draft Commission Notice on Horizontal Mergers provided that a transaction *was* likely to raise serious doubts (justifying the Commission in taking the case into Phase II) if it leads to an HHI of 2,000 or more and an increase in HHI of 150 or more in a market for relatively homogenous goods; see paras 16 and 27.
[22] See, e.g. Case COMP/M.3625 *Blackstone / Acetex* [2005] O.J. L312/60, paras 85, 86, 105, 123 and 137.
[23] Verouden, "The Role of Market Shares and Market Concentration Indices in the European Commission's Guidelines on the Assessment of Horizontal Mergers Under the EC Merger Regulation" (available at *www.ftc.gov/bc/mergerenforce/presentations/040217verouden.pdf*).

in all cases and provided a clear and informative distinction between cases in which substantive competition concerns would arise and those in which they would not; for this reason, the Commission added the "special circumstances" exceptions, enabling it to set higher thresholds (in particular, higher deltas) than would otherwise have been the case. Further, the Commission tailored the HHI thresholds in the Notice so that there were no contradictions with the market share thresholds.[24]

4–037   Secondly, the concentration ratio, *CRn*, identifies the market share held by the largest "n" companies in the market, e.g. CR4 measures the total share held by the largest four companies in the market.[25] The Commission regularly refers to concentration ratios.[26] However, they have significant limitations: they provide no information about the distribution of market shares amongst the companies included in the ratio or about companies excluded from the ratio; they are also arbitrary in the sense that the choice of the number of companies included can significantly affect the ratio.

If the market operates as a cartel comprising the "n" largest firms and the remaining suppliers act as a competitive fringe, then the loss of total welfare is proportionate to CRn.[27] If it does not, the predictive power of CRn is reduced.

Thirdly, the *Lerner Index* is the ratio of price minus marginal cost against price. In a perfectly competitive market the ratio is nil (since price is set at marginal cost), and the object of the Lerner Index is to provide a direct measure of the extent to which the market in question diverges from the perfectly competitive model. It is little used in merger control because of lack of reliable data on marginal costs. Furthermore, the essential question in merger control is whether post-merger prices will be higher than the prices which would be likely to prevail in the absence of the merger and not

---

[24] Verouden also stated that the market share thresholds are not applicable when analysing coordinated effects, whereas the HHI thresholds are applicable generally. However, see n.9 to para.4–035 above.

[25] The research suggests that concentration makes little difference to price, provided that CR4 is below 50%: see Scherer & Ross, *Industrial Market Structure and Economic Performance* (3rd edn, Houghton Mifflin Co, 1990), p.423, n.45. See also Carlton & Perloff, *Modern Industrial Organization* (4th edn, Addison-Wesley, 2005), p.266.

[26] See the Notice on Horizontal Mergers, n.17 (stating that the ratio is usually calculated using the leading three or four firms) and, e.g. Case COMP/M.1628 *TotalFina / Elf* [2001] O.J. L143/1, para.199; Case COMP/M.1693 *Alcoa / Reynolds* [2002] O.J. L58/25, para.21; and Case COMP/M.2498 *UPM-Kymmene / Haindl* [2002] O.J. L233/38, para.115. The US Department of Justice "Merger Guidelines", May 30, 1968 (now superseded), focused on CR4. The Australian Merger Guidelines, June 1999 (*www.accc.gov.au/content/item.phtml?itemId=719436&nodeId=file43a1f42c7eb63&fn=Merger%20Guidelines.pdf*), para.5.95, use CR4. The New Zealand Merger Guidelines, 2004 (*www.comcom.govt.nz/Publications/ContentFiles/Documents/MergersandAcquisitionsGuidelines.PDF*), para.5.3, use CR3.

[27] Areeda, Hovenkamp & Solow, *Antitrust Law* (2nd edn, Aspen Law & Business, 1998), Vol.IV, para.931d2.

whether prices will diverge from those which would subsist in a perfectly competitive market.[28]

---

[28] See generally, Martin, *Advanced Industrial Economics* (2nd edn, Blackwell, 2002), Ch.6. The difficulties in identifying marginal costs referred to above have caused researchers to seek alternative sources of data: see generally, Martin, *Advanced Industrial Economics* (2nd edn, Blackwell, 2002), pp.199 to 215. Some economists have used a ratio of price minus average variable cost to price, although this leads to serious biases: see Carlton & Perloff, *Modern Industrial Organization* (4th edn, Addison-Wesley, 2005), p.254. Others have sought approximations of marginal cost by identifying the increase in costs incurred by a company over a period and dividing that figure by the company's increase in output during that period: Cabral, *Introduction to Industrial Organization* (The MIT Press, 2000), p.6. Others again have sought indirectly to measure the competitiveness of an industry, e.g. by analysing how companies react to changes in marginal cost (e.g. an increase in a tax which is payable on a per unit basis) or shifts in the demand curve: for further details see Carlton & Perloff, *Modern Industrial Organization* (4th edn, Addison-Wesley, 2005), pp.277 to 279.

CHAPTER 5

THE COUNTERFACTUAL

5.1 INTRODUCTION

5–001 The Commission cannot prohibit a concentration unless it establishes that the transaction will result in a significant impediment to effective competition.[1] The counterfactual provides a rigorous means of identifying the effects of the merger, and thereby establishing whether there is a *causal link* between the transaction and any loss of consumer welfare. This Chapter describes the use of the counterfactual (s.5.2) and discusses its application when there are two or more mergers in contemplation in the same market at the same time (s.5.3). The application of the counterfactual in the particular situation when one of the merging parties is likely to exit from the market is discussed in Ch.17 (The Failing Firm Defence).

5.2 THE COUNTERFACTUAL

5–002 The Commission described the position as follows in the Notice on Horizontal Mergers:

"In assessing the competitive effects of a merger, the Commission compares the competitive conditions that would result from the notified

---

[1] The Court of First Instance has confirmed that a merger may only be prohibited under the ECMR if it has the "direct and immediate" effect of (as the substantive test then stood) creating or strengthening a dominant position: Case T-102/96 *Gencor v Commission* [1999] E.C.R. II-753, para.94 and Case T-342/ 99 *Airtours plc v Commission* [2002] E.C.R. II-2585, para.58. The Court of First Instance also emphasised in *Airtours*, at para.82, that, "If there is no significant change in the level of competition obtaining previously, the merger should be approved because it does not restrict competition". See also Case T-282/02 *Cementbouw Handel & Industrie v Commission*, not yet reported, judgment of February 23, 2006, paras 269 and 270.

merger with the conditions that would have prevailed without the merger. In most cases, the competitive conditions existing at the time of the merger constitute the relevant comparison for evaluating the effects of a merger. However, in some circumstances, the Commission may take into account future changes to the market that can reasonably be predicted. It may, in particular, take account of the likely entry or exit of firms if the merger did not take place when considering what constitutes the relevant comparison".[2]

More specifically, issues of causation are most clearly analysed by identi- **5–003** fying separately:

(a) the *pre-merger* state of the market[3];

(b) whether the pre-merger state of the market would have been likely to change *in the absence of the merger*[4] and, if so, in what respects (the way in which the market is predicted to operate in the absence of the merger is the *counterfactual*);

(c) the likely post-merger state of the market; and

(d) the differences between steps (b) and (c) (i.e. the effects of the merger).

The counterfactual principle has seven specific consequences for merger **5–004** control.[5]

(a) The Commission does not have power under the ECMR to intervene to address concerns about the general market structure, i.e. issues which exist independently of the merger.[6] The Commission has

---

[2] Para.9.
[3] In Case T-342/99 *Airtours plc v Commission* [2002] E.C.R. II-2585, the Court of First Instance stated, at para.82, that "the level of competition obtaining in the relevant market at the time when the transaction is notified is a decisive factor in establishing whether a collective dominant position has been established". The Commission had argued that the way in which the market operated previously was not a significant factor in merger appraisal (see para.81).
[4] The UK Office of Fair Trading's Substantive Merger Guidelines, May 2003 (*www.oft.gov.uk*), provide, at para.3.24, "In most cases, the best guide to the appropriate counterfactual will be prevailing conditions of competition. However, the OFT may need to take into account likely and imminent changes in the structure of competition in order to reflect as accurately as possible the nature of the rivalry without the merger. Examples of such circumstances may include the following. [1] Where a firm is about to enter or exit the market. Similarly, the OFT may also take account of committed expansion plans by existing competitors. [2] Where changes in the regulatory structure of the market, such as market liberalisation, or tighter environmental constraints, will change the nature of competition".
[5] See also Case COMP/M.2547 *Bayer / Aventis Crop Science* [2004] O.J. L107/1, para.324 (new product launches). The Commission failed to apply the counterfactual principle in setting the test for merger-specific efficiencies (see n.75 to para.18–015) and in formulating the test for the failing firm defence (see s.17.5 below).
[6] See, e.g. Case COMP/M.3178 *Bertelsmann / Springer / JV*, paras 157 and 159.

power to intervene only to address issues which are *"merger specific"*.[7]

(b) A merger may be prohibited *even if prices are likely to fall* following the transaction if it can be shown that prices would have fallen further or faster in the absence of the transaction. This is because the counterfactual, against which the effects of the merger are judged, is one in which prices would have fallen further or faster. In this scenario, the merger harms consumers just as much as if prices had risen following the transaction.[8]

(c) The Commission does not have power to intervene to prohibit a transaction[9] if it does *not materially increase the acquiring party's influence or control* over the target.

    (i) Most mergers involving a change from *"joint"* to *"sole"* control are approved on the basis that the acquiring party already exercises decisive influence over the target.[10] Exceptionally, in *KLM / Martinair (II)*[11] the Commission proposed to prohibit a change from joint to sole control by KLM in Martinair, but the parties abandoned the transaction before a formal prohibition decision was adopted. The Commission noted[12] that the change from joint to sole control "would have materially reduced Martinair's remaining independence from KLM, with serious consequences for competition. The Commission considered that the operation would have allowed KLM to fully integrate the operations of Martinair with those of its subsidiary Transavia. KLM (principally through its subsidiary, Transavia) already supplied a substantial share of the supply of 'holiday' flights—whether on chartered or scheduled services—to tour

---

[7] The remedies for any merger specific issues may involve the correction of market flaws; see para.20–103 below.

[8] See the Notice on Horizontal Mergers, n.7.

[9] Or to approve it only subject to commitments.

[10] See, e.g. Case COMP/M.2588 *Rheinbraun Brennstoff / SSM Coal* (a company holding joint control acquired sole control in circumstances in which the acquirer also had joint control over a competitor of the target; the Commission found that the other company holding joint control over the competitor would wish to maintain the competitor's independence and the merger therefore did not increase the risk of alignment of behaviour between the two companies; para.12); Case COMP/M.2761 *BP / Veba Oel* (approving a change from joint to sole control on the grounds that it would not change the market structure because: "There are no indications that the presence of E.ON in the Veba Oel joint venture could have led to a market behaviour on the part of Veba Oel different from a behaviour under sole control by BP ... [T]here are no indications that E.ON had any specific own interests differing from those of BP with regard to the competitive behaviour of Veba Oel, which could have translated into a different business strategy on the part of Veba"; para.13); and Case COMP/M.3161 *CVRD / Caemi* (when considering a change from joint to sole control, the Commission examined whether the interests of the jointly controlling parents diverged and the extent to which the party giving up joint control was in practice engaged in the management or strategy of the joint venture; paras 34 and 35).

[11] Case COMP/M.1328.

[12] XXIXth Annual Report on Competition Policy, 1999.

operators in the Netherlands. Martinair is an equally significant competitor in this market, and together the two airlines supply around two thirds of it".[13]

(ii) *Coca-Cola Enterprises / Amalgamated Beverages Great Britain*[14] involved the acquisition by The Coca-Cola Company ("TCCC") of control over a British bottler. The Commission found that the merger would have allowed TCCC to become completely vertically integrated, but that there was not enough evidence to conclude with sufficient certainty that the transaction would lead to an appreciable strengthening of the British bottler's dominant position in the British cola market because TCCC already exerted substantial influence, if not joint control, over the British bottler's commercial strategy.

(iii) In *First / Keolis / TPE JV*[15] the Commission found that an agreement between First and Keolis did not have the effect of coordinating their competitive behaviour within the meaning of Art.2(4) of the ECMR[16] because the parents had already entered a joint venture to coordinate their activities on the market. The decision is noteworthy because the existing joint venture had *not* been notified or approved under the ECMR.

(d) A merger may not be prohibited even if conditions of competition decline following the transaction, if conditions of competition would have declined at least to the same extent if the transaction had not occurred.[17] For example, *Deloitte & Touche / Andersen (UK)*[18] involved a reduction from five to four players in the market for audit and accounting services for quoted and large companies. The Commission cleared the transaction on the grounds that a causal link between the concentration and a possible situation of collective dominance could be excluded and relied on two propositions in reaching this conclusion. First, the reduction from five to four players was inevitable because the Andersen network was disin-

---

[13] The *KLM / Martinair* case is also discussed in Loriot, Menzes & Koch, "Commission revises notices following adoption of the new merger regulation", *Competition Policy Newsletter*, Autumn 2004, 47 at p.48. It is now generally possible to make a short form notification of a merger involving a change from joint to sole control, but a full notification may be required when the former joint venture is integrated into the group or network of its remaining single controlling shareholder and the disciplining effects exercised by the potentially diverging incentives of the different controlling shareholders are removed and its strategic market position could be strengthened; see the Commission Notice on a simplified procedure for treatment of certain concentrations under Council Regulation (EC) No 139/2004 [2005] O.J. C56/32, paras 5(d) and 9.

[14] Case IV/M.794.

[15] Case COMP/M.3273, para.13.

[16] See Ch.13 below.

[17] See also Ch.17 below.

[18] Case COMP/M.2810, paras 44, 45 and 49. See also Case COMP/M.2816 *Ernst & Young France / Andersen France*; Case COMP/M.2824 *Ernst & Young / Andersen Germany*; and Areeda, Hovenkamp & Solow, *Antitrust Law* (2nd edn, Aspen Law & Business, 1998), Vol.IVA, para.963a3.

tegrating in the aftermath of the Enron scandal. Secondly, "no other scenario could be established, which would be less harmful for competition on the market ... (it is considered that other scenarios can be established for the market which is under consideration in this decision, given its specific characteristics, in particular that only a very limited number of companies is there operating, and that there is no realistic possibility of penetration following an acquisition by a new entrant) ... [If] the transaction proposed did not take place for any conceivable reason ... only two possible alternative scenarios to the proposed transaction can be established. These two scenarios are [1] the take-over by Andersen UK by one of the other remaining Big Four auditing and accounting firms; [2] no take-over takes place and the existing clients would be dispersed between the remaining Big Four firms (with two scenarios for the attribution of shares)". The Commission examined the two scenarios (i.e. the counterfactuals to the concentration) in detail before concluding that a causal link was not established.[19]

(e) A merger may not be prohibited if it reduces (or does not aggravate) a pre-existing competition issue. For example, in *Logista / Etinera / Terzia*[20] the sale of a monopoly distributor of tobacco from a large producer of tobacco to a smaller producer of tobacco *reduced* the incentive to discriminate against rival upstream producers of tobacco and the transaction was accordingly cleared. It would have been necessary to carry out a vertical effects analysis if the distributor had been independently owned prior to the merger.

(f) A merger may not be prohibited if the acquiring party could achieve the same result through its own independent conduct (i.e. without merging). For example, in *YLE / TDF / Digita / JV*[21] the Commission found that the merger would not "itself necessarily" lead to or facilitate price increases, i.e. the transaction did not alter Digita's ability as a *de facto* monopolist to raise prices. Similarly, in *De Beers / LVMH*[22] the Commission found that the creation of a joint venture in retailing diamond jewellery "would not lead to a significant strengthening of De Beers' already existing dominant position in the global market for rough diamonds" as De Beers could have altered its branding strategy by introducing a new brand without the proposed joint venture.

(g) In analysing the market, the Commission is bound to take into account likely future developments. For example, in *TUI / CP Ships*[23]

---

[19] Paras 49 to 60.
[20] Case COMP/M.3553.
[21] Case COMP/M.2300, para.40.
[22] Case COMP/M.2333 [2003] O.J. L29/40, paras 112 to 114.
[23] Case COMP/M.3863, n.26.

a third party had served notice to terminate its membership of a shipping consortium and was therefore not considered as part of the consortium for the purposes of assessing the proposed merger.[24]

5.3 OTHER TRANSACTIONS

(a) Parallel mergers

The counterfactual principle is of particular relevance if there are two or **5–005** more mergers in contemplation in the same market at the same time. Four conclusions arise from an application of the counterfactual analysis to *parallel mergers* (i.e. mergers which are in contemplation in the same market, but which involve different suppliers).

(a) If there are two proposed mergers, A and B, and the Commission is considering proposed merger A, it is required to take account of proposed merger B (since it has to predict the way in which the market would develop in the absence of merger A in order to identify the counterfactual).[25]

　　(i) In *Nestlé / Perrier*[26] the Commission stated: "In its assessment of the proposed merger, the Commission must take into account any existing agreement, the implementation of which would have an appreciable effect on the future market structure".[27]

---

[24] In Case COMP/M.2547 *Bayer / Aventis Crop Science* [2004] O.J. L107/1 the Commission took account, at paras 21 and 22, of the effects of an EC Directive which was likely to result in the withdrawal from the market of a large number of plant protection products. The Commission appears to have misapplied a counterfactual analysis in Case COMP/M.3280 *Air France / KLM* (appeal pending in Case T-177/04 *easyJet Airline Company v Commission*). In that case, at para.59, the Commission considered an argument that a third party airline intended to join an alliance but stated that its admittance to the alliance was "not a fact" and "it would not be appropriate to take it into consideration" in the merger investigation. (The Commission also noted that if the third party airline were to enter relevant agreements, these could be reviewed by the relevant competition authorities.) Further, the Commission stated, at para.124, that it could not take into account potential entry on an airline route because "it is a future and merely hypothetical fact".

[25] See also Case IV/M.1532 *BP Amoco / Arco* [2001] O.J. L18/1, para.28; Case IV/M.1578 *Sanitec / Sphinx* [2000] O.J. L294/1 (para.149, in which the Commission noted, in presenting market share data, that if a separate announced merger proceeded, the parties to that transaction would have a substantial market share); and Case COMP/M.3752 *Verizon / MCI* (the Commission assumed that a parallel merger would proceed and found that no competition concerns would arise even if it did; paras 81 and 98 to 106). See also the Commission's press release in *Time Warner / EMI* (IP/00/617).

[26] Case IV/M.190 [1992] O.J. L356/1.

[27] Para.37. The case involved an *overlapping merger* (see para.5–007 below) and the Commission took account of an agreement entered by the proposed purchaser to sell a mineral water brand if the notified concentration proceeded to completion (i.e. implementation). The Commission assessed the transaction both on the basis that the disposal proceeded and that it did not (see paras 108 and 132).

      (ii)   In *Air Liquide / BOC*[28] the Commission carried out its investigation in parallel with a second ECMR analysis.[29]

(b) If the parties to either or both mergers offer commitments then, in determining whether to approve merger A (as amended by any commitments), the Commission must take account of the likely treatment of merger B (as amended by any commitments). In the following two sets of cases involving parallel mergers, both merging parties offered similar undertakings and the decisions are consistent with the principle set out above.

      (i)   In *BP / E.ON*[30] and *Shell / DEA*[31] the Commission prepared near-identical decisions and considered the remedies offered in the two concentrations together.

      (ii) It is clear from *VEBA / VIAG*[32] that the same analysis applies when the parallel merger is considered by national competition authorities. The Commission cleared the *VEBA* case subject to undertakings, having concluded that the undertakings submitted *in the two cases* (the second was considered by the German authorities) were sufficient to resolve the competition issues.

(c) If the Commission has jurisdiction in relation to proposed mergers A and B and determines that only one of the mergers may proceed, then, logically, the first one which is *decided*[33] should be approved because, in assessing the likelihood of the second occurring, the Commission will take account of the question of whether it is likely to grant approval to the second.

(d) If the second merger falls outside the Commission's jurisdiction, then the Commission must predict the likely treatment of the second merger by any other antitrust authorities. The Commission can be expected to establish this by liaising with those authorities.[34] If the other authorities are likely to prohibit the second transaction if the Commission approves the first, then the position is as described in sub-para.(c) above. The position is more complex if the other antitrust authorities are likely to permit the second merger even if the

---

[28] Case COMP/M.1630 *Air Liquide / BOC* [2004] O.J. L92/1.

[29] Para.39. The competitive assessment of *Air Liquide / BOC* did not turn on whether the other merger proceeded (see, e.g. para.117, noting that the current number of suppliers could be reduced from seven to six or five).

[30] Case COMP/M.2533 [2002] O.J. L276/31.

[31] Case COMP/M.2389 [2003] O.J. L15/35.

[32] Case COMP/M.1673 [2001] O.J. L188/1, para.62 ("it is conceivable, not to say probable, that [the second transaction] will be declared exempt within the applicable forecast period [so] this change in market structure must be taken into account in the assessment of the planned merger of VEBA and VIAG").

[33] Merger decisions are based on an analysis of the market at the date of the decision and not at some earlier date (e.g. the date of any merger agreement or the date of the notification).

[34] In some cases, their analysis of the second transaction will not be sufficiently far advanced for them to be able to express an informed view.

Commission approves the first. If the Commission's assessment is that only one transaction may proceed then, logically, it is required to prohibit the first transaction in this situation.

The Commission has not made a final decision in any cases falling within **5–006** sub-paras 5–005(c) or (d). It perhaps came closest in *Price Waterhouse / Coopers & Lybrand* which was, for a time, considered in parallel with a proposal by KPMG and Ernst & Young to merge. The Commission "found it appropriate to analyse the proposed PW/C&L concentration within the context of the KPMG/E&Y operation since under the Merger Regulation the effects of the merger operations are assessed in a perspective which is projected in the future of the market, taking into account not only the changes brought about by the merger itself but also making allowance for future development such as new entrants, liberalisation, product innovation and so on ..."[35] In that case, the Commission reached the preliminary view that the two mergers taken together would result in a situation of collective dominance.[36] However, since the KPMG/Ernst & Young merger was called off, the Commission was able to clear the remaining merger without undertakings.

If both merger notifications had remained active and neither party proposed any remedies, then the Commission ought to have adopted the approach identified in para.5–005(c) above.

(a) Prohibiting both transactions would produce an incoherent outcome because the Commission would have no grounds for prohibiting a subsequent third merger in the same market or, indeed, a fresh merger between one of the original two sets of merging parties.[37] It is also noteworthy that if both transactions are prohibited in this situation, then there is scope for competitors to seek to block a transaction by themselves announcing a merger.[38]

(b) Permitting the merger that has the greatest customer benefits[39] is inconsistent with the framework of the ECMR. The Commission is

---

[35] Case IV/M.1016 [1999] O.J. L50/27, para.108.

[36] Para.110.

[37] See generally Stadler, " 'Conflicting Mergers': Combined Assessment or Priority Rule?" [2003] E.C.L.R. 321.

[38] For discussion of the strategic aspects of sequential mergers, see Jacobs, "Second Order Oligopoly Problems with International Dimensions: Sequential Mergers, Maverick Firms and Buyer Power" [2001] *The Antitrust Bulletin* 537. Sullivan & Grimes, *The Law of Antitrust: An Integrated Handbook* (West, 2000), comment, at p.600: "Sometimes, a rival may see a follow-the-leader merger as a way of thwarting the merger of its major rival. When the Coca-Cola Company announced the proposed acquisition of Dr. Pepper, Pepsi quickly announced that it would acquire Seven-Up in a tactical move widely perceived as seeking to reduce the chances that Coca-Cola would receive antitrust clearance for its acquisition. The Federal Trade Commission successfully forestalled both acquisitions".

[39] This is a variant on the argument by Schmidt, "Spotting the Elephant in Parallel Mergers: First Past the Post, or Combined Assessment?" [2003] E.C.L.R. 183, p.186 that the Commission should in this situation "clear the one that is most beneficial to competition".

empowered to prohibit mergers that significantly impede effective competition but, on the hypothetical facts, either merger in isolation would not have had such an effect. There is no provision in the ECMR which provides for a more general customer benefits analysis in the case of a "tie".[40]

(b) Overlapping mergers

5–007 The counterfactual is also relevant when assessing overlapping mergers, i.e. mergers which are in contemplation in the same market and which involve the same supplier, e.g. if one of the parties to the first proposed transaction is in the process of acquiring or disposing of another business in the same market through a second transaction. The Commission applies the counterfactual principle in assessing proposed *acquisitions* (and analyses the first transaction on the assumption that the second will proceed), but is cautious about assuming that proposed *disposals* will proceed (because, once approval for the first transaction has been obtained, the merging party may have an *incentive*[41] to renege on the disposal agreement if retaining the business will result in its acquiring substantial market power).[42]

(a) In *Industri Kapital / Perstorp*[43] the Commission's press release,[44] announcing that the case had been taken into a detailed Phase II investigation, stated: "The impact of the proposed acquisition of Industri Kapital of Dyno is under investigation under a separate procedure. Consequently, the assessment of Industri Kapital's acquisition over Perstorp has to be based on the assumption that Dyno already forms part of the Industri Kapital group".

(b) In *Ahlström / Andritz*[45] the Commission took note of the fact that the purchaser had signed an agreement to sell a business which gave rise to the bulk of the overlap. The Commission cleared the transaction on the basis that it did not raise competition concerns provided that the disposal was completed, and indicated that if the disposal were not completed "the Commission may revoke the present decision and

---

[40] See Stadler, "'Conflicting Mergers': Combined Assessment or Priority Rule?" [2003] E.C.L.R. 321, at p.328.
[41] Whether the merging party has the *ability* to renege on the disposal agreement depends in particular on the terms of the sale agreement and the attitude of the counterparty.
[42] See also Case COMP/M.3355 *Apollo / JP Morgan / PrimaCom* (one of the joint acquirers was in the process of selling a competing business; the Commission approved the transaction, but proceeded on the basis that the joint acquirer *retained* ownership of the competing business; para.7) and Case COMP/M.3809 *Siemens / Flender*, para.25 (two overlapping acquisitions by Siemens; the Commission calculated market shares assuming that the other transaction also proceeded in order to assess the maximum harm to competition that could arise).
[43] Case COMP/M.1963.
[44] IP/00/698.
[45] Case COMP/M.1930, para.81.

re-examine the transaction". The Commission could instead have accepted undertakings from the purchaser to dispose of the business.[46]

(c) Applying the counterfactual to parallel and overlapping mergers

The question arises whether the second transaction is *sufficiently far* **5–008** *advanced* to be taken into account for the purposes of the Commission's counterfactual analysis. On a counterfactual analysis, if the second transaction is likely to occur, then it ought to be factored into the analysis, but if it is not (as will normally be the case with transactions that have not passed the planning stage), it should be disregarded. The decision in *Industri Kapital 97 Ltd | Superfos A/S*[47] is consistent with this approach (although the Commission's reasoning is slightly different). The parties informed the Commission of their intention to purchase another company but the Commission did not take account of this plan in considering the transaction because it had not yet been implemented.

It may also be necessary to determine whether two transactions are *sufficiently close to one another chronologically* that the latter should be taken into account for the purposes of the counterfactual analysis. Logically, the decision whether to approve a merger is made on the basis of the information available as at the date of that decision and a recently announced merger ought therefore to be taken into account. However, there are strict deadlines for making decisions under the ECMR[48] and if the new information emerged so shortly before the deadline[49] that the Commission could not carry out a proper assessment, then it should be entitled to disregard it.[50]

---

[46] Provided that it first established that the transaction would have created or strengthened a dominant position (as the substantive test then stood) if the disposal were not completed.

[47] Case COMP/M.1748, at para.10.

[48] In the case of parallel mergers, the power under ECMR, Art.10.4 (to suspend the timetable whilst information is requested under Art.11) is not available because the need to obtain additional information would not arise as a result of circumstances for which one of the undertakings involved in the concentration is responsible.

[49] The argument in the text is stronger in the case of deadlines in a second phase inquiry because, when a case is being considered in the first phase, the Commission has the option to open a second phase inquiry to consider the relevance of the recently announced transaction if that transaction creates "serious doubts" regarding the compatibility of the concentration with the common market.

[50] See also Schmidt, "Spotting the Elephant in Parallel Mergers: First Past the Post, or Combined Assessment?" [2003] E.C.L.R. 183, at p.189 who argues that the answer depends on the ability of the Commission to carry out a proper assessment and on procedural fairness to both parties (i.e. their right to be heard).

CHAPTER 6

MARKET OPERATION

6.1 INTRODUCTION

6–001 Every market is unique[1] and the Commission takes account of the specific ways in which the market operates in carrying out its functions under the ECMR.[2] In particular, the Notice on Horizontal Mergers states that, "the Commission interprets market shares in the light of likely market conditions, for instance, if the market is highly dynamic in character and if the market structure is unstable due to innovation or growth".[3]

This Chapter summarises some of the principal economic models of market operation (s.6.2) and discusses dynamic effects (i.e. changes in the market over time) (s.6.3), the nature of the competitive interaction between rival suppliers (s.6.4), the effects of EU procurement and harmonising legislation (s.6.5), and the scope to create "national champions" under the ECMR (s.6.6).

6.2 PRINCIPAL ECONOMIC MODELS OF MARKET OPERATION

6–002 An economic model is an attempt to describe reality in simplified form. A model with good descriptive powers can be used to predict the impact on market performance of changing a variable (e.g. reducing the number of suppliers by one following a merger). Perfect competition, monopoly and

---

[1] See generally Porter, *Competitive Strategy* (The Free Press, 1998 edn), Ch.8.
[2] For an example of a decision in which the Commission examined carefully the way in which the market operated, see Case COMP/M.1741 *MCI WorldCom / Sprint* [2003] O.J. L300/1, paras 71 to 83.
[3] Para.15.

Cournot's and Bertrand's models of oligopoly were considered in s.1.3 above.

The 2002 draft Commission Notice on Horizontal Mergers, emphasised[4] the importance of establishing the "main parameters of competition" in the market and distinguished markets in which competition occurs primarily in output or capacity (reflecting the Cournot model)[5] and markets in which competition occurs primarily in price (reflecting the Bertrand model).[6] These passages were omitted from the final version of the Notice on Horizontal Mergers.

The remainder of this section describes the Stackelberg leader-follower model, limit pricing[7] and game theory.

(a) The Stackelberg leader-follower model

The Stackelberg leader-follower model applies when the leading firm **6–003** chooses its output and the competitors in the market then select their own outputs in the light of the leader's decision. The leader is able to predict how its competitors will react and its role as leader allows it to profit relative to the Cournot equilibrium.[8] The model is important because many industries are characterised by leadership by one company. The Stackelberg leader-follower model suggests that the market in such situations may be operating less effectively, judged in terms of allocative efficiency and economic welfare, than other oligopolistic markets.[9] A merger in such a market is likely to lead the merged group to reduce its output (relative to the sum of the two merging firms' outputs) and rivals to increase their output.[10]

(b) Limit pricing theory

The Cournot, Bertrand and Stackelberg leader-follower models of oligopoly **6–004** all assume that producers aim to maximise their profits in the short run, i.e.

---

[4] Para.17.
[5] See paras 1–019 to 1–021 above.
[6] See para.1–022 above.
[7] These models are discussed in detail in numerous industrial organisation and microeconomics texts, including Carlton & Perloff, *Modern Industrial Organization* (4th edn, Addison-Wesley, 2005); Varian, *Intermediate Microeconomics: A Modern Approach* (5th edn, W W Norton & Co, 1999); Cabral, *Introduction to Industrial Organization* (The MIT Press, 2000); Shy, *Industrial Organization* (The MIT Press, 1995); Martin, *Advanced Industrial Economics* (2nd edn, Blackwell, 2002); Scherer & Ross, *Industrial Market Structure and Economic Performance* (3rd. edn, Houghton Mifflin Co, 1990); and Tirole, *The Theory of Industrial Organization* (The MIT Press, 1988).
[8] Carlton & Perloff, *Modern Industrial Organization* (4th edn, Addison-Wesley, 2005), pp.176 to 180.
[9] See Shy, *Industrial Organization* (The MIT Press, 1995), pp.104 to 107.
[10] See Europe Economics, "Study on Assessment Criteria for Distinguishing between Competitive and Dominant Oligopolies in Merger Control", Report for the European Commission, p.11.

in making sales in the period immediately following the decision to set particular outputs or prices. However, most producers aim to maximise long run profits (although the extent to which producers *discount* the value of uncertain future profit streams varies). This insight led to the development of theories of *limit pricing* which suggest that oligopolists will independently recognise that the best way to maximise short run profits is to set prices and aggregate outputs at the same level as a monopoly producer; but that in doing so, the oligopolists are likely to encourage new entry into the market which is likely to reduce future profits. *Limit pricing* theory[11] suggests that producers will set prices below the monopoly level but at a level which either deters any entry or limits the incentives to enter. A supplier engages in limit pricing if it sets its price and output at a level such that there is insufficient demand for a rival firm to enter the market profitably.[12]

(c) Game theory

6–005 Game theory seeks to predict the outcome of strategic interaction between agents when decisions by one agent directly affect the *pay-offs* received by other agents as well as itself.[13] Game theory is capable of modelling oligopolistic markets in which a decision by one supplier to increase output affects not only its own profits but those of its rivals.[14]

The Cournot, Bertrand and the Stackelberg leader-follower models of oligopoly are all models of *static equilibrium*, i.e. they proceed on the basis that producers make a once-and-for-all decision about their operation on the market.[15] However, in practice, producers keep their market operation under constant review and are frequently receiving updated information

---

[11] See in particular Viscusi, Vernon & Harrington, *Economics of Regulation and Antitrust* (3rd edn, The MIT Press, 2000), pp.169 to 178.

[12] Carlton & Perloff, *Modern Industrial Organization* (4th edn, Addison-Wesley, 2005), p.360. The central criticism of the theory is that producers make decisions on entry on the basis of predictions of *post-entry prices* and not of *pre-entry prices,* with the consequence that pre-entry prices are relevant only as a mechanism for signalling to potential entrants the likely post-entry price. The counter-argument is that the entrant is likely to have limited information about incumbents' costs and limit pricing can therefore play a role in shaping the entrant's perceptions of those costs. See generally, Besanko, Dranove & Shanley, *Economics of Strategy* (2nd edn, John Wiley & Sons Inc, 2000), pp.340 to 346 and Oster, *Modern Competitive Strategy* (3rd edn, Oxford UP, 1999), pp.289 to 292 and 297.

[13] Shy, *Industrial Organization* (The MIT Press, 1995), p.11. See generally, Varian, *Intermediate Microeconomics: A Modern Approach* (5th edn, W W Norton & Co, 1999), Ch.28; Dixit & Nalebuff *Thinking Strategically* (W W Norton & Co, 1991); and Nalebuff & Brandenburger, *Co-opetition* (HarperCollinsBusiness, 1997 edn.).

[14] In game theory each agent has an *action set* (i.e. a range of possible choices of action) and a *pay-off* function which maps a return (typically profits or welfare) against each possible action in the light of the possible actions to be taken by other agents. When one particular action will always maximise an agent's pay-off, no matter what the choices of the other agents, it is a *dominant action.* When the choice of a particular action is a dominant action for each of the agents, the game is in *equilibrium in dominant actions.* A *Nash equilibrium* arises if no agent would gain by deviating from the outcome of a particular game, provided that each other agent adheres to its previous strategy.

[15] i.e. they are *one-shot games.*

about the conduct of their competitors, whether by analysing their market prices, bidding against them or otherwise.

This has led economists to analyse oligopoly as a *repeated game*, i.e. through **6–006** models which seek to capture the fact that each time producers make market decisions they factor in the most up-to-date information on how their competitors are behaving and analyse their competitors' likely reactions to the new decision. Formally, a repeated game is a one-shot game which is repeated for several periods with the repeated game being played once in each period[16] and a *supergame* is an infinitely-repeated game. In this respect, repeated interaction game theory seems to capture very closely the way in which oligopolistic markets operate in practice. Agents are able to adopt *strategies* in repeated games.[17] These games closely mimic the decisions which are taken by members of cartels or members of oligopolies which, through tacit coordination, mimic to a greater or lesser extent the outcome in a cartelised market.[18]

The practical difficulty with such a theory is that the model of the way in which producers factor in these *dynamic* changes is extremely sensitive to small changes in the underlying assumptions about producer behaviour, with the consequence that predictions of whether, following a merger, an industry will be characterised by limited competition with price and output near to the monopoly level or by intense competition with price and output near to the perfectly competitive level can be difficult to make with any sense of assurance.

6.3 DYNAMIC EFFECTS: CHANGES IN THE MARKET OVER TIME

(a) Expanding markets

If a market is expanding rapidly, this may facilitate new entry with the **6–007** consequence that high market shares may not confer market power.[19] For

---

[16] Shy, *Industrial Organization* (The MIT Press, 1995), p.28.

[17] e.g. a trigger strategy involves adhering to the cooperative outcome provided that all other players adhered to the cooperative strategy in the previous game; a tit-for-tat strategy involves playing what the opponent played in the last round. In a competition organised by Robert Axelrod to write a computer programme to play the Prisoners' Dilemma game, the tit-for-tat strategy won: see Shy, *Industrial Organization* (The MIT Press, 1995), p.33.

[18] For examples of game theoretic models see Martin, *Advanced Industrial Economics* (2nd edn, Blackwell, 2002), generally, and, in particular, at p.70.

[19] See, e.g. Case COMP/M.1947 *ABN AMRO Lease Holding / Dial Group* (annual growth rate of 33% facilitated new entry; paras 14 and 15); Case COMP/M.2706 *Carnival Corporation / P&O Princess* [2003] O.J. L248/1 (the Commission press release, IP/02/1141, stated that "the high recent and projected growth rate in cruise markets would, in itself, constitute a significant competitive constraint on the incumbent cruise operators as high growth rates provide an incentive for new operators to enter the market"); Case COMP/M.3486 *Magna / New Venture Gear* (the Commission expected the market to double in size in the near future which would have been likely to bring opportunities to all suppliers, potentially affecting market positions, and might have induced new entry; para.46); and Case COMP/M.3816 *Apax / Mölnlycke* (the Commission found that growth rates of over 20% per annum made the market very attractive to suppliers and ensured effective competition; para.43). It also important to consider the *rate of change* of growth rates: see Porter, *Competitive Strategy* (The Free Press, 1998 edn), p.238.

example, in *Gerling | NCM*[20] the merged group's share of the Swedish *del credere* insurance market would have been 60 to 70 per cent, but the Commission found that the market was small and had grown by 60 to 65 per cent in the preceding five years and that such growth would facilitate new entry and enable new entrants to attain substantial market shares in a short period.[21] By contrast, in *WorldCom | MCI*[22] the Commission rejected an argument that the rapid growth of the internet would prevent the merged group from exercising market power in the provision of top level or "universal" Internet connectivity because new entry was unlikely at that level given the network effects which would operate to the merged group's benefit.[23]

(b) Static or declining markets

6–008 If a market is *static*, new entry is less likely because a new entrant would have to win business from existing suppliers.

If a market is *declining*, the merged group is less likely[24] to enjoy market power if other competitors are chasing volumes[25] and/or customers are switching to other products.[26] If exit barriers are high, competition may be ferocious, particularly if assets are sold at under-value but remain within the industry, because the purchasers of such assets will face different incentives from the incumbents, in particular to cut prices.[27] In *Framatome | Siemens | Cogema JV*[28] the Commission commented that: "future demand for spent-fuel racks in the EEA is both limited and decreasing. In those circumstances, it appears difficult for any market player to offer spent-fuel racks at less than competitive conditions."

---

[20] Case COMP/M.2602.
[21] Paras 44 and 45. See also Case IV/M.126 *Accor | Wagons-Lits* [1992] O.J. L204/1; Case IV/M.222 *Mannesmann | Hoesch* [1993] O.J. L114/34, para.106; and Case IV/M.970 *TKS | ITW Signode | Titan* [1998] O.J. L316/33.
[22] Case IV/M.1069 [1999] O.J. L116/1.
[23] See s.6.4(e) below.
[24] It remains possible for a supplier to exploit market power in a declining market; see Case COMP/M.3751 *Novartis | Hexal*, p.9.
[25] See, e.g. Case COMP/M.3431 *Sonoco | Ahlstrom* [2005] O.J. L159/13, para.97. For discussion of the way in which exit occurs from declining markets, see Phlips edn, *Applied Industrial Economics* (Cambridge UP, 1998), p.12 and Chs 4 and 5 and Martin, *Advanced Industrial Economics* (2nd edn, Blackwell, 2002), pp.369 to 371. For empirical evidence of the history of entry and exit, see Martin, pp.371 to 377. There may be efficiency gains from mergers in declining markets in terms of optimal consolidation and retirement of assets (see Ch.18 below for the relevance of efficiency arguments under the ECMR). For a strategic perspective on competing in declining markets, see Porter, *On Competition* (The Harvard Business Review book series, 1998), Ch.4 and Porter, *Competitive Strategy* (The Free Press, 1998 edn), Ch.12.
[26] See, e.g. the UK Competition Commission Report on *BASF AG | Takeda Chemical Industries Ltd*, Cm. 5209, para.2.112. If markets are declining, companies with in-house capabilities may commence sales in the market: see Case COMP/M.1597 *Castrol | Carless | JV*, para.28.
[27] See Porter, *Competitive Strategy* (The Free Press, 1998 edn), pp.259 to 266.
[28] Case COMP/M.1940 [2001] O.J. L289/8, para.145.

(c) New markets

If the merger will enable the merged group to develop a new product,[29] it **6–009** may result in the merged group holding market power. This will depend in particular on barriers to entry, any first-mover advantage (e.g. through supply-side economies of scale, including learning-by-doing, and demand-side economies of scale through network effects)[30] and the extent to which the first-mover can adopt pricing strategies to retain that advantage.[31] However, a significant impediment to effective competition will arise only if the merged group's market power will be more than merely transient.[32] Indeed, there are numerous examples of products which enjoyed 100 per cent market shares but were overtaken by competitors, including CP/M, WordStar and VisiCalc.[33]

In *Vodafone Airtouch / Mannesmann*[34] the Commission defined the market as the provision of advanced seamless pan-European mobile tele-communications services because there was consumer demand for such services,[35] even though they could not be provided at the date of the decision for technical reasons.[36] The Commission found that the merged group would be the only mobile operator able to supply such services in the short to medium term, which was taken as three to five years,[37] would be more attractive to customers than its rivals[38] and would have an incentive to refuse access to its network or to provide access on unattractive terms.[39] The Commission concluded that the merger would create a dominant position[40] but cleared the concentration following the provision of undertakings intended to allow third parties non-discriminatory access to the merged group's integrated network.[41] The undertakings applied for three years.

---

[29] See generally Porter, *Competitive Strategy* (The Free Press, 1998 edn), Ch.10; OFT Economic Discussion Paper, "Innovation and Competition Policy", Charles River Associates, March 2002 (note that the views in the paper do not necessarily reflect those of the OFT); Bishop & Caffarra, "Merger control in 'new markets'" [2001] E.C.L.R. 31; and Evans, Padilla & Ahlborn, "Competition Policy in the New Economy: is European Competition Law up to the Challenge?" [2001] E.C.L.R. 156.

[30] See Shapiro & Varian, *Information Rules: A Strategic Guide to the New Economy* (Harvard Business School Press, 1999), p.273.

[31] For discussion of pricing strategies, see Shapiro & Varian, *Information Rules: A Strategic Guide to the New Economy* (Harvard Business School Press, 1999), p.30.

[32] See Case 85/76 *Hoffmann-La Roche v Commission* [1979] E.C.R. 461.

[33] Shapiro & Varian, *Information Rules: A Strategic Guide to the New Economy* (Harvard Business School Press, 1999), p.32. For further examples, see Oster, *Modern Competitive Strategy* (3rd edn, Oxford UP, 1999), p.316.

[34] Case COMP/M.1795.

[35] Para.21.

[36] Para.13.

[37] Para.44.

[38] Para.45.

[39] Para.46.

[40] Para.48.

[41] Paras 58 and 59.

6–010   The following cases also gave rise to concerns in "new" markets.[42]

(a) *Vodafone | Vivendi | Canal+*[43] involved the developing national markets for TV-based internet portals and the developing national and European markets for mobile phone-based internet portals. The parties provided commitments to allow customers to access third party portals and to change the default portal (themselves or by authorising a third party portal operator).

(b) *Vivendi | Canal + | Seagram*[44] involved the emerging pan-European market for portals and the emerging market for online music delivery. The Commission accepted an undertaking from Vivendi to provide rival portals with access to Universal's online music content for five years.

(c) *AOL | Time Warner*[45] involved the emerging market for internet music delivery online. The Commission was concerned that the merged group would become gatekeeper to this nascent market but accepted commitments aimed at severing the links between AOL and Bertelsmann, Europe's leading media company.

(d) *BSkyB | KirchPayTV*[46] raised issues in the emerging market for digital interactive television services. The Commission was concerned that the merger would allow KirchPayTV to enter this market at the same time as or before rival operators and to raise the barriers to entry for third parties. The merger was cleared after the parties provided undertakings intended to lower barriers to entry.

(e) *DaimlerChrysler | Deutsche Telekom | JV*[47] involved the emerging market for traffic telematics systems for transport and logistics undertakings (such systems are used to exchange information between truck operators and vehicles, to improve fleet management). The joint venture was formed to develop on behalf of the German Republic an onboard unit to be supplied *free of charge* to those liable to pay a truck toll. However, the parties planned to add traffic

---

[42] See also Case IV/M.469 *MSG Media Service*; Case COMP/M.2028 *ABB | Bilfinger | MVV Energie | JV*; Case COMP/M.2547 *Bayer | Aventis Crop Science* [2004] O.J. L107/1 (taking account of R&D capabilities in assessing future competition in a current production market and future markets; para.18); and Case COMP/M.3314 *Air Liquide | Messer Targets* (even in an emerging market, a combined share of 70 to 80% was a strong indication of the creation of a dominant position; para.78). In relation to Case IV/M.490 *Nordic Satellite Distribution* [1996] O.J. L53/20, the Commission stated in its XXVth Annual Report on Competition Policy, 1995, at para.133: "As the markets affected are currently in a transitional phase the Commission acted to ensure that these future markets would not be foreclosed".
[43] Case COMP/JV.48.
[44] Case COMP/M.2050, paras 22 and 26.
[45] Case COMP/M.1845 [2001] O.J. L268/28.
[46] Case COMP/JV.37.
[47] Case COMP/M.2903 (appeal pending in Case T-269/03 *Socratec (Satellite Navigation Consulting, Research & Technology) v Commission*).

telematics functionality to the unit. The Commission found that this would create a dominant position for the joint venture in traffic telematics because it was unlikely that truck operators would then *pay* to add a second unit with traffic telematics capacity.[48]

By contrast, in other cases involving new markets, the Commission has applied the reasoning set out above in relation to growing markets, namely that the evolving nature of the market will facilitate new entry. For example,[49] in *GE / Instrumentarium*[50] the Commission considered the emerging market for digital mammography and ruled out concerns on the basis that many companies were then entering the market. Similarly, in *Bertelsmann / Burda / Springer-HOS-MM*[51] the Commission considered the undeveloped market for online medical information services but cleared the transaction without undertakings because of the presence of actual competitors and potential entrants.[52] Finally, in *TXU Europe / EDF-London Investments*[53] the Commission found that the joint venture would supply the entirety of the new market for utility network management and operation services but the transaction was approved as the market remained open for future competition and the first mover's strong position was therefore only temporary.

(d) Innovation

The existence and extent of innovation[54] in a market may be relevant to the **6–011** merger appraisal in several respects.

    (a) The merger may affect competition in innovation. The question of whether a merger will increase the rate or scope of innovation to the benefit of consumers, or reduce it, is fact-specific and a detailed

---

[48] Para.51.

[49] See also Case IV/M.986 *Agfa-Gevaert / Du Pont* [1998] O.J. L211/22 (a merger between two of the three suppliers in a relatively new market was cleared because recent entry had been successful and other suppliers were also entering the market; paras 87 to 92); Case COMP/ M.2471 *Accenture / Lagardere / JV* (emerging market for consulting and development services for interactive television editors); and Case COMP/M.3090 *Volkswagen / Offset / Crescent / LeasePlan / JV* (the market was at an early stage of development and had grown by over 50% in the previous two years; although the merger created high market shares, the Commission granted approval; para.21).

[50] Case COMP/M.3083 [2004] O.J. L109/1, para.285.

[51] Case IV/M.972; and Case IV/M.973 *Bertelsmann / Burda-HOS Lifeline*.

[52] See also Case IV/M.57 *Digital / Kienzle*, para.20.

[53] Case COMP/JV.36, paras 37 to 40.

[54] See generally Porter, *Competitive Strategy* (The Free Press, 1998 edn), Ch.8; Porter, *Competitive Advantage* (The Free Press, 1998 edn), Ch.5; OFT Economic Discussion Paper, "Innovation and Competition Policy", Charles River Associates, March 2002 (note that the views in the paper do not necessarily reflect those of the OFT); OECD, "Merger Review in Emerging High Innovation Markets" DAFFE/COMP (2002) 20; Rapp, "The Misapplication of the Innovation Market Approach to Merger Analysis" (1995) 64 *Antitrust Law Journal* 19; and Evans, Padilla & Ahlborn, "Competition Policy in the New Economy: is European Competition Law up to the Challenge?" [2001] E.C.L.R. 156.

analysis is required before it can be concluded that a merger will have an adverse effect on competition by reducing innovation.[55]

(b) When innovations are the subject of trade, they may comprise antitrust markets, e.g. for licensing technology.[56]

(c) Innovations may result in new markets, even though trade has yet to occur.[57]

(d) The merged group's technology may be relevant to an assessment of its market power.[58]

(e) The extent of innovation in a market may affect the Commission's appraisal. If a market is characterised by a *high rate of product innovation*[59] then relatively high market shares of the current gen-

---

[55] This is discussed further in para. 7–014 below.

[56] See para.3–054 above.

[57] See paras 6–009 and 6–010 above. In particular, in the pharmaceutical industry, products which are not yet on the market but are at an advanced stage of development (pipeline products) may be identified: Case COMP/M.1846 *Glaxo Wellcome / SmithKline Beecham*, paras 70 to 72. In assessing competition on future markets the Commission focuses on products which are likely to come to market within three years (compounds in Phase III): *Glaxo Wellcome*, para.190.

[58] In Case T-5/02 *Tetra Laval BV v Commission* [2002] E.C.R. II-4381, the Court of First Instance rejected the Commission's finding that the merged group's research programmes were an indicator that it would hold a dominant position, stating, at para.233: "It has not been shown in the contested decision that the applicant is in a better position than its various competitors on this market". (The Court of First Instance's decision was upheld on appeal on the basis of reasoning not relating to this issue in Case C-12/03P *Commission v Tetra Laval BV*, not yet reported, judgment of February 15, 2005.) See also Case IV/M.774 *Saint-Gobain / Wacker-Chemie / NOM* [1997] O.J. L247/1; Case IV/M.877 *Boeing / McDonnell Douglas* [1997] O.J. L336/16; and Case COMP/M.1630 *Air Liquide / BOC* [2004] O.J. L92/1, paras 92 to 97.

[59] Innovation is the search for new products and processes. The issue of innovation is a contentious one within merger control, because merger control has a tendency to focus on *static efficiency* and, in particular, the question of whether the merged group will have power profitably to raise prices following completion (i.e. implementation) of the transaction. For an explanation of why static performance has been accorded greater weight by antitrust authorities than dynamic performance, see Areeda, Hovenkamp & Solow, *Antitrust Law* (2nd edn, Aspen Law & Business, 1998), Vol.IV, para.918. However, some economists, notably Joseph Schumpeter, believe that the growth of national economies is much more dependent on *dynamic efficiency* through the development of new products and processes. If correct, this raises the question of whether merger control is blocking transactions which would contribute materially to the growth of the economy. Compare Areeda, Hovenkamp & Solow, *Antitrust Law* (2nd edn, Aspen Law & Business, 2000), Vol.IIA, para.407d. Incumbent firms have a greater incentive than new entrants to pursue *gradual innovation*, where the innovation does not displace the previous product, because they will benefit from the continuing sales of the pre-existing product and sales of the innovative one. By contrast, monopolists may have a lower incentive than new entrants to pursue *drastic innovation*, where the innovative product renders the existing one obsolete, because a monopolist has a pre-invention stream of monopoly profits which it wishes to protect. A non-monopolist has no such stream of monopoly profits and therefore has a greater incentive to innovate in order to establish one. This is known as the *replacement effect*. See Cabral, *Introduction to Industrial Organization* (The MIT Press, 2000), pp.294 and 298; Oster, *Modern Competitive Advantage* (3rd edn, Oxford UP, 1999), p.124 (discussing a possible evolution from competition for market share to competition for *opportunity share* in new and emerging markets); Besanko, Dranove & Shanley, *Economics of Strategy* (2nd edn, John Wiley & Sons Inc, 2000), pp.491 to 495; and

eration of products may not confer market power.[60] The issue is whether competition is occurring predominantly *in* the market (most obviously, on the price, quality and terms on which goods and services are supplied)[61] or *for* the market (i.e. "winner takes all") through the development of new products and functions (with price a less important competitive factor).[62] In particular, if the market structure is likely to change radically in the short to medium term, then the harm to consumer welfare in creating or strengthening market power in the market as it currently stands may not be substantial *provided* that the conditions of competition in the market following the step-change prompted by innovation will not be substantially influenced by market power held in the market as it currently stands. For example, in *Philips / Agilent Health Care Solutions*[63] the Commission found that market positions in the provision of cardiology machinery were largely determined by innovation and did not remain stable over time. In *Hoffmann-La Roche / Boehringer Mannheim*[64] the Commission recognised that in technology-driven markets a careful analysis must be made of the likely development of market dynamics, but found on the facts that the market was stable without volatility in market shares or a change in market leadership for many years.

(f) If one of the merging parties is not active in a market but is developing a new technology, the merger may significantly impede effective competition by eliminating an important potential competitor.[65]

Scherer & Ross, *Industrial Market Structure and Economic Performance* (3rd edn, Houghton Mifflin Co, 1990), p.660. The importance of research and development expenditure in an industry can be measured by the ratio of its research and development expenditure to output sales in comparison with other industries: see Shy, *Industrial Organization* (The MIT Press, 1995), p.221 for comparators.

[60] See the Notice on Horizontal Mergers, para.15 and, e.g. Case IV/M.57 *Digital / Kienzle*, para.20; Case IV/M.354 *American Cyanamid / Shell*, para.33; Case IV/M.821 *Baxter / Immuno*; and Case COMP/M.2609 *HP / Compaq*, para.39. See also Case T-5/02 *Tetra Laval BV v Commission* [2002] E.C.R. II-4381, para.131 (Tetra Laval "has argued convincingly since these are emerging technologies, the market shares calculated by reference to existing products are not very reliable") (the decision was upheld on appeal on the basis of reasoning not relating to this issue in Case C-12/03P *Commission v Tetra Laval BV*, not yet reported, judgment of February 15, 2005).

[61] In which case, an orthodox market share analysis is appropriate.

[62] See OFT Economic Discussion Paper, "Innovation and Competition Policy", Charles River Associates, March 2002 (note that the views in the paper do not necessarily reflect those of the OFT), paras 7.3 to 7.23. Compare the Commission's observation that it has *not* found that competition in innovative markets is largely for the market and market power is undermined quickly by other innovations (see "Merger Review in Emerging High Innovation Markets", OECD, DAFFE/COMP(2002)20, p.161; although compare the views of the Secretariat at p.7).

[63] Case COMP/M.2256, paras 31 and 32.

[64] Case IV/M.950 [1998] O.J. L234/14, para.135.

[65] See, e.g. Case COMP/M.2416 *Tetra Laval / Sidel* (decision of January 13, 2003), para.99.

(e) Naturally concentrated markets

6–012 In *Siemens / Italtel*[66] the Commission found that the market for the supply of switches was naturally concentrated because customers had a preference for using small numbers of technologies in a system and the product had a life cycle of 15 years, and concluded: "A high concentration of the supply of public switching systems is the normal consequence of the basic rationale underlying demand for these products."[67]

6.4 COMPETITIVE INTERACTION

6–013 The outcome of a market, in terms of its effects on consumer welfare, may be crucially affected by the way in which rivalry occurs in the market, i.e. by the nature of competitive interaction.[68] This section examines the importance of pricing strategies (s.(a)), costs (s.(b)), the nature of the products (s.(c)), contractual terms (s.(d)), network effects (s.(e)), two-sided markets (s.(f)), tender or bidding markets (s.(g)), derived demand (s.(h)), connected markets (s.(i)) and not-for-profit organisations (s.(j)).

(a) Pricing

6–014 Whilst most markets involve competition on price, intense competition could occur on non-price grounds.[69] The Commission may therefore need to determine whether competition in the market is occurring wholly or largely on parameters other than price. For example, in *TotalFina / Elf*[70] the Commission found that fuel was a fungible product, despite attempts by oil companies to differentiate their service stations, indicating that any competition in the market would of necessity occur on price.

If price is a relevant competitive parameter—as is almost invariably the case—then it may be relevant to analyse the following categories of evidence

---

[66] Case IV/M.468 [1995] O.J. L161/27, para.43. See also the discussion of research and development expenditure in para.50.

[67] Similarly, in Case COMP/M.3820 *Avnet / Memec*, paras 39 and 40, the Commission noted that the Slovenian market was relatively small and therefore would not support a large number of suppliers; this explained why its structure was more concentrated than other national markets. See also para.16–009 below.

[68] This is readily illustrated by game theory: see Dixit & Nalebuff, *Thinking Strategically* (W W Norton & Co, 1991), p.44, explaining that the outcome of bargaining depends crucially on who gets to make an offer to whom (i.e. the rules of the game) and what happens if the parties fail to reach agreement.

[69] Such competition may promote other aspects of consumer welfare, namely quality, variety or innovation. It is commonly a profit-maximising strategy for suppliers to compete on non-price criteria, such as quality, reliability and new product development.

[70] Case COMP/M.1628 [2001] O.J. L143/1, paras 192 to 195.

to understand the way in which the market operates and the likely effects of a merger.

(i) Pre-merger pricing strategies The following *pricing strategies* may be **6–015** distinguished.

(a) *Price leadership* occurs when one supplier sets its price and the other suppliers generally follow suit.[71] Price leadership reduces competition in the market and may lead to the emergence of coordinated effects or non-coordinated effects.

(b) *Parallel pricing* occurs when rival suppliers follow any supplier which changes its price (and, in contrast to price leadership, the first supplier to change is not always the same).[72] The effects of parallel pricing, in terms of dampening competition in the market, are similar to those of price leadership.

(c) *Geographic pricing schemes* may comprise: *zone prices*, when the price is uniform within particular areas (e.g. Scotland); *basing point systems*, when the price is set at a base price plus the cost of shipping from a specified place of delivery[73]; and *uniform free on board* prices when the delivered price is equal to the ex-works price plus actual transport costs.[74]

If a merger is likely to increase the scope for the merged group to act as a *price leader*, with its competitors acting as *price takers* (i.e. following rather than challenging price increases), then the merged group is likely to enjoy market power as the risk of an aggressive response from smaller suppliers is reduced.[75] Similarly, the dampening of competition which occurs in markets characterised by parallel pricing makes it more likely that a merger will result in the merged group enjoying market power.

---

[71] Scherer & Ross, *Industrial Market Structure and Economic Performance* (3rd edn, Houghton Mifflin Co, 1990), pp.248 to 250 distinguish *dominant firm price leadership, collusive price leadership* and *barometric price leadership* (when the price leader acts as a barometer of market conditions setting prices which would have emerged in any event under competitive conditions).

[72] See Phlips edn, *Applied Industrial Economics* (Cambridge UP, 1998), p.15.

[73] Such a system was used for the pricing of steel in the USA until the 1920s—the "Pittsburgh-plus" system. Producers, whether manufacturing in Pittsburgh or not, used the system, which tended to facilitate coordinated effects.

[74] Sometimes producers offer a choice of an ex-works or a delivered price.

[75] See Case COMP/M.1672 *Volvo / Scania* [2001] O.J. L143/74, para.288; Case COMP/M.1806 *Astra Zeneca / Novartis* [2004] O.J. L110/1, para.223; Case COMP/M.2187 *CVC / Lenzing*, [2004] O.J. L82/20, para.173; and Case COMP/M.2420 *Mitsui / CVRD / Caemi* [2004] O.J. L92/50, para.207. In the UK Competition Commission's report on *Kingfisher Plc / Dixons Group Plc*, Cm. 1079, May 23, 1990, emphasis was placed on the fact that the merging parties were in very direct competition and the remainder of the market tended to follow their prices with the result that a merger would eliminate the main form of price competition in the market.

6–016 **(ii) The merging parties' prices** If one of the merging parties sets prices which are lower than the other, one issue is whether the merged group will adopt the higher pricing strategy, leading to price increases.[76] In *France Telecom / Orange*[77] France Telecom controlled a Belgian mobile telephony provider which set high tariffs when it faced a single competitor but was forced to reduce them significantly when Orange entered the market. The Commission concluded that, since Orange had played an important role in breaking the previous duopolistic pricing behaviour, there were serious doubts as to the compatibility of the concentration with the common market. In *Imperial Tobacco / Reemtsma Cigarettenfabriken GmbH*[78] the Commission emphasised, in finding serious doubts about the transaction, that the target company fully occupied the segment of the market in which new entry was most likely and controlled brands "that appear to discipline the market".

6–017 **(iii) The merging parties' pricing incentives** In *BP / E.ON*[79] the Commission was concerned that the merger (together with a parallel merger) would eliminate the only independent, non-integrated suppliers from the merchant market for ethylene: "The increase in market power may even go beyond the mere gain of market shares since DEA and Veba have been of particular importance for the market in their role as ethylene producers without downstream interests and independent price settlers. The transactions would therefore not only lead to pure formal changes in market share figures, but would considerably affect the market structure in substantive terms."[80]

6–018 **(iv) Pricing trends as evidence of competitive conditions** In *Solvay / Montedison-Ausimont*[81] the Commission relied on pricing data as an indication that competition in the market was not particularly intense, noting that selling prices tended to remain stable over time when they would have been expected to fall as the products in question required substantial initial investment.

Conversely, in *Krupp / Thyssen / Riva / Falck / Tadfin / AST*[82] the Commission found that price falls in the face of increasing consumption

---

[76] See also Case COMP/M.2187 *CVC / Lenzing* [2004] O.J. L82/20, para.232 and Case COMP/M.3314 *Air Liquide / Messer Targets* (Air Liquide's internal documents showed that it had an aggressive expansion policy and the market test confirmed that it had offered significantly lower prices; the Commission found that Air Liquide's incentive to increase its customer base would be substantially weakened through the acquisition of a significant incumbent supplier; paras 88 to 90).
[77] Case COMP/M.2016, paras 26 to 28.
[78] Case COMP/M.2779, paras 52, 55 and 56.
[79] Case COMP/M.2533 [2002] O.J. L276/31.
[80] Para.46.
[81] Case COMP/M.2690, para.43.
[82] Case IV/M.484 [1995] O.J. L251/13, para.61.

provided a clear indication of existing price competition in the market.[83] Further, in *MAN / Auwärter*[84] the Commission found that there was, prior to the merger, effective competition on the German city bus market despite a high level of supply-side concentration, noting that "prices on the city bus market have remained essentially stable, which in view of recent improvements in technology and equipment translates into an actual price cut."[85]

(v) A comparison of prices in different markets If prices are lower in area A   **6–019** than in areas B and C, and one of the merging parties is active only in area A, one issue is whether the activities of the party in question have caused the lower prices in area A, and, if so, whether this factor will be lost as a result of the merger.[86] In comparing prices of specific products between jurisdictions, it is important to allow for general differences in price in the sector in question.[87] In *Exxon / Mobil*[88] the Commission compared the prices of fuel on the motorway network and in the off-motorway market, took account of differing costs, and concluded that the players on the motorway market seemed to have reached a supra-competitive equilibrium. The Commission also compared the margins from service stations in Luxembourg and France and found that the high margins in the former suggested a substantial deficit of competition on the market.[89]

(vi) The effects of previous mergers on prices If the purchaser has previously   **6–020** raised prices after completing acquisitions, this suggests (weakly) that prices may rise after the notified transaction.

---

[83] In Case IV/M.737 *Ciba-Geigy / Sandoz* [1997] O.J. L201/1, the Commission stated, at para.74, that price rises broadly in line with inflation were not an indicator of the scope for dominant behaviour. In Case COMP/M.2547 *Bayer / Aventis Crop Science* [2004] O.J. L107/1 the Commission noted, at para.595, that price reductions did not necessarily imply that margins had been reduced as production may have become more efficient.

[84] Case COMP/M.2201 [2002] O.J. L116/35, para.26. The Commission also relied on the fact that the merging parties were making losses.

[85] In compiling price series in cases where the quality of the product changes over time (e.g. cars, computers), it may be necessary to carry out *hedonic price analysis*, which strips out the effect of quality changes.

[86] In the United Kingdom, see the Director General of Fair Trading's advice in *Grundfos Holding AG / Myson Pumps*, October 11, 2000 (*http://www.oft.gov.uk/Business/Mergers+FTA/Decisions/index.htm*).

[87] See Case COMP/M.2044 *Interbrew / Bass* rejecting, at para.48, direct comparisons between Member States. In *The Supply of Recorded Music*, Cm. 2599, June 23, 1994, the UK Competition Commission found that CDs were more expensive in the United Kingdom than the US but the difference was in line with the general difference in prices of manufactured leisure goods. It is also important to allow for taxes and to use an appropriate exchange rate. The UK Competition Commission also acknowledged the difficulties in international price comparisons in *Domestic Electrical Goods*, Cm. 3675, July 1997, para.2.95.

[88] Case IV/M.1383 [2004] O.J. L103/1, para.552. See also paras 663 to 669.

[89] Para.634.

6–021 **(vii) The way in which price is set** If there is a single firm price,[90] the merged group may be deterred from reducing price to win new business as it will have to extend the price reduction to its other customers. By contrast, if the merged group can price discriminate, it will have a greater incentive to cut price to win new business as it will not have to take account of reduced revenues from other customers.[91]

If a supplier sets a single price and customers choose to buy or not, an analysis of the effect of the merger involves assessing the incentives on the merged group to alter that single price. On the other hand, if a supplier negotiates prices individually, an analysis of the effect of the merger may focus largely on understanding the effects of the merger on those negotiations.[92]

(b) Costs

6–022 The Commission considers whether the merged group's cost structure will create incentives for it to maintain or increase output (thereby maintaining or decreasing prices, other things being equal). In *Carnival Corporation / P&O Princess*[93] the Commission relied, in finding that the transaction would not create a dominant position, on the parties' incentives to expand sales because the high fixed costs of the cruise industry meant that the profit-maximising strategy was to arrive at, or close to, 100 per cent capacity utilisation, stating that: "The basic economics of the cruise industry provide considerable incentives to arrive at 100% or close to 100% capacity utilisation. This is due to the fact that—once capacity is set—the marginal costs are very low. Nearly all costs are fixed costs and only costs such as for food are variable costs. These costs are largely outweighed by the on-board revenue generated by each passenger."

---

[90] Much economic theory proceeds on the assumption that there is a *single market price* (i.e. all customers pay the same price for the product) and that the *market clears* (i.e. supply and demand are brought into balance) by changes in market price. However, empirical observation suggests that this is not true: popular concerts, films and plays are often sold out well in advance of performance; and retailers who have made buying errors frequently leave prices unchanged until the sales. These are examples of price rigidity, which sometimes arises because of the costs of changing prices (including in particular, the costs of tracking market conditions, reprinting price lists and loss of customer goodwill in increasing price). When prices are rigid, the market may "clear" by suppliers increasing their inventory, suppliers increasing delivery times (common in the car market) or customers delaying consumption. See Carlton & Perloff, *Modern Industrial Organization* (4th edn, Addison-Wesley, 2005), Ch.17.

[91] See paras 1–006 and 1–011 above.

[92] Muris, speech of January 15, 2003, "Improving the Economic Foundations of Competition Policy" (available at *www.ftc.gov/speeches/muris/improveconfoundatio.htm*), observed that: "the key institutions are the determinants of the specifics of competition in each industry. For example, how do transactions occur, and what are their determinants? Can the process be properly approximated as an auction, and, if so, what kind? Are transactions negotiated? Are suppliers 'qualified,' and what does this qualification involve? What is the nature of supplier/buyer relationships? How important are long-term relationships? What information do the transacting parties possess that is relevant to the transaction's outcome?"

[93] Case COMP/M.2706 [2003] O.J. L248/1, paras 238 and 251.

If switching costs are high and price discrimination is not possible, suppliers with larger market shares have an incentive to raise prices (to exploit their existing customer bases) whereas suppliers with no or smaller market shares have an incentive to compete more aggressively (to win lucrative new business). In this situation, a merger between two larger suppliers may have less effect on consumers than a merger involving a relatively smaller supplier. If switching costs are high and price discrimination is possible, then all suppliers may compete aggressively to win new business whilst exploiting any existing customer base.[94]

Similarities in costs have been described as the "key component" in assessing whether two or more suppliers have sufficiently similar incentives to give rise to coordinated effects.[95]

(c) Products

This section distinguishes several types of goods and services. *Durable* **6–023** *goods*[96] are goods which last over several periods. In markets for durable goods: customers generally have a choice between new and second-hand goods[97]; customers which already own the product have a choice between extending the life of their existing goods or purchasing a replacement; customers which intend to spread the use of the goods over several periods, have the choice to delay purchases[98]; and suppliers of durable goods which require secondary products (e.g. toner for photocopiers) have an incentive to price the durable good competitively to win the customer if they are able to lock-in the customer to using their secondary products.[99] These factors may[1] make a durable goods market hard to monopolise by providing viable choices for customers other than purchasing from the monopoly supplier and tend to mean that a durable goods monopolist will maximise its profits by renting the goods rather than selling (as renting eliminates the second-hand market, prevents customers from extending the useful life of the

---

[94] See para.7–011 below. For a detailed discussion of the effects of switching costs, see OFT Economic Discussion Paper 5, "Switching Costs", NERA, April 2003 (note that the views in the paper do not necessarily reflect those of the OFT).

[95] See para.8–022 below.

[96] See generally Areeda, Hovenkamp & Solow, *Antitrust Law* (2nd edn, Aspen Law & Business, 2000), Vol.IIA, para.573; Carlton & Perloff, *Modern Industrial Organization* (4th edn, Addison-Wesley, 2005), Ch.15; Shy, *Industrial Organization* (The MIT Press, 1995), Ch.12; and Porter, *Competitive Strategy* (The Free Press, 1998 edn), p.168.

[97] See para.3–050 above.

[98] Producers, for their part, have to decide how long durable goods should last for. There is substantial debate on the question of whether a monopoly producer of durable goods has an incentive to reduce their durability: see Shy, *Industrial Organization* (The MIT Press, 1995), p.315.

[99] See para.3–044 above and Shapiro & Varian, *Information Rules: A Strategic Guide to the New Economy* (Harvard Business School Press, 1999), pp.118 to 121 and 145 to 147.

[1] It is necessary to examine who controls the stock of second-hand goods.

product, and removes the incentive to defer purchasing).[2] In *KNP / Bühr-mann-Tetterode / VRG*[3] the Commission noted that customers took account, in purchasing goods, of the scope to sell them in the second-hand market and found that the fact that only certain brands of goods could be sold into a well developed second-hand market created a barrier to entry for suppliers of other brands.

Goods are *homogeneous* when they are perfect substitutes and purchasers perceive no differences[4] between the offerings of rival firms.[5] By contrast, *differentiated* goods are regarded by customers as having different attributes. A distinction can be drawn between *horizontal differentiation*—when different products appeal to different tastes and some customers may prefer one taste and others a second (e.g. sweetened or unsweetened breakfast cereals)—and *vertical differentiation* when, other things being equal, all customers would prefer one product over another (e.g. all customers would, other things being equal, prefer a computer with more memory than less). If the parties supply differentiated products, market shares may provide information of limited weight, as they do not reflect the "closeness" of the competition between the parties.[6]

6–024　　The following categories of goods may also be distinguished[7]: *convenience goods*, such as sweets, where the costs of carrying out a price comparison are disproportionate relative to the benefits, given the low prices of the goods[8]; *shopping goods*, such as carpets, where purchases are infrequent, prices are high relative to average earnings and many customers are willing to shop around before making a purchase[9]; *inspection goods*, such as artwork, whose quality can be determined by examination; and *experience goods*, such as wine, whose quality is uncertain and can be determined only upon consumption.[10] Markets for experience goods are typically characterised by

---

[2] This is known as the Coase Conjecture. See the discussion in Dixit & Nalebuff, *Thinking Strategically* (W W Norton & Co, 1991), p.166. The Coase Conjecture does not hold in all circumstances: see Shy, *Industrial Organization* (The MIT Press, 1995), p.85.

[3] Case IV/M.291 [1993] O.J. L217/35, para.28.

[4] However, Shapiro, "Mergers With Differentiated Products", speech of November 9, 1995 (*http://www.usdoj.gov/atr/public/speeches/shapiro.spc.htm*) observed: "To a greater or lesser degree, virtually all markets involve some element of product differentiation. Even in a classic homogeneous-goods market—such as the market for an agricultural commodity or for a specific chemical compound—producers often attempt to differentiate themselves based on product quality, reliability, or customer service".

[5] See OECD "Glossary of Industrial Organisation Economics and Competition Law" (*www.oecd.org/dataoecd/8/61/2376087.pdf*).

[6] See s.7.3 below.

[7] Producers may make goods for *stock* or, alternatively, only following an *order*. When goods are produced for stock, producers can benefit from economies of scale in production and can respond quickly to orders. On the other hand, production to order reduces the need for working capital and may enable the suppliers to offer customised products on demand.

[8] In such markets there may not be a single price.

[9] Scherer & Ross, *Industrial Market Structure and Economic Performance* (3rd edn, Houghton Mifflin Co, 1990), p.7.

[10] Porter, *Competitive Advantage* (1998 edn, The Free Press), pp.142 and 145, explains that buyers decide whether to purchase on the basis of *use criteria* (such as product quality and features) and *signalling criteria* (such as reputation and advertising) and signalling criteria are most important in relation to products such as experience goods.

asymmetry of information, as sellers (unlike buyers) commonly *are* able to determine the quality of the goods or services. For example, many professional services are experience goods. Further, if purchasers of, e.g. used cars cannot distinguish between good and poor quality vehicles, both will sell at the same price, with the result that bad products will drive out good (because good products will be undervalued by the market and owners of such goods will be less willing to sell).[11] In experience goods markets, customers commonly place reliance on the reputation of the seller; for example, it is impossible to know in advance what quality of food will be served by a restaurant but customers who have previously been served good food at a restaurant will rely on that experience in deciding whether to eat there again. In general, if *search costs* (including an imputed money value for the time spent searching) are low, then prices will be lower and closer to a single price (since suppliers which increase price will lose significant custom). By contrast, as search costs increase, prices tend to increase and the differences between prices offered by different suppliers tend to increase.[12] When some customers have high search costs and others low, it is possible that a market equilibrium exists[13] with some suppliers charging high prices and others low prices; in that situation, customers with high search costs would buy from the first available source whilst others would shop around.

(d) Contractual terms

Buying decisions may be affected by contractual terms such as after-sales **6–025** service and warranties. Terms of this type serve to define the product that is being acquired.

Other contractual terms have strategic effects on the way that the market operates.[14] For example, some contracts include "meeting competition" clauses (which provide that a customer which finds a supplier willing to offer a better price is to be released from the contract unless the supplier is willing to match the price) or "most favoured customer" clauses (which provide that the supplier is not supplying the goods at more favourable prices to any other customer).

Evidence that suppliers are able to negotiate contractual terms that are heavily skewed in their favour in comparison with market practice may itself suggest that the suppliers enjoy market power. In *Boeing / McDonnell Douglas*[15] the Commission regarded the fact that Boeing had concluded exclusive supply agreements with three major airlines as confirming that

---

[11] See Carlton & Perloff, *Modern Industrial Organization* (4th edn, Addison-Wesley, 2005), pp.443 and 445. If bad products drive out good, the result is a *market for lemons*.
[12] See Shy, *Industrial Organization* (The MIT Press, 1995), p.426.
[13] This can be simulated through *tourists-locals models*: see Cabral, *Introduction to Industrial Organization* (The MIT Press, 2000), pp.218 and 219.
[14] See para.8–044 below.
[15] Case IV/M.877 [1997] O.J. L336/16.

Boeing held a dominant position, as the airlines in question would not have signed long-term exclusive supply agreements unless the supplier was dominant. The Commission was concerned that, following the merger, the merged group would conclude similar agreements and accepted commitments not to enforce the existing exclusivity provisions and not to enter any new exclusive supply agreements.[16] The Commission has expressed similar concerns in relation to loyalty schemes and rebates.[17]

(e) Network effects

6–026 Network effects[18] arise when the value a potential purchaser places on a good depends on the number of other consumers of the good. Network effects are *demand-side economies of scale*. It is possible to distinguish *direct network effects*, where the benefit of the network to a customer depends directly on the number of other customers who are linked to the network (e.g. telephone networks and postal services); and *indirect network benefits* where the number of other customers on the network affects the price of goods and services offered to each user (e.g. the fact that there are more users of Microsoft's operating systems than Apple's means that there is a greater range of software and books for Microsoft's system).[19]

There are several specific characteristics of network industries that affect the way in which competition occurs.[20] First, demand in network industries depends critically on *customer expectations* of future network size; in particular, customers may be willing to pay more to join a network which they expect to become very extensive.[21] Secondly, there may be a *critical mass* of customers which, once achieved, enables the network to build up. This has the consequence that technologies with strong network effects may exhibit

---

[16] Paras 68 to 71. See also Case IV/M.9 *Fiat Geotech / Ford New Holland* (exclusive purchasing agreement) and Case IV/M.582 *Orkla / Volvo* (long-term exclusive supply agreements).

[17] See Case IV/M.190 *Nestlé / Perrier* [1992] O.J. L356/1 (rebate schemes) and Case IV/M.784 *Kesko / Tuko*, [1997] O.J. L110/53.

[18] See generally Shy, *The Economics of Network Industries* (Cambridge UP, 2001); Shapiro & Varian, *Information Rules: A Strategic Guide to the New Economy* (Harvard Business School Press, 1999); OFT Economic Discussion Paper, "Innovation and Competition Policy", Charles River Associates, March 2002 (note that the views in the paper do not necessarily reflect those of the OFT); Bishop and Caffarra, "Merger Control in 'New Markets'" [2001] E.C.L.R. 31; Evans, Padilla & Ahlborn, "Competition Policy in the New Economy: is European Competition Law up to the Challenge?" [2001] E.C.L.R. 156; Gladwell, *The Tipping Point* (Abacus, 2000); *www.inforules.com* and *www.sims.berkeley.edu/resources/infoecon*.

[19] See Carlton & Perloff, *Modern Industrial Organization* (4th edn, Addison-Wesley, 2005), pp.391 and 391; the discussion of *Microsoft / Liberty Media / Telewest* in the Commission's press release IP/00/733; and Bishop and Caffarra, "Merger Control in 'New Markets'" [2001] E.C.L.R. 31, at p.32.

[20] In addition, network industries commonly have high sunk costs and low marginal costs, which tends to require suppliers to price discriminate in order to recover the sunk costs: see Shapiro & Varian, *Information Rules: A Strategic Guide to the New Economy* (Harvard Business School Press, 1999). This is particularly true of *information goods*, where the majority of the costs may be incurred in producing the first copy.

[21] Cabral, *Introduction to Industrial Organization* (The MIT Press, 2000), p.312.

long lead times followed by very rapid expansion.[22] Thirdly, network industries are characterised by *positive feedback*: successful suppliers become progressively more attractive to potential customers as their customer-base expands.[23] Fourthly, markets characterised by "network effects" may *tip*,[24] i.e. demand for one network may become so large that demand for rival networks declines rapidly to zero and the industry becomes *locked-in*[25] to one of the technologies. For example, as use of VHS as a home video format grew, the indirect network benefits (in terms of range of videotapes available to rent and buy) grew, and eventually Betamax disappeared as a format. Fifthly, the third and fourth points mean that the decisions of early adopters may have a very substantial or determinative effect on the outcome of the industry, i.e. competition is a dynamic process which is *path dependent*.[26]

Sixthly, the consequences of network compatibility,[27] as opposed to incompatibility, are ambiguous in economic terms. In particular, prior to the market tipping, suppliers of incompatible systems may compete more intensively in an attempt to win the standards battle,[28] become the standards setter and enjoy monopoly profits at the post-standards battle stage. Whilst customers benefit from price competition prior to tipping, this may be characterised as a "down payment" on future lock-in.[29] Farrell & Shapiro comment: "The underlying principle guiding antitrust law is the protection of competition as a *process*. If a single firm is victorious and gains a monopoly position based on offering low prices and superior product quality, the competitive process has worked just fine."[30] However, whilst the antitrust authorities will not intervene to prevent a company from winning the standards battle through superior efficiency, they may prevent a resolution of the battle through merger, as the merger may cut short the period of intense competition which would otherwise enhance consumer welfare.[31]

---

[22] Shapiro & Varian, *Information Rules: A Strategic Guide to the New Economy* (Harvard Business School Press, 1999), p.13.

[23] Shapiro & Varian, *Information Rules: A Strategic Guide to the New Economy* (Harvard Business School Press, 1999), pp.173 and 174.

[24] See OFT Economic Discussion Paper, "Innovation and Competition Policy", Charles River Associates, March 2002 (note that the views in the paper do not necessarily reflect those of the OFT), para.3.31.

[25] *Lock-in* arises when the costs of switching from one brand of technology to another are substantial. Shapiro & Varian, *Information Rules: A Strategic Guide to the New Economy* (Harvard Business School Press, 1999), p.117 summarise types of lock-in and the associated switching costs.

[26] Cabral, *Introduction to Industrial Organization* (The MIT Press, 2000), p.316.

[27] If the output of one manufacturer can be operated or used by goods produced by other manufacturers then they are *compatible*. For example, all compact discs are compatible with all CD players; but the same is not true of DVDs.

[28] See Shapiro & Varian, *Information Rules: A Strategic Guide to the New Economy* (Harvard Business School Press, 1999), Ch.9.

[29] Shapiro & Varian, *Information Rules: A Strategic Guide to the New Economy* (Harvard Business School Press, 1999), pp.233 and 234.

[30] Shapiro & Varian, *Information Rules: A Strategic Guide to the New Economy* (Harvard Business School Press, 1999), p.301.

[31] See OFT Economic Discussion Paper, "Innovation and Competition Policy", Charles River Associates, March 2002 (note that the views in the paper do not necessarily reflect those of the OFT), paras 7.16 to 7.20.

By contrast, suppliers of compatible systems have no hope of tipping the market in their favour and therefore do not have the same incentives as suppliers of incompatible systems to compete aggressively to win market share. But they have less scope to engage in product differentiation and, other things being equal, reduced levels of product differentiation lead to greater price competition. Accordingly, the effect of openness is that consumers have reduced choice and do not benefit from intense price competition to win the standards battle but they avoid the risk of being stranded if they fail to pick the winner of the standards battle, enjoy maximum network benefits, face reduced risk of lock-in and benefit from ongoing price competition.[32] Openness is common when several products must work together[33] and when no single supplier is sufficiently strong to dictate the technology standards.[34]

Seventhly, the importance of *customer expectations* has the consequence that network industries may be characterised by *excess inertia* (when customers fail to switch to a superior technology out of fear of becoming stuck with useless hardware)[35] or *excess momentum*[36] (when customers switch to a new technology in the expectation that others will do so even though it offers little, if any, advantage).[37] In the software industry, a wish to influence customer expectations has led suppliers to announce the forthcoming release of new products without any real expectation that the release date announced could be met (*vapourware*).

6–027 In *WorldCom / MCI*[38] the Commission found that network effects would serve to protect the merged group from challenge: "Because of the specific features of network competition and the existence of network externalities which make it valuable for customers to have access to the largest network, MCI WorldCom's position can hardly be challenged once it has obtained a dominant position. The more its network grows, the less need it has to interconnect with competitors and the more need they have to interconnect with the merged entity ... The merger might well create a 'snowball effect', in that MCI WorldCom would be better placed than any of its competitors to capture future growth through new customers, because of the attractions for any new customer of direct connection with the largest network, and the relative unattractiveness of competitors' offerings owing to the threat of disconnection or degradation of peering which MCI WorldCom's compe-

---

[32] See generally Shapiro & Varian, *Information Rules: A Strategic Guide to the New Economy* (Harvard Business School Press, 1999), pp.223 to 237.

[33] The need for different components to interface successfully with one another means that suppliers in network industries have an incentive to cooperate as well as compete.

[34] Shapiro & Varian, *Information Rules: A Strategic Guide to the New Economy* (Harvard Business School Press, 1999), p.199.

[35] The digital radio industry is anxious not to fall within this category.

[36] See Cabral, *Introduction to Industrial Organization* (The MIT Press, 2000), p.324 and Farrell & Saloner, "Installed base and compatibility: innovation, product pronouncements and predation", (1986) 76 *American Economic Review* 940.

[37] New versions of computer software may fall within this category.

[38] Case IV/M.1069 [1999] O.J. L116/1. See also Case COMP/M.1795 *Vodafone Airtouch / Mannesmann*.

titors must constantly live under. As a result, the merger might provide MCI WorldCom with the opportunity to enlarge its market share still further."[39] In *Vivendi / Canal+ / Seagram*[40] the Commission was concerned about the combination of Vizzavi's position on the emerging market for portals with Universal's music content. It predicted that Vizzavi would attract a large customer base which would, in turn, attract the other four major music labels to license their content via Vizzavi, with the consequence that: "the addition of Universal's music content to the very large distribution structure of Vivendi and Canal+ is likely to create [a] network effect to the detriment of competitors and to consumers. Customers risk to be 'walled in' and to pay higher prices for the services due to the lack of competition." Accordingly, the Commission found that there were serious doubts whether the transaction would lead to the creation of a dominant position on the emerging pan-European market for portals and the emerging market for online music.

(f) Two-sided markets

In a two-sided market,[41] an assessment of the profitability of a change in the price of one side of the market depends not only on the effects of the change in price on the side in question, but also the knock-on effects on the second side. For example, a newspaper which increases its cover price will find that this affects not only the profitability of its sales to readers, but also the profitability of its advertising activities as advertisers' willingness to pay will be affected if the rise in cover price reduces circulation.[42] This makes the exercise of assessing the effect of the merger on the merged group's incentives and abilities to raise prices somewhat more complex.[43] It also means that mergers may have beneficial effects on some groups of consumers (e.g. by lowering advertising rates) whilst having adverse effects on others (e.g. increasing cover prices).[44] **6–028**

---

[39] Paras 126 and 131. The Commission suggested, at para.126, that the network may become an "essential facility".

[40] Case COMP/M.2050, paras 51 to 67. See also Case COMP/M.1845 *AOL / Time Warner* [2001] O.J. L268/28, paras 69 and 85.

[41] See para.3–046 for a discussion of the meaning of two-sided markets and market definition in such cases.

[42] In two-sided markets, suppliers compete according to the *structure* of their offering (e.g. a free newspaper with extensive advertising may be competing against a paid for title with relatively little advertising); see "Media Mergers", OECD, DAFFE/COMP(2003)16, p.8.

[43] The essential question, namely whether the merged group will have the incentive and ability to raise prices, remains identical.

[44] See the discussion in "Media Mergers", OECD, DAFFE/COMP(2003)16, p.20. Compare the inability, as part of an assessment of efficiencies, to trade-off efficiency gains for one group of customers against detriments to another; see para.18–022 below.

(g) Tender or bidding markets

6–029 *Tender or bidding markets* may be more competitive than other markets for three principal reasons.[45] First, intense competition is possible with very few suppliers, in particular if the volumes at stake in the tender account for a large proportion of the bidding companies' sales and the industry is characterised by high fixed costs.[46] More generally, in tender markets, competition may be "for" the market, not "in" the market. This means that historic market shares based on sales may be a very poor indicator of a merged group's market power[47] and explains why, in genuine "bidding markets", market shares are calculated on the basis of the number of credible players.[48] Secondly, the fact that suppliers can generally charge different prices to different customers in tender markets increases the incentive to compete aggressively for a single contract, as a supplier can reduce prices to one customer without having to make similar reductions to others. Thirdly, in tender markets, companies with no or limited sales can have a significant effect on market price, e.g. a "maverick" supplier with new capacity may bid very aggressively to win share to use the new capacity.

On the other hand, the 2002 draft Commission Notice on Horizontal Mergers noted[49] that there may be bidding contests in which the merging firms are likely to be one another's most credible competitors: "This could be the case when the merging parties are the two bidders with the lowest costs and where no other bidders have sufficiently low costs to exercise a competitive constraint on the winning bidder." In such a case, the merged group may have power profitably to increase prices (i.e. non-coordinated effects may arise, which may justify a prohibition decision).

In predicting the effects of a merger on a bidding market, an analogy can be drawn with the extensive literature on auction theory, because prices in auctions are also determined through a bidding process.[50] In particular, in private value auctions (when each bidder has a confidential, personal valuation of the subject of the auction which may differ from those of other bidders), an increase in the number of bidders is associated with an increase in competition (and conversely, a reduction in the number of bidders through a merger reduces the intensity of competition), but in common value auctions (when the subject of the auction has the same value to each

---

[45] On the other hand, tender markets provide frequent opportunities for interaction between competitors, which may facilitate tacit coordination.

[46] See Case COMP/M.3512 *VNU / WPP / JV*, finding that a merger reducing the number of credible competitors from four to three did not raise competition concerns, because customers organised auctions that were well adapted to the market setting; paras 22, 23, 25 and n.7.

[47] See, e.g. Case COMP/M.2036 *Valeo / Labinal*, paras 26, 27, 29 and 34.

[48] See para.4–006 above.

[49] Para.39. This paragraph was not included in the final version of the Notice.

[50] See Carlton & Perloff, *Modern Industrial Organization* (4th edn, Addison-Wesley, 2005), pp.338 and 339 and, for a more detailed account, Klemperer *Auctions: Theory and Practice* (Princetown University Press, 2004) and ABA Section of Antitrust Law, *Econometrics* (ABA Publishing, 2005), Ch.IX.

bidder, although the value is unknown when bids are submitted), an increase in the number of bidders may not increase competition (because bidders fear the winner's curse, namely that the more bidders there are, the more likely it is that the winning bidder will have overpaid).[51]

The Commission has examined tender or bidding markets in many **6–030** cases.[52] For example, in *Pirelli / BICC*[53] the Commission noted that: "In the [market in question], tenders take place infrequently, while the value of each individual contract usually is very significant. Contracts are typically awarded to a single successful bidder (so-called 'winner-takes-all' principle). Strong incentives therefore exist for all competitors to bid aggressively for each contract." In *Price Waterhouse / Coopers & Lybrand*[54] the Commission examined national markets for audit and accounting services to large companies. The Commission first considered the parties' shares of the markets measured by value and concluded that the merged group would not enjoy excessive market power. However, it then proceeded, in addition, to analyse tender offers in the market, stating: "the norm is for an audit appointment to be renewed over many years and to be long-term, even lasting several decades. This lack of market fluidity means that in addition to market shares relating to a single year, it is necessary to examine tender offers and bidding data over a longer period in order to appraise more fully the nature and extent of the competitive process in the Big Six market for large companies. The Commission's investigation has revealed that although tender offers are not a frequent occurrence, when a client does decide that a change of auditor may be appropriate and launches a tender process, there is competition in the form of bids from other members of the Big Six. Clients are well-informed buyers and are well aware of price, quality and value in relation to the service offered. The fact that normally three or four members of the Big Six make offers when tenders are launched makes it clear that to an extent clients are able to use the implicit threat of going to tender to constrain the power of their incumbent auditor."

In *Alcoa / Reynolds*[55] the Commission emphasised that in a tender situation where every bidder has capacity to supply the whole market, the winner will be the company with the lowest average cost and that company will set its bid just below the closest rival's average cost, with the consequence that a merger between the companies with the lowest and next-lowest average costs will lead to price increases to just below the third-best bidder's average cost. The parties in that case argued that in markets with a capacity constraint, tenders result in prices close to the average costs of the bidder with the *highest* costs. However, the Commission found on the facts that Reynolds had spare capacity and therefore an incentive to bid below

---

[51] See Olley, "Applying the Lessons of Auction Theory to the Analysis of Mergers in Bidding Markets" (available at *http://www.nera.com/NewsletterIssue/AT_Insights_082505_final.pdf*).
[52] See para.7–006(a) below.
[53] Case COMP/M.1882 [2003] O.J. L70/35, para.79.
[54] Case IV/M.1016 [1999] O.J. L50/27, paras 85 to 94.
[55] Case COMP/M.1693 [2002] O.J. L58/25, paras 52 to 54.

that level, with the consequence that the merger would result in increased prices.

(h) Derived demand

6–031 The nature of competition in markets downstream of the one in which the merging parties sell may affect the merged group's ability to increase its prices or otherwise exercise market power. For example, in *Du Pont / ICI*[56] the merging parties produced fibres which were used in the production of carpets. In the retail market for carpets, goods produced using the fibres produced by the parties competed against goods produced from other materials. The Commission concluded: "This degree of overlap at retail level results in significant indirect competitive pressure on the prices of carpet fibres. This indirect pressure amounts to a significant constraint on the competitive behaviour of the nylon fibre suppliers." By contrast, in *VEBA / VIAG*[57] the parties supplied cyanuric chlorine to, amongst others, producers of maize herbicides which competed with Novartis (which self-supplied cyanuric chlorine); the parties argued that the downstream competition to which their customers were subject would limit the merged group's ability to raise price; the Commission rejected the argument, noting that it only applied to some customers and that the limit on price increases would be the level at which the customers exited the market, which still left substantial room for manoeuvre.[58]

(i) Connected markets

6–032 The Commission has in several cases found that a number of separate product or geographic markets are connected and the question of whether the merged group will enjoy market power in one market depends in part on its activities in other, neighbouring markets. For example, in *Mercedes-Benz / Kässbohrer*[59] the Commission examined three markets together in the light

---

[56] Case IV/M.214 [1993] O.J. L7/13, para.46.
[57] Case COMP/M.1673 [2001] O.J. L188/1, para.171.
[58] In Case COMP/M.2533 *BP / E.ON* [2002] O.J. L276/31, in the context of an analysis of possible vertical foreclosure, the Commission rejected, at paras 93 and 94, an argument that the fact that the market in which their customers sold was competitive would limit the merged group's scope to raise prices to those customers because they would not be able to pass on their increased input costs: "According to the Commission's market investigation it may be the case that the producers of ethylene derivatives in certain market situations will not be able to pass the increased raw material cost on to their customers due to the competition which they face from producers located outside the ARG + and imports of the ethylene downstream product. However, such a limit for the increase of ethylene prices does not change the general incentives of the merged entities as, even if the ethylene prices cannot be increased above a certain limit, the merged parties would share the incentives to increase prices up to this limit, gain the profits of the downstream derivatives producers and reduce their competitiveness compared to their own ethylene derivative units".
[59] Case IV/M.477 [1995] O.J. L211/1.

of the considerable links between them. In *Nordbanken / Postgirot*[60] the Commission identified various separate markets for financial products but emphasised that services to end customers were linked as they used the same distribution networks (in that case branch offices, telephone and internet banking) with the consequence that: "market power for these services at the national level arises mainly at the distribution level (access to a customer base) rather than the product generation level. The assessment, therefore, has to take account of competitors' market positions within each individual product market as well as their position across the product range."[61]

(j) Not-for-profit organisations

Not-for-profit entities *may* have different incentives[62] from profit-maximis- **6–033** ing companies[63] and it is important to analyse whether any differences affect the assessment of the impact of the merger on competition.[64] In *Danish Crown / Vestjyske Slagterier*[65] the Commission considered the merged group's position in the Danish market for the purchase from farmers of live pigs for slaughtering and did not identify any concerns about the merged group's ability to extract monopsonistic profits from its suppliers because, as a cooperative, any profits were returned to its farmer-members. *YLE /*

---

[60] Case COMP/M.2567.
[61] Para.38.
[62] For discussion of the relevance of the merged group's *incentives*, see para.2–022 above.
[63] See Thomas, "Do Not-For-Profit Firms Behave Differently?", 2005 (available via *http://www.nera.com/NewsletterIssue/Insights_September_October_2005_FINAL.pdf*); Brennan & Cuomo, "The 'Nonprofit Defense' in Hospital Merger Antitrust Litigation" [1999] *Antitrust* 13; and Eisenstadt, "Hospital Competition and Costs: the Carilion Case", published as Ch.2 of Kwoka & White eds., *The Antitrust Revolution* (3rd edn, Oxford UP, 1999) (but omitted from the 4th edn, Oxford UP, 2004), discussing *US v Carilion Health System* 707 F. Supp.840 (Western District of Virginia, 1989), a case involving a merger of two hospitals. The New Zealand Merger Guidelines, 2004 (*http://www.comcom.govt.nz/Publications/ContentFiles/Documents/MergersandAcquisitionsGuidelines.PDF*), para.5.1, state: "the Commission and the courts have examined the extent to which corporate form may affect business behaviour and competition. In no case to date have they held that the corporate form of an entity would by itself provide such a restraint as to alleviate any market power concerns. The Commission has accepted that the shareholder-suppliers of a co-operative can be in a position to prevent, or at least curtail, the exercise of any power that would be against their interest".
[64] Brennan & Cuomo, "The 'Nonprofit Defense' in Hospital Merger Antitrust Litigation" [1999] *Antitrust* 13, comment, at pp.18 and 19, in relation to US practice: "To make the claim credible, defendants must come forward with factual evidence that shows the court why the hospital's nonprofit status imposes a lasting institutional constraint on the exercise of market power. To this end, evidence that courts have favourably considered includes: pricing studies ... documented hospital 'mission statements' ... along with proof of the mission's implementation ... evidence that board members ... are highly resistant to rising health care costs; and [evidence of efficiency gains]. [Counter-arguments include]: the upredictability of how future board members will run the institution ... the possibility of a for-profit hospital acquiring the nonprofit hospital and changing its incentives ... the human nature of administrators to 'strive for the last penny' when it may enhance their job rating or salary potential; [and] the limited oversight board members may provide over administrators on a day-to-day basis".
[65] Case IV/M.1313 [2000] O.J. L20/1, paras 128 and 192.

TDF / Digita / JV[66] involved a transaction in which TDF would acquire joint control of Digita, which was formerly solely controlled by a not-for-profit organisation, YLE. Third parties argued that the differing incentives facing TDF as a commercial profit-maximiser meant that the merger would strengthen YLE's existing dominant position. However, the Commission rejected these arguments as it was not possible to establish that the merger would necessarily lead to or facilitate price increases and price discrimination as Digita, a monopolist, already had the ability to increase prices.

6.5 EU PROCUREMENT AND HARMONISING LEGISLATION

6–034 When national markets are in a state of transition to pan-European markets under the influence of EU procurement or harmonisation legislation,[67] the prospects for future liberalisation may mean that high national market shares do not confer market power. Mario Monti, then the Commissioner for Competition Policy, stated that: "It may be of interest to note that when such a transition is detected on the basis of evidence submitted by the parties (or elsewhere found in the investigation), the Commission will normally assess the market as national, but may be less concerned with moderately high market shares. Regarding steel tubes, in the *Mannesmann / Hoesch* merger case, the market for certain steel tubes used in various industrial applications was defined as national in scope (Germany). Despite high degrees of concentration, the merger was still cleared, inter alia, with reference to ongoing trends towards a transition to a wider market (partly owing to the European procurement directives)."[68]

6.6 NATIONAL CHAMPIONS

6–035 A merger may not be justified on the grounds that it will create a national champion, capable of competing effectively on the global stage. This was affirmed by the Commission in its press release[69] in relation to the *Schneider Electric / Legrand* decision in which the Commission blocked a merger

---

[66] Case COMP/M.2300, paras 39 and 40.
[67] In Case COMP/M.3352 *VW / Hahn + Lang*, the Commission took account of liberalisation of the market for motor vehicle parts through EC regulation in approving a transaction which created relatively high shares in the supply of original spare parts to independent repair shops and end customers.
[68] Mario Monti, then the Commissioner for Competition Policy, "Market Definition as a cornerstone of EU Competition Policy", speech of October 5, 2001 (*http://europa.eu.int/comm/competition/speeches/index_2001.html*).
[69] IP/01/1393, October 10, 2001.

between two French producers of electrical equipment (although its decision was subsequently overturned on other grounds)[70]:

> "This prohibition must be seen in the wider context of the merging of two companies originating in one and the same Member State with a view to creating a 'national champion'. Such a merger cannot be authorised unless the conditions of effective competition, ensuring in particular fair prices for consumers, continue to apply or are rapidly restored. In some of the proposed mergers of this type already dealt with by the Commission, such as that between *TotalFina* and *Elf*, this proved possible on the basis of substantial remedies, while in other cases, such as *Volvo / Scania* and the present case, it proved impossible."[71]

Subsequently, the Commissioner for Competition Policy, Neelie Kroes, rejected a suggestion from the Industry Commissioner, Gunter Verheugen, that the merger rules should be amended to facilitate the creation of *European* champions, stating that there was "no need to talk about champions. That is, I think, a thing of the past."[72]

---

[70] Case T-310/01 *Schneider Electric SA v Commission* [2002] E.C.R. II-4071.
[71] See also the speech of Mario Monti, then the Commissioner for Competition Policy, at the International Competition Network Conference of September 28 and 29, 2002, "Analytical Framework for Merger Review" (*www.europa.eu.int/comm/competition/speeches/index_2002.html*) and Bernitz & Gutu, "The Effect of EU Merger Policy on Large Multinationals Based in Sweden and Other Smaller EU Member States: Is the Policy Discriminatory?" [2003] E.C.L.R. 19.
[72] *Financial Times*, January 26, 2005, p.8. See also *Financial Times*, March 16, 2006, p.5.

CHAPTER 7

HORIZONTAL MERGERS: NON-COORDINATED EFFECTS

7.1 INTRODUCTION

7–001 *Non-coordinated effects*[1] arise when, as a result of a merger, the merged group is able profitably to increase price or reduce quality, choice or innovation through its own acts without the need for a cooperative response from competitors.[2] If the merged group adopts such strategies, rivals may follow,[3] at least to an extent,[4] with the consequence that any anti-

---

[1] See generally the International Competition Network, "Analysis of Merger Guidelines", Ch.3, "Unilateral Effects" (*http://www.internationalcompetitionnetwork.org/seoul/amg_chap3-unilateral.pdf*).

[2] See also the discussion of the scope of "non-coordinated effects" in the UK Office of Fair Trading's Substantive Merger Guidelines, May 2003 (*www.oft.gov.uk*), para.4.7 and n.21. In a narrow sense, non-coordinated effects arise when the actions of the merged group and the significant impediment to effective competition occur in a single antitrust market. In this narrow sense, non-coordinated effects are distinct from vertical effects and conglomerate effects (see Chs 11 and 12) as those theories of competitive harm arise when power in one market is leveraged into a second. In a broader sense, non-coordinated effects arise when effective competition is significantly impeded by the merged group *in its own right*, whether the market power and competitive harm arise in the same or different markets.

[3] See the Notice on Horizontal Mergers, para.24. More particularly, a merger *shifts* the best reaction function of the merging parties (when compared with the aggregate best reaction functions of the two suppliers separately), which may lead it to increase its price, *and* if the merged group's prices change, this alters the best reactions of the competitors (without shifting their best reaction functions); see further Fingleton, "Does Collective Dominance Provide Suitable Housing for All Anti-Competitive Oligopolistic Mergers?" published in the 2002 *Annual Proceedings of the Fordham Corporate Law Institute*, p.181 at p.183.

[4] Competitors' prices generally do not rise by as much as the merged group's and, for this reason, the Commission focuses its attention, in non-coordinated effects cases, on the likelihood of price rises *by the merged group*; see Kühn, "Closing Pandora's Box? Joint Dominance After the Airtours Judgment", published as Ch.3 of *The Pros and Cons of Merger Control* by the Swedish Competition Authority in 2002 (and available at *http://www.kkv.se/bestall/pdf/skrift_proscons.pdf*), p.42.

competitive effects of the merger are felt across the whole market (and not just by the merged group's customers).[5]

The Notice on Horizontal Mergers identifies three principal theories of competitive harm which may arise in non-coordinated effects cases when the parties have overlapping activities. First, if the merged group has a large market share, it is more likely to possess market power (see s.7.2 below). Secondly, if the merging parties supply *differentiated products* (i.e. products which consumers perceive to have different attributes from rival products), then a merger may allow the merged group profitably to raise its prices if the parties are close competitors, because the merger removes an important competitive constraint that each merging party was exercising on the other (s.7.3). Thirdly, if the merging parties' competitors are unlikely to increase supply if price increases (for example, if they face *capacity constraints*), then the merged group may be able profitably to raise prices by reducing its own output (s.7.4). The Notice on Horizontal Mergers also identifies other factors which, whether considered separately or together, may lead the Commission to conclude that the merger is likely materially to harm consumers (s.7.5). This Chapter also examines a more controversial issue, namely whether the fact that a merger creates efficiencies may form part of a theory of competitive harm, although this issue is not raised directly in the Notice on Horizontal Mergers (s.7.6).

7.2 MERGING FIRMS HAVE LARGE MARKET SHARES

The larger the merged group's market share, the more likely it is to enjoy **7–002** market power, and the larger the increment in market share arising from the merger, the more likely the merger is to significantly increase the merged group's market power.[6] Whilst high market shares do not comprise, in themselves, decisive proof that the merged group will hold market power, they comprise important evidence. The Notice on Horizontal Mergers describes the position as follows: "Although market shares and additions of market shares only provide first indications of market power and increases in market power, they are normally important factors in the assessment."[7] The calculation and significance of market shares is discussed in detail in s.4.2 above.

---

[5] It is to capture this point that the Commission uses the term "non-coordinated effects" to describe such theories of competitive harm, rather than "unilateral effects"). See generally Ivaldi *et al*, "The Economics of Unilateral Effects", 2003, Interim Report for DG Competition (available via *http://europa.eu.int/comm/competition/mergers/review/the_economics_of_unilateral_effects_en.pdf*), pp.23 to 25.
[6] Notice on Horizontal Mergers, para.27.
[7] Para.27.

7.3 DIFFERENTIATED PRODUCTS

7–003   In markets[8] involving *differentiated products*[9] (i.e. products which consumers perceive to have different attributes from rival products)[10] the intensity of competition between brands or physical locations[11] may vary across the market. This means that an orthodox market share analysis, which ascribes equal value to every unit of sales of products which fall within the market

---

[8] See generally Areeda, Hovenkamp & Solow, *Antitrust Law* (2nd edn, Aspen Law & Business, 1998), Vol.IV, para.914; ABA Section of Antitrust Law, *Market Power Handbook* (ABA Publishing, 2005), pp.103 to 110; Bishop & Lofaro, "Assessing Unilateral Effects in Practice—Lessons from GE / Instrumentarium" [2005] E.C.L.R. 205; Völcker, "Mind the Gap: Unilateral Effects Analysis Arrives in EC Merger Control" [2004] E.C.L.R. 395; Shapiro, "Mergers with Differentiated Products" [1996] *Antitrust* 23; Overstreet, Keyte & Gayle, "Understanding Econometric Analysis of the Price Effects of Mergers Involving Differentiated Products" [1996] *Antitrust* 30; Werden, "Demand Elasticities in Antitrust Analysis" (1998) 66 *Antitrust Law Journal* 363, at pp.406 to 409; Rubinfeld, "Market Definition with Differentiated Products: The Post / Nabisco Cereal Merger" (2000) 68 *Antitrust Law Journal* 163; Baker & Coscelli, "The Role of Market Shares in Differentiated Product Markets" [1999] E.C.L.R. 412; Baker & Wu, "Applying the Market Definition Guidelines of the European Commission" [1998] E.C.L.R. 273, at pp.277 and 278; Starek & Stockum, "What Makes Mergers Anticompetitive? 'Non-coordinated Effects' Analysis Under the 1992 Merger Guidelines" (1995) 63 *Antitrust Law Journal* 801; Berry & Waldfogel, "Do Mergers Increase Product Variety? Evidence from Radio Broadcasting" [2001] *The Quarterly Journal of Economics* 1009; Scherer & Ross, *Industrial Market Structure and Economic Performance* (3rd edn, Houghton Mifflin Co, 1990), Ch.16; Porter, *Competitive Advantage* (1998 edn, The Free Press), Chs 4 and 7; Oster, *Modern Competitive Advantage* (3rd edn, Oxford UP, 1999), Ch.5; Tirole, *The Theory of Industrial Organization* (The MIT Press, 1988), pp.96 to 100; Martin, *Advanced Industrial Economics* (2nd edn, Blackwell, 2002), pp.106 to 116; the US Horizontal Merger Guidelines, 1992 (amended in 1997) (*www.usdoj.gov/atr/public/guidelines/hmg.htm*), para.2.21; and the New Zealand Merger Guidelines, 2004 (*http://www.comcom.govt.nz/ Publications/ContentFiles/Documents/MergersandAcquisitionsGuidelines.PDF*) (para.3.2, noting the artificiality of market definition in cases of differentiated products and contemplating focusing instead on a direct analysis of the likely effect of the transaction on localised prices). Porter, *Competitive Advantage* (The Free Press, 1998 edn), p.3, has observed that product differentiation is one of the two main forms of competitive advantage. Since variety or choice is one of the components of consumer welfare, a merger which *enhances* product differentiation might be regarded as both positive for consumer welfare *and* a profit-maximising strategy. However, the Commission, in its decisions on product differentiation, has focused on cases which will not increase consumer choice but may enable the merged group profitably to increase the prices of its existing products.

[9] See the Notice on Horizontal Mergers, n.32. Porter, *Competitive Advantage* (The Free Press, 1998 edn), p.120, comments, "A firm differentiates itself from its competitors when it provides something unique that is valuable to buyers beyond simply offering a low price ... Differentiation leads to superior performance if the price premium achieved exceeds any added costs of being unique".

[10] In Case COMP/M.1628 *TotalFina / Elf* [2001] O.J. L143/1, the Commission found that fuel was a fungible product, despite attempts by oil companies to differentiate their service stations; this finding led to the conclusion that competition in the market occurred on price; paras 192 to 195.

[11] Analytically, spatial differentiation is no different from differentiation in other product characteristics. However, in Case COMP/M.3593 *Apollo / Bakelite*, at para.69, the Commission considered an argument that the parties had complementary activities as they tended to sell in different Member States but rejected it on the grounds that this was irrelevant once an EEA market had been identified.

definition, may be misleading.[12] If the merging parties' products are not regarded by customers as close substitutes, then relatively high market shares may not be indicative of market power.[13] By contrast, if the merging parties' products are seen by customers as the next best alternatives to one another, then the merged group may enjoy market power with market shares that, in an orthodox market share analysis, would not be regarded as a potential source of market power.[14] The Notice on Horizontal Mergers states that a merger may significantly impede effective competition "by eliminating important competitive constraints on one or more firms, which consequently would have increased market power, without resorting to coordinated behaviour".[15] In *Siemens / Drägerwerk / JV*,[16] having found that the parties' products were one another's closest substitutes, the Commission stated: "The merging of the two product ranges within the joint venture would enable the parties to charge higher prices in as much as a large part of the customers lost as a result of the price increase by one of the parties would switch to products made by the other party".

A merger between rival suppliers of products A and B is likely to result in **7–004** increases in the price of A if the merged group has the incentive and ability to raise the price of A.[17]

(a) The merged group's *incentive* to raise the price of product A depends, in particular, on the following three factors.

    (i) The *closeness of substitution* between products A and B,[18] in the light, in particular, of their product attributes, geographic location or perceived quality or reliability. The Notice on Horizontal Mergers states: "The higher the degree of sub-

---

[12] See Shapiro, "Mergers with Differentiated Products" [1996] *Antitrust* 23; Rubinfeld, "Market Definition with Differentiated Products: The Post / Nabisco Cereal Merger" (2000) 68 *Antitrust Law Journal*, 163, at 181; Baker & Coscelli, "The Role of Market Shares in Differentiated Product Markets" [1999] E.C.L.R. 412, at 413 and 414; and Baker & Wu, "Applying the Market Definition Guidelines of the European Commission" [1998] E.C.L.R. 273, at p.277. Vickers, "Competition Economics and Policy", speech of October 3, 2002 (*http://www.oft.gov.uk/News/Speeches + and + articles/2002/index.htm*), referred to the "pitfall [of] the 'zero-one' fallacy—the tendency, once 'the market' is defined, to think of all products within it as extremely substitutable for the products at the centre of concern, and those products beyond the boundaries as irrelevant. In reality matters are of varying degrees, and the useful tool of market definition must be employed with this in mind".

[13] See e.g. Case COMP/M.2201 *MAN / Auwärter* [2002] O.J. L116/35, para.28.

[14] However, in cases involving differentiated products, the Commission generally still takes market shares into account as they reflect real purchasing decisions by customers in a given year; see Case COMP/M.3083 *GE / Instrumentarium* [2004] O.J. L109/1, paras 123, 124 and 272.

[15] Para.22(a).

[16] Case COMP/M.2861 [2003] O.J. L291/1, para.103.

[17] See the Notice on Horizontal Mergers, paras 28 to 30.

[18] See the Notice on Horizontal Mergers, para.28. Starek & Stockum, "What Makes Mergers Anticompetitive? 'Non-coordinated Effects' Analysis Under the 1992 Merger Guidelines" (1995) 63 *Antitrust Law Journal* 801 emphasise, at pp.806 and 807, that the likelihood of market power arising is reduced when competition occurs across several product characteristics rather than just one.

stitutability between the merging firms' products, the more likely it is that the merging firms will raise prices significantly".[19] The incentive to increase prices arises because, prior to the merger, a producer of A, in deciding whether to increase price, has to take account of lost revenues from customers switching to other products, B, C and D, as well as the gain in revenue through higher charges to the customers which continue to purchase A. However, when the producer of A merges with the producer of B, the loss of revenue arising from an increase in the price of A is partly offset by the fact that some of the customers lost from A will switch to B. If B is regarded by customers as a very good substitute for A,[20] then the scope for the merged group profitably to increase the price of A is substantially increased.

(ii) The *gross margin* earned on B. The higher the gross margin, the greater the profit earned on each sale of B which is gained as a result of customers switching from A.[21]

(iii) *Efficiency gains.* The merged group's *most profitable* strategy may be to increase its sales of A to take advantage of efficiency gains arising from the merger.[22] If so, the merged group will not have an incentive to raise the price of A.

(b) The merged group would not have the *ability* profitably to raise the price of A in particular in the following circumstances.

(i) *Rival suppliers' products* may be sufficiently close substitutes for the products supplied by the merging parties to defeat an attempt by the merged group profitably to raise the price of A.[23] If C or D are regarded by customers as close substitutes for A, then an attempt by the merged group profitably to raise the price of A is more likely to be defeated by switching to rival suppliers.[24]

(ii) Actual and potential rival suppliers may have the incentive[25]

---

[19] Para.28.

[20] In particular if a substantial number of customers regard A and B as their first and second choices.

[21] See the Notice on Horizontal Mergers, para.28; Shapiro, "Mergers with Differentiated Products" [1996] *Antitrust* 23; and the OFT Economic Discussion Paper, "Innovation and Competition Policy", Charles River Associates, March 2002 (note that the views in the paper do not necessarily reflect those of the OFT), para.7.12.

[22] See Ch.18 and Shapiro, "Mergers with Differentiated Products" [1996] *Antitrust* 23, at p.24.

[23] Notice on Horizontal Mergers, para.28 and n.37.

[24] See Baker & Coscelli, "The Role of Market Shares in Differentiated Product Markets" [1999] E.C.L.R. 412, at p.414.

[25] See the Notice on Horizontal Mergers, para.30 (emphasising that rivals may not have an incentive to reposition their products because of the risks and sunk costs involved or if the potential new line is less profitable than the current line). The US Horizontal Merger Guidelines, 1992 (amended in 1997) (*www.usdoj.gov/atr/public/guidelines/hmg.htm*) state, at para.2.21, that: "Substantial non-coordinated price elevation in a market for differentiated products requires that there be a significant share of sales in the market accounted for by

and ability to *enter* the market as suppliers of close substitutes, or to *reposition*[26] their products as closer substitutes[27] for A, in a way which is timely,[28] likely and sufficient to defeat any attempt profitably to raise the price of A. The scope for repositioning may be affected by: those characteristics of the merging parties' products which are most important in distinguishing them from rival products; the costs and difficulties facing rivals in emulating those key characteristics and in particular whether emulation involves significant sunk costs or delay; and whether the ability to emulate successfully is dependent on the availability of economies of scale or scope in advertising.[29]

The same effect may also allow the merged group profitably to increase the price of B.[30]

The Commission may prohibit a merger (or clear it only subject to **7–005** undertakings) on the basis of concerns about the loss of competition in the supply of differentiated products even if the parties are not one another's *closest* competitors. This is clear both from the Notice on Horizontal Mergers, which identify a risk of price increases when the parties are "close competitors"[31] (as opposed to "closest" competitors), and the Commission's decisions. In particular, in *Air Liquide / Messer Targets*,[32] the Commission stated: "Although Linde has been Messer's closest competitor insofar as it

---

[26] See the US Horizontal Merger Guidelines, 1992 (amended in 1997) (*www.usdoj.gov/atr/public/guidelines/hmg.htm*), n.23. Testing the scope for repositioning of products by rivals requires evidence on the characteristics of the products and the flexibility of the production process; see the International Competition Network, "ICN Investigative Techniques Handbook for Merger Review", June 2005 (*http://www.internationalcompetitionnetwork.org/handbook_5-5.pdf*), p.61. Product repositioning may reduce the diversion ratio between the products of the merging parties. In deciding where to position its product, a supplier will take account of the direct effects of product positioning (in general, the "closer" a product is positioned to a rival, the greater the volume of business which will be won from that rival) and the strategic effects (in general, the more "distant" a product is positioned away from a rival, the less intense the price competition between them): see Cabral, *Introduction to Industrial Organization* (The MIT Press, 2000), p.216.

[27] The effect of product repositioning by rivals is to reduce the cross-price elasticity between the merging firms' products and to add product variety (which benefits consumers).

[28] In Case COMP/M.2861 *Siemens / Drägerwerk / JV* [2003] O.J. L291/1, para.105, the Commission disregarded possible repositioning by a competitor on the grounds that it was not likely to occur over the one to two year time period relevant for the competition assessment.

[29] See Baker & Coscelli, "The Role of Market Shares in Differentiated Product Markets" [1999] E.C.L.R. 412, at p.418.

[30] For a more detailed discussion, see Europe Economics, "Study on Assessment Criteria for Distinguishing between Competitive and Dominant Oligopolies in Merger Control", Report for the European Commission, 2001, pp.58 to 62.

[31] Para.28. See also Werden, "Demand Elasticities in Antitrust Analysis" (1998) 66 *Antitrust Law Journal*, 363, at p.408.

[32] Case COMP/M.3314, para.74. See also Case COMP/M.3083 *GE / Instrumentarium* [2004] O.J. L109/1, para.244, n.151 (rejecting an argument that competitive concerns would arise only if the parties were one another's closest substitutes) and Federal Trade Commission and Department of Justice, "Commentary on the Horizontal Merger Guidelines", 2006 (available via *www.ftc.gov/os/2006/03/CommentaryontheHorizontalMergerGuidelinesMarch2006.pdf*), pp.27 and 28.

was considered as the second best supplier in most instances where Messer was awarded a tonnage contract, Air Liquide was nevertheless a close competitor to Messer".

7–006 The intensity of the competition between suppliers of differentiated goods can be analysed or measured using seven main overlapping techniques or categories of evidence.[33]

(a) A *bidding study*[34] may be used in cases involving tender markets.[35] A bidding study involves identifying for all, all substantial, or a representative sample of bids, who bid, who won the contract and the prices bid. This may show, for example, that: the merging parties tended not to bid against one another; when they did, there was always a third bidder present; when they did, they did not submit the lowest and next lowest prices; and/or prices were lower whenever a third bidder was present.[36] This technique was used for example[37] in *Boeing / McDonnell Douglas*[38] to show that when McDonnell Douglas did not bid, prices were on average 7.6 per cent higher. In *GE /*

---

[33] The Notice on Horizontal Mergers states, at para.29: "When data are available, the degree of substitutability may be evaluated through customer preference surveys, analysis of purchasing patterns, estimation of the cross-price elasticities of the products involved, or diversion ratios. In bidding markets, it may be possible to measure whether historically the submitted bids by one of the merging parties have been constrained by the presence of the other merging party". See also Baker & Coscelli, "The Role of Market Shares in Differentiated Product Markets" [1999] E.C.L.R. 412, at p.415; Baker & Wu, "Applying the Market Definition Guidelines of the European Commission" [1998] E.C.L.R. 273, at p.277; and the UK Office of Fair Trading's Substantive Merger Guidelines, May 2003 (*www.oft.gov.uk*), n.23. The International Competition Network, "ICN Investigative Techniques Handbook for Merger Review", June 2005 (*http://www.internationalcompetitionnetwork.org/handbook_5-5.pdf*), p.60, contemplates the use of price correlation studies to assess the potential for non-coordinated increases in prices by measuring the price correlations between a product and its rivals, on the basis that, other things being equal, a merger between suppliers of products which have a higher price correlation is more likely to lead to price increases because the correlations suggest that they are closer competitors; for more general discussion of price correlation, see para.3–014 above.

[34] See also sub-para.(e) below.

[35] See paras 6–029 and 6–030 above. See also ABA Section of Antitrust Law, *Econometrics* (ABA Publishing, 2005), pp.240 to 244.

[36] See the 2002 draft Commission Notice on Horizontal Mergers, para.14 (this text was not included in the final version of the Notice).

[37] See also Case IV/M.580 *ABB / Daimler Benz* [1997] O.J. L11/1 (the Commission carried out its own bidding study by contacting customers; paras 78 and 79); Case COMP/M.1741 *MCI WorldCom / Sprint* [2003] O.J. L300/1, para.208; Case COMP/M.1882 *Pirelli / BICC* [2003] O.J. L70/35; Case COMP/M.2201 *MAN / Auwärter* [2002] O.J. L116/35 (the bidding study showed that the involvement or non-involvement of the target had no detectable effect on prices; para.31); Case COMP/M.2816 *Ernst & Young France / Andersen France*, para.60 and Table 3; Case COMP/M.3436 *Continental / Phoenix*, para.136; Case COMP/M.2861 *Siemens / Drägerwerk / JV* [2003] O.J. L291/1, paras 94 to 102 and 132 to 140; Case COMP/M.3486 *Magna / New Venture Gear* (the bidding study did not indicate that the parties were the closest substitutes for a substantial proportion of customers; para.61); Case COMP/M.3641 *BT / Infonet* (bidding data did not show that the parties were close competitors; para.16); Case COMP/M.3653 *Siemens / VA Tech*; and Case COMP/M.4003 *Ericsson / Marconi* (the bidding study showed that the merging parties were not one another's closest competitors; para.24).

[38] Case IV/M.877 [1997] O.J. L336/16, para.58. See Bishop, "The Boeing / McDonnell Douglas Merger" [1997] E.C.L.R. 417.

Instrumentarium[39] the Commission carried out very extensive bidding studies to assess the closeness of competition on markets for medical equipment; it sought to identify the frequency with which the market players encountered one another, the number of occasions on which they faced no other competitor and (separately) one other competitor, the closeness of substitution, and the possible impact of the merger on prices.

(b) *Diversion ratios*[40] identify the proportion of sales of a product, A, which would be lost to another product, B, if the price of A increased[41] (i.e. it identifies customers' second preferred choices).[42] More particularly, a diversion ratio would commonly be used to assess the extent to which an increase in price of one brand by 5 to 10 per cent would lead to switching to a second brand. This can be calculated econometrically if good data are available (e.g. supermarket scanner or panel[43] data) but survey evidence[44] can also be used. If the goods in the market are regarded as approximately equivalent in terms of product positioning, then a crude diversion ratio can be constructed by assuming that the lost sales will be distributed between other brands in direct proportion to the market shares held by the brands in question.[45]

(c) *Survey* evidence[46] may be used to assess customers' preferences for particular *characteristics*[47] in products, provided that valid sampling procedures are used and the questions are framed neutrally.[48] This approach proceeds on the assumption that customers choose the product which offers the best combination of the characteristics they

---

[39] Case COMP/M.3083 [2004] O.J. L109/1, paras 125, 131, 133, 134 (finding in one market that Instrumentarium appeared to bid lower when GE was present and Philips tended to bid lower when both Instrumentarium and GE were present), 142, 149, 224, 244 and 273. See also Loriot, Rouxel & Durand, "GE / Instrumentarium: a practical example of the use of quantitative analyses in merger control", *Competition Policy Newsletter*, Spring 2004, p.58.

[40] Shapiro, "Mergers with Differentiated Products" [1996] *Antitrust* 23, suggests that a rough indicator of possible anti-competitive non-coordinated effects may be obtained by multiplying the diversion ratio by the gross margin.

[41] See the Notice on Horizontal Mergers, n.39.

[42] See Baker & Coscelli, "The Role of Market Shares in Differentiated Product Markets" [1999] E.C.L.R. 412, at p.417 and Shapiro "Mergers with Differentiated Products" (1996) 10(2) *Antitrust* 23.

[43] Data collected over time from a group of repeat purchasers.

[44] See sub-para.(c) below.

[45] Europe Economics, "Study on Assessment Criteria for Distinguishing between Competitive and Dominant Oligopolies in Merger Control", Report for the European Commission, 2001, p.61.

[46] See, e.g. Case IV/M.430 *Procter & Gamble / VP Schickedanz (II)* [1994] O.J. L354/32, para.50 and Case COMP/M.2861 *Siemens / Drägerwerk / JV* [2003] O.J. L291/1, paras 88 to 90 and 123 to 126.

[47] Those preferences can be depicted on a product map, which illustrates customers' perceptions of the product based on its differing characteristics. See, e.g. Oster, *Modern Competitive Advantage* (3rd edn, Oxford UP, 1999), pp.264 and 265.

[48] See Shapiro, "Mergers with Differentiated Products" [1996] *Antitrust* 23, at p.25.

are searching for (rather than purchasing goods for their own sake). It involves asking customers to rank the factors which they consider in purchasing a product. If the most important characteristics are common to the products supplied by a group of competitors, this suggests that there is intense competition between them; but if the most important characteristics are available only by purchasing certain products, then competition between products with the key characteristics and those without may not be substantial.[49] In *Johnson & Johnson / Guidant*[50] the Commission asked customers of the merging parties to identify the first and second next best alternatives to the products they currently purchased and used the responses to conclude that the parties were one another's closest competitors. In *Continental / Phoenix*[51] the Commission asked customers and competitors to rank manufacturers in six categories (such as technical competence/innovation, quality/reliability and customer service/support) and found that the merging parties tended to rank first and second, indicating that the merger would result in the loss of Continental's strongest competitor from the market.

(d) *Merger simulation*[52] may be used to predict directly the likely effect of the merger on price. In *Volvo / Scania*[53] the Commission instructed economists to seek to measure directly the likely effects of the merger on the prices charged by heavy truck producers in various national markets. The study pointed to serious competition problems, but the Commission did not rely on it in reaching its decision to prohibit the transaction because of the novelty of the approach and disputes about the validity of the study.[54]

(e) Other *econometric techniques* may also be used, in particular when bidding data is available. For example, in *GE / Instrumentarium*[55] the

---

[49] See Case COMP/M.3093 *INA / AIG / SNFA* (notification withdrawn during a phase II investigation) as described by Rouxel, Emberger & Koch, "INA / AIG / SNFA", *Competition Policy Newsletter*, Summer 2004, p.75 (the Commission carried out a survey asking customers to rank the importance of seven criteria and to rank each supplier against those criteria; the results showed that customers perceived the merging parties to be the strongest competitors with respect to many criteria).

[50] Case COMP/M.3687, paras 265, 266 and 270 and n.146.

[51] Case COMP/M.3436, paras 121, 122 and 135.

[52] See para.19–006 below.

[53] Case COMP/M.1672 [2001] O.J. L143/74, paras 72 to 75. The study was based on a nested logit model. See further, Ivaldi & Verboven, "Quantifying the Effects from Horizontal Mergers in European Competition Policy", 2002 (available via *http://idei.fr/doc/by/ivaldi/iv_merger_v04.pdf*).

[54] There is substantial academic literature on the estimation of non-coordinated effects in retail chain mergers. See Baker, Coscelli & Van Dijk, "Non-coordinated Effects in Retail Chain Mergers: an Application to Supermarkets" [2002] E.C.L.R. 180, which summarises earlier work and identifies a method for the assessment of competitive constraints at the store level.

[55] Case COMP/M.3083 [2004] O.J. L109/1, paras 166 to 186, 227, 228, 247, 248, 277 and 278.

Commission ran multiple regressions[56] to seek to identify the likely effect of the merger on price in the light of the bidding data it collated. The parties supplied different types of medical equipment and tenders were invited for a wide variety of different specifications, so the Commission measured the price impact by examining the *discounts*[57] proposed by the suppliers.

(f) *Shock analysis* can be used to assess the effects of previous launches of new products or similar significant changes in the operation of the market.[58] In *Piaggio / Aprilia*[59] the Commission assessed issues of closeness of competition in the supply of scooters below 50cc. Aprilia's sales dropped significantly when it developed financial difficulties and reduced its production. The Commission identified the models which benefited most from this reduction in supply, finding that a Piaggio product benefited from the largest increase in market share. Similarly, in *Philip Morris / Papastratos*[60] the failure of a premium cigarette brand led the market shares to migrate to other premium brands and not to brands in the low priced segment.

(g) *Internal documents*, such as business plans, competitor analysis and marketing studies, may reveal the parties' own perceptions about the relative market positions of the different products or the extent to which different rivals' prices are taken into account in determining price.[61]

In addition to the cases described above, the Commission has considered **7–007** issues of product differentiation in numerous decisions.[62]

---

[56] Regression analysis is a statistical technique which seeks to identify the extent to which a particular outcome is influenced by specified factors. See Bishop & Walker, *The Economics of EC Competition Law* (2nd edn, Sweet & Maxwell, 2002), Ch.15; ABA Section of Antitrust Law, *Econometrics* (ABA Publishing, 2005), Ch.1; OFT Research Paper "Quantitative Techniques in Competition Analysis", LECG, Ch.8 (note that the views in the paper do not necessarily represent those of the OFT); and Kennedy, "A Guide to Econometrics" (4th edn, Blackwell, 1998), pp.269, 270, 286 and 287.

[57] See also Case COMP/M.3216 *Oracle / PeopleSoft* [2005] O.J. L218/6, para.142, discussing the treatment in the econometric analysis of automatic volume discounts.

[58] See the International Competition Network, "ICN Investigative Techniques Handbook for Merger Review", June 2005 (*http://www.internationalcompetitionnetwork.org/handbook_5-5.pdf*), p.61. For discussion of the use of shock analysis in market definition, see para.3–022.

[59] Case COMP/M.3570.

[60] Case COMP/M.3191, para.27.

[61] See, e.g. Case COMP/M.2861 *Siemens / Drägerwerk / JV* [2003] O.J. L291/1, paras 91 to 93 and 127 to 131.

[62] See, e.g. Case IV/M.430 *Procter & Gamble / VP Schickedanz (II)* [1994] O.J. L354/32; Case IV/M.623 *Kimberly-Clark / Scott* [1996] O.J. L183/1 (the Commission noted, at para.193, that if the merged group were to increase the prices of its branded products, the loss of sales would be at least partially compensated for by increased sales of its private label goods); Case IV/M.794 *Coca Cola Enterprises / Amalgamated Beverages Great Britain*; Case IV/M.1133 *Bass plc / Saison Holdings BV*; Case IV/M.1596 *Accor / Colony / Blackstone / Vivendi*; Case COMP/M.1892 *Sarah Lee / Courtaulds* (the Commission emphasised, at para.40, in finding that the transaction could create a dominant position, that each of the merging parties produced a "must stock" brand); Case COMP/M.2033 *Metso / Svedala* [2004] O.J. L88/1 (the Com-

(a) In *Masterfoods / Royal Canin*[63] the Commission identified a separate antitrust market for pet food but focused on the parties' activities in the speciality segment, finding that the parties had high combined shares in that segment, private label competitors had less impact, and the parties owned the most important individual brands. It concluded: "The merged entity's strengths as regards top selling brands is likely to add to the market power that stems from its market shares".[64]

(b) In *Volvo / Renault VI*[65] the parties presented evidence in the form of a "shock analysis" which tended to show that they were not one another's closest competitors. The evidence was based on studying the effects of a price increase by Volvo that was not matched by rival suppliers. The effects on demand arising from this price increase suggested that suppliers other than the target were seen as good substitutes for Volvo's products.

(c) Similarly, in *Imperial Tobacco / Reemtsma Cigarettenfabriken GmbH*[66] the Commission emphasised that prices and brand posi-

mission found that the merging parties were one another's closest competitors relying on: its market investigation, which showed that most customers could only name the merging parties as suppliers of turnkey contracts and, when asked to name rival equipment suppliers, could name none or quoted a limited number and stated that they suffered from substantial competitive disadvantages; the fact that the vast majority of suppliers sourced from both merging parties; and statements from several customers that their procurement policy was based on competition between the merging parties; paras 163 to 168); Case COMP/M.2197 *Hilton / Accor / Forte / Travel Services / JV*; Case COMP/M.2537 *Philips / Marconi Medical Systems*, para.31; Case COMP/M.2569 *Interbrew / Beck's*; Case COMP/M.2609 *HP / Compaq* (the Commission concluded, at para.43, on the basis of an analysis of the parties' products, that they were not one another's closest competitors in the provision of servers); Case COMP/ M.2706 *Carnival Corporation / P&O Princess* [2003] O.J. L248/1 (the Commission regarded the distinction between luxury, premium and economy cruises "as relevant for the assessment of brand positioning and the closeness of competition between different products", para.126; in analysing this issue the Commission considered, amongst other evidence, brand positioning, brand awareness, evidence from a supplier's internal papers and a survey which asked past cruise customers to identify the brand which they viewed as the closest alternative to the one they had chosen, paras 134 to 152); Case COMP/M.2922 *Pfizer / Pharmacia* (doctors regarded third parties' products as closer substitutes in calcium antagonist plain drugs; para.77); Case COMP/M.3418 *General Dynamics / Alvis*, para.23 (ruling out competitive concerns as the parties were not one another's closest competitors); Case COMP/M.3658 *Orkla / Chips* (the parties were one another's closest competitors by brand positioning and recipe; the Commission's concerns were resolved by commitments); Case COMP/M.3765 *Amer / Salomon* (the parties were not close competitors of one another, based on information regarding consumers' preferences obtained from the market test; paras 76 and 84); Case COMP/M.3770 *Lufthansa / Swiss* (the parties were one another's closest substitutes, creating a risk of post-merger price increases; paras 76 and 88); COMP/M.3803 *EADS / Nokia* (the parties were not one another's closest competitors as evidenced by a bidding study and an analysis of the different standards used in the parties' products; paras 39 to 41); Case COMP/ M.3942 *Adidas / Reebok* (the parties were not close competitors in athletic footwear; paras 37 to 49); and Case COMP/M.3943 *Saint-Gobain / BPB* (the parties' products were not close substitutes; para.106).

[63] Case COMP/M.2544, paras 43 to 49.
[64] Para.49 (discussing the French market).
[65] Case COMP/M.1980, para.34.
[66] Case COMP/M.2779, paras 37 to 39 and 49 to 57.

tioning differed in the market, and focused on the parties' activities in the low price segment (whilst recognising that this did not comprise a separate market because there was actual competition between brands positioned in the premium and low priced segments).

(d) In *Philips / Agilent Health Care Solutions*[67] the Commission found that the merging parties were not one another's closest substitutes in the light of a survey of competitors and a bidding study.

(e) In *Barilla / BPL / Kamps*[68] the Commission relied on "estimates submitted by retail chains and competitors" in concluding that the parties were one another's closest competitors, and confirmed that there was no scope for product repositioning by competitors.

(f) In *Volvo / Scania*[69] the Commission concluded that the merging parties were one another's closest competitors on the basis that: "Both ... are Swedish makes and are generally perceived as the expression of quality products, offering globally a reliable service. An examination of Volvo's and Scania's respective market shares clearly shows their essentially parallel positions throughout the whole of Europe".

7.4 COMPETITORS ARE UNLIKELY TO INCREASE SUPPLY IF PRICE INCREASES

If rival suppliers are unlikely to expand production in the short to medium **7–008** term, then the merged group may have an incentive to reduce its output with the aim of raising prices.[70] A horizontal merger increases the merged group's incentive to adopt such a strategy, because the merged group will have a larger base of sales on which to benefit from the higher margins arising from the increase in price.

Rival suppliers may be unlikely to expand production because they face capacity constraints (if the expansion of capacity would not be timely, likely and sufficient[71]) or if existing spare capacity is not cost effective.[72] The competitive constraint posed by rival suppliers is discussed in detail in Ch.14 below.

This theory of competitive harm is most likely to arise in the case of

---

[67] Case COMP/M.2256, paras 33 and 34.
[68] Case COMP/M.2817, paras 34 to 37.
[69] Case COMP/M.1672 [2001] O.J. L143/74, para.80.
[70] Notice on Horizontal Mergers, para.32 and Case COMP/M.2187 *CVC / Lenzing* [2004] O.J. L82/20, paras 162 to 170.
[71] See the Notice on Horizontal Mergers, n.45, stating that, when analysing the scope for competitors to add new capacity, the Commission applies by analogy the principles relevant to new entry (see Ch.16).
[72] Notice on Horizontal Mergers, para.34.

homogeneous goods (i.e. goods which are identical), but the Commission has emphasised that it may also be important when suppliers provide differentiated goods.[73]

In *Total / Sasol / JV*[74] the Commission emphasised, when opening a second phase investigation, that rival suppliers of paraffin waxes and micro waxes were capacity constrained.[75] By contrast,[76] in *UCB / Solutia*,[77] the Commission ruled out competition concerns because competitors had spare capacity and an incentive to expand output if prices rose because they enjoyed increasing returns to scale. Similarly, in *Blackstone / Acetex*[78] the Commission found that capacity would increase faster than projected demand and would therefore be sufficient to defeat any attempt to increase prices.

7.5 OTHER FACTORS WHICH MAY GIVE RISE TO NON-COORDINATED EFFECTS

7–009 The Notice on Horizontal Mergers identifies three other factors which, taken separately or together,[79] may lead to a finding that a merger is likely to lead to a significant impediment to effective competition.

(a) Limited possibilities of switching supplier

7–010 If customers have *limited possibilities of switching supplier*, then the merged group may have greater power to increase prices.[80] Customers may be restricted in their ability to switch supplier because there are few alternative suppliers[81] or there are switching costs.[82]

In the former case, customers may be harmed by a merger if it occurs between competitors from whom they dual or multiple sourced,[83] or if they

---

[73] Notice on Horizontal Mergers, para.35. Compare the 2002 draft Commission Notice on Horizontal Mergers, para.30 which focused on the situation when goods are "relatively homogeneous". See para.6–023 above for discussion of homogeneous and differentiated goods.

[74] Case COMP/M.3637.

[75] The parties subsequently abandoned the transaction. See press releases IP/05/425 and IP/05/478.

[76] See also Case COMP/M.3687 *Johnson & Johnson / Guidant*, paras 169 and 182 and Case COMP/M.3943 *Saint-Gobain / BPB*, para.105.

[77] Case COMP/M.3060, para.43.

[78] Case COMP/M.3625 [2005] O.J. L312/60, paras 95 and 115.

[79] Notice on Horizontal Mergers, para.26 (referring to the points discussed in ss 7.2 to 7.4 above as well as the three factors discussed in s.7.5 of the text). See also para.20 of the Notice, identifying "special circumstances" which are exceptions to the HHI safe harbours.

[80] Notice on Horizontal Mergers, para.31.

[81] See Case IV/M.877 *Boeing / McDonnell Douglas* [1997] O.J. L336/16, para.70.

[82] See Case IV/M.986 *Agfa Gevaert / DuPont* [1998] O.J. L211/22, paras 63 to 71.

[83] Notice on Horizontal Mergers, para.31.

otherwise relied on competition between the merging parties to protect their interests.

(a) If customers *dual or multiple source*, the elimination of a competitor through a merger may result in some customers being unable to maintain as many sources of supply as they wish.[84] On the other hand, the fact that customers dual source means that they have a ready means of assessing whether prices offered by the merged group are reasonable and, subject to capacity constraints, it is relatively easy to switch suppliers.[85] In *VIAG | Continental Can* the Commission stated that customers' dual or triple sourcing policies meant that they could "easily play off one supplier against another". In *Sanitec | Sphinx*[86] the Commission noted that dual or triple sourcing meant that: "customers were usually familiar with more than one producer. For the suppliers this means that they have the necessary customer contacts and do not need to build their customer base from scratch, as in the case of new entry. Therefore, should the parties raise prices, customers could switch a large part of ceramic sanitary ware currently sourced from the parties to other suppliers."[87] By contrast, single sourcing is common when it results in significant cost savings. For example, in *Volvo | Scania*[88] the Commission found that smaller truck operators had a preference for single-sourcing as this reduced the costs of maintenance and training of personnel, primarily drivers.[89]

(b) In *Oracle | PeopleSoft*[90] the Commission examined the effect of a merger on a market in which contracts were awarded through ten-

---

[84] See Case COMP/M.2187 *CVC | Lenzing* [2004] O.J. L82/20, para.214.

[85] See also Case IV/M.430 *Procter & Gamble | VP Schickedanz (II)* [1994] O.J. L354/32 (customers were unlikely to dual source following the transaction as this would involve de-listing an established premium brand supplied by the merged group in favour of an untried new product; para.171); Case IV/M.1286 *Johnson & Johnson | Depuy* (customers "generally perform a dual sourcing policy under which they prefer to be supplied by more than one supplier, in order to avoid a dependency relationship. This mechanism allows them to keep a certain competitive pressure"; para.35); Case COMP/M.1939 *Rexam | American National Can* (an argument based on buyer power through dual-sourcing was rejected because 50 to 60% of Rexam's customers used a single source and the merged group would have been able to price discriminate between the sophisticated and non-sophisticated customers; para.26); Case COMP/M.2199 *Quantum | Maxtor*, para.17; Case COMP/M.2348 *Outokumpu | Norzink* (the Commission focused on customers which did not dual source and considered whether the merged group could discriminate against them; para.27); Case COMP/M.2498 *UPM-Kymmene | Haindl* [2002] O.J. L233/38, para.62; Case COMP/M.2690 *Solvay | Montedison-Ausimont*, para.125; and Case COMP/M.2816 *Ernst & Young France | Andersen France*, para.69.

[86] Case IV/M.1578 [2000] O.J. L294/1.

[87] Para.151.

[88] Case COMP/M.1672 [2001] O.J. L143/74.

[89] Para.115. See also Case IV/M.291 *KNP | Bührmann-Tetterode | VRG* [1993] O.J. L217/35 (sole sourcing of printing presses, because of training costs and a need to carry spare parts, operated as a barrier to entry; para.24)

[90] Case COMP/M.3216 [2005] O.J. L218/6, paras 197 to 205.

ders. It ran multiple regressions on data regarding suppliers' bidding behaviour and found that the number of suppliers bidding did not influence the outcome, nor did the presence of a particular supplier. The Commission noted that the outcome could have resulted from low data quality or biases in its selection,[91] but nevertheless approved the transaction (taking account also of the fact that the sophisticated purchasers structured the tenders to maximise their buying power, the market would still contain more bidders following the merger than buyers normally invited to tender, and a very strong competitor would remain).

7–011 Switching costs[92] are costs which are incurred in switching supplier, but not in remaining with the existing supplier (e.g. the time cost and hassle involved in switching between providers of banking current accounts). The effects of switching costs on competition in general and merger appraisal in particular are subtle.[93]

(a) If switching costs are present, suppliers can price above cost to existing customers. Further, it is attractive for suppliers to win new customers (as they can then charge them prices above cost).

(b) This means that if switching costs are present, suppliers which can price discriminate will generally charge higher prices to existing customers and lower prices to new customers; but if price discrimination is not possible, then suppliers with a large customer base will charge higher prices (to earn profits from existing customers) whereas suppliers with a smaller customer base will charge lower prices (because they do not fear a loss of profits from existing customers and they are seeking to build up a customer base).

(c) The extent to which switching costs are present can be examined by comparing the prices charged to old and new customers (if price discrimination is possible) or comparing companies' shares of supply to old and new customers (if price discrimination is not possible).[94]

(d) When switching costs are present in start-up markets, competition may be very intense as all suppliers have small customer bases, but prices are likely to rise as the market matures.[95]

---

[91] See also the discussion in para.203 of other possible explanations for the results.
[92] See para.6–022 above. For a detailed discussion of the effects of switching costs, see OFT Economic Discussion Paper 5, "Switching Costs", NERA, April 2003 (note that the views in the paper do not necessarily reflect those of the OFT).
[93] This paragraph draws on OFT Discussion Paper 5, "Switching Costs", NERA, April 2003 (note that the views in the paper do not necessarily reflect those of the OFT), Chs 1 and 4 and paras 7.102 to 7.118.
[94] Switching costs may be evidenced by disparities in shares of supply.
[95] However, the higher prices in the mature market may be compensated, at least in part, by the initial phase of intense competition.

(e) Switching costs may discourage new entry in mature markets, but they have two entry-inducing features: if their presence makes the market profitable, the incentive to enter is increased; and switching costs can facilitate entry when suppliers cannot price discriminate because incumbents are not likely to react aggressively to entry.

(f) When considering the effects of switching costs on the merger appraisal process, the issue is not whether there are switching costs (as these are not caused by the merger), but whether a merger in the market characterised by switching costs is likely to harm consumers. If price discrimination is not possible, a merger between two larger suppliers may have less effect on competition than a merger involving a relatively *smaller* supplier. Further, when price discrimination is not possible, a merger during the *start-up* phase may have a greater effect on the intensity of competition than a merger during the mature phase.

(b) Merged group's ability to hinder expansion

If the merged group is able to hinder expansion by competitors, this may **7–012** allow it to raise prices, harming consumers. Section 7.4 above discusses the scope for the merged group profitably to raise its prices if rival suppliers are unable to increase supply. The merged group's ability to hinder expansion may come from a variety of sources, including control over inputs, intellectual property rights (such as patents), distribution channels or infrastructure.[96] The Notice on Horizontal Mergers emphasises that, in assessing the merged group's ability to hinder expansion by its rivals, the Commission will take into account the financial strength of the merged group relative to its rivals.[97]

(c) Loss of an important competitive force or a "maverick"

If the merger eliminates an *important competitive force* (sometimes referred **7–013** to as a "maverick"), this may harm consumers. The Notice on Horizontal Mergers states that a supplier may have greater significance than its market share suggests if it is particularly *innovative* or is a *recent entrant*.[98] The loss

---

[96] Notice on Horizontal Mergers, para.36. These factors may also give rise to a theory of competitive harm based on *vertical foreclosure* (see Ch.11 below) (e.g. refusal to supply an essential input). However, the Commission appears to have included this list of factors in a discussion of horizontal mergers because they may contribute to a finding that the merged group will, as a result of the reduction in *horizontal* competition arising from the merger, have the power to act in ways which materially harm consumers.

[97] Notice on Horizontal Mergers, para.36 and n.52, citing Case T-156/98 *RJB Mining v Commission* [2001] E.C.R. II-337. See s.7.6(c) below.

[98] Notice on Horizontal Mergers, paras 37 and 38.

through a merger of such a supplier is more likely to harm consumers if the market is already concentrated.[99]

The two specific categories identified in the Notice on Horizontal Mergers (innovative suppliers and recent entrants) are discussed further below. However, there are other respects in which a merger can harm consumers through the loss of an important competitive force or a "maverick". In particular,[1] if the target's products are regarded by consumers as close substitutes for the purchaser's, but the target's prices are lower (e.g. because it has lower production costs or an aggressive policy of expansion),[2] then the merger may significantly reduce the competitive constraints faced by the purchaser.[3] Further, a supplier with a relatively smaller market share may have a greater incentive to adopt an aggressive strategy to increase that share to benefit from economies of scale and build up an installed base,[4] or if it is competing in a market where products are homogeneous and market prices are decided by output decisions by producers.[5]

7–014 **(i) Loss of innovation competition** It is difficult to predict the effect of mergers on the incentive to *innovate*.[6] A merger may enable the merged group to

---

[99] Notice on Horizontal Mergers, para.37. See also Case IV/M.877 *Boeing | McDonnell Douglas* [1997] O.J. L336/16, para.58 and Case COMP/M.2568 *Haniel | Ytong* [2003] O.J. L111/1, para.126.

[1] ABA Section of Antitrust Law, *Market Power Handbook* (ABA Publishing, 2005), pp.95 and 96, states: "The factors that might lead a firm to act as a maverick include: particularly high or low costs; a differing technology that allows the firm to take better advantage of scale economies; atypically large excess capacity; differentiated products that can be substitutes for rivals' offerings but that cause the firm to face a demand that differs from that of its rivals; differing costs of punishing a defector to an agreement; differing probabilities of being detected as a defector; and differing levels of vertical integration". See also p.96, discussing the scope to model maverick behaviour.

[2] See para.16–016(b) above (and, for a general discussion of competition involving differentiated products, s.7.3 above).

[3] See Case COMP/M.2187 *CVC | Lenzing* [2004] O.J. L82/20 (the Commission emphasised that the transaction would eliminate the one player in the market which had significantly increased its capacity in the years preceding the merger; see paras 143 and 162; further, the merger would have combined suppliers with the highest quality standards which were present in all segments of the market; see para.161 and n.138); Case COMP/M.3314 *Air Liquide | Messer Targets* (Air Liquide's internal documents showed that it had an aggressive expansion policy and the market test confirmed that it had offered significantly lower prices; the Commission found that Air Liquide's incentive to increase its customer base would have been substantially weakened through the acquisition of a significant incumbent supplier; paras 88 to 90); and Case COMP/M.3436 *Continental | Phoenix*, paras 134 and 140.

[4] See Case COMP/M.2861 *Siemens | Drägerwerk | JV* [2003] O.J. L291/1, paras 122 and 142.

[5] See Case COMP/M.3130 *Arla Foods | Express Dairies*, para.69: "In markets where products are homogeneous and market prices are decided by the output decisions by the producers, the incentive to compete is closely linked to the market share of the company. Aggressive pursuit of market share is likely to depress margins generally in the market. In particular firms with large volumes will lose from a decrease in margins. The merged entity is thus likely to have weaker incentives to compete aggressively to win or defend their market share than Arla and Express had individually before the merger".

[6] See generally Davis, "Innovation Markets and Merger Enforcement: Current Practice in Perspective" (2003) 71 *Antitrust Law Journal* 677; ABA Section of Antitrust Law, *Market Power Handbook* (ABA Publishing, 2005), pp.113 and 114; and Gotts & Rapp, "Antitrust Treatment of Mergers Involving Future Goods", *Antitrust*, Fall 2004, 100. For discussion of market definition in cases of innovation markets, see para.3–053 above.

bring new innovations to market *more quickly*, for example through the pooling of physical and intellectual capital. In this case, the effect of the merger on innovation is beneficial to customers. By contrast, a merger between two companies with similar "pipeline" products may reduce the pressure on the merged group to innovate (e.g. if the merged group finds it more profitable to reap the rewards from existing products rather than pressing to develop the next generation, once the rivalry which was driving the innovation process is diminished through the merger). The Notice on Horizontal Mergers recognises that the effect of a merger on the incentive to innovate is ambiguous and dependent on the facts,[7] and the Commission has tended to focus its concerns about mergers reducing innovation on transactions in the pharmaceutical sector when one of the parties has a pipeline product which is likely to compete with the other's existing or pipeline products.[8] The caution which should be exercised when using innovation market analysis to challenge mergers was emphasised by US Federal Trade Commission Chairman, Timothy J Muris, in a statement accompanying a decision to close an investigation into a merger to monopoly amongst rival innovators[9]; he emphasised that "economic theory and empirical investigations have not established a general causal relationship between innovation and competition"[10] and a very careful factual investigation was therefore required to discriminate between mergers with pro-competitive effects on innovation and those with anti-competitive effects.[11] This point was also recognised by the Commission in *Areva / Urenco / ETC JV*[12] when it stated: "Innovation markets are usually dependent on a large number of uncertain parameters and therefore often do not justify regulatory intervention. This is particularly true in a case ... where the new product cycle is between 10 and 20 years".

(ii) Mergers involving recent entrants In principle, if the system of EC merger control is to be coherent, then the treatment of mergers involving recent   **7–015**

---

[7] Notice on Horizontal Mergers, para.38. See also the discussion in "Merger Review in Emerging High Innovation Markets", OECD, DAFFE/COMP(2002)20, p.8 and Davis, "Innovation Markets and Merger Enforcement: Current Practice in Perspective" (2003) 71 *Antitrust Law Journal* 677, at pp.681 and 696.

[8] See, e.g. Case IV/M.1846 *Glaxo Wellcome / SmithKline Beecham*, para.188. In Case IV/M.737 *Ciba-Geigy / Sandoz* [1997] O.J. L201/1, the Commission noted that the merged group would have twice as large a potential as the next largest competitor in crop protection research and development but concluded that rival companies had the necessary "critical mass" to provide effective competition.

[9] *Genzyme Corporation / Novazyme Pharmaceuticals Inc* (the press release is available at *www.ftc.gov/opa/2004/01/genzyme.htm* and Chairman Muris's statement is available at *www.ftc.gov/os/2004/01/murisgenzymestmt.pdf*).

[10] The Chairman was quoting the FTC Staff Report, "Anticipating the 21st Century: Competition Policy in the New High-Tech, Global Marketplace", May 1996, Vol.1, Ch.7, p.16.

[11] The Chairman also emphasised that, except in extraordinary circumstances, innovation markets should only be considered in cases in which the number of competitors is very small.

[12] Case COMP/M.3099, para.52.

entrants ought to dovetail[13] with that of the loss of potential competition (see Ch.9) as there may only be a marginal difference between a very likely entrant (a supplier on the cusp of entry) and a recent entrant.[14] Indeed, in *Johnson & Johnson / Guidant*[15] the Commission identified Guidant as a supplier which would probably have developed into a key player in the absence of the merger, but did not find a significant impediment to effective competition in the market in question because other new entrants were likely to exert a sufficient competitive constraint to compensate for the loss of competition from Guidant.[16]

7.6 EFFICIENCIES GENERATED BY THE MERGER AND OTHER ASPECTS OF THE MERGED GROUP'S MARKET POSITION

(a) Whether efficiencies resulting from the merger may contribute to a prohibition decision

7–016 The question of whether efficiencies generated by a merger may be relied on by the Commission as a ground for prohibiting a transaction has proven hugely controversial and the debate is continuing.

The issue can be examined by imagining a conglomerate merger (i.e. one which does not give rise to horizontal or vertical effects) and assuming that the transaction will not allow the merged group to leverage market power from one market into a second (compare Ch.12 below) but will generate significant production cost savings through economies of scope. In broad terms, the Commission could adopt one of three possible approaches to such a case:

(a) The Commission could examine whether the efficiencies are likely to significantly impede effective competition *directly*, by conferring an advantage on the merged group *compared with its competitors*.

(b) The Commission could examine whether the efficiencies are likely to

---

[13] The treatment would not be expected to be identical because, in the case of actual entry, there is no need to discount the prospect that entry will not in fact occur.

[14] In Case COMP/M.3108 *Office Depot / Guilbert*, where one of the parties was expected to grow organically in the absence of the merger, the Commission carried out an analysis which was similar to that in a loss of potential competition case; see paras 34 to 41.

[15] Case COMP/M.3687, paras 114, 115 and 165.

[16] This analysis would have been equally applicable if Guidant had been identified as a potential competitor, rather than an actual competitor. Further, in *Johnson & Johnson*, when considering a different market, the Commission dealt with actual competitors and potential entrants in the same analysis, stating, at para.196, that "it seems unlikely that remaining competitors and potential entrants can constitute a sufficient and timely competitive constraint such as to prevent a unilateral increase in prices by the merged entity".

significantly impede effective competition *indirectly*, by making entry or expansion by competitors more difficult.

(c) The Commission could approve the transaction, without considering the points identified in sub-paras (a) and (b) above, on the grounds that the efficiencies are likely to benefit consumers by leading to lower prices,[17] creating an incentive for competitors to respond (and even if the efficiencies do not benefit consumers, the efficiencies will not harm them). On this view, there is no "efficiency offence".

The Commission's approach to this issue has varied from time to time. For example, in its XXIst Annual Report on Competition Policy, 1991, the Commission focused on whether the merged group would have "advantages over competitors" including through efficiencies (reflecting the approach summarised in sub-para.(a) above)[18] but, in the following year's Annual Report, it stated that competitive advantages arising from efficiencies should not be held against the merged group, although they could contribute to the erection of entry barriers (shifting the Commission's position to the one described in sub-para.(b) above).[19]

However, in its decisions since the publication of the 1992 Report, the **7-017**

[17] At least in so far as they relate to marginal or variable costs.
[18] The Commission's XXIst Annual Report on Competition Policy, 1991, stated, at pp.363 and 364, that, in appraising horizontal mergers, it analysed (amongst other factors): "the market position of the merged firm (market share and other advantages over competitors) ... Other advantages over competitors considered in the market position of the merged firm were: financial strength, technological expertise, higher production capacities, wider product range giving the possibility of package deals or cross-subsidization, distribution network, exclusive access to distribution channels, long-term supply agreements with customers, etc". See also Jones & González-Díaz (ed. by Overbury), *The EEC Merger Regulation* (Sweet & Maxwell, 1992), pp.157 and 158 ("Efficiencies that result from a merger can therefore be seen by the Commission as likely to contribute to a finding of dominance") and the Commission guidelines on market analysis and the assessment of significant market power under the Community regulatory framework for electronic communications networks and services [2002] O.J. C165/3 (identifying economies of scale and economies of scope, amongst others, as evidence of the existence of a dominant position; para.78). See, generally, the discussion of impediments to imitation in Besanko, Dranove & Shanley, *Economics of Strategy* (2nd edn, John Wiley & Sons Inc, 2000), pp.457 to 465. See also Oster, *Modern Competitive Advantage* (3rd edn, Oxford UP, 1999), pp.27 and 28.
[19] The Commission's XXIInd Annual Report on Competition Policy, 1992, para.250, stated: "The assessment also has to take into account other competitive advantages or disadvantages of the merged firm compared to remaining competitors such as: the financial power of the merged firm, scale economies, other cost advantages, product range, access to technology, position in terms of quality and technology, brand image resulting from long standing and high advertising, vertical integration, etc. Without holding such competitive advantages against the merged firm, one has to take into account that they can contribute to the erection of entry barriers for other competitors and therefore lead to the creation of market power in the hands of the merged firm. If this is not the case and barriers to entry are low, these competitive advantages are generally pro-competitive and, under the pressure of competition, the merged firm will have to allow consumers a fair share of the resulting benefit". Compare Röller, Stennek & Verboven, "Efficiency Gains from Mergers", The Research Institute of Industrial Economics, Working Paper No. 543, 2000 (available at *http://www.iui.se/wp/ Wp543/IUIWp543.pdf*), who state, at p.85: "if the cost reduction is big enough, the merger may imply that competitors are driven out of the market, or that new entry is blocked. In this sense, cost savings may be anti-competitive".

Commission has focused on the competitive advantages enjoyed by the merged group, not so much in determining the extent of any barriers to entry, but as a *direct* indicator of whether the merged group would hold a dominant position (reverting to the approach set out in sub-para.7–016(a) above).[20]

The 2002 draft Commission Notice on Horizontal Mergers identified a range of factors, including economies of scale and the merged group's distribution and sales network, as relevant to the market power held by the merged group and continued: "Some of the factors ... are likely to benefit the customers of the paramount firm ... However, they may also make it difficult for competitors, either individually or in the aggregate, to effectively constrain the paramount firm to a sufficient degree. For instance, they may make expansion of smaller firms or entry of new competitors difficult. The Commission will thus examine whether the merging firms will face sufficient residual competition to make it unprofitable to increase prices or decrease output".[21] The approach in the draft involved a proposed switch to the position summarised in sub-para.7–016(b) above.

However, these passages were *not* included in the final version of the Notice on Horizontal Mergers and the Commission has since stated that it "welcomes efficiencies as a means to foster dynamic competition and increasing competitiveness leading to economic progress. Therefore, there is clearly no efficiency offence in EU merger review".[22] This position is summarised in sub-para.7–016(c) above.

The Commission's statements that "there is no efficiency offence" are at odds with the decision of the Court of First Instance in *BaByliss v Commission*[23] (an appeal against the decision in *SEB / Moulinex*[24]), which stated that the merged group might be capable of types of anti-competitive behaviour other than price increases: "In particular, the concentration will enable SEB-Moulinex to make economies of scale and implement various rationalisation measures, thus generating a reduction in costs of which it could take advantage to reduce prices or allow retailers a bigger margin in order to increase its market share". This sentence implies that the Commission has a duty to prohibit mergers which directly benefit consumers by lowering prices and appears to reflect a belief that the objective of competition law is to protect rivalry (rather than consumers).[25]

7–018   If the Court's statement in *BaByliss* is treated as anomalous, on the grounds that the Court could not have intended through a single paragraph to shift the focus of EC merger control from the protection of consumers to

---

[20] See para.7–019 below.
[21] Paras 21 and 22.
[22] OECD, "Substantive Criteria Used for the Assessment of Mergers", DAFFE/COMP (2003) 5, p.313.
[23] Case T-114/02 [2003] E.C.R. II-1279, para. 360. See also para.18–008 below.
[24] Case COMP/M.2621.
[25] See s.2.2 above.

the protection of rivalry, then the Commission's current position appears to be as follows.

(a) The Commission will *not* use its powers under the ECMR to protect competitors against more efficient rivals. This means that a merger whose sole effect is to generate efficiencies (e.g. lowering production costs) will not be prohibited. In the "hard" case, this means that a merger would be approved, even if the Commission predicted that it was likely to lead to exit by competitors, provided that the merged group was not likely to pursue a leveraging strategy. This contrasts with the position under the 2002 draft Commission Notice on Horizontal Mergers, which contemplated that a merger that was likely to harm consumers by marginalising or eliminating competitors—even in the absence of a leveraging strategy—would be prohibited. However, if there is no efficiency offence, then such a merger must be permitted because it has no anti-competitive effects, in the same way that organic growth is not anti-competitive, even if one supplier's success leads others to exit from the market.

(b) The Commission *will* take efficiencies into account as part of its normal appraisal of the merger's effects (whether horizontal, vertical or conglomerate). If the Commission were to adopt a rule that it would disregard all efficiencies generated by the merger, this would be artificial (it would be examining the market but knowingly disregarding certain aspects of its operation) and arbitrary (generating a good deal of pointless debate about whether certain factors were to be treated as "efficiencies"). This means, for example, that when examining a horizontal merger, it may be relevant to take into account possible efficiencies when assessing the likelihood that new entry will prevent the merged group from raising its prices. Similarly, the efficiencies generated by a merger may give the merged group the ability to pursue a predatory pricing policy.[26] However, the crucial point here is that the Commission will intervene to prohibit a transaction (or approve it subject to undertakings) only if it is likely to reduce horizontal competition or facilitate a leveraging strategy (in

---

[26] In Case T-114/02 *BaByliss v Commission* [2003] E.C.R. II-1279 the Court of First Instance, in a paragraph discussing possible economies of scale or rationalisation, stated that the merger might have an anti-competitive effect because the merged group might be able to induce retailers to de-list its competitors (a potential exclusionary strategy); see para.360. The paper submitted by the Commission to the OECD roundtable on "Portfolio Effects in Conglomerate Mergers", OECD, DAFFE/COMP(2002)5 stated at p.243: "short-term strategic price reductions cannot be considered as efficiencies in the sense that they do not correspond to a sustainable reduction in the cost of production of the merged firm, likely to be passed on permanently to customers and consumers".

the case of vertical and conglomerate mergers), i.e. the merger would not be prohibited simply because it generates efficiencies.[27]

The discussion below should be read in the light of the Commission's current thinking, as many of the decisions were taken during a period when the Commission's attitude to efficiencies was less benign.

(b) Economies of scale or other efficiencies

7–019 Historically, the Commission has objected to transactions in part because they generate economies of scale or other efficiencies.[28]

(a) In *Aerospatiale | Alenia | de Havilland*[29] the merger would have given

---

[27] Drauz, "Unbundling *GE | Honeywell*: the Assessment of Conglomerate Mergers Under EC Competition Law", published in the 2001 *Annual Proceedings of the Fordham Corporate Law Institute*, p.183, argued that "the conglomerate aspects of mergers may constitute an additional factor, either aggravating or mitigating, to existing horizontal and/or vertical effects". The approach set out in the text receives some support from the decision of the Court of First Instance in Case T-210/01 *General Electric Company v Commission*, not yet reported, judgment of December 14, 2005, paras 183 to 189, 193, 229 and 241, in which the Court emphasised that the fact that the merged group would benefit from GE Group's AAA credit rating, had not been identified by the Commission as a free standing ground for prohibiting the merger but instead was an adjunct to other factors supporting the conclusion that GE held a pre-merger dominant position on the market for jet engines.

[28] See, e.g. Case IV/M.85 *Elf | Occidental*; Case IV/M.197 *Solvay-Laporte | Interox*; Case IV/M.290 *Sextant | BGT-VDO*; Case IV/M.426 *Rhône-Poulenc | Cooper*; Case IV/M.603 *Crown Cork & Seal | Carnaud Metalbox* [1996] O.J. L75/8 (the merged group would have benefited from flexibility in production; para.64); Case IV/M.774 *Saint-Gobain | Wacker-Chemie | NOM* [1997] O.J. L247/1 (customer efficiencies may also arise through *technical integration of products* when the merged group is able to offer consistent technical compositions across its range; para.178); Case IV/M.833 *The Coca-Cola Company | Carlsberg A/S* [1998] O.J. L145/41 (if the merged group has a wide product range, its unit costs of distribution may be reduced, enabling it to offer the best terms to any third party seeking distribution services; para.68); Case IV/M.856 *British Telecom | MCI (II)* [1997] O.J. L336/1 (international voice telephony services between the United Kingdom and the US); Case IV/M.1681 *Akzo Nobel | Hoechst Roussel Vet* (customer efficiencies may arise through the creation of a *one stop shop* where customers may be induced to buy all of their requirements from a single supplier; see para.32); Case COMP/M.1853 *EDF | EnBW* (pan-European supplier); Case COMP/M.1972 *Granada | Compass* (the Commission noted, at para.27, that the merged group would benefit from scale economies in purchasing, although the transaction was cleared because competitors would provide a sufficient competitive constraint despite their cost disadvantages); Case COMP/M.2033 *Metso | Svedala* [2004] O.J. L88/1 (availability of economies of scale could enable the merged group, as the largest supplier, to engage in targeted competitive actions against its rivals and further tighten its grip on the market; paras 137 to 139); Case COMP/M.2220 *GE | Honeywell* [2004] O.J. L48/1 (relying, at para.163, on the fact that GE had a large fleet in service and *customers* therefore benefited from economies of scale in continuing to purchase from GE because of the "commonality" issues explained in para.147) (prohibition decision upheld on appeal in Case T-210/01 *General Electric Company v Commission*, not yet reported, judgment of December 14, 2005); Case COMP/M.2420 *Mitsui | CVRD | Caemi* [2004] O.J. L92/50 (the merged group would have had the lowest production costs in the market; para.177); Case COMP/M.2431 *Allianz | Dresdner* (combination of strong distribution networks in "bancassurance"); and Case COMP/M.2530 *Südzucker | Saint Louis Sucre* [2003] O.J. L103/1 (pan-European supplier).

[29] Case IV/M.53 [1991] O.J. L334/42.

the parties a range of products across each of the commuter plane markets (20 to 39 seats; 40 to 59 seats; and 60 seats and over). The Commission found that being active in each of these sectors conferred an advantage: "This logic flows from the fixed costs borne by the carrier for each aircraft manufacturer dealt with by that carrier. These costs include the fixed costs of pilot and mechanic training as well as the costs of maintaining different in-house inventories of parts and the fixed costs of dealing with several manufacturers when ordering parts stocked only by the individual manufacturers themselves".

(b) In *Boeing / McDonnell Douglas*[30] the transaction would have resulted in the merged group becoming the only manufacturer to offer a complete range of large commercial aircraft. The Commission concluded that the economies of scope available to the merged group would have strengthened the merged group's dominant position: "Where a large fleet in service is combined with a broad product range, the existing fleet in service can be a key factor which may often determine decisions of airlines on fleet planning or acquisitions. Cost savings arising from commonality benefits, such as engineering spares inventory and flight crew qualifications, are very influential in an airline's decision-making process for aircraft type selections and may frequently lead to the acquisition of a certain type of aircraft even if the price of competing products is lower".

However, if the analysis in s.(a) above is correct, then the Commission will rely on economies of scale or other efficiencies against the interests of the merging parties only in limited circumstances.

(c) The merged group's financial resources

Mergers may provide access to greater capital ("deep pockets")[31] which **7–020** could be used, for example, to finance substantial investments in a capital intensive industry or advertising in a consumer goods industry[32] or to fund a strategy of hindering expansion by competitors.[33] The 2002 draft Commission Notice on Horizontal Mergers provided that the merged group's privileged access to specific inputs, such as physical or financial capital, may be taken into account in determining the extent of its market power, noting that: "In the large majority of cases financial strength is unlikely to be an issue. However, in some cases it may be one of the factors that contribute to

[30] Case IV/M.877 [1997] O.J. L336/16.
[31] Art.2(1) of the ECMR requires the Commission to take into account, in its merger appraisal, the "economic and financial power" of the undertakings concerned in the concentration.
[32] Case IV/M.430 *Procter & Gamble / VP Schickedanz (II)* [1994] O.J. L354/32, para.160.
[33] Notice on Horizontal Mergers, para.36.

a merger giving rise to competition concerns, in particular in those cases where (i) finance is relevant to the competitive process in the industry under review, (ii) there are significant asymmetries between competitors in terms of their internal financing capabilities and (iii) particular features of the industry make it difficult for firms to attract external funds".[34] However, these passages were not included in the final version of the Notice.

This relevance of the merged group's financial resources has arisen in numerous cases including[35] *General Electric / Honeywell*[36] in which the Commission noted[37] that: "In addition to having enormous financial means available in-house, GE's unmatchable balance sheet size offers other major advantages to GE businesses ... GE is able to take more risk in product development programmes than any of its competitors. This ability to absorb product failures without jeopardising its future ability to compete and develop new products in an industry characterised by long term investments is crucial". On appeal, the Court of First Instance in *General Electric Company v Commission*[38] stated that "competition law does not impose

---

[34] Para.21.
[35] See also Case IV/M.43 *Magneti Marelli / CEAC* [1991] O.J. L222/38 (the merged group would hold a dominant position in part because of "the financial strength of the new entity and that of its parent companies and its greater access to the lead market"; para.16(b)); Case IV/M.139 *VIAG / EB Brühl* (para.18; and see also the discussion in Commission's XXVIIth Annual Competition Report, 1997, p.184); Case IV/M.196 *Volvo / Procordia*, para.12; Case IV/M.580 *ABB / Daimler Benz* [1997] O.J. L11/1 ("Even if the financial strength of the undertakings is not such on its own as to allow proper conclusions to be drawn as to their competitive achievement potential, the economic strength underlying the size of the undertakings in conjunction with the current market position and the investment necessary on rail technology markets, on which research and development are important, is a general indication of a considerable competitive lead over other suppliers"; para.64); Case IV/M.877 *Boeing / McDonnell Douglas* [1997] O.J. L336/16, paras 53 to 82; Case COMP/JV.37 *BSkyB / Kirch-PayTV*, para.50; Case COMP/M.1630 *Air Liquide / BOC* [2004] O.J. L92/1, paras 150, 151 and 190; and Case COMP/M.2925 *Charterhouse / CDC / TDF* (in which the Commission stated, at para.40, that: "it cannot be excluded that TDF's financial situation might improve as a result of its integration with the triple-A credit rated CDC. However, at least so far as the present case is concerned, financial strength could only contribute, in combination with other elements, to the creation or strengthening of a dominant position as a result of which competition will be significantly impeded ... [The] horizontal and vertical effects of the concentration are not indicative of any creation or strengthening of a dominant position. Therefore, even if TDF's financial situation were to be improved following the change of control, there are no indications that it could lead to the creation or strengthening of a dominant position on any existing or emerging market"). In Case IV/M.1040 *Wolters Kluwer / Reed Elsevier* the Commission opened a detailed second phase inquiry, which was subsequently terminated when the parties abandoned the transaction, in part because: "the parties' strength across ... a wide-ranging series of closely related markets, and the resulting very large size of the merged entity— several times larger than any other publisher of professional information in the Community—was a further source of concern. In the Commission's view such a market structure could prevent the maintenance of competition in the supply of legal, fiscal and scientific information, with a consequent adverse effect on prices. In addition, there could be a foreclosure effect, since the combination of the parties' financial resources and their ownership of copyright material would be likely to discourage investment by existing and potential competitors"; see the Commission's XXVIIIth Annual Report on Competition Policy, 1998, para.154.
[36] Case COMP/M.2220, [2004] O.J. L48/1, paras 107 to 120 and 345.
[37] At para.108.
[38] Case T-210/01, not yet reported, judgment of December 14, 2005, para.185.

penalties on undertakings merely on account of their size or their financial resources" but found that the Commission was entitled to take account of GE's AAA credit rating as part of its overall assessment of whether GE held a pre-merger dominant position in the supply of jet engines.[39]

The decision of the Court of First Instance supports the analysis of the treatment of efficiencies set out in para.7–018 above.[40]

---

[39] See paras 201, 202, 229 and 241.
[40] The European Commission's paper for the OECD roundtable on "Portfolio Effects in Conglomerate Mergers" OECD, DAFFE/COMP(2002)5, states, at p.239: "Competitive concerns in conglomerate mergers may be reinforced in the case of the accretion to the merged firm of considerable financial strength". The Bundeskartellamt's assessment of the position in Germany (see the paper prepared for the International Competition Network's Analytical Framework Sub-group, available at *www.internationalcompetitionnetwork.org*) is that: "it is not the increase in financial strength as such that leads to the deterioration of market structures. The likelihood of anti-competitive impact should be examined, i.e. whether resources are likely to be of relevance for predatory and disciplinary strategies or as barriers to entry".

CHAPTER 8

COORDINATED EFFECTS

8.1 INTRODUCTION

8–001 If a merger enables the companies remaining in the market to increase their profits by actions which depend for their success on cooperative responses from other suppliers[1] (i.e. tacitly to coordinate[2] their activities),[3] they may be

---

[1] See generally: Europe Economics, "Study on Assessment Criteria for Distinguishing between Competitive and Dominant Oligopolies in Merger Control", Final Report for the European Commission, May 2001 (available via *www.eer.co.uk*); Ivaldi *et al*, "The Economics of Tacit Collusion", Report for DG Competition, March 2003 (available via *http://europa.eu.int/ comm/competition/mergers/review/the_economics_of_tacit_collusion_en.pdf*); OECD, "Oligopoly", Best Practice Roundtable, October 1999, DAFFE/CLP(99)25 (available via *www.oecd.org*); OFT Research Paper, "Merger Appraisal in Oligopolistic Markets", NERA, 1999 (note that the views expressed in OFT Research Papers do not necessarily represent those of the OFT) (available via *www.oft.gov.uk*); the International Competition Network, "Analysis of Merger Guidelines", Ch.4, "Coordinated Effects Analysis Under International Merger Regimes" (available via *http://www.internationalcompetitionnetwork.org/seoul/amg_ chap4_coordinated.pdf*); Jenny, "Collective Dominance and the EC Merger Regulation", published in the 2001 *Annual Proceedings of the Fordham Corporate Law Institute*, p.361; Kantzenbach, Kottmann & Krüger, "New Industrial Economics and Experiences From European Merger Control—New Lessons About Collective Dominance", March 1995 (prepared on behalf of the Commission but not necessarily representing the Commission's official position); Tirole, *The Theory of Industrial Organization* (The MIT Press, 1988), Ch.6; Scherer & Ross, *Industrial Market Structure and Economic Performance* (3rd edn, Houghton Mifflin Co, 1990), Chs 6, 7 and 10; Martin, *Advanced Industrial Economics* (2nd edn, Blackwell, 2002), Ch.10; Carlton & Perloff, *Modern Industrial Organization* (4th edn, Addison-Wesley, 2005), pp.379 to 386; Besanko, Dranove & Shanley, *Economics of Strategy* (2nd edn, John Wiley & Sons Inc, 2000), Ch.9; Porter, *Competitive Strategy* (The Free Press, 1998 edn), pp.17 to 23 and Chs 4 and 5; Porter, *Competitive Advantage* (The Free Press, 1998 edn), Ch.6; Motta, "EC Merger Policy and the Airtours Case" [2000] E.C.L.R. 199; Christensen & Rabassa, "The Airtours decision: Is there a new Commission approach to collective dominance?" [2001] E.C.L.R. 227; Nicholson & Cardell, "Airtours v Commission: Collective Dominance Contained?", paper presented to EC Merger Control Conference on November 8, 2002; Kloosterhuis, "Joint Dominance and the Interaction Between Firms" [2001] E.C.L.R. 79; Haupt, "Collective Dominance Under Article 82 E.C. and E.C. Merger Control in the Light of the *Airtours* Judgment" [2002] E.C.L.R. 434; Black, "Collusion and Co-ordination in EC Merger Control" [2003] E.C.L.R. 408; Nikpay & Houwen, "Tour de Force or a Little Local Tur-

able to increase prices or reduce quality, choice or innovation, thereby mimicking, wholly or partly, the monopoly[4] or cartel outcome.[5] Such a situation is commonly referred to as one of collective or joint dominance.

This Chapter seeks to identify criteria for distinguishing oligopolies in which such cooperation is likely to occur from those in which it is not. As Götz Drauz has noted: "The crucial point that antitrust regulators are called to reflect on is to distinguish between 'good' and 'bad' oligopolies or, in other words, to focus on whether or not a merger is likely to create or strengthen a dominant oligopoly".[6] This is not straightforward

---

bulence? A Heretical View on the *Airtours* Judgment" [2003] E.C.L.R. 193; Rabassa, "Joint Ventures as a Mechanism that May Favour Co-ordination: An Analysis of the Aluminium and Music Mergers" [2004] E.C.L.R. 771; Baxter Dethmers, "Collective Dominance Under EC Merger Control—After Airtours and the Introduction of Unilateral Effects is there Still a Future for Collective Dominance" [2006] E.C.L.R. 148; Kühn, "Closing Pandora's Box? Joint Dominance After the Airtours Judgment", published as Ch.3 of *The Pros and Cons of Merger Control* by the Swedish Competition Authority in 2002 (available via *http://www.kkv.se/ bestall/pdf/skrift_proscons.pdf*); James, "Rediscovering Coordinated Effects", speech to the American Bar Association, August 13, 2002 (available from *www.usdoj.gov*); Dick, "Strengthening the Micro Foundations for Coordinated Interaction in Merger Analysis" (*http://www.usdoj.gov/atr/public/workshops/docs/202659.htm*); US Horizontal Merger Guidelines, 1992 (amended in 1997) (*www.usdoj.gov/atr/public/guidelines/hmg.htm*), s.2; and US Non-Horizontal Merger Guidelines, 1984 (*http://www.usdoj.gov/atr/public/guidelines/ 2614.htm*), s.4.22. In the US, the focus of merger control has historically been on coordinated effects (and non-coordinated effects were not mentioned in the US Horizontal Merger Guidelines until the 1992 edition). See also Federal Trade Commission and Department of Justice, "Commentary on the Horizontal Merger Guidelines", 2006 (available via *www.ftc.gov/os/2006/03/CommentaryontheHorizontalMergerGuidelinesMarch2006.pdf*), pp 18 to 25.

[2] Through independent decision-taking, i.e. without expressly colluding with competitors. Express collusion will generally infringe EC or national competition laws. On the question of whether a merger may be prohibited because it increases the likelihood of *express* collusion, see Areeda, Hovenkamp & Solow, *Antitrust Law* (2nd edn, Aspen Law & Business, 1998), Vol.IV, para.917. This Chapter does not examine coordination through express collusion. By contrast, the US Horizontal Merger Guidelines, 1992 (amended in 1997) (*www.usdoj.gov/atr/ public/guidelines/hmg.htm*) treat coordinated effects as including tacit or express collusion whether or not the conduct is lawful or unlawful; para.2.1.

[3] Coordination may relate to, e.g. price, fixed price differentials, capacity, down-time, market shares or customer or territorial restrictions.

[4] Fingleton, "Does Collective Dominance Provide Suitable Housing for All Anti-Competitive Oligopolistic Mergers?", published in the 2002 *Annual Proceedings of the Fordham Corporate Law Institute*, p.181 at p.189, points out that the definition of coordinated effects is closely modelled on single firm dominance, the defining feature being that the firms act as if they enjoyed a monopoly and adopt a common policy.

[5] See the US Horizontal Merger Guidelines, 1992 (amended in 1997) (*www.usdoj.gov/atr/public/ guidelines/hmg.htm*), s.2.1. Robert D. Willig, "Merger Analysis, Industrial Organisation Theory, and Merger Guidelines", in (1991) *Brookings Papers: Microeconomics* 281, at p.293, states: "Coordinated effects are changes in the actions of the merging firms that would be profitable for them as a result of the merger only if the changes are accompanied by altera- tions in the actions of the non-parties that are motivated in part by fear of reprisals". Ivaldi *et al*, "The Economics of Unilateral Effects", 2003, Interim Report for DG Competition (available via *http://europa.eu.int/comm/competition/mergers/review/the_economics_of_ unilateral_ effects_en.pdf*), state, at p.17: "The fundamental idea behind all models of tacit collusion is that firms may have an incentive to set a price higher than they would otherwise wish, because of the fear that if they do not do so, other firms will react by setting lower prices in the future".

[6] Götz Drauz, "Recent Developments in the Assessment of Dominance", in *EC Merger Con- trol: Ten Years On* (International Bar Association, 2000), p.109, at p.110.

because[7] it involves predicting how two or more companies will *interact*,[8] bearing in mind that each producer will recognise that its best choices depend on the choices made by its competitors.[9] In general, if the interactions between the principal operators in the market result in their recognising that the long-term gains of cooperation outweigh the short term gains of competing, then a stable supra-competitive equilibrium will result, i.e. the producers will coordinate to produce an outcome which mimics wholly or partly the outcome which a monopoly firm would adopt.[10]

8–002   The decision of the Court of First Instance in *Airtours plc v Commission*[11] to quash the Commission's decision in *Airtours / First Choice*,[12] which prohibited the transaction on the grounds of coordinated effects, emphasises two points. First, a transaction cannot be blocked *merely* because it reduces the number of players in an oligopolistic market or it takes place in a market in which companies determine their strategies in the light of predictions about their competitors' strategies.[13] Secondly, in cases of coordinated effects, the Commission is required to provide "convincing evidence"[14] before proceeding to a prohibition decision.[15] This is a demanding standard

---

[7] It is also complicated by the fact that data *rejecting* an hypothesis of coordinated effects tends to be stronger than data *supporting* an hypothesis of coordinated effects (because such data is often also *consistent* with a competitive outcome); see Scheffman & Coleman, "Quantitative Analyses of Potential Competitive Effects From a Merger" (*http://www.usdoj.gov/atr/public/workshops/docs/202661.htm*).

[8] An assessment of non-coordinated effects also involves an analysis of the ways in which competitors will act as a constraint on the merged group's behaviour, but the starting point in non-coordinated effects cases is the position of the merged group.

[9] A further complicating factor is that oligopolies may have multiple equilibria, i.e. there may be several outcomes in an oligopolistic market, each of which may result in none of the suppliers having an incentive to change its competitive choices, so long as none of the other suppliers changes its choices. Game theory cannot predict which of multiple equilibria will result: see the discussion in Europe Economics, "Study on Assessment Criteria for Distinguishing between Competitive and Dominant Oligopolies in Merger Control", Final Report for the European Commission, May 2001, at p.20.

[10] This involves companies making their decisions on the basis of profits to be made both in the short run *and* in the future.

[11] Case T-342/99 [2002] E.C.R. II-2585. See also Overd, "After the Airtours Appeal" [2002] E.C.L.R. 375.

[12] Case IV/M.1524 [2000] O.J. L93/1.

[13] Interaction is the hallmark of oligopoly and companies are permitted to adapt their market behaviour intelligently to the competitive conditions they face; see *Cooperative Vereniging Suiker Unie UA v European Commission* [1975] E.C.R. 1663. However, in Case IV/M.1524 *Airtours / First Choice* [2000] O.J. L93/1 (which was quashed on appeal), the Commission stated, at para.54, that: "It is sufficient that the merger makes it rational for the oligopolists, in adapting themselves to market conditions, to act—individually—in ways which will substantially reduce competition between them, and as a result of which they may act, to an appreciable extent, independently of competitors, customers and consumers".

[14] Para.63. The Court of First Instance found, at para.294, that the decision was "vitiated by a series of errors of assessment as to factors fundamental to any assessment of whether a collective dominant position might be created". See s.2.5(b) above for a more general discussion of the standard of proof which the Commission ought to discharge before prohibiting a transaction.

[15] In Case IV/M.165 *Alcatel / AEG* the Commission noted, at para.32, that there is no presumption under the ECMR that coordinated effects will result from a merger and it "would have to demonstrate in all cases that effective competition could not be expected on structural grounds between the leading companies in a highly concentrated market". In Case IV/M.1016

given the uncertainties inherent in predicting how companies will interact[16] and the need to establish a causal link between the transaction and the coordinated effects.[17]

Recital 25 of the revised ECMR makes clear that the adoption of a significant impediment of effective competition test was not intended to alter the treatment of coordinated effects under the ECMR.[18]

Non-coordinated and coordinated effects are *mutually inconsistent*[19] **8–003** because non-coordinated effects arise when the merged group enjoys market power in its own right (i.e. without depending for its success on cooperative responses from other suppliers), whereas coordinated effects depend for their success on cooperative responses from other suppliers. It follows that a merger may result in non-coordinated effects *or* in coordinated effects but both cannot occur at once. This straightforward analytical distinction between non-coordinated effects and coordinated effects is subject to three caveats. First, merger control under the ECMR is inherently forward-looking or prophylactic. The uncertainty inherent in any predictive exercise means that the Commission might find that there was a prospect that the merger would result in *either* non-coordinated or coordinated effects. Secondly, a merger may result in non-coordinated *and* coordinated effects occurring sequentially. Götz Drauz posited the following example:

"Consider that the acquired firm is a 'maverick' and/or the closest competitor of the acquirer. By acquiring its 'maverick' and/or closest competitor, the merged firm has an incentive for a non-coordinated price increase on products where the target's pricing constrained its own. At the

---

Price Waterhouse / Coopers & Lybrand [1999] O.J. L50/27, the Commission acknowledged, at para.104, that the judgment of the Court of Justice in Joined Cases C-68/94 and C-30/95 *France v Commission* [1998] E.C.R. I-1375 emphasised the onus on the Commission to establish that coordinated effects will result from a concentration, and stated that the evidence as to the lack of effective competition and the weakness of competitive pressure from other suppliers must be very strong.

[16] The predictions of oligopoly models are very sensitive to changes in the underlying assumptions: see, e.g. OFT Research Paper, "Merger Appraisal in Oligopolistic Markets", NERA, 1999 (note that the views expressed in OFT Research Papers do not necessarily represent those of the OFT), p.9. Carlton & Perloff, *Modern Industrial Organization* (4th edn, Addison-Wesley, 2005), p.189, state: "Because all these models are logically consistent, one cannot choose between them on purely theoretical grounds. One can ask, however, whether their assumptions are reasonable or whether their predicted outcomes are consistent with actual market outcomes".

[17] Jenny, "Collective Dominance and the EC Merger Regulation", Paper for the 28th Annual Fordham Conference on International Antitrust Law and Policy, states: "economists can establish that in certain circumstances the probability of departure from the cooperative oligopoly equilibrium is lower when there are many oligopolists than when there are only a few. Consequently, everything else being equal, the probability that the oligopolists will arrive at a cooperative equilibrium is greater after the merger than before. However, economists cannot predict with great precision whether this probability is high or low or the precise effect that the structural change of the industry has on this possibility".

[18] See para.2–015 above.

[19] Europe Economics, "Study on Assessment Criteria for Distinguishing between Competitive and Dominant Oligopolies in Merger Control", Final Report for the European Commission, May 2001, pp.vi, 62 and 63.

same time, the elimination of the 'maverick' and/or closest competitor improves the chances of coordinated pricing among the remaining competitors. What is interesting to note in this example is that a merger may produce both non-coordinated and coordinated effects, without one excluding the other. In reality, the two effects may not be simultaneous: the non-coordinated effects would appear in the first place, whereas coordinated behaviour would become rational for the remaining market players afterwards".[20]

Thirdly, whilst the analytical distinction between non-coordinated and coordinated effects can be readily drawn, the difference in practice may not be substantial because the unilateral action which is the hallmark of non-coordinated effects may be dependent for its success upon, or at least result in, a change in output or prices[21] by competitors.[22] For example, if the merged group is expected to continue to act as price leader following the transaction, this suggests that the competitive constraint posed by rivals on the merged group's ability to exercise market power is weak and, other things being equal, means that non-coordinated effects are more likely, i.e. that a decision taken unilaterally by the merged group to increase its prices is more likely to be profitable.[23] However, the presence in the market of a price leader may also facilitate coordinated effects in the sense that both the leader and the followers enjoy enhanced profits by choosing to follow the price leader rather than setting prices independently—such an arrangement may form part of a coordinated effects analysis.[24]

---

[20] "Recent Developments in the Assessment of Dominance" in *EC Merger Control: Ten Years On* (International Bar Association, 2000), p.109, at 113.

[21] The UK Office of Fair Trading's Substantive Merger Guidelines, May 2003 (*www.oft.gov.uk*), provide, at para.4.10: "Though the profits from non-coordinated effects are generally captured by the merging parties, rival firms can also benefit from reductions in competitive pressures as a result of a merger. Even if rival firms pursue the same competitive strategies that they did prior to the merger, this can result in their increasing prices in the wake of a merger".

[22] See, for discussion, the UK Office of Fair Trading's Substantive Merger Guidelines, May 2003 (*www.oft.gov.uk*), n.21.

[23] In Case COMP/M.2420 *Mitsui / CVRD / Caemi* [2004] O.J. L92/50 the merged group's role as likely price leader was found to contribute to the creation or strengthening of a dominant position through non-coordinated effects (see paras 207 and 209). See also Case IV/M.582 *Orkla / Volvo* [1996] O.J. L66/17 (company's position as price leader would be exacerbated by the merger; paras 100 and 101); Case COMP/M.1628 *TotalFina / Elf* [2001] O.J. L143/1 (the merged group's competitors would not be able significantly to increase sales of LPG and would therefore have an incentive to follow the merged group's price; the Commission made a finding of sole firm dominance; paras 300, 301 and 343); Case COMP/M.1672 *Volvo / Scania* [2001] O.J. L143/74, para.288; Case COMP/M.1806 *Astra Zeneca / Novartis* [2004] O.J. L110/1, para.223; and Case COMP/M.2187 *CVC / Lenzing* [2004] O.J. L82/20, para.173.

[24] This example serves to emphasise that an analysis of the merged group's inter-relationship with its competitors is important in both non-coordinated and coordinated effects analysis. See also the UK Competition Commission's Merger References Guidelines, March 2003 (*www.competition-commission.org.uk*), para.3.28. In Case IV/M.1383 *Exxon / Mobil* [2004] O.J. L103/1 price leadership by the "A-brands" was taken into account in finding that a merger would result in the creation of a joint dominant position by the suppliers of the A-brands (paras 592 and 610 to 612). If the merged group could not profitably raise prices if its competitors acted independently, then the example given in the text is best analysed as one of coordinated effects.

The remainder of this Chapter describes the test for identifying coordinated effects (s.8.2) and discusses the methodology to be applied in analysing coordinated effects issues (s.8.3), before describing each of the relevant steps in the analysis, namely identifying the nature of the potential coordination (s.8.4), determining whether coordinated effects were present prior to the merger (s.8.5), identifying the members of the candidate oligopoly (s.8.6), determining whether the participants are able to reach terms of coordination (s.8.7), assessing whether deviations from the coordinated strategy can be monitored effectively (s.8.8), identifying a deterrent mechanism to "punish" cheating on the coordinated outcome (s.8.9), determining whether the coordination would be defeated by the actions of outsiders, such as the competitive fringe, new entrants or customers (s.8.10), and identifying a causal link between the merger and any coordinated effects (s.8.11). The remainder of the Chapter then discusses three specific issues, namely the relevance to a coordinated effects analysis of capacity information (s.8.12), structural links between the coordinating parties (s.8.13), and historic cartel activity (s.8.14).

8.2 THE TEST FOR IDENTIFYING COORDINATED EFFECTS

The Court of First Instance has stated that[25]:   **8–004**

"in the case of an alleged collective dominant position, the Commission is ... obliged to assess, using a prospective analysis of the reference market, whether the concentration which has been referred to it leads to a situation in which effective competition in the relevant market is significantly impeded by the undertakings involved in the concentration and one or more other undertakings which together, in particular because of factors giving rise to a connection between them, are able to adopt a common policy on the market and act to a considerable extent independently of their competitors, their customers, and also of their consumers".[26]
"A collective dominant position significantly impeding effective com-

---

[25] See also Case T-374/00 *Verband der freien Rohrwerke v Commission* [2003] E.C.R. II-2275, para.121 (a concentration under the ECSC) and Case T-193/02 *Piau v Commission*, not yet reported, judgment of January 26, 2005, para.111 (Art.82). The European Court of Justice has ruled that the Commission may investigate coordinated effects under the ECMR (as well as non-coordinated effects): Joined Cases C-68/94 and C-30/95 *France v Commission* [1998] E.C.R. I-1375. The Court stated at para.166: "Article 2, in referring to 'a concentration which creates or strengthens a dominant position', does not itself exclude the possibility of applying the Regulation to cases where concentrations lead to the creation or strengthening of a collective dominant position, that is, a dominant position held by the parties to the concentration together with an entity not a party thereto".

[26] Joined Cases C-68/94 and C-30/95 *France v Commission* [1998] E.C.R. I-1375, para.163; Case T-102/96 *Gencor v Commission* [1999] E.C.R. II-753, para.163; and Case T-342/99 *Airtours plc v Commission* [2002] E.C.R. II-2585, para.59.

petition in the common market or a substantial part of it may thus arise as the result of a concentration where, in view of the actual characteristics of the relevant market and of the alteration in its structure that the transaction would entail, the latter would make each member of the dominant oligopoly, as it becomes aware of common interests, consider it possible, economically rational, and hence preferable, to adopt on a lasting basis a common policy on the market with the aim of selling at above competitive prices, without having to enter into an agreement or resort to a concerted practice within the meaning of Article 81 EC ... and without any actual or potential competitors, let alone customers or consumers, being able to react effectively".[27]

8–005 More specifically, a merger may be prohibited (or cleared only subject to undertakings) if, but only if, the following five criteria are met.[28]

(a) It is possible to *reach terms of coordination*[29] without any need for express collusion (i.e. coordination is *feasible*). This requires both that:

   (i) there is a *reference point* or points (e.g. price, output or market shares) around which terms of coordination can be reached[30]; and

   (ii) there is sufficient *transparency* that all participants can identify the relevant reference point without any need for express collusion.[31]

(b) The coordinating firms are able to *monitor deviations*,[32] i.e. there is sufficient *transparency* that the coordinating firms can identify whether the terms of coordination are being complied with.

(c) There is a credible *deterrent mechanism*.[33] Producers have an *incentive* to tacitly coordinate (i.e. the tacitly coordinated outcome is stable, so that suppliers do not deviate from it) only when they are deterred

---

[27] Case T-342/99 *Airtours plc v Commission* [2002] E.C.R. II-2585, para.61.
[28] The US Horizontal Merger Guidelines, 1992 (amended in 1997) (*www.usdoj.gov/atr/public/guidelines/hmg.htm*) state, at para.2.1: "Successful coordinated interaction entails reaching terms of coordination that are profitable to the firms involved and an ability to detect and punish deviations that would undermine the coordinated interaction". The New Zealand Merger Guidelines, 2004 (*http://www.comcom.govt.nz/Publications/ContentFiles/Documents/MergersandAcquisitionsGuidelines.PDF*), note, at para.9.1: "In broad terms, effective co-ordination can be thought of as requiring three ingredients: collusion, detection and retaliation". The evolution of the Commission's thinking on coordinated effects is summarised in Nicholson & Cardell, "Airtours v Commission: Collective Dominance Contained?", paper presented to EC Merger Control Conference on November 8, 2002.
[29] Notice on Horizontal Mergers, para.41.
[30] If there is no reference point, collusion is possible only through express agreement, i.e. the formation of an unlawful cartel.
[31] If there is insufficient transparency, collusion is possible only through express agreement, i.e. the formation of an unlawful cartel.
[32] Notice on Horizontal Mergers, para.41.
[33] Notice on Horizontal Mergers, para.41.

from deviating from the coordinated outcome. The existence of a credible mechanism to act as a deterrent to deviation is crucial because participants in a tacitly coordinating market generally benefit in the short run by *cheating* on the arrangement. In particular, whenever price is raised above the competitive level, producers tend to have an incentive to increase their individual output to benefit from sales at the increased price, and it is therefore necessary to examine carefully whether producers will choose not to cheat because they fear a credible retaliatory threat outweighing the short run gains from cheating.[34]

(d) The coordinated outcome would not be defeated by the *actions of outsiders*.[35] Producers have the *ability* to raise prices[36] through tacit coordination only if the coordinated output can be imposed on the market without being defeated, e.g. by buyer power, new entry or the activities of fringe producers who are active in the market but are not engaged in tacit coordination.

(e) There is a *causal link* between the merger and the coordinated effects.[37]

In determining whether the five criteria in para.8–005 are satisfied, a wide **8–006** range of market characteristics may be relevant. These characteristics are commonly presented as a "check list". However, the presence or absence of one or more of the characteristics on the "check list" is not determinative of the question of whether coordinated effects are likely to result from the merger.[38] Rather, the issue is whether the market characteristics taken together, and bearing in mind their interaction,[39] indicate that the five criteria are satisfied.[40] Furthermore, the differing characteristics may have opposing effects on different dimensions of rival suppliers' incentives and

---

[34] As Phlips observes in *Applied Industrial Economics* (Cambridge UP, 1998), p.27: "Deviation does not occur when it leads to future losses, due to retaliation, which are larger than the immediate gains from deviating". See Case COMP/M.1741 *MCI WorldCom / Sprint* [2003] O.J. L300/1, para.261 and paras 279 to 282.

[35] Notice on Horizontal Mergers, para.41.

[36] Or reduce quality, variety or innovation.

[37] Notice on Horizontal Mergers, para.42.

[38] Case COMP/M.2498 *UPM-Kymmene / Haindl* [2002] O.J. L233/38, at para.77. Europe Economics, "Study on Assessment Criteria for Distinguishing between Competitive and Dominant Oligopolies in Merger Control", Final Report for the European Commission, May 2001, at p.29, take a slightly different approach from the one in the text, identifying six "necessary criteria" for coordinated effects and a wide range of "factors that contribute to the necessary criteria" which correspond to the common "check list". The necessary criteria identified by Europe Economics are: (1) very few firms; (2) repeated interaction; (3) barriers to entry; (4) capacity to reach a mutually acceptable equilibrium; (5) ease of detection of cheating; and (6) enforcement of compliance.

[39] OECD, "Oligopoly", Best Practice Roundtable, October 1999, DAFFE/CLP(99)25 (*www.oecd.org*), p.31.

[40] See Areeda, Hovenkamp & Solow, *Antitrust Law* (2nd edn, Aspen Law & Business, 1998), Vol.IV, para.944f.

abilities to coordinate.[41] Such an all-encompassing appraisal[42] is criticised by Areeda, Hovenkamp & Solow[43]: "Our own conclusion is that identifying these criteria in the specific case, making the relevant measurements and assigning weights, and predicting the true 'likelihood' that collusion will occur in the postmerger market are nearly impossible in most situations. If that is so, adding the criteria offers little or no promise of increased accuracy while making merger legality much less predictable than it would be if simpler criteria were used".

8.3 METHODOLOGY IN ANALYSING COORDINATED EFFECTS

8–007 In determining whether a concentration will significantly impede effective competition through coordinated effects, the Commission adopts a four-stage *methodology*.[44]

(a) The Commission first identifies a theory of coordination for investigation.

---

[41] OECD, "Oligopoly", Best Practice Roundtable, October 1999, DAFFE/CLP(99)25 (*www.oecd.org*), p.31. See also Europe Economics, "Study on Assessment Criteria for Distinguishing between Competitive and Dominant Oligopolies in Merger Control", Final Report for the European Commission, May 2001, at p.37; and Kühn, "Closing Pandora's Box? Joint Dominance After the Airtours Judgment", published as Ch.3 of *The Pros and Cons of Merger Control* by the Swedish Competition Authority in 2002 (and available at *www.kkv.se/bestall/pdf/skrift_proscons.pdf*), p.59. The empirical evidence is summarised at OECD, "Oligopoly", Best Practice Roundtable, October 1999, DAFFE/ CLP(99)25 (*www.oecd.org*), p.237.

[42] See para.1–027(d) above.

[43] Areeda, Hovenkamp & Solow, *Antitrust Law* (2nd edn, Aspen Law & Business, 1998), Vol.IV, para.916a.

[44] As a complementary methodology, Europe Economics, "Study on Assessment Criteria for Distinguishing between Competitive and Dominant Oligopolies in Merger Control", Final Report for the European Commission, May 2001, pp.46 and 47, suggest a "step-wise" approach by asking the following questions.

(a) Is the market highly concentrated with few suppliers?
(b) Are there barriers to entry?
(c) Does the market operate through the repeated interaction of "patient players" (i.e. suppliers who value profits in future periods sufficiently highly to allow predictions of profitability in future periods to affect decisions taken in the current period; if this is not the case, then the supplier will not be deterred by the threat of retaliation in future periods)?
(d) Is the market a mature one with low innovation and low uncertainty?
(e) Is the market transparent, with homogeneous goods and symmetry of supplies?
(f) Are there any factors to counteract tacit coordination, in particular strong buyer power or maverick suppliers?

If the answers to any of (a) to (e) are "no" then, in general, coordinated effects are unlikely.

(b) The next stage is to assess whether coordinated effects were occurring on the market prior to the merger.

(c) The Commission then identifies the members of the oligopoly,[45] to distinguish the suppliers which may have an incentive to engage in tacit coordination from those which are outside the oligopoly and are therefore part of the competitive fringe.[46]

(d) Fourthly, the Commission applies the test for coordinated effects set out in para.8–005 above.[47]

8.4 THE NATURE OF COORDINATION

The first stage in the analysis is to identify the type or types of coordination **8–008** for investigation. Commonly, coordination involves increases in price, but coordination is in principle possible on any competitive parameter (e.g. allocating customers, reducing output, not increasing capacity, closing capacity, or research and development).[48]

8.5 WHETHER COORDINATED EFFECTS ARE PRESENT PRIOR TO THE MERGER

(a) The Airtours decision

A thorough analysis of historic market operation is essential to a coordi- **8–009** nated effects analysis because it provides information about the counter-factual, i.e. the way in which the market would have operated in the absence

---

[45] The word "oligopoly" is used in two senses: its normal sense is to identify a market where there are few suppliers and each of the suppliers recognises its inter-dependence with the other suppliers. In this paragraph of the text, "oligopoly" is used to refer to the suppliers which are engaged in tacit coordination, in contrast to rival suppliers which are active in the market but form part of the competitive fringe.

[46] A supplier's incentive to join an oligopoly will depend on the trade-off between an increased profit share (if prices rise then suppliers will often generate increased profits from the higher prices) as compared with the gains available from increasing output if the market price is increased by the members of the oligopoly.

[47] Commission paper tabled at OECD, "Oligopoly", Best Practice Roundtable, October 1999, DAFFE/CLP(99)25 (*www.oecd.org*), p.213, at pp.217 to 221.

[48] See Ivaldi *et al*, "The Economics of Tacit Collusion", Report for DG Competition, March 2003 (available via *http://europa.eu.int/comm/competition/mergers/review/the_economics_of_tacit_collusion_en.pdf*), Ch.IV, discussing coordination on parameters other than price. In *Carnival / Princess* and *Royal Caribbean / Princess*, the US FTC considered the scope for coordination on (separately) price, quality and capacity reductions and whether the transaction might substantially lessen competition through "maverick theory" (under which an acquisition could make coordinated interaction more likely or more effective by eliminating an industry "maverick") (see *www.ftc.gov/os/2002/10/cruisestatement.htm*).

of the merger.[49] In *Airtours plc v Commission*[50] the Court of First Instance emphasised that if the merger does not result in any "significant change" in the level of competition, then the merger should be approved. The Commission has recognised the importance of establishing the level of competition prior to the merger, stating: "It is . . . necessary to first analyse the past level of competition in order to determine whether an oligopolistically dominant position already existed in the pre-merger situation. Furthermore, an analysis of the level of competition in the market in the past can also provide important information as to whether a merger is likely to lead to the creation of a dominant position. On this basis it is then assessed which impact the merger has on competition in the market".[51] Accordingly, in *Sony | BMG*[52] the Commission started its analysis of coordinated effects by considering whether there was evidence of a coordinated price policy in the previous three or four years.

(b) The practical importance of a finding of pre-merger coordinated effects

8–010 Commonly, the most important single issue in a case involving coordinated effects is whether there has been coordination prior to the merger. If there has, then the issue facing the Commission is relatively tractable, namely whether the merger renders coordination easier, more stable or more effective.[53] Other things being equal, a reduction in the number of coordinating suppliers is likely to make it easier to reach terms of coordination or monitor deviations,[54] but it may reduce the merged group's incentives to coordinate (e.g. by creating an asymmetry in costs structures).[55] This implies that if the Commission identifies pre-merger coordinated effects, then it is likely (but not inevitable) that a transaction involving a party within the coordinating group will be found to create a significant impediment to effective competition. Indeed, in the 2002 draft Commission Notice on Horizontal Mergers, the Commission stated that: "It is unlikely that the

---

[49] See Ch.5 above.

[50] Case T-342/99 [2002] E.C.R. II-2585, para.82. See also paras 75, 76 and 92 (placing substantial weight on the Commission's finding that the transaction created rather than strengthened a dominant position).

[51] Commission paper tabled at the OECD "Oligopoly" Best Practice Roundtable, October 1999, DAFFE/CLP(99)25 (*www.oecd.org*), p.213 at p.219. See also Case IV/M.190 *Nestlé | Perrier* [1992] O.J. L356/1, in which the Commission emphasised that, when a market is highly concentrated with weakened price competition, the maintenance or development of whatever competition remains on the market requires particular protection and any structural operation restricting further the scope for competition "has to be judged severely"; para.118.

[52] Case COMP/M.3333 [2005] O.J. L62/30 (appeal pending in Case T-464/04 Impala v Commission), para.69.

[53] Notice on Horizontal Mergers, para.39. See further para.8–055 below.

[54] A merger involving a member of the competitive fringe may increase the coordinating group's ability profitably to raise prices by reducing the competitive constraints that they face.

[55] See para.8–022 below.

Commission would approve a merger if coordination were already taking place prior to the transaction unless it determines that the merger is likely to disrupt such coordination".[56] The language proved controversial[57] and was omitted from the *final* version of the Notice, but it is clear that the Commission will place substantial weight on such a finding.[58]

However, if there has not been coordination prior to the merger, the issue **8–011** is altogether more complex, namely whether the change brought about the merger increases the likelihood of coordination[59] *notwithstanding that coordination has not occurred to date.* If the merger involves a maverick company which had prevented coordination in the past, this will be straightforward.[60] But in other cases the exercise is almost impossible as Areeda, Hovenkamp & Solow explained in the passage quoted in para.8–006 above. The position is further complicated because the distinction (which was the basis for the Court of First Instance's decision in *Airtours*[61]) between markets in which there is pre-merger coordination and those in which there is not, is more theoretical than real. In practice, markets generally do not "tip" from not exhibiting coordinated effects to doing so; in reality, they generally pass through a spectrum ranging from very weak or loose coordination to more extensive coordination and a merger may cause the market to pass further along the spectrum towards more extensive coordination. A similar point[62] has been made by Götz Drauz, in the following terms:

"In the *Airtours* case, the CFI basically said that if the market has been competitive, then we simplify by saying that the market was 'white'. Now, let us look at what the market is with three players—has the market which has previously been white, now become black? [The Commission's] main argument was that the market with four players was already reduced in competition, and the change from four integrated players to three integrated players had an effect of making collusive behaviour a real possibility".[63]

---

[56] Para.41.
[57] See Robert & Hudson, "Past Co-ordination and the Commission Notice on the Appraisal of Horizontal Mergers" [2004] E.C.L.R. 163.
[58] Para.43 of the final version provides in part: "Evidence of past coordination is important if the relevant market characteristics have not changed appreciably or are not likely to do so in the near future".
[59] Notice on Horizontal Mergers, para.39. See further para.8–055 below.
[60] Notice on Horizontal Mergers, para.42.
[61] Case T-342/99 *Airtours plc v Commission* [2002] E.C.R. II-2585.
[62] See also Fingleton, "Does Collective Dominance Provide Suitable Housing for All Anti-Competitive Oligopolistic Mergers?" published in the 2002 *Annual Proceedings of the Fordham Corporate Law Institute*, p.181 at p.185, noting that the authority must show that the merger is the *straw that breaks the camel's back*, i.e. coordinated effects did not arise prior to the merger despite a preponderance of "plus factors", yet they are likely to arise after the merger.
[63] "Collective Dominance Under the European Merger Control Regulation: The Implications of the Airtours Case", ABA Section of Antitrust Law "Brown Bag" Programme (available at *www.abanet.org/antitrust/source/11-02/airtours.pdf*). In fact, the Commission accepted in its pleadings that the market was sufficiently competitive prior to the merger.

This point is illustrated by the Commission's decision in *Sony / BMG*.[64] The Commission found that the markets for recorded music "display certain features which indicate a conduciveness to collective dominance" but concluded that it did not have sufficient evidence to prove that the five majors held a collective dominant position in the past. It then considered whether the merger would *create* a collective dominant position and noted that a reduction in the number of majors from five to four would reduce the number of bilateral competitive relationships from ten to six, which would in principle facilitate monitoring of the respective markets. However, the Commission concluded that it had "not found sufficient evidence to prove that the reduction of the majors from five to four represents a change substantial enough to result in the likely creation of collective dominance. In particular, the Commission has not found sufficient evidence that a reduction from five to four majors would facilitate transparency and retaliation to such an extent that the creation of a collective dominant position of the remaining four majors has to be anticipated".

(c) Evidence[65]

8–012 (i) Similarities in price movements In general, similarities in price movements[66] are consistent both with a highly competitive market and one in which coordinated effects are present. Therefore, evidence that rivals' prices are similar or tend to move together is *not* in itself evidence of coordinated effects. However, evidence that rivals' price movements bear little relationship with one another *is* evidence that coordinated effects on price are *not* present.[67] More specifically, pre-merger coordinated effects on price can

---

[64] Case COMP/M.3333 [2005] O.J. L62/30 (appeal pending in Case T-464/04 *Impala v Commission*), para.157.

[65] Commission paper tabled at OECD, "Oligopoly", Best Practice Roundtable, October 1999, DAFFE/CLP(99)25 (www.oecd.org) p.213, at pp.219 and 220. The Commission's paper also mentions the past existence of excess capacity. If there is excess capacity within the market, this is consistent with pre-merger coordinated effects, where the excess capacity was necessary to support a deterrent mechanism involving an expansion of output. However, excess capacity can also be explained by numerous other matters which do not involve coordinated effects, and this is therefore a weak indicator. For discussion, see the International Competition Network, "ICN Investigative Techniques Handbook for Merger Review", June 2005 (www.internationalcompetitionnetwork.org/handbook_5-5.pdf), p.61.

[66] In Case COMP/M.3333 *Sony / BMG* [2005] O.J. L62/30 (appeal pending in Case T-464/04 *Impala v Commission*), para.73, the Commission analysed average wholesale net prices, list prices and discounts to test for evidence of pre-merger coordinated effects.

[67] See the UK Competition Commission, "Merger References: Competition Commission Guidelines", CC2, June 2003 (*www.competition-commission.org.uk/rep_pub/rules_ and_ guide/ pdf/15073compcommguidance2final.pdf*), para.3.43. Götz Drauz, in "Recent Developments in the Assessment of Dominance", published in *EC Merger Control: Ten Years On* (International Bar Association, 2000) p.109, at p.112, noted that: "the evaluation of the past level of competition—by looking at the variations of market shares and prices over a long period of time—will help us to understand the likely impact of certain operations on competitors' future conduct and make assumptions with regard to their likely reactions. In cases such as *Exxon / Mobil* and *Airtours / First Choice*, we had to analyse carefully previous price wars and their consequence on prices". Compare Case IV/M.190 *Nestlé / Perrier* [1992] O.J. L356/1, where the Commission identified a series of parallel price increases.

be ruled out if there is evidence that prices vary significantly across competitors (controlling for observable differences, such as order size).[68]

Nevertheless, it is possible to test *positively* for historic coordinated effects on price, using a range of evidence.

(a) Markets in which coordinated effects on price are present generally show greater "stickiness" of prices[69] and variations in inventory and order backlog than markets without coordinated effects.[70]

(b) If coordinated effects on price are present, then an increase in price by one supplier would *not* necessarily lead to an increase in market shares for rivals; by contrast, in a competitive market, if one supplier increases its prices, rivals generally gain market share (as well as increasing their prices).[71]

(c) Excessive profits are a positive indicator of coordinated effects.[72]

(d) The use of facilitating practices, such as delivered pricing, is a positive indicator of coordinated effects if there are no other explanations for the practices.[73]

(e) Finally, Scheffman, Coate & Silva[74] state: "Another approach to prove coordination/collusion has been to look for differences in prices or margins (or netbacks) across products or geography that appear to be inconsistent with competitive arbitrage. Such evidence is then used in support of an argument that there must be some sort of coordinated price discrimination already occurring in the market".

---

[68] See Scheffman & Coleman, "Quantitative Analyses of Potential Competitive Effects From a Merger" (*http://www.usdoj.gov/atr/public/workshops/docs/202661.htm*).

[69] The UK Competition Commission, "Merger References: Competition Commission Guidelines", CC2, June 2003 (*http://www.competition-commission.org.uk/rep_pub/rules_and_guide/pdf/15073compcommguidance2final.pdf*), para.3.43, describes the point as follows: "prices in competitive conditions, though tending to the same level, are, over time, likely to exhibit significant variation as they respond to changing supply and demand conditions. This is less likely to be the case with oligopoly pricing, because the incentive not to depart from an established level of high prices will to some extent dampen the responsiveness of prices to costs and demand changes".

[70] Scherer & Ross, *Industrial Market Structure and Economic Performance* (3rd edn, Houghton Mifflin Co, 1990), pp.270 and 273.

[71] See the International Competition Network, "ICN Investigative Techniques Handbook for Merger Review", June 2005 (*http://www.internationalcompetitionnetwork.org/handbook_5-5.pdf*), p.63.

[72] The UK Competition Commission, "Merger References: Competition Commission Guidelines", CC2, June 2003 (*http://www.competition-commission.org.uk/rep_pub/rules_and_guide/pdf/15073compcommguidance2final.pdf*), para.3.43, identifies excessive profits as a positive indicator of the possible presence of coordinated effects. See para.19–005 below for a discussion of the calculation of profitability.

[73] See para.8–021 below.

[74] "20 Years of Merger Guidelines Enforcement at the FTC: An Economic Perspective" (available at *www.usdoj.gov/atr/hmerger/11255.htm*).

8–013 (ii) Past evidence of suppliers' ability to increase prices In *Nestlé | Perrier*[75] the Commission found that there was a low cross-price elasticity of demand in the French mineral water market between national still mineral waters and local waters, which facilitated price increases, and the production cost-price margin was very high, indicating that prices were probably already at a supra-competitive level.[76]

8–014 (iii) Past evidence of retaliation In *Sony | BMG*[77] the Commission examined whether there was evidence of retaliation, in particular through a temporary return to competitive behaviour or the exclusion of the deviator from compilation joint ventures and agreements.

8–015 (iv) Other evidence Coordination on market sharing may be evidenced by stability of market shares in the face of changes in relative prices or qualities.

Coordination on customer allocation or bidding behaviour may partly be evidenced by low customer churn and/or bidding patterns which are not reasonably explicable other than by the existence of coordination on customer allocation.[78]

8.6 THE MEMBERS OF THE CANDIDATE OLIGOPOLY

8–016 The Commission has stated:

"Whether a company belongs to the fringe or is part of the oligopoly depends on the specific market circumstances. This assessment has to be based on the particular circumstances of the market in question. Capacity or access to key raw materials may, for example, in some cases be used to determine which companies are part of the oligopoly and which companies are part of the fringe ... However, depending on the circumstances, in some markets even smaller players may be able to compete on an equal footing with the largest suppliers. In such markets such smaller firms would have the possibility to act as 'maverick firms', and would have to be considered as competitors in the same sense as the oligopolists, and not simply as belonging to the fringe. In short, the oligopoly will include all those firms who as a group have the ability to raise prices above the

---

[75] Case IV/M.190 [1992] O.J. L356/1, paras 60 and 61.
[76] Compare the emphasis on excessive *profits* in para.8–012(c) above.
[77] Case COMP/M.3333 O.J. [2005] L62/30 (appeal pending in Case T-464/04 *Impala v Commission*), para.114.
[78] For more general discussion of the use of historic shares and tender patterns as evidence of coordinated effects, see the International Competition Network, "ICN Investigative Techniques Handbook for Merger Review", June 2005 (*www.internationalcompetition network.org/handbook_5-5.pdf*), p.64.

competitive level and who, if left out, would make it impossible for the others to achieve the anti-competitive outcome".[79]

In *UPM-Kymmene / Haindl*[80] the Commission was persuaded to exclude from the candidate oligopoly a company which had expanded its market share significantly over a number of years, on the basis that the Commission doubted whether it would change its strategy following the merger and follow an approach of tacit coordination.

Kühn argues that the candidate oligopoly should comprise firms with similar incentives to collude and its members should therefore have similar asset structures to one another and different asset structures from firms outside the group. He recommends proxying the asset distributions by looking at the firms' market shares and treating firms as sufficiently similar to form part of a candidate oligopoly if their market shares are closely comparable.[81]

The definition of the coordinating group is important in particular because, other things being equal, it is more difficult to sustain coordinated effects as the number of coordinating firms increases; but the larger the competitive fringe, the more likely it is to defeat any attempted coordination. There is no hard-and-fast rule on the proportion of the market that must be supplied by the coordinating firms if coordinated effects are to be identified. Christensen & Rabassa argued[82] that less than complete coordination is sufficient and proposed that the test should be whether the coordination was equivalent in effect to that sustainable by a company holding a position of sole firm dominance (with the consequence that coordination might need to be complete with combined market shares at around 40 per cent but would need to be less extensive at higher levels of combined market share). Subsequently, in *Verizon / MCI*[83] the Commission doubted whether a combined share of less than 50 per cent presented a sufficient level of concentration to result in a duopoly structure prone to coordinated effects. Baxter and Dethmers[84] observed that "if the combined market position of fringe rivals is greater than 20 per cent and if such rivals are not subject to

---

[79] Commission paper tabled at OECD, "Oligopoly", Best Practice Roundtable, October 1999, DAFFE/CLP(99)25 (*www.oecd.org*), p.213, at pp.216 to 217.
[80] Case COMP/M.2498 [2002] O.J. L233/38, para.141 (dealing also with the position of a second candidate oligopolist).
[81] Kühn, "Closing Pandora's Box? Joint Dominance After the Airtours Judgment", published as Ch.3 of *The Pros and Cons of Merger Control* by the Swedish Competition Authority in 2002 (and available at *http://www.kkv.se/bestall/pdf/skrift_proscons.pdf*), p.56.
[82] "The Airtours decision: Is there a new Commission approach to collective dominance?" [2001] E.C.L.R. 227, p.228. The authors noted that, at the time they wrote, there were no European Commission decisions identifying the extent to which coordination must occur before a finding of collective dominance may be made.
[83] Case COMP/M.3752, paras 100 and 101.
[84] "Collective Dominance Under EC Merger Control—After Airtours and the Introduction of Unilateral Effects is there Still a Future for Collective Dominance" [2006] E.C.L.R. 148, at p.156.

any significant barriers to expansion, the Commission is unlikely to dismiss the existence of a competitive fringe".

8.7 REACHING TERMS OF COORDINATION

(a) Introduction

8–017 If there is no reference point around which producers can make their business decisions, then there is no scope for tacit coordination, since no supplier can have any assurance that the variable on which it is focusing is the same as the one being focused on by its competitors.[85] The Notice on Horizontal Mergers describes the position in the following terms:

> "Coordination is more likely to emerge if competitors can easily arrive at a common perception as to how the coordination should work. Coordinating firms should have similar views regarding which actions would be considered to be in accordance with the aligned behaviour and which would not".[86]

(b) Terms of coordination will only emerge if they are profitable

8–018 A tacitly coordinated outcome will often enhance the profits of the participants. For example, tacit coordination on price will increase profits, provided that the gains in terms of increased revenues on units which are sold (and any savings in costs associated with a reduction in output) are more than offset by the loss in revenue arising from the loss of some sales following the price increase. The question of whether a price increase will be profitable therefore depends in particular on the elasticity of demand at the prevailing price and suppliers' cost functions.

However, terms of coordination will not arise if they are not profitable for *each* of the participants. For example, in *Mitsui / CVRD / Caemi*[87] the Commission found that there was no incentive for suppliers to split the market geographically (*chacun chez soi*) because growth was expected to differ by region. Similarly, in *Verizon / MCI*[88] the Commission rejected coordinated effects concerns because the parties would not have an incentive to pursue a strategy that was not expected to lead to a balanced increase in profits for each of the participants.

---

[85] The difficulties of identifying terms of coordination were first emphasised by George Stigler, "A Theory of Oligopoly" (1964) 44 Journal of Political Economy.
[86] Para.44.
[87] Case COMP/M.2420 [2004] O.J. L92/50, para.236.
[88] Case COMP/M.3752, paras 104 and 105.

In assessing a supplier's incentive to engage in tacit coordination,[89] it may be instructive to analyse the critical loss, i.e. the proportion of sales which, if lost following a price increase, would render the price increase unprofitable. If marginal costs are very low (e.g. in a network where adding a subscriber has virtually nil cost), then a price increase of 5 per cent might be unprofitable if sales declined by, say, 5.5 per cent. By contrast, where marginal costs are high, a price increase of 5 per cent might be unprofitable only if sales were to decline by, say, 15 per cent. The analysis may be important because the lower the figure the more cautious a supplier is likely to be about raising price.

(c) Type of product

The ready comparability of products[90] assists the formulation and applica- **8–019** tion[91] of a tacitly coordinated arrangement because competition in such circumstances tends to focus on price.[92] Customer surveys may be relevant in determining whether a product is *homogeneous*,[93] i.e. whether customers base their purchasing decisions on a range of factors or focus exclusively on price. More generally, if value and volume data is available by customer or by transaction, then the net price per unit can be compared (controlling for observable differences between customers, e.g. location and order size) to assess the extent to which prices vary between customers and/or suppliers; if

---

[89] Case COMP/M.2389 *Shell / DEA* [2003] O.J. L15/35, paras 105 to 111.

[90] The extent of product homogeneity is also relevant in analysing whether suppliers have an incentive to cheat: a supplier which prices below its rivals would expect to win a greater share if the products are homogeneous; but, equally, any punishment through retaliatory price reductions is likely to be more effective in cases of homogeneous products (see s.8.9 below). Martin, *Advanced Industrial Economics* (2nd edn, Blackwell, 2002), comments, at p.313: "Product differentiation reduces the incremental profit to be gained by departing from a joint-profit maximizing configuration because product differentiation insulates rivals' markets and reduces the extent to which a single firm can lure rivals' customers into its own market".

[91] See Scherer & Ross, *Industrial Market Structure and Economic Performance* (3rd edn, Houghton Mifflin Co, 1990), pp.279 and 282.

[92] See the Notice on Horizontal Mergers, para.45 and Ivaldi *et al*, "The Economics of Tacit Collusion", Report for DG Competition, March 2003 (available via *http://europa.eu.int/comm/competition/mergers/review/the_economics_of_tacit_collusion_en.pdf*), pp.45 to 47. See also Case IV/M.1016 *Price Waterhouse / Coopers & Lybrand* [1999] O.J. L50/27, para.100; Case IV/M.1383 *Exxon / Mobil*, [2004] O.J. L103/1, para.467; Case COMP/M.2389 *Shell / DEA*, [2003] O.J. L15/35; and Case COMP/M.2499 *Norske Skogg / Parenco / Walsum* [2002] O.J. L233/38, para.79. In Case COMP/M.1673 *VEBA / VIAG* [2001] O.J. L188/1, the product, electricity, was homogeneous, but the Commission contemplated the possibility of the merged group and RWE continuing to share customers geographically using the former geographical monopolies as reference points; para.80. For the possibility of coordinated *price discrimination*, see Areeda, Hovenkamp & Solow, *Antitrust Law* (2nd edn, Aspen Law & Business, 1998), Vol.IV, para.927e.

[93] See para.6–023 above for discussion of the distinction between homogeneous and differentiated products. Issues of market definition may be crucial in determining product homogeneity as the wider the product market, in general, the lower the degree of product homogeneity.

the variation is significant, then it will be more difficult to reach terms of coordination.[94]

Tacit coordination may nevertheless occur in markets for differentiated goods.[95] First, tacit coordination on price may still arise, although it is less likely[96] because competition in such cases occurs across more parameters than price. Secondly, the oligopolists may adopt facilitating practices as described in s.(d) below. Thirdly, tacit coordination may occur on other variables, such as customer allocation[97] or market share. For example, in *Airtours plc v Commission*[98] the Court of First Instance emphasised that "for the purposes of determining whether there is a collective dominant position, the stability of historic market shares is a factor conducive to the development of tacit collusion, inasmuch as it facilitates division of the market instead of fierce competition, each operator referring to its historic market share in order to fix its production in proportion thereto". Similarly, in *BP / E.ON*[99] the Commission found that a possible reference point was the allocation of customers on the basis of established supply relationships and the geographic proximity of the customer to the producer. However, coordination by way of market division[1] is easier if customers have simple characteristics, enabling the coordinating firms readily to allocate customers between them, e.g. if it is easy to identify each customer's supplier and the

---

[94] See Scheffman & Coleman, "Quantitative Analyses of Potential Competitive Effects From a Merger" (*http://www.usdoj.gov/atr/public/workshops/docs/202661.htm*).

[95] Case IV/M.190 *Nestlé / Perrier* [1992] O.J. L356/1, para.128.

[96] In Case COMP/M.3216 *Oracle / PeopleSoft* [2005] O.J. L218/6, para.213, the Commission stated: "In ... a market in which the transparency is reduced, in particular, by the very heterogeneous products, a coordination of the competitive behaviour of vendors would be difficult to achieve. Nevertheless, the Commission does not exclude that coordination could be conceivable in such a market if there were only two players and no outsiders could destablize such a duopoly". See also Case IV/M.206 *Rhône-Poulenc / SNIA*, para.24.

[97] See the Notice on Horizontal Mergers, para.46 (noting that market division is easier if customers have characteristics—such as geography, customer type or historic trading relationship—which allow the coordinating firms readily to allocate them); the Commission paper tabled at OECD, "Oligopoly", Best Practice Roundtable, October 1999, DAFFE/CLP(99)25 (*www.oecd.org*) p.213, at pp.217 and 218; and Europe Economics, "Study on Assessment Criteria for Distinguishing between Competitive and Dominant Oligopolies in Merger Control", Final Report for the European Commission, May 2001, p.32. Scheffman & Coleman, "Quantitative Analyses of Potential Competitive Effects From a Merger" (*http://www. usdoj.gov/atr/public/workshops/docs/202661.htm*) note that, in assessing whether there has been, or is likely to be, coordinated effects on customer allocation, it is important to identify the proportion of sales which shifts between suppliers each year.

[98] Case T-342/99 [2002] E.C.R. II-2585, para.111. In that case, the Court of First Instance found that the Commission had been wrong to examine the stability of market shares excluding growth by acquisition because the Commission had, in other parts of its decision, recognised that the size of the undertakings and their degree of vertical integration exercised a significant influence on the nature of competition in the market, with the consequence that acquisitions "may be taken to be indicative of strong competition between those operators, which make further acquisitions to avoid being outdistanced by their main competitors in key areas in order to take full advantage of economies of scale"; para.113.

[99] Case COMP/M.2533 [2002] O.J. L276/31, para.95.

[1] Coordination on *procurement* markets may involve the allocation of input markets to different suppliers, so that each supplier is able to exercise buyer power without facing significant competition; see Peter Carstensen, "Buyer Power and Merger Analysis—The Need for Different Metrics" (*www.ftc.gov/bc/mergerenforce/presentations/040217carstensen.pdf*).

coordination device is the allocation of existing customers to their incumbent supplier.[2]

The Commission's approach is exemplified by the following cases.[3]   **8–020**

(a) In *Exxon / Mobil*[4] the Commission found that petrol was a homogeneous good: "It is probably one of the few commodities where customers (motorists) are unable to point to any difference between two different brands of motor fuel, in terms of characteristics and performance". The parties' argument that their products were differentiated as customers selected their supplier on the basis of their total offering including, e.g. the range of products in the shop or the availability of a car wash, was rejected in the light of surveys showing that purchases of fuel were determined by location and price.

(b) However, in *BP Amoco / Castrol*[5] international marine lubricants contracts were found to be *heterogeneous* because they involved a bundle of products (lubricants of different grades), volumes, services (such as engine performance monitoring) and locations (since marine lubricants may need to be collected at any port globally).

(c) In *Price Waterhouse / Coopers & Lybrand*[6] the Commission found that audit services were relatively homogeneous as any audit involved elements specified by national regulations and institutional self-regulation and the "Commission's investigation has revealed that the

---

[2] See the Notice on Horizontal Mergers, para.46.
[3] See also Case IV/M.190 *Nestlé / Perrier* [1992] O.J. L356/1 (mineral waters); Case IV/M.1432 *Agfa-Gevaert / Sterling* (X-ray films, para.32); Case COMP/M.1524 *Airtours / First Choice* [2000] O.J. L93/1 (short-haul package holidays) (annulled on appeal in Case T-342/99 *Airtours plc v Commission* [2002] E.C.R. II-2585); Case COMP/M.1663 *Alcan / Alusuisse* [2002] O.J. L90/1 (lithographic sheet); and Case COMP/M.1673 *VEBA / VIAG* [2001] O.J. L188/1 (electricity). In Case IV/M.619 *Gencor / Lonrho* [1997] O.J. L11/30 (decision upheld on appeal in Case T-102/96 *Gencor v Commission* [1999] E.C.R. II-753), the transaction involved a commodity sold in a global market to standardised specifications with the result that there was a single reference point, namely the global price; the Commission prohibited the transaction on the grounds of coordinated effects. Other commodities cases include Case IV/M.308 *Kali und Salz / MdK / Treuhand* [1994] O.J. L186/38, para.57 and Case IV/M.1517 *Rhodia / Donau Chemie / Albright & Wilson*, para.52. Götz Drauz, "Recent Developments in the Assessment of Dominance", printed in *EC Merger Control: Ten Years On* (International Bar Association, 2000), p.109, at p.111, stated: "In reality, very few products are completely homogeneous. Therefore, the question that has to be posed is whether or not the nature and the pricing of the products are differentiated. Take, for example, markets like mandatory accounting services in Price Waterhouse or short haul holiday packages in Airtours. In both cases, the markets were characterised by a stagnant demand growth and a very low level of innovation. In the eyes of customers, the products offered by different firms can look surprisingly similar (think of a 4-star hotel, at the seaside, with golf facilities, etc). Or think, for instance, of bidding markets. Certain goods or services offered by different suppliers may appear to be highly differentiated. But in the course of the bidding process, they will become homogeneous since the tender will contain concrete product specifications".
[4] Case IV/M.1383 [2004] O.J. L103/1, paras 467 to 472.
[5] Case COMP/M.1891, para.36(a). See also Case COMP/M.1597 *Castrol / Carless* (virgin / reclaimed oils; para.33).
[6] Case IV/M.1016 [1999] O.J. L/50, p.27, para.100.

vast majority of clients consider all members of the Big Six to be interchangeable".

(d) In *Sony / BMG*[7] the parties argued that recorded music was heterogeneous because each music release was unique. The Commission accepted that there was an element of heterogeneity in the market (because the prices charged varied depending on the content of the recording) but emphasised that the format was homogeneous (with CD albums predominating) and the way that albums were priced and marketed on the wholesale level was quite standardised.

(d) Facilitating practices

8–021 Product heterogeneity can be overcome by devices which facilitate coordination.[8] The following techniques are commonly used:[9]

(a) *Price leadership*—where industry practice is to follow price changes by the price leader, coordinated effects may be facilitated. In *Exxon / Mobil*[10] price leadership by suppliers of the "A-brands" was taken into account in finding that a merger would result in the creation of a dominant position held jointly by the suppliers of the A-brands. In examining whether price leadership is present, it is relevant to consider in particular whether price increases and decreases are announced publicly (or in a similar form, e.g. through the use of headline price increase letters sent to all customers), which supplier initiates price changes, whether price changes are followed, and the relationship between actual prices and announced prices.[11]

---

[7] Case COMP/M.3333 [2005] O.J. L62/30 (appeal pending in Case T-464/04 *Impala v Commission*), para.110.

[8] See Scherer & Ross, *Industrial Market Structure and Economic Performance* (3rd edn, Houghton Mifflin Co, 1990), p.282.

[9] See the Notice on Horizontal Mergers, para.47. See also OECD, "Oligopoly", Best Practice Roundtable, October 1999, DAFFE/CLP(99)25 (*www.oecd.org*), pp.27 to 29. The role of facilitating practices is also recognised in the US Horizontal Merger Guidelines, 1992 (amended in 1997) (*www.usdoj.gov/atr/public/guidelines/hmg.htm*), s.2.11.

[10] Case IV/M.1383 [2004] O.J. L103/1, paras 592 and 610 to 612. See also Besanko, Dranove & Shanley, *Economics of Strategy* (2nd edn, John Wiley & Sons Inc, 2000), at p.314. (Price leadership may also form part of a non-coordinated effects analysis: see, e.g. Case IV/M.582 *Orkla / Volvo* [1996] O.J. L66/17 (a company's position as price leader would be exacerbated by the merger; paras 100 and 101); Case COMP/M.1628 *TotalFina / Elf* [2001] O.J. L143/1 (the merged group's competitors would not be able significantly to increase sales of LPG and would therefore have an incentive to follow the merged group's price; finding of sole firm dominance; paras 300, 301 and 343); Case COMP/M.1672 *Volvo / Scania* [2001] O.J. L143/74, para.288; Case COMP/M.1806 *Astra Zeneca / Novartis* [2004] O.J. L110/1, para.223; Case COMP/M.2187 *CVC / Lenzing* [2004] O.J. L82/20, para.173; and Case COMP/M.2420 *Mitsui / CVRD / Caemi* [2004] O.J. L92/50, para.207.)

[11] See Scheffman & Coleman, "Quantitative Analyses of Potential Competitive Effects From a Merger" (*www.usdoj.gov/atr/public/workshops/docs/202661.htm*).

(b) Use of *focal point pricing*[12]—including: *price lining*, which is common in retailing (e.g. pricing at £8.99, £9.99 and £10.99); *round number discounts*, when prices are invariably quoted as a round number (e.g. 5 per cent or 10 per cent) off the list price; and *rule-of-thumb pricing*, when prices are calculated on a standard basis (e.g. cost-plus pricing or with a view to securing a particular profit margin on the transaction). In *multi-product formula pricing*, the price of one product is used as the basis for calculating others. In *Exxon / Mobil*[13] the Luxembourg government set a *maximum* price per grade of motor fuels. The Commission found that the seven main motor fuel retailers systematically adapted their prices to the maximum price and described the maximum price as functioning "like a cartel benchmark". The existence of the focal point provided by the government had the consequence that the merger would have created or strengthened a dominant position held by *seven* suppliers.

(c) The use of *headline price increases* (when prices are increased by the same percentage for all customers irrespective of their order size or mix) or *list prices* may facilitate coordination, although whether they do so will depend on whether changes in prices are incorporated consistently across customer groups.[14]

(d) Consistent use of *delivered pricing*—under which the price is quoted inclusive of freight so that the producer absorbs the transport cost, which eliminates uncertainty about how prices are calculated and provides a focal point for tacit collusion.[15]

(e) Use of *uniform* free-on-board pricing—which severely restricts suppliers' ability to price competitively (because they cannot cut prices to certain customers without factoring in the loss of profits from the price reduction when applied to all other customers). Thisse & Vives have therefore argued that if such pricing is observed in practice it may be because it serves as a coordinating device.[16]

---

[12] A focal point is an outcome which stands out as self-evident from a variety of possible outcomes.

[13] Case IV/M.1383 [2004] O.J. L103/1, paras 635, 640 and 644.

[14] See Scheffman & Coleman, "Quantitative Analyses of Potential Competitive Effects From a Merger" (*http://www.usdoj.gov/atr/public/workshops/docs/202661.htm*). Compare the UK Competition Commission report on *DS Smith plc / Linpac Containers Ltd* (*http://www. competition-commission.org.uk/rep_pub/reports/2004/fulltext/492.pdf*), 2004, para.5.59, discussing the use of headline price increase letters.

[15] *Basis point pricing* is a type of delivered pricing system which arises when prices are quoted subject to the addition of freight at market rates from a specified location (e.g. ex-Birmingham) even if the seller produces elsewhere (e.g. London). See Areeda, Hovenkamp & Solow, *Antitrust Law* (2nd edn, Aspen Law & Business, 1998), Vol.IV, para.944e2 and Carlton & Perloff, *Modern Industrial Organization* (4th edn, Addison-Wesley, 2005), p.381.

[16] Thisse & Vives, "Spatial Pricing Schemes" (1988) 78 *American Economic Review* 122. See also Besanko, Dranove & Shanley, *Economics of Strategy* (2nd edn, John Wiley & Sons Inc, 2000), pp.315 to 317.

(f) Standardisation of product features—which reduces the extent of product heterogeneity and increases the chances of coordinated effects.

(g) Formation of *strategic groups* or *clusters* following similar strategies—when producers differ in a substantial number of areas (e.g. building a brand reputation through advertising or offering full after-sales support). This may facilitate coordinated effects amongst those producers forming part of a particular strategic group or cluster.[17]

(e) Similarity in costs structures

8–022 If parties have similar costs structures,[18] they have similar pricing and output incentives, which increases the chances of their reaching terms of coordination.[19] By contrast, if suppliers have different cost structures, they have different incentives, with a low cost supplier generally preferring a lower price and higher output than other suppliers.[20] Suppliers' cost structures have been described as the "key component"[21] in assessing asym-

---

[17] Scherer & Ross, *Industrial Market Structure and Economic Performance* (3rd edn, Houghton Mifflin Co, 1990), pp.284 and 285.

[18] Notice on Horizontal Mergers, para.48. The Commission also considers whether the parties have similar portfolios of customers (Case COMP/M.1741 *MCI WorldCom / Sprint* [2003] O.J. L300/1, para.265) and/or similar ranges and qualities of service and product portfolios (Case COMP/M.1741 *MCI WorldCom / Sprint* [2003] O.J. L300/1, para.267 and Case COMP/ M.2268 *Pernod Ricard / Diageo / Seagram Spirits*, para.22). Contrast Case COMP/M.2348 *Outokumpu / Norzink*, para.22.

[19] See the Notice on Horizontal Mergers, para. 48; Ivaldi *et al*, "The Economics of Tacit Collusion", Report for DG Competition, March 2003 (available via *http://europa.eu.int/ comm/competition/mergers/review/the_economics_of_tacit_collusion_en.pdf*), pp.35 to 40; and Case IV/M.1383 *Exxon / Mobil* [2004] O.J. L103/1, para.476. See also Case IV/M.190 *Nestlé / Perrier* [1992] O.J. L356/1, para.125; Case COMP/M.1571 *New Holland / Case* para.45; Case COMP/M.1663 *Alcan / Alusuisse* [2002] O.J. L90/1, para.94; and Scherer & Ross, *Industrial Market Structure and Economic Performance* (3rd edn, Houghton Mifflin Co, 1990), pp.238 and 239.

[20] See Case COMP/M.2348 *Outokumpu / Norzink*, para.21; Case COMP/M.2965 *Staples / Guilbert* (ruling out coordinated effects, at para.20, on the grounds that the parties in question would have different cost structures and different incentives); and Case COMP/M.3625 *Blackstone / Acetex* [2005] O.J. L312/60, paras 99, 129 and 130 (rivals used different technologies and had different plant sizes, creating different costs structures and incentives; further, there were different levels of vertical integration, as evidenced by comparing the rivals' respective capacities and merchant market shares, which also created different incentives). See also Europe Economics, "Study on Assessment Criteria for Distinguishing between Competitive and Dominant Oligopolies in Merger Control", Final Report for the European Commission, May 2001, p.31.

[21] Kantzenbach, Kottmann & Krüger, "New Industrial Economics and Experiences From European Merger Control—New Lessons About Collective Dominance", March 1995 (prepared on behalf of the Commission but not necessarily representing the Commission's official position), p.61.

metry[22] of interests because any supplier enjoying a persistent cost advantage is likely to have an incentive to engage in aggressive competitive behaviour.

It follows that, other things being equal, a merger which *increases the costs asymmetry*[23] is likely to *reduce* the scope for tacit coordination.[24]

However, as well as examining the scope for tacit coordination on price, which is likely to be defeated by asymmetric cost structures, it is important to consider the scope for tacit coordination on other variables, such as market sharing and, separately, the likelihood of the development of price leadership with the low cost supplier assuming the role of leader.[25]

The depth of the Commission's analysis of the cost structures of candidate oligopolists has varied between cases.[26]   **8–023**

(a) In *Airtours / First Choice*[27] the Commission found that the operators had similar cost structures as they flew to the same destinations, used largely the same hotels and all needed a high load factor.

(b) In *UPM-Kymmene / Haindl*[28] the Commission analysed in great detail the cost structures, including marginal costs,[29] of the main suppliers, using data on costs per machine obtained from questionnaires and industry data.[30]

(c) In *BP / E.ON*[31] the Commission relied on the findings of "industry consultants" about the maximum difference in production costs between the most and least economic plants in support of a finding that there was a strong similarity in costs between the candidate duopolists.

---

[22] See Case IV/M.190 *Nestlé / Perrier* [1992] O.J. L356/1 (the Commission noted, at para.125, that "significant differences in costs can reasonably be considered an element that would hinder the implementation of tacit parallel behaviour"); Case IV/M.315 *Mannesmann / Vallourec / Ilva* [1994] O.J. L102/15, para.68; and Case COMP/M.2201 *MAN / Auwärter* [2002] O.J. L116/35. See also Besanko, Dranove & Shanley, *Economics of Strategy* (2nd edn, John Wiley & Sons Inc, 2000), pp.307 to 312.

[23] In particular, the costs asymmetry may be increased by efficiencies created by the merger.

[24] See also Scherer & Ross, *Industrial Market Structure and Economic Performance* (3rd edn, Houghton Mifflin Co, 1990), p.285.

[25] Europe Economics, "Study on Assessment Criteria for Distinguishing between Competitive and Dominant Oligopolies in Merger Control", Final Report for the European Commission, May 2001, pp.27 and 31.

[26] See also Case IV/M.190 *Nestlé / Perrier* [1992] O.J. L356/1 and Case IV/M.358 *Pilkington-Techint / SIV* [1994] O.J. L158/24, para.41.

[27] Case IV/M.1524 [2000] O.J. L93/1, paras 99 and 100. The Court of First Instance annulled the Commission's decision because of errors by the Commission in assessing the evidence: see Case T-342/99 *Airtours plc v Commission* [2002] E.C.R. II-2585.

[28] Case COMP/M.2498 [2002] O.J. L233/38.

[29] Para.89 (although the Commission was able to assume that average variable costs were a good proxy for marginal costs given that the industry did not link the operating rate of a machine to its individual costs; para.90). Raw materials and energy were taken as variable and labour as fixed costs in the Commission's analysis; para.90 and n.36.

[30] Paras 89 to 94 and n.34. The Commission used external economists for these purposes.

[31] Case COMP/M.2533 [2002] O.J. L276/31, para.73.

(f) Complexity of the terms of coordination

8–024 If the terms of coordination are simple (e.g. the price of a homogeneous product)[32] then coordination is more likely. By contrast, if the terms are complex, it is less likely that a coordinated outcome will be achievable without express collusion. For example, tacit coordination on investment in expensive new capacity may be complicated by a need to determine the order in which suppliers should invest in new capacity and the gaps between each addition.[33] The 2002 draft Commission Notice on Horizontal Mergers provided that, for these purposes, the "terms of coordination" includes both the type of coordination and the implicit rules governing the coordination[34] but this passage was *not* included in the final version of the Notice.

(g) Transparency of the reference point

8–025 Tacit coordination is feasible only when there is sufficient *transparency*[35] for all participants to be able to identify the relevant reference point without the need for express collusion. This was recognised in *Exxon / Mobil*[36] when the Commission stated that: "Market transparency is ... one of the basic conditions characterising markets conducive to oligopoly. [Such] transparency allows the players on the market to converge towards a given price with no need of explicit coordination. Accordingly, price transparency can be expected to lead to price parallelism between the undertakings present on the market".[37] Similarly, in *Airtours plc v*

---

[32] In Case COMP/M.1741 *MCI WorldCom / Sprint* [2003] O.J. L300/1 the Commission indicated, at para.263, that in a tender market with high barriers to entry: "if there was parallel behaviour, this would centre around the bidding process and the ability to offer competitive services to the companies requiring those services. In such a case, collusion will not take place on prices but on who wins the bid (and who has won what bids)".

[33] The example is based on COMP/M.2498 *UPM-Kymmene / Haindl* [2002] O.J. L233/38.

[34] Para.43. The "terms" therefore include determining the actions which would be regarded as "cheating" and the "punishment" to be administered in such cases by the other members of the oligopoly. See also para.49.

[35] See Case IV/M.165 *Alcatel / AEG*, para.21; Case IV/M.704 *Unilever / Diversey*, para.22; Case IV/M.1016 *Price Waterhouse / Coopers & Lybrand* [1999] O.J. L50/27 para.100; Case IV/M.1245 *Valeo / ITT Industries*, para.54; Case IV/M.1313 *Danish Crown / Vestjyske Slagterier* [2000] O.J. L20/1, para.176; Case COMP/M.1882 *Pirelli / BICC* [2003] O.J. L70/35, para.91; Case COMP/M.1891 BP *Amoco / Castrol*, para.36; Case COMP/M.2097 *SCA / Metsä Tissue*, para.149; Case COMP/M.2389 *Shell / DEA* [2003] O.J. L15/35, paras 112 to 115; Case COMP/M.2972 *DSM / Roche Vitamins* [2004] O.J. L82/73 (the Commission found that monitoring was extremely difficult because prices were negotiated privately and relatively infrequently and information provided by customers was imprecise and not always reliable; para.76); and Case COMP/M.3060 *UCB / Solutia* (the Commission found that there was not transparency because prices and quantities were not observable and prices were very variable, with frequent volume and other discounts; para.46).

[36] Case IV/M.1383 [2004] O.J. L103/1, para.474.

[37] The Commission also observed, at para.474 (in relation to the importance of transparency to the deterrent mechanism), that "the transparency of the market is an essential condition for an oligopoly to function effectively". The Commission has also stated that market transparency "is normally deemed to be a necessary condition for oligopolistic dominance, since the members of the oligopoly will not otherwise be able to detect and punish 'unfair' competitive behaviour": Commission paper tabled at OECD, "Oligopoly", Best Practice Roundtable, October 1999, DAFFE/CLP(99)25 (*www.oecd.org*), p.213, at p.217.

Commission[38] the Court of First Instance stressed that "the fact that a market is sufficiently transparent to enable each member of the oligopoly to be aware of the conduct of the others is conducive to the creation of a collective dominant position".[39]

It is not necessary for the market to be transparent in all respects. Rather, it is sufficient if the market is transparent with respect to key parameters, typically, but not invariably, price[40] and output.[41] More particularly, for tacit coordination to occur, the market must be transparent in respect of the criterion—whether price,[42] output, customer allocation, down-time, etc.—which is the reference point. This means that if the reference point is, for example, customer allocation, then it is irrelevant that the market is not transparent on other variables (e.g. price and output).[43]

In principle, tacit coordination remains possible even if the market is not transparent on the variable which forms the reference point, *provided* that

---

[38] Case T-342/99 [2002] E.C.R. II-2585.

[39] Para.156. The Court of First Instance (in the context of an allegation of coordinated effects in relation to capacity) noted, at para.159: "it is appropriate to ascertain, first, whether each of the large tour operators will be able, when making its crucial capacity decisions during the planning period, to find out with any degree of certainty what those of its main competitors are. Only if there is sufficient transparency will an operator be able to estimate the total capacity decided upon by the other members of the alleged oligopoly and then be in a position to be sure that by planning its capacity in a given way it is adopting the same policy as them and hence will have an incentive to do so". Dixit & Nalebuff, *Thinking Strategically* (W W Norton & Co, 1991), comment, at p.97, that "collusion focuses on the more transparent dimensions of choice, and competition shifts to the less observable ones: we call this the Law of Increasing Opaqueness".

[40] In Case IV/M.315 *Mannesmann / Vallourec / Ilva* [1994] O.J. L102/15, the Commission noted, at para.94, that: "pricing behaviour, as well as the fact that the main suppliers have commercial contacts on a regular basis with the same customers, further strengthens this transparency and enables each competitor to have a good knowledge of the other competitors' prices. The degree of transparency would be sufficient for each of the two principal producers to find out rapidly if the other one was not following the tacitly agreed pricing behaviour by decreasing prices so as to put greater volumes onto the market". By contrast, in Case IV/ M.337 *Knorr-Bremse / Allied Signal* the Commission stressed, at para.45, that "the lack of transparency in prices resulting from the fact that suppliers negotiate individually with vehicle manufacturers, together with the importance of non-price criteria (such as quality, delivery and technical competence), means that overall coordinated behaviour would be extremely difficult".

[41] Götz Drauz, "Recent Developments in the Assessment of Dominance", printed in *EC Merger Control: Ten Years On* (International Bar Association, 2000), p.109, at p.111. The US Horizontal Merger Guidelines, 1992 (amended in 1997) (*www.usdoj.gov/atr/public/guidelines/ hmg.htm*) provide, at s.2.11: "Terms of coordination need not perfectly achieve the monopoly outcome in order to be harmful to consumers. Instead, the terms of coordination may be imperfect and incomplete—inasmuch as they omit some market participants, omit some dimensions of competition, omit some customers, yield elevated prices short of monopoly levels, or lapse into episodic price wars—and still result in significant competitive harm".

[42] Case COMP/M.2499 *Norske Skog / Parenco / Walsum* [2002] O.J. L233/38, paras 86 to 87.

[43] See Case COMP/M.2533 *BP / E.ON* [2002] O.J. L276/31, at para.103: "The Commission's concerns mainly relate to the fear that the two new entities will not actively compete for the other's current customers, which are mainly linked by long term contracts, and therefore engage in a market sharing based on continuity and geographic proximity. For this kind of tacit market sharing, no individually detailed contract data and transparency is necessary". See also Case T-342/99 *Airtours plc v Commission* [2002] E.C.R. II-2585, in which the Court of First Instance emphasised, at para.157, in considering the issue of transparency, that the alleged coordinated effects related to capacity and not price.

the market is transparent on other criteria which form a good proxy for the reference point; e.g. tacit coordination on price may be possible if the market is transparent on customer purchases and market shares, so long as these variables form a good substitute for direct information on pricing.[44]

8–026 Transparency[45] may arise most obviously if producers provide advance notice of price changes[46] but equally if, for example in bidding markets, tenders[47] are frequent and customers commonly report other bids to rivals as part of the negotiating process[48] or through openness[49] in a public procurement process.[50] It may also arise[51] through public speeches or other "cheap talk",[52] publication of price lists,[53] use of transparent exchanges such as world metal exchanges,[54] industry associations,[55] trade magazines,

---

[44] See by analogy the Notice on Horizontal Mergers, para.50. See also Europe Economics, "Study on Assessment Criteria for Distinguishing between Competitive and Dominant Oligopolies in Merger Control", Final Report for the European Commission, May 2001, at p.33.

[45] See also the Notice on Horizontal Mergers, para.47. See generally OECD, "Oligopoly", Best Practice Roundtable, October 1999, DAFFE/ CLP(99)25 (*www.oecd.org*), pp.27 to 29.

[46] See Kwoka & White eds., *The Antitrust Revolution* (4th edn, Oxford UP, 2004), case 9 (see also case 7 of the 3rd edn, Oxford UP, 1999).

[47] In Case IV/M.1539 *CVC / Danone / Gerresheimer* the Commission found that the market was not transparent although competitive tendering occurred; para.33. See also Case COMP/ M.1597 *Castrol / Carless / JV*, para.42.

[48] See Case IV/M.190 *Nestlé / Perrier* [1992] O.J. L356/1 and Case COMP/M.1939 *Rexam / American National Can*, para.24. In *Rexam* the Commission also relied on the fact that the parties had compiled a bidding study as an indicator that the market was transparent; para.24, n.10. In other cases, the Commission has found that the use of bidding processes reduced transparency: Case IV/M.1245 *Valeo / ITT Industries*, para.54; Case IV/M.1432 *Agfa-Gevaert / Sterling*, para.26; and Case COMP/M.1597 *Castrol / Carless*, para.32. For discussion of the circumstances in which coordinated effects may occur in tender markets, see Case COMP/ M.2201 *MAN / Auwärter* [2002] O.J. L116/35, para.35. On the facts of that case, there was no specific criterion on the basis of which the two market leaders might tacitly coordinate their competitive behaviour; see paras 37 to 49.

[49] Ivaldi *et al*, "The Economics of Tacit Collusion", Report for DG Competition, March 2003 (available via *http://europa.eu.int/comm/competition/mergers/review/the_economics_of_tacit_collusion_en.pdf*) note, at p.62, that sealed bid auctions generate less information than public descending procurement auctions.

[50] Case IV/M.580 *ABB / Daimler Benz* [1997] O.J. L11/1, para.89.

[51] See the Notice on Horizontal Mergers, para.51.

[52] See the Notice on Horizontal Mergers, para.51 (and the 2002 draft Commission Notice on Horizontal Mergers, para.52 for more detailed discussion about the exchange of information through the press). In Case COMP/M.2498 *UPM-Kymmene / Haindl* [2002] O.J. L233/38, the Commission referred to statements by executives about down-time quoted in an industry journal; para.72.

[53] Travel brochures provide almost complete transparency on price: Case COMP/M.1524 *Airtours / First Choice* [2000] O.J. L93/1 (annulled on appeal in Case T-342/99 *Airtours plc v Commission* [2002] E.C.R. II-2585). See also Case IV/M.315 *Mannesmann / Vallourec / Ilva* [1994] O.J. L102/15, para.83; Case IV/M.1494 *Sair Group / AOM*, para.34; Case COMP/ M.1571 *New Holland / Case*, para.45; and Case COMP/M.3333 *Sony / BMG* [2005] O.J. L62/ 30 (appeal pending in Case T-464/04 *Impala v Commission*), para.76 (list prices of recorded music were transparent as they were published in the majors' catalogues). In Case IV/M.603 *Crown Cork & Seal / Carnaud Metalbox* [1996] O.J. L75/38, the Commission noted that the "food can market is sufficiently transparent to allow anti-competitive parallel behaviour, even in the absence of price lists, since in a concentrated market it is possible to deduce the pricing behaviour of a competitor by analysing the contracts it gains".

[54] Case IV/M.619 *Gencor / Lonrho* [1997] O.J. L11 p.30 (decision upheld on appeal in Case T-102/96 *Gencor v Commission* [1999] E.C.R. II–753).

[55] Case IV/M.1383 *Exxon / Mobil* [2004] O.J. L103/1, para.474.

published statistical information,[56] obligations on publicly quoted companies to announce substantial capacity additions,[57] swap transactions,[58] regulatory intervention,[59] use of contractual terms such as "most favoured customer" or "meeting competition" clauses,[60] if one year's output is directly related to the previous year's or if the price of a single product is used in an industry as a reference in setting the prices of a range of others. Links between the parties may also increase transparency, e.g. making competitors more aware of one another's strategy, cost structure and plans.[61]

It may be possible to test the degree of transparency in the market.[62] For example, transparency on price can be tested if the merging parties recorded estimates of one another's prices to particular customers, by comparing those estimates with the actual prices.[63]

Vertical mergers may increase transparency by enabling companies to monitor market conditions more easily (e.g. if a retailer purchases a wholesaler which also supplies competing retailers).[64] The US Non-Horizontal Merger Guidelines[65] indicate that such effects are unlikely unless the upstream market has an HHI[66] of over 1800 and a large percentage of

---

[56] Case IV/M.1383 *Exxon / Mobil* [2004] O.J. L103/1, para.474. In Case COMP/M.2498 *UPM-Kymmene / Haindl* [2002] O.J. L233/38, the Commission noted that, even though market prices were published, individual transaction prices were not transparent because the final net price was dependent on retroactive price rebates; paras 86 and 87. Similarly, in Case IV/M.358 *Pilkington-Techint / SIV* [1994] O.J. L158/24, the use of substantial and variable discounts substantially reduced transparency.

[57] Case COMP/M.1524 *Airtours / First Choice* [2000] O.J. L93/1 (annulled on appeal in Case T-342/99 *Airtours plc v Commission* [2002] E.C.R. II-2585).

[58] Case COMP/M.3314 *Air Liquide / Messer Targets*, para.94.

[59] As seems to have occurred when the Danish competition authority decided to publish statistics on transaction prices for certain grades of ready mixed concrete: see Europe Economics, "Study on Assessment Criteria for Distinguishing between Competitive and Dominant Oligopolies in Merger Control", Final Report for the European Commission, May 2001, at p.68.

[60] See the discussion in Dixit & Nalebuff, *Thinking Strategically* (W W Norton & Co, 1991), pp.102 to 104 and Nalebuff & Brandenburger, *Co-opetition* (HarperCollinsBusiness, 1997 edn), pp.156 to 171. When collating evidence, contracts should be analysed across customers and suppliers to identify the prevalence of such clauses; see the International Competition Network, "ICN Investigative Techniques Handbook for Merger Review", June 2005 (*www.internationalcompetitionnetwork.org/handbook_5-5.pdf*), p.63.

[61] See the Notice on Horizontal Mergers, para.51. See also Case IV/M.1383 *Exxon / Mobil* [2004] O.J. L103/1, para.480. Equally, individually negotiated contracts can limit transparency (Case IV/M.818 *Cardo / Thyssen*, para.33) as can price variations reflecting individual customer specifications (Case IV/M.1539 *CVC / Danone / Gerresheimer*, para.33).

[62] The Court of First Instance's judgment in Case T-342/99 *Airtours plc v Commission* [2002] E.C.R. II-2585 emphasises that the Commission must investigate the precise nature and quality of the information which is available, criticising, at para.173, the general assertion that information about competitors would be disseminated because tour operators negotiated with the same hotels. In Case COMP/M.2690 *Solvay / Montedison-Ausimont* the Commission used as evidence of transparency the level of detail in the parties' response to a request by the Commission for information about capacity expansions in the market; para.47 and n.10.

[63] See Scheffman & Coleman, "Quantitative Analyses of Potential Competitive Effects From a Merger" (*www.usdoj.gov/atr/public/workshops/docs/202661.htm*).

[64] See Case IV/M.1517 *Rhodia / Donau Chemie / Albright & Wilson*, para.71.

[65] The US Non-Horizontal Merger Guidelines, 1984 (*www.usdoj.gov/atr/public/guidelines/2614.htm*), para.4.221.

[66] See s.4.3 above.

the upstream product would be sold through vertically integrated retail outlets after the merger. Conversely, vertical integration may reduce market transparency because of difficulties in assessing internal transfer prices amongst the vertically integrated players.

(h) Other factors affecting the ability to reach terms of coordination

8–027 **(i) The number of coordinating firms** It is harder[67] to reach terms of coordination[68] between large numbers of suppliers[69] because there is greater scope for disagreement on the tacitly coordinated outcome.[70] The general rule was identified in *Price Waterhouse / Coopers & Lybrand*[71] as follows: "From a general viewpoint, collective dominance involving more than three or four suppliers is unlikely simply because of the complexity of the inter-relationships involved, and the consequent temptation to deviate; such a situation is unstable and untenable in the long term".[72]

Tacit coordination may arise between *some* but not all of the suppliers in the market. For example, tacit coordination may arise between three suppliers

---

[67] In Case IV/M.1016 *Price Waterhouse / Coopers & Lybrand* [1999] O.J. L50/27, the Commission acknowledged, at para.105, that the European Court of Justice had held in Joined Cases C-68/94 and C-30/95 *France v Commission* [1998] E.C.R. I-1375 that a high level of concentration in an oligopolistic market is not in itself determinative of the question of whether coordinated effects are likely to occur. In Case IV/M.779 *Bertelsmann / CLT*, the Commission found that, even though CLT/UFA and Kirch had a combined market share of TV advertising of around 88%, there was effective competition in the market. HHI data was used in Case COMP/M.1524 *Airtours / First Choice* [2000] O.J. L93/1, at para.139 (annulled on appeal in Case T-342/99 *Airtours plc v Commission* [2002] E.C.R. II-2585). Note, however, that HHI data may be misleading: e.g. other things being equal, a merger which results in increased asymmetry in suppliers' costs reduces the likelihood of a tacitly coordinated outcome whilst increasing the HHI. In *Airtours* the Commission also identified, at para.143, the number of competitive relationships and the number of bilateral links in which one of the parties would not participate. See also Case COMP/M.3333 *Sony / BMG* [2005] O.J. L62/3 (appeal pending in Case T-464/04 *Impala v Commission*), para.157, noting that a reduction in the number of suppliers from five to four leads to an increase in transparency as the number of bilateral competitive relationships falls from ten to six (but ruling out coordinated effects on other grounds).

[68] See also para.8–037 below on the difficulties of monitoring coordination between larger numbers of suppliers.

[69] See the Notice on Horizontal Mergers, para.45. See also Areeda, Hovenkamp & Solow, *Antitrust Law* (2nd edn, Aspen Law & Business, 1998), Vol.IV, para.925. Under German merger control (Act Against Restraints of Competition), three or fewer undertakings with a combined market share of at least 50% and five or fewer undertakings with a combined market share of at least two-thirds are *presumed* to jointly hold a dominant position. The merging parties may rebut this presumption. In Case T-374/00 *Verband der freien Rohrwerke and others v Commission* [2003] E.C.R. II-2275, the Court of First Instance confirmed, at para.121, that the mere fact that three undertakings together held a very large share of market was not in itself proof of coordinated effects.

[70] i.e. the probability of divergent preferences increases with the number of suppliers.

[71] Case IV/M.1016 [1999] O.J. L50/27, para.103.

[72] In Case COMP/M.3216 *Oracle / PeopleSoft* [2005] O.J. L218/6, para.209, the Commission stated: "among seven credible bidders a common understanding as regards a softening of price competition and a slow-down of product improvements appears difficult to reach and to sustain".

each holding 30 per cent of the market, notwithstanding that there are 10 other suppliers—the competitive fringe—each holding 1 per cent of the market. For discussion of the proportion of the market that must be supplied by the coordinating firms if coordinated effects are to be identified, see s.8.6 above.

(ii) The benefits of not coordinating If there is a small number of large **8–028** contracts (and particularly if there is little or no transparency),[73] then there is a substantial incentive on each firm to try to win the business represented by each such contract.[74] The incentive to cut prices increases as the size of the contract increases relative to the size of the market. For example, in *Pilkington-Techint / SIV*[75] motor manufacturers tended to single-source their supplies of glass, with the consequence that each order involved a very substantial amount of business for the glass manufacturers, giving them a substantial incentive to seek to win each contract. Similarly, in *SNECMA / TI*[76] customers' preferences for long-term contracts for the supply of aircraft landing gear was an indicator against a finding of coordinated effects.[77] In *Pirelli / BICC*[78] the Commission stated that: "The bidding structure (infrequent, high-value contracts) prevailing in the … market makes conscious parallel behaviour unattractive, because the benefit of winning each contract is likely to outweigh potential future gains from collusion". Finally, in *Exxon / Mobil*[79] the Commission found that hypermarkets had historically acted as aggressive price cutters in the UK fuel retailing market but predicted that they would change strategy to follow the pricing decisions of the oil majors for several reasons, including the hypothesis that experience had taught them that the benefits of not coordinating were limited: the "hypermarkets have learnt that any aggressive pricing will be followed by the majors, even if that entails severe losses in the retail sector. In such a case, there would be no incentive for price reductions, as they would not result in higher market shares but lower profits".

---

[73] See Case IV/M.390 *Akzo / Nobel*, para.18.
[74] See Case COMP/M.2201 *MAN / Auwärter* [2002] O.J. L116/35, para.48: "the smaller the number of invitations to tender and the larger the number of buses asked for at the same time per invitation to tender, the more unlikely it is that either of the two market leaders will be prepared to relinquish the contract in favour of the other". See also Case COMP/M.3512 *VNU / WPP / JV*, para.30.
[75] Case IV/M.358 [1994] O.J. L158/24.
[76] Case IV/M.368.
[77] Contrast Case IV/M.1539 *CVC / Danone / Gerresheimer* in which the short duration of supply contracts was found to facilitate switching between suppliers.
[78] Case COMP/M.1882 [2003] O.J. L70/35, para.82.
[79] Case IV/M.1383 [2004] O.J. L103/1, para.734.

8–029 **(iii) Market growth** Suppliers are arguably[80] less likely to reach terms of coordination when the market in question is growing rapidly[81] as the incentive to win contracts, which may generate large potential profits, is likely to outweigh any gains from coordination. By contrast, stagnant[82] or slow-growing markets are arguably more likely to be subject to tacit coordination as there are reduced incentives to compete.[83] Coordinated effects are arguably[84] less likely in cases of declining markets (if the suppliers have excess capacity and are incentivised to compete on price)[85] and in markets where there is great uncertainty about future trends.[86]

---

[80] Contrast Ivaldi *et al*, "The Economics of Tacit Collusion", Report for DG Competition, March 2003 (available via *http://europa.eu.int/comm/competition/mergers/review/the_economics_of_tacit_collusion_en.pdf*), who state, at pp.26 and 27: "collusion is easier to sustain when short-term gains from deviation are small compared with the cost of future retaliation. This implies that: For a fixed number of market participants, collusion is easier to sustain in growing markets, where today's profits are small compared with tomorrow's costs". At p.28, the authors point out that the assumption that the number of market participants remains fixed may not hold in a growing market. See also Kühn, "Closing Pandora's Box? Joint Dominance After the Airtours Judgment", published as Ch.3 of *The Pros and Cons of Merger Control* by the Swedish Competition Authority in 2002 (available via *www.kkv.se/bestall/pdf/skrift_proscons.pdf*), who argues at p.55 that it is not possible to quantify the impact of demand growth on the likelihood of coordination in any particular case.

[81] See the Notice on Horizontal Mergers, para.45; Case IV/M.1440 *Lucent Technologies / Ascend Communications* (in which the Commission found, at para.18, that the merger was unlikely to result in coordinated effects as the market was technology-driven and rapidly expanding); and Case COMP/M.3333 *Sony / BMG* [2005] O.J. L62/30 (appeal pending in Case T-464/04 *Impala v Commission*) (ruling out coordinated effects concerns in the emerging market for online music; paras 168 and 169). See also Europe Economics, "Study on Assessment Criteria for Distinguishing between Competitive and Dominant Oligopolies in Merger Control", Final Report for the European Commission, May 2001, p.76.

[82] See Case COMP/M.1663 *Alcan / Alusuisse* [2002] O.J. L 90/1, para.96.

[83] There is also little attraction to potential entrants and cheating is easier to detect. See the Commission paper tabled at OECD, "Oligopoly", Best Practice Roundtable, October 1999, DAFFE/CLP(99)25 (*www.oecd.org*), p.213, at p.218. In Case IV/M.165 *Alcatel / AEG* (power cables) and Case IV/M.603 *Crown Cork & Seal / Carnaud Metalbox* [1996] O.J. L75/38 (food cans), the Commission found the markets to be mature. See also Case IV/M.315 *Mannesmann / Vallourec / Ilva* [1994] O.J. L102/15; Case IV/M.422 *Unilever France / Ortiz Miko*, para.51; Case IV/M.619 *Gencor / Lonrho* [1997] O.J. L11/30 (decision upheld on appeal in Case T-102/96 *Gencor v Commission* [1999] E.C.R. II-753); Case IV/M.1313 *Danish Crown / Vestjyske Slagterier* [2000] O.J. L20/1, para.176; Case COMP/M.1524 *Airtours / First Choice* [2000] O.J. L93/1 (annulled on appeal in Case T-342/99 *Airtours plc v Commission* [2002] E.C.R. II-2585); and Case COMP/M.1673 *VEBA / VIAG* [2001] O.J. L188/1 (electricity, para.82).

[84] Contrast Ivaldi *et al*, "The Economics of Tacit Collusion", Report for DG Competition, March 2003 (available via *http://europa.eu.int/comm/competition/mergers/review/the_economics_of_tacit_collusion_en.pdf*), who state, at p.27: "collusion is more difficult to sustain in declining markets, where tomorrow's profits (with our without retaliation) will be small anyway".

[85] Case IV/M.308 *Kali und Salz / MdK / Treuhand* [1994] O.J. L186/38 (where demand for potash declined by 30% between 1988 and 1993) and Case COMP/M.1597 *Castrol / Carless*.

[86] Case IV/M.726 *Bosch / Allied Signal*. Compare Ivaldi *et al*, "The Economics of Tacit Collusion", Report for DG Competition, March 2003 (available via *http://europa.eu.int/comm/competition/mergers/review/the_economics_of_tacit_collusion_en.pdf*), pp.29 to 32, concluding that: "demand fluctuations hinder collusion and more so when fluctuations are deterministic (as in the case of seasonal cycles) rather than random".

(iv) Innovation Markets characterised by substantial product innovation[87] **8–030** are less prone to coordinated effects because there is less scope to reach terms of coordination which the parties are incentivised to adhere to in the long term.[88] Conversely, markets involving mature technology which is unlikely to undergo significant innovation are more likely to be subject to coordinated effects.[89] In *Exxon / Mobil*[90] the Commission stated: "The lack of technological innovation is another feature typical of a market conducive to oligopoly and is directly linked to the homogeneity issue. Without innovation, competitors have no other choice than competing on price. Also, low technological innovation ensures that the nature of competition (and the homogeneity of products) will not substantially change in the near future". It may be possible to measure the extent of innovation by, for example, calculating the proportion of sales which are accounted for by products introduced in the previous, say, three years.[91]

Nevertheless, the presence of product innovation is not decisive and, indeed, coordination may be possible on research and development.[92] The Commission has stated[93]: "It cannot be excluded that oligopolistic dominance can be found in markets with high rates of product and/or process innovation. An indication could be stable market shares in markets with high rates of innovation. However, industries with high rates of process and/

---

[87] See para.6–011 above and Case IV/M.1298 *Kodak / Imation*, para.60; Case COMP/M.1838 *BT / ESAT*, para.14; Case COMP/M.2111 *Alcoa / British Aluminium*, para.14; and Case COMP/M.2537 *Philips / Marconi Medical Systems*.

[88] See the Notice on Horizontal Mergers (para.45); Ivaldi *et al*, "The Economics of Tacit Collusion", Report for DG Competition, March 2003 (available via *http://europa.eu.int/ comm/competition/mergers/review/the_economics_of_tacit_collusion_en.pdf*), pp.32 to 35; and the OFT Economic Discussion Paper, "Innovation and Competition Policy", Charles River Associates, March 2002 (note that the views in the paper do not necessarily reflect those of the OFT), paras 7.13 and 7.14.

[89] See Case IV/M.190 *Nestlé / Perrier* [1992] O.J. L356/1; Case IV/M.308 *Kali und Salz / MdK / Treuhand* [1994] O.J. L186/38; Case IV/M.315 *Mannesmann / Vallourec / Ilva* [1994] O.J. L102/15, paras 78 and 94; Case IV/M.619 *Gencor / Lonrho* [1997] O.J. L11/30 (decision upheld on appeal in Case T-102/96 *Gencor v Commission* [1999] E.C.R. II-753); and Case IV/M.1016 *Price Waterhouse / Coopers & Lybrand* [1999] O.J. L50/27, para.100.

[90] Case IV/M.1383 [2004] O.J. L103/1, para.473.

[91] See Scheffman & Coleman, "Quantitative Analyses of Potential Competitive Effects From a Merger" (*www.usdoj.gov/atr/public/workshops/docs/202661.htm*).

[92] See Europe Economics, "Study on Assessment Criteria for Distinguishing between Competitive and Dominant Oligopolies in Merger Control", Final Report for the European Commission, May 2001, at p.34.

[93] The Commission's position is more cautious than that of Europe Economics in "Study on Assessment Criteria for Distinguishing between Competitive and Dominant Oligopolies in Merger Control", Final Report for the European Commission, May 2001, who state, at p.79: "We believe that in markets subject to rapid and unpredictable technological change it will be difficult to sustain tacit collusion even when concentration is high and there are other facilitating factors such as similar cost structures. It is important that the analysis is a dynamic one. However, it is particularly difficult to predict the pace and impact of technological change and to assess the likelihood that a dramatic change is just around the corner. In this respect, it is understandable that the Commission takes a cautious position when attaching weight to technological change as a factor making coordinated behaviour harder".

or product innovation are normally assumed unlikely to be conducive to oligopolistic dominance".[94]

8–031 **(v) Extent of repeated interaction** The extent to which the market involves repeated interaction affects the ability of suppliers to reach terms of coordination.[95] Europe Economics note that: "By setting choice variables such as price, quantity or advertising levels in subsequent periods, firms can find out what triggers an aggressive reaction by rivals and what is met by cooperation. Using this trial-and-error method, firms can arrive at a collusive equilibrium without any communication".[96]

8–032 **(vi) Similarities in market shares** The Notice on Horizontal Mergers identifies symmetry in market shares as a factor which may increase the ease of reaching terms of coordination.[97] However, this is a much less significant

---

[94] Commission paper tabled at OECD, "Oligopoly", Best Practice Roundtable, October 1999, DAFFE/CLP(99)25 (*www.oecd.org*), p.213, at p.218. For a discussion of differing rates of innovation in a production process as opposed to the end product, see Case COMP/M.2498 *UPM-Kymmene / Haindl* [2002] O.J. L233/38, paras 106 to 107.

[95] See Ivaldi *et al*, "The Economics of Tacit Collusion", Report for DG Competition, March 2003 (available via *http://europa.eu.int/comm/competition/mergers/review/the_economics_of_tacit_collusion_en.pdf*), pp.19 to 22, concluding: "Frequent interaction and frequent price adjustments facilitate collusion".

[96] Europe Economics, "Study on Assessment Criteria for Distinguishing between Competitive and Dominant Oligopolies in Merger Control", Final Report for the European Commission, May 2001, at p.22.

[97] Para.48. The Commission has traditionally placed substantial weight on similarities in market shares as an indicator of the likelihood of a tacitly coordinated outcome: in Case IV/M.315 *Mannesmann / Vallourec / Ilva* [1994] O.J. L102/15, the Commission noted, at para.55, that the incentive to engage in anti-competitive parallel behaviour increases both with the level of concentration and the symmetry of market shares. See also Case IV/M.190 *Nestlé / Perrier* [1992] O.J. L356/1; Case IV/M.619 *Gencor / Lonrho* [1997] O.J. L11/30 (decision upheld on appeal in Case T-102/96 *Gencor v Commission* [1999] E.C.R. II-753); Case COMP/M.1681 *Akzo Nobel / Hoechst Roussel Vet*; Case COMP/M.1741 *MCI WorldCom / Sprint* [2003] O.J. L300/1; Case COMP/M.1939 *Rexam / American National Can*; Case COMP/M.2499 *Norske Skog / Parenco / Walsum* [2002] O.J. L233/38; Case COMP/M.2690 *Solvay / Montedison-Ausimont*, para.46; Case COMP/M.2810 *Deloitte & Touche / Andersen (UK)* ("In principle symmetry in market shares could be one of the elements considered to make a market structure conducive to sustainable tacit collusion"; para.58); and Case COMP/M.3625 *Blackstone / Acetex* [2005] O.J. L312/60, para.118. The Commission has also relied on the lack of symmetry in market shares: see, e.g. Case IV/M.422 *Unilever France / Ortiz Miko*, para.51; Case IV/M.1223 *Tyco International / US Surgical Corp.*, para.11; Case IV/M.1230 *Glaverbel / PPG*, paras 20 and 21; Case IV/M.1440 *Lucent Technologies / Ascend Communications*, para.18; Case IV/M.1491 *Robert Bosch / Magneti Marelli*, para.29; Case COMP/M.1571 *New Holland / Case*, para.45; Case COMP/M.1681 *Akzo Nobel / Hoechst Roussel Vet*, para.73; Case COMP/M.1663 *Alcan / Alusuisse* [2002] O.J. L90/1, para.94; Case COMP/M.1882 *Pirelli / BICC* [2003] O.J. L70/35, para.83; and Case COMP/M.3216 *Oracle / PeopleSoft* [2005] O.J. L218/6, para.210. See also Kühn, "Closing Pandora's Box? Joint Dominance After the Airtours Judgment", published as Ch.3 of *The Pros and Cons of Merger Control* by the Swedish Competition Authority in 2002 (and available at *www.kkv.se/bestall/pdf/skrift_proscons.pdf*), pp.57 and 58 for discussion of potential positive tests for identifying coordinated effects based on market shares.

indicator of a coordinated outcome than similarities in cost structure.[98] The Commission has commented:

"market shares do not need to be completely symmetric in order for oligopolistic dominance to take place. It is quite conceivable that a merger will lead to one or more oligopolists being stronger than the other members in the oligopoly. In some situations there will even be a leader of the oligopoly. The important issue in the assessment of the symmetry of market shares is whether the market shares indicate a sufficient degree of similarity in incentives and retaliation possibilities".[99]

Furthermore, in *Exxon / Mobil*[1] the Commission stated[2]:

"In some of the national markets ... market shares are unevenly distributed among the various players. However this factor should not be regarded as precluding in itself the possibility of oligopolistic dominance. This is because, although symmetry of market shares provides additional incentives for parallel behaviour, it cannot be considered to be a prerequisite for such parallel behaviour to exist. For instance, even in presence of market share asymmetries, there can be symmetries of costs. This is the case in motor fuel retailing where the most important economies of scale are reached at the level of the station site. And similarly, the oligopoly members may feel that they have a fair share of the market and that they perceive each other as being on an 'equal footing' and having comparable strength. They would have therefore little to win and much to lose from aggressive competitive actions".

(vii) **Price elasticity** When industry demand is inelastic[3] at the prevailing **8–033**

---

[98] Notice on Horizontal Mergers, para.48, emphasising the importance of symmetry in costs structures. See also Ivaldi *et al*, "The Economics of Tacit Collusion", Report for DG Competition, March 2003 (available via *http://europa.eu.int/comm/competition/mergers/review/ the_economics_of_tacit_collusion_en.pdf*), p.15: "when market shares are asymmetric in a given industry, one should suspect that firms have different (marginal) costs and/or provide differentiated goods or services. But then, the relevant question becomes the impact of these more profound asymmetries in cost or product range or quality".

[99] Commission paper tabled at OECD, "Oligopoly", Best Practice Roundtable, October 1999, DAFFE / CLP(99)25 (*www.oecd.org*), p.213, at p.218.

[1] Case IV/M.1383 [2004] O.J. L103/1, para.477.

[2] For examples of cases in which coordinated effects were identified but market shares were *not* symmetrical, see Case IV/M.1313 *Danish Crown / Vestjyske Slagterier* [2000] O.J. L20/1; Case IV/M.1524 *Airtours / First Choice* [2000] O.J. L93/1 (annulled on appeal in Case T-342/99 *Airtours plc v Commission* [2002] E.C.R. II-2585); and Case COMP/M.3314 *Air Liquide / Messer Targets* (absence of symmetrical market shares not sufficient to rule out coordinated effects; para.102). See also the discussion in Case COMP/M.2498 *UPM-Kymmene / Haindl* [2002] O.J. L233/38, at para.81.

[3] See Case IV/M 1016 *Price Waterhouse / Coopers & Lybrand* [1999] O.J. L50/27 (paras 96 and 97); Case COMP/M.1628 *TotalFina / Elf* [2001] O.J. L143/1 ("The lack of incentives to engage in price competition is further weakened by the price inelasticity of demand"; para.206); Case COMP/M.2097 *SCA / Metsä Tissue*, para.148; Case COMP/M.2499 *Norske Skog / Parenco / Walsum* [2002] O.J. L233/38, para.88; and Case COMP/M.3130 *Arla Foods / Express Dairies* (the Commission found that demand for the products was very inelastic and it was therefore likely that the parties would have an incentive to coordinate; para.80).

price, there is a greater incentive to parallel behaviour as the potential gains from coordination are increased.[4] The Commission has analysed the position as follows: "In general terms, if demand is price inelastic, there is a higher incentive to parallel behaviour. As total demand volumes will not decrease significantly in the case of price increases, there is therefore a strong incentive for the market players to engage in supra-competitive pricing".[5]; low price elasticity "creates an incentive for anti-competitive parallel behaviour, since all suppliers would lose by engaging in price competition".[6]

8–034 **(viii) Multi-market contacts** The presence of the same competitors on several markets[7] may enable them tacitly to coordinate their activities by sharing markets (i.e. the existence of multi-market contact may provide further terms for tacit coordination).[8]

8–035 **(ix) Vertical integration** If the players in a market are vertically integrated[9] to the same extent,[10] the likelihood of tacit collusion is increased as it is more

---

[4] See Ivaldi et al, "The Economics of Tacit Collusion", Report for DG Competition, March 2003 (available via http://europa.eu.int/comm/competition/mergers/review/the_economics_of_tacit_collusion_en.pdf), p.50. Whilst techniques exist formally to estimate price elasticity, the Commission has in several cases proceeded on an informal basis. This point is noted by Europe Economics, "Study on Assessment Criteria for Distinguishing between Competitive and Dominant Oligopolies in Merger Control", Final Report for the European Commission, May 2001, p.83. See Case IV/M.190 Nestlé / Perrier [1992] O.J. L356/1, para.124; Case IV/M.1016 Price Waterhouse / Coopers & Lybrand [1999] O.J. L50/27, para.99; Case IV/M.1524 Airtours / First Choice [2000] O.J. L93/1, para.98 (annulled on appeal in Case T-342/99 Airtours plc v Commission [2002] E.C.R. II-2585); and Case COMP/M.2690 Solvay / Montedison-Ausimont, para.49. By contrast, formal techniques were used in Case IV/M.619 Gencor / Lonrho [1997] O.J. L11/30 (decision upheld on appeal in Case T-102/96 Gencor v Commission [1999] E.C.R. II-753) (where the Commission found that demand for platinum in its three major fields of use was inelastic at then-current prices because there were virtually no substitutes) and Case COMP/M.2498 UPM-Kymmene / Haindl [2002] O.J. L233/38 (where the Commission used an external economist to estimate a simple model of supply and demand in the light of previous academic research into the industry; para.88 and n.34).
[5] Case IV/M.1383 Exxon / Mobil [2004] O.J. L103/1, para.479. See also Case IV/M.190 Nestlé / Perrier [1992] O.J. L356/1, para.124 and Case COMP/M.1673 VEBA/VIAG [2001] O.J. L188/1, para.83.
[6] Case IV/M.619 Gencor / Lonrho [1997] O.J. L11/30 (decision upheld on appeal in Case T-102/96 Gencor v Commission [1999] E.C.R. II-753), para.149. See also Case IV/M.315 Mannesman / Vallourec / Ilva [1994] O.J. L102/15, para.56. Contrast Case IV/M.399 Rhône Poulenc / SNIA / Nordfaser, paras 25 and 26.
[7] Case COMP/M.2499 Norske Skog / Parenco / Walsum [2002] O.J. L233/38, paras 95 to 99.
[8] See Ivaldi et al, "The Economics of Tacit Collusion", Report for DG Competition, March 2003 (available via http://europa.eu.int/comm/competition/mergers/review/the_economics_of_tacit_collusion_en.pdf), pp.48 to 50 and Scherer & Ross, Industrial Market Structure and Economic Performance (3rd edn, Houghton Mifflin Co, 1990), p.312. For criticism of use of "multi-market contact" as a criterion in assessing coordinated effects, see Kühn, "Closing Pandora's Box? Joint Dominance After the Airtours Judgment", published as Ch.3 of The Pros and Cons of Merger Control by the Swedish Competition Authority in 2002 (and available at http://www.kkv.se/bestall/pdf/skrift_proscons.pdf), p.50.
[9] See also the UK Office of Fair Trading's Substantive Merger Guidelines, May 2003 (www.oft.gov.uk) (para.5.5) and Chen, "On vertical mergers and their competitive effects" (2001) 32 RAND Journal of Economics 667.
[10] Case COMP/M.2389 Shell / DEA [2003] O.J. L15/35, paras 84 and 85.

likely that the companies will share similar cost structures and their strategic interests will tend to coincide at every level.[11]

The mergers in *BP / E.ON*[12] and *Shell / DEA*[13] were considered together by the Commission and would have eliminated the two non-integrated suppliers of ethylene, thereby removing the only independent price setters from the market (since vertically integrated suppliers took account of their downstream interests in setting prices for the merchant market). The Commission found that: "Both mergers lead to the disappearance of the only independent sellers on the merchant market for ethylene via the integration of Veba and DEA in fully vertically integrated international companies with strong interests in the downstream derivatives market. It is this structural change, to which the combination of BP and Veba contributes in equal terms, which leads to a competitive situation in the market ultimately resulting in the creation of collective dominance".[14]

However, in *Airtours plc v Commission*[15] the Court of First Instance acknowledged that an increased level of vertical integration in the short-haul package tours market was pro-competitive, in the context of an investigation into coordinated effects, as it increased efficiency and reduced the interdependence of the large tour operators.

8.8 MONITORING DEVIATIONS

Whenever price is raised above the competitive level, producers tend to have an incentive to increase their individual output to benefit from sales at the increased price, and coordinated effects are therefore sustainable only if producers have an incentive not to cheat. The incentive not to cheat arises from the existence of a credible deterrent mechanism (which is discussed in s.8.9 below), but it is a necessary condition for the operation of a successful deterrent mechanism that suppliers can monitor deviations from the coordinated outcome, so that they know when to retaliate.[16] It follows that transparency (which is essential if the parties are to reach terms of coordination as discussed in s.8.7(g) above) also permits the monitoring of competitors' behaviour, without the need for express collusion, to verify whether any supplier is cheating on the tacitly coordinated arrangement.[17] The US

8–036

---

[11] See Areeda, Hovenkamp & Solow, *Antitrust Law* (2nd edn, Aspen Law & Business, 1998), Vol.IVA, para.1007.
[12] Case COMP/M.2533 [2002] O.J. L276/31.
[13] Case COMP/M.2389 [2003] O.J. L15/35.
[14] Case COMP/M.2533 *BP / E.ON* [2002] O.J. L276/31, para.49.
[15] Case T-342/99 [2002] E.C.R. II-2585, para.106. See also para.284.
[16] Notice on Horizontal Mergers, para.49. See also Ivaldi *et al*, "The Economics of Tacit Collusion", Report for DG Competition, March 2003 (available via *http://europa.eu.int/comm/competition/mergers/review/the_economics_of_tacit_collusion_en.pdf*), pp.22 to 26.
[17] See the Notice on Horizontal Mergers, paras 49 to 51 and Scherer & Ross, *Industrial Market Structure and Economic Performance* (3rd edn, Houghton Mifflin Co, 1990), p.215.

Horizontal Merger Guidelines state that, "if information about specific transactions or individual price or output levels is available routinely to competitors, it may be difficult for a firm to deviate secretly".[18]

In *Airtours plc v Commission*[19] the Court of First Instance identified as a necessary condition for a finding of coordinated effects that: "each member of the dominant oligopoly must have the ability to know how the other members are behaving in order to monitor whether or not they are adopting the common policy ... it is not enough for each member of the dominant oligopoly to be aware that interdependent market conduct is profitable for all of them but each member must also have a means of knowing whether the other operators are adopting the same strategy and whether they are maintaining it. There must, therefore, be sufficient market transparency for all members of the dominant oligopoly to be aware, sufficiently precisely and quickly, of the way in which the other members' market conduct is evolving".[20]

8–037   Monitoring is more difficult if *more suppliers are involved*.[21] However, in markets which are very transparent, reciprocal monitoring may be possible between numerous players and, indeed, the European Commission found a position of collective dominance held by seven companies in Luxembourg in *Exxon / Mobil*.[22] In that case, the Commission stated: "it is undisputed that the higher the number of firms participating in an oligopoly, the higher is the risk of defection in the oligopoly. Nonetheless, standard antitrust economics suggest that an oligopoly can function also in less concentrated markets. This is the case when the transparency of the market in terms of price is such that a reciprocal monitoring is easily possible even between numerous players on the market".[23]

---

[18] The US Horizontal Merger Guidelines, 1992 (amended in 1997) (*www.usdoj.gov/atr/public/ guidelines/hmg.htm*), para.2.12. See also Case IV/M.1383 *Exxon / Mobil* [2004] O.J. L103/1, para.474.

[19] Case T-342/99 [2002] E.C.R. II-2585, para.62. In *Airtours*, the Court of First Instance (in the context of an allegation of coordinated effects in relation to capacity) noted, at para.159: "The degree of transparency is also important for the purposes of permitting each member of the oligopoly subsequently to detect alterations made by the others as regards capacity, to distinguish deviations from the common policy from mere adjustments consequent upon volatility of demand and, finally, to ascertain whether it is necessary to reach to any such deviations by punishing them".

[20] In Case COMP/M.2201 *MAN / Auwärter* [2002] O.J. L116/35, the Commission stated, at paras 50 and 52, that "the large number of criteria governing the award of contracts in the present case makes any coordination difficult, and in the long term it would undermine the stability of any supposed coordinated behaviour ... Consequently the companies concerned can scarcely verify to what extent the other market leader has deviated from the postulated coordinated behaviour. This would, however, be a necessary precondition for any retaliatory behaviour between them and for maintenance of the postulated tacit coordination".

[21] See para.8–027 above and Ivaldi *et al*, "The Economics of Tacit Collusion", Report for DG Competition, March 2003 (available via *http://europa.eu.int/comm/competition/mergers/ review/the_economics_of_tacit_collusion_en.pdf*), pp.12 to 14; Scherer & Ross, *Industrial Market Structure and Economic Performance* (3rd edn, Houghton Mifflin Co, 1990), pp.277 and 278; and Europe Economics, "Study on Assessment Criteria for Distinguishing between Competitive and Dominant Oligopolies in Merger Control", Final Report for the European Commission, May 2001, at pp.21 and 22.

[22] Case IV/M.1383 [2004] O.J. L103/1, para.649.

[23] Para.466.

It is more difficult to detect cheating in a *growing market*[24] (since it is more **8–038** difficult to determine whether changes in a rival supplier's position are a result of developments in the market or of cheating).[25] The Court of First Instance in *Airtours plc v Commission*[26] summarised the position as follows: "economic theory regards volatility of demand as something which renders the creation of a collective dominant position more difficult. Conversely, stable demand, thus displaying low volatility, is a relevant factor indicative of the existence of a collective dominant position, in so far as it makes 'deviations from the common policy' (that is, cheating) more easily detectable, by enabling them to be distinguished from capacity adjustments intended to respond to expansion or contraction in a volatile market".

Contractual terms can facilitate the monitoring of deviations.[27] For example, "most favoured customer" clauses,[28] under which the producer promises to extend to the customer any more favourable terms agreed with other purchasers,[29] can facilitate monitoring of deviations as competitors need only identify one or two of a supplier's actual prices to monitor the entirety of that supplier's prices if most favoured customer clauses are signed by most customers.[30] Similarly, "meeting competition" clauses,[31] under which a buyer who finds a more favourable price during the currency of the contract is entitled to terminate the contract unless the supplier matches the new price, can increase transparency on deviations, because customers have an incentive to monitor prices in the market and pass on information to suppliers.

The existence of *similar cost structures* increases the ease of monitoring, **8–039** because a supplier faced with a fall in profitability has to determine whether this arose from something outside the supplier's control, a mistake by a rival supplier, or cheating on the tacitly coordinated outcome; this assessment is

---

[24] See the discussion in Europe Economics, "Study on Assessment Criteria for Distinguishing between Competitive and Dominant Oligopolies in Merger Control", Final Report for the European Commission, May 2001, at p.17. The Commission found that detection of cheating was easy in Case COMP/M.1741 *MCI WorldCom / Sprint* [2003] O.J. L300/1, para.280.

[25] Case IV/M.1383 *Exxon / Mobil* [2004] O.J. L103/1, para.475. See also Case COMP/M.1838 *BT / ESAT* and Case COMP/M.2016 *France Télécom / Orange*.

[26] Case T-342/99, para.139.

[27] In para. 51 the Notice on Horizontal Mergers refers to the use of facilitating practices (e.g. meeting competition or most-favoured customer clauses and cross directorships) to enable suppliers to monitor deviations.

[28] See the discussion in Dixit & Nalebuff, *Thinking Strategically* (W W Norton & Co, 1991), pp.102 to 104; Nalebuff & Brandenburger, *Co-opetition* (HarperCollinsBusiness, 1997 edn), pp.156 to 171; Besanko, Dranove & Shanley, *Economics of Strategy* (2nd edn, John Wiley & Sons Inc, 2000), pp.314 and 315; and Holt & Scheffman, "Facilitating Practices: the effects of advance notice and best-price policies" (1987) 18 *RAND Journal of Economics* 187.

[29] See Viscusi, Vernon & Harrington, *Economics of Regulation and Antitrust* (3rd edn, The MIT Press, 2000), p.131, n.34.

[30] See Martin, *Advanced Industrial Economics* (2nd edn, Blackwell, 2002), p.329.

[31] For a discussion of the effects of "take or pay" contracts and rebate programmes such as "frequent flyer" programmes, see Nalebuff & Brandenburger, *Co-opetition* (HarperCollins-Business, 1997 edn), pp 173 to 187.

easier in cases involving similar cost structures because, other things being equal, each of the suppliers ought to be operating in the same way.[32]

Monitoring may be possible *even if there is not transparency across the whole market*. For example, in *Sony / BMG*[33] the Commission noted that the large number of albums could complicate monitoring of a tacit agreement on recorded music, but emphasised that majors needed only to monitor the pricing points of a limited number of best selling albums to account for most sales.

The Notice on Horizontal Mergers emphasises[34] that transparency may be affected by *the way the market works* (e.g. there is greater transparency when transactions occur on public exchanges than when they occur through confidential bilateral discussions) and that the key question for the purposes of monitoring deviations is whether suppliers can infer from the information they receive that cheating has occurred (e.g. if demand is volatile a supplier may not be able to determine whether a loss of sales arose as a result of cheating by rivals or because of a reduction in customers' requirements).

8.9 DETERRENT MECHANISMS

(a) Generally

8–040 Generally, if suppliers engage in tacit coordination, then it will be profitable for any one of them to "cheat". For example, in cases of coordinated effects on price, it will generally be profitable for a supplier to reduce its prices below the tacitly coordinated level to increase its sales. If suppliers were able to cheat with impunity, then a tacitly coordinated outcome would not be sustainable. However, suppliers may be incentivised to comply with the tacitly coordinated outcome by the threat of retaliation in cases of cheating.[35]

In *Airtours plc v Commission*[36] the Court of First Instance identified as a condition of a finding of coordinated effects:

"the situation of collective dominance must be sustainable over time, that is to say, there must be an incentive not to depart from the common policy on the market. ... [It] is only if all the members of the dominant oligopoly maintain the parallel conduct that all can benefit. The notion of

---

[32] See Europe Economics, "Study on Assessment Criteria for Distinguishing between Competitive and Dominant Oligopolies in Merger Control", Final Report for the European Commission, May 2001, p.31.
[33] Case COMP/M.3333 [2005] O.J. L62/30 (appeal pending in Case T-464/04 *Impala v Commission*), para.111.
[34] Para.50.
[35] See the Notice on Horizontal Mergers, para.52 and Martin, *Advanced Industrial Economics* (2nd edn, Blackwell, 2002), p.295.
[36] Case T-342/99 [2002] E.C.R. II-2585, para.62.

retaliation in respect of conduct deviating from the common policy is thus inherent in this condition. In this instance, the parties concur that, for a situation of collective dominance to be viable, there must be adequate deterrents to ensure that there is a long-term incentive in not departing from the common policy, which means that each member of the dominant oligopoly must be aware that highly competitive action on its part designed to increase its market share would provoke identical action by others, so that it would derive no benefit from its initiative".[37]

(b) The scope of the obligation to identify a deterrent mechanism

In *Airtours plc v Commission*[38] the Court of First Instance stated:　　　**8–041**

"the situation of collective dominance must be sustainable over time, that is to say, there must be an incentive not to depart from the common policy on the market ... [It] is only if all the members of the dominant oligopoly maintain the parallel conduct that all can benefit. The notion of retaliation in respect of conduct deviating from the common policy is thus inherent in this condition.[39]

It is ... important to ascertain whether the individual interests of [the alleged collectively dominant oligopolists] (maximising profits while competing with the whole range of operators) outweigh the common interests of the members of the alleged dominant oligopoly (restricting capacity in order to increase prices and make supra-competitive profits). That would be the case if the absence of deterrents induced an operator to depart from the common policy, taking advantage of the absence of competition essential to that policy, so as to take competitive initiatives and derive benefit from the advantages inherent therein ... The fact that there is scope for retaliation goes some way to ensuring that the members of the oligopoly do not in the long run break ranks by deterring each of them from departing from the common course of conduct. In that context, the Commission must not necessarily prove that there is a specific 'retaliation mechanism involving a degree of severity', but it must none the less establish that deterrents exist, which are such that it is not worth the while of any member of the dominant oligopoly to depart from the common course of conduct to the detriment of the other oligopolists".[40]

---

[37] The US Non-Horizontal Merger Guidelines, 1984 (*www.usdoj.gov/atr/public/guidelines/2614.htm*), state, at para.2.1: "Successful coordinated interaction entails reaching terms of coordination that are profitable to the firms involved and an ability to detect and punish deviations that would undermine the coordinated interaction. Detection and punishment of deviation ensure that coordinating firms will find it more profitable to adhere to the terms of coordination than to pursue short term profits from deviating, given the costs of reprisal".

[38] Case T-342/99 [2002] E.C.R. II-2585.

[39] Para.62.

[40] Paras 193 to 195.

8–042 It follows that the Commission is required to establish that a deterrent mechanism exists without particularising every aspect of that mechanism[41] (notwithstanding its statements in *Airtours / First Choice*[42] that "where ... there are strong incentives to reduce competitive action, coercion may be unnecessary"[43] and, more emphatically, "it is not necessary to show that there would be a strict punishment mechanism").[44] This conclusion is reflected in the Notice on Horizontal Mergers which states that: "Coordination is not sustainable unless the consequences of deviation are sufficiently severe to convince coordinating firms that it is in their best interests to adhere to the terms of coordination".[45]

(c) The incentives to comply with the coordinated outcome

8–043 **(i) The nature of the deterrent mechanism** The US Horizontal Merger Guidelines state that: "Credible punishment ... may not need to be any more complex than temporary abandonment of the terms of coordination by other firms in the market".[46] However, more sophisticated deterrent mechanisms may be equally effective, perhaps occurring in markets other than the market[47] in which deviation occurred.[48] Retaliation may take place, for example, through a *cross-parry* (when a company responds to a rival's strategy in one market by taking action in a second market in which the rival is also present) or a *fighting brand* (strategically targeted at the rival's brand).[49] In *Airtours / First Choice*[50] the Commission emphasised the scope for retaliation through links between the parties in distribution and charter

---

[41] See the discussion in Nikpay & Houwen, "Tour de Force or a Little Local Turbulence? A Heretical View on the *Airtours* Judgment" [2003] E.C.L.R. 193, at p.198.

[42] Case IV/M.1524 [2000] O.J. L93/1.

[43] Para.55.

[44] Para.150.

[45] Para.52.

[46] The US Horizontal Merger Guidelines, 1992 (amended in 1997) (*www.usdoj.gov/atr/public/guidelines/hmg.htm*), para.2.12.

[47] In Case COMP/M.2498 *UPM-Kymmene / Haindl* [2002] O.J. L233/38 the Commission stated, at para.99, that "multi-market contacts may influence strategic behaviours and may tend to substantially increase the sustainability of coordination on the markets".

[48] See the Notice on Horizontal Mergers, para.55 (noting that the retaliation could take many forms, including the cancellation of joint ventures or other forms of cooperation or selling of shares in jointly owned companies). See also Case IV/M.190 *Nestlé / Perrier* [1992] O.J. L356/1, para.123 and Case IV/M.619 *Gencor / Lonrho* [1997] O.J. L11/30 (decision upheld on appeal in Case T-102/96 *Gencor v Commission* [1999] E.C.R. II-753) and Case IV/M.1383 *Exxon / Mobil* [2004] O.J. L103/1, para.487.

[49] In Case COMP/M.1628 *TotalFina / Elf* [2001] O.J. L143/1, at para.205, the Commission identified multi-market contact concerns in stating: "The extent of each network of motorway service stations means that each brand has service stations located directly before or directly after service stations owned by each of its competitors. An aggressive policy focused on a single section of motorway could lead to reprisals on other sections". See also Europe Economics, "Study on Assessment Criteria for Distinguishing between Competitive and Dominant Oligopolies in Merger Control", Final Report for the European Commission, May 2001, pp.35, 85 and 89.

[50] Case IV/M.1524 [2000] O.J. L93/1, paras 143 and 153.

airline seats, although the Court of First Instance found that, on the facts of the case, the deterrent mechanisms identified by the Commission would not be capable of coming into play because of a lack of transparency in the market.[51]

The precise nature of any deterrent mechanism will depend on the reference point around which tacit coordination is expected to operate and the incentives of the parties to comply. In *BP / E.ON*[52] the Commission stated:

"as a general point, the necessity and sophistication of a retaliation mechanism cannot be analysed without taking the incentives and abilities to deviate from a behavioural pattern into account. The retaliation mechanism must be sufficiently plausible and effective to counterbalance the existing degree of probability and incentives to deviate in the market situation of the individual case. In the present case, the parties' argument related to the long term nature of the contracts also applies to the possibilities to deviate. The possibilities for retaliation occur with the same frequency as the possibilities [of] deviation, and therefore are sufficiently frequent and effective. In addition, if in the parties' view market interaction is relatively slow and infrequent compared to other markets, then the possibilities for deviation in the first place are as well, and underpin the probability and stability of the market sharing pattern".[53]

(ii) The incentive to comply A supplier will have an incentive to comply with **8–044** the coordinated outcome if[54]:

(a) the chances of cheating being *detected* are high and the delay between cheating and punishment is short[55]; as explained in s.8.8 above, retaliation is possible only if cheating is detected and, the longer the delay before detection, the greater the scope to profit from cheating;

(b) retaliation is *possible*,[56] i.e. the other oligopolists can take action which will result in the supplier being worse off following its decision

---

[51] Case T–342/99 *Airtours plc v Commission* [2002] E.C.R. II-2585, paras 197 to 199.
[52] Case COMP/M.2533 [2002] O.J. L276/31.
[53] Para.111.
[54] See Ivaldi *et al*, "The Economics of Tacit Collusion", Report for DG Competition, March 2003 (available via *http://europa.eu.int/comm/competition/mergers/review/the_economics_of_tacit_collusion_en.pdf*), pp.6 to 8 and 17 to 21 and Besanko, Dranove & Shanley, *Economics of Strategy* (2nd edn, John Wiley & Sons Inc, 2000), pp.303 to 307.
[55] See the Notice on Horizontal Mergers, para.53; Case COMP/M.1741 *MCI WorldCom / Sprint* [2003] O.J. L300/1, para.280; and Case COMP/M.3512 *VNU / WPP / JV*, para.30.
[56] See Case IV/M.1313 *Danish Crown / Vestjyske Slagterier* [2000] O.J. L20/1 para.177; Case COMP/M.1741 *MCI WorldCom / Sprint* [2003] O.J. L300/1, para.261; Case COMP/M.2389 *Shell / DEA* [2003] O.J. L15/35, paras 116 to 125; Case COMP/M.2499 *Norske Skog / Parenco / Walsum* [2002] O.J. L233/38, para.132; and Case COMP/M.3197 *Candover / Cinven / BertelsmannSpringer*, para.46. Punishment through retaliatory price cuts is likely to be more effective in cases of homogeneous products.

to cheat (e.g. by increasing output and flooding the market, thereby reducing market price); and

(c) the retaliatory threat is *credible*,[57] i.e. the prospective cheat will conclude that the other oligopolists, behaving rationally, will choose to invoke the retaliatory mechanism even though they may suffer as a result in the short-term.

Contractual clauses can blunt the incentives to cheat. For example, "most favoured customer" clauses reduce the gains from cheating because a price cut agreed with one customer will trigger an obligation to reduce prices to other customers, increasing the total cost of the price reduction. "Meeting competition" clauses also reduce the incentives to cheat by cutting prices as a potential price cutter will be aware that the incumbent is contractually obliged to match the price reduction (or release the customer). Price matching clauses, under which a supplier commits to match or beat competitors' prices (e.g. lowest price pledges such as, "We will not be undercut") have the same effects.[58]

(d) Chances of detection and speed of punishment

8–045 The efficacy of the retaliatory mechanism depends on the chances of cheating being detected and the speed with which detection and punishment occur. The more rapid the detection and punishment, the greater the incentive to adhere to the tacitly coordinated outcome without cheating. Conversely, if detection and punishment are slow, there are greater opportunities to cheat.[59] More specifically, a stable coordinated outcome is likely if, but only if, the chances of detection multiplied by the punishment exceed the gains from cheating.[60] The issue of "monitoring deviations", which was considered in s.8.8 above, is therefore of crucial importance.

Repeated interaction is essential if tacit coordination is to occur. If there

---

[57] See the Notice on Horizontal Mergers, para.52; Case COMP/M.1939 *Rexam | American National Can*, para.24; Case COMP/M.3314 *Air Liquide | Messer Targets* (selective under-cutting as a credible retaliatory mechanism; para.97); and Case COMP/M.3729 *EDF | AEM | Edison*, para.100.

[58] See Martin, *Advanced Industrial Economics* (2nd edn, Blackwell, 2002), p.330.

[59] See the Notice on Horizontal Mergers, para.53 (noting that if the market is characterised by infrequent, large orders, then the gains from cheating may be large, certain and immediate and the losses from being punished may be small and uncertain and only materialise after some time). See also the US Horizontal Merger Guidelines, 1992 (amended in 1997) (*www.usdoj. gov/atr/public/guidelines/hmg.htm*), para.2.12.

[60] See the 2002 draft Commission Notice on Horizontal Mergers, para.62 (this passage was omitted from the *final* version of the Notice) and Europe Economics, "Study on Assessment Criteria for Distinguishing between Competitive and Dominant Oligopolies in Merger Control", Final Report for the European Commission, May 2001, p.25. Scherer & Ross, *Industrial Market Structure and Economic Performance* (3rd edn, Houghton Mifflin Co, 1990), observe, at p.308, that: "The longer the adverse consequences of rival retaliation can be forestalled, the more attractive undercutting the accepted price structure becomes. A common method of attempting to delay retaliation is to grant price concessions secretly".

were no repeated interaction, then each supplier would have an incentive to cheat, since there would be no punishment for deviation, and all other suppliers would be aware of this. Similarly, a supplier which believes that there is a good prospect that it will exit from a market has a reduced incentive to engage in tacit coordination. This is because, in determining strategy in a repeated game, a supplier must identify its *discount factor*, i.e. the value it places on £1 of income in a future period. If the discount value is low (i.e. £1 in a future period is worth relatively little to the supplier, e.g. because it believes that it may by then have left the market) then a supplier's incentive to engage in tacit coordination to increase returns in future periods is reduced: its incentive is to maximise profitability in the short run.

(e) The deterrent mechanism must eliminate the gains from cheating

If the deterrent mechanism is to be effective, then the punishment must be **8–046** powerful, i.e. it must, at the very least, eliminate the gains made by the cheater prior to the imposition of the retaliatory mechanism.[61] If the gains from cheating are high,[62] the threatened punishment must be stronger in order to maintain the stability of the coordinated outcome. Conversely, a weaker punishment mechanism may be sufficient if the gains from cheating are limited.[63]

---

[61] See the Notice on Horizontal Mergers, para.52 (and the 2002 draft Commission Notice on Horizontal Mergers, para.62).

[62] The more successful the coordinated effects, the greater the gains from cheating, e.g. if the price increases, additional sales become more profitable and suppliers have a greater incentive to increase their output. Ivaldi *et al*, "The Economics of Tacit Collusion", Report for DG Competition, March 2003 (available via *http://europa.eu.int/comm/competition/mergers/review/the_economics_of_tacit_collusion_en.pdf*), explain, at p.12, that the gains from cheating are higher and the benefits of coordinating lower as the number of oligopoly suppliers increases (because increasing the number of oligopolists reduces the profit share available to each coordinating firm). See also Europe Economics, "Study on Assessment Criteria for Distinguishing between Competitive and Dominant Oligopolies in Merger Control", Final Report for the European Commission, May 2001, p.21 and Besanko, Dranove & Shanley, *Economics of Strategy* (2nd edn, John Wiley & Sons Inc, 2000), p.303.

[63] Peter Carstensen argues that the incentive to cheat in the case of coordination on *procurement* markets is lower than the incentive to cheat on *supply* markets because, on supply markets, suppliers gain by cheating (e.g. increasing output to benefit from the higher prices brought about by the coordination), whereas on procurement markets customers always have a common interest in keeping prices for inputs low (unless demand for the input exceeds supply at the prevailing price); see "Buyer Power and Merger Analysis—The Need for Different Metrics" (*www.ftc.gov/bc/mergerenforce/presentations/040217carstensen.pdf*). For a contrary view, see Schwartz, "Should Antitrust Assess Buyer Market Power Differently than Seller Market Power?" (*www.ftc.gov/bc/mergerenforce/presentations/040217schwartz.pdf*). The Commission considered the scope for coordinated effects on a procurement market in Case COMP/M.3130 *Arla Foods / Express Dairies*, paras 58 and 59.

(f) The credibility of the retaliatory threat

8-047 If the retaliatory threat is not credible[64] (i.e. suppliers could not, or would not want to invoke it if a deviation occurred), it will not deter cheating, because a supplier considering whether to cheat will calculate that the other oligopolists will accommodate its actions rather than retaliating.[65]

For example, the most straightforward deterrent mechanism (an increase in output by the oligopolists which reduces market price) requires that the oligopolists have spare capacity.[66] In *Outokumpu | Norzink*[67] the Commission observed that: "Capacity constraints affect tacit coordination principally because in the absence of excess capacity, firms cannot impose a very impressive threat for retaliation on potential deviators".

In *UPM-Kymmene | Haindl*[68] the prospect of the oligopolists themselves investing in new production facilities as a punishment for cheating on a tacitly coordinated policy limiting such investment[69] was found to lack credibility because of its cost.[70] (In addition, the punishment could not serve to reverse the cheat's conduct in future periods[71] and nor could the effect of the punishment be limited in time.)[72] However, in the same case, the Commission considered the scope for tacit coordination on down-time (which could be used to reduce effective capacity in the industry and maintain prices) and found, following a careful examination of the ability and incentives of the other suppliers, that the punishment threat *was* credible. In particular, the Commission established that the competitors had sufficient capacity to retaliate by increasing available capacity if cheating occurred and noted: "When a competitor deviates, the remaining top-suppliers can take aggressive actions without having to change prices for all their remaining customers. This may induce some customers to switch from

---

[64] Case COMP/M.1939 *Rexam/American National Can*, para.24.

[65] See the Notice on Horizontal Mergers, para.54. See also Case IV/M.1298 *Kodak | Imation*, para.57 and Case COMP/M.1741 *MCI WorldCom | Sprint* [2003] O.J. L300/1, para.261.

[66] In Case COMP/M.1681 *Akzo Nobel | Hoechst Roussel Vet*, the Commission noted, at para.47, that the substantial overcapacity of the three players could be used as a means of retaliation.

[67] Case COMP/M.2348, para.17.

[68] Case COMP/M.2498 [2002] O.J. L233/38.

[69] Frontier Economics, Competition Bulletin, January 2002, "Unrepeatable Games" (*www.frontier-economics.com*), note that in cases of coordination on new capacity: (a) the set of credible punishments is smaller because investments are permanent and the costs of inflicting punishment would therefore be substantial; and (b) the deviator can limit the size of the punishment because if it invests in sufficient capacity to fill the "capacity gap" completely then active counter-investment would be irrational and the deviator will benefit from its status as first mover. See Case COMP/M.2499 *Norske Skog | Parenco | Walsum* [2002] O.J. L233/38, paras 127 to 139.

[70] Para.135.

[71] The cheat would still have the capacity available to it. By contrast, when tacit coordination occurs on price, a price-cutter may be induced to raise the price for future periods.

[72] The punishment would leave the other suppliers with a permanent excess of capacity. By contrast, when tacit coordination occurs on price, punishment by flooding the market and reducing the market price may be limited in time and prices may be increased for future periods. See the 2002 draft Commission Notice on Horizontal Mergers, paras 66 and 67 (these paragraphs were not included in the *final* version of the Notice).

the other top-suppliers, and may drive down the price paid by important customers of the deviator. Moreover ... in a period of low demand, capacities are available if needed to support retaliation. These capacities may be used to target important customers of a deviator without affecting the whole market".[73]

The existence of *similar cost structures* increases the risk of retaliation,[74] and therefore the likelihood of compliance with the tacitly coordinated outcome, because each company will be aware that its competitors can match its competitive actions[75]; conversely, retaliation is normally more difficult against a supplier which has a lower cost base than its competitors.[76]

Substantial *switching costs* reduce the risk of retaliation, because they increase the cost and difficulty of retaliation.[77]

(g) Market operation

A market in which coordinated effects occurs may be characterised by bouts **8–048** of intense price competition as retaliation occurs in the market. Indeed, there are suggestions that only industries involving tacit or express coordination generate price wars.[78]

8.10 REACTIONS OF OUTSIDERS

(a) Introduction

In *Airtours plc v Commission*[79] the Court of First Instance stated that: **8–049**

"to prove the existence of a collective dominant position to the requisite legal standard, the Commission must ... establish that the foreseeable

---

[73] Para.138.
[74] Case COMP/M.1939 *Rexam / American National Can*, para.24.
[75] Case IV/M.1383 *Exxon / Mobil* [2004] O.J. L103/1, para.476.
[76] Commission paper tabled at OECD, "Oligopoly", Best Practice Roundtable, October 1999, DAFFE / CLP(99)25 (*www.oecd.org*), p.213, at p.218.
[77] See OFT Economic Discussion Paper 5, "Switching Costs", NERA, April 2003 (note that the views in the paper do not necessarily reflect those of the OFT), paras 1.12, 7.20 to 7.38, 7.119 and 7.120 (noting, however, that in general switching costs have an ambiguous effect on the likelihood of coordinated effects). See also para.7–011 above.
[78] Europe Economics, "Study on Assessment Criteria for Distinguishing between Competitive and Dominant Oligopolies in Merger Control", Final Report for the European Commission, May 2001, p.34. For a general survey see Martin, *Advanced Industrial Economics* (2nd edn, Blackwell, 2002), p.314.
[79] Case T-342/99 [2002] E.C.R. II-2585.

reaction of current and future competitors, as well as of consumers, would not jeopardise the results expected of the common policy".[80]

"to prove conclusively the existence of a collective dominant position in this instance, the Commission should ... have established that the foreseeable reactions of current and future competitors and consumers would not jeopardise the results expected from the large tour operators' common policy. In this case, that implies that where the large tour operators, for anti-competitive purposes, reduce available capacity to a level below what is required to adjust to anticipated trends in demand, such a reaction must not be offset by their current competitors, smaller operators, any potential competitors, tour operators with a presence in other countries or on the long-haul market, or their customers (United Kingdom consumers) reacting in such a way as to render the dominant oligopoly unviable".[81]

The Notice on Horizontal Mergers summarises the position as follows: "For coordination to be successful, the actions of non-coordinating firms and potential competitors, as well as customers, should not be able to jeopardise the outcome expected from coordination".[82]

(b) The competitive fringe

8–050   Coordinated effects will not arise if the firms which are outside the candidate oligopoly[83] are able to defeat any coordinated outcome.[84]

As noted above in s.8.6 above, it is necessary to distinguish the suppliers which form part of the candidate oligopoly from those which form part of the competitive fringe. Having identified the members of the competitive fringe, it is necessary to determine whether the fringe suppliers could

---

[80] Para.62. Further, at para.192, the Court emphasised that "the prospective analysis of the market necessary in any assessment of an alleged collective dominant position must not only view the position statically at a fixed point in time—the point when the transaction takes place and the structure of competition is altered—but must assess it dynamically, with regard in particular to its internal equilibrium, stability, and the question as to whether any parallel anti-competitive conduct to which it might give rise is sustainable over time".

[81] Para.210.

[82] Para.56.

[83] i.e. the coordinating group.

[84] See generally Scherer & Ross, *Industrial Market Structure and Economic Performance* (3rd edn, Houghton Mifflin Co, 1990), Ch.10 (discussing pricing incentives facing oligopolists concerned about new entry by fringe players or expansion by existing fringe suppliers). See also Case IV/M.315 *Mannesmann / Vallourec / Ilva* [1994] O.J. L102/15 (coordinated price increases would be defeated by Japanese competitors; paras 112 to 115); Case COMP/M.1741 *MCI WorldCom / Sprint* [2003] O.J. L300/1 (coordination through mutual accommodation in tender markets would be defeated by competitors; paras 272 to 302); Case COMP/M.1882 *Pirelli / BICC* [2003] O.J. L70/35, para.88; Case COMP/M.2499 *Norske Skog / Parenco / Walsum* [2002] O.J. L233/38, paras 140 to 148; and Case COMP/M.3829 *Maersk / PONL*, para.59.

undermine the tacitly coordinated outcome (whether relating to price, market share, customer allocation,[85] etc.).[86]

The Notice on Horizontal Mergers notes that coordination aimed at reducing overall capacity in the market would be defeated if non-coordinating firms have the ability and incentive to increase their own capacities sufficiently to offset the reduction or to render the reduction unprofitable.[87] In *UPM-Kymmene / Haindl*[88] the Commission investigated the possibility of tacit coordination on down-time but concluded that the fringe players could undermine such a strategy[89] by increasing production when the oligopolists chose to shut down their machines temporarily,[90] having satisfied itself that the fringe suppliers had sufficient, readily-available capacity to expand.[91] Conversely, in *Exxon / Mobil*[92] a price war initiated by independent fuel retailers was regarded as unlikely, in part because the independents purchased fuel from the oil majors who formed part of the oligopoly, with the consequence that a strategy of aggressive competition might jeopardise their future supply arrangements.

In cases where tacit coordination occurs on price, fringe suppliers will **8–051** generally have an incentive to increase their output as the market price increases to make more sales at the higher prevailing price. If the fringe faces no or low *barriers to expansion*, it may defeat the attempted price increase by increasing output to such an extent that price is reduced.[93] In *Airtours plc v Commission*[94] the Court of First Instance stated that: "it must be made clear that the issue here is not whether a small tour operator can reach the size necessary for it to compete effectively with the integrated tour operators by

---

[85] See Case COMP/M.2389 *Shell / DEA* [2003] O.J. L15/35, paras 105 to 111.

[86] See Case IV/M.190 *Nestlé / Perrier* [1992] O.J. L356/1 (the Commission stated, at para.129, that producers of local spring and national mineral waters were "too small and dispersed to constitute a significant alternative to national waters" and none would constrain the prices of the duopoly); Case IV/M.580 *ABB / Daimler Benz* [1997] O.J. L11/1 (the Commission stated boldly, at para.63, that: "Market shares of 67% to 100% achieved by only two undertakings are an indication of a dominant position on the part of both undertakings together vis-à-vis those outside the duopoly"); and Case COMP/M.1741 *MCI WorldCom / Sprint* [2003] O.J. L300/1 (the Commission found, at paras 283 to 290, that smaller competitors and new entrants to the market would not be able to challenge the parallel behaviour).

[87] Para.56.

[88] Case COMP/M.2498 [2002] O.J. L233/38. See also Case COMP/M.2420 *Mitsui / CVRD / Caemi* [2004] O.J. L92/50 (customers could defeat coordination on pricing by settling with "fringe" suppliers as they had done in the past; para.234).

[89] See also Case IV/M.1539 *CVC / Danone / Gerresheimer*, para.38. Contrast: Case IV/M.190 *Nestlé / Perrier* [1992] O.J. L356/1; Case IV/M.308 *Kali und Salz / MdK / Treuhand* [1994] O.J. L186/38; and Case COMP/M.1524 *Airtours / First Choice* [2000] O.J. L93/1 (annulled on appeal in Case T-342/99 *Airtours plc v Commission* [2002] E.C.R. II-2585).

[90] Para.142.

[91] Para.147. Often the competitive fringe will face barriers to expansion which prevent them from defeating any tacitly coordinated outcome.

[92] Case IV/M.1383 [2004] O.J. L103/1, para.673.

[93] However, if only one or two fringe suppliers can expand to reach the scale of the larger firms, those firms may have an incentive to join the oligopoly: see Europe Economics, "Study on Assessment Criteria for Distinguishing between Competitive and Dominant Oligopolies in Merger Control", Final Report for the European Commission, May 2001, at p.30.

[94] Case T-342/99 [2002] E.C.R. II-2585.

challenging them for their places as market leaders. Rather, it is a question of whether, in the anti-competitive situation anticipated by the Commission, the hundreds of smaller operators already present on the market, taken as a whole, can respond effectively to a reduction in capacity put on to the market by the large tour operators to a level below estimated demand by increasing their capacity to take advantage of the opportunities inherent in a situation of overall under-supply and whether they can thereby counteract the creation of a collective dominant position".[95]

(c) New entry

8–052 Oligopolists will not be able profitably to implement a tacitly coordinated strategy[96] if it would be defeated by new entry[97] which is timely, likely and sufficient to prevent the exercise of market power.[98] In *Airtours plc v Commission*,[99] the Court of First Instance stated: "It should ... be borne in mind that ... what is important here is not whether there is scope for potential competitors to reach a sufficient size to compete on an equal footing with the large tour operators, but simply whether there is scope for such competitors to take advantage of opportunities afforded by the large operators restricting capacity put onto the relevant market to below a competitive level".[1]

---

[95] Para.213. See also para.266 (in which the Court of First Instance made the same point in relation to potential entry by tour operators operating in territories outside the United Kingdom).

[96] See Ivaldi *et al*, "The Economics of Tacit Collusion", Report for DG Competition, March 2003 (available via *http://europa.eu.int/comm/competition/mergers/review/the_economics_of_tacit_collusion_en.pdf*), pp.16 to 19, concluding: "Collusion cannot be sustained in the absence of entry barriers and it is more difficult to sustain, the lower the entry barriers".

[97] Entry barriers were found to be high in Case IV/M.190 *Nestlé / Perrier* [1992] O.J. L356/1; Case IV/M.358 *Pilkington-Techint / SIV* [1994] O.J. L158/24; Case IV/M.619 *Gencor / Lonrho* [1997] O.J. L11/30 (decision upheld on appeal in Case T-102/96 *Gencor v Commission* [1999] E.C.R. II-753); Case IV/M.1430 *Vodafone / Airtouch*, paras 27 to 28; Case COMP/M.1524 *Airtours / First Choice* [2000] O.J. L93/1 (annulled on appeal in Case T-342/99 *Airtours plc v Commission* [2002] E.C.R. II-2585); Case COMP/M.1663 *Alcan / Alusuisse* [2002] O.J. L90/1, paras 99 to 100; Case COMP/M.1741 *MCI WorldCom / Sprint* [2003] O.J. L300/1, paras 205 and 263; Case COMP/M.2389 *Shell / DEA* [2003] O.J. L15/35, paras 126 to 131; and Case COMP/M.2533 *BP / E.ON* [2002] O.J. L276/31, paras 63 and 67. The Commission noted the absence of potential competition in Case IV/M.1313 *Danish Crown / Vestjyske Slagterier* [2000] O.J. L20/1, para.174. For an example of a case involving low barriers to entry, see Case IV/M.1517 *Rhodia / Donau Chemie / Albright & Wilson*, paras 58 and 77. See also Case IV/M.1432 *Agfa-Gevaert / Sterling*, para.29; Case IV/M.1467 *Rohm and Haas / Morton*; and Case COMP/M.1838 *BT / ESAT*, para.15.

[98] See Case IV/M.315 *Mannesman / Vallourec / Ilva* [1994] O.J. L102/15, paras 116 to 124; Case IV/M.704 *Unilever / Diversey*, paras 26 to 28; Case IV/M.737 *Ciba-Geigy / Sandoz* [1997] O.J. L201/1, para.303; Case IV/M.1127 *Nestle / Dalgety* para.31; Case IV/M.1298 *Kodak / Imation*, para.60; Case IV/M.1383 *Exxon / Mobil* [2004] O.J. L103/1 para.48; and Case COMP/M.1835 *Monsanto / Pharmacia & Upjohn*, paras 84 to 87. New entry was found to be unlikely in Case COMP/M.2097 *SCA / Metsä Tissue*, paras 159, 163, 176, 186, 211, 221, 234 and 244.

[99] Case T-342/99 [2002] E.C.R. II-2585.

[1] Para.266.

(d) Countervailing buyer power

If buyers[2] have substantial power,[3] a tacitly coordinated outcome is less **8–053** likely[4] because of the difficulty in ensuring implementation[5] of the coordinated arrangements.[6] For example, by concentrating purchases with one supplier or entering long-term contracts, a large buyer may make coordination unstable by creating an incentive for a coordinating firm to deviate to win a significant piece of business.[7] The Commission has observed: "The ability of oligopolists to raise prices can be constrained by countervailing buyer power of customers. Powerful and concentrated customers may either prevent the oligopolists from engaging in parallel behaviour or provide a sufficient incentive to deviate from collusion and compete. This can be done in two ways. Firstly, customers may be able to play off suppliers against one another with a credible threat to switch between them. A short term switch would only be possible if the other suppliers have enough spare capacity to fill the large order. A second strategy would be the development of a new supplier or a credible threat to produce the good in question in-house".[8]

---

[2] See generally Ch.15.

[3] In particular, tacit coordination on price may be defeated by customers' ability to switch to other suppliers. In Case T–342/99 *Airtours plc v Commission* [2002] E.C.R. II-2585, the Court of First Instance emphasised, at para.274, that, "the fact that consumers do not have significant buyer power because they act in isolation must not be confused with the question of whether they would be able to react to a price rise brought about by the large tour operators restricting capacity put onto the market to an anti-competitive level". In that case, the Court of First Instance found that the Commission had underestimated the role that might be played by consumers comparing prices and switching to smaller tour operators; paras 274 and 275. The Commission found that customers did not have buyer power in Case COMP/M.2097 *SCA / Metsä Tissue* but they did in Case COMP/M.3680 *Alcatel / Finmeccanica / Alcatel Alenia Space & Telespazio*, para.113.

[4] See Ivaldi *et al*, "The Economics of Tacit Collusion", Report for DG Competition, March 2003 (available via *http://europa.eu.int/comm/competition/mergers/review/the_economics_of_tacit_collusion_en.pdf*), p.53; Case IV/M.1230 *Glaverbel / PPG*, para.26; Case IV/M.1245 *Valeo / ITT Industries* para.54; Case IV/M.1363 *DuPont / Hoechst / Herberts*, para.37; Case COMP/M.1891 *BP Amoco / Castrol* para.36; and Case COMP/M.2348 *Outokumpu / Norzink* paras 26 to 28. In Case COMP/M.1532 *BP Amoco / Arco*, the market investigation showed that "typical concession contracts between governments and explorers-producers prohibit the latter from limiting their output".

[5] Or uniform implementation.

[6] Case IV/M.1383 *Exxon / Mobil* [2004] O.J. L103/1, para.486. However, it should also be noted that a more fragmented buyer side increases the scope for cheating to be detected: Europe Economics, "Study on Assessment Criteria for Distinguishing between Competitive and Dominant Oligopolies in Merger Control", Final Report for the European Commission, May 2001, p.84.

[7] Notice on Horizontal Mergers, para.57.

[8] Commission paper tabled at OECD, "Oligopoly", Best Practice Roundtable, October 1999, DAFFE / CLP(99)25 (*www.oecd.org*), p.213, at pp.220 and 221. The Commission noted the absence of countervailing buyer power in Case IV/M.315 *Mannesmann / Vallourec / Ilva* [1994] O.J. L102/15 para.126; Case IV/M.818 *Cardo / Thyssen* para.32; Case IV/M.1313 *Danish Crown / Vestjyske Slagterier* [2000] O.J. L20/1 para.174; Case COMP/M.1663 *Alcan / Alusuisse* [2002] O.J. L90/1 para.104; and Case COMP/M.1741 *MCI WorldCom / Sprint* [2003] O.J. L300/1, paras 291 and 292. See the discussion in Europe Economics, "Study on Assessment Criteria for Distinguishing between Competitive and Dominant Oligopolies in Merger Control", Final Report for the European Commission, May 2001, pp.35, 36, 84 and 85. In Case COMP/M.1882 *Pirelli / BICC* [2003] O.J. L70/35, the Commission noted, at

In *Knorr-Bremse | Allied Signal*[9] the threat of commencing in-house production gave rise to buyer power. Similarly, in *Enso | Stora*[10] the possibility of customers sponsoring new entry was found to confer buyer power.

8–054 However, concentration on the buyer side is not sufficient in itself to conclude that tacit coordination is unlikely.[11] The Commission has stated: "A highly concentrated demand side, however, does not necessarily imply countervailing buyer power. In ... *Nestle | Perrier* the Commission concluded that even the large French retail chains were unable to countervail the emerging duopoly of mineral water producers. Moreover, even when there is, in the extreme, a bilateral oligopoly, the market structure may be at best neutral in cases where the intermediate firms face competition downstream or worse in that the intermediate firms may either pass on the price increase or even add their own supracompetitive margin (double marginalisation problem)".[12]

8.11 CAUSATION

8–055 The Notice on Horizontal Mergers states that a causal link exists if, as a result of the merger:

(a) it is significantly more likely that firms which were not previously coordinating their behaviour would begin to do so; or

(b) coordination would be easier, more stable or more effective for firms which were coordinating prior to the merger.[13]

Point (a) above is materially different from the formulation of the test adopted by the Commission in *Sony | BMG*,[14] which post-dates the adoption

---

para.90, that utilities had "various possibilities to thwart attempts of conscious parallel behaviour among bidders". See also Case IV/M.165 *Alcatel | AEG Kabel* para.25; Case IV/M.818 *Cardo | Thyssen*; Case IV/M.1363 *DuPont | Hoechst | Herberts* para.37; and Case IV/M.1491 *Robert Bosch | Magneti Marelli* para.28. Contrast: Case IV/M.190 *Nestlé | Perrier* [1992] O.J. L356/1 para.84; Case IV/M.619 *Gencor | Lonrho* [1997] O.J. L11/30, para.150 (decision upheld on appeal in Case T–102/96 *Gencor v Commission* [1999] E.C.R. II–753); and Case COMP/M.2498 *UPM-Kymmene | Haindl* [2002] O.J. L233/38 paras 100 to 105.

[9] Case IV/M.337.

[10] Case IV/M.1225 [1999] O.J. L254/9, para.91. See also Case IV/M.556 *Zeneca | Vanderhave*, paras 22 and 23.

[11] Baxter and Dethmers, "Collective Dominance Under EC Merger Control—After Airtours and the Introduction of Unilateral Effects is there Still a Future for Collective Dominance" [2006] E.C.L.R. 148, comments, at p.153, that buyer power has rarely been accepted as a factor rebutting a finding of coordinated effects.

[12] Commission paper tabled at OECD, "Oligopoly", Best Practice Roundtable, October 1999, DAFFE / CLP(99)25 (*www.oecd.org*), p.213, at p.220.

[13] Notice on Horizontal Mergers, paras 22(b) and 39.

[14] Case COMP/M.3333 [2005] O.J. L62/30 (appeal pending in Case T-464/04 *Impala v Commission*), para.157.

of the Notice. In that case, the Commission concluded that it had "not found sufficient evidence to prove that the reduction of the majors from five to four represents a change substantial enough to result in the likely creation of collective dominance". If the Commission is required to show that coordinated effects are "likely" to occur following the merger, then it must establish that the chances of their occurring are greater than 50 per cent (because the use of the word "likely" connotes a balance of probabilities test). By contrast, if the Commission is simply required to show that coordinated effects are "significantly more likely" to occur following the merger (as the Notice on Horizontal Mergers suggests), then it need only show that the chances of coordinated effects have increased significantly as a result of the merger and, accordingly, an increase from, say, 5 per cent to 35 per cent might well satisfy this criterion (although it would not satisfy a "likelihood" test).[15]

The importance of this issue is emphasised by the observation by Ivaldi *et al* (emphasis added): "Short of determining whether collusion will indeed occur, *a highly difficult if not impossible task*, the merger control office can however address a different but still relevant question: will the merger create a situation where collusion becomes more likely, that is, will collusion significantly be easier to sustain in the post-merger situation?"[16]

Many of the factors relevant to an assessment of coordinated effects are **8–056** likely to be unaffected by the merger. However, the merger may render coordinated effects more likely, for example because there are fewer suppliers,[17] the merger involves a maverick company whose incentives will be changed making it less competitive following the merger, or the merger renders competitors' costs structures more symmetrical.[18] Further, the merger may affect market transparency, product differentiation, characteristics of demand, multi-market contact or the operation of the market, all of which may have an effect on the likelihood of coordination.[19]

---

[15] See s.2.5(b) above for discussion of the standard of proof.

[16] Ivaldi *et al*, "The Economics of Tacit Collusion", Report for DG Competition, March 2003 (available via *http://europa.eu.int/comm/competition/mergers/review/the_economics_of_tacit_collusion_en.pdf*), p.64. Kühn, "Closing Pandora's Box? Joint Dominance After the Airtours Judgment", published as Ch.3 of *The Pros and Cons of Merger Control* by the Swedish Competition Authority in 2002 (and available at *www.kkv.se/bestall/pdf/skrift_proscons.pdf*), p.44, describes the causation issue as follows: "has the merger made it more or less credible to make the implicit promises of future collusion and threats of punishments that sustain collusive (or parallel) behaviour?"

[17] See the discussion in Kühn, "Closing Pandora's Box? Joint Dominance After the Airtours Judgment", published as Ch.3 of *The Pros and Cons of Merger Control* by the Swedish Competition Authority in 2002 (and available at *www.kkv.se/bestall/pdf/skrift_proscons.pdf*), p.45.

[18] Notice on Horizontal Mergers, para.42.

[19] See Ivaldi *et al*, "The Economics of Tacit Collusion", Report for DG Competition, March 2003 (available via *http://europa.eu.int/comm/competition/mergers/review/the_economics_of_tacit_collusion_en pdf*), p.69.

Conversely, a merger may render coordinated effects less likely in particular by increasing the asymmetry in costs structures.[20]

More particularly, an acquisition by a company forming part of the candidate oligopoly of an important "maverick" player (or an aggressive competitor) may have an impact on competition out of proportion to the impact on market share.[21] For example, in *Gencor / Lonrho*[22] the merger would have eliminated from the market Lonrho which had been a vigorous competitor.[23] For these purposes a "maverick"[24] is a supplier that has a history of preventing or disrupting coordination (e.g. by failing to follow price increases) or has characteristics (e.g. a materially different costs structure) that give it incentives to favour different strategic choices than its coordinating competitors.[25] In assessing whether a supplier operates as a maverick, it may be possible to compare situations in which the supplier is present (e.g. particular geographic markets or tenders for particular contracts) with those in which it is not, in order to assess the effects of the supplier's activities.[26] It is also important to analyse *why* a firm operates as a maverick (e.g. whether it has significant excess or low cost capacity or whether its costs structure creates materially different incentives from those facing other suppliers).[27]

8–057   The Commission will also examine the impact of a merger between oligopolists *on the members of the competitive fringe*. In *Airtours / First Choice*[28] one concern was that the merger would reduce the availability of charter airline seats to fringe suppliers, reducing their ability to act as a competitive constraint outside the oligopoly, although the Court of First Instance found that this conclusion was incorrect on the facts of that case.[29]

A transaction involving members of the competitive fringe may create or

---

[20] See para.8–022 above and Kühn, "Closing Pandora's Box? Joint Dominance After the Airtours Judgment", published as Ch.3 of *The Pros and Cons of Merger Control* by the Swedish Competition Authority in 2002 (and available at *www.kkv.se/bestall/pdf/skrift_proscons.pdf*), pp.46 and 57. Kühn concludes, at p.57: "The increased asymmetry argument should therefore always be accepted as a defense against the claim of creating or strengthening a collective dominant position".

[21] Notice on Horizontal Mergers, para.42.

[22] Case IV/M.619 [1997] O.J. L11/30 (decision upheld on appeal in Case T-102/96 *Gencor v Commission* [1999] E.C.R. II-753).

[23] See also Case COMP/M.2016 *France Télécom / Orange*, para.28 and Case COMP/M.3314 *Air Liquide / Messer Targets*, paras 122 and 123.

[24] The Canadian Merger Guidelines, 2004 (*www.competitionbureau.gc.ca/PDFs/2004%20MEGs.Final.pdf*), state, at n.75: "A maverick is a firm that has a disproportionate incentive to deviate from coordinated behaviour". Ivaldi *et al*, "The Economics of Tacit Collusion", Report for DG Competition, March 2003 (available via *http://europa.eu.int/comm/competition/mergers/review/the_economics_of_tacit_collusion_en.pdf*) define a maverick, at p.40, as "a firm with a drastically different cost structure, which is thus unwilling to participate to a collusive action"; see also the discussion at p.55.

[25] Notice on Horizontal Mergers, para.42.

[26] See Scheffman & Coleman, "Quantitative Analyses of Potential Competitive Effects From a Merger" (*www.usdoj.gov/atr/public/workshops/docs/202661.htm*).

[27] See Scheffman & Coleman, "Quantitative Analyses of Potential Competitive Effects From a Merger" (*www.usdoj.gov/atr/public/workshops/docs/202661.htm*).

[28] Case COMP/M.1524 [2000] O.J. L93/1, paras 78, 79 and 83.

[29] Case T-342/99 *Airtours plc v Commission* [2002] E.C.R. II-2585, paras 229 to 251.

strengthen a position of *collective dominance held by third parties* not forming part of the concentration.[30] In *EnBW / EDP / Cajastur / Hidro-cantábrico*[31] one of the companies acquiring joint control of the Spanish utility Hidrocantábrico was jointly controlled by the French electricity company, EDF. The Commission identified EDF as the main competitor to the existing Spanish electricity generators and concluded that its indirect interest in Hidrocantábrico would reduce EDF's incentives to promote or accept a substantial expansion in interconnection capacity between France and Spain. The Commission therefore found that the concentration would strengthen a dominant position held jointly by Endesa and Iberdrola.

The US Non-Horizontal Merger Guidelines state[32] that the elimination of a disruptive *buyer* in a downstream market (i.e. vertical integration) is unlikely to result in adverse competitive consequences unless the upstream market is generally conducive to collusion and the disruptive firm is significantly more attractive to sellers than the other firms in its market.[33]

8.12 CAPACITY

(a) Introduction

Suppliers' capacity may be relevant to the analysis of tacit coordination in **8–058** four specific respects.[34]

(a) Symmetry in spare capacity or over-capacity[35] may affect the likelihood of tacit coordination.

(b) Symmetry in actual capacity[36] may affect the likelihood of tacit coordination.

(c) The reference point for a tacitly coordinated outcome may be suppliers' capacity.

(d) The introduction of new capacity by a rival supplier may result in

---

[30] See para.2–023 above.

[31] Case COMP/M.2684, paras 33 and 37. See also Case COMP/M.2434 *Grupo Villar Mir / EnBW / Hidroélectrica del Cantábrico* [2004] O.J. L48/86.

[32] The US Non-Horizontal Merger Guidelines, 1984 (*www.usdoj.gov/atr/public/guidelines/2614.htm*), para.4.222.

[33] See Areeda, Hovenkamp & Solow, *Antitrust Law* (2nd edn, Aspen Law & Business, 1998), Vol.IVA, paras 1001 and 1006.

[34] See generally Ivaldi *et al*, "The Economics of Tacit Collusion", Report for DG Competition, March 2003 (available via *http://europa.eu.int/comm/competition/mergers/review/the_economics_of_tacit_collusion_en.pdf*), pp. 41 to 45. Areeda, Hovenkamp & Solow, *Antitrust Law* (2nd edn, Aspen Law & Business, 1998), Vol.IV, argue, at para.944e3, that, since excess capacity can point both towards and against a finding of coordinated effects, it is virtually useless as a factor in analysing mergers.

[35] Case COMP/M.1939 *Rexam / American National Can*, para.24.

[36] Case COMP/M.2389 *Shell / DEA* [2003] O.J. L15/35, para.83.

"continuous price competition", in which case a merger is unlikely to lead to coordinated effects.[37]

(b) Symmetry in over-capacity

8–059 Suppliers' over-capacity may have the following effects.

(a) If all of the oligopoly suppliers are operating at or near full capacity, the suppliers have a lower incentive and ability to cheat if they cannot expand their output.[38] However, if there are tight capacity constraints, it may not be possible to identify a deterrent mechanism.[39]

(b) If one supplier has substantial over-capacity but others do not, the likelihood of tacit coordination is reduced, since the supplier with over-capacity has an incentive to reduce prices to win business but others do not.[40] In *Schmalbach-Lubeca / Rexam*[41] the Commission found that "the asymmetric distribution of the suppliers' capacity and spare capacity indicates the absence of an oligopolistic market equilibrium, which would make collusive behaviour unsustainable over the medium to long term".

(c) By contrast, if the players have symmetric over-capacity,[42] each may have a similar incentive not to compete, on the basis that any price reduction can be matched quickly by competitors, establishing an effective retaliatory mechanism.

It follows that a merger which *increases the over-capacity asymmetry* is likely to *reduce* the scope for coordinated effects, other things being equal.[43]

(c) Actual capacity

8–060 There are suggestions that the supplier with the smallest capacity share has the least incentive to enter a tacitly coordinated arrangement and the

---

[37] Case COMP/M.2314 *BASF / Eurodiol / Pantochim* [2002] O.J. L132/45, paras 74 to 76.

[38] Europe Economics, "Study on Assessment Criteria for Distinguishing between Competitive and Dominant Oligopolies in Merger Control", Final Report for the European Commission, May 2001, p.34.

[39] See Kühn, "Closing Pandora's Box? Joint Dominance After the Airtours Judgment", published as Ch.3 of *The Pros and Cons of Merger Control* by the Swedish Competition Authority in 2002 (available via *www.kkv.se/bestall/pdf/skrift_proscons.pdf*), p.55.

[40] Case IV/M.358 *Pilkington-Techint / SIV* [1994] O.J. L158/24. Similarly, unevenly distributed capacities are an indicator that the market will not facilitate coordinated effects: see Case IV/M.390 *Akzo / Nobel Industrier*, para.18 and Case IV/M.1517 *Rhodia / Donau Chemie / Albright & Wilson*, para.71.

[41] Case COMP/M.2542, para.18.

[42] Case COMP/M.1939 *Rexam / American National Can*, para.24.

[43] For this reason, focusing on HHIs may be misleading in examining coordinated effects.

greatest incentive to cheat because it is likely to derive the smallest share of the increase in profits arising from coordination whilst having the greatest incentive to increase output (because, if a smaller supplier were to increase its output by a specified percentage, it would have a relatively smaller impact on the market price than a larger supplier).[44] If this model accurately reflects market operation, it suggests that a merger not involving the smaller players within the oligopoly may create fewer concerns (if any) than a merger involving one or more of the smaller players within the oligopoly.

(d) Tacit coordination on capacity

The Commission has analysed the scope for tacit coordination with capacity **8–061** as the reference point in the following cases.[45]

(a) *Airtours / First Choice*[46] related to the UK market for short-haul package holidays. The Commission found that a reduction in the number of large players from four to three would have increased the scope for coordination, particularly to avoid over-capacity. Suppliers had to set their capacity (in terms of numbers of charter flights, hotel rooms, etc.) well in advance (up to one year) in a market in which over-capacity resulted in deep discounting (because the suppliers' costs were largely sunk and it was therefore important for them to sell all of the units) which, in turn, caused customers to delay their purchases in future periods to take advantage of the discounts. The Commission's decision was annulled by the Court of First Instance, which found that the Commission had made several errors in its appraisal of the evidence.[47] In any event, *Airtours* was an unusual case as the decisions on new investment were made regularly and

---

[44] Frontier Economics, Competition Bulletin, January, 2002, "Fearful asymmetry" (*www.frontier-economics.com*).

[45] See Ivaldi *et al*, "The Economics of Tacit Collusion", Report for DG Competition, March 2003 (available via *http://europa.eu.int/comm/competition/mergers/review/the_economics_of_tacit_collusion_en.pdf*), pp.59 to 61; Porter, *Competitive Strategy* (The Free Press, 1998 edn), Ch.15; Kühn, "Closing Pandora's Box? Joint Dominance After the Airtours Judgment", published as Ch.3 of *The Pros and Cons of Merger Control* by the Swedish Competition Authority in 2002 (available via *http://www.kkv.se/bestall/pdf/skrift_proscons.pdf*), p.55 (noting that if capacity decisions are irreversible, collusion in reducing capacity investments may not be feasible); and Scheffman & Coleman, "Quantitative Analyses of Potential Competitive Effects From a Merger" (*www.usdoj.gov/atr/public/workshops/docs/202661.htm*) (noting that if capacity can be altered incrementally, e.g. through de-bottlenecking, then transparency as to actual capacity may be reduced).

[46] Case COMP/M.1524 [2000] O.J. L93/1.

[47] Case T-342/99 *Airtours plc v Commission* [2002] E.C.R. II-2585, para.294. By the time of the hearing, there was little difference between the parties on the *legal principles* applicable to cases of coordinated effects (see in particular para.62) and the Court's decision therefore does not preclude the Commission from finding on proper evidence that a transaction is likely to give rise to coordination in setting capacity.

were applicable only for a short period (i.e. the holiday season). In the more normal case of investment by a manufacturer, the investment is commonly durable and irreversible, with the consequence that investment decisions affect the ongoing operation of the market.

(b) In *UPM-Kymmene / Haindl*[48] the Commission considered the scope for tacit coordination on investment in new capacity[49] through a process of announcements and counter-announcements of plans to install new paper machines. After a detailed inquiry, the Commission found that this was highly improbable because of a lack of transparency and the absence of a credible punishment threat. Indeed, tacit coordination on new capacity is likely to be complicated in most cases by the "first-mover" advantages enjoyed by the first supplier to add to its investment.[50]

(c) In *Mitsui / CVRD / Caemi*[51] the Commission concluded that a punishment mechanism which responded to unauthorised capacity expansion with further capacity expansion was not necessarily lacking in credibility given the high levels of expected market growth.[52] However, it found that coordination on capacity expansion would not be likely to work effectively because expansion of the industry involved small numbers of large investments which were difficult to coordinate without express collusion, the product was differentiated, growth rates were expected to differ by regions, and customers could threaten the stability of the arrangement.

(d) In *Areva / Urenco / ETC JV*[53] the joint venture agreement provided that any increase in capacity by either Areva or Urenco required the approval of both parties. The Commission found that the parents would choose a level of capacity that maximised their joint profit and concluded that this would result in increases in prices (because there was a significant link between capacity and price in the market). The transaction was approved only after these veto rights were removed.

---

[48] Case COMP/M.2498 [2002] O.J. L233/38.
[49] Case COMP/M.2499 *Norske Skog / Parenco / Walsum* [2002] O.J. L233/38, paras 127 to 139.
[50] See Europe Economics, "Study on Assessment Criteria for Distinguishing between Competitive and Dominant Oligopolies in Merger Control", Final Report for the European Commission, May 2001, p.27.
[51] Case COMP/M.2420 [2004] O.J. L92/50, paras 238 to 246.
[52] The arguments deployed against such a punishment mechanism were that it would harm all suppliers, capacity exerts long-term effects on the market, and the punishment would not affect the maverick's behaviour as it would be committed to using the capacity it had installed; para.240.
[53] Case COMP/M.3099, paras 157, 158, 164, 175 and 191.

8.13 STRUCTURAL LINKS

Links[54] between the parties are not necessary for a finding of coordinated **8–062** effects[55] but they *may* increase the likelihood of tacit coordination.[56] Such links may comprise partial cross-shareholdings,[57] cross-directorships, joint shareholdings,[58] partial ownership by third parties, family links with economic consequences, joint ventures,[59] alliances,[60] shared ownership of distribution channels or supplies, model conditions of supply drawn up by a common trade association, cooperative research and development agreements,[61] cross-licences, involvement in sector regulation,[62] etc.

The Commission has commented: "Such links may reduce the competitive zeal between the oligopolists, they may represent potential means of retaliation and depending on the circumstances such links would also result in a certain common commercial interest in the market in question. Therefore, the impact of a merger in terms of whether it creates or gives a different

---

[54] The Commission found structural links in Case IV/M.1313 *Danish Crown | Vestjyske Slagterier* [2000] O.J. L20/1, para.117 and Case IV/M.1430 *Vodafone | AirTouch*, para.28.

[55] This was confirmed in Case T-102/96 *Gencor v Commission* [1999] E.C.R. II-753 when the Court of First Instance stated, at para.276: "There is no reason whatsoever in legal or economic terms to exclude from the notion of economic links the relationship of interdependence existing between the parties to a tight oligopoly within which, in a market with the appropriate characteristics, in particular in terms of market concentration, transparency and product homogeneity, those parties are in a position to anticipate one another's behaviour and are therefore strongly encouraged to align their conduct in the market, in particular in such a way as to maximise their joint profits by restricting production with a view to increasing prices". This passage was quoted in Case T-342/99 *Airtours plc v Commission* [2002] E.C.R. II-2585, para.60.

[56] See Ivaldi *et al*, "The Economics of Tacit Collusion", Report for DG Competition, March 2003 (available via *http://europa.eu.int/comm/competition/mergers/review/the_economics_of_tacit_collusion_en.pdf*), p.53.

[57] See, e.g. Case COMP/M.1673 *VEBA | VIAG* [2001] O.J. L188/1, para.78.

[58] See, e.g. Case COMP/M.1673 *VEBA | VIAG* [2001] O.J. L188/1, para.79.

[59] See Ivaldi *et al*, "The Economics of Tacit Collusion", Report for DG Competition, March 2003 (available via *http://europa.eu.int/comm/competition/mergers/review/the_economics_of_tacit_collusion_en.pdf*), p.54; Case IV/M.1332 *Thomson | Lucas*, para.16; Case COMP/M.1663 *Alcan | Alusuisse* [2002] O.J. L90/1 (Norf joint venture); Case COMP/M.2389 *Shell | DEA* [2003] O.J. L15/35; Case COMP/M.2499 *Norske Skog | Parenco | Walsum* [2002] O.J. L233/38, paras 95 to 99; and Case COMP/M.3099 *Areva | Urenco | ETC JV*, para.195. For a detailed discussion of the scope for joint ventures to facilitate coordinated effects, see Rabassa, "Joint Ventures as a Mechanism that May Favour Co-ordination: An Analysis of the Aluminium and Music Mergers" [2004] E.C.L.R. 771 (arguing, at pp.772 and 773, that the principal mechanisms by which joint ventures may facilitate coordinated effects are: limitation of independent decision-making through the ownership structure and control over key assets, exchange of information within the joint venture, and the use of joint ventures as part of the deterrent mechanism).

[60] See, e.g. Case COMP/M.3765 *Amer | Salomon*, paras 135, 138, 155 and 156 (agreement with a competitor providing for exchange of commercially sensitive information and granting influence over competitive behaviour) and Case COMP/M.3829 *Maersk | PONL* (shipping alliances; paras 40 to 43, 76 to 79, 97, 98, 120 to 122, 130 to 134, 140 to 142, 148 to 151 and 157 to 161).

[61] See Case IV/M.1245 *Valeo | ITT Industries*, para.54.

[62] Case IV/M.1016 *Price Waterhouse | Coopers & Lybrand* [1999] O.J. L50/27, paras 101 and 102.

quality to such structural links needs to be assessed. However, structural links are not a necessary condition for a finding of oligopolistic dominance".[63]

8–063 It follows that structural links between the parties are relevant to an analysis of coordinated effects insofar as a *mechanism* can be identified through which the links may affect the candidate oligopolists' incentive and ability to tacitly coordinate.[64]

(a) In *Airtours plc v Commission*[65] the Court of First Instance emphasised, in annulling the Commission's decision, that: "the Commission has not explained why what it regards as commercial links (purchase of airline seats from the others and sale of its own products in agencies owned by the others) must be explained solely in terms of strong economic links between the major operators ... and cannot simply be explained on the ground that it is profitable to maintain those links in a competitive situation, given that the major tour operators are economic units, firmly entrenched in several markets within the industry and that it is in their interest to be profitable and to maximise their revenues in those markets as a whole".

(b) Contacts between competitors may result in similar cost structures,[66] as the Commission found with the joint export company in *Danish Crown | Vestjyske Slagterier*.[67]

(c) Partial ownership and inter-locking directorships may alter the oligopolists' incentives to coordinate.[68]

---

[63] Commission paper tabled at OECD, "Oligopoly", Best Practice Roundtable, October 1999, DAFFE/CLP(99)25 (*www.oecd.org*), p.213, at p.218. The text follows closely the wording in the Commission's decision in Case IV/M.1383 *Exxon | Mobil* [2004] O.J. L103/1, para.480.

[64] See also Case IV/M.190 *Nestlé | Perrier* [1992] O.J. L356/1 (the joint reaction by two of the three existing suppliers of bottled water in France to a bid by a third party for Perrier was regarded by the Commission as a joint entry deterrence action; para.127). In Case T-342/99 *Airtours plc v Commission* [2002] E.C.R. II-2585, the Court of First Instance found, at para.91, that: "the fact that to some extent (30 to 40% of the shares) the same institutional investors are found in [the three companies alleged to form part of the collectively dominant oligopoly] cannot be regarded as evidence that there is already a tendency to collective dominance in the industry ... [There] is no suggestion ... that the group of institutional shareholders forms a united body controlling those quoted companies or providing a mechanism for exchange of information between the three undertakings".

[65] Case T-342/99 [2002] E.C.R. II-2585, para.285. See also para.289.

[66] Symmetry in costs structures is an important indicator of the likelihood of tacit coordination: see s.8.7(e) above. See also Case COMP/M.2499 *Norske Skog | Parenco | Walsum* [2002] O.J. L233/38, paras 89 to 94.

[67] Case IV/M.1313 [2000] O.J. L20/1. See also Case COMP/M.1939 *Rexam | American National Can*, para.24.

[68] See Europe Economics, "Study on Assessment Criteria for Distinguishing between Competitive and Dominant Oligopolies in Merger Control", Final Report for the European Commission, May 2001, p.41, and OECD, "Oligopoly", Best Practice Roundtable, October 1999, DAFFE/CLP(99)25 (*www.oecd.org*), p.213, at pp.241 and 242.

(d) Commercial contact between oligopolists may increase transparency. A provision in a contract between Interbrew and Scottish & Newcastle for meetings to occur between the two major brewers and suppliers of premium lager in the United Kingdom was deleted whilst the Commission was examining the notification in *Interbrew / Beck's*,[69] enabling it to clear the transaction without conditions.[70]

8.14 EVIDENCE OF HISTORIC CARTEL ACTIVITY

There is controversy over the weight, if any, to be placed on evidence of **8–064** previous cartel activity in a market when assessing coordinated effects.[71] The existence of such activity[72] may be taken as an indicator that the parties have an *incentive* to coordinate[73] or that *market conditions are conducive* to coordinated effects.[74] On the other hand, it is reasonable to assume that senior managers[75] at companies will nowadays[76] choose to form an unlawful cartel (creating attendant risks of fines, damages actions and, in some jurisdictions, criminal penalties for individuals) only if they cannot achieve the same result lawfully through coordinated effects; this tends to suggest that the existence of previous cartel activity is a pointer *against* a finding of coordinated effects in the absence of evidence that conditions have materially change since the cartel ended (or will materially change as a result of the merger).[77] It has therefore been argued that limited weight should be placed on previous evidence of cartel activity,[78] and the Commission has

---

[69] Case COMP/M.2569.
[70] *Financial Times*, October 27/28, 2001, p.17.
[71] See generally Robert & Hudson, "Past Co-ordination and the Commission Notice on the Appraisal of Horizontal Mergers" [2004] E.C.L.R. 163 and Federal Trade Commission and Department of Justice, "Commentary on the Horizontal Merger Guidelines", 2006 (available via www.ftc.gov/os/2006/03/CommentaryontheHorizontalMergerGuidelinesMarch2006.pdf), pp.22 to 24.
[72] In the absence of any material changes in market structure.
[73] Case COMP/M.3314 *Air Liquide / Messer Targets*, paras 92 and 123.
[74] US Horizontal Merger Guidelines, 1992 (amended in 1997) (*www.usdoj.gov/atr/public/guidelines/hmg.htm*), s.2.1. See also Areeda, Hovenkamp & Solow, *Antitrust Law* (2nd edn, Aspen Law & Business, 1998), Vol.IV, para.944b.
[75] Some cartel activity is organised by middle and junior managers and sales personnel who may not assess whether similar results could be achieved through coordinated effects.
[76] The point made in the text may not have been true in the 1960s or 1970s when the culture of compliance with antitrust laws was less firmly established within Europe.
[77] See Robert & Hudson, "Past Co-ordination and the Commission Notice on the Appraisal of Horizontal Mergers" [2004] E.C.L.R. 163, at p.167.
[78] See Europe Economics, "Study on Assessment Criteria for Distinguishing between Competitive and Dominant Oligopolies in Merger Control", Final Report for the European Commission, May 2001, p.89: "the Commission should be rather cautious in putting weight on ... past collusive behaviour". See also Dick, "Strengthening the Micro Foundations for Coordinated Interaction in Merger Analysis", available at *www.usdoj.gov/atr/public/workshops/docs/202659.htm*.

CHAPTER 9

LOSS OF POTENTIAL COMPETITION AND MERGERS IN NEIGHBOURING MARKETS

9.1 INTRODUCTION

The Notice on Horizontal Mergers states[1]: "A merger with a potential **9–001** competitor can generate horizontal anti-competitive effects, whether coordinated or non-coordinated, if the potential competitor significantly constrains the behaviour of the firms active in the market".[2] It follows that the elimination of potential competition from a merging party is a "theory of competitive harm" or a possible ground for objecting to a transaction.[3] This Chapter discusses the loss of potential competition in a market in which the other merging party is present (s.9.2) and the separate question of whether a merger between suppliers in neighbouring markets might significantly impede effective competition (s.9.3).

9.2 LOSS OF POTENTIAL COMPETITION

(a) General

The loss of a potential competitor through a merger may harm competition[4] **9–002**
through one of two distinct mechanisms. First, the merger may harm *actual*

---

[1] Para.59.
[2] The Form CO requires (see para.6.3(a)) the notifying parties to identify markets on which "any of the parties to the concentration has a market share larger than 25% and any other party to the concentration is a potential competitor into that market". The Form CO states, also at para.6.3(a): "A party may be considered a potential competitor, in particular, where it has plans to enter a market, or has developed or pursued such plans in the past two years".
[3] See generally Areeda & Turner, *Antitrust Law* (Aspen Law & Business, 1980), Vol.V, s.11B–2.
[4] For discussion of the legal question of whether a merger may be prohibited on the basis of loss of potential competition when one of the merging parties already has a monopoly, see para.2–024 above, considering the decision of the Court of First Instance in Case T-87/05 *EDP v Commission* not yet reported, judgment of September 21, 2005.

potential competition, and might therefore result in a lost opportunity for improvement in market performance. In general, the most likely *actual* potential competitors are those which possess assets that could easily be used to enter the market without incurring significant sunk costs,[5] e.g. companies active in neighbouring product or geographic markets or those which have in place a distribution system comparable to suppliers in the market in question. The loss of potential competition through a merger may be material if one of the merging parties was likely to incur the necessary sunk costs to enter the market in a relatively short period of time.[6] Secondly, the merger may harm *perceived* potential competition if the perceived threat of entry from the target is already constraining activity in the market, in particular if the incumbents are practising *limit pricing*[7] (i.e. pricing at a level below the short run profit-maximising level in order to avoid creating an incentive for potential competitors to enter the market). Such potential competition may be perceived irrespective of whether the potential competitor has any plans to enter.[8] *Perceived potential competition*[9] is unlikely to affect the prices of *existing suppliers* unless existing suppliers cannot rapidly reduce their prices in response to entry. If they can, a potential entrant would not assume that post-entry prices will be the same as pre-entry prices, and existing suppliers are therefore unlikely to engage in limit pricing.

The elimination of *actual* or *perceived* potential competition is unlikely to harm consumer welfare if:

(a)   the market is not concentrated—as rival suppliers will, through the competitive process, protect consumer welfare;

(b)   in the case of actual potential competition, entry by the merging party is unlikely—as the effect of the merger on market performance is remote; or

(c)   conditions for entry are favourable—consumers will be protected by

---

[5] Notice on Horizontal Mergers, para.59.
[6] Notice on Horizontal Mergers, para.59. A distinction may be drawn between: *product extension mergers* between firms which sell non-competing products but which may use related marketing or distribution channels and *market extension mergers* between firms which supply similar products in different geographic markets.
[7] See para.6–004 above.
[8] It is difficult to establish an effect on market operation from perceived potential competition; see Areeda & Turner, *Antitrust Law* (Aspen Law & Business, 1980), Vol.V, para.1120e.
[9] The Australian Merger Guidelines, June 1999 (*www.accc.gov.au/content/item.phtml? itemId= 719436&nodeId=file43a1f42c7eb63&fn=Merger%20Guidelines.pdf*), para.5.127, consider the circumstances in which perceived potential competition is likely, stating: "where purchases are one-off, such as building services, actual entry may be required before there is any impact on current conduct, since high prices today are unlikely to deter tomorrow's customers. However, for goods which are subject to repeat purchases and significant customer loyalty, potential entry is more likely to have an impact on current conduct, which has the potential to lose customers in the future. Product life is also important. Customers may choose to extend the life of their existing durable goods rather than buy new ones if the price is too high. In such markets, entry need not occur as swiftly to be effective".

entry from third parties[10] which would be likely, timely and sufficient to defeat any attempted exercise of market power by the merged group.[11]

Conversely, loss of potential competition is a concern in markets which are **9–003** highly concentrated, with high barriers to entry and where one of the merging parties is *well placed* to enter the market and *better placed* than all or most other potential entrants.[12] The Notice on Horizontal Mergers provides:

"For a merger with a potential competitor to have significant anti-competitive effects, two basic conditions must be fulfilled. First, the potential entrant must already exert a significant constraining influence or there must be a significant likelihood that it would grow into an effective competitive force. Evidence that a potential competitor has plans to enter a market in a significant way could help the Commission to reach such a conclusion. Second, there must not be a sufficient number of other potential competitors, which could maintain sufficient competitive pressure after the merger".[13]

The Commission's analysis therefore involves assessing the incentives and abilities of each of the candidate entrants (including the merging party) and the likely development of competition on the market. The Commission may examine the internal documents not only of the potential entrants (to assess their plans) but also of the incumbent merging party (to identify the suppliers that it regards as the most likely entrants).[14]

(b) The Commission's decision in Air Liquide / BOC

Air Liquide / BOC[15] was a case involving harm to *actual* potential compe- **9–004** tition from a market extension merger. The transaction involved a merger of

---

[10] For discussion about forecasting potential entrants, see Porter, *Competitive Strategy* (1998 edn, The Free Press), p.50.
[11] Götz Drauz has commented, "Recent Developments in the Assessment of Dominance" published in *EC Merger Control: Ten Years On* (International Bar Association, 2000), p.109, at p.117: "in concentrated markets with high barriers to entry, the Commission will not hesitate to challenge concentrations that would remove an important source of potential competition, and thereby strengthen an existing dominant position. This obviously does not mean that we will challenge any merger with an effect on potential competition. But we will, in the same way as applying potential competition as a defence, be concerned when a merger would remove the possibility of potential entry or expansion that in a timely, likely and sufficient manner could have constrained an existing dominant position".
[12] For discussion of the evidential difficulties associated with cases involving loss of potential competition, see Areeda & Turner, *Antitrust Law* (Aspen Law & Business, 1980), Vol.V, para.1121.
[13] Para.60.
[14] See Case COMP/M.3695 *BT / Radianz*, para.30.
[15] Case COMP/M.1630 [2004] O.J. L92/1.

substantial suppliers of bulk and cylinder gases in neighbouring geographic markets, France and the United Kingdom/Ireland. The Commission found that the merger would create or strengthen a dominant position in the supply of bulk and cylinder gases in the United Kingdom/Ireland as it would eliminate Air Liquide as an actual potential entrant.[16] In analysing the issue, the Commission found that BOC had dominant positions in the United Kingdom/Ireland[17] (and the markets were therefore highly concentrated) and barriers to entry were high.[18] It also found that Air Liquide was *well placed* to enter BOC's home markets[19] in the light of Air Liquide's strong capability to overcome the barriers to entry into the market by setting up a production and distribution infrastructure given: its financial strength and technological expertise[20]; its record as the most successful entrant in other European markets for industrial gases[21]; and internal Air Liquide documents demonstrating that Air Liquide had considered supplying the United Kingdom when consulted by a customer.[22] Finally, the Commission found that Air Liquide was *better placed* than any competitor successfully to sustain such market entry. The Commission identified four other companies with the ability to enter the markets in the United Kingdom/Ireland or to expand in those markets but concluded that their competitive strength, especially when weighed against the incumbent BOC's market power, was much more limited than Air Liquide's. The Commission found that: "Air Liquide is therefore the only credible potential competitor. In conclusion, potential competition in the markets for cylinder and bulk gases in the United Kingdom and Ireland depends on Air Liquide's continuing presence as an independent competitor. Once the incumbent (BOC) and the strongest potential entrant (Air Liquide) were merged, this competitive pressure would be lost".[23]

The Commission also found that the merger would eliminate potential competition from BOC in Air Liquide's home market in France for the supply of bulk and cylinder gases. It concluded that BOC was a potential competitor "having demonstrated that it can establish a bulk and cylinder

---

[16] Paras 152 and 201 to 222. The Commission's analysis focused exclusively on Air Liquide's incentive and ability to enter the markets in the United Kingdom/Ireland and it is therefore to be inferred that the Commission's decision was based on *actual* potential competition rather than *perceived* potential competition. If the case were one of *perceived* potential competition, the focus would have been on *competitors'* assessments of the likelihood of Air Liquide entering the market.

[17] Paras 154 to 168.

[18] The Commission noted, at para.209, that: "the main barriers to entry consist of the capital investment and operating expenses involved in establishing and sustaining a production and distribution infrastructure, in the acquisition of a sufficient customer base to justify that expenditure, and in the financing of operative losses during a start-up period until the newly established business becomes profitable".

[19] Paras 201 and 219.

[20] Paras 214, 216 and 217.

[21] Para.203.

[22] Para.203.

[23] Paras 219 and 220.

gases business in continental Europe"[24] but did not analyse whether there were any other credible competitors into the market or whether BOC enjoyed an entry advantage in comparison with those competitors.

(c) The Commission's other decisions

The Commission has also considered whether transactions raise substantive **9–005** concerns through the elimination of one of the merging parties as a potential competitor in the following cases.[25]

(a) *Glaxo Wellcome / SmithKline Beecham*[26] involved the pharmaceutical industry, where a distinction is drawn between drugs which are on the market (pharmaceutical specialities) and drugs which are under development (pipeline products). Pipeline products pass through three phases before coming to market and there is a risk of failure at each phase.[27] The Commission was concerned about the elimination of potential competition in the supply of treatments for chronic obstructive pulmonary disease, finding that Glaxo Wellcome had a 35 to 45 per cent share in the diagnosis categories in which the parties' pipeline products were mostly indicated. The Commission's approach in this case is significant because it focused on Phase III compounds, which are likely to be launched on the market within *three years*, to the exclusion of Phase II compounds, which are likely

---

[24] Para.198.
[25] See also Case IV/M.53 *Aerospatiale / Alenia / de Havilland* [1991] O.J. L334/42, para.31; Case IV/M.833 *The Coca-Cola Company / Carlsberg A/S* [1998] O.J. L145/41 (elimination of potential competition in brands); Case IV/M.950 *Hoffmann-La Roche / Boehringer Mannheim* [1998] O.J. L234/14 (the transaction strengthened a dominant position by eliminating "the best placed potential entrant to the European markets"; paras 140 to 142); Case COMP/ M.1403 *Astra / Zeneca* (the Commission identified Zeneca as the only likely source of competition in a market, relying on the fact that it had concluded an exclusive worldwide agreement (except for Japan) to license-in a competitive product; paras 83 and 84); Case COMP/M.2530 *Südzucker / Saint Louis Sucre* [2003] O.J. L103/1 (the merger would eliminate a potential competitor to Südzucker in geographic areas close to Saint Louis Sucre's home market in France; paras 80 to 125); Case COMP/JV.37 *BSkyB / KirchPayTV* (News International, which owned a stake in BSkyB, was found *not* to be a credible actual potential competitor in the pay-TV market in Germany; paras 71 and 72); Case COMP/M.2803 *Telia / Sonera*, paras 75 to 77; Case COMP/M.2876 *NewsCorp / Telepiù* [2004] O.J. L110/73 (Telecom Italia was found not to be a credible potential competitor in the Italian pay-TV market as it was exiting full scale operations and had no commercial incentive to reactivate its cable network to offer full scale pay-TV services; paras 295 and 297); Case COMP/M.3149 *Procter & Gamble / Wella* (considering whether Procter & Gamble had been "the most likely and most credible" potential entrant; para.44); Case COMP/M.3280 *Air France / KLM* (appeal pending in Case T-177/04 *easyJet Airline Company v Commission*) (loss of the "most likely" potential competitor; para.92; see also paras 119 and 120); Case COMP/M.3695 *BT / Radianz* (BT was not "the most important and the most likely entrant"); and Case COMP/M.3817 *Wegener / PCM / JV* (the Commission relied on a previous failed attempt at entry in finding that PCM was unlikely to enter in the future if the merger did not proceed; para.52).
[26] Case COMP/M.1846.
[27] Para.70.

to be launched within *four to five years* and which have a higher failure rate.[28] Also, the Commission was unable to judge which of the potential new products was likely to succeed and therefore accepted an undertaking to outlicense one of the parties' products *if* competing Phase III pipeline compounds for the treatment in question failed.[29] The Commission was not concerned about the elimination of potential competition in asthma treatments because at least one competing product was likely to be launched before SmithKline Beecham's and a large number of competitors had Phase II pipeline products for asthma.[30]

(b) In *EDF / EnBW*[31] the Commission found that the merger would eliminate one of the *most likely* and *strategically best placed* potential entrants into the market for the supply of electricity to large customers in France, given that EnBW's supply area had a common border with France, there were electricity interconnectors joining EnBW's supply area with EDF's, and EnBW had access to generation capacity in France.

(c) In *Telia / Telenor*[32] the national telephone operators in Sweden and Norway were regarded as the most likely entrants into one another's national markets, in circumstances in which no other company had the business incentives, commitment and experience to replace that level of competition.

(d) In *Swissair / Sabena*[33] the Commission identified Sabena as the "most likely and significant" potential entrant to the Brussels-Bern route because a Treaty between Belgium and Switzerland designated Swissair and Sabena as the only airlines permitted to fly on that route.

(e) In the second *Tetra Laval / Sidel*[34] decision (following the Court of First Instance's judgment quashing the original prohibition decision), the Commission found that the merger would create a dominant position in high-capacity SBM machines by combining Sidel's existing strong position (share of 50 to 60 per cent by installed capacity) with Tetra Laval's "Tetra Fast" technology which had been patented and was being developed for use on SBM machines. The Commission found that no other competitor had technology in the pipeline which showed comparable promise and that barriers to

---

[28] Para.190.
[29] Para.195.
[30] Para.177.
[31] Case COMP/M.1853, paras 51 to 68.
[32] Case COMP/M.1439 [2001] O.J. L40/1, paras 148 to 154.
[33] Case IV/M.616, paras 27 to 30. The Commission cleared the transaction on the basis of a declaration by the Swiss and Belgian governments to take steps to amend the Treaty so that rival airlines could operate on the route in question; paras 42 to 44.
[34] Case COMP/M.2416 (decision of January 13, 2003), para.99.

entry and expansion were high. It therefore identified serious doubts regarding the creation of a dominant position in high-capacity SBM machines.[35]

(f) In *Pfizer / Pharmacia*[36] the Commission identified serious doubts regarding the loss of potential competition from Pharmacia to Pfizer's erectile dysfunction drug, Viagra. The Commission found that Viagra did not face any credible actual competition[37] and many competitors' products in development could not be launched if Pfizer's patent claims were upheld in litigation that was pending at the date of the Commission's decision. Pharmacia's pipeline products were not affected by the patent litigation. The Commission found that Pharmacia had the "greatest potential" of the companies whose pipeline products were not affected by the patent claims even though Pharmacia's products were at an early stage of development, as the other companies were smaller and most lacked any experience in the erectile dysfunction market.

(g) In *ENI / EDP / GDP*[38] the Commission found that the merger would strengthen a dominant position in a wholesale electricity market by preventing the entry of "the most timely, likely and effective" rival, and in a retail electricity market by removing the "most likely and effective" or "best placed" potential entrant. In the retail market, the Commission emphasised that the merged group would be able to offer "dual fuel" (i.e. a mixed bundle of gas and electricity from the same supplier) and found that this would enable the merged group to retain customers more easily and that other players were unlikely to be able to match this offer within a relatively short period of time.[39]

(d) The approach of the US agencies

The US agencies adopt a single structural analysis, analogous to the **9–006** approach applied to horizontal mergers, in analysing harm to both *actual* potential competition and *perceived* potential competition.[40] They apply a set of four objective factors designed to identify cases in which harmful effects are plausible, and use those factors to filter cases which require

---

[35] The Commission's decision did not describe the concerns as involving a loss of potential competition (referring instead to the fact that the merger might raise barriers to entry, foreclose competitors and/or reduce the merged group's incentive to license).

[36] Case COMP/M.2922, paras 79 to 91.

[37] The Commission placed particular weight on Pfizer's high market shares; see para.91.

[38] Case COMP/M.3440 [2005] O.J. L302/69, paras 363, 450, 458 and 460 (prohibition upheld on appeal in Case T-87/05 *EDP v Commission*, not yet reported, judgment of September 21, 2005, on grounds which did not call into question the finding that the dominant positions on electricity markets would be strengthened).

[39] Paras 467 to 469.

[40] *The US Non-Horizontal Merger Guidelines, 1984 (www.usdoj.gov/atr/public/guidelines/2614. htm)*, s.4.1.

detailed investigation from those which do not.[41] First, *market concentration*: the US agencies believe that adverse competitive effects are likely only if overall concentration or the largest firm's market share is high. If the HHI[42] in the market in question is less than 1800, then a challenge is unlikely (in the absence of indicators of coordinated effects). Secondly, *general conditions of entry*: if entry barriers are low, the elimination of a potential entrant is unlikely to be a concern even if entry is marginally easier for one of the firms. Thirdly, *the target firm's entry advantage*: if the target has an entry advantage which is shared by no or few other firms, the elimination of potential competition is more likely to be a concern. The US Non-Horizontal Merger Guidelines[43] indicate that a challenge based on potential competition is unlikely "if the entry advantage ascribed to the acquiring firm (or another advantage of comparable importance) is also possessed by three or more other firms". However, a merger may still be challenged if the evidence of likely actual entry by the acquiring firm is particularly strong: "In such cases, the [US] Department [of Justice] will determine the likely scale of entry, using either the firm's own documents or the minimum efficient scale of the industry. The Department will then evaluate the merger much as it would a horizontal merger between a firm the size of the likely scale of entry and the acquired firm".[44] Fourthly, the *acquired firm's market share*: if the acquired firm has a relatively small market share then the acquisition may have competitive effects analogous to new entry. The US authorities' policy is generally not to challenge a "potential competition merger" when the acquired firm has a market share of 5 per cent or less. The likelihood of challenge increases as the target's market share increases and is likely when it is 20 per cent or more if the other conditions are satisfied.[45]

9.3 MERGERS IN NEIGHBOURING MARKETS

9–007 S.9.2 above analysed the possible effects of a merger in terms of eliminating actual or perceived potential competition from one of the merging parties *in a relevant antitrust market*. This section analyses the distinct question of whether a significant impediment to effective competition in a relevant antitrust market, A, may arise through the acquisition of a company active

---

[41] The US Non-Horizontal Merger Guidelines, 1984 (*www.usdoj.gov/atr/public/guidelines/2614. htm*), paras 4.131 to 4.135.
[42] See s.4.3 above for details of the HHI.
[43] The US Non-Horizontal Merger Guidelines, 1984 (*www.usdoj.gov/atr/public/guidelines/2614. htm*).
[44] The US Non-Horizontal Merger Guidelines, 1984 (*www.usdoj.gov/atr/public/guidelines/2614. htm*), para.4.133.
[45] The US authorities will also consider the efficiencies expected from the merger: the US Non-Horizontal Merger Guidelines, 1984 (*www.usdoj.gov/atr/public/guidelines/2614.htm*), para.4.135.

in a neighbouring antitrust market, B.[46] In particular, if the merged group holds a monopoly in market A, then its pricing will be constrained by the actions of competitors in neighbouring markets and, in principle, if the merger eliminates an important competitive constraint in a neighbouring market, then it may enable the merged group profitably to increase prices in market A, significantly impeding effective competition in that market. The issue raised in this section is sometimes described as *associative links* theory. The Court of First Instance considered this issue in *Tetra Laval BV v Commission*[47] and concluded, in reasoning upheld on appeal,[48] that the Commission had jurisdiction to prohibit a merger if it strengthened a dominant position because it eliminated a competitive constraint posed by a supplier in a neighbouring market.

In determining whether a significant impediment to effective competition **9–008** in market A arises through the acquisition of a supplier in neighbouring market B, it is necessary to consider:

(a) the extent of competition in market A; the greater the competitive constraints posed by rival suppliers in market A, the less the significance of competition from products outside the relevant market;

(b) the extent to which competition from suppliers in market B constrains suppliers' decisions in market A; if products in market B are a weak substitute for those in market A, then the reduction in competition from market B through the merger may not have a significant effect on competition in market A;

(c) the extent of competition in market B; if rival suppliers in market B are likely to be able to replicate the pre-merger competitive constraint notwithstanding the merger, then the merger will not have any competitive effect; in *Tetra Laval BV v Commission*[49] the Court of First Instance found that the Commission had not adequately explained why rival suppliers on the neighbouring market, B, would no longer form an effective competitive constraint, and concluded that the Commission had not demonstrated that the elimination of competition from the target would strengthen a dominant position in

---

[46] It may also be necessary to examine whether the merged group could leverage market power from market A into market B (see Ch.12) and whether the merged group would enjoy original market power in a concentric market comprising products A and B (notwithstanding that separate antitrust markets are also identified for products A and B); see para.3–002(b) above. Mergers between suppliers active in neighbouring markets may also result in multi-market contact, facilitating coordinated effects (see Ch.8 above).

[47] Case T-5/02 [2002] E.C.R. II-4381, paras 322 and 323.

[48] Case C-12/03P *Commission v Tetra Laval BV*, not yet reported, judgment of February 15, 2005, paras 125 to 131.

[49] Case T-5/02 [2002] E.C.R. II-4381, para.324. At para.328, the Court stated: "If the pressure from Sidel were to disappear, the contested decision does not explain why, if Sidel's competitors had not been marginalised through successful leveraging, the other companies active in the PET equipment markets would no longer be able to promote the advantages of PET to Tetra's customers on the carton markets".

market A; this decision was upheld on appeal in *Commission v Tetra Laval BV*,[50] in which the European Court of Justice ruled that a merger could not be prohibited merely by demonstrating the existence of a dominant position and a loss of potential competition, because the loss of potential competition might be compensated by other factors, such as the reactions of competitors; and

(d) the extent to which the merged group's activities in market A are constrained by competition from markets other than market B; a company active in market A may face competitive constraints from more than one neighbouring market and, accordingly, the elimination of a competitive constraint in one neighbouring market may not be sufficient significantly to impede effective competition.

---

[50] Case C-12/03P, not yet reported, judgment of February 15, 2005, paras 125 to 131. See also the Opinion of Advocate General Tizzano of May 25, 2004, para.153.

CHAPTER 10

THE MERGED GROUP'S BUYER POWER

10.1 INTRODUCTION

A concentration may significantly impede effective competition in the **10–001** *acquisition* of goods or services (as distinct from their supply).[1] In other words, the creation or strengthening of market power in a *procurement market*[2] is a "theory of competitive harm" or a possible ground for objecting to a transaction.[3]

The exercise of buyer power on a procurement market[4] has important

---

[1] See generally OFT Research Paper, Dobson, Waterson & Chu, "The Welfare Consequences of Buyer Power", 1998 (note that the views expressed in OFT research papers do not necessarily represent the views of the OFT); Areeda, Hovenkamp & Solow, *Antitrust Law* (2nd edn, Aspen Law & Business, 1998), Vol.IVA, s.9F; and the Australian Merger Guidelines, June 1999 (*http://www.accc.gov.au/content/item.phtml?itemId=719436&nodeId= file43a1f42c7eb63&fn=Merger%20Guidelines.pdf*), paras 5.20 to 5.22 and 5.131. For analysis of the bargaining power of suppliers, see Porter, *Competitive Strategy* (1998 edn, The Free Press), pp.27 to 29.

[2] For discussion of market definition in procurement markets, see para.3–055 above.

[3] Dobson Consulting, "Buyer Power and its Impact on Competition in the Food Retail Distribution Sector of the European Union", May 1999, IV/98/ETD/078, p.3, state, "buyer power is viewed ... as arising from the ability of retail firms to obtain from suppliers more favourable terms than those available to other buyers or would otherwise be expected under normal competitive conditions".

[4] A monopsony is the converse of a monopoly and a monopsonist selling into a *competitive downstream market* has an incentive to reduce its demand to avoid bidding up the market price (in the same way that a monopolist has an incentive to reduce output in order not to drive down the market price). This results in demand and prices in the upstream market which are below the perfectly competitive level and causes a deadweight welfare loss. Further, if the monopsonist also holds a *monopoly in the downstream market* (i.e. the market on which the goods are sold), it will have an incentive to *further* reduce its purchases to restrict downstream sales and generate monopoly profits. This is because each time the monopsonist/monopolist increases its purchases/sales, it *bids up* the price paid in the monopsony market and *drives down* the price received in the monopoly market, creating a double incentive to restrict purchases/sales. Finally, when a *monopsonist purchases from a monopolist*, the seller will attempt to raise prices above the competitive level and the buyer to lower them below it. In such cases, the outcome is unclear and will depend on the relative bargaining strength of the parties; the implications for consumer welfare are ambiguous.

implications for consumers in the downstream market: if the merged group uses its *market power*[5] to drive down the price paid in the procurement market by reducing its purchases, it must, of necessity,[6] reduce its *sales* on the downstream market since it has fewer goods to sell.[7] Therefore, if the downstream market is not competitive, the exercise of buyer power on a *procurement* market may lead to a loss of consumer welfare on the *downstream* market, as prices on the downstream market may be increased by the shortage of supply.[8] Mergers which create procurement power therefore have important implications not merely for the merged group's suppliers but also for their customers.[9]

10–002   The Notice on Horizontal Mergers states:

"On the one hand, a merger that creates or strengthens the market power of a buyer may significantly impede effective competition, in particular by creating or strengthening a dominant position. The merged firm may be in a position to obtain lower prices by reducing its purchase of inputs. This may, in turn, lead it also to lower its level of output in the final product market, and thus harm consumer welfare. Such effects may in particular arise when upstream sellers are relatively fragmented ... On the other hand, increased buyer power may be beneficial for competition. If increased buyer power lowers input costs without restricting downstream competition or total output, then a proportion of these cost reductions are likely to be passed onto consumers in the form of lower prices."[10]

---

[5] If the merged group reduces its input prices because of *efficiencies* (e.g. lower transport costs per unit) rather than market power, then the merged group will have an incentive to increase its output, which will lower price and benefit consumers: see Schwartz, "Buyer Power Concerns and the *Aetna-Prudential* Merger", speech of 1999 (available from *http://www.usdoj.gov/atr/public/speeches/3924.htm*).

[6] Assuming that the merged group simply sells the goods it acquires, as is the case in most retail markets (compare an industrial context where the merged group may be able to substitute one input for another in an industrial process).

[7] The increase in buyer power may also reduce the upstream suppliers' incentives to invest, ultimately harming consumers by reducing product quality or choice.

[8] For discussion of the trade off between increased procurement power and efficiencies generated by the merger, see Peter Carstensen, "Buyer Power and Merger Analysis—The Need for Different Metrics" (*www.ftc.gov/bc/mergerenforce/presentations/040217carstensen.pdf*).

[9] In two UK cases, the Competition Commission identified concerns that if the merged group obtained better terms from its suppliers, those suppliers would have to increase their prices to other customers; see *British United Provident Association / Community Hospitals Group*, Cm 5003, para.2.180(b) and *Safeway / Wm Morrison Supermarkets*, Cm 5950, para.2.218. Majumdar criticises these decisions on the grounds that, if the suppliers could profitably raise their prices to other customers, they would have done so irrespective of the merger, but describes a model under which such "waterbed" effects could be observed, the essential feature being that the merged group's rivals reduce their demand for inputs (because the merged group wins a larger share of the downstream market as it negotiates better prices) which reduces the constraint posed by potential entrants that have a reduced incentive to enter the input market; see Majumdar, "Waterbed Effects and Buyer Mergers" (available via *www.ccp.uea.ac.uk/public_files/workingpapers/CCP05-7.pdf*).

[10] Paras 61 and 62. The Notice on Horizontal Mergers also states, at para.61: "Competition in the downstream markets could also be adversely affected if, in particular, the merged entity were to use its buyer power vis-à-vis its suppliers to foreclose its rivals". The concerns identified in this sentence involve vertical effects; the relevant principles are discussed in Ch.11 below.

10.2 CONDITIONS FOR THE EXERCISE OF BUYER POWER

There are three principal conditions[11] for the exercise of buyer power. First, **10–003** buyer power can be exercised only if supply is *not perfectly elastic*. If supply is perfectly elastic, changes in quantities purchased have no effect on price because suppliers can, without cost, redirect their efforts to producing other products.[12] The scope to exercise buyer power increases as the elasticity of supply falls. Secondly, buyer power can be exercised only if the buyer or buyers in question represent a *substantial proportion of purchases* in the market— otherwise their purchases will not have a significant effect on the market price. However, whilst market share is important, a high market share does not, in itself, create significant buyer power. Thirdly, buyer power can only be exercised in the long run if there are *barriers to entry* into the buyers' market—otherwise the monopsony profits will be eroded by new entry.[13]

10.3 DECISIONS OF THE COMMISSION

In assessing whether a merger significantly impedes effective competition as **10–004** a result of the merged group's position on a procurement market, the Commission focuses on whether the merged group's buyer power is likely to lead to the elimination or marginalisation of competitors in the downstream market (i.e. the market on which the goods purchased by the merged group are sold) leading, in time, to detriments to consumer welfare because of the reduction in the intensity of competition. The Commission is *not* directly concerned about the implications of the enhanced procurement power held

---

[11] See the OFT Research Paper, Dobson, Waterson & Chu, "The Welfare Consequences of Buyer Power", 1998, p.13 (note that the views expressed in OFT research papers do not necessarily represent the views of the OFT).

[12] See generally Areeda, Hovenkamp & Solow, *Antitrust Law* (2nd edn, Aspen Law & Business, 1998), Vol.IVA, para.981a.

[13] Carlton & Perloff, *Modern Industrial Organization* (4th edn, Addison-Wesley, 2005), comment, at p.109: "Monopsony is most likely in markets where resources are specialized to a few uses. Moreover, even if resources are initially specialized to one use, as with a piece of custom-designed machinery (or a plant in a specific location serving a single buyer), monopsony may not persist in the long run. The reason is that no one will make new custom-designed machinery (or new investments in a plant) for a specific buyer if they earn a depressed return compared to what they can earn from making other machines (or building a plant elsewhere). In other words, few resources are specialised in the long run, and therefore it is unlikely that monopsony can persist in the long run. Another way to explain the preceding point is as follows. If resources are not specialized to a particular market in the long run, then the long-run supply curve tends to be flat ... [A] flat long run supply curve is most likely to occur when the market uses only a relatively small fraction of the total consumption of its inputs. Long-run monopsony power is impossible if the long-run supply curve is flat because price cannot be lowered below the competitive price".

by the merged group for companies supplying the merged group, as any detriment suffered by those suppliers does not affect consumer welfare (since, in the procurement market, the consumer is the merged group).[14] In determining whether consumers in the downstream market will suffer harm, the Commission considers in particular:

(a) whether the merger results in a substantial enhancement in buyer power (in particular, whether there are substantial overlaps in the goods purchased by the merging parties and whether post-merger joint purchasing would be practicable);

(b) whether suppliers to the merged group, taken in aggregate,[15] enjoy market power and in particular whether they can sell their goods to alternative outlets (as the availability of alternative outlets may confer power on the suppliers by giving them a genuine alternative to dealing with the merged group)[16];

(c) whether the merged group holds substantial market power in the downstream market and, in particular, whether an attempt to increase prices in the downstream market by restricting sales would be defeated by rivals[17]; and

(d) whether competitors in the downstream market can realistically seek to negotiate terms of supply comparable to those enjoyed by the merged group, whether alone or through joint purchasing schemes.

The Commission has also developed a "spiral theory", namely that a company which obtains a leading position in a procurement market may enter a virtuous spiral (from the company's perspective) whereby the

---

[14] For discussion whether, in the US, harm to final consumers is necessary for antitrust concerns to arise, see Schwartz, "Buyer Power Concerns and the *Aetna-Prudential* Merger", speech of 1999 (available from *www.usdoj.gov/atr/public/speeches/3924.htm*). See also Peter Carstensen, "Buyer Power and Merger Analysis—The Need for Different Metrics" (*www.ftc.gov/bc/ mergerenforce/presentations/040217carstensen.pdf*) (arguing that if customers appropriate most of the wealth generated by the upstream activity, this harms competition in the upstream market because the attractiveness of entry or innovation is eliminated) and Schwartz, "Should Antitrust Assess Buyer Market Power Differently than Seller Market Power?" (*www.ftc.gov/ bc/mergerenforce/presentations/040217schwartz.pdf*).

[15] In the Commission's XXVIth Annual Report on Competition Policy 1996, para.147, the Commission stated: "the key issue is not the possible dependence of single individual suppliers. What is decisive is the extent to which suppliers have on average the possibility to substitute supplies to the retailer in question by supplies to other buyers".

[16] e.g. if the companies supplying the procurement market can sell internationally.

[17] In the United Kingdom, the Director General of Fair Trading's advice on *Enterprise Inns / Laurel Pub Group Ltd*, June 5, 2002 (*www.oft.gov.uk/Business/Mergers + FTA/Decisions/ index.htm*), analysed whether a merger between operators of pubs might substantially lessen competition in the procurement market supplied by brewers and commented: "provided that competition among pubs at a local level remains strong, any price reductions that a larger pub company did manage to obtain from a brewer may be expected to be passed on to tenants in lower wholesale prices or subsidised rents and on to consumers in the form of lower retail prices ... [Price] reductions, if they are passed on to customers through competition, are to be welcomed".

improved terms negotiated in purchasing markets enable the company to win a larger share of the downstream market enabling it to negotiate better terms in the procurement market, and so forth, leading, ultimately, to the elimination or marginalisation of competitors in the downstream market.[18]

In the following cases, the Commission considered whether the merger **10–005** would lead to an increase in the buyer power of the merged group.[19]

(a) In *Kesko / Tuko*[20] the Commission found that the merged group's buyer power would further reinforce its dominant position on the downstream retail and cash-and-carry markets by enabling it to employ strategies which would have the long-term effect of further weakening the position of its competitors.[21] The Commission did *not* identify any concerns about the implications of the transaction for companies supplying the merged group.[22]

(b) In *Rewe / Billa*[23] the Commission considered whether the acquisition

---

[18] See the discussion of Case IV/M.1221 *Rewe / Meinl* [1999] O.J. L274/1, in para.10–005(f) below.

[19] See also Case IV/M.603 *Crown Cork & Seal / Carnaud Metalbox* [1996] O.J. L75/38 (procurement of tinplate and tinfree steel products: paras 88 to 95); Case IV/M.1085 *Promodes / Catteau* (the Commission approved a merger between French supermarkets in the light of the alternative outlets open to suppliers, in particular sales to the French buyer collectives; paras 22 to 26); Case IV/M.1086 *Promodes / S21 / Gruppo GS* (Italian supermarkets); Case IV/M.1087 *Promodes / Simago*; Case IV/M.1439 *Telia / Telenor* [2001] O.J. L40/1, para.277; Case IV/M.1529 *Havas Advertising / Media Planning* (media buying; compare Case COMP/M.2000 *WPP Group / Young & Rubicam* and Case COMP/M.2415 *Interpublic / True North*, para.11); Case COMP/M.1716 *Gehe / Herba* (pharmaceutical wholesaling); Case COMP/M.1832 *Ahold / ICA Förbundet / Canica*, paras 19 to 24; Case COMP/M.1904 *Carrefour / Gruppo GS* (procurement of daily consumer goods); Case COMP/M.2002 *Preussag / Thomson* (procurement of hotel accommodation in resort destinations; paras 7, 11 and 12); Case COMP/M.2050 *Vivendi / Canal+ / Seagram* (procurement of first-window premium films; paras 43 to 50); Case COMP/M.2161 *Ahold / Superdiplo*, paras 32 to 34; Case COMP/M.2228 *C&N / Thomas Cook* (procurement of holiday accommodation; para.8); Case COMP/M.2300 *YLE / TDF / Digita / JV* (procurement of radio transmission and distribution equipment; para.34); Case COMP/JV.37 *BSkyB / KirchPayTV* (acquisition of broadcasting rights; paras 42 to 44); Case COMP/M.2330 *Cargill / Banks* (purchase of oilseed rape; para.19); Case COMP/M.2425 *Coop Norden* (daily consumer goods; paras 12 and 13); Case COMP/M.2473 *Finnforest / Moelven Industrier* (wood procurement; paras 10 to 12); Case COMP/M.2483 *Group Canal+ / RTL / GJCD / JV* (acquisition of football broadcasting rights); Case COMP/M.2604 *ICA Ahold / Dansk Supermarked / JV* (daily consumer goods; para.14); Case COMP/M.2747 *Ondeo-Thames Water / Water Portal* (procurement of water-related products and services; paras 11 to 13); and Case COMP/M.2706 *Carnival Corporation / P&O Princess* [2003] O.J. L248/1 (procurement of ships; "the Commission has received no evidence that competing cruise companies would be prevented from having access to the shipyards or from receiving deliveries according to agreed timetables. This has not happened in the past and there is no evidence that it will happen in the future. Therefore the investigation has not shown that the merger could lead to any foreclosure effects for other cruise ship buyers"; para.274). For the US position see, in particular, Schwartz, Economics Director of Enforcement, Antitrust Division, US Department of Justice, "Buyer Power Concerns and the *Aetna-Prudential* Merger" (available from *www.usdoj.gov/atr/public/speeches/speech_schwartz.htm*).

[20] Case IV/M.784 [1997] O.J. L110/53.

[21] Paras 152 and 153.

[22] This is consistent with an approach to merger control which focuses exclusively on *consumer welfare* and does not accord weight directly to allocative efficiency: see s.2.2 above.

[23] Case IV/M.803.

of an Austrian food retailer by a German food retailer raised concerns about enhancement of the merged group's buyer power. The Commission concluded that it did not in the light in particular of: the relatively small size of the Austrian retail market (which had the consequence that the enhancement in buyer power was limited); the fact that the merged group's buying policy would have to take account of differences in customer preferences between Austria and Germany; the products where customer preferences were similar in Austria and Germany tended to be supplied by large international companies; two other companies had activities in Germany and Austria and could therefore carry out joint purchasing; and there was another strong competitor in Austrian food retailing.

(c)   In *Boeing / McDonnell Douglas*[24] the Commission found that suppliers of parts would be reliant on the merged group and might therefore give it priority over its main rival, Airbus, which could significantly weaken the competitive position of Airbus relative to Boeing.

(d)   In *Intermarché / Spar*[25] the Commission allowed the merger despite accepting that it would enhance buyer power. This was because the merged group would compete with other similar buyers and the affected upstream suppliers were essentially international-scale producers of "Eurobrand"[26] products (similar to the "must have" brands referred to in *Promodes / Casino* below) which would have sufficient power to counterbalance the merged group's buyer power.

(e)   *Promodes / Casino*[27] involved a merger of two French retailers. The Commission focused on the parties' buyer power on the grounds that the terms negotiated might affect competition in the downstream retailing market.[28] (Again, the Commission was not concerned about the implications of the transaction for the suppliers to the merged group as such.) In analysing these issues, the Commission took account of the parties' shares of the downstream retail market. It also focused on the position of large-scale buyer collectives.[29] The transaction was approved on the grounds that: suppliers were often of significant size; some supplied "must have" brands (conferring power on them); the suppliers had numerous other substantial customers (in particular the other buyer collectives) in addition to the merged group[30]; and there was no evidence that the merged group's buyer

---

[24] Case IV/M.877 [1997] O.J. L336/16, paras 106 to 108.
[25] Case IV/M.946, para.13
[26] The Commission described the brands in this way at para.15.
[27] Case IV/M.991.
[28] Para.14.
[29] Paras 33 to 38.
[30] Para.47.

power would prove detrimental to the final consumer (as opposed to the upstream sellers).[31]

(f) In *Rewe / Meinl*[32] the Commission found that the retail merger would create or strengthen a dominant position on nine Austrian procurement markets for daily consumer goods. The merged group would represent on average 29 per cent of suppliers' turnover in circumstances in which the responses to questionnaires sent out by the Commission indicated that suppliers could switch on average only 22 per cent of turnover to other channels.[33] This meant that suppliers would have a high degree of dependency on the merged group. The Commission was concerned about a *spiral effect* of the merged group's ever-increasing buyer power, and required Rewe and Meinl to give substantial undertakings to allay their concerns. The Commission stated:

"The exercise of buyer power which leads to the securing of a more favourable purchase deal is not to be considered *per se* detrimental to the economy as a whole. Especially where the supplier side is itself highly concentrated and powerful, buyers are faced with effective competition in their own selling market and hence are compelled to pass on any savings to their own customers, buyer power can prevent monopoly or oligopoly profits from being earned on the supply side. However, if the powerful buyer himself occupies in his selling market a strong position which is no longer kept sufficiently in check by the competition, any savings can no longer be expected to be passed on to customers. In the retail trade there is a close interdependence between the distribution market and the procurement market. Retailers' shares of the distribution market determine their procurement volume: the bigger the retailer's share of the distribution market, the larger the procurement volume. And the larger the procurement volume, the more favourable as a rule are the buying conditions which the trader obtains from his suppliers. Favourable buying conditions can in turn be used in various ways to improve one's position in the distribution market (sometimes through internal or external growth, but also through low-price strategies targeted at competitors). The improved position in the distribution market is itself reflected in a further improvement in buying conditions, and so on.

The spiral described above leads to ever-higher concentration both in distribution markets and in procurement markets. In the short term, final consumers may benefit from the process, as there may be a period of intense (predatory) competition in the

---

[31] Para.45.
[32] Case IV/M.1221 [1999] O.J. L274/1, paras 71 to 117.
[33] Para.101.

distribution market during which the powerful buyer/trader is forced to pass on his savings to consumers. But this will last only until such time as a structure (in this case, an individual dominant position) is arrived at in the distribution market which leads to a clear reduction in competitive intensity. At this stage, any consideration for the final consumer goes by the board, as he is left with few alternatives."[34]

(g) In *Carrefour / Promodes*[35] the Commission considered the *spiral effect* identified in *Rewe / Meinl*. The Commission's concern was again that this would cause prices to consumers to fall initially, but to rise in the long run as the buyer power of some supermarkets would eliminate competitors, enabling the remaining buyers to raise prices in their downstream markets.[36] There was also a concern that when the loss of a contract to supply the merged group would result in the supplier risking insolvency (the *threat point*), the merged group would enjoy excessive buyer power. The Commission permitted the transaction to proceed because it felt that the effects mentioned would depend upon a number of factors which were as yet unknown.[37] However, the Commission noted that future supermarket mergers would be carefully scrutinised.[38]

(h) In *Danish Crown / Vestjyske Slagterier*[39] the Commission found that the merger would lead to the creation of a dominant position on the Danish market for the purchase of live pigs for slaughtering. The Commission was *not* concerned about the scope for the merged group to extract monopsonistic profits from its suppliers because the parties were owned by their members and any profits would therefore be paid to their farmer-members. Rather, the Commission was concerned that: farmers would have a reduced choice of slaughterhouses; the merged group would control innovation in the Danish pig industry; and the merged group could drive out of business private slaughterhouses by offering to pay prices above market rates to farmers which currently trade with such slaughterhouses.

(i) In *NewsCorp / Telepiù*[40] the Commission analysed a merger to near monopoly in the Italian pay-TV market, which would have resulted in the merged group acting as a near monopsony purchaser of certain types of audio-visual television content in Italy. The Commission found that:

---

[34] Paras 71 to 73.
[35] Case IV/M.1684.
[36] Para.46.
[37] Para.88.
[38] Para.104.
[39] Case IV/M.1313 [2000] O.J. L20/1, paras 20, 21, 128 and 192.
[40] Case COMP/M.2876 [2004] O.J. L110/73, para.173.

"following the merger the bargaining position of the smaller independent suppliers of channels will be weakened due to the absence of alternative platforms to the combined entity. This could indirectly harm consumers' welfare, should the merged entity decide to stop purchasing rights to TV channels or exert its monopsonistic power to such an extent that some TV channel providers exit the market, due to unsustainable economic conditions. If that were to be the case, consumers would enjoy a greatly reduced choice of products and freedom of choice."

Again, the Commission focused on the effects of the merger on consumers and did *not* identify any concerns about the implications of the transaction for companies supplying the merged group.

CHAPTER 11

VERTICAL ISSUES

11.1 INTRODUCTION

(a) Definition

11–001 A company[1] is vertically integrated[2] if it is active in two or more successive stages of the production or distribution process.[3]

---

[1] See generally: Church, "The Impact of Vertical and Conglomerate Mergers on Competition", 2004 (report for DG Competition) (available via *http://europa.eu.int/comm/competition/mergers/others/merger_impact.pdf*); Tirole, *The Theory of Industrial Organization* (The MIT Press, 1988), Ch.4; Perry, "Vertical Integration: Determinants and Effects", published as Ch.4 of Schmalensee & Willig eds., *Handbook of Industrial Organization*, (North-Holland, 1989) Vol.1; RBB Economics, "The Efficiency-Enhancing Effects of Non-Horizontal Mergers", 2005 (report for the Commission DG for Enterprise and Industry) (available via *http://europa.eu.int/comm/enterprise/library/lib-competition/doc/non_horizontal_mergers.pdf*); Carlton & Perloff, *Modern Industrial Organization* (4th edn, Addison-Wesley, 2005), Ch.12; Areeda, Hovenkamp & Solow, *Antitrust Law* (2nd edn, Aspen Law & Business, 1998), Vol.IVA, Ch.10; Scherer & Ross, *Industrial Market Structure and Economic Performance* (3rd edn, Houghton Mifflin Co, 1990), Ch.14; Martin, *Advanced Industrial Economics* (2nd edn, Blackwell, 2002), pp.404 to 408; Cabral, *Introduction to Industrial Organization* (The MIT Press, 2000), Ch.11; Porter, *Competitive Strategy* (The Free Press, 1998 edn), Ch.14; Porter, *Competitive Advantage* (The Free Press, 1998 edn), Ch.9; Scheffman, "The Application of Raising Rivals' Costs Theory to Antitrust" [1992] The Antitrust Bulletin 187; Reiffen & Vita, "Comment: Is There New Thinking on Vertical Mergers?" (1995) 63 *Antitrust Law Journal*, 917; Salop, "Anticompetitive Overbuying by Power Buyers" (2005) 72 *Antitrust Law Journal* 669 (discussing the scope for exclusionary overbuying strategies, in particular *predatory overbuying* intended to eliminate rival purchasers of inputs from the input market and *raising rivals' costs overbuying* intended to raise rivals' input costs to gain market power in the output market); and the OFT Economic Discussion Paper, "Innovation and Competition Policy", Charles River Associates, March 2002 (note that the views in the paper do not necessarily reflect those of the OFT), paras 7.24 to 7.26. The Commission has a long-standing intention to publish a notice on non-horizontal mergers; see Mario Monti, then Commissioner for Competition Policy, speech, "Review of the EC Merger Regulation—the Reform Package", November 7, 2002, Brussels (*www.europa.eu.int/comm/competition/speeches/index_2002.html*); press release IP/02/1856; and Philip Lowe, Director General of DG Competition, speech, "The future shape of European merger control", Brussels, February 17, 2003 (*http://europa.eu.int/comm/competition/speeches/*).

[2] "Upstream" or "backward" integration refers to the purchase by a company of a supplier of its inputs (e.g. the acquisition by a producer of a supplier of raw materials). "Downstream" or "forward" integration refers to the purchase by a company of a purchaser of its outputs (e.g.

(b) Ambiguous effects of vertical integration on consumer welfare

Vertical integration[4] may have as its motivation or consequence effects **11–002** which are *positive* or at least *ambiguous* from the perspective of maximising consumer welfare including[5]: lowering transaction costs; addressing information uncertainty[6]; providing an assurance of supply of key inputs[7];

---

the acquisition by a producer of a distributor). This categorisation is potentially misleading as the relationships can be reversed relatively easily; e.g. instead of selling goods to distributors, a manufacturer could "purchase" distribution services by appointing a commercial agent so that the manufacturer retains ownership of the goods until final sale and the distributor receives a fee for each successful transaction: Kwoka & White eds., *The Antitrust Revolution* (4th edn, Oxford UP, 2004), p.323.

[3] This approach is consistent with the definition of vertical affected markets in the Form CO, s.6. Such markets exist when "one or more of the parties to the concentration are engaged in business activities in a product market, which is upstream or downstream of a product market in which any other party to the concentration is engaged, and any of their individual or combined market shares at either level is 25% or more, regardless of whether there is or is not any existing supplier/customer relationship between the parties to the concentration". A narrower approach is to distinguish between vertical integration in a narrow sense (when internal exchanges, i.e. exchanges based on management decision, are used in place of market exchanges) and vertical "combination" (when a company is active in two or more successive stages of the production or distribution process but the relationship between the two stages is governed by market exchanges rather than management decisions). (Perry, "Vertical Integration: Determinants and Effects", published as Ch.4 of Schmalensee & Willig eds., *Handbook of Industrial Organization*, (North-Holland, 1989) Vol.1, p.185, states that: "A firm can be described as vertically integrated if it encompasses two single-output production processes in which either (1) the entire output of the 'upstream' process is employed as part or all of the quantity of one intermediate input into the 'downstream' process, or (2) the entire quantity of one intermediate input into the 'downstream' process is obtained from part or all of the output of the 'upstream' process. This includes the more restrictive criterion that the entire output of the upstream subsidiary be employed as all of the quantity of one intermediate input into the downstream process. However, both categorizations rule out the case in which most of the output of the upstream process is employed as most of the input in the downstream process. This case is best described as 'partial' vertical integration because some of the output of the upstream process is sold to other buyers and some of the intermediate input for the downstream process is purchased from other suppliers".) Since the Commission's analysis under the ECMR is *prospective*, it is not surprising that it should adopt the wider approach in defining vertical affected markets, thereby avoiding the need to make an up-front determination as to whether the merged group will proceed with vertical integration in a narrow sense or with vertical combination. However, the Commission recognises the distinction between vertical integration in a narrow sense and vertical combination, as it has relied on a finding that the merged group would operate as a vertical combination as a ground for finding that the transaction would not result in any foreclosure effects; see para.11–014 below.

[4] The same analysis applies to vertical restraints as the effects of vertical integration can generally be emulated by contract.

[5] See Porter, *Competitive Strategy* (The Free Press, 1998 edn), pp.303 to 309. See further s.11.2 below.

[6] See Martin, *Advanced Industrial Economics* (2nd edn, Blackwell, 2002), p.406 and Perry, "Vertical Integration: Determinants and Effects", in Schmalensee & Willig eds., *Handbook of Industrial Organization*, (North-Holland, 1989) Vol.1, Ch.4, pp.208 to 211.

[7] This is important when price is not the only method by which goods are allocated, i.e. when the market does not or may not clear at prevailing prices. When the market clears effectively, vertical integration is not necessary in order to obtain an assurance of supplies. See the discussion in Perry, "Vertical Integration: Determinants and Effects", in Schmalensee & Willig eds., *Handbook of Industrial Organization*, (North-Holland, 1989) Vol.1, Ch.4, pp.206 to 208.

avoiding successive mark-ups by successive monopolists; saving costs through technological economies of integration[8]; eliminating free riding by discount retailers who benefit from the pre-sales service or investment in advertising by full-price retailers; eliminating opportunistic behaviour[9]; or eliminating market power.

On the other hand, exceptionally[10] vertical integration may have as its motivation or consequence effects which are *negative* from a consumer welfare perspective, including allowing the merged group to eliminate existing competition; prevent new entry; engage in price discrimination; or avoid regulatory restrictions.[11]

(c) Decisions of the Community Courts

11–003 Recent decisions of the Community Courts have made it more difficult for the Commission to intervene in vertical mergers and, when substantive issues arise, the Commission is now less likely to require remedies involving the transfer of a market position.[12]

  (a) In *General Electric Company v Commission*[13] the Court of First Instance emphasised that the Commission faced issues of proof[14] in vertical mergers that are similar to those in conglomerate mergers because the harmful consequences to consumers arise in each case only if the merged group adopts a particular course of conduct:

> "In those circumstances, the Commission had the onus to provide convincing evidence to support its conclusion that the merged entity would probably behave in the way foreseen. If it did not behave in that way, the combination of the positions of the two parties to the merger on neighbouring but distinct markets could not have led to the creation or strengthening of dominant posi-

---

[8] e.g. by producing steel and steel sheet in the same or neighbouring factories to eliminate the costs of reheating the steel to make the sheet, or combining pulping and newsprint production to eliminate the costs of drying and reconstituting.

[9] e.g. a manufacturer may not wish to invest in maintenance equipment unless it can ensure that the equipment is not used to maintain rivals' products.

[10] RBB Economics, "The Efficiency-Enhancing Effects of Non-Horizontal Mergers", 2005 (report for the Commission DG for Enterprise and Industry) (available via *http://europa. eu.int/comm/enterprise/library/lib-competition/doc/non_horizontal_mergers.pdf*) argue, at p.3: "In general, non-horizontal mergers will be pro-competitive and such exclusionary behaviour can occur only under very stringent conditions ... In short, anti-competitive non-horizontal mergers are the exception rather than the rule". See also Church, "The Impact of Vertical and Conglomerate Mergers on Competition", 2004 (report for DG Competition) (available via *http://europa.eu.int/comm/competition/mergers/others/merger_impact.pdf*), Ch.7.

[11] These issues, amongst others, are analysed in ss.11.3 to 11.6 of this Chapter.

[12] The Commission has shown greater flexibility to accept remedies other than the transfer of a market position in vertical mergers and, in particular, has commonly accepted access remedies, as explained in Ch.20.

[13] Case T-210/01, not yet reported, judgment of December 14, 2005, paras 67 to 69.

[14] For a more general discussion of the standard of proof, see s.2.5(b).

tions, since those respective positions of the parties would not have had any commercial impact on one another".

(b) The Court's decision in *General Electric*[15] is also important in establishing that the Commission must carry out a careful factual assessment to determine whether the merged group will have an *incentive* to adopt the conduct which is hypothesised,[16] as well as the *ability* to do so.

(c) Finally, this Chapter should also be read in the light of the discussion in s.2.7(a) of the relevance of Art.82 to the Commission's merger under the ECMR, and in s.20.6 of the Commission's duty to take account of "behavioural" or conduct remedies (e.g. a commitment to supply on terms fixed by agreement or, in default of agreement, by pendulum arbitration). It is now clear that the Commission is required to take account of the merged group's legal obligations under Art.82 (to an extent) and of any behavioural or conduct commitments offered.

(d) Consistent application of antitrust law

The issues raised by vertical integration are similar to those raised by ver- **11–004** tical restraints and, in economic terms, a vertical merger can be characterised as a series of vertical restraints such as exclusive dealing and distribution, resale price maintenance and quantity forcing.[17] Further, the principal ground for objecting to vertical and conglomerate mergers is identical at an overarching level, namely that the merged group may use power in one market to leverage into a second.[18] It is important that antitrust laws treat structures which have equivalent economic effects in a consistent way, to avoid creating incentives for companies to adopt inefficient structures simply to obtain advantages in antitrust treatment.

(e) Vertical effects flow-chart

Fig.11.1 below summarises the Commission's approach to vertical and **11–005** conglomerate effects.

---

[15] Case T-210/01, not yet reported, judgment of December 14, 2005.
[16] i.e. whether such a strategy is the most profitable available to the merged group.
[17] Bishop & Walker, *The Economics of EC Competition Law* (2nd edn, Sweet & Maxwell, 2002), p.288. See generally the Commission's Guidelines on Vertical Restraints [2000] O.J. C 291/1.
[18] Further, vertically related components are often economic complements and it may be difficult in practice to distinguish vertical and conglomerate mergers in this context. Case COMP/M.1879 *Boeing / Hughes*, is a good example of a case which could be characterised as a merger between suppliers of complementary goods (as the Commission described the case in para.81) but, equally, could be regarded as one involving vertical integration.

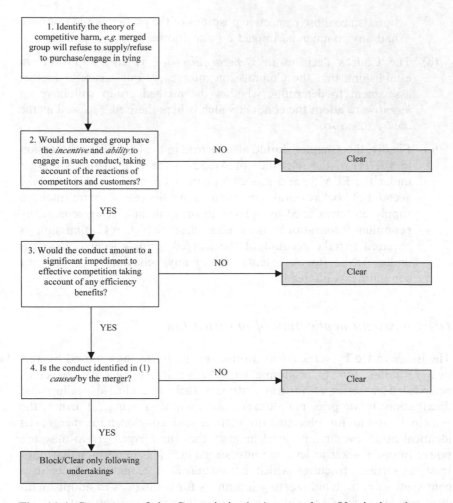

Fig. 11.1: Summary of the Commission's Approach to Vertical and Conglomerate Issues

The remainder of this Chapter is organised as follows: s.11.2 identifies possible efficiencies in vertical mergers, and the remaining sections analyse several theories of competitive harm that may be relevant when examining vertical mergers, namely upstream foreclosure / refusal to supply / raising rivals' costs (s.11.3), downstream foreclosure / refusal to purchase (s.11.4), foreclosure of new entry (s.11.5), and other concerns arising from vertical integration (s.11.6).

11.2 POSSIBLE EFFICIENCIES IN VERTICAL MERGERS

(a) Introduction

This section[19] examines in outline[20] two consequences of vertical integration **11–006** which may result in efficiency gains, namely reduction in transaction costs and elimination of double marginalisation in cases of successive monopolies.

(b) Transaction costs

All companies must decide whether to produce particular goods themselves **11–007** or purchase from third parties.[21] Purchasing from third parties may generate transaction costs.[22] Such costs tend to be high when one of the parties expects the other to engage in opportunistic behaviour.[23] In any event, when such behaviour is expected, it is impossible to provide for all eventualities in the agreement.[24] Transaction costs may also be high when extensive coordination is required (e.g. agreements between rival suppliers of connected transport systems) or there is substantial uncertainty. Vertical integration is a means of eliminating[25] high transaction costs and is rational and efficient

---

[19] Constant returns to scale are assumed through this section.

[20] For an authoritative survey, see RBB Economics, "The Efficiency-Enhancing Effects of Non-Horizontal Mergers", 2005 (report for the Commission DG for Enterprise and Industry) (available via *http://europa.eu.int/comm/enterprise/library/lib-competition/doc/non_horizontal_mergers.pdf*), Ch.3.

[21] See generally, Williamson, "Transaction Cost Economics", in Schmalensee & Willig eds., *Handbook of Industrial Organization* (North-Holland, 1989), Vol.1, Ch.3.

[22] Much economic theory proceeds on the *assumption* that transaction costs are nil.

[23] Opportunistic behaviour is likely in cases of "asset specificity", where investment in assets which are dedicated to a particular purchaser results in a bilateral monopoly. Williamson, "Transaction Cost Economics", in Schmalensee & Willig eds., *Handbook of Industrial Organization*, (North-Holland, 1989) Vol.1, Ch.3, describes the issue as follows, at pp.142 and 143: "Asset specificity has reference to the degree to which an asset can be redeployed to alternative uses and by alternative users without sacrifice of productive value. This has a relation to the notion of sunk cost ... [Asset] specificity distinctions of five kinds have been made: (1) site specificity, as where successive stations are located in a cheek-by-jowl relation to each other so as to economize on inventory and transportation expenses; (2) physical asset specificity, such as specified dies that are required to produce a component; (3) human asset specificity that arises in a learning-by-doing fashion; (4) dedicated assets, which are discrete investments in general purpose plant that are made at the behest of a particular customer; and (5) brand name capital". See also Besanko, Dranove & Shanley, *Economics of Strategy* (2nd edn, John Wiley & Sons Inc, 2000), pp.148 to 153.

[24] It is commonly said that parties form *incomplete contracts* because of the *bounded rationality* of the individuals negotiating them.

[25] Tapered integration (i.e. partial integration) may also generate many of these benefits: see Perry, "Vertical Integration: Determinants and Effects", in Schmalensee & Willig eds., *Handbook of Industrial Organization* (North-Holland, 1989), Vol.1, Ch.4, pp.216 and 217.

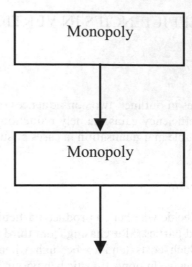

Fig. 11.2: Successive Monopolies

whenever the costs of obtaining an integrated supply are lower than the costs of obtaining a supply in the market.[26]

(c) Double marginalisation

11–008 A merger of successive monopolies when the downstream monopoly uses goods produced by the upstream monopoly as its only input (see Fig.11.2) will reduce the market price and enhance consumer welfare by eliminating the "double marginalisation" issue.[27]

The double marginalisation issue is illustrated in Fig.11.3. It arises because the upstream monopolist will set a profit-maximising price (i.e. will set its output at a level where its marginal revenue is equal to its marginal cost, MC_1) and the downstream monopolist will *then* set its profit-maximising price, but the cost of purchasing from the upstream monopolist will form part of the downstream monopolist's marginal cost, MC_2, leading

---

[26] Coase, *The Firm, The Market and The Law* (The University of Chicago Press, 1988), p.7 (summarising an article, "The Nature of the Firm", published in 1937 and reprinted as Ch.2 of *The Firm, The Market and The Law*), explains the point as follows: "although production could be carried out in a completely decentralized way by means of contracts between individuals, the fact that it costs something to enter those transactions means that firms will emerge to organize what would otherwise be market transactions whenever their costs were less than the costs of carrying out the transactions through the market. The limit to the size of the firm is set where its costs of organizing a transaction become equal to the cost of carrying it out through the market. This determines what the firm buys, produces and sells". For a summary of the costs and benefits of using the market, see Besanko, Dranove & Shanley, *Economics of Strategy* (2nd edn, John Wiley & Sons Inc, 2000), p.112.

[27] See Areeda & Hovenkamp, *Antitrust Law* (2nd edn, Aspen Law & Business, 2002), Vol.IIIA, para.758.

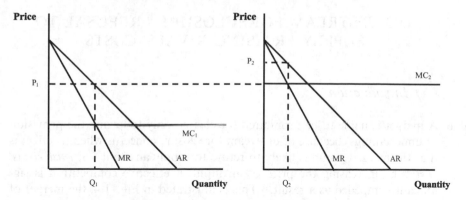

Fig. 11.3: The Double Marginalisation Issue

to a final price, P_2, which reflects the successive mark-ups (or double marginalisation) of the two monopolists.

If the two monopolists merge, the merged group will determine its output **11–009** on the basis of the marginal cost of *producing* the upstream good, MC_1 (and not the higher marginal cost of *purchasing* the good at a price which includes a monopoly profit, MC_2), which will result in an increased output and lower prices than in the non-integrated situation. Vertical integration in this case eliminates the *externality* which arises when the downstream monopolist fails to take into account the monopoly profit made by the upstream monopolist in determining the optimal output for the downstream market.[28]

---

[28] The double marginalisation issue does not arise when the *upstream or the downstream market is competitive* (i.e. price is set at marginal cost) provided that the downstream supplier uses as its *only input* goods produced by the upstream supplier. In such cases the vertical relationship does not give rise to an externality which can be internalised through a merger. Equally, a merger between such companies will not result in any increase in price or reduction in consumer welfare and there is therefore no justification for blocking a merger in this category (assuming that none of the effects identified in ss.11.3 to 11.6 is also present). See Tirole, *The Theory of Industrial Organization* (The MIT Press, 1988), p.175. Further, where there is a *monopoly producer in the upstream market* and the *downstream retail market is monopolistically competitive* (i.e. the retailers are themselves differentiated and consumer welfare therefore depends not just on price but also on the number of retailers), the economic models are ambiguous on the question of whether vertical integration leads to a welfare gain or loss in terms of retail diversity. The research is reviewed in Perry, "Vertical Integration: Determinants and Effects", in Schmalensee & Willig eds., *Handbook of Industrial Organization* (North-Holland, 1989), Vol.1, Ch.4, pp.200 to 203. However, it is clear that in this case there is in any event a welfare gain arising from the elimination of double marginalisation since in a monopolistically competitive market suppliers enjoy some market power arising from the differentiated nature of their products.

11.3 UPSTREAM FORECLOSURE / REFUSAL TO SUPPLY / RAISING RIVALS' COSTS

(a) Introduction

11–010 A merger is liable to be prohibited (or cleared only following the provision of undertakings) because of upstream foreclosure concerns when its effect is that the merged group is likely to refuse to supply an input[29] or *raise rivals' costs*[30] by increasing the price of an input, if effective competition is significantly impeded as a result.[31] This is illustrated in Fig.11.4: the merger of companies A and B may lead company A to cease to supply or to increase prices in its terms of supply to rivals 1 and 2.

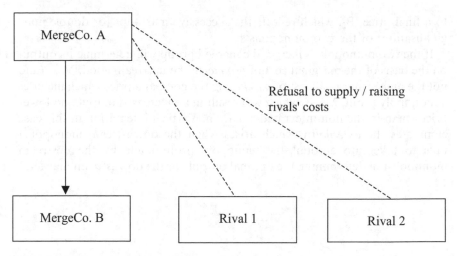

Fig. 11.4: Upstream Foreclosure

(b) The test for analysing upstream foreclosure issues

11–011 (i) A four-stage analysis In *Telia / Sonera*[32] the Commission stated: "In assessing whether [a vertical foreclosure issue] is significant, it is necessary to establish not only that the merged entity will have the *incentive* to foreclose,

---

[29] This may arise directly if the supplier refuses to enter a contract or indirectly if, e.g. it designs its products to be incompatible with rival downstream suppliers' products.

[30] See Viscusi, Vernon & Harrington, *Economics of Regulation and Antitrust* (3rd edn, The MIT Press, 2000), p.226.

[31] The essence of upstream foreclosure is that the merged group's actions in the upstream market are profitable *because of their effects on the downstream market*.

[32] Case COMP/M.2803, para.91.

but also whether it has the *ability* to do so, and whether it will have *any significant effect* on competition on the market in question". Underlying this statement[33] is a four-stage analysis[34]:

(a) identify the leveraging conduct;

(b) analyse whether the merged group will have an incentive and the ability to pursue such conduct;

(c) identify the foreclosure effect, if any, arising from the leveraging conduct; and

(d) assess whether there is a causal link between any foreclosure effect and the merger.

These issues are considered in ss.(ii) to (v) below. Ss.(vi) to (viii) discuss several legal issues that arise in the context of a vertical effects analysis.

(ii) Identify the leveraging conduct The first stage in analysing upstream[35] **11–012** foreclosure[36] issues[37] is to identify the behaviour which the merged group

---

[33] See generally Church, "The Impact of Vertical and Conglomerate Mergers on Competition", 2004 (report for DG Competition) (available via *http://europa.eu.int/comm/competition/ mergers/others/merger_impact.pdf*), pp.vi to xv and s.3.2 and Scheffman, "The Application of Raising Rivals' Costs Theory to Antitrust" [1992] *The Antitrust Bulletin* 187 (and in particular the discussion of the policy implications of raising rivals' costs theory, at pp.204 to 206).

[34] See also RBB Economics, "The Efficiency-Enhancing Effects of Non-Horizontal Mergers", 2005 (report for the Commission DG for Enterprise and Industry) (available via *http:// europa.eu.int/comm/enterprise/library/lib-competition/doc/non_horizontal_mergers.pdf*), pp.123 and 124.

[35] For discussion of market definition in cases of vertical foreclosure, see Areeda, Hovenkamp & Solow, *Antitrust Law* (2nd edn, Aspen Law & Business, 2000), Vol.IIA, para.570.

[36] Bork, *The Antitrust Paradox* (1993 edn, The Free Press, 1978), p.228, saw no justification for the antitrust authorities intervening to block vertical mergers, emphasising the importance of focusing on opportunity cost rather than on book values: "It is impossible for a firm actually to sell to itself for less than it sells to an outside firm because the real cost of any transfer from the manufacturing unit to the retailing unit includes the return that could have been made on a sale to an outsider. No matter what the bookkeeper writes down as the transfer price, the real cost is always the opportunity foregone. (If a garment manufacturer spends $50 to make a dress, could sell it for $100, but chooses to give it to his wife, the cost to him is $100, not $50, and the fact cannot be altered by any number he chooses to put in his books)". However, Bork's view is not now widely held and a great deal of recent research has been devoted to identifying circumstances in which vertical integration may have a harmful effect on consumer welfare. Notwithstanding this research, it is noteworthy that Tirole, *The Theory of Industrial Organization* (The MIT Press, 1988), p.193, commented that: "Though market foreclosure is a 'hot' issue among those concerned with antitrust proceedings and with regulation, economists still have a very incomplete understanding of its motivations and effects".

[37] Under the ECMR, information on vertical relationships is required only if the merged group will have a share of at least 25%. in the upstream or the downstream market (Form CO, s.6), implying that no serious issues are expected in cases that do not cross that threshold.

might adopt in order to exclude or marginalise competitors.[38] Commonly, the theory of competitive harm is based on a refusal to supply or an increase in price. However,[39] in *Boeing | Hughes*[40] the Commission examined six potentially adverse effects of the transaction, including the possibility that the merged group might design its satellites to fit optimally with its launchers. In *GE | Instrumentarium*[41] the concern was that the merged group might use its significant market power in anaesthesia machines to raise the costs of rival suppliers of equipment that interfaces with such machines by withholding or degrading cooperation.

11–013   **(iii) Whether the merged group will have the incentive and ability to pursue the leveraging conduct** The second stage is to determine whether the merged group will have the *incentive* and *ability* to engage in upstream foreclosure. This requires the Commission to consider whether upstream foreclosure would be the *profit-maximising* strategy for the merged group and, if so, whether it would be *practicable* to implement such a strategy.

In *Boeing | Hughes*[42] the Commission stated that it "is necessary to examine whether the merged entity would gain more through additional launch service contracts than it would lose through lost satellite contracts, if it were to engage in such behaviour".

The importance of analysing the effects of the merged group's strategy on its profits was confirmed in *General Electric Company v Commission*[43] when the Court of First Instance placed great emphasis on the need for the Commission to provide convincing evidence that the merged group would have an incentive to adopt the hypothesised course of conduct. It stated that evidence might be derived from economic studies analysing the likely

---

[38] In Case T-5/02 *Tetra Laval BV v Commission* [2002] E.C.R. II-4381, the Court of First Instance implicitly accepted the Commission's contention, at para.180 (in the context of a conglomerate merger), that it may be sufficient for the Commission to establish that competitors would be marginalised (as opposed to excluded): see paras 281 and 306. (The decision was upheld on appeal on the basis of reasoning not relating to this issue in Case C-12/03P *Commission v Tetra Laval BV*, not yet reported, judgment of February 15, 2005.)

[39] See also Case COMP/M.1751 *Shell | BASF | JV—Project Nicole* (scope for the joint venture to control, at least to a degree, the polypropylene technologies available to competitors; para.32); Case COMP/M.2197 *Hilton | Accor | Forte | Travel Services JV* (scope for the merged group to discriminate in favour of its subsidiaries in the provision of *information*; para.31); Case COMP/M.2315 *The Airline Group | NATS* (in which the Commission identified carefully the conduct in question before proceeding to the subsequent stages of the analysis; para.34); Case COMP/M.2803 *Telia | Sonera* (raising, or not decreasing, charges; application of technical standards; use of inconvenient interconnection points; degrading quality of termination; and the offering of technical add on services only to Sonera; para.90); and Case COMP/M.2861 *Siemens | Drägerwerk | JV* [2003] O.J. L291/1 (scope to make access to interfaces more difficult, or to design equipment so that it could only be combined with other equipment supplied by the merging parties; para.151).

[40] Case COMP/M.1879 [2004] O.J. L63/53, para.82.

[41] Case COMP/M.3083 [2004] O.J. L109/1, paras 288, 290, 311, 312, 313 and 218 and n.209.

[42] Case COMP/M.1879 [2004] O.J. L63/53, para.83. See also Case COMP/M.3696 *E.ON/MOL*, para.400.

[43] Case T-210/01, not yet reported, judgment of December 14, 2005, paras 295 to 297. (See also para.327 regarding the conglomerate aspects of the merger.)

development of the market and demonstrating the merged group's incentives, but added that the categories of evidence are not closed and in some cases the "simple economic and commercial realities of the particular case may constitute the convincing evidence required by the case-law".

An assessment of the merged group's incentives and abilities to pursue the **11–014** leveraging strategy requires a very careful analysis of the way in which the market operates on a case-by-case basis,[44] taking account, in particular, of the following factors.[45]

(a) The impact of a vertical foreclosure strategy on the merged group's revenues and costs.[46]

(b) The scope for the merged group to *profit in the downstream market* from the changes in the competitive conditions in that market resulting from its upstream foreclosure strategy.[47] In general terms, an upstream foreclosure strategy may be profitable because it:

   (i) forces downstream rivals to exit from the market, reducing the competitive constraints on the merged group in the downstream market and enabling it to exercise market power in its own right by profitably raising prices[48];

   (ii) raises the cost of marginal *industry* production,[49] which may force downstream rivals to reduce their output and raise their

---

[44] Compare Scheffman, "The Application of Raising Rivals' Costs Theory to Antitrust" [1992] *The Antitrust Bulletin* 187, identifying, at pp.189 and 190, three principles which determine whether a raising rivals' costs strategy would be profitable.

[45] The factors listed overlap in part.

[46] Refusal to supply an input may lead to losses resulting from the reduced sales of the input but gains in terms of increased sales and profits in the downstream market and reduced costs in the upstream market. It may be difficult to ascribe financial values to strategic objectives, such as the prospect of inducing a rival to leave the market. See also Motta, *Competition Policy Theory and Practice* (2004, Cambridge UP), pp.375 to 377; the speech of Richard Parker, Senior Deputy Director, Bureau of Competition, FTC, "Global Merger Enforcement", September 28, 1999 (*www.ftc.gov/speeches/other/barcelona.htm*); and Scheffman, "The Application of Raising Rivals' Costs Theory to Antitrust" [1992] *The Antitrust Bulletin* 187, at pp.190 and 199 to 202.

[47] See Case COMP/M.3333 *Sony / BMG* [2005] O.J. L62/30 (appeal pending in Case T-464/04 *Impala v Commission*), paras 163 and 174 (ruling out vertical foreclosure concerns on the grounds that there was no evidence that it would be a profitable strategy), and Case COMP/ M.3696 *E.ON/MOL*, paras 420, 432 and 671.

[48] See, e.g. Case COMP/M.2903 *DaimlerChrysler / Deutsche Telekom / JV* (appeal pending in Case T-269/03 *Socratec (Satellite Navigation Consulting, Research & Technology) v Commission*), para.59, contemplating that the merged group could refuse to grant access to its upstream platform and use that platform to develop its own downstream business.

[49] Scheffman, "The Application of Raising Rivals' Costs Theory to Antitrust" [1992] *The Antitrust Bulletin* 187, at pp.190 to 195, gives as an example an industry in which there are three suppliers, A, B and C, with constant average and marginal costs. A and B have lower costs than C but A and B face capacity constraints and cannot supply the whole market. In those circumstances, the price in the market is determined by C's marginal costs. Accordingly, if A or B can raise C's marginal costs (which comprise the "cost of marginal industry production") then the market price will increase (in the face of a downward sloping demand curve) even if A's and B's costs are unchanged. The same conclusion may apply when all producers are marginal; see pp.197 to 199.

prices, enabling the merged group to win downstream market share by undercutting its rivals and/or profitably to increase its downstream prices in the "shadow" of its downstream rivals' price increases; and/or

(iii) deprives downstream rivals of economies of scale,[50] increasing their marginal costs, with the consequences described in sub-para.(ii).

Conversely, the merged group would have no incentive to pursue an upstream foreclosure strategy if it led to no change in the market price in the downstream market (in particular, if demand in the downstream market is perfectly or highly elastic)[51] *and* created no strategic benefits (in terms, e.g. of increasing the likelihood of a downstream rival exiting from the market).

In *Alcan / Pechiney (II)*,[52] Pechiney held a dominant position in the licensing of smelter technology to third parties. The Commission considered the incentives for the merged group to refuse to license third parties or raise the licence fees, finding that the merged group was unlikely to become dominant in the supply of aluminium (the downstream market) and would therefore not be able profitably to raise prices in that market by reducing its own output. However, by refusing to license or increasing the licence fees, the merged group could raise its rivals' costs because fewer new smelters would be installed[53] (keeping marginal high cost smelters in operation) and new smelters that were installed with inferior technology would operate with higher variable costs (which would be likely to increase the market price).[54]

(c) The scope for *downstream* actual and potential *competitors* to defeat or restrict the scope for the merged group to raise prices or gain share

---

[50] e.g. if the upstream merging party is the leading producer of hi-fi systems and it acquires a downstream retail chain, it may choose to terminate its distribution agreements with rival downstream retail chains, which may reduce the total volumes of hi-fi equipment traded by the rival downstream retail chains, potentially depriving those rivals of economies of scale.

[51] See Scheffman, "The Application of Raising Rivals' Costs Theory to Antitrust" [1992] *The Antitrust Bulletin* 187, at pp.189 and 190.

[52] Case COMP/M.3225, paras 40 to 44. In Case COMP/M.3923 *AMI / Eurotecnica* the Commission opened a phase II investigation because of concerns that the merged group would refuse to license technology hampering entry into the downstream market and controlling the expansion projects of current competitors; see press release IP/05/1306; the parties subsequently abandoned the transaction.

[53] The Commission predicted that licensees would have to pay higher fees to the merged group (reducing the likelihood that the investment would be made) or would obtain the licence from a third party (which would mean that the licensee produced aluminium at a lower output and a higher cost).

[54] In order to assess the merged group's incentives to pursue a raising rivals' costs strategy it would be necessary to estimate the loss of profits in the upstream licensing market and compare it with the potential additional profits to be earned in the downstream aluminium market.

in the downstream market.[55] For example, it is important to consider the counter-strategies open to existing rivals. Further, if the downstream market price increases, this may create an incentive for new entry.[56]

(d) The viability of actual and potential *competitors* in the *upstream* market taking account, in particular, of their available *capacities* and *costs*.[57] Upstream foreclosure can generally be ruled out if rival upstream suppliers could readily expand[58] output to supply the needs of downstream rivals of the merged group *and* would do so at the prices[59] which the upstream merging party would have charged had the merger not occurred. By contrast, an upstream foreclosure strategy may be practicable if its effect is that downstream rivals are unable to access an essential input or are able to do so only at prices higher than those the upstream merging party would have charged had the merger not occurred.[60]

(e) The *buyer power* enjoyed by rival downstream producers which might be employed to defeat an attempted foreclosure strategy.[61] In

---

[55] In Case COMP/M.3686 *Honeywell / Novar*, paras 57 and 59, the Commission considered the incentive for the merged group to use its upstream position to squeeze out *one* of its downstream rivals (i.e. the single downstream rival which sourced from the upstream merging party prior to the merger). However, the Commission concluded that such a strategy was unlikely to be profitable because the merged group had a low downstream share and, even if one of the downstream rivals could be excluded, a large part of its share would be likely to be captured by other downstream rivals. For a more general discussion of simulations of the potential vertical competition issues in this case, see Rouxel, "Honeywell / Novar: When it Comes to Fire, Vertical has a Taste of the Horizontal", *Competition Policy Newsletter*, Summer 2005, p.63.

[56] This point is closely connected to the third stage of the analysis (i.e. foreclosure), which is discussed in para.11–015 below.

[57] See, e.g. Case COMP/M.3064 *Ahlström Capital / Capman / Nordkalk*, para.36; Case COMP/M.3136 *GE / Agfa NDT* (the merged group was the clear market leader on the upstream markets but "credible competitors" were also present; para.44); and Case COMP/M.3465 *Syngenta CP / Advanta*, para.97. Compare Case COMP/M.3809 *Siemens / Flender* in which the Commission stated, at para.29, in ruling out an upstream foreclosure concern, that adding an additional upstream supply would take 18 to 24 months "at a cost that is below the 5% to 10% price increase used as the standard test for a hypothetical monopolist". (See also para.33.)

[58] The merged group is likely to have a reduced demand for the input from third parties if it pursues an upstream foreclosure strategy and this factor (taken in isolation) will tend to *reduce* the price of the input for downstream rivals; see Motta, *Competition Policy Theory and Practice* (2004, Cambridge UP), p.373.

[59] The upstream rivals' prices will depend in part on their costs in comparison with those of the upstream merging party.

[60] Areeda, Hovenkamp & Solow, *Antitrust Law* (2nd edn, Aspen Law & Business, 1998), Vol.IVA, para.1008, comment: "The theory [of raising rivals' costs] must be reserved for markets in which *either* (1) economies of scale are very significant, or (2) the particular input in question is sold by firms with widely different costs". See also Martin, *Advanced Industrial Economics* (2nd edn, Blackwell, 2002), p.245.

[61] In Case COMP/M.3649 *Finmeccanica / BAES Avionics and Communications*, para.30 and Case COMP/M.3735 *Finmeccanica / AMS*, para.30, the Commission found that the UK Ministry of Defence had sufficient leverage to prevent the merged group from foreclosing its avionics competitors.

appraising a vertical merger, it is important, in particular, to identify any switching costs and to examine carefully customers' reactions to any previous attempts by the upstream merging party to increase its prices.

(f) *Current purchasing patterns* within the market.[62] For example, if, prior to the merger, downstream rivals to the merged group sourced exclusively from upstream rivals to the merged group (and not the upstream merging party), the inference is that foreclosure would not be practicable because downstream rivals would be able to continue to rely on their existing sources of supply following the merger[63] *unless* there is evidence, for example:

(i) that the presence of the upstream merging party on the upstream market as an actual or potential rival bidder materially influenced the terms of supply obtained by the downstream rivals; or

(ii) of likely changes in the market, such as the exit of rival upstream suppliers or growth in demand by downstream rivals which could not be met by capacity-constrained upstream rivals.

(g) Any *differences in the volume of the input* produced by the merged group in the upstream market and its requirements in the downstream market. For example, if the merged group's downstream requirements comprise a small proportion of its upstream outputs, a strategy of refusing to supply downstream rivals is unlikely to be profitable because the upstream business will not have an outlet for a large part of its production.[64] In *RMC / Rugby*[65] the Commission found that the merged group would have an incentive to continue to supply cement to rival downstream producers of ready mixed concrete because the merged group would consume only a small pro-

---

[62] In COMP/M.3593 *Apollo / Bakelite*, the majority of the upstream company's sales were made via independent distributors and the vast majority of those distributors' sales were for uses other than as inputs for products which competed with the downstream company. The Commission was unable to conclude clearly that the merged group would have an incentive to raise the price to the independent distributors as this may not have been profitable given the extensive use of the input for purposes not competing with the downstream business; see para.153. See also Case COMP/M.3064 *Ahlström Capital / Capman / Nordkalk*, para.39.

[63] See Case COMP/M.1789 *INA / LuK* (no downstream foreclosure because, prior to the merger, LuK had purchased exclusively from INA and other downstream producers would have adequate alternative sources of supply; paras 15 to 21); Case COMP/M.2438 *SES / Stork / Fokker Space* (prior to the merger, the upstream product was not sold to any third parties and there was therefore no risk of actual foreclosure of supplies; para.19); and Case COMP/ M.3722 *Nutreco / Stolt-Nielsen / Marine Harvest JV*, para.44.

[64] See, e.g. Case COMP/M.3081 *Michelin / Viborg*, para.28; Case COMP/M.3136 *GE / Agfa NDT* (GE accounted for less than 5% of Agfa's output and any anti-competitive behaviour in relation to Agfa's business was likely to cause it substantial damage); Case COMP/M.3142 *CVC / Danske Traelast*, para.28; Case COMP/M.3558 *Cytec / UCB—Surface Specialties*, para.31; and Case COMP/M.3943 *Saint-Gobain / BPB*, paras 57 and 78.

[65] Case COMP/M.1759, para.18.

portion of its output of cement (i.e. the merged group's *volume throughputs* differed radically in the two markets) and third party sales were therefore essential for RMC to earn a return on its investment in Rugby. Similarly, in *Lafarge / Blue Circle*[66] the Commission found that the vertical links between the upstream cement and aggregates markets and the downstream concrete products markets in the United Kingdom did not justify prohibiting the transaction, in part because the merged group's downstream requirements for cement would be less than its total production.[67]

(h) The *proportion of the downstream selling price* accounted for by the upstream input. If the price of the upstream input is trivial relative to the price of the downstream product, an upstream foreclosure strategy is likely to be ineffective because the upstream supplier would be unable to influence significantly the downstream market price (save in exceptional circumstances in which very large increases in the price of the input would not lead downstream rivals to switch to, or companies to develop, rival products). The essence of upstream foreclosure is that the merged group's actions in the upstream market are profitable *because of their effects on the downstream market*—and it follows that an upstream foreclosure strategy is viable only if it can be used to raise the downstream market price materially (or expand the merged group's share of the downstream market). For example,[68] in *ICI / Tioxide*[69] the Commission established that the upstream product, titanium oxide, represented less than 20 per cent of the costs of the downstream paint market, limiting the gains available to the merged group through its vertical integration. Similarly, in *SES / Stork / Fokker Space*[70] the Commission found that the upstream product represented only about 5 per cent of the costs of the downstream product, and concluded: "Consequently, the possible leverage from this component on the downstream market ... is very limited". By contrast, the Court of First Instance in *General Electric*

---

[66] Case COMP/M.1874, para.18.

[67] In addition, in the United Kingdom more than half of the cement supply would remain outside the merged entity. (The Commission also identified vertical concerns as the merged group would have held 90% of the Danish cement market and would have been one of two significant suppliers in the downstream roofing tiles market. The parties undertook to divest Lafarge's roofing tile business.)

[68] See also Case COMP/M.2738 *GEES / Unison* (the Commission ruled out a theory of vertical foreclosure, at para.20, on the basis that: "Owing to the low input costs that these products represent in the overall price of the engine, any possible price increase could not materially affect the ability of rival engine OEMs to compete in the down-stream markets"); Case COMP/M.3267 *CRH / Cementbouw* (an upstream foreclosure strategy could *at most* increase the price of rivals' downstream products by around 1%, enabling the Commission to exclude any concerns; para.26); and Case COMP/M.3680 *Alcatel / Finmeccanica / Alcatel Alenia Space & Telespazio* (the impact of any increase in the price of the upstream component on the price of the downstream product would be minimal; para.102).

[69] Case IV/M.23.

[70] Case COMP/M.2438, para.19.

Company v Commission[71] found that a foreclosure strategy would have been in the merged group's interests in part *because* an engine starter accounted for a very small proportion of the total costs of the engine, meaning that the profits foregone through reduced sales of engine starters would have been small and likely to be outweighed by increased profits in the supply of jet engines.

(i) The *extent of vertical integration* in the market. This has two aspects. First, the viability of an upstream foreclosure strategy may depend on whether rival upstream suppliers are themselves vertically integrated and whether they are pursuing strategies of upstream foreclosure. Secondly, if the merging parties or their competitors had an opportunity, prior to the merger, to adopt an upstream foreclosure strategy, it is important in appraising a vertical merger to examine the effects of such a strategy if it were adopted and, if it were not, to consider whether the merger creates new incentives to do so.

(j) The *practicability* of implementing an upstream foreclosure strategy, in the light of industry regulation,[72] market practice,[73] the merged group's internal organisation, or the terms of joint ventures to which it is party.[74] For example, in *Sovion / HMG*[75] the merged group was under a regulatory obligation to collect and process abattoir by-products and therefore would not have been able to pursue a foreclosure strategy based on a refusal to collect or process abattoir by-products for rival slaughterhouses. Similarly, in *Thorn EMI / Virgin Music*[76] the Commission found that industry regulation would preclude the merged group from refusing to grant licences for the exploitation of musical works held by the merged group. Finally, in *The Airline Group / NATS*[77] the Commission found that discrimination by a supplier of air traffic services in favour of its airline shareholders would not be practicable because of a lack of common interest between the parents and the existence of a regulatory structure governing en route air traffic services.

(k) Whether the merged group would have an *incentive to continue to*

---

[71] Case T-210/01, not yet reported, judgment of December 14, 2005, para.299.
[72] See s.2.7(b) above.
[73] In Case COMP/M.3083 *GE / Instrumentarium* [2004] O.J. L109/1, para.311, the Commission found that a strategy of degrading cooperation with suppliers of medical equipment which wanted their products to interface with the merged group's anaesthesia equipment would be practicable because there was an ever-increasing need for interfacing and cooperation was necessary for this to occur.
[74] In Case COMP/M.3267 *CRH / Cementbouw*, the upstream activity was carried out in a joint venture with a third party and the third party would have no commercial interest in supplying the downstream business at below cost; para.26.
[75] Case COMP/M.3605 (appeal pending in Case T-151/05 *Nederlandse Vakbond Varkenshouders v Commission*), paras 116 and 117. (See also paras 128 and 129 regarding possible cross-subsidisation.)
[76] Case IV/M.202.
[77] Case COMP/M.2315, paras 35 and 36.

supply third parties on reasonable terms notwithstanding the merger.[78] In *Elf / Occidental*,[79] *VIAG / EB-Brühl*[80] and *Péchiney / VIAG*[81] the Commission found that, because of industry practice or the particular geographic locations of the merged group's facilities, the parties would continue to be active on the market, with the consequence that upstream foreclosure was unlikely to occur.[82]

(l) Whether the merger will generate any *efficiency gains* affecting the merged group's incentives.[83]

In summary, it is crucial in a vertical foreclosure case to compare[84] the loss of profit arising from reduced upstream sales with the profit associated with the anticipated gains in the downstream market (in terms of increased prices, higher market share or both). For example, if rival upstream suppliers have spare capacity, then the merged group may need significantly to reduce its sales in the upstream market in order to produce a foreclosure effect which, depending on the margins associated with upstream sales, may involve a significant loss of profits, making a foreclosure strategy less attractive. Similarly, if the merged group has a relatively small share of the downstream market, it may derive relatively little profit from a strategy which successfully raises price in that market (as the benefits will be obtained mainly by downstream rivals).

(iv) Foreclosure The third stage is to determine whether an upstream fore- **11–015** closure strategy would have a *significant effect* on the downstream market.[85] In other words, in order to establish that a merger creates vertical competition concerns justifying a prohibition decision or the acceptance of commitments, it is *not* sufficient merely to show that the merged group is likely to adopt an upstream foreclosure strategy; it is *also* necessary to establish that such a strategy would have significant effects on the downstream market and therefore on consumers.[86] More particularly, the mere fact that

---

[78] Compare Areeda, Hovenkamp & Solow, *Antitrust Law* (2nd edn, Aspen Law & Business, 1998), Vol.IVA, para.1004b, recommending an irrebuttable presumption of self-dealing.

[79] Case IV/M.85.

[80] Case IV/M.139.

[81] Case IV/M.198.

[82] See also Case COMP/M.3542 *Sony Pictures / Walt Disney / ODG / MovieCo*, finding that, in order for the platform to be successful, it would have to be kept open to all content providers (enabling the Commission to rule out vertical foreclosure concerns); see para.16.

[83] See Ch.18 below.

[84] By constructing a model to assess the costs and benefits of the hypothesised foreclosure strategy.

[85] See also para.12–011 below, considering the same issue in the context of conglomerate mergers.

[86] RBB Economics, "The Efficiency-Enhancing Effects of Non-Horizontal Mergers", 2005 (report for the Commission DG for Enterprise and Industry) (available via *http://europa.eu.int/comm/enterprise/library/lib-competition/doc/non_horizontal_mergers.pdf*), comment, at pp.123 and 124: "A price reduction can be said to marginalize competitors only if, at any given price level, the competitive constraint currently provided by the rivals at that price

a merger leads to a re-ordering of vertical supply relationships does not in itself prove that the merger is anti-competitive (irrespective of the extent to which the displaced downstream rivals face economic losses as a result of that re-ordering). Indeed, even if it were shown that the merger would be likely to lead to the exit or marginalisation of downstream competitors (taking account of their potential counter-strategies) this would not, in itself, be sufficient to satisfy this third criterion; it would be necessary *also* to show that new entry or re-entry would not be timely, likely and sufficient to protect consumer welfare.[87]

For example, in *Sovion / HMG*[88] the Commission calculated that an increase of 10 per cent in the merged group's charges for processing certain materials would raise rival slaughterhouses' costs by less than 0.16 per cent and found that such a limited increase would not affect competition between slaughterhouses to an appreciable extent. Similarly, in *The Airline Group / NATS*[89] the Commission found that discrimination (i.e. raising rivals' costs) was practicable to a limited extent, but that this was not sufficient to justify finding that the merger would create or strengthen a dominant position: "NATS could give preference to calls coming from other airports in the London area. Again in this case the market investigation has shown that even if flights to/from London would be discriminated, given the transparency of the system, this kind of discrimination could not be so systematic as to create or strengthen a dominant position in any city pair to/from London".

11–016 **(v) Causation** The final stage is to establish whether there is a *causal link* between the merger and any foreclosure effect.[90]

11–017 **(vi) The relevance of the switch to a significant impediment to effective competition test** Prior to the change in the substantive test contained in the revised ECMR,[91] the need to establish that a merger created or strengthened a dominant position created a potentially difficult hurdle in cases involving upstream foreclosure. This is because the substantive test under Regulation 4064/89 (namely whether the merger created or strengthened a dominant position as a result of which effective competition would be significantly

---

level were to be reduced following a temporary price reduction ... [P]rices will increase and consumers will be harmed ... only ... if competitors are marginalised to such an extent so as to be forced to withdraw permanently from the market". This approach is adopted in Case COMP/M.3589 *Körber / Winkler & Dünnebier*, para.17. Contrast Case COMP/M.3696 *E.ON/ MOL*, para.403.

[87] See generally Ch.16.
[88] Case COMP/M.3605 (appeal pending in Case T-151/05 *Nederlandse Vakbond Varkenshouders v Commission*), para.121.
[89] Case COMP/M.2315, para.36.
[90] See generally Ch.5 (discussing the counterfactual).
[91] See s.2.2 above.

impeded in the common market or a substantial part of it) was not well-suited to analysing cases in which the theory of competitive harm is that actions will be taken in one market (the upstream market) to obtain advantage in a second (the downstream market). The main effects of an upstream foreclosure strategy are felt in the downstream market and, as explained in para.11–019 below, consumers may be harmed in this situation without creating or strengthening a dominant position in the downstream market.[92] The change in the substantive test brought about by the revisions to the ECMR (so that the operative part is whether the merger will lead to a significant impediment to effective competition in the common market or a substantial part of it) *arguably* eliminates this *legal* impediment to intervention in vertical mergers.[93]

(vii) Whether substantial market power upstream (i.e. an upstream dominant   11–018
position) is a necessary condition for finding upstream foreclosure If the merged group lacks substantial market power (i.e. a dominant position) in the upstream market,[94] then any attempt to engage in upstream foreclosure

---

[92] See the discussion in the first edition of this work at paras 5–15 to 5–18; Case COMP/M.2861 *Siemens / Drägerwerk / JV* [2003] O.J. L291/1, para.152 (considering the possible creation or strengthening of a dominant position in either the upstream or the downstream markets); and Case COMP/M.3225 *Alcan / Pechiney (II)* (finding that the merger would *not* create or strengthen a dominant position in the downstream market and identifying serious doubts on the basis of a possible strengthening of the existing upstream dominant position; paras 40 to 44).

[93] There remains some doubt because recital 25 refers to the fact that the change in the substantive test was intended to extend the Commission's jurisdiction when compared with the dominance test only as regards anti-competitive effects arising from non-coordinated behaviour. However, as discussed in para.2–015 above, the expression "non-coordinated behaviour" covers all theories of competitive harm apart from coordinated effects and therefore ought to apply to vertical and conglomerate effects (although it is fair to observe that the debate surrounding the change to the substantive test focused on the possible existence of "gaps" in the Commission's jurisdiction to prohibit *horizontal* mergers and this is reflected, e.g. in Völcker, "Mind the Gap: Unilateral Effects Analysis Arrives in EC Merger Control" [2004] E.C.L.R. 395, p.404, who states at n.64, that the effect of recital 25 is that the Commission has no greater powers to challenge vertical or conglomerate mergers).

[94] The UK Competition Commission's Merger References Guidelines, March 2003 (*www.competition-commission.org.uk*) state, at para.3.64: "Generally, a vertical merger will only raise competition concerns when the firms involved are able to exercise a substantial level of market power in one or more markets along the supply chain". The International Competition Network Analytical Framework Sub-group, "The Analytical Framework for Merger Control" (available at *www.internationalcompetitionnetwork.org/afsguk.pdf*), para.40(b), provides that vertical integration "may in some circumstances reduce competitive constraints faced by the merged firm as a result of increased barriers to entry, raising rivals costs, substantial market foreclosure or an increased likelihood of collusion. This risk is, however, unlikely to arise except in the presence of existing market power or in markets where there is already significant vertical integration/restraints". The UK Office of Fair Trading's Substantive Merger Guidelines, May 2003 (*www.oft.gov.uk*), adopt, at para.3.8, language which is materially the same as that in "The Analytical Framework for Merger Control" and, at para.5.3, identify concerns about upstream and downstream foreclosure when: "rivals lack a reasonable alternative to the vertically integrated firm. In this circumstance, rivals may either be deprived of access altogether or might be allowed to obtain the product or the facility only at unfavourable prices, thereby lessening rivalry in the market". The Australian Merger Guidelines, June 1999 (*www.accc gov.au/content/item.phtml?itemId−719436&nodeId−file43a1f42 c7eb63*

will be defeated,[95] e.g. by customers switching to suppliers with spare capacity which can supply at the price the upstream merging party would have charged had the merger not occurred.[96] It follows that substantial market power upstream (i.e. an upstream dominant position) is a necessary condition for finding upstream foreclosure.

However, the Commission's decisions on this issue under Regulation 4064/89 (which required the Commission to show that the merger created or strengthened a dominant position) are not consistent.[97]

(a) In *Tetra Laval / Sidel*,[98] in a section headed "Vertical effects", the

---

&fn = *Merger%20Guidelines.pdf*), para.5.151, provide: "Vertical relationships and vertical mergers will raise concerns only if there is a concentrated industrial structure at one or more of the related or integrated stages of production or distribution". It is, however, clear that consumer welfare may be adversely affected in cases in which the upstream supplier has substantial market power falling short of monopoly. Perry, "Vertical Integration: Determinants and Effects", in Schmalensee & Willig eds., *Handbook of Industrial Organization* (North-Holland, 1989), Vol.1, Ch.4, comments, at p.197: "A dominant firm need not acquire all of the scarce resources in order to effectively raise the costs of its actual or potential rivals. By leaving the open market thin, competitors may be unable to expand without significantly driving up the input price, they may be subject to higher prices set by the fewer remaining suppliers, or they may incur higher transaction costs from having to negotiate contracts with suppliers. [For example, in a case of successive duopolies, by] acquiring one of the upstream firms, a downstream firm can disadvantage and reduce the profits of its competitor by forcing it to rely on an upstream monopolist for the input". Accordingly, concerns arise here if rival suppliers are forced to use more costly or less efficient alternatives.

[95] The converse question arises in the case of downstream foreclosure, namely whether the Commission is entitled to object to a merger on the grounds of downstream foreclosure if the merged group will not hold a dominant position in the downstream market; see s.11.4 below.

[96] See Areeda & Hovenkamp, *Antitrust Law* (2nd edn, Aspen Law & Business, 2002), Vol.IIIA, para.756a and Viscusi, Vernon & Harrington, *Economics of Regulation and Antitrust* (3rd edn, The MIT Press, 2000), pp.223 to 229.

[97] See, e.g. Case IV/M.81 *VIAG / Continental Can* (the Commission found that vertical integration between a supplier of aluminium and a supplier of packaging would not lead to upstream foreclosure because of the existence of alternative non-integrated suppliers of aluminium); Case IV/M.197 *Solvay-Laporte / Interox*; Case IV/M.221 *ABB / BREL* (a merger between a supplier of railway vehicles and an upstream supplier was cleared as there was considerable buyer power and the industry was characterised by over-capacity); Case IV/M.1381 *Imetal / English China Clays*, para.69; Case COMP/M.1745 *EADS*, paras 100 and 101; Case COMP/M.1879 *Boeing / Hughes* [2004] O.J. L63/53 (the Commission found, at paras 40 and 44, that there were adequate alternative suppliers in the upstream market for satellite equipment and therefore cleared the transaction without undertakings; as regards the separate question of the proposed integration between satellites and launch services, the Commission found, at paras 84 to 101, that the merged group would not be able to foreclose other suppliers, given the sophistication and buyer power of customers and the fact that rival suppliers were credible suppliers and, having substantial sunk costs, had the incentive to cut prices to win share if necessary; this relationship is probably properly characterised as a merger between suppliers of complementary goods, although the principles applicable to conglomerate and vertical mergers are the same at an overarching level since both involve the merged group leveraging market power from one market into a second); and Case COMP/M.2574 *Pirelli / Edizione / Olivetti / Telecom Italia* (the Commission established that, although the merged group would be the largest supplier of telecommunication cables in Italy, its downstream rivals could be assured of supplies from important players such as Corning, Alcatel and Lucent; the concentration therefore did not create or strengthen a dominant position).

[98] Case COMP/M.2416 [2004] O.J. L43/13, para.322 (decision of October 30, 2001). The Court of First Instance quashed the Commission's decision in Case T-5/02 *Tetra Laval BV v Commission* [2002] E.C.R. II-4381, but the Court's analysis of vertical issues, at paras 133 to

Commission found that: "to the extent that Sidel is not dominant in [the upstream market], inter-brand competition would not be significantly affected. If, however, Sidel became dominant in [the upstream market], this could allow the merged entity to dominate the [downstream market], by engaging in [specified practices] in particular by marginalising [downstream competitors] and offering combined packages of [the upstream and downstream products]".

(b) In *Hilton / Accor / Forte / Travel Services JV*,[99] the Commission noted that: "There may only be a risk of foreclosure in the [downstream] markets if it were shown that the parents have sufficient market power in the [upstream] market".

(c) In *Telia / Sonera*,[1] the Commission stated: "The competitive concerns [relating to vertical foreclosure] can be limited to markets (i) that are vertically related to another market where either Telia or Sonera have a dominant position (condition 1) and (ii) where the other party is present (condition 2)".

(d) Further, in *AOL / Time Warner*,[2] the Commission stated that: "A company holding a dominant position in the [upstream market] would be in a position to play the gamekeeper's role dictating the conditions for [delivery in the downstream market] by refusing to license or threatening to withhold the rights".

(e) However, in *Vivendi / Canal+ / Seagram*[3] the Commission considered a proposed merger between Canal+ (Europe's largest pay-TV operator with dominant positions in five national markets in the EC) and Universal (one of seven major US film studios which produce and co-produce premium films).[4] The Commission did not suggest that Universal held a dominant position in any markets prior to the merger. The Commission identified two theories of competitive harm arising from the combination of film production and pay-TV services. The first theory was that, following the merger, Universal would refuse to license pay-TV operators other than Canal+, which, the Commission found, would be likely to strengthen Canal+'s position as a pay-TV operator.[5] This reasoning implies that a refusal to supply by a non-dominant upstream operator can strengthen a dominant position held by the merged group in a downstream market. However, if the merged group did not hold a dominant

141, turned on the commitments offered by Tetra Laval and not the Commission's analysis of the vertical issues absent the commitments. (The Court of First Instance's decision was upheld on appeal on the basis of reasoning not relating to this issue in Case C-12/03P *Commission v Tetra Laval BV*, not yet reported, judgment of February 15, 2005.)

[99] Case COMP/M.2197, para.31.
[1] Case COMP/M.2803, para.80.
[2] Case COMP/M.1845 [2001] O.J. L268/28, para.25.
[3] Case COMP/M.2050.
[4] Para.39 and the tables following para.41.
[5] Para.43.

position in the upstream market, it is not clear why downstream competitors of Canal+ in the supply of pay-TV services could not simply obtain content from one or more of the other six major studios. In the light of this analytical difficulty with the Commission's analysis,[6] the implication that upstream foreclosure is possible notwithstanding the absence of a dominant position in the upstream market is of doubtful validity. The second theory of competitive harm identified by the Commission was also based on foreclosure of access by rival pay-TV operators to content from major US film studios. The Commission found that, in addition to controlling Universal's licensing policy, the merged group would be able to influence those studios with which Universal co-financed films (with the consequence that it was highly likely that Universal would obtain the rights for those territories where Canal+ held a dominant position) and would also be able to influence Twentieth Century Fox by virtue of Vivendi's 25 per cent stake in BSkyB, the largest shareholder of which was The News Corporation (which controlled Twentieth Century Fox). The Commission found that the transaction would create or strengthen Canal+'s dominant position in national pay-TV markets *not* because Universal would hold a dominant position in the upstream market (taking account of its position as both producer and co-producer of films) but because the transaction would *enhance Canal+'s bargaining position* as against the US studios and, by using that power to negotiate exclusive deals, Canal+'s competitors in the downstream pay-TV market would be foreclosed.[7] The case therefore seems to be one in which the merger would have created a dominant position on a *procurement* market and is not authority for the proposition that upstream foreclosure may arise when the merged group does not hold a dominant position on the upstream market.[8]

11–019 **(viii) The relevance of the competitiveness of the downstream market in cases of upstream foreclosure** The question of whether the Commission must *also* establish that the merged group will hold substantial market power (i.e. a dominant position) in the downstream market (or, at least, that the downstream market is not competitive) in order to prohibit[9] a transaction on the

---

[6] Further, the argument was dealt with summarily in just five lines and the reasoning was not essential to the Commission's decision given the second theory of competitive harm identified in the text. Also, the case was cleared in Phase I on the basis of undertakings and the Commission was therefore applying a "serious doubts" test, rather than asking itself whether (as the substantive test then stood) it was more likely than not that the merger would create or strengthen a dominant position as a result of which effective competition would be significantly impeded.

[7] Paras 43 to 50.

[8] The parties undertook for a period of five years not to grant Canal+ "first window" rights covering more than 50% of Universal's production or co-production and to divest Vivendi's stake in the British pay-TV company, BSkyB.

[9] Or to clear the transaction only following the provision of undertakings.

grounds of upstream foreclosure[10] is also controversial.[11] In principle, the merged group will not have the incentive and ability to engage in upstream foreclosure, *unless* it would *profit in the downstream market* from the changes in the competitive conditions in that market resulting from such a strategy. As noted above,[12] an upstream foreclosure strategy may be profitable because it forces downstream rivals to exit from the market (reducing the competitive constraint on the merged group in the downstream market and enabling it to exercise market power in its own right by profitably raising prices) *or* raises downstream rivals' costs (either through increases in the price of the input or by depriving the downstream rivals of economies of scale). The first source of profits is available only if, following the implementation of the upstream foreclosure strategy, the merged group holds substantial market power (i.e. a dominant position) in the downstream market (otherwise attempts by the merged group to increase prices in the downstream market would be defeated), but the second may be available even if the downstream market is generally competitive. This conclusion is supported by Scheffman,[13] who comments: "*the profitability of* [raising rivals' costs] *does not generally require that the predator(s) have power over price in the market for its output.* The [raising rivals' costs] predator's ability to raise the market price derives from its power to raise industry marginal costs relative to its average costs. This requires that the [raising rivals' costs] predator have power over price for some input that is critical to its rivals".[14]

The conclusion that it is *not* necessary to establish that the merged group will hold substantial market power (i.e. a dominant position) in the downstream market[15] in order to prohibit a transaction on the grounds of upstream foreclosure is supported by the following cases.

(a) In *Alcan / Pechiney (II)*[16] the Commission found that the merger would not create or strengthen a dominant position in the downstream market (and therefore that the merged group would not be able profitably to raise prices in that market by restricting its output) but nevertheless found that an upstream foreclosure strategy might[17]

---

[10] The converse question arises in cases of downstream foreclosure.

[11] See Areeda & Hovenkamp, *Antitrust Law* (2nd edn, Aspen Law & Business, 2002), Vol.IIIA, paras 759c and 1004c.

[12] See para.11–014(b).

[13] "The Application of Raising Rivals' Costs Theory to Antitrust" [1992] *The Antitrust Bulletin* 187, at p.196.

[14] By contrast, the incentive to engage in *predatory pricing* depends on the company's ability profitably to reduce *its own* output in the market from which competitors have been excluded and therefore requires that the merged group has a dominant position in that market. For discussion of strategies available when the merged group *has* market power in the downstream market, see Scheffman, "The Application of Raising Rivals' Costs Theory to Antitrust" [1992] *The Antitrust Bulletin* 187, at p.203.

[15] For upstream foreclosure cases in which the Commission focused, under the old test, on whether a dominant position would be created or strengthened in the *downstream* market, see the first edition of this work, para.5–18.

[16] Case COMP/M.3225, paras 40 to 44.

be profitable by raising rivals' costs (as discussed in para.11–014(b) above).

(b) In *BP / E.ON*,[18] which was decided under Regulation 4064/89, the parties made specific arguments about the test to be applied in analysing cases of the alleged raising of rivals' costs: "According to the parties, the incentives and the ability successfully to raise rivals' costs by raising the price of a necessary input depend on two conditions: (i) sufficient market power upstream; and (ii) an appreciable market share shift to their downstream divisions by raising the costs of downstream non-integrated competitors. Furthermore, according to the parties the share shift in the downstream markets must lead to the gaining or strengthening of market power in the downstream derivatives market, so that prices can be raised in those markets".[19] The Commission found that the question of whether the parties would achieve a dominant position on the downstream market was *not* relevant and focused instead on whether the merger created or strengthened a dominant position in the upstream market.[20]

11–020 However, in *Tetra Laval BV v Commission*[21] the Court of First Instance focused on whether the merged group could, through a leveraging strategy, create or strengthen a dominant position on the *leveraged* market.[22] The Court's exclusive focus on the *leveraged* market raises some doubts regarding the analysis set out above. Nevertheless, if necessary, *Tetra Laval* can be distinguished on the basis that it arose under the old substantive test[23]

---

[17] The case was resolved in phase I and the Commission had therefore only reached the stage of "serious doubts" and, judging from the terms of the decision, had not sought to model the potential gains in profits in the downstream market against the loss of profits in the upstream market.

[18] Case COMP/M.2533 [2002] O.J. L276/31.

[19] Para.88.

[20] Para.89. See also para.92. At paras 93 and 94, the Commission rejected an argument that the fact that the market in which their customers sold (i.e. the market downstream of the downstream market analysed for the purposes of a vertical foreclosure assessment) was competitive would limit the merged group's ability to raise prices to those customers because they would not be able to pass on their increased input costs: "According to the Commission's market investigation it may be the case that the producers of ethylene derivatives in certain market situations will not be able to pass the increased raw material cost on to their customers due to the competition which they face from producers located outside the ARG+ and imports of the ethylene downstream product. However, such a limit for the increase of ethylene prices does not change the general incentives of the merged entities as, even if the ethylene prices cannot be increased above a certain limit, the merged parties would share the incentives to increase prices up to this limit, gain the profits of the downstream derivatives producers and reduce their competitiveness compared to their own ethylene derivative units".

[21] Case T-5/02 [2002] E.C.R. II-4381, paras 148, 153, 154, 251, 254, 281 and 291. (The Court of First Instance's decision was upheld on appeal on the basis of reasoning not relating to this issue in Case C-12/03P *Commission v Tetra Laval BV*, not yet reported, judgment of February 15, 2005.)

[22] The case arose under the dominance test and involved conglomerate issues (although these are analytically identical to vertical issues at an overarching level as both involve the leveraging of market power from one market into a second).

[23] Compare the discussion of recital 25 to the revised ECMR in para.2–015 above.

and the Commission therefore needed to establish that the merger would create or strengthen a dominant position on either the upstream or the downstream market.

11.4 DOWNSTREAM FORECLOSURE / REFUSAL TO PURCHASE

(a) Introduction

A merger is liable to be prohibited (or cleared only following the provision **11–021** of undertakings) because of downstream foreclosure concerns when its effect is that the merged group is likely to refuse to *purchase* an output from rival upstream suppliers, if effective competition is significantly impeded as a result.[24] This is illustrated in Fig.11.5: the merger of companies A and B may lead company A to cease purchasing from suppliers 1 and 2 or to reduce its purchases.

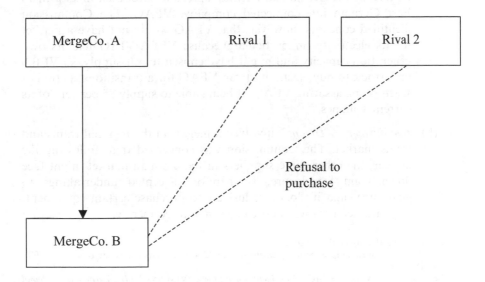

Fig. 11.5: Downstream Foreclosure

---

[24] The essence of downstream foreclosure is that the merged group's actions in the downstream market are profitable *because of their effects on the upstream market*. See generally Church, "The Impact of Vertical and Conglomerate Mergers on Competition", 2004 (report for DG Competition) (available via *http://europa.eu.int/comm/competition/mergers/others/merger_ impact.pdf*), pp.xv to xix and s.3.3

(b) The test for analysing downstream foreclosure issues

11–022 The four stages for analysing upstream foreclosure issues[25] are equally applicable to the analysis of downstream foreclosure issues. In particular, an *incentive* to engage in downstream foreclosure arises if the merged group is able to deprive rival upstream producers of significant *economies of scale* (because they are no longer able to sell to the merged group's downstream business), increasing their costs and, potentially, their prices, and excluding or marginalising them from the upstream market.[26]

(c) The Commission's approach

11–023 The Commission has considered downstream foreclosure in the following cases.[27]

(a) *VEBA / VIAG*[28] involved the German market for electricity supply at the interconnected level. In order to eliminate duopoly concerns, the parties (and RWE whose acquisition of VEW was considered in parallel by the German authorities) agreed to sever their links with an East German interconnected company, VEAG. The Commission identified concerns, however, that VEAG would not have a market for its electricity, in particular because VEBA/VIAG had its own generation capacity and might have chosen to self-supply, so VEBA undertook to buy electricity from VEAG for a transitional period of seven years, assuring VEAG of being able to supply 75 per cent of its current volumes.

(b) *Bombardier / ADtranz*[29] involved a merger in the regional trains and trams market. The Commission was concerned that, following the merger, the other three suppliers in the German market might face downstream foreclosure. It therefore accepted undertakings to guarantee capacity load, exclusively to purchase certain equipment, to guarantee turnover and to continue to cooperate.

---

[25] See paras 11–012 to 11–016 above.

[26] See Areeda, Hovenkamp & Solow, *Antitrust Law* (2nd edn, Aspen Law & Business, 1998), Vol.IVA, para.1008.

[27] See also: Case IV/M.81 *VIAG / Continental Can*; Case IV/M.553 *RTL / Veronica / Endemol* [1996] O.J. L294/14 (an appeal was dismissed in Case T–221/95 *Endemol Entertainment Holding BV v Commission* [1999] E.C.R. II–1299); Case IV/M.603 *Crown Cork & Seal / Carnaud Metalbox* [1996] O.J. L75/38; Case COMP/M.2149 *T-Online International / TUI / C&N Touristic* (notification withdrawn, but details of the Commission's provisional findings are printed in *Competition Policy Newsletter*, June 2002, p.57); Case COMP/M.3809 *Siemens / Flender* (no further foreclosure of upstream rivals from supplying the downstream merging party because the downstream merging party purchased all of its requirements from the upstream merging party prior to the merger; para.30); and Case COMP/M.3943 *Saint-Gobain / BPB*, paras 56 and 58.

[28] Case COMP/M.1673 [2001] O.J. L188/1.

[29] Case COMP/M.2139.

(c)   In *The Coca-Cola Company / Kar-Tess Group (Hellenic Bottling)*[30] the Commission authorised a merger between the bottling interests of Hellenic Bottling (controlled by Kar-Tess Group ("Kar-Tess")) and Coca-Cola Beverages ("CCB", controlled by The Coca-Cola Company ("TCCC")). Kar-Tess and Hellenic each had interests in Frigoglass, a supplier of food and beverage coolers which are used to display cooled soft drinks in retail outlets. The Commission found that rival suppliers of food and beverage coolers might have been foreclosed from supplying to bottlers who distributed TCCC products. The Commission accepted a commitment that Hellenic would sell its stake in Frigoglass.

(d)   In *INA / LuK*[31] the merged group would have accounted for over 90 per cent of sales in the downstream market but the Commission found that downstream foreclosure would not occur because the upstream product was also sold for other applications, before the merger LuK had purchased the input exclusively from INA, and other downstream producers would have adequate sources of supply.

(e)   In *RMC / Rugby*[32] the Commission found that, even if the merged group chose to source cement exclusively from internal sources in particular local geographic markets for ready mixed concrete, there would be no exclusionary effect because any reduction in local demand would be offset by increased demand elsewhere from other ready mixed concrete manufacturers or even other RMC plants.

(f)   In *Imetal / English China Clays*[33] downstream foreclosure was ruled out because, even if the merged group ceased to purchase from independent suppliers, it was unlikely that the viability of any such suppliers would be prejudiced.

11.5 FORECLOSURE OF NEW ENTRY

Vertical integration may create a barrier to entry if potential entrants need **11–024** to enter two markets rather than one. The US Non-Horizontal Merger Guidelines[34] identify a concern that vertical integration may create barriers

---

[30] Case COMP/M.1683.
[31] Case COMP/M.1789, paras 15 to 21.
[32] Case COMP/M.1759, para.19.
[33] Case IV/M.1381, para.70.
[34] The US Non-Horizontal Merger Guidelines, 1984 (*www.usdoj.gov/atr/public/guidelines/ 2614.htm*). Areeda & Hovenkamp, *Antitrust Law* (2nd edn, Aspen Law & Business, 2002), Vol.IIIA, comment, at para.755c (see also paras 756c3 and 761d): "Vertical integration can create entry barriers by effectively requiring new entrants to come in at two market levels rather than one; this problem is most severe when scale economies are significantly different at the two levels; for example, bundling film and developing it by the monopolist requires the aspiring film developer to become a film producer as well". See generally Areeda, Hovenkamp

to entry when three conditions are satisfied. First, it is necessary for a new entrant wishing to enter the primary market also to enter the secondary (i.e. vertically connected) market. Two-level entry will *not* be necessary when there is sufficient unintegrated capacity in the secondary market. Secondly, the need to enter the secondary market makes entry into the primary market significantly more difficult and less likely to occur. If entry into the secondary market is easy, vertical integration will not foreclose entry to the primary market. Simultaneous entry may be harder if the cost of capital for entering the secondary market is higher or there are substantial economies of scale in the secondary market.[35] Thirdly, the structure and performance of the primary market is otherwise conducive to non-competitive performance (otherwise increased difficulty of entry is unlikely to affect its performance).

11.6 OTHER CONCERNS ARISING FROM VERTICAL INTEGRATION

(a) Coordinated effects

11–025 Vertical integration may increase the likelihood or intensity of coordinated effects, for example by increasing transparency if the merger has the effect that all the coordinating suppliers are active in the downstream market, allowing information exchange (e.g. if a producer buys a distributor which also serves rival suppliers), removing a disruptive buyer or increasing multi-market contact.[36] These issues are discussed in Ch.8 above.[37]

(b) Price discrimination

11–026 Price discrimination is possible only when the supplier can prevent arbitrage, i.e. sale by customers purchasing at low prices (i.e. high elasticity customers) to customers who are required by the supplier to pay high prices (i.e. low elasticity customers). Vertical integration may allow the merged

---

& Solow, *Antitrust Law* (2nd edn, Aspen Law & Business, 1998), Vol.IVA, para.1011. See also the Canadian Merger Guidelines, 2004 (*www.competitionbureau.gc.ca/PDFs/2004%20MEGs. Final.pdf*), paras 10.2 to 10.4.

[35] e.g. if brewers only supply pubs which they own, then a new entrant to the pub market would need also to set up a brewery, which is a substantial barrier to entry because economies of scale in the brewing market are more extensive than those in the pub market.

[36] See Church, "The Impact of Vertical and Conglomerate Mergers on Competition", 2004 (report for DG Competition) (available via *http://europa.eu.int/comm/competition/mergers/others/merger_impact.pdf*), pp.xliv to xlvii and ss.5.2; and RBB Economics, "The Efficiency-Enhancing Effects of Non-Horizontal Mergers", 2005 (report for the Commission DG for Enterprise and Industry) (available via *http://europa.eu.int/comm/enterprise/library/lib-competition/doc/non_horizontal_mergers.pdf*), pp.13 and 14.

[37] See also the Canadian Merger Guidelines, 2004 (*www.competitionbureau.gc.ca/PDFs/2004%20MEGs.Final.pdf*), paras 10.5 to 10.7.

group to prevent arbitrage by purchasing suppliers in the low price/high elasticity market. This may enable the merged group to charge high prices to high price/low elasticity customer groups without fear of being undermined by arbitrage.[38]

(c) Information

The motivation for, or consequence of, vertical integration may be that one **11–027** of the merging parties obtains valuable private information. A distinction can be drawn between two categories of information.[39] First, valuable private information about the target's business (e.g. in cases of downstream integration into retail markets, detailed knowledge of customer sensitivity to price increases). Obtaining access to such information through a merger is likely to increase productive efficiency and is therefore unobjectionable unless any of the exclusionary effects described in ss.11.3 to 11.6 are likely. Secondly, information relating to the proposed acquirer's competitors, e.g. if a retailer purchases a wholesaler, the retailer may be able to obtain information about the products which are being purchased by rival retailers. The Commission may be concerned in such cases that the merger will raise rivals' costs (as they may seek alternative sources of supply to avoid disclosure of the information) and/or facilitate coordinated effects or exclusionary conduct in the light of the information about the activities of competitors.[40] In *ENI / EDP / GDP*[41] the Commission found that EDP's dominant position on the market for wholesale gas would be strengthened through the merger because it would know the gas costs of its competitors (in circumstances where gas costs are around 70 per cent of the variable

---

[38] See Perry, "Vertical Integration: Determinants and Effects", in Schmalensee & Willig eds., *Handbook of Industrial Organization* (North-Holland, 1989), Vol.1, Ch.4, pp.192 to 196. Areeda & Hovenkamp, *Antitrust Law* (2nd edn, Aspen Law & Business, 2002), Vol IIIA, argue, at para.756b5, that "price discrimination resulting from vertical integration is not readily classifiable as good or bad. Because most of the other effects seem insubstantial, output effects govern the general economic appraisal. As a general proposition, price discrimination is desirable if it expands output and undesirable if it lowers output, but such a determination cannot easily be made in particular cases. Nevertheless, price discrimination resulting from vertical integration should generally be regarded as more likely to be beneficial rather than adverse. This entails that antitrust should not condemn vertical integration simply because it facilitates price discrimination". See also Areeda, Hovenkamp & Solow, *Antitrust Law* (2nd edn, Aspen Law & Business, 1998),Vol.IVA, para.1012.

[39] See the speech of Richard Parker, Senior Deputy Director, Bureau of Competition, FTC, "Global Merger Enforcement", September 28, 1999 (*www.ftc.gov/speeches/other/barcelona.htm*).

[40] See Case COMP/M.1673 *VEBA / VIAG* [2001] O.J. L188/1, para.106; Case COMP/M.2510 *Cendant / Galileo*, (concluding that the information obtained would not, given the way in which contracts were negotiated, confer a competitive advantage; paras 26(c), 29 and 37); Case COMP/M.3101 *Accor / Hilton / Six Continents / JV*, paras 16 and 17; and Case COMP/ M.3943 *Saint-Gobain / BPB*, paras 79 and 80.

[41] Case COMP/M.3440 [2005] O.J. L302/69, paras 368, 369 and 378 (prohibition upheld on appeal in Case T-87/05 *EDP v Commission*, not yet reported, judgment of September 21, 2005, on grounds which did not call into question the finding that the dominant positions on electricity markets would be strengthened).

costs of producing electricity) and its competitors' daily requirements for gas. This issue was also raised in *Boeing / Hughes*[42] where it was alleged that: "As a satellite manufacturer, HSC receives competitively sensitive information relating to the launch vehicles with which its satellites will be integrated. Although that information is usually protected by confidentiality clauses, HSC might use it to the detriment of third party launch service operators".[43] The parties offered undertakings—in particular that HSC would not pass on any non-public information relating to launchers or satellites[44]—but the Commission cleared the transaction without undertakings, impliedly finding that the concerns expressed by third parties about confidential information were not of sufficient magnitude to justify a finding that the merger would create or strengthen a dominant position (as the substantive test then stood).

(d) Avoidance of regulatory constraints

11–028 Vertical integration may allow a regulated entity to acquire the supplier of its fixed or variable inputs, which may make it hard for regulators to assess the market value of those supplies (enabling the regulated entity to inflate its allowable costs). Further, vertical integration may allow a regulated entity to avoid its regulatory constraints, e.g. by switching capital or revenues out of the regulated business into the upstream business.

(e) Reduced incentive to engage in research and development

11–029 In certain markets, suppliers that are not vertically integrated cooperate on research and development with upstream suppliers or downstream customers and, as part of that cooperation, share confidential information. The Commission may be concerned that a vertical merger would reduce the incentive to share information (which might reduce research and development and might ultimately harm consumers) because of concerns that it will be shared with a competing business.[45]

---

[42] Case COMP/M.1879 [2004] O.J. L63/53.
[43] Para.82(e).
[44] Para.102.
[45] See RBB Economics, "The Efficiency-Enhancing Effects of Non-Horizontal Mergers", 2005 (report for the Commission DG for Enterprise and Industry) (available via *http:// europa.eu.int/comm/enterprise/library/lib-competition/doc/non_horizontal_mergers.pdf*), p.14 (noting that the merged group may not have such an incentive and the effects on consumers are ambiguous).

CHAPTER 12

CONGLOMERATE ISSUES

12.1 INTRODUCTION

(a) General

Conglomerate issues[1] arise in mergers[2] between parties which are not actual **12–001** or potential competitors of one another (horizontal mergers), and where neither produces a good which is, or could be, used by the other (vertical mergers).[3]

---

[1] See Church, "The Impact of Vertical and Conglomerate Mergers on Competition", 2004 (report for DG Competition) (available via *http://europa.eu.int/comm/competition/mergers/others/merger_impact.pdf*); Völcker, "Leveraging as a Theory of Competitive Harm in EU Merger Control" (2003) 40 C.M.L.Rev. 581; RBB Economics, "The Efficiency-Enhancing Effects of Non-Horizontal Mergers", 2005 (report for the Commission DG for Enterprise and Industry) (available via *http://europa.eu.int/comm/enterprise/library/lib-competition/doc/non_horizontal_mergers.pdf*); and Nalebuff, "Bundling, Tying and Portfolio Effects", 2003 (DTI Economics Paper) (available via *www.dti.gov.uk/ccp/topics2/pdf2/bundle1.pdf*). For a strategic perspective on diversification, see Oster, *Modern Competitive Advantage* (3rd edn, Oxford UP, 1999), Ch.10 and Porter, *Competitive Advantage* (The Free Press, 1998 edn), Chs 9, 10 and 12. The Commission has a long-standing intention to publish a notice on non-horizontal mergers; see Mario Monti, then Commissioner for Competition Policy, speech, "Review of the EC Merger Regulation—the Reform Package", November 7, 2002, Brussels (*www.europa.eu.int/comm/competition/speeches/index_2002.html*); press release IP/02/1856; and Philip Lowe, Director General of DG Competition, speech, "The future shape of European merger control", Brussels, February 17, 2003 (*http://europa.eu.int/comm/competition/speeches/*).

[2] The Form CO, para.6.3(c), requires the notifying parties to identify situations in which they are present on closely related neighbouring markets and the individual or combined market shares of the parties in any one of these markets is 25% or more; the Form CO describes product markets as closely related neighbouring markets when the products are complementary to each other or when they belong to a range of products that is generally purchased by the same set of customers for the same end use.

[3] The analysis of conglomerate issues is bedevilled with terminological differences. The issues discussed in this Chapter are also commonly referred to as "leveraging issues", "portfolio effects" and "range effects". Nothing turns on the terminology and the Chapter analyses these connected points under the umbrella heading "conglomerate issues". As a definitional issue, this book treats a reduction of potential competition as giving rise to possible horizontal non-

405

(b) Ambiguous effects of conglomerate mergers on consumer welfare

12–002 Conglomerate mergers may have as their motivation or consequence effects which are *positive* or at least *ambiguous* from the perspective of maximising consumer welfare. When a conglomerate merger occurs between two suppliers of complementary goods (i.e. products where demand for one is positively correlated to demand for the other), the merged group generally has an incentive to *reduce* its prices, which benefits consumers. The incentive arises because lowering the price of complementary good A increases demand for complementary good B and if the suppliers of A and B merge then the merged group benefits from increased sales of A *and* B if it lowers the price of A (whereas prior to the merger, it only benefited from increased sales of A). In addition, conglomerate mergers may lower transaction costs, give rise to productive efficiencies (e.g. through economies of scope), increase pricing efficiency and/or prevent profit expropriation.[4]

On the other hand, conglomerate mergers may harm consumers in certain circumstances, in particular by marginalising or eliminating competitors. However, this is the exception rather than the rule[5] and requires a fact-specific assessment of the merged group's incentives and abilities to pursue particular strategies and the effects of those strategies on competitors and, ultimately, consumers.

(c) Decisions of the Community Courts

12–003 Recent decisions of the Community Courts have made it more difficult for the Commission to intervene in conglomerate mergers and, when substantive issues arise, the Commission is now less likely to require remedies involving the transfer of a market position.

---

coordinated effects (see Ch.9 above) on the basis that this is essentially an issue relating to activity in a specific market. Equally, the question of whether a conglomerate merger increases *multi-market contact*, and might therefore increase the chances of coordinated effects, is dealt with in Ch.8.

[4] For an authoritative survey of efficiencies in conglomerate mergers see RBB Economics, "The Efficiency-Enhancing Effects of Non-Horizontal Mergers", 2005 (report for the Commission DG for Enterprise and Industry) (available via *http://europa.eu.int/comm/enterprise/library/lib-competition/doc/non_horizontal_mergers.pdf*), Ch.4. See also Church, "The Impact of Vertical and Conglomerate Mergers on Competition", 2004 (report for DG Competition) (available via *http://europa.eu.int/comm/competition/mergers/others/merger_impact.pdf*), Ch.7.

[5] RBB Economics, "The Efficiency-Enhancing Effects of Non-Horizontal Mergers", 2005 (report for the Commission DG for Enterprise and Industry) (available via *http://europa.eu.int/comm/enterprise/library/lib-competition/doc/non_horizontal_mergers.pdf*) argue, at p.3: "In general, non-horizontal mergers will be pro-competitive and such exclusionary behaviour can occur only under very stringent conditions ... In short, anti-competitive non-horizontal mergers are the exception rather than the rule". Compare Nalebuff, "Bundling, Tying and Portfolio Effects", 2003 (DTI Economics Paper) (available via *www.dti.gov.uk/ccp/topics2/pdf2/bundle1.pdf*), pp.9 to 11.

(a) In *Tetra Laval BV v Commission*[6] the Court of First Instance confirmed that the Commission has power under the ECMR to prohibit
conglomerate mergers, but emphasised that such transactions are
generally neutral or even beneficial for competition and, accordingly,
"the proof of anti-competitive conglomerate effects of such a merger
calls for a precise examination, supported by convincing evidence, of
the circumstances which allegedly produce those effects". On appeal,
the European Court of Justice[7] upheld the Court of First Instance's
reasoning on this point,[8] adding[9]: "The analysis of a 'conglomerate-
type' concentration is a prospective analysis in which, first, the
consideration of a lengthy period of time in the future and, secondly,
the leveraging necessary to give rise to a significant impediment to
effective competition mean that the chains of cause and effect are
dimly discernible, uncertain and difficult to establish".[10]

(b) The Court of First Instance's decision in *General Electric Company v
Commission*[11] emphasised that the Commission must carry out a
careful factual assessment to determine whether the merged group
will have an *incentive* to adopt the conduct which is hypothesised,[12] as
well as the *ability* to do so.

(c) This Chapter should also be read in the light of the discussion in
s.2.7(a) of the relevance of Art.82 to the Commission's assessment
under the ECMR, and in s.20.6 of the Commission's duty to take
account of "behavioural" or conduct remedies (e.g. a commitment
not to engage in tying). It is now clear that the Commission is
required to take account of the merged group's legal obligations
under Art.82 (to an extent) and of any behavioural or conduct
commitments.

More generally, Commission officials have emphasised that in more recent
cases the Commission is "adopting a cautious attitude when assessing the
risk of foreclosure effects stemming from bundling strategies",[13] which
serves to emphasise that earlier decisions on conglomerate mergers may be
of limited value as indicators of the Commission's current approach.

---

[6] Case T-5/02 [2002] E.C.R. II-4381, paras 148 to 155.
[7] Case C-12/03P *Commission v Tetra Laval BV*, not yet reported, judgment of February 15,
2005.
[8] See para.45.
[9] Para.44.
[10] Subsequently, in Case T-210/01 *General Electric Company v Commission*, not yet reported,
judgment of December 14, 2005, paras 65, 66 and 69, the Court of First Instance followed the
approach in the *Tetra Laval* cases.
[11] Case T-210/01, not yet reported, judgment of December 14, 2005.
[12] i.e. whether such a strategy is the most profitable available to the merged group.
[13] Bacchiega, Dionnet, Todino & MacEwen, "Johnson & Johnson / Guidant: Potential Competition and Unilateral Effects in Innovative Markets", *Competition Policy Newsletter*,
Autumn 2005, p.87

(d) Grounds for intervention in conglomerate mergers

12–004 The principal ground for intervention in conglomerate mergers is that the merger will allow the merged group to leverage market power in one market ("the leveraging market") into a second ("the leveraged market") to the detriment of consumers ("leveraging").[14] In this respect, the analysis of vertical and conglomerate mergers is identical at an overarching level,[15] as each focuses on the connections between two distinct markets, the scope to use a position in one market for advantage in a second, and the implications of such strategies for consumers.[16] The similarity between vertical and conglomerate mergers is most striking when the conglomerate merger involves a combination of producers of *complementary goods*[17] (i.e. products where demand for one is positively correlated to demand for the other)[18] because goods sold in vertically connected markets are also generally complements.

---

[14] Drauz, "Unbundling *GE / Honeywell*: the Assessment of Conglomerate Mergers Under EC Competition Law", published in the 2001 *Annual Proceedings of the Fordham Corporate Law Institute*, p.183, states: "In general, conglomerate mergers will raise concerns when they make the leverage of market power possible, thus having as their effect or object to foreclose the market to effective competition".

[15] The application of the overarching principles differs between vertical and conglomerate mergers. Völcker, "Leveraging as a Theory of Competitive Harm in EU Merger Control" (2003) 40 C.M.L.Rev. 581, comments, at p.586, that vertical cases generally involve raising rivals' costs whereas leveraging practices potentially affect rivals by diverting demand to the merged group, lowering rivals' profits. RBB Economics, "The Efficiency-Enhancing Effects of Non-Horizontal Mergers", 2005 (report for the Commission DG for Enterprise and Industry) (available via *http://europa.eu.int/comm/enterprise/library/lib-competition/doc/non_horizontal_ mergers.pdf*) note, at p.p.5 and 6 (see also n.20), that in vertical mergers the downstream company generally combines the two goods, whereas in conglomerate mergers integration is left to the customer.

[16] Drauz, "Unbundling *GE / Honeywell*: the Assessment of Conglomerate Mergers Under EC Competition Law", published in the 2001 *Annual Proceedings of the Fordham Corporate Law Institute*, p.183, states: "As far as the exclusionary effects of conglomerate mergers are concerned, there is a clear parallel to be made with vertical effects, since in economic terms the exclusion mechanism in the context of vertical integration functions in a similar way as in the context of a merger of complements".

[17] Porter, *Competitive Advantage* (The Free Press, 1998 edn), pp.418 to 421, identified the following advantages from controlling complementary goods: improving buyer performance and thus differentiating; improving the perception of value; optimal pricing; reducing marketing and selling costs; sharing other activities; and raising mobility barriers.

[18] The following categories of complementary goods may be distinguished.

    (a) Economic complements are products which are consumed together, such as fish and chips, or produced together, such as petrol and lubricants.

    (b) Commercial complements include goods forming part of a range which must be carried by distributors, such as different types of spirits.

    (c) Technical complements are goods which, for technical reasons, must be consumed together, such as computer operating systems and programs.

    (d) Perfect complements are always consumed together in fixed proportions, e.g. left and right shoes.

    (e) "Stochastically dependent" products exist when demand for the two goods is positively correlated but the goods are not economic, commercial or technical complements, e.g. consumers with the highest demand for spreadsheets may have also have the highest demand for database programmes.

The Commission has stated repeatedly that there is no "efficiency offence" under the ECMR[19] and this implies that the Commission will *not* use its powers under the ECMR simply to protect competitors against more efficient rivals (e.g. because the merger provides access to greater resources or economies of scale). However, as explained in s.7.6 above, the Commission *does* take efficiencies into account as part of its normal appraisal of the merger's effects (whether horizontal, vertical or conglomerate).[20] This means, for example, that when examining a horizontal merger, it may be relevant to take into account possible efficiencies when assessing the likelihood that new entry would prevent the merged group from raising its prices.[21]

(e) Organisation of the Chapter

S.12.2 identifies the generic criteria which must be established to prove **12–005** leveraging. The remainder of the Chapter reviews conglomerate issues by category: tying, pure bundling and mixed bundling (s.12.3), other theories of leverage (s.12.4), portfolio power (s.12.5), and reduced incentives to engage in research and development (s.12.6).[22]

12.2 GENERIC TREATMENT OF CONGLOMERATE ISSUES—LEVERAGING

(a) The test for assessing conglomerate issues

In *Johnson & Johnson / Guidant*,[23] the Commission described its approach to **12–006** bundling issues in mergers as follows: "In order to assess the risk of fore-

---

[19] See para.18–008 below.

[20] Drauz, "Unbundling *GE / Honeywell*: the Assessment of Conglomerate Mergers Under EC Competition Law", published in the 2001 *Annual Proceedings of the Fordham Corporate Law Institute*, p.183, argued that "the conglomerate aspects of mergers may constitute an additional factor, either aggravating or mitigating, to existing horizontal and/or vertical effects".

[21] In Case T-114/02 *BaByliss v Commission* [2003] E.C.R. II-1279 the Court of First Instance, in a paragraph discussing possible economies of scale or rationalisation, stated that the merger might have an anti-competitive effect because the merged group might be able to induce retailers to de-list its competitors (a potential exclusionary strategy); see para.360. The approach in the text receives some support from the decision of the Court of First Instance in Case T-210/01 *General Electric Company v Commission*, not yet reported, judgment of December 14, 2005, paras 183 to 189, 193, 229 and 241, in which the Court emphasised that the fact that the merged group would benefit from GE Group's AAA credit rating had not been identified by the Commission as a free standing ground for prohibiting the merger but instead was an adjunct to other factors supporting the conclusion that GE held a pre-merger dominant position on the market for jet engines.

[22] Economies of scale and financial resources ("deep pockets") (both of which are a source of efficiency and not an independent, free-standing theory of competitive harm) are analysed in s.7.6 above.

[23] Case COMP/M.3687, para.339. See also Bacchiega, Dionnet, Todino & MacEwen, "Johnson & Johnson / Guidant: Potential Competition and Unilateral Effects in Innovative Markets", *Competition Policy Newsletter*, Autumn 2005, p.87.

closure effects arising from the merger, the Commission has considered whether the merging entity has the ability and incentive to engage in bundling practices and if so, whether such a strategy could give rise to foreclosure effects".

The four-fold test[24] inherent in this formulation (identify the conduct in issue, consider whether the merged group will have the incentive and ability to pursue it, assess whether it will have a foreclosure effect, and determine whether there is a causal link between the foreclosure effect and the merger) is adopted in the text below.[25]

12–007   However, the Commission adopted a more nuanced formulation in *GE /Amersham*[26]:

> "for commercial bundling to result in foreclosure of competition it is necessary that the merged entity is able to leverage its pre-merger dominance in one product to another complementary product. In addition, for such a strategy to be profitable, there must be a reasonable expectation that rivals will not be able to propose a competitive response, and that their resulting marginalisation will force them to exit the market. Finally, once rivals have exited the market, the merged firm must be able to implement unilateral price increases and such increases need to be sustainable in the long term, without being challenged by the likelihood of new rivals entering the market or previously marginalised ones re-entering the market".

The *Amersham* formulation is excessively narrow insofar as it purports to summarise the circumstances in which the Commission would prohibit a transaction because of concerns about conglomerate effects. In particular, as the Commission has recognised in cases involving vertical effects, a leveraging strategy may be profitable without creating an ability to imple-

---

[24] See also RBB Economics, "The Efficiency-Enhancing Effects of Non-Horizontal Mergers", 2005 (report for the Commission DG for Enterprise and Industry) (available via *http://europa.eu.int/comm/enterprise/library/lib-competition/doc/non_horizontal_mergers.pdf*), pp.123 and 124. For a longer formulation, see "Portfolio Effects in Conglomerate Mergers", OECD, DAFFE/COMP(2002)5, pp.8 and 9.

[25] The approach in the text is consistent with the judgment of the Court of First Instance in Case T-5/02 *Tetra Laval BV v Commission* [2002] E.C.R. II-4381, in which the Court examined the merged group's ability to engage in leveraging (at paras 192 to 199, under the heading "The possibility of leveraging"), its incentive to engage in leveraging (at paras 200 to 216), the methods which might be used by the merged group in pursuit of its leveraging strategy (at paras 217 to 224) and the foreseeable effects of the leveraging strategy (at paras 225 to 307). The Opinion of Advocate General Tizzano in Case C-12/03P *Commission v Tetra Laval BV*, noted, at para.114, the Commission's view that, in order to establish a leveraging case, it is necessary to show that the merged group has the "means and incentives" to engage in abuses permitting it to oust its competitors from the market (a somewhat lower test than that described in the text as the Commission's formulation does not consider whether any exclusion would be likely to harm consumers). (The Court of First Instance's decision was upheld on appeal on the basis of reasoning not relating directly to this issue in Case C-12/03P *Commission v Tetra Laval BV*, not yet reported, judgment of February 15, 2005.)

[26] Case COMP/M.3304, para.37.

ment unilateral price increases[27] and (as the Commission recognised elsewhere in the *Amersham* decision itself) a leveraging strategy may be possible without excluding competitors, so long as they are marginalised.[28]

(b) Identify the leveraging conduct

It is first necessary to identify the conduct that the merged group might **12–008** adopt as part of a leveraging strategy. This might involve, for example, offering customers the option to purchase two or more products for less than the aggregate of the individual prices (mixed bundling), designing products so that they are not compatible with rivals' products (technical tying) or engaging in predatory pricing.

(c) Whether the merged group will have the incentive and ability to pursue the leveraging conduct

The second stage is to assess whether the merged group will have the **12–009** *incentive*[29] and *ability* to leverage its position in one market into a second.

In *General Electric Company v Commission*[30] the Court of First Instance stated: "it was for the Commission to establish not only that the merged entity had the ability to transfer those practices to the markets for avionics and non-avionics products but also, on the basis of convincing evidence, that it was likely that the merged entity would engage in such conduct".[31] The likelihood of the merged group adopting a particular strategy can be determined only by assessing whether it would have an incentive to adopt that conduct, and in particular by determining whether this would be the merged group's *most profitable* strategy. The Court stated that evidence of the merged group's incentives could be derived, for example, from internal company documents (e.g. documents describing the settled intention of the

---

[27] See para.11–014(b) above and, for a more detailed analysis, para.12–010(b)(ii) below.
[28] See para.12–012 below.
[29] See, generally, Besanko, Dranove & Shanley, *Economics of Strategy* (2nd edn, John Wiley & Sons Inc, 2000), Ch.8. See also Nalebuff & Brandenburger, *Co-opetition* (HarperCollins Business, 1997 edn), who identify cooperation with "complementors" as a key creator of value; A is a complementor of B if consumers value B's products more highly when they have A's product as well as B's (e.g. suppliers of computer software are complementors of suppliers of computer hardware).
[30] Case T-210/01, not yet reported, judgment of December 14, 2005, para. 327.
[31] Para.405. The Court also observed, at para.466: "the Court must determine whether the Commission has established that the merged entity would not only have the capability to engage in the bundling practices described in the contested decision but also, on the basis of convincing evidence, that it would have been likely to engage in those practices after the merger" and stated that "the fact that the merged entity could have made a strategic decision to such effect is not sufficient to establish that it would in fact have done so". See also paras 447 (emphasising the importance of assessing the merged group's incentives) and 470.

board of directors) or an economic analysis showing that such behaviour would be in the merged entity's commercial interests.[32]

Further, in addition to the passages from *Johnson & Johnson / Guidant* quoted in para.12–006 above, the importance of examining whether the merged group will have both the incentive and the ability to engage in a leveraging strategy, was emphasised by the Commission in the following cases.

(a) In *GE / Amersham*[33] the Commission stated that its investigation examined "whether or not the merged entity may acquire, as a direct and immediate result of the merger, the ability and economic incentive to foreclose competition, by leveraging its pre-merger market power from one market to another through exclusionary practices, such as bundling and/or tying".[34]

(b) *Boeing / Hughes*[35] involved (essentially) a merger between a supplier of satellites, HSC, and a supplier of satellite launch services, Boeing. The Commission identified a number of steps which the merged group could take to try to leverage its position from one market into another, such as designing launchers so that they only worked with the merged group's satellites[36] and continued: "It appears that, although the behaviour ... might theoretically lead HSC's customers to favour Boeing's launch services, it could also undermine HSC's competitiveness on the satellite market ... In that context, it is necessary to examine whether the merged entity would gain more through additional launch service contracts than it would lose through lost satellite contracts, if it were to engage in such behaviour".[37] The Commission concluded on the facts that the merged group would not have both the incentive and the ability to tie or bundle, in particular because customers placed a large premium on the ability to use a number of launchers and not just one.[38]

---

[32] Para.333.
[33] Case COMP/M.3304, para.37.
[34] Para.31. See also para.43, rejecting the possibility that the merged group might engage in forced bundling on the grounds that it lacked the economic incentive to do so. In addition to the passage quoted in para.12–007 above, the Commission focused on whether the strategy would be profitable (i.e. whether the merged group would have an *incentive* to adopt it) taking account of the reactions of competitors (i.e. whether the merged group would have the *ability* to implement the strategy).
[35] Case COMP/M.1879 [2004] O.J. L63/53. This case is discussed by Lafaro & Ridyard, "Beyond Bork: New Economic Theories of Exclusion in Merger Cases" [2002] E.C.L.R. 151.
[36] Para.82.
[37] Para.83.
[38] Para.87.

(c)   In *Tetra Laval / Sidel*[39] the Commission analysed the acquisition by a supplier of carton packaging systems of a supplier of PET packaging systems under the heading, "Ability and incentive to leverage".

Determining whether the merged group will have the incentive and ability to **12–010** pursue a leveraging strategy will depend to a material extent on the type of leveraging that is being investigated. For example, a leveraging strategy may involve tying, pure bundling, mixed bundling, full-line forcing, exclusive dealing, predatory pricing or cross-subsidisation. These theories of competitive harm are considered in ss.12.3 to 12.5 of this Chapter. However, at a generic level, the merged group's incentive and ability to pursue a leveraging strategy may be affected by the following factors.[40]

(a)   Leveraging will not be profitable in the absence of *substantial market power* (i.e. a dominant position[41]) *in the leveraging market.*[42]

(i)   In *Tetra Laval / SIG*,[43] a decision post-dating the implementation of the significant impediment to effective competi-

---

[39] Case COMP/M.2416 [2004] O.J. L43/13 (decision of October 30, 2001), para.359. The Commission's decision was quashed by the Court of First Instance in Case T-5/02 *Tetra Laval BV v Commission* [2002] E.C.R. II-4381 (upheld on appeal in Case C-12/03P *Commission v Tetra Laval BV*, not yet reported, judgment of February 15, 2005), but the analysis by the Community Courts did not cast doubt on the principle identified in the text.

[40] It is also relevant to consider the rate of growth in the leveraged market: see Case T-5/02 *Tetra Laval BV v Commission* [2002] E.C.R. II-4381, para.201 (the decision was upheld on appeal on the basis of reasoning not relating to this issue in Case C-12/03P *Commission v Tetra Laval BV*, not yet reported, judgment of February 15, 2005).

[41] Under the former substantive test (namely whether the merger would create or strengthen a dominant position), a legal issue arose when considering conglomerate mergers, namely whether a merger which satisfied the four criteria set out in the text might be prohibited on the grounds that it strengthened a dominant position on the *leveraging* market or whether it was necessary for the Commission to establish that the merger created or strengthened a dominant position on the *leveraged* market. This issue was discussed in the context of upstream foreclosure in the case of vertical integration (see paras 11–018 and 11–019 above) and the conclusion was that it is *sufficient* to establish that the transaction will strengthen a dominant position on the *leveraging market* (but a transaction *may* also be prohibited if it creates or strengthens a dominant position on the leveraged market).

[42] Compare Drauz, "Unbundling *GE / Honeywell*: the Assessment of Conglomerate Mergers Under EC Competition Law", published in the 2001 *Annual Proceedings of the Fordham Corporate Law Institute*, p.183, who states, at p.185: "the existence of market power or dominance in at least one of the pre-merger complementary products is a necessary condition for the likelihood and the profitability of leveraging practices". See also p.188. Further, the Commission, in a paper tabled at the OECD roundtable, "Portfolio Effects in Conglomerate Mergers", OECD, DAFFE/COMP(2002)5 stated, at p.239: "To date, the European Commission has challenged the leveraging effects of conglomerate mergers only when market power has pre-existed before the merger in at least one of the markets composing the combined product range". The words "To date" at the start of the quoted passage should probably not be read as implying that the Commission proposes to challenge transactions on conglomerate grounds where the merged group does not have a dominant position in any individual product market. Nevertheless, in a merger involving both horizontal and conglomerate aspects, where the horizontal aspects create a dominant position, it may also be necessary to consider whether that dominant position could be used to leverage market power into other markets.

[43] Case COMP/M.3746, para.76(1).

tion test, the Commission ruled out a leveraging concern on the grounds that the merged group would not hold a position of market power in either market.

(ii) In *GE / Amersham*[44] the Commission stated that a finding of pre-merger dominance is generally required in order to find that leveraging is likely.

(iii) In *Boeing / Hughes*[45] the Commission noted that "even launch service competitors who expressed concerns admit that, in the absence of substantial market power on the satellite market, the [conglomerate effects] could not profitably take place".

(iv) Similarly, in *BT / AT&T*[46] the Commission rejected an argument that BT would tie sales of the joint venture's products and its own products on the grounds that "the joint venture will not hold a dominant position on any of the markets in which it will be active, so any tying of BT's services to those offered by the joint venture could not lead to any increase in market power, since any advantage that BT could obtain from the creation of the joint venture could be matched by other UK operators either on their own or in conjunction with the joint venture's competitors".

Other things being equal, if the merged group has a stronger dominant position in the leveraging market, it is more likely to have the ability and incentive to pursue a leveraging strategy.[47]

(b) The impact of a leveraging strategy on the *merged group's profits*.[48]

(i) In general, a leveraging strategy involves sacrificing profits in one market with the objective of increasing profits in a second market by an amount which exceeds the profits lost in the first. This means that an assessment of the merged group's incentive to adopt a leveraging strategy requires a careful analysis of the profits foregone in the first market and the likely increase in profits in the second. In *General Electric Company v Commission*[49] the Court of First Instance criticised the Commission for failing properly to carry out this balancing exercise when assessing the merged group's incentives to engage in bundling. The Court stated: "to extend the practices at issue to [other

---

[44] Case COMP/M.3304, para.21. See also paras 31, 37 and 38.
[45] Case COMP/M.1879 [2004] O.J. L63/53, para.93.
[46] Case COMP/JV.15, para.163.
[47] See Case T-5/02 *Tetra Laval BV v Commission* [2002] E.C.R. II-4381, para.197 (the decision was upheld on appeal on the basis of reasoning not relating to this issue in Case C-12/03P *Commission v Tetra Laval BV*, not yet reported, judgment of February 15, 2005).
[48] In Case COMP/M.3304 *GE / Amersham*, para.43 (see also para.59), the Commission found that the merged group would not have an incentive to engage in "forced bundling" in particular because many sales would be lost, making the move unprofitable. See also Case COMP/M.3978 *Oracle / Siebel*, para.39.
[49] Case T-210/01, not yet reported, judgment of December 14, 2005, paras 338, 353 and 420.

markets] would have been rational commercial behaviour following the merger only in so far as the revenues which the merged entity was likely to derive from those practices would have offset that potential cost. It follows that the Commission was not entitled to regard it as logical or inevitable that the merged entity would extend those practices to the" other markets.

(ii) The merged group may be able to increase its *profits* using a leveraging strategy,[50] in particular by the following means: through increased or more profitable sales calculated across both the leveraging and leveraged markets; by forcing rivals to exit from the leveraged market; by deterring potential entrants; or by raising rivals' costs in the leveraged market, in particular by depriving them of economies of scale. It follows that a leveraging strategy may be profitable through mechanisms going beyond the implementation of unilateral price increases, and the formulation in *GE / Amersham* quoted in para.12–007 above is unduly narrow. This is confirmed by the cases on vertical integration in which leveraging strategies have been identified which are profitable notwithstanding the absence of substantial market power in the leveraged market.[51]

(c) The links between the products and in particular[52]:

(i) the extent to which demand for the products is *complementary*; if the products are strong complements then, in general, tying and bundling strategies are more likely to be profitable[53];

(ii) whether there is *customer overlap*; unless there is a material group of customers with demand for both products, a strategy based on encouraging or forcing customers to purchase both products will very probably fail[54];

(iii) whether the products are *typically purchased together*; if they are not, it is more difficult to encourage or force customers to

---

[50] The success of a leveraging strategy may depend on the merged group's ability to *pre-commit* to that strategy: see Whinston, "Tying, Foreclosure and Exclusion" (1990) 80 *American Economic Review* 837, at pp.839 and 840.

[51] See para.11–014(b) above.

[52] See Case T-5/02 *Tetra Laval BV v Commission* [2002] E.C.R. II-4381, paras 196 and 198 (the decision was upheld on appeal on the basis of reasoning not relating to this issue in Case C-12/03P *Commission v Tetra Laval BV*, not yet reported, judgment of February 15, 2005). See also Völcker, "Leveraging as a Theory of Competitive Harm in EU Merger Control" (2003) 40 C.M.L.Rev. 581, pp.597 to 599.

[53] See Case COMP/M.3304 *GE / Amersham* and Case COMP/M.3732 *Procter & Gamble / Gillette*, para.117.

[54] See, e.g. Case COMP/M.3314 *Air Liquide / Messer Targets* (bundling concerns ruled out because of doubts whether a significant proportion of customers required both of the products; para.66) and Case COMP/M.3687 *Johnson & Johnson / Guidant* (bundling is not possible if the customers for the two products are not generally the same; para.342).

purchase both[55]; for example,[56] in *Tetra Laval / SIG*[57] a full line forcing concern was ruled out on the grounds that there was no evidence that customers tended to purchase two or more of the products together;

(iv) whether the products are typically purchased by the *same individuals* through *similar procedures*; if not, an attempt to link their purchase is likely to fail[58];

(v) whether customers are *willing to purchase bundled products*; if they require a full range, they may reject attempts to link the purchase of two or more products.[59]

(d) In considering the merged group's incentive and ability to pursue a leveraging strategy, the Commission will also consider the extent to which this *occurred prior to the merger*.[60] In particular, if the merging parties or their competitors had an opportunity, prior to the merger, to adopt a leveraging strategy, it is important to examine the effects of such a strategy if it was adopted and, if it was not, to consider whether the merger creates a different incentive and ability to do so.[61]

(e) The *competitive constraints* posed by actual and potential competitors and buyer power. Such constraints may mean that the merged group lacks the ability successfully to implement a leveraging strategy.

(i) In *Tetra Laval BV v Commission*[62] the Court of First Instance described the intensity of competition in the leveraged market as "fundamental" and concluded that "it has not been shown that the number of sales could reach a level which could threaten the strong competition prevailing on the [leveraged] market".

(ii) In *GE / Amersham*[63] the Commission found that rivals could respond to any bundling strategy adopted by the merged group through a range of counter-strategies including price reduc-

---

[55] Suppliers could seek to link the purchase of two or more products that are acquired at different times, e.g. by the use of retroactive discounts.

[56] See also Case COMP/M.3304 *GE / Amersham*, para.35 and Case T-210/01 *General Electric Company v Commission*, not yet reported, judgment of December 14, 2005, para.413.

[57] Case COMP/M.3746, paras 71 and 74.

[58] See, e.g. Case COMP/M.3304 *GE / Amersham*, para.35 and Case T-210/01 *General Electric Company v Commission*, not yet reported, judgment of December 14, 2005, para.410.

[59] For example, wholesalers may have a strong preference to carry a full range of products; see Case COMP/M.2397 *BC Funds / Sanitec*.

[60] See, e.g. Case COMP/M.3304 *GE / Amersham*, para.35.

[61] Völcker, "Leveraging as a Theory of Competitive Harm in EU Merger Control" (2003) 40 C.M.L.Rev. 581, at p.599, argues that the absence of pre-merger combined offers should create a rebuttable presumption that such offers are inimical to the way an industry functions.

[62] Case T-5/02 [2002] E.C.R. II-4381, para.245. See also para.294. (The decision was upheld on appeal on the basis of reasoning not relating to this issue in Case C-12/03P *Commission v Tetra Laval BV*, not yet reported, judgment of February 15, 2005.)

[63] Case COMP/M.3304, para.39.

tions, offering similar bundles (through "teaming" or counter-mergers) and technological leapfrogging as a result of innovation.[64] The Commission also found that a mixed bundling strategy would be unlikely to be profitable even if rivals exited from a Member State, because barriers to entry or re-entry in a specific Member State were not significant.[65]

(iii) In *Procter & Gamble / Gillette*[66] the Commission found that rivals had similar product ranges and retailers could exercise buyer power.

(iv) In *Tetra Laval / SIG*[67] the Commission emphasised that competitors with significant positions would remain in the market following the merger and would be able to offer as broad a portfolio of products as the merged group.

(f) The *practicability* of implementing a leveraging strategy. For example, in *General Electric Company v Commission*[68] the Court of First Instance found that the Commission had erred in failing to recognise that a joint venture partner would have no interest in making financial sacrifices to allow the merged group to favour its own products through a bundling strategy.

(g) Any *efficiencies* generated by the merger may affect the merged group's incentives.[69]

(d) Foreclosure

Thirdly, if so,[70] will the conduct in question have a *significant effect* through **12–011** the elimination or marginalisation of competitors?[71]

There are three strands to the foreclosure analysis.[72]

(a) The first issue is whether competitors are likely to be excluded or

---

[64] See also Case COMP/M.3687 *Johnson & Johnson / Guidant* (bundling strategy could be matched successfully by a number of competitors; para.341).
[65] Para.41.
[66] Case COMP/M.3732, paras 121 to 130.
[67] Case COMP/M.3746, para.75.
[68] Case T-210/01, not yet reported, judgment of December 14, 2005, paras 147, 458 and 459.
[69] See Ch.18.
[70] i.e. if the merged group will have the incentive and ability to pursue the leveraging conduct.
[71] Drauz, "Unbundling *GE / Honeywell*: the Assessment of Conglomerate Mergers Under EC Competition Law", published in the 2001 *Annual Proceedings of the Fordham Corporate Law Institute*, p.183, states, at p.188: "the Commission also assesses ... whether tying has as a consequence the reduction of competition in the markets, as a result of the foreclosure, marginalisation or elimination of competing suppliers".
[72] See generally Völcker, "Leveraging as a Theory of Competitive Harm in EU Merger Control" (2003) 40 C.M.L.Rev. 581, pp.602 to 608 and RBB Economics, "The Efficiency-Enhancing Effects of Non-Horizontal Mergers", 2005 (report for the Commission DG for Enterprise and Industry) (available via *http://europa.eu.int/comm/enterprise/library/lib-competition/doc/non_horizontal_mergers.pdf*), pp.123 and 124

marginalised by the strategy, e.g. by inducing exit, deterring entry or discouraging investment by competitors in research and development.[73]

(b) The second is whether competitors and/or customers have available counter-strategies to respond to the merged group's leveraging. In the case of competitors, the counter-strategy may involve merging or entering "teaming" agreements. Customers can maintain two or more suppliers or otherwise support relatively weaker suppliers to maintain competition in the market.

(c) The third arises if exit or foreclosure is predicted, and involves considering whether new entry or re-entry will be timely, likely and sufficient to prevent the merged group from materially harming consumers.[74]

12–012 In the passage from *GE / Amersham*[75] quoted in para.12–007 above, the Commission focused on the question of whether rivals would *exit* from the market, without considering the scope for the merged group to *marginalise* its rivals. However:

(a) in other parts of the decision the Commission considered the marginalisation issue (as well as exit)[76];

(b) focusing on exit appears unduly narrow when compared with the cases on vertical effects[77]; and

(c) in *Tetra Laval BV v Commission*[78] the Court of First Instance implicitly accepted the Commission's contention that marginalisation (i.e. falling short of exclusion) was sufficient to justify blocking a transaction.

---

[73] In Case COMP/M.3314 *Air Liquide / Messer Targets*, foreclosure was ruled out because customers would benefit from any reductions in prices (through a bundling strategy) and even in the longer term customers would still be able to switch to alternative suppliers; para.66.

[74] See generally Ch.16.

[75] Case COMP/M.3304, para.37.

[76] Para.40.

[77] See para.11–014(b) above. Contrast RBB Economics, "The Efficiency-Enhancing Effects of Non-Horizontal Mergers", 2005 (report for the Commission DG for Enterprise and Industry) (available via *http://europa.eu.int/comm/enterprise/library/lib-competition/doc/non_horizontal_mergers.pdf*), pp.123 and 124: "A price reduction can be said to marginalize competitors only if, at any given price level, the competitive constraint currently provided by the rivals at that price level were to be reduced following a temporary price reduction ... [P]rices will increase and consumers will be harmed ... only ... if competitors are marginalised to such an extent so as to be forced to withdraw permanently from the market".

[78] Case T-5/02 [2002] E.C.R. II-4381, paras 180, 281 and 306. (The decision was upheld on appeal on the basis of reasoning not relating to this issue in Case C-12/03P *Commission v Tetra Laval BV*, not yet reported, judgment of February 15, 2005.)

(e) Causation

Finally, it is necessary to determine whether there is a causal link between **12–013** the merger and the adverse effects identified at the second and third stages.[79] For example, in *Tetra Laval / SIG*[80] the Commission emphasised that the transaction brought about only marginal changes in Tetra's incentives. Similarly, in *Akzo Nobel / Hoechst Roussel Vet*[81] the Commission found that the transaction did not lead to any significant "portfolio effects" in adding a single vaccine to a range of more than 50.[82]

12.3 TYING, PURE BUNDLING AND MIXED BUNDLING

(a) Introduction[83]

Tying is the practice of requiring a purchaser of one good, A, to purchase a **12–014** distinct second good, B. A and B may be consumed in variable proportions (in contrast to, e.g. left and right shoes which are consumed in fixed proportions). For example, earlier in its existence, IBM leased mainframe computers and required lessees to purchase from IBM their requirements for punch cards which were used to input data. The effect of the tie was that IBM could levy higher charges on more intensive users by charging high prices for punch cards.[84]

Tying is most profitable if consumer valuations of the two goods are positively correlated, i.e. if consumers who place the greatest value on good

---

[79] See generally Ch.5 above.
[80] Case COMP/M.3746, para.76(2).
[81] Case COMP/M.1681, para.104.
[82] See also Case IV/M.794 *Coca-Cola Enterprises / Amalgamated Beverages Great Britain*, para.209; Case COMP/M.1601 *Allied Signal / Honeywell* [2001] O.J. L152/1 (the Commission noted, at para.113, that competition to supply certain products already took place on an integrated basis with the consequence that the merger could not create portfolio power in those areas); and Case COMP/M.1683 *The Coca-Cola Company / Kar-Tess Group (Hellenic Bottling)*, para.30.
[83] See generally Areeda, Hovenkamp & Solow, *Antitrust Law* (2nd edn, Aspen Law & Business, 2000), Vol.IIA, para.519; Areeda & Turner, *Antitrust Law* (Aspen Law & Business, 1980), Vol.V, s.11C–2; Church, "The Impact of Vertical and Conglomerate Mergers on Competition", 2004 (report for DG Competition) (available via *http://europa.eu.int/comm/competition/mergers/others/merger_impact.pdf*), pp.xix to xl and ss.4.1 to 4.3; the OFT Economic Discussion Paper, "Innovation and Competition Policy", Charles River Associates, March 2002 (note that the views in the paper do not necessarily reflect those of the OFT), paras 5.37 to 5.69; and Nalebuff, "Bundling, Tying and Portfolio Effects", 2003 (DTI Economics Paper) (available via *www.dti.gov.uk/ccp/topics2/pdf2/bundle1.pdf*), pp.9 to 11. For a strategic perspective, see Porter, *Competitive Advantage* (The Free Press, 1998 edn), Ch.12.
[84] In this example, tying is a *metering device*.

A also place the greatest value on good B.[85] Terminologically, the "tying product" is the vital component that the merged group would refuse to sell independently of its other products.

Pure bundling is the practice of selling two goods, A and B, as a single package when A and B are *not* sold separately.[86] For example, a restaurant which offers a set menu but not *à la carte* is engaged in pure bundling. Pure bundling is most profitable if consumer valuations of the two goods are negatively correlated,[87] i.e. if consumers who place the greatest reservation price[88] on good A, place the lowest reservation price on good B.[89] If consumer X is willing to pay £4 for good A and £6 for good B and consumer Y is willing to pay £6 for good A and £4 for good B, then a monopoly supplier of goods A and B has a choice of pricing strategies. If it sells goods A and B separately for £6 each, it will sell one unit of each giving a total revenue of £12. If it sells goods A and B separately for £4 each, it will sell two units of each giving a total revenue of £16. But if it bundles A and B as a package for £10 it will sell two bundles giving a total revenue of £20. Bundling is the profit-maximising strategy in this case because customers place different valuations on the individual components of the package (with the consequence that the producer must reduce its price to increase sales of the individual components) but identical valuations on the package as a whole, and bundling reduces the dispersion of willingness to pay.

Mixed bundling arises when the supplier offers both the single package and the separate goods. A restaurant is engaged in mixed bundling if it offers both a set and an *à la carte* menu. In a mixed bundle, the set must be offered at a lower price than the sum of the component parts, otherwise customers would have no incentive to buy the bundle. It may be profitable to engage in mixed bundling when consumer valuations are negatively correlated and marginal costs are low.[90] Mixed bundling provides greater choices to the customer whilst increasing the scope for the producer to extract consumer surplus. In particular, if a producer offers a pure bundle, then the customer must choose either to buy the bundle or to buy nothing;

---

[85] This is because the monopolist can extract increased rents from more intensive users through a tied price structure than through the next best alternative which is a two-part tariff using a fixed fee and a variable price (see para.1–007 above for discussion). Tying allows the supplier to place greater reliance on the variable fee and therefore minimises the loss of customers who are put off by the need to pay a fixed fee.

[86] Pure bundling may take the form of *technical bundling* under which the individual components function effectively only as part of the bundled system and are incompatible with components supplied by rival companies.

[87] And if the marginal costs of production are low. If marginal costs are low the producer has an incentive to seek to increase output through sales of the bundled product: see "Portfolio Effects in Conglomerate Mergers", OECD, DAFFE/COMP(2002)5, at p.35.

[88] A reservation price is the highest price that a customer would be willing to pay for a unit of the good. If the price offered to the customer exceeds her reservation price, she will not buy; if it is below, she will buy and her consumer surplus will be the difference between the price paid and the reservation price; see para.1–003 above.

[89] Goods A and B may nevertheless be complementary goods.

[90] See the discussion in Carlton & Perloff, *Modern Industrial Organization* (4th edn, Addison-Wesley, 2005), pp.324 to 328.

but if the producer offers a mixed bundle, A + B, and sells A and B separately, a customer has four choices: to buy the bundle, A separately, B separately or nothing.[91]

(b) The Chicago School

Members of the Chicago School have argued that there is no *incentive* to **12–015** engage in tying or pure bundling because "there is only one monopoly profit" and a company holding a monopoly can maximise its returns through the sale of the monopolised product without needing to tie or bundle the supply of the monopolised product with a second product. This is certainly true in some circumstances (e.g. an attempt to tie from a monopoly market to a competitive market with constant returns to scale) and the analysis remains the general rule.[92]

However, there is a rapidly developing body of economic models in which a supplier may have an incentive to tie or bundle, including[93] the following three situations.

(a) The *Cournot effect* (also known as the *elimination of double marginalisation*) arises in the sale of complementary goods, A and B. If A and B are sold by separate producers and the producer of A cuts its price, then this will result in increased sales of both A (from which the producer of A benefits) and B (as B is a complement of A). If the

---

[91] See the OFT Economic Discussion Paper, "Innovation and Competition Policy", Charles River Associates, March 2002 (note that the views in the paper do not necessarily reflect those of the OFT), para.5.46, arguing that mixed bundling is likely to increase consumer welfare, in particular, because it is likely to increase the sales of the good.

[92] See RBB Economics, "The Efficiency-Enhancing Effects of Non-Horizontal Mergers", 2005 (report for the Commission DG for Enterprise and Industry) (available via *http://europa. eu.int/comm/enterprise/library/lib-competition/doc/non_horizontal_mergers.pdf*), pp.14 and 15.

[93] For details see Nalebuff, "Bundling, Tying and Portfolio Effects", 2003 (DTI Economics Paper) (available via *www.dti.gov.uk/ccp/topics2/pdf2/bundle1.pdf*), pp.9 to 11 and Chs 3, 4 and 6 (distinguishing between efficiency reasons to bundle (cost reductions, quality improvement and reducing pricing inefficiencies) and strategic reasons to bundle (entry deterrence, mitigation of competition, gain competitive advantage and price obfuscation)); Church, "The Impact of Vertical and Conglomerate Mergers on Competition", 2004 (report for DG Competition) (available via *http://europa.eu.int/comm/competition/mergers/others/ merger_impact.pdf*), pp.xix to xl and ss.4.1 to 4.3; Carlton & Perloff, *Modern Industrial Organization* (4th edn, Addison-Wesley, 2005), pp.322 to 333; "Portfolio Effects in Conglomerate Mergers", OECD, DAFFE/COMP(2002)5, at p.31; and RBB Economics, "The Efficiency-Enhancing Effects of Non-Horizontal Mergers", 2005 (report for the Commission DG for Enterprise and Industry) (available via *http://europa.eu.int/comm/enterprise/library/ lib-competition/doc/non_horizontal_mergers.pdf*), pp.15 to 19. Porter, *Competitive Advantage* (The Free Press, 1998 edn), pp.426 to 429, identifies the following competitive advantages (i.e. incentives) to pure bundling (and tying): economies of providing the bundle; increased differentiation (by providing more bases for differentiation, a high-performing interface, optimised package performance or one-stop shopping); enhanced opportunities for price discrimination; increased entry/mobility barriers; and mitigated rivalry. Conversely, the risks of bundling identified by Porter, at pp.429 and 430, are: diversity of buyer needs; buyer ability to assemble the bundle; specialist ability to provide parts of the bundle on more favourable terms; and bundling through coalitions.

producers of A and B merge, then the *externality* which arises from the fact that the producer of B benefits from the reduction in the price of A is *internalised*, with the consequence that the merged group has a *greater* incentive to cut the prices of A and B than separate suppliers of the two products because it obtains greater benefit from the price cut.[94]

(b) Efficiency savings may be available. Economies of scope may arise when the complementary products use common inputs, common distribution channels or have common marketing or promotional needs. If there are substantial economies of scale in the *tied* or *bundled* product, then the producer may benefit by tying or bundling because its total sales of the tied or bundled product will increase, and the economies of scale will reduce the unit costs of producing the tied or bundled product.

(c) Selling a bundle of products may result in less intense competition than component-by-component pricing, since the suppliers are offering differentiated products where price comparison is less straightforward.

(c) Incentive and ability to tie or bundle

12–016 In *General Electric / Honeywell*[95] the Commission found that the merged group would have the *incentive* and *ability* to bundle General Electric ("GE") and Honeywell products and services.[96] The Commission referred expressly to the "Cournot effect of bundling"[97] and found that the merged group might engage in mixed bundling or pure bundling including technical bundling.[98] The Court of First Instance overturned the Commission's reasoning on conglomerate effects in *General Electric Company v Commission*,[99]

---

[94] The Cournot effect will exist or be significant only if pre-merger prices were above the competitive level in at least one of the complements; see "Portfolio Effects in Conglomerate Mergers", OECD, DAFFE/COMP(2002)5, at p.8.

[95] Case COMP/M.2220 [2004] O.J. L48/1. See also Giotakos, Petit, Garnier & de Luyck, "General Electric / Honeywell—An Insight into the Commission's Investigation and Decision", *Competition Policy Newsletter*, October 2001, p.5 and Pflanz & Caffarra, "The Economics of G.E. / Honeywell" [2002] E.C.L.R. 115.

[96] Para.349. The Commission analysed economic models in its deliberations but did not rely on them in its final decision; para.352.

[97] Paras 374 to 376.

[98] The Commission stated, at paras 353 and 354: "As a result of the proposed merger, the merged entity will be able to price its packaged deals in such a way as to induce customers to buy GE engines and Honeywell [avionics] over those of competitors, thus increasing the combined share of GE and Honeywell on both markets. This will occur as a result of the financial ability of the merged entity to cross-subsidise discounts across the products composing the packaged deal ... [The] merged entity can also be expected to engage in technical bundling—that is, to make its products available only as an integrated system that is incompatible with competing individual components". Contrast Case COMP/M.1601 *Allied Signal / Honeywell* [2001] O.J. L152/1, paras 112, 113 and 118 to 121.

[99] Case T-210/01, not yet reported, judgment of December 14, 2005, paras 366 to 473.

finding that the Commission had not identified convincing evidence that the merged group would have an incentive to adopt a bundling strategy. More particularly, the Court emphasised that pure bundling is precluded in cases in which different people make the purchasing decisions for the two products[1] and is more difficult when the purchasing decisions are made at different times.[2] It also emphasised that pure bundling could have harmful commercial consequences because some customers might choose not to buy from the merged group when they would have bought the tying product had it been available separately, and criticised the Commission for failing to assess whether the likely lost profits were outweighed by potential increases in profits arising from the pure bundling strategy.[3] The Court found that the Commission had provided no evidence that there was a real likelihood that the merged group would have an incentive to adopt a mixed bundling strategy following the transaction and therefore did not uphold the Commission's reasoning on the Cournot effect.[4] Finally, the Court emphasised that the Commission had failed to take account of the fact that GE's joint venture partner would not share GE's incentive to favour the interests of the remainder of GE's business.[5]

The Commission also considered whether the merged group would have **12–017** the incentive and ability to engage in tying or bundling[6] in the following cases.

(a) In *GE / Amersham*[7] the Commission considered whether the merged group would have the incentive and ability to engage in mixed bundling or pure bundling of GE's diagnostic equipment (e.g. scanners) with Amersham's diagnostic pharmaceuticals (which are used to enable certain diagnostic equipment to image the health

---

[1] Para.410.
[2] Para.413.
[3] Para.420.
[4] Paras 449, 453 (relying in part on statements by an economics consultancy retained by one of the complainants and published after the Commission had reached its decision) and 456.
[5] Paras 458 and 459.
[6] In Case COMP/M.2397 *BC Funds / Sanitec* the Commission found, at para.17, that the merged group would not have an incentive to engage in pure bundling "in case wholesalers were not prepared to take the whole range". See also Case IV/M.950 *Hoffmann La Roche / Boehringer Mannheim* [1998] O.J. L234/14 (the merger would strengthen a dominant position through the possibility of successful bundling; para.142); Case COMP/M.1845 *AOL / Time Warner* [2001] O.J. L268/28 (leverage by agreeing to distribute competitors' products on AOL's distribution network only if the competitors accepted AOL's technology; para.57); Case COMP/M.2291 *VNU / AC Nielsen* (no concerns about possible bundling because bundling played a minor role in the market; paras 36 to 39); Case COMP/M.2547 *Bayer / Aventis Crop Science* [2004] O.J. L107/1, paras 521 and 522; Case COMP/M.2803 *Telia / Sonera*, paras 108 to 112; Case COMP/M.3182 *Scottish & Newcastle / HP Bulmer* (no scope to leverage from the UK cider market to the UK beer market because the cider market was around one-twentieth the size of the beer market; para.42); and Case COMP/M.3751 *Novartis / Hexal* (the Commission considered it likely that the merged group would bundle branded and generic pharmaceuticals, blocking shelf space for rivals; it should be noted that this case involved bundling of *substitute* products; see p.11).
[7] Case COMP/M 3304, paras 31 to 60.

status of the body). The Commission stated that "the analysis of potential market power leveraging becomes redundant when there is no or limited complementarity between the products assessed". It examined a wide range of different strategies and ruled them out on different grounds. Mixed bundling was ruled out on the grounds that combined offers of equipment and pharmaceuticals were unusual (reducing the prospects of a successful bundling strategy), neither party had a dominant position prior to the merger, competitors would be able to implement counter-strategies, rivals would not be marginalised or forced to exit and, even if they were, the merged group was likely to face entry or re-entry preventing it from profitably raising prices. Pure bundling was unlikely to be profitable because GE would deprive itself of sales of diagnostic pharmaceuticals to current users of non-GE equipment. Further, it would not be feasible technically to reduce or eliminate the interconnectivity of the merged group's future products with rivals'.

(b) In *Procter & Gamble / Gillette*[8] the Commission considered the scope to engage in bundling of the parties' wide range of consumer brands. The Commission stated: "Regarding in particular pure bundling, anticompetitive conglomerate effects are more likely to arise when the two merging parties offer goods which are highly complementary in demand".[9] Concerns about possible bundling were ruled out as rivals had broad product ranges, retailers were able to exercise buyer power through a variety of mechanisms, previous Procter & Gamble acquisitions had not resulted in anti-competitive practices, and customers might benefit from portfolio efficiencies. The Commission also examined whether Procter & Gamble's role as "category manager" for retailers (providing advice on product selection and shelf positioning) might allow it to favour its own products. The Commission investigated the evidence regarding category management and found that retailers were capable of preventing bias by the manager in favour of the manager's own products.

(c) *BSkyB / KirchPayTV*[10] raised two tying issues. The first arose from the fact that the markets for pay-TV and digital interactive television services were complementary.[11] KirchPayTV had a monopoly in the German pay-TV market and, following the merger, would have been the only entity able to offer pay-TV in combination with digital interactive television services, with the consequence that consumers would have been likely to purchase both services from KirchPayTV

---

[8] Case COMP/M.3732, paras 115 to 151. See also Kloc-Evison, Larsson Haug & Siebert, "Procter & Gamble / Gillette: the Role of Economic Analysis in Phase I cases", *Competition Policy Newsletter*, Autumn 2005, p.43.
[9] Para.117.
[10] Case COMP/JV.37.
[11] Para.40.

to avoid the cost or inconvenience of having two boxes. The Commission found that KirchPayTV would have had an incentive to refuse to license the digital interactive television services technology to other service providers, which would have lead to the creation of a dominant position on the market for digital interactive television services for KirchPayTV.[12] The second issue was whether Kirch might have used its dominant position *in Germany* for the purchase of broadcasting rights to require suppliers of such rights to sell exclusively to BSkyB *in the United Kingdom.* The Commission dismissed this concern on the facts, finding that such coordination would have been difficult in practice because output deals for film rights and exclusive sports rights were generally long-term and might not have expired at the same time in different territories; furthermore, such behaviour would have created a risk that rights holders would develop their own television channels.[13]

(d) *Astra Zeneca | Novartis*[14] involved an overlap in the supply of (amongst other products) fungicides. The Commission noted that fungicides could be supplied "straight" for "tank-mixing" by customers or as a pre-mixed "formulated" product. The Commission found that the merged group would have had an incentive to withdraw one of the leading "straight" products and replace it with formulated products to eliminate the scope for competitors to supply other products for tank-mixing with the leading straight product, and that the concentration therefore created a dominant position.

(e) In *Allied Signal | Honeywell*[15] the Commission found that the merged group would have had strong positions in the supply of a number of avionics products which have to be integrated with an aircraft's terrain avoidance warning system ("TAWS"). The Commission found that the merged group could have strengthened its position in the supply of the other avionics by refusing to supply the information required for rival suppliers to integrate their products with the merged group's TAWS product. The Commission accepted undertakings to ensure that Honeywell products maintained open standards.

(f) *Tetra Pak | Alfa-Laval*[16] involved a merger between suppliers of complementary goods, namely equipment for processing milk and juice and equipment for packaging milk and juice. The Commission

---

[12] Paras 78 to 80.
[13] Para.88.
[14] Case COMP/M.1806 [2004] O.J. L110/1, para.223. See generally paras 202 to 222. The Commission reached similar conclusions in relation to herbicides, at para.363. See also para.362, noting that actual or potential parties to development and cooperation agreements with the merged group would be adversely affected by the merged group's incentive to use its own products in developing ready mix formulations.
[15] Case COMP/M.1601 [2001] O.J. L152/1, paras 101 to 103.
[16] Case IV/M.68 [1991] O.J. L290/35, s.4.

found that the merged group would not have been able to increase the difficulty of entry or penetration of actual or potential competitors because the two categories of machine were distinct and separate in commercial and technical terms. In particular, the interface between the two types of machines was not complicated in technical terms and there was therefore no risk that Alfa-Laval aseptic processing machines could have been made difficult to interface with packaging machines other than those of Tetra Pak.

(d) The exclusionary effects of tying or bundling

12–018 Tying or bundling may have the object or effect of eliminating or marginalising competitors.[17] In particular, there is a developing body of economic models which indicate that tying or bundling may be profitable for exclusionary reasons, for example when economies of scale are available in the tied market or through entry deterrence.[18]

In *General Electric / Honeywell*[19] the Commission found that the merged group's ability to engage in mixed, pure and technical bundling would have adverse effects on competitors: "The ability of the merged entity to cross-subsidise its various complementary activities and to engage in profitable forms of packaged sales will have an adverse effect on the profitability of competing producers of avionics and non avionics products, as a result of market share erosion. This is likely to lead to market exit of existing competitors and market foreclosure both over the short term, insofar as price is below average variable cost, and over the longer term, insofar as competitors would be unable to cover their fixed costs if they were to remain active and to proceed with the new investment in R&D so as to compete viably and in the future".[20] The Commission did not suggest that the merged group would necessarily engage in predatory pricing, but rather that the merged group would have an incentive and the ability to *reduce* its prices on bundled

---

[17] See Nalebuff, "Bundling, Tying and Portfolio Effects", 2003 (DTI Economics Paper) (available via *www.dti.gov.uk/ccp/topics2/pdf2/bundle1.pdf*), pp.9 to 11; Church, "The Impact of Vertical and Conglomerate Mergers on Competition", 2004 (report for DG Competition) (available via *http://europa.eu.int/comm/competition/mergers/others/merger_impact.pdf*), pp.xix to xl and ss.4.1 to 4.3; and Martin, *Advanced Industrial Economics* (2nd edn, Blackwell, 2002), p.439. However, in general, increasing the volumes of products sold *increases* consumer welfare: see the OFT Economic Discussion Paper, "Innovation and Competition Policy", Charles River Associates, March 2002 (note that the views in the paper do not necessarily reflect those of the OFT), paras 5.43 and 5.46.

[18] See generally OFT Economic Discussion Paper, "Innovation and Competition Policy", Charles River Associates, March 2002 (note that the views in the paper do not necessarily reflect those of the OFT), paras 5.59 to 5.61; and "Portfolio Effects in Conglomerate Mergers", OECD, DAFFE/COMP(2002)5, at pp.31 to 33 and 223.

[19] Case COMP/M.2220 [2004] O.J. L48/1. See also: Giotakos, Petit, Garnier & de Luyck, "General Electric / Honeywell—An Insight into the Commission's Investigation and Decision", *Competition Policy Newsletter*, October 2001, p.5 and Pflanz & Caffarra, "The Economics of G.E. / Honeywell" [2002] E.C.L.R. 115.

[20] Para.398.

products following the merger. In general, reductions in prices serve to promote consumer welfare and the Commission's concerns were therefore premised on a prediction that competitors would be eliminated or marginalised.[21] However, when the effect of the Commission's conclusion is to deprive consumers of gains in terms of lower prices at least in the short and medium term (leaving to one side the consequences for the merging parties), any conclusion that a transaction is likely to result in the exclusion of competitors in circumstances falling short of predation ought to be supported by highly particularised evidence and reasoning, to avoid any suspicion that the analysis is based on self-serving statements by rival suppliers which would suffer competitive disadvantage if the merged group reduced prices to consumers. Since the Court of First Instance in *General Electric Company v Commission*[22] rejected the Commission's findings regarding the merged group's incentives to adopt a leveraging strategy, it expressly declined to consider the findings that competitors would be foreclosed.

By contrast, in *BC Funds / Sanitec*[23] the Commission found that the merged group would have the ability to engage in mixed bundling of ceramic sanitary ware, taps and mixers but cleared the transaction on the grounds that mixed bundling "could not squeeze competitors out of the market" because competitors could also offer full ranges, wholesalers typically sourced from multiple suppliers, and wholesalers could rearrange the product mix and sell products either individually or in packages.

12.4 OTHER THEORIES OF LEVERAGE

(a) Introduction

Conglomerate mergers may result in the merged group having the incentive **12–019** and ability to adopt any of a range of practices which have similar effects to tying, pure bundling or mixed bundling in that each may harm consumers by eliminating or marginalising competitors.[24]

    (a) *Full-line forcing* arises when a supplier puts pressure on a customer to take the whole range of goods offered by the supplier, e.g. by

---

[21] Pflanz & Caffara, "The Economics of G.E. / Honeywell" [2002] E.C.L.R. 115, at p.117, comment: "the prediction of exit is a much more hazardous prediction than the prediction of short run post-merger price increases (as in a horizontal merger)—not least because of the extended time-scale involved, and the reliance on assumptions about general economic conditions, the success of future products, etc". Compare the UK Competition Commission's Merger References Guidelines, March 2003 (*www.competition-commission.org.uk*), para.3.71.

[22] Case T-210/01, not yet reported, judgment of December 14, 2005, para.471.

[23] Case COMP/M.2397, para.19.

[24] See also Case IV/M.877 *Boeing / McDonnell Douglas* [1997] O.J. L336/16, para.64 (leverage through spare parts and maintenance business).

threatening to withdraw supplies of the "must have" or desirable parts of the range.[25]

(b) *Exclusive dealing* arises when a supplier obtains from a customer a commitment not to trade with rival suppliers. In *Boeing / McDonnell Douglas*[26] the Commission was concerned that, by broadening its customer base from 60 per cent to 84 per cent of fleet in service, the merged group might have had greater scope to persuade airlines to enter exclusive supply arrangements.[27]

(c) The merged group may be able to use the revenues generated by its "must have" brands or products, which face limited competition, to *cross-subsidise* its secondary brands or products, which face more substantial competition.[28] A cross-subsidisation strategy may be implemented, for example, through "loss leadership" or system pricing, such as subsidising the price of razors but charging premiums for blades. In *Boeing / McDonnell Douglas*[29] the Commission found that, following the merger: "Boeing would have opportunities, where it thought appropriate, to set prices at zero-profit or below-cost levels within the mid-size segment [where competition was stronger], financed by the higher margins achieved in the smallest and largest segments". Similarly,[30] in *Danish Crown / Vestjyske Slagterier*[31] the merged group would have been the only slaughterhouse selling fresh beef and pork on the Danish market and the Commission found that it could have introduced discounting schemes relating to the total volume of beef and pork sold, enabling it to push the sale of pork using beef as a lever and vice versa. Cross-subsidisation is rational only if it will result in the exit of competitors in circumstances in which the subsidiser can recoup its losses by increasing price.

---

[25] See Case IV/M.836 *Gillette / Duracell* (combining Gillette's personal grooming, stationery and small electrical and electronic appliances businesses with Duracell's consumer batteries business) and Case COMP/M.3746 *Tetra Laval / SIG*, paras 69 to 75. See also "Portfolio Effects in Conglomerate Mergers", OECD, DAFFE/COMP(2002)5, p.35.

[26] Case IV/M.877 [1997] O.J. L336/16.

[27] The Commission also found that the combination of the parties' civil, military and space businesses would have strengthened the merged group's negotiating position with its suppliers. See also "Portfolio Effects in Conglomerate Mergers", OECD, DAFFE/COMP(2002)5, p.35.

[28] See Case T-5/02 *Tetra Laval BV v Commission* [2002] E.C.R. II-4381, para.217 (the decision was upheld on appeal on the basis of reasoning not relating to this issue in Case C-12/03P *Commission v Tetra Laval BV*, not yet reported, judgment of February 15, 2005). See also Case COMP/M.1630 *Air Liquide / BOC* [2004] O.J. L92/1, paras 194 and 195. Porter, *Competitive Advantage* (The Free Press, 1998 edn), pp.437 and 438, identifies the following factors as favouring cross-subsidisation: sufficient price sensitivity in the base good; sufficient price insensitivity in the profitable good; strong connection between the profitable and base good; and barriers to entry in the market in which the profitable good is sold. Conversely, the risks identified by Porter, at pp.438 and 439, are: buyer cherry-picking; substitutes for the profitable good; buyer vertical integration; and specialist (focused) competitors.

[29] Case IV/M.877 [1997] O.J. L336/16, para.78.

[30] See also Case IV/M.938 *Guinness / Grand Metropolitan* [1998] O.J. L288/24, para.99.

[31] Case IV/M.1313 [2000] O.J. L20/1, para.196.

(d) A conglomerate merger may increase the probability of exclusion through *predatory pricing*.[32] Predatory pricing is rational only if it will result in the exit of competitors in circumstances in which the predator can recoup its losses by increasing price. The UK Office of Fair Trading's Substantive Merger Guidelines[33] state that: "In rare cases, a conglomerate merger may also make predatory behaviour more feasible, especially where competition is localised so that firms only face a competitive threat on a few brands or a few geographic markets at any one time ... Such behaviour is likely only when the merging firms already have market power in some markets and where barriers to entry are already relatively high, so that the short run losses can be recouped by higher prices in the long run". In *P&O Stena Line (Holding) Ltd*[34] the Commission considered whether P&O could have used its monopoly in one market to cross-subsidise a campaign of predatory pricing in other markets in which it faced competition, but concluded that it would lack the ability to do so, because it would have to target several competitors, some of which had substantial financial backing and/or were vertically integrated and, in any event, barriers to entry to those markets were low.

(e) An ability to *control information* may be used strategically to eliminate or marginalise competitors.

The general principles described in s.12.2 above apply to each of these "theories of competitive harm".

12.5 PORTFOLIO POWER OR RANGE EFFECTS

(a) The scope of portfolio power theories

Portfolio power[35] arises[36] when the market power derived by the merged **12–020**

---

[32] See Case IV/M.53 *Aerospatiale | Alenia | de Havilland* [1991] O.J. L334/42 and Case COMP/ M.3746 *Tetra Laval | SIG*, para.76(2). See also Martin, *Advanced Industrial Economics* (2nd edn, Blackwell, 2002), pp.246, 263 and 273 and Areeda & Turner, *Antitrust Law* (Aspen Law & Business, 1980), Vol.V, para.1136. Predatory pricing as a theory of competitive harm is very closely related to cross-subsidisation.

[33] May 2003 (*www.oft.gov.uk*), para.6.5.

[34] Case COMP/M.2838, paras 19 and 20.

[35] In the early days of the ECMR, the Commission seems not to have regarded portfolio effects as potentially harmful to competition. In Case IV/M.184 *Grand Metropolitan | Cinzano* the Commission stated, at para.13: "The operation does not produce any appreciable effects in any other of the abovementioned beverage sectors, whether analysing it from a narrow [or] wider definition of the market. It will simply enable IDV to offer a wider range of brands than before". Operating in two or more connected markets may result in efficiency gains in terms of reduced transaction costs and sale and distribution economies: see Areeda & Turner, *Antitrust Law* (Aspen Law & Business, 1980), Vol.V, para.1109d3. Compare the UK Competition Commission's Merger References Guidelines, March 2003 (*www.competition-commission.*

group from its presence in two or more separate markets *exceeds* the power derived from those markets separately.[37] It is best regarded as[38] a theory of leverage, the issue being whether the merged group can profitably leverage market power in one of the markets into a second by tying, pure bundling, mixed bundling, full line forcing, exclusive dealing, cross-subsidisation, predatory pricing and/or the control of information.[39] In this form, portfolio power does not comprise a separate theory of competitive harm but is simply a convenient label for a collection of leveraging theories.[40]

---

org.uk), para.3.69. See also Nalebuff, "Bundling, Tying and Portfolio Effects", 2003 (DTI Economics Paper) (available via *www.dti.gov.uk/ccp/topics2/pdf2/bundle1.pdf*), p.11; Church, "The Impact of Vertical and Conglomerate Mergers on Competition", 2004 (report for DG Competition) (available via *http://europa.eu.int/comm/competition/mergers/others/merger_ impact.pdf*), pp.xli to xliv and s.4.4; Baker & Ridyard, "Portfolio Power: A Rum Deal?" [1999] E.C.L.R. 181; Watson, "Portfolio Effects in EC Merger Law" [2003] *The Antitrust Bulletin* 781; and Case T-114/02 *BaByliss SA v Commission* [2003] E.C.R. II-1279, paras 345 to 365.

[36] This section does not discuss "range effects" which arise from the exercise by customers of *buyer power*. These arguments, which derive from Case COMP/M.2621 *SEB / Moulinex*, are discussed in Ch.15.

[37] In Case IV/M.938 *Guinness / Grand Metropolitan* [1998] O.J. L288/24, the Commission also considered portfolio effects *within* a market, noting, at para.99, that "a deep portfolio of whiskey brands, spread out across the various quality and price segments, confers considerable price flexibility and marketing opportunities".

[38] For other views on the proper scope of portfolio power, see paras 6–14 and 6–15 of the first edition of this work.

[39] These theories of leverage are described in ss.12.3 and 12.4 above.

[40] See Nalebuff, "Bundling, Tying and Portfolio Effects", 2003 (DTI Economics Paper) (available via *www.dti.gov.uk/ccp/topics2/pdf2/bundle1.pdf*), Ch.7 (arguing that the term "portfolio effects" is unhelpful and does not disclose a distinct theory of competitive harm). The Irish Competition Authority's "Guidelines for Merger Analysis", December 2002 (*www.tca.ie*), at para.6.7, adopt the approach described in the text: "The theory is that market power is created because the firm is better able to leverage its products by tying, bundling or other means (e.g. it can use its strength across a range of markets to force buyers to obtain all inputs from it, thereby increasing market share). There are a number of important limitations on the application of this theory for a finding of SLC.

(a) First, it can only be applied to the merger of complementary goods. If the products are substitutes the merger should be classified as horizontal and treated accordingly. If the products are unrelated (i.e., neither substitutes nor complements), it is difficult to see how leverage could occur.

(b) Second, in the case of complements, the merger may be efficiency-enhancing so that portfolio effects, if they exist, could easily be outweighed by pro-competitive factors.

(c) Third, the bringing together of different product lines may result in (or be motivated by) economies of scope for the merging firm, whereby the total production cost is lowered. Any harm to rivals arising from the increased efficiency resulting would not be harmful to competition.

(d) Fourth, it requires that there is already an element of market power in at least one of the markets".

The Irish authority's requirement that the products in question are *complements* may be unnecessarily limiting: the Court of First Instance identified possible scope for leveraging in cases of *substitutes* in Case T-5/02 *Tetra Laval BV v Commission* [2002] E.C.R. II-4381, at para.196 ("leveraging may be carried out when the products in question are ones which the customer finds suitable for the same end use") (the decision was upheld on appeal on the basis of reasoning not relating to this issue in Case C-12/03P *Commission v Tetra Laval BV*, not yet reported, judgment of February 15, 2005).

In its decisions, the Commission has identified[41] nine potential sources of **12–021** market power available to a supplier offering a portfolio of products, namely that the merged group may enjoy[42]:

(a) greater flexibility to structure prices, promotions and discounts,[43] including the use of price discrimination[44];

(b) greater potential for bundling[45] or tying[46];

(c) greater scope to threaten to refuse to supply[47];

(d) greater scope to influence retailers' decisions on stocking, display of goods or use of generic products (e.g. which brand to use when the customer orders "a whisky") and over the timing of promotions[48];

(e) greater scope to cross-subsidise secondary brands from best-selling brands[49];

---

[41] See also Case 85/76 *Hoffmann-La Roche* [1979] E.C.R. 461 (evidence that the company supplied a range of vitamins was, on the facts, not material to the question of whether it held a dominant position for the purposes of Art.82; paras 45 and 46). In Case IV/M.1371 *Ahlström / Kvaerner* the notification was withdrawn the day before the Commission planned to issue a prohibition decision. In its XXIXth Annual Report on Competition Policy, 1999, the Commission stated, at para.164: "The Commission also sought to prohibit the operation on the ground that the parties would have become the only viable full-line supplier in the chemical pulping sector, providing incentives and the ability to cross-subsidise in an anticompetitive manner between products where it would have had a dominant market position and those for which it would face more competition, and also to tie products in competitive markets to those for other pulp mill equipment, in which it would have had a dominant position". In addition, the merged group's range of activities may create multi-market contacts which deter competitors from competing aggressively for fear of reprisals in different markets; see Case COMP/M.1630 *Air Liquide / BOC* [2004] O.J. L92/1, paras 102, 192 and 193; Case COMP/M.1853 *EDF / EnBW*, paras 69 and 71; Case COMP/M.2187 *CVC / Lenzing* [2004] O.J. L82/20, para.182; and Case COMP/M.2530 *Südzucker / Saint Louis Sucre* [2003] O.J. L103/1.

[42] See generally Case IV/M.214 *Du Pont / ICI* [1993] O.J. L7/3, para.41; Case IV/M.580 *ABB / Daimler Benz* [1997] O.J. L11/1, para.65; Case COMP/M.2033 *Metso / Svedala* [2004] O.J. L88/1, paras 131 to 134 and 194; and Case COMP/M.2547 *Bayer / Aventis Crop Science* [2004] O.J. L107/1, paras 449, 476 and 987.

[43] Case IV/M.938 *Guinness / Grand Metropolitan* [1998] O.J. L288/24, paras 40 and 101. See also Case IV/M.794 *Coca-Cola Enterprises / Amalgamated Beverages Great Britain* ("the ability to offer the most wide-ranging overrider discounts and other promotional measures to customers ... designing promotional measures to boost the Coca-Cola brand"; para.208); Case COMP/M.1630 *Air Liquide / BOC* [2004] O.J. L92/1, paras 99 and 194; and Case COMP/M.2268 *Pernod Ricard / Diageo / Seagram Spirits*, para.23.

[44] Case COMP/M.2187 *CVC / Lenzing* [2004] O.J. L82/20, para.182.

[45] In Case COMP/JV.37 *BSkyB / KirchPayTV*, at paras 78 to 80, the Commission found that, if KirchPayTV were to enter the market for digital interactive television services, this might foreclose the market to other entrants because KirchPayTV would be the only supplier offering a single box providing both pay-TV and digital interactive television services (since it had a monopoly in pay-TV).

[46] Case IV/M.938 *Guinness / Grand Metropolitan* [1998] O.J. L288/24, paras 40 and 100. See also Case IV/M.53 *Aerospatiale / Alenia / de Havilland* [1991] O.J. L334/42, para.31 and Case COMP/M.2220 *GE / Honeywell* [2004] O.J. L48/1, para.163 (although the Court of First Instance overturned the Commission's reasoning on this issue in Case T-210/01 *General Electric Company v Commission*, not yet reported, judgment of December 14, 2005).

[47] Case IV/M.938 *Guinness / Grand Metropolitan* [1998] O.J. L288/24, para.40.

[48] Case IV/M.938 *Guinness / Grand Metropolitan* [1998] O.J. L288/24, para.101.

[49] Case IV/M.938 *Guinness / Grand Metropolitan* [1998] O.J. L288/24, para.99.

(f)   greater scope to use secondary brands tactically, not as a revenue source, but as a means of competing against other competitors' main brands by, e.g. granting non-negligible overall volume rebates[50];

(g)   greater scope to use brand proliferation to exclude rivals or prevent new entry; the Commission noted: "Greater portfolio diversity and the subsequent listing of the parties' weaker brands reduce the opportunities for competing suppliers whose products may be then delisted by retailers"[51];

(h)   greater scope to offer "one-stop-shopping" or single-sourcing[52]; and

(i)   the benefits of economies of scale and scope in sale, marketing and distribution activities.[53]

Points (a) to (g) are connected[54] in the sense that each comprises a mechanism by which the merged group can use its powerful brands to "pull through"[55] its secondary brands, in particular by securing listing opportu-

---

[50] Case COMP/M.2268 *Pernod Ricard / Diageo / Seagram Spirits*, para.23.
[51] Case COMP/M.2268 *Pernod Ricard / Diageo / Seagram Spirits*, para.24.
[52] See Case IV/M.938 *Guinness / Grand Metropolitan* [1998] O.J. L288/24, para.101. See also Case IV/M.17 *MMB / Aérospatiale* (range of helicopters); Case IV/M.53 *Aérospatiale / Alenia / de Havilland* [1991] O.J. L334/42 (range of commuter aircraft; paras 32 and 33); Case IV/M.603 *Crown Cork & Seal / Carnaud Metalbox* [1996] O.J. L75/38, para.62; Case IV/M.774 *Saint-Gobain / Wacker-Chemie / NOM* [1997] O.J. L247/1 (range of silicon carbide grades for abrasives and refractories; paras 178, 179 and 224); Case IV/M.794 *Coca-Cola Enterprises / Amalgamated Beverages Great Britain* para.193; Case IV/M.833 *The Coca-Cola Company / Carlsberg A/S* [1998] O.J. L145/41 (the Commission found, at para.69, that for customers it was an advantage to be able to purchase a complete portfolio from a single supplier as it involved fewer deliveries); Case IV/M.877 *Boeing / McDonnell Douglas* [1997] O.J. L336/16 (range of aircraft; paras 38 and 41); Case IV/M.890 *Blokker / Toys 'R' Us (II)* [1998] O.J. L316/1 (range of retail formulae; para.62); Case IV/M.984 *Du Pont / ICI* (range of nylon carpet fibres); Case COMP/M.1339 *ABB / Elsag Bailey* (range of technical applications for process analysers); Case COMP/M.1853 *EDF / EnBW* (pan-European supplier, paras 85 to 89); and Case COMP/M.2530 *Südzucker / Saint Louis Sucre* [2003] O.J. L103/1 (pan-European deals). In Case COMP/M.1630 *Air Liquide / BOC* [2004] O.J. L92/1, at paras 88 to 91, the Commission found that there were separate market for tonnage and bulk gases but that the merged group could leverage its strong position in the bulk market into the tonnage market because of the knowledge and customer relationships obtained through its activities in the bulk market. The Commission also found that holding a strong position in the tonnage market conferred advantages on a company seeking to compete in the bulk market: paras 166 to 168. Compare Areeda & Turner, *Antitrust Law* (Aspen Law & Business, 1980), Vol.V, para.1109d2, discussing the arguments that the merged group can provide a one-stop service and may have better knowledge of its customers.
[53] Case IV/M.938 *Guinness / Grand Metropolitan* [1998] O.J. L288/24, para.40. In Case IV/M.794 *Coca-Cola Enterprises / Amalgamated Beverages Great Britain*, the Commission identified, at para.208, as an advantage of a wide portfolio, the fact that the merged group would enjoy scale economies in purchasing, production and distribution. Similarly, in Case IV/M.833 *The Coca-Cola Company / Carlsberg A/S* [1998] O.J. L145/41, the Commission found, at para.68, that the merged group's range of brands would enable it to operate the lowest cost distribution system and reach the highest number of customers; see also para.69. See also Case COMP/M.1630 *Air Liquide / BOC* [2004] O.J. L92/1 (the merged group would have lower distribution costs; see paras 70 to 77, 166 to 168 and 177 to 179).
[54] Indeed, they overlap.
[55] Case IV/M.938 *Guinness / Grand Metropolitan* [1998] O.J. L288/24, para.99.

nities and resisting possible de-listings. Further, if applied robustly, points (a) to (g) are each capable of giving rise to competitive harm by leverage; in particular, the application of the umbrella term "portfolio power" does not free the Commission from the obligation to apply the generic principles of leverage described in s.12.2 above. By contrast, points (h) and (i) do *not* disclose a theory of competitive harm: such facilities or savings do not lead to any direct harm to consumers and are therefore not a reason, as such, for objecting to a merger as explained in s.7.6 above.[56]

The question arises whether a transaction may be regarded as *creating* a **12–022** dominant position[57] in a market because of portfolio effects, even if the parties' activities in that market do not overlap and the party active in the market prior to the merger did not hold a dominant position. This seems possible in principle, since the essence of portfolio power is that the whole is worth more than the sum of the parts,[58] and was confirmed in *Guinness / Grand Metropolitan*[59] when the Commission found that the transaction *created* a dominant position in a market in which the parties' activities did not overlap.[60]

---

[56] See Areeda & Turner, *Antitrust Law* (Aspen Law & Business, 1980), Vol.V, para.1109d. Nevertheless, in its XXVIIth Annual Report on Competition Policy, 1997, the Commission focused, at p.55, on the benefits to the owner of portfolios of brands (as opposed to the potential exclusionary strategies which the owner might pursue) and noted that: "The question of the potential impact of range effects on competition, which is particularly important with regard to daily consumer goods, such as drinks, arises in connection with the additional benefits that may accrue to the owners of dominant brand names". The UK Director General of Fair Trading noted in his advice on *SMG / Scottish Radio Holdings* of June 21, 2001 (*www.oft.gov.uk/Business/Mergers+FTA/Decisions/index.htm*), that: "Portfolio power is said to exist when the market power derived from a combined portfolio of brands ... exceeds the sum of its parts so that power could be created or strengthened over and above the consequences of any increase in market share in individual markets. Such power could potentially be increased where: (1) the firms' offerings are more attractive because they offer a wider range of products; (2) economies of scale and scope are realised; (3) there is greater potential for tying products; and (4) the threat of refusal to supply is more potent ... The first two grounds are generally more likely to benefit than harm customers unless, perhaps, they also create strategic entry barriers". See also Baker & Ridyard, "Portfolio Power: A Rum Deal?" [1999] E.C.L.R. 181.

[57] The adoption of the significant impediment to effective competition test ought to overcome some of the more arcane issues of interpretation arising from the dominance test, but it should be noted that recital 25 of the revised ECMR states that the new test is not intended to expand the Commission's jurisdiction except in relation to anti-competitive effects arising from "non-coordinated behaviour". As discussed in para.2–015 above, the phrase "non-coordinated behaviour" seems to cover all theories of competitive harm apart from coordinated effects and would therefore be applicable to cases of conglomerate effects.

[58] In Case IV/M.833 *The Coca-Cola Company / Carlsberg A/S* [1998] O.J. L145/41, the Commission stated, at para.67, that the merged group's portfolio "gives each of the brands in the portfolio greater market power than if they were sold on a 'stand-alone' basis".

[59] Case IV/M.938 [1998] O.J. L288/24, para.117.

[60] Case IV/M.938 *Guinness / Grand Metropolitan* [1998] O.J. L288/24, also confirms that a dominant position may be created or strengthened through portfolio power in markets for acquired brands *or retained brands*; see paras 96, 117 and 118 and Table 5.

(b) Applying leveraging theory to portfolio power cases

12–023 The general principles described in s.12.2 above apply to portfolio power theories.

More particularly, in assessing whether the merged group will have an *incentive* to adopt a leveraging strategy involving portfolio effects, it is relevant to consider[61] the *links between the products* as explained in para.12–010(c) above.

(a) In *Akzo Nobel / Hoechst Roussel Vet*[62] the Commission identified possible portfolio power concerns when products in different markets could be used in combination for certain indications or after one another in a treatment process[63] but ruled them out when the parties' products were sold to different customer groups.[64]

(b) In *INA / FAG*[65] the merged group would have been a full range supplier of bearings but the Commission dismissed concerns about portfolio power in part because customers generally bought bearings separately from different suppliers.

(c) In *Newell / Rubbermaid*[66] the Commission ruled out portfolio power because "the product markets in which the portfolio is held, widely diverge from each other thus making tying sales or predatory pricing unprofitable".

(d) In *Allied Signal / Honeywell*[67] the Commission dismissed concerns that the merged group would bundle avionics and non-avionics on the grounds that there was "no natural link" between the products and that packages including both avionics and non-avionics were rare.

The merged group's incentives to adopt a leveraging strategy involving portfolio effects will also be affected by the *costs of implementing* such a strategy. For example, in *UIAG / Carlyle / Andritz*[68] the transaction was

---

[61] The Commission has in some cases acknowledged that, in the absence of leverage, the ability to supply a range of products is beneficial to consumers or at least neutral from their perspective. For example, in Case COMP/M.1601 *Allied Signal / Honeywell* [2001] O.J. L152/1, the Commission stated, at para.112, that: "As long as ... technical integration does not lead to foreclosure effects, improved technical inter-operability may generally be considered to be in the interests of customers".
[62] Case COMP/M.1681.
[63] Paras 40 and 41.
[64] Paras 32 and 102.
[65] Case COMP/M.2608, para.34.
[66] Case IV/M.1355, para.19.
[67] Case COMP/M.1601 [2001] O.J. L152/1, para.121.
[68] Case COMP/M.1736, para.13.

cleared in part because there would have been substantial costs in adapting the parties' products to be compatible with one another.[69]

In analysing whether the merged group will have the *ability* to adopt a **12–024** leveraging strategy involving portfolio effects (see s.12.2(c) above),[70] the Commission stated in *Guinness / Grand Metropolitan*[71]: "The strength of [the advantages conferred by a portfolio of brands], and their potential effect on the competitive structure of the market, depends on a number of factors, including ... the market shares of the various brands, particularly in relation to the shares of competitors; the relative importance of the individual markets in which the parties have significant shares and brands across the range of product markets in which the portfolio is held; and/or the number of markets in which the portfolio holder has a brand leader or the leading brand. In addition the strength of a portfolio effect has to be considered in the context of the relative strength of competitors' brands and their portfolios".[72] More particularly, the merged group's ability to pursue a leveraging strategy involving portfolio effects may be affected by the following factors.

(a) The Commission has repeatedly stated that portfolio effects arise only if the merged group has at least one "must stock" brand (which may be taken as an approximation for holding a dominant position).[73] For example, in *Akzo Nobel / Hoechst Roussel Vet*[74] the Commission identified possible portfolio power concerns when at least one of the products was a "must stock" item.[75] Similarly, in *Allied Signal / Honeywell*,[76] the Commission identified portfolio power concerns arising from the merged group's *monopoly* in the provision of one item of avionics equipment and its strong positions in other, closely connected, equipment. By contrast, in *Newell /*

---

[69] By contrast, in Case IV/M.794 *Coca-Cola Enterprises / Amalgamated Beverages Great Britain* the Commission found, at para.148, that the merged group's portfolio of soft drinks would allow it to structure its discounts to maximise volume and discourage switching.

[70] The UK Office of Fair Trading's Substantive Merger Guidelines, May 2003 (*www.oft.gov.uk*), s.6

[71] Case IV/M.938 [1998] O.J. L288/24, paras 41 and 42.

[72] The Commission takes account of historic exclusionary conduct in the market (see, e.g. Case IV/M.938 *Guinness / Grand Metropolitan* [1998] O.J. L288/24, para.100) but this is not decisive, as the issue is whether the effect of the merger is to create or enhance such opportunities on a prospective basis. See also COMP/M.2495 *Haniel / Fels* [2003] O.J. L103/36 (merger led to wider product range but did not give the merged group additional power to raise prices).

[73] In Case IV/M.833 *The Coca Cola Company / Carlsberg A/S* [1998] O.J. L145/41, the Commission concluded that "the inclusion of strong beer and packaged water brands, such as those of Carlsberg, in the beverage portfolio gives each of the brands in the portfolio greater market power than if they were sold on a 'stand-alone' basis". Similarly, in Case COMP/ M.2268 *Pernod Ricard / Diageo / Seagram Spirits* portfolio effects were ruled out in certain territories because the merged group's market positions in different spirits markets were not "sufficient to give rise to significant portfolio effects"; paras 32, 34 and 35.

[74] Case COMP/M.1681, paras 40 and 41.

[75] See also Case IV/M.938 *Guinness / Grand Metropolitan* [1998] O.J. L288/24, para.41.

[76] Case COMP/M.1601 [2001] O.J. L152/1, para.114.

Rubbermaid[77] the Commission ruled out portfolio power because the parties did not have "any significant market power" in any of their product lines. In *The Coca-Cola Company / Nestle / JV*[78] the joint venture distributed iced tea and the Commission found that: "No portfolio effects in favour of TCCC's CSDs / cola-flavoured products would arise from the concentration as iced tea is far from being a 'must stock' product in Spain, being still a novel product in that country with volumes very small compared to other soft drinks and other countries". Similarly, in *INA / FAG*[79] one of the reasons for rejecting portfolio power concerns was that the merged group lacked sufficient market power profitably to engage in tying.

(b) If competitors can readily *match the breadth or quality* of the merged group's product range, then portfolio effects will generally not arise.[80]

   (i) In *Guinness / Grand Metropolitan*, in finding that portfolio effects arose, the Commission emphasised that the "competitors have weaker portfolios and fewer strong brands".[81]

   (ii) In *Akzo Nobel / Hoechst Roussel Vet*[82] the Commission ruled portfolio effects out when rival suppliers had similar attractive portfolios.

   (iii) In *INA / FAG*[83] the merged group would have been a full range supplier of bearings, but the Commission dismissed concerns about portfolio power in part because other suppliers also offered a full range. The Commission also stated that the portfolio effects arising from the parties' product ranges "would have to be weighed against the economies of scale generated by product specialists that produce a limited number of products in high quantities".

As regards new entrants, the existence of portfolio power may itself result in barriers to entry (e.g. arising from economies of scale or scope) which reduces the likelihood of potential competition.[84]

---

[77] Case IV/M.1355, para.19.

[78] Case COMP/M.2276, para.37 (see also paras 43 and 44).

[79] Case COMP/M.2608, para.34.

[80] See also Case IV/M.794 *Coca-Cola Enterprises / Amalgamated Beverages Great Britain* (para.147, emphasising that CCSB had the widest portfolio of any soft drinks producer in Great Britain); Case COMP/M.2568 *Haniel / Ytong* [2003] O.J. L111/1 (the merger combined a monopoly in one market with strong positions in neighbouring markets; the transaction was approved on the basis of undertakings); and Case COMP/M.3816 *Apax / Mölnlycke* (para.36).

[81] Case IV/M.938 [1998] O.J. L288/24, para.103. See also para.116.

[82] Case COMP/M.1681, paras 98 and 103.

[83] Case COMP/M.2608, para.34.

[84] See, e.g. Case IV/M.794 *Coca-Cola Enterprises / Amalgamated Beverages Great Britain* (as Coca-Cola was a "must stock" item, potential competitors had difficulty obtaining access to shelf space; para.190) and Case IV/M.938 *Guinness / Grand Metropolitan* [1998] O.J. L288/24 ("as a result of the creation of GMG ... entry of new products is likely to become more difficult"; para.113). See generally s.7.6 above.

(c) *Buyer power* may prevent a merged group from pursuing a strategy based on leveraging through portfolio power. For example,[85] in *Allied Signal | Honeywell*[86] the Commission rejected an argument that the merged group could exclude competitors by engaging in pure bundling, in part because customers had considerable engineering capability and would allow bundling only if it was to their own advantage. Further, customers could retaliate against unwanted bundling by the merged group in relation to products where third party suppliers were available and there was evidence that customers broke up packages by "mixing and matching" products from various suppliers.[87]

(d) In *Akzo Nobel | Hoechst Roussel Vet*[88] the Commission ruled portfolio effects out when *national regulatory systems* placed an obligation on the merged group's customers to carry all products of all suppliers.[89]

(e) In *SEB | Moulinex*,[90] which involved national markets for different types of small electrical household appliances, the Commission adopted a *rule of thumb* that portfolio effects could be ruled out when the product markets in which the merged group had a share exceeding 40 per cent did not represent more than 35 per cent of the parties' aggregate turnover.[91] However, in *Pernod Ricard /Allied Domecq*,[92] the Commission did not apply the rule of thumb identified in *SEB | Moulinex* on the grounds that the market setting was different.[93] In that case, the Commission ruled out portfolio power concerns on the basis that there was no evidence that the new entity

---

[85] See also Case IV/M.938 *Guinness | Grand Metropolitan*, [1998] O.J. L/288/24 (paras 104 to 111, discussing countervailing buyer power and para.112, discussing the scope for parallel trade) and Case IV/M.1335 *Dana | Glacier Vandervell* (the Commission rejected portfolio power concerns on the grounds that *customers* were increasingly moving towards the sourcing of comprehensive product packages; para.15; the inference is that the merger was regarded as a reaction to customers' requirements rather than a source of possible exclusionary power).

[86] Case COMP/M.1601 [2001] O.J. L152/1, para.113.

[87] The Commission took account of the low proportion of Allied Signal's bids which were not broken as evidence of the difficulty in pure bundling; para.120.

[88] Case COMP/M.1681, paras 32 and 41.

[89] Similarly, in Case COMP/M.1601 *Allied Signal | Honeywell* [2001] O.J. L152/1, the Commission relied, at paras 113 and 120, in rejecting a portfolio power argument, on the fact that standardisation of product interfaces was widespread in the industry, which reduced the scope to bundle products through proprietary interfaces.

[90] Case COMP/M.2621, para.83.

[91] This part of the Commission's reasoning was not called into question by the Court of First Instance in Case T-114/02 *BaByliss v Commission* [2003] E.C.R. II-1279; see paras 341 and 351 (the Court found that the Commission had not discharged the standard of proof when ruling out concerns in certain territories on the basis of buyer power, which the Commission confusingly described as a "range effect"; see paras 352 to 363).

[92] Case COMP/M.3779, paras 74 to 79 and n.30.

[93] Generally, the Commission is required to analyse the particular circumstances relating to each market affected by a concentration and the Commission is therefore reluctant to adopt or apply rigid rules of thumb. The decision in *SEB | Moulinex* should therefore be regarded as exceptional.

was likely to engage in anti-competitive practices and most smaller spirits producers who replied on the market test had not indicated that they would be foreclosed from distribution.

12.6 REDUCED INCENTIVES TO ENGAGE IN RESEARCH AND DEVELOPMENT

12–025 In certain markets, suppliers of complementary goods cooperate on research and development and, as part of that cooperation, share confidential information. The Commission may be concerned that a conglomerate merger would reduce the incentive to share information (which might reduce research and development and might ultimately harm consumers) because of concerns that it will be shared with a competing business.[94]

---

[94] See RBB Economics, "The Efficiency-Enhancing Effects of Non-Horizontal Mergers", 2005 (report for the Commission DG for Enterprise and Industry) (available via *http://europa. eu.int/comm/enterprise/library/lib-competition/doc/non_horizontal_mergers.pdf*), p.14 (noting that the merged group may not have such an incentive and the effects on consumers are ambiguous).

CHAPTER 13

COORDINATION IN JOINT VENTURES

13.1 INTRODUCTION

(a) The effects of joint ventures on competition

Joint ventures[1] may have the following effects on competition: **13–001**

(a) The management structures adopted by most joint ventures involve the application of decisions on competitive variables, such as price, output and advertising, to *all* businesses contributed to the joint venture, eliminating any pre-merger competition between them.[2]

(b) A parent which is active in a market which is the same as, or connected with, the market in which the joint venture is active, has an incentive to use its control over *both* the joint venture and *separately* its own business to maximise its *aggregate*[3] profits, reducing competition between the parent and the joint venture.[4]

---

[1] See generally Werden, "Antitrust Analysis of Joint Ventures: An Overview" (1998) 66 *Antitrust Law Journal* 701; Bresnahan & Salop, "Quantifying the Competitive Effects of Production Joint Ventures" (1986) 4 *International Journal of Industrial Organisation* 155; Martin, *Advanced Industrial Economics* (2nd edn, Blackwell, 2002), pp.414, 455 and 462; and Rabassa, "Joint Ventures as a Mechanism that May Favour coordination: An Analysis of the Aluminium and Music Mergers" [2004] E.C.L.R. 771.
[2] See Werden, "Antitrust Analysis of Joint Ventures: An Overview" (1998) 66 *Antitrust Law Journal* 701, at p.722.
[3] i.e. its share of profits from the joint venture and the profits from any wholly owned businesses.
[4] Bresnahan & Salop, "Quantifying the Competitive Effects of Production Joint Ventures" (1986) 4 *International Journal of Industrial Organisation* 155, state: "By its very nature, a horizontal joint venture involves financial interest among competitors. This occurs because the profits of the joint venture are shared by the parent stockholders, which reduces the parent's private incentive to expand output and thereby lower price toward the competitive level. A second, related issue concerns the management control over the pricing and output decisions of the joint venture. Just as the parents' financial interest makes competition against

(c) The joint venture may increase the likelihood of coordinated effects (i.e. collective dominance) or it may make coordination (i.e. collective dominance) easier, more stable or more effective for the firms involved.

(d) The joint venture may facilitate coordination in the activities of the parents.

(e) The agreements comprising the joint venture may include restrictions on competition.

(f) The formation of the joint venture may generate efficiencies, in particular through economies of scale and scope, improved use of existing assets, restructuring of assets, elimination of free-riding, efficient risk-sharing and the elimination of double marginalisation.[5]

Under the ECMR, which applies to certain joint ventures,[6] issues (a) and (b) are addressed by considering whether the formation of the joint venture will result in a significant impediment to effective competition ("the SIEC

---

the joint venture unprofitable, competitive moves by the joint venture against the parents are also self-destructive. In order to prevent unprofitable competition by the joint venture entity against its parent corporations, the parents have a private incentive to structure the joint venture agreement in a way that removes the discretion of the joint venture management over these competitive instruments and replaces discretion with either control by the parents or with a formula that determines price or output".

[5] See Rabassa, "Joint Ventures as a Mechanism that May Favour coordination: An Analysis of the Aluminium and Music Mergers" [2004] E.C.L.R. 771, at pp.771 and 772; and Werden, "Antitrust Analysis of Joint Ventures: An Overview" (1998) 66 *Antitrust Law Journal* 701, at p.702. For discussion of double marginalisation see s.11.2(c) above.

[6] Before the amendments to the ECMR which were made in 1997 and came into force on March 1, 1998 (pursuant to Council Regulation (EC) No. 1310/97 of June 30, 1997 amending Regulation (EEC) No 4064/89 on the Control of Concentrations Between Undertakings [1997] O.J. L180/1) a distinction was drawn between cooperative and concentrative joint ventures. The former were examined under Regulation 17/62 ([1962] O.J. L13/204) and the latter under the ECMR. Prior to the coming into force of the 1997 amendments, a merger that gave rise to cooperative concerns might require clearance under the ECMR and notification under Art.81. The 1997 amendments eliminated this distinction, with the consequence that "full function" joint ventures which meet the turnover thresholds are assessed exclusively under the ECMR. A full function joint venture is one which "perform[s] on a lasting basis all the functions of an autonomous economic entity": ECMR, Art.3(2). More specifically, the Commission Notice on the Concept of Full-Function Joint Ventures [1998] O.J. C66/1, states, at para.12: "[the concept of a full functionality] means that a joint venture must operate on a market, performing the functions carried out by undertakings operating on the same market. In order to do so the joint venture must have a management dedicated to its day-to-day operations and access to sufficient resources including finance, staff, and assets (tangible and intangible) in order to conduct on a lasting basis its business activities within the area provided for in the joint venture agreement". The 1997 amendments allowed the ECMR to operate as a "one-stop shop", as noted in recital 2 of Regulation 1310/97. Other advantages for the parties from this amendment include the fact that they benefit from more stringent time limits under the ECMR and ECMR clearance is generally permanent rather than temporary (in contrast to the general position under Art.81(3)). The "one-stop shop" principle has been retained in the revised ECMR. However, it does *not* extend to cases in which there is an express agreement between the parents to coordinate their behaviour which is not directly related and necessary for the establishment of the joint venture: such agreements must be the subject of a separate decision as noted in Case IV/JV.22 *Fujitsu / Siemens*, para.77.

issue").[7] Issue (c) is addressed in Ch.8. Issue (d), namely whether the joint venture has as its object or effect the coordination of competitive behaviour between the parents ("the coordination issue"),[8] is governed by Arts 2(4) and 2(5) of the revised ECMR[9] and is the subject of the remainder of this Chapter. Issue (e) is governed by the rules on ancillary restraints[10] and Art.81 EC generally and is outside the scope of this book. Issue (f) is relevant to the first five issues.[11]

(b) The relationship between Arts 2(4) and 2(5) of the ECMR and coordinated effects

The relationship between coordinated effects/collective dominance (issue (c) above) and Arts 2(4) and 2(5) (issue (d) above) is complex. The European Court of Justice in *Compagnie Maritime Belge Transports v Commission*[12] stated: **13–002**

---

[7] The SIEC issue involves examining whether the merger of the businesses contributed by the parents to the joint venture is likely to give rise to horizontal non-coordinated effects, coordinated effects, vertical issues or conglomerate issues. These issues are analysed in Chs 7, 8, 11 and 12. See also Nye, "Can a Joint Venture Lessen Competition more than a Merger?" (1992) 40 *Economics Letters* 487.

[8] The coordination issue is sometimes described as involving "spill-over effects": see the Commission's XXVIIIth Annual Report on Competition Policy, 1998, insert 7, para.3.

[9] A legal issue arises, namely whether a review under Arts 2(4) and 2(5) of the revised ECMR is limited to assessing whether the merger is likely to result in coordination between two or more of the parents of the joint venture or extends also to coordination between one or more of the parents and the joint venture itself. On the former approach, possible coordination between the joint venture's parents on the one hand and the joint venture on the other is assessed as part of the SIEC issue; on the latter approach such coordination is considered as part of the coordination issue (or as part of both the SIEC and coordination issues). There are strong arguments that the former approach is correct. First, the text of Art.2(4) refers to the coordination of the competitive behaviour "of undertakings that remain independent" and a joint venture which is jointly controlled by two or more other entities is not properly described as "independent". (The contrary argument is that a joint venture subject to the ECMR may be regarded as "independent" in the sense that it operates as a "full function" entity.) Secondly, the text which was replaced by Art.2(4) of the ECMR in 1997 referred expressly to coordination between the parents and the joint venture (Art.3(2) of Regulation 4064/89, prior to its amendment in 1997, referred to "coordination of the competitive behaviour between the parties themselves or between them and the joint venture"), suggesting that the decision to omit such references in 1997 (and to maintain the omission in the revised ECMR) was deliberate. Finally, from a purposive perspective, there can be no doubt that the Commission ought to have power to examine the effect on competition of one or both of the parent companies retaining businesses operating in the same market as the joint venture; but such an analysis can take place in examining the SIEC issue. In Case COMP/M.3099 *Areva | Urenco | ETC JV*, para.222 and Case COMP/M.3178 *Bertelsmann | Springer | JV*, para.164 the Commission discussed the application of Art.2(4) in general terms but solely with reference to coordination between the parents (and did not refer to possible coordination between one or more of the parents and the joint venture itself).

[10] See the Commission notice on restrictions directly related and necessary to concentrations [2001] O.J. C188/5.

[11] See generally Ch.18.

[12] Joined Cases C-395/96P and C-396/96P [2000] E.C.R. I-1445, paras 44 and 45.

"an agreement, decision or concerted practice (whether or not covered by an exemption under Article [81(3)] of the Treaty) may undoubtedly, where it is implemented, result in the undertakings concerned being so linked as to their conduct on a particular market that they present themselves on that market as a collective entity vis-à-vis their competitors, their trading partners and customers. The existence of a collective dominant position may therefore flow from the nature and terms of an agreement, from the way in which it is implemented and, consequently, from the links or factors which give rise to a connection between undertakings which result from it".

The existence of a joint venture may therefore be relevant both to an assessment of coordinated effects/collective dominance and to an appraisal under Arts 2(4) and 2(5) of possible coordination between the parents. However, any coordinated effects/collective dominance are assessed as part of the SIEC issue (even if the only parties to the candidate coordinated effects/collective dominance are the parents of the joint venture), whilst an appraisal under Arts 2(4) and 2(5) of possible coordination between the parents is governed by the principles in Arts 81(1) and (3). It is more difficult for notifying parties to establish that there is no infringement of Art.81 than to establish that there is no significant impediment to effective competition.

The tension arises[13] because agreements that appreciably restrict competition are presumed to be unlawful under Art.81(1) unless the parties can demonstrate that they have countervailing efficiency benefits as described in Art.81(3), whereas mergers are presumed to generate some efficiencies with the consequence that they are treated more benignly than restrictive agreements (even though a merger can be regarded as an agreement providing for coordination between the parties on all competitive parameters, including hard core cartel activity such as price fixing and market sharing).[14]

Nevertheless, in practice, the Commission does not appear to have drawn a significant distinction between a coordinated effects/collective dominance analysis and an assessment of coordination under Arts 2(4) and (5). For example, in *Areva / Urenco / ETC JV*[15] the Commission carried out a detailed analysis of whether the merger might result in coordinated effects/

---

[13] The Commission's "Memorandum on the Problem of Concentration in the Common Market", EC Competition Series, Study No.3, 1966, concluded that Art.81 could not be applied uniformly to cartels and mergers as its application in both contexts would either result in the prohibition of too many mergers or the allowing of too many cartels; see further Hildebrand, *The Role of Economic Analysis in the EC Competition Rules* (Kluwer, 2002), p.71.

[14] See para.1–025 above.

[15] Case COMP/M.3099, para.224 (see also para.145, in which the Commission did not distinguish between concerns relating to a significant impediment to effective competition and concerns regarding coordination under Art.2(4) of the ECMR). The Commission's approach in this case was logical since the threshold for intervention in reliance on coordinated effects/collective dominance theory is *higher* than the threshold under Arts 2(4) and 2(5) of the ECMR and if the former is satisfied the latter ought also to be satisfied. Nevertheless, the summary nature of the assessment of the coordination issue under Art.2(4) of the ECMR suggested that the Commission did not draw a rigorous distinction between the two analyses.

collective dominance involving the parents and stated that the same facts gave rise to serious doubts under Art.2(4).

13.2 COORDINATION OF BEHAVIOUR

(a) General

The coordination issue is addressed in Arts 2(4) and 2(5) of the revised **13–003** ECMR[16]:

"To the extent that the creation of a joint venture constituting a concentration ... has as its object or effect the coordination of the competitive behaviour of undertakings that remain independent, such coordination shall be appraised in accordance with the criteria of Article 81(1) and (3) of the Treaty, with a view to establishing whether or not the operation is compatible with the common market.

In making this appraisal, the Commission shall take into account in particular:

— whether two or more parent companies retain, to a significant extent, activities in the same market as the joint venture or in a market which is downstream or upstream from that of the joint venture or in a neighbouring market closely related to this market;
— whether the coordination which is the direct consequence of the creation of the joint venture affords the undertakings concerned the possibility of eliminating competition in respect of a substantial part of the products or services in question".

If there is no evidence that the *object* of the joint venture is to coordinate the **13–004** parents' activities,[17] it is necessary to assess the *effects* of the joint venture. In *Bertelsmann / Springer / JV*[18] the Commission stated: "A restriction of competition under Article 81(1) of the Treaty is established when the coordination of the parent companies' competitive behaviour is likely and appreciable and results from the creation of the joint venture".[19] Applying this test involves six separate issues, which are discussed below.

---

[16] See also recital 27 to the ECMR.
[17] The Commission commonly rules out the possibility that the *object* of the joint venture is the coordination of the parents' activities in fairly summary terms. See, e.g. Case COMP/M.3099 *Areva / Urenco / ETC JV*, para.223; Case COMP/M.3178 *Bertelsmann / Springer / JV*, para.166; and Case COMP/M.3333 *Sony / BMG* [2005] O.J. L62/30 (appeal pending in Case T-464/04 *Impala v Commission*), para.178.
[18] Case COMP/M.3178, para.164.
[19] This form of words has been used consistently; for an early example, see Case COMP/JV.1 *Telia / Telenor / Schibsted*, para.28.

(b) Identifying the markets for analysis

13–005 The first stage is to identify the markets for analysis in the light of the *nexus*[20] between the candidate market for coordinated effects and the market in which the joint venture is or will be active. This requires an analysis of the parents' activities in the market in which the joint venture will be active and markets which are upstream, downstream or closely related to that market.[21] Coordinated effects can be ruled out if the parents are not currently active[22] or potential competitors[23] in any such markets. By contrast, in *Wegener / PCM / JV*[24] the parents were planning to retain to a significant extent activities in the same market as the joint venture, creating a risk that the joint venture might have as its effect the coordination of the competitive behaviour of the undertakings concerned.

(c) Identifying the mechanism for coordination

13–006 The second stage is to identify the mechanism through which coordination may occur. Coordination may occur across any competitive parameters, including price, output, expansion of capacity, allocation of customers, allocation of markets, the exchange of commercially sensitive information,[25] the discriminatory treatment of third parties impeding their market access,[26] or the entering of exclusive supply obligations to create a barrier to entry.[27]

(d) Assessing the parents' incentive and ability to engage in coordination

13–007 The third stage is to determine whether coordination is likely,[28] which depends on whether the parents will have the *incentive* and *ability* to adopt the mechanism identified in the second stage.

In some cases, the transaction documentation provides expressly for coordination, in which case it is straightforward to establish the parents'

---

[20] The nexus may arise through physical proximity: see Case COMP/JV.23 *Telefónica / Portugal Telecom / Médi Telecom*, para.27.

[21] See the ECMR, Art.2(5).

[22] In Case COMP/M.3464 *Kesko / ICA / JV*, para.63, the parents did not retain outside the joint venture any businesses which competed with one another and concerns under Art.2(4) of the ECMR were therefore ruled out. See also Case COMP/JV.19 *KLM / Alitalia*, paras 61 and 62; Case COMP/M.2982 *Lazard / IntesaBCI / JV*, para.28; and Case COMP/M.3856 *Boeing / Lockheed Martin / United Launch Alliance JV*, paras 15 to 19.

[23] Coordination issues may arise if the parents are *potential* competitors on the market in question: see Case COMP/JV.28 *Sydkraft / HEW / Hansa Energy Trading*, para.27.

[24] Case COMP/M.3817, para.62.

[25] See, e.g. Case COMP/M.3101 *Accor / Hilton / Six Continents / JV*, paras 24 to 28.

[26] In Case IV/M.1327 *NC / Canal+ / CDPQ / BankAmerica* the Commission accepted undertakings to ensure that one of the parties did not discriminate, in a neighbouring geographic market, in favour of an entity controlled by one of the other parties.

[27] OECD roundtable on "Competition Issues in Joint Ventures", OECD, DAFFE/ CLP(2000)33, Commission paper, "Competition Issues in Joint Ventures", at p.129.

[28] See s.2.5(b) above.

ability to coordinate (and probably also their incentive to coordinate).[29] In most cases, however, an assessment of the parties' incentives and abilities to coordinate is based on a more general analysis of their respective commercial positions.

The parents are unlikely to have a material incentive to coordinate if the joint venture is relatively unimportant when compared with their retained activities. By contrast, coordination between parents is, in general, more likely if the turnover of the joint venture is high relative to the turnover of the existing activities of at least one of the parents, since that parent will have an incentive not to compete actively against its joint venture partner for fear of reprisals through the joint venture. For example,[30] in *Boeing / Lockheed Martin / United Launch Alliance JV*[31] the joint venture accounted for a small part of the parents' overall activities, and of their activities in the sector in question. It therefore did not create a strong incentive on the parents to align their activities outside the joint venture. Similarly, in *Bertelsmann / Springer / JV*[32] the Commission considered whether the formation of a printing joint venture might lead to coordination between the parents in the upstream market for the publishing of magazines, but found that the incentives to coordinate were weak, since printing costs accounted for less than 15 per cent of the total costs of a magazine, and the revenues from the joint venture were expected to be relatively small when compared with the parents' revenues from publishing magazines. By contrast, in *Wegener / PCM / JV*[33] the joint venture was relatively significant when compared with the parents' remaining publishing interests and the Commission relied on this factor in identifying serious doubts regarding possible coordination of competitive behaviour.

If an assessment of the significance of the joint venture to the parties does not rule out the prospect of coordination, it is necessary to carry out a general assessment of the operation of the market to assess the parents' incentives and abilities to pursue the coordinated strategy. The issues arising at this stage are similar[34] to those arising in coordinated effects/collective dominance analysis which were described in Ch.8.[35]

---

[29] See Case COMP/M.3099 *Areva / Urenco / ETC JV*.

[30] See also, e.g. Case COMP/JV.23 *Telefónica / Portugal Telecom / Médi Telecom*, para.29; Case COMP/M.2851 *Intracom / Siemens / STI*, para.44; Case COMP/M.3464 *Kesko / ICA / JV*, para.63; Case COMP/M.3542 *Sony Pictures / Walt Disney / ODG / MovieCo*, para.18 (finding that the joint venture would not change the incentives of the content providers to compete against one another).

[31] Case COMP/M.3856, para.14.

[32] Case COMP/M.3178, paras 167 to 169.

[33] Case COMP/M.3817, para.62.

[34] However, as noted in para.13–002 above, there is a tension in the use of the significant impediment of effective competition standard in assessing coordinated effects/collective dominance (as described in Ch.8) and the use of Arts 81(1) and (3) in an assessment under Arts 2(4) and 2(5) of the ECMR.

[35] In Case COMP/M.2851 *Intracom / Siemens / STI*, para.44, the Commission found that the parties lacked an incentive to coordinate in part because their activities (in terms of total EEA sales and distribution of activities geographically) were asymmetric.

13–008   The following factors in particular may be relevant to an assessment of the parents' *incentives* to coordinate:

(a) The impact of a coordination strategy on each of the parents' *expected profit streams*. If the coordination strategy is not profit-maximising for one of the parents, it will have no incentive to pursue the strategy.

(b) High concentration levels and symmetrical market shares[36] are likely to encourage coordination between the parties.[37]

(c) The way that the market operates may create an incentive for at least one of the parents to compete rather than coordinating. For example, markets involving small numbers of high value contracts tend not to be conducive to coordination because each party has a strong incentive to win the business.[38] Similarly, in *Ericsson / Nokia / Psion*[39] the Commission took account of the product's position in the production chain, noting that the manufacturers' ability to add a great deal of functionality to the product (the operating system) before it was sold meant that the incentive to coordinate on price was diminished: each manufacturer hoped to add sufficient value to the product to obtain a competitive advantage. Finally, in *Intracom / Siemens / STI*[40] the fact that innovation played an important role in the market pointed against a finding of coordination.

13–009 Even if the parents have an incentive to coordinate, they may not have the *ability* to do so.

(a) *Actual and potential*[41] rivals may be able to defeat or restrict the coordinated strategy.[42] For example,[43] in *Telia / Telenor / Schibsted*[44] the Commission found that coordinated effects were unlikely when barriers to entry were low and switching costs were low. In *Boeing / Lockheed Martin / United Launch Alliance JV*[45] the Commission found that there was significant overcapacity and the market was

---

[36] Compare para.8–032 above (emphasising that similarities in costs structures are more important than similarities in market shares when considering incentives to coordinate).

[37] See Case COMP/JV.22 *Fujitsu / Siemens*, para.63. Concentration levels are also relevant to the parents' *abilities* to coordinate; see para.13–009 below.

[38] See, e.g. Case COMP/M.1413 *Thomson-CSF / Racal Electronics*, para.31.

[39] Case IV/JV.6, para.35.

[40] Case COMP/M.2851, para.43.

[41] See Case COMP/JV.1 *Telia / Telenor / Schibsted*, para.42.

[42] If the parties' combined market shares are low, concerns regarding Arts 2(4) and 2(5) can be ruled out: see, e.g. Case COMP/M.3858 *Lehman Brothers / SCG / Starwood / Le Meridien*, para.24.

[43] See also Case COMP/M.2851 *Intracom / Siemens / STI*, para.43.

[44] Case IV/JV.1, para.44.

[45] Case COMP/M.3856, para.26. The Commission was equally not persuaded that the parents would have the ability to adopt a predation strategy to successfully force out the other leading supplier; see paras 30 to 34.

highly competitive with each supplier having an incentive to seek to increase its number of launches because the industry operated with high fixed costs. It concluded that if the parents sought to cooperate by raising prices this would probably be defeated by expansion by rivals which would not have an incentive to follow the parents' strategy.

(b) Customers may use their *buyer power* to frustrate the attempted coordination.[46]

(c) The parents may be unable to implement the coordination strategy in the light, for example, of third party rights or the organisation of the market. In *Boeing / Lockheed Martin / United Launch Alliance JV*[47] the Commission found that a coordinated strategy would be more difficult to implement because Boeing would have to persuade a partner in a separate joint venture to follow the strategy in question. Similarly, in *Sony / BMG*[48] concerns about possible coordination between the parents' music publishing businesses were ruled out on the grounds that collecting societies (and not the parties) carried out the main administration of publishing rights and fixed royalties in agreement with publishers, authors and composers.

(e) Appreciability

The fourth stage is to determine whether any coordination is likely to have **13–010** an *appreciable* effect on competition, bearing in mind in particular the coordinating parties' market shares,[49] the viability of actual and potential competitors and buyer power.[50] This issue is very closely connected to the question of the parents' *ability* to engage in coordination which is discussed in para.13–009 above.

(f) Causation

The fifth stage is to determine whether there is a *causal link* between the **13–011** creation of the joint venture and the likelihood of coordination.

---

[46] See Case COMP/JV.21 *Skandia / Storebrand / Pohjola* (the role of independent brokers in resisting price increases; para.45); Case COMP/JV.36 *TXU Europe / EDF-London Investments* (customer vigilance; para.48); and Case COMP/M.2851 *Intracom / Siemens / STI* (para.43).
[47] COMP/M.3856, para.23. See also paras 34 and 35.
[48] Case COMP/M.3333 [2005] O.J. L62/30 (appeal pending in Case T-464/04 *Impala v Commission*), para.179.
[49] See Case IV/JV.1 *Telia / Telenor / Schibsted*, para.41.
[50] See Case COMP/M.1413 *Thomson-CSF / Racal Electronics*, para.34.

(a) In *Telefónica | Portugal Telecom | Médi Telecom*[51] the Commission noted the prior existence of a general cooperation agreement (which had been notified to it) and concluded that the current absence of competition between the parents was unrelated to the existence of the joint venture.[52]

(b) In *First | Keolis | TPE JV*[53] the Commission found that an agreement between First and Keolis did not have the effect of coordinating their competitive behaviour within the meaning of Art.2(4) of the ECMR because the parents had already entered a joint venture to coordinate their activities on the market. The decision is noteworthy because the existing joint venture had *not* been notified or approved under the ECMR.

(c) In *Boeing | Lockheed Martin | United Launch Alliance JV*[54] the Commission considered whether the parties could engage in a strategy of jointly raising prices or, alternatively, of seeking to exclude competitors through predatory pricing, but found that there was no causal link between the joint venture and the parties' incentives and abilities to adopt either of the strategies.

(g) Art.81(3) analysis

13–012 The sixth stage arises if the Commission finds that the merger will have as its object or effect the coordination of the parents' activities contrary to Art.81(1). In such a situation, the arrangement can be justified only if the criteria in Art.81(3) are satisfied. In practice, the Commission has not carried out an Art.81(3) analysis as in each of the cases in which coordination concerns arose, the parties offered commitments to eliminate the concerns.[55]

---

[51] Case COMP/JV.23, para.29.
[52] However, the Commission has indicated that the mere prior existence of links between the parents does not automatically imply that there is no causation under Arts 2(4) and 2(5): see the Commission's XXVIIIth Annual Report on Competition Policy, 1998, insert 7, para.11.
[53] Case COMP/M.3273, para.13.
[54] Case COMP/M.3856, paras 20, 24 and 29.
[55] See Case IV/JV.15 *BT | AT&T*; Case IV/JV.22 *Fujitsu | Siemens*; Case IV/M.1327 *NC | Canal+ | CDPQ | BankAmerica*; Case COMP/M.3099 *Areva | Urenco | ETC JV*; and Case COMP/M.3817 *Wegener | PCM | JV*.

CHAPTER 14

COMPETITION FROM ACTUAL RIVALS

14.1 INTRODUCTION

The merged group may not have substantial market power because of the **14–001** competitive constraints posed by actual[1] rival suppliers.[2] In *Metso / Svedala*[3] the Commission stated that "it is necessary to examine whether the pressure of those suppliers could substantially constrain the competitive behaviour of the merged entity".[4]

This Chapter discusses the principles that the Commission applies in assessing the strength of the competitive constraints posed by rival suppliers. S.14.2 describes the main general categories of evidence which are used by the Commission. S.14.3 describes in more detail the Commission's approach

---

[1] See Ch.16 below for discussion of the competitive constraints posed by *potential* rival suppliers (i.e. new entry).

[2] See generally Porter, *Competitive Strategy* (1998 edn, The Free Press), Ch.3. At the most basic level, in Case COMP/M.1578 *Sanitec / Sphinx* [2000] O.J. L294/1, the main European suppliers were active in Belgium/Luxembourg but some were absent from the Nordic region. The Commission identified concerns in the Nordic region but not in Belgium/Luxembourg.

[3] Case COMP/M.2033 [2004] O.J. L88/1, para.141.

[4] In the Commission's XXIst Annual Report on Competition Policy, 1991, p.364, the Commission noted that: "Potential competition from established competitors or from entirely new entry and barriers preventing such competition play a significant role in the appraisal of mergers". Further, at p.365, the Commission identified six categories of potential competition (covering both actual rivalry from suppliers and new entry), namely: expansion of capacity by established competitors; potential imports from another geographic market; switching of production from a neighbouring product market; entirely new entry into the market; self-supply by purchasers; and potential competition from a downstream market. In Case T-114/02 *BaByliss v Commission* [2003] E.C.R. II-1279, the Court of First Instance stated, at para.329: "The presence of competitors is likely to modify, or even eliminate, the combined entity's dominant position only if those competitors hold a strong position which acts as a genuine counterweight". (The passage is misleading in the sense that the role of competitors is an *integral* part of an assessment of whether the merged group holds a dominant position and not a factor which *eliminates* a dominant position or, under the revised ECMR, a significant impediment to effective competition.) See also Case T-282/02 *Cementbouw Handel & Industrie v Commission*, not yet reported, judgment of February 23, 2006, para.212.

to determining whether competitors comprise viable alternatives to the merged group. Finally, s.14.4 discusses the weight to be placed on links between the merged group and its competitors, as these may *reduce* the incentive for the rival to compete aggressively against the merged group.

14.2 ASSESSING THE STRENGTH OF COMPETITION FROM RIVALS

(a) General

14–002 A merger will not significantly impede effective competition if an attempt by the merged group profitably to raise prices (or reduce quality, innovation or choice) would be defeated by switching to rival suppliers, i.e. if such switching would be likely, timely and sufficient to defeat the attempted exercise of market power. When assessing the strength of competition from rival suppliers, the Commission generally starts by considering market share and concentration data and the results of any bidding studies.

(b) Market shares

14–003 The Notice on Horizontal Mergers states that market shares[5] provide a useful first indication of the importance of the merging parties' competitors.[6]

In assessing the significance of the competitive constraints posed by rivals, the Commission pays particular attention to the *gap*, if any, between the market shares of the merged group and its largest rival.[7] In *CVC / Lenzing*[8] the Commission emphasised that "the relationship between the market shares of the undertakings involved in the concentration and their competitors, especially those of the next largest, is relevant evidence of the existence of a dominant position". In *Metso / Svedala*[9] the gap between the merged group's market share and the shares of its leading competitors was treated as *decisive* on the question of whether the merged group would hold a dominant position, the Commission stating that: "The mere difference in market shares means that [the leading competitors] will not be in a position significantly to constrain the parties' competitive behaviour".

---

[5] The calculation and significance of market share data is considered in detail in s.4.2 above.
[6] Para.14.
[7] See, e.g. Case IV/M.12 *Varta / Bosch* [1991] O.J. L/320, p.26; Case COMP/M.1339 *ABB / Elsag Bailey*; Case IV/M.1286 *Johnson & Johnson / DuPuy*; Case COMP/M.1672 *Volvo / Scania* [2001] O.J. L143/74 (noting, at para.106, that the merged group would have a share 14.5 times larger than the next largest competitor on the market in question); and Case COMP/M.2947 *Verbund / EnergieAllianz* [2004] O.J. L92/91 (appeal pending in Case T-350/03 *Wirschaftskammer Karnten and best connect Ampere Strompool v Commission*), paras 106 and 128. See also Case T-282/02 *Cementbouw Handel & Industrie v Commission*, not yet reported, judgment of February 23, 2006, paras 201 and 202.
[8] Case COMP/M.2187, para.138.
[9] Case COMP/M.2033 [2004] O.J. L88/1, para.197.

(c) Concentration data

In analysing the strengths of competitors, the Commission also takes **14–004**
account of concentration data, in particular HHI scores and deltas, which
provides information about the overall structure of the market and in
particular the extent to which a few large firms control supplies or purchases.[10] For example, in *Continental / Phoenix*[11] the Commission found that
the HHI score and delta indicated that the merger would give the merged
group competitive room for manoeuvre which the remaining competitors
would be unable to limit effectively.

(d) Bidding studies

In tender markets, the Commission may examine the significance of parti- **14–005**
cular competitors or categories of competitors by investigating how often
they are invited to bid and how frequently they are successful.[12] For
example,[13] in *Group 4 Falck / Securicor*[14] the Commission emphasised that
competitor A regularly competed in tenders against Securicor and won a
large proportion of contracts, including for accounts where it was not the
incumbent supplier, and found that A would remain an effective competitor
following the merger.

14.3 VIABILITY OF ALTERNATIVE SOURCES
OF SUPPLY

(a) General

In determining whether competitors will provide an effective competitive **14–006**
constraint on the merged group, the Commission examines whether they
provide *viable* alternative sources of supply for customers.[15] If they do, the
merged group will be unable profitably to raise its prices as customers will
switch, or threaten to switch, suppliers. Analytically, as noted earlier,
determining whether competitors will provide a viable alternative source of
supply through expansion raises the same issues as an assessment of whether

---

[10] See the Notice on Horizontal Mergers, para.14. The calculation and significance of concentration data, including HHI scores and deltas, is discussed in detail in s.4.3 above.

[11] Case COMP/M.3436, para.120.

[12] The operation of tender markets and the use of bidding studies is discussed in detail in paras
6–029, 6–030 and 7–006 above.

[13] See also, e.g. Case COMP/M.2947 *Verbund / EnergieAllianz* [2004] O.J. L92/91 (appeal
pending in Case T-350/03 *Wirschaftskammer Karnten and best connect Ampere Strompool v
Commission*), para.63 and Case COMP/M.3803 *EADS / Nokia*, para.38.

[14] Case COMP/M.3396, para.142.

[15] See, e.g. Case COMP/M.1628 *TotalFina / Elf* [2001] O.J. L143/1, para.44 (concluding that a
competitor identified by the notifying parties might not be viable).

new entry[16] will prevent the merged group from exercising market power, namely that expansion from existing competitors must be *likely, timely and sufficient* to defeat the attempt to exercise market power.[17] The application of these principles to expansion by existing competitors has a number of aspects, which are considered in this section.

(b) Incentive to expand output

14–007 Viable competitors have an *incentive* to expand, i.e. they would find it profitable and strategically desirable to expand sales by winning new business if the merged group sought to exercise market power.

Competitors may lack the incentive to expand in particular in the following circumstances.[18]

(a) Their costs structures mean that expanding output would not increase their profits. This could arise, for example, if:

    (i) their marginal costs of production rise significantly as output increases even though capacity is available (e.g. if it is necessary to switch from a double to a triple shift system)[19];

    (ii) their production facilities are inferior or operate at relatively higher costs[20]; or

    (iii) they lack economies of scale which are available to the merged group.[21]

---

[16] See Ch.16.

[17] This point is recognised in the UK Office of Fair Trading's Substantive Merger Guidelines, May 2003 (*www.oft.gov.uk*), which provide, at para.4.17: "Entry by new competitors or expansion by existing competitors may be sufficient in time, scope, and likelihood to deter or defeat any attempt by the merging parties or their competitors to exploit the reduction in rivalry flowing from the merger".

[18] The US Horizontal Merger Guidelines, 1992 (amended in 1997) (*www.usdoj.gov/atr/public/guidelines/hmg.htm*) state, at para.2.22, that non-party expansion is unlikely if those firms face binding capacity constraints that could not be economically relaxed within two years or if existing excess capacity is significantly more costly to operate than capacity currently in use. The Australian Merger Guidelines, June 1999, para.5.136 (*www.accc.gov.au/content/item.phtml?itemId=719436&nodeId=file43a1f42c7eb63&fn=Merger%20Guidelines.pdf*), state: "many distribution services tend to be characterised by high fixed costs and low variable costs over a large range of output, which can promote intense rivalry even between a small number of players. In other industries, costs rise sharply when full capacity is approached. If the merged firm has the majority of capacity, the ability of remaining firms to inhibit price increases is likely to be limited. However, the costs of capacity expansion also need to be considered, which can sometimes differ markedly from the costs of new entry".

[19] This issue was identified by the UK Competition Commission in *BASF AG / Takeda Chemical Industries Ltd*, Cm. 5209, July 2001, at para.2.112.

[20] See, e.g. Case IV/M.754 *Anglo American Corporation / Lonrho* [1998] O.J. L149/21, paras 111 and 117 and Case COMP/M.3099 *Areva / Urenco / ETC JV*, para.111.

[21] Case IV/M.986 *Agfa-Gevaert / Du Pont* [1998] O.J. L211/22, para.61. As noted in s.7.6 above, the fact that a merger will result in economies of scale is not a free-standing theory of competitive harm that could justify prohibiting a merger but, in considering the viability of actual or potential competition, economies of scale may operate as a barrier to expansion or entry.

(b) They can deploy their assets more profitably for other purposes. In *Bertelsmann / Springer / JV*[22] the Commission considered whether rival printers would switch from printing advertisements to printing magazines if the merged group sought to raise its charges for printing magazines. The Commission calculated the contribution margins of printing different products, found that printing advertisements gave the lowest contribution margin, and therefore concluded that printers would seek to switch capacity away from printing advertisements into printing magazines if the opportunity arose.

(c) They are precluded from expanding their sales by quota or treaty and therefore have no incentive to compete intensively to gain share.[23]

(c) Ability to expand output

If competitors are to be a viable alternative source of supply to the merged group, they must have the ability to expand,[24] either through existing spare capacity or the ability readily to add new[25] capacity.[26] The Notice on Horizontal Mergers considers markets in which firms are unlikely to increase supply if price increases, stating:

14–008

"When market conditions are such that the competitors of the merging parties are unlikely to increase their supply substantially if prices increase, the merging firms may have an incentive to reduce output below the combined pre-merger levels, thereby raising market prices ... Such output

---

[22] Case COMP/M.3178, paras 125 to 128.

[23] See, e.g. Case COMP/M.3099 *Areva / Urenco / ETC JV*, para.106.

[24] More particularly, a competitor which lacks available capacity will have little incentive to compete aggressively against the merged group because, in order to win new business, it will have to turn away existing customers, and it will generally be more profitable for a capacity-constrained supplier largely to follow price increases by the merged group than to adopt a strategy of undercutting the merged group because the competitor will be unable to service all the customers attracted by its lower prices.

[25] It is also possible to expand capacity through de-bottlenecking, which involves replacing those parts of a production line which prevent production from being increased: see, e.g. Case COMP/M.2187 *CVC / Lenzing* [2004] O.J. L82/20, n.112.

[26] In Case COMP/M.3178 *Bertelsmann / Springer / JV*, para.106, in assessing the effect of the merger on the market for the printing of magazines, the Commission identified the following issues: "(1) whether competitors currently have sufficient spare capacity to replace these sales to a significant extent, (2) whether competitors could make available such capacity by shifting their capacity to the printing of magazines, (3) whether planned capacity extensions will make available further capacity and (4) whether potential competitors could contribute to making available further capacity for the printing of magazines in the event of a price increase". See also, e.g. Case IV/M.12 *Varta / Bosch* [1991] O.J. L320/26; Case IV/M.355 *Rhône-Poulenc / Snia*; Case IV/M.906 *Mannesmann / Vallourec*; and Case COMP/M.3056 *Celanese / Degussa / European Oxo Chemicals* [2004] O.J. L38/47. The US Horizontal Merger Guidelines, 1992 (*amended in 1997*) (*www.usdoj.gov/atr/public/guidelines/hmg.htm*) identify, at para.2.22, differences in capacities as a source of non-coordinated effects (and see Starek & Stockum, "What Makes Mergers Anticompetitive? 'Non-coordinated Effects' Analysis Under the 1992 Merger Guidelines" (1995) 63 *Antitrust Law Journal* 801, at pp.820 and 821).

expansion is, in particular, unlikely when competitors face binding capacity constraints and the expansion of capacity is costly or if existing excess capacity is significantly more costly to operate than capacity currently in use".[27]

14–009 The issue of competitors' abilities to *expand output using existing capacity*[28] has been analysed by the Commission in a series of cases, including the following:

(a) In *Rexam / American National Can*[29] the Commission stated: "the remaining competitor . . . is capacity-constrained. In this context, [the competitor] may not have any incentive to engage in price-cutting, since it will not be able to capture market share by supplying more customers in the market than it does today. In these circumstances, the parties will have the incentive to behave independently and to charge supra-competitive prices".

(b) Similarly, in *Mitsui / CVRD / Caemi*[30] the Commission stated: "Should CVRD attempt to raise . . . prices . . . customers could only defeat that price rise by obtaining larger quantities from other producers. However, the results of the Commission's investigation indicate that this is to a large extent not possible".

(c) Conversely, in *Friesland Coberco / Nutricia*[31] the Commission found that the "available spare capacity in the dairy industry would considerably constrain any efforts by the parties to increase prices as a result of the transaction".

(d) In *Kali und Salz / Solvay / JV*[32] the Commission cleared a transaction involving combined shares of 50 to 60 per cent given the general overcapacity in the sector, noting in its press release that: "The situation of overcapacity in the salt sector means that competitors will be able to increase production for other applications".

(e) In *Danish Crown / Flagship Foods*[33] the Commission emphasised that spare capacity could be used at short notice and without incurring additional costs.

---

[27] Paras 32 and 34.

[28] *De facto* maximum capacity may be less than theoretical maximum capacity because of a need for down-time for technical maintenance and switching between products; see, e.g. the discussion in Case COMP/M.2187 *CVC / Lenzing* [2004] O.J. L82/20, paras 156 and 157. In Case COMP/M.2345 *Deutsche BP / Erdölchemie* the Commission took the capacity utilisation rate that was attained in a year in which prices were very high as a "maximum"; para.47.

[29] Case COMP/M.1939, para.25.

[30] Case COMP/M.2420 [2004] O.J. L92/50, para.183.

[31] Case COMP/M.2399, para.27.

[32] Case COMP/M.2176, para.41; and see the press release IP/02/34.

[33] Case COMP/M.3401, para.11 (see also para.33).

(f) Finally, in *Aster 2 / Flint Ink*[34] the Commission emphasised that there was significant excess capacity in the industry which would allow competitors to increase their production in the very short term without incurring significant costs. The Commission stressed that each of the competitors had sufficient spare capacity readily to supply any account in Europe.

Competitors may be unable to expand (whether using existing or additional **14–010** capacity) if they have limited financial strength,[35] are restricted by contractual commitments, such as debt covenants,[36] lack parent company support,[37] or have weak management.[38] Further, if vertical integration provides a competitive advantage and the merged group is vertically integrated whilst competitors are not, this may result in a barrier to expansion.[39] Conversely,[40] competitors with low market shares may be highly effective if they are committed to expanding their presence in the market and have access to funding to drive the expansion.[41]

(d) Credible alternatives for customers

If the Commission establishes that competitors have the incentive and **14–011** ability to expand their output, it is then necessary to consider *whether they have the ability to win new business from the merged group* if it seeks to exercise market power. This requires that customers regard the competitors as *credible* alternatives, i.e. at least some customers[42] would be willing to switch to the competitors in response to an attempt by the merged group to exercise market power. In *Industri Kapital (Nordkem) / Dyno*,[43] in considering whether rival suppliers would form an adequate competitive con-

---

[34] Case COMP/M.3886, para.27.

[35] See, e.g. Case COMP/M.2220 *GE / Honeywell* [2004] O.J. L48/1, paras 302 to 304 (prohibition decision upheld on appeal on the basis of its horizontal effects in Case T-210/01 *General Electric Company v Commission*, not yet reported, judgment of December 14, 2005). In Case IV/M.580 *ABB / Daimler Benz* [1997] O.J. L11/1, competitors other than Siemens were dependent on collaboration with either the merged group or Siemens, with the consequence that the parties and Siemens had even greater market strength than their market shares suggested; para.61.

[36] Porter, *Competitive Strategy* (1998 edn, The Free Press), p.53.

[37] See Porter, *Competitive Strategy* (1998 edn, The Free Press), pp.53 and 54, noting the importance also of examining why the parents entered the business and the relationship between the business and other group companies.

[38] See Porter, *Competitive Strategy* (1998 edn, The Free Press), pp.64 and 65.

[39] See, e.g. Case COMP/M.2220 *GE / Honeywell* [2004] O.J. L48/1, para.307 (prohibition decision upheld on appeal on the basis of its horizontal effects in Case T-210/01 *General Electric Company v Commission*, not yet reported, judgment of December 14, 2005).

[40] It is also relevant to consider whether competitors might be encouraged to add additional capacity by customers, which can sponsor expansion by entering long-term agreements in advance of an investment being made (giving the investor a secure income stream to justify the capital expenditure).

[41] See, e.g. Case IV/M.42 *Alcatel / Telettra* [1991] O.J. L122/48.

[42] The question of how many customers must be willing to switch is discussed in s.(e) below.

[43] Case COMP/M.1813 [2001] O.J. L154/41, para.129.

straint on the merged group, the Commission borrowed from the SSNIP test, which is used to define the relevant antitrust market, stating: "Customers have indicated that they have switched suppliers in the past and can do so if facing a price increase of 5% to 10%".

Competitors' credibility as alternative suppliers to the merged group may be affected by a range of factors including the following:

(a) If competitors' goods are regarded by customers as *second-rate* or inferior or delivery is unreliable,[44] then customers' incentives to switch supplier are reduced and the merged group is more likely to enjoy market power.[45]

(b) If competitors' *brands* are regarded by customers as operating in different segments of the market from the merged group's, then they may form only a limited competitive constraint.[46] In *SCA / Metsä Tissue*[47] the Commission distinguished "premium" and "basic" brands and relied on survey evidence to establish that the parties' brands were better known than their closest competitor's in concluding that the competitor would have to invest in a major promotional effort to increase its market share. More generally, the Commission has in some cases distinguished between "first-tier", "second-tier" and "local" competitors to emphasise their respective competitive significance.[48]

(c) If the merged group will supply a *wider range of products or a wider range of geographic markets* than its competitors *and* the breadth of product range or geographic coverage affects purchasers' choice of suppliers, then competitors may not be regarded as a viable alternative to the merged group.[49]

---

[44] Case IV/M.774 *Saint-Gobain / Wacker-Chemie / NOM* [1997] O.J. L247/1, para.119.

[45] See, e.g. Case IV/M.53 *Aerospatiale / Alenia / de Havilland* [1991] O.J. L334/42 (alternatives not satisfying western certification standards were not regarded as viable; paras 57 to 62) and Case COMP/M.2187 *CVC / Lenzing* [2004] O.J. L82/20 (a Russian producer was not regarded by customers as reliable; para.202). In Case COMP/M.1741 *MCI WorldCom / Sprint* [2003] O.J. L300/1, the Commission sought to assess the credibility of competitors by asking customers and competitors to rank suppliers against various criteria; para.241.

[46] See the discussion of markets involving differentiated products in s.7.3 above.

[47] Case COMP/M.2097, paras 82 and 83.

[48] See, e.g. Case COMP/M.2097 *SCA / Metsä Tissue*, para.39. In Case COMP/M.1628 *Total-Fina / Elf* [2001] O.J. L143/1, the Commission also identified three categories of market player at para.200.

[49] See, e.g. Case IV/M.214 *Du Pont / ICI* [1993] O.J. L7/3; Case IV/M.774 *Saint-Gobain / Wacker-Chemie / NOM* [1997] O.J. L247/1 (range of silicon carbide grades for abrasives and refractories; paras 178, 179 and 224); Case IV/M.986 *Agfa-Gevaert / Du Pont* [1998] O.J. L211/22, paras 61 and 76; Case COMP/M.2187 *CVC / Lenzing* [2004] O.J. L82/20, para.200; and Case COMP/M.2220 *GE / Honeywell* [2004] O.J. L48/1, paras 305 and 306 (prohibition decision upheld on appeal on the basis of its horizontal effects in Case T-210/01 *General Electric Company v Commission*, not yet reported, judgment of December 14, 2005). Conversely, if competitors have wider product ranges, a merger of complementary suppliers may be pro-competitive in enabling the merged group to "catch up" with its competitors: see, e.g. Case IV/M.818 *Cardo / Thyssen*.

(d) In some markets, suppliers must reach a *critical mass* before customers regard them as a viable alternative source of supply. For
example, in an industry characterised by network effects,[50] customers
may be unwilling to switch to a recent entrant until the entrant's
customer base is sufficiently developed.[51]

Finally, competitors may be able to operate as a stronger countervailing
force by entering "teaming" arrangements between themselves.[52]

(e) Sufficiency of competitor activity

The Commission will consider whether activity by competitors would be **14–012**
sufficient to defeat an attempt by the merged group to exercise market
power.[53] For example, in *Bertelsmann / Springer / JV*[54] the Commission
found that printing magazines involved high fixed costs and suppliers generally required as high a level of capacity utilisation as possible. This meant
that the merged group could only afford to lose a limited proportion of sales
if it wanted to increase its profitability by raising prices, and the Commission found that competitors would probably be able to defeat any price
increase by raising their own sales by at least this amount.

(f) Competition from outside the market

By defining the product and geographic markets on which suppliers com- **14–013**
pete, the Commission distinguishes direct and immediate constraints on the
merged group from more tangential constraints. However, *suppliers from
outside the market* may exercise an important influence on the conduct of the
merged group[55] and, especially when taken with other factors, may prevent
the merged group from exercising market power.[56]

---

[50] See paras 6–026 and 6–027 above.

[51] In Case IV/M.737 *Ciba-Geigy / Sandoz* [1997] O.J. L201/1, the Commission concluded that
the merged group would not have a dominant position in research and development despite its
strong relative position in crop protection research and development because enough other
large companies had the necessary "critical mass".

[52] See, e.g. Case COMP/M.3920 *France Télécom / Amena*, para.50 and Case COMP/M.3304 *GE
/ Amersham*.

[53] If price discrimination is possible, then the merger would result in a significant impediment to
effective competition if the merged group could materially increases prices to some customers,
even if it could not raise prices to *all* customers; see para.15–009 below.

[54] Case COMP/M.3178, para.139. See the discussion of "critical loss analysis" in para.3–031.

[55] Vickers, "Competition Economics and Policy", speech of October 3, 2002 (*www.oft.gov.uk/
News/Speeches + and + articles/2002/index.htm*), refers to the "pitfall [of] the 'zero-one' fallacy—the tendency, once 'the market' is defined, to think of all products within it as extremely
substitutable for the products at the centre of concern, and those products beyond the
boundaries as irrelevant. In reality matters are of varying degrees, and the useful tool of
market definition must be employed with this in mind".

[56] See also Case IV/M.72 *Sanofi / Sterling Drug* (competition from products outside the product
market was taken into account in clearing the transaction); Case IV/M.430 *Procter & Gamble
/ VP Schickedanz (II)* [1994] O.J. L354/32, paras 161 to 165; Case IV/M.906 *Mannesmann /*

(a) In *Bertelsmann / Springer / JV*[57] the Commission identified Germany as the relevant geographic market for the supply of magazine printing services but, in clearing the transaction, placed significant weight on potential competition from foreign printers located fairly close to the German border.

(b) In *Mercedes-Benz / Kässbohrer*[58] the Commission identified separate antitrust markets for different types of buses but added: "the fluid boundaries between the segments [which had been found not to comprise a single market] and the flexibility on the supply side means that the competitive positions of the suppliers on the individual relevant markets are relative. In assessing the impact of the merger, these market segments cannot be considered in isolation. Rather, competitive conditions and the position of the suppliers on the overall market must also be taken into account".

(c) In *Schering / Gehe-Jenapharm*[59] the Commission found that the geographic markets (for pharmaceutical products) were national, but parallel imports (i.e. supplies from outside the relevant geographic market) nevertheless constituted an important constraint on the parties' behaviour.

(d) In *CVC / Lenzing*[60] the Commission noted that: "Despite the fact that it is appropriate to identify distinct product markets, there can be a certain degree of substitutability between [products] belonging to neighbouring product markets".

(e) In *Blokker / Toys 'R' Us (II)*[61] the Commission acknowledged that "to some extent the specialised toy outlets do face competition from other outlets outside the market selling toys, in particular in the toy season".

Vallourec; Case IV/M.997 *Swedish Match / KAV* (the Commission found that the geographic market was not wider than the EEA but took account of imports, in particular from Turkey, as exerting significant pressure on the producers situated in the EEA); Case COMP/M.2690 *Solvay / Montedison-Ausimont* (noting that market shares had to be considered with care because "there exist numerous substitutes to peracetic acid" (although the substitutes differed by application); paras 102 and 111).
[57] Case COMP/M.3178, paras 140 to 153.
[58] Case IV/M.477 [1995] O.J. L211/1, para.22.
[59] Case IV/M.781.
[60] Case COMP/M.2187 *CVC / Lenzing* [2004] O.J. L82/20, para.178, although the market investigation showed that, on the facts of that case, the competitive constraint from neighbouring markets was weak; see para.180.
[61] Case IV/M.890 [1998] O.J. L316/1, para.79.

14.4 LINKS BETWEEN THE MERGED GROUP AND ITS COMPETITORS

(a) General

The merged group may have links to its competitors, in particular through **14–014** shareholdings, cross-directorships,[62] contractual links or, indeed, because the competitors are acting together to make a joint bid for target business with the intention of dividing that business between them. Those links may affect the way in which the linked suppliers compete with the merged group following the transaction. This section should be read with para.4–022 above, which discusses the calculation of market shares when a merging party has an interest falling short of sole control in a rival supplier.

(b) Can the Commission take account of cross-shareholdings which do not confer control?

In assessing *shareholdings* held by the merging parties in their competitors, **14–015** the first question is whether the shareholding must confer control or some other specified level of influence before it may be taken into account by the Commission. In *Kesko Oy v Commission*[63] the Court of First Instance rejected such an approach, stating:

"The applicant argues, in essence, that the Commission was not entitled to aggregate the market shares of the Kesko and Tuko retailers for the purposes of assessing the effects of the concentration in issue without establishing that Kesko and Tuko had 'control' over those retailers within the meaning of Article 3 of Regulation No 4064/89, and that, since the only 'concentration' within the meaning of Article 3 was that between Kesko and Tuko, the assessment of the effect of that concentration should necessarily have been limited to the market in which Kesko and Tuko operate, namely the wholesale market.

It must be stated in that regard that Article 3 of Regulation No 4064/89 merely defines the criteria governing the existence of a 'concentration'. By contrast, where, in a proceeding under Article 22(3) of Regulation No 4064/89, the Commission finds that an operation does indeed constitute a concentration within the meaning of Article 3, its assessment of the question whether that concentration creates or strengthens a dominant position as a result of which effective competition would be significantly impeded within the territory of the Member State concerned must take

---

[62] For the US rules on cross-directorships, see Areeda & Turner, *Antitrust Law* (Aspen Law & Business, 1980), Vol.V, Ch.13.
[63] Case T-22/97 [1999] E.C.R. II-3775, paras 137 to 140.

account of the conditions laid down by Article 2(1)(a) and (b) of Regulation No 4064/89, in accordance with the first sentence of Article 22(4) of that regulation.

Thus, the Commission was not in any way bound, when assessing the effect of the concentration at issue on competition, to apply the control test referred to in Article 3 of Regulation No 4064/89 in order to determine whether the market shares of Kesko and Tuko should be aggregated. Having established the existence of the concentration between Kesko and Tuko, the Commission was required to take into account all the facts of the present case, including, in particular, the links between, on the one hand, Kesko and Tuko and, on the other, their respective retailers, in order to assess whether that concentration created or strengthened a dominant position as a result of which effective competition would be significantly impeded on the relevant Finnish markets. By the same token, the Commission was under no obligation to limit its appraisal solely to the wholesale market, since it had concluded that the concentration between Kesko and Tuko would also affect the retail market in daily consumer goods, having regard to the close links existing between, on the one hand, Kesko and Tuko and, on the other, their retailers".

This passage was relied on in *BSkyB / KirchPayTV*,[64] where the issue was whether the Commission should consider the activities of News Corporation, which indirectly held a share of 39.7 per cent in BSkyB (i.e. the issue in *BSkyB* related to interests held *in* the merging parties rather than *by* the merging parties).[65] The Commission did not need to reach a conclusion on the question of whether News Corporation controlled BSkyB because News Corporation accepted, in the light of the Court's decision in *Kesko*, that its shareholding in BSkyB could be taken into account by the Commission in making its appraisal of the market.[66]

14–016 Further, in the Commission's XXIVth Annual Report on Competition Policy, 1994,[67] the Commission stated that it "takes account of any structural links between the parties to the concentration and third parties within the same sector of activity, even if such links do not mean that the parties concerned have control, within the meaning of the Regulation, over such third parties".

---

[64] Case COMP/JV.37.

[65] See also ECMR, Art.5(4) for the rules on calculation of turnover.

[66] Para.8. On the question of the economic incentives created by minority interests, see also para.89. In Case COMP/M.2532 *FIAT / Italenergia / Montedison* the Commission did not take account of EDF's interest in Italenergia, the proposed purchaser of Montedison, because EDF did not have a controlling position in Italenergia as it was limited in both ordinary and extraordinary shareholders' meetings to casting 2% of the votes: see the discussion by Mario Monti, then the Commissioner for Competition, in a speech, "The single energy market: the relationship between competition policy and regulation", March 7, 2002 (*www.europa.eu.int/comm/competition/speeches/index_2002.html*).

[67] Para.300.

The importance of taking account of cross-shareholdings falling short of control was described in detail by the Commission in *Exxon / Mobil*[68]:

"It is indeed a well established principle under mainstream antitrust economics that, generally, the existence of links between two competing undertakings in the form of a significant interest stake of one in the other may change their incentives to compete. First, a link of this nature creates a strong financial interest of one firm in its competitor's welfare. This automatically can alter the dynamics of the competitive game as one firm is less interested in competing against the other than in finding a common strategy profitable for both. In addition, such a link can secure access to commercially sensitive information. This in turn renders the competitive conduct of each undertaking vis-à-vis the other more transparent and thus susceptible to be easily anticipated and monitored. Also, and perhaps more importantly, a link of this nature may put one undertaking in a position that enables it to influence the strategic choices of its competitor towards decisions in line with the common interest. Finally, a link of this kind has a disciplinary effect as it can expose one firm to possible retaliations of the other in the case of disagreement. All these factors may push the undertakings concerned towards a convergence of their commercial policies. It should be noted that the conduct described above is for each of the undertakings concerned absolutely rational as they are based on a profit-maximising perspective".

(c) The weight to be placed on cross-shareholdings which confer control

In *Exxon / Mobil*[69] the parties argued that Mobil had no involvement in the **14–017** day-to-day governance of a joint venture notwithstanding its joint control and that the merged group and the joint venture would have every incentive to continue to compete vigorously with each other. This was rejected: "the Commission is to assume the worst possible scenario for antitrust purposes, that is to say the alignment of the competitive strategies of Exxon / Mobil and [the joint venture] as a result of the joint control of the former over the latter".[70]

---

[68] Case IV/M.1383 [2004] O.J. L103/1, para.452.
[69] Case IV/M.1383 [2004] O.J. L103/1, paras 447 to 458.
[70] The Commission also stated, at para.449, that: "In order to ascertain the existence of a dominant position, the relations between the JV and the parents are considered on the basis of the generally correct assumption that they achieve some form of integration and that the parent company is in a position to control the commercial policy of its JV, so that from a competition point of view they are to be viewed as being not in competition with each other". Similarly, in Case IV/M.269 *Shell / Montecatini* [1994] O.J. L332/48, the Commission, at para.59, rejected an argument that a subsidiary of one of the parties should be treated as an autonomous economic entity irrespective of the question of whether the subsidiary in fact competed with other group companies because: "Under the provisions of [the ECMR], a fully-owned subsidiary must be considered to fall under the ultimate control of the parent company of the group".

(d) The weight to be placed on cross-shareholdings which do not confer control

14–018 There are four possible approaches to ascribing weights to cross-shareholdings in competitors which do not confer control. The first approach is to acknowledge that cross-shareholdings falling short of control may affect competition but to make a qualitative assessment of their significance in general terms (the "qualitative approach"). The Commission has in numerous cases found that stakes held by the merging parties in one or more of their competitors and/or cross-directorships will result in diminished competition between the merged group and the competitors in question. Such finding is also implicit in the numerous decisions by the Commission to include some or all of a rival supplier's share along with the merged group's own share when calculating market shares (see para.4–022 above). The following cases are also illustrative of this approach.[71]

(a) In *Allianz / Dresdner*[72] the merger would have created a strong "bancassurance" group. Between them, Allianz and Dresdner held 32.3 per cent of the shares in Münchener Rück, which formed part of a rival "bancassurance" group. The Commission expressed concerns about this cross-shareholding but cleared the transaction after accepting undertakings that the merging parties would reduce their joint holdings in Münchener Rück to 20.5 per cent.[73]

(b) In *Generali / INA*[74] directors of the merging parties were also members of the boards and/or executive committees of rival insurers. The Commission was concerned that such interlocking directorships might facilitate coordination in competitive behaviour and accepted undertakings to eliminate them.[75]

---

[71] See also Case IV/M.269 *Shell / Montecatini* [1994] O.J. L332/48 (noting the prevalence of joint venture links between the merging parties and their competitors and accepting an undertaking to dissolve a joint venture; paras 106 and 114); Case IV/M.1082 *Allianz / AGF* (considering a range of links between AGF and Coface which together created a risk that the two companies would not compete on the market; paras 46 to 56). However, in Case COMP/M.1745 *EADS* the Commission noted, at para.146, that the merged group would have substantially different stakes in three joint ventures, two of which were jointly controlled by another company with potentially different incentives, leading to the conclusion that "it is possible that some of the joint ventures [will] still compete with each other after the present transaction".
[72] Case COMP/M.2431.
[73] See also Case IV/M.942 *VEBA / Degussa* [1998] O.J. L201/102 (in which the Commission required the merged group to sell its stake in a joint venture when the evidence was that the merged group would be able to learn about its competitor's pricing through the joint venture); Case COMP/M.1673 *VEBA / VIAG* [2001] O.J. L188/1 (elimination of links with competitors); and Case COMP/M.2139 *Bombardier / Adtranz* [2002] O.J. L69/50 (commitment to terminate a joint venture between one of the merging parties and a competitor).
[74] Case COMP/M.1712.
[75] See also Case IV/M.1082 *Allianz / AGF*, in which the Commission accepted commitments to reduce the merged entity's shareholding in a rival supplier of *del credere* insurance and to remove personal links between the merged group and the rival supplier.

(c) In *Thyssen / Krupp*[76] Thyssen was one of the four European suppliers of escalators. Krupp had sold its escalator supply business to one of the other three European suppliers, Kone, and had not retained any direct escalator supply activities, but held a 10 per cent shareholding in Kone, had rights to acquire further shares, held a seat on the Kone board and had entered mutual non-competes with Kone. The Commission was concerned about the combination of Thyssen's existing business with Krupp's links with Kone and required undertakings to ensure that the merged group and Kone remained independent competitors.

(d) In *Solvay / Montedison-Ausimont*[77] the target was party to a 50/50 joint venture with a competitor and the Commission found that the links between the merged group and the competitor, in terms of the shared participation in the joint venture, a supply contract and information sharing, would lead the merged group and the competitor to behave as a single entity.

(e) In *United Airlines / US Airways*[78] the Commission was concerned about the reduction in competition between one of the merging parties and the second merging party's contractual partner. United Airlines was linked to Lufthansa as both were members of the Star Alliance and were party to an extensive transatlantic cooperation agreement. The Commission relied on these links in identifying concerns about the substantial reduction in competition between US Airways and Lufthansa (i.e. United Airlines' contractual partner): "the competitive effects of the proposed transaction will not only consist in the elimination of competition between US Air and United. In view of the extensive co-operation between United and Lufthansa (or SAS) on transatlantic routes, the notified concentration is also analysed as substantially reducing the competition previously existing between US Air and Lufthansa on transatlantic services".[79]

(f) *Air Liquide / BOC*[80] involved a joint offer by Air Liquide and Air Products for BOC on the basis of an agreement between the joint offerors to divide the BOC assets between them. The Commission was concerned that: "in order to be able to bid for, and subsequently split up BOC, both Air Liquide and Air Products may have to

---

[76] Case IV/M.1080.
[77] Case COMP/M.2690, para.86.
[78] Case COMP/M.2041.
[79] Paras 35 to 38. See also Case IV/M.646 *Repola / Kymmene* (membership of a joint sales organisation marketing the paper products of its members on a worldwide basis; paras 53 and 54; the Commission accepted a commitment not to sell paper products through the joint sales agency); Case IV/M.1651 *Maersk / Sea-Land* (shipping conferences; para.18); Case COMP/M.2391 *CVC / Cinven / Assidomän* (taking account of Kappa's alliance with DS Smith and SAICA in the market for corrugated cases; para.50); and Case COMP/M.2672 *SAS / Spanair* (airline alliances; paras 30 to 35).
[80] Case COMP/M.1630 [2004] O.J. L92/1.

acquire extensive knowledge of BOC's activities and have extensive contact with each other. This may endanger the confidentiality of information relating to each other's operations, and thus effective competition between the companies".[81]

14–019 The second approach is to recognise that cross-shareholdings can affect competition and to identify a method of measuring the importance of those interests (a "quantification approach"). In the Notice on Horizontal Mergers, the Commission stated[82] that in markets with cross-shareholdings or joint ventures the Commission may use a modified HHI and referred to its decision in *Exxon / Mobil*.[83] In that case, the Commission adopted a quantification approach, stating that: "a reinforcement of the equity links between companies on the same market increases the possibility for the use of market power. In order to appreciate the level of concentration in this market pre-merger and the impact of the merger, the Commission has estimated HHI indices that take into account the existence of cross shareholdings among most of the players in that market. The calculation was based on the work of Bresnahan and Salop".

Bresnahan and Salop[84] developed a "modified" HHI ("MHHI") to measure the effect of an acquisition of a non-controlling stake in a competitor.[85] Under a normal HHI calculation, the delta (i.e. the increase in HHI through the merger) is twice the product of the merging parties' market shares. Under MHHI the delta is the ownership share expressed as a decimal (e.g. a 15 per cent stake is expressed as 0.15) multiplied by the product of the merging parties' market shares. For example, a merger between two companies with market shares of 30 and 25 per cent will result in an HHI delta of $2 \times 30 \times 25 = 1,500$. But if one of the companies takes a 5 per cent non-

---

[81] Para.234.
[82] See n.25.
[83] Case IV/M.1383 [2004] O.J. L103/1, para.256.
[84] "Quantifying the Competitive Effects of Production Joint Ventures" (1986) 4 *International Journal of Industrial Organisation* 155. The authors comment, at pp.155 and 156: "By its very nature, a horizontal joint venture involves financial interest among competitors. This occurs because the profits of the joint venture are shared by the parent stockholders, which reduces the parent's private incentive to expand output and thereby lower price toward the competitive level. A second, related issue concerns the management control over the pricing and output decisions of the joint venture. Just as the parents' financial interest makes competition against the joint venture unprofitable, competitive moves by the joint venture against the parents are also self-destructive. In order to prevent unprofitable competition by the joint venture entity against its parent corporations, the parents have a private incentive to structure the joint venture agreement in a way that removes the discretion of the joint venture management over these competitive instruments and replaces discretion with either control by the parents or with a formula that determines price or output". See the discussion in Temple Lang, "Two important merger regulation judgments: the implications of Schneider-Legrand and Tetra Lavel-Sidel" (2003) EL Rev 259, at pp.269 to 271.
[85] In addition to identifying a MHHI in the case of a "silent financial interest" (i.e. a non-controlling stake), Bresnahan & Salop also articulate, at pp.158 to 168, MHHI formulae applicable in the case of: (a) control by one parent; (b) full ownership by one parent; (c) limited joint control; (d) partial merger; (e) competitor-based output formula; (f) transfer-price formula with control by distributing parent; and (g) transfer-price formula with limited joint control.

controlling stake in the other, the MHHI delta is $0.05 \times 30 \times 25 = 37.5$. This is a substantially different approach: "The difference between changes in the HHI and MHHI arises from the difference between the factors that are used to multiply the products of the merging firm's shares. The product of the market shares is multiplied by 2 in calculating the HHI to take into account the fact that each firm is effectively a half-owner of the other and has full control over its output. The product of the market shares is multiplied by the partial ownership share in calculating the MHHI to take into account the fact that one firm has a partial ownership interest in its rival and neither firm has any control over the output of the other".[86]

The third approach is to carry out a detailed analysis of the effect of the **14–020** cross-shareholding on the incentives of the merged group to compete ("a detailed incentives analysis") in the light of the possible distortive effects identified in *Exxon / Mobil*[87] in the passage quoted in para.14–016 above. Taking, by way of example, the specific question of whether a merged group with a non-controlling share in a competitor would have an incentive to increase its price, it would be necessary for the Commission to examine the merged group's loss of revenues as sales are reduced following the increase in price; its increased profits on the retained sales which are made at higher prices; and the increased share of profits as a non-controlling shareholder in the competitor which may be expected if customers switch from the merged group to the competitor in response to the merged group's price increase.[88] The incentive on the merged group to raise its prices will be greater in particular if[89]: it has a greater shareholding in the competitor, as the merged group will derive a greater share of the increased profits of the competitor; the competitor has a high market share because, other things being equal, the competitor would expect to obtain a greater proportion of the customers who switch from the merged group in response to the merged group's price increase; the merged group has a high market share, because the higher price is applied to more units of output; and/or the merged group can exercise influence over the competitor's prices so that it can be confident that the competitor will raise its prices as well.

The fourth approach is to wholly exclude from the analysis cross-shareholdings which do not confer control ("an all-or-nothing approach"). An all-or-nothing approach is not consistent with the Court of First Instance's decision in *Kesko Oy* and leaves out of account the potential effects on

---

[86] Besen, Murdoch, O'Brien, Salop and Woodbury, "Vertical and Horizontal Ownership in Cable TV: Time Warner-Turner (1996)", in Kwoka & White, eds., *The Antitrust Revolution* (3rd edn, Oxford UP, 1999), p.452, at pp.466 and 467 (this case study was omitted from the 4th edn, Oxford UP, 2004).

[87] Case IV/M.1383 [2004] O.J. L103/1.

[88] See, by analogy, the discussion in s.7.3 above of techniques for predicting the effects on price of mergers in cases involving differentiated products.

[89] See Besen, Murdoch, O'Brien, Salop and Woodbury, "Vertical and Horizontal Ownership in Cable TV: Time Warner-Turner (1996)" in Kwoka & White, eds., *The Antitrust Revolution* (3rd edn, Oxford UP, 1999), p.452 at pp.465 and 466 (this case study was omitted from the 4th edn, Oxford UP, 2004).

competition of cross-shareholdings falling short of control that were identified by the Commission in *Exxon / Mobil*. However, in *AXA / GRE*,[90] in determining whether to take account of one of the parties' 34.8 per cent stake in a competitor, the Commission asked itself whether the party could exercise *decisive influence* over the competitor. Similarly, in *Elkem / Sapa*,[91] Alcoa was the largest shareholder in Elkem with a 35.2 per cent stake but did not have control (i.e. *Elkem* was a case involving shareholdings *in* one of the merging parties rather than *by* one of the merging parties). The Commission stated that: "The market shares of Alcoa can, therefore, not be added to those of Elkem / Sapa in the market for soft alloy extrusions in which both Alcoa and Sapa are strong players". Finally, in *Jefferson Smurfit / Kappa*[92] the Commission ruled out concerns arising from Jefferson Smurfit's interest in one of Kappa's competitors on the grounds that Jefferson Smurfit could not exercise control or decisive influence over that competitor.

[90] Case COMP/M.1453, paras 20 and 24
[91] Case COMP/M.2404, para.21.
[92] Case COMP/M.3935, paras 33 to 38.

CHAPTER 15

COUNTERVAILING BUYER POWER

15.1 INTRODUCTION

Buyer power[1] arises when customers can readily adopt strategies which **15–001** would defeat any attempt by the merged group to exercise market power.[2] More particularly, buyer power comprises "the bargaining strength that the buyer has vis-à-vis the seller in commercial negotiations due to its size, its commercial significance to the seller and its ability to switch to alternative suppliers".[3] In *The Coca-Cola Company / Carlsberg A/S*[4] the Commission stated that "in an assessment of dominance the question is whether there is sufficient countervailing buyer power to neutralise the market power of the parties".

The importance of buyer power as a constraint is emphasised by an empirical review carried out by the economics consultancy, NERA, of transactions which had been subject to review under UK merger control. NERA concluded that: "Buyer power emerged as one of the strongest constraints on market power in the cases examined ... Post-merger

---

[1] See generally Areeda, Hovenkamp & Solow, *Antitrust Law* (2nd edn, Aspen Law & Business, 1998), Vol.IV, para.943; Nordemann, "Buying Power and Sophisticated Buyers in Merger Control Law: The Need for a more Sophisticated Approach" [1995] E.C.L.R. 270; Porter, *Competitive Strategy* (1998 edn, The Free Press), pp.27 to 29; Dobson & Waterson, "Countervailing Power and Consumer Prices" (1997) *The Economic Journal* 418; Steptoe, "The Power-Buyer Defense in Merger Cases" (1993) 61 *Antitrust Law Journal* 493; and Besanko, Dranove & Shanley, *Economics of Strategy* (2nd edn, John Wiley & Sons Inc, 2000), pp.363, 364 and 382.

[2] The Notice on Horizontal Mergers states, at para.64: "Countervailing buyer power in this context should be understood as the bargaining strength that the buyer has vis-à-vis the seller in commercial negotiations due to its size, its commercial significance to the seller and its ability to switch to alternative suppliers".

[3] Notice on Horizontal Mergers, para.64.

[4] Case IV/M.833 [1998] O.J. L145/41, para.81.

developments have justified the authorities' decisions in most cases".[5]

15–002   However,[6] buyer power in itself is *rarely*[7] sufficient to justify clearing a transaction without undertakings when the merger results in very high market shares because, in such cases, customers generally cannot defeat attempts by the merged group to exercise market power.[8] In other words, in contrast to the position in the case of new entry,[9] buyer power does not generally "trump" the presumption that high market shares are associated with market power. For example, in *Solvay / Montedison-Ausimont*[10] the main persalts customers were large detergents companies (Procter & Gamble, Unilever, Henkel and Reckit-Benckiser) who adopted policies of multi-sourcing, but the Commission rejected an argument based on buyer power because it was doubtful whether the purchasers could exercise buyer power given the reduction in choice arising from the merger.[11] Buyer power tends therefore to be relevant to merger appraisal in moderate to highly concentrated markets or in combination with other factors which together serve as a competitive constraint on the activities of the merged group.

The remainder of this Chapter describes the principles applied by the Commission when assessing buyer power (s.15.2) before analysing some of the leading cases on this issue (s.15.3).

---

[5] OFT Research Paper, "Merger Appraisal in Oligopolistic Markets", NERA, November 1999, at p.69 (note that the views in the paper do not necessarily represent those of the OFT). By contrast, a regression analysis of a large sample of ECMR decisions taken during the period January 1, 2000 to June 30, 2002 did not find buyer power significant in determining the outcome of notifications, but this may have been due to the quality of the data; see Lindsay, Lecchi & Williams, "Econometrics Study into European Commission Merger Decisions Since 2000" [2003] E.C.L.R. 673, at p.681.

[6] Further, in a subsequent empirical study of UK second phase merger decisions, Price WaterhouseCoopers concluded that the UK Competition Commission had found it more difficult to predict when buyer power was likely to act as a significant competitive constraint (when compared with its assessment of when new entry was likely to act as a significant competitive constraint); see "Ex Post Evaluation of Mergers", Report Prepared for the OFT, DTI and Competition Commission, March 2005 (available via *www.oft.gov.uk/NR/rdonlyres/ 4E8F 41F9-5D96-4CD4-8965-8DDA26A64DA8/0/oft767.pdf*), paras 1.12 to 1.14 and 5.44 to 5.70.

[7] However, see the discussion below of Case IV/M.1225 *Enso / Stora* [1999] O.J. L254/9 (which involved an "exceptional market structure"; see para.97).

[8] See Case COMP/M.3680 *Alcatel / Finmeccanica / Alcatel Alenia Space & Telespazio* (a merger to monopoly was not justified by the presence of significant buyer power; para.86). Further, the UK Office of Fair Trading's Substantive Merger Guidelines, May 2003 (*www.oft.gov.uk*), make this point, at para.4.28: "Logically, buyers will also be constrained in their ability to exercise buyer power if there are no remaining alternative suppliers to which they could turn".

[9] See Ch.16 below.

[10] Case COMP/M.2690, para.89.

[11] See also Case COMP/M.3436 *Continental / Phoenix*, para.213 and Case COMP/M.3465 *Syngenta CP / Advanta*, para.51.

15.2 ASSESSING BUYER POWER

(a) General

In assessing the buyer power of the merged group's *customers*, the principles **15–003** applicable to the assessment of the buyer power *of the merged group* discussed above in Ch.10 are equally valid. More specifically, in its decisions on buyer power, the Commission has taken account in particular of the following four factors[12]:

(a) the existence of viable alternatives or credible threats;

(b) whether buyers have an incentive to act;

(c) symmetry between the buyer and supplier sides; and

(d) the role of smaller customers.

These factors are analysed in the remainder of this section.

(b) Existence of viable alternatives or credible threats

First, buyer power arises when a customer has *viable alternatives* or can **15–004** make other credible threats to obtain advantage in its negotiations with the supplier. In the absence of credible alternatives or other sources of leverage, a customer, no matter how large,[13] will not enjoy buyer power. Those alternatives or sources of leverage may arise from[14]:

(a) the customer's ability to switch[15] to other suppliers of the product (inside or outside the geographic market)[16] or other products (e.g. a

---

[12] The Commission has also considered whether there is an imbalance in the commercial relationship between the buyers and sellers: see Case COMP/M.2220 *GE / Honeywell* [2004] O.J. L48/1, paras 227 and 228 (prohibition decision upheld on appeal on the basis of its horizontal effects in Case T-210/01 *General Electric Company v Commission*, not yet reported, judgment of December 14, 2005).

[13] The Notice on Horizontal Mergers states (at para.65) that large and sophisticated customers are more likely to possess buyer power than smaller firms in a fragmented industry. However, the Notice does not rule out the possibility that, on appropriate facts, small customers will enjoy material buyer power.

[14] Buyer power may also arise through forming or threatening to form a purchasing collective or contractual terms (e.g. that the supplier should meet any better quotation obtained by the customer). On the other hand, the buyer may not in practice be able to obtain an advantage if the seller has restricted its ability to offer better terms by entering most favoured customer clauses with other purchasers. (A supplier acting strategically may deliberately accept such restrictions so that it can credibly demonstrate to customers that it cannot offer them better terms).

[15] Switching costs are typically lower if products are standardised.

[16] See the Notice on Horizontal Mergers, para.65. See also Case IV/M.42 *Alcatel / Telettra* [1991] O.J. L122/48, paras 39 and 40.

purchaser which dual sources[17] may[18] be able credibly to threaten to switch demand to the other supplier unless that supplier is known by the first supplier to be capacity-constrained)[19];

(b) sponsorship of new entry[20] (e.g. awarding a long-term contract in advance of the supplier commencing construction of a new factory);

(c) starting own-production[21] or increasing own-production[22];

(d) delaying purchases[23];

(e) threats to switch suppliers of other products supplied by the merged group or of products supplied by the merged group in other geographic markets[24];

---

[17] Conversely, a merger may *create* or *increase* market power by undermining a dual-sourcing strategy; see the Notice on Horizontal Mergers, para.31 and PricewaterhouseCoopers, "Ex Post Evaluation of Mergers", Report Prepared for the OFT, DTI and Competition Commission, March 2005 (available via *www.oft.gov.uk/NR/rdonlyres/4E8F41F9-5D96-4CD4-8965-8DDA26A64DA8/0/oft767.pdf*), para.1.13.

[18] In Case COMP/M.3687 *Johnson & Johnson / Guidant*, the Commission stated, at para.238: "multiple sourcing does not necessarily translate in the absence of competition concerns. Customers can source from multiple suppliers as long as there is a sufficient number of them to choose from". See also para.270, in which the Commission concluded that the fact that the merging parties were one another's closest competitors in a differentiated product market undermined the argument that the merger did not give rise to competition concerns because customers tended to dual source.

[19] One issue is whether the customers are *aware* of the other potential suppliers.

[20] See the Notice on Horizontal Mergers, para.65. See also Case COMP/M.1882 *Pirelli / BICC* [2003] O.J. L70/35, para.76 and Case COMP/M.3732 *Procter & Gamble / Gillette*, para.123. Baker & Lofaro, "Buyer Power and the Enso / Stora Decision" [2000] E.C.L.R. 187, at pp.188 and 189, raise the question of whether the threat of sponsoring new entry is less potent when there would be a time lag before entry occurs and conclude that, in cases of delay, the time lag may be counterbalanced by the length of time the capacity would be in competition with the merged group.

[21] See the Notice on Horizontal Mergers, para.65 and, e.g. Case COMP/M.3035 *Berkshire Hathaway / Converium / Gaum / JV*, para.43. See also Scherer & Ross, *Industrial Market Structure and Economic Performance* (3rd edn, Houghton Mifflin Co, 1990), p.530.

[22] See, e.g. Case COMP/M.2358 *Flextronics / Ericsson*, para.12 (the Commission found that the most significant customers were "sophisticated buyers with significant in-house production capabilities providing them with an effective competitive alternative to outsourcing") and Case COMP/M.3351 *ArvinMeritor / Volvo (Assets)*, para.13. For a summary of the benefits of "tapered integration" (when a company produces some of its requirements in-house and purchases the balance in the market), see Besanko, Dranove & Shanley, *Economics of Strategy* (2nd edn, John Wiley & Sons Inc, 2000), p.183.

[23] See the UK Office of Fair Trading's Substantive Merger Guidelines, May 2003 (*www.oft. gov.uk*), para.4.27.

[24] In Case COMP/M.2621 *SEB / Moulinex* the Commission found that a merger of suppliers of small domestic electrical goods did not give rise to substantive concerns in certain geographic markets on the grounds that any attempt by the merged group to exercise market power in the supply of those categories of goods where the merged group had high market shares would be defeated because customers could reduce their purchases of categories of goods where the merged group's market share was lower. The Commission referred to this type of buyer power as a "range effect". In that case the Commission cleared the merger without commitments in Member States in which the sales of the merged group in product markets with shares exceeding 40% accounted for less than 10% of the merged group's total sales in that Member State. In Case T-114/02 *BaByliss v Commission* [2003] E.C.R. II-1279, at paras 352 to 363, the

(f) threats to compete aggressively in other markets in which purchasers and suppliers are both active[25];

(g) awarding contracts through tenders,[26] particularly if the tenders can be designed to improve the efficiency of the market[27];

(h) entering short-term contracts with suppliers[28];

(i) monitoring costs[29];

(j) in the case of retailers, delisting[30] or positioning the supplier's products in less favourable parts of the shop[31]; and

(k) an awareness of the vulnerabilities or "threat points"[32] of the supplier, in particular if those vulnerabilities make it clear to both parties that the seller will lose more than the buyer[33] from a failure to reach an agreement[34] (e.g. if the supplier has high fixed costs[35] and is

---

Court of First Instance overturned this part of the Commission's decision in particular on the grounds that the Commission had not demonstrated that the merged group's customers were likely to exercise buyer power in this way.

[25] Case COMP/M.2399 *Friesland Coberco | Nutricia*, para.25.

[26] See, e.g. Case COMP/M.2690 *Solvay | Montedison-Ausimont*, para.125; Case COMP/M.3216 *Oracle | PeopleSoft* [2005] O.J. L218/6, para.205 (noting that buyers of software were very sophisticated and used a range of techniques to exert competitive pressure on the bidders); and Case COMP/M.3680 *Alcatel | Finmeccanica | Alcatel Alenia Space & Telespazio*, para.73. In Case IV/M.950 *Hoffmann-La Roche | Boehringer Mannheim* [1998] O.J. L234/14, the Commission found, at para.104, that the use of calls to tender would not increase the countervailing power of customers to a large extent because they were used relatively infrequently and requests for tenders were generally for small volumes organised by regional purchasing organisations.

[27] See PriceWaterhouseCoopers, "Ex Post Evaluation of Mergers", Report Prepared for the OFT, DTI and Competition Commission, March 2005 (available via *www.oft.gov.uk/NR/rdonlyres/4E8F41F9-5D96-4CD4-8965-8DDA26A64DA8/0/oft767.pdf*), para.5.51, contemplating that the efficiency of the market could be improved by removing information asymmetries or internalising externalities. See also the Report's more general discussion of the role of incentives in the exercise of buyer power at paras 5.65 to 5.70.

[28] See, e.g. Case COMP/M.2690 *Solvay | Montedison-Ausimont*, para.125.

[29] See, e.g. Case COMP/M.3680 *Alcatel | Finmeccanica | Alcatel Alenia Space & Telespazio*, paras 73 and 109.

[30] See, e.g. Case COMP/M.3732 *Procter & Gamble | Gillette*, para.127 (noting that retailers had de-listed the parties' "must stock" brands).

[31] See the UK Office of Fair Trading's Substantive Merger Guidelines, May 2003 (*www.oft.gov.uk*), para.4.27.

[32] PriceWaterhouseCoopers, "Ex Post Evaluation of Mergers", Report Prepared for the OFT, DTI and Competition Commission, March 2005 (available via *www.oft.gov.uk/NR/rdonlyres/4E8F41F9-5D96-4CD4-8965-8DDA26A64DA8/0/oft767.pdf*), suggest, at para.5.50, that measurement of whether threat points are strong or weak is difficult, particularly when switching costs are high.

[33] The seller will of course be searching for vulnerabilities on the part of the buyer, e.g. if the buyer requires the product for important downstream activities and the seller is the most attractive source of supply then the seller may be better positioned to accommodate delays in reaching agreement.

[34] This involves a comparison of the next best alternatives to an agreement for both the purchaser and the seller.

[35] PriceWaterhouseCoopers, "Ex Post Evaluation of Mergers", Report Prepared for the OFT, DTI and Competition Commission, March 2005 (available via *www.oft.gov.uk/NR/rdonlyres/4E8F41F9-5D96-4CD4-8965-8DDA26A64DA8/0/oft767.pdf*) state, at para.5.51, that buyer

dependent on the customer for volumes which enable it to cross the break-even point[36]; this arises most obviously when the buyer purchases a large proportion of the supplier's output; in such cases a threat to switch small but strategic volumes of business may confer substantial bargaining power).[37]

15–005 In determining whether a buyer has credible alternative suppliers to the merged group[38] the Commission considers whether customers have information about other suppliers,[39] the importance of product branding,[40] the availability of close substitutes,[41] and whether the supplier has the status of an "unavoidable trading partner".[42] In *Nestlé / Perrier*[43] the merging parties, which supplied bottled water, argued that retailers would exercise coun-

---

power may be increased if purchasers have good sources of information about suppliers' costs; at para.5.60 they discuss a case in which buyer power was substantial because the purchasers insisted on "open-book" contracts (giving the purchasers information about the supplier's costs) and devoted significant effort to the monitoring of performance.

[36] Or if the supplier's ability to sell complementary or future products to the purchaser or to sell to other buyers is dependent on making the sale.

[37] In Case COMP/M.3732 *Procter & Gamble / Gillette*, para.125, the Commission noted that retailers provide important "gatekeeper" functions for suppliers of consumer brands because retailers which carry the brand ensure that customers remain familiar with it.

[38] See Case COMP/M.2097 *SCA / Metsä Tissue*, para.87. In this case the dominant sellers had around 80 to 90% of the market. The Commission therefore found that buyers had no adequate choice of alternative suppliers. In Case IV/M.1578 *Sanitec / Sphinx* [2000] O.J. L294/1, the Commission noted, at para.221, that "in order to exercise buying power, wholesalers must have viable alternative suppliers they could switch to". See also Case COMP/M.1882 *Pirelli / BICC* [2003] O.J. L70/35, para.75; Case COMP/M.2498, *UPM-Kymmene / Haindl* [2002] O.J. L233/38; and Case T-282/02 *Cementbouw Handel & Industrie v Commission*, not yet reported, judgment of February 23, 2006, paras 231 and 232; Case COMP/M.2499 *Norske Skog / Parenco / Walsum* [2002] O.J. L233/38, paras 102 and 105.

[39] See Case IV/M.1524 *Airtours / First Choice* [2000] O.J. L93/1, para.124. In this case (which was quashed on appeal for reasons not affecting the Commission's conclusions on this issue in Case T-342/99 *Airtours plc v Commission* [2002] E.C.R. II-2585), it was found that market imperfections ("the difficulty of comparing competing products from the limited information available in tour operators' brochures, and the 'sight unseen' nature of holiday purchases") limited any buyer power that the consumers might have.

[40] See Case COMP/M.2097 *SCA / Metsä Tissue*, para.89. The Commission noted that, for branded products, switching volumes between suppliers can only be a credible threat if other comparable brands are available. See also Case IV/M.623 *Kimberly-Clark / Scott* [1996] O.J. L183/1, para.186(i); Case IV/M.794 *Coca-Cola Enterprises / Amalgamated Beverages Great Britain*, paras 140 and 182; Case IV/M.833 *The Coca-Cola Company / Carlsberg A/S* [1998] O.J. L145/41, para.81; and Case COMP/M.3149 *Procter & Gamble / Wella* (finding that buyer power was limited when manufacturers offered strong or well-performing brands that retailers must have in order to offer their customers a competitive assortment of brands; para.57).

[41] See Case COMP/M.2314 *BASF / Eurodiol / Pantochim* [2002] O.J. L132/45, para.115. The Commission noted that "customers in the market investigation consider that they have no buyer power, because [the product] is in short supply and there is little choice of who to buy from".

[42] In Case COMP/M.2220 *GE / Honeywell* [2004] O.J. L48/1, at para.227, the Commission noted that large airlines were not likely or willing to exert significant buyer power against General Electric as a supplier of jet engines because the airlines required spare parts, licences and repair services from General Electric which made General Electric an "unavoidable trading partner" (prohibition decision upheld on appeal on the basis of its horizontal effects in Case T-210/01 *General Electric Company v Commission*, not yet reported, judgment of December 14, 2005).

[43] Case IV/M.190 [1992] O.J. L356/1, para.80.

tervailing buyer power, but the Commission rejected this: "In other cases decided by the Commission where buying power was one of the elements creating a counterweight, the products involved were generally intermediary products or products where long-term contracts or cooperation agreements for development of the products were involved which can create a more balanced seller-buyer relationship, provided the buyers are sufficiently concentrated. This is not the case for bottled waters which are widely used consumer products where the retailers only reflect the demands of consumers".

(c) Whether buyers have an incentive to act

Secondly, the Commission considers whether buyers have an *incentive to switch* supplier if price is increased.[44] If purchasers can pass through increases in price to their customers, they may have little incentive to resist increases in price. In *BaByliss v Commission*[45] the Court of First Instance found that the Commission had not demonstrated that buyer power would act as an effective countervailing force because the exercise of buyer power by the customers (retailers of small household electrical goods) was no more plausible than an agreement between those customers and the manufacturers to maximise their respective interests.[46] **15–006**

Further, the Notice on Horizontal Mergers, states that: "it may be important to pay particular attention to the incentives of buyers to utilise their buyer power. For example, a downstream firm may not wish to make an investment in sponsoring new entry if the benefits of such entry in terms of lower input costs could also be reaped by its competitors".[47]

Buyers generally have a greater incentive to exercise any power that they may have in the following three circumstances: **15–007**

(a) When the buyer's purchases represent a large proportion of its input costs, the buyer will generally be more price-sensitive and more willing to shop around.[48]

(b) When the end-product market is itself competitive, there will com-

---

[44] See Case IV/M.1225 *Enso / Stora* [1999] O.J. L254/9, para.91; contrast Case COMP/JV.55 *Hutchison / RCPM / ECT* [2003] O.J. L223/1, para.122.

[45] Case T-114/02 [2003] E.C.R. II-1279, paras 357 and 358.

[46] See also Case IV/M.430 *Procter & Gamble / VP Schickedanz (II)* [1994] O.J. L354/32, para.170; Case IV/M.623 *Kimberly-Clark / Scott* [1996] O.J. L183/1, para.194; and Case IV/M.754 *Anglo American Corporation / Lonrho* [1998] O.J. L149/21, para.120. See also Areeda, Hovenkamp & Solow, *Antitrust Law* (2nd edn, Aspen Law & Business, 1998), Vol.IV, para.943b.

[47] Para.66.

[48] PriceWaterhouseCoopers, "Ex Post Evaluation of Mergers", Report Prepared for the OFT, DTI and Competition Commission, March 2005 (available via *www.oft.gov.uk/NR/rdonlyres/4E8F41F9-5D96-4CD4-8965-8DDA26A64DA8/0/oft767.pdf*) note, at paras 5.51 and 5.62, that buyer power may be increased if the purchaser devotes substantial effort to the negotiations.

monly[49] be no or limited scope to pass through increases in input costs.[50]

(c) When there is competition in a downstream market, a purchaser of an input used to produce *one of the products* sold on that market *but not others* is more likely to restrain the conduct of the supplier of the input,[51] because the purchaser has an incentive to control costs which cannot be passed on.

(d) Symmetry between the buyer and supplier sides

15–008 Thirdly, the Commission investigates whether concentration on the buyer side is *symmetrical* with concentration on the supplier side.[52]

(e) The role of smaller customers

15–009 Fourthly, the Commission considers the positions of *all* customers not just the larger ones.[53] It examines the welfare of each buyer separately and not simply the stronger or even a majority of buyers and it does not seek to balance benefits to certain buyers against detriments to others. The Notice on

---

[49] If the downstream market is perfectly competitive *and* the increase in upstream cost affects all downstream producers (i.e. the cost is "common") then the increase in cost will be passed on in full by the downstream producers (as it will serve simply to increase the marginal costs facing the downstream industry).

[50] In Case COMP/M.1940 *Framatome / Siemens / Cogema / JV* [2001] O.J. L289/8, the Commission noted, at para.130, that utilities had substantial buyer power, emphasising that: "With the current liberalisation process of the energy markets, the majority of [the merged group's customers] are required to lower their costs". In Case COMP/M.1882 *Pirelli / BICC* [2003] O.J. L70/35, the Commission noted, at para.49, that deregulation of utilities markets had increased utilities' incentives to bargain aggressively with their suppliers.

[51] Case IV/M.214 *Du Pont / ICI* [1993] O.J. L7/13. See also Case COMP/M.2187 *CVC / Lenzing* [2004] O.J. L82/20, paras 183 to 192.

[52] See Case IV/M.833 *The Coca-Cola Company / Carlsberg A/S* [1998] O.J. L145/41, para.81; Case IV/M.1157 *Skanska / Scancem* [1999] O.J. L183/1 (noting that the substantial proportions of each customer's requirements purchased from Scancem revealed that customers were significantly more dependent on Scancem than vice versa; para.89); Case IV/M.1225 *Enso / Stora* [1999] O.J. L254/9, para.97; Case IV/M.1517 *Rhodia / Donau Chemie / Albright & Wilson*, para.55; Case COMP/M.1630 *Air Liquide / BOC* [2004] O.J. L92/1, paras 117 and 119; Case COMP/JV.55 *Hutchison / RCPM / ECT* [2003] O.J. L223/1, para.119; Case COMP/ M.3431 *Sonoco / Ahlstrom* [2005] O.J. L159/13, para.90; and Case COMP/M.3687 *Johnson & Johnson / Guidant*, para.238. See also Case IV/M.1313 *Danish Crown / Vestjyske Slagterier* [2000] O.J. L20/1 (for the customers, the merging parties supplied a "must stock" product; whereas the merging parties had the option to export and were therefore not nearly so dependent on their customers as their customers were on them; para.173); Case COMP/ M.3680 *Alcatel / Finmeccanica / Alcatel Alenia Space & Telespazio* (merger to monopoly not justified by the presence of significant buyer power; para.86); and Case T-282/02 *Cementbouw Handel & Industrie v Commission*, not yet reported, judgment of February 23, 2006, paras 231 and 232.

[53] There is, though, a materiality threshold in the ECMR in the sense that a transaction can only be prohibited if it results in effective competition being *significantly* impeded in the common market or a substantial part of it: see s.2.4(d) above.

Horizontal Mergers states[54]: "Countervailing buyer power cannot be found to sufficiently off-set potential adverse effects of a merger if it only ensures that a particular segment of customers, with particular bargaining strength, is shielded from significantly higher prices or deteriorated conditions after the merger".[55] Further, in *Nestlé / Perrier*[56] the Commission stated: "In the enforcement of the competition rules, the Commission must also pay attention to the protection of the weaker buyers. Even if some buyers might have a certain buying power, in the absence of sufficient competitive pressure on the market, it cannot be excluded that Nestlé and BSN apply different conditions of sale to the various buyers". Similarly, in *SCA / Metsä Tissue*[57] the Commission found that "even if the largest customers would be able to exercise some countervailing buyer power this would not protect smaller customers, and the new entity would still be able to raise prices above the pre-merger level". By contrast, in *Procter & Gamble / Gillette*[58] the Commission considered the position of smaller retailers but ruled out any concerns. In *Aster 2 / Flint Ink*[59] the Commission noted that smaller customers bundled their purchasing requirements to increase their leverage.

Buyer power arguments are of little or no relevance in markets in which price discrimination is possible. In such markets, the more powerful buyers may be able to protect their positions but the weaker purchasers will generally not benefit from the powerful buyers' negotiating position.

15.3 LEADING DECISIONS ON BUYER POWER

(a) Commission decisions

The leading case on buyer power is *Enso / Stora*.[60] In that case, the merged **15–010** group's share of the liquid packaging board market would have been between 50 and 70 per cent.[61] However, the merger was cleared, principally because of the buyer power of the three main customers. The Commission stated: "the merger will result in a market structure with one large and two smaller suppliers facing one large and two smaller buyers. This is a rather

---

[54] Para.67.
[55] The equivalent text in the 2002 draft Commission Notice on Horizontal Mergers (para.77, citing Case IV/M.1225 *Enso / Stora* [1999] O.J. L254/9, paras 95 and 96) contemplated that smaller purchasers may in certain circumstances benefit from the exercise of buyer power by the larger purchasers: "The Commission may conclude that buyer power is sufficient to prevent a creation or strengthening of a dominant position as a result of which effective competition would be significantly impeded if the smaller customers without buyer power will not be faced with significantly higher prices or deteriorated conditions after the merger".
[56] Case IV/M.190 [1992] O.J. L356/1, para.78.
[57] Case COMP/M.2097.
[58] Case COMP/M.3732, paras 128 to 130.
[59] Case COMP/M.3886, para.26.
[60] Case IV/M.1225 [1999] O.J. L254/9. See also Baker & Lofaro, "Buyer Power and the Enso / Stora Decision" [2000] E.C.L.R. 187.
[61] Para.74.

exceptional market structure. On balance, the Commission considers that the buyers in these rather special market circumstances have sufficient countervailing buyer power to remove the possibility of the parties exercising market power".[62] The Commission examined carefully the incentives facing the suppliers and the customers and concluded that the relationship was one of "mutual dependency".[63] In particular, it was hard, for technical reasons, for customers to switch supplier[64] but, on the other hand, the three customers placed orders large enough to fill at least one board machine in an industry in which high rates of utilisation were needed to achieve satisfactory levels of profitability[65]; Tetra Pak could sponsor new entry or expansion[66]; the two smaller customers sourced strategic volumes from the US[67]; and customers had an incentive to control their input costs as liquid packaging board represented a substantial proportion of the final selling price of the output.[68] The Commission also considered whether the merged group would be able to exercise market power in its dealings with the two smaller customers (as opposed to the largest, Tetra Pak), but dismissed this, stating: "in the case of Elopak and SIG Combibloc, it also has to be considered that the parties will have an incentive to have both companies as major players in the market in order to not to become completely dependent on Tetra Pak. Therefore, while the concern that Elopak and SIG Combibloc could be disadvantaged by the merger in comparison with Tetra Pak is not completely removed, it also has to be recognised that the countervailing buyer power of Tetra Pak will for this reason, to a certain extent, spill over to Elopak and SIG Combibloc as well".[69]

15–011   The Commission also considered buyer power arguments in the following cases.

(a) In *Air Liquide / BOC*[70] the Commission emphasised that the supply-side was highly concentrated even before the merger, in contrast to the demand side, which was much less concentrated.[71] It also found on the facts that customer procurement strategies and contract award procedures[72] did not confer substantial buyer power on the merged group's customers,[73] in particular because an incumbent supplier which had already invested in infrastructure on the customer's site would be able to make the most economical offer[74] and would have greater knowledge of the customer.[75]

---

[62] Para.97.
[63] Para.86.
[64] Para.86
[65] Paras 90 and 94.
[66] Para.91.
[67] Para.94.
[68] Para.91.
[69] Para.96.
[70] Case COMP/M.1630 [2004] O.J. L92/1.
[71] Paras 117 and 119.
[72] Contrast Case IV/M.692 *Electrowatt / LandisGyr* and Case IV/M.1298 *Kodak / Imation*.
[73] Paras 121 to 144.
[74] Para.134.
[75] Para.133.

(b) In *Hutchison / RCPM / ECT*[76] the Commission emphasised that the "concentration on the customer side, such as it may be, must in any event be compared to the concentration existing on the supply side". The Commission also emphasised that port handling charges, which would be set by the merged group, were "only one, and not the most important, factor when shipping lines choose which port to call at". The fact that other factors were important or more important meant that "there will often be a large amount of manoeuvre for the terminal operators to raise the port handling charges, without this increase being sufficient to justify a change of port for the shipping lines".

(c) In *Danish Crown / Vestjyske Slagterier*[77] the Commission recognised that two buyers between them had a substantial market share (over 50 per cent in Denmark) and were able to purchase on more favourable terms than the smaller purchasers, but found that this did not mean that there was sufficient countervailing power to prevent the emergence of a dominant position since: the sellers could export their products; the sellers were dominant not only on the market for Danish pork but also on the closely related market for Danish beef; and Danish pork was a "must stock" item in a Danish supermarket.

(d) In *Nestlé / Perrier*[78] the Commission found that purchasers lacked buyer power as the merged group supplied "must stock" brands, which had no available substitutes.[79] The Commission also focused on the price increases achieved by the suppliers in the four years preceding the merger as evidence that there was no effective countervailing buyer power in the market.

(e) In *UPM-Kymmene / Haindl*[80] and *Norske Skog / Parenco / Walsum*[81] the Commission focused on the high break-even utilisation rate and noted that when demand was low or there was over-capacity this would give customers higher countervailing buyer power.[82] However, the Commission found that customers' *ability to switch* in these cases was limited by the time and cost involved. This analysis was supported by the fact that customers ranked continuing business relationship ahead of price as the most important factor in their choice of

---

[76] Case COMP/JV.55 [2003] O.J. L223/1, paras 119 and 122.

[77] Case IV/M.1313 [2000] O.J. L20/1, paras 172 and 173.

[78] Case IV/M.190 [1992] O.J. L356/1.

[79] See also Case COMP/M.1578 *Sanitec / Sphinx* [2000] O.J. L294/1. Baker & Coscelli, "The Role of Market Shares in Differentiated Product Markets" [1999] E.C.L.R. 412, at p.418, argue that, even in the case of "must stock" brands, retailers can reduce the shelf space provided to the brand in question and promote rival products. See also Baker & Wu, "Applying the Market Definition Guidelines of the European Commission" [1998] E.C.L.R. 273, at p.276.

[80] Case COMP/M.2498 [2002] O.J. L233/38.

[81] Case COMP/M.2499 [2002] O.J. L233/38.

[82] Para.66.

supplier[83] and, in order to win new business, suppliers had to offer significant discounts.[84] Further, the Commission found that customers purchasing large volumes would find it difficult to switch.[85] These factors all served to limit the extent of the buyer power in the case.

(f) In *General Electric / Honeywell*[86] the Commission focused on the market shares and balance in the commercial relationship between buyers and sellers. Since the supplier of aircraft engines, General Electric, also supplied customers with essential spare parts and repair services, they lacked bargaining power.[87]

(g) In *Pirelli / BICC*[88] four major buyers represented between 70 and 100 per cent of sales in various countries. The Commission found that possible seller power was counterbalanced by buyer power because "the demand side is dominated by sophisticated customers, purchasing power cables in a bidding process". The Commission noted that the bidding process was conducted in such a way that "strong incentives exist for all competitors to bid aggressively for each contract".

(h) In *Lucas / Eaton*[89] an ability to switch to own production was found to confer buyer power, although the purchasers in that case generally produced the product in-house in any event as well as purchasing in the market.

(i) In *CVC / Lenzing*[90] the Commission noted that: "Whilst it may be surprising to note that even big tampons manufacturers have insufficient buying power to effectively constrain the independence of competitive behaviour of the merged entity, it should be considered that these companies are to a large extent 'locked in' by high switching costs. Even though the big tampons manufacturers belong to industrial groups many times larger than the viscose producers, they will have no other choice than to source their supplies with the merged entity...". This passage confirms that buyer power does not depend on the mere size of the purchaser.

(j) In *Guinness / Grand Metropolitan*[91] the Commission identified the

[83] Para.102.
[84] Para.104.
[85] Para.105.
[86] Case COMP/M.2220 [2004] O.J. L48/1 (prohibition decision upheld on appeal on the basis of its horizontal effects in Case T-210/01 *General Electric Company v Commission*, not yet reported, judgment of December 14, 2005).
[87] Para.227.
[88] Case COMP/M.1882 [2003] O.J. L70/35, paras 77 to 80.
[89] Case IV/M.149, para.37(b).
[90] Case COMP/M.2187 [2004] O.J. L82/20, para.223.
[91] Case IV/M.938 [1998] O.J. L288/24, para.68. The passage quoted is a summary of the Commission's Statement of Objections; see also the subsequent discussions in paras 69 to 78.

following criteria as necessary for the existence of countervailing buyer power in consumer markets as a means of preventing the creation or strengthening of a dominant supply position at a higher level in the distribution chain: "The retail and wholesale customers must include several who are each responsible for a significant share of sales by the dominant supplier and by his competitors and have the necessary technical facilities and bargaining skills to put that advantage to use in the buying process. Crucially, there must be alternative suppliers capable of offering an equivalent range of products on equally favourable terms and conditions and the retailer or wholesaler must have effective power to delist brands if the terms on which he is offered them are not satisfactory".

(b) The BaByliss decision

The Court of First Instance's decision in *BaByliss v Commission*[92] raises a **15–012** legal issue about the scope to rely on buyer power in approving a concentration. The Court stated that, insofar as the Commission had concluded that the merged group's customers would be able to *penalise* the merged group's exercise of market power, this would involve the customers *preventing the abuse* of a dominant position rather than preventing the *emergence* of a dominant position and the ECMR (under the substantive test as it then stood) was concerned with the prevention of the creation or strengthening of a dominant position and not the abuse of one. However, this point is more semantic than real: if the merged group's customers are able effectively to penalise attempts to exercise market power then they will not suffer as a result of the merger.

---

[92] Case T-114/02 [2003] E.C.R. II-1279, para.362.

CHAPTER 16

NEW ENTRY

16.1 INTRODUCTION

16–001 If entry[1] into a market[2] is sufficiently easy then a merger is unlikely to create any substantive competition concerns.[3] More particularly, the Commission will clear a transaction, even if the merged group will enjoy high market shares, if any attempt by the merged group[4] to increase price or reduce quality, variety or innovation would be defeated by new entry by rival suppliers.[5]

This Chapter discusses the principles applied by the Commission in assessing possible new entry in s.16.2 and describes barriers to entry separately in s.16.3.

---

[1] See generally, the International Competition Network, "Analysis of Merger Guidelines", Ch.5, "Assessment of Market Entry and Expansion (Barriers to Entry)" (*www.international competitionnetwork.org/seoul/amg_chap5_barriers.pdf*); ABA Section of Antitrust Law, *Market Power Handbook* (ABA Publishing, 2005), Ch.VII; Besanko, Dranove & Shanley, *Economics of Strategy* (2nd edn, John Wiley & Sons Inc, 2000), pp.362, 363, 380 and 381; and Federal Trade Commission and Department of Justice, "Commentary on the Horizontal Merger Guidelines", 2006 (available via *www.ftc.gov/os/2006/03/CommentaryontheHorizontalMergerGuidelinesMarch2006.pdf*), Ch.3. Art.2(1) of the ECMR requires the Commission, in appraising concentrations, to take account of "potential competition from undertakings located either within or outwith the Community".

[2] It is important to distinguish new entry as a source of potential competition *to* the merged group from the elimination through the merger of potential competition *from* one of the merging parties which is a theory of competitive harm, i.e. a possible ground for objecting to transactions (see Ch.9).

[3] Notice on Horizontal Mergers, para.68.

[4] Whether through coordinated effects or non-coordinated effects.

[5] Church & Ware, *Industrial Organization A Strategic Approach* (McGraw-Hill, 2000), pp.728 and 729 argue that the fact that the merger is occurring is evidence that new entry will not be sufficient to overcome any anti-competitive effects of the merger, because a merger will not be privately profitable unless there are entry barriers, even if there are efficiency gains.

16.2 RELEVANT PRINCIPLES

(a) Test of likely, timely and sufficient

In order to defeat attempts by the merged group profitably to raise price or **16–002** reduce quality, variety or innovation, new entry must be *likely, timely and sufficient* in its magnitude and scope to deter or defeat any potential anti-competitive effects of the merger.[6] In *Nestlé / Perrier*[7] the Commission explained the test in the following terms:

"To address the question of potential competition it needs to be examined whether there exists competitively meaningful and effective entry that could and would be likely to take place so that such entry would be capable of constraining the market power of the [merged group]. The question is not whether new local water suppliers or foreign firms can merely enter by producing and selling bottled water but whether they are likely to enter and whether they would enter on a volume and price basis which would quickly and effectively constrain a price increase or prevent the maintenance of a supra-competitive price. The entry would have to occur within a time period short enough to deter the company(ies) concerned from exploiting their market power".

The Commission focuses on the likely reactions of potential entrants in the event that the merged group seeks to exercise market power and *not* simply on the question of whether barriers to entry to the market are high or low—although an assessment of barriers to entry forms an important *part* of the Commission's analysis.

---

[6] See the Notice on Horizontal Mergers, para.68. The Commission's formulation is consistent with the US Horizontal Merger Guidelines, 1992 (amended in 1997) (*www.usdoj.gov/atr/ public/guidelines/hmg.htm*), s.3.0. The New Zealand Merger Guidelines, 2004 (*www.com com.govt.nz/Publications/ContentFiles/Documents/MergersandAcquisitionsGuidelines.PDF*), para.6.3, refer to the test as "the let test" (i.e. entry of new participants in response to the exercise of market power must be *likely*, sufficient in *extent* and *timely*). See also the UK Office of Fair Trading's Substantive Merger Guidelines, May 2003 (*www.oft.gov.uk*) ("Entry by new competitors or expansion by existing competitors may be sufficient in time, scope, and likelihood to deter or defeat any attempt by the merging parties or their competitors to exploit the reduction in rivalry flowing from the merger"; para.4.17; see also para.4.20). See also Baker, "Responding to Developments in Economics and the Courts: Entry in the Merger Guidelines", 2002, (available at *www.usdoj.gov/atr/hmerger/11252.htm*). Shepherd, Shepherd & Shepherd, "Sharper Focus: Market Shares in the Merger Guidelines" [2000] *Antitrust Bulletin* 835, at pp.859 to 862 criticise the focus in the US Horizontal Merger Guidelines on potential entrants as turning attention from the centre of the market to its periphery.
[7] Case IV/M.190 [1992] O.J. L356/1, para.91.

(b) Likelihood of entry

16–003 There are three principal and connected elements to the assessment of the *likelihood of entry*.[8]

    (a) Fundamentally, entry is unlikely unless it would be profitable.[9]

        (i) If entry is possible without incurring any sunk costs (i.e. if barriers to entry and exit are nil), then uncommitted, "hit and run" entry will occur in response to any attempt by incumbents to exercise market power—such "uncommitted entry" is closely connected with the concept of contestable markets.[10] It is rarely observed.

        (ii) However, suppliers in other markets which already possess production facilities that could be used to enter the market in question may choose to enter in response to an increase in price provided that the difference in profitability between entry and non-entry prior to the merger is small.[11]

        (iii) If entrants incur sunk costs, then their decisions whether to enter will depend in particular on their predictions of their costs,[12] the post-entry market price and their likely sales, taking account of the strategic reactions of incumbents.[13]

        (iv) The decision by such committed entrants to enter the market will affect the market price.[14] The Notice on Horizontal Mergers addresses this issue as follows: "For entry to be likely, it must be sufficiently profitable taking into account the price effects of injecting additional output into the market and the potential responses of the incumbents. Entry is thus less likely if it would only be economically viable on a large scale, thereby resulting in significantly depressed price levels. And entry is likely to be more difficult if the incumbents are able to protect their market shares by offering long-term contracts or giving targeted pre-emptive price reductions to those customers that

---

[8] See Besanko, Dranove & Shanley, *Economics of Strategy* (2nd edn, John Wiley & Sons Inc, 2000), p.329 and Werden & Froeb, "The Entry-Inducing Effects of Horizontal Mergers: An Exploratory Analysis" (1998) *The Journal of Industrial Economics* 525.

[9] See generally Baker, "Responding to Developments in Economics and the Courts: Entry in the Merger Guidelines", 2002 (available at *www.usdoj.gov/atr/hmerger/11252.htm*) and Areeda, Hovenkamp & Solow, *Antitrust Law* (2nd edn, Aspen Law & Business, 2000), Vol.IIA, para.422a.

[10] See para.16–018 below.

[11] The Notice on Horizontal Mergers, para.73.

[12] In assessing possible new entry, the Commission may need to carry out a careful analysis of the costs of the different options for entry; see, e.g. Case COMP/M.3687 *Johnson & Johnson / Guidant*, paras 216 to 232.

[13] Entry is less likely if the costs and risks of failure are high: Notice on Horizontal Mergers, para.69.

[14] In predicting post-entry market conditions, a new entrant may be influenced by the available capacity held by the incumbents.

the entrant is trying to acquire".[15] The US solution to determining the post-entry market price is to assume that it is the same as the pre-merger market price in the absence of other evidence,[16] on the grounds that, if the new entry is sufficient to prevent the exercise of market power by the merged group, then prices will not be elevated beyond the pre-merger level.

(v)   A committed entrant will also consider carefully the source of its sales; they may arise, in particular, from reductions in output by incumbents (as the incumbents seek to increase the market price),[17] growth in the market, or winning business from the incumbents. The Notice on Horizontal Mergers provides: "The expected evolution of the market should be taken into account when assessing whether or not entry would be profitable. Entry is more likely to be profitable in a market that is expected to experience high growth in the future than in a market that is mature or expected to decline. Scale economies or network effects may make entry unprofitable unless the entrant can obtain a sufficiently large market share".[18] The US authorities[19] seek to identify the *minimum viable scale*, namely the smallest average annual sales which the entrant must persistently achieve for profitability at pre-merger prices.[20] The rationale is that a company is unlikely to incur sunk costs in entering a market if the smallest sales volume which must be consistently achieved in order to be profitable at post-entry market prices is larger than the likely available sales.

---

[15] Para.82.

[16] There is no inconsistency in assessing new entry on the assumption that post-entry prices are the same as pre-merger prices notwithstanding that entry had not occurred pre-merger. The US Horizontal Merger Guidelines, 1992 (amended in 1997) (*www.usdoj.gov/atr/public/guide lines/hmg.htm*), s.3.0 explain: "A merger having anticompetitive effects can attract committed entry, profitable at premerger prices, that would not have occurred premerger at these same prices. But following the merger, the reduction in industry output and increase in prices associated with the competitive effect of concern may allow the same entry to occur without driving market prices below premerger levels."

[17] See the US Horizontal Merger Guidelines, 1992 (amended in 1997) (*www.usdoj.gov/atr/public/ guidelines/hmg.htm*), n.32.

[18] Para.72

[19] The US approach seeks to avoid an abstract analysis of barriers to entry, which are difficult to quantify in the time periods available on a merger investigation. See the US Horizontal Merger Guidelines, 1992 (amended in 1997) (*www.usdoj.gov/atr/public/guidelines/hmg.htm*), s.3.3. Compare the UK Office of Fair Trading's Substantive Merger Guidelines, May 2003 (*www.oft.gov.uk*), para.4.21.

[20] The minimum viable scale is likely to be high if: the fixed costs of entry are large; the fixed costs of entry are largely *sunk* (i.e. costs which must be invested in order to enter the market but which would not be recovered through their redeployment on exit)—sunk costs typically include research and development, regulatory approvals, testing, market-specific technology and production facilities, advertising and arguably *brand proliferation*; the marginal costs of production are high at low levels of output; there are delays in winning market acceptance leading to under-utilisation of plant; there are cost or demand advantages for incumbents such as intellectual property rights, customer loyalty (whether generally or through long-term exclusivity deals) or access to scarce raw materials; and/or customer switching costs are high.

(vi) In *Skanska / Scancem*[21] the Commission proceeded on the assumption that the costs of commencing production of ready-mixed concrete were low, but continued: "it must however be remembered that there already exists a significant overcapacity on the Swedish market, and that the market is not forecast to grow significantly in the near future. A new entrant would therefore have to take significant sales from the existing players in order to establish itself. An entrant would also have to consider that Skanska, given its control over the main raw material, cement, would be in an excellent position to affect its possibilities of making a sufficient return on the investment. Moreover, given the already existing overcapacity, and the fact that a ready-mixed plant cannot readily be used to produce other goods, any investment in new production capacity would largely be a sunk cost". By contrast, in *Carnival Corporation / P&O Princess*[22] the Commission found that the growth in the market would create incentives for new entry (and expansion) which would limit the impact of barriers to entry.

(b) In determining the likelihood of entry, the Commission examines carefully any barriers to entry[23] and the history of previous actual, attempted and threatened entry and exit.[24] The Notice on Horizontal Mergers defines barriers to entry as specific features of the market which give incumbent firms advantages over potential competitors.[25] Barriers to entry and the history of previous entry are considered in s.16.3 below.[26]

(c) The Commission seeks to identify any evidence of *planned* entry or entry which *might* occur if the merged group sought to raise prices, and places substantial weight on the responses of potential entrants to questions asking how they would react in such circumstances.[27]

---

[21] Case IV/M.1157 [1999] O.J. L183/1, para.140.

[22] Case COMP/M.2706 [2003] O.J. L248/1, para.155; see also para.197.

[23] It also takes account of any matters which facilitate entry. For example, in Case COMP/M.3819 *Daimler Chrysler / MAV*, Commission Regulation (EC) No 1400/2002 of 31 July 2002 on the application of Article 81(3) of the Treaty to categories of vertical agreements and concerted practices in the motor vehicle sector [2002] O.J. L203/30, was found to have liberalised the distribution of spare parts for motor cars, facilitating market entry.

[24] Notice on Horizontal Mergers, para.70. For further discussion of the evidence that can be obtained from past episodes of entry, see the International Competition Network, "ICN Investigative Techniques Handbook for Merger Review", June 2005 (*www.international competitionnetwork.org/handbook_5-5.pdf*), p.61.

[25] Para.70.

[26] In Case COMP/M.3436 *Continental / Phoenix*, the Commission focused on the question of whether it was possible to enter the market without considerable investment cost (concluding that it was); paras 216 to 218.

[27] Companies with existing investments in similar or neighbouring markets are more readily accepted as likely entrants. See, e.g. Case IV/M.591 *Dow / Buna* (transaction cleared in part because of "potential supply by producers who normally manufacture for captive use only"; paras 24 and 28); Case IV/M.942 *VEBA / Degussa* [1998] O.J. L201/102 (companies producing mainly or entirely for their own use might increase or begin sales to third parties if market

For example,[28] in *Industri Kapital / Perstorp (II)*[29] the Commission consulted manufacturers in other territories to assess whether they would consider supplying the geographic market in question and relied on their negative responses in finding that there was limited potential competition. There is a danger in placing undue weight on the responses of third parties to hypothetical questions about their plans which are asked in the context of an ongoing investigation, because third parties may choose to respond strategically, allowing their evidence to be coloured by their commercial judgment about whether the merger would benefit them. It is therefore important that survey evidence is supplemented by objective analysis. By contrast, the US agencies apply the new entry analysis *without* attempting to identify the potential entrants.[30]

(c) *Timeliness*

The following factors are taken into account in considering the issue of **16–004** timeliness:

(a) Timeliness is important because existing players will enjoy greater market power if there are substantial delays whilst new entrants enter the market. Further, new entrants will be deterred from entering if the existing players have a long time to respond to the threat.

(b) The Commission assesses whether entry would be sufficiently quick and sustained to deter or defeat the exercise of market power.[31] The time period depends on the characteristics and dynamics of the market and the specific capabilities of potential entrants[32] but the

---

[28] conditions are attractive enough; para.63); Case IV/M.1094 *Caterpillar / Perkins Engines* (the Commission identified, at para.36, integrated companies whose production was mainly captive as potential entrants); and Case COMP/M.2690 *Solvay / Montedison-Ausimont* (entry into a chemicals market by chemicals distributors was regarded as likely; para.113).

See also Case IV/M.330 *McCormick / CPC / Rabobank / Ostrmann* (survey of potential entrants had not identified any with "concrete plans" to enter; paras 73 to 76).

[29] Case COMP/M.2396, para.78.

[30] US Horizontal Merger Guidelines, 1992 (amended in 1997) (*www.usdoj.gov/atr/public/guidelines/hmg.htm*), s.3.1.

[31] Notice on Horizontal Mergers, para.74.

[32] See, e.g. Case IV/M.430 *Procter & Gamble / VP Schickedanz (II)* [1994] O.J. L354/32, para.178 and Case IV/M.774 *Saint-Gobain / Wacker-Chemie / NOM* [1997] O.J. L247/1. In Case COMP/M.1693 *Alcoa / Reynolds* [2002] O.J. L58/25, which was decided in May 2000, the Commission noted that production at a new plant was scheduled to commence in 2005 at the earliest and commented, at para.31: "This is clearly outside the time frame used by the Commission to assess the impact of potential competition on a proposed merger." In Case COMP/M.2033 *Metso / Svedala* [2004] O.J. L88/1 the Commission found, at para.156, that there was no indication that the merged group's position "could be substantially challenged in the short to medium term by the prospect of new entry."

Notice on Horizontal Mergers states that entry is normally only considered timely if it occurs within two years.[33]

(c) Timeliness may be affected by planning, design, management, permits, licences, other approvals, construction, debugging, operation of production facilities, promotion, marketing, distribution, customer testing, etc.[34]

(d) Evidence of the steps and time taken for previous entry or expansion may be relevant in assessing timeliness.

(d) Sufficiency

16–005 Even if new entry will be both likely and timely, it may nevertheless not be *sufficient* in its magnitude and scope to counteract the merged group's attempt to exercise market power. The Notice on Horizontal Mergers states: "Entry must be of sufficient scope and magnitude to deter or defeat the anti-competitive effects of the merger. Small-scale entry, for instance into some market 'niche', may not be considered sufficient".[35] In *Skanska / Scancem*[36] the Commission described the importance of the sufficiency criterion as follows: "the relevant question is not only whether new entry is possible, but also whether it is likely to be on a scale sufficient to restrict Skanska from behaving largely independently of its competitors following the concentration".[37] More particularly, entry by one or more suppliers will be sufficient if it fills the gap between the competitive output[38] and the post-merger out-

---

[33] Para.74. In principle, the issue is not when entry is likely to occur, but when the *effects* of actual or threatened entry arise. For example, if construction of a plant takes five years (i.e. outside the period generally analysed) but the capacity will remain for several decades, exerting a significant influence over the operation of the market, then incumbents may alter their market behaviour significantly if they become aware of discussions between a major customer and a potential entrant about the possibility of the former sponsoring construction of a new plant by entering a significant long-term contract before building commences. In the US, timely entry generally involves a significant market impact within two years of initial planning, although the period may be extended in cases of durable goods if customers are willing to defer purchases beyond two years if a company provides significant evidence of commitment to enter: see the US Horizontal Merger Guidelines, 1992 (amended in 1997) (*www.usdoj.gov/atr/public/guidelines/hmg.htm*), s.3.2. The UK Office of Fair Trading's Substantive Merger Guidelines, May 2003 (*www.oft.gov.uk*), para.4.23, identify a two year period.

[34] US Horizontal Merger Guidelines, 1992 (amended in 1997) (*www.usdoj.gov/atr/public/guidelines/hmg.htm*), s.3.1.

[35] Para.75.

[36] Case IV/M.1157 [1999] O.J. L183/1, para.184.

[37] See also the Commission's XXIst Annual Report on Competition Policy, 1991, p.365. Strictly, in the case of a merger which significantly impedes effective competition by *strengthening* a dominant position, the issue is whether new entry would be sufficient to preclude the merged group from acting independently of market pressure to any greater extent than it could prior to the merger.

[38] Strictly, the question is whether entry will fill the gap between the likely output in the absence of the merger and the likely post-merger output.

put.[39] On the other hand, entry will not be sufficient if, for example, the merged group controls essential assets, or the product is differentiated and the new entrant's product is not in direct competition with the merged group's products.[40]

(e) New entry as a "trump"

When these three criteria are satisfied, new entry from potential competitors **16–006** to the merged group may operate as a genuine "trump" to the presumption that high market shares confer market power,[41] i.e. even a merger to monopoly would be approved if new entry would be likely, timely and sufficient to defeat any attempt by the merged group to increase prices or reduce quality, variety or innovation. A regression analysis of a large sample of ECMR decisions taken during the period January 1, 2000 to June 30, 2002 concluded that if barriers to entry are low then even mergers involving high market shares are cleared.[42] The Commission's approach is illustrated by the following decisions:

(a) In *Mercedes-Benz / Kässbohrer*[43] the Commission placed decisive weight on potential competition in clearing the transaction: "The potential competition from foreign bus suppliers on the German market is of decisive importance if there is to be sufficient competitive control of the freedom of manoeuvre of Mercedes-Benz after the merger. This potential competition embraces both an expected

---

[39] Areeda, Hovenkamp & Solow, *Antitrust Law* (2nd edn, Aspen Law & Business, 2000), Vol.IIA, para.422c. See also the US Horizontal Merger Guidelines, 1992 (amended in 1997) (*www.usdoj.gov/atr/public/guidelines/hmg.htm*) ("where the competitive effect of concern is not uniform across the relevant market, in order for entry to be sufficient, the character and scope of entrants' products must be responsive to the localized sales opportunities that include the output reduction associated with the competitive effect of concern"; para.3.4); the Australian Merger Guidelines, June 1999 (*www.accc.gov.au/content/item.phtml?itemId = 719436&nodeId = file43a1f42c7eb63&fn = Merger%20Guidelines.pdf*), para.5.125; and the New Zealand Merger Guidelines, 2004 (*www.comcom.govt.nz/Publications/ContentFiles/Documents/Mergers andAcquisitionsGuidelines.PDF*), para.6.3.

[40] US Horizontal Merger Guidelines, 1992 (amended in 1997) (*www.usdoj.gov/atr/public/guide lines/hmg.htm*), s.3.4.

[41] The Notice on Horizontal Mergers is somewhat equivocal on the question whether new entry is a "trump" in all cases: see the reference to the merger being "unlikely" to pose any concerns in para.68. The US Horizontal Merger Guidelines, 1992 (amended in 1997) (*www.usdoj.gov/ atr/public/guidelines/hmg.htm*), s.3.0, provide: "A merger is not likely to create or enhance market power or to facilitate its exercise, if entry into the market is so easy that market participants, after the merger, either collectively or unilaterally could not profitably maintain a price increase above pre-merger levels ... In markets where entry is that easy (i.e., where entry passes the tests of timeliness, likelihood and sufficiency), the merger raises no antitrust concern and ordinarily requires no further analysis". See also Newman, edn, *The New Palgrave Dictionary of Economics and the Law* (1998 edn, Palgrave Macmillan), definition of "horizontal mergers" by Hay, stating that: "A necessary condition for the adverse effects of monopoly to occur is the presence of some barriers to entry; otherwise, the higher prices will simply induce new firms to enter ... [If] entry barriers are very low, even high concentration should not produce any significant anti-competitive effect".

[42] Lindsay, Lecchi & Williams, "Econometrics Study into European Commission Merger Decisions Since 2000" [2003] E.C.L.R. 673, at p.681.

[43] Case IV/M.477 [1995] O.J. L211/1, para.79.

increase in current imports into the German market, and hence a strengthening of the market position of those foreign suppliers who are already present in the German market, and imports from suppliers who will enter the market".

(b) In *Western Power Distribution / Hyder*[44] the Commission found that, even if the geographic market were defined narrowly and the merging parties therefore had a monopoly or near-monopoly, the transaction would not create or strengthen a dominant position because barriers to entry were very low and there were significant numbers of potential competitors.

(c) In *Mannesmann / Hoesch*[45] the Commission found that "there is strong evidence that the parties concerned may achieve upon completion of the concentration a liberty of action that is not immediately fully controlled by existing competitors" but cleared the transaction because of the high probability of new entry which would quickly erode the merged group's position on the market.

(d) Finally, in *HP / Compaq*[46] the Commission cleared in Phase I a transaction in which the merged group would hold a market share of 85 to 95 per cent in Personal Digital Assistants ("PDAs") because barriers to entry were low and credible competitors had announced future launches of PDAs.

16.3 BARRIERS TO ENTRY

(a) Definition

16–007 If barriers to entry[47] into a market are low,[48] then potential competition from new entrants is more likely (and, indeed, may be more timely).[49] Bain's definition of a barrier to entry is "the extent to which, in the long run,

---

[44] Case COMP/M.1949, para.22

[45] Case IV/M.222 [1993] O.J. L114/34, paras 92 and 112 to 114.

[46] Case COMP/M.2609, para.38.

[47] See generally OFT Research Paper, "Barriers to Entry and Exit in UK Competition Policy", London Economics, 1994 (note that the views in the paper do not necessarily represent those of the OFT); Scherer & Ross, *Industrial Market Structure and Economic Performance* (3rd edn, Houghton Mifflin Co, 1990), Chs 4 and 10; Porter, *Competitive Strategy* (The Free Press, 1998 edn), pp.7 to 17; Porter, *Competitive Advantage* (The Free Press, 1998 edn), Ch.3; Besanko, Dranove & Shanley, *Economics of Strategy* (2nd edn, John Wiley & Sons Inc, 2000), Ch.10; Areeda, Hovenkamp & Solow, *Antitrust Law* (2nd edn, Aspen Law & Business, 2000), Vol.IIA, s.4C; Oster, *Modern Competitive Advantage* (3rd edn, Oxford UP, 1999), Ch.4 and p.297; Tirole, *The Theory of Industrial Organization* (The MIT Press, 1988), Ch.8; and OECD, "Barriers to Entry", DAF/COMP (2005) 42 (available via *www.oecd.org/dataoecd/43/49/36344429.pdf*).

[48] Barriers to entry may be assessed either subjectively (i.e. as high, medium or low based on a review of the industry) or using a variety of objective measurements. A detailed analysis is contained in OFT Research Paper, "Barriers to Entry and Exit in UK Competition Policy", London Economics, 1994 (note that the views in the paper do not necessarily represent those of the OFT). See further s.(d) below.

[49] Low entry barriers may also result in a broader market definition on the supply-side: see Ch.3 above.

established firms can elevate their selling prices above minimal average costs of production and distribution ... without inducing potential entrants to enter the industry".[50] This approach is based on the theory of limit pricing, i.e. the higher the entry barriers, the greater the scope for the incumbent suppliers to raise prices above the competitive level without inducing entry.[51] The Commission's view[52] that barriers to entry are specific features of the market which give incumbents advantages over potential entrants is consistent with Bain's approach. Ultimately, however, the debate about the definition of a barrier to entry is somewhat arid and the focus in any merger case should be on the way in which the market will develop, and in particular on whether new entry would be likely, timely and sufficient to counteract any anti-competitive strategy adopted by the merged group.[53]

In examining barriers to entry, a distinction can be drawn between legal advantages, technical advantages, strategic incumbent advantages and impediments to entry.[54] *Legal advantages* include regulatory barriers, such as requirements to obtain a licence in order to carry on a particular category of business. For example, in *Vodafone Airtouch / Mannesmann*[55] the need to

---

[50] *Industrial Organization* (2nd edn, John Wiley & Sons, 1970), p.233.

[51] See para.6–004 above and Martin, *Advanced Industrial Economics* (2nd edn, Blackwell, 2002), p.341. More narrowly, Stigler stated that "a barrier to entry may be defined as a cost of producing (at some or every rate or output) which must be borne by firms which seek to enter an industry but is not borne by firms already in the industry": *The Organization of Industry* (Richard D Irwin, 1968), p.67; and see also Carlton & Perloff, *Modern Industrial Organization* (4th edn, Addison-Wesley, 2005), p.77. On this basis, economies of scale are *not* a barrier to entry provided that new entrants operate on the same cost curves as incumbents. For example, an incumbent—as well as a new entrant—must establish and maintain a brand identity in a consumer goods market with the consequence that advertising expenditure would be a barrier to entry on Bain's but not Stigler's view. It is clear that the Commission treats economies of scale as a barrier to entry (see the Notice on Horizontal Mergers, para.71(b), and the Commission's XXIInd Annual Report on Competition Policy, 1992, para.250), leading to the conclusion drawn in the text that the Commission follows Bain's definition of a barrier to entry rather than Stigler's. Areeda, Hovenkamp & Solow, *Antitrust Law* (2nd edn, Aspen Law & Business, 2000), Vol.IIA, para.420c, also prefer Bain's definition because Stigler's definition would exclude features of the market which in fact impede new entry. (Most narrowly, Bork defines barriers to entry as artificial inhibitions on entry *which do not reflect superior efficiency*: Bork, *The Antitrust Paradox* (1993 edn, The Free Press, 1978), pp.195 and 311. Bork regards the only true barriers to entry as exclusionary practices and contends that the characterisation of, e.g. advertising and brand proliferation, as barriers to entry damages the economy by suppressing efficiency.) The terminological debate about the definition of a barrier to entry can be avoided by focusing on costs of entry as opposed to barriers to entry: see Martin, *Advanced Industrial Economics* (2nd edn, Blackwell, 2002), p.343.

[52] See the Guidelines on Horizontal Mergers, para.70. The UK Office of Fair Trading's Substantive Merger Guidelines, May 2003 (*www.oft.gov.uk*), para.4.21, track closely Bain's definition. See also the Australian Merger Guidelines, June 1999 (*www.accc.gov.au/content/item.phtml?itemId = 719436&nodeId = file43a1f42c7eb63&fn = Merger%20Guidelines.pdf*), para.5.116 and the New Zealand Merger Guidelines, 2004 (*www.comcom.govt.nz/Publications/ContentFiles/Documents/MergersandAcquisitionsGuidelines.PDF*), para.6.2, both of which treat economies of scale as a barrier to entry. Compare Case T-282/02 *Cementbouw Handel & Industrie v Commission*, not yet reported, judgment of February 23, 2006, para.219.

[53] See generally Carlton, "Why Barriers to Entry are Barriers to Understanding" (2004) 94 *American Economic Review* 466.

[54] See the Guidelines on Horizontal Mergers, para.71.

[55] Case COMP/M.1795, para.28.

obtain a licence from a national regulator in order to provide mobile tele-communications services was regarded as an obvious barrier to entry.[56] Such barriers to entry are straightforward to analyse and are not considered further in this section. *Technical advantages* include preferential access to essential facilities, natural resources, innovation and research and development, intellectual property rights, economies of scale and scope and distribution and sales networks. *Strategic advantages* benefit the first mover or incumbent suppliers and include investing in excess capacity and advertising. (In practice, the distinction between technical and strategic advantages is not straightforward and the two categories are treated together in s.(b) below.) Finally, *impediments to entry* delay but do not prevent entry.

(b) Technical and strategic advantages

16–008　Strategic[57] or first mover advantages may arise through either the structure of the industry (*exogenous* barriers to entry) or the activities of incumbents (*endogenous* barriers to entry).[58] The distinction between exogenous and endogenous barriers to entry is important because suppliers can act strategically by seeking to create endogenous barriers as a defence to new entry. In considering endogenous barriers to entry, Scherer & Ross have commented that to create a commitment to deter entry into the market (i.e. to act strategically by creating endogenous barriers to entry): "(1) an incumbent's investment must be durable, that is, it must be in place long enough to constrain the entrant; (2) it must be irreversible—otherwise the potential entrant could reasonably expect the incumbent to disregard its aggressive posture post-entry; and (3) its implications must be clear to the entrant, that is, the entrant must be able to observe the investment and recognize that entry following the investment is unlikely to be profitable".[59]

16–009　　The following technical and strategic advantages can be distinguished. First, if a first mover in an industry incurs substantial *sunk costs* (i.e. costs

---

[56] See also Case IV/M.1383 *Exxon / Mobil* [2004] O.J. L103/1, para.557 (construction of new service stations was controlled by the French highway authorities).

[57] Salop distinguished strategic and innocent entry barriers: Salop, "Strategic Entry Deterrence" (1979) *American Economic Review* 335. A strategic move is one which is intended to alter the perceptions of others in favour of the person making the move by purposefully limiting the person's freedom of action: see Dixit & Nalebuff, *Thinking Strategically* (W W Norton & Co, 1991), p.120 and Besanko, Dranove & Shanley, *Economics of Strategy* (2nd edn, John Wiley & Sons Inc, 2000), Ch.8. For a strategic perspective on exclusionary strategies, see Porter, *Competitive Advantage* (1998 edn, The Free Press), Ch.14.

[58] Industries characterised by high levels of endogenous investment in advertising and/or research and development tend to be associated with high levels of concentration no matter how large the market: see, in particular, Sutton, *Sunk Costs and Market Structure: Price Competition, Advertising, and the Evolution of Concentration* (The MIT Press, 1991).

[59] *Industrial Market Structure and Economic Performance* (3rd edn, Houghton Mifflin Co, 1990), p.381.

which cannot be recovered on exit)[60] this may act as a barrier to entry.[61] This is because, having sunk those costs, the incumbent will find it rational to stay in the market so long as its revenues cover its variable costs. By contrast a new entrant, faced with the prospect of incurring the same sunk costs, will only enter if it predicts that its revenues will also cover its fixed costs of entry.

Secondly, if incumbents benefit from *economies of scale*,[62] this may result in barriers to entry.[63] Areeda, Hovenkamp & Solow comment[64]: "economies

---

[60] Cabral states in *Introduction to Industrial Organization* (The MIT Press, 2000), pp.21 and 22: "A sunk cost is an investment in an asset with no alternative use (also referred to as 'specific asset'). In other words, a sunk cost is an asset with no opportunity cost".

[61] See, e.g. Case IV/M.190 *Nestlé / Perrier* [1992] O.J. L356/1, para.33.

[62] See Porter, *Competitive Advantage* (1998 edn, The Free Press), pp.70 and 71. "Supply-side economies of scale" (as distinct from "demand-side economies of scale" or "network effects") may fall into the following categories.

(a) *Product-specific* economies, e.g. publishing thousands of copies of a newspaper results in lower unit costs than publishing a single copy because the costs of editorial and setting up the production line can be spread across more copies. Similarly, a dynamic scale economy may arise through *learning-by-doing*, i.e. the more times that a specific task has been carried out the quicker it becomes. When data is available, it is possible to calculate a *learning rate*, i.e. an elasticity of average costs with respect to cumulated output. The existence of learning-by-doing economies may allow a supplier which is protected from competition by a patent to maintain a strong position after the expiry of the patent: see the discussion in Cabral, *Introduction to Industrial Organization* (The MIT Press, 2000), pp.246, 268 and 301. It also helps to explain why suppliers of a new product may price at low levels to win volume to try to build up economies through learning-by-doing, which will enable them to resist subsequent attempts to enter the market.

(b) *Plant-specific* economies, e.g. energy costs tend to rise at a lower rate than vessel size: Carlton & Perloff, *Modern Industrial Organization* (4th edn, Addison-Wesley, 2005), p.38. Similarly, economies of massed reserves may mean that opening additional lines does not result in any increase in the need to hold spare parts because random events tend to cancel one another out as the number of events increases: see Carlton & Perloff, *Modern Industrial Organization* (4th edn, Addison-Wesley, 2005), p.38; this is sometimes referred to as the *law of large numbers*. There may also be economies of scope when the costs of producing two outputs together is lower than the costs of producing them separately.

(c) *Multi-plant* economies, e.g. by permitting greater specialisation. A company which produces a range of products at identical plants may benefit from multi-plant economies if it is able to benefit from longer production runs at each plant, reducing the need for downtime to re-set the machines.

For discussion about estimating economies of scale, see Besanko, Dranove & Shanley, *Economics of Strategy* (2nd edn, John Wiley & Sons Inc, 2000), pp.102 to 108. See generally Areeda, Hovenkamp & Solow, *Antitrust Law* (2nd edn, Aspen Law & Business, 2000), Vol.IIA, para.408c.

[63] Economies of scale may result in:

(a) a high *minimum viable scale* of entry, i.e. the lowest volume of sales which would need to be achieved to justify entry into the market; the US Horizontal Merger Guidelines, 1992 (amended in 1997) (*www.usdoj.gov/atr/public/guidelines/hmg.htm*), s.3.3, define minimum viable scale as "the smallest annual level of sales that the committed entrant must persistently achieve for profitability at pre-merger prices";

(b) a high *minimum efficient scale,* i.e. the lowest output necessary to minimise average cost; alternatively, the minimum efficient scale may be regarded as the minimum scale at which the firm's average cost is close to (say within 10%) the minimum average cost: see Cabral, *Introduction to Industrial Organization* (The MIT Press, 2000), p.244.

[64] Areeda, Hovenkamp & Solow, *Antitrust Law* (2nd edn, Aspen Law & Business, 1998), Vol.IV, para.941b. See also para.941f.

of scale are best considered as a qualifying entry barrier for merger purposes even though they may not be so considered for other purposes. The relevant question is not whether economies of scale are a good thing or whether firms should be encouraged to pursue all available economies. The antitrust policy answer must be affirmative to both. But in the merger case the question is whether a merger generating no provable efficiencies should be permitted where the result is increased concentration protected from new entry by significant economies of scale. A negative answer to that question is calculated to produce the maximum amount of competition consistent with the presence of scale economies". In *Metso / Svedala*[65] economies of scale were identified as a barrier to entry, the Commission noting that: "This would place any newcomer at a cost-disadvantage in relation to well-established producers, particularly since the newcomer would have to offer a complete range of products of various sizes and performance". If the minimum viable scale and/or the minimum efficient scale[66] is large relative to the total size of the market, this suggests that the industry will support one (*natural monopoly*) or a few (*natural oligopoly*) producers.[67] In *Interbrew / Bass*[68] the Commission noted that "most other European beer markets are smaller than that in the UK, and it is therefore to be expected that the markets would be more concentrated". Similarly, the commitments accepted by the Commission in *Air France / Sabena*[69] to resolve concerns about concentration on the Brussels/Paris-Ankara and Brussels/Paris-Budapest routes provided for the multi-designation of other airlines, provided that minimum volume thresholds were reached: "Taking into account, however, the relatively weak volume of traffic on these routes and the necessity to have a minimum number of passengers in order to ensure the exploitation of the route, multi-designation will only start if a threshold of 100,000 passengers annually on each of them is exceeded". Enrique González-Díaz commented: "This seems to amount to the acceptance of the natural monopoly theory in the context of merger control".[70]

16–010   Thirdly, if products are differentiated by *advertising*[71] this may[72] create a

---

[65] Case COMP/M.2033 [2004] O.J. L88/1, para.160.

[66] Oster, *Modern Competitive Advantage* (3rd edn, Oxford UP, 1999), comments, at p.65: "Long-term survival at a scale less than MES requires some factor that permits the firm to charge a premium price. Product differentiation and locational monopoly are two possible effects".

[67] For a detailed discussion of the measurement of such cost-scale relationships see Scherer & Ross, *Industrial Market Structure and Economic Performance* (3rd edn, Houghton Mifflin Co, 1990), pp.111 to 118. See also para.6–012 above.

[68] Case COMP/M.2044, para.40.

[69] Case IV/M.157, para.37.

[70] Case note, European Competition Law, para.9(c) (published in Van Gerwen (coordinator), *Merger Control Reporter* (Kluwer Law International)).

[71] See Carlton & Perloff, *Modern Industrial Organization* (4th edn, Addison-Wesley, 2005), Ch.14; Martin, *Advanced Industrial Economics* (2nd edn, Blackwell, 2002), Ch.6; Cabral, *Introduction to Industrial Organization* (The MIT Press, 2000), pp.226 to 234; and Oster, *Modern Competitive Advantage* (3rd edn, Oxford UP, 1999), pp.272 to 274. Porter, Competitive Advantage (1998 edn, The Free Press), p.142 explains that buyers decide whether to purchase on the basis of *use criteria* (such as product quality and features) and *signalling criteria* (such as reputation and advertising). Advertising has a variety of implications for a market:

barrier to entry[73] as advertising is a sunk cost.[74] Three types of advertising may be distinguished. *Informative advertising* provides information about a product or its price. *Persuasive advertising* seeks to change customer preferences by building up potential customers' emotional "pull" towards the brand. *Comparison advertising* involves one supplier advertising its goods in comparison with those of other suppliers, e.g. an airline flying from London to Barcelona might publish its fares and those of rival airlines to support a claim that the advertiser offers the best value.[75] The significance of advertising in an industry can be measured by identifying the ratio of advertising expenditure to turnover.[76] The Commission has identified advertising as a barrier to entry in a number of cases. In *Kimberly-Clark / Scott*[77] the Commission noted that advertising was a sunk cost which added to the cost of entry,[78] adding: "Moreover, advertising expenditure and market share is self-reinforcing. On the one hand, there is the virtuous circle where high market share allows high profitability to engage in sustained advertising to support the brand. On the other hand, there is a vicious circle where low market share means low profits and inadequate resources to implement the

---

(a) advertising may be a barrier to entry;

(b) advertising may be a signal of product quality, because a supplier of high quality goods gains more through advertising since new customers are more likely to become repeat customers (i.e. to provide a source of revenue to repay the costs of the advertising) if product quality is high;

(c) advertising product characteristics may increase product differentiation and therefore dampen the intensity of competition;

(d) advertising prices clearly increases competition on price; and

(e) in principle, if comparison advertising is widely used within an industry *and* the criteria chosen for comparison are central to the purchasing decision (e.g. in the case of airlines, price, rather than, say, choice of free newspapers) then it is an indicator that the market is operating competitively.

[72] In Case IV/M.938 *Guinness / Grand Metropolitan* [1998] O.J. L288/24, the Commission identified *restrictions* on advertising as a barrier to entry, stating at para.62: "Restrictions on advertising favour incumbents, whose products are known to customers and so require less advertising, against entrants, whose products are by definition unknown to customers".

[73] In some markets, however, the first mover has to incur costs in persuading customers to use the product which subsequent entrants do not need to incur.

[74] Further, advertising has cumulative as well as current effects with the consequence that incumbents will continue to derive a benefit from historic investment in advertising which, in turn, increases the level of advertising required for a new entrant to be successful. Advertising is determined by companies in the market (i.e. it is *endogenous*) and may therefore be used as a defence to entry: for an empirical analysis of "first mover" advantage in advertising, see Sutton, *Sunk Costs and Market Structure: Price Competition, Advertising, and the Evolution of Concentration* (The MIT Press, 1991), Ch.9. Investment in advertising may allow a company to benefit from economies of scope known as "umbrella branding" which enable a company to introduce new products in reliance on its existing brand reputation; see Besanko, Dranove & Shanley, *Economics of Strategy* (2nd edn, John Wiley & Sons Inc, 2000), p.336.

[75] This type of advertising is regulated within the EU to ensure that the comparisons are fair and verifiable.

[76] See Scherer & Ross, *Industrial Market Structure and Economic Performance* (3rd edn, Houghton Mifflin Co, 1990), p.436. In principle, advertising intensity is likely to be higher if demand is sensitive to advertising (i.e. there is a high advertising elasticity of demand) but not sensitive to price (i.e. there is a low price elasticity of demand): Cabral, *Introduction to Industrial Organization* (The MIT Press, 2000), pp.227 and 228.

[77] Case IV/M.623 [1996] O.J. L183/1.

[78] Para.211.

necessary advertising campaign to boost flagging sales".[79] Similarly, in *Nestlé / Perrier*[80] the Commission found that there was heavy advertising of brands in the French water market with the consequence that establishing a new brand would require heavy sunk investment and could take a long time. In *Procter & Gamble / VP Schickedanz (II)*[81] the Commission reviewed a number of consumer research studies which showed a high degree of brand loyalty and found that such loyalty acted as a barrier to entry in a market which was not growing rapidly as an entrant would have to win share from incumbents. Barriers to entry arising from brand loyalty may be lower outside consumer goods markets. In *Mercedes-Benz / Kässbohrer*[82] the Commission referred expressly to *Procter & Gamble / VP Schickedanz (II)* in commenting that: "Unlike in the consumer goods sphere, where purchasers tend to show less price sensitivity ... purchasers of industrial capital goods normally base their purchase decisions on a cost-benefit analysis". The Commission added: "The existence of a multiple sourcing strategy for a considerable part of the demand decreases the importance of brand loyalty as a market entry barrier".

16–011   Fourthly, *brand proliferation* may be a barrier to entry because any new entrant with a single brand is likely to be able to win market share primarily from the brands which are closest in characteristics to the new entrant's and the larger the number of brands, the smaller the likely share of the market held by any single brand and available to be won by the new entrant. A similar effect arises in relation to geographic markets through a *plant* or *outlet proliferation* strategy.[83] For example, in *Nestlé / Perrier*[84] the Commission noted that "the multiplicity of existing brands makes the establishment of a new one more difficult (access to the media at the appropriate moment) and involves a high level of risk, in particular in view of the national image attached to [existing] brands". In *Exxon / Mobil*[85] the Commission found that the "saturation" of the French service station market reduced the possibility of creating new outlets and therefore comprised a barrier to entry.[86] Brand, plant and outlet proliferation are endogenous.[87]

---

[79] Para.145.

[80] Case IV/M.190 [1992] O.J. L356/1, para.33.

[81] Case IV/M.430 [1994] O.J. L354/32, paras 125 to 130.

[82] Case IV/M.477 [1995] O.J. L211/1, paras 83 and 86.

[83] See Scherer & Ross, *Industrial Market Structure and Economic Performance* (3rd edn, Houghton Mifflin Co, 1990), pp.396 to 404.

[84] Case IV/M.190 [1992] O.J. L356/1, para.33.

[85] Case IV/M.1383 [2004] O.J. L103/1, para.558. See also para.641.

[86] Similarly, in the US, in *Staples / Office Depot* 970 F Supp 1066, United States District Court of Columbia, 1997, it was suggested that the three US office superstore operators had "saturated" many local retail markets leaving little or no room for additional stores. See Dalkir & Warren-Boulton, "Prices, Market Definition, and the Effects of Merger: Staples-Office Depot (1997)", in Kwoka & White eds., *The Antitrust Revolution* (4th edn, Oxford UP, 2004), at p.64. That case was also characterised by barriers to entry arising from economies in local and national advertising.

[87] See OFT Research Paper, "Barriers to Entry and Exit in UK Competition Policy", London Economics, 1994 (note that the views in the paper do not necessarily represent those of the OFT), p.12 and Scherer & Ross, *Industrial Market Structure and Economic Performance* (3rd edn, Houghton Mifflin Co, 1990), pp.404 to 407.

Fifthly, *research and development* expenditure may be a substantial barrier to entry.[88] The significance of research and development in an industry can be measured by identifying the ratio of research and development expenditure to turnover.[89] If substantial development costs are required in order to enter a market and the market is declining, new entry is unlikely because a new supplier would not be able to spread its development costs over a sufficient product volume.[90] An incumbent may invest in research and development strategically to have a "stock" of new products in place to launch in the event of attempted entry.[91]

Sixthly, *excess capacity* may be an endogenous barrier to entry if it **16–012** involves sunk costs because it may reduce the marginal cost of production, giving the incumbent greater scope and incentive to cut prices in response to entry, i.e. the lower the incumbent's marginal cost the greater its incentive to *increase* output and, commensurately, the greater the incentive for any new entrant to produce *less*. The Commission has regularly identified excess capacity[92] as a barrier to entry.[93]

Seventhly, a barrier to entry may arise if new entrants face *higher costs of capital*, whether because they pose more risk than incumbents or the capital market does not operate perfectly.[94] However, absolute costs of entry are *not* a barrier to entry.[95] In *Carnival Corporation / P&O Princess*[96] the absolute

---

[88] See, e.g. Case IV/M.468 *Siemens / Italtel* [1995] O.J. L161/27 para.50; Case COMP/M.2547 *Bayer / Aventis Crop Science* [2004] O.J. L107/1 ("In markets subject to intensive R&D, potential entry cannot be generally expected in the short to medium term, firstly because of the length of time required for development of equally effective substances, and, secondly, due to the costs involved in the development of a product capable of competing with the new or improved one"; para.15); and Case COMP/M.2690 *Solvay / Montedison-Ausimont* (the fact that it was necessary to carry out many years of testing before a product would be accepted by customers was regarded as a barrier to entry; para.32).

[89] Case IV/M.468 *Siemens / Italtel* [1995] O.J. L161/27, para.50. See generally, Sutton, *Technology and Market Structure* (The MIT Press, 1998).

[90] Case COMP/M.1601 *Allied Signal / Honeywell* [2001] O.J. L152/1, paras 70 and 71.

[91] See Case COMP/M.1813 *Industri Kapital (Nordkem) / Dyno* [2001] O.J. L154/41.

[92] OFT Research Paper, "Barriers to Entry and Exit in UK Competition Policy", London Economics, 1994 (note that the views in the paper do not necessarily represent those of the OFT), p.11. See also Viscusi, Vernon & Harrington, *Economics of Regulation and Antitrust* (3rd edn, The MIT Press, 2000), pp.178 to 182.

[93] See, e.g. Case IV/M.603 *Crown Cork & Seal / Carnaud Metalbox* [1996] O.J. L75/38, para.79; Case COMP/M.1693 *Alcoa / Reynolds* [2002] O.J. L58/25, para.121; Case COMP/M.1813 *Industri Kapital (Nordkem) / Dyno* [2001] O.J. L154/41 ("Given this excess capacity [the parties] could use the threat of a temporary capacity increase as a deterrent to discourage new entry"; para.100); and Case COMP/M.1940 *Framatome / Siemens / Cogema / JV* [2001] O.J. L289/8, paras 79 to 84. However, entry deterrence is not the only motive for holding excess capacity: see Martin, *Advanced Industrial Economics* (2nd edn, Blackwell, 2002), p.237 (and see generally pp.227 to 239, 272 and 273).

[94] See Scherer & Ross, *Industrial Market Structure and Economic Performance* (3rd edn, Houghton Mifflin Co, 1990), p.126. Bork, *The Antitrust Paradox* (1993 edn, The Free Press, 1978), p.320, has a different perspective: "Capital requirements exist and certainly inhibit entry—just as talent requirements for playing professional football exist and inhibit entry. Neither barrier is in any sense artificial or the proper subject of special concern for antitrust policy". Bork also notes, at p.147, that the capital market is not imperfect if banks refuse to make unprofitable loans.

[95] Contrast Porter, *Competitive Strategy* (1998 edn, The Free Press), p.9.

[96] Case COMP/M.2706 [2003] O.J. L248/1, paras 182 and 183.

cost of new ships ran into hundreds of millions of pounds but "in terms of their competitive effects the magnitude of these costs matters less than the question of whether or not operators could recoup these costs on exit, in other words, whether or not these costs are sunk".

16–013   Eighthly, a need to provide distribution and service networks may constitute a barrier to entry, e.g. purchasers of cars, trucks or computers may require access to a local servicing facility creating an entry barrier. In *Volvo / Scania*[97] the Commission found that buyers of heavy trucks required a local service network and the costs of establishing a viable network were high relative to the likely returns. Similarly,[98] in *Kimberly-Clark / Scott*[99] the Commission emphasised the difficulties for manufacturers of consumer goods in obtaining access to shelf space in supermarkets. By contrast, if a new entrant can use an existing third party distribution network, this may facilitate new entry. In *Gerling / NCM*[1] the Commission stated: "Due to the importance of intermediaries, distribution expenditure requirements are lower in Sweden. This can facilitate new market entry . . ." Also, in *The Post Office / TPG / SPPL*[2] the Commission found that the presence of consolidators in the UK market for outbound cross-border business mail meant that barriers to entry were low[3] whilst their absence in the Netherlands contributed to a finding that barriers to entry were high in the Dutch market.[4]

Ninthly, other barriers to entry include switching costs (e.g. if existing suppliers have created loyalty incentives,[5] package deals or exclusive arrangements),[6] high concentration,[7] market maturity,[8] network effects,[9] vertical foreclosure (in particular, incumbents may operate in a way which

---

[97] Case COMP/M.1672 [2001] O.J. L143/74.
[98] Case IV/M.784 *Kesko / Tuko* [1997] O.J. L110/53 (the merged group would have held a dominant position in a retail market in part because of its control of premises); Case IV/M.1439 *Telia / Telenor* [2001] O.J. L40/1 (scope to refuse entry to local telecommunications loops); and Case COMP/M.1571 *New Holland / Case* (distribution and sales networks for agricultural machinery and construction equipment).
[99] Case IV/M.623 [1996] O.J. L183/1, para.213. See also Case IV/M.190 *Nestlé / Perrier* [1992] O.J. L356/1, para.32 (access to shelf space as a barrier to entry).
[1] Case COMP/M.2602, para.47.
[2] Case COMP/M.1915 [2004] O.J. L82/1.
[3] As a new entrant could gain access to many business customers by winning a contract with a single consolidator; para.77.
[4] Paras 74 to 83 and 113 to 116.
[5] In Case COMP/M.1628 *TotalFina / Elf* [2001] O.J. L143/1, the Commission found that a system of deposits on LPG bottles and a contractual prohibition on distributors accepting gas bottles from other producers increased barriers to entry; para.291.
[6] See, e.g. Case IV/M.190 *Nestlé / Perrier* [1992] O.J. L356/1 (wholesale annual rebates as a barrier to entry; para.95) and Case IV/M.986 *Agfa-Gevaert / Du Pont* [1998] O.J. L211/22 (package deals, tying and exclusivity provisions; paras 63 to 71).
[7] In Case IV/M.190 *Nestlé / Perrier* [1992] O.J. L356/1, the Commission stated, at para.98 (see also para.34): "High concentration in itself is a barrier to entry because it increases the likelihood and the efficiency of single or concerted reaction by the established firms against newcomers with a view to defending the acquired market positions and profitability".
[8] Case COMP/M.1813 *Industri Kapital (Nordkem) / Dyno* [2001] O.J. L154/41, para.100.
[9] See paras 6–026 and 6–027 above and Areeda, Hovenkamp & Solow, *Antitrust Law* (2nd edn, Aspen Law & Business, 2000), Vol.IIA, para.421f.

acts as a barrier to entry by restricting access to inputs, e.g. by purchasing suppliers or through long-term exclusivity or matching rights terms in contracts) and a belief on the part of potential entrants that incumbents may engage in predation.[10]

(c) Entry impediments

Entry impediments[11] delay entry and enable incumbents to earn excess profits in the period between the decision to enter and actual entry. They may arise, e.g. from a need to set up production facilities, obtain necessary approvals and, if there are long-term contracts in place, obtain contracts. **16–014**

(d) Analysis of barriers to entry in practice

Analysis of barriers to entry—and in particular, quantification—is very difficult, particularly in the time periods available under the ECMR. This section identifies categories of evidence which are commonly regarded as probative in determining the extent of barriers to entry. First, the *history of previous actual, attempted and threatened entry* and exit is relevant to an analysis of barriers to entry. In particular, successful true new entry—as opposed to entry through acquisition[12]—*suggests*[13] that entry barriers are not high. The fact that new entry has not occurred in the past is consistent *both* with entry barriers being high *and* with the market price being at competitive levels (reducing the incentive to enter). In assessing true new entry it is important to understand the motivation behind the entry attempt,[14] how rapidly it occurred, and the effects it had on profits and prices. Potential entry may be clear, e.g. from announcements by potential competitors or through their applications for planning permission. If entry barriers are believed to be low it is instructive to analyse entry and *survival rates*[15] over specified periods, typically three and seven years. **16–015**

Secondly, changes in market conditions are relevant to an appraisal of

---

[10] Such beliefs may be based on past activity or a prediction of the likelihood of predation. Predation is most likely to succeed if the incumbent has a large market share, price cuts can be targeted effectively at the new entrant and the new entrant will have difficulty accessing capital to fund it through the period of predatory behaviour.

[11] See Oster, *Modern Competitive Advantage* (3rd edn, Oxford UP, 1999), p.82.

[12] Porter, *Competitive Strategy* (1998 edn, The Free Press), p.7, argues that: "Companies diversifying through acquisition into the industry from other markets often use their resources to cause a shake-up ... Thus acquisition into an industry with intent to build market position should probably be viewed as entry even though no new entity is created".

[13] Areeda, Hovenkamp & Solow, *Antitrust Law* (2nd edn, Aspen Law & Business, 2000), Vol.IIA, note at para.422e that, "if the minimum efficient scale is large, entry that was profitable for one firm may no longer be profitable for another. Thus, to demonstrate low barriers conclusively, entry must be recurring and achieve significant market shares".

[14] e.g. was it a diversification from a neighbouring market?

[15] The period of time which the entrant traded in the market.

barriers to entry. If, for example, there is evidence of deregulation or the collapse of a cartel, this may alter the analysis of barriers to entry.

Thirdly, economists have surveyed a number of industries to seek to determine the shapes of companies' cost curves.[16] The surveys tend to be based on *engineering studies* of the costs of constructing a plant to minimum efficient scale or *survivorship studies* which proceed on the assumption that if a certain size of plant is efficient, then, over time, all plants in the industry should approach that size as operators of plants of other sizes either invest in their plant or exit from the industry.[17] Such surveys are not generally possible within the timescales available under the ECMR.

16–016   Fourthly, as noted above, there is a number of specific measurements which can be carried out in the context of the merger analysis. These include in particular, advertising intensity (the ratio of advertising expenditure to sales), and research and development intensity (the ratio of research and development expenditure to sales).

Fifthly, if profits are persistently high without attracting entry, this suggests that there are barriers to entry,[18] since entry would be expected if investment is likely to generate an economic profit.

(e) Barriers to expansion

16–017   Barriers to expansion affect the ability of existing suppliers to increase their capacity. In general they are closely related to barriers to entry. However, some industries (such as petroleum refining) involve high sunk costs of entry but the costs of expanding output of a particular product may be low.[19]

(f) Barriers to exit and contestable markets

16–018   Barriers to *exit* from a market are relevant because new *entry* is less likely when the costs of exit are high, since the risks of attempted entry are increased. Exit barriers include: *sunk costs*, e.g. through investment in durable and specialised assets; the fixed costs of exit, such as redundancy payments to staff; and strategic barriers, e.g. if a presence in the market in question is necessary to provide a full range service to customers.

---

[16] See Martin, *Advanced Industrial Economics* (2nd edn, Blackwell, 2002), pp.376 and 377 (and see also pp.371 to 376).

[17] Carlton & Perloff, *Modern Industrial Organization* (4th edn, Addison-Wesley, 2005), pp.40 to 42.

[18] The Commission took account of Volvo's margins in finding that its acquisition of Scania would create a dominant position in Sweden: Case COMP/M.1672 *Volvo / Scania* [2001] O.J. L143/74, paras 144 and 145. Carlton & Perloff, *Modern Industrial Organization* (4th edn, Addison-Wesley, 2005), pp.245 to 246, observe: "testing whether long-run profits are positive is a test of free entry, not of (perfect) competition. Free entry guarantees that long-run profits equal zero, but not that price equals marginal cost".

[19] See generally Case COMP/M.2498 *UPM-Kymmene / Haindl* [2002] O.J. L233/38, paras 108 to 111.

When barriers to entry and exit are absent, a market may be a *contestable market*,[20] i.e. a market which is completely open to potential competition and which would have a competitive outcome even if there were only one supplier. In such markets, incumbents will, in making their pricing decisions, take account of uncommitted entrants which would be likely to respond to price increases by "hit and run" entry. A contestable market exists when three conditions are met. First, there are potential entrants. Secondly, sunk costs are nil and potential entrants have the same costs as incumbents. Thirdly, potential entrants will gain an advantage from entering, e.g. because the contracts in question are substantial in terms of value or duration.[21] The parties argued unsuccessfully that markets were contestable in *Volvo / Scania*[22] and *SCA / Metsä Tissue*.[23] By contrast, the UK Competition Commission found that the supply of helicopter services to offshore oil and gas facilities was a contestable market in *CHC Helicopter Corporation / Helicopter Services Group ASA*.[24] However, an empirical study of the effects of UK mergers found that the competitive constraint following that merger arose from *actual* entry rather than the mere *threat* of entry.[25]

---

[20] See Scherer & Ross, *Industrial Market Structure and Economic Performance* (3rd edn, Houghton Mifflin Co, 1990), pp.374 to 377; Carlton & Perloff, *Modern Industrial Organization* (4th edn, Addison-Wesley, 2005), p.76; Porter, *Competitive Strategy* (1998 edn, The Free Press), pp.259 to 266; and Martin, "The Theory of Contestable Markets" (available at *www.blackwellpublishers.co.uk/martin*).

[21] Viscusi, Vernon & Harrington, *Economics of Regulation and Antitrust* (3rd edn, The MIT Press, 2000), pp.160 and 161.

[22] Case COMP/M.1672 [2001] O.J. L143/74, para.268.

[23] Case COMP/M.2097, para.187.

[24] Cm. 4556, January, 2000. Similarly, the UK Director General of Fair Trading's advice in *EasyJet / NewGo*, July 10, 2002 (*www.oft.gov.uk/Business/Mergers + FTA/Decisions/index. htm*), recommended clearing a transaction involving shares of 90% on some airline routes on the grounds that the markets were "contestable" with at least one substantial competitor and entry barriers which were not high.

[25] PriceWaterhouseCoopers, "Ex Post Evaluation of Mergers", Report Prepared for the OFT, DTI and Competition Commission, March 2005 (available via *www.oft.gov.uk/NR/rdonlyres/ 4F8F41F9-5D96-4CD4-8965-8DDA26A64DA8/0/oft767.pdf*), para.1.11.

CHAPTER 17

THE FAILING FIRM DEFENCE

17.1 INTRODUCTION

17–001 If the Commission anticipates that consumer welfare will decline following a merger, it may nevertheless approve the transaction on the grounds that one of the parties is a failing firm[1] and the deterioration in the competitive structure will not be *caused* by the merger.[2] The failing firm defence is therefore very closely related to the "counterfactual" principle, which was discussed in Ch.5 above.[3]

This Chapter describes the current test for the failing firm defence as set out in the Notice on Horizontal Mergers (s.17.2), describes the evolution of

---

[1] See generally Areeda, Hovenkamp & Solow, *Antitrust Law* (2nd edn, Aspen Law & Business, 1998), Vol.IV, s.9D-1; Pitofsky, "Proposals for Revised United States Merger Enforcement in a Global Economy" (1982) 81 *Georgetown Law Journal* 195; Sohn, "Failing and Flailing Firms: Merger Analysis in a time of Recession, Changing Technology, and International Competition" (1992) 61 *Antitrust Law Journal* 155; Correia, "Re-examining the Failing Company Defense" (1996) 64 *Antitrust Law Journal* 683; Mason & Weeds, "The Failing Firm Defence: Merger Policy and Entry" (available via *http://repec.org/res2003/Mason.pdf*); and Baccaro, "Failing Firm Defence and Lack of Causality: Doctrine and Practice in Europe of Two Closely Related Concepts" [2004] E.C.L.R. 11. The US Horizontal Merger Guidelines, 1992 (amended in 1997) (*www.usdoj.gov/atr/public/guidelines/hmg.htm*), s.5, define the failing firm defence as arising when: the failing firm will be unable to meet its financial obligations in the near future; it will not be able to reorganise successfully under insolvency legislation; it has made good faith efforts to seek alternative purchasers who would keep the assets in the market and would raise less substantial competition issues; and, without the merger, the assets would leave the market. The Guidelines state that similar arguments can be made for "failing divisions".

[2] Notice on Horizontal Mergers, para.89.

[3] The UK Office of Fair Trading's Substantive Merger Guidelines, May 2003 (*www.oft.gov.uk*), state, at para.4.36, that if one of the parties to the merger is a failing firm: "the counterfactual might need to be adjusted to reflect the likely failure of one of the parties and the resulting loss of rivalry". Areeda, Hovenkamp & Solow, *Antitrust Law* (2nd edn, Aspen Law & Business, 1998), Vol.IVA, para.963a3, raise the question of whether the target's financial difficulties might lead to a transaction being cleared in circumstances falling short of a failing firm defence; for the position under the ECMR, see Case COMP/M.2810 *Deloitte & Touche / Andersen (UK)*, paras 44, 45 and 49, which is discussed in para.17–010 below.

the test (s.17.3), reviews the Commission's more recent decisions (s.17.4) and assesses whether the test is drawn too narrowly (s.17.5).

17.2 THE NOTICE ON HORIZONTAL MERGERS

The Notice on Horizontal Mergers provides[4]: **17–002**

"The Commission considers the following three criteria as relevant for the application of a 'failing firm defence'. First, the allegedly failing firm would in the near future be forced out of the market because of financial difficulties if not taken over by another undertaking. Second, there is no less anti-competitive alternative purchaser than the notified concentration. Third, in the absence of a merger, the assets of the failing firm would inevitably exit the market".

In *NewsCorp / Telepiù*[5] the Commission explained that the rationale for the third criterion was that the first two criteria do not completely rule out the possibility of third parties acquiring the assets if the failing firm becomes insolvent. Such an acquisition of assets would have similar competitive effects to a merger.

The Notice on Horizontal Mergers also states that the burden of proof is on the notifying parties.[6]

17.3 THE EVOLUTION OF THE TEST

(a) The Commission's approach prior to BASF

In *Kali und Salz / MdK / Treuhand*[7] the Commission identified three criteria **17–003** which, if proven, establish the defence. First, in the absence of the merger or acquisition, the merging or acquired company would disappear from the market in the near future ("failing firm").[8] Secondly, merger with or

---

[4] Para.90.
[5] Case COMP/M.2876 [2004] O.J. L110/73.
[6] Para.91. For discussion of the standard of proof, see para.2–031(c) above.
[7] Case IV/M.308 [1994] O.J. L186/38, paras 70 to 90.
[8] The Canadian Merger Guidelines, 2004 (*www.competitionbureau.gc.ca/PDFs/2004% 20MEGs.Final.pdf*), para.9.4, discuss categories of evidence which may be relevant to the issue of whether the target is likely to fail. Scheffman, Coate & Silva, "20 Years of Merger Guidelines Enforcement at the FTC: An Economic Perspective" (available at *www.usdoj.gov/ atr/hmerger/11255.pdf*), state: "In a number of cases the FTC has undertaken a variety of accounting and economic analyses to determine the financial health of one of the merging parties. These analyses include: reviewing cash flow forecasts to determine whether financial obligations will be met in short term, analyzing operating statements to render an opinion on what impact exiting a market has on corporate cash flow and profitability post exit, evaluating

acquisition by another company which would result in less damage to the competitive structure of the market can be practically ruled out. And thirdly, there is evidence that, if the merging or acquired company were to disappear from the market, virtually all of its market share would go to its merger partner or acquirer. On the facts, the Commission found that the defence was established. MdK's losses were covered by a public body, the Treuhand, but the Commission accepted that it was a failing firm, not least because ongoing funding was prohibited by the rules on State aids. Neither an investment bank appointed as part of the privatisation procedure nor the Commission in its review of the market was able to identify any alternative purchaser for MdK, even combined with substantial aid by the Treuhand. In the unusual circumstances of this case, the third criterion identified by the Commission in the passage quoted above was also satisfied: if MdK ceased trading it could reasonably be expected that all of its market share would shift to Kali und Salz because this was the only other supplier in the German potash market.

The Commission's decision was appealed to the European Court of Justice, which upheld the existence of a failing firm defence.[9] The Court adopted a broader formulation of the test than the Commission, stating that a concentration could be approved "if the *competitive structure* resulting from the concentration would deteriorate in similar fashion even if the concentration did not proceed".

In *Aerospatiale / Alenia / de Havilland*[10] the defence was rejected because there was no likelihood that Boeing would close down de Havilland if the merger failed: although it had expressed a preference to sell de Havilland, the parties were not the only potential purchasers. In *Saint-Gobain / Wacker-Chemie / NOM*[11] the defence failed because the Commission felt that there were alternative solutions and, even if there were not, the competitive situation for customers would be better if Wacker-Chemie's silicon carbide activities ceased rather than being transferred to the proposed purchasers.[12]

(b) The BASF decision

17–004 In *BASF / Eurodiol / Pantochim*[13] the Commission refined the approach it had developed in *Kali und Salz*. Pantochim and Eurodiol had been placed

---

cost allocation methods to assure appropriate costs have been allocated to failing assets, performing standard financial statement analyses of a firm or division which is anticipating exit, and assessing alternative buyers or other financing opportunities".

[9] Joined Cases C-68/94 and C-30/95 *France v Commission* [1998] E.C.R. I-1375, paras 112 to 116.

[10] Case IV/M.53 [1991] O.J. L334/42, para.31.

[11] Case IV/M.774 [1997] O.J. L247/1, paras 247 to 259.

[12] See also Case IV/M.877 *Boeing / McDonnell Douglas* [1997] O.J. L336/16, paras 57 to 61 (and see Bishop, "The Boeing / McDonnell Douglas Merger" [1997] E.C.L.R. 417); Case IV/M.890 *Blokker / Toys 'R' Us (II)* [1998] O.J. L316/1, paras 109 to 113; Case IV/M.993 *Bertelsmann / Kirch / Premiere* [1999] O.J. L53/1, para.71 (rejecting a failing division defence); and Case IV/M.1221 *Rewe / Meinl* [1999] O.J. L274/1, paras 66 to 69 (rejecting a failing division defence).

[13] Case COMP/M.2314 [2002] O.J. L132/45.

under the Belgian pre-bankruptcy regime. BASF was able to establish that the first and second limbs of the Commission's traditional three-stage test were satisfied but could not show that, if the target businesses were closed, it would acquire *all* of their market share.[14] However, the Commission accepted BASF's argument that, in the light of the decision of the European Court of Justice in *Kali und Salz*, the criteria should be refined into a four-stage test[15]:

(a) the acquired undertaking would in the near future be forced out of the market if not taken over by another undertaking[16];

(b) there is no less anti-competitive alternative purchaser;

(c) the assets to be acquired would inevitably exit the market if not taken over by another undertaking; and

(d) the deterioration of the competitive structure through the merger is at least no worse than in the absence of the merger.

On the facts,[17] the Commission found that, if the target businesses were closed, a subsequent restart would be unlikely, there would be significant capacity shortages, a long lead-time for the construction of new capacity and, therefore, adverse effects on market conditions for a considerable transitional period as a direct consequence of the exit of the target's capacity. It also found that, following the merger, BASF would not have an incentive to raise price as its business plans demonstrated that the target plants had to be operated at or near full capacity in order to achieve profitability. The Commission concluded that: "the customer may expect better supply conditions and prices after the merger than under a bankruptcy scenario where the assets of Eurodiol are taken off the market ... [The] deterioration of the competitive structure resulting from the notified operation will be less significant than in the absence of the merger".[18]

The first three criteria identified by the Commission in *BASF* are reflected in the passage from the Notice on Horizontal Mergers quoted in para.17–002 above.

17–005

---

[14] Para.151.

[15] Paras 142 and 143.

[16] It is unclear how significant the risk of failure must be and how remote the prospects of successful restructuring. Areeda, Hovenkamp & Solow, *Antitrust Law* (2nd edn, Aspen Law & Business, 1998), Vol.IV, advocate, at para.953c, a criterion that insolvency or bankruptcy is imminent or highly probable.

[17] Paras 144 to 163.

[18] Paras 162 and 163. In Case COMP/M.2621 *SEB / Moulinex* the Commission rejected a failing firm argument, at para.41, on the grounds that third parties might, in the absence of the merger, have acquired some of the Moulinex brands and restored all or part of Moulinex' competition capacity. (However, the Commission referred the French aspects of the transaction to the French authorities, which *accepted* the failing firm defence; see the discussion in Case T-119/02 *Royal Philips Electronics NV v Commission* [2003] E.C.R. II-1433, para.346.)

17.4 THE COMMISSION'S MORE RECENT DECISIONS

(a) NewsCorp / Telepiù

17–006 In *NewsCorp / Telepiù*[19] the Commission considered a merger to near monopoly[20] between two suppliers of pay-TV services[21] in Italy, Telepiù and Stream, which had both incurred heavy losses in the period 1991 to 2001.[22] NewsCorp argued that, in the absence of the merger, it was likely to close Stream and claimed, therefore, that the merger should be approved unconditionally[23] because the failing firm defence was available.

The Commission noted that Stream was jointly controlled by NewsCorp and Telecom Italia, which meant that NewsCorp was relying on the failure of part of the acquiring company (not the target, which is the more usual situation) and, furthermore, was relying on the failure of a *division* (and not the whole of NewsCorp). It stated: "The importance of proving lack of causality is even greater in the case of a claimed 'failing division' which is actually the acquiring company".[24]

17–007 The Commission then considered the three criteria for the application of the failing firm defence which are now set out in the Notice on Horizontal Mergers.[25]

(a) It rejected NewsCorp's claim that Stream would have been forced out of the market if not taken over by another undertaking, seemingly[26] on the grounds that the case involving a failing division and there was no risk of NewsCorp being forced out of the market. (This

---

[19] Case COMP/M.2876 [2004] O.J. L110/73. See also Baccaro, "The Commission closes probe into pay-TV industry in Italy approving Newscorp / Telepiù deal", *Competition Policy Newsletter*, Summer 2003, p.8; Pereira, "Recent Consolidation in the European pay-TV sector", *Competition Policy Newsletter*, Summer 2003, p.29; Baccaro, "Failing Firm Defence and Lack of Causality: Doctrine and Practice in Europe of Two Closely Related Concepts" [2004] E.C.L.R. 11; and Caffara & Coscelli, "Merger to Monopoly: NewsCorp / Telepiù" [2003] E.C.L.R. 625.

[20] See paras 103 and 114.

[21] See also Case COMP/M.2845 *Sogecable / Canalsatélite / Via Digital*, in which a failing firm argument was rejected in a Spanish pay-TV merger (see paras 110 to 117).

[22] However, the Commission noted some more recent improvements, in particular a reduction in the ratio of total programming costs to total subscription revenues and an increase in the number of subscribers following successful attempts to combat privacy; see paras 87, 97 and 98.

[23] In this respect, NewsCorp's argument could be said to "prove too much".

[24] See paras 211 and 212.

[25] Paras 213 to 220.

[26] It is clear from para.220 of the decision that the argument was rejected, but the reasoning at paras 213 to 215 is opaque. In particular, the suggestion that Stream could be turned around is attributed to third parties and the Commission does not express a view on its credibility. The account given in the text is based on Pereira, "Recent Consolidation in the European pay-TV sector", *Competition Policy Newsletter*, Summer 2003, p.29 at p.35 and Baccaro, "Failing Firm Defence and Lack of Causality: Doctrine and Practice in Europe of Two Closely Related Concepts" [2004] E.C.L.R. 11, at p.22.

reasoning implies that a failing division defence would *always* fail unless it could be shown that the sale of the division was necessary to prevent the parent company becoming insolvent[27].)

(b) It also rejected the argument that there was no less anti-competitive purchaser on the grounds that neither NewsCorp nor Telecom Italia had ever invited public offers for the business. NewsCorp had argued that there were no purchasers with synergies large enough to turn the business around and had relied in support of this argument on an expert report from JP Morgan.[28]

(c) The Commission left open the third issue (whether, in the absence of a merger, the assets of the failing firm would inevitably exit from the market) as it had found against NewsCorp on the first two criteria.

However, having rejected the failing firm defence, the Commission added[29]: **17–008**

"the risk of Stream exiting the market, if it were to materialise, would be a factor to take into account when assessing the present merger. The Commission further considers that an authorisation of the merger subject to appropriate conditions will be more beneficial to consumers than a disruption caused by a potential closure of Stream".

The reasoning on this crucial point of policy is extremely brief and the case is probably best understood as one in which a merger to near monopoly *as amended by the commitments* was less harmful to consumers than the counterfactual (in which there was a material risk that one of the pay-TV operators, Stream, would exit from the market)[30] and the merger was therefore approved on the basis of a counterfactual analysis, taking account of the customer benefits *brought about by the commitments* (which might be described in a broad sense as efficiencies).[31]

Given the brevity of the Commission's reasoning, it is useful to examine **17–009**

---

[27] The reasoning is flawed because the basis of the failing firm defence (namely that there is no causal link between the merger and the detriment to competition) is equally applicable to a failing division and it is therefore illogical to make the defence available in one situation but not the other. In any event, if the failing firm defence is not available for arbitrary, technical reasons, a counterfactual analysis should lead the Commission to reach the same result.

[28] The Commission should have carried out a market test to identify whether NewsCorp was incorrect in reaching the conclusion that there were no potential purchasers for Stream, since there is little point in requiring parties to incur costs in seeking to sell a business that no rational purchaser would buy.

[29] Para.211.

[30] Caffara & Coscelli, "Merger to Monopoly: NewsCorp / Telepiù" [2003] E.C.L.R. 625 refer, at p.627, to the emergence of an "ailing-but-not-yet failing" defence.

[31] Caffara & Coscelli, "Merger to Monopoly: NewsCorp / Telepiù" [2003] E.C.L.R. 625 comment, at p.626: "Merger control is being used to impose *ex ante* regulation that could not readily be imposed through general competition law".

subsequent comment on the case by the Commission and its senior officials.[32]

(a) The Commission's XXXIIIrd Annual Report on Competition Policy, 2003, stated[33] that an authorisation subject to conditions would be more beneficial to consumers than a prohibition "followed most probably by the closure of Stream by its owners". The Commission's decision did *not* state that Stream would "most probably"[34] have closed in the absence of a decision approving the merger. The statement implies that on a counterfactual analysis, the merger per-haps[35] ought to have been cleared, since it was more likely than not that Stream would have left the market in any event.

(b) Philip Lowe, Director General of DG Competition, said: "The solution took due account of the circumstances of the case and was pragmatic because neither Telepiù nor Stream, the pay-TV operators present so far, had ever been profitable. There was accordingly a strong risk that one of them would exit the market in any event, with all negative consequences for Italian pay-TV subscribers that this would have entailed".[36] Philip Lowe's reference to the decision being "pragmatic" may reflect the fact that consumers would have suffered if the transaction had been prohibited (since it was likely that one of the operators would have left the market, creating a great deal of hassle for consumers in migrating to the other supplier), and would also have suffered (in a somewhat artificial respect) if the Commission had accepted the failing firm defence, because the transaction would then have been cleared unconditionally (which would have deprived consumers of the benefits of the remedies package which was negotiated).[37]

---

[32] See also Commission press release IP/03/478; "Media Mergers", OECD, DAFFE/ COMP(2003)16, p.294; Ungerer, speech, "Application of Competition Law to Media—Some Recent Issues", June 22, 2004 (*http://europa.eu.int/comm/competition/speeches/text/ sp2004_019_en.pdf*); and Baccaro, "Failing Firm Defence and Lack of Causality: Doctrine and Practice in Europe of Two Closely Related Concepts" [2004] E.C.L.R. 11, at p.22.
[33] Para.270.
[34] See also Baccaro, "The Commission closes probe into pay-TV industry in Italy approving Newscorp / Telepiù deal", *Competition Policy Newsletter*, Summer 2003, p.8, at p.9 (also using the expression "most probably") and the Commission's press release, IP/03/478 (which refers to the "likely closure of Stream").
[35] The issues which arise are: (a) whether the standard of proof is the balance of probabilities (see s.2.5(b) above); and (b) whether the reallocation of assets on closure would have resulted in a less anti-competitive outcome than the merger, an issue that the Commission left open in the case itself.
[36] Speech, "Media Concentration and Convergence: Competition in Communications", 13 January, 2004 (*http://europa.eu.int/comm/competition/speeches/text/sp2004_002_en.pdf*).
[37] Consumers would not have been harmed as a result of the merger if the failing firm defence had been available as the defence is premised on the absence of a causal link between the merger and any harm to consumers.

(b) Andersen

Deloitte & Touche | Andersen (UK)[38] involved a reduction from five to four **17–010** players in the market for audit and accounting services for quoted and large companies. The Commission cleared the transaction on the grounds that a causal link between the concentration and a possible situation of collective dominance could be excluded and relied on a counterfactual analysis (proceeding on the basis that a reduction from five to four players was inevitable because the Andersen network was disintegrating in the aftermath of the Enron scandal, and finding that there was no less harmful scenario for competition than the merger).[39] The Commission did *not* even refer in the decision to the failing firm defence (presumably because the transaction did not satisfy its terms).

(c) BLU

In *Pirelli | Edizione | Olivetti | Telecom Italia*,[40] Edizione undertook to **17–011** dispose of its shareholding in BLU as a condition of approval of the merger, but it was unable to find a purchaser and the Commission agreed to substitute a new set of undertakings for the original commitments. The new commitments provided for the break-up of BLU's assets and distribution to the remaining players in the market, with the customer base being transferred in its entirety to the smallest supplier. Baccaro has drawn an analogy between the principles applied by the Commission in that case (which involved a comparison of the detriments to competition arising from implementation of the revised undertakings with those arising from an insolvency of BLU) and the failing firm defence.[41] In particular, whilst BLU's assets would not have exited from the market in the absence of the restructuring, it was likely that the leading operator would have acquired at least part of its customer base if BLU became insolvent, meaning that the likely distribution of assets following an insolvency proceeding could have resulted in a greater detriment to consumer welfare than the "break up" approved by the Commission in accepting the revised undertakings.

---

[38] Case COMP/M.2810, paras 44, 45 and 49. See also Case COMP/M.2816 *Ernst & Young France | Andersen France*; Case COMP/M.2824 *Ernst & Young | Andersen Germany*; and Areeda, Hovenkamp & Solow, *Antitrust Law* (2nd edn, Aspen Law & Business, 1998), Vol.IVA, para.963a3.

[39] For further details of the counterfactual analysis, see para.5–004(d) above.

[40] Case COMP/M.2574 as explained in Baccaro, "Failing Firm Defence and Lack of Causality: Doctrine and Practice in Europe of Two Closely Related Concepts" [2004] E.C.L.R. 11, at pp.18 and 19.

[41] See p.19.

17.5 WHETHER THE FAILING FIRM TEST IS DRAWN TOO NARROWLY

17–012 This section argues that the criteria for the failing firm defence set out in the Notice on Horizontal Mergers are drawn too narrowly, since the defence is based on the principle that the Commission should not prohibit mergers which do not *cause* any detriments to consumers because conditions of competition would be *at least as bad* if the merger did not proceed,[42] but the Notice requires the notifying parties to prove more than the absence of causation in order to establish the defence.

    (a) The criterion that the failing firm would be forced out of the market "in the near future" if not taken over by another undertaking reflects a concern that customers should not be deprived of the benefits of competition from the target firm for a material time (if it would, in the absence of the merger, have remained in the market for longer than "the near future"). However, in other circumstances, the Commission is willing to permit mergers to proceed which cause harm to consumers over a period longer than "the near future", so long as consumers do not suffer in the longer term. In particular, when considering new entry, it is *not* necessary to show that the merged group would be deterred from raising prices by the threat of entry; it is sufficient to show that any attempt by the merged group to exercise market power would be defeated by *timely* new entry, which normally means entry within two years,[43] a longer period than "the near future". There is no principled basis for permitting relatively short term harm to consumers in cases when the analysis is based on new entry but not when it is based on the failing firm defence.

    (b) Further, the criterion that in the absence of a merger, the assets of the failing firm would inevitably exit from the market requires the notifying party to prove additional facts beyond showing that the merger is not the cause of any significant impediment to competition in the market.[44] For example, if the assets would be purchased by a party raising competition issues at least as serious as those raised by the notifying party, then the failing firm defence would not be available even though an absence of causation was established. Similarly, if the assets would remain in the industry but the purchaser would operate them at low level of intensity, this may harm consumers more than an acquisition by the notifying party (particularly

---

[42] See the decision of the European Court of Justice in Joined Cases C-68/94 and C-30/95 *France v Commission* [1998] E.C.R. I-1375, para.110 and the Notice on Horizontal Mergers, para.89.
[43] See para.16–004 above.
[44] The question of the relevant standard of proof under the ECMR is discussed in para.2–031(c) above.

if prices are heavily influenced by available capacity and the purchaser can demonstrate that it would not close the capacity and
would operate it intensively).

The fact that the failing firm defence is drawn too narrowly may explain why **17–013**
the Commission has decided cases involving firms in severe financial difficulty on the basis of other criteria. In particular, the Commission's analysis
in *Deloitte & Touche / Andersen (UK)*[45] was based on an assessment of the
counterfactual and *not* a failing firm analysis. Nevertheless, the Commission
cited this decision as an illustration of the "failing firm" defence in the 2002
draft Commission Notice on Horizontal Mergers,[46] although these references are *not* included in the *final* version of the Notice. The inference is that
the Commission found that there was no causal link between the merger and
any reduction in competition but the failing firm defence was not available.

---

[45] Case COMP/M.2810, paras 44, 45 and 49.
[46] See n.51.

CHAPTER 18

EFFICIENCY GAINS

18.1 INTRODUCTION

(a) General

18–001 The proper role of efficiencies[1] in the appraisal of mergers[2] has been the

---

[1] See generally Areeda, Hovenkamp & Solow, *Antitrust Law* (2nd edn, Aspen Law & Business, 1998), Vol.IVA, s.9E; Gotts & Goldman, "The Role of Efficiencies in M&A Global Antitrust Review: Still in Flux?", published in the 2002 *Annual Proceedings of the Fordham Corporate Law Institute*, p.201; Röller, Stennek & Verboven, "Efficiency Gains from Mergers", The Research Institute of Industrial Economics, Working Paper No. 543, 2000 (available at *www.iui.se/wp/Wp543/IUIWp543.pdf*); Stennek & Verboven, "Merger Control and Enterprise Competitiveness—Empirical Analysis and Policy Recommendations", The Research Institute of Industrial Economics, Working Paper No 556, 2001 (available at *www.iui.se/wp/Wp556/IUIWp556.pdf*); "The Efficiency Defense and the European System of Merger Control", a study prepared for the Directorate General of Economics and Financial Affairs, No. 5, 2001 (*http://europa.eu.int/comm/economy_finance/publications/european_economy/2001/eers0501_en.pdf*); the International Competition Network, "Analysis of Merger Guidelines", Chapter 6, "Efficiencies" (*www.internationalcompetitionnetwork.org/seoul/amg_chap6_efficiencies.pdf*); RBB Economics, "The Efficiency-Enhancing Effects of Non-Horizontal Mergers", 2005 (report for the Commission DG for Enterprise and Industry) (available via *http://europa.eu.int/comm/enterprise/library/lib-competition/doc/non_horizontal_mergers.pdf*); Venit, "The Role of Efficiencies in Merger Control", paper presented to the EC Merger Control Conference on November 8, 2002; Leary, "Efficiencies and Antitrust: A Story of Ongoing Evolution", speech of November 8, 2002 (*www.ftc.gov/speeches/leary/efficienciesand antitrust.htm*); Gerard, "Merger Control Policy: How to Give Meaningful Consideration to Efficiency Claims?" [2003] C.M.L.Rev. 1367; Luescher, "Efficiency Considerations in European Merger Control—Just Another Battle Ground for the European Commission, Economists and Competition Lawyers?" [2004] E.C.L.R. 72; Leary, "An Inside Look at the *Heinz* Case" [2002] *Antitrust* 32; Kolasky, "Lessons from Baby Food: the Role of Efficiencies in Merger Review" [2002] *Antitrust* 82; Bian & McFetridge, "The Efficiencies Defence in Merger Cases: Implications of Alternative Standards" (2000) 33 *Canadian Journal of Economics* 293; Kolasky & Dick, "The Merger Guidelines and the Integration of Efficiencies into Antitrust Review of Horizontal Mergers" (available at *www.usdoj.gov/atr/hmerger/11254.htm*); de la Mano, "For the Customer's Sake: The Competitive Effects of Efficiencies in Merger Control", Enterprise Papers No. 11; Werden, "An Economic Perspective on the Analysis of Merger Efficiencies" [1997] *Antitrust* 12; Farrell & Shapiro, "Scale Economies and Synergies

most controversial topic in the history of the ECMR. The debate has focused on two issues.[3] The first is whether the fact that a merger is expected to result in efficiency gains for the merged group may be relied on as a ground for prohibiting the transaction (or clearing it only on the provision of undertakings). This issue is analysed in s.7.6 above. The second is whether, and if so to what extent, the generation of efficiency gains should be taken into account by the Commission as a factor weighing in favour of approving the merger. This Chapter focuses on the second issue.

This section considers the rationale for treating efficiency gains as a positive factor in merger appraisal and identifies a number of approaches that could be adopted by merger authorities in assessing efficiency gains. Section 18.2 surveys the Commission's historic treatment of efficiencies. Section 18.3 describes the approach to efficiency gains in the revised ECMR. Finally, s.18.4 analyses the practical issues which arise in taking efficiency gains into account when appraising mergers.

(b) Rationale for treating efficiency gains as a positive factor in merger appraisal

The rationale for taking account of efficiencies resulting from mergers as a **18–002** factor weighing in favour of an approval decision is threefold. First, the

---

in Horizontal Merger Analysis" (2001) 68 *Antitrust Law Journal* 685; Brodley, "Proof of Efficiencies in Mergers and Joint Ventures" (1996) 64 *Antitrust Law Journal* 575; Yde & Vita, "Merger Efficiencies: Reconsidering the 'Passing-On' Requirement" (1996) 64 *Antitrust Law Journal* 735; Stockum, "The Efficiencies Defense for Horizontal Mergers: What is the Government's Standard?" (1993) 61 *Antitrust Law Journal* 829; Hausman & Leonard, "Efficiencies from the Consumer Viewpoint" (1999) 7 *George Mason Law Review* 707; Conrath & Widnell, "Efficiency Claims in Merger Analysis: Hostility or Humility?" (1999) 7 *George Mason Law Review* 685; Pitofsky, "Proposals for Revised United States Merger Enforcement in a Global Economy" (1982) 81 *Georgetown Law Journal* 195; Froeb & Werden, "A Robust Test for Consumer Welfare Enhancing Mergers Among Sellers of a Homogeneous Product" (1998) 58 *Economics Letters* 367; Noel, "Efficiency Considerations in the Assessment of Horizontal Mergers Under European and U.S. Antitrust Law" [1997] E.C.L.R. 458; Camesasca, "The Explicit Efficiency Defence in Merger Control: Does it Make the Difference?" [1999] E.C.L.R. 14; Kattan, "Efficiencies and Merger Analysis" (1994) 62 *Antitrust Law Journal* 513; Kocmut, "Efficiency Considerations and Merger Control—Quo Vadis, Commission?" [2006] E.C.L.R. 19; Ross & Winter, "The Efficiency Defense in Merger Law: Economic Foundations and Recent Canadian Developments" (2005) 72 *Antitrust Law Journal* 471 and Federal Trade Commission and Department of Justice, "Commentary on the Horizontal Merger Guidelines", 2006 (available via *www.ftc.gov/os/2006/03/CommentaryontheHorizontalMergerGuidelinesMarch2006.pdf*), Ch.4.
[2] For discussion of different types of efficiencies, see the Appendix to "The Merger Guidelines and the Integration of Efficiencies into Antitrust Review of Horizontal Mergers", Kolasky & Dick, 2002 (available at *www.usdoj.gov/atr/hmerger/11254.pdf*); Areeda, Hovenkamp & Solow, *Antitrust Law* (2nd edn, Aspen Law & Business, 2000), Vol.IIA, para.402b; Röller, Stennek & Verboven, "Efficiency Gains from Mergers", The Research Institute of Industrial Economics, Working Paper No. 543, 2000 (available at *www.iui.se/wp/Wp543/IUIWp543.pdf*), pp.12 to 22; and Stennek & Verboven, "Merger Control and Enterprise Competitiveness—Empirical Analysis and Policy Recommendations", The Research Institute of Industrial Economics, Working Paper No 556, 2001 (available at *www.iui.se/wp/Wp556/IUIWp556.pdf*), pp.11 to 16.
[3] Efficiencies may also be relevant to an assessment of the merged group's incentives, in particular to tacitly collude or pursue a leveraging strategy; see Chs 8, 11 and 12 above.

basis for treating mergers more benignly than cartels, notwithstanding that both eliminate price competition between previously independent companies, is that mergers generate efficiencies.[4] Secondly, efficiencies may contribute to achieving the goals of an antitrust system—whether promoting consumer welfare, total welfare or efficiency—and therefore provide a genuine benefit to society. Thirdly, efficiencies which *increase* competition in the market are unambiguously to be encouraged.

(c) Options for giving positive effect to efficiency gains

18–003 Efficiency gains may be treated positively by antitrust authorities through one or more of the following mechanisms.[5]

(a) A *presumptive approach* gives positive weight in the merger appraisal process to efficiency gains (by treating mergers more benignly than cartels and setting safe-harbours based on market shares or concentration levels below which transactions generally will not be challenged) but does *not* allow any direct analysis of efficiencies as part of that process, on the grounds that it is impossible in practice properly to adjudicate on such issues.[6]

(b) Under an *increasing rivalry standard*, efficiencies may be taken into account in so far as they *increase* competition within the market. For example, a merger of two inefficient suppliers, each of which acted as a price-follower on the market, might result in the creation of a company able to compete actively on price and exert greater competitive pressure on its larger competitors.[7]

---

[4] See para.1–025 above. However, the ideological coherence of a system which treats mergers more benignly than cartels is called into question by the conclusions in a working paper co-authored (prior to his appointment) by Lars-Hendrik Röller, the first Chief Competition Economist at DG COMP. Röller, Stennek & Verboven, "Efficiency Gains from Mergers", The Research Institute of Industrial Economics, Working Paper No. 543, 2000 (available at *www.iui.se/wp/Wp543/IUIWp543.pdf*) conclude a literature review, at pp.9 and 35, by stating that "there seems to be no support for a general presumption that mergers create efficiency gains".

[5] See generally the decision of the Canadian Competition Tribunal in *The Commissioner of Competition v Superior Inc*, April 4, 2002, paras 84 to 113 (the decision was upheld on appeal by the Canadian Federal Court of Appeal on January 31, 2003) and Bian & McFetridge, "The Efficiencies Defence in Merger Cases: Implications of Alternative Standards" (2000) 33 *Canadian Journal of Economics* 293.

[6] Bork, *The Antitrust Paradox* (1993 edn, The Free Press, 1978), states, at p.219: "Williamson was wrong in proposing an efficiency defense in merger cases, since the elements of the trade-off between output restriction and efficiency gain cannot be studied directly. The trade-off must be estimated indirectly through economic reasoning. Market shares that may or may not be created by merger can then be expressed in general legal rules".

[7] See the UK Office of Fair Trading's Substantive Merger Guidelines, May 2003 (*www.oft. gov.uk*), para.4.30.

(c) A *price standard*[8] requires the antitrust authority to determine whether any efficiencies will ensure that post-merger prices are no higher than they would have been in the absence of the merger. In particular, a merger may result in the merged group having the *ability* profitably to reduce its output and increase prices because of the reduction in rivalry brought about by the merger, but the merged group may nevertheless have an *incentive* to increase its output, thereby reducing prices, if the merger results in efficiency gains which reduce the merged group's marginal costs, as a profit-maximising firm will increase its output until its marginal revenue is equal to its marginal cost.[9] In other words, whilst reducing output may be *more* profitable than the merging parties' pre-merger strategies, efficiencies may ensure that the *most* profitable strategy for the merged group is to increase output, which reduces price. There are four principal criticisms of a price standard.[10] First, it is difficult in practice to carry out a precise trade-off between market power and efficiencies in order to predict the effect of the merger on price.[11] Secondly, by

---

[8] The US Horizontal Merger Guidelines, 1992 (amended in 1997) (*www.usdoj.gov/atr/public/ guidelines/hmg.htm*), para.4, provide: "The Agency will not challenge a merger if cognizable efficiencies are of a character and magnitude such that the merger is not likely to be anti-competitive in any relevant market. To make the requisite determination, the Agency considers whether cognizable efficiencies likely would be sufficient to reverse the merger's potential to harm consumers in the relevant market, e.g. by preventing price increases in that market. In conducting this analysis, the Agency will not simply compare the magnitude of the cognizable efficiencies with the magnitude of the likely harm to competition absent the efficiencies. The greater the potential adverse competitive effect of a merger ... the greater must be cognizable efficiencies in order for the Agency to conclude that the merger will not have an anticompetitive effect in the relevant market". This passage is commonly regarded as applying a price or broad consumer welfare standard but compare Kolasky & Dick, "The Merger Guidelines and the Integration of Efficiencies into Antitrust Review of Horizontal Mergers" (available at *www.usdoj.gov/atr/hmerger/11254.htm*), characterising the approach in the US Horizontal Merger Guidelines as a "hybrid consumer welfare / total welfare model". See also Werden, "An Economic Perspective on the Analysis of Merger Efficiencies" [1997] *Antitrust* 12, at p.14. (Compare the US Supreme Court's statement in *FTC v Procter & Gamble* 386 US 568 (1967): "Possible economies cannot be used as a defense to illegality".) The New Zealand Merger Guidelines, 2004 (*www.comcom.govt.nz/Publications/ContentFiles/Documents/Mergersand AcquisitionsGuidelines.PDF*), adopted a price standard at para.7.4. See also the UK Office of Fair Trading's Substantive Merger Guidelines, May 2003 (*www.oft.gov.uk*), para.4.31. The UK Competition Commission's Merger References Guidelines, March 2003 (*www.competition-commission.org.uk*), identify the availability of an efficiency defence and adopt a price standard, at para.4.41: "The prospective cost reductions must be expected to result in prices lower than if the merger did not take place. This must be the case notwithstanding the scope to charge higher prices because of the reduction in competitive pressures in the market".

[9] See Europe Economics, Report for the European Commission, "Study on Assessment Criteria for Distinguishing between Competitive and Dominant Oligopolies in Merger Control", May 2001, p.56 (and see also p.53) and Farrell & Shapiro, "Horizontal Mergers: an Equilibrium Analysis" (1990) 80 *American Economic Review* 107.

[10] See Areeda, Hovenkamp & Solow, *Antitrust Law* (2nd edn, Aspen Law & Business, 1998), Vol.IVA, paras 971d and 976c.

[11] Compare Froeb & Werden, "A Robust Test for Consumer Welfare Enhancing Mergers Among Sellers of a Homogeneous Product" (1998) 58 *Economics Letters* 367, identifying a simple calculation to determine the reduction in marginal cost necessary to off-set the incentive to reduce output in the case of homogenous products.

focusing on the implications of the transaction for prices,[12] a price standard neglects the other important aspects of consumer welfare, namely innovation and variety or choice. Thirdly, very few mergers satisfy a price standard, with the consequence that adopting such a test accords very little practical significance to efficiency gains arising from mergers.[13] Fourthly, a price standard is ambiguous when some prices rise and others fall.[14]

(d) A *broad consumer welfare standard* is closely related to a price standard but recognises that consumer welfare may be affected not merely by price (and its concomitant, quality) but also innovation and variety or choice.[15] Under a broad consumer welfare standard, a merger would be permitted provided that its aggregate effect on consumer welfare is neutral or beneficial. A merger which would be likely to increase prices might nevertheless satisfy this test if the antitrust authority adjudged that benefits to consumers in terms of choice or innovation outweighed the detriment arising from increases in price.[16] There are two principal criticisms of the broad consumer welfare standard.[17] The first is that there are practical difficulties in trading off market power and efficiency and in trading off the different facets of consumer welfare. Secondly, as is the case with a price standard, a broad consumer welfare standard provides a very limited practical role for efficiency gains in merger appraisal.

(e) A *total welfare standard* examines whether the effect of any efficiency savings is to confer a net benefit on consumers and producers taken in aggregate. This is the basis of Williamson's "naïve trade-off" model.[18] It treats redistribution of wealth between consumers and

---

[12] For these purposes, quality is an aspect of price.

[13] See Bian & McFetridge, "The Efficiencies Defence in Merger Cases: Implications of Alternative Standards" (2000) 33 *Canadian Journal of Economics*, 293 at p.301 (see also pp.314 and 315).

[14] See Werden, "An Economic Perspective on the Analysis of Merger Efficiencies" [1997] *Antitrust* 12, at p.13 (observing, at n.11, that the use of average prices raises the question of whether the weight to be used is pre-merger or post-merger quantities).

[15] The introduction of new and improved products are sometimes described as "demand-side efficiencies" (in contrast to cost-side efficiencies). Whilst cost-side efficiencies may not be of any benefit to consumers, demand-side efficiencies *always* benefit consumers (because they gain through increased choice arising from the availability of new and improved products). See generally Evans & Padilla, "Demand-side Efficiencies in Merger Control", 26 *World Competition: Law and Economics Review*, Summer 2003.

[16] See the discussion in the Canadian Competition Tribunal in *The Commissioner of Competition v Superior Propane Inc*, April 4, 2002, paras 214 and 331 (the decision was upheld on appeal by the Canadian Federal Court of Appeal on January 31, 2003). Further, it is arguable that a merger which is liable to increase prices might be approved under a broad consumer welfare standard if the acquisition of a failing firm would result in customers continuing to be supplied during the process of change or the acquirer committed to honour existing warranties.

[17] Use of a broad consumer welfare standard addresses two of the criticisms of a price standard, as it takes account of variety or choice and innovation as well as price and quality issues and is able to deal with cases in which some prices rise and others fall.

[18] See paras 1–023 and 1–024 above.

producers as neutral and is not consistent with the Commission's focus, in applying EC antitrust rules, on consumer welfare.

(f) A *balancing weights approach* takes account of both consumer and producer welfare but addresses distributional concerns by placing greater weight on losses of consumer welfare than on gains in producer welfare.[19] As in the case of a total welfare standard, such an approach is not open to the Commission given its objective of maximising consumer welfare.

The operation of the broad consumer standard is illustrated in Fig. 18.1 below.

18.2 THE HISTORIC TREATMENT OF EFFICIENCY ARGUMENTS UNDER THE ECMR

(a) Legislative history

The 1989 draft of the ECMR[20] permitted mergers to be approved when they **18–004** "contribute to the attainment of the basic objectives of the Treaty in such a

---

[19] In Canada an "efficiency defence" is available if the company can demonstrate that the merger has brought about or is likely to bring about gains in efficiency that will be greater than, and will offset, the anti-competitive effects of the merger *and* that the gains in efficiency would not be likely to be achieved in the absence of the merger. In *The Commissioner of Competition v Superior Propane Inc*, the Tribunal's decision of August 30, 2000 was overturned by the Federal Court of Appeal in a judgment of April 4, 2001 and the case was remitted to the Tribunal, which took a second decision on April 4, 2002. (The second decision was upheld on appeal by the Canadian Federal Court of Appeal on January 31, 2003.) The case raised the question of how to quantify the anti-competitive effects of a transaction. In its first decision, the Tribunal applied a total welfare standard, leaving out of the analysis any shift from consumer to producer surplus (i.e. transfers from consumers to shareholders through price increases). The Court overturned this decision, finding that a total welfare standard was too narrow and suggesting instead that the Tribunal use a balancing weights approach in a form somewhat broader than that described in sub-para.(f) of the text under which an assessment of the anti-competitive effects of the merger would be based on a range of factors including the deadweight welfare loss, any shift from consumer to producer surplus, loss of variety of products and the prevention of competition or creation of a monopoly in some markets. In its second decision, the Tribunal noted that Canadian competition law focuses on efficiency and not consumers and that a broad consumer welfare standard would unduly limit the ambit of the efficiency defence. The Tribunal applied the balancing weights standard suggested by the Court, taking account of deadweight welfare loss and attributing a value to the redistributive effects of the merger. The Tribunal's decision was upheld on appeal. See further the Canadian Merger Guidelines, 2004, (*www.competitionbureau.gc.ca/PDFs/2004%20MEGs.Final.pdf*), part 8. Following the *Superior Propane* decision, the Canadian Competition Bureau appointed an Advisory Panel on Efficiencies which reported in August 2005 (the report is available at *www.competitionbureau.gc.ca/PDFs/FinalPanelReport Efficiencies_e.pdf*), concluding in particular that Parliament should define the standard to be applied in weighing efficiency gains against competition effects and that an efficiencies defence should not be available in the case of merger to monopoly.

[20] [1989] O.J. C22/14, recital 16. See also the 1988 draft at [1988] O.J. C130/4.

515

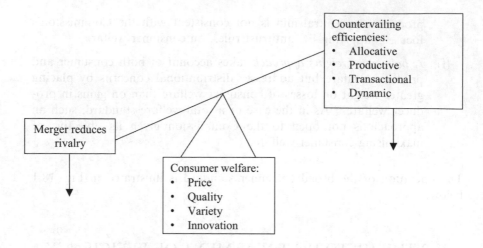

Fig. 18.1: The Efficiency Balance

way that, on balance, their economic benefits prevail over the danger they cause to competition". However, such language was omitted from the final version of the original ECMR.

(b) Early treatment of efficiency issues under the ECMR

18–005 There are suggestions that in certain early cases under the ECMR the Commission gave positive weight to efficiency gains in appraising mergers, without articulating, in any clear sense, the principles it was applying.[21] For example, in *Air France / Sabena*[22] the transaction created monopolies on the Brussels-Lyon, Brussels-Nice and Brussels-Paris routes but, on the Brussels-Paris route, the parties planned to increase the frequencies of flights by introducing a shuttle service which better responded to the needs of transit passengers. The Commission required more onerous commitments in relation to the Brussels-Lyon and Brussels-Nice routes (namely withdrawal by one of the parties from each of the routes) than the Brussels-Paris route (the granting of rights for other Community carriers to operate on the route), in part because the merger would result in the introduction of a "Brussels-Paris shuttle which the parties contemplate will be of benefit to consumers". Enrique González-Díaz commented: "In reaching the conclusion that the operation would not result in the creation or strengthening of a dominant position the Commission also took into account, for the first time, at least in

---

[21] Camesasca, "The Explicit Efficiency Defence in Merger Control: Does it Make the Difference?" [1999] E.C.L.R. 14, at pp.25 and 26, identifies a series of cases in which efficiencies may have been taken into account in the decision to clear a transaction or in determining the acceptability of commitments.

[22] Case IV/M.157, paras 30 to 32.

a positive way, the creation of efficiencies in terms of an increase in the frequency of services offered as a result of the setting up of a shuttle service between Paris and Brussels".[23]

In *Aerospatiale | Alenia | de Havilland*[24] the Commission appeared to identify circumstances in which efficiency gains could be given positive weight in merger appraisal. However, it excluded from its analysis efficiencies which were not merger-specific and therefore refused to take account of cost savings arising from better management of certain aspects of de Havilland's internal operation on the grounds that such savings could be achieved by de Havilland's existing owner or any other potential acquirer, and found that cost savings of around 0.5 per cent of the turnover of the combined group were insufficient to contribute to the development of technical and economic progress within the terms of Art.2(1)(b)[25] of the ECMR.[26] The Commission subsequently confirmed that its analysis in *de Havilland* "did offset the static efficiency gains to the parties against both the loss of consumer welfare and the longer term possibilities for technical progress which would have been afforded by the merger".[27]

However, in a consistent line of subsequent cases, the Commission **18–006** rejected arguments that efficiency gains should be treated positively, either because the arguments were not made out on the facts of the case or on the grounds that Art.2(1)(b) of the ECMR did not permit such factors to be taken into account in cases involving the creation or strengthening of a dominant position.

(a) In *MSG Media Service*[28] unquantified efficiency gains were found to be irrelevant because Art.2(1)(b) of the ECMR provides that technical and economic progress is relevant only if no obstacle is formed to competition and the transaction formed such an obstacle.

(b) *Nordic Satellite Distribution*[29] also involved a prohibition decision since the merger would have created obstacles to competition as well

---

[23] Case note, European Competition Law, para.9(b) (published in Van Gerven (coordinator), *Merger Control Reporter* (Kluwer Law International)).

[24] Case IV/M.53 [1991] O.J. L334/42, paras 65 to 69.

[25] Art.2(1) of the ECMR provides that, "In making [its] appraisal, the Commission shall take into account ... (b) ... the development of technical and economic progress provided that it is to consumers' advantage and does not form an obstacle to competition". The text is unchanged in the revised ECMR.

[26] Further, in Case IV/M.126 *Accor | Wagons-Lits* [1992] O.J. L204/1, claims of cost savings were rejected as unproven and the Commission found that any savings could be achieved without a merger, adding that the market had a low elasticity of demand and the merged group would have no incentive to pass on to customers any gains; paras 25 to 28.

[27] Commission paper at the OECD Roundtable, "Competition Policy and Efficiency Claims in Horizontal Agreements", OCDE/GD(96)65, p.55. See also Noel, "Efficiency Considerations in the Assessment of Horizontal Mergers Under European and U.S. Antitrust Law" [1997] E.C.L.R. 458, pp.512 and 513.

[28] Case IV/M.469.

[29] Case IV/M.490 [1996] O.J. L53/20.

as creating efficiencies, with the result that the conditions in Art.2(1)(b) of the ECMR were not met.[30]

(c) In *Saint-Gobain / Wacker-Chemie / NOM*[31] the Commission accepted that the merger would generate synergies but found that there was no mechanism for those synergies to be passed on to customers. It also emphasized that the purchasers of the merged group's products (producers of abrasive and refractory products) had higher levels of employment and added more value than the upstream producers with the consequence that "the overall effect of the operation would be likely to be more harmful than beneficial".

(d) In *Gencor / Lonrho*[32] the Commission found that the main effect of the merger would be to increase the market power of the merged entity and, if there were any synergies, they would not benefit consumers as the merger would form an obstacle to competition.

(e) In *Danish Crown / Vestjyske Slagterier*[33] the Commission stated that: "the Commission may take account of the development of technical and economic progress only to the extent that it is to consumers' advantage and does not form an obstacle to competition. The creation of a dominant position in the relevant markets ... therefore, means that the efficiencies argument put forward by the parties cannot be taken into account in the assessment of the present merger".

(c) The Commission's more recent analysis

18–007 In 1996, the Commission's position was that: "There is no real legal possibility of justifying an efficiency defence under the Merger Regulation".[34]

However, by September 2000, the Commission's position had evolved, with Götz Drauz, then the Director of the Merger Task Force, stating:

"I would not exclude that efficiency-type arguments could tilt the balance in borderline cases. (And by borderline cases I do not mean those that would lead to a monopoly or near monopoly.) Clearly, any party who wants to claim important efficiencies should be able to substantiate such claims. Moreover, I believe that such a party should provide reasonable evidence that the purpose of the transaction is to achieve the claimed

---

[30] A similar conclusion was reached in Case IV/M.993 *Bertelsmann / Kirch / Premiere* [1999] O.J. L53/1, para.122.
[31] Case IV/M.774 [1997] O.J. L247/1, para.246.
[32] Case IV/M.619 [1997] O.J. L11/30, para.214 (decision upheld on appeal in Case T–102/96 *Gencor v Commission* [1999] E.C.R. II–753).
[33] Case IV/M.1313 [2000] O.J. L20/1, para.198.
[34] Commission paper at the OECD Roundtable, "Competition Policy and Efficiency Claims in Horizontal Agreements", OCDE/GD(96)65, p.53.

efficiencies and not simply to gain market power. Finally, it would seem reasonable to require evidence that the efficiencies cannot be achieved through other, less restrictive means, and that a pass-on to customers will be highly likely. These may be tough criteria to meet, but unless they are met I find it difficult to envisage a case where the creation or strengthening of dominance would be outweighed by efficiency gains".[35]

In the aftermath of the public debate on *General Electric / Honeywell*,[36] **18–008** Mario Monti, then the Commissioner for Competition Policy, said:

"I would like ... to refute the assertion that the European Commission, when dealing with conglomerate mergers, is in fact applying what has been dubbed an 'efficiency offence'. Indeed, we distinguish clearly between—on the one hand—mergers leading to price reductions that are the result of strategic behaviour on the part of a dominant firm, the purpose of which is to eliminate or marginalize competitors with a view to exploiting consumers in the medium term, and—on the other—mergers which will objectively lead to significant and durable efficiency gains that are likely to be passed on to the consumer. By 'efficiency gain' I do not refer to any cost reduction resulting from the merger, but the types of efficiencies which are relevant for antitrust authorities that is a long-term and structural reduction in the marginal cost of production and distribution, which comes as a direct and immediate result of the merger, which cannot be achieved by less restrictive means and which reasonably will be passed on to the consumer on a permanent basis, in terms of lower prices or increased quality. When the merging parties do not provide a clearly articulated and quantified defence in terms of efficiencies ... it is much harder for an antitrust authority to clear a transaction that is likely to lead to foreclosure effects, because if foreclosure takes place and competitors are marginalised, there is no guarantee that prices are going to be maintained at least over the medium and longer term, at the low level that the merged entity might strategically set them at in order to foreclose competition".[37]

The Green Paper on the Review of the ECMR[38] invited views on the proper role and scope of efficiency considerations in the field of merger control.[39] In

---

[35] "Recent Developments in the Assessment of Dominance", in *EC Merger Control: Ten Years On* (International Bar Association, 2000), p.109, at p.119.
[36] Case COMP/M.2220 [2004] O.J. L48/1 (prohibition decision upheld on appeal on the basis of its horizontal effects analysis in Case T-210/01 *General Electric Company v Commission*, not yet reported, judgment of December 14, 2005).
[37] Speech of November 14, 2001, "Antitrust in the US and Europe: a History of Convergence" (*www.europa.eu.int/comm/competition/speeches/index_2001.html*). The Commissioner repeated the fact that there is no "efficiency offence" under the ECMR in a subsequent speech, "Review of the EC Merger Regulation—Roadmap for the reform project", Brussels, June 4, 2002 (*www.europa.eu.int/comm/competition/speeches/index_2002.html*).
[38] COM(01) 745/6 final, December 11, 2001.
[39] Para.172.

a speech commenting on the responses received to the Green Paper, the then Commissioner for Competition Policy, Mario Monti, noted that most respondents considered that there should be an "efficiency defence" that could mitigate a finding of dominance and stated that he shared that approach. He continued: "Many respondents to the Green Paper favour a 'restrictive' approach, namely that the efficiencies must be merger-specific, must be likely to be passed on to consumers, must not be mere cost-savings but 'real' reductions in the marginal cost of production, and that the burden of proving the efficiencies should lie with the merging parties. A minority of respondents favour a more 'liberal' approach, some indicating, for example, that there should be no bias in favour of efficiencies which benefit consumers over producers, and some arguing that there is no convincing reason why efficiencies should be merger-specific. We will deal with these questions and define our position more precisely in relation to the treatment of efficiencies in the [Commission] market power guidelines".[40]

18–009   The Commission provided evidence regarding efficiency issues to the UK House of Lords Select Committee on the European Union. The Committee's report states[41]:

"The Commission explained that 'one of the main streams of thought behind the merger review' was 'to give more explicit and predictable recognition to efficiency considerations.' It said that if a merger brought efficiencies, and it could be expected that these efficiencies would be passed on to consumers, this was something to be taken into account ... The Commission ... did not think that there was 'an objection in principle' to efficiencies being taken into consideration in the ECMR dominance test. They ... stressed that the dominance test was 'dominance plus' and 'on that basis' felt 'more confident about looking in a more prospective and dynamic way at efficiencies' ... The Commission confirmed that under its proposed efficiencies test the parties would have to show that the efficiencies would be passed on to the consumer. The Commission admitted that, once it had ruled that a merger would create or strengthen a dominant position, it would be difficult to demonstrate that the remaining elements of competition were such that they would 'lead to a transfer of wealth or benefits to the consumer.' The Commission, therefore, thought that in future any efficiency defence would be used 'rather exceptionally' ".

---

[40] Speech by Mario Monti, then the Competition Commissioner, "Review of the EC Merger Regulation—Roadmap for the reform project", Brussels, June 4, 2002 (*www.europa.eu.int/comm/competition/speeches/index_2002.html*). The then Commissioner added: "in my view it is appropriate to maintain a touch of 'healthy scepticism' with regard to efficiency claims, particularly in relation to transactions which appear to create competition problems".

[41] Thirty-second Report, "The Review of the EC Merger Regulation", July 23, 2002, HL Paper 165 (available at *www.parliament.the-stationery-office.co.uk/pa/ld200102/ldselect/ldeucom/165/16501.htm*), paras 166, 170 and 178.

Mario Monti, then the Commissioner for Competition Policy, in a speech of **18–010** November 7, 2002, stated[42]:

"We are of the opinion that an explicit recognition of merger-specific efficiencies is possible without changing the present wording of the substantive test in the Merger Regulation. Article 2(1)(b) of the Merger Regulation provides a clear legal basis in that respect ... The guidelines should say that the Commission intends to carefully consider any efficiency claim in the overall assessment of the merger, and may ultimately decide that, as a consequence of the efficiencies the merger brings about, the merger does not create or strengthen a dominant position as a result of which effective competition would be significantly impeded. A note of caution, however: efficiency claims should only be accepted when the Commission is in a position to conclude with sufficient confidence that the efficiencies generated by the merger will enhance the incentive of the merged entity to act pro-competitively for the benefit of consumers, because the efficiencies generated by the merger will either outweigh any adverse effects on consumers or make these effects unlikely. For the Commission to reach such a conclusion, the efficiencies would have to be of direct benefit to consumers, as well as being merger-specific, substantial, timely, and verifiable. The burden of proof should moreover rest on the parties, including the burden of demonstrating that the efficiencies are of such a magnitude as to outweigh the negative effects of the merger on competition. The draft guidelines will also indicate that it is very unlikely that efficiencies could be accepted as sufficient to permit a merger leading to monopoly or quasi-monopoly to be cleared".

On December 12, 2002, the Commission published the Proposed Amended and Re-stated ECMR and stated in the explanatory memorandum that: "The Commission is of the opinion that it is legally possible to deal explicitly with the issue of efficiencies under the present substantive test and with the present and proposed wording of the Merger Regulation".[43] The Commission referred specifically to Art.2(1)(b) of the ECMR in support of this proposition.[44] Consistently with this view, the 2002 draft Commission Notice on Horizontal Mergers, published on the same date, stated that efficiencies are taken into account under the ECMR in the assessment of horizontal mergers and identified the principles which would be applied in appraising such claims.[45]

---

[42] "Review of the EC Merger Regulation—the Reform Package", November 7, 2002, Brussels (*www.europa.eu.int/comm/competition/speeches/index_2002.html*).

[43] Para.60 of the explanatory memorandum.

[44] Notwithstanding this analysis, the Commission proposed to insert a new recital into the ECMR confirming that "it is appropriate to take account of any substantiated likely efficiencies put forward by the undertakings concerned".

[45] Paras 87 to 95. On February 17, 2003, Philip Lowe, Director General of DG Competition, in a speech in Brussels, "The future shape of European merger control" (*http://europa.eu.int/comm/competition/speeches/*), stated. "efficiencies generated by a merger may enhance the

On April 2, 2003 the Commission approved a merger to near monopoly subject to behavioural undertakings in *Newscorp / Telepiù*[46] on the grounds that "an authorisation of the merger subject to appropriate conditions will be more beneficial to consumers than a disruption caused by a potential closure of Stream". Although the decision does not contain an orthodox analysis of efficiency gains, it recognises that customer benefits may be accorded positive weight in the appraisal of mergers.[47]

(d) Input from academic economists

18–011 An important working paper from 2000 co-authored by Lars Hendrik Röller, who subsequently became the first Chief Competition Economist at DG COMP, concluded from a literature review that there was no support for a general presumption that mergers create efficiency gains, but some mergers do create efficiencies and benefit consumers through lower prices (with around 30 to 70 per cent of cost savings being passed on). The authors concluded that the presence and magnitude of efficiency gains should therefore be examined on a case-by-case basis.[48]

Subsequently, in 2001, Stennek and Verboven (who were co-authors of the working paper mentioned above) published a review of the empirical evidence on economies of scale, concluding that the exploitation of scale economies is a source of substantial cost savings in some but not all industries, and they are often present at low volumes of output but exhausted at larger volumes. They concluded: "the variability of scale economies across industries and different output volumes support the idea that cost savings should be evaluated on a case-by-case basis, i.e. an efficiency defence".[49]

In 2002, Neven and Röller stated that "the objective of protecting consumer welfare and the Commission's apparent neglect of efficiency considerations would be hard to square with the fact that most mergers are allowed. Indeed, if no efficiency is ever taken into account, all horizontal

---

incentive of the merged group to act pro-competitively, thereby counteracting the effects on competition which the merger might otherwise have". On April 20, 2004, in its Communication "A Pro-Active Competition Policy for a Competitive Europe" (available via *http:// europa.eu.int/comm/competition/publications/proactive/en.pdf*), the Commission stated: "The purpose of the merger control rules is not to stand in the way of necessary and efficiency-enhancing restructuring, but to ensure that those mergers are stopped or modified that would harm competition".

[46] Case COMP/M.2876, [2004] O.J. L110/73, paras 221 and 325.
[47] This case is discussed in s.17.4(a) above.
[48] Röller, Stennek & Verboven, "Efficiency Gains from Mergers", The Research Institute of Industrial Economics, Working Paper No. 543, 2000 (available at *www.iui.se/wp/Wp543/ IUIWp543.pdf*), pp.35, 42 and 53.
[49] Stennek & Verboven, "Merger Control and Enterprise Competitiveness—Empirical Analysis and Policy Recommendations", The Research Institute of Industrial Economics, Working Paper No 556, 2001 (available at *www.iui.se/wp/Wp556/IUIWp556.pdf*), pp.5 and 32 to 44. See also p.43, noting that in many industries concentration has gone further than would seem to be justified based on economies of scale alone.

mergers should be prohibited".[50] The authors surmised that the Commission assumed a certain level of efficiencies, enabling it to clear the majority of notified transactions (although this observation should be compared with the analysis in the working paper from 2000 discussed above), and concluded that the failure by the Commission systematically to evaluate efficiencies in each case could involve bias in the Commission's decisions.

18.3 THE TREATMENT OF EFFICIENCY GAINS UNDER THE REVISED ECMR

Recital 29 to the revised ECMR provides, in part: 18–012

"In order to determine the impact of a concentration on competition in the common market, it is appropriate to take account of any substantiated and likely efficiencies put forward by the undertakings concerned. It is possible that the efficiencies brought forward by the concentration counteract the effects on competition, and in particular the potential harm to consumers, that it might otherwise have and that, as a consequence, the concentration would not significantly impede effective competition, in particular as a result of the creation or strengthening of a dominant position".

Recital 29 makes clear that the Commission must give positive effect to efficiency gains. It also requires the Commission to apply either a price standard or a broad consumer welfare standard, but does not restrict the Commission to one or the other approach.

The Notice on Horizontal Mergers states that the Commission will approve a merger if the efficiencies arising from the merger enhance the incentive and ability of the merged group to act pro-competitively for the benefit of consumers, thereby counteracting the potential harm to consumers which might otherwise have arisen.[51] In this sense, therefore, efficiency gains form part of an analysis of the competitive effects of the merger rather than constituting a separate "efficiency defence". In order to qualify, the efficiencies must benefit consumers and be merger-specific and verifiable.[52]

The Form CO now includes a section on efficiency gains (s.9.3). The **18–013** accompanying notes make clear that completion of this section is voluntary.

---

[50] Neven & Röller, "Discrepancies Between Markets and Regulators: An Analysis of the First Ten Years of EU Merger Control", published as Ch.2 of *The Pros and Cons of Merger Control* by the Swedish Competition Authority in 2002 (and available at *www.kkv.se/bestall/pdf/ skrift_proscons.pdf*), p.22. See also para.1–025 above which discusses the rationale for treating mergers more benignly than cartels.
[51] Paras 76 and 77.
[52] Para.78. These criteria are discussed in the text below.

However, parties wishing the Commission to consider from the outset[53] whether efficiency gains generated by the merger are likely to enhance the incentive and ability of the merged group to act pro-competitively for the benefit of consumers are required to provide detailed information and underlying documentation in support of their claims.[54]

No mergers have yet been approved on the basis of efficiency gains of the type described in recital 29 of the revised ECMR. Whilst the Commission has in several cases taken account in a general sense of the efficiency gains arising from transactions,[55] the significant practical role for efficiency gains has, to date, been in the area of remedies: the Commission has accepted less intrusive remedies in several cases in order to protect efficiency gains that were expected to benefit consumers, as explained in s.20.4(c)(ii) below.[56]

18.4 SPECIFIC ISSUES IN ANALYSING EFFICIENCY GAINS

(a) Benefit to consumers

18–014 The Notice on Horizontal Mergers[57] states that efficiencies must be of benefit to consumers[58] if they are to be ascribed positive weight in the merger appraisal process: "The relevant benchmark in assessing efficiency claims is

---

[53] DG Competition's "Best Practices on the conduct of EC merger control proceedings" recommend, at para.18, that, where appropriate, notifying parties provide evidence of efficiency gains at the pre-notification stage because such claims are likely to require extensive analysis.

[54] For details of the evidence required by the Commission, see the Notice on Horizontal Mergers, para.88.

[55] See, e.g. Case COMP/M.3664 *Repsol Butano | Shell Gas (LPG)* (the Commission placed weight on the pro-competitive aspects of the transaction, arising in part from the generation of efficiencies; paras 33 to 35); Case COMP/M.3732 *Procter & Gamble | Gillette* (the Commission placed general weight on possible "portfolio efficiencies" arising from the transaction; see para.131); and Case COMP/M.3886 *Aster 2 | Flint Ink* (customers expected the merged group to generate cost and R&D synergies which could make it a stronger rival to a substantial existing supplier and confirmed the parties' claim that the merger resulted from a need for global reach; para.22). Further, the Commission has investigated why there has been relatively little cross-border merger activity in the financial sector; it carried out the investigation in part because of concerns that the benefits of scale (i.e. efficiencies) were not being realised; see press release IP/05/1386.

[56] The decisions include Case COMP/M.3099 *Areva | Urenco | ETC JV* in which the Commission doubted whether the specific efficiency effects claimed by the parties were "merger specific" (para.220), but took account of general efficiency gains in appraising the remedies (paras 242 and 243).

[57] Paras 79 to 84.

[58] See Hausman & Leonard, "Efficiencies from the Consumer Viewpoint" (1999) 7 *George Mason Law Review* 707 (describing a model which can be used to estimate the proportion of marginal cost savings which will be passed through to customers) and Yde & Vita, "Merger Efficiencies: Reconsidering the 'Passing-On' Requirement" (1996) 64 *Antitrust Law Journal* 735.

that consumers will not be worse off as a result of the merger".[59] Consumers may benefit in particular from lower prices or new or improved products.[60]

The question arises whether efficiencies generated by a merger must operate *exclusively* for the benefit of consumers (i.e. whether they must be passed on *in their entirety*) or whether a transaction may be cleared in reliance on efficiency considerations when the efficiencies are *shared* between producers and consumers, provided that consumers receive direct benefits.[61] The latter approach is to be preferred for two reasons. First, in applying a price standard or a broad consumer welfare standard, the focus is on the impact of the transaction on consumers, in which case the question of whether producers benefit is irrelevant, provided that the effect of the transaction is neutral or beneficial to consumers. Secondly, at a practical level, it is highly unlikely that a profit-maximising company would ever pass on to consumers the entirety of any efficiency savings,[62] and including a requirement to pass-on *all* efficiency savings to consumers would therefore render the efficiencies analysis of no practical relevance.[63] Accordingly, the

---

[59] Notice on Horizontal Mergers, para.79.

[60] Notice on Horizontal Mergers, paras 80 and 81. The scope for customers to benefit from lower prices through economies of scale is well-established (albeit difficult to prove), but the effects of mergers on incentives to engage in research and development and advertising are less well-established (see Stennek & Verboven, "Merger Control and Enterprise Competitiveness—Empirical Analysis and Policy Recommendations", The Research Institute of Industrial Economics, Working Paper No 556, 2001 (available at *www.iui.se/wp/Wp556/IUIWp556.pdf*), pp.14 and 15 for discussion).

[61] Prior to the publication of the 2002 draft Commission Notice on Horizontal Mergers, the then Commissioner for Competition Policy, Mario Monti, and the then Director of the Merger Task Force, Götz Drauz, confirmed that efficiencies which serve only to benefit the merging parties are excluded from the analysis: see paras 18–008 ("passed on to the consumer on a permanent basis") and 18–007 ("a pass-on to customers will be highly likely") above. Indeed, it is inherent in the choice of a price standard or a broad consumer welfare standard that efficiencies which serve solely to benefit producers are disregarded. Götz Drauz, then the Director of the Merger Task Force, "Recent Developments in the Assessment of Dominance", published in *EC Merger Control: Ten Years On* (International Bar Association, 2000), p.109 at p.118, has noted that: "efficiencies in the form of cost savings that will not be passed on to the merging firm's customers are irrelevant for the assessment. A more difficult situation is when a merger may lead to the introduction of new products or technology".

[62] Areeda, Hovenkamp & Solow, *Antitrust Law* (2nd edn, Aspen Law & Business, 1998), Vol.IVA, identify, at para.971b, three situations in which efficiency savings would be passed on in their entirety to customers: (a) when the market is competitive *and* rivals obtain the same efficiencies as the merged group; (b) when the supplier faces a vertical demand curve in the relevant price range; and (c) when price regulation requires a complete transfer of the benefits. Röller, Stennek & Verboven, "Efficiency Gains from Mergers", The Research Institute of Industrial Economics, Working Paper No. 543, 2000 (available at *www.iui.se/wp/Wp543/IUIWp543.pdf*), p.53, note empirical evidence suggesting that 30 to 70% of cost savings would be expected to be passed on.

[63] Equally, it is fallacious to suggest that a monopolist would choose to pass on *none* of the benefits of any reductions in marginal cost because it does not face any competition. The monopolist maximises its profits by setting its output or price such that its marginal revenue is equal to its marginal cost. If its marginal cost is reduced then it will profitably increase its output until its marginal revenue is equal to marginal cost and the effect of increasing output in the face of a downward sloping demand curve is that price will fall.

real issue is whether the efficiency gains from the transaction will be suffi-cient that the merged group has no *incentive* to exercise market power.[64]

The issue of passing-on benefits to consumers also raises the question of whether efficiencies which have longer-term benefits for consumers, such as innovation and research and development, may be taken into account in the merger appraisal. It is clear from the Notice on Horizontal Mergers[65] that efficiencies which lead to new or improved products (i.e. through innovation or research and development) are considered and the consumer benefits need not arise immediately, although the weight to be ascribed to any effi-ciencies will be reduced the longer they are projected into the future.[66]

(b) Merger-specific efficiencies

18–015 It is clear from the Commission's decision in *Aerospace / Alenia / de Havilland*[67] and the Notice on Horizontal Mergers that the Commission will exclude from its analysis any efficiencies which are not merger-specific. The Notice on Horizontal Mergers provides[68] that: "Efficiencies are relevant to the competitive assessment when they are a direct consequence of the notified merger and cannot be achieved to a similar extent by less anti-competitive alternatives. In these circumstances, the efficiencies are deemed to be caused by the merger and thus, merger-specific. It is for the merging parties ... to demonstrate that there are no less anticompetitive, realistic and attainable alternatives ... which preserve the claimed efficiencies. The Commission only considers alternatives that are reasonably practical in the business situation faced by the merging parties having regard to established business practices in the industry concerned". The Form CO requires parties wishing to rely on efficiency gains to identify "the reason why the party or parties could not achieve the efficiency to a similar extent by means other than through the concentration proposed, and in a manner that is not likely to raise competition concerns".[69]

The Commission's reference to *realistic and attainable* alternatives may be compared to:

---

[64] This implies that there is a "sliding scale" for assessing efficiencies: the greater the merged group's *ability* to exercise market power in the light of a structural analysis of the market, the more extensive must be the efficiencies in order to demonstrate that the merged group's *incentives* will be to take actions which do not harm consumer welfare; see the Notice on Horizontal Mergers, para.84. See also the comments of Götz Drauz, then the Director of the Merger Task Force, quoted in para.18–007 above (limiting the relevance of efficiency gains to borderline cases).

[65] Para.81.

[66] The US Horizontal Merger Guidelines 1992 (amended in 1997) (*www.usdoj.gov/atr/public/guidelines/hmg.htm*), n.37, do not require that the benefits to consumers are passed-on immediately and instead state that "delayed benefits from efficiencies (due to delay in the achievement of, or the realization of consumer benefits from efficiencies) will be given less weight because they are less proximate and more difficult to predict".

[67] Case IV/M.53 [1991] O.J. L334/42.

[68] Para.85.

[69] Para.9.3(iv).

(a) the test of *practicability* articulated by the then Commissioner for Competition Policy, Mario Monti ("cannot be achieved by less restrictive means")[70] and then the Director of the Merger Task Force, Götz Drauz ("cannot be achieved through other, less restrictive means")[71] in speeches prior to the adoption of the Notice on Horizontal Mergers[72]; and

(b) the US Horizontal Merger Guidelines, which refer[73] to efficiencies which are likely to be accomplished through the proposed merger and *unlikely* in practice in the business situation facing the merging firms to be accomplished in the absence of either the proposed merger or another means having comparable anti-competitive effects.[74] It remains to be determined whether the Commission's reference to "realistic" efficiencies is treated as synonymous with the US test of likelihood.[75]

---

[70] See para.18–008 above.

[71] See para.18–007 above.

[72] There are many reasons why efficiencies which are *practicable* may never be pursued by companies. In particular, investment in capacity in a static or declining market may depress the market price whilst a merger generally will not (as it will not increase industry capacity); and obtaining efficiencies through joint ventures or other contracts may raise hold-up concerns or give rise to other transaction costs. See generally Kolasky & Dick, "The Merger Guidelines and the Integration of Efficiencies into Antitrust Review of Horizontal Mergers" (available at *www.usdoj.gov/atr/hmerger/11254.htm*) and Areeda, Hovenkamp & Solow, *Antitrust Law* (2nd edn, Aspen Law & Business, 1998), Vol.IVA, para.973.

[73] The US Horizontal Merger Guidelines, 1992 (amended in 1997) (*www.usdoj.gov/atr/public/guidelines/hmg.htm*), para.4.

[74] The US Horizontal Merger Guidelines, 1992 (amended in 1997) (*www.usdoj.gov/atr/public/guidelines/hmg.htm*), n.35, make clear that if the merger enables an efficiency to be achieved more rapidly, then the timing advantage is a merger-specific efficiency. See also Stockum, "The Efficiencies Defense for Horizontal Mergers: What is the Government's Standard?" (1993) 61 *Antitrust Law Journal* 829 (arguing, at p.839, that if the merger enables an efficiency to be obtained at a lower cost then the cost advantage is a merger-specific efficiency). Areeda, Hovenkamp & Solow, *Antitrust Law* (2nd edn, Aspen Law & Business, 1998), Vol.IVA, recommended excluding as not merger-specific claimed management efficiencies (para.974b2) and unattributed reductions in personnel (para.974b3; the exclusion of this latter category of claimed efficiencies is also supported on the ground that layoffs may not be evidence of efficiencies in any event). The proposed treatment of management efficiencies is consistent with the Commission's in *de Havilland*; see para.18–005 above.

[75] In principle, the test of *likelihood* is to be preferred. The question of whether efficiencies are merger-specific is relevant in identifying the counterfactual against which the effects of the merger are appraised. If the merging parties are *likely* to take steps to realise the efficiencies if the merger does not proceed then there is no causal link between the merger and the generation of the efficiencies. Conversely, if the efficiencies are unlikely to be generated in the absence of the merger then prohibiting a merger on the grounds that it would be practicable for the parties to achieve efficiencies (notwithstanding that in all likelihood in practice they will not) is liable to harm consumer welfare. See s.2.5(b) above (standard of proof) and Ch.5 (the counterfactual). Compare Hausman & Leonard, "Efficiencies from the Consumer Viewpoint" (1999) 7 *George Mason Law Review* 707, arguing that mergers which lead to lower prices should be approved irrespective of whether the specific tests applied in appraising efficiencies are satisfied. They criticise the approach in the US Horizontal Merger Guidelines, 1992 (amended in 1997) (*www.usdoj.gov/atr/public/guidelines/hmg.htm*), on the grounds that it "can and does harm consumer welfare because it trades off relatively certain welfare gains (generated by the merger under consideration) to speculative potential welfare gains (generated by the hypothetical alternative means suggested by the Agencies)".

(c) Verifiable

18–016 Efficiency claims are hard to adjudicate upon for three reasons.[76] First, the evidence relating to possible efficiencies generally lies wholly or largely within the possession of the merging parties.[77] Secondly, efficiency claims are prospective and, as predictions, are inherently uncertain. Thirdly, the uncertainty is compounded by the fact that many mergers fail,[78] i.e. the efficiency gains anticipated by the merging parties commonly do not materialise. The Commission has therefore indicated that it will disregard efficiencies unless they are verifiable[79] and has placed the burden of proof[80]

---

[76] See Brodley, "Proof of Efficiencies in Mergers and Joint Ventures" (1996) 64 *Antitrust Law Journal* 575 (advocating a two-stage process involving an initial screening to determine whether the transaction is likely to generate efficiencies and a post-implementation review to identify the actual efficiency outcome).

[77] This generally applies to efficiencies at the level of the merging firms, but not to "industry level efficiencies", e.g. if the merger alters the research and development incentives for the competitors; see Röller, Stennek & Verboven, "Efficiency Gains from Mergers", The Research Institute of Industrial Economics, Working Paper No. 543, 2000 (available at *www.iui.se/wp/ Wp543/IUIWp543.pdf*), p.84.

[78] The numerous studies of the effects of mergers suggest that a substantial proportion is not successful: see, e.g. Scherer & Ross, *Industrial Market Structure and Economic Performance* (3rd edn, Houghton Mifflin Co, 1990), pp.97 to 141. Oster, *Modern Competitive Advantage* (3rd edn, Oxford UP, 1999), pp.232 to 236, describes the principal difficulties as arising from the "interaction problem" (namely integrating the merging businesses) and the "inspection problem" (namely that a company will sell a business only if the purchaser places a higher value on that business than the vendor, yet the vendor is much better placed to identify the proper value of the business, with the consequence that some acquisitions may fail because of errors in valuation by the acquirer). See also the International Competition Network Analytical Framework Sub-group, "The Analytical Framework for Merger Control" (available at *www.internationalcompetitionnetwork.org/afsguk.pdf*), para.5.

[79] The Notice on Horizontal Mergers, paras 86 to 88. See also Case IV/M.126 *Accor / Wagons-Lits* [1992] O.J. L204/1; the comments of Götz Drauz, then the Director of the Merger Task Force, quoted in para.18–007 above (referring to a need to "substantiate" claims); and the speech of the then Commissioner for Competition Policy, Mario Monti, "Review of the EC Merger Regulation—the Reform Package", November 7, 2002, Brussels (*www.europa.eu.int/ comm/competition/speeches/index_2002.html*). The US Horizontal Merger Guidelines, 1992 (amended in 1997) (*www.usdoj.gov/atr/public/guidelines/hmg.htm*) note, at para.4, the difficulties in verifying claimed efficiency gains and state that they will not be considered if they are vague or speculative or cannot be verified by reasonable means.

[80] In terms of evidence, Scheffman, Coate & Silva, "20 Years of Merger Guidelines Enforcement at the FTC: An Economic Perspective" (available at *www.usdoj.gov/atr/hmerger/11255.htm*), summarise practice in the US FTC as follows: "FTC accountants have also had a very important role in assessing potential efficiencies. The types of analyses performed may typically include: reviews of material costs and related contracts to assess savings related to quality purchases, reviews of labor costs and related union agreements to assess savings related to head count reductions, reviews of labor rates and anticipated reductions to see if actual reductions look realistic based on current manufacturing requirements and reviews of machine run rates and capacity schedules to assess whether it is likely for plant consolidation to result in anticipated cost savings. In addition, FTC accountants may perform cost/volume/ profit analyses evaluating shifts of production from one facility to another, and undertake research into current industry practices for comparison of claims that only a merger will allow achievement of operational efficiencies". See also Kattan, "Efficiencies and Merger Analysis" (1994) 62 *Antitrust Law Journal* 513, at p.533. At a practical level:

(a) the Commission may prefer evidence of efficiencies contained in real implementation plans, papers for the notifying parties' board and briefings prepared by the notifying

on the notifying party.[81]

In terms of a methodology for assessing efficiency gains, there are two principal options.[82] First, a *quantitative* analysis seeks to identify the *minimum required efficiencies* necessary to ensure (in the case of a price standard) that the merger will not result in an increase in prices relative to likely prices in the absence of the merger, and quantifies the *qualifying efficiencies*[83] to determine whether the latter outweigh the former.[84] Secondly, a *qualitative* approach seeks to take account at a more impressionistic level (recognising the difficulties in quantification) of whether the efficiency gains are sufficient to ensure that the merger will not significantly impede effective competition.[85] Such an approach is consistent with the Commission's qualitative

party to its lenders ahead of evidence generated specifically for the purposes of the merger appraisal process;

(b)　it may be instructive to examine whether the notifying party has previously made acquisitions and, if so, whether it delivered any claimed efficiency gains (whether such claims were made to antitrust authorities or the financial markets); and

(c)　in determining whether efficiencies are merger-specific, it may be important to document the transaction costs associated with the alternatives to merger.

[81] Notice on Horizontal Mergers, para.87.

[82] See Conrath & Widnell, "Efficiency Claims in Merger Analysis: Hostility or Humility?" (1999) 7 *George Mason Law Review* 685 (noting, at pp.693 and 694, that merger simulations may assist in overcoming the perception that balancing efficiencies with market power is like "subtracting apples from oranges"). The creation or strengthening of market power may have effects on customers going beyond possible increases in price by the merged group. In particular, rival suppliers may raise their own prices in the "shadow" of the merged group's price increase. Conversely, efficiency benefits may be felt by rival suppliers and not just the merged group. Kattan, "Efficiencies and Merger Analysis" (1994) 62 *Antitrust Law Journal* 513 and Roberts & Salop, "Efficiencies in Dynamic Merger Analysis" (1996) 19 *World Competition Law and Economic Review* 5, note that efficiencies generated by the merging parties may "diffuse" through to rival suppliers, creating a net benefit to consumers in excess of the benefits enjoyed by the merged group. There is an analogy here with innovations in product design which are commonly copied by rivals notwithstanding intellectual property laws. However, efficiencies which can be copied by rivals may only rarely be "merger-specific". Further, the efficiencies generated by mergers may be less visible to competitors than innovations in product design and the diffusion process may therefore not occur or occur more slowly.

[83] For discussion of the methodology in calculating qualifying efficiencies, see Stennek & Verboven, "Merger Control and Enterprise Competitiveness—Empirical Analysis and Policy Recommendations", The Research Institute of Industrial Economics, Working Paper No 556, 2001 (available at *www.iui.se/wp/Wp556/IUIWp556.pdf*), pp.5, 6 and 32 to 44. In the US, such efficiencies are assessed net of costs produced by the merger or incurred in achieving the efficiencies. (See also "The Efficiency Defense and the European System of Merger Control", a study prepared for the Directorate General of Economics and Financial Affairs, No. 5, 2001 (*http://europa.eu.int/comm/economy_finance/publications/european_economy/2001/eers0501_en. pdf*), p.92.)

[84] See Röller, Stennek & Verboven, "Efficiency Gains from Mergers", The Research Institute of Industrial Economics, Working Paper No. 543, 2000 (available at *www.iui.se/wp/Wp543/ IUIWp543.pdf*), pp. 10 and 92; and Dalkir & Warren-Boulton, "Prices, Market Definition, and the Effects of Merger: Staples-Office Depot (1997)", published in Kwoka & White eds., *The Antitrust Revolution* (4th edn, Oxford UP, 2004), p.52, at p.65.

[85] The US Horizontal Merger Guidelines, 1992 (amended in 1997) (*www.usdoj.gov/atr/public/ guidelines/hmg.htm*), state: "The Agency will not challenge a merger if cognizable efficiencies are of a character and magnitude such that the merger is not likely to be anticompetitive in any relevant market. To make the requisite determination, the Agency considers whether cognizable efficiencies likely would be sufficient to reverse the merger's potential to harm consumers in the relevant market, e.g. by preventing price increases in that market. In con-

approach in most cases to *all* other issues in merger appraisal.[86] Nevertheless, the Commission has indicated that: "Where reasonably possible, efficiencies ... should ... be quantified".[87] Philip Lowe, Director General of DG Competition, has observed:

"I would like to point out that quantitative analysis should not become a *sine qua non* for the analysis of efficiencies (or for the analysis of possible anticompetitive effect, for that matter). Often the relevant cost and demand data will not be available with sufficient precision or reliability to allow for precise estimation of the likely price effect of a merger. Nor will it very often be possible to determine, on the basis of demand data alone, precisely what the minimum required efficiencies should be for positive effects to result from a merger. In the majority of efficiency cases we will have, if anything, to resort to more qualitative assessments of the welfare impact. This is why, I think, our guiding principle that efficiencies are more likely to make a difference when they are shown to be substantial and the possible anticompetitive effects that might otherwise occur are small, is a reasonable one. I interpret these words as meaning that when precise cost and demand data are not available to allow for a precise quantitative estimation and comparison, for the Commission to allow an efficiency defence argument, it must be possible to foresee a *clearly* identifiable positive impact on consumers, not a marginal one".[88]

In assessing the extent to which costs savings will be passed on, it is important to assess whether the savings involve variable or fixed costs (the former are more likely to be passed on), the intensity of competition (the more competition there is, the more savings will be passed on), the elasticity of demand (pass on is likely to be limited if there is margin absorption arising from an increasing price elasticity of demand), the slope of the marginal cost function (if marginal costs are increasing, e.g. because of capacity constraints, pass on is likely to be limited), and the merged group's market share (pass on is typically higher for firms with intermediate market shares, i.e. neither very large nor very small).[89]

---

ducting this analysis, the Agency will not simply compare the magnitude of the cognizable efficiencies with the magnitude of the likely harm to competition absent the efficiencies. The greater the potential adverse competitive effect of a merger ... the greater must be cognizable efficiencies in order for the Agency to conclude that the merger will not have an anticompetitive effect in the relevant market".

[86] Arguably, the real issue in appraising efficiency arguments is whether the notifying party has presented a credible explanation of why the merger will have substantial consumer benefits, e.g. in terms of more dynamic competition or the introduction of new products.

[87] Notice on Horizontal Mergers, para.86.

[88] Philip Lowe, Director General of DG Competition, speech, "The future shape of European merger control", Brussels, February 17, 2003 (*http://europa.eu.int/comm/competition/speeches/*).

[89] See Röller, Stennek & Verboven, "Efficiency Gains from Mergers", The Research Institute of Industrial Economics, Working Paper No. 543, 2000 (available at *www.iui.se/wp/Wp543/IUIWp543.pdf*), pp.86 and 103 and Stennek & Verboven, "Merger Control and Enterprise Competitiveness—Empirical Analysis and Policy Recommendations", The Research Institute

The following categories of evidence, amongst others, may be relevant to an assessment of efficiency claims: information about costs and synergies, internal documents from the parties, previous industry studies (if any) and merger simulations.

(d) Substantial efficiencies

The Notice on Horizontal Mergers provides that efficiencies will be ascribed **18–017** positive weight in the appraisal of a transaction only if they are "substantial".[90] This is consistent with Areeda, Hovenkamp & Solow's[91] recommendation to ignore *minor* efficiencies on the basis that "ordinary" efficiencies are already taken into account in that antitrust treats mergers more benignly than cartels, notwithstanding that both eliminate competition between previously independent companies.[92] The Notice on Horizontal Mergers also confirms that the greater the possible negative effects on competition arising from a transaction, the more that the Commission has to be sure that the claimed efficiencies are substantial.[93]

(e) Timely

The Commission will only ascribe positive weight to efficiencies if they are **18–018** timely and has stated that "the later the efficiencies are expected to materialise in the future, the less weight the Commission can assign to them".[94]

(f) Disregarding anti-competitive strategies

The Commission will not consider as qualifying cost reductions, savings **18–019** which result from anti-competitive reductions in output.[95]

---

of Industrial Economics, Working Paper No 556, 2001 (available at *www.iui.se/wp/Wp556/IUIWp556.pdf*), pp.6 to 9 and 45 to 76. At pp.109 to 113, Röller, Stennek & Verboven discuss the scope to construct a model which takes account of both the price effect and any countervailing efficiencies. At pp.76 to 87, Stennek & Verboven discuss methods of quantifying pass on using data on prices, marginal or variable costs and (possibly) sales for several firms within the industry.

[90] Para.79.

[91] *Antitrust Law* (2nd edn, Aspen Law & Business, 1998), Vol.IVA, para.974.

[92] Such an approach is supported by the Commission's decision in *de Havilland*; see para.18–005 above. See also para.1–025 above.

[93] Para.84. Philip Lowe, Director General of DG Competition, speech, "The future shape of European merger control", Brussels, February 17, 2003 (*http://europa.eu.int/comm/competition/speeches/*), stated: "efficiencies are more likely to make a difference when they are substantial and the possible anti-competitive effects that might otherwise occur are small".

[94] Notice on Horizontal Mergers, para.83.

[95] Notice on Horizontal Mergers, para.80. See also the comments of Götz Drauz, then the Director of the Merger Task Force, quoted in para.18–007 above (stating that a party wishing to rely on efficiency gains ought to provide evidence that the purpose of the transaction is to

(g) A preference for reductions in marginal or variable costs

18–020 The Notice on Horizontal Mergers states[96] that "cost efficiencies that lead to reductions in variable or marginal costs are more likely to be relevant to the assessment of efficiencies than reductions in fixed costs; the former are, in principle, more likely to result in lower prices for consumers".[97] The Commission's *preference* for efficiencies which reduce marginal or variable costs reflects the view that efficiencies which reduce the merged group's *fixed* costs and not its *variable* costs[98] do not create the same incentive on the merged group to increase its output and reduce its price. However, the Notice on Horizontal Mergers does not *exclude* from the analysis efficiencies which reduce fixed costs. This may reflect the fact that[99] in the long run all costs are variable, the distinction between fixed and variable costs is not clear-cut (e.g. fixed costs which are subject to depreciation may, on analysis, be variable), and prices may in practice take account of amortisation of fixed costs.[1]

---

achieve the claimed efficiencies and not simply to gain market power). If the merged group were to seek to exercise market power by reducing output in an attempt to increase prices, then it would, in general, save costs. However, such savings are not qualifying efficiencies as they are inherent in the exercise of market power rather than a counter-weight to such exercise. Similarly, a reduction in marketing expenditure arising from the elimination of rivalry is not a qualifying efficiency. See also Röller, Stennek & Verboven, "Efficiency Gains from Mergers", The Research Institute of Industrial Economics, Working Paper No. 543, 2000 (available at *www.iui.se/wp/Wp543/IUIWp543.pdf*), p.83; the US Horizontal Merger Guidelines, 1992 (amended in 1997) (*www.usdoj.gov/atr/public/guidelines/hmg.htm*), para.4; and Kolasky & Dick, "The Merger Guidelines and the Integration of Efficiencies into Antitrust Review of Horizontal Mergers" (available at *www.usdoj.gov/atr/hmerger/ 11254.htm*).

[96] Para.91. See also para.94.

[97] Kolasky argues that the focus on efficiencies which reduce marginal costs is not appropriate for markets characterised by high rates of innovation (in contrast to a smokestack industry) and that a merger in such a market which allows very short-term price increases may enhance competition by enhancing the merged group's ability to fund research and development (see *www.usdoj.gov/atr/public/workshops/docs/202670.htm*).

[98] In *FTC v H J Heinz Co* 246 F.3d 708 (DC Cir 2001) the US DC Circuit Court considered an efficiency argument raised by Heinz on its proposed purchase of rival baby food producer, Beech-Nut. Heinz argued that the transaction would enable it to switch production from Beech-Nut's inefficient plant to Heinz's new plant which had spare capacity, claiming that the costs of processing Beech-Nut's food could be reduced by 43% if production were switched to Heinz's facilities. The US DC District Court concluded that the calculation of any savings should be based on the reduction in the *merged group's* variable costs rather than that of *the target's.*

[99] See Areeda, Hovenkamp & Solow, *Antitrust Law* (2nd edn, Aspen Law & Business, 1998), Vol.IVA para.974d and RBB Economics, "The Efficiency-Enhancing Effects of Non-Horizontal Mergers", 2005 (report for the Commission DG for Enterprise and Industry) (available via *http://europa.eu.int/comm/enterprise/library/lib-competition/doc/non_horizontal_ mergers.pdf*), p.11. See also Röller, Stennek & Verboven, "Efficiency Gains from Mergers", The Research Institute of Industrial Economics, Working Paper No. 543, 2000 (available at *www.iui.se/wp/Wp543/IUIWp543.pdf*), who state, at p.26: "In a dynamic setting, when new entry may occur, it may be possible that also fixed cost savings have an impact on prices".

[1] Stockum, "The Efficiencies Defense for Horizontal Mergers: What is the Government's Standard?" (1993) 61 *Antitrust Law Journal* 829, notes, at p.844, that costs which are fixed in the short run are, in the long run, relevant to firms' pricing and concludes that "it may be more appropriate to focus on long-term marginal cost, which includes more than simple

The Commission's focus, in its Notice, on costs savings has been criticised on the grounds that many of the most important synergies generated by non-horizontal mergers are the result of synergies arising from the combination of complementary assets, rather than direct costs savings as such.[2]

(h) Remaining competition

The Notice on Horizontal Mergers emphasises that the incentive on the **18–021** merged group to pass on efficiency gains to consumers is often linked to the competitive constraint posed by rival suppliers remaining on the market and potential entrants.[3] The Commission has also stated that a merger to monopoly is highly unlikely to be permitted on efficiency grounds[4] (although see para.18–010 above).

(i) Efficiencies arising in markets other than the one in which market power is created or strengthened

The Notice on Horizontal Mergers provides[5] that any efficiencies should "in **18–022** principle, benefit consumers in those relevant markets where" competition problems arise.[6] In other words, the Notice contemplates that it will *not* be possible to trade off gains to consumers in one market against losses in a second market.[7]

---

marginal production costs, on which only the most myopic firm would focus". See also Werden, "An Economic Perspective on the Analysis of Merger Efficiencies" (1997) 11 *Antitrust* 12, at p.13.

[2] See RBB Economics, "The Efficiency-Enhancing Effects of Non-Horizontal Mergers", 2005 (report for the Commission DG for Enterprise and Industry) (available via *http:// europa.eu.int/comm/enterprise/library/lib-competition/doc/non_horizontal_mergers.pdf*), p.105.

[3] Para.84.

[4] Notice on Horizontal Mergers, para.84.

[5] Para.79.

[6] See also Case T-87/05 *EDP v Commission*, not yet reported, judgment of September 21, 2005, where the Court of First Instance stated, at para.236, "the Commission cannot agree to declare the concentration compatible with the common market owing to the beneficial effects for competition on one of the sectors in question while ignoring the negative effects on the other sector".

[7] This seems correct in principle since the contrary approach implies a trade-off between one category of customers and a second (*except* in the unusual case in which products in the two markets in question are invariably sold together as pure bundles). Concerns are sometimes expressed that ruling out the scope for trading off benefits in one market against detriments in a second may be inefficient if the merger gives rise to competition concerns in a small market but the efficiency gains are substantial and relate to a much larger market; in this case, it *may* be appropriate to adopt a more flexible approach to remedies in the smaller market in order to ensure that the merger proceeds so that consumers in the larger market benefit (see s.20.4(c)(ii) below). The terms of the Notice can be compared with remarks at the EC Merger Control Conference, held in Brussels on November 7 and 8, 2002 (i.e. prior to the publication of the 2002 draft Commission Notice on Horizontal Mergers), by Claude Rakovsky of DG Competition, who had contemplated that efficiencies arising in markets other than the one in which the competition concerns arise might be taken into account provided that the goods were

By contrast, the US Horizontal Merger Guidelines provide that[8]: "the Agency normally assesses competition in each relevant market affected by a merger independently and normally will challenge the merger if it is likely to be anticompetitive in any relevant market. In some cases, however, the Agency in its prosecutorial discretion will consider efficiencies not strictly in the relevant market, but so inextricably interlinked with it that a partial divestiture or other remedy could not feasibly eliminate the anticompetitive effect in the relevant market without sacrificing the efficiencies in the other market(s). Inextricably linked efficiencies rarely are a significant factor in the Agency's determination not to challenge a merger. They are most likely to make a difference when they are great and the likely anticompetitive effect in the relevant market(s) is small".[9]

(j) Other issues

18–023 Several commentators[10] have sought to determine whether particular categories of efficiency (e.g. savings in corporate headquarters) are capable

---

complements (e.g. milk and butter). Further, it is sometimes suggested that such a trade-off should be permitted when there is a single customer in each of the markets in question (e.g. a national ministry of defence). For further discussion, see Röller, Stennek & Verboven, "Efficiency Gains from Mergers", The Research Institute of Industrial Economics, Working Paper No. 543, 2000 (available at *www.iui.se/wp/Wp543/IUIWp543.pdf*), pp.83 and 84.

[8] The US Horizontal Merger Guidelines, 1992 (amended in 1997) (*www.usdoj.gov/atr/public/guidelines/hmg.htm*), n.36. See also Areeda, Hovenkamp & Solow, *Antitrust Law* (2nd edn, Aspen Law & Business, 1998), Vol.IVA, para.972 (noting, at para.972c, the situation in which concerns about the creation through merger of market power in a very small market might be outweighed by tiny efficiency gains in a very large, connected market in which the merger would not create market power).

[9] See Kolasky & Dick, "The Merger Guidelines and the Integration of Efficiencies into Antitrust Review of Horizontal Mergers" (available at *www.usdoj.gov/atr/hmerger/11254.htm*) and Kolasky's comments at the FTC/DOJ Joint Workshop on Merger Enforcement (available at *www.usdoj.gov/atr/public/workshops/docs/202670.htm*).

[10] See Areeda, Hovenkamp & Solow, *Antitrust Law* (2nd edn, Aspen Law & Business, 1998), Vol.IVA, para.975; Porter, *Competitive Advantage* (The Free Press, 1998 edn), pp.324 and 325 (and see generally Ch.9); and Werden, "An Economic Perspective on the Analysis of Merger Efficiencies" (1997) 11 *Antitrust* 12 (distinguishing "unidirectional" rationalisation, which may occur if, e.g. the merger allows one of the parties' plants to be shut down, saving fixed costs and reducing variable costs if the retained plants are more efficient, and "bidirectional" rationalisation, which may occur if production for each merging party may be moved into capacity formerly owned by the other, e.g. by operating longer production runs to supply the merged group's broader customer-base). Compare the US Horizontal Merger Guidelines, 1992 (amended in 1997) (*www.usdoj.gov/atr/public/guidelines/hmg.htm*), para.4. The Irish Competition Authority's Guidelines for Merger Analysis, December 2002 (available at *www.tca.ie*), state at paras 5.10, 5.12 and 5.13: "The nature of potential efficiencies must be identified. Each case is considered on its merits. As a general indication, however, efficiencies that may be considered include:

    (a) Efficiencies that are likely to increase price rivalry (e.g. increase cost heterogeneity thus making tacit collusion more difficult, or enable two smaller firms to take on larger rivals);

    (b) Savings relating to more efficient purchasing processes;

    (c) Efficiencies that arise because competition is destructive (e.g. cherry picking) can be considered, although such arguments are likely to arise only in a very small number of markets;

of satisfying the tests described above. For example,[11] Farrell & Shapiro[12] distinguish simple scale economies (which they suggest should be treated with scepticism in particular because the merging parties are likely to have an incentive to expand output unilaterally if substantial economies are available and, if they are not, it is doubtful whether customers will benefit from the realisation of limited economies) and genuine efficiencies based on the close integration of specific, hard-to-trade assets owned by the merging

---

(d) Efficiencies that arise because of network effects in demand (e.g. standardisation); and
(e) Efficiencies due to technology transfer . . .

Efficiencies that are generally not considered are:

(a) Savings due to the integration of administration or head office functions;
(b) Input price reductions related to buyer power;
(c) Efficiencies related to economies of scale and scope that do not involve marginal cost reductions; and
(d) Efficiencies that may reduce price in one market cannot compensate for price increases in another.

In general, efficiencies that can be shown to reduce marginal (as opposed to fixed) costs will be treated more sympathetically as it is more probable that part of any reduction gets passed on to consumers as lower prices. This may be the case even in monopoly situations, although pass-through of cost reduction is generally higher the more rivalry is higher. Economic theory is less clear on the extent to which lower fixed costs are passed through as lower prices, especially if rivalry is not strong".

[11] Areeda, Hovenkamp & Solow, *Antitrust Law* (2nd edn, Aspen Law & Business, 1998), Vol.IVA para.970e, distinguish *real economies* (which may be taken into account) and *pecuniary economies* (which may not). Real economies involve true resource savings, such as reductions in the unit cost of producing goods, and are a genuine benefit to society. By contrast, pecuniary economies are economic advantages obtained by the merged group but which involve a transfer of wealth from third parties (such as benefits derived from buyer power or tax advantages) and provide no benefit to society. See also Röller, Stennek & Verboven, "Efficiency Gains from Mergers", The Research Institute of Industrial Economics, Working Paper No. 543, 2000 (available at *www.iui.se/wp/Wp543/IUIWp543.pdf*), p.83. The Australian Merger Guidelines, June 1999 (*www.accc.gov.au/content/item.phtml?itemId =719436&nodeId=file43a1f42c7eb63&fn=Merger%20Guidelines.pdf*), para.6.40, *exclude* from the analysis pecuniary savings from increased bargaining power, which simply result in a wealth transfer without creating any real resource savings. See also the Irish Competition Authority's Guidelines for Merger Analysis, December 2002 (available at *www.tca.ie*), quoted above. The references to *real economies* and *pecuniary economies* are unhelpful as they divert attention from the effect of the merger on consumers towards an analysis of the position of producers. Compare Hausman & Leonard, "Efficiencies from the Consumer Viewpoint" (1999) 7 *George Mason Law Review* 707, at pp.720 and 721: "Two problems arise with this argument. First, it is inconsistent with the argument that the part of productive efficiencies that are not passed on to consumers, but only increase producer surplus (profit), should not be taken into account. If increases in producer surplus should not be counted, decreases in producer surplus should not be counted either. But the more important problem is that this argument once again loses sight of consumers, the ultimate beneficiaries of the antitrust laws. When prices decrease to consumers as a result of 'pecuniary efficiencies' . . . the outcome is pro-competitive. In our view, this outcome should end the inquiry. The question should be the welfare effects for consumers, not the welfare effects for input suppliers. Otherwise the Agencies can and will reject mergers that are pro-competitive in that they increase consumer welfare".
[12] Farrell & Shapiro, "Scale Economies and Synergies in Horizontal Merger Analysis" (2001) 68 *Antitrust Law Journal* 685.

parties.[13] Farrell & Shapiro's insight arises from an application of established principles but is noteworthy because of the widespread expectation that economies of scale would readily qualify as efficiency gains.

---

[13] Farrell & Shapiro describe such efficiencies as "synergies" and note that they allow the merged group to produce on a different production function from either of the merging parties (rather than simply producing at a different point on an existing production function).

CHAPTER 19

OTHER EVIDENCE OF THE LIKELY EFFECTS OF THE MERGER ON CONSUMERS

19.1 INTRODUCTION

This Chapter discusses seven categories of evidence that relate *directly* to the question of whether the merger is likely to harm consumers. The categories of evidence discussed in this Chapter therefore differ to an extent[1] from those that allow the Commission to build up its own understanding of the way that the market operates and to make a qualitative prediction about the likely effects of the merger (see Chs 3 to 18 above).

19–001

19.2 CATEGORIES OF EVIDENCE

(i) Stock market announcements In assessing whether the merged group will have market power, it can be instructive to analyse stock market reactions to merger announcements.[2] In particular, purchasers of shares are generally aware that if a merger will lead to price increases in markets supplied by the merged group, then this will benefit both the merging parties *and* their competitors and, accordingly, the prices of shares in *all* companies active in the market would be expected to rise on announcement of such a transaction. Equally, purchasers of shares are generally aware that if a merger will

19–002

---

[1] The difference is one of degree. In particular, the use of merger simulations involves analysing the likely effects of the merger quantitatively (the Commission's normal approach is to carry out the analysis qualitatively).

[2] See generally Martin, *Advanced Industrial Economics* (2nd edn, Blackwell, 2002), pp.215 to 217 and Scherer & Ross, *Industrial Market Structure and Economic Performance* (3rd edn, Houghton Mifflin Co, 1990), pp.167 to 170. Analysis of stock market reactions supposes that such markets are efficient, i.e. that changes in the prices of shares reflect changing information about the underlying prospects for the business.

lead to cost savings for the parties without facilitating price increases, then the merged group will benefit but its competitors will, other things being equal, suffer from reduced profits and, accordingly, on the announcement of such a transaction, the price of shares in the merged group would be expected to rise but the price of shares in competitor companies would be expected to fall. Accordingly, if the stock market's reaction to news of a merger is to mark down the price of competitors' shares, this *suggests* that the market regards the merger as giving rise to cost savings rather than opportunities to increase prices.[3] Similarly, a merger which increases efficiency ought, other things being equal, to lead to an increase in the price of shares in *customer* companies, whereas one which increases market power ought to lead to shares in *customer* companies being marked down by the market. In applying such an analysis, it is necessary[4] to strip out from the analysis the "noise" caused by general movements in share prices[5] by predicting what the price of the competitors' shares would have been in the absence of the merger announcement (e.g. by using a market index). It is also important to analyse carefully the time-frame for the analysis. For example, if there is substantial delay between the announcement of the deal and the final decision by the antitrust authority, one approach is to examine the returns across the whole of the period but another is to focus on the reaction of the market to the release of information about the merger during "event windows".[6]

The potential importance of analysis of stock market announcements is illustrated by the fact that the Commission's first Chief Competition Economist co-authored a study of ECMR decisions based on stock market effects. Duso, Neven and Röller[7] analysed 164 ECMR decisions by assessing the effect of the announcement of the merger on the share prices[8] of competitors. Their principal conclusions were: the Commission cleared

---

[3] This is true of horizontal mergers, but not necessarily of conglomerate mergers (where rivals' profitability would be reduced if the merged group successfully adopted a leveraging strategy, although this would not be in the interests of consumers). In addition, the analysis assumes that competitors will not be weakened to such an extent that they leave the industry, and that the merger does not affect the competitiveness of competitors (which is possible in particular if there is technological spillover, so that some of the efficiency gains from the merger also operate for the benefit of competitors).

[4] The extent to which this is possible is subject to debate.

[5] Share prices can also change significantly as a result of market speculation about *other* transactions (e.g. the announcement of a bid by A for B may reduce the likelihood that A will bid for C, reducing C's share price; but it may increase the likelihood that D will bid for E, increasing E's share price) and such speculative effects on the share prices of C and E may predominate over the competition effects arising from A's proposed acquisition of B (i.e. the likely effects of the merger on the future profitability of C and E).

[6] Both approaches can be used to determine whether they corroborate one another.

[7] "The Political Economy of European Merger Control: Evidence using Stock Market Data", April 2003 (*http://econ.lse.ac.uk/events/papers/sticio-130603.pdf*). See also Neven & Röller, "Discrepancies Between Markets and Regulators: An Analysis of the First Ten Years of EU Merger Control", published as Ch.2 of *The Pros and Cons of Merger Control* by the Swedish Competition Authority in 2002 (and available at *www.kkv.se/bestall/pdf/skrift_proscons.pdf*).

[8] Stock market data provides an independent assessment of the competition consequences of the transaction which does not depend on information from, or analysis by, the Commission.

transactions which the stock market regarded as anti-competitive in about 23 per cent of cases and prohibited mergers which the stock market regarded as pro-competitive in 4 out of 14 cases (28 per cent).[9]

(ii) Price/concentration analysis In seeking to identify the effect of a merger **19–003** on competition, it may be relevant to identify whether there is a relationship between price and the level of concentration in the market. *Price/ concentration analysis* is commonly used in local retail markets and involves comparing conditions of competition in a series of different markets and identifying the variables which affect price levels. If the studies show that concentration in the local market does not affect price, this suggests that the merged group will not enjoy market power. The analysis is complicated by a need to isolate the effects of concentration from the numerous other differences between local markets, such as sales volumes, product mix and the costs of marketing, distribution, staff and premises.[10] Further, in order to carry out the study, the products must be comparable. In markets for homogeneous products this is straightforward. When companies (such as retailers) supply numerous products the technique can be carried out for representative products separately or a basket or index of representative products.[11] Finally, when suppliers compete on quality and service, a positive price/concentration relationship could be due to the competitive superiority of the offering, rather than a lack of competition in the market.[12] In *Staples / Office Depot*[13] the US FTC analysed a number of local markets for the retail of office supplies and found that, where Staples was present but the other office superstores were not, prices were 13 per cent higher than in markets where Staples, Office Depot and Office Max were all present.[14]

---

[9] Pro-competitive deals were more likely to be curtailed if none of the merging companies had its headquarters in a large Member State (France, Germany, Italy, Spain or the UK) and if they occurred in the transport, storage and communication industry. Anti-competitive deals were more likely to be approved if one of the merging parties had its headquarters in a large Member State or if the geographic market definition were wider than national.

[10] Newmark, "Price-Concentration Studies: There You Go Again" (*www.usdoj.gov/atr/public/ workshops/docs/202603.htm#N_4_*) argues that it is not possible to control for these differences and that price/concentration analysis is therefore fundamentally flawed.

[11] For details of other technical issues associated with price concentration studies, see Bishop & Walker, *The Economics of EC Competition Law* (2nd edn, Sweet & Maxwell, 2002), pp.425 to 430.

[12] See Newmark, "Price-Concentration Studies: There You Go Again" (*www.usdoj.gov/atr/ public/workshops/docs/202603.htm#N_4_*).

[13] *Federal Trade Commission v Staples Inc*, 970 F Supp 1066, United States District Court of Columbia, 1997. See Kwoka & White eds., *The Antitrust Revolution* (4th edn, Oxford UP, 2004) (Case 2) and Baker, "Econometric analysis in FTC v. STAPLES", speech of July 17, 1997 (revised March 31, 1998) (available at *www.ftc.gov/speeches/other/stspch.htm*).

[14] The methodology involved in price/concentration analysis can be applied in other contexts. For example, it can be used in any situations in which the number of competitors varies, e.g. if there has been previous entry into or exit from the market, or if the number of competitors bidding for a contract varies from tender to tender. Further, if the question arises whether supermarkets form part of the same market as convenience stores, it would be possible to run multiple regressions to assess whether the presence of a convenience store within, say, 400 metres of a supermarket has any effect on the profits or prices of the supermarket; if the effect

19–004 **(iii) Motives** The Commission[15] may analyse the parties' *motives* for merging.[16] If the parties cannot identify any motive for the transaction, the inference may be that the merger is driven by a desire to acquire market power. By contrast, if the merger is motivated by matters which are not dependent on the creation or enhancement of market power,[17] such an inference is avoided, although the Commission must of course examine whether the *effect* of the merger is to create or enhance market power.

19–005 **(iv) Past profitability** Past profitability of the merging parties or the market is sometimes taken as an indicator of pre-merger market power.[18] Areeda, Hovenkamp & Solow[19] comment on the use of past profitability as an indicator of market power: "persistent excess returns can sometimes prove durable, individually-held market power for a firm that is the only producer

---

is significant, this suggests that convenience stores poses a direct competitive constraint on supermarkets; for further discussion of this example, see Harkrider, "The Use of Econometrics in Antitrust Analysis", available at *http://admin.avhlawyers.com/FSL5CS/Published Works/Econometrics.pdf*, pp.11 to 16.

[15] It is clearly instructive for the parties' advisers to understand the economic and business drivers for the transaction as those drivers will, in all likelihood, shed light on the way in which the market operates.

[16] See the discussion in Kwoka & White, eds., *The Antitrust Revolution* (3rd edn, Oxford UP, 1999), at p.61 (this case study was omitted from the 4th edn, Oxford UP, 2004); Areeda, Hovenkamp & Solow, *Antitrust Law* (2nd edn, Aspen Law & Business, 1998), Vol.IVA, para.964; Oster, *Modern Competitive Advantage* (3rd edn, Oxford UP, 1999), pp.225 to 231; and Cabral, *Introduction to Industrial Organization* (The MIT Press, 2000), pp.277 and 278.

[17] e.g. if the target firm has capacity but the purchaser does not, then the merger may enable the purchaser to avoid expensive capacity expansion. Similarly, if the target is regarded by customers as the least attractive supplier in the market, then the buyer may be able to improve the quality of the product and apply its branding.

[18] See, generally, OFT Economic Discussion Paper 6, "Assessing Profitability in Competition Policy Analysis", OXERA, July 2003 (note that the views in the paper do not necessarily represent those of the OFT); OFT Research Paper, "The Assessment of Profitability by Competition Authorities", Martin Graham and Anthony Steel, February 1997 (note that the views in the paper do not necessarily represent those of the OFT); Carlton & Perloff, *Modern Industrial Organization* (4th edn, Addison-Wesley, 2005), Ch.8; Martin, *Advanced Industrial Economics* (2nd edn, Blackwell, 2002), Ch.6; ABA Section of Antitrust Law, *Econometrics* (ABA Publishing, 2005), pp.321 to 335; ABA Section of Antitrust Law, *Market Power Handbook* (ABA Publishing, 2005), pp.147 to 159; Clarke, *Industrial Economics* (Blackwell, 1985), p.100; and DG Competition Discussion Paper on the Application of Article 82 of the Treaty to Exclusionary Abuses, December 2005, para.26; and OFT Economic Discussion Paper, "Innovation and Competition Policy", Charles River Associates, March 2002 (note that the views in the paper do not necessarily reflect those of the OFT), paras 5.121 to 5.127 (arguing that it is rarely, if ever, possible to infer market power from data about firm profitability because: accounting profits do not measure economic profits; not all economic profits are monopoly profits; and there are problems identifying the relevant cost of capital for risky projects, survivorship bias and other practical problems). In practice, profitability is commonly analysed using return on capital employed or return on sales. For criticism, see Lind & Walker, "The (Mis)use of Profitability Analysis in Competition Law Cases" [2004] E.C.L.R. 439 (arguing that profits may be evidence of innovation or efficiency—as opposed to market power—and it is virtually impossible in practice to measure the economic profitability of a product line in a complex business).

[19] *Antitrust Law* (2nd edn, Aspen Law & Business, 2000), Vol.IIA, para.516a. Scarcity rents arise when owners of valuable resources (e.g. houses in central London) benefit from prices above average total cost but cannot influence market prices by restricting output.

of a physically distinguishable product or that has produced a very high and relatively stable portion of the output of that product. We are talking of economic returns rather than accounting returns, and emphasize that capital must be valued at its replacement cost, assets must generally be valued at their opportunity cost, and so-called scarcity rents must be included as a cost. Moreover, the firm's returns must be greater than any reasonable estimate of normal returns, and excess returns must have continued longer than required for new capacity to enter the industry in competition with the established firm".[20] The UK Competition Commission relies on excess profits in an industry as an indicator of pre-merger coordinated effects.[21] The Commission's approach is exemplified by the following cases:

(a) In *Mitsui / CVRD / Caemi*[22] the Commission relied on presentations to analysts identifying high profit margins and returns on capital as evidence of "the presence of substantial rigidities in the [market], enabling the major producers to enjoy very comfortable profits".

(b) By contrast, in *Tyco / Mallinckrodt*[23] the Commission took account of falling prices and profit margins in deciding to clear the transaction.

(c) In *Skanska / Scancem*[24] the Commission found that falling profit margins did not indicate the absence of market power, as they could be explained in the cement industry by cyclical down-turns leading to reduced capacity utilisation in an industry with significant economies of scale.

(v) **Merger simulations** In general,[25] the Commission seeks to determine **19–006** whether a transaction will significantly impede effective competition by carrying out a structural analysis of the features of the market and the way in which it operates. When using this approach, the Commission makes a qualitative assessment of the effects of the merger in the light of the available evidence (which may include quantitative analysis relating to one or more of the issues in the case, such as price correlation analysis).

However, the Commission may seek to supplement[26] such a structural

---

[20] It is important also to examine the reason for any persistent economic profits. If, for example, a firm enjoys such profits by virtue of its superior distribution system, the profits may be consistent with a market in which competition is operating effectively.

[21] See the UK Competition Commission, "Merger References: Competition Commission Guidelines", CC2, June 2003 (*www.competition-commission.org.uk/rep_pub/rules_and_guide/pdf/15073compcommguidance2final.pdf*), para.3.43 and Ch.8 above.

[22] Case COMP/M.2420 [2004] O.J. L92/50, para.51.

[23] Case COMP/M.2074, para.21.

[24] Case IV/M.1157 [1999] O.J. L183/1, para.81.

[25] See generally Scheffman, Coate & Silva, "20 Years of Merger Guidelines Enforcement at the FTC: An Economic Perspective" (available at *www.usdoj.gov/atr/hmerger/11255.htm*).

[26] Econometric analysis is not a substitute for a proper analysis of the structure of the market: see Baker, "Econometric analysis in *FTC v. STAPLES*", speech of July 17, 1997 (revised March 31, 1998) (available at *www.ftc.gov/speeches/other/stspch.htm*). In any event, there appears to be a legal obligation on the Commission to define an antitrust market before a transaction may be prohibited: see para.3–001 above.

analysis using a merger simulation, i.e. an economic model designed to estimate *directly* whether the merged group would have the power profitably to increase prices following completion (i.e. implementation) of the transaction. The model assumes a particular form of competition in the market (e.g. Bertrand competition) and requires data about prices, sales and elasticities.[27] In general terms, the following techniques are available.[28]

(a) An *estimation of demand system* seeks to specify a full set of demand and supply equations for all products and suppliers, enabling extensive modelling of post-merger market operation. Data for such an analysis is rarely available,[29] leading to the use of the following simplified models of consumer demand.[30]

(i) The antitrust logit model requires data on market shares, a measure of substitutability between products, and an estimate of market demand elasticity. However, it assumes that when

[27] The data requirements vary by model, with more straightforward models requiring less data.
[28] For an account commissioned by DG Competition, see Epstein & Rubinfeld, "Technical Report—Effects of Mergers Involving Differentiated Products", 2004, Report for DG Competition (available via *http://europa.eu.int/comm/competition/mergers/others/effects_mergers_involving_differentiated_products.pdf*), Ch.I. See also ABA Section of Antitrust Law, *Econometrics* (ABA Publishing, 2005); Keyte & Gayle, "Understanding Econometric Analysis of the Price Effects of Mergers Involving Differentiated Products" [1996] *Antitrust* 30; Harkrider, "The Use of Econometrics in Antitrust Analysis" (available via *http://admin.avhlawyers.com/FSL5CS/PublishedWorks/Econometrics.pdf*); ABA Section of Antitrust Law, *Market Power Handbook* (ABA Publishing, 2005), pp.142 to 144; Motta, *Competition Policy Theory and Practice* (2004, Cambridge UP), pp.125 to 134; Werden & Froeb, "Calibrated Economic Models Add Focus, Accuracy and Persuasiveness to Merger Analysis", published as Ch.4 of *The Pros and Cons of Merger Control* by the Swedish Competition Authority in 2002 (available via *www.kkv.se/bestall/pdf/skrift_proscons.pdf*), pp.70 to 78; Dubow, Elliott & Morrison, "Unilateral Effects and Merger Simulation Models" [2004] E.C.L.R. 114; Church & Ware, *Industrial Organization A Strategic Approach* (McGraw-Hill, 2000), p.733; Hausman, Leonard & Zona, "A Proposed Method for Analyzing Competition Among Differentiated Products" (1992) 60 *Antitrust Law Journal* 889; Hausman, Leonard & Zona, "Competitive Analysis with Differentiated Products" (1994) 34 *Annales d'Economique et Statistique* 159; Werden, "A Robust Test for Consumer Welfare Enhancing Mergers Among Sellers of Differentiated Products" (1996) XLIV *The Journal of Industrial Economics* 409; Baker, "Noncoordinated Competitive Effects Theories in Merger Analysis" [1997] *Antitrust* 21; Baker & Coscelli, "The Role of Market Shares in Differentiated Product Markets" [1999] E.C.L.R. 412, at pp.416 and 417; Baker & Wu, "Applying the Market Definition Guidelines of the European Commission" [1998] E.C.L.R. 273, at p.277; and US FTC Bureau of Economics Working Paper, "Demand System Estimation and its Application to Horizontal Merger Analysis" (available at *www.ftc.gov/be/workpapers/wp246.pdf*).
[29] In the US, demand estimation is done in a small minority of cases (see William Kolasky, Deputy Assistant Attorney General, "'Sound Economics and Hard Evidence': The Touchstones of Sound Merger Review", speech of June 14, 2002; available at *www.usdoj.gov*). Data is required on consumer demand, producers' costs, profit margins and interaction between products in the market: see Overstreet, Keyte & Gayle, "Understanding Econometric Analysis of the Price Effects of Mergers Involving Differentiated Products" [1996] *Antitrust* 30. The data requirements may be satisfied in particular if supermarket scanner information or panel data (collected over time from a group of repeat purchasers) is available.
[30] This summary is based on Epstein & Rubinfeld, "Technical Report—Effects of Mergers Involving Differentiated Products", 2004, Report for DG Competition (available via *http://europa.eu.int/comm/competition/mergers/others/effects_mergers_involving_differentiated_products.pdf*), pp.2 and 3.

customers switch away from a good, they switch to other goods in proportion to the market shares held by those goods.[31] This independence of irrelevant alternatives ("IIA") assumption generally does not hold in cases involving differentiated products.[32]

(ii) Almost Ideal Demand Systems ("AIDS") require detailed price and revenue data (generally from scanner data) but do not make the IIA assumption.

(iii) Proportionality-calibrated AIDS ("PCAIDS") are simplified versions of AIDS that make the IIA assumption[33] and require only market share data, an estimate of the market's elasticity of demand and an estimate of price elasticity for a single brand in the market.

In a technical report for DG Competition, Epstein & Rubinfield explained why ALM and PCAIDS will lead to different predicted price effects and recommended that both models are used to provide approximate upper and lower bounds on the price effects of the transaction.[34]

(b) *Residual demand analysis* seeks to identify the shape of a firm's residual demand curve. Post-merger price increases may be identified by estimating the residual demand curves facing the merging parties separately and the residual demand curve which would face the merged group.[35]

The Commission has carried out merger simulations in a series of cases.   **19–007**

(a) In *Oracle / PeopleSoft*[36] the Commission carried out a merger simulation on the assumption that the merger reduced the number of viable suppliers from three to two. Oracle subsequently established that the number of viable suppliers was larger and the Commission

---

[31] i.e. the cross-price elasticities for all goods with respect to the price of any other good are the same.

[32] The logit model can overcome this issue through the use of nests; see Epstein & Rubinfeld, "Technical Report—Effects of Mergers Involving Differentiated Products", 2004, Report for DG Competition (available via *http://europa.eu.int/comm/competition/mergers/others/ effects_mergers_involving_differentiated_products.pdf*), p.5.

[33] The PCAIDS model can overcome this issue through the use of nests; see Epstein & Rubinfeld, "Technical Report—Effects of Mergers Involving Differentiated Products", 2004, Report for DG Competition (available via *http://europa.eu.int/comm/competition/mergers/ others/effects_mergers_involving_differentiated_products.pdf*), p.5.

[34] See Epstein & Rubinfeld, "Technical Report—Effects of Mergers Involving Differentiated Products", 2004, Report for DG Competition (available via *http://europa.eu.int/comm/ competition/mergers/others/effects_mergers_involving_differentiated_products.pdf*), p.11 (see also p.24). The software provided to the Commission with the report allows for a comparison to be made between the predictions of the two models; see p.12.

[35] See Areeda, Hovenkamp & Solow, *Antitrust Law* (2nd edn, Aspen Law & Business, 2000), Vol.IIA, para.521.

[36] Case COMP/M.3216 [2005] O.J. L218/6, paras 191 to 196.

accepted that, since one of the main assumptions had been invalidated, it could not rely on the results of the model. However, the Commission made a number of more general observations about the utility of merger simulations:

> "The Commission agrees that the use of simulation models depends critically on the ability of the model to adequately capture the fundamental mechanisms that drive the behaviour of the different market participants and that, in principle, the assessment as to whether that is the case in any particular case may be a subject of debate ... [The] debate over which simplifications to accept in the model should not obscure the fact that any prospective analysis of the effect of a merger will inherently be based on assumptions. A prediction of the effect of a merger made within the framework of a model is based on a high degree of transparency regarding the logical consistency of the prediction as well as its underlying assumptions ... The Commission therefore maintains as a general point that this kind of simulation model can be a useful tool in assisting the Commission in making the economic assessment of the likely impact of a merger".

(b) In *Lagardère / Natexis / VUP*[37] the Commission simulated the effect of the merger and found that list prices would rise by around 5 per cent.

(c) In *Philip Morris / Papastratos*[38] the Commission relied in part on the fact that a merger simulation model supplied by the parties indicated that the merger would not result in significant increases in price.

19–008 The use of merger simulations is controversial for three main reasons. First, they are based on an assumption about the way in which competition occurs (a Bertrand model is usually used).[39] Secondly, the IIA assumption (if made) is a strong assumption.[40] Thirdly, merger simulations are incomplete in the sense that, depending on their specifications, models do not take account of at least some of the following: customer responses; buyer power; new entry; repositioning; other strategic competitor responses; and efficiencies. These factors therefore need to be addressed outside the model. However, the fact that creators of models specify their assumptions clearly can facilitate

---

[37] Case COMP/M.2978 [2004] O.J. L125/54 (appeal pending in Case T-279/04 *Editions Odile Jacob SAS v Commission*), paras 700 to 707.

[38] Case COMP/M.3191, para.32.

[39] Epstein & Rubinfeld, "Technical Report—Effects of Mergers Involving Differentiated Products", 2004, Report for DG Competition (available via *http://europa.eu.int/comm/ competition/mergers/others/effects_mergers_involving_differentiated_products.pdf*), pp.21 and 22, identify several circumstances in which it would be misleading to use a model based on the assumption of Bertrand competition.

[40] See Epstein & Rubinfeld, "Technical Report—Effects of Mergers Involving Differentiated Products", 2004, Report for DG Competition (available via *http://europa.eu.int/comm/ competition/mergers/others/effects_mergers_involving_differentiated_products.pdf*), pp.22 and 23.

informed debate about the effects of the merger (and in particular whether the assumptions are consistent with empirical evidence about the operation of the market)[41] and the use of models shifts the focus from intuition to calculation.[42]

(vi) The effects of previous mergers If previous mergers led to price increases, **19–009** this suggests, other things being equal, that a further reduction in the number of suppliers through merger would be likely to lead to further price increases.[43]

(vii) Whether customers object to the merger If customers do not object to a **19–010** transaction, this suggests, without being decisive, that it is unlikely to lead to higher prices, reduced service quality or a loss of choice or innovation, as customers would often be able to assess whether such results were likely and to object if they were. However, there are several reasons why customers may choose not to object even though a merger is anti-competitive. First, customers may lack the skills to assess the effects of the merger and to prepare a complaint. This applies in particular in consumer goods markets, where there are non-expert customers and each customer's expenditure on the products is so small that it would not be worthwhile for them to object. By contrast, in a business-to-business context with sophisticated purchasers, the absence of customer complaints is more telling.[44] Secondly, customers may not have an incentive to object even if the merger is anti-competitive. For example, if all customers are affected to the same extent and increases in prices can be passed on, customers may gain little from objecting. Thirdly,

---

[41] This requires that the model is treated as *a* source of information about the likely effects of the merger (and not a "black box" which provides *the* answer to the question of whether the merger will result in increases in prices).

[42] See Werden & Froeb, "Calibrated Economic Models Add Focus, Accuracy and Persuasiveness to Merger Analysis", published as Ch.4 of *The Pros and Cons of Merger Control* by the Swedish Competition Authority in 2002 (and available at *www.kkv.se/bestall/pdf/skrift_proscons.pdf*), pp.63 and 64.

[43] See the International Competition Network, "ICN Investigative Techniques Handbook for Merger Review", June 2005 (*www.internationalcompetitionnetwork.org/handbook_5-5.pdf*), p.61. See also para.6–020 above.

[44] See, e.g. Case COMP/M.1854 *Emerson Electric / Ericsson Energy Systems*, para.9; Case COMP/M.1891 *BP Amoco / Castrol*, para.41; Case COMP/M.1930 *Ahlström / Andritz*, para.86; Case COMP/M.2020 *Metsä-Serla Modo* (see press release IP/00/913); Case COMP/M.2602 *Gerling / NCM*, para.48; Case COMP/M.3090 *Volkswagen / Offset / Crescent / LeasePlan / JV*, para.24; Case COMP/M.3280 *Air France / KLM* (appeal pending in Case T-177/04 *easyJet Airline Company v Commission*), para.132; Case COMP/M.3351 *ArvinMeritor / Volvo (Assets)*, para.15; Case COMP/M.3752 *Verizon / MCI*, para.80; Case COMP/M.3779 *Pernod Ricard / Allied Domecq*, para.26; Case COMP/M.3789 *Johnson Controls / Robert Bosch / Delphi SLI*, para.17; Case COMP/M.3874 *CVC / Ruhrgas Industries*, para.39; and Case COMP/M.3943 *Saint-Gobain / BPB*, para.118. In Case COMP/M.3732 *Procter & Gamble / Gillette*, the Commission emphasised that the fact that many large retailers had not objected was "not in itself sufficient" to remove all competition concerns; in that case, other retailers *had* objected; see para.113.

customers may be fearful of retaliation from the merged group if objections are made to the merger or, alternatively, customers may use the merger control process to curry favour with the merging parties by cooperating with them (e.g. sharing information received from the Commission and making clear to the notifying party that the customer is providing evidence which supports the notifying party's interests).

In *General Electric Company v Commission*[45] the appellant emphasised that the purchasers of jet engines, Boeing and Airbus, did not oppose the merger. Both were expert purchasers who had a significant incentive to object if they expected the merger to harm their interests and, as unavoidable trading partners, would presumably not fear retaliation from GE. However, the Court of First Instance declined to place weight on this fact: "This lack of opposition could be explained by a number of different reasons, including the possibility, advanced by the Commission at the hearing, that Boeing and Airbus do not have a marked interest in reducing the price of engines inasmuch as the relatively high level of prices affects them both equally. Moreover, giving significant weight to a lack of opposition would be tantamount to holding that an undertaking's customers can determine, by means of a kind of private merger control, whether their supplier is in a dominant position on a given market".[46]

---

[45] Case T-210/01, not yet reported, judgment of December 14, 2005, para.278.

[46] This passage is unfortunate. The Commission's conjecture would be true only if Boeing and Airbus both knew that they paid the same price to General Electric. Since prices of airline engines are presumably subject to individual private negotiation, this would be correct only if both had most favoured customer clauses in their supply contracts (which was not suggested in the Court of First Instance's judgment). Further, the Court's observations about the dangers of setting up a system of "private merger control" lose sight of the fact that the ECMR is intended to protect consumers and if they have sufficient expertise to conclude that their interests will not be harmed, it is unnecessary for the Commission to intervene.

CHAPTER 20

REMEDIES

20.1 INTRODUCTION

(a) General

If a merger creates substantive competition issues but the parties propose **20–001**
commitments[1] which satisfactorily resolve those issues, the Commission is
bound to approve the merger. The process of accepting commitments is very
important because the vast majority of cases which raise material issues are
cleared on the basis of commitments, rather than being prohibited. Indeed,
in the period from the coming into force of Regulation 4064/89 to December
31, 2005, 209 concentrations were approved on the basis of commitments,
compared with 23 which were prohibited,[2] a ratio of 9:1. At the same time,
the area of remedies is very dynamic and the Commission's approach is

---

[1] See generally Lévêque & Shelanski (eds), *Merger Remedies in American and European Union
Competition Law* (Edward Elgar, 2003); "Merger Remedies", OECD, DAF/COMP(2004)21;
International Competition Network, "Merger Remedies Review Project", June 2005 (avail-
able via *www.internationalcompetitionnetwork.org/ICN_Remedies_StudyFINAL5-10.pdf*);
"Statement of Federal Trade Commission's Bureau of Competition on Negotiating Merger
Remedies", April 2003 (available via *www.ftc.gov/bc/bestpractices/bestpractices030401.htm*);
US Department of Justice, "Antitrust Policy Guide to Merger Remedies", October 2004
(available via *www.usdoj.gov/atr/public/guidelines/205108.htm*); and Holmes & Turnbull,
"Remedies in Merger cases: Recent Developments" [2002] E.C.L.R. 499. Claude Rakovsky,
"Remedies: A Few Lessons From Recent Experience", published in *EC Merger Control: Ten
Years On* (International Bar Association, 2000), p.135, at pp.137 and 138, notes that there are
some cases where no remedy is possible including, e.g.:

  (a)   cases in which the merged group is much bigger than any other competitor and there is
        no viable divestment package;
  (b)   cases involving substantial vertical links which cannot be reduced or eliminated; and
  (c)   joint dominance cases in which the only credible purchasers are themselves part of the
        joint dominant position.

[2] Including four cases in which the Commission took measures against completed transactions
under Art.8(4) of the ECMR.

evolving rapidly,[3] in particular in the light of emerging evidence on the design, implementation and effectiveness of commitments that the Commission has accepted in the past.

20–002 The principal steps in the relatively recent evolution of the Commission's approach to remedies are as follows:

(a) The Commission significantly increased the transparency of its approach to remedies by publishing a Notice on Remedies on December 21, 2000 ("the Notice on Remedies").[4]

(b) The Commission sought to improve the consistency of its approach to remedies by establishing, in April 2001, a new Enforcement Unit dedicated to advising on the acceptability and implementation of remedies.

(c) In 2003, the Commission released model texts for commitments submitted under the ECMR and for the trustee mandate[5] (together, "the Model Texts") and published best practice guidelines.[6]

(d) In October 2005, the Commission published a DG Competition staff paper, "Merger Remedies Study"[7] (the "Merger Remedies Study") which reviewed the design and implementation of 96 separate remedies accepted in 40 cases over the period from 1996 to 2000.

The Commission has announced plans to amend the Notice on Remedies.[8]

(b) Burden of proof

20–003 In general, the burden is on the Commission to show that the concentration will significantly impede effective competition in the common market or in a

---

[3] For this reason, this Chapter focuses on remedies which have been accepted since the adoption of the Notice on Remedies or were accepted shortly before it.

[4] Commission Notice on remedies acceptable under Council Regulation (EEC) No.4064/89 and under Commission Regulation (EC) No.447/98 [2001] O.J. C68/3.

[5] The Model Texts were published on May 2, 2003. For an explanation of the "trustee mandate" see s.20.13(b) below.

[6] "Best Practice Guidelines: The Commission's Model Texts for Divestiture Commitments and the Trustee Mandate under the EC Merger Regulation". See also the speech of Mario Monti, then the Commissioner for Competition Policy, "The Commission notice on merger remedies—one year after", January 18, 2002 (*www.europa.eu.int/comm/competition/speeches/index_2002.html*) and the Commission's XXXIst Annual Report on Competition Policy, 2001, paras 290 and 291.

[7] The study is available via *http://europa.eu.int/comm/competition/mergers/others/remedies_study.pdf*. See also Kopke, "Merger Remedies Study", *Competition Policy Newsletter*, Autumn 2005, p.3.

[8] See, e.g. Drauz, "Merger Remedies", speech to the BIICL 3rd Annual Merger Control Conference, December 6, 2004 and Commission press release IP/05/1327.

substantial part of it.[9] In *EDP v Commission*[10] the Court of First Instance ruled that the provision of commitments by a notifying party[11] does not alter this general rule, i.e. the burden of showing that the concentration *as modified by the commitments* significantly impedes effective competition *remains on the Commission* in such a situation.[12]

(c) Remedies in phases I and II

Remedies may be accepted in phase I[13] or phase II, but the Commission's **20–004** approach differs between the two[14] because it has not, in a phase I investigation, carried out an in-depth market investigation and the remedies must clearly rule out any "serious doubts" held by the Commission about the compatibility of the concentration with the common market.[15] By contrast, in phase II, once the Commission has carried out an in-depth market investigation,[16] the issue is whether the remedies eliminate the significant impediment to effective competition.[17] In practice, this means that, in order for the Commission to accept remedies in phase I, the parties must generally[18] demonstrate that the competition concerns identified by the

---

[9] See s.2.5(a) above for more general discussion of the burden of proof.

[10] Case T-87/05, not yet reported, judgment of September 21, 2005, paras 62 to 65, observing that the Notice on Remedies, para.6 (which states that it "is the ultimate responsibility of the parties to show that the proposed remedies ... eliminate the creation or strengthening of ... a dominant position") does not alter the legal position set out in the text. The Court of First Instance confirmed, at para.80, that when the Commission receives a set of commitments, it does not need to recommence its analysis as though the transaction had been notified anew in the form amended by the commitments.

[11] The obligation is on the parties to devise a remedies package which addresses the Commission's concerns and not on the Commission to specify to the parties what is required; see Case T-210/01 *General Electric Company v Commission*, not yet reported, judgment of December 14, 2005, para.52. Further, the Commission is not required, before making its final decision, to identify to the notifying parties its current thinking on the means of resolving the problems it has identified in the statement of objections; see Case T-209/01 *Honeywell International Inc v Commission*, not yet reported, judgment of December 14, 2005, para.99.

[12] The Court added, at para.200, that the transaction must be approved if the commitments produce "a competitive adjustment outweighing the significant impediment to effective competition caused by the concentration as notified".

[13] If the notifying parties offer commitments, the time period for a phase I decision is extended from 25 working days to a total of 35 working days; ECMR, Art.10(1).

[14] See also the Commission's XXXIst Annual Report on Competition Policy, 2001, para.301 (non-standard remedies are more likely to be accepted in Phase II when there is sufficient time for the efficacy of the proposals to be examined).

[15] ECMR, Art.6(1)(c).

[16] For the position when remedies are offered in phase II before completion of the market investigation, see Case COMP/M.2861 *Siemens / Drägerwerk / JV* [2003] O.J. L291/1, para.4 (see also para.110) and Case COMP/M.3099 *Areva / Urenco / ETC JV*, paras 221, 224 and 235.

[17] The Notice on Remedies, para.10.

[18] In Case T-158/00 *ARD v Commission* [2003] E.C.R. II-3825, para.181, the Court of First Instance rejected a challenge to a decision to accept a complex package of behavioural commitments in phase I, on the grounds that the appellant had not established that the Commission had made a manifest error in its conclusion that the competition problem was readily identifiable and could be remedied easily.

Commission have been wholly eliminated, normally by divesting one of the merging parties' businesses in the markets in issue.[19]

(d) Structure of this Chapter

20–005 In s.20.2, this Chapter describes two important empirical studies of the effectiveness of remedies. The US Federal Trade Commission's study was published in 1999 and influenced the drafting of the Commission's Notice on Remedies. The Merger Remedies Study involved a detailed appraisal by DG Competition staff of 96 separate remedies adopted under the ECMR and is set to exert a significant influence over the Commission's future policy on the acceptance of commitments. Section 20.3 describes a taxonomy of remedies. Section 20.4 discusses the principles which apply in determining whether a remedy is suitable, as they appear from the Notice on Remedies, the Commission's decisions and judgments of the Community Courts. Section 20.5 analyses the types of remedies which are typically accepted to address particular theories of competitive harm. Section 20.6 discusses the distinction which is sometimes drawn between structural and behavioural remedies. Sections 20.7 to 20.11 describe the Commission's approach to the five following substantive types of remedies: transfers of businesses; transfers of intellectual property rights; exit from a joint venture; the grant of access; and other remedies. The Chapter then describes the Commission's approach to different procedural types of remedies, including "fix it first" remedies, "crown jewels" and conditional remedies (s.20.12). Finally, there is discussion of other aspects of the remedies process (s.20.13) and the options for structuring transactions when remedies are likely to be required (s.20.14).

---

[19] Recital 30 to the revised ECMR states, in part: "It is also appropriate to accept commitments before the initiation of proceedings where the competition problem is readily identifiable and can easily be remedied". In Case T-114/02 *BaByliss v Commission* [2003] E.C.R. II-1279, the Court of First Instance stated, at para.169: "there is no material difference between the commitments made in phase I and those in phase II although, as an in-depth market study is not carried out in phase I, the former must not only permit such a conclusion, but must also be sufficient to rule out clearly any serious doubt on the point". The Court of First Instance made a similar point in Case T-119/02 *Royal Philips Electronics NV v Commission* [2003] E.C.R. II-1433, at para.79, concluding that "commitments entered into during the Phase I procedure must constitute a direct and sufficient response capable of clearly excluding the serious doubts expressed". In the context of Case COMP/M.1751 *Shell / BASF / JV—Project Nicole* the Commission commented (see press release IP/00/313) that: "the package of commitments to which the parties have committed ... in order to remedy the Commission's concerns in this case is highly complex, especially given that an in-depth investigation has not been carried out. Such a complex package can only be accepted at this stage because the parties have been open with the Commission about the problems that this operation would raise, they discussed the problems and potential remedies with the Commission before submitting formal notification of the operation, and they have subsequently cooperated at all stages of the investigation. Without such cooperation, it is highly unlikely that the Commission's concerns about the operation could have been eliminated at this stage".

20.2 EMPIRICAL STUDIES OF THE EFFECTIVENESS OF REMEDIES

(a) The FTC Divestiture Study

The Commission has acknowledged that the approach in the Notice on **20–006** Remedies was influenced by the US Federal Trade Commission's study on the divestiture process[20] (the "FTC Divestiture Study").[21] The FTC Divestiture Study involved an evaluation of the success of remedies in 35 cases in which consent orders involving the divestiture of assets or the licensing of intellectual property were entered between 1990 and 1994. The FTC reached the following general conclusions.[22]

(a) Divestitures generally produce viable competitors in the relevant markets.

(b) The merging parties have an incentive to identify "marginally acceptable buyers" and may engage in strategic conduct to preclude the purchaser from competing effectively after the acquisition.

(c) Most buyers of divested assets lack sufficient information to avoid mistakes in the course of their acquisitions, with the consequence that the antitrust authorities cannot rely on the buyer's analysis of what is required in identifying the scope of the business or assets to be divested.

(b) The Merger Remedies Study

In the light of the FTC Divestiture Study,[23] DG Competition commissioned **20–007** a staff paper[24] studying the design, implementation and effectiveness of 96 remedies in 40 cases decided between 1996 and 2000. The Merger Remedies Study was published in October 2005 and was based principally on interviews with the parties, purchasers, trustees and others (and therefore did not involve fully fledged market investigations). It reached the following principal conclusions:

---

[20] "A Study of the Commission's Divestiture Process" (1999, available at *www.ftc.gov* under "Publications—Antitrust"). On April 2, 2003, the US Federal Trade Commission published a "Statement of the Federal Trade Commission's Bureau of Competition on Negotiating Merger Remedies" (*www.ftc.gov/bc/bestpractices/bestpractices030401.htm*).

[21] Speech of Mario Monti, then the Commissioner for Competition Policy, "The Commission notice on merger remedies—one year after", January 18, 2002 (*www.europa.eu.int/comm/competition/speeches/index_2002.html*).

[22] FTC Divestiture Study, p.8.

[23] See p.11 of the Merger Remedies Study.

[24] The paper does not represent the views of the European Commission: see p.3 of the Merger Remedies Study.

(a) 79 per cent of the 84 divestiture remedies raised one or more serious design and/or implementation issues. More particularly, 21 of the 84 remedies raised serious issues regarding the scope of the divested business which were not resolved, and 12 raised such issues regarding the suitability of the purchaser.[25]

(b) 57 per cent of the remedies analysed were "effective", 24 per cent were "partially effective", 7 per cent were "ineffective", and in 12 per cent of cases, the position was unclear.[26]

(c) The Commission's press release also emphasised the Study's conclusions about the need to ensure interim preservation until divestiture and to ensure effective monitoring of implementation of the remedies.[27]

In releasing the results of the Study, the Commissioner for Competition Policy, Neelie Kroes, stated that its findings would influence the Commission's future approach to remedies, adding: "It is the merging companies, not their customers, who should bear the risks of potentially inadequate remedies".[28]

Several more general points should be noted regarding the Study. First, the cases were decided before publication of the Notice on Remedies, the Model Texts and the best practice guidelines.[29] Some of the difficulties identified by the Study might have been avoided had these documents been applicable at the time. Secondly, evidence provided in surveys may not be reliable. For example, a purchaser which had not made a success of the divestment business might wrongly attribute that lack of success to deficiencies in the remedies package rather than a lack of management skill. Thirdly, the market outcome may be affected by factors other than the remedies package.[30]

20.3 A TAXONOMY OF REMEDIES

(a) The Merger Remedies Study

20–008 The Merger Remedies Study distinguished the following substantive types of remedies.[31]

---

[25] See p.140. Other unresolved serious issues included: third party involvement (2), carve-out issues (9), interim preservation (5) and transfer (10).
[26] See pp.169 to 171.
[27] IP/05/1327.
[28] IP/05/1327.
[29] See p.12.
[30] See p.16.
[31] Merger Remedies Study, pp.18 and 19.

(a) Commitments to *transfer a market position* through *transfers of businesses or assets*. These remedies seek to recreate the competitive strength of a business in the hands of a suitable purchaser.

(b) Commitments to *transfer a market position* through *transfers of intellectual property rights*. These remedies involve the divestiture or grant of a long-term exclusive licence with infinite duration or until the expiry of patent protection and have the same aims as transfers of businesses or assets.

(c) Commitments to *exit from a joint venture*, by transferring joint control of the business to a third party.

(d) Commitments to grant *access* to key assets in order to reduce barriers to entry. The Study distinguished: granting access to infrastructure or technical platforms; granting access to technology via licences or other intellectual property rights; and termination of exclusive vertical agreements.

(e) *Other* remedies.

This Chapter adopts the taxonomy used in the Merger Remedies Study.[32]

(b) Different procedural forms of remedy

In addition, remedies can be distinguished according to their *procedural* **20–009** *form*; in particular, whilst most remedies involve commitments to implement specific actions following completion (i.e. implementation) of the notified concentration, other types of remedies include "fix it first" commitments (when a contract to transfer a market position must be signed before completion (i.e. implementation) of the notified concentration may occur), "crown jewels" remedies (when a failure to implement specific actions by a particular date triggers an obligation to undertake other, more onerous actions); and conditional remedies (when the obligation to take specific actions becomes operative only if certain criteria are satisfied). These different procedural forms are discussed in s.20.12 below.

---

[32] For a taxonomy of behavioural remedies, see International Competition Network, "Merger Remedies Review Project", June 2005 (available via *www.internationalcompetitionnetwork. org/ICN_Remedies_StudyFINAL5-10.pdf*), para.3.22.

20.4 GENERAL PRINCIPLES RELEVANT TO THE SELECTION OF AN APPROPRIATE REMEDY

(a) The importance of clarity and transparency

20–010 The choice of principles to be applied in assessing whether a proposed package of commitments is suitable to resolve the substantive issues created by a transaction is of great practical importance. For example, there is clearly a greater willingness on the part of the Commission to accept remedies that do not involve the transfer of a market position (e.g. access remedies) in cases raising vertical or conglomerate issues than those involving horizontal overlaps, but it is important to understand when divestments will be required in vertical effects cases[33] and when remedies falling short of divestment will be acceptable in horizontal overlaps cases. Similarly, in cases involving international brands and national markets, when a significant impediment to effective competition arises in one geographic market but not others, the question arises whether it is sufficient to transfer the brand in the Member State in question rather than throughout the EEA. The answers to these questions (and others like them) are important, both in determining whether the ECMR is successful in its objective of maintaining consumer welfare and because they may have significant financial consequences for the parties involved. For these reasons, the principles which are applied in assessing whether a remedy is suitable should be clear and transparent.

(b) The Notice on Remedies

20–011 The Notice on Remedies identifies three criteria which must be satisfied if a remedy is to be acceptable to the Commission, namely that the proposal:

(a) clearly[34] prevents[35] the significant impediment to effective competition[36];

---

[33] Rey argues that regulators' experience suggests that access remedies may perform better than divestments, especially when fixed costs are high and there are few participants; see Lévêque & Shelanski (eds), *Merger Remedies in American and European Union Competition Law* (Edward Elgar, 2003), p.131.

[34] The Notice on Remedies, para.32: "Where the parties submit proposed remedies that are so extensive and complex that it is not possible for the Commission to determine with the required degree of certainty that effective competition will be restored in the market, an authorisation decision cannot be granted". The Commission refers as examples to Case COMP/M.1672 *Volvo / Scania* [2001] O.J. L143/74 and Case COMP/M.1741 *MCI WorldCom / Sprint* [2003] O.J. L300/1. The point was also emphasised by Mario Monti, then the Commissioner for Competition Policy, in a speech of June 26 2000, (*www.europa.eu.int/comm/competition/speeches/index_2000.html*). For a criticism of this approach, see Cornelius Canenbley, "Remedies under EC Competition Law: Finding the Right Cure", published in *EC Merger Control: Ten Years On* (International Bar Association, 2000), p.273.

[35] Recital 30 of the ECMR refers to the entire elimination of the competition problem.

[36] The Notice on Remedies, para.9 (which was drafted with reference to the substantive test under Regulation 4064/89). See also Götz Drauz, "Conglomerate and Vertical Mergers in the Light of the Tetra Judgment", *Competition Policy Newsletter*, Summer 2005, p.35 at p.39,

(b) can be implemented effectively[37] and within a short period[38]; and

(c) does not, other than in exceptional circumstances,[39] require any additional monitoring once it has been implemented.[40]

In applying the "clear prevention" criterion (para.(a)), it is necessary to understand precisely why the transaction creates a significant impediment to effective competition and what steps would eliminate those effects. In this respect, the process of "designing" a remedies package is pre-eminently fact-specific.[41] For example, in *BaByliss v Commission*[42] the appellant argued that the Commission had been wrong to accept a commitment to license a trade mark, but the Court upheld that decision on the grounds that trade marks were of "vital importance" in the sector in question and were one of the "main factors" in final consumers' choices,[43] whereas a transfer of tangible assets would have had only a marginal effect on the structure of competition.[44] Similarly, in airline mergers, the main barrier to entry has commonly

---

stating that, in appraising remedies, the Commission asks itself whether, "assuming the remedy works properly, does it fully address the competition problem in its entirety? It must be sufficiently complete in scope and not leave any room for doubts or 'exceptions'".

[37] The US Department of Justice, "Antitrust Policy Guide to Merger Remedies", October 2004 (available via *www.usdoj.gov/atr/public/guidelines/205108.htm*) notes, in s.II, that: "A remedy is not effective if it cannot be enforced". At s.III.A, the Policy Guide describes speed, certainty, cost and efficiency as important measures of effectiveness and identifies four costs of "conduct remedies" (see s.20.6 below) (direct monitoring costs, costs arising from attempts by the merged group to undermine the spirit of the remedy, costs in terms of restraining behaviour which may be pro-competitive (as in certain restrictions on discrimination) and costs in terms of restricting the merged group's ability to adapt to changing market conditions). Rey distinguishes two elements of enforceability, simplicity and monitorability; see Lévêque & Shelanski (eds), *Merger Remedies in American and European Union Competition Law* (Edward Elgar, 2003), pp.132 to 134.

[38] The Notice on Remedies, para.10. See also the Notice on Remedies, para.8: "the Commission will take into account the fact that any remedy, so long as it remains a commitment which is not yet fulfilled, carries with it certain uncertainties as to its eventual outcome. This general factor must be taken into consideration by the parties when presenting a remedy to the Commission".

[39] Notice on Remedies, n.10, referring to Case IV/M.877 *Boeing / McDonnell Douglas* [1997] O.J. L336/16.

[40] Notice on Remedies, para.10. In Case T-158/00 *ARD v Commission* [2003] E.C.R. II-3825, the Court of First Instance stated, at para.211, that the relevant section of the Notice on Remedies should not be read as prohibiting *any* monitoring by the Commission of the performance of commitments; instead, it is intended to ensure that the commitments will not require permanent monitoring *once implemented*.

[41] See the US Department of Justice, "Antitrust Policy Guide to Merger Remedies", October 2004 (available via *www.usdoj.gov/atr/public/guidelines/205108.htm*), which states, at s.II, that "the staff should satisfy itself that there is a close, logical nexus between the recommended remedy and the alleged violation—that the remedy fits the violation and flows from the theory of competitive harm".

[42] Case T-114/02 [2003] E.C.R. II-1279, paras 169 to 173 and 191 to 195.

[43] The Court stated, at para.191, that "the relevant question is ... whether [the] commitments were, in the present case, capable of preventing the emergence or strengthening of a dominant position".

[44] The Court also stated, at para.209, that the question, when assessing the adequacy of the remedies, was whether the licensees would be able to establish or strengthen their own position as effective competitors of SEB.

been identified as the scarcity of take-off and landing rights, and the Commission has therefore tailored the remedies around these assets.[45]

More generally, a significant distinction can be drawn between those remedies which are intended to *create an effective competitor directly*, by transferring a market position (generally through the divestment of a business), and those which are intended to *facilitate new entry*.[46] In principle, the distinction turns on whether a remedy intended to facilitate new entry would be likely to eliminate the significant impediment to effective competition, i.e. whether, in the light of the remedy, new entry would be likely, timely and sufficient to counteract the competition issues arising from the transaction.[47] For example, in some cases involving loss of potential competition, the remedy has involved the transfer of a market position through a divestment, whereas in others, remedies designed to facilitate new entry have been accepted.[48] By contrast, in most cases involving horizontal overlaps, the remedy has been divestment (as this is usually best suited[49] to restoring the competitive intensity which has been lost as a result of the concentration) but other remedies, including licensing of intellectual property, have accepted when they adequately restore effective competition (e.g. if the principal barrier to entry lies in ownership of intellectual property rights).[50]

20–012   Götz Drauz, then Deputy Director General, DG Competition, described the Commission's approach to the "effective implementation" and "monitoring" criteria (paras (b) and (c)) in the context of behavioural remedies,[51] in the following terms:

> "... can non-compliance be detected easily and is the remedy 'self-policing' without the need for continued monitoring by the Commission? This is a crucial element with regard to behavioural remedies, which typically translate into many individual commercial interactions on the market that cannot—and indeed should not—be followed by the Commission in detail. And ... assuming non-compliance is detected, would Commission intervention still be timely? If a violation of the commitment can only be detected when it has taken place, this speaks against the suitability of the remedy".[52]

---

[45] See, e.g. Case COMP/JV.19 *KLM / Alitalia*; Case COMP/M.3280 *Air France / KLM* (appeal pending in Case T-177/04 *easyJet Airline Company v Commission*); and Case COMP/M.3770 *Lufthansa / Swiss*.

[46] e.g. through the "sponsorship" of new entry falling short of a divestment, the elimination of contractual provisions which restrict entry, the correction of market flaws or the "creation of product space" in the market which new entrants can fill.

[47] See Ch.16.

[48] See s.20.5(c) below.

[49] However, see the discussion of the proportionality principle in s.(c) below.

[50] See s.20.8 below.

[51] See s.20.6 below.

[52] Götz Drauz, "Conglomerate and Vertical Mergers in the Light of the Tetra Judgment", *Competition Policy Newsletter*, Summer 2005, p.35 at p.39.

As regards the "monitoring" criterion (para.(c)), in *ARD v Commission*[53] the Court of First Instance stated that remedies which require ongoing monitoring are not inconsistent with the Notice on Remedies, so long as the monitoring is carried out *by third parties* (e.g. through a system of arbitration) rather than by the Commission itself. For example, in *Verbund / Energie Allianz*[54] the Austrian regulator, E-Control, was willing to monitor the fulfilment of the commitments as the Commission's trustee. Similarly, in *Areva / Urenco / ETC JV*[55] the firewall provisions in the commitments were to be monitored by the joint venture's auditor and in *NewsCorp / Telepiù*[56] a complex set of behavioural commitments was accepted in the light of proposed monitoring by the Italian Communication Authority and the merged group's agreement to submit to a private arbitration system.

(c) Other relevant factors

In addition to the factors listed in the Notice on Remedies, the decisions of **20–013** the Community Courts and the Commission reveal several other criteria which are relevant to the decision whether to accept the proposed commitments.[57]

(i) Proportionality *Proportionality* is a general principle of EC law which is **20–014** applicable when designing merger remedies. Indeed, recital 30 of the revised ECMR states that "commitments should be proportionate to the competition problem".[58] Consistently with this recital, the Court of First Instance and the Commission have taken proportionality issues into account in a series of cases.[59]

---

[53] Case T-158/00 [2003] E.C.R. II-3825, para.295.

[54] Case COMP/M.2947 [2004] O.J. L92/91, para.154.

[55] Case COMP/M.3099, para.232. In addition, the Euratom Supply Agency assumed a more general monitoring role as explained in para.233.

[56] Case COMP/M.2876 [2004] O.J. L110/73, para.259.

[57] In Case COMP/M.2621 *SEB / Moulinex*, one of the commitments was intended to maintain production at a site in order to preserve jobs, but on appeal the commitments were not challenged on this point (see Case T-114/02 *BaByliss v Commission* [2003] E.C.R. II-1279, para.238).

[58] See also recital 6 of the revised ECMR, which provides that: "In accordance with the principles of subsidiarity and proportionality set out in Article 5 of the Treaty, this Regulation does not go beyond what is necessary in order to achieve the objective of ensuring that competition in the common market is not distorted, in accordance with the principle of an open market economy with free competition".

[59] See also the Notice on Remedies (noting at para.26 that access remedies may be appropriate when a divestiture of a business is impossible, citing Case COMP/M.877 *Boeing / McDonnell Douglas*); the Merger Remedies Study (which stated, at p.32: "Re-branding remedies have been found acceptable when the share of the problem market vis-à-vis the total brand equity (or trademark equity) was very small and therefore a divestiture (via an exclusive licence or an assignment) of the brand or trademark seemed disproportionate"); Case COMP/M.2876 *NewsCorp / Telepiù* [2004] O.J. L110/73 (emphasising that the remedies were adequate and proportionate, paras 232 and 239); and Case COMP/M.3770 *Lufthansa / Swiss* (emphasising,

(a) In *BaByliss v Commission*,[60] the Court of First Instance ruled that the Commission was bound to accept the least onerous set of remedies which was likely to resolve the competition concerns, referring expressly to the principle of proportionality.[61]

(b) In *Piaggio / Aprilia*[62] the Commission accepted a commitment to make physical supplies of a four-stroke engine to resolve serious doubts arising from overlaps in the supply of scooters up to 50cc in Italy, and did *not* insist on divestments, in part because this would have been disproportionate, affecting a number of markets in which no competition concerns were identified.[63]

(c) In *Apollo / Bakelite*[64] the Commission identified serious doubts arising from horizontal overlaps in the supply of phenolic resins for three particular end-uses, but accepted commitments under which a customer could, during the five years following completion (i.e. implementation) of the notified concentration, nominate another EEA producer to whom the merged group would grant a royalty-free licence for the technology used in that customer's products. The Commission found that this would significantly reduce customers' switching costs (and noted that it would increase their bargaining power as against the merged group), and concluded that a divestment remedy would have been disproportionate because phenolic resins were made in reactors and production plants that were also used to

---

at para.202, the need for the remedy to be proportionate). Further, in Case COMP/M.3091 *Konica / Minolta*, at paras 4 to 6 and 52 to 54, the Commission found that Konica controlled Sekonic, a company listed on the Tokyo Stock Exchange, in which Konica held a 37.97% shareholding. It identified serious doubts arising from the combination of the photometer activities of Sekonic and Minolta, but accepted that it was not possible (or very difficult) to sell Minolta's photometer business. The commitments provided for the sale of Konica's interest in Sekonic to Sekonic and a range of third parties, with the consequence that the remedies did not involve the *transfer* of a market position (in the form of a controlling interest in Sekonic) but simply eliminated the overlap in the parties' activities. The decision does not discuss the reasons for this approach but, presumably, the Commission concluded that Sekonic was a viable competitor in its own right and there was no need for any third party to hold control over it (with the consequence that it would be disproportionate to insist on the transfer of a market position).

[60] Case T-114/02 [2003] E.C.R. II-1279, paras 169 to 173.

[61] See also "Merger Remedies", OECD, DAF/COMP(2004)21, p.253 in which the European Commission's paper stated that it fully supported the principle that remedies should be the least restrictive means to effectively eliminate the competition concerns posed by a merger. At p.255, the Commission's paper stated that quasi-structural remedies may be accepted instead of divestiture remedies "if a clear-cut divestiture appears disproportionate and the fall-back solution is capable of restoring effective competition on the market".

[62] Case COMP/M.3570.

[63] See Todino, "First Experiences with the New Merger Regulation: Piaggio / Aprilia", *Competition Policy Newsletter*, Spring 2005, p.79, at p.83. The Commission also took account of the fact that the availability of the engine would enable some of the rivals to exercise a more effective competitive constraint, the principal asset in the market was the brand (rather than manufacturing capacity), the parties had no plants to divest, rival suppliers had existing spare capacity and were therefore not concerned to acquire plants and the market test did not press for divestment.

[64] COMP/M.3593.

produce a variety of other resins and the parties' sales of phenolic resins for the three end uses accounted for less than 10 per cent of their total sales of phenolic resins and less than 5 per cent of their total sales of resins.[65]

(d) In the Commission's second substantive decision in *Tetra Laval / Sidel*[66] (following the Court of First Instance's judgment quashing the original prohibition decision),[67] the Commission accepted a remedy involving the licensing on a non-discriminatory basis of the families of patents covering the Tetra Fast technology (to resolve concerns regarding the loss of potential competition arising from the combination of Sidel's existing strong position in high capacity SBM machines and Tetra Laval's unique and important technology), stating that it would have been disproportionate to require the divestiture (through an exclusive licence) of the technology.

(e) Separately, in the Commission's second substantive decision in *Tetra Laval / Sidel*,[68] Tetra Laval also claimed that it had been unable to identify a purchaser for its Dynaplast subsidiary (the sale of which would have resolved a horizontal issue) and had therefore closed the business. Tetra Laval offered commitments to assign the intellectual property rights which had been used or were capable of being used by Dynaplast and to divest assets and personnel used for technical service and maintenance. The Commission stated that an assignment of the intellectual property rights was necessary (but did *not* make this a condition or obligation of the decision) and simply "took note"[69] of the technical service and maintenance commitments. The Commission's decision did *not* analyse the question of whether the sale of *Sidel's* business was appropriate. One *possible* explanation is that such a remedy was considered disproportionate because Tetra Laval's Dynaplast subsidiary had already been shut down at the time of the Commission's decision. However, it remains to be seen whether the Commission would accept a commitment to shut down a business which had not already been closed (rather than requiring a divestment) if the parties could demonstrate that a buyer for that business would not be available.[70]

---

[65] Paras 157 to 162.
[66] Case COMP/M.2416 (decision of January 13, 2003), paras 115 to 118.
[67] Case T-5/02 *Tetra Laval BV v Commission* [2002] E.C.R. II-4381 (upheld on appeal in Case C-12/03P *Commission v Tetra Laval BV*, not yet reported, judgment of February 15, 2005).
[68] Case COMP/M.2416 (decision of January 13, 2003), paras 120 and 121.
[69] See s.20.13(h) below.
[70] In the Merger Remedies Study, at p.123, the DG Commission staff were very critical of a decision to approve a transaction subject to the withdrawal of a product with a significant market presence from the market, emphasising that it reduced consumer choice and destroyed value in circumstances where divestment seemed feasible.

(f) In *Reuters / Telerate*[71] the Commission identified serious doubts because there was a horizontal overlap in the parties' activities in the supply of market data platforms ("MDPs"). However, the Commission accepted a remedy involving the grant of a global exclusive licence for Telerate's MDP technology. The Commission did not insist on a divestiture[72] because Telerate had a limited share of the MDP market, its products were normally sold as part of a bundle and a purchaser of its MDP assets would face relatively higher costs.

(g) In *Johnson & Johnson / Guidant*[73] the Commission accepted commitments to divest a business even though the undertaking did not include manufacturing or R&D facilities. The Commission emphasised that Johnson & Johnson's manufacturing and R&D operated on a worldwide basis and the manufacturing plant also produced products other than the overlapping product. It found that requiring Johnson & Johnson to sell these assets would be disproportionate, in the light of commitments to assist the purchaser in building up its own manufacturing capabilities and to support the purchaser during a transitional period.

(h) In *Alcatel / Finmeccanica / Alcatel Alenia Space & Telespazio*[74] the parties argued that it would not be feasible to divest one of the parties' businesses in a particular area because it was not a stand-alone business and could not be carved-out from other activities. The Commission considered whether the parties should be required to divest a larger manufacturing unit but found that this would be disproportionate, since the product in question would account for a negligible part of the turnover of the business being sold. It therefore accepted a remedy (for a merger to monopoly) under which the parties committed to grant a technology licence to a single purchaser, to reduce the effort and cost involved in that purchaser developing rival products.

(i) In *Gerling / NCM*[75] the Commission permitted the purchaser, in providing an undertaking to dispose of credit insurance businesses in the Netherlands and Denmark, to exclude policies issued for international customers covering several territories on the grounds that the exclusion related only to large multi-national customers and was "justified by the fact that the divestiture of a part of an international

---

[71] Case COMP/M.3692, paras 29 to 35.
[72] Some respondents on the market test argued that divestiture was appropriate to eliminate the overlap and avoid any risk that the licensee would be dependent on the licensor.
[73] Case COMP/M.3687, as explained in Bacchiega, Dionnet, Todino & MacEwen, "Johnson & Johnson / Guidant: Potential Competition and Unilateral Effects in Innovative Markets", *Competition Policy Newsletter*, Autumn 2005, p.87, at pp.93 and 94.
[74] Case COMP/M.3680, paras 76, 120 to 125 and 130.
[75] Case COMP/M.2602, para.56.

policy is not feasible without affecting the remaining parts of the policy".

The broader question raised by the cases discussed above is when the **20–015** transfer of a market position through a divestment will be disproportionate. Generally, when a horizontal merger creates or enhances market power, the merged group can exercise that market power in many different ways (not only raising prices, but reducing the quality of service in subtle but important respects, reducing innovation or limiting consumer choice) meaning that remedies which seek to regulate ongoing "conduct" in the market will not resolve the competition concerns. By contrast, in cases raising vertical or conglomerate issues, if the conduct which the merged group might adopt is clear (e.g. refusing to supply) then it may be disproportionate to require divestment if less intrusive remedies can be devised which will prevent such conduct.[76] The *Piaggio*, *Apollo* and *Reuters* cases are unusual because they involved horizontal mergers in which the remedy did not create a new competitor[77] but instead created conditions in which rival competitors might be able to become more effective (*Piaggio*), consumers would have increased buyer power through a reduction in switching costs (*Apollo*), or a licensee would have the opportunity to develop a competing business (*Reuters*). The circumstances in which the strengthening of rivals or buyer power will be sufficient to resolve a case involving horizontal overlaps remain somewhat opaque. (As explained in s.(ii) below, horizontal mergers may be approved on the basis of commitments falling short of the transfer of a market position when this serves to *benefit consumers*, as is clear from a series of airline mergers,[78] *NewsCorp / Telepiù*[79] and, arguably, *Alcatel / Finmeccanica / Alcatel Alenia Space & Telespazio*.)[80]

A further question is whether the proportionality principle requires the Commission to be more open to remedies falling short of divestment in fast-moving markets in which the competition problems are likely to have a *short* duration[81] *or* if there is less certainty about the way that the market will develop, creating a greater risk that divestment remedies would in fact be unnecessary.[82]

---

[76] See generally ss.20.6, 20.10 and 20.11 below.
[77] In contrast to the brand licensing cases discussed in s.20.8 below, which are effectively divestments but where the relevant assets necessary to transfer a business as a going concern are intellectual property rather than physical assets.
[78] See n.45 above.
[79] Case COMP/M.2876 [2004] O.J. L110/73.
[80] Case COMP/M.3680.
[81] See UK Competition Commission, "Application of Divestiture Remedies in Merger Inquiries: Competition Commission Guidelines", December 2004 (available via *www.competition-commission.org.uk/rep_pub/rules_and_guide/pdf/divestiture_remedies_guidance.pdf*), para.1.8 and International Competition Network, "Merger Remedies Review Project", June 2005 (available via *www.internationalcompetitionnetwork.org/ICN_Remedies_StudyFINAL5-10.pdf*), para.3.24.
[82] See para.20–089 below and "Merger Remedies", OECD, DAF/COMP(2004)21, pp.8 and 25.

20–016 (ii) The benefits of the transaction for consumers The Commission has taken account of the *benefits of the transaction for consumers* in assessing proposed commitments.[83] In particular, the Commission has preferred a remedies package that captures such benefits to one which does not.[84]

(a) In a significant proportion of cases raising vertical issues, the Commission has accepted access remedies[85] rather than insisting on divestments[86] and this preference may be explained,[87] at least in part,[88] by a recognition that vertical mergers commonly generate efficiencies[89] and structural remedies may deprive consumers of the benefits of those efficiencies.

(b) The Notice on Remedies[90] noted that exclusive licensing may be preferred to divestiture when divestiture would impede efficient, ongoing research.

(c) In *Lufthansa / Swiss*[91] the Commission stated: "it is imperative in this case to strike a balance between the need to i) allow potential competition on these hub-to-hub routes; and ii) ensure that the efficiencies that the parties can derive from their networks are not disrupted, thus harming the consumers' interests".

(d) In *Air France / KLM*[92] the Commission placed great emphasis in its press release on the benefits of the transaction for consumers, through access to new destinations and routes, costs savings and service improvements, and accepted a relatively complex package of commitments.

---

[83] Indeed, the purpose of a remedies system is arguably to enable parties to generate benefits from mergers for the benefit of consumers without adversely affecting conditions of competition; see also International Competition Network, "Merger Remedies Review Project", June 2005 (available via *www.internationalcompetitionnetwork.org/ICN_Remedies_StudyFINAL5-10.pdf*), para.1.4 and the US Department of Justice, "Antitrust Policy Guide to Merger Remedies", October 2004 (available via *www.usdoj.gov/atr/public/guidelines/205108.htm*), s.III(E)(2) (identifying the circumstances in which efficiencies could justify the adoption of conduct relief).

[84] See the US Department of Justice, "Antitrust Policy Guide to Merger Remedies", October 2004 (available via *www.usdoj.gov/atr/public/guidelines/205108.htm*), stating, at s.II, that: "Effective remedies preserve the efficiencies created by a merger, to the extent possible, without compromising the benefits that result from maintaining competitive markets".

[85] See s.20.10 below.

[86] See "Merger Remedies", OECD, DAF/COMP(2004)21, p.10.

[87] This is the explanation given in UK Competition Commission, "Application of Divestiture Remedies in Merger Inquiries: Competition Commission Guidelines", December 2004 (available via *www.competition-commission.org.uk/rep_pub/rules_and_guide/pdf/divestiture_remedies_guidance.pdf*), para.1.8.

[88] The proportionality principle may also be relevant as explained above.

[89] See s.11.2 above.

[90] Para.28.

[91] Case COMP/M.3770, para.202.

[92] Case COMP/M.3280, as explained in press release IP/04/194 (appeal pending in Case T-177/04 *easyJet Airline Company v Commission*).

(e) In *Areva / Urenco / ETC JV*[93] the Commission emphasised that the joint venture would allow Areva to produce enriched uranium more economically by giving it access to a superior technology, making it a more competitive player. The Commission accepted a complex package of commitments (including firewall arrangements to be monitored by the joint venture's auditor), stating: "In these specific circumstances, the Commitments submitted by the parties directly address the serious doubts arising from specific features of the concentration and modify the concentration in such a way as to specifically remove those serious doubts. However, the Commitments leave the positive effects arising from the concentration as such untouched".

(f) In *NewsCorp / Telepiù*[94] the Commission approved a merger to near monopoly in the Italian pay-TV market on the basis of a complex package of remedies which could be said not to satisfy the criteria in the Notice on Remedies summarised in sub-paras (b) and (c) of para.20–011 above, stating that "an authorisation of the merger subject to appropriate conditions will be more beneficial to consumers than a disruption caused by a potential closure of Stream". The remedies package was intended to create the conditions for actual competition to subsist and/or potential competition to emerge, in particular by lowering barriers to entry.[95]

(g) In *Alcatel / Finmeccanica / Alcatel Alenia Space & Telespazio*[96] the Commission accepted a commitment to grant a single licence of a package of technology rather than insisting on a divestment to remedy a merger to monopoly.[97] The Commission focused on proportionality issues when analysing the remedy[98] but its willingness to accept licensing as a solution to a merger to monopoly also appears to have been influenced by efficiency considerations. In particular, the Commission prefaced its analysis of the substantive issues in the case by noting that both the European Commission and the European Space Agency had called for consolidation in the European space industry to concentrate research and development efforts.[99]

(h) In *DaimlerChrysler / Deutsche Telekom / JV*[1] the Commission accepted remedies involving third party access to a gateway asset (an

---

[93] Case COMP/M.3099, paras 242 and 243. (The decision to take account of efficiency gains when appraising remedies is significant because the Commission doubted whether the specific efficiency effects claimed by the parties were "merger specific"; para.220.)
[94] Case COMP/M.2876 [2004] O.J. L110/73, paras 221 to 261.
[95] Para.228.
[96] Case COMP/M.3680, paras 76 and 125.
[97] The merger also gave rise to vertical effects arising from the same overlap; see paras 93 and 94.
[98] See para.121.
[99] Para.68.
[1] Case COMP/M.2903, as explained in press release IP/03/594 (appeal pending in Case T-269/03 *Socratec (Satellite Navigation Consulting, Research & Technology) v Commission*).

onboard unit for trucks which was installed for free in order to collect tolls, but which could also be used to provide telematics services), rather than preventing the use of the unit for onboard telematics services, on the grounds that such a remedy would have disadvantaged consumers, who would have been forced to pay for a second unit for telematics services.

20–017 **(iii) The overall effect of the remedies package on consumers** The Commission has taken account of the *overall effect of the remedies package on consumers* in assessing proposed commitments.[2] For example,[3] the Commission sought in *Nestlé / Ralston Purina*[4] to avoid a situation in which the remedies package might have resulted in customer confusion because it split the ownership of a trademark between two rival suppliers. The Commission stated that the remedy aimed to avoid "a situation where the ownership of the involved pet food brands would be permanently split in different parts of the Community".[5] The Commission also relied on customer confusion in *Procter & Gamble / Gillette*[6] when explaining why it had insisted that Procter & Gamble grant a licence of the co-brands used on the divested battery toothbrush business *throughout the EEA* and not just in those territories where they were marketed by Procter & Gamble prior to the merger.

20–018 **(iv) The effect of the remedies on technical and economic progress** The Commission takes account of the effect of the remedies package on technical and economic progress, as reflected in Art.2(1)(b) of the ECMR. In the Commission's second substantive decision in *Tetra Laval / Sidel*[7] (following the Court of First Instance's judgment quashing the original prohibition decision[8]), it accepted a remedy based on the licensing to third parties of technology on non-discriminatory terms, and stated that this was preferable to an assignment of that technology, in part because an assignment might

---

[2] See also International Competition Network, "Merger Remedies Review Project", June 2005 (available via *www.internationalcompetitionnetwork.org/ICN_Remedies_StudyFINAL5-10.pdf*), noting, at para.2.6, that remedies packages may create their own adverse effects, e.g. a price cap may discourage market entry.

[3] In Case COMP/M.2876 *NewsCorp / Telepiù* [2004] O.J. L110/73, para.241, the Commission accepted a package of remedies intended to facilitate entry when approving a merger to near monopoly in the Italian pay-TV market. When considering commitments regarding the merged group's dealings with movie studios on future deals, the Commission rejected a proposal put forward by third parties on the grounds that it would involve a disproportionate shift in bargaining power to the studios, to the detriment of potential new entrants (i.e. the proposal would have partly undermined the objective of the set of remedies, namely to facilitate new entry, which would have harmed consumers).

[4] Case COMP/M.2337.

[5] Commission press release IP/01/1136.

[6] Case COMP/M.3732, para.156.

[7] Case COMP/M.2416 (decision of January 13, 2003), para.121.

[8] Case T-5/02 *Tetra Laval BV v Commission* [2002] E.C.R. II-4381 (upheld on appeal in Case C-12/03P *Commission v Tetra Laval BV*, not yet reported, judgment of February 15, 2005).

delay the introduction of the new technology to the market, which would be contrary to the aim of maintaining technical and economic progress provided that it is to consumers' advantage and does not form an obstacle to competition.

(v) Compatibility with the competition rules In *BaByliss*,[9] the Court of First **20–019** Instance stated that "the Commission cannot ... approve commitments which are contrary to the competition rules laid down in the Treaty inasmuch as they impair the preservation or development of effective competition in the common market".

(vi) No power to "over-remedy" Finally, it follows from the structure of the **20–020** ECMR (under which the Commission is obliged to approve a concentration if the remedies resolve the competition problem created by the transaction), that the Commission does not have power to "over-remedy" by seeking wider remedies than are necessary[10] or using the merger control process to improve competition within a market.[11]

20.5 SELECTION OF REMEDIES BY THEORY OF COMPETITIVE HARM

The types of remedies which are typically regarded as resolving competition **20–021** concerns vary according to the theory of competitive harm.

---

[9] Case T-114/02 *BaByliss v Commission* [2003] E.C.R. II-1279, para.421. The Court made the same point in Case T-119/02 *Royal Philips Electronics NV v Commission* [2003] E.C.R. II-1433, para.215.

[10] The US Department of Justice, "Antitrust Policy Guide to Merger Remedies", October 2004 (available via *www.usdoj.gov/atr/public/guidelines/205108.htm*) makes the point, in s.II, that doing so would unjustifiably restrict companies and may raise prices to consumers (by depriving the merging parties of efficiencies which would otherwise have benefited consumers). It adds: "the purpose of a remedy is not to enhance pre-merger competition but to restore it".

[11] In "Merger Remedies", OECD, DAF/COMP(2004)21, p.7, the OECD Secretariat states: "Remedies should not be used to 'improve' deals that do not rise to the level of a violation, or to make the competitive landscape better than it was before the transaction. Competition authorities should not use merger review to engage in industrial policy or to become a market regulator, even if the outcome of such an intervention could be more desirable from a competition point of view". See also p.253, in which the Commission stated that it fully supported the principle that competition authorities should not use merger review to engage in industrial planning. A similar point is made in International Competition Network, "Merger Remedies Review Project", June 2005 (available via *www.internationalcompetitionnetwork. org/ICN_Remedies_StudyFINAL5-10.pdf*), para.1.6.

(a) Non-coordinated effects (horizontal overlaps)

20–022 In non-coordinated effects cases involving the elimination of actual competition in supply (i.e. horizontal overlaps), the normal remedy is the transfer of a market position whether through the disposal or shares or assets (s.20.7 below) or the transfer of intellectual property rights (s.20.8 below). In a small number of cases, the transfer of a market position has been regarded as disproportionate and/or destructive of efficiencies that would otherwise have benefited consumers and a lesser remedy has been accepted (as explained in s.20.4(c) above).

(b) Coordinated effects

20–023 Remedies in cases raising coordinated effects issues need to reflect the fact that the concerns in such cases relate to the interaction between the merged group and at least one of its competitors and are not focused (as is the case with non-coordinated effects involving horizontal overlaps) on the conduct of the merged group.[12] Further, any divestiture may *itself* result in coordinated effects (for example because the sale is to a member of the oligopoly, it increases multi-market contact, or the purchaser chooses to "join the club", particularly in cases in which the purchaser is dependent on the merged group for transitional support). If the merger eliminates a "maverick" supplier, then divestiture of a different business (or the same business to, or with, different management) may not restore conditions of competition.[13]

The Commission discussed the issue of remedies in cases of coordinated effects in its XXIXth Annual Report on Competition Policy, 1999,[14] noting that: "The number of prospective purchasers is reduced by the need to exclude, as a rule, the other oligopolists, although suitable acquirers may still be found".

20–024 There are numerous cases in which coordinated effects concerns were addressed by undertakings involving the transfer of a market position.[15] In

---

[12] In non-coordinated effects cases, customers may be harmed not only by the actions of the merged group but also by the *reactions* of competitors, e.g. if competitors react to an increase in prices by the merged group by raising their own prices or to a reduction in output by reducing their output. However, if the remedies remove the incentive and/or ability of the merged group materially to change its competitive behaviour (in particular by increasing prices or reducing output) then the competitors will not face a material change in behaviour by the merged group to which they could react.

[13] See Europe Economics, "Study on Assessment Criteria for Distinguishing between Competitive and Dominant Oligopolies in Merger Control", May 2001, Executive Summary, p.v (and see the substantive discussion at pp.102 to 116); "Merger Remedies", OECD, DAF/COMP(2004)21, p.23; and Motta, Polo & Vasconcelos in Lévêque & Shelanski (eds), *Merger Remedies in American and European Union Competition Law* (Edward Elgar, 2003), at pp.113 to 114.

[14] Para.176.

[15] See, e.g. Case IV/M.1383 *Exxon / Mobil* [2004] O.J. L103/1 (in relation to the retail motor fuel market); Case COMP/M.1571 *New Holland / Case* (where a divestiture was supported by a commitment to allow dealers to freely sell the products manufactured by the purchaser of the

other cases,[16] the features of the market (in particular structural links or facilitating practices) which meant that the merger was likely to result in coordinated effects were found to be[17] capable of elimination through undertakings.[18]

(a) In *Danish Crown / Vestjyske Slagterier*[19] one of the Commission's concerns was that the merger would have created a duopolistic dominant position in the supply of fresh pork meat in supermarkets. The Commission accepted a package of undertakings including a commitment to abolish the pig quotation system (which was intended[20] to reduce the transparency of the market, increase price competition, and increase the scope for differences in costs to emerge between the merged group and the other duopolist) and dissolve the co-ownership of an export company (removing the structural links[21] between the parties and the other duopolist).[22]

(b) In *Nestlé / Perrier*[23] the Commission found that the transaction was likely to result in coordinated effects, in part because of transparency in the market. One element of the remedy was a commitment not to provide certain data on sales volume which is less than one year old to any trade association.

(c) In *EnBW / EDP / Cajastur / Hidrocantabrico*[24] the Commission found that the acquisition by EnBW, EDP and Cajastur of joint control over the Spanish utility company, Hidrocantabrico would have strengthened the existing dominant position held collectively by Endesa and Iberdrola (neither of which was involved in the notified concentration) because EDF, which jointly controlled EnBW, would, as a result of the transaction, no longer have an incentive to expand the electricity interconnection capacity between France and Spain.

---

divested assets); Case COMP/M.1939 *Rexam / American National Can* (beverage cans); and Case COMP/M.3314 *Air Liquide / Messer Targets* (divestment removed the symmetry in market shares and therefore the serious doubts regarding possible coordinated effects; para.212).

[16] The Merger Remedies Study, p.122, analysed six cases where the remedies were designed to address coordinated effects concerns and stated that most were dealt with through divestiture commitments or commitments to sever influence in a competitor, but exceptionally the Commission had accepted commitments to stop information flow between competitors.

[17] Contrast *Alcan / Pechiney / Alusuisse*, Commission press release IP/00/258.

[18] See also Case IV/M.308 *Kali und Salz / MdK / Treuhand* [1994] O.J. L186/38 (which involved commitments by the purchaser to withdraw from an export cartel and to establish its own distribution organisation; para.64) and Case COMP/M.3829 *Maersk / PONL* (withdrawal from shipping conferences and shipping consortia to resolve coordinated effects issues; paras 176 and 177).

[19] Case IV/M.1313 [2000] O.J. L20/1, paras 236 and 237.

[20] The remedy was not successful, as explained in the Merger Remedies Study, pp.122 and 123.

[21] Commitments to remove structural links are commonplace in addressing issues of the merged group's market power.

[22] Para.236.

[23] Case IV/M.190 [1992] O.J. L356/1, para.136.

[24] Case COMP/M.2684, paras 33 and 37.

The effect of the merger would therefore have been the elimination of the existing Spanish electricity generators' main potential independent competitor. The transaction was approved when EDF and the French grid operator, EDF/RTE, submitted undertakings to take all necessary steps to increase capacity on the interconnector connecting France and Spain to about 4,000 MW from an existing 1,100 MW.[25]

(d) In *Amer / Salomon*[26] the Commission identified serious doubts that the merger would result in coordinated effects, in particular in the light of an extensive cooperation agreement between Salomon and a competitor, but accepted commitments to amend that agreement to remove provisions for exchange of information on prices, costs and commercial behaviour and other clauses limiting the independence of behaviour.

(e) In *Areva / Urenco / ETC JV*[27] the Commission accepted commitments to remove the parties' veto rights over capacity increases, to reinforce firewalls to prevent information flows between the parties and the joint venture, and to provide information to the Euratom Supply Agency so that it could, if necessary, take corrective action by increasing third party imports.

(c) Loss of potential competition

25 When the theory of competitive harm arises from the elimination of *potential competition*, there is, by definition, no overlapping business which may be divested. Nevertheless, in *Air Liquide / BOC*[28] the remedy for the elimination of potential competition involved the divestiture of sufficient businesses to reduce BOC's share below the level of market dominance[29] and create a new competitive force.[30] In *Pfizer / Pharmacia*[31] the Commission identified serious doubts regarding the loss of potential competition in the erectile dysfunction market and accepted commitments by Pfizer to transfer both of Pharmacia's *products in development*.

However, in other cases in which potential competition concerns were

---

[25] Para.50.
[26] Case COMP/M.3765, paras 135 to 138, 155, 156 and 173 to 175.
[27] Case COMP/M.3099, paras 226 to 248.
[28] Case IV/M.1630.
[29] This explanation of the remedies appears in Cornelius Canenbley, "Remedies under EC Competition Law: Finding the Right Cure", in *EC Merger Control: Ten Years On* (International Bar Association, 2000), p.269, at p.274. Canenbley adds: "In a nutshell, it can be said that a loss of potential competition was counterbalanced by the gain of more actual competition".
[30] It is clear that if, following the divestitures, the merged group does not hold a dominant position, then the elimination of potential competition cannot be said to have created or strengthened a dominant position (although it could of course still result in a significant impediment to effective competition).
[31] Case COMP/M.2922.

raised, remedies based on facilitating new entry have been accepted. For example,[32] in the second substantive decision in *Tetra Laval / Sidel*[33] (following the overturning of the Commission's original prohibition decision) the Commission identified a loss of potential competition in high-capacity SBM machines (evidenced by the fact that Tetra was well advanced in developing new technology), but accepted remedies based on the grant of open access to the technology in question.

(d) Procurement power

In cases involving the elimination of actual competition in procurement markets, the normal remedy is the transfer of a market position,[34] although by analogy with the cases discussed in s.(a) above involving non-coordinated effects in the *supply* of goods or services, lesser remedies may sometimes be accepted on proportionality or consumer benefit grounds.[35]   **20–026**

(e) Vertical issues

A wide range of different types of remedies has been accepted to resolve vertical issues. In some cases, the remedy has involved the divestiture of the upstream or downstream business, severing the vertical link and eliminating the competition problem. However, applying the proportionality principle reflected in *BaByliss*,[36] if the parties offer a less intrusive remedy which nevertheless eliminates the competition concern, the Commission is bound to accept that remedy. Such commitments typically comprise access remedies (in particular the grant of access to infrastructure, technical platforms or technology, or the termination of exclusive vertical agreements) (see s.20.10 below) but they also include a wide range of other remedies such as assuring a third party that the merged group will make certain purchases (see s.20.11 below).   **20–027**

(f) Conglomerate issues

Conglomerate issues are analytically very similar to vertical issues, as explained in Ch.12 above, and the same wide range of remedies accepted in vertical effects cases is in principle available to resolve conglomerate cases.[37]   **20–028**

---

[32] See also Case COMP/M.1853 *EDF / EnBW*; Case COMP/M.2434 *Grupo Villar Mir / EnBW / Hidroélectrica del Cantábrico* [2004] O.J. L48/86; and Case COMP/M.2530 *Südzucker / Saint Louis Sucre* [2003] O.J. L103/1.

[33] Case COMP/M.2416 (decision of January 13, 2003), paras 99 and 120 to 122.

[34] See, e.g. Case IV/M.1221 *Rewe / Meinl* [1999] O.J. L274/1, para.123.

[35] See s.20.4(c) above.

[36] See s.20.4(c) above.

[37] See s.20.6 below for discussion of the relevance of behavioural commitments.

(g) Coordination in joint ventures

20–029 When the competition concerns arise from possible coordination in joint ventures as described in Arts 2(4) and 2(5) of the revised ECMR, the transfer of a market position may not be necessary if a less intrusive remedy is available which nevertheless satisfies the criteria set out in s.20.4 above. For example,[38] in *Wegener / PCM / JV*[39] the Commission identified concerns regarding possible coordination in the sale of advertising space and accepted undertakings from Wegener to sell its advertising space separately. It also accepted ring-fencing commitments under which the joint venture would appoint a supervisory board, would not share certain information with its shareholders, and would have its advertising prices approved by the supervisory board.

20.6 THE DISTINCTION BETWEEN BEHAVIOURAL AND STRUCTURAL REMEDIES

20–030 **(i) Distinction between behavioural and structural remedies generally immaterial** A distinction is sometimes drawn between remedies which are "behavioural"[40] and those which are "structural".[41] However, the question of whether the remedy is categorised as "behavioural" or "structural" is *immaterial*: the question in each case is whether the remedy in question satisfies the criteria described in s.20.4 above. The Court of First Instance stated in *Gencor Ltd v Commission*[42] that:

---

[38] In Case COMP/M.3099 *Areva / Urenco / ETC JV*, para.241, the Commission accepted commitments to remove the parties' veto rights over capacity increases and to reinforce firewalls to prevent information flows to address concerns under Art.2(4) of the ECMR.

[39] Case COMP/M.3817, paras 62 and 68 to 70.

[40] Behavioural commitments are more common when the competition issue involves an inability to access technology or infrastructure; see further OECD, "Merger Review in Emerging High Innovation Markets" DAFFE/COMP (2002) 20, especially pp.29 to 31, 164 and 165.

[41] International Competition Network, "Merger Remedies Review Project", June 2005 (available via *www.internationalcompetitionnetwork.org/ICN_Remedies_StudyFINAL5-10.pdf*), para.3.25 (and see Appendix A, paras 3 and 4), draws a distinction between remedies which *control outcomes* (e.g. a price cap) and those which facilitate competition, for example by improving the information available to buyers. See also the discussion of the use of conduct relief in US Department of Justice, "Antitrust Policy Guide to Merger Remedies", October 2004 (available via *www.usdoj.gov/atr/public/guidelines/205108.htm*), s.III(E). See generally Frontier Economics, "Surgery or Medicine? The Use of Behavioural Remedies in Merger Control", September 2005 (available via *www.frontier-economics.com/bulletins/en/72.pdf*).

[42] Case T-102/96 [1999] E.C.R. II-753, paras 318 and 319. See also Case T-114/02 *BaByliss v Commission* [2003] E.C.R. II-1279, paras 170 and 191; Case T-5/02 *Tetra Laval BV v Commission* [2002] E.C.R. II-4381, para.161 (upheld on appeal in Case C-12/03P *Commission v Tetra Laval BV*, not yet reported, judgment of February 15, 2005, para.85); and Case T-87/05 *EDP v Commission* not yet reported, judgment of September 21, 2005, paras 99 and 100. (Compare Case T-158/00 *ARD v Commission* [2003] E.C.R. II-3825, para.199, emphasising that the remedies in the case in question were structural and not behavioural as they were intended to resolve a structural problem, namely market access by third parties. If the Court

"under the Regulation the Commission has power to accept only such commitments as are capable of rendering the notified transaction compatible with the common market. In other words, the commitments offered by the undertakings concerned must enable the Commission to conclude that the concentration at issue would not create or strengthen a dominant position within the meaning of Article 2(2) and (3) of the Regulation.

The categorisation of a proposed commitment as behavioural or structural is therefore immaterial. It is true that commitments which are structural in nature, such as a commitment to reduce the market share of the entity arising from a concentration by the sale of a subsidiary, are, as a rule, preferable from the point of view of the Regulation's objective, inasmuch as they prevent once and for all, or at least for some time, the emergence or strengthening of the dominant position previously identified by the Commission and do not, moreover, require medium or long-term monitoring measures. Nevertheless, the possibility cannot automatically be ruled out that commitments which prima facie are behavioural, for instance not to use a trademark for a certain period, or to make part of the production capacity of the entity arising from the concentration available to third-party competitors, or, more generally, to grant access to essential facilities on non-discriminatory terms, may themselves also be capable of preventing the emergence or strengthening of a dominant position".

(ii) Distinction between conduct and quasi-structural remedies Within behavioural remedies, a distinction can usefully be drawn between "conduct" remedies (which concern the ongoing activities of a firm on the market) and "quasi-structural" remedies (which involve a single behavioural step and may be equivalent to a "structural" remedy in effecting a long-term alteration in the structure of the market), such as the grant of an exclusive licence. Quasi-structural remedies are regularly accepted by the Commission when they meet the criteria set out in s.20.4 above.   **20–031**

The more difficult issue is whether, and under what circumstances, "conduct" remedies are acceptable. A *general* conduct undertaking not to abuse a dominant position is not, in itself, an acceptable remedy even if monitoring of the commitment is straightforward, because the purpose of the ECMR is to prevent a significant impediment to effective competition, in particular through the creation or strengthening of a dominant position, and not to provide for the ongoing regulation of any such dominant positions once created or strengthened.[43]

---

had properly applied *Gencor* to this issue, it would have treated the question of whether the remedies should be classified as structural or behavioural as irrelevant). In its Notice on Remedies, para.9, the Commission summarises the relevant parts of the *Gencor* decision and concludes that the question of whether remedies which are not structural are acceptable "has to be determined on a case-by-case basis".

[43] See Case T-102/96 *Gencor Ltd v Commission* [1999] E.C.R. II-753, paras 316 and 317 and Case T-158/00 *ARD v Commission* [2003] E.C.R. II-3825, para.221. In any event, in the case of a merger creating or strengthening a position of *original* market power, the merged group may be able to harm consumer welfare through a wide range of strategies (increasing price,

20–032 However, if the Commission's theory of competitive harm in a case is that the merged group will adopt a *particular* strategy[44] (e.g. tying or bundling),[45] then a conduct commitment is in principle capable of resolving that concern

reducing quality, delaying innovation, limiting choice, etc.) and it is difficult to envisage circumstances in which undertakings could be devised which are adequate to deal with all of the respects in which such power may be exercised. Contrast Case IV/M.1225 *Enso / Stora* [1999] O.J. L254/9, in which a pricing commitment was not formally accepted by the Commission but (curiously—see further s.20.13(h) below) the commitment was relied on in concluding that the merger would not create or strengthen a dominant position; paras 96 and 101. The Australian Merger Guidelines, June 1999 (*www.accc.gov.au/content/item.phtml?itemId=719436&nodeId=file43a1f42c7eb63&fn=Merger%20Guidelines.pdf*), para.7.13, state that "the Commission prefers structural remedies, but where these are not feasible it may consider proposals for behavioural undertakings, taking account of the regulatory costs in balancing the likely public benefit and detriment". The UK Office of Fair Trading's Substantive Merger Guidelines, May 2003 (*www.oft.gov.uk*), state at para.8.10: "The OFT will consider behavioural undertakings where it considers that divestment would be impractical, or disproportionate to the nature of the concerns identified". Compare the UK Competition Commission's Merger References Guidelines, March 2003 (*www.competition-commission.org.uk*), para.4.17, identifying three categories of remedy which will be considered, including "remedies aimed at excluding or limiting the possibility that the merged firm will take advantage of the increased market power resulting from the merger to behave anti-competitively or to exploit its customers or suppliers".

[44] Such concerns generally arise in cases of *exclusionary* market power, in particular through vertical and conglomerate effects. However, the theory of harm in a vertical or conglomerate effects merger may not be based on a prediction that the merged group would adopt a particular course of conduct; see Götz Drauz, "Conglomerate and Vertical Mergers in the Light of the Tetra Judgment", *Competition Policy Newsletter*, Summer 2005, p.35 at p.37.

[45] In cases prior to the Court of First Instance's decision in Case T-5/02 *Tetra Sidel BV v Commission* [2002] E.C.R. II-4381 (upheld on appeal in Case C-12/03P *Commission v Tetra Laval BV*, not yet reported, judgment of February 15, 2005), in which bundling or tying has been in issue, the Commission's approach varied.

(a) In Case IV/M.794 *Coca-Cola Enterprises / Amalgamated Beverages Great Britain* the Commission accepted undertakings from Coca-Cola Enterprises not to include tying provisions relating to the purchase of cola-flavoured beverages in agreements concluded or renewed with customers in Great Britain. Tying provisions were described by the Commission as provisions making the supply of products or the availability or size of rebates or other advantages conditional on a customer purchasing one or more additional beverages and purchasing one or more products: see the Commission's XXVIIth Annual Report on Competition Policy, 1997, pp.186 and 187.

(b) In Case IV/M.877 *Boeing / McDonnell Douglas* [1997] O.J. L336/16, the Commission accepted undertakings not to establish any link between the sale of Boeing aircraft and access to the McDonnell Douglas fleet.

(c) Similarly, in Case COMP/M.1601 *Allied Signal / Honeywell* [2001] O.J. L152/1, the Commission accepted, at paras 114 and 128, undertakings including a commitment that the parties would not pursue an active policy of selling avionics and non-avionics jointly. (See also Case COMP/M.1845 *AOL / Time Warner* [2001] O.J. L268/28, in which the Commission took note of a commitment not to engage in tying, at para.90, but the obligation did not form part of the formal commitments annexed to the decision.)

(d) By contrast, in Case COMP/M.2220 *GE / Honeywell* [2004] O.J. L48/1 (prohibition decision upheld on appeal on the basis of its horizontal effects in Case T-210/01 *General Electric Company v Commission*, not yet reported, judgment of December 14, 2005), which raised concerns about the scope for the merged group to eliminate competitors by engaging in mixed bundling, the Commission rejected undertakings not to engage in bundling, stating, at para.530: "The undertakings not to engage in bundling practices are submitted in relation to the concerns on the use by the merged entity of its vertical integration and financial strength and its ability to engage in product bundling. However, they are purely behavioural and as such cannot constitute the basis for a clear elimination of the said concerns".

(See also Case COMP/M.1741 *MCI WorldCom / Sprint* [2003] O.J. L300/1, paras 402 and 403.)

provided that it satisfies the other criteria (in particular monitoring) identified in s.20.4 above. Indeed, the Commission is bound by the European Court of Justice's decision in *Commission v Tetra Laval BV*[46] to *take into account*[47] any behavioural commitments, including conduct commitments, in determining whether the merged group is likely to act in a manner which could result in a significant impediment to effective competition. Further, in *ARD v Commission*[48] the Court of First Instance stated that the question of whether the commitments reflect obligations contained in Art.82 is irrelevant, the issue being whether the commitments are capable of resolving the issues created by the merger.[49]

Consistently with this approach, the Commission has in several cases accepted remedies which were "conduct" commitments but which prevented the competition issue from arising. For example,[50] in *Wegener / PCM / JV*[51] commitments to sell advertising space separately and to "ring-fence" the joint venture company were accepted.

On the other hand, Götz Drauz has stated[52]: "The judgment [of the European Court of Justice in *Tetra*] does not suggest that the Commission has to be in principle satisfied with such promises in leveraging scenarios to eliminate competition concerns. Such an approach would be contrary to the Court's conclusions on Art.82 ... If the Court concludes that illegality and fines under Art.82 are not sufficient to reliably stop undertakings from engaging in leveraging practices, why should a mere promise to respect Art.82 make such a substantial difference? The additional risk of a revocation of the merger clearance decision does not appear to add much".

---

[46] Case C-12/03P *Commission v Tetra Laval BV*, not yet reported, judgment of February 15, 2005. The case involved an appeal against the decision of the Court of First Instance in Case T-5/02 *Tetra Laval BV v Commission* [2002] E.C.R. II-4381, in which the Court of First Instance concluded, at para.161, that "the fact that the applicant offered commitments regarding its future conduct is also a factor which the Commission should have taken into account in assessing whether it was likely that the merged entity would act in a manner which could result in the creation of a dominant position on one or more of the relevant PET equipment markets". On appeal, the European Court of Justice upheld the Court of First Instance's decision on this point, confirming, at paras 85 to 89, that the *Gencor* decision meant that it was not open to the Commission to refuse to accept "behavioural" commitments as a matter of principle and the Commission was required to "take into account" any commitments as to future conduct when assessing the likelihood that the merged group would act in a way that would make it possible to create a dominant position. (See also Advocate General Tizzano's Opinion of May 25, 2004, at para.126.)

[47] The Commission may of course conclude on the evidence that, notwithstanding the commitments provided by the notifying party, it is likely that the merged group would act in a way which significantly impedes effective competition.

[48] Case T-158/00 [2003] E.C.R. II-3825, para.201.

[49] The Court also emphasised, at paras 202, 203 and 209, that the commitments offered far greater legal certainty than enforcement of general obligations under Art.82.

[50] See also Case COMP/M.2876 *NewsCorp / Telepiù* [2004] O.J. L110/73, paras 222 to 325.

[51] Case COMP/M.3817, paras 62 and 68 to 70.

[52] "Conglomerate and Vertical Mergers in the Light of the Tetra Judgment", *Competition Policy Newsletter*, Summer 2005, p.35 at p.38.

20–033 **(iii) Use of conduct remedies in support of a structural solution** In addition, the Commission may accept "conduct" remedies in support of a structural solution or to protect consumers in the interim whilst a market is being liberalised. For example, in *Verbund / Energie Allianz*[53] the Commission accepted a price cap to operate during the period of transition until there was full competition on the market (for power supply in Austria) to limit the potential cost risk for customers. In *Air France / KLM*[54] the Commission accepted a commitment that, whenever the merged entity published a reduced fare on the Paris-Amsterdam route, it would apply an equivalent reduction on the Lyon-Amsterdam route (for so long as there was no competition on that route). The Commission explained that this would deter predatory pricing on the Paris-Amsterdam route (by making it more expensive) and would protect consumers on the Lyon-Amsterdam route in the period prior to entry by a rival.[55]

20.7 TRANSFERRING A MARKET POSITION—TRANSFERS OF BUSINESSES OR ASSETS

(a) Introduction

20–034 In the majority of cases, the competition concern arising from the merger is based on non-coordinated effects theory, namely that as a result of the merger the merged group will hold original market power in its own right. In such cases, the primary remedy is (adopting the language of the Merger Remedies Study) an undertaking to transfer a market position, i.e. to divest a business in the market in question.

Indeed, the Notice on Remedies states: "Where a proposed merger [gives rise to competition concerns], the most effective way to restore effective competition, apart from prohibition, is to create the conditions for the emergence of a new competitive entity or for the strengthening of existing competitors via divestiture".[56]

20–035 The Merger Remedies Study[57] found that of 64 "transfer remedies" from 1996 to 2000 that were evaluated, 56 per cent were effective, 25 per cent

---

[53] Case COMP/M.2947 [2004] O.J. L92/91, para.153.
[54] Case COMP/M.3280 (appeal pending in Case T-177/04 *easyJet Airline Company v Commission*), paras 158(g) and 166.
[55] See also Case COMP/M.3770 *Lufthansa / Swiss*, para.197(f).
[56] Notice on Remedies, para.13.
[57] See p.134. As explained on p.132, "effective" remedies clearly achieved their competition objective, "partially effective" remedies experienced design and implementation issues which were not fully resolved three to five years after the divestiture and may have partially affected the competitiveness of the divested business, and "ineffective" remedies failed to restore competition as foreseen in the Commission's conditional clearance decision. See also p.129, noting that the shares of the divested business decreased in 44% of cases whilst they increased in only 18% of cases (remaining stable in 34% of cases and disappearing in 4% of cases).

partially effective, 6 per cent ineffective, and in 13 per cent of cases the outcome was unclear. The Study[58] also found that the 17 "divestiture commitments"[59] that were considered "partially effective" suffered from serious design and/or implementation issues concerning: the scope of the divested business (in all 17 cases), carving out the divestment business (in eight cases), the suitability of the purchaser (in nine cases), the involvement of affected third parties (in two cases), interim preservation of the divested business and holding it separate (in four cases), and the transfer of the business (in nine cases).[60]

In terms of structuring remedies involving the transfer of a market position, the Merger Remedies Study stated[61]:

"The Study identified the following considerations which need to be fully analysed by the Commission before it can determine the correct scope of the divestiture package: (1) upstream and downstream links between the divested business and parts of the parties' retained business; (2) geographic scope of a viable and competitive divested business as compared to the geographic scope of the relevant market which may not be the same; (3) critical size or mass of the divestiture package; (4) considerations of product cycle effects such as the divestiture of mature products to compete against the parties' retained innovative new generation products; and (5) IPR issues".

(b) Divestiture of a business

The divestiture of a business may occur through a sale of shares or assets. **20–036** Sales of assets range from the transfer of the full package of assets necessary to carry on a business to the transfer of selected assets which may facilitate new entry. The remainder of this section analyses in detail the Commission's approach to sales of shares or "full packages" of assets (although the scope to exclude certain assets from the divestment package in discussed in s.(e)(ii)

---

[58] See p.126.

[59] Comprising 16 transfer remedies and one remedy involving exit from a joint venture.

[60] These findings are consistent with studies by the UK Competition Commission ("Application of Divestiture Remedies in Merger Inquiries: Competition Commission Guidelines", December 2004, available via *www.competition-commission.org.uk/rep_pub/rules_and_guide/ pdf/divestiture_remedies_guidance.pdf*, para.2.4) and the International Competition Network (Merger Remedies Review Project", June 2005, available via *www.internationalcompetition network.org/ICN_Remedies_StudyFINAL5-10.pdf*, para.3.9) which identified three main risks associated with divestment commitments: composition risks arise if the divestiture package is not appropriately configured (meaning that the business cannot be sold or cannot be operated as a viable business in the hands of the purchaser); purchaser risks arise if the business is not sold to a buyer which will operate the business as an effective competitor; and asset risks arise if the divestiture package deteriorates prior to sale (e.g. losing customers or key staff).

[61] See pp.140 and 141. See also the Study's proposed improvements to current practice at pp.142 and 143.

below).[62] Such sales are the paradigm remedy and many aspects of the Commission's approach in this area are applicable equally to the other types of remedy discussed in subsequent sections of this Chapter.

The Commission has published model divestiture commitments ("the model Divestiture Commitments"), a model trustee mandate ("the model Trustee Mandate")[63] and "Best Practice Guidelines: the Commission's Model Texts for Divestiture Commitments and the Trustee Mandate under the EC Merger Regulation" ("Best Practice Guidelines"). The Best Practice Guidelines make clear that the Commission regards the draft Divestiture Commitments and the model Trustee Mandate as providing a "framework" for the discussion of remedies.[64]

(c) Clear identification of the business to be transferred

20–037 It is necessary to identify clearly *the business to be transferred*.[65] The model Divestiture Commitments require the notifying party to describe the legal and functional structure of the divestment business and to identify specifically the assets and personnel included in the divestment business.[66] When assets are used within the business but are not intended to form part of the divestment business, the parties are required to identify them specifically.[67] If a remedy is vague (e.g. giving the divesting party a discretion about which customers should be transferred) it will not be acceptable.[68]

(d) A viable business

20–038 **(i) Introduction** The objective of a remedy involving the transfer of a market position through divestment is to replace the competitive intensity lost as a result of the merger, and this requires that the purchaser should have the incentive and ability to compete as intensively as the operator of the business which is being sold. The Notice on Remedies states[69]: "The divested activities must consist of a *viable business* that, if operated by a suitable purchaser, can compete effectively with the merged entity on a lasting

---

[62] See also s.20.11 below for discussion of transfers of selected assets.

[63] The model Divestiture Commitments and the model Trustee Mandate.

[64] The Best Practice Guidelines, paras 2 and 4 to 6. In practice, strong grounds are required to persuade the Commission's case teams to depart from the terms of the models.

[65] Notice on Remedies, para.46. The business may be located outside the EU: see, e.g. Case IV/M.1381 *Imetal / English China Clays* (which involved the divestment of a kaolin plant in the US to address concerns about the impact of the concentration on the global market for kaolin) and Case COMP/M.2690 *Solvay / Montedison-Ausimont* (disposal of a plant in Alabama, USA; para.193).

[66] The model Divestiture Commitments, para.4 and the Schedule.

[67] Notice on Remedies (para.46) and the Schedule to the model Divestiture Commitments (para.3). See s.(e)(ii) below for discussion of the scope to exclude certain assets from the divestiture package.

[68] See, e.g. Case COMP/M.3314 *Air Liquide / Messer Targets*, paras 190 and 211 (the Commission insisted on specific remedies to prevent the divesting party from "cherry picking" the more attractive customers for itself).

[69] Para.14.

basis".[70] For example,[71] in *SCA / Metsä Tissue*[72] a proposed plant disposal was rejected on the grounds that the new owner would not have sufficient capacity to compete aggressively in markets in which the merged group would otherwise hold a dominant position.[73]

In addition to the factors discussed in the remainder of this section, the viability of the divestment business may be affected in particular by a failure to include all necessary assets (s.(e) below) or a failure to include a full line of products or sufficient activities to benefit from economies of scale or scope (s.(f) below).

The Notice on Remedies confirms that the business to be transferred should be "the most appropriate" one.[74] This might be the purchaser's, for example in the case of a hostile bid where the bidder lacks sufficient knowledge about the target's structure and operations properly to identify a viable business to be sold.[75]

(ii) Preference for existing businesses The Notice on Remedies states[76]: 20–039 "Normally, a viable business is an *existing* one ... In proposing a viable business for divestiture, the parties must take into account the uncertainties and risks related to the transfer of a business to a new owner. These risks may limit the competitive impact of the divested business, and, therefore,

---

[70] The Merger Remedies Study found that one or more serious issues concerning the scope of the divested business were identified in 79% of the 84 analysed divestiture remedies; see p.23. The main inadequacy involved the omission of key assets (see p.140).

[71] In Case COMP/M.1715 *Alcan / Pechiney* the parties sought to address the Commission's concerns about the concentration before deciding to withdraw their notification. The discussions between the parties and the Commission were summarised in a press release (IP/00/258) issued after the notification was withdrawn: (a) a proposal to divest capacity at a rolling mill would not have been acceptable because the purchaser would have become a wholesaler rather than a producer and was therefore unlikely to become a viable competitor; (b) the Commission would have rejected a proposal to sell plants which were "reportedly not viable or are high cost facilities which were meant to be shut down anyway"; (c) a proposal to sell plants where "the full transfer of the divested business and the integration and establishment process would take a number of years to complete" would not have been acceptable; and (d) the Commission would have rejected a proposal to sell a production line without transferring customer contracts or providing non-compete or non-solicitation clauses. See now the model Divestiture Commitments, para.10 (non-solicitation clause) and the Best Practice Guidelines, para.24 (explaining that non-solicitation clauses should normally apply for two years and that the Commission *may* request the inclusion of non-compete clauses in the commitments). Compare US Department of Justice, "Antitrust Policy Guide to Merger Remedies", October 2004 (available via *www.usdoj.gov/atr/public/guidelines/205108.htm*), s.III(E)(1) strongly disfavouring the use of non-competes on vendors of divestment businesses. See also Case COMP/M.1601 *Allied Signal / Honeywell* [2001] O.J. L152/1, para.131 and the Commission's XXXIst Annual Report on Competition Policy, 2001, para.300.

[72] Case COMP/M.2097, paras 187 and 252.

[73] See also the Merger Remedies Study, p.24, noting that serious issues concerning the scope of the remedy had been identified when the divested business lacked critical size, i.e. it was too small to be an effective competitor in anybody's hands (except perhaps a significant, established competitor which would be likely to raise separate competition concerns).

[74] The Notice on Remedies, para.16. See also the US Department of Justice, "Antitrust Policy Guide to Merger Remedies", October 2004 (available via *www.usdoj.gov/atr/public/guidelines/205108.htm*), n.15.

[75] The Notice on Remedies, para.16.

[76] Para.14.

may lead to a market situation where the competitive concerns of the Commission will not necessarily be eliminated".[77]

20–040 **(iii) Carve-out remedies commonly, but not invariably, accepted** Commonly, a divestment remedy requires that the business being sold is carved out[78] of the seller's business. Indeed, of the 84 divestiture remedies from 1996 to 2000 examined in the Merger Remedies Study, 60 per cent required an extensive carving out of assets.[79] (The remainder did not because the divested businesses were already operating to a large extent on a stand-alone basis.)

Nevertheless, the Commission has rejected proposed remedies on the grounds that the business to be sold is too heavily integrated with the merging parties' businesses to be carved out into a viable competitor. This occurred in *Exxon | Mobil*,[80] in which the Commission did not accept the proposed divestiture of Mobil's aviation lubricants business, because: "Mobil's activities are integrated within the Mobil group. Mobil produces its own ester base stock and also produces five proprietary additives. It did not appear to be possible to offer Mobil's blending facility as it was part of a wider complex. Respondents to the Commission's market test therefore indicated their doubts as to the capacity of a purchaser of Mobil's aviation lubricants business to operate as a viable competitive force able to constrain Exxon Mobil's actions". The parties therefore offered instead to sell Exxon's aviation lubricants business, which was accepted by the Commission. Similar concerns about integration led the Commission to reject the proposed divestiture of Sprint's internet business in *MCI WorldCom | Sprint*.[81] The Commission stated that the proposal "was insufficient as it would not re-establish, with sufficient certainty as to its effect, immediate and effective competition in the market for top-level Internet connectivity".[82] Finally, in *Airtours | First Choice*[83] a proposed divestiture was

---

[77] The FTC Divestiture Study, p.10, supports the conclusion that a divestiture of an ongoing business is more likely to result in a viable operation than the divestiture of selected assets designed to facilitate entry.
[78] i.e. legally and physically separated.
[79] See p.73.
[80] Case IV/M.1383 [2004] O.J. L103/1, para.860.
[81] Case COMP/M.1741 [2003] O.J. L300/1.
[82] The Commission's XXXth Annual Report on Competition Policy, 2000, p.185. At para.339 of the decision, the Commission emphasised that, given the high growth of the internet and the importance attached by customers to quality of service, it was important that any proposed business for divestiture should be in a position to compete fully and effectively from the date of transfer of ownership. The Commission's concerns about the proposed commitments are described at paras 340 to 409 of the decision. The earlier divestment of MCI's internet business to Cable & Wireless was not successful (as explained by Jenny in Lévêque & Shelanski (eds), *Merger Remedies in American and European Union Competition Law* (Edward Elgar, 2003), at p.203) and this undoubtedly encouraged the Commission to treat subsequent proposals with caution. (Contrast Case COMP/M.3680 *Alcatel | Finmeccanica | Alcatel Alenia Space & Telespazio*, para.127, emphasising that a similar package of remedies in a previous case had been successful.)
[83] Case COMP/M.1524 [2000] O.J. L93/1 (overturned on appeal on other grounds in Case T-342/99 *Airtours plc v Commission* [2002] E.C.R. II-2585).

rejected on the grounds that the assets had not previously constituted an integrated business (although the Commission also emphasised that the scale of the divestiture was limited and the buyer would be at a competitive disadvantage as it would not be vertically integrated).

The Merger Remedies Study identified a number of issues arising from the process of carving out the divested business.[84] **20–041**

(a) It found that there were fewer problems during transfer if the divestment business belonged to the target, because the notifying party did not already possess sensitive business information regarding the target and had fewer possibilities to alter or degrade the business during the interim period.

(b) When there were shared assets, these needed to be replicated and the complexity of this exercise was frequently underestimated, particularly in the case of shared IT systems.

(c) Allocating intellectual property rights and know-how posed major problems and could be very time-consuming.

(d) Monitoring of the carve-out could be crucial to the effectiveness of the remedy, even in the case of an up-front buyer. Investment banks typically lack the expertise necessary to monitor carve-outs.

(e) The commitments did not impose on the parties an obligation to carry out a timely, full and best effort carve-out.

(iv) "Mix and match" remedies not usually accepted The Commission is very cautious about accepting "mix and match" remedies comprising assets from two or more parties because this creates additional risks as to the viability and efficiency of the divestment business.[85] For example, in *Group 4 Falck / Securicor*,[86] the Commission rejected a "mix and match" remedy including customers from both merging parties' businesses in particular because there were doubts about its viability and a risk that the parties had selected customers that were less interesting or could more easily be recaptured by the parties. The Commission's cautious approach is supported by the outcome of the FTC Divestiture Study.[87] However, such remedies have been accepted in specific circumstances.[88] There may be greater scope to construct a "mix and match" remedy if the notifying party offers a "fix it first" **20–042**

---

[84] See pp.73 to 79 (and pp.150 to 153).
[85] The Notice on Remedies, para.17.
[86] Case COMP/M.3396, paras 151 and 153.
[87] p.38. See also US Department of Justice, "Antitrust Policy Guide to Merger Remedies", October 2004 (available via *www.usdoj.gov/atr/public/guidelines/205108.htm*), s.III(C).
[88] The Notice on Remedies, para.17, referring to Case IV/M.603 *Crown Cork & Seal / Carnaud Metalbox* [1996] O.J. L75/38.

commitment, as this addresses the risk that a suitable purchaser might not be found.[89]

20–043 **(v) Divestment business must normally operate on a "stand-alone" basis** The Notice on Remedies states[90]: "Normally, a viable business is ... one that can operate on a *stand-alone-basis*, which means independently of the merging parties as regards the supply of input materials or other forms of co-operation other than during a transitory period".[91] For example, in *Degussa / Laporte*[92] the Commission carefully established that the purchaser would have access to an essential input before approving the commitments. In cases when the purchaser would not have such access, the Commission has more recently[93] followed the approach in the Notice on Remedies and rejected remedies involving ongoing cooperation, whilst accepting remedies that assured the buyer of access to inputs without such cooperation. In *CVC / Lenzing*[94] the notifying party proposed to grant a non-exclusive patent licence and enter a toll-manufacturing agreement[95] for up to five years. The Commission was concerned that the licensee's ability to commence production in a two to three year period would depend on the merged group's technical support and pricing strategy. Further, the toll-manufacturing agreement would have resulted in the merged group having access to the licensee's business strategy, costs, sales and customers in circumstances in which the licensee could not compete on quality of technical service (as it would be dependent on the merged group) or price (as it would have to pay the merged group's production cost plus a fee, putting it at a cost dis-

---

[89] See Case COMP/M.2544 *Masterfoods / Royal Canin*.

[90] Para.14.

[91] See also the Merger Remedies Study, pp.23 and 24 (issues arising from vertical dependence on the vendor, e.g. for critical inputs, after sales service or other critical assets; the Study also identified issues regarding unresolved intellectual property rights issues). Further, the FTC Divestiture Study noted, at p.28, that: "Establishing a viable competitor requires a thorough understanding of the operations of the business. The order must ensure that the buyer has access to the necessary technology, suppliers, distribution channels and other essential business elements".

[92] Case COMP/M.2277, para.51.

[93] By contrast, in Case IV/M.938 *Guinness / Grand Metropolitan* [1998] O.J. L288/24, a decision taken *prior* to publication of the Notice on Remedies, the undertakings to divest whisky brands included a commitment, insofar as whisky indispensable to the blending of the brands could only be sourced from distilleries owned by the merged group, to continue to supply such whisky to the purchaser if requested on reasonable arm's length commercial terms; the obligation was supported by an arbitration clause; para.183.

[94] Case COMP/M.2187 *CVC / Lenzing* [2004] O.J. L82/20.

[95] A proposal to enter a toll-manufacturing agreement was also rejected by the Commission following market-testing in Case COMP/M.2277 *Degussa / Laporte*, para.49; the notifying party modified the commitment to provide for a full divestiture of assets. In its earlier decision in Case IV/M.1517 *Rhodia / Donau Chemie / Albright & Wilson* the Commission had accepted an irrevocable commitment to enter into toll-manufacturing agreements (supported, in one of the markets, by a commitment to provide a list of customers) (paras 82 and 83). For an example of toll-manufacturing forming part of an acceptable commitment to license intellectual property rights, see Case COMP/M.2547 *Bayer / Aventis Crop Science* [2004] O.J. L107/1, paras 1105 and 1106.

advantage relative to the merged group). The proposal was not accepted by the Commission.[96] By contrast, in *Solvay / Montedison-Ausimont*[97] the competition issue arose in the persalts market because the target was party to a 50/50 joint venture with a competitor. Solvay undertook to dispose of the target's 50 per cent holding *and* either to dispose of a business making a raw material used in the production of persalts or, if divestment were not possible, to amend the toll-manufacturing agreement between the target and the joint venture so that no competition concerns would arise. The Commission regarded the package of commitments as essential to avoid a situation in which the joint venture depended on a competitor, Solvay, for the supply of an essential input, and in which Solvay could obtain access to confidential information about the joint venture's activities on the persalts market.[98]

(vi) Product cycle effects may undermine viability The Merger Remedies 20–044 Study identified serious issues regarding the scope of divestment packages in cases in which demand was likely to shift from the divested product to other, newer products which were being retained by the merging parties and had greater strategic importance and better future business prospects.

(vii) Strategic behaviour by the vendor of the divestment business A business 20–045 may not be viable if the seller is able, following the sale, to engage in *strategic behaviour* to damage the buyer's business. The FTC Divestiture Study reports an example in which the seller used confidential information to undermine the buyer's introduction of a new product by simultaneously introducing a similar product.[99]

(viii) Notifying party can choose between two equally viable remedies If there 20–046 are two equally viable remedies (e.g. divestment of either of the merging parties' businesses) then in principle the notifying party can choose the remedy as it would be disproportionate[1] to require it to pursue one if the other is also adequate. However, it seems likely that the Commission will adopt a more cautious approach in the future when assessing the adequacy of remedies and this will reduce the notifying party's choice in some cases. This is because the Merger Remedies Study[2] found that divestments of "just the overlap" were effective in 43 per cent of cases, effective after later

---

[96] Paras 264 to 268.
[97] Case COMP/M.2690, paras 183 and 189.
[98] See also Case COMP/M.3314 *Air Liquide / Messer Targets*, para.187 (divestment of a source of industrial gases).
[99] The FTC Divestiture Study, p.18.
[1] See s.20.4(c) above.
[2] See p.35.

additions in a further 14 per cent of cases and "risky/doubtful" in 43 per cent of cases. This is a relatively low success rate when read in the context of the statement by the Commissioner for Competition Policy, Neelie Kroes, that: "It is the merging companies, not their customers, who should bear the risks of potentially inadequate remedies".[3] The Study found[4] that a remedy was more likely to be effective where the divested business was relatively self-contained, with stand-alone characteristics that would support its long-term viability. The Commission may in the future show greater inclination to reject divestments not satisfying these criteria. Indeed, in a supermarket merger raising a series of local overlap issues, the UK Competition Commission[5] refused to allow the purchaser to choose which store to divest in four instances, ruling that divestment of the purchaser's existing store would be "significantly inferior" to divestment of the acquired store as it had a "significantly greater" risk of not attracting a suitable purchaser.

(e) All necessary assets should be included in the divestment package

20–047 **(i) General** In order to ensure that the divestment business is viable,[6] the divestiture package must, subject to s.(ii) below, include all[7] of the elements which are necessary for the business to act as a viable competitor on the market, in particular research and development,[8] production, distribution, sales and marketing activities, intellectual property rights, goodwill, assets, personnel (including personnel working for the divestment business and providing support services, such as information technology and research

---

[3] IP/05/1327.

[4] See p.35.

[5] *Somerfield Plc / Wm Morrison Supermarkets Plc*, September 2005 (available via *www.competition-commission.org.uk/rep_pub/reports/2005/fulltext/501.pdf*), para.11.22 (this part of the Competition Commission's analysis was challenged unsuccessfully in the UK Competition Appeal Tribunal in Case 1051/4/8/05 *Somerfield plc v Competition Commission* [2006] CAT 4).

[6] See generally US Department of Justice, "Antitrust Policy Guide to Merger Remedies", October 2004 (available via *www.usdoj.gov/atr/public/guidelines/205108.htm*), s.III(B). The International Competition Network, "Merger Remedies Review Project", June 2005 (available via *www.internationalcompetitionnetwork.org/ICN_Remedies_StudyFINAL5-10.pdf*), states, at para.3.10: "In general a suitable divestiture package may be defined as the smallest operating unit of a business, (e.g. a subsidiary or a division) that contains all the relevant operations pertinent to the area of competitive overlap and that can compete successfully on a stand alone basis". The same text is used in the UK Competition Commission, "Application of Divestiture Remedies in Merger Inquiries: Competition Commission Guidelines", December 2004 (available via *www.competition-commission.org.uk/rep_pub/rules_and_guide/pdf/divestiture_remedies_guidance.pdf*), para.3.1.

[7] For discussion of criticisms regarding the selection of assets in the US, see Baer & Redcay in Lévêque & Shelanski (eds), *Merger Remedies in American and European Union Competition Law* (Edward Elgar, 2003), at pp.60 to 62.

[8] See, e.g. Case COMP/M.3225 *Alcan / Pechiney (II)*, para.163(ii). In Case COMP/M.2972 *DSM / Roche Vitamins* [2004] O.J. L82/73, the notifying party committed to transfer existing research and development projects relating to the divestment business *or* at the purchaser's request and subject to the Commission's prior approval, to complete one specific research and development project on behalf of the purchaser.

and development), supply and sales agreements (with appropriate guarantees about their transferability), customer lists, third party service agreements and technical assistance.[9] The model Divestiture Commitments require the party providing the undertakings to confirm that the divestment business includes all assets which contribute to its current operation or are necessary to ensure its viability and competitiveness and all personnel retained by the divestment business (including shared personnel).[10]

The FTC Divestiture Study revealed that potential purchasers of divest- **20–048** ment businesses are commonly *not* well-placed to identify what needs to be included as part of the divestiture package[11] in order to create a viable business: "Especially in orders that require the divestiture of less than an entire business, the buyers lack important information about the business that is being divested. This lack, this industry ignorance, is not the result of carelessness, of a failure to perform due diligence, or of poor judgment; it is an inherent characteristic of entering a new business".[12] The Study gave as examples cases in which: the seller of the divestment business had encouraged customers to stockpile goods in advance of the divestiture; the buyer had not realised that the seller could control the buyer's manufacturing costs through the supply of a key raw material; and the buyer had refused to supply crucial raw materials because the antitrust authority's order did not require such supply.[13] It concluded that: *buyers* of divestment businesses commonly lack buyer power, notwithstanding the seller's status as forced seller, because they perceive there to be multiple buyers interested[14]; buyers commonly overestimate the value of the assets because of a false assumption that a purchase from a forced seller will be a bargain[15]; and buyers sometimes reduce the value of the divestment package by offering favourable terms to the seller in the hope of being chosen as the purchaser.[16]

The FTC Divestiture Study also found that the transfer of confidential business information can be the most difficult aspect of a divestiture and recommended considering the inclusion of obligations on the seller to grant the buyer rights to all related technology, rights to technical assistance, rights to inspect the seller's facilities in operation, and the right to seek to employ selected people from the merged group who have important knowledge.[17]

---

[9] The Notice on Remedies, paras 46 and 47. See also the Merger Remedies Study, pp.23 to 45 (scope of the divestment business) and 80 to 86 (transfer of the divested business).

[10] The model Divestiture Commitments para.4 (read with the definition of "Personnel" in Section A) and the Schedule. See also the Best Practice Guidelines, paras 18 and 19.

[11] For discussion of whether the interests of the purchaser of the divestment business are more closely aligned with the *merging parties* under the original concentration, rather than with the Commission, see Farrell in Lévêque & Shelanski (eds), *Merger Remedies in American and European Union Competition Law* (Edward Elgar, 2003), at pp.95 to 98.

[12] p.15.

[13] pp.20 to 23.

[14] p.23.

[15] p.25.

[16] p.25.

[17] pp.36 and 37.

The Merger Remedies Study noted that some sellers use the divestment process to "off-load" unproductive staff by transferring them with the divestment business, which has worked against the effectiveness of the remedy.[18]

20–049 **(ii) When specific assets may be excluded from the divestment package** The US Federal Trade Commission's Bureau of Competition has said that it is *not* necessary to include assets when there is evidence that the assets are readily available to any likely purchaser.[19] For example, if any buyer likely to be acceptable would have its own research and development unit, it would not be necessary to transfer research and development resources.[20] Similarly, if third party contract manufacturing is readily and competitively available, it may not be necessary to transfer manufacturing plants.[21] These principles are reflected in the Commission's decisions. In *Johnson & Johnson / Guidant*[22] Johnson & Johnson sourced its guidewires from an OEM manufacturer. The Commission accepted commitments to divest this business without any manufacturing capability on the grounds that the divestment business would be viable because many guidewire suppliers sourced from OEM manufacturers. Similarly, in *Metso / Svedala*[23] the omission of a production facility was accepted by the Commission because the facilities included in the divestment package could take on production from the omitted plant and the parties agreed to produce under licence from the retained plant during the interim period. In a second market, the omission of dedicated production facilities and personnel was accepted on the grounds that this was not necessary as orders were too infrequent to render dedicated facilities economic.

20–050 **(iii) Granting the purchaser the option to require the inclusion of an asset** The Commission sometimes accepts remedies under which the purchaser chooses whether it wishes to purchase certain specified assets. The advantage of such an arrangement is that the purchaser can acquire the assets if it believes it needs them, but is not saddled with them if it concludes that it does not. This can be particularly important when the potential buyers fall into different

---

[18] See p.43.
[19] See also US Department of Justice, "Antitrust Policy Guide to Merger Remedies", October 2004 (available via *www.usdoj.gov/atr/public/guidelines/205108.htm*), s.III(C) (requiring clear evidence that the relevant assets are in the possession of, or readily obtainable in a competitive market by, the potential purchaser, and referring as examples to general accounting or computer programming services) and the Canadian Competition Bureau's draft "Information Bulletin on Merger Remedies in Canada", October 2005 (available via *www.competition bureau.gc.ca/PDFs/info_bulletin_mergerremedies_051017_e.pdf*), paras 15 and 16.
[20] This issue arises in particular with human resources, accounting and distribution functions.
[21] "Statement of Federal Trade Commission's Bureau of Competition on Negotiating Merger Remedies", April 2003 (available via *www.ftc.gov/bc/bestpractices/bestpractices030401.htm*).
[22] Case COMP/M.3687, paras 358(a) and 359.
[23] Case COMP/M.2033 [2004] O.J. L88/1, paras 232, 235 and 236.

classes, some of which already own certain essential assets and others of which do not. However, the Merger Remedies Study identified risks regarding such arrangements because the economic interests of the sellers and purchasers typically did not coincide with the objectives of the Commission and the vendor might favour purchasers which indicated from the outset that they did not require the additional assets.[24]

(f) Divestment of "more than the overlap"

(i) Commission requires a broader divestment In order to ensure that there is **20–051** a viable business which can be sold to create an effective competitor, it may be necessary to include in the divestment package businesses which do not form part of the market in which competition issues were identified,[25] for example to enable the purchaser to offer a full line of products, to benefit from economics of scale or scope, or to avoid a situation in which the purchaser has ongoing dependence on the vendor.[26] Indeed, the Merger Remedies Study stated[27]: "there are a large number of situations where a divestiture of larger than the overlapping businesses would have been necessary in order to secure an effective remedy".

(a) In *Sanitec / Sphinx*[28] the competition concerns related to the ceramic sanitary ware market (alternatively, the markets for WCs, WC cisterns and washbasins) and the markets for bathtubs and shower screens. However, Sanitec undertook to divest an entire business, whose products included taps and mixers (where no competition concerns had been identified). The Commission was concerned that the purchaser of the divested business should have an opportunity to buy these lines so that it could offer a *full range* of products and would therefore be a viable competitor.

(b) In *TotalFina / Elf*[29] the Commission market-tested a proposal to dispose of assets to eliminate the competition concerns. The market test identified concerns about the viability of the proposed remedy

---

[24] See p.42.
[25] The Notice on Remedies, para.17. The Commission's approach is consistent with the approach in the US: see *Olin Corp v FTC* 986 F.2d 1295 (9th Cir. 1993). See generally "Merger Remedies", OECD, DAF/COMP(2004)21, pp.23 and 256 and US Department of Justice, "Antitrust Policy Guide to Merger Remedies", October 2004 (available via *www.usdoj.gov/atr/public/guidelines/205108.htm*), s.III(C).
[26] See also Case COMP/M.3687 *Johnson & Johnson / Guidant*, para.358(b). The FTC Divestiture Study identified, at pp.18 and 19, difficulties in cases in which a purchaser required a *full line* of products to operate as a viable competitor, or required on an ongoing basis crucial raw materials held by the party providing the undertakings.
[27] See p.40.
[28] Case IV/M.1578 [2000] O.J. L294/1, para.313.
[29] Case COMP/M.1628 [2001] O.J. L143/1.

and the parties therefore offered a broader divestment of a company going well beyond the elimination of the specific overlaps.

(c) In *Unilever / Amora-Maille*[30] the concerns related to the merged group's position in France in the supply of mayonnaise, salad dressings and other cold dressings. The divestiture of the Bénédicta brand covered other products (such as mustard) and all territories where the mark was registered (not just France). The rationale for this requirement was that the new entrant would need to offer the *full range* of Bénédicta products and would need to be present internationally in order to compete effectively with Unilever.[31]

(d) In *Unilever / Bestfoods*[32] the undertakings, which were structured as a brand divestiture, covered the whole range of products sold under the brands in question, not just the product-lines where specific competition concerns had been identified. The Commission noted that: "This should ensure that the respective purchasers will not only acquire the present market share attached with the above-mentioned portfolios but also their full brand value together with the access to the customer base attached to them".[33] The divestiture package was estimated to involve businesses with an annual turnover of Euros 500 million.[34]

(e) In *Degussa / Laporte*,[35] in order to address concerns about specific types of cationic reagents and monomers, the notifying party agreed to divest the entirety of Laporte's cationic reagents and monomers businesses.[36]

(f) In *Nestlé / Ralston Purina*[37] the Commission took account, in determining the appropriate remedy, of the *interests of consumers*, going beyond their interests in the maintenance of effective competition. The remedy was aimed at "avoiding a situation where the ownership of the involved pet food brands would be permanently split in different parts of the Community".[38]

(g) In *Buhrmann / Samas*,[39] the notifying party agreed to sell an entire

---

[30] Case COMP/M.1802.
[31] See Claude Rakovsky, "Remedies: A Few Lessons From Recent Experience", published in *EC Merger Control: Ten Years On* (International Bar Association, 2000), p.135, at p.139.
[32] Case COMP/M.1990.
[33] Commission press release IP/00/1076.
[34] See the Commission's XXXth Annual Report on Competition Policy, 2000, p.175.
[35] Case COMP/M.2277.
[36] It is not clear from the Commission's decision or the accompanying press release whether the concern which led to a requirement to divest activities in markets not giving rise to competition concerns arose because production of the affected and non-affected products was *integrated* or because customers required a *full range* and the creation of a viable competitor therefore required that the divestment business comprise a full range.
[37] Case COMP/M.2337.
[38] Commission press release IP/01/1136.
[39] Case COMP/M.2286.

Dutch contract-stationing business, although the competition concerns were limited to the provision of office supplies to larger customers. The Commission considered that the wider sale was necessary to ensure that the remedy was viable because if only part of the business had been sold, the distribution centre and sales organisation would not have been profitable and the purchaser would have lacked buyer power compared with the pre-merger position.

(h) In *DSM / Roche Vitamins*[40] the Commission stated that any remedy could not be limited to the overlapping product but had to include others which had to date been developed, produced, sold and distributed together with the overlapping product.

(i) In *Cytec / UCB—Surface Specialties*[41] the Commission found that it would not be possible to carve out a viable business producing only the product which gave rise to the competition concerns. The notifying party therefore provided a broader commitment.

(j) In *Group 4 Falck / Securicor*[42] the Commission insisted on the inclusion in the remedies package of an additional product (which did not raise competition concerns in itself), because a viable competitor had to be able to offer the full range.

The Merger Remedies Study found[43] that divestiture commitments including "more than the overlap" were more effective than those comprising "just the overlap" or "less than the overlap".

(ii) Parties choose a broader divestment In *DSM / Roche Vitamins*[44] the   **20–052** notifying party broadened the scope of the divestiture commitment on "industrial and commercial" grounds by adding an additional product.[45] Separately, once a divestiture commitment has been accepted, the Commission is willing for the parties to add other assets to make the package more attractive to purchasers.[46]

---

[40] Case COMP/M.2972 [2004] O.J. L82/73, para.90.
[41] Case COMP/M.3558, para.42.
[42] Case COMP/M.3396, para.148.
[43] See p.36.
[44] Case COMP/M.2972 [2004] O.J. L82/73, para.91.
[45] Two concerns arise from such a voluntary expansion of the remedies package. The first is that purchasers that would operate as effective competitors in the market in which the competition concerns arose might be deterred from buying by the inclusion of the additional business. Secondly, purchasers may be more interested in the additional business, creating a risk that the buyer will not operate as an effective competitor in the markets in which the competition concerns arose. See generally the Merger Remedies Study, p.30.
[46] The Notice on Remedies, para.21 and n.25, referring to the divestment process in Case IV/M.1532 *BP Amoco / Arco* [2001] O.J. L18/1. See also the Best Practice Guidelines para.18 and the Merger Remedies Study, p.29. Indeed, a senior Commission official has suggested that it is arguable that, if the parties are unable to sell the divestiture business, then they have an *obligation* to add other assets spontaneously to make the package more attractive to buyers so

(g) Divestment of "less than the overlap"

20–053 **(i) Divestments in cases in which a dominant position is created** If a trans-action creates a dominant position, the question arises as to whether any divestment must eliminate the overlap between the parties or whether it is sufficient that the commitments remove sufficient overlap to ensure that the transaction does not create a dominant position. In principle, if the remedy offered by the notifying party prevents the creation of a dominant position *and* avoids any significant impediment to effective competition (which could exist even though a dominant position is not created) *and* is a satisfactory remedy meeting the criteria set out in s.20.4 above,[47] then the merger must be cleared.[48] However, the Merger Remedies Study[49] examined seven cases (from 1996 to 2000) in which the Commission accepted remedies involving divestiture of "less than the overlap" (reasoning that the resulting market share would remain below the dominance threshold which was then applicable) and found that such remedies were often ineffective or risky, whilst recognising that the sample size may have been too small to draw definitive conclusions.

20–054 **(ii) Divestment of a strong business** If the divested business is strong, with good potential to expand, it may comprise a suitable remedy even though its sale does not entirely eliminate the overlap in the parties' activities. For example, in *The Post Office / TPG / SPPL*[50] the Commission found that a divestiture of The Post Office's international outbound mail business in the Netherlands would *not* lead to the creation of a viable competitor. However, the Commission accepted as a remedy the divestiture of TPG's international outbound mail business in the Netherlands even though its market share was smaller than The Post Office's, with the consequence that the joint venture's market share would be increased as a result of the concentration. The Commission's analysis was that, notwithstanding the position in terms of market share, the strength of TPG's business at least outweighed the increase in market share with the consequence that, following the dives-titure, the position of TPG in the Netherlands would not be strengthened.

that they can comply with their undertaking to dispose of the divestiture business in accor-dance with the timetable set out in the commitments: see Claude Rakovsky, "Remedies: A Few Lessons From Recent Experience", published in *EC Merger Control: Ten Years On* (International Bar Association, 2000), p.135, at p.142.

[47] If it were not possible to divest as a viable business parts of either of the parties' businesses, then the only satisfactory remedy might be divestment of the whole of one of the parties' businesses. For example, in Case COMP/M.2547 *Bayer / Aventis Crop Science* [2004] O.J. L107/1 the effect of the divestiture package was to reduce the merged group's market share in one market to 10 to 20%, well below the threshold for dominance.

[48] See, e.g. Case COMP/M.2547 *Bayer / Aventis Crop Science* [2004] O.J. L107/1 (the remedy would "bring down market shares to an acceptable level"; para.1106). See also Case COMP/ ECSC 1351 *Usinor / Arbed / Aceralin*, para.242.

[49] See pp.37 and 38.

[50] Case COMP/M.1915 [2004] O.J. L82/1, para.152.

(iii) Divestments leaving a trivial overlap Logically, if a merger resulting in a **20–055** trivial increment in market position does not give rise to a significant impediment to effective competition, then a divestment which does not entirely eliminate the overlap but leaves a trivial overlap ought to be acceptable (so long as it satisfies the other criteria for suitable remedies). For example,[51] in *Sanitec / Sphinx*[52] the Commission noted that the divestments removed most of the overlap between the parties and the retention of the remainder of the business would not lead to any strengthening of Sanitec's dominant position on the market in question.[53]

(h) Retention by the divesting party of an interest in the divested business

In general, a party undertaking to sell a business will be required to sell the **20–056** entirety of its interest in that business.[54] However, there are exceptions, including the following cases.[55]

---

[51] See also Case COMP/M.3314 *Air Liquide / Messer Targets*, para.185 and Case COMP/ M.3544 *Bayer Healthcare / Roche (OTC Business)*, para.58.

[52] Case IV/M.1578 [2000] O.J. L294/1.

[53] Para.254. See also Case IV/M.1069 *WorldCom / MCI* [1999] O.J. L116/1, para.161 and Case COMP/M.2922 *Pfizer / Pharmacia*, para.155.

[54] See the International Competition Network Analytical Framework Sub-group, "The Analytical Framework for Merger Control" (available at *www.internationalcompetition network.org/afsguk.pdf*), para.73 and n.24 for discussion.

[55] In Case IV/M.890 *Blokker / Toys 'R' Us (II)* [1998] O.J. L316/1 (a completed transaction in which the Commission exercised its powers under Art.8(4) of the ECMR, rather than accepting commitments under Art.8(2)) the Commission found that the transaction was not compatible with the common market but permitted Blokker to retain a minority shareholding in Toys 'R' Us, noting, at para.132: "The Commission ... acknowledges that, in the light of the specific circumstances of the case, in particular the poor performance of the Toys 'R' Us business in the Netherlands since its establishment in 1993, there may be difficulties in attracting a third party to purchase the whole of the Toys 'R' Us business. For this reason, the Commission considers that the continued presence of Blokker in the form of a 20% minority shareholding in combination with the active presence of Blokker on the management board of Speelhoorn can, at least for a certain period of time, serve both to demonstrate the confidence of Blokker in the future viability of the company and to guarantee the development of the company into a viable business within this period". The Commission required Blokker to eliminate its active presence on the management board of Speelhoorn once the viability of the company was established; see para.133. In contrast to the Commission's approach in *Blokker / Toys 'R' Us (II)* of preferring to make an order under Art.8(4) of the ECMR rather than accepting commitments in a completed transaction, in Case IV/M.754 *Anglo American Corporation / Lonrho* [1998] O.J. L149/21, discussed in the text at sub-para.(a) below, the Commission stated, at para.125, that "as the concentration has already been implemented, and in order to avoid any unnecessary harm to AAC and its related companies, it is considered to be appropriate to permit AAC greater flexibility by allowing it to put in place its undertaking on its terms rather than imposing the same terms by way of an Article 8(4) order". See also Case IV/M.931 *Neste / IVO* (undertaking to sell down from a 75% holding to 25% to resolve vertical issues; paras 57 and 61); Case COMP/M.1693 *Alcoa / Reynolds* [2002] O.J. L58/25 (the Commission accepted a commitment to divest a 25% production share in a smelter used to produce high-purity P0404 aluminium; the stake was sufficient to produce more than the annual requirements of the downstream customer who faced potential vertical foreclosure as a result of the merger; see para.137); Case COMP/M.2283 *Schneider / Legrand* (the Commission's divestment decision of January 30, 2002, reported in Commission press

(a) In *Anglo American Corporation / Lonrho* an acquisition by Anglo American Corporation ("AAC") of shares in Lonrho was approved conditional upon AAC reducing its shareholding to less than 10 per cent so that it could not exercise decisive influence over Lonrho.[56]

(b) In *Nordbanken / Postgirot*[57] the concentration would have resulted in Nordbanken acquiring full control of the Postgirot payment system as well as a significant shareholding in Bankgirot, the other main giro payment system in Sweden. The Commission accepted an undertaking to reduce Nordbanken's holding in Bankgirot to 10 per cent on the basis that, at this level, Nordea would no longer have decisive influence.

(c) In *Pirelli / Edizione / Olivetti / Telecom Italia*[58] the Commission accepted a commitment from Edizioni to transfer exclusive control of Autostrade Telecomunicazioni to one or more independent third parties "with the possibility of maintaining, subject to the approval of the Commission, only a minority participation in the Italian backbone operator".[59]

(i) The purchaser of the divestment business

20–057 **(i) The purchaser standards** The Commission will require that any divestment business is sold to a *suitable purchaser*.[60] A suitable purchaser must be approved by the Commission[61] and satisfy three conditions known as the "purchaser standards".[62]

(a) The purchaser must be a viable existing or potential competitor,

---

release IP/02/173, (which was subsequently overturned on appeal in Case T-77/02 *Schneider Electric SA v Commission* [2002] E.C.R. II-4201, as the Court of First Instance quashed the prohibition decision), regarding a deal which had been completed (i.e. implemented), provided that Schneider could retain a 5% stake in Legrand (based on a modified-HHI calculation) (this decision is criticised in Temple Lang, "Two Important Merger Regulation Judgments: The Implications of Schneider-Legrand and Tetra Laval-Sidel" (2003) 28 *European Law Review* 259, at pp.269 to 271)); Case COMP/M.2431 *Allianz / Dresdner* (reduction of shareholding to 20.5%); and the Commission's XXXIst Annual Report on Competition Policy, 2001, para.297. Finally, Volvo was able to retain shares in Scania notwithstanding the Commission's finding that the merger was not compatible with the common market (although it subsequently agreed to sell the retained shares in Case IV/M.1980 *Volvo / Renault*, para.29).
[56] See the Commission's XXVIIth Annual Report on Competition Policy, 1997, p.188.
[57] Case COMP/M.2567, para.60.
[58] Case COMP/M.2574. The remedies in this case were subsequently replaced; see Baccaro, "Failing Firm Defence and Lack of Causality: Doctrine and Practice in Europe of Two Closely Related Concepts" [2004] E.C.L.R. 11, at pp.18 and 19.
[59] Commission press release, IP/01/1299.
[60] The Notice on Remedies, para.19.
[61] In the US, the FTC's authority to approve the divestiture buyer was approved in *West Texas Transmission LP v Enron Corp* 1998 WL 156330, 1989–1 Trade Cas. (CCH) para.68,424 (W.D. Tex. 1988).
[62] See the Notice on Remedies (para.49) and the model Divestiture Commitments (para.14).

possessing the financial resources and proven expertise and having the incentive to maintain and develop the divested business as a viable and active competitive force in competition with the parties and other competitors.[63]

(b) The purchaser must be independent of, and unconnected to, the parties.

(c) The purchaser must neither be likely to create competition concerns nor give rise to a risk that the implementation of the commitments will be delayed and must in particular reasonably be expected to obtain all necessary approvals from the relevant competition and regulatory authorities for the acquisition of the divestment business.

(ii) The operation of the purchaser standards The Merger Remedies Study[64] **20–058** identified two remedies in which the choice of the wrong purchaser was considered the single most important cause of the remedy's ineffectiveness and nine in which the choice of a less than optimal purchaser raised issues and may have contributed to reducing the competitiveness of the divested business.

The Commission market tests the draft undertakings before accepting them. If the indications from the market are that there are no suitable purchasers available, then divestiture undertakings will be rejected.[65]

The Commission's approach to the application of the purchaser standards is not transparent as it has made its decision on an application for approval public in very few cases. The exceptional cases in which the Commission's decision was made public include its refusal to approve a purchaser of around 70 petrol stations in France under commitments provided in *TotalFina / Elf*[66] and its approval of the sale by Anglo American of a majority of its shares in Lonrho to Johannesburg Consolidated Investment. In addition, the Merger Remedies Study refers[67] to a case in which the Commission objected to a proposal by the parties to dispose of shares through an initial public offering on a stock exchange, on the grounds that this was likely to weaken the competitive position of the divested business. An appeal to the Court of First Instance is pending against the decision following *Lagardère / Natexis / VUP*[68] to approve Wendel as a suitable purchaser.[69] A further appeal is pending in *Scania AB v Commission*[70]

---

[63] Divestment remedies to resolve coordinated effects concerns can raise difficult questions about the suitability of proposed purchasers; see s.20.5(b) and "Merger Remedies", OECD, DAF/COMP(2004)21, p.23.

[64] See p.98.

[65] Compare para.20–014(e) above.

[66] Case COMP/M.1628 [2001] O.J. L143/1. See para.20–063 below.

[67] See p.68.

[68] COMP/M.2978 [2004] O.J. L125/54.

[69] Case T-452/04 *Editions Odile Jacob SAS v Commission* (pending).

[70] Case T 248/04.

against a decision following *Volvo / RVI*[71] to allow Volvo to transfer a substantial holding in Scania to a new company; whilst the Commission imposed conditions with the aim of ensuring that the new company was independent of Volvo, Scania claims that Renault and Volvo will obtain information about, and influence over, Scania's business.

The burden is on the parties or the trustee to demonstrate to the Commission that the purchaser[72] meets the requirements of the commitments.[73] Occasionally, the parties have discharged the burden *prior* to finalisation of the commitments, enabling them to undertake to divest the business in question to one or more *named purchasers* (or another purchaser approved by the Commission and meeting the purchaser standards).[74]

20–059 The FTC Divestiture Study reached the following conclusions on the identity of the purchaser:

"*The knowledge and experience of the buyer makes a difference* ... the weakness of some of the buyers appears to have resulted from their lack of knowledge. Some paid too much. Some were dependent for assistance on the respondent. Many made other mistakes. The most successful buyers appear to be the ones that knew the most about what they were buying. Frequently, the most knowledgeable and best buyer was the fringe competitor or an entrant expanding geographically ... In other cases, suppliers or distributors knew enough to be very good buyers...

The degree of the buyer's commitment to the market may make a difference The staff has insisted on a demonstration of commitment by would-be buyers ... [In one case, staff] discouraged a proposal that would have allowed the buyer to borrow money from the respondent. Had that loan been allowed, the buyer might have made profits during the period of the supply contract and then walked away from the deal with a net profit when the supply arrangement ended. Instead, staff recommended the divestiture contract only after the owner of [the firm] personally guaranteed the funding. With such a commitment, the only way the buyer could expect to recoup his investment was to plan to operate the business for a period that was longer than the supply contract ... It is difficult to insist on equivalent ways to commit large firms ... For this reason, staff examines the business plan of large firms with special reference to their own criteria, seeking to understand how the acquisition is justified internally. For these firms, the internal bureaucratic approval systems may represent a commitment sufficient to support the divestiture ...

---

[71] Case COMP/M.1980.
[72] Experience suggests that the Commission's assessment of the suitability of a proposed purchaser is affected by the availability of other potential purchasers, i.e. a purchaser might be acceptable if there are no better alternatives but not acceptable if there are. Contrast the US Department of Justice, "Antitrust Policy Guide to Merger Remedies", October 2004 (available via *www.usdoj.gov/atr/public/guidelines/205108.htm*), s.IV(D), stating that it does not "compare" purchasers.
[73] The Notice on Remedies, para.58.
[74] See s.20.14 below.

The size of the buyer may make a difference, such that smaller buyers should not be presumed to be less competitive buyers ... Partly, the better record of smaller firms appears to be due to commitment. The owners had risked their own money and were therefore more determined to succeed".[75]

The FTC Divestiture Study also noted that buyers' interests are different from the competition authority's,[76] giving as an example a firm which: "acquired the divested assets as part of a multi-year plan to create a business that it would be profitable to resell. It placed few demands on its managers, and thus the assets had little competitive vigor".[77] Other cases identified in the FTC Divestiture Study include one in which the disposal was structured so that the result was implicit partnership, rather than competition, between the firms, and a second in which the purchaser obtained a complete product line through the acquisition but used it to compete in the sale of its other products and not the sale of the product in the market which concerned the FTC.[78]

(iii) Financial resources The Merger Remedies Study found[79] that the **20–060** financial resources criterion was particularly important in cases in which the divested business required sustained future investment or when the purchaser was a small company.

(iv) Proven expertise In certain cases, the Commission has required parties to **20–061** agree to more particularised criteria regarding the expertise of the purchaser than those set out in s.(i) above. For example,[80] in *Masterfoods / Royal Canin*[81] the parties agreed to sell only to a purchaser with sufficient financial resources and research and development capabilities and with proven expertise in the branded pet food market. Such standards would preclude, for example, a sale to a private equity house with no existing pet food business but proven expertise in managing businesses. Similarly, in *Barilla /*

---

[75] FTC Divestiture Study, pp.34 and 35.
[76] For a more radical view of the extent of the divergence, see Farrell in Lévêque & Shelanski (eds), *Merger Remedies in American and European Union Competition Law* (Edward Elgar, 2003), pp.95 to 98.
[77] FTC Divestiture Study, p.27.
[78] FTC Divestiture Study, pp.26 and 27.
[79] p.102.
[80] See also Case COMP/M.2621 *SEB / Moulinex* (discussed in para.20–082(a) below); Case COMP/M.2876 *NewsCorp / Telepiù* [2004] O.J. L110/73 (the commitments provided that the purchaser of the divested business must be a company willing to include pay-TV broadcasting of one or more channels in its business plan after the switchover from analogue to digital terrestrial television in Italy; para.256); Case COMP/M.3420 *GIMD / Socpresse* (in which the Commission emphasised that it would seek to ensure that the purchaser of the divested publication had sufficient credibility in the publishing industry to ensure the credibility of the title and effective long-term competition in the market).
[81] Case COMP/M.2544, para.102.

BPL / Kamps[82] the parties included in the undertakings a clause that "the Purchaser shall be reasonably involved in the food sector and in the sector for branded products". Finally, in *Air Liquide / Messer Targets*,[83] the Commission insisted that the purchaser should be active in the relevant market because the remedies involved an aggregation of assets and there were important barriers to entry.

More generally, the Merger Remedies Study found[84] that certain industrial sectors require a greater degree of specialised expertise than others. In particular, innovation-driven markets require very specific research and development expertise that is rarely available in the jobs market. The Study therefore recommended that purchasers in such markets should themselves possess such expertise.

20–062 There has been ongoing controversy about whether, and in what circumstances, *financial buyers* can be suitable purchasers.

(a) In the Best Practice Guidelines, the Commission stated[85] that the purchaser standards "can be met by either industrial or financial investors. The latter must demonstrate the necessary management capabilities and proven expertise can in particular be met by financing a management buy-out".

(b) The Merger Remedies Study found[86] that issues of expertise tended to arise less frequently when the divestment was of a stand-alone business, adding: "in those cases there may be less of a need for the purchaser to supplement specific expertise". It referred to two cases (from 1996 to 2000) in which financial investors had been suitable purchasers and noted that the Commission had evaluated the expertise of both the financial investor and the proposed management (i.e. the existing management) in assessing the suitability of the purchaser.[87]

(c) However, in its XXXIst Annual Report on Competition Policy, 2001,[88] the Commission stated that, in the case of a sale to a financial buyer: "certain factors could raise difficulties. For example, it is important that the buyer and seller are independent from each other, hence the seller should not have significant loans provided by the buyer, nor indeed should the buyer be in receipt of significant loans from or under obligations towards the selling party. Furthermore,

---

[82] Case COMP/M.2817, Undertakings, para.19.
[83] Case COMP/M.3314, para.219.
[84] See p.100. The Study also noted that some purchasers and sellers highlighted the importance of identifying purchasers with good market knowledge and a familiarity with the dynamics of the regulatory environment in the EEA.
[85] Para.27
[86] See pp.101 and 102 (and p.161).
[87] The Study noted that interviewees had argued that the financial buyer's exit plans would be the single most important factor to consider in assessing suitability.
[88] Para.314.

the Commission has to assess whether the financial investor has the necessary business expertise to develop or maintain the business as an active competitive force. This is especially important when the buyer is taking a majority stake in the divested business". Nevertheless, the Commission acknowledged that "the circumstances of each individual case have to be taken into account"[89] and it seems that the key issue in each case is not whether a buyer is categorised as "financial", but whether it is independent of the divesting party and its business plan and track record demonstrate that it will operate as an effective competitor.

(d) The Commission approved a financial buyer in *Carrefour / Promodes*.[90]

(e) In *Alcan / Pechiney (II)*[91] third parties argued that financial buyers may not have the incentive or ability to develop the divestment business beyond the short term and Alcan agreed to strengthen the purchaser standards to specify that the future purchaser must be shown to have a strategic commitment to the competitiveness and development of the business, including product development and R&D.

(v) Incentive to compete The Merger Remedies Study noted[92] that the **20–063** assessment of the buyer's incentives to compete is based "primarily" on the basis of "a business plan which should set out detailed plans for the operation of the divested business by the proposed purchaser. The Commission also regularly requires an opinion of the trustee".[93] Claude Rakovsky of DG Competition has commented: "We have to make an assessment of the incentives to compete of would-be acquirers, examine and discuss their business plans and try to understand, from their perspective, the rationale of the transaction they propose to enter. This is a difficult exercise and there are no guarantees, in a moving market, that the acquirer

---

[89] See the Commission's XXXIst Annual Report on Competition Policy, 2001, para.314.
[90] Case COMP/M.1684. The approval is recorded in the Commission's XXXIst Annual Report on Competition Policy, 2001, para.314. At para.312, the Commission noted, in relation to Case COMP/M.1628 *TotalFina / Elf* [2001] O.J. L143/1, that the divestiture of an LPG business to a financial purchaser *and* a US company with LPG activities was approved. See also the case study summarised in the FTC Divestiture Study, p.17.
[91] Case COMP/M.3225, paras 162, 163, 170 and 171 (and see para.19(b) of the commitments). The commitments do not expressly preclude a sale to a financial buyer, but they are drafted in terms that a financial buyer might find difficult to satisfy.
[92] See p.102.
[93] See also Case COMP/M.3225 *Alcan / Pechiney (II)*, para.171 (stating that a purchaser without convincing business plans would not normally be considered an acceptable purchaser) and Case COMP/M.3692 *Reuters / Telerate*, paras 31 and 32 (although the remedy in that case was the licensing of intellectual property rather than the transfer of shares or assets). Compare the US Department of Justice, "Antitrust Policy Guide to Merger Remedies", October 2004 (available via *www.usdoj.gov/atr/public/guidelines/205108.htm*), s.IV(D).

will stick to its initial business plan ... However, the Commission should not, in my view, hesitate to reject a potential buyer, even if it is a viable and independent business, if there are doubts about its commitment to compete: such an approach does not amount to interventionist industrial policy".[94]

In *TotalFina / Elf*[95] the parties undertook to divest around 70 petrol stations in France. The Commission rejected the parties' proposed group of purchasers on the grounds that they did not have the incentive to bring competition to the market.[96] The Commission accepted a second group of buyers including the large supermarket group, Carrefour, which, following completion (i.e. implementation), announced a reduction in petrol prices on French motorways.[97]

If the potential purchaser intends to make significant *captive use* of the output of the divestment business (i.e. to use the acquired business for self-supply), the Commission may regard the purchaser as unsuitable "because this limits the quantities available for the free market and therefore the competitive force of the purchaser".[98]

20–064　　The Merger Remedies Study observed[99] that some of the cases which were reviewed indicated that *smaller and/or new entrant* purchasers sometimes have a *greater* incentive to develop a product in competition with the merging parties than a large, established market player.[1] On the other hand, three of the six "ineffective" remedies identified by the Study involved smaller or new entrant purchasers (who may lack expertise or financial resources).[2]

The Merger Remedies Study noted[3] that the purchaser may have a reduced incentive to compete when it obtains the divested business for *free or at a negative price*. Indeed, a sale at less than the liquidation value *may* be evidence that the purchaser intends to liquidate the assets and exit from the

---

[94] Claude Rakovsky, "Remedies: A Few Lessons From Recent Experience", published in *EC Merger Control: Ten Years On* (International Bar Association, 2000), p.135, at p.144.

[95] Case COMP/M.1628 [2001] O.J. L143/1.

[96] Speech of Mario Monti, then the Commissioner for Competition Policy, "The Commission notice on merger remedies—one year after", January 18, 2002 (*www.europa.eu.int/comm/competi tion/speeches/index_2002.html*). See also the Commission's XXXIst Annual Report on Competition Policy, 2001, para.311. An appeal against the Commission's decision was rejected in Case T-342/00 *Petrolessence SA v Commission* [2003] E.C.R. II-1161 (see in particular, paras 101 to 120). The Court accorded the Commission a broad range of discretion in selecting the purchaser for the divested business, stating that the Court would intervene only if the Commission's assessment were "manifestly erroneous" or "clearly mistaken".

[97] Speech of Mario Monti, then the Commissioner for Competition Policy, "The Commission notice on merger remedies—one year after", January 18, 2002 (*www.europa.eu.int/comm/competition/speeches/index_2002.html*).

[98] Case COMP/M.2277 *Degussa / Laporte*, para.56.

[99] See p.104.

[1] Existing competitors might be deterred from developing new products by the risk of reducing the profit stream from their existing products. A new entrant or a smaller rival would not face this constraint, either at all or to the same extent. See also the FTC Divestiture Study, quoted in para.20–059 above.

[2] See pp.161 and 162.

[3] See p.103.

market, which would destroy the efficacy of the remedies.[4] Further, a buyer at a low price might be able to obtain an adequate return without developing an effective competitor, with the consequence that the remedy would fail.[5]

In general, the Commission will be sceptical whether a buyer who is not "*on risk*" through the investment of its own capital meets the purchaser standard of having an incentive to compete. Such concerns were also identified in the FTC Divestiture Study (see para.20–059 above).[6]

(vi) Independence Claude Rakovsky of DG Competition summarised the **20–065** Commission's application of the "independent and unconnected" criterion as follows: it "evidently transcends the mere capitalistic relations between the merged parties and the potential acquirer and includes, in principle, any sort of personnel links or economic relations (e.g. distribution, supply). In practice this condition may be difficult to meet in certain oligopolistic industries or in sectors (e.g. insurance, banking, civil aviation) where competitors are linked by some degree of cooperation. Basically the Commission must be convinced that the seller will not be in a position to influence the acquirer's behaviour".[7]

(vii) No competition concerns Any necessary antitrust approvals for the **20–066** purchase of the divestment business[8] may be from the Commission alone, the Commission and other national authorities or from national authorities alone. This may mean that the competitive effects of a sale to a particular purchaser are considered both by the Commission (in applying the purchaser standards) and the competition authorities of one or more Member States (applying their national competition law to a transaction below the ECMR thresholds).

---

[4] See "Merger Remedies", OECD, DAF/COMP(2004)21, p.28 and the US Department of Justice, "Antitrust Policy Guide to Merger Remedies", October 2004 (available via *www.usdoj.gov/atr/public/guidelines/205108.htm*), ss.IV(D) and (E).

[5] See "Statement of Federal Trade Commission's Bureau of Competition on Negotiating Merger Remedies", April 2003 (available via *www.ftc.gov/bc/bestpractices/bestpractices 030401.htm*).

[6] See also "Statement of Federal Trade Commission's Bureau of Competition on Negotiating Merger Remedies", April 2003 (available via *www.ftc.gov/bc/bestpractices/bestpractices 030401.htm*), noting that: "A buyer that requires seller financing may not be financially sound". The Statement also discusses, at n.15, structures involving a small initial payment and subsequent payments. The US Department of Justice also strongly disfavours seller finance for reasons set out in "Antitrust Policy Guide to Merger Remedies", October 2004 (available via *www.usdoj.gov/atr/public/guidelines/205108.htm*), s.IV(G).

[7] Claude Rakovsky, "Remedies: A Few Lessons From Recent Experience", published in *EC Merger Control: Ten Years On* (International Bar Association, 2000), p.135, at pp.143 and 144.

[8] See the Notice on Remedies, para.60 and the Merger Remedies Study, pp.106 and 107.

20–067 **(viii) Other issues relating to the purchaser standards** The Commission may grant approval to the identity of the buyer subject to the provision of undertakings. In particular, in *Anglo American Corporation / Lonrho*[9] the Commission approved the identity of the purchaser of the divestment shares "provided that certain undertakings were given to ensure that AAC and [the purchaser of the divestment shares] would be completely independent".[10] However, the Commission[11] does not currently require purchasers of divested businesses to commit to retain them or to operate them for a specific period.[12]

(j) When it is necessary to sell the business to a single purchaser

20–068 The Commission may require the divestiture to be made to a *single* purchaser. Indeed, the Commission has stated: "For viability considerations and in order to preserve pre-merger levels of competition, the Commission usually ... prefers that the divested business is sold to a single purchaser".[13] A split sale may, for example, deprive the purchasers of economies of scale or scope, or create difficulties in integration.

In *Nestlé / Ralston Purina*[14] the parties agreed to divest to one suitable purchaser per country. By contrast, in *Masterfoods / Royal Canin*[15] the commitment was to sell the divestment businesses internationally "en bloc" to a single purchaser.[16] The inference from the decision is that the Commission concluded that only a single purchaser would be able to transform the divestment businesses into a coherent and viable competitor. Similarly, in *Air Liquide / Messer Targets*[17] the notifying party committed to sell two businesses that were closely intertwined to the same purchaser.

In *SEB / Moulinex*[18] the commitments permitted the grant of trade mark licences (which were intended to have similar effects to a divestiture) to

---

[9] Case IV/M.754 [1998] O.J. L149/21.

[10] See the Commission's XXVIIth Annual Report on Competition Policy, 1997, p.188.

[11] For details of a similar policy on the part of the US Department of Justice (subject to a caveat) see "Antitrust Policy Guide to Merger Remedies", October 2004 (available via *www.usdoj.gov/atr/public/guidelines/205108.htm*), s.IV(F). Compare the FTC Divestiture Study, p.v.

[12] However, in Case COMP/M.3692 *Reuters / Telerate*, para.33, in which the remedy for a horizontal overlap was an undertaking to license intellectual property rights to facilitate the development of a new competitor, the commitments provided that if the licensee failed to use the licence effectively or the business relying on the licence was unsuccessful or economically unviable, the *merging parties* were required to transfer the licence to a second licensee under the same terms and conditions as those agreed with the first licensee.

[13] See the Commission's paper in "Merger Remedies", OECD, DAF/COMP(2004)21, p.256.

[14] Case COMP/M.2337, para.60.

[15] Case COMP/M.2544, paras 90, 99 and 102.

[16] See also Case COMP/M.2547 *Bayer / Aventis Crop Science* [2004] O.J. L107/1 (sale in a single package of the target's entire European seed treatment business; para.1130).

[17] Case COMP/M.3314. Paras 216 and 217 record the comments of third parties. The press release (IP/04/342) identifies the Commission's reason for requiring a single purchaser as being that the two businesses were intimately intertwined.

[18] Case COMP/M.2621, commitments s.1(c), third sub-para.

different licensees in different Member States. On appeal, the Court of First Instance[19] upheld this part of the Commission's decision on the grounds that the existence of different licensees would not threaten the *viability* of the licensees as competitors (because the geographic markets were national, the licences were exclusive, and parallel imports were minimal).

In *Lagardère | Natexis | VUP*[20] the commitments provided that if Lagardère wished to sell the divestment businesses to two or more purchasers, it would need to meet four additional criteria designed to ensure that a split disposal nevertheless addressed the vertical and conglomerate issues raised by the merger.[21]

(k) Whether it is necessary to sell the business to the purchaser offering the highest price

For the time being, an undertaking selling a business pursuant to commitments agreed with the Commission has a certain leeway to sell to a purchaser which does not offer the highest price, but nevertheless meets the purchaser standards.[22] The Merger Remedies Study states[23]: "Normally the Commission is interested in the sales price only insofar as it might impact on the success of the remedy, e.g. by not creating sufficient incentives to compete (sales price too low), or by disabling the purchaser from making necessary investments in the business (sales price too high)". It follows that the Commission (with assistance from the trustee) will wish, during the process of approving the purchaser, to understand the reason for not selling to a bidder offering a higher price. Some reasons (such as concerns over possible delays and risk about whether the purchaser would proceed to signing) would be of equal concern to the Commission. However, the Commission would be concerned if there were evidence that the purchaser would not have an incentive to compete intensely or that the notifying party was acting strategically in seeking to sell to a weaker or more accommodating rival and, in this situation, would be likely to reject the proposed

20–069

---

[19] Case T-119/02 *Royal Philips Electronics NV v Commission* [2003] E.C.R. II-1433, paras 169 to 175.

[20] Case COMP/M.2978 [2004] O.J. L125/54 (appeal pending in Case T-279/04 *Editions Odile Jacob SAS v Commission*), paras 991 and 1001 to 1003.

[21] See also Boeshertz, Kleiner, Nouet, Petit, Von Koppenfels & Rabassa, "Lagardère / Natexis / VUP: big deal in a small world", *Competition Policy Newsletter*, Spring 2004, p.8, at p.14.

[22] Indeed, the party selling the business is not currently required to adopt a particular format for the sale process and in particular is not required to provide a public notification of an auction process (see the Merger Remedies Study, p.148; but note the concerns identified by the Study and suggested changes to the Commission's approach at pp.149 and 150). Compare the view of the US Department of Justice, "Antitrust Policy Guide to Merger Remedies", October 2004 (available via *www.usdoj.gov/atr/public/guidelines/205108.htm*), s.IV(D): "Ideally, assets should be held by those who value them the most and, in general, the highest paying, competitively acceptable bidder will be the firm that can compete with the assets most effectively".

[23] See p.104

purchaser.[24] Indeed, the Merger Remedies Study noted[25] that "some sellers may have abused the lack of transparency in the divestiture process to propose a weaker purchaser to the Commission as the only possible proposal ... Parties sometimes may have preferred foregoing a higher one off present sales price for potentially higher longer term anticipated gains resulting from a weaker competitor". On the other hand, there are situations where the fact that a purchaser is willing to pay the highest price may be evidence that the purchaser is *not* suitable; in particular, if there are coordinated effects, the party with the highest willingness to pay might be the most likely to continue coordinated effects after the divestment has completed (i.e. been implemented).[26] The law on this issue may change as an appeal to the Court of First Instance is pending against the decision following *Lagardère / Natexis / VUP*[27] to approve Wendel as a suitable purchaser, in which the appellant claims that the sale process was discriminatory and anti-competitive and the Commission wrongly failed to ensure that the sale process was transparent, objective and non-discriminatory.[28]

(1) Time limits

20–070 The model Divestiture Commitments distinguish[29] an initial divestiture period and an extended divestiture period. During the initial period, the party providing the undertaking is free to seek a buyer (subject to the supervision of a monitoring trustee). However, if an agreement to sell the divestment business is not signed within this period, the divestiture trustee is given an irrevocable and exclusive mandate to sell the divestment business within the extended divestiture period at no minimum price.[30] Further, the divestiture trustee will be empowered to include in the sale agreement "such customary representations and warranties and indemnities as are reasonably required to effect the Sale".[31]

---

[24] See para.20–057 for details of the purchaser standards.
[25] See p.70 (and p.149).
[26] See "Merger Remedies", OECD, DAF/COMP(2004)21, pp.27 and 28 (also raising the possibility that the party with the highest willingness to pay may be intending to divert the assets to an alternative use and identifying a concern that a purchaser which over-pays may lack sufficient working capital to be an effective competitor and/or may be forced into insolvency). The US Department of Justice, "Antitrust Policy Guide to Merger Remedies", October 2004 (available via *www.usdoj.gov/atr/public/guidelines/205108.htm*), s.IV(E) identifies a general concern that a purchaser willing to pay a high price may be paying a premium for market power.
[27] COMP/M.2978 [2004] O.J. L125/54.
[28] Case T-452/04 *Editions Odile Jacob SAS v Commission* (pending).
[29] Para.1.
[30] The model Divestiture Commitments (para.30) and the model Trustee Mandate (para.11).
[31] The model Trustee Mandate, para.11.

The Best Practice Guidelines indicate[32] that the initial divestiture period is normally around six months[33] and the extended divestiture period a further period of three to six months, although the periods may require modification depending on the particular circumstances of the case. In deciding whether to modify the normal periods, the Commission will take the following factors into account[34]:

(a) the time needed to prepare the business for divestment (a longer period may be required for a complicated assets deal than a straightforward share sale);

(b) the number of potential acquirers; and

(c) the speed with which an industry is changing (e.g. in technology markets, the market conditions may change very rapidly, creating concerns about long divestiture periods).

In addition, the Commission has placed weight on the need to safeguard the interests of staff in the divestment business[35] and the existence of contractual restrictions that were expected to give rise to delays in the divestment process.[36]

The Merger Remedies Study noted[37] that excessively *short* divestiture periods can pose problems because the parties may not have sufficient time

---

[32] Para.15. In almost all cases, the time period allowed to the party providing the undertakings to sign an agreement for the sale of the divestment business is redacted from the public version of the Commission's decision on the grounds that it is commercially sensitive (as a potential purchaser which knows the final deadline for divestment may behave opportunistically). For exceptions, see Case COMP/M.1601 *Allied Signal / Honeywell* [2001] O.J. L152/1 (divestments within six months; paras 126 and 127) and Case COMP/M.1663 *Alcan / Alusuisse* [2002] O.J. L90/1 (where the commitment was to sell a business within a nine month period which could be extended by agreement of the Commission for a further three months; in the event that divestment had not been effected by Alcan by the end of the ninth or the twelfth month as the case may be, Alcan was to give an irrevocable mandate to a trustee to sell the business within a period of three months with no minimum price; paras 130, 135 and 141). In the Merger Remedies Study, the average divestiture period in the sample of analysed commitments to transfer a market position (dating from 1996 to 2000 and therefore pre-dating the publication of the Notice on Remedies) was 7.6 months; see p.110.

[33] See also the Commission's paper in "Merger Remedies", OECD, DAF/COMP(2004)21, p.257, stating that the first divestiture period does not usually exceed six months. Compare the US Department of Justice, "Antitrust Policy Guide to Merger Remedies", October 2004 (available via *www.usdoj.gov/atr/public/guidelines/205108.htm*), s.IV(C), stating that the purchaser is normally given 60 to 90 days to identify a purchaser.

[34] Claude Rakovsky, "Remedies: A Few Lessons From Recent Experience", published in *EC Merger Control: Ten Years On* (International Bar Association, 2000), p.135, at p.141.

[35] See Case COMP/M.2650 *Haniel / Cementbouw / JV (CVK)* [2003] O.J. L282/1 (appeal dismissed in Case T-282/02 *Cementbouw Handel & Industrie v Commission*, not yet reported, judgment of February 23, 2006) (this case involved a retroactive approval; Commission press release IP/02/933 states: "The Commission has recognised that the companies involved will need time to comply with the commitment given, with a view in particular to safeguarding the interests of the affected CVK staff, and agreed to grant an appropriate deadline").

[36] See Case COMP/M.3314 *Air Liquide / Messer Targets*, para.218.

[37] p.109 (and, more generally, pp.162 and 163).

to find a suitable purchaser, buyers may not have sufficient time to carry out adequate due diligence, and buyers have greater scope to act strategically.

20–071   The Commission is willing to *extend* the time period for divestments[38] when the delay arises for "reasons independent from the willingness of the parties" and provided that "genuine efforts by the parties are proved".[39] However, in *Volvo / Renault RVI*[40] the Commission refused to extend a deadline for Volvo to sell certain shares in Scania. It appointed an independent expert who concluded that a share placement at the price then expected would not noticeably impact on Volvo's ability to invest and borrow or on its independence and, in any event, the Commission reaffirmed that a party giving undertakings has no legitimate expectation to any minimum price.

If a party appeals against an *order* requiring it to unwind a transaction,[41] the Commission may be willing to extend the deadline to allow the appeal to be determined first.[42]

(m) Interim preservation of the business

20–072 The Commission is concerned to ensure that the competitive force of the divestment business is not reduced pending sale and the undertakings must therefore provide for the maintenance of the independence, economic viability, marketability and competitiveness of the business.[43] In addition, the divestment business must be held separately from the merging parties' retained businesses, both to support the more general interim preservation provisions discussed above and so that it will have a chance to exercise some independent competitive standing on the market prior to its sale.[44]

---

[38] The Merger Remedies Study reported, at p.112, that in 30% of cases reviewed (18 of the analysed remedies) deadlines were extended once or several times.

[39] Speech of Mario Monti, then the Commissioner for Competition Policy, "The Commission notice on merger remedies—one year after", January 18, 2002 (*www.europa.eu.int/comm/competition/speeches/index_2002.html*). An extension was granted in Case COMP/M.1684 *Carrefour / Promodes* because, despite Carrefour's genuine efforts, the shareholding could not be sold within the time specified: see the Commission's XXXIst Annual Report on Competition Policy, 2001, para.313.

[40] Case COMP/M.1980, "Implementation of The Scania Undertaking" (available via *http://europa.eu.int/comm/competition/mergers/cases/additional_data/348610.pdf*). In Case T-163/03 *Scania AB v Commission* (pending), Scania challenged the Commission's refusal to take action to enforce the undertaking given by Volvo and to enforce an immediate divestment. In Case T-248/04 *Scania AB v Commission* (pending), Scania brought a further challenge to the delay in enforcing the undertaking.

[41] In contrast to a commitment which is provided by the parties and accepted by the Commission.

[42] The Commission granted such an extension in Case COMP/M.2283 *Schneider / Legrand*; see *Financial Times*, May 31, 2002, p.29. See also the formulation of the time limits for divestment in Case COMP/M.2568 *Haniel / Ytong* [2003] O.J. L111/1, paras 141 and 142.

[43] The Notice on Remedies, paras 50 and 51. See also the model Divestiture Commitments, para.5.

[44] See the Merger Remedies Study, p.59.

The Merger Remedies Study[45] found that 37 per cent of remedies (involving 31 separate remedies) raised implementation issues regarding the interim preservation of the business.[46] The difficulties arose, in particular,[47] because vendors degraded tangible and intangible assets (most notably the know-how of the personnel and the business's order book), deprived the purchaser of sales volumes by front loading sales immediately prior to completion (i.e. implementation) of the divestment, and failed to support investment programmes or customer relationship management.[48] The Study also found[49] that preservation measures typically became more complex when the business being sold was not a stand-alone business.

The following specific points arise regarding the interim preservation of **20–073** the business.

(a) It is necessary to keep the divestment business separate from the merged business and ensure that it is separately managed. It is particularly important to ensure that confidential information does not flow from the divestment business to the party who provided the undertakings.[50] The model Divestiture Commitments require[51] the party providing the undertakings to appoint a "hold separate manager" who is employed by the divestment business to manage the day-to-day business under the supervision of the monitoring trustee.[52] Interim preservation commitments may include behavioural obligations such as the operation of "firewalls".[53] The Commission accepted that a hold-separate arrangement was *not* required in a case involving a commitment to sell to an upfront buyer.[54]

(b) The remedies will seek to ensure that the tangible and intangible assets of the divestment business are maintained.[55]

(c) It is necessary to maintain the competitiveness of the business in

---

[45] See p.56 (and pp.145 to 148).

[46] The Merger Remedies Study found, at pp.59, 60, 62 and 64, that implementation of hold-separate provisions was variable (indeed, the meaning of "hold separate" was not well understood by trustees) and was particularly problematic in the case of divestments of interests in joint ventures when the joint venture was not a stand-alone business.

[47] pp.57 to 59.

[48] At pp.147 and 148, DG Competition staff identified 10 specific issues regarding the monitoring of the interim preservation and hold-separate provisions in commitments.

[49] p.57.

[50] Claude Rakovsky, "Remedies: A Few Lessons From Recent Experience", published in *EC Merger Control: Ten Years On* (International Bar Association, 2000), p.135 at p.142. See the model Divestiture Commitments, para.12.

[51] Para.7.

[52] The Merger Remedies Study identifies, at p.67, a number of attributes and behaviours of effective hold-separate managers.

[53] See, e.g. Case COMP/M.2268 *Pernod Ricard / Diageo / Seagram Spirits*.

[54] Case COMP/M.1915 *The Post Office / TPG / SPPL* [2004] O.J. L82/1, paras 163 and 164.

[55] See the model Divestiture Commitments, paras 4(a) and 5.

particular by making available sufficient resources for the development of the business, on the basis of the existing business plans.[56]

(n) Post-completion transitional support for the purchaser

20–074 The Remedies Notice states that the divested business must be a viable business that can be operated on a stand-alone basis without ongoing cooperation with the merging parties other than during a transitional arrangement.[57] When transitional support is required from the divesting parties following completion (i.e. implementation) of the divestiture sale, in order to ensure that the purchaser can operate as an effective competitor, this must be specified in detail in the undertakings.[58] Transitional support may include, for example, short-term supply arrangements, technical assistance or a waiver of contractual terms which lock in customers.

The Merger Remedies Study[59] found that technical assistance or interim services had been crucial to the success of some remedies and that toll-manufacturing remedies could "perhaps work satisfactorily as supplementary remedies in support of divestiture remedies". However, it noted that purchasers emphasised the need for pricing to be cost-based and found that transitional arrangements could create a temporary dependence of the purchaser on the parties, allowing the parties to influence the purchaser's competitive behaviour, creating information links, and making the divested business vulnerable to misconduct or neglect by the parties.

20–075 The FTC Divestiture Study also examined this issue and reached similar conclusions.

(a) The Study stated: "The case studies indicate that relationships between the buyer of divested assets and the respondent, which continue beyond the transfer of the divested assets, may increase the vulnerability of the buyers of the divested assets, particularly in those cases in which the divested assets comprise less than an on-going business. However, the continuing relationships between the buyer and respondent may often have been critical to the success of the buyer of the divested assets ... [In] six cases, continuing relationships

---

[56] See the model Divestiture Commitments, para.5(b). For detailed commitments on the provision of funding, see Case COMP/M.1795 *Vodafone Airtouch / Mannesmann*, divestment undertaking, clause 18.

[57] Para.14.

[58] See the model Divestiture Commitments, para.4. For an example of complex transitional arrangements, see Case COMP/M.1915 *The Post Office / TPG / SPPL* [2004] O.J. L82/1, paras 153 to 155. See also the detailed discussion in "Statement of Federal Trade Commission's Bureau of Competition on Negotiating Merger Remedies", April 2003 (available via *www.ftc.gov/bc/bestpractices/bestpractices030401.htm*).

[59] pp.44 and 45. See also p.141 (noting that transitional arrangements were not considered problematic if the links they created did not continue beyond reasonable time limits) and p.142 (recording that purchasers regularly pointed out that pricing of transitional agreements needed to be cost-based).

such as supply contracts or technical assistance obligations were not only helpful to the buyer but were critical to the subsequent success of the buyer".[60]

(b) The Study identified several instances of sellers engaging in strategic behaviour to impede the success of the buyer, e.g. by purportedly complying with an obligation to provide technical assistance by sending an employee with no previous experience along with the divested equipment, by supplying late, providing poor quality goods or service, or providing technical assistance which was unhelpful.[61]

(c) The Study also noted that in cases of normal commercial contracts, parties are able to structure the agreement to provide for incentives for the successful transfer of the business, whereas in the case of divestments the seller has an incentive to frustrate the success of the purchaser with the consequence that: "Unless respondents' incentives can be altered, it is likely that most respondents will do only what is necessary to achieve a consent order and avoid civil penalties. Given the level of support which is necessary for many orders, that minimal effort may not be sufficient to obtain the remedies ordered by the Commission".[62]

(d) The Study found that when problems arose in transitional support, buyers rarely raised their concerns with the antitrust authorities out of fear that, if they complained, the seller would reduce the quality of the service still further.[63]

In *MCI-WorldCom / Sprint*[64] the Commission was concerned about the **20–076** viability of Sprint's internet business, as it was closely intertwined with Sprint's traditional telecoms activities. Sprint offered a series of transitional support agreements but the Commission was concerned that they were so complex that they made the effectiveness of the implementation of the remedy more uncertain and it therefore prohibited the transaction.[65] The Commission also took account of difficulties in the implementation of similar remedies in *WorldCom / MCI*.[66]

Whilst transitional support is normally limited to the short term, in *GE /*

---

[60] FTC Divestiture Study, p.12.
[61] FTC Divestiture Study, p.18.
[62] FTC Divestiture Study, p.19. See also p.31, proposing that interim supply contracts include provision for consequential damages.
[63] FTC Divestiture Study, p.26.
[64] Case COMP/M.1741 [2003] O.J. L300/1.
[65] See the discussion in Claude Rakovsky, "Remedies: A Few Lessons From Recent Experience", in *EC Merger Control: Ten Years On* (International Bar Association, 2000), p.135, at pp.138 and 139.
[66] Case IV/M.1069 [1999] O.J. L116/1.

Instrumentarium[67] the Commission accepted commitments under which GE agreed to supply certain equipment to the purchaser for periods of up to 10 years to increase its viability, in particular by enabling it to participate in tenders for the supply of systems. Similarly, in *Verbund / EnergieAllianz*[68] Verbund committed to divest its controlling shareholding in a company selling electricity to large customers and agreed to supply electricity to the purchaser for at least four years. The Commission stated that this supply commitment removed the risks of purchasing electricity in the market and meant that the buyer did not itself need to organise the electricity supply. Finally, in *Pfizer / Pharmacia*[69] the Commission accepted a commitment to transfer a product in development to a named transferee (to remedy serious doubts regarding a loss of potential competition) but this was supported by a commitment by Pfizer to provide financial and technical support to the transferee to preserve the viability of the project.[70]

(o) Prohibition on buying back the assets in cases of divestitures

20–077 The Notice on Remedies states[71] that, even in the absence of specific provision in the undertakings, a company which has provided commitments to sell a business cannot re-acquire the whole or parts of it "unless the Commission has previously found that the structure of the market has changed to such an extent that the absence of influence over the divested business is no longer necessary to render the concentration compatible with the common market".[72] However, undertakings accepted by the Commission now routinely include provision that the parties will not subsequently re-acquire any influence over any shareholding in the divestment business without prior Commission approval.[73] In an exceptional case, the undertaking itself may identify the circumstances in which parts of the divested business may be transferred back to the party providing the commitment.[74]

---

[67] Case COMP/M.3083 [2004] O.J. L109/1, paras 325 to 329. In general, however, long-term relationships between the seller and buyer of the divestment business are undesirable because they involve ongoing connections between competitors which can lead to a dampening of competition.
[68] Case COMP/M.2947 [2004] O.J. L92/91, para.148.
[69] Case COMP/M.2922, para.153.
[70] On its face, this decision appears anomalous when compared with the normal policy of not encouraging ongoing relationships between the seller and the buyer of the divestment business as explained in para.20–074 above.
[71] Para.49.
[72] The legal basis for this proposition is not clear. The Commission may regard the obligation in the commitment to divest as subject to an implied undertaking not to reacquire the divested business (subject to obtaining the Commission's consent).
[73] See the model Divestiture Commitments, para.3 (limiting the prohibition on re-purchasing without prior Commission waiver to a period of 10 years from the date of the Commission's decision to approve the transaction subject to commitments), The Best Practice Guidelines, para.17 and, e.g. Case COMP/M.2533 *BP / E.ON* [2002] O.J. L276/31, Annex 1, clause 12.
[74] In Case COMP/M.2547 *Bayer / Aventis Crop Science* [2004] O.J. L107/1 the notifying party committed to divest a business on a worldwide basis (para.1062) but, outside Europe and the US, the parties had the right to negotiate a licence-back, provided that such negotiations could not occur until after divestment had been completed, and subject to the approval by the Commission of the terms of the licence; para.1066.

20.8 TRANSFERRING A MARKET POSITION— TRANSFER OF INTELLECTUAL PROPERTY RIGHTS

(a) When the transfer of intellectual property rights will provide an appropriate remedy

As noted in para.20–034 above, the primary divestiture remedy is the sale of **20–078** a business comprising all of the assets necessary to effect an immediate transfer of market share to the purchaser. However, there are exceptions where the divestiture of intellectual property rights[75] (falling short of such an all-encompassing package) will adequately resolve the competition concerns. This arises if intellectual property rights are the "critical component for facilitating entry",[76] with the consequence that their transfer[77] will enable an effective competitor to emerge, ensuring that the merger does not result in a significant impediment to effective competition.[78]

(b) Pharmaceuticals mergers

The Notice on Remedies states: "the Commission may accept licensing **20–079** arrangements (preferably exclusive licences without any field-of-use restrictions on the licensee) as an alternative to divestiture where, for instance, a divestiture would have impeded efficient, on-going research. The Commission has used this approach in mergers involving, for example, the pharmaceutical industry".[79]

---

[75] See "Statement of Federal Trade Commission's Bureau of Competition on Negotiating Merger Remedies", April 2003 (available via *www.ftc.gov/bc/bestpractices/bestpractices 030401.htm*) and the OFT Economic Discussion Paper, "Innovation and Competition Policy", Charles River Associates, March 2002 (note that the views in the paper do not necessarily reflect those of the OFT), paras 7.28 and 7.29.

[76] See "Statement of Federal Trade Commission's Bureau of Competition on Negotiating Merger Remedies", April 2003 (available via *www.ftc.gov/bc/bestpractices/bestpractices 030401.htm*).

[77] A "transfer" generally involves an assignment or the grant of an *exclusive* licence (whereas access remedies, which are discussed in s.20.10 below, typically involve non-exclusive licences). See also the International Competition Network, "Merger Remedies Review Project", June 2005 (available via *www.internationalcompetitionnetwork.org/ICN_Remedies_StudyFINAL5-10.pdf*), para.3.18, which draws a distinction between assignments or licences which do not involve an ongoing connection between the parties (and in particular do not involve royalty payments or the provision of upgrades) and are effectively structural and those in which there is an ongoing relationship. At para.3.20 the authors discuss a range of factors which may affect the design of a remedy involving intellectual property rights.

[78] See Steptoe & Balto, "The FTC's Use of Innovative Merger Remedies" [1995] *Antitrust* 16, identifying four categories of case in which the US FTC might accept alternatives to simple structural relief, namely those involving innovation and research and development, reputation, distribution and inputs.

[79] Notice on Remedies, para.29. In Case COMP/M.2139 *Bombardier / Adtranz* [2002] O.J. L69/50, the Commission accepted an undertaking to grant an exclusive non-transferable licence of the rights and tangible and intangible assets (excluding certain patents) to the design,

More specifically, in mergers of pharmaceutical and analogous companies,[80] issues may arise in the supply of particular products in cases in which there are no research and development facilities, manufacturing assets, or employees dedicated to the production of the products. In such cases, the Commission has been willing to accept divestiture packages comprising transfers or grants of irrevocable exclusive licences[81] of intellectual property rights (patents, trade marks and know-how)[82] and public authority authorisations[83] or the grant of exclusive distribution rights,[84] in some cases supported by a commitment to supply or engage in toll-manufacturing.[85]

20–080   In *Novartis / Hexal*[86] the Commission accepted commitments involving "*branding plus*", i.e. the grant of an exclusive right to use a trademark in a territory for products covered by a marketing authorisation provided that the licensee used a suffix or prefix indicating its name.

Brand splitting may create viability issues in pharmaceuticals mergers (see further para.20–084 below). For example, in *Bayer Healthcare / Roche (OTC Business)*[87] the Commission accepted "crown jewels" remedies[88] involving the sale of a brand in Austria, provided that the divestment would be extended to cover the entire EEA if a viable purchaser for the brand in Austria were not identified in a specified period.

---

production and marketing in the EU of a particular type of single car railway vehicle product combined with a non-compete provision; Annex, clause 1(h). For discussion of the relative merits of mandatory licences and partial forfeitures of intellectual property rights, see "Merger Review in Emerging High Innovation Markets", OECD, DAFFE/COMP(2002)20, p.30. For the criticism that licensing diminishes the licensor's incentive to continue product development, see Dunlap, "A Practical Guide to Innovation Markets", *Antitrust*, Summer 1995, 21 at p.26.

[80] See the discussion in the FTC Divestiture Study, pp.40 to 42.

[81] "Statement of Federal Trade Commission's Bureau of Competition on Negotiating Merger Remedies", April 2003 (available via *www.ftc.gov/bc/bestpractices/bestpractices030401.htm*) emphasises that performance-based payments such as royalties are disfavoured because they tend to skew competitive incentives or result in disclosure of competitively sensitive information. The US Department of Justice, "Antitrust Policy Guide to Merger Remedies", October 2004 (available via *www.usdoj.gov/atr/public/guidelines/205108.htm*), s.III(D) also notes, at n.22, that royalties tend to increase the purchaser's profit-maximising price (in contrast to fully paid up licences).

[82] See Case COMP/M.2547 *Bayer / Aventis Crop Science* [2004] O.J. L107/1, paras 1105 and 1106 and Case COMP/M.3751 *Novartis / Hexal*, pp.19 and 36.

[83] See, e.g. Case COMP/M.1835 *Monsanto / Pharmacia & Upjohn*; Case COMP/M.1846 *Glaxo Wellcome / SmithKline Beecham* Annex, Undertaking—Monocid, s.II; Case COMP/M.1878 *Pfizer / Warner Lambert*, Annex, Dilzem Commitment, s.IIA; Case COMP/M.3544 *Bayer Healthcare / Roche (OTC Business)*, para.59; and Case COMP/M.3751 *Novartis / Hexal*, p.36.

[84] See, e.g. Case COMP/M.1403 *Astra / Zeneca*, para.93.

[85] See, e.g. Case COMP/M.3544 *Bayer Healthcare / Roche (OTC Business)*, Remedies, Sch.1, para.4(d) and Sch.2, para.4.

[86] Case COMP/M.3751, p.38.

[87] Case COMP/M.3544, para.58 and Remedies, Sch.1, para.5

[88] See s.20.12(a) below.

(c) Consumer goods mergers

(i) Sometimes no need to transfer production facilities If the Commission **20–081** judges that the economic value of the business lies in the brand, it may not require the transfer of production facilities because a brand transfer may be sufficient to ensure the emergence of an effective competitor as the following cases illustrate.

(a) In *SEB / Moulinex*[89] the Commission accepted a commitment based on the licensing of a trade mark without the transfer of any tangible assets. The Court of First Instance[90] upheld the Commission's decision on this point on the grounds that trade marks were of vital importance to the sector (many of the producers had outsourced their production and only retained brands, sales forces and marketing teams) and were one of the main factors in the final consumers' choices. The Court stated that the transfer of tangible assets in that case would have had only a marginal effect on the structure of competition.

(b) In *Procter & Gamble / Wella*[91] the Commission accepted commitments involving the assignment or grant of an exclusive licence of trademarks (supported by a *commitment to supply* and the transfer of other intellectual property rights, know-how and recipes) without the transfer of any production facilities on the grounds that trademarks were considered of "major importance" in order to compete in the hair care business.

(c) In *Honeywell / Novar*[92] the Commission accepted a commitment to grant an exclusive licence of a trade mark for a fire alarm product for a specified period of time[93] supported by a prohibition on Honeywell marketing any fire alarm systems in the territory for that period plus a further black-out period[94]; in addition, Honeywell agreed to transfer key personnel, existing commercial relationships and assets, to grant a technology licence, and to enter a *transitional supply contract*.

(d) In *Nestlé / Ralston Purina*[95] the divestment of brands and commercial

---

[89] Case COMP/M.2621.
[90] Case T-114/02 *BaByliss v Commission* [2003] E.C.R. II-1279, paras 173 and 192.
[91] Case COMP/M.3149, paras 60 and 61.
[92] COMP/M.3686, para.68.
[93] The period is not identified in the non-confidential version of the decision.
[94] The period is not identified in the non-confidential version of the decision.
[95] Case COMP/M.2337, paras 70 and 71. This commitment was provided in relation to the Greek and Italian markets where Ralston Purina had no production facilities and mainly imported pet food products from other European countries.

relationships was supported by a *commitment to supply* the products in question at cost during the production period.[96]

(e) In *Unilever / Bestfoods*[97] one of the remedies was a commitment to dispose of a brand and to grant an *option* enabling the purchaser of the brand to acquire manufacturing facilities.

(f) Similarly, in *Imperial Tobacco / Reemtsma Cigarettenfabriken GmbH*[98] the Commission identified serious doubts about the transaction because the purchaser would acquire control over own label cigarette brands that appeared to discipline the whole market[99] (through the target's ownership of the trademarks for a large proportion of own label sales), but cleared the transaction on the provision of undertakings to assign the trade marks to distributors on request. The Commission concluded that such commitments would enable distributors to switch suppliers, freeing them from dependence on the merged group, and enabling them to compete independently.

20–082 **(ii) Remedies through licensing of brands** In a brand divestiture, it is not always necessary to *assign* the brands, particularly when the merging parties sell other products under the brands in question, provided that re-branding by the purchaser is practicable.[1]

(a) In *SEB / Moulinex*[2] the Commission accepted a commitment to grant an exclusive licence to use the Moulinex brand for five years for the sale of small electric household appliances in specified territories and SEB agreed not to reintroduce the Moulinex brand into those territories for a further three years after the expiry of the exclusive licence. On appeal, the Court of First Instance[3] stated that the question, when assessing the adequacy of the remedies, was whether the licensees would be able to establish or strengthen their own

---

[96] In other cases, the transfer of a brand has been combined with a transfer of production assets; see, e.g. Case COMP/M.2544 *Masterfoods / Royal Canin* and Case COMP/M.2337 *Nestlé / Ralston Purina*, paras 67 to 69 and 71.

[97] Case COMP/M.1990, paras 125 to 131 and 177.

[98] Case COMP/M.2779, paras 59 to 63.

[99] The main interest of supermarkets and cash-and-carry outlets in selling own label cigarettes was to have a product that fixed the bottom price for cigarettes to constrain the pricing of the manufacturers' brands; para.55.

[1] See also Case COMP/M.1990 *Unilever / Bestfoods* (the Commission accepted an undertaking involving the "transfer of the product only and licence for use of the current endorser brand to allow rebranding by the purchaser"; paras 137 and 139); Case COMP/M.2817 *Barilla / BPL / Kamps* (non-renewable licence to use the brand for a finite period; Undertakings, para.2); and Case COMP/M.3732 *Procter & Gamble / Gillette* (in which Procter & Gamble agreed to divest its "SpinBrush" battery toothbrush business in the EEA *and* agreed to grant a two year exclusive licence—followed by a four year black-out period—of the "co-brands" used on the SpinBrush battery toothbrush covering the whole of the EEA; paras 152 to 156).

[2] Case COMP/M.2621.

[3] Case T-114/02 *BaByliss v Commission* [2003] E.C.R. II-1279.

position as effective competitors of SEB.[4] It found that they would, for two main reasons. First, on the question of duration, the Court placed great weight on the fact that the average life of the products in question is three years, emphasising that the commitments would cover a period equal to about three product life cycles and that the "black-out" period would be equal to at least one product life cycle.[5] The Court contrasted this with *Schneider / Legrand*[6] (in which the market test showed that around seven years would be required to complete the trade mark substitution,[7] but the commitments involved an offer to use the trade marks only for three years) and compared it with *Kimberly-Clark / Scott*[8] (in which a licence for a maximum of ten years and a five year "black-out" period were justified because of the difficulties of introducing a new brand of toilet paper, kitchen towels and paper tissues).[9] Secondly, the purchaser standards required that the licensees should be operators with their own trade mark which could be used in association with the Moulinex trade mark, but not operators whose principal activities were retail sales. The Court found that the limitations were capable of effectively ensuring that the licensees would become effective competitors within the period provided for in the commitments.[10] The Court therefore concluded that the commitments were likely to enable the licensees to induce customers of Moulinex products to migrate to their own brand.[11]

(b) *Procter & Gamble / Wella*[12] also involved a five year licensing period followed by a three year black-out period.[13]

(c) In *Masterfoods / Royal Canin*[14] the Commission accepted commitments which did not include the divestment of certain pet food brands but comprised royalty-free licences for three years from the closing of the transaction to enable the purchaser to re-brand; in addition, the parties undertook not to re-introduce the licensed brands within ten years from the closing of the transaction.

However, the Merger Remedies Study[15] found that five of the nine temporary licensing remedies which were examined (all arising in the period **20–083**

---

[4] Para.209.
[5] Paras 215 and 216.
[6] Case COMP/M.2283 [2004] O.J. L101/1.
[7] Para.226.
[8] Case IV/M.623 [1996] O.J. L183/1.
[9] Para.225.
[10] Paras 206 and 221.
[11] Paras 193 to 195 and 205 to 226.
[12] Case COMP/M.3149, paras 60 and 61.
[13] In relation to two of the brands, Procter & Gamble maintained an option whether to grant an exclusive licence or to assign the brand; see para.60.
[14] Case COMP/M.2544, para.89.
[15] See p.31.

1996 to 2000) experienced problems, and in three of the nine cases the issues remained unresolved and affected the viability of the remedy. The Study identified two important disadvantages: "First, the stronger the particular brand or trademark, the higher the inherent risks to the effectiveness. Second, temporary licences were liable to create uncomfortable brand splitting situations, either geographically or between different (range) products in the same geographic area". It also stated[16]:

> "Re-branding remedies have been found acceptable when the share of the problem market vis-à-vis the total brand equity (or trademark equity) was very small and therefore a divestiture (via an exclusive licence or an assignment) of the brand or trademark seemed disproportionate ... Of the three remedies that can be classified as effective at least one also showed serious transfer losses. The risks entailed in the migration of a product to a different brand or trademark can thus be qualified as fairly high".[17]

20–084 **(iii) Brand splitting may create viability issues** The Commission seeks to ensure that ownership of a brand is not split[18] when doing so might prevent the divested business from being viable because of indirect competition from the same brand in the hands of the merged group.[19] In the Merger Remedies Study, the DG Competition staff team noted that brand splitting had given rise to serious issues in cases in which a business in a neighbouring and closely related market had not been included in the divestment package.[20]

In *Unilever / Bestfoods*,[21] in describing the undertakings provided in relation to the food service sector, the Commission stated: "Unilever will in each case divest the whole product portfolio currently marketed under the ... brands [in question] and will not retain any products under those portfolios ... The potential purchaser will acquire the entire product portfolio

---

[16] See p.32.

[17] It is unclear whether the more recent cases accepting such remedies have proven successful (e.g. because the Commission now has greater experience in structuring remedies and has since developed its thinking in particular through the Notice on Remedies and the Model Texts).

[18] For discussion of general concerns about allowing split access to intellectual property rights, including brands, see US Department of Justice, "Antitrust Policy Guide to Merger Remedies", October 2004 (available via *www.usdoj.gov/atr/public/guidelines/205108.htm*), s.III(D).

[19] Case COMP/M.2337 *Nestlé / Ralston Purina*, para.68. In Case T-119/02 *Royal Philips Electronics NV v Commission* [2003] E.C.R. II-1433, the Court of First Instance considered an argument that the commitments accepted by the Commission in Case COMP/M.2621 *SEB / Moulinex* were defective because the licensees under the commitments would not be protected against parallel trade; the Court analysed the market structure and concluded that it was not evident that the commitments were capable of substantially increasing parallel trade (paras 82 to 104).

[20] See pp.24 and 31 (and the case study at pp.25 and 26).

[21] Case COMP/M.1990, paras 177 and 181. The Commission also accepted an undertaking by Unilever to dispose of a particular wet pasta brand in Germany *and* to re-brand all of its wet pasta sauces sold elsewhere in the EEA under that brand; para.144.

[associated with the brands being disposed of] ... These conditions will ensure that the brand value is not diminished as a result of the divestiture".

In *Procter & Gamble / Wella*[22] the notifying party undertook to grant the right to use the trademarks which had been licensed not only in the hair care product categories in which the serious doubts arose (e.g. shampoos) but in *all* other hair care product categories (e.g. conditioners) in which the parties were not active in the Member State at the date of the decision. This was because the market test had indicated that it was "preferable" for a prospective licensee to obtain a licence across all hair care segments in order for the brand to constitute a viable business.

(iv) Brand splitting and consumer protection issues In the *Nestlé / Ralston* **20–085** *Purina*[23] press release the Commission emphasised that the remedy was "in the interests of consumers, by avoiding a situation where the ownership of the involved ... brands would be permanently split in different parts of the Community". This statement suggests that the Commission was concerned that, when the rights to use the same trademark are owned by independent companies, there is a danger of customer confusion as the brand can no longer be relied on as an indicator of origin and the incentive on the producers to maintain quality standards may be reduced. If correct, this would imply that in cases involving international brands but national geographic markets, a significant impediment to effective competition in *one* national market arising from ownership of a particular brand could only be remedied by selling that brand across *all* EEA Member States. However, the Commission's statement appears to be inconsistent both with a judgment of the European Court of Justice and a subsequent decision by the Commission. The European Court of Justice in *Ideal Standard*[24] ruled that A, an owner of a trade mark in one EC Member State, can rely on that trade mark to prevent imports of goods which were marketed by B under the same trade mark in a different Member State even though A assigned the trade mark to B for use in that state, provided that A severed its ability to control the quality of the products sold by B. So long as any commitments were consistent with this decision (involving an assignment of the trade mark and no ongoing quality control), then action by the assignor or the assignee to prevent parallel trade would be compatible with EC competition law,[25] and in many cases would eliminate or significantly reduce the risk of customer

---

[22] Case COMP/M.3149, paras 60 and 61.
[23] Case COMP/M.2337.
[24] Case C-9/93 *IHT Internationale Heiztechnik GmbH v Ideal Standard GmbH* [1994] E.C.R. I-2789, paras 40 to 62.
[25] It would be necessary to assess whether the arrangements in question created a risk of collusion under Art.81, but a clean break ought to eliminate concerns arising, e.g. from the existence of a market sharing agreement (which the European Court of Justice referred to expressly in *Ideal Standard*, at para.59) or the scope for ongoing marketing discussions or approval processes.

confusion. Further,[26] in *Bayer Healthcare / Roche (OTC Business)*[27] the Commission accepted the divestment of a brand in one Member State (subject to a "crown jewel" remedy[28] of divestment of the brand in the EEA if the disposal in the single Member State were not implemented within a specified period) seemingly without considering customer confusion issues.[29]

20–086 **(v) Brand splitting and coordination issues** In *BaByliss v Commission*[30] the appellant argued that splitting the right to use the Moulinex trade mark in different Member States created a risk of coordination between SEB-Moulinex and the licensee or licensees. The Court of First Instance rejected this on the grounds that the markets were national and the same trade mark could be used by different, independent operators in different Member States and developed by them without any need for coordination with SEB or the other licensees. The Court implied that concerns about coordination would arise[31] if the licensee were not independent of the licensor, the licensor and licensee were active in markets which overlapped (e.g. neighbouring product markets) and/or if the licensor had the right to carry out quality control over the licensee's products.[32]

20.9 COMMITMENTS TO EXIT FROM A JOINT VENTURE

20–087 If the competition concern arises because one of the merging parties jointly controls a joint venture,[33] then the remedy is straightforward in principle,[34]

---

[26] However, customer confusion issues were relied on in Case COMP/M.3732 *Procter & Gamble / Gillette* to justify a wider remedy; see para.156.

[27] Case COMP/M.3544, para.58 and the remedies, Schedule 1.

[28] See s.20.12(a) below.

[29] The remedy involved the "right" to use the trade marks (see the remedies, Schedule 1, para.4(b)(iii)) and it is therefore unclear whether it involved an assignment, an exclusive licence or either.

[30] Case T-114/02 [2003] E.C.R. II-1279, paras 244 to 253.

[31] If coordination between the licensor and licensee (or between licensees) is likely, then it is unlikely that the remedy could be regarded as viable (because it will not restore conditions of competition).

[32] At paras 412 to 425, the Court also rejected an argument that the terms of the commitments themselves facilitated geographic market sharing. See also Case COMP/M.3692 *Reuters / Telerate*, para.33 (the licence was not royalty-bearing and did not include any clauses which could conceivably have created a risk of dependency by the licensee on the licensor; paras 26 and 33).

[33] e.g. because of non-coordinated effects concerns arising out of the merged group's ability to both control its own business and influence the joint venture, or if the joint venture would facilitate coordinated effects.

[34] Pending the transfer, it may be necessary to replace the divesting party's representatives on the joint venture's board with trustees; see by analogy Case COMP/M.3653 *Siemens / VA Tech*.

namely to exit from the joint venture.[35] For example, in *Solvay / Montedison-Ausimont*[36] the competition issue arose in the persalts market because the target was party to a 50/50 joint venture with a competitor and Solvay undertook to dispose of the target's 50 per cent holding. Similarly, in *Hutchison / RCPM / ECT*,[37] ECT agreed to divest its minority shareholding in a joint venture.[38] Finally, in *Verbund / Energie Allianz*[39] the Commission accepted a commitment to transfer to an independent trustee the rights derived from a holding in a joint venture (apart from the right to dividends) and the rights derived from the shareholders' agreement. This appears to demonstrate that the principal concern in such cases is to deprive the merging parties of influence over the joint venture rather than to transfer the holding to a third party (although there may be cases in which a transfer to a third party is necessary in order for the joint venture to remain a viable competitor).

20.10 ACCESS REMEDIES

(a) Introduction

The Notice on Remedies states: **20–088**

"First, there may be situations where a divestiture of a business is impossible. Second, competition problems can also result from specific features, such as the existence of exclusive agreements, the combination of networks ('network effects') or the combination of key patents. In such circumstances, the Commission has to determine whether or not other types of remedy may have a sufficient effect on the market to restore effective competition.

The change in the market structure resulting from a proposed concentration can cause existing contractual arrangements to be inimical to effective competition. This is in particular true for exclusive long-term supply and distribution agreements if such agreements will limit the market potential available for competitors. Where the merged entity will

---

[35] Commitments to exit from a joint venture have been relatively successful (in large part because the purchaser is often the other joint venture partner who knows the business well, can preserve it in the interim, and is able to exert a competitive constraint as soon as the divestment is completed or even before), as explained in the Merger Remedies Study, pp.132, 134 and 135.

[36] Case COMP/M.2690, paras 183 and 189.

[37] Case COMP/JV.55, paras 132 and 133.

[38] It also agreed to take measures to enable the joint venture to handle third party business, in particular by releasing it from contractual restrictions, and providing capacity to enable it to operate as an independent handler.

[39] Case COMP/M.2947 [2004] O.J. L92/91, paras 112 (showing that there was joint control), 144 and 151.

have a considerable market share, the foreclosure effects resulting from *existing exclusive agreements* may contribute to the creation of a dominant position. In such circumstances the termination of existing exclusive agreements may be considered appropriate to eliminate the competitive concerns if there is clearly no evidence that de facto exclusivity is being maintained.

The change in the market structure resulting from a proposed concentration can lead to major barriers or impediments to entry into the relevant market. Such barriers may arise from control over infrastructure, in particular networks, or key technology including patents, know-how or other intellectual property rights. In such circumstances, remedies may aim at facilitating market entry by ensuring competitors will have *access to the necessary infrastructure* or *key technology*".

20–089 The Merger Remedies Study identified three types of access remedies[40]:

(a)   the granting of access to infrastructure or technical platforms;

(b)   the granting of access to technology via licences or other intellectual property rights; and

(c)   the termination of exclusive vertical agreements.

The Study examined 10 access remedies (accepted during the period 1996 to 2000) and found that in five of the cases, later market developments had not confirmed the necessity of the remedy.[41] Whilst this is a very small sample, the finding raises the question of whether the Commission has "over-remedied" certain cases (requiring commitments, when none was necessary).[42]

The Merger Remedies Study concluded[43]:

"the following conditions appear important in designing workable access remedies: (1) non-exclusive licences granting access to critical assets, such as IPRs, should be offered and granted to a sufficient number of potential users; (2) licences should clearly spell out the field of use, the correct territorial dimension, a sufficient period of time to make access to the assets worthwhile, and should be granted under terms that make access commercially feasible (in particular, the costs of the licence must not be too high); (3) such commitments should not contain clauses that could adversely affect the competitive outcome, by for example, conveying competitive advantages to the licensors (such as information on the sales volumes and/or values of the licensees); (4) licences should not facilitate

---

[40] p.19.
[41] pp.114 and 164.
[42] For discussion of the effectiveness of the access remedies, see the Merger Remedies Study, pp.127, 132 and 134.
[43] p.165.

co-ordination of the competitive behaviour of the grantor and its beneficiaries; and (5) interviewed parties consistently pointed out the need for
review clauses in commitments involving the grant of access. By providing
for a response to unexpected market developments, a review clause can
ensure that the impact of the Commission's intervention on the parties in
such cases is limited".

(b) Access to infrastructure or technical platforms

The following are examples of cases in which the remedy was designed to **20–090**
provide access to infrastructure or technical platforms (falling short of the
transfer of a market position).[44]

(a) In *BSkyB / KirchPayTV*[45] the Commission was concerned that the
acquisition by BSkyB of joint control over KirchPayTV would create
or strengthen KirchPayTV's dominant position, as BSkyB would be
able to provide additional resources and know-how. The remedies
were designed to lower barriers to entry to the pay-TV market and
prevent KirchPayTV from leveraging its dominance in the provision
of pay-TV into the market for digital interactive services. The
undertakings provided for the grant of access by interested third
parties to KirchPayTV's technical platform so that the third parties
could develop interactive applications for KirchPayTV's "d-box".
(They also provided for the use of KirchPayTV's technology[46] by
competing platforms so that third party providers of digital interactive television services could establish their own technical platform
and compete with KirchPayTV by offering access to KirchPayTV's
pay-TV services.) The commitments provided for arbitration in the
event of a disagreement with a third party.

(b) *NewsCorp / Telepiù*[47] involved a merger to near-monopoly in the
Italian pay-TV market. The package of commitments included
undertakings to grant access to NewsCorp's DTH platform and
access to the application program interface, to facilitate possible new
entry.

(c) In *Shell / DEA*[48] the concern was that the merger (together with a
separate transaction) would create a duopoly in the supply of ethylene on the ARG+ pipe network. Shell undertook to grant third

---

[44] See also Case COMP/M.3410 *Total / Gaz de France* (access to gas transmission network and
storage facilities). The Merger Remedies Study emphasised, at p.116, the importance of
affordable access fees in cases in which the remedy involves access to infrastructure or
technical platforms.
[45] Case COMP/JV.37.
[46] See s.(c) below.
[47] Case COMP/M.2876 [2004] O.J. L110/73, paras 225(h), 257 and 258.
[48] Case COMP/M.2389 [2003] O.J. L15/35.

party access to an import facility for a specified volume of ethylene for 10 years. The terms on which third parties were to be granted access were identified in a model agreement which formed part of the undertakings (reducing the risk of the remedy being frustrated by a failure by the party providing the undertaking to offer reasonable terms).

(d) *Telia / Telenor*[49] involved a proposed merger between the former national telephone operators in Sweden and Norway. One part of the remedies accepted by the Commission was the provision of local loop unbundling in both countries to ensure that third parties could supply final users of telecommunications services.

(e) In *BP / E.ON*[50] the Commission identified a concern that the merged group would prevent certain customers from accessing the free market for ethylene through its control of the pipelines for delivery of the ethylene. The parties committed to guarantee access to the connection pipeline for those dependent customers. The assurance was to supply on reasonable terms and conditions and, in the event of a disagreement, on terms and conditions set by an independent arbitrator.

(f) In *DaimlerChrysler / Deutsche Telekom / JV*[51] the Commission found that adding traffic telematics capacity to equipment which was to be provided free to those liable to pay a truck toll would have given the joint venture a gatekeeper role (as truck operators were unlikely then to pay to add a second unit). The Commission accepted commitments to provide non-discriminatory third party access to the equipment (supported by structural changes, in particular the formation of an independent telematics gateway company).

(g) In *Vodafone Airtouch / Mannesmann*[52] the Commission found that the merged group would be able to provide a seamless pan-European mobile telecommunications service which would be very difficult to replicate in the short to medium term. The remedies were designed to ensure that third parties could provide such services, thereby preventing the emergence of a dominant position. The commitments were very detailed and included[53] a commitment to provide third party access to roaming agreements and wholesale arrangements. The pricing and quality of the service provided to third parties was to be non-discriminatory and the undertakings provided for a fast-track dispute resolution process.

---

[49] Case COMP/M.1439 [2001] O.J. L40/1.
[50] Case COMP/M.2533 [2002] O.J. L276/31, para.147 and Annex II.
[51] Case COMP/M.2903 (appeal pending in Case T-269/03 *Socratec (Satellite Navigation Consulting, Research & Technology) v Commission*), paras 67 to 77.
[52] Case COMP/M.1795, paras 58, 60 and the undertakings provided in the case.
[53] Vodafone also committed not to enter exclusive roaming agreements.

(h) In *Exxon / Mobil*[54] the Commission found that an existing dominant position in the storage of natural gas in southern Germany would be strengthened, as Mobil had concession rights which could be converted into storage facilities. By providing for third party access to Mobil's concession rights, the remedy was designed to ensure that the barriers to entry into the market for storage of natural gas were not increased. Exxon committed to offer to enter binding agreements with third parties for the sale of all of Mobil's rights to the reservoirs suitable for conversion into storage facilities, up to a certain limit of gas volume. Although this commitment was similar in form to a standard divestiture commitment, there were two important differences arising from the fact that the purpose of the remedy was to address barriers to entry rather than the merged group's market position. First, the obligation was to *offer* to enter into binding contracts, but not to find a buyer at any price. In other words, the undertakings could be satisfied even if no sale occurred, provided that the offer were made. Secondly, access was to be at a fair market price to be settled by expert valuers in the event of disagreement. This is different from the normal divestiture obligation, which ultimately requires a sale at any price.

(c) Access to technology

The Merger Remedies Study concluded[55]:   **20–091**

"the Study tends to suggest that remedies to have access to technology or IPRs have only worked in a limited number of instances. The Study suggests that, in order to be effective, licences: (1) are offered and granted to a sufficient number of (potential) licensees; (2) have the field of use defined sufficiently broadly for (potential) licensees; (3) have the correct territorial scope for (potential) licensees; (4) are granted for a sufficient period of time to make access to the assets worthwhile; (5) are granted under terms that make access commercially attractive, in particular ensuring that the costs of the licence allow the licensee to effectively compete in the market; (6) are not encumbered by third party rights or

---

[54] Case IV/M.1383 [2004] O.J. L103/1, paras 838 to 840 and Annex, para.50.
[55] p.120. See para.20–089 above for the Merger Remedies Study's conclusion regarding access remedies as a whole (as opposed to access to technology in particular). At p.118, the Study identified access terms as the single most important element in the effectiveness of licensing remedies: onerous terms can discourage or hinder access; some schemes can convey sensitive information to the licensor or deter the licensee from competing; pre-determined prices can pose problems attracting new licensees as the date for expiry of the patent approaches; "non-discrimination" and "fair market value" clauses can be useful but interviewees emphasised the importance of appropriate dispute resolution mechanisms because it is not easy to determine whether a licensor has been guilty of discrimination or whether a proposed charging structure is above fair market value.

restrictions; (7) do not convey any new competitive advantage to the licensor, such as the dissemination of commercially sensitive information on sales volumes of the licensee; and (8) do not facilitate co-ordination between the licensor and the licensee (e.g. co-licensing in an oligopolistic market structure)".

20–092 The following are examples of cases in which the remedy involved the grant of access to technology through licences or other intellectual property rights.[56]

(a) In *Air Liquide / BOC*[57] the Commission accepted commitments to license all of BOC's patented technology to third parties on request on reasonable and non-discriminatory terms. The object of these provisions was to lessen the concerns arising from the combination of technologies.

(b) In *Allied Signal / Honeywell*[58] the Commission was concerned that rival suppliers of terrain awareness warning systems ("TAWS") might not have been able to arrange for their products to *interface* with the merged group's avionics. The parties undertook to provide third party suppliers of TAWS with all licences and interface specification data necessary to facilitate such interfacing.

(c) Similarly, in *Siemens / Drägerwerk / JV*[59] the Commission accepted a set of *interfacing* commitments in order to eliminate vertical foreclosure concerns regarding the interoperability between anaesthesia and ventilation equipment on the one hand and patient monitors on the other. The Commission accepted similar remedies in *GE / Instrumentarium*.[60]

(d) In *EADS*[61] the concern was that the merged group would be a monopoly supplier of components which it used in a downstream business, creating a risk that the merged group would refuse to supply a rival operator in the downstream market. The Commission accepted undertakings designed to facilitate new entry into the upstream components markets through the grant of *non-exclusive*

---

[56] See also Case IV/M.877 *Boeing / McDonnell Douglas* [1997] O.J. L336/16, para.117 (commitment to license on a non-exclusive, reasonable royalty-bearing basis any "government-funded" patent which could be used in the manufacture or sale of commercial jet aircraft); Case COMP/JV.37 *BSkyB / KirchPayTV* (discussed in para.20–090(a) above, which involved the grant of access to technology as well as the grant of access to a platform); and Case COMP/M.3225 *Alcan / Pechiney (II)*, para.150 (grant of a non-exclusive licence of technology to remedy concerns about possible upstream foreclosure by refusing to license or raising the licence fees; para.150; see also para.153 for a remedy involving the "divestment" of designs subject to a right to use the designs for its own purposes free of royalty).
[57] Case COMP/M.1630, paras 296(f) and 297.
[58] Case COMP/M.1601 [2001] O.J. L152/1, para.128.
[59] Case COMP/M.2861 [2003] O.J. L291/1, para.156.
[60] Case COMP/M.3083 [2004] O.J. L109/1, paras 352 and 353.
[61] Case COMP/M.1745.

intellectual property rights, the provision of technical assistance *or* the transfer of employees, and the transfer of contracts with the downstream competitor (with that competitor's agreement).[62]

(e) In *Shell / BASF—Project Nicole*[63] the Commission found that the combination of a suite of patents with the market position of the joint venture raised serious doubts about the effect of the operation. The Commission accepted commitments to license the patents to all third parties who wished to license them directly and not to assert those patents against third parties who wished to license the technology from other operators in the technology market.[64] The commitments provided that the licences "will be granted on non-discriminating, arm's length terms and conditions" and provided that, in the event of disagreement on consideration, the issue would be settled by "pendulum" arbitration under which each party submits a single proposal to an arbitration panel, which is obliged to choose one or other of the two proposals.[65]

(f) In *Ciba-Geigy / Sandoz*[66] the Commission was concerned that the merged group would control an active ingredient needed by competitors to develop a category of products (insect growth regulators). The Commission accepted undertakings to provide *non-exclusive* licences for the active ingredient and physical supplies until the licensees could begin production (subject to a long-stop date). This remedy was intended to facilitate competition in the insect growth regulators market and assure supplies of the active ingredient to competitors in that downstream market.

(g) In the Commission's second substantive decision in *Tetra Laval / Sidel*[67] (following the Court of First Instance's judgment quashing the original prohibition decision),[68] the Commission accepted a commitment to offer on a non-discriminatory basis licences of the patents relating to the Tetra Fast technology for a fixed flat fee, subject to "pendulum" arbitration in the event of a failure by Tetra Laval and the licensee to agree.

(h) In *Alcatel / Finmeccanica / Alcatel Alenia Space & Telespazio*[69] the parties committed to provide a single licence of a technology package

---

[62] Appendix 2. A similar remedy was accepted in Case COMP/M.1636 *MMS / DASA / Astrium* [2003] O.J. L314/1 to address analogous concerns.
[63] Case COMP/M.1751.
[64] See para.55, fourth indent. For similar undertakings, see Case IV/M.950 *Hoffmann-La Roche / Boehringer Mannheim* [1998] O.J. L234/14 and Case COMP/M.1671 *Dow Chemicals / Union Carbide* [2001] O.J. L245/1, para.176.
[65] Commitments, s.2B(3).
[66] Case IV/M.737 [1997] O.J. L201/1.
[67] Case COMP/M.2416, (decision of January 13, 2003), paras 120 to 122.
[68] Case T-5/02 *Tetra Laval BV v Commission* [2002] E.C.R. II-4381 (upheld on appeal in Case C-12/03P *Commission v Tetra Laval BV*, not yet reported, judgment of February 15, 2005).
[69] Case COMP/M.3680, paras 76, 117 and 118.

to a third party, to reduce the effort and cost necessary for the third party to develop rival products and become a credible supplier (to overcome a merger to monopoly). This commitment was supported on a transitional basis by a commitment to supply the equipment at pre-merger prices, subject to arbitration by the European Space Agency in case of dispute.

(i) *NewsCorp / Telepiù*[70] involved a merger to near-monopoly in the Italian pay-TV market. The package of commitments included undertakings to grant to third parties licences for NewsCorp's conditional access system on a fair and non-discriminatory basis.

(d) Termination of exclusive vertical agreements

20–093 The Commission accepted remedies[71] intended to reduce the effect of exclusivity provisions on the operation of the market in the following cases.[72]

(a) In *Agfa-Gevaert / Dupont*[73] the Commission found that the merger would have created a dominant position in a market in which the merging parties had both entered exclusive, package and tying contracts with customers, distributors and suppliers which made it difficult for competitors to win business. The remedy was to cancel the exclusivity provisions and release suppliers from certain restrictions in order to *increase inter-brand competition*.[74] The Commission did not consider divestment a suitable remedy on the facts: "Consideration was given to potential divestment and sale to a third party or third parties of certain production facilities or production lines ... Such a measure would, however, not sufficiently address the competition concerns, as the structure of the market would not be significantly affected".[75]

---

[70] Case COMP/M.2876 [2004] O.J. L110/73, para.225(i).
[71] The Merger Remedies Study examined one remedy involving the termination of exclusive vertical relationships (from the period 1996 to 2000) and found that it had failed, as suppliers did not have an incentive to exploit the new sales opportunities because of design flaws in the remedy; see p.120.
[72] See also Case IV/M.1467 *Rohm and Haas / Morton* (three-year commitment not to distribute on an exclusive basis within the EU any dry film photo resists made by other manufacturers). In Case COMP/M.1672 *Volvo / Scania* [2001] O.J. L143/74, a proposed remedy involving opening the dealer and service networks was rejected on the grounds that its efficacy had not been demonstrated; para.341. Contrast the "statement" referred to in para.78 and attached as Annex 5 to the decision in Case IV/M.477 *Mercedes-Benz / Kässbohrer* [1995] O.J. L211/1, and the remedies accepted in Case COMP/M.1571 *New Holland / Case*, at paras 77, 81 and 86.
[73] Case IV/M.986 [1998] O.J. L211/22.
[74] See the Commission's XXVIIIth Annual Report on Competition Policy, 1998, pp.192 and 193.
[75] Para.111.

(b) In *BT / ESAT*[76] the Commission's concerns related to the distribution of global telecommunications products in Ireland. The Commission accepted undertakings designed to open up the Irish market to competition through new entry or strengthening the position of the existing suppliers by granting a right to a third party to terminate an exclusive distribution agreement and *not renewing* a separate distribution agreement.

(c) In *Boeing / McDonnell Douglas*[77] the Commission accepted commitments by Boeing not to enter any new exclusive supply agreements for a specified period and not to enforce existing ones.[78]

(d) In *Danish Crown / Vestjyske Slagterier*[79] the Commission found that the merger would have created a dominant position on the market for the *purchase* of live pigs for slaughter, but accepted commitments to allow members of the merged group, which was a cooperative, to supply pigs to other slaughterers, subject to maximum limits and procedural requirements (and to permit members to leave the cooperative on 12 months' notice), on the grounds that this would ensure that the transaction did not result in foreclosure of the Danish market.

(e) *NewsCorp / Telepiù*[80] was a merger to near-monopoly in the Italian pay-TV market. The Commission accepted a package of commitments, including the grant to rights owners of a power unilaterally to terminate contracts entered with the merging parties and the waiver of exclusive rights for certain TV platforms and formats (e.g. pay-per-view). The package also restricted the merged group's ability to enter *future* exclusive contracts.[81]

(f) In *EnBW / ENI / GVS*[82] the parties undertook to grant a right of early termination of supply contracts. This was intended to make substantial volumes of gas *demand* available in the market earlier than would have been possible under the long-term supply contracts,[83] which was expected to contribute to increased competition.

---

[76] Case COMP/M.1838, paras 31 and 32.
[77] Case IV/M.877 [1997] O.J. L336/16.
[78] These commitments were subject to exceptions and formed part of a package; see para.116.
[79] Case IV/M.1313 [2000] O.J. L20/1, paras 234 and 235.
[80] Case COMP/M.2876 [2004] O.J. L110/73, paras 225(a) to (c) and 230 to 232.
[81] Paras 225(d) to (f) and 233 to 238.
[82] Case COMP/M.2822 [2003] O.J. L248/51, paras 61 to 72.
[83] See also Case COMP/M.2947 *Verbund / Energie Allianz* [2004] O.J. L92/91 (grant of unilateral right to early termination to of large customers' electricity supply contracts to assist in removing obstacles to entry; para.162).

20.11 OTHER REMEDIES

(a) Introduction

20–094 This section describes the principal categories of remedies that have been accepted by the Commission but which do not fit into the taxonomy set out in the Merger Remedies Study and adopted for the purposes of organising this Chapter. Some of the categories described below are reasonably similar to those already considered, in particular severing influence in a competitor (s.(b), which is similar to withdrawal from a joint venture); the transfer of specific assets (other than the transfer of intellectual property rights) to transfer a market position (s.(c), which is similar to the Commission's category of commitments to transfer a market position); termination of distribution agreements (s.(d), which in certain cases has the same effect as a commitment to transfer a market position); and the supply of goods or services to eliminate vertical foreclosure concerns or facilitate entry (s.(e), which the Commission could have included in its category of access commitments). By contrast, the creation of product space (s.(f)), other remedies designed to facilitate new entry (s.(g)), the assurance of purchases from third parties (s.(h)), the correction of market flaws (s.(i)), and other remedies (s.(j)) are genuine outliers which belong in a residual, "other" category and serve to emphasise that the process of formulating an acceptable remedy is a bespoke process depending on the particular circumstances of the transaction and the markets involved.

(b) Commitments to sever influence in a competitor

20–095 The Merger Remedies Study[84] noted that commitments to sever influence in a competitor are designed to ensure that the competitor competes freely with the merged entity. The remedies may include[85] termination or amendment of agreements with competitors, the surrender or restriction of representation

---

[84] See p.121.
[85] See, e.g. Case COMP/M.2879 *Wallenius Lines / Wilhelmsen / Hyundai Merchant Marine* (the Commission accepted commitments to terminate a shipping conference (a contractual arrangement with effects which are in certain respects analogous to a joint venture) and not to enter a similar one for a specified period without the prior consent of the Commission; paras 66 to 69); Case COMP/M.3322 *Polestar / Prisa / Inversiones Ibersuizas / JV* (one of the joint venture partners held a 10% stake in a competitor and had the right to appoint a director; the transaction was approved subject to the sale of that stake); Case COMP/M.3765 *Amer / Salomon* (remedies to convert a widespread cooperation agreement with a competitor into a supply agreement, removing provisions for exchange of information on prices, costs and commercial behaviour and other clauses limiting independence of behaviour; paras 173 to 175); Case COMP/M.3770 *Lufthansa / Swiss* (termination of airline alliance agreements; para.197(g)); Case COMP/M.3829 *Maersk / PONL* (withdrawal from shipping conferences and shipping consortia; paras 176 and 177); and Case COMP/M.3863 *TUI / CP Ships* (withdrawal from shipping conferences; para.62).

or voting rights in a competitor, and commitments to divest a non-controlling[86] stake in a rival.

(c) Transfer of specific assets (other than the transfer of intellectual property rights) to transfer a market position

Ss.20.7 and 20.8 described remedies which were intended to transfer a **20–096** market position by transferring a business (in the form of shares or assets) or intellectual property rights. In some cases, a remedy may be available involving the transfer of specific assets other than intellectual property rights. This arises when the real value in the business is derived from particular assets and transferring those assets will create a viable competitor, ensuring that the merger does not result in a significant impediment to effective competition.

For example,[87] in *KLM / Alitalia*[88] the parties intended to form a joint venture involving their scheduled passenger air transport and cargo air transport activities. The joint venture would have had a monopoly on the Amsterdam-Milan and Amsterdam-Rome routes. The undertakings were intended to remove barriers to entry and facilitate the effective entry of a competitor so that the alliance would be constrained by the competitive threat of entry after the merger. The Commission commented: "In the present case, the usual remedies accepted by the Commission to prevent the creation or reinforcement of a dominant position (i.e. the divestiture of assets) are not suitable. The divestiture of assets used to provide the transport service in the routes between the Netherlands and Italy would not automatically lead to a reduction of the market share of the alliance. In addition, the mere divestiture of tangible and intangible assets would not guarantee that such assets would be used in competition with the alliance in the two markets in question. Planes and crews, for instance, can be used to provide transport services on a wide number of routes".[89] The undertakings comprised in particular: the surrender of specified numbers of slots at specified times at the airports in question if any new entrant were unable to obtain the slots needed through normal procedures; a commitment that, for every daily return flight ("frequency") introduced by a new entrant, the parties would *reduce* their own frequencies by one, up to a maximum of 40 per cent of the frequencies[90]; and a commitment to offer to enter blocked space agreements and interline agreements with any new entrant, to admit

---

[86] The divestment of controlling stakes is addressed in s.20.7 (sole control) and s.20.9 (joint control).

[87] In Case COMP/M.3570 *Piaggio / Aprilia* an obligation to supply a four-stroke engine was accepted as a remedy for issues in the 50cc scooter market in Italy, on the grounds that this would enable some rivals to exert a more effective competitive influence and divestment would be disproportionate.

[88] Case COMP/JV.19, para.68.

[89] Para.68.

[90] The commitment was also subject to other limitations.

the entrant to their Frequent Flyer Programme and to ensure that the new entrant was listed on the first page of the Computerised Reservation System.[91] The commitments are noteworthy because they involved detailed provisions designed to accommodate entry into the market.[92] Subsequently, in *Air France / KLM*[93] the Commission accepted a similar set of remedies, adapted in particular to deal with concerns regarding hub dominance.[94]

20–097   Similarly, in *British Telecom / MCI*[95] the Commission found that the proposed merger was liable to create or strengthen a dominant position on the market for international voice-telephony services between the United Kingdom and the US. The issue arose because there was a relative shortage of transmission facilities and the merged group would have had a substantial share of the available capacity. The Commission accepted remedies involving offers to sell certain assets used for United Kingdom-US transmission (and offering third party access on non-discriminatory terms to other assets).

The FTC Divestiture Study found that: "divestitures of selected assets can succeed. Where the Commission [i.e. the FTC] determines that the divestiture of an on-going business is undesirable because it would destroy the efficiencies of a merger, the case studies indicate ways that the higher risks associated with a partial divestiture can be reduced ... [T]hese risks can be reduced by affording greater protection to the buyer of the divested assets by including provisions requiring the use of auditor trustees, rights to hire employees, rights to technical assistance, and supply contracts".[96]

(d) Termination of distribution agreements

20–098   In *Pfizer / Pharmacia*[97] one of the merging parties was a *distributor* of a particular product. The Commission accepted commitments to *discontinue selling* that product and transfer any relevant rights or assets to the original licensor or one or more designated third parties. Pfizer presented this as a "divestment" by termination of the distribution agreement.[98] Subsequently, in *Pernod Ricard / Allied Domecq*[99] the Commission accepted the

---

[91] COMP/JV.19, para.69.

[92] In a straightforward divestiture of a business, the provision of a non-compete covenant by the vendor also involves the accommodation of entry into the market.

[93] Case COMP/M.3280 (appeal pending in Case T-177/04 *easyJet Airline Company v Commission*), paras 158 and 161.

[94] See also Case IV/M.259 *British Airways / TAT*; Case IV/M.616 *Swissair / Sabena*; Case COMP/M.2041 *United Airlines / US Airways* (congestion at Frankfurt and Munich airports was seen as a barrier to entry or expansion and the commitment was to make slots available at those airports); and Case COMP/M.3770 *Lufthansa / Swiss*, paras 188 to 205.

[95] Case IV/M.353.

[96] FTC Divestiture Study, p.12.

[97] Case COMP/M.2922, para.155 and Remedies, Sch.2.

[98] This is logical if: (a) the distributor cannot assign the distribution agreement as of right; and (b) the licensor would appoint a new distributor (or carry out the distribution itself) which would be as effective a competitor as the merging party.

[99] Case COMP/M.3779, paras 83 and 88.

discontinuance or termination of agency agreements as remedies which would eliminate the competition concerns identified by the Commission (presumably on the basis that the owner of the brands would be expected to appoint another agent or distributor, effectively transferring the market position).

(e) The supply of goods or services to eliminate vertical foreclosure concerns or facilitate entry

In cases in which there are concerns that the merged group will *refuse to* **20–099** *supply* particular goods[1] or the scope for *new entry* is reduced by the merged group's control over particular goods, the remedy may involve a commitment to make the goods available. The effect of remedies of this kind is similar to the granting of access to infrastructure, technical platforms or intellectual property rights[2]; the cases discussed below differ simply in the sense that the barrier to entry did not involve any of the three categories of assets specified in the Merger Remedies Study.

(a) In *Apollo / Bakelite*[3] the Commission was concerned that the upstream business would refuse to supply downstream competitors. The remedy involved the grant to customers of the right to purchase 100 per cent of their then current annualised purchasing volumes, increasing by 5 per cent per year, at a price based on a formula approved by the Commission, for a duration of seven years, with an obligation on the merged group to negotiate in good faith using best efforts to reach an agreement with customers within three months of completion (i.e. implementation) of the notified concentration.[4]

(b) In *EDF / EnBW*[5] the Commission found that the merger might have strengthened EDF's dominant position in the market for the supply of electricity to the liberalised market in France through the elimination of a potential competitor, the potential for retaliation in Germany against competitors in France, and the strengthening of EDF's position as a pan-European supplier. The remedies included a commitment by EDF to make available to competitors, for a period of five years (extendable by the Commission depending on the development of the French market), specified generation capacity through virtual power plants and back-to-back agreements to existing co-generation power purchase agreements. The capacity was to

---

[1] The analysis in the text is equally applicable to services.
[2] See s.20.10 above.
[3] Case COMP/M.3593.
[4] Para.165.
[5] Case COMP/M.1853.

be made available through auctions under the supervision of a trustee.

(c) In *Südzucker / Saint Louis Sucre*[6] the issues were similar to those in *EDF / EnBW* (i.e. loss of potential competition, increased scope for retaliation, and the merged group's unique ability to offer pan-European deals). The remedy was to make a specified volume of "quota sugar" available at EU intervention prices. This was regarded as likely to facilitate entry by an independent trader into the German sugar market.

(f) The creation of "product space" to facilitate new entry

20–100 The Commission has on occasion accepted commitments to free "product space" in the expectation that this will facilitate new entry.[7]

(a) In *RTL / Veronica / Endemol*[8] the Commission was concerned that the joint venture would strengthen an existing dominant position on the Dutch TV production market. The Commission accepted an undertaking to convert one of the joint venture's channels from a general interest to a news channel. The rationale was that this change would create "more room for competing general interest channels".[9]

(b) In *Telekom Austria / Libro*[10] Telekom Austria held an existing dominant position in the supply of fixed telephony networks in Austria. It proposed to acquire joint control over Libro, which had an outstanding application for a licence to supply such services in Austria. The Commission accepted an undertaking to *renounce* the licence to avoid a further strengthening of the dominant position (in particular by adding Libro's marketing skills to Telekom Austria's existing dominant position).

(g) Other remedies designed to "sponsor" new entry (not falling within the "access" category)

20–101 The following are examples of cases in which the remedy was designed to "sponsor" new entry (but which do not fall within the "access" category

---

[6] Case COMP/M.2530 [2003] O.J. L103/1, paras 157 to 177.
[7] See also Case T-158/00 *ARD v Commission* [2003] E.C.R. II-3825, paras 315 to 319 (upholding a remedy intended to create space for third parties to supply).
[8] Case IV/M.553 [1996] O.J. L294/14 (an appeal was dismissed in Case T-221/95 *Endemol Entertainment Holding BV v Commission* [1999] E.C.R. II-1299).
[9] The Commission's XXVIth Annual Report on Competition Policy, 1996, p.185.
[10] Case COMP/M.1747.

discussed in s.20.10 above or the supply of goods or services or the creation of product space discussed in ss.(e) and (f) above).[11]

(a) *NewsCorp / Telepiù*[12] involved a merger to near-monopoly in the Italian pay-TV market. The package of commitments included undertakings to allow third parties to distribute the merged group's content on certain platforms for a price calculated on a "retail minus" basis.

(b) In *Vivendi / Canal+ / Seagram*[13] the concentration had effects in the markets for pay-TV, portals and online music. The package of remedies included commitments to grant rival portals access to Universal's online music content for five years[14] and not to grant Canal Plus "first window" rights (i.e. for pay-TV broadcast after release in cinema and video but before free-to-air television) for films covering more than 50 per cent of Universal's production and co-production. The Commission agreed to review the undertakings after three years, given that the market might evolve rapidly in a short period. The Commission stated that the undertakings had a structural effect because they provided for access to Universal's music content.

(c) In *Reuters / Telerate*[15] the Commission accepted a remedy involving the grant of a global exclusive licence for Telerate's market data platforms technology in the belief that this would enable the licensee to develop a business to rival the merged group. The Commission did not envisage that the licence would be sufficient to transfer a market position (in contrast to remedies involving the assignment or licensing of intellectual property rights in pharmaceutical cases and mergers involving consumer brands).[16] The Commission recognised that the licensee would need to make significant investments (and

---

[11] See the Commission's XXXIst Annual Report on Competition Policy, 2001, paras 302 and 303 (noting that no such remedies had been accepted during Phase I in 2001 (in contrast to the position in 2000) but had continued to be accepted in Phase II, which "may reflect a greater degree of caution from the Commission following the adoption of the remedies notice").

[12] Case COMP/M.2876 [2004] O.J. L110/73, paras 225(g) to (c) and 246 to 253.

[13] Case COMP/M.2050, paras 72 to 79.

[14] The commitment not to discriminate (which was supported by a dispute resolution clause) was as follows: "Universal undertakes to provide access to its music content on a non-discriminatory basis which shall mean that Universal shall not discriminate in favour of Vizzavi in the supply of music for downloading or streaming online to its subscribers in the EEA such that any differences in the conditions, including price and terms, upon which the music is made available to Vizzavi and the conditions, including price and terms, upon which such music content is made available to competitors of Vizzavi shall be based on objective reasons and not on the basis that Vizzavi and Universal are both affiliated through common ownership with Vivendi. For the purposes of this Undertaking, objective reasons include but are not limited to the security of the systems operated by such competitors ... the quality of their technology ... and their creditworthiness".

[15] Case COMP/M.3692, paras 29 to 35.

[16] See s.20.8 above.

investigated whether it was likely to do so) and that the licensee might fail to either launch a product or make it successful (and the commitments provided that the merged group would have to transfer the licence to a third party on equivalent terms in such a situation).

(d) In *Telia / Sonera*[17] the Commission identified concerns in the markets for mobile telecommunications services and corporate communications services, but accepted a commitment to divest a business in a *neighbouring* market, namely a cable television network, on the grounds that "in the medium to long term, the commitment to divest Telia's cable TV network would enhance the emergence of an alternative fixed network to the local loop in Sweden". (However, the Commission acknowledged that the divestiture was "only a medium to long term solution" and "would alone not be a sufficient remedy" and accepted additional commitments, which it described as "partly behavioural", to create a legal separation between the parties' fixed and mobile networks[18] and, for a period limited to three years, to grant non-discriminatory access to their networks.)

(e) In *EDF / Louis Dreyfus*[19] the Commission was concerned that the creation of an electricity trading joint venture might have restricted or delayed the entry of competing suppliers of electricity into the French market, once France complied with its obligations under the Electricity Directive by introducing competition. The remedies involved the implementation of measures to prevent the joint venture from assisting EDF in relation to eligible customers (i.e. those for which there would be potential competition following the implementation of the Electricity Directive) in France and a prohibition on transferring know-how or relevant information from the joint venture to EDF.

(f) In *Vodafone / Vivendi / Canal Plus*[20] the parties proposed to form a joint venture to establish the Vizzavi internet portal. The Commission identified concerns in the developing national markets for TV-based internet portals and mobile telephone-based internet portals. The remedies involved ensuring that customers could access third party portals and change the default portal themselves or through a third party portal operator.

---

[17] Case COMP/M.2803, paras 125 to 144.
[18] The rationale for this provision was that "third parties consider it to be very important to have clear interfaces between service and network operations, in both fixed and mobile telephony services, in order to apply and to monitor the application of the legal obligations as regards cost oriented pricing" (para.135).
[19] Case COMP/M.1557.
[20] Case COMP/JV.48.

(h) Assurance of purchases from third parties

In *Bombardier / ADtranz*[21] the concentration would have led to the creation **20–102** of a dominant position in the supply of regional trains and trams in Germany. In order to strengthen the position of the independent players in those markets, the merged group committed to: guarantee capacity load for one competitor for a transitional period; exclusively use specific equipment manufactured by a second; guarantee a certain volume of business with that supplier for a specified period; and continue to cooperate with a third competitor for a specified period on certain projects.

(i) Correction of market flaws

In some cases the Commission has accepted remedies intended to correct **20–103** "flaws" in market operation to facilitate the development of effective competition.[22]

(a) In *VEBA / VIAG*[23] the concern was that the merger (together with a separate transaction) would create a duopoly on the German market for electricity from the interconnector grid. One component of a package of remedies was a commitment not to charge a transmission fee which would otherwise have been payable in certain circumstances by users of the transmission system. The fee had acted as a deterrent to imports.

(b) In *Grupo Villar Mir / EnBW / Hidroeléctrica del Cantábrico*[24] the Commission was concerned that the merger would strengthen an existing position of collective dominance on the Spanish wholesale electricity market. The remedy was a commitment to increase substantially the capacity of the electricity interconnector between France and Spain so that trade in electricity between the two states could increase.

In *EDP v Commission*[25] the appellant argued that the Commission had misused its powers by requiring commitments aimed at liberalising the gas

---

[21] Case COMP/M.2139 [2002] O.J. L69/50.
[22] In Case COMP/M.1672 *Volvo / Scania* [2001] O.J. L143/74, a commitment to use best efforts to seek the abolition of the Swedish cab crash test (which tended to result in the Swedish market being isolated from other EEA markets) was rejected on the basis that the power to abolish lay with the Swedish Government, which had not indicated that the test would be removed; para.339. See also Case IV/M.774 *St Gobain / Wacker Chemie / NOM* [1997] O.J. L247/1, in which a commitment to withdraw support for anti-dumping measures was rejected, as the decision whether to remove the measures was for the Council and the undertaking did not in any way modify the concentration; paras 261 and 262.
[23] Case COMP/M.1673 [2001] O.J. L188/1.
[24] Case COMP/M.2434 [2004] O.J. L48/86.
[25] Case T-87/05, not yet reported, judgment of September 21, 2005, paras 86 and 91.

and electricity markets. The Court of First Instance rejected this argument on the grounds that the entry of competitors was an important way of resolving the competition issues arising from the merger.

(j) Other remedies

20–104 **(i) Other remedies for vertical effects** In some cases involving vertical issues, remedies have been accepted which do not involve the transfer of a market position, the grant of access or any of the other categories of remedy discussed in this residual section.[26]

    (a) In *Alcatel / Thomson CSF-SCS*[27] the competition concern was that the merged group would be a monopoly supplier of components which it used in a downstream business, creating a risk that it would refuse to supply a rival operator in the downstream business. The competition issue was therefore identical to the one in *EADS* (see para.20–092(d) above). In *EADS*, the remedy was to facilitate new entry by offering a non-exclusive intellectual property licence. However, in *Alcatel* the Commission accepted a remedy based on the insertion of an arbitration clause into the supply agreement with the downstream competitor.

    (b) In *PTT Post / TNT / GD Express Worldwide*[28] the competition issue was that the merged group might have discriminated against companies wishing to use its postal or telecommunications networks. The Commission found that this possibility was largely eliminated by the regulatory framework but accepted undertakings not to cross-subsidise or discriminate against competitors.

20–105 **(ii) Ring-fencing and firewalls commitments** The Commission has occasionally accepted commitments providing for ring-fencing or the introduction or strengthening of firewalls. For example, in *Wegener / PCM / JV*[29] the

---

[26] See the US Department of Justice, "Antitrust Policy Guide to Merger Remedies", October 2004 (available via *www.usdoj.gov/atr/public/guidelines/205108.htm*), s.III(E)(2), discussing the scope to use firewall provisions, fair dealing provisions, transparency provisions and others (including competitive-rule joint ventures (intended to ensure that competitors have access to essential assets on competitive terms), non-compete clauses, long-term supply agreements and restrictions on reacquisition of scarce personnel assets). The Australian Merger Guidelines, June 1999 (*www.accc.gov.au/content/item.phtml?itemId=719436&nodeId=file43a1f42c7eb63&fn=Merger%20Guidelines.pdf*), para.7.11, provide, in relation to vertical mergers: "In some cases the Commission's concerns may be able to be addressed by way of quasi-structural undertakings like ring fencing and access undertakings".

[27] Case IV/M.1185.

[28] Case IV/M.843, paras 39 to 46. Contrast Case COMP/M.1672 *Volvo / Scania* [2001] O.J. L143/74, at para.346 (rejecting a commitment not to discriminate against dealers taking on a new brand as "too vague and impossible to monitor effectively").

[29] Case COMP/M.3817, paras 62 and 68 to 70.

Commission accepted ring-fencing commitments to resolve concerns about possible coordination between the joint venture's parents under Art.2(4) of the ECMR. The undertakings provided that the joint venture would appoint a supervisory board, would not share certain information with its shareholders and would have its advertising prices approved by the supervisory board. Further, in *Areva / Urenco / ETC JV*[30] the Commission accepted detailed remedies regarding firewalls as part of a package of commitments to eliminate concerns based on coordinated effects and Art.2(4) of the ECMR. The commitments were to be monitored by the auditor of the joint venture.

(iii) Other specific "conduct" commitments In several cases, the Commission **20–106** has accepted specific commitments regarding the merged group's conduct. For example, in *Wegener / PCM / JV*[31] the Commission accepted undertakings from Wegener to sell its advertising space separately.

20.12 CROWN JEWELS, FIX IT FIRST AND CONDITIONAL REMEDIES

(a) Alternative and "crown jewels" remedies

In its Notice on Remedies[32] the Commission recognised that implementation **20–107** of the parties' preferred divestiture option might be uncertain or difficult in the light, for example, of third party rights of pre-emption[33] or uncertainty as to the transferability of key contracts, intellectual property rights or employees. In those circumstances, the Notice on Remedies states that the Commission is willing to accept the parties' preferred divestiture option *provided*[34] that an alternative is available which is at least equally-suited to restore effective competition and a clear timetable is identified for implementation of one of the two sets of remedies.[35]

In practice, the Commission has been willing to accept remedies drafted in the alternative in numerous cases, seemingly without establishing whether

---

[30] Case COMP/M.3099, paras 232 and 238.
[31] Case COMP/M.3817, paras 62 and 68 to 70.
[32] The Notice on Remedies, para.22. See also the Merger Remedies Study, pp.52 to 55.
[33] The Commission may accept undertakings by a joint venture partner to terminate the joint venture even though doing so may affect the interests of third parties: Joined Cases C-68/94 and C-30/95 *France v Commission* [1998] E.C.R. I-1375 and Case COMP/M.1693 *Alcoa / Reynolds* [2002] O.J. L58/25, para.133. Contrast: *Alcan / Pechiney / Alusuisse*, Commission press release IP/00/258. See s.20.13(d) below discussing third party consents.
[34] And provided, also, that it is otherwise compatible with the principles summarised in s.20.4 above.
[35] The Notice on Remedies, para.23.

the criteria in the Notice on Remedies are satisfied.[36] By accepting alternative remedies, the Commission may reduce opportunistic behaviour by potential purchasers in circumstances where, in the absence of alternatives and as a forced seller, the divesting party lacks bargaining power.[37]

20–108   The Commission also considers[38] the use of *"crown jewels"* undertakings, a particular type of alternative remedy in which the party providing the undertakings commits to sell a specific business within a set period and, in the event that a sale agreement is not concluded within that period, commits instead to sell a *more valuable* business.[39] Such an approach increases the incentive on the divesting party to make a rapid sale of the first business and increases the flexibility of the Commission if, e.g. the definition of the viable business is not clear-cut and depends partly on the identity of the purchaser[40] or if there are doubts about whether the first remedy is a viable business for which suitable purchasers will emerge. On the other hand, the Merger Remedies Study noted that such undertakings can prolong the divestiture period if the first proposed option is not successful and increase uncertainty and costs as the interim preservation and hold separate arrangements must be applied to both divestment businesses.[41]

"Crown jewels" remedies have been used by the Commission in several cases.[42]

---

[36] The cases include Case IV/M.291 *KNP / Bührmann Tetterode / VRG*; Case IV/M.873 *Bank Austria / Creditanstalt*; Case IV/M.938 *Guinness / Grand Metropolitan* [1998] O.J. L288/24, para.190; Case IV/M.1182 *Akzo Nobel / Courtaulds*; Case IV/M.1453 *AXA / GRE*, paras 34 and 35; Case IV/M.1467 *Rohm and Haas / Morton*, para.41; Case COMP/M.1571 *New Holland / Case*, para.87; Case COMP/M.1671 *Dow Chemical / Union Carbide* [2001] O.J. L245/1, para.173; Case COMP/M.1806 *Astra Zeneca / Novartis* [2004] O.J. L110/1, para.470; Case COMP/M.1813 *Industri Kapital (Nordkem) / Dyno* [2001] O.J. L154/41 (paras 133 and 135 to 137; see also the Commission press release IP/00/753 noting that: "By accepting alternative undertakings the Commission has taken a novel approach. Alternative divestiture undertakings facilitate the divestiture process and increase the chances of finding a buyer for a business to be divested"); Case COMP/M.1846 *Glaxo Wellcome / SmithKline Beecham*, para.219; Case COMP/M.2533 *BP / E.ON*, para.137; Case COMP/M.2547 *Bayer / Aventis Crop Science* [2004] O.J. L107/1, paras 1143 and 1144; Case COMP/M.2690 *Solvay / Montedison-Ausimont*, para.183; and Case COMP/M.3225 *Alcan / Pechiney (II)*, paras 150 and 155.

[37] By contrast, in *Alcan / Pechiney / Alusuisse*, Commission press release IP/00/258, the Commission was critical of the provision of remedies in the alternative.

[38] See the Commission's XXXIst Annual Report on Competition Policy, 2001, para.299 ("it is a form of commitment which the Commission expects to see more of in the future"). However, in its paper in "Merger Remedies", OECD, DAF/COMP(2004)21, the Commission stated, at p.257, that "crown jewels" remedies were used only in a limited number of cases in which the Commission had doubts as to the viability or saleability of the divested business.

[39] See the Merger Remedies Study, p.52.

[40] See Claude Rakovsky, "Remedies: A Few Lessons From Recent Experience", in *EC Merger Control: Ten Years On* (International Bar Association, 2000), p.135, at p.142 and the FTC Divestiture Study, pp.30 and 31.

[41] p.145.

[42] See also Case COMP/M.1813 *Industri Kapital (Nordkem) / Dyno* [2001] O.J. L154/41, para.132; Case COMP/M.2922 *Pfizer / Pharmacia*; and Case COMP/M.3544 *Bayer Healthcare / Roche (OTC Business)* (if a suitable purchaser for the business in Austria were not found, the divestment was extended to cover the whole of the EEA; para.58 and Remedies, Sch.1, para.5(a)).

(a) Mario Monti, then the Commissioner for Competition Policy, summarised the Commission's assessment of the position in *Nestlé / Ralston Purina*[43] as follows: "In this case, the first alternative was the licensing of Nestlé's Friskies brand in Spain. If this licensing alternative is not implemented either by a fixed date or the date on which the notified operation is closed, then the option to license Nestlé's Friskie's brands would no longer be available to the parties and the second alternative ('the crown jewel') would have to be implemented. The second alternative, which involves the divestiture of the 50% shareholding of Ralston Purina in the Spanish joint venture with Agrolimen (Gullina Blanca Purina JV), consists of a larger and more easily saleable package compared to the licensing of Nestlé's Friskie's brand".[44]

(b) In *Johnson & Johnson / Guidant*[45] the notifying party committed to divest the overlapping product line or, if that failed, to divest the business which included the overlapping product line along with others. The market test had raised doubts about the viability of a business limited to the overlapping product line but the Commission found that the "crown jewel" solution safeguarded against any failure of the first remedy.

In addition to the concerns expressed in the Merger Remedies Study, the use **20–109** of "crown jewels" remedies is sometimes criticised[46] on the grounds that they can lead to the implementation of remedies which are wider than is necessary to resolve the competition issues,[47] which may be disproportionate and may deprive consumers of benefits that would otherwise arise from the transaction. Further, if "crown jewel" commitments are accepted, at least two businesses (rather than just one) face the possibility of divestment, which increases the uncertainty over the implementation of the remedies (which may lead to a loss of customers and key staff) and delays integration of both businesses, which may delay the realisation of customer benefits.[48] Further, such remedies can promote strategic behaviour on the part of potential purchasers of divestment assets, as they attempt to delay negotiations to trigger the "crown jewel" provisions. Finally, the use of "crown

---

[43] Case COMP/M.2337.
[44] Speech of Mario Monti, then the Commissioner for Competition Policy, "The Commission notice on merger remedies—one year after", January 18, 2002 (*www.europa.eu.int/comm/competition/speeches/index_2002.html*). In that case, the "crown jewel" element of the remedy was in fact implemented.
[45] Case COMP/M.3687, para.360.
[46] See also the US Department of Justice, "Antitrust Policy Guide to Merger Remedies", October 2004 (available via *www.usdoj.gov/atr/public/guidelines/205108.htm*), s.IV(H), strongly disfavouring the use of "crown jewel" provisions. Compare Baer & Redcay in Lévêque & Shelanski (eds), *Merger Remedies in American and European Union Competition Law* (Edward Elgar, 2003), at p.62.
[47] See "Merger Remedies", OECD, DAF/COMP(2004)21, p.9.
[48] See "Merger Remedies", OECD, DAF/COMP(2004)21, p.29.

jewels" remedies creates a risk that the purchaser of the divested assets is principally interested in the ancillary assets (rather than those which are being sold to remedy the competition concerns).[49]

(b) "Fix it first" remedies

20-110 In cases in which the viability of the divestiture package depends to a large extent on the identity of the purchaser or the Commission doubts whether a purchaser will be found,[50] it may require an up-front buyer by adopting a "fix it first"[51] approach under which completion (i.e. implementation) of the transaction may not occur until a contract to sell the divestment business has been signed.[52] The Commission has stated that, although there is some evidence that the use of "fix it first" remedies may contribute to shorter divestiture deadlines, it intends for proportionality reasons to require such remedies only when there are doubts about whether the proposed remedy can be implemented.[53] The Merger Remedies Study identified[54] the advantages of "fix it first" remedies as being that they tend to speed up the divestiture process, provide a strong assurance that the competition issues will be resolved, and reduce the risk of degradation of the divested business during the interim period, in particular when the business to be sold belongs to the target. On the other hand, the seller's wish to speed up the divestiture process can result in its failing to pursue an adequate sales procedure, which can affect the future viability and competitiveness of the divested business.

In the US, the FTC Divestiture Study found that the use of "fix it first" remedies[55] reduces the likelihood of customers being harmed whilst waiting for divestiture, ensures that there is a satisfactory purchaser, "shifts the costs of delaying the divestiture from the public to respondents", avoids problems of "commingling" and implements the policy of the Hart-Scott-Rodino Act by preventing, rather than remedying, competitive harm.[56] In its Statement

---

[49] See UK Competition Commission, "Application of Divestiture Remedies in Merger Inquiries: Competition Commission Guidelines", December 2004 (available via *www.competition-commission.org.uk/rep_pub/rules_and_guide/pdf/divestiture_remedies_guidance.pdf*), para.3.7.

[50] In its paper in "Merger Remedies", OECD, DAF/COMP(2004)21, the Commission stated, at p.257, that "fix it first" remedies were used only in a limited number of cases where the Commission had doubts as to the viability or saleability of the divested business.

[51] Note that the expression "fix it first remedy" is sometimes used in the US to refer to a remedy which is completed (i.e. implemented) by the parties in order to avoid the need for a consent decree (and is used in contra-distinction to "up-front buyers", where a consent decree provides that the transaction cannot be completed (i.e. implemented) until the divestment business has been sold).

[52] See the Notice on Remedies (para.20), the model Divestiture Commitments (para.1) and the Best Practice Guidelines (para.16).

[53] See the Commission's paper in "Merger Remedies", OECD, DAF/COMP(2004)21, at p.258. The Commission's approach addresses the substantive criticisms of the use of "fix it first" remedies by Baer & Redcay in Lévêque & Shelanski (eds), *Merger Remedies in American and European Union Competition Law* (Edward Elgar, 2003), at pp.57 and 58.

[54] pp.107 and 108.

[55] See n.51 above.

[56] pp.39 and 42.

on Negotiating Merger Remedies of April 2, 2003,[57] the FTC stated that, if the parties seek to divest a package of assets comprising less than an autonomous, ongoing business, the Bureau would usually require an up-front buyer; however, post-closing divestitures are contemplated in other cases and the FTC does not have a formal "fix it first" policy.[58]

Remedies involving *up-front buyers* have been adopted[59] under the ECMR **20–111** in the following cases.[60]

(a) In *Bosch / Rexroth*[61] the Commission was concerned that allowing Bosch to complete the acquisition before signing a contract for the sale of the divestment business would allow it to win back market share, preventing the purchaser from being an effective competitor. The Commission's analysis was that: "If Bosch was to sell its radial piston pumps business to a 'weak' buyer AFTER acquiring Rexroth AG, the market leader in axial piston pumps, it would have been able to win back gradually the market shares lost through the sale. Bosch's strong customer relations in the industrial hydraulics field would have been sufficient to persuade such customers to switch from radial to axial piston pumps. The Commission therefore imposed that the merger was not put into effect until a suitable buyer

---

[57] Available via *www.ftc.gov/bc/bestpractices/bestpractices030401.htm#In%20cases%20 requiring.*
[58] The US Department of Justice, "Antitrust Policy Guide to Merger Remedies", October 2004 (available via *www.usdoj.gov/atr/public/guidelines/205108.htm*), s.IV(A) states that the DOJ does not discourage acceptable "fix it first" remedies but does not have a policy of insisting on them.
[59] It is not clear whether the Commission *required* up-front buyers in each of the cases cited. In particular, notifying parties may occasionally *prefer* to remedy the issues up front to eliminate the risk that an acceptable purchaser for the divested business is not willing to pay the price expected by the notifying parties.
[60] See also Case COMP/M.2337 *Nestlé / Ralston Purina* (the first of two alternative remedies was available only in the event that the parties signed an agreement *prior* to completion (i.e. implementation) of the notified transaction; see speech of Mario Monti, then the Commissioner for Competition Policy, "The Commission notice on merger remedies—one year after", January 18, 2002, available via *www.europa.eu.int/comm/competition/speeches/index_2002. html*); Case COMP/M.2544 *Masterfoods / Royal Canin* (the parties proposed an up-front buyer solution, committing to suspend implementation of the concentration until they had signed a binding sale and purchase agreement with a purchaser approved by the Commission; para.90 and commitments, paras 9 to 13; as there might be a delay between signing the agreement to sell the divested assets and completion of the divestment, the commitments entered by the parties extended to the preservation of viability, marketability and competitiveness of the divestment business and imposed hold-separate obligations on the parties); Case COMP/M.2947 *Verbund / Energie Allianz* [2004] O.J. L92/91 (paras 143 and 157); Case COMP/M.3136 *GE / Agfa NDT* (in which, at the time of the Commission's decision, GE had *already* entered an agreement to sell the divestment business, subject to approval by the Commission and the US FTC; the Commission approved the identity of the buyer in its decision and described the sale as involving an "up-front buyer" and therefore not requiring hold-separate or ring-fencing provisions; see paras 48 to 53; it is not clear whether the Commission would have required an up-front buyer in this case if GE had not itself identified one); and Case COMP/M.3687 *Johnson & Johnson / Guidant* ("crown jewels" remedy combined with an up-front buyer in the light of the US Federal Trade Commission's requirements; para.360).
[61] Case COMP/M.2060 [2004] O.J. L43/1.

was found, leading Bosch to propose Moog, a strong competitor in Europe, very quickly".[62]

(b) In *The Post Office | TPG | SPPL*[63] the parties undertook to sell TPG's Dutch outbound international mail business. The Commission concluded that the success of the divestiture would depend to a large extent on the characteristics of the purchaser, which would need to establish its own network for the upstream and downstream services that would cease to be provided by TPG after a transitional period and would also need to generate the necessary amount of mail volume to enable it to offer competitive prices. The Commission therefore accepted an up-front purchaser proposal that put the risk of divestiture on the notifying parties. The parties were required to identify the purchaser and obtain the Commission's approval within a short time period, otherwise the conditional decision would no longer stand.

(c) In *DSM | Roche Vitamins*[64] the remedies provided for an up-front buyer because the transferability and viability of the divested business (and therefore the success of the remedies in restoring effective competition) depended to a large extent on the identity of the purchaser. Indeed, in that case, if the remedy had failed, there would have been no significant competition whatsoever.

(d) In *Sonoco | Ahlstrom*[65] the market test indicated that a management buyout of the divestment business would not resolve the competition issues, and a sale to a large company with existing activities in the core business was necessary. As there were uncertainties about whether an acceptable buyer would be available, the Commission required an up-front buyer to ensure the viability of the business.

In *DaimlerChrysler | Deutsche Telekom | JV*[66] the Commission allowed the parties to complete their joint venture but required that the third party access regime for the gateway asset was operating before the parties could benefit from their vertical integration by using the gateway asset themselves. The remedies were therefore analogous in some respects to cases involving up-front buyers.

---

[62] Commission press release, IP/00/1457.

[63] Case COMP/M.1915 [2004] O.J. L82/1, paras 154, 155 and 161; see also Commission press release, IP/01/364. The Commission's decision was taken on March 14, 2001 and the Commission accepted Swiss Post International as a suitable purchaser on June 14, 2001 (see the Commission's XXXIst Annual Report on Competition Policy, 2001, para.306).

[64] Case COMP/M.2972 [2004] O.J. L82/73, paras 80, 90 and 94.

[65] Case COMP/M.3431 [2005] O.J. L159/13, paras 111, 112 and 121.

[66] Case COMP/M.2903 (appeal pending in Case T-269/03 *Socratec (Satellite Navigation Consulting, Research & Technology) v Commission*), paras 68 and 76.

(c) Conditional remedies

In *Glaxo Wellcome | SmithKline Beecham*[67] the Commission accepted a **20–112** remedy which took effect only in the event that rival sources of potential competition in the pharmaceutical market failed to develop into actual competitors. The Commission regarded the case as depending on its "very special circumstances", namely that there were competing compounds at Phase III of development. Phase III commences three years before the pharmaceutical product is marketed, but there is a 50 per cent chance of failure and it was therefore unclear at the date of the Commission's decision whether the merged group would face effective competition.[68]

20.13 OTHER ASPECTS OF THE REMEDIES PROCESS

(a) Legal status of the Notice on Remedies

The legal status of the Notice on Remedies was clarified in the Court of First **20–113** Instance's decision in *BaByliss v Commission*.[69] The Commission argued that the Notice was "devoid of any binding legal obligation" but the Court found that, having published the Notice, the Commission was bound to apply it, subject to limited exceptions, stating: "The Commission is bound by notices which it issues in the area of supervision of concentrations, provided they do not depart from the rules in the Treaty and from [the ECMR] ... Moreover, the Commission cannot depart from rules which it has imposed on itself".[70]

---

[67] Case COMP/M.1846, paras 70, 195 and 222.
[68] See the discussion of the use of conditional remedies in high innovation markets which are characterised by high levels of uncertainty in "Merger Review in Emerging High Innovation Markets", OECD, DAFFE/COMP(2002)20, p.10. See also "Merger Remedies", OECD, DAF/COMP(2004)21, pp.20, 21 and 255, discussing the use of contingent remedies which come into operation if conditions of competition deteriorate. In the OFT Economic Discussion Paper, "Innovation and Competition Policy", Charles River Associates, March 2002 (note that the views in the paper do not necessarily reflect those of the OFT), it is suggested, at para.7.31, that in dynamic markets in which there is a good deal of uncertainty it may be possible to prepare undertakings which become operative in specified circumstances (e.g. obliging the merged group to maintain open access in the event that it becomes dominant).
[69] Case T-114/02 [2003] E.C.R. II-1279, para.143.
[70] The decision in *BaByliss* was effectively confirmed by the Court of First Instance (without referring to the *BaByliss* decision or the reasoning contained in it) in Case T-210/01 *General Electric Company v Commission*, not yet reported, judgment of December 14, 2005, para.516 ("As regards the alleged failure to comply with the notice on market definition, it is appropriate to observe at the outset that the Commission may not depart from rules which it has imposed on itself ... Thus, to the extent that the notice on market definition lays down in mandatory terms the method by which the Commission intends to define markets in the future and does not retain any margin of assessment, the Commission must indeed take account of the provisions of the notice").

(b) The roles of the trustees

20–114 The Commission almost invariably requires the parties to appoint monitoring and divestiture trustees.[71] The monitoring trustee and the divestiture trustee may be the same person.[72] The terms on which trustees are typically appointed are included in the model Trustee Mandate.[73]

The *monitoring trustee* carries out four distinct functions: monitoring the interim preservation arrangements, overseeing the hold-separate and ring-fencing arrangements, monitoring the carve-out arrangements and monitoring the divestiture process.[74] The monitoring trustee is, typically, an accounting firm, an insolvency administrator or an industry consultant.[75] Historically, investment banks have also taken on this role, but the Merger Remedies Study found that they lack the expertise to carry out certain of the functions.[76] The *divestiture trustee* will be given an irrevocable and exclusive mandate to sell the divestment business during the extended divestiture period.

(c) The "review clause"

20–115 Commitments now include a "review clause",[77] providing that the Commission may, upon request[78] from the parties showing good cause, grant an extension of the time periods foreseen in the commitments or waive, modify, or substitute in exceptional circumstances, one or more of the undertakings

---

[71] See the Notice on Remedies (para.52), the model Divestiture Commitments (paras 16 to 21) and the Merger Remedies Study, pp.61, 87 to 97, 145 to 148 and 154 to 159. The Commission's XXXIst Annual Report on Competition Policy, 2001, para.293, noted that trustees were employed in all but one of the cases which involved conditional clearance in 2001. In a paper from 2004, the Commission stated that trustees have not been appointed in a "limited number of smaller and seemingly straightforward cases", including Case COMP/M.2431 *Allianz / Dresdner Bank* (which was cleared in 2001) and Case COMP/M.3091 *Konica / Minolta* (2003); see "Merger Remedies", OECD, DAF/COMP(2004)21, p.256 and n.18 on p.260.

[72] See the Notice on Remedies (para.55).

[73] The provisions on conflicts of interest (paras 20 to 23), remuneration (para.24) and indemnities (para.25) are particularly noteworthy. See also the model Divestiture Commitments, paras 16 to 33 and the Merger Remedies Study, pp.93 and 94.

[74] See the Merger Remedies Study, p.90. The monitoring trustee may in certain circumstances be required to exercise the shareholder rights held by the party providing the undertakings or to appoint members to the board of the divestment business if it is a separate company: see the model Divestiture Commitments (para.8), the model Trustee Mandate (para.6(d)) and the Best Practice Guidelines (para.17).

[75] The FTC Divestiture Study refers, at p.30, to the appointment of individuals with technical knowledge of the industry to perform this role.

[76] See pp.91 and 92.

[77] The model Divestiture Commitments, para.34. See, e.g. Case COMP/M.1915 *The Post Office / TPG / SPPL* [2004] O.J. L82/1, Appendix 2, para.12 and Case COMP/M.2337 *Nestlé / Ralston Purina*, Commitments, clause 24.

[78] The request must be accompanied by a report from the monitoring trustee.

in the commitments.[79] The Commission is very cautious about any suggestion that the scope of the divestment business should be curtailed, but is willing to consider such applications, for example if a potential purchaser does not wish to acquire the entire business as it already has the necessary personnel and infrastructure.[80] In *Shell / Montecatini*[81] Shell provided undertakings to sell certain businesses, subsequently sold other businesses, and then requested the Commission to amend its original decision given this change of circumstances. The Commission found that the subsequent sale by Shell meant that the sale of the divestment business was no longer required and amended its original decision by revoking the conditions relating to the sale of the divestment business.[82] In *Hoechst / Rhône-Poulenc*[83] the Commission agreed to amend a set of commitments to allow the parties to substitute the disposal of one business for another; both of the disposals eliminated the overlap and the Commission found that insisting on the disposal of the first business could seriously prejudice its future survival (as it was in financial difficulties and needed restructuring). Finally, in *Pirelli / Edizione / Olivetti / Telecom Italia*,[84] Edizione undertook to dispose of its shareholding in BLU as a condition of approval of the merger but was unable to find a purchaser and the Commission agreed to substitute a completely new set of undertakings for the original commitments. The new commitments provided for the break-up of BLU's assets and distribution to the remaining players in the market with the customer base being transferred in its entirety to the smallest remaining supplier.

Commitments may also include bespoke clauses providing an ongoing role for the Commission, for example to release parties from a continuing conduct commitment or to extend a commitment.[85]

---

[79] For a bespoke review clause taking into account the possibility that a Member State reviewing the same merger following a referral back might impose commitments which were inconsistent with commitments accepted by the Commission, see Case COMP/M.2621 *SEB / Moulinex*, commitments, s.2(g) (and the discussion on appeal in Case T-119/02 *Royal Philips Electronics NV v Commission* [2003] E.C.R. II-1433, paras 181 to 195, in which a challenge to this part of the commitments was rejected on procedural grounds).

[80] Case COMP/M.1915 *The Post Office / TPG / SPPL* [2004] O.J. L82/1, para.162. See also para.20–049 above.

[81] Case IV/M.269 [1994] O.J. L332/48.

[82] Although the Commission's decision pre-dated the adoption of the model Divestiture Commitments, it made reference to the possibility of such a review. In particular, para.118 of the Commission's decision noted that the undertakings provided that: "The parties reserve their rights under Community law to request the Commission to review the whole or any specific undertakings relating to PP technology set out above". See also the Commission's XXVIIth Annual Report on Competition Policy, 1997, p.184.

[83] Case COMP/M.1378 (decision of January 30, 2004), paras 20 and 36. For discussion of earlier amendments to the commitments in that case, see paras 7 and 8.

[84] Case COMP/M.2574, as explained in Baccaro, "Failing Firm Defence and Lack of Causality: Doctrine and Practice in Europe of Two Closely Related Concepts" [2004] E.C.L.R. 11, at pp.18 and 19.

[85] See, e.g. Case COMP/M.2947 *Verbund / EnergieAllianz* [2004] O.J. L92/91, para.145(a).

(d) Third party consents

20–116 (i) General Implementation of the remedies proposed by the parties may require consent from a third party. The Merger Remedies Study stated[86]: "The Commission ... normally require[s] the parties offering the commitments to implement the remedy fully, regardless of third party rights". It nevertheless found[87] that when third parties were in a position to prevent or impede the implementation of remedies that affected them, their actions had frequently led to delays in implementation and difficulties in securing their agreement had frequently been underestimated.

20–117 (ii) Rejection of necessary remedies conditional on third party consents The starting point is that the Commission requires that commitments are implemented and a commitment which is essential to resolve the competition concerns but which may not be implemented because it is conditional on the grant of consent from a third party is not acceptable. In *General Electric Company v Commission*[88] the Court of First Instance stated that the Commission needed to conclude "with certainty" that it would be possible to implement the commitments and it followed that if a failure by a third party to provide a necessary consent would preclude implementation of the commitments, the Commission was bound to reject them. Applying this test, the Court upheld the Commission's decision to reject a commitment that was subject to approvals under United States export control rules on the grounds that the commitment might never have been implemented.[89] However, there is a range of solutions to this issue.

20–118 (iii) Acceptance of absolute obligations notwithstanding the need for third party consents In *Air Liquide / Messer Targets*[90] the notifying party committed to transfer a third party contract even though it required the consent of a third party in order to do so. The Commission *accepted* the commitment, stating: "The Commission underlines that the above divestitures are conditions to the clearance of the proposed transaction". This meant that the notifying party took the risk of the third party refusing to grant consent.

20–119 (iv) Other solutions to the issue of third party consents In some cases, the issue of third party consents can be resolved *before the Commission accepts the commitments*. In *Exxon / Mobil*[91] as part of the market test of the remedies

---

[86] See p.143.
[87] See pp.46, 143 and 144.
[88] Case T-210/01, not yet reported, judgment of December 14, 2005, paras 555 and 557.
[89] Paras 615 and 617.
[90] Case COMP/M.3314, para.175.
[91] Case IV/M.1383 [2004] O.J. L103/1, para.836.

package, the Commission ascertained whether necessary third party consents would be granted.

In others, the Commission can establish that the exercise by the third party of its rights would *not affect the viability of the remedy*. For example, in *The Coca-Cola Company / Carlsberg A/S*[92] the Commission noted, in relation to a commitment to dispose of shares in a company, that the other shareholders in that company had rights of first refusal over those shares but that it would be acceptable for the sale to proceed to one of those shareholders.

The Commission has in several cases accepted *alternative* commitments.[93] In principle such commitments are acceptable provided that either alternative would adequately resolve the competition concerns and one of them is not conditional on the obtaining of a third party's consent. For example, in *TotalFina / Elf*[94] the notifying party offered a commitment to sell certain service stations on the basis that, if a particular station could not be transferred because a necessary third party consent was not available, the notifying party would sell to another purchaser or substitute the station in question with another.

The Commission has in several cases accepted *qualified* commitments. In **20–120** principle, such commitments are acceptable provided that they would adequately resolve the competition concerns even in the face of third party obstruction or opportunistic behaviour.

(a) In *WorldCom / MCI*[95] the parties were concerned that a commitment to transfer *all* of the contracts of the divestment business would result in opportunistic behaviour by customers whose contracts contained prohibitions on assignment without prior customer consent. The Commission accepted a commitment to transfer contracts representing a specified percentage of the divestment business's turnover and, where contracts could not be transferred, to put the traffic on to the acquirer's network and pay a specified proportion of revenues to the acquirer. It emphasised that its main concern was to ensure that the customers transferred did not migrate back to the divesting party and noted that the non-compete provisions forming part of the commitments ought to have achieved this.

(b) More recently, in *NewsCorp / Telepiù*[96] the notifying party committed to supply audio-visual content to third parties as part of a "wholesale offer". NewsCorp required consents from the holders of intellectual property rights in the content in order to make such supplies and committed to exercise "best endeavours" to obtain these consents

---

[92] Case IV/M.833 [1998] O.J. L145/41, para.115.
[93] See s.20.12(a) above.
[94] Case COMP/M.1628 [2001] O.J. L143/1, para.335.
[95] Case IV/M.1069 [1999] O.J. L116/1, paras 154 to 157.
[96] Case COMP/M.2876 [2004] O.J. L110/73, para.249.

and, if they were not available, to take reasonable steps to provide a full package of content, including the provision of suitable alternative content.

(c) Similarly, in *Alcatel / Finmeccanica / Alcatel Alenia Space & Telespazio*[97] the parties offered to license a technology package to a third party. Some of the intellectual property rights were owned by national space agencies. The Commission accepted a firm commitment from the parties to license their intellectual property rights and a "best efforts" commitment to obtain approval from the space agencies to transfer the remaining intellectual property rights.

(d) In *Bayer / Aventis Crop Science*[98] the Commission accepted a commitment to transfer as many as possible of Aventis's third party distribution agreements and to discontinue the remainder.[99]

(e) Commitments given in earlier cases

20–121 The Commission may also take account of commitments provided to the Commission by one of the merging parties *in an earlier case*.[1] Indeed, the Court of First Instance has indicated that the Commission is under a duty to take account of existing commitments if requested to do so by the notifying party.[2]

If a concentration adversely affects the implementation of commitments provided to the Commission in an earlier case, then the parties to the concentration will need to offer remedies to ensure the effective implementation of those commitments. For example,[3] in *Mitsui / CVRD / Caemi*,[4] Mitsui and CVRD provided commitments in the context of their acquisition of joint control over Caemi. When CVRD acquired sole control over Caemi, it assumed full responsibility for complying with those commitments.[5]

If a concentration renders commitments given in an earlier case unnecessary or potentially anti-competitive, the Commission will release the party that gave the earlier undertaking from its commitments. For example, in *Siemens / VA Tech*[6] the Commission released a third party from a

---

[97] Case COMP/M.3680, para.124.
[98] Case COMP/M.2547 [2004] O.J. L107/1, para.1141.
[99] See also paras 1147 and 1151 (noting commitments by the notifying party which applied in the event that a third party consent was not provided).
[1] See Case COMP/M.2305 *Vodafone Group PLC / Eircell*, para.9.
[2] Case T-5/02 *Tetra Laval BV v Commission* [2002] E.C.R. II-4381, paras 220 to 222 (the decision was upheld on appeal on the basis of reasoning not relating directly to this issue in Case C-12/03P *Commission v Tetra Laval BV*, not yet reported, judgment of February 15, 2005).
[3] See also Case COMP/M.2761 *BP / Veba Oel*, paras 15 and 16 and Case COMP/JV.56 *Hutchinson / ECT*.
[4] Case COMP/M.2420 [2004] O.J. L92/50.
[5] Case COMP/M.3161 *CVRD / Caemi*.
[6] Case COMP/M.3653.

commitment to purchase certain products from VA Tech, to avoid creating a link between Siemens and that third party.

(f) Commitments to resolve two or more cases

The Commission has accepted undertakings designed to resolve competition concerns arising from the notified concentration *and* an earlier concentration which the Commission was investigating to determine whether it ought to have been notified.[7] **20–122**

(g) Clearance without accepting the commitments (or all of them)

The Commission may approve a transaction without accepting commitments which have been offered by the parties.[8] It may also accept some but not all of the commitments provided by the parties.[9] **20–123**

(h) Status of different types of commitments and consequences of breach

In its decisions, the Commission now distinguishes clearly between[10]: **20–124**

---

[7] Case IV/M.1157 *Skanska / Scancem* [1999] O.J. L183/1, paras 208 and 211 ("While the cement restructuring does not directly address the competition concerns arising from the [notified] transaction, that undertaking resolves the Commission's doubts with respect to the [earlier] transaction and would therefore in combination with [another element of the undertakings] obviate the need to pursue that investigation further, provided that the undertakings are complied with").

[8] See, e.g. Case COMP/M.2079 *Raytheon / Thales / JV*, para.76; Case COMP/M.2201 *MAN / Auwärter*; Case COMP/M.2510 *Cendant / Galileo* (see press release IP/01/1307); Case COMP/ M.2745 *Shell / Enterprise Oil* (see "Merger Remedies", OECD, DAF/COMP(2004)21, p.254 for confirmation that remedies were offered but the case was cleared unconditionally); Case COMP/M.3148 *Siemens / Alstom Gas and Steam Turbines* (remedies were submitted to support an application for a derogation from the prohibition on implementing mergers, but withdrawn by the parties after the Commission advised them that remedies were not required to rule out any "serious doubts"); Case COMP/M.3182 *Scottish & Newcastle / HP Bulmer*, paras 35 and 38; and Case COMP/M.3664 *Repsol Butano / Shell Gas (LPG)*, n.2.

[9] See, e.g. Case COMP/M.1628 *TotalFina / Elf* [2001] O.J. L143/1 (para.330, noting a commitment without its being a condition for declaring the concentration compatible with the common market); Case COMP/M.2416 *Tetra Laval / Sidel* (decision of January 13, 2003), paras 113 (recording that the commitments were offered on the understanding that the Commission could accept any or all of them), and 118 and 119; and Case COMP/M.2420 *Mitsui / CVRD / Caemi* [2004] O.J. L92/50, para.255. In Case COMP/M.4035 *Telefónica/0Z*, the notifying party offered two sets of undertakings, the second of which would apply only if the first was not sufficient to obtain clearance in phase 1; para.68.

[10] The ECMR, recitals 30 and 31, provides: "It should be expressly provided that the Commission may attach to its decision conditions and obligations in order to ensure that the undertakings concerned comply with their commitments in a timely and effective manner so as to render the concentration compatible with the common market ... The Commission should have at its disposal appropriate instruments to ensure the enforcement of these commitments and to deal with situations where they are not fulfilled".

(a) the *conditions* of the decision (commonly, commitments to sell specified businesses), breach of which results in the Commission's
decision being automatically void; and

(b) *obligations* (such as implementing steps), breach of which may result
in the Commission using its powers to withdraw the clearance decision[11] and/or to impose fines and periodic penalty payments.[12]

The Commission has not, to date, declared a clearance decision void
because of a failure to comply with a commitment to divest a business,
although the press has reported indications of an intention to do so.[13]

In addition, the Commission sometimes "takes note" of commitments. In
some cases, it is clear that the commitments in question are not intended to
be binding.[14] In others, however, the Commission relies on the commitments
in reaching its decision, indicating that it expects them to be complied with
and yet, by failing to make them conditions or obligations, the Commission
very likely lacks a remedy in the event of breach. For example,[15] in its second
decision in *Tetra Laval / Sidel*[16] (following the overturning by the Court of
First Instance of the Commission's original prohibition decision) the
Commission found that the vertical issues arising from Tetra Laval's
activities as a pre-forms producer had been resolved by their sale, but "took
note" of Tetra Laval's commitment not to resume the commercial sale of
PET pre-forms in the EEA and certain other states for a specified period
(which might be extended by the Commission in certain circumstances). This
commitment was not described as a condition or obligation but the decision
was drafted in terms which implied that Tetra Laval was expected to comply
with it.[17] Similarly, in *Verbund / EnergieAllianz*,[18] the Commission "took

---

[11] ECMR, Art.8(6)(b).

[12] See the ECMR, recital 31 and Arts 14(2)(d) and 15(1)(c).

[13] *Financial Times*, May 28, 2002, reported, at p.26: "Mario Monti, the competition commis-
sioner, has urged the Benettons and the Italian government to do more to look for a buyer for
Blu. Last week, he warned that Brussels could revoke its clearance of the takeover of Telecom
Italia by Pirelli and the Benetton family. The deal was conditional on the sale of Blu." (In fact,
the Commission agreed to accept a substitute set of commitments in that case; see Baccaro,
"Failing Firm Defence and Lack of Causality: Doctrine and Practice in Europe of Two
Closely Related Concepts" [2004] E.C.L.R. 11, at pp.18 and 19.)

[14] See Joined Cases T-125/97 and T-127/97 *The Coca-Cola Company v Commission* [2000] E.C.R.
II-1733, para.106.

[15] See also, e.g. Case IV/M.1225 *Enso / Stora* [1999] O.J. L254/9 (in which a pricing commitment
was not formally accepted by the Commission but the commitment was relied on in concluding that the merger would not create or strengthen a dominant position; paras 96 and
101); Case COMP/M.2876 *NewsCorp / Telepiù* [2004] O.J. L110/73, para.324; and Case
COMP/M.3083 *GE / Instrumentarium* [2004] O.J. L109/1, para.330.

[16] Case COMP/M.2416 (decision of January 13, 2003), paras 103, 119 and 125. See also the press
release, IP/03/36.

[17] In contrast to para.123, in which the Commission stated that it did not need to consider certain
remedies because it had not identified serious doubts on the points which the remedies sought
to address. The Commission also "took note" of commitments regarding the divestiture of
Tetra Laval's SBM business even though it found that one part of the commitments (regarding
intellectual property rights) was "necessary"; see para.118. The "necessary" part of the
commitments was not made a condition or obligation of the clearance decision; see para.125.

[18] Case COMP/M.2947 [2004] O.J. L92/91, para.150.

note" of a commitment offered by Verbund to sell its minority holdings in two companies, expressly stated that the commitment would not be a condition or obligation of the clearance decision (implying that the parties were not bound by it) but the decision was drafted in terms[19] that contemplated that the commitment would in fact be implemented.[20]

(i) Declarations from the competent authorities of Member States

The Commission takes account of declarations provided by the competent **20–125** authorities of Member States, although these are not binding in a formal sense.[21] For example, in *DaimlerChrysler / Deutsche Telekom / JV*[22] the Commission took account of an "undertaking" from the German Federal Ministry of Transport, Construction and Housing that it would not discriminate on costs against third party providers of telematics equipment when compared with the joint venture (which was contracted to provide services to the German Republic). Similarly, in *Verbund / EnergieAllianz*[23] the Commission took note of an indication from the Austrian Minister for Economic Affairs and Labour regarding the immediate implementation of certain provisions in a directive. In *Swissair / Sabena*[24] the Commission identified Sabena as the "most likely and significant" potential entrant on to the Brussels-Bern route because a Treaty between Belgium and Switzerland designated Swissair and Sabena as the only airlines permitted to fly on that route. However, the transaction was cleared on the basis of a declaration by the *Swiss and Belgian governments* to take steps to amend the Treaty so that rival airlines could operate on the route in question. Similarly, declarations from the French and Belgian governments were taken into account in *Air France / Sabena*.[25] Finally, in *Air France / KLM*[26] the Commission received

---

[19] Para.150 stated that "Verbund's commitment to divest its minority holding in Unsere Wasserkraft and MyElectric will mean that these undertakings will be unaffected by any influence and financial interest on behalf of the merged entity and will be able to compete with it on the market to supply power to small customers".

[20] See also para.156. In press release IP/03/825 the Commission stated that it "took note" of commitments regarding the removal of existing bottlenecks and the development of interconnectors, but the decision itself contemplated that the undertakings would be binding as they would help to ensure that the remedies package contributed to the real removal of the competition concerns identified in the decision.

[21] In any event, formal commitments cannot be accepted from third parties in the light of Case T-158/00 *ARD v Commission* [2003] E.C.R. II-3825, in which the Court of First Instance stated, at para.341: "the Commission ... cannot accept a commitment imposed on a third party to the proposed concentration as part of a decision adopted under" the ECMR.

[22] Case COMP/M.2903 (appeal pending in Case T-269/03 *Socratec (Satellite Navigation Consulting, Research & Technology) v Commission*), para.70.

[23] Case COMP/M.2947 [2004] O.J. L92/91, para.156 and press release IP/03/825.

[24] Case IV/M.616, paras 27 to 30 and 42 to 44.

[25] Case IV/M.157, paras 32, 36 and 50.

[26] Case COMP/M.3280 (appeal pending in Case T-177/04 *easyJet Airline Company v Commission*), paras 102, 103, 155 and 163.

declarations from the competent authorities of France and the Netherlands that certain regulatory barriers would not be triggered on long-haul routes and concluded: "The Commission has taken note of these declarations, which form an integral part of its assessment".[27]

(j) International cooperation

20–126 The Commission commonly consults with other antitrust authorities. For example,[28] in *Metso / Svedala*[29] the Commission and the US FTC cooperated closely and were able to request very similar undertakings and arrange to approve the buyer of the divestment business at the same time.[30] The EU and US "Best Practices" for coordinating merger reviews[31] emphasise that the merging parties should work with both the EU and US agencies to minimise the risk of inconsistent remedies or subsequent difficulties in interpretation.

20.14 STRUCTURING TRANSACTIONS WHEN REMEDIES ISSUES ARE EXPECTED

20–127 Notifying parties which anticipate that a concentration will give rise to a significant impediment to effective competition have several options when structuring the transaction.[32]

---

[27] See also Case COMP/M.3770 *Lufthansa / Swiss*, paras 42 and 189.

[28] Cooperation with the US Federal Trade Commission occurred in Case COMP/M.2922 *Pfizer / Pharmacia*, in which the divestments were made on a worldwide basis as described in the Commission's XXXIIIrd Annual Report on Competition Policy, 2003, para.236. Cooperation involving the Canadian authorities occurred in Case COMP/M.2337 *Nestlé / Ralston Purina*. In Case IV/M.1381 *Imetal / English China Clays* the Commission accepted a commitment to dispose of a plant in the US and noted that a similar requirement would be made by the US Department of Justice, stating, at para.81: "For the precise identification of the kaolin plant as well as the calciners to be divested the Commission is content to accept the plant and calciners named in the consent decree which will be stipulated between Imetal and the DOJ, so long as the criteria set out above are satisfied". The Commission also identified a plant to be divested in the event that Imetal failed to reach agreement with the DOJ.

[29] Case COMP/M.2033 [2004] O.J. L88/1.

[30] Speech of Mario Monti, then the Commissioner for Competition Policy, "The Commission notice on merger remedies—one year after", January 18, 2002 (*www.europa.eu.int/comm/competition/speeches/index_2002.html*). See generally European Commission "Report from the Commission to the Council and the European Parliament on the application of agreements between the European Communities and the Government of the United States of America and the Government of Canada regarding the application of their competition laws", COM (02) 505 final, September 17, 2002, in particular at para.1.21.

[31] Commission press release of October 30, 2002 (IP/02/1591). See also the US FTC's press release of the same date.

[32] The scope to "warehouse" the acquired business with a bank through an arrangement under which the ultimate purchaser provides funds for the bank to make the acquisition (without making a filing under the ECMR, in reliance on the exception in Art.3(5)(a) for purchases by financial institutions of securities on a temporary basis with a view to reselling them) and the

First, the transaction may be structured so that the business which would create competition concerns if acquired by the notifying party is instead purchased by a third party which does not raise any competition concerns. A purchase by a third party as part of a genuine split sale will normally[33] prevent the competition issues from arising, avoids the need to obtain approval from the Commission for the identity of the purchaser and the terms of the sale, and eliminates the risk of delays (whether small, through the modest extensions to the timetable which occur when remedies are proposed, or large if the Commission requires a "fix it first" remedy).[34] In *Kayserberg SA v Commission*[35] the Court of First Instance stated: "the parties to the concentration in question clearly intended to exclude VPS's business relating to infant hygiene, that is to say baby nappies, from the subject-matter of the concentration since that business was intended to be sold to a third party concomitantly with the authorization of the concentration. Under the acquisition agreements notified to the Commission, that business was to be separated from VPS and transferred to a trustee, already designated at the time of the notification, with a mandate to ensure its sale to a third party within a short period of time following the completion of the acquisition of VPS by P&G ... Consequently, since there was no lasting and actual transfer of control of that business to P&G, the business was not covered by the concentration plan submitted to the Commission for its examination".

Similar issues arise when the relevant remedies do not involve divestments. In *Banco Santander / Abbey National*[36] the purchaser stated in its

---

bank agrees to transfer the acquired business once approval is obtained under the ECMR for that transfer (or otherwise to hold the acquired business to the ultimate purchaser's order) is under challenge in the Court of First Instance in Case T-279/04 *Editions Odile Jacob SAS v Commission* (appeal against the decision in Case COMP/M.2978 *Lagardère / Natexis / VUP* [2004] O.J. L125/54). This structure is therefore of doubtful legality pending a favourable ruling from the Court of First Instance.

[33] However, recital 21 of the ECMR now provides that transactions which are linked by condition and are therefore closely connected are treated as a single concentration. If the on-sale is conditional on completion of the main agreement (as will usually be the case), the Commission may seek to challenge a split sale structure that causes a significant impediment to effective competition. For example, imagine that there are two suppliers of widgets, A and B. B is part of a wider group, X. A purchases X and structures the purchase as a split sale so that B is purchased by C. C has no interest in the widgets market but wishes to use the B's assets in the production of blodgets. The effect of the merger is that A obtains a monopoly in the widgets market, but A never obtains decisive influence over B because of the split sale structure. A less extreme example arises if C will operate the assets in the widgets market but is not expected to be such an aggressive competitor as B was when owned by X (e.g. because C requires part of the widgets output for its downstream activities and therefore chooses to compete less aggressively for third party business), such that C would not have met the purchaser standards if approval had been required under a divestment commitment.

[34] See the discussion in Baer & Redcay in Lévêque & Shelanski (eds), *Merger Remedies in American and European Union Competition Law* (Edward Elgar, 2003), at pp.61 and 62.

[35] Case T-290/94 [1997] E.C.R. II-2137, para.190.

[36] Case COMP/M.3547, paras 11 and 14 (and see also press release IP/04/1105). See also Case COMP/M.2245 *Metsä-Serla / Zanders* in which the Commission identified, at para.23, concerns based on Zanders' sales and marketing agreements with third parties, but the parties put a formal end to the agreements, which eliminated the competition concerns.

notification that, subject to completion (i.e. implementation) of the notified concentration, it had agreed to modify its cooperation agreement with a UK bank, Royal Bank of Scotland, in particular to terminate the representation on each other's board of directors. The Commission treated the termination of the cooperation agreement as "a fact" in its appraisal and approved the transaction unconditionally.[37]

20–128   Secondly, the notifying party may purchase the entire business (meaning that remedies are required to resolve the competition issues), having already entered an agreement to sell the divestment business in the event that such a sale is required in order to obtain approval from the European Commission.[38] The advantage of this structure is that the notifying party avoids the status of "forced seller", but is able to retain the business if, for example, the Commission does not identify competition concerns or requires different remedies. In *GE / Agfa NDT*,[39] at the time of the Commission's decision, GE had *already* entered an agreement to sell the divestment business, subject to approval by the Commission and the US FTC; the Commission approved the identity of the buyer in its decision and described the sale as involving an "up-front buyer". The Commission's decision in *Akzo Nobel / Courtaulds*[40] is a variant on this approach, as the parties entered an orthodox post-completion (i.e. post-implementation) commitment, but undertook to sell to Dexter (Courtaulds' current partner) *or* an independent purchaser approved by the Commission.[41]

20–129   Thirdly, the notifying party may purchase the entire business and agree to a "fix it first" remedy which precludes the notifying party from completing (i.e. implementing) the notified concentration until after signing an agreement to sell the divestment business to a purchaser approved by the Commission. In general, notifying parties seek to avoid "fix it first" remedies as they delay completion (i.e. implementation), which can trigger "drop dead" dates in the sale and purchase agreement, delay the integration process, and risk damage to the target business (e.g. through loss of customers or key staff) as a result of the uncertainty in the meantime. However, one

---

[37] The curiosity about this approach is that Banco Santander would have been free to sign a fresh cooperation agreement with Royal Bank of Scotland after the Commission approved the concentration and the Commission's remedy in such a situation would be limited to taking action under Art.81.

[38] Such a sale ought to be made conditional on the approval by the Commission of the purchaser's identity.

[39] Case COMP/M.3136, paras 48 to 53.

[40] Case IV/M.1182.

[41] See also Case COMP/M.2922 *Pfizer / Pharmacia* (commitment to transfer a product in development to a named transferee; para.153); Case COMP/M.3436 *Continental / Phoenix*, para.220; and Case COMP/M.3692, *Reuters / Telerate* (the Commission accepted a licensing remedy based on a licence to a named licensee, i.e. the identity of the licensee was effectively approved as part of the decision assessing the notified concentration; see paras 29 to 35). In Case COMP/M.3465 *Syngenta CP / Advanta* the notifying party agreed to divest Advanta's European seeds business and a few days later the Commission approved the acquisition of that business by a third party in Case COMP/M.3506 *Fox Paine / Advanta*, enabling Syngenta to fulfil the undertakings that it had provided (see the Commission's XXXIVth Annual Report on Competition Policy, 2004, paras 253 to 258).

important advantage of "fix it first" remedies is that the notifying parties are able to establish with certainty the price at which the divestment business will be sold. For example, a joint venture may only be viable if the price obtained on a sale of the divestment business reaches a certain threshold, and the parties can avoid assuming the risk that the proceeds fail to meet that threshold by using a "fix it first" remedy. The same issue arises in a purchase, although it is usually more difficult commercially to negotiate a clause allowing completion (i.e. implementation) to be delayed until a sale agreement had been signed pursuant to a "fix it first" remedy.

Fourthly, the notifying party may purchase the entire business and agree **20–130** to a normal divestment remedy under which the sale agreement is signed after the notified concentration is completed (i.e. implemented). This occurs in the vast majority of remedies cases, because:

(a) notifying parties are often not willing to agree to sell businesses if they believe that there is a reasonable prospect of retaining them in the debate with the Commission;

(b) it is not normally possible to sell businesses owned by the target until after the notified concentration has been completed (i.e. implemented)[42] and notifying parties seem to have at least some preference to sell target assets (because there is no integration risk with businesses which are already owned);

(c) attempting to sell a business during the notification process may be interpreted as an admission by the Commission that competition issues arise (creating difficulties if a buyer is not found);

(d) there may be resourcing issues associated with carrying out a sale during the process of notifying the Commission.

The main risks of proceeding along this orthodox route are: **20–131**

(a) the divested business may be sold for a lower price than expected;

(b) the divested business can only be sold to a buyer approved by the Commission, which reduces the number of potential purchasers (which may reduce the proceeds from the auction)[43]; and

(c) if the disposal business is not divested to a suitable purchaser, then the notifying party will be in breach of a condition and the approval will be void. Historically, the Commission has tended to seek practical solutions in cases in which remedies prove difficult to

---

[42] Occasionally, a vendor under the notified concentration may be willing to allow the warranties on that sale to be passed on to the purchaser of the divestment business and may also allow the purchaser of the divestment business to carry out due diligence (i.e. accessing the relevant parts of the data room, visiting any plants and questioning management).

[43] It also reduces or eliminates the scope to act strategically on the sale (e.g. by selling to a buyer which is likely to run the business less aggressively).

implement, but there is a risk that this flexibility encourages strategic behaviour and there is a realistic prospect that the Commission will make greater use of its powers under the ECMR in the future.

INDEX